CollegeBoard

SAT

THE OFFICIAL STUDY GUIDE

FOR ALL SAT SUBJECT TESTS™

SECOND EDITION

The College Board
New York, N.Y.

About the College Board

The College Board is a mission-driven not-for-profit organization that connects students to college success and opportunity. Founded in 1900, the College Board was created to expand access to higher education. Today, the membership association is made up of over 6,000 of the world's leading educational institutions and is dedicated to promoting excellence and equity in education. Each year, the College Board helps more than seven million students prepare for a successful transition to college through programs and services in college readiness and college success — including the SAT® and the Advanced Placement Program®. The organization also serves the education community through research and advocacy on behalf of students, educators, and schools.

For further information, visit www.collegeboard.org.

Copies of this book are available from your bookseller or may be ordered from College Board Publications at store.collegeboard.org or by calling 800-323-7155.

Editorial inquiries concerning this book should be addressed to the College Board, SAT Program, 250 Vesey Street, New York, New York 10281.

ISBN-13: 978-0-87447-975-1

Printed in the United States of America

Distributed by Macmillan

9 10 11 12 13 14 15 21 20 19 18 17 16

CONTENTS

The SAT Subject Tests™

About SAT Subject Tests

SAT Subject Tests™ are a valuable way to help you show colleges a more complete picture of your academic background and interests. Each year, nearly one million Subject Tests are taken by students throughout the country and around the world to gain admission to the leading colleges and universities in the United States.

SAT Subject Tests are one-hour exams that give you the opportunity to demonstrate knowledge and showcase achievement in specific subjects. They provide a fair and reliable measure of your achievement in high school — information that can help enhance your college admission portfolio. Subject Tests are also a great way for you to let colleges know that you are interested in specific subjects or majors.

This book provides information and guidance to help you study for and familiarize yourself with each of the Subject Tests. It contains actual, previously administered tests and official answer sheets that will help you get comfortable with the tests' format, so you feel better prepared on test day.

The Benefits of SAT Subject Tests

SAT Subject Tests let you put your best foot forward, allowing you to focus on subjects that you know well and enjoy. They can help you differentiate yourself in a competitive admission environment by providing additional information about your knowledge of and interest in particular subjects. Many colleges also use Subject Tests for course placement and selection; some schools allow you to place out of introductory courses by taking certain Subject Tests.

Subject Tests are flexible and can be tailored to your strengths and areas of interest. These are the **only** national admission tests where **you** choose the tests that best showcase your achievements and interests. You select the Subject Test(s) and can take up to three tests in one sitting. With the exception of listening tests, you can even decide to change the subject or number of tests you want to take on the day of the test. This flexibility can help you be more relaxed on test day.

Who Should Consider Subject Tests?

Anyone can take an SAT Subject Test to highlight his or her knowledge of a specific subject. SAT Subject Tests may be especially beneficial for certain students:

REMEMBER

Subject Tests are a valuable way to help you show colleges a more complete picture of your academic achievements.

- Students applying to colleges that require or recommend Subject Tests — be aware that some schools have additional Subject Test requirements for certain students, majors or programs of study
- Students who wish to demonstrate strength in specific subject areas
- Students who wish to demonstrate knowledge obtained outside a traditional classroom environment (e.g., summer enrichment, distance learning, weekend study, etc.)
- Students looking to place out of certain classes in college
- Students enrolled in dual-enrollment programs
- Home-schooled students or students taking courses online
- Students who feel that their course grade may not be a true reflection of their knowledge of the subject matter

Who Requires the SAT Subject Tests?

Most college websites and catalogs include information about admission requirements, including which Subject Tests are needed or recommended for admission. Schools have varying policies regarding Subject Tests, but they generally fall into one or more of the following categories:

- Required for admission
- Recommended for admission
- Required or recommended for certain majors or programs of study (e.g., engineering, honors, etc.)
- Required or recommended for certain groups of students (e.g., home-schooled students)
- Required, recommended or accepted for course placement
- Accepted for course credit
- Accepted as an alternative to fulfill certain college admission requirements
- Accepted as an alternative to fulfill certain high school subject competencies
- Accepted and considered, especially if Subject Tests improve or enhance a student's application

In addition, the College Board provides a number of resources where you can search for information about Subject Test requirements at specific colleges.

- Visit the websites of the colleges and universities that interest you.
- Visit College Search at www.collegeboard.org.
- Purchase a copy of *The College Board College Handbook*.

Some colleges require specific tests, such as mathematics or science, so it's important to make sure you understand the policies prior to choosing which Subject Test(s) to take. If you have questions or concerns about admission policies, contact college admission officers at individual schools. They are usually pleased to meet with students interested in their schools.

Subject Tests Offered

SAT Subject Tests measure how well you know a particular subject area and your ability to apply that knowledge. SAT Subject Tests aren't connected to specific textbooks or teaching methods. The content of each test evolves to reflect the latest trends in what is taught in typical high school courses in the corresponding subject.

The tests fall into five general subject areas:

	Languages	
English	**Reading Only**	**Languages with Listening**
Literature	French	Chinese
History	German	French
United States History	Italian	German
World History	Latin	Japanese
Mathematics	Modern Hebrew	Korean
Mathematics Level 1	Spanish	Spanish
Mathematics Level 2		
Science		
Biology E/M		
Chemistry		
Physics		

What the SAT Subject Tests Cover

The SAT Subject Tests are one-hour tests that assess content knowledge and interpretation and problem-solving skills acquired through high school course work.

Subject	Description	Course Work Preparation
U.S. History	• Assesses knowledge of and ability to use material commonly taught in U.S. history and social studies courses in high school • Covers political, economic, social, intellectual and cultural history as well as foreign policy from pre-Columbian history to the present	• One-year college-preparatory U.S. history course
World History	• Assesses understanding of key developments in global history, the application and weighing of evidence, and the ability to interpret and generalize • Covers the development of major world cultures, from ancient times to the present, in all historical fields: political and diplomatic, intellectual and cultural, and social and economic	• One-year college-preparatory world history course
Literature	• Assesses how well the student has learned to read and interpret literature • Covers poetry, prose and drama in English and American literature from the Renaissance to the present	• Three or four years of college-preparatory literary study
Mathematics Level 1	• Assesses mathematics knowledge through the first three years of college-preparatory mathematics course work	• Three years of college-preparatory mathematics • Two years of algebra • One year of geometry
Mathematics Level 2	• Assesses mathematics knowledge through the first three years of college-preparatory mathematics course work and precalculus	• More than three years of college-preparatory mathematics • Two years of algebra • One year of geometry • Elementary functions (precalculus) and/or trigonometry

Subject	Description	Course Work Preparation
Biology E/M (Ecological/Molecular)	• Assesses understanding of general biology • Covers knowledge of fundamental concepts, application and interpretation skills • Biology E: Focuses on biological communities, populations and energy flow • Biology M: Focuses on biochemistry, cellular structure and processes, such as respiration and photosynthesis	• One-year college-preparatory course in biology • One-year course in algebra and familiarity with simple algebraic concepts such as ratios and direct and inverse proportions • Laboratory experience (helpful)
Chemistry	• Covers the major concepts of chemistry and the ability to apply these concepts in problem-solving scenarios • Requires the ability to organize and interpret results obtained by observation and experimentation	• One-year college-preparatory course in chemistry • Familiarity with simple algebraic relationships and applying these to solving word problems • Familiarity with concepts of ratio and direct and inverse proportions, exponents, and scientific notation • Laboratory experience (helpful)
Physics	• Assesses the understanding of the major concepts of physics and the ability to apply physical principles to solve specific problems	• One-year college-preparatory physics course • Laboratory experience (helpful) • Familiarity with simple algebraic, trigonometric and graphical relationships, as well as the concepts of ratio and proportion, and applying these to physics problems • Familiarity with the metric system
Foreign Language Tests		
French, German, Italian, Latin, Modern Hebrew, Spanish, Chinese with Listening, French with Listening, German with Listening, Japanese with Listening, Korean with Listening, Spanish with Listening	• Assesses the ability to read by testing vocabulary use, language structure and comprehension of a variety of texts • Listening tests assess listening comprehension	• Two to four years of study in high school or the equivalent, or two years of strong preparation

Who Develops the Tests

The SAT Subject Tests are part of the SAT® Program of the College Board, a mission-driven not-for-profit organization of more than 5,900 of the world's leading educational institutions. Every year, the College Board helps more than seven million students prepare for a successful transition to college through programs and services in college readiness and college success.

Each subject has its own test development committee, typically composed of teachers and college professors appointed for the different Subject Tests. The test questions are written and reviewed by each Subject Test Committee, under the guidance of professional test developers. The tests are rigorously developed, highly reliable assessments of knowledge and skills taught in high school classrooms.

Deciding to Take an SAT Subject Test

Which Tests Should You Take?

The SAT Subject Tests that you take should be based on your interests and academic strengths. The tests are a great way to indicate interest in specific majors or programs of study (e.g., engineering, pre-med, cultural studies).

You should also consider whether the colleges that you're interested in require or recommend Subject Tests. Some colleges will grant an exemption from or credit for a freshman course requirement if a student does well on a particular SAT Subject Test. Below are some things for you to consider as you decide which test(s) to take.

Think through your strengths and interests

- List the subjects in which you do well and that truly interest you.
- Think through what you might like to study in college.
- Consider whether your current admission credentials (high school grades, SAT scores, etc.) highlight your strengths.

Consider the colleges that you're interested in

- Make a list of the colleges you're considering.
- Take some time to look into what these colleges require or what may help you stand out in the admission process.
- Use College Search on collegeboard.org to look up colleges' test requirements.
- If the colleges you're interested in require or recommend SAT Subject Tests, find out how many tests are required or recommended and in which subjects.

Take a look at your current and recent course load

- Have you completed the required course work? The best time to take SAT Subject Tests is at the end of the course, when the material is still fresh in your mind.

- Check the recommended preparation guidelines for the Subject Tests that interest you to see if you've completed the recommended course work.
- Try your hand at some SAT Subject Test practice questions on collegeboard.org or in this book.

Don't forget, regardless of admission requirements, you can enhance your college portfolio by taking Subject Tests in subject areas that you know very well.

If you're still unsure about which SAT Subject Tests to take, talk to your teacher or counselor about your specific situation. You can also find more information about SAT Subject Tests on collegeboard.org.

When to Take the Tests

We generally recommend that you take Subject Tests after you complete the relevant course work, prior to your senior year of high school, if possible. This way, you will already have your Subject Test credentials complete, allowing you to focus on your college applications in the fall of your senior year. If you are able to, take Subject Tests as close to the end of the course as possible, when the content is still fresh in your mind.

Since not all Subject Tests are offered on every test date, be sure to check when the Subject Tests that you're interested in are offered and plan accordingly.

You should also balance this with college application deadlines. If you're interested in applying Early Decision or Early Action to any college, many colleges advise that you take the SAT Subject Tests by October or November of your senior year. For regular decision applications, some colleges will accept SAT Subject Test scores through the December or January administration. Use College Search on collegeboard.org to look up policies for specific colleges.

This book suggests ways you can prepare for each of the SAT Subject Tests. Before taking a test in a subject you haven't studied recently, ask your teacher for advice about the best time to take the test. Then review the course material thoroughly over several weeks.

How to Register for the Tests

There are several ways to register for the SAT Subject Tests.

- Visit the College Board's website at www.collegeboard.org. Most students choose to register for Subject Tests on the College Board website.
- Register by telephone (for a fee) if you have registered previously for the SAT or an SAT Subject Test. Call, toll free from anywhere in the United States, 866-756-7346. From outside the United States, call 212-713-7789.

- If you do not have access to the Internet, registration forms are available in *The Paper Registration Guide for the SAT and SAT Subject Tests*. You can find the booklet in a guidance office at any high school or by writing to:

  The College Board
  SAT Program
  P.O. Box 025505
  Miami, FL 33102

When you register for the SAT Subject Tests, you will have to indicate the specific Subject Tests you plan to take on the test date you select. You may take one, two or three tests on any given test date; your testing fee will vary accordingly. Except for the Language Tests with Listening, you may change your mind on the day of the test and instead select from any of the other Subject Tests offered that day.

Student Search Service®

The Student Search Service® helps colleges find prospective students. If you take the PSAT/NMSQT, the SAT, an SAT Subject Test, or any AP Exam, you can be included in this free service.

Here's how it works: During SAT or SAT Subject Test registration, indicate that you want to be part of the Student Search. Your name is put in a database along with other information such as your address, high school grade point average, date of birth, grade level, high school, e-mail address, intended college major and extracurricular activities.

Colleges and scholarship programs then use the Student Search to help them locate and recruit students with characteristics that might be a good match with their schools.

Here are some points to keep in mind about the Student Search Service:

- Being part of Student Search is voluntary. You may take the test even if you don't join Student Search.
- Colleges participating in the Search do not receive your exam scores. Colleges can ask for the names of students within certain score ranges, but your exact score is not reported.
- Being contacted by a college doesn't mean you have been admitted. You can be admitted only after you apply. The Student Search Service is simply a way for colleges to reach prospective students.
- Student Search Service will share your contact information only with approved colleges and scholarship programs that are recruiting students like you. Your name will never be sold to a private company or mailing list.

Keep the Tests in Perspective

Colleges that require Subject Test scores do so because the scores are useful in making admission or placement decisions. Schools that don't have specific Subject Test policies generally review Subject Test scores during the application process because the scores can give a fuller picture of your academic achievement. The Subject Tests are a particularly helpful tool for admission and placement programs because the tests aren't tied to specific textbooks, grading procedures or instruction methods but are still tied to curricula. The tests provide level ground on which colleges can compare your scores with those of students who come from schools and backgrounds that may be far different from yours.

It's important to remember that test scores are just one of several factors that colleges consider in the admission process. Admission officers also look at your high school grades, letters of recommendation, extracurricular activities, essays and other criteria. Many colleges indicate that Subject Test results often help strengthen a student's college application. Try to keep this in mind when you are preparing for and taking Subject Tests.

Score Choice™

In March 2009, the College Board introduced Score Choice™, a feature that gives you the option to choose the scores you send to colleges by test date for the SAT® and by individual test for the SAT Subject Tests — at no additional cost. Designed to reduce your test day stress, Score Choice gives you an opportunity to show colleges the scores you feel best represent your abilities. Score Choice is optional, so if you don't actively choose to use it, all of your scores will be sent automatically with your score report. Since most colleges only consider your best scores, you should still feel comfortable reporting scores from all of your tests.

REMEMBER

Score Choice gives you an opportunity to show colleges the scores you feel best represent your abilities.

More About collegeboard.org

collegeboard.org is a comprehensive tool that can help you be prepared, connected and informed throughout the college planning and admission process. In addition to registering for the SAT and SAT Subject Tests, you can find information about other tests and services, try The Official SAT Question of the Day™, browse the College Board Store (where you can order *The Official SAT Subject Tests in U.S. and World History Study Guide*™ or *The Official SAT Subject Tests in Mathematics Levels 1 & 2 Study Guide*™), and send e-mails with your questions and concerns. collegeboard.org also contains free practice questions for each of the 20 SAT Subject Tests. These are an excellent supplement to this Study Guide and can help you be even more prepared on test day.

Once you create a free online account, you can print your SAT admission ticket, see your scores and send them to schools.

Which colleges are right for you? College Search at www.collegeboard.org has two ways to help you. The College MatchMaker lists colleges that meet all of your needs. If you are already familiar with a school, use College QuickFinder for updates of essential information. Both methods help you find the latest information on more than 3,800 colleges, as well as easy access to related tools.

How will you pay for college? While you're at the College Board website, look at the Financial Aid EasyPlanner, to help you organize your finances. It can help you find answers to such questions as: What does the school of your choice cost? How much can you save? How much can you and your family afford to pay? How much can your family afford to borrow for your education? What scholarships are available to you?

How to Do Your Best on the SAT Subject Tests

Get Ready

Give yourself several weeks before the tests to read the course materials and the suggestions in this book. The rules for the SAT Subject Tests may be different than the rules for most of the tests you've taken in high school. You're probably used to answering questions in order, spending more time answering the hard questions and, in the hopes of getting at least partial credit, showing all your work.

When you take the SAT Subject Tests, it's OK to move around within the test section and to answer questions in any order you wish. Keep in mind that the questions go from easier to harder. You receive one point for each question answered correctly. For each question that you try but answer incorrectly, a fraction of a point is subtracted from the total number of correct answers. No points are added or subtracted for unanswered questions. If your final raw score includes a fraction, the score is rounded to the nearest whole number.

Avoid Surprises

Know what to expect. Become familiar with the test and test-day procedures. You'll boost your confidence and feel a lot more relaxed.

- **Know how the tests are set up.** All SAT Subject Tests are one-hour multiple-choice tests. The first page of each Subject Test includes a background questionnaire. You will be asked to fill it out before taking the test. The information is for statistical purposes only. It will not influence your test score. Your answers to the questionnaire will assist us in developing future versions of the test. You can see a sample of the background questionnaire for each Subject Test at the start of each test in this book.
- **Learn the test directions.** The directions for answering the questions in this book are the same as those on the actual test. Some tests, such as the Subject Test in Chemistry, may have specialized directions. If you become familiar with the directions now, you'll leave yourself more time to answer the questions when you take the test.
- **Study the sample questions.** The more familiar you are with the question formats, the more comfortable you'll feel when you see similar questions on the actual test.
- **Get to know the answer sheet.** At the back of this book, you'll find a set of sample answer sheets. The appearance of the answer sheets in this book may differ from the answer sheets you see on test day.

- **Understand how the tests are scored.** You get one point for each right answer and lose a fraction of a point for each wrong answer. You neither gain nor lose points for omitting an answer. Hard questions count the same amount as easier questions.
- For additional details, see **www.collegeboard.org/subjecttests.**

A Practice Test Can Help

Find out where your strengths lie and which areas you need to work on. Do a run-through of a Subject Test under conditions that are close to what they will be on test day.

- **Set aside an hour so you can take the test without interruption.** You will be given one hour to take each SAT Subject Test.
- **Prepare a desk or table that has no books or papers on it.** No books, including dictionaries, are allowed in the test room.
- **Read the instructions that precede the practice test.** On test day, you will be asked to do this before you answer the questions.
- **Remove and fill in an answer sheet from the back of this book.** You can use one answer sheet for up to three Subject Tests.
- **Use a clock or kitchen timer to time yourself.** This will help you to pace yourself and to get used to taking a test in 60 minutes.

The Day Before the Test

It's natural to be nervous. A bit of a nervous edge can keep you sharp and focused. Below are a few suggestions to help you be more relaxed as the test approaches.

Do a brief review on the day before the test. Look through the sample questions, answer explanations and test directions in this book or on the College Board website. Keep the review brief; cramming the night before the test is unlikely to help your performance and might even make you more anxious.

The night before test day, prepare everything you need to take with you. You will need:

- your admission ticket
- an acceptable photo ID (see page 14)
- two No. 2 pencils with soft erasers (Do not bring pens or mechanical pencils.)
- a watch without an audible alarm
- an approved calculator with fresh batteries (if you are taking a Mathematics Subject Test)
- a snack
- a portable CD player with earphones that is in working order (if you are taking a Language with Listening Test)

REMEMBER

You are in control.

Come prepared.

Pace yourself.

Guess wisely.

Know the route to the test center and any instructions for finding the entrance.

Check the time your admission ticket specifies for arrival. Arrive a little early to give yourself time to settle in.

Get a good night's sleep.

Acceptable Photo IDs

- Driver's license (with your photo)
- State-issued ID
- Valid passport
- School ID card
- Student ID form that has been prepared by your school on school stationery and includes a recognizable photo and the school seal, which overlaps the photo (go to www.collegeboard.org for more information)

The most up-to-date information about acceptable photo IDs can be found on collegeboard.org.

REMINDER **What I Need on Test Day**

Make a copy of this box and post it somewhere noticeable.

I Need	I Have
Appropriate photo ID	______
Admission ticket	______
Two No. 2 pencils with clean soft erasers	______
Watch (without an audible alarm)	______
Calculator with fresh batteries (if you are taking a Mathematics Subject Test)	______
Snack	______
Bottled water	______
Directions to the test center	______
Instructions for finding the entrance on weekends	______
Portable CD player with earphones (Language with Listening test-takers only)	______

I am leaving the house at ____________ a.m.

****Be on time or you can't take the test.****

On Test Day

You have good reason to feel confident. You're thoroughly prepared. You're familiar with what this day will bring. You are in control.

Keep in Mind

You must be on time or you can't take the test. Leave yourself plenty of time for mishaps and emergencies.

Think positively. If you are worrying about not doing well, then your mind isn't on the test. Be as positive as possible.

Stay focused. Think only about the question in front of you. Letting your mind wander will cost you time.

Concentrate on your own test. The first thing some students do when they get stuck on a question is to look around to see how everyone else is doing. What they usually see is that others seem busy filling in their answer sheets. Instead of being concerned that you are not doing as well as everyone else, keep in mind that everyone works at a different pace. Your neighbors may not be working on the question that puzzled you. They may not even be taking the same test. Thinking about what others are doing distracts you from working on your own test.

Making an Educated Guess

Educated guesses are helpful when it comes to taking tests with multiple-choice questions; however, making random guesses is not a good idea. To correct for random guessing, a fraction of a point is subtracted for each incorrect answer. That means random guessing — guessing with no idea of an answer that might be correct — could lower your score. The best approach is to eliminate all the choices that you know are wrong. Make an educated guess from the remaining choices. If you can't eliminate any choices, move on.

REMEMBER

All correct answers are worth one point, regardless of the question's difficulty level.

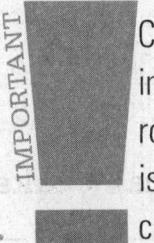

IMPORTANT

Cell phone use is prohibited in the test center or testing room. If your cell phone is on, your scores will be canceled.

10 Tips FOR TAKING THE TEST

1. **Read carefully.** Consider all the choices in each question. Avoid careless mistakes that will cause you to lose points.
2. **Answer the easy questions first.** Work on less time-consuming questions before moving on to the more difficult ones.
3. **Eliminate choices that you know are wrong.** Cross them out in your test book so that you can clearly see which choices are left.
4. **Make educated guesses or skip the question.** If you have eliminated the choices that you know are wrong, guessing is your best strategy. However, if you cannot eliminate any of the answer choices, it is best to skip the question.
5. **Keep your answer sheet neat.** The answer sheet is scored by a machine, which can't tell the difference between an answer and a doodle. If the machine mistakenly reads two answers for one question, it will consider the question unanswered.
6. **Use your test booklet as scrap paper.** Use it to make notes or write down ideas. No one else will look at what you write.
7. **Check off questions as you work on them.** This will save time and help you to know which questions you've skipped.
8. **Check your answer sheet regularly.** Make sure you are in the right place. Check the number of the question and the number on the answer sheet every few questions. This is especially important when you skip a question. Losing your place on the answer sheet will cost you time and even points.
9. **Work at an even, steady pace and keep moving.** Each question on the test takes a certain amount of time to read and answer. Good test-takers develop a sense of timing to help them complete the test. Your goal is to spend time on the questions that you are most likely to answer correctly.
10. **Keep track of time.** During the hour that each Subject Test takes, check your progress occasionally so that you know how much of the test you have completed and how much time is left. Leave a few minutes for review toward the end of the testing period.

IMPORTANT! If you erase all your answers to a Subject Test, that's the same as a request to cancel the test. All Subject Tests taken with the erased test will also be canceled.

7 Ways TO PACE YOURSELF

1. Set up a schedule. Know when you should be one-quarter of the way through and halfway through. Every now and then, check your progress against your schedule.

2. Begin to work as soon as the testing time begins. Reading the instructions and getting to know the test directions in this book ahead of time will allow you to do that.

3. Work at an even, steady pace. After you answer the questions you are sure of, move on to those for which you'll need more time.

4. Skip questions you can't answer. You might have time to return to them. Remember to mark them in your test booklet, so you'll be able to find them later.

5. As you work on a question, cross out the answers you can eliminate in your test book.

6. Go back to the questions you skipped. If you can, eliminate some of the answer choices, then make an educated guess.

7. Leave time in the last few minutes to check your answers to avoid mistakes.

REMEMBER

Check your answer sheet. Make sure your answers are dark and completely filled in. Erase completely.

After the Tests

Most, but not all, scores will be reported online several weeks after the test date. A few days later, a full score report will be available to you online. You can request a paper score report too, which arrives later. Your score report will also be mailed to your high school and to the colleges, universities and scholarship programs that you indicated when you registered or on the correction form attached to your admission ticket. The score report includes your scores, percentiles and interpretive information.

How the Tests Are Scored

Each test is scored slightly differently depending on how many answer choices there are. See specific Subject Test chapters in this book for more information. The total score for each test is on a 200- to 800-point scale. All questions on the Subject Test are multiple choice.

Each correct answer receives one point. Each incorrect answer is subtracted as follows:

- ¼ point for subtracted for each five-choice question
- ⅓ point subtracted for each four-choice question
- ½ point subtracted for each three-choice question
- 0 points subtracted for questions you don't answer

What's Your Score?

Scores are available for free at www.collegeboard.org several weeks after each Subject Test is given. You can also get your scores — for a fee — by telephone. Call customer service at 866-756-7346 in the United States. From outside the United States, call 212-713-7789.

Some scores may take longer to report. If your score report is not available online when expected, check back the following week. If you have requested a paper score report and you have not received it by eight weeks after the test date (by five weeks for online reports), contact customer service by phone at 866-756-7346 or by e-mail at sat@info.collegeboard.org.

Should You Take the Tests Again?

Before you decide whether or not to retest, you need to evaluate your scores. The best way to evaluate how you really did on a Subject Test is to compare your scores to the admission or placement requirements, or average scores, of the colleges to which you are applying. You may decide that with additional work you could do better taking the test again.

Contacting the College Board

If you have comments or questions about the tests, please write to us at The College Board SAT Program, P.O. Box 025505, Miami, FL 33102, or e-mail us at sat@info.collegeboard.org.

Chapter 1

Literature

Purpose

The Subject Test in Literature measures how well you have learned to read literary works from different periods and cultures. There is no prescribed or suggested reading list.

Format

This one-hour test consists of approximately 60 multiple-choice questions based on six to eight reading selections. About half of the selections are poetry and half are prose. Selections include complete short poems or excerpts from various works, including longer poems, stories, novels, nonfiction writing, and drama.

You are not expected to have read or studied particular poems or passages that appear on the test. Extensive knowledge of literary terminology is not essential, but the test does assume a good working knowledge of basic terminology.

All questions are based on selections from original works written in English from the Renaissance to the present. The date printed at the end of each passage or poem is the original publication date, or in some cases, the estimated date of composition. The set of 4 to 12 questions per selection may cover these aspects of a text:

- Interpret themes and meanings of a text
- Understand both denotations and connotations of words in context
- Recognize the structure of a text, including genre, development, and organization
- Respond to a writer's use of language, including diction, imagery, and figurative language, and to its effect on the reader
- Analyze aspects of narration, including narrative voice, tone, and point of view
- Analyze poetry in terms of speaker, audience, occasion, and purpose
- Understand characterization in narrative and dramatic selections

Content

All of the questions are five-choice completion questions, which fall into three categories:

- Regular multiple-choice questions ask you to choose the best response
- NOT or EXCEPT questions ask you to select the inappropriate choice from five choices
- Roman numeral questions ask you which statement or combination of statements may be the best response

Source of Questions	Approximate Percentage of Test*
English Literature	40–50%
American Literature	40–50%
Other Literature Written in English	0–10%
Chronology	
Renaissance and 17th Century	30%
18th and 19th Centuries	30%
20th Century	40%
Genre	
Poetry	40–50%
Prose	40–50%
Drama	0–10%

* The distribution of passages may vary in different editions of the test. The chart above indicates typical or average content.

The Subject Test in Literature included in this book contains 61 questions based on seven selections—"A Divine Mistress" by Thomas Carew, an excerpt from *Middlemarch* by George Eliot, an excerpt from *Our Country's Good* by Timberlake Wertenbaker, an excerpt from the *Autobiography of Benjamin Franklin*, an excerpt from *Invisible Man* by Ralph Ellison, "Of English Verse" by Edmund Waller, and "Daybreak" by Gary Soto. As frequently happens when tests are composed of lengthy sets of questions based on relatively few selections, the distribution of passages in a particular test differs somewhat from the typical or average content summarized in the chart. The test in this book, for example, contains one more selection from English Literature than from American Literature.

How to Prepare

- Close, critical reading in English and American literature from a variety of historical periods and genres
- Reading of complete novels and plays, not just excerpts
- Working knowledge of basic literary terminology, such as *speaker, tone, image, irony, alliteration*, and *stanza*

- Three or four years of literary study at the college-preparatory level
- Independent, critical reading of poetry, prose, and drama
- There is no suggested reading list

Score

The total score is reported on the 200-to-800 scale.

Sample Questions

The James Merrill poem below and many of the questions that follow it are fairly easy; however, some of the other passages and questions used in the Subject Test in Literature are likely to be more difficult.

James Merrill was a twentieth-century American poet; therefore, according to the content chart on page 20, all of the questions on this poem would be classified as American Literature, Twentieth Century, Poetry.

The directions used in the test book precede the poem.

Directions: This test consists of selections from literary works and questions on their content, form, and style. After reading each passage or poem, choose the best answer to each question and fill in the corresponding circle on the answer sheet.

Note: Pay particular attention to the requirement of questions that contain the words NOT, LEAST, or EXCEPT.

Questions 1–6. Read the following poem carefully before you choose your answers.

Kite Poem

"One is reminded of a certain person,"
Continued the parson, settling back in his chair
With a glass of port, "who sought to emulate
The sport of birds (it was something of a chore)
By climbing up on a kite. They found his coat
Two counties away; the man himself was missing."

His daughters tittered: it was meant to be a lesson
To them—they had been caught kissing, or some such nonsense,
The night before, under the crescent moon.
So, finishing his pheasant, their father began
This thirty-minute discourse ending with
A story improbable from the start. He paused for breath,

Having shown but a few of the dangers. However, the wind
Blew out the candles and the moon wrought changes
Which the daughters felt along their stockings. Then,
Thus persuaded, they fled to their young men
Waiting in the sweet night by the raspberry bed,
And kissed and kissed, as though to escape on a kite.

1. The attitude of the parson (line 2) toward the "certain person" (lines 1–6) is one of
   (A) admiration
   (B) anxiety
   (C) disdain
   (D) curiosity
   (E) grief

Choice (C) is the correct answer to question 1. In order to warn his daughters of the danger of imprudent behavior, the parson uses the tale of the person who climbed up on a kite. It is unlikely, given this purpose, that he would feel either "admiration," "anxiety," "curiosity," or "grief" for the man, and nothing in the poem suggests that the parson had any of these feelings. His attitude is one of disdain for a person whose behavior he regards as foolish.

2. The descriptive detail "settling back in his chair/With a glass of port" (lines 2–3) underscores the parson's
   (A) authority
   (B) complacency
   (C) hypocrisy
   (D) gentleness
   (E) indecisiveness

Choice (B) is the correct answer to question 2. The poem suggests that the parson is a rather rigid, formal man focused on his own comforts and ignorant of his daughters' needs. It can be inferred from the context that complacency—unaware self-satisfaction—is one element of his character. There is no evidence in the poem that the parson is either hypocritical, gentle, or indecisive. Out of context, the quotation from the poem might be interpreted as behavior associated with someone in a position of authority. In context, however, the parson is more notable for his lack of authority—his daughters titter when he lectures and ignore his advice.

3. The chief reason the parson's daughters "tittered" (line 7) is that they
   (A) were embarrassed to have been caught kissing
   (B) knew where the missing man in their father's story was
   (C) wanted to flatter their father
   (D) did not take their father's lecture seriously
   (E) took cruel pleasure in the kite flyer's disaster

Choice (D) is the correct answer to question 3. It is the most plausible explanation of why the daughters "tittered"—they did not take their father's lecture seriously. This view is supported by the daughters' actions—as soon as their father paused for breath, they did what his "thirty-minute discourse" warned them not to do. There is no indication in the poem that choices (B) or (E) are true, and if the daughters had wanted to flatter their father, as choice (C) claims, they certainly would not have tittered during his serious lecture. If choice (A) were true, it is unlikely that the daughters would have "fled to their young men" so quickly the second time.

4. The speaker's tone suggests that the reader should regard the parson's "thirty-minute discourse" (line 11) as
   (A) scholarly and enlightening
   (B) serious and important
   (C) entertaining and amusing
   (D) verbose and pedantic
   (E) grisly and morbid

Choice (D) is the correct answer to question 4. The speaker's tone suggests that the reader should regard the parson's "thirty-minute discourse" as "verbose and pedantic." The parson is presented as one who speaks at length, telling "improbable" stories and taking 30 minutes to show "but a few of the dangers" he wanted to warn his daughters about. He uses lengthy phrases such as "emulate/The sport of birds" when a simple verb such as "fly" would have sufficed. The parson might well have intended his discourse to seem "scholarly and enlightening," choice (A), and "serious and important," choice (B), but neither the daughters nor the speaker suggests that the parson succeeded, and the reader has no reason to assess the effectiveness of the discourse differently from the speaker and the daughters. The reader may be entertained and amused by the speaker's account of the discourse, but that response is not the same as being amused by the discourse itself, as choice (C) states. Choice (E) is implausible.

5. The daughters are "persuaded" (line 16) by
   (A) their own fear of danger
   (B) the fate of the kite flyer
   (C) their own natural impulses
   (D) the parson's authority
   (E) respect for their father

Choice (C) is the correct answer to question 5. The daughters are "persuaded" by their own natural impulses. According to the poem, "the moon wrought changes/Which the daughters felt along their stockings" (lines 14–15). These natural impulses were, ironically, more persuasive than the long discourse delivered by their father in an attempt to dissuade them. The daughters, like the kite flyer, are attracted to the possibility of "escape on a kite" (line 18) and are not deterred by solemn and tedious warnings of danger.

6. All of the following are elements of opposition in the development of the poem EXCEPT
   (A) indoors . . outdoors
   (B) talking . . kissing
   (C) caution . . adventure
   (D) work . . play
   (E) settling back . . flying

Choice (D) is the correct answer to question 6. It is the only opposition that is not evident in the poem. Actions such as "climbing up on a kite" and "kissing...under the crescent moon" might be regarded as forms of play, but the poem really does not offer any contrasting examples of work. Choices (A), (B), (C), and (E) illustrate the contrasting actions and attitudes of the parson on the one hand and the daughters or the kite flyer, or both, on the other.

Literature Subject Test

Practice Helps

The test that follows is an actual, previously administered SAT Subject Test in Literature. To get an idea of what it's like to take this test, practice under conditions that are much like those of an actual test administration.

- Set aside an hour when you can take the test uninterrupted.
- Sit at a desk or table with no other books or papers. Dictionaries, other books, or notes are not allowed in the test room.
- Tear out an answer sheet from the back of this book and fill it in just as you would on the day of the test. One answer sheet can be used for up to three Subject Tests.
- Read the instructions that precede the practice test. During the actual administration you will be asked to read them before answering test questions.
- Time yourself by placing a clock or kitchen timer in front of you.
- After you finish the practice test, read the sections "How to Score the SAT Subject Test in Literature" and "How Did You Do on the Subject Test in Literature?"
- The appearance of the answer sheet in this book may differ from the answer sheet you see on test day.

LITERATURE TEST

The top portion of the page of the answer sheet that you will use to take the Literature Test must be filled in exactly as illustrated below. When your supervisor tells you to fill in the circle next to the name of the test you are about to take, mark your answer sheet as shown.

● Literature	○ Mathematics Level 1	○ German	○ Chinese Listening	○ Japanese Listening
○ Biology E	○ Mathematics Level 2	○ Italian	○ French Listening	○ Korean Listening
○ Biology M	○ U.S. History	○ Latin	○ German Listening	○ Spanish Listening
○ Chemistry	○ World History	○ Modern Hebrew		
○ Physics	○ French	○ Spanish	**Background Questions:** ① ② ③ ④ ⑤ ⑥ ⑦ ⑧ ⑨	

After filling in the circle next to the name of the test you are taking, locate the Background Questions section, which also appears at the top of your answer sheet (as shown above). This is where you will answer the following Background Questions on your answer sheet.

BACKGROUND QUESTIONS

Please answer the two questions below by filling in the appropriate circle in the Background Questions box on your answer sheet. <u>The information you provide is for statistical purposes only and will not affect your test score.</u>

Answer <u>both</u> questions on the basis of the authors and works read in your English classes in grade 10 to the present.

<u>Question I</u>

How many semesters of English courses that were predominantly devoted to the study of literature have you taken from grade 10 to the present? (If you are studying literature in the current semester, count the current semester as a full semester.) Fill in only <u>one</u> circle of circles 1-3.

- One semester or less —Fill in circle 1.
- Two semesters —Fill in circle 2.
- Three semesters or more —Fill in circle 3.

<u>Question II</u>

Of the following, which content areas made up a significant part (at least 10 percent) of the literature you read in your English classes in grades 10-12 ? Fill in as many circles as apply.

- British and/or North American writers writing before 1800 —Fill in circle 4.
- European writers in translation —Fill in circle 5.
- African American and Black writers —Fill in circle 6.
- Ethnic American writers (Hispanic American, Asian American, American Indian, etc.) —Fill in circle 7.
- Latin American writers in translation —Fill in circle 8.
- Writers from Africa or India writing in English —Fill in circle 9.

When the supervisor gives the signal, turn the page and begin the Literature Test. There are 100 numbered circles on the answer sheet and 61 questions in the Literature Test. Therefore, use only circles 1 to 61 for recording your answers.

LITERATURE TEST

Directions: This test consists of selections from literary works and questions on their content, form, and style. After reading each passage or poem, choose the best answer to each question and fill in the corresponding circle on the answer sheet.

Note: Pay particular attention to the requirement of questions that contain the words NOT, LEAST, or EXCEPT.

Questions 1-7. Read the following poem carefully before you choose your answers.

A Divine Mistress

In Nature's pieces still I see
Some error that might mended be;
Something my wish could still remove,
Alter or add; but my fair love
Was framed by hands far more divine,
For she hath every beauteous line.
Yet I had been far happier
Had Nature, that made me, made her.
Then likeness might (that love creates)
Have made her love what now she hates;
Yet, I confess, I cannot spare
From her just shape the smallest hair;
Nor need I beg from all the store
Of heaven for her one beauty more.
She hath too much divinity for me:
You gods, teach her some more humanity.

(c. 1640)

1. Which of the following best restates the meaning of lines 1 and 2 ?
   (A) The natural world contains imperfections.
   (B) The natural world has only the meaning that poets give it.
   (C) The natural world has been systematically destroyed by humans.
   (D) The natural world was an accident of divinity.
   (E) The poetic imagination can create or destroy the natural world.

2. The word "framed" in line 5 is particularly appropriate in this context because it suggests the woman's
   (A) deceitfulness and evil intentions
   (B) imagination and fertility
   (C) virtue and benevolence
   (D) fickleness and ethereal nature
   (E) physical shape and aesthetic completeness

3. Which of the following could be substituted for "had been" (line 7) without changing the meaning?
   (A) was
   (B) will be
   (C) have been
   (D) would have been
   (E) ought to be

4. All of the following contrasts appear in the first ten lines of the poem EXCEPT
   (A) nature and divinity
   (B) error and perfection
   (C) similarity and difference
   (D) love and hate
   (E) innocence and experience

GO ON TO THE NEXT PAGE

5. Which of the following best states the wish of the speaker in lines 7-14 ?
   (A) He wants the woman to be even more beautiful than she is.
   (B) He wants the woman to ignore other men.
   (C) He wants the woman to be both beautiful and accessible.
   (D) He does not want the woman to love him in the same way he loves her.
   (E) He does not want the woman to be so vain.

6. The speaker's tone in lines 15-16 is best described as
   (A) bitter sarcasm
   (B) amused indifference
   (C) dignified solemnity
   (D) playful exasperation
   (E) cold rationality

7. The unannounced intention of the speaker in this poem is to
   (A) commend a woman for her impeccable virtue
   (B) praise a woman for her unequaled beauty
   (C) make a woman more receptive to his passion
   (D) delude a woman into thinking that he loves her
   (E) flatter a woman so that she will have a better opinion of herself

GO ON TO THE NEXT PAGE

Questions 8-17. Read the following passage carefully before you choose your answers.

He had not had much foretaste of happiness in his previous life. To know intense joy without a strong bodily frame, one must have an enthusiastic soul. Mr. Casaubon had never had a strong bodily frame, and his soul was sensitive without being enthusiastic: it was too languid to thrill out of self-consciousness into passionate delight; it went on fluttering in the swampy ground where it was hatched, thinking of its wings and never flying. His experience was of that pitiable kind which shrinks from pity, and fears most of all that it should be known: it was that proud narrow sensitiveness which has not mass enough to spare for transformation into sympathy, and quivers thread-like in small currents of self-preoccupation or at best of an egoistic scrupulosity. And Mr. Casaubon had many scruples: he was capable of a severe self-restraint; he was resolute in being a man of honour according to the code; he would be unimpeachable by any recognised opinion. In conduct these ends had been attained; but the difficulty of making his *Key to all Mythologies* unimpeachable weighed like lead upon his mind; and the pamphlets—or "Parerga"[1] as he called them—by which he tested his public and deposited small monumental records of his march, were far from having been seen in all their significance. He suspected the Archdeacon of not having read them; he was in painful doubt as to what was really thought of them by the leading minds of Brasenose,[2] and bitterly convinced that his old acquaintance Carp had been the writer of that depreciatory recension which was kept locked in a small drawer of Mr. Casaubon's desk, and also in a dark closet of his verbal memory. These were heavy impressions to struggle against, and brought that melancholy embitterment which is the consequence of all excessive claim: even his religious faith wavered with his wavering trust in his own authorship, and the consolations of the Christian hope in immortality seemed to lean on the immortality of the still unwritten *Key to all Mythologies.*

(1871)

[1] Greek term for supplementary or secondary works

[2] a college at Oxford

8. The passage is best described as an example of

(A) character analysis
(B) historical commentary
(C) allegorical drama
(D) interior monologue
(E) political satire

9. By the end of the passage, Casaubon emerges as

(A) crude and inconsiderate
(B) insecure and self-centered
(C) temperamental and rebellious
(D) sensitive but self-confident
(E) ambitious but generous

10. In the context of the passage, the image of the fluttering bird "thinking of its wings and never flying" (lines 8-9) is most suggestive of

(A) Casaubon's lifelong aversion to physical activities
(B) Casaubon's control over his imagination and emotions
(C) the limiting effect of Casaubon's self-consciousness
(D) the nobility of Casaubon's physical and mental striving
(E) the liberating influence of Casaubon's scholarly intellect

11. Casaubon's struggle to make "his *Key to all Mythologies* unimpeachable" (lines 20-21) can be best viewed as an example of his

(A) dedication to an outdated code of honor
(B) enthusiasm only for intellectual pursuits
(C) unrealistic expectations of achievement
(D) rivalry with the Archdeacon
(E) tendency toward procrastination

GO ON TO THE NEXT PAGE

12. The phrase "tested his public" (line 23) means that Casaubon
    (A) tried the patience of those who were eagerly waiting for his *Key to all Mythologies*
    (B) evaluated his popularity with the general reading public
    (C) examined the public on its knowledge of mythological literature
    (D) attempted to confirm publicly the validity of his scholarly project
    (E) compared the public's reaction to his pamphlets with that of the scholarly community

13. The statement "These were . . . excessive claim" (lines 33-36) can be best interpreted as
    (A) a paraphrase of the negative responses to Casaubon's work
    (B) a generalization about human nature applicable to Casaubon's personality
    (C) an allusion to Casaubon's earlier years of unhappiness
    (D) a denunciation of harsh critics like Carp
    (E) a plea for sympathy for Casaubon

14. The repeated reference to smallness—"shrinks" (line 10), "has not mass enough" (line 12), "small currents" (line 14), "small monumental records" (line 24), and "small drawer" (lines 31-32)—has the cumulative effect of reinforcing the theme of Casaubon's
    (A) aptitude for analyzing only the small details in his life
    (B) intellectual and emotional limitations
    (C) modesty and lack of idealism
    (D) heroic struggle against the weight of public opinion
    (E) inability to live up to his reputation as an eminent scholar

15. In context, the comment "the consolations of the Christian hope in immortality seemed to lean on the immortality of the still unwritten *Key to all Mythologies*" (lines 37-40) suggests the narrator's belief that
    (A) Casaubon's scholarly work would be a contribution to the Christian community
    (B) Casaubon hoped that his work, when completed, would be as widely read as the Bible
    (C) Casaubon relied desperately on his religious faith to help him complete his manuscript
    (D) the importance Casaubon ascribed to his work was greatly inflated
    (E) the suffering and humiliation endured by Casaubon would make his work immortal

16. Which of the following references is NOT metaphorical but actually describes a physical act performed by Casaubon?
    (A) "fluttering in the swampy ground" (lines 7-8)
    (B) "quivers thread-like in small currents" (lines 13-14)
    (C) "weighed like lead" (line 21)
    (D) "deposited small monumental records of his march" (line 24)
    (E) "locked in a small drawer" (lines 31-32)

17. The narrator's attitude toward Casaubon is primarily one of
    (A) ambivalence
    (B) puzzlement
    (C) revulsion
    (D) bitter disparagement
    (E) incisive criticism

GO ON TO THE NEXT PAGE

Questions 18-27. Read the following dramatic excerpt carefully before you choose your answers.

In this scene, the somewhat inebriated officers of an eighteenth-century Australian penal colony debate the merits of Second Lieutenant Ralph Clark's proposal to stage a play—George Farquhar's "The Recruiting Officer"—using the convicts as actors.

REVEREND JOHNSON: What is the plot, Ralph?

RALPH: It's about this recruiting officer and his friend, and they are in love with these two young ladies from Shrewsbury and after some difficulties, they marry them.

REV. JOHNSON: It sanctions Holy Matrimony then?

RALPH: Yes, yes, it does.

REV. JOHNSON: That wouldn't do the convicts any harm. I'm having such trouble getting them to marry instead of this sordid cohabitation they're so used to.

ROSS: Marriage, plays, why not a ball for the convicts!

CAMPBELL: Euuh. Boxing.

ARTHUR PHILLIP: Some of these men will have finished their sentence in a few years. They will become members of society again, and help create a new society in this colony. Should we not encourage them now to think in a free and responsible manner?

TENCH: I don't see how a comedy about two lovers will do that, Arthur.

ARTHUR PHILLIP: The theatre is an expression of civilisation. We belong to a great country which has spawned great playwrights: Shakespeare, Marlowe, Jonson, and even in our own time, Sheridan. The convicts will be speaking a refined, literate language and expressing sentiments of a delicacy they are not used to. It will remind them that there is more to life than crime, punishment. And we, this colony of a few hundred will be watching this together, for a few hours we will no longer be despised prisoners and hated gaolers. We will laugh, we may be moved, we may even think a little. Can you suggest something else that will provide such an evening, Watkin?

DAWES: Mapping the stars gives me more enjoyment, personally.

TENCH: I'm not sure it's a good idea having the convicts laugh at officers, Arthur.

CAMPBELL: No. Pheeoh, insubordination, heh, ehh, no discipline.

ROSS: You want this vice-ridden vermin to enjoy themselves?

COLLINS: They would only laugh at Sergeant Kite.

RALPH: Captain Plume is a most attractive, noble fellow.

REV. JOHNSON: He's not loose, is he Ralph? I hear many of these plays are about rakes and encourage loose morals in women. They do get married? Before, that is, before. And for the right reasons.

RALPH: They marry for love and to secure wealth.

REV. JOHNSON: That's all right.

TENCH: I would simply say that if you want to build a civilisation there are more important things than a play. If you want to teach the convicts something, teach them to farm, to build houses, teach them a sense of respect for property, teach them thrift so they don't eat a week's rations in one night, but above all, teach them how to work, not how to sit around laughing at a comedy.

ARTHUR PHILLIP: The Greeks believed that it was a citizen's duty to watch a play. It was a kind of work in that it required attention, judgement, patience, all social virtues.

TENCH: And the Greeks were conquered by the more practical Romans, Arthur.

COLLINS: Indeed, the Romans built their bridges, but they also spent many centuries wishing they were Greeks. And they, after all, were conquered by barbarians, or by their own corrupt and small spirits.

TENCH: Are you saying Rome would not have fallen if the theatre had been better?

GO ON TO THE NEXT PAGE

RALPH (*very loud*): Why not? (*Everyone looks at him and he continues, fast and nervously.*) In my own small way, in just a few hours, I have seen something change. I asked some of the convict women to read me some lines, these women who behave often no better than animals. And it seemed to me, as one or two—I'm not saying all of them, not at all—but one or two, saying those well-balanced lines of Mr. Farquhar, they seemed to acquire a dignity, they seemed—they seemed to lose some of their corruption. There was one, Mary Brenham, she read so well, perhaps this play will keep her from selling herself to the first marine who offers her bread—

FADDY (*under his breath*): She'll sell herself to him, instead.

ROSS: So that's the way the wind blows—

CAMPBELL: Hooh. A tempest. Hooh.

RALPH: (*over them*): I speak about her, but in a small way this could affect all the convicts and even ourselves, we could forget our worries about the supplies, the hangings and the floggings, and think of ourselves at the theatre, in London with our wives and children, that is, we could, euh—

ARTHUR PHILLIP: Transcend—

RALPH: Transcend the darker, euh—transcend the—

JOHNSTON: Brutal—

RALPH: The brutality—remember our better nature and remember—

COLLINS: England.

RALPH: England.

(1988)

18. The positions articulated by Reverend Johnson and Arthur Phillip are alike in that both men

    (A) believe that great art is defined by its morality
    (B) assume the convicts will value the beliefs of the characters they observe
    (C) see entertainment as a distraction that will pacify the convicts
    (D) think that presenting harsh social realities will lead to moral reformation
    (E) rely on empirical evidence for their credibility

19. Arthur Phillip's invocation of Shakespeare, Marlowe, Jonson, and Sheridan (lines 23-25) can be most aptly described as

    (A) an irrefutable argument about the value of drama
    (B) a pedantic display of expert learning
    (C) an irrelevant aside
    (D) an appeal to a tradition of national culture
    (E) a justification of lovers' comedies

20. The arguments advanced about performing a play invoke all of the following issues EXCEPT the

    (A) representation of immoral behavior
    (B) desirability of reforming convicts
    (C) values of the colonizing country
    (D) possibility of transcending local circumstances
    (E) merit of staging plays about convicts

21. If Tench's position in lines 52-59 is valid, then, by contrast, the views of Ralph and Arthur Phillip are

    (A) without historical precedent
    (B) not sufficiently pragmatic
    (C) morally irresponsible
    (D) philosophically questionable
    (E) self-interested

22. The tone of Tench's question in lines 70-71 can best be described as

    (A) sardonically contentious
    (B) dispassionately curious
    (C) sympathetically supportive
    (D) personally offended
    (E) humorously credulous

GO ON TO THE NEXT PAGE

This passage is reprinted for your use in answering the remaining questions.

In this scene, the somewhat inebriated officers of an eighteenth-century Australian penal colony debate the merits of Second Lieutenant Ralph Clark's proposal to stage a play—George Farquhar's "The Recruiting Officer"—using the convicts as actors.

REVEREND JOHNSON: What is the plot, Ralph?

RALPH: It's about this recruiting officer and his friend, and they are in love with these two young ladies from Shrewsbury and after some difficulties, they marry them.

REV. JOHNSON: It sanctions Holy Matrimony then?

RALPH: Yes, yes, it does.

REV. JOHNSON: That wouldn't do the convicts any harm. I'm having such trouble getting them to marry instead of this sordid cohabitation they're so used to.

ROSS: Marriage, plays, why not a ball for the convicts!

CAMPBELL: Euuh. Boxing.

ARTHUR PHILLIP: Some of these men will have finished their sentence in a few years. They will become members of society again, and help create a new society in this colony. Should we not encourage them now to think in a free and responsible manner?

TENCH: I don't see how a comedy about two lovers will do that, Arthur.

ARTHUR PHILLIP: The theatre is an expression of civilisation. We belong to a great country which has spawned great playwrights: Shakespeare, Marlowe, Jonson, and even in our own time, Sheridan. The convicts will be speaking a refined, literate language and expressing sentiments of a delicacy they are not used to. It will remind them that there is more to life than crime, punishment. And we, this colony of a few hundred will be watching this together, for a few hours we will no longer be despised prisoners and hated gaolers. We will laugh, we may be moved, we may even think a little. Can you suggest something else that will provide such an evening, Watkin?

DAWES: Mapping the stars gives me more enjoyment, personally.

TENCH: I'm not sure it's a good idea having the convicts laugh at officers, Arthur.

CAMPBELL: No. Pheeoh, insubordination, heh, ehh, no discipline.

ROSS: You want this vice-ridden vermin to enjoy themselves?

COLLINS: They would only laugh at Sergeant Kite.

RALPH: Captain Plume is a most attractive, noble fellow.

REV. JOHNSON: He's not loose, is he Ralph? I hear many of these plays are about rakes and encourage loose morals in women. They do get married? Before, that is, before. And for the right reasons.

RALPH: They marry for love and to secure wealth.

REV. JOHNSON: That's all right.

TENCH: I would simply say that if you want to build a civilisation there are more important things than a play. If you want to teach the convicts something, teach them to farm, to build houses, teach them a sense of respect for property, teach them thrift so they don't eat a week's rations in one night, but above all, teach them how to work, not how to sit around laughing at a comedy.

ARTHUR PHILLIP: The Greeks believed that it was a citizen's duty to watch a play. It was a kind of work in that it required attention, judgement, patience, all social virtues.

TENCH: And the Greeks were conquered by the more practical Romans, Arthur.

COLLINS: Indeed, the Romans built their bridges, but they also spent many centuries wishing they were Greeks. And they, after all, were conquered by barbarians, or by their own corrupt and small spirits.

TENCH: Are you saying Rome would not have fallen if the theatre had been better?

GO ON TO THE NEXT PAGE

RALPH (*very loud*): Why not? (*Everyone looks at him and he continues, fast and nervously.*) In my own small way, in just a few hours, I have seen something change. I asked some of the convict women to read me some lines, these women who behave often no better than animals. And it seemed to me, as one or two—I'm not saying all of them, not at all—but one or two, saying those well-balanced lines of Mr. Farquhar, they seemed to acquire a dignity, they seemed—they seemed to lose some of their corruption. There was one, Mary Brenham, she read so well, perhaps this play will keep her from selling herself to the first marine who offers her bread—

FADDY (*under his breath*): She'll sell herself to him, instead.

ROSS: So that's the way the wind blows—

CAMPBELL: Hooh. A tempest. Hooh.

RALPH: (*over them*): I speak about her, but in a small way this could affect all the convicts and even ourselves, we could forget our worries about the supplies, the hangings and the floggings, and think of ourselves at the theatre, in London with our wives and children, that is, we could, euh—

ARTHUR PHILLIP: Transcend—

RALPH: Transcend the darker, euh—transcend the—

JOHNSTON: Brutal—

RALPH: The brutality—remember our better nature and remember—

COLLINS: England.

RALPH: England.

(1988)

23. Faddy's interruption (lines 85-86) of Ralph's reflections functions as which of the following?

    I. A comic aside
    II. A cynical deflation of pretension
    III. A reprimand for poor taste

    (A) I only
    (B) III only
    (C) I and II only
    (D) I and III only
    (E) I, II, and III

24. Ross's comment in line 87 most probably refers to his

    (A) appreciation of Faddy's sense of humor
    (B) assessment of Mary Brenham's character
    (C) perception of Ralph's underlying motives
    (D) recognition of the validity of Ralph's argument
    (E) indifference to the topic at hand

25. The moral effect of speaking the well-written language of the play is most persuasively argued by

    (A) Reverend Johnson
    (B) Tench
    (C) Campbell
    (D) Collins
    (E) Ralph

26. The characters want to "remember . . . England" (lines 99-102) because for them England is

    (A) no longer the country that Shakespeare knew
    (B) the ideal civilization
    (C) the home of the theatre's most skilled performers
    (D) a reminder of their authority
    (E) the country in which comedy serves a social purpose

27. The excerpt thematically explores the

    (A) history of drama in recent centuries
    (B) importance of wholesome entertainment
    (C) need for reform in government
    (D) nature and purpose of drama itself
    (E) tendency of people everywhere to engage in acting

GO ON TO THE NEXT PAGE

Questions 28-35. Read the following passage carefully before you choose your answers.

I believe I have omitted mentioning that in my first Voyage from Boston, being becalm'd off Block Island, our People set about catching Cod and hawl'd up a great many. Hitherto I had stuck to my Resolution of not eating animal Food; and on this Occasion, I consider'd with my Master Tryon,* the taking every Fish as a kind of unprovok'd Murder, since none of them had or ever could do us any Injury that might justify the Slaughter. All this seem'd very reasonable. But I had formerly been a great Lover of Fish, and when this came hot out of the Frying Pan, it smelt admirably well. I balanc'd some time between Principle and Inclination: till I recollected, that when the Fish were opened, I saw smaller Fish taken out of their Stomachs: Then thought I, if you eat one another, I don't see why we mayn't eat you. So I din'd upon Cod very heartily and continu'd to eat with other People, returning only now and then occasionally to a vegetable Diet. So convenient a thing it is to be a *reasonable Creature*, since it enables one to find or make a Reason for every thing one has a mind to do.

(1791)

* The author of a book espousing vegetarianism

28. As it is used in line 13, "Inclination" means

(A) leaning, bending
(B) slant, slope
(C) bowing, nodding
(D) disposition, preference
(E) decision, determination

29. Which of the following best describes the tone of the sentence "Then thought I, if you eat one another, I don't see why we mayn't eat you" (lines 15-16) ?

(A) Witty
(B) Inquiring
(C) Critical
(D) Defiant
(E) Sincere

30. As used in lines 20-21, the phrase "find or make a Reason for" means

(A) show enthusiasm for
(B) understand the outcome of
(C) think of an excuse to justify
(D) examine the motivation behind
(E) weigh the advantages and disadvantages of

31. In the final sentence of the passage, the speaker can be best described as

(A) humorously self-aware
(B) objective and matter-of-fact
(C) slightly befuddled
(D) selfish and immodest
(E) thoroughly disillusioned

GO ON TO THE NEXT PAGE

32. Which statements about the speaker's vegetarianism can be inferred from the passage?

    I. It had been adopted in response to reading Tryon's book.
    II. It was based on a concern for the just treatment of animals.
    III. It was chosen because it seemed to be rational behavior.

    (A) I only
    (B) II only
    (C) I and II only
    (D) II and III only
    (E) I, II, and III

33. Which of the following shows the use of hyperbole?

    (A) "great many" (line 4)
    (B) "Murder" (line 7) and "Slaughter" (line 9)
    (C) "Injury" (line 8) and "reasonable" (line 9)
    (D) "admirably well" (line 12)
    (E) "very heartily" (line 17)

34. The tone of the final sentence is established by which of the following?

    I. The use of the word "convenient"
    II. The italicization of "*reasonable Creature*"
    III. The use of the phrase "to find or make a Reason"

    (A) II only
    (B) I and II only
    (C) I and III only
    (D) II and III only
    (E) I, II, and III

35. The speaker actually abandons vegetarianism because the speaker

    (A) cannot find a reasonable argument for continuing it
    (B) has never been convinced by the arguments for it
    (C) is convinced that the big fish deserves to be eaten
    (D) loves cod more than meat
    (E) has an appetite that outweighs abstract principles

GO ON TO THE NEXT PAGE

Questions 36-44. Read the following passage carefully before you choose your answers.

I am not ashamed of my grandparents for having been slaves. I am only ashamed of myself for having at one time been ashamed. About eighty-five years ago they were told that they were free, united with others of our country in everything pertaining to the common good, and, in everything social, separate like the fingers of the hand. And they believed it. They exulted in it. They stayed in their place, worked hard, and brought up my father to do the same. But my grandfather is the one. He was an odd old guy, my grandfather, and I am told I take after him. It was he who caused the trouble. On his deathbed he called my father to him and said, "Son, after I'm gone I want you to keep up the good fight. I never told you, but our life is a war and I have been a traitor all my born days, a spy in the enemy's country ever since I give up my gun back in the Reconstruction. Live with your head in the lion's mouth. I want you to overcome 'em with yeses, undermine 'em with grins, agree 'em to death and destruction, let 'em swoller you till they vomit or bust wide open." They thought the old man had gone out of his mind. He had been the meekest of men. The younger children were rushed from the room, the shades drawn and the flame of the lamp turned so low that it sputtered on the wick like the old man's breathing. "Learn it to the younguns," he whispered fiercely; then he died.

But my folks were more alarmed over his last words than over his dying. It was as though he had not died at all, his words caused so much anxiety. I was warned emphatically to forget what he had said and, indeed, this is the first time it has been mentioned outside the family circle. It had a tremendous effect upon me, however. I could never be sure of what he meant. Grandfather had been a quiet old man who never made any trouble, yet on his deathbed he had called himself a traitor and a spy, and he had spoken of his meekness as a dangerous activity. It became a constant puzzle which lay unanswered in the back of my mind. And whenever things went well for me I remembered my grandfather and felt guilty and uncomfortable. It was as though I was carrying out his advice in spite of myself. And to make it worse, everyone loved me for it. I was praised by the most lily-white men of the town. I was considered an example of desirable conduct—just as my grandfather had been. And what puzzled me was that the old man had defined it as *treachery*. When I was praised for my conduct I felt a guilt that in some way I was doing something that was really against the wishes of the white folks, that if they had understood they would have desired me to act just the opposite, that I should have been sulky and mean, and that that really would have been what they wanted, even though they were fooled and thought they wanted me to act as I did. It made me afraid that some day they would look upon me as a traitor and I would be lost. Still I was more afraid to act any other way because they didn't like that at all. The old man's words were like a curse. On my graduation day I delivered an oration in which I showed that humility was the secret, indeed, the very essence of progress. (Not that I believed this —how could I, remembering my grandfather?—I only believed that it worked.) It was a great success. Everyone praised me and I was invited to give the speech at a gathering of the town's leading white citizens. It was a triumph for our whole community.

(1952)

36. The narrator's central concern in the passage is

(A) curiosity about his family history
(B) uneasiness about his family's care of his dying grandfather
(C) frustration with the limitations imposed by his parents
(D) a sense of being betrayed by the leading citizens of the town
(E) uncertainty about how he should act

37. The simile of the hand (line 7) suggests

(A) acceptance of change in social worlds
(B) a rationale for a segregated social system
(C) a symbol of racial pride
(D) hard work as the basis for economic prosperity
(E) a physical basis for similarities and differences

GO ON TO THE NEXT PAGE

38. In the context of lines 1-9, the narrator is suggesting that his grandparents
    (A) built an ideal life after they had been freed
    (B) were proud of the efforts they made to achieve their freedom
    (C) appeared to have adopted socially approved values
    (D) were unusual among the former slaves of their generation
    (E) lived in the past rather than the present

39. The grandfather's injunction "to overcome 'em with yeses, undermine 'em with grins" (lines 18-19) asks for
    (A) optimism in the face of adversity
    (B) resignation when change is impossible
    (C) subtle imitation as a way to gain favor
    (D) seeming acquiescence as a means of rebellion
    (E) unforced graciousness toward defeated opponents

40. The fact that the narrator has never, before now, mentioned his grandfather's dying words outside the family circle suggests that he has
    (A) been deliberately disrespectful to his grandfather
    (B) felt that the words were entrusted to him
    (C) concluded that no one would be interested in them
    (D) not bothered to think about them
    (E) felt profoundly anxious about them

41. The lifelong behavior and the deathbed words of his grandfather, taken together, puzzle the narrator because they
    (A) imply that the grandfather was not devoted to his family
    (B) require the narrator to assume a position of leadership
    (C) seem to reflect contradictory impulses
    (D) prove that direct confrontations are undesirable
    (E) suggest that unqualified victory is attainable

42. It can be inferred from the passage that the grandfather regarded what he called treachery as
    (A) an affirmative act, because the deception allows you to prevail
    (B) a useless act, because those who are betrayed are too obtuse to notice
    (C) an innocent act, because no one is misled by it
    (D) an honorable act, because the behavior exhibited is friendly and agreeable
    (E) an unintentional act, because no one would knowingly engage in such dangerous behavior

43. By "worked" (line 64), the narrator means
    (A) pleased the leading citizens of the community
    (B) brought about intellectual progress
    (C) shocked the graduating class
    (D) encouraged frank discussion of bias
    (E) openly challenged racist assumptions

44. In the context of the passage, the sentence "It was a triumph for our whole community" (line 67) suggests that
    (A) the triumph was not necessarily what it seemed
    (B) humility and triumph are irreconcilable
    (C) the grandfather's battle has temporarily been halted
    (D) formal education will reduce racial discrimination
    (E) the nature of language is essentially deceptive

GO ON TO THE NEXT PAGE

Questions 45-51. Read the following poem carefully before you choose your answers.

Of English Verse

Poets may boast, as safely vain,
Their works shall with the world remain;
Both, bound together, live or die,
The verses and the prophecy.

But who can hope his lines should long
Last in a daily changing tongue?
While they are new, envy prevails;
And as that dies, our language fails.

When architects have done their part,
The matter may betray their art;
Time, if we use ill-chosen stone,
Soon brings a well-built palace down.

Poets that lasting marble seek
Must carve in Latin or in Greek;
We write in sand, our language grows,
And, like the tide, our work o'erflows.

Chaucer[1] his sense can only boast,
The glory of his numbers lost!
Years have defaced his matchless strain,
And yet he did not sing in vain.

The beauties which adorned that age,
The shining subjects of his rage,[2]
Hoping they should immortal prove,
Rewarded with success his love.

This was the generous poet's scope,
And all an English pen can hope,
To make the fair approve his flame,
That can so far extend their fame.

Verse, thus designed, has no ill fate
If it arrive but at the date
Of fading beauty; if it prove
But as long-lived as present love.

(1668)

[1] Fourteenth-century poet whose works, written in Middle English, reflect features that English has lost

[2] Poetic inspiration

45. In the context of lines 5-8, "fails" presents the English language as

(A) possessing a vocabulary too narrow to express the richness of human experience
(B) reflecting the central weakness of a society consumed by jealousy of talent
(C) containing too few beauties of sound for spoken poetry to please listeners
(D) imitating the worst features of languages like Latin and Greek
(E) undergoing too many transformations to preserve all the original qualities of a poem

46. In the argument of the poem, the function of the third stanza is to show that

(A) the art of poetry is superior to the art of architecture
(B) architecture requires artistic skills as great as those of poetry
(C) worldly pomp is subject to the power of time
(D) art lasts only as long as its materials do
(E) the choice of subject may determine the usefulness of a work of art

47. In the fourth stanza, all of the following words are used metaphorically EXCEPT

(A) "Poets" (line 13)
(B) "marble" (line 13)
(C) "carve" (line 14)
(D) "sand" (line 15)
(E) "o'erflows" (line 16)

48. In line 14, the speaker refers to Latin and Greek because

(A) classical civilization is noted for its marble temples and statues
(B) they are thought of as unchanging languages
(C) the greatest poetry has been written in Latin and Greek
(D) time renders all languages obsolete
(E) the inscriptions on tombs are frequently written in Latin and Greek

GO ON TO THE NEXT PAGE

49. In lines 15-16, "grows" implies that English does which of the following?

(A) Becomes more refined in its vocabulary.
(B) Changes inevitably with the passage of time.
(C) Alters imperceptibly to reflect social transformations.
(D) Evolves away from its original purity and simplicity.
(E) Gains a new power of expression.

50. According to lines 29-32, what trait does "Verse" share with "fading beauty" and "present love" ?

(A) Sentimental appeal to nostalgic temperament
(B) Dazzling effect on the speaker
(C) Lack of recognition by fashionable society
(D) Beauty that must endure hardship before triumphing
(E) Value that can last only a limited time

51. Which of the following does the poem most frequently employ?

(A) Hyperbole
(B) Apostrophe
(C) Antithesis
(D) Euphemism
(E) Metaphor

GO ON TO THE NEXT PAGE

Questions 52-61. Read the following poem carefully before you choose your answers.

Daybreak

In this moment when the light starts up
In the east and rubs
The horizon until it catches fire,

We enter the fields to hoe,
Row after row, among the small flags of onion,
Waving off the dragonflies
That ladder the air.

And tears the onions raise
Do not begin in your eyes but in ours,
In the salt blown
From one blister into another;

They begin in knowing
You will never waken to bear
The hour timed to a heart beat,
The wind pressing us closer to the ground.

When the season ends,
And the onions are unplugged from their sleep,
We won't forget what you failed to see,
And nothing will heal
Under the rain's broken fingers.

(1977)

52. The tone of the poem is best described as one of

(A) shock
(B) anxiety
(C) rationalization
(D) bitterness and pain
(E) resignation and apathy

53. The basic opposition in the poem is between

(A) the employed and the unemployed
(B) time and timelessness
(C) worker and consumer
(D) misery and elation
(E) machines and laborers

54. In light of the poem as a whole, the figurative language of the first stanza sets a scene with an image of

(A) peace
(B) creativity
(C) affection
(D) friction
(E) chaos

55. The effect of lines 14 and 15 is to

(A) illustrate the conditions that the workers have to endure
(B) show how nature both helps and hinders those who work in the fields
(C) suggest that while nature is changeable, human will is constant
(D) imply that those who study nature will eventually realize their own shortcomings
(E) suggest that workers who have pride in what they do can withstand adversity

56. The relation between the third and fourth stanzas might best be described as a

(A) change from one explanation for the tears to another
(B) contrast between experienced and anticipated pain
(C) progression in time from the past to the present
(D) movement from the concerns of consumers to the concerns of workers
(E) shift in tone from acceptance to denial

57. In line 17, "unplugged from their sleep" means

(A) planted
(B) cultivated
(C) harvested
(D) consumed
(E) replenished

GO ON TO THE NEXT PAGE

58. Which of the following will not "heal" (line 19) ?

I. The problems of the workers
II. The tears of "you"
III. The rift between "we" and "you"

(A) I only
(B) I and II only
(C) I and III only
(D) II and III only
(E) I, II, and III

59. In context, the image of the "rain's broken fingers" (line 20) calls attention to the

(A) decreasing profit margin of farming
(B) disappointment of the workers when a crop is poor
(C) difficulty of the workers' situation
(D) inconveniences that adverse weather conditions produce in modern life
(E) failure of science in predicting the weather

60. The physical labor the speaker describes is presented as

(A) an occupation that ruthlessly exploits natural resources
(B) a difficult but satisfying way of earning a living
(C) an opportunity to be at one with nature
(D) a way of life that is about to become outdated
(E) a painful and unappreciated endeavor

61. The speaker suggests that the "you" referred to in the poem can best be characterized as

(A) ignorant or unseeing
(B) sentimental and foolish
(C) greedy or wasteful
(D) physically exhausted
(E) emotionally unstable

STOP

IF YOU FINISH BEFORE TIME IS CALLED, YOU MAY CHECK YOUR WORK ON THIS TEST ONLY. DO NOT TURN TO ANY OTHER TEST IN THIS BOOK.

ACKNOWLEDGMENTS

From *NEW AND SELECTED POEMS* by Gary Soto © 1995. Reprinted by permission of Chronicle Books, San Francisco.

How to Score the SAT Subject Test in Literature

When you take an actual SAT Subject Test in Literature, your answer sheet will be "read" by a scanning machine that will record your response to each question. Then a computer will compare your answers with the correct answers and produce your raw score. You get one point for each correct answer. For each wrong answer, you lose one-fourth of a point. Questions you omit (and any for which you mark more than one answer) are not counted. This raw score is converted to a scaled score that is reported to you and to the colleges you specify.

Worksheet 1. Finding Your Raw Test Score

STEP 1: Table A on the following page lists the correct answers for all the questions on the Subject Test in Literature that is reproduced in this book. It also serves as a worksheet for you to calculate your raw score.

- Compare your answers with those given in the table.
- Put a check in the column marked "Right" if your answer is correct.
- Put a check in the column marked "Wrong" if your answer is incorrect.
- Leave both columns blank if you omitted the question.

STEP 2: Count the number of right answers.

Enter the total here: ________________

STEP 3: Count the number of wrong answers.

Enter the total here: ________________

STEP 4: Multiply the number of wrong answers by .250.

Enter the product here: ______________

STEP 5: Subtract the result obtained in Step 4 from the total you obtained in Step 2.

Enter the result here: _______________

STEP 6: Round the number obtained in Step 5 to the nearest whole number.

Enter the result here: _______________

The number you obtained in Step 6 is your raw score.

Table A

Answers to the Subject Test in Literature and Percentage of Students Answering Each Question Correctly

Question Number	Correct Answer	Right	Wrong	Percentage of Students Answering the Question Correctly*	Question Number	Correct Answer	Right	Wrong	Percentage of Students Answering the Question Correctly*
1	A			94	32	E			44
2	E			75	33	B			50
3	D			75	34	E			40
4	E			81	35	E			41
5	C			44	36	E			86
6	D			32	37	B			66
7	C			55	38	C			46
8	A			84	39	D			60
9	B			69	40	E			50
10	C			68	41	C			79
11	C			57	42	A			57
12	D			20	43	A			66
13	B			33	44	A			49
14	B			49	45	E			70
15	D			34	46	D			57
16	E			59	47	A			75
17	E			41	48	B			74
18	B			62	49	B			55
19	D			52	50	E			50
20	E			57	51	E			75
21	B			52	52	D			78
22	A			38	53	C			75
23	C			55	54	D			52
24	C			33	55	A			63
25	E			75	56	A			29
26	B			70	57	C			82
27	D			70	58	C			68
28	D			72	59	C			66
29	A			54	60	E			85
30	C			82	61	A			88
31	A			69					

* These percentages are based on an analysis of the answer sheets of a representative sample of 12,064 students who took the original administration of this test and whose mean score was 579. They may be used as an indication of the relative difficulty of a particular question.

Answer explanations for the Subject Test in Literature can be found on page 50.

Finding Your Scaled Score

When you take SAT Subject Tests, the scores sent to the colleges you specify are reported on the College Board scale, which ranges from 200–800. You can convert your practice test score to a scaled score by using Table B. To find your scaled score, locate your raw score in the left-hand column of Table B; the corresponding score in the right-hand column is your scaled score. For example, a raw score of 21 on this particular edition of the Subject Test in Literature corresponds to a scaled score of 500.

Raw scores are converted to scaled scores to ensure that a score earned on any one edition of a particular Subject Test is comparable to the same scaled score earned on any other edition of the same Subject Test. Because some editions of the tests may be slightly easier or more difficult than others, College Board scaled scores are adjusted so that they indicate the same level of performance regardless of the edition of the test taken and the ability of the group that takes it. Thus, for example, a score of 400 on one edition of a test taken at a particular administration indicates the same level of achievement as a score of 400 on a different edition of the test taken at a different administration.

When you take the SAT Subject Tests during a national administration, your scores are likely to differ somewhat from the scores you obtain on the tests in this book. People perform at different levels at different times for reasons unrelated to the tests themselves. The precision of any test is also limited because it represents only a sample of all the possible questions that could be asked.

Table B

Scaled Score Conversion Table

Subject Test in Literature

Raw Score	Scaled Score	Raw Score	Scaled Score	Raw Score	Scaled Score
61	800	32	590	3	350
60	800	31	580	2	350
59	800	30	570	1	340
58	790	29	560	0	330
57	790	28	550	-1	320
56	780	27	550	-2	320
55	770	26	540	-3	310
54	760	25	530	-4	300
53	750	24	520	-5	290
52	750	23	510	-6	280
51	740	22	510	-7	280
50	730	21	500	-8	270
49	720	20	490	-9	260
48	710	19	480	-10	250
47	710	18	470	-11	240
46	700	17	470	-12	230
45	690	16	460	-13	220
44	680	15	450	-14	210
43	680	14	440	-15	200
42	670	13	430		
41	660	12	430		
40	650	11	420		
39	640	10	410		
38	640	9	400		
37	630	8	390		
36	620	7	390		
35	610	6	380		
34	600	5	370		
33	590	4	360		

How Did You Do on the Subject Test in Literature?

After you score your test and analyze your performance, think about the following questions:

Did you run out of time before reaching the end of the test?

If so, you may need to pace yourself better. For example, maybe you spent too much time on one or two hard questions. A better approach might be to skip the ones you can't answer right away and try answering all the questions that remain on the test. Then if there's time, go back to the questions you skipped.

Did you take a long time reading the directions?

You will save time when you take the test by learning the directions to the Subject Test in Literature ahead of time. Each minute you spend reading directions during the test is a minute that you could use to answer questions.

How did you handle questions you were unsure of?

If you were able to eliminate one or more of the answer choices as wrong and guess from the remaining ones, your approach probably worked to your advantage. On the other hand, making haphazard guesses or omitting questions without trying to eliminate choices could cost you valuable points.

How difficult were the questions for you compared with other students who took the test?

Table A shows you how difficult the multiple-choice questions were for the group of students who took this test during its national administration. The right-hand column gives the percentage of students that answered each question correctly.

A question answered correctly by almost everyone in the group is obviously an easier question. For example, 84 percent of the students answered question 8 correctly. But only 20 percent answered question 12 correctly.

Keep in mind that these percentages are based on just one group of students. They would probably be different with another group of students taking the test.

If you missed several easier questions, go back and try to find out why: Did the questions cover material you haven't yet reviewed? Did you misunderstand the directions?

Answer Explanations for the Literature Subject Test

1. Choice (A) is the correct answer. In lines 1 and 2, the speaker asserts that "In Nature's pieces still I see/Some error that might mended be." By "Nature's pieces," the speaker means things created by Nature, such as landscapes, creatures, objects; in other words, aspects of the natural world. By saying "still I see/Some error that might mended be," then, the speaker is indicating that, upon observing the natural world, he perceives flaws or imperfections that might be repaired or corrected. The best way to restate the meaning of lines 1 and 2 is to say that the natural world contains imperfections.

2. Choice (E) is the correct answer. In this context, "framed" means shaped or constructed by fitting and uniting the parts of a structure. The word "framed" is particularly appropriate because the poem characterizes the woman as a perfect form or structure: "She hath every beauteous line" and a "just shape." Indeed, the metaphor of a workshop runs throughout the poem: Unlike "Nature's pieces" (objects constructed by Nature), which contain errors "that might mended be," and unlike the speaker, who was also "made" by Nature, the speaker's "fair love/Was framed by hands far more divine" and has a "just shape" that could not be improved despite access to "all the store/Of heaven" (in other words, heaven's warehouse). The woman is described throughout the poem as an aesthetic object perfectly constructed, or "framed."

3. Choice (D) is the correct answer. In lines 7–8, the speaker claims that he "had been far happier/Had Nature, that made me, made her." In other words, the speaker wishes that his "fair love," instead of having been "framed by hands far more divine," or made with no flaws, had been made by Nature. According to the logic of the poem, all of "Nature's pieces" are imperfect ("In Nature's pieces still I see/Some error that might mended be"). If the woman were flawed instead of perfect, the speaker is claiming, then she might have loved him back ("Then likeness might (that love creates)/Have made her love what now she hates"). In short, if the woman had been made by Nature, with flaws, the speaker would have been far happier. "Had been" could be replaced with "would have been" without changing the meaning of the line.

4. Choice (E) is the correct answer. There is no reference in the first ten lines of the poem to either innocence or experience. The other contrasts are all present. Nature and divinity are contrasted in lines 1–8, as the speaker explains that his "fair love/ Was framed by hands far more divine" than those of Nature ("Yet I had been far happier/Had Nature, that made me, made her"). The contrast between Nature and divinity is also a contrast between error and perfection, as "Nature's pieces" each contain "Some error," while the woman, "framed by hands far more divine ... hath every beauteous line." Lines 9–10 feature contrasts between similarity and difference and between love and hate: "Then likeness might (that love creates)/Have made her love what now she hates." In other words, were the speaker and his "fair love" similar to each other (flawed, made by Nature) rather than different (she is perfect, made by divine hands), she might have loved him rather than hated him.

5. Choice (C) is the correct answer. The speaker presents two contradictory wishes in lines 7–14. On the one hand, he wishes that his "fair love" were flawed rather than perfect, because then she might love him rather than hate him ("I had been far happier/Had Nature, that made me, made her./Then likeness might (that love creates)/Have made her love what now she hates"). In short, he wants her to be accessible to him; or, in other words, to love him back. On the other hand, the speaker is so pleased with the woman's perfect beauty, her "just shape," that he is unwilling to see her flawed in any way: "Yet I confess, I cannot spare/From her just shape the smallest hair." In other words, he wants her to maintain her perfect beauty, but, at the same time, wishes that she might somehow become accessible to him, despite his flaws.

6. Choice (D) is the correct answer. The speaker concludes the poem by claiming "She hath too much divinity for me" and exhorting the "gods" to "teach her some more humanity." These lines refer back to the earlier claim that, because the speaker is made by Nature and is thus flawed, and his "fair love" is made by "hands far more divine" and is thus perfect, the two of them cannot be together. Taken together, the lines serve as an affectionate critique of the woman's resistance to the speaker's advances: since, as the poem has shown, the woman has "too much divinity" to listen to a flawed, human speaker, he asks the "gods" to teach her "humanity." This creates an amusing paradox: "gods" cannot teach "humanity" to a person, and, moreover, a human being cannot really have "too much divinity." The speaker's tone would best be described as one of "playful exasperation," or good-humored irritation.

7. Choice (C) is the correct answer. The speaker is using the poem to pay the woman an extravagant compliment and make the case that they should be together. The crux of the poem is the speaker's assertion that even though his "fair love['s]" beauty, her perfection, prevents her from loving him, he still admires her so much that he would not wish her to be any less beautiful. In indicating his willingness to sacrifice his own

happiness in order to safeguard the perfection of the woman he loves, the speaker is openly praising the woman's beauty. However, his unannounced intention is to put himself forward—to show how much he admires her, how cleverly he can praise her, how beautiful he can make her appear in a poem—with the goal of winning her favor, or making her more receptive to his passion for her.

8. Choice (A) is the correct answer. The passage is best described as an example of character analysis; it describes in detail the qualities of one character, Mr. Casaubon. The passage briefly touches on Mr. Casaubon's physical features ("never had a strong bodily frame") but focuses primarily on his personality and behavior. The passage reveals, among other things, that Mr. Casaubon "had not had much foretaste of happiness in his previous life"; that he "had many scruples," "was capable of a severe self-restraint," and "was resolute in being a man of honour"; that he was disappointed by and suspicious of responses to "the pamphlets" he seems to have written and distributed; and that "his religious faith wavered with his wavering trust in his own" ability to write. The primary purpose of the passage is to give the reader a clear understanding of Mr. Casaubon's personality and motivations.

9. Choice (B) is the correct answer. Lines 14–15 refer to Casaubon's "self-preoccupation" and "egoistic scrupulosity," and the remainder of the passage gives evidence to support the description of Casaubon as an insecure and self-centered man. The passage indicates that Casaubon's trouble with the book he was trying to write "weighed like lead upon his mind" and that he felt his pamphlets "were far from having been seen in all their significance." We learn that Casaubon "suspected the Archdeacon of not having read" the pamphlets and that he "was bitterly convinced that his old acquaintance" had written a "depreciatory recension"—that is, that someone he knew well had written a disparaging and belittling review and revision of his work. We also learn that Casaubon's suspicions left him with "melancholy embitterment" and, ultimately, "wavering trust in his own authorship." Clearly, Casaubon has uncertainties about himself and is completely absorbed with his own interests and desires. On the other hand, Casaubon does not seem to be particularly crude, rebellious, self-confident, or generous.

10. Choice (C) is the correct answer. The reference to the bird occurs during a discussion of Casaubon's soul. The passage explains that Casaubon's soul "was too languid to thrill out of self-consciousness into passionate delight; it went on fluttering in the swampy ground where it was hatched, thinking of its wings and never flying." The passage makes it clear that Casaubon is uncomfortably aware of himself as an object of the observation of others; he is determined to "be unimpeachable by any recognised opinion," he feels "painful doubt as to what was really thought of [his works] by the leading minds of Brasenose," and he experiences "wavering trust in his own authorship" as he worries about what others think. In the context of the

passage as a whole, the image of the bird that flutters, "thinking of its wings and never flying," primarily suggests the limiting effect of Casaubon's self-consciousness. The image suggests that Casaubon's awareness of himself and of others' judgments holds him back from experiencing "passionate delight" in his life.

11. Choice (C) is the correct answer. The passage indicates that Casaubon is "resolute in being a man of honour according to the code" and determined to "be unimpeachable by any recognised opinion." In other words, Casaubon expects himself to be completely honorable and thus avoid any criticism from others. The author indicates that "In conduct these ends had been attained"—in other words, Casaubon was free from any criticism of his choices and behavior in his personal life. However, Casaubon was striving to make the book he is trying to write, *Key to all Mythologies*, "unimpeachable," or faultless, as well, and this effort "weighed like lead upon his mind." Casaubon is trying to do the impossible: write a book that no reader will criticize. Clearly, Casaubon has unrealistic expectations of achievement.

12. Choice (D) is the correct answer. In lines 22–26 we learn that "the pamphlets ... by which [Casaubon] tested his public ... were far from having been seen in all their significance." The passage goes on to indicate that Casaubon "suspected the Archdeacon of not having read them" and "was in painful doubt as to what was really thought of them by the leading minds of Brasenose." It is clear that he expected the Archdeacon and the scholars ("leading minds") of an important college to read his pamphlets and recognize their "significance." In this context, the phrase "tested his public" suggests that Casaubon had distributed pamphlets in the hope that important officials and scholars, not general readers, would confirm publicly the validity of his scholarly project.

13. Choice (B) is the correct answer. The passage explains that Casaubon "suspected the Archdeacon of not having read" his pamphlets, and was also "in painful doubt as to what was really thought of them by ... leading minds" and "bitterly convinced" that someone he knew well had written negative things about them. In lines 33–36, the passage states that "These were heavy impressions to struggle against, and brought that melancholy embitterment which is the consequence of all excessive claim." This statement contains a generalization about human nature; it suggests that people who ask for or expect too much ("excessive claim") end up being bitterly disappointed ("melancholy embitterment"). This generalization clearly applies to Casaubon. Casaubon expected people to see the "significance" of his writings and to consider them flawless and "unimpeachable," and he became bitter and sad when his work received very little recognition.

14. Choice (B) is the correct answer. Throughout the passage, references to smallness serve to reinforce the theme of Casaubon's limitations in two areas: intellect and emotion. Casaubon's emotional limitations are described in detail: the reader learns that he is the kind of person who "shrinks from pity" and that his "sensitiveness ... has not mass enough to spare for transformation into sympathy" and simply "quivers thread-like in small currents of self-preoccupation." In other words, Casaubon withdraws when others show him pity and is unable to feel emotions—such as sympathy—for others because he is self-preoccupied, or absorbed in himself and his own concerns. Casaubon's intellectual limitations are also emphasized; the passage describes Casaubon's pamphlets as containing "small monumental records of his march" and explains that Casaubon keeps a negative response to his work ("that depreciatory recension") locked away "in a small drawer" of his desk. Although Casaubon has grand ambitions, it seems that he has made little progress and has attracted little attention for his intellectual work. The passage presents a "small" man who is limited both emotionally and intellectually.

15. Choice (D) is the correct answer. In lines 37–40, the narrator comments that "the consolations of the Christian hope in immortality seemed to lean on the immortality of the still unwritten *Key to all Mythologies*"—in other words, Casaubon's hope of an eternal afterlife seemed to lean on, or depend on, his success in creating an "unimpeachable" or faultless work that could live forever. Casaubon does possess some religious faith, but it is subordinate to his feelings about the book he is trying to write: "even his religious faith wavered with his wavering trust in his own authorship." These comparisons between Casaubon's religious faith and his "still unwritten" book show that the narrator believes that Casaubon was greatly inflating the importance of the book. Along with the earlier comment about Casaubon's "excessive claim," or overly high expectations, the comment about "immortality" reveals that Casaubon had unrealistic and overly grand beliefs concerning his writings.

16. Choice (E) is the correct answer. The passage makes many metaphorical references. The statement about Casaubon's soul "fluttering in the swampy ground" and "never flying" is meant to portray Casaubon's soul as restrained and held back; the narrator does not mean that Casaubon's soul is actually in a swamp, making fluttering motions. The comment that Casaubon's "sensitiveness ... quivers thread-like in small currents of self-preoccupation" is also metaphorical; indeed, sensitiveness is an emotional attribute, not a physical object that could quiver or tremble. When the narrator comments that the difficulty in creating an "unimpeachable" work "weighed like lead upon [Casaubon's] mind," he or she means that Casaubon was preoccupied and disheartened by the difficulty, not that the difficulty was physically heavy and pushed down on him. Finally, the statement that Casaubon "deposited small monumental records of his march" in his pamphlets simply means that Casaubon recorded his meager intellectual progress through his writing, not that he created objects and physically placed them in his pamphlets. Only the reference to something

"locked in a small drawer" describes a physical act performed by Casaubon; the narrator means that Casaubon literally kept a copy of a negative review of his work ("that depreciatory recension") "locked in a small drawer of [his] desk."

17. Choice (E) is the correct answer. The narrator's attitude toward Casaubon is primarily one of incisive criticism; he or she offers a direct, unsentimental critique. Casaubon is presented as someone who has never experienced "intense joy" because his soul is "languid," or weak and listless; who "shrinks from pity" and cannot offer "sympathy" to others because of his "self-preoccupation" and "egoistic scrupulosity"; and who is concerned with "self-restraint" and being "unimpeachable," or faultless, "by any recognised opinion" in both his behavior and his work. Casaubon is also revealed to be petty and weak: he "suspected" important figures of overlooking the "significance" of his writings, kept a negative review "locked in a small drawer," and experienced "melancholy embitterment." Although the narrator is critical of Casaubon, he or she does not seem to be disgusted or bitter; the narrator also does not seem to have mixed feelings or experience any confusion. Rather, the narrator is calm and straightforward as he or she criticizes Casaubon's personality and behavior.

18. Choice (B) is the correct answer. Both Reverend Johnson and Arthur Phillip assume that the convicts will value, and be influenced by, the beliefs of the play's characters. Johnson asks in lines 6–7 if the play "sanctions," or approves of, "Holy Matrimony," or marriage, and indicates in lines 9–11 that the play's emphasis on marriage "wouldn't do the convicts any harm." In lines 46–49, Johnson reiterates his concern with the play's attitude toward marriage and sexuality: "I hear many of these plays ... encourage loose morals. ... They do get married? Before, that is, before." Johnson clearly assumes that the men will be influenced by the beliefs presented in the play; otherwise, it is unlikely that he would care so much about the messages the play was sending. Likewise, Arthur Phillip assumes that the play will have a direct impact on those involved with its production; as he says in lines 15–19, "Some of these men will have finished their sentence in a few years. ... Should we not encourage them now to think in a ... responsible manner?" And in lines 28–33, referring to the play, he says, "It will remind them that there is more to life than crime, punishment. ... We will laugh, we may be moved, we may even think a little." Phillip clearly feels that the ideas expressed in the play will be valued by the convicts, stimulating them emotionally and intellectually, and ultimately improving their lives.

19. Choice (D) is the correct answer. In lines 15–19, Arthur Phillip defends the decision to put on the play by pointing out that the convicts will "in a few years ... help create a new society in this colony. Should we not encourage them now to think in a ... responsible manner?" When Tench retorts, "I don't see how a comedy about two lovers will do that," Phillip explains, "The theatre is an expression of civilization. We belong to a great country [England] which has spawned great playwrights:

Shakespeare, Marlowe, Jonson, and even ... Sheridan." By mentioning that England, a great country, has a tradition of great playwrights, Phillip is implying that there a link between being involved in plays and creating a great society or country—a link that has particular relevance to English citizens. Phillip is making an appeal to a tradition of national culture: because England, their home country, values the theatre, they should value the theatre—even if they are just "despised prisoners and hated gaolers" in an Australian penal colony.

20. Choice (E) is the correct answer. There is no indication in the excerpt that the play to be performed is about convicts. Rather, the play is described as a romantic comedy about an "officer and his friend" who are "in love with these two young ladies ... and after some difficulties, they marry them." All of the other issues are discussed. Reverend Johnson is concerned about possible representation of immoral behavior in the play; he says about one of the play's characters, "He's not loose, is he Ralph? I hear many of these plays ... encourage loose morals" (lines 46–48). Phillip, Tench, and others are interested in reforming the convicts; Phillip argues in lines 17–19 that the men "will become members of society again. ... Should we not encourage them now to think in a free and responsible manner?" Phillip, Ralph, and Collins all refer directly or indirectly to the colonizing country, England, and its values (lines 23, 93, 101–102). And Phillip and Ralph explicitly discuss in lines 92–96 the possibility of transcending local circumstances: "we could forget our worries ... the hangings and the floggings, and think of ourselves at the theatre, in London."

21. Choice (B) is the correct answer. Tench's position, as expressed in lines 52–59, is that "if you want to build a civilization there are more important things than a play ... teach them to farm, to build houses ... but above all, teach them how to work, not how to sit around laughing at a comedy." Tench is focused on the practical skills the convicts need to learn in order to be productive citizens; in other words, his views are pragmatic—concerned with practical affairs rather than intellectual or artistic ones. Unlike Ralph and Arthur Phillip, who are arguing in favor of performing a play, Tench does not see the importance of plays, or the value in "laughing at a comedy." According to Tench, the view that the convicts should spend their time being involved in a play is not sufficiently pragmatic.

22. Choice (A) is the correct answer. A "sardonically contentious" tone is disdainfully or derisively argumentative. In lines 60–70, the men are arguing about whether a society should value the arts or focus primarily on practical affairs. When Arthur Phillip brings up the art-loving Greeks, asserting that the Greeks believed that watching a play "was a citizen's duty. ... a kind of work," Tench has a witty comeback: "[T]he Greeks were conquered by the more practical Romans." Collins then jumps in on Phillip's side, arguing that the Romans were perhaps too practical; they "spent many centuries wishing they were Greeks" and were eventually conquered, perhaps

"by their own corrupt and small spirits." Tench, who finds the implications of this argument to be absurd, responds provocatively, "Are you saying Rome would not have fallen if the theatre had been better?" Tench is not just making a point in an argument; he is doing so sardonically, emphasizing the implications of Collins's argument in a disdainful or derisive way.

23. Choice (C) is the correct answer. In lines 72–84, Ralph argues earnestly for the value of the play, describing how "some of the convict women. ... seemed to acquire a dignity" upon reading some of its lines. Ralph identifies one of the women by name ("Mary Brenham") and claims that "she read so well, perhaps this play will keep her from selling herself to the first marine who offers her bread." Faddy responds, "She'll sell herself to him [Ralph], instead." In other words, Mary Brenham's "dignity" may be a sham; her actual motive may be to seduce Ralph for her own advantage. The stage directions indicate that Faddy is speaking "under his breath," or quietly (so as not to be heard by Ralph), so the statement could certainly be characterized as a comic aside, or a humorous utterance meant to be inaudible to someone. Further, Faddy's statement clearly qualifies as a cynical deflation of pretension. By suggesting that Mary Brenham may be deceiving Ralph, and that Ralph's attraction to the woman may be less noble than he portrays it to be, Faddy is contemptuously undermining Ralph's idealistic scenario. Finally, it would not be appropriate to call Faddy's comment a reprimand for poor taste. Faddy is not severely reproving or censuring Ralph; indeed, Faddy's comment is not even meant to be heard by Ralph.

24. Choice (C) is the correct answer. Following Ralph's earnest defense of the value of staging a play, and Faddy's cynical aside, Ross reflects, "So that's the way the wind blows—." Ross has only spoken twice in the scene, but both lines have shown his deep skepticism regarding Ralph's plans for the play: he asks, incredulously, "Marriage, plays, why not a ball for the convicts!" (lines 12–13) and "You want this vice-ridden vermin to enjoy themselves?" (lines 41–42). The reader can infer from these comments that Ross is suspicious of Ralph's idealistic view of the convicts. Ross's comment in line 87, on the other hand, suggests that he now understands just what Ralph's motives are—and finds them consistent with his generally dark view of the situation. Ross, like Faddy, seems to believe that Ralph's plan may be motivated by a romantic interest in the women convicts, especially Mary Brenham—not by idealism.

25. Choice (E) is the correct answer. Ralph argues in lines 79–82 that reading the play's lines aloud can have a positive moral effect on the convicts: "saying those well-balanced lines of Mr. Farquhar, they seemed to acquire a dignity ... to lose some of their corruption." The only other character in the excerpt to address the benefits of speaking the language of the play is Arthur Phillip, who approves of the fact that the convicts "will be speaking a refined, literate language and expressing sentiments of a delicacy they are not used to." The benefits of reciting the language of Farquhar's play

are not mentioned by Reverend Johnson, Tench, Campbell, or Collins. All of these characters comment, directly or indirectly, on the effects of the play in general—Tench, for example, says that "there are more important things than a play"—but only Ralph and Arthur Phillip discuss the effects of actually speaking lines from the play, as opposed to merely watching it.

26. Choice (B) is the correct answer. The characters in the play, officers assigned to an Australian penal colony, clearly idealize their home country, England. The men's allegiance to England is clear from Arthur Phillip's statement in lines 23–24: "We belong to a great country which has spawned great playwrights" (including the English icon, Shakespeare). Ralph also reveals the great value the men place on England, arguing that the play could help them "forget our worries about the supplies, the hangings and the floggings, and think of ourselves at the theatre, in London with our wives and children." The excerpt ends with overlapping comments from Arthur Phillip, Johnston, Ralph, and Collins; these comments suggest that, to the officers, Australia is "darker" and "brutal," but one can "transcend" it with thoughts of "our better nature" and "England"—the ideal civilization.

27. Choice (D) is the correct answer. The excerpt utilizes a "play-within-a-play" conceit. That is, the characters in the play are themselves planning to put on a play, and in the process they discuss the value of plays. This multilayered dramatic situation provides the author the opportunity to examine different ideas about drama. When Reverend Johnson speculates in the beginning of the excerpt about the importance of the play's messages ("That wouldn't do the convicts any harm"), viewers are invited to think about the effects of this play's messages. When Arthur Phillip indicates that "for a few hours we will no longer be despised prisoners and hated gaolers. ... we may be moved, we may even think a little," his words could also refer to the experience of the audience watching this play. Do plays have positive moral effects? Are they useful at all? Is a belief in the value of drama really just a cover for other, selfish motivations? The excerpt asks all of these questions in such a way that they could apply to Farquhar's play or to this one, and in so doing offers a rich exploration of the nature and purpose of drama.

28. Choice (D) is the correct answer. The speaker, a vegetarian who had previously "stuck to [a] Resolution of not eating animal Food," describes being tempted by the smell of some freshly cooked fish, "hot out of the Frying Pan." He or she describes the feeling of indecision: "I balanc'd some time between Principle and Inclination." In this context, "principle" refers to a rule of conduct the speaker tried to follow—in other words, his or her resolution not to eat meat. "Inclination," on the other hand, clearly refers to disposition or preference—what the speaker preferred to do in this instance. The speaker mentions inclination again at the end of the passage, describing the convenience of being able to "make a Reason for every thing one has a mind to do."

Despite attempting to follow the principle of vegetarianism, the speaker had in this instance a "mind"—that is, a disposition, a preference, an inclination—to eat fish, so he or she came up with a reason to do so.

29. Choice (A) is the correct answer. In this part of the excerpt, the hungry speaker smells some freshly cooked fish, "hot out of the Frying Pan," and is tempted to break his or her "Resolution of not eating animal Food." Eventually, recalling that fish eat other fish, the speaker makes a decision: "Then thought I, if you eat one another, I don't see why we mayn't eat you. So I din'd upon Cod very heartily." The tone of this sentence is best described as "witty," or cleverly playful. Although the issue of meat-eating is a serious one for many people, the situation the speaker imagines—a person arguing with a fish he or she is about to eat—is humorous rather than serious. None of the other options reflect the lighthearted tone of the sentence.

30. Choice (C) is the correct answer. After telling the story of how he or she gave in to temptation and "din'd upon Cod very heartily," despite having a "Resolution of not eating animal Food," the speaker concludes with a satirical reflection: "So convenient a thing it is to be a reasonable Creature, since it enables one to find or make a Reason for every thing one has a mind to do." In other words, people who have "a mind," or a desire or inclination, to do something, are always able to come up with a reason or excuse to justify the thing they want to do. The speaker is referring to the conclusion he or she draws in lines 15–16: "If you [fish] eat one another, I don't see why we mayn't eat you." According to the speaker, this "Reason" was really just an excuse to justify the thing he or she wanted to do: eat the fish.

31. Choice (A) is the correct answer. The speaker tells the story of how he or she broke a "Resolution of not eating animal Food" and "din'd upon Cod very heartily." After explaining his or her reasoning ("If you [fish] eat one another, I don't see why we mayn't eat you"), the speaker concludes by remarking how "convenient" it is to be able to "find or make a Reason for every thing one has a mind to do." The speaker is being humorously self-aware, poking fun at his or her use of logic to justify what he or she clearly wanted to do all along: eat the fish, which was "hot out of the Frying Pan" and "smelt admirably well." The humor of the statement comes from its play on words: the phrase "reasonable creature" typically means someone who acts with sound or logical judgment, but the speaker twists it to mean someone who acts according to desire or inclination, and then finds a principle or "Reason" to justify the action.

32. Choice (E) is the correct answer. All three statements can be inferred from information provided in lines 5–9 of the passage. Explaining his or her "Resolution of not eating animal Food," the speaker states, "I consider'd with my Master Tryon, the taking every

Fish as a kind of unprovok'd Murder, since none of them ... could do us any injury." As Tryon was the author of a book "espousing," or promoting, vegetarianism, it can be inferred that the speaker had read Tryon's book and had adopted vegetarianism in response. Second, the speaker's (and Tryon's) defense of vegetarianism seems based chiefly on a concern that meat-eating is unfair to animals; the "unprovok'd Murder" argument says that it is unfair to kill an animal that cannot kill you. Finally, the speaker asserts in line 9 that "All this seem'd very reasonable." In other words, the speaker practiced vegetarianism because it seemed to be rational behavior.

33. Choice (B) is the correct answer. "Hyperbole" is exaggeration for effect. The speaker's use of the term "Murder" to characterize the killing of fish could be described as an exaggeration. Murder is defined as the killing of a human being, so the term does not technically apply to this situation; however, the speaker is not simply misusing the word. Rather, he or she is making a deliberate overstatement—exaggerating for effect. The speaker's use of the term "Slaughter" could also be interpreted as hyperbole. Even though one definition of slaughter is the killing of animals for food, slaughter is more commonly used to indicate a massacre, or a particularly heinous or brutal slaying—and most readers would not interpret the killing of fish for food as a massacre. Such readers would see the use of the term "slaughter" in this context as an exaggeration.

34. Choice (E) is the correct answer. The final sentence reads, "So convenient a thing it is to be a reasonable Creature, since it enables one to find or make a Reason for every thing one has a mind to do." The tone of the sentence, which might be described as witty, satirical, or ironic, is established by each of the sentence's elements, working in unison. The speaker is poking fun at himself or herself and at the pretensions of human beings in general (so-called "reasonable Creatures") who may say they are acting on principle or according to logic, but are in fact making up reasons to justify their desires or inclinations. The word "convenient" implies that thinking of oneself as "reasonable" is really just a convenience that allows one to act a certain way, rather than a fact. In addition, the italicization of the phrase "reasonable Creature" and the use of the phrase "to find or make a Reason" work together as a play on words: the phrase "reasonable creature" typically means someone with inherently sound or logical judgment, but the speaker twists it to mean someone who creates a principle or "Reason" to justify an action taken to satisfy a desire.

35. Choice (E) is the correct answer. The speaker shows in the passage how his or her appetite—his or her "Inclination," or what he or she "has a mind to do"—wins out over his or her "Resolution," or "Principle," of vegetarianism. First, the speaker presents the abstract principles supporting vegetarianism and indicates that "All this seem'd very reasonable." But then, in line 10, something changes: "I had formerly been a great Lover of Fish, and when this came hot out of the Frying Pan, it smelt admirably well." The remainder of the passage shows the witty and self-aware speaker

creating a justification for satisfying his or her appetite: "Then thought I, 'If you [fish] eat one another, I don't see why we mayn't eat you.'" The final sentence confirms that appetite, rather than a rational shift in principles, has been the determining factor; the speaker remarks that human beings are always able to find reasons to justify "every thing one has a mind"—or stomach—"to do."

36. Choice (E) is the correct answer. The narrator explains that while on "his deathbed," his grandfather, a former slave, gave the narrator's father certain instructions: "[A] fter I'm gone I want you to keep up the good fight. ... Live with your head in the lion's mouth. I want you to overcome [the enemy] with yeses, undermine 'em with grins ... Learn it to the younguns." The rest of the passage clarifies that the grandfather was encouraging his son and other young family members to undermine "the enemy"—"the white folks"—by always being agreeable and positive. The narrator explains that his grandfather's instructions became "a constant puzzle which lay unanswered" and caused him to question his own behavior. The narrator indicates that he "was considered an example of desirable conduct," but was "puzzled" by the fact that his grandfather had considered such behavior "treachery." He adds that he was troubled by the idea that "the white folks" might "look upon [him] as a traitor" if they "understood" what he was doing, but that he was "afraid to act any other way because they didn't like that at all." Clearly, the narrator is not sure how he is supposed to act: Is he supposed to follow his grandfather's advice even though it makes him feel guilty, or should he act some other way? This question is the narrator's central concern.

37. Choice (B) is the correct answer. After stating that his grandparents were once slaves, the narrator explains, "About eighty-five years ago they were told that they were free, united with others of our country in everything pertaining to the common good, and, in everything social, separate like the fingers of the hand." The narrator uses a simile, saying that socially, people of different races were at this time separated from one another as fingers are separated from one another on a hand. This simile suggests a rationale for the segregated social system: Different races could and should work together as a single unit for "the common good" of the country, just as the hand can function as an autonomous body part, but (according to the theory of segregation) the races should remain separate in social matters, just as the fingers on a hand are separate from one another. As the passage later demonstrates, this system was offensive to minority groups, and to the grandfather in particular.

38. Choice (C) is the correct answer. In the beginning of the passage, the narrator explains that his grandparents had been slaves, but, "Eighty-five years ago they were told that they were free, united with others of our country in everything pertaining to the common good, and, in everything social, separate like the fingers of the hand." He goes on to add, "And they believed it. They exulted in it. They stayed in their place, worked hard, and brought my father up to do the same." By stating that they

"worked hard," the narrator indicates that his grandparents met the expectation of working with others for "the common good"; in saying that they "stayed in their place," the narrator suggests that his grandparents kept themselves socially "separate" from "others of our country," as a segregated society expected them to do. In these lines, the narrator suggests that his grandparents appeared to have adopted the values society deemed appropriate for them—though we later learn that the narrator's grandfather saw his compliance as "treachery" and himself as "a traitor and a spy," suggesting that the grandfather followed but did not truly believe in these hypocritical values.

39. Choice (D) is the correct answer. The narrator explains that while on his deathbed, his grandfather issued certain instructions to his son—instructions on how to "keep up the good fight" against "the [enemy]." Two of the grandfather's injunctions are "to overcome 'em with yeses" and to "undermine 'em with grins." In other words, the grandfather is ordering his son to rebel through seeming acquiescence, or through seeming to be compliant and submissive; he asserts the need to weaken and subvert ("undermine") and ultimately win against ("overcome") the enemy by being accommodating ("yeses") and positive ("grins"). The grandfather is not encouraging his son to be optimistic or to imitate the enemy, but rather to merely have the appearance of cooperating with the enemy while ultimately seeking to change the system.

40. Choice (E) is the correct answer. The narrator recounts his grandfather's dying words, which included instructions on how to "keep up the good fight" against "the [enemy]" and "Live with your head in the lion's mouth." The narrator then explains that he "was warned emphatically to forget what [his grandfather] had said," adding that "indeed, this is the first time it has been mentioned outside the family circle." The fact that the narrator has not previously mentioned his grandfather's dying words to anyone other than family members suggests that he has felt profoundly anxious, or uneasy, about them. In fact, the narrator suggests that other family members also felt uneasy about the grandfather's words: "his words caused so much anxiety." He goes on to reveal just how anxious the dying words have made him, explaining that he would remember the words "whenever things went well" and would then feel "guilty and uncomfortable." The narrator even goes so far as to say that "the old man's words were like a curse."

41. Choice (C) is the correct answer. In lines 35–40, the narrator explains, "Grandfather had been a quiet old man who never made any trouble, yet on his deathbed he had called himself a traitor and a spy, and he had spoken of his meekness as a dangerous activity. It became a constant puzzle which lay unanswered in the back of my mind." These lines highlight the contradiction between the lifelong behavior and the deathbed words of the narrator's grandfather. On the one

hand, the grandfather was "an example of desirable conduct," worked hard, and didn't cause trouble; this behavior seems to reflect an impulse to be agreeable and to work in cooperation with others. On the other hand, the grandfather announced that he had been a traitor and a spy and that he saw his good behavior and conduct as a dangerous form of "treachery"; these words seem to reflect an impulse to conquer others—to "overcome" and "undermine" the enemy by only appearing to be compliant ("yeses," "grins"). The narrator makes it clear that he is puzzled by the contradiction between his grandfather's behavior and his grandfather's words.

42. Choice (A) is the correct answer. While on his deathbed, the grandfather stated that "our life is a war" and that he had "been a traitor all [his] born days" and "a spy in the enemy's country." The grandfather had been "the meekest of men," the "quiet old man who never made any trouble," and "an example of desirable conduct"—but he described his meekness and good conduct as "treachery." The description of his behavior as treachery suggests that the grandfather had just pretended to be acquiescent and compliant; he was actually working to weaken and conquer the enemy. With his dying words, the grandfather suggested that his son and "the younguns"—the younger people in the family—could prevail against the enemy by being deceptive in the same way he had been: They should "overcome [the enemy] with yeses, undermine 'em with grins, agree 'em to death and destruction, let 'em swoller you till they vomit or bust wide open." The passage suggests that the grandfather viewed his treachery as an affirmative, or positive, act because the deception could lead to triumph over the enemy.

43. Choice (A) is the correct answer. The narrator tells us that his grandfather encouraged his son and other family members to be treacherous by pretending to be compliant ("overcome 'em with yeses, undermine 'em with grins"). Although the narrator explains that this advice caused him to be anxious and to question his own behavior, he also indicates that his "desirable conduct" paid off: "everyone loved me for it." At the end of the passage, the narrator relates his experience on the day he graduated: "I delivered an oration in which I showed that humility was the secret, indeed, the very essence of progress. (Not that I believed this—how could I, remembering my grandfather?—I only believed that it worked.)" The context makes it clear that by saying he believed humility "worked," the narrator means that he was able to please the leading citizens of the community by being modest and deferential. Indeed, even the narrator's speech about humility pleased others; the narrator says that the speech "was a great success" and that "Everyone praised [him] and [he] was invited to give the speech at a gathering of the town's leading white citizens."

44. Choice (A) is the correct answer. The "triumph" to which the narrator refers is his graduation day speech, "in which [he] showed that humility was the secret, indeed, the very essence of progress." The narrator explains that the speech "was a great

success" and that "Everyone praised [him] and [he] was invited to give the speech at a gathering of the town's leading white citizens." He then adds, "It was a triumph for the whole community." However, as the passage shows, this triumph was not necessarily what it seemed. The narrator admits in lines 63–65 that he did not believe the sentiments he expressed in the speech ("Not that I believed this ... I only believed that it worked"). Earlier in the paragraph he mentions the guilt and anxiety that he felt "whenever things went well for me." In the context of the passage, it is clear that the so-called triumph did not feel like a triumph to the narrator, who is struggling to understand the ramifications of his grandfather's assertion that success in the white world was a kind of "treachery."

45. Choice (E) is the correct answer. Lines 1–4 refer to the common poetic theme of achieving lasting fame, or immortality, through one's writing, describing poets who boast that "Their work shall with the world remain." Lines 5–8 question this possibility for poets who write in English: "But who can hope his lines should long/Last in a daily changing tongue?/While they are new, envy prevails;/And as that dies, our language fails." The rapidly changing nature of the English language is the main concern of the poem. As the speaker says in lines 15–16, "We write in sand, our language grows,/And, like the tide, our work o'erflows": Poets writing in English, in other words, cannot hope for the permanence of those who "carve in Latin or in Greek." In the context of lines 5–8, then, "our language fails" when the poet's lines become dated. A poet may be envied when he or she publishes a new poem, but as the months and years pass ("as that [newness] dies"), the poet ceases to be envied because the language "fails" to communicate any longer. The speaker presents English as a language that changes so much, so quickly, that the original qualities of an "old" poem can only be understood or appreciated when the poem is "new."

46. Choice (D) is the correct answer. In the third stanza (lines 9–12), the speaker further develops the argument that the English language is too changeable to support immortal poetry. Here the poet speaks of architects, saying that when they have "done their part," or performed their work, the "matter"—or materials—that they have used "may betray their art." The next two lines support this thesis: If the architect uses poor materials ("ill-chosen stone"), the ravages of time "soon [bring] a well-built palace down." Buildings, like poetry, only last as long as the stuff of which they are made. The analogy suggests that the English language—"a daily changing tongue"—is an "ill-chosen" material for poets who wish to achieve immortality through their poems. Time changes the English language so much, and so quickly, that it renders an English poem impossible to read after a relatively short amount of time—just as a building constructed of less durable materials may be impossible to live in after a short amount of time. Art lasts only as long as its materials do.

47. Choice (A) is the correct answer. The words "marble," "carve," "sand," and "o'erflows" are all used figuratively in the fourth stanza of the poem, and all of them refer metaphorically to the artistic process. The word "Poets," however, is used to denote just what it says: people who write poetry. Lines 13–14 ("Poets that lasting marble seek/Must carve in Latin or in Greek") use the terminology of sculpture to refer metaphorically to the act of writing poetry: "marble" represents poetry or language, and "carve" represents writing. Lines 15–16 ("We write in sand, our language grows,/And, like the tide, our work o'erflows") also refer to the act of writing poetry, but this time the speaker uses the metaphor of forming letters on a beach. Poets do not literally write in "sand," and there is no actual tide of water that "o'erflows" and wipes out their efforts.

48. Choice (B) is the correct answer. In this poem, the speaker develops an argument about the unsuitability of the ever-changing English language as a medium for timeless poetry. In lines 13–14, the speaker continues a metaphor that treats poetry as though it were architecture, saying that "Poets that lasting marble seek/Must carve in Latin or in Greek." Latin and ancient Greek were the languages utilized by the great Roman and Greek poets of the classical era; early versions of the Bible were also written in Greek. Some English poets continued to write in Latin and ancient Greek in the 1600s, as did some legal and religious officials. The main difference between these languages and English is that Latin and ancient Greek were no longer spoken languages and were not subject to change. Thus, any poem written in these unchanging, "lasting" languages would be as indestructible as marble.

49. Choice (B) is the correct answer. In these lines, the speaker continues the argument that a changeable, still-evolving language such as English is an inappropriate medium for immortal poetry. The speaker contrasts poetry written in Latin or Greek ("lasting marble") with poetry written in English, saying, "We write in sand, our language grows/And like the tide, our work o'erflows." Writing in English, then, is like writing in the sand on a beach: As "our language grows," the words we have previously written are wiped away by the incoming tide—the growing, changing language. The inevitable evolution of the language renders work written in an earlier version of the language difficult to read and understand. As a result, the speaker implies, poetry written in English only lasts a short time; it is impossible to achieve poetic immortality writing in English.

50. Choice (E) is the correct answer. The speaker, having just spoken of Chaucer's ability to celebrate "The beauties which adorned that age," says in lines 26–28 that "all an English pen can hope" is "To make the fair approve his flame/That can so far extend their fame." In other words, given the changing nature of the English language, poets should focus on the limited goal of impressing the beautiful women of the era. Lines 29–32 continue the theme: "Verse, thus designed, has no ill fate/If it arrive but at the date/Of fading beauty." Beauty fades, of course, but poetry can temporarily preserve

that beauty, and will still serve a purpose, however limited, "if it prove/But as long-lived as present love." Like beauty and love, poems may not last forever, but they are nonetheless worthwhile.

51. Choice (E) is the correct answer. In this context, a metaphor consists simply of speaking of one thing in terms of another thing in order to make a comparison between the two. This poem uses many such comparisons: the comparison between architecture and poetry (lines 9–12); the related comparisons between poetry and stone carving on the one hand, and writing in sand on the other (lines 13–16); and the complicated set of comparisons between poetry that can only last for a short time and "fading beauty" and "present love" (lines 29–32). It might be said that the entire poem is developed through the use of metaphor. None of the other devices is used with any frequency. Some might say that the speaker uses "hyperbole," or exaggeration, in his or her praise of Chaucer's "matchless strain," but hyperbole is not a regular feature of the poem. Neither "apostrophe," the address to an absent person or concept, or "euphemism," the substitution of an agreeable expression for a disagreeable one, is used at all. The speaker does occasionally use "antithesis," or opposition between two things (most notably the opposition between carving in marble and writing in sand), but metaphor is employed far more frequently than antithesis in the poem.

52. Choice (D) is the correct answer. The poem is full of images of desolation: "tears the onions raise"; "the salt blown/From one blister into another"; "The wind pressing us closer to the ground"; "nothing will heal/Under the rain's broken fingers." The narrator is speaking of working in the fields at dawn, "when the light starts up/In the east"—apparently a bleak experience, made even worse by the speaker's anger at an unnamed antagonist ("You will never waken ... We won't forget what you failed to see"). The tone of the poem is one of bitterness, hopelessness, and emotional pain.

53. Choice (C) is the correct answer. The speaker, in describing working in the fields at sunrise, addresses someone as "you," while speaking of the workers as "we": "We enter the fields to hoe ... And tears the onions raise/Do not begin in your eyes but in ours." Here the speaker invokes the familiar image of getting tears in one's eyes while chopping onions, but says the tears first form in "our"—the workers'—eyes, implying that the "you" is someone chopping onions, i.e., the consumer. Further supporting this interpretation are the other statements addressed to "you," both of which refer to the hard work involved in harvesting the onions: "You will never waken to bear/The hour timed to a heart beat" and "We won't forget what you failed to see." The basic opposition in the poem is between the workers, who harvest the onions, and the consumers, who enjoy the onions without acknowledging the pain others endured to produce them.

54. Choice (D) is the correct answer. The first stanza (lines 1–3) imagines the sunrise as a fire started by the old-fashioned method of rubbing sticks together: "the light ... rubs/The horizon until it catches fire." This image of literal "friction" sets the stage for the poem by suggesting that apparently natural occurrences, such as the sunrise, or the harvesting of onions, are actually the products of difficult labor or clashing forces. This image is consistent with the theme of friction and discord in the poem, which features the bitter opposition between the workers and the consumers who "will never waken to bear/The hour timed to a heart beat." The image presented in the first stanza is not of creativity, peace, affection, or chaos.

55. Choice (A) is the correct answer. In these lines, the speaker mentions two things that the addressee will "never waken to bear," or never have to experience first thing in the morning: "The hour timed to a heart beat" (presumably the carefully measured hour for which the worker is paid) and "The wind pressing us closer to the ground" (the harsh wind of the fields). Together these images convey a sense that the workers are being constrained or pushed down by the brutal demands of their task. Lines 14 and 15 illustrate the difficult conditions endured by the workers.

56. Choice (A) is the correct answer. In the third stanza, the speaker says that the tears "Do not begin in your eyes but in ours,/In the salt blown/From one blister into another," suggesting that the workers' tears are caused in part by physical pain (their hands are blistered from working with the onions). But then in the fourth stanza, the speaker says that the tears "begin in knowing/You will never waken to bear/The hour timed to a heart beat"—in other words, the tears are caused by the workers' feelings of unfairness and oppression (they know that "You," the consumer, will never suffer as they do). The stanzas are linked by the verb "begin," which suggests that the source of the tears is the topic of both stanzas. The relation between the third and fourth stanzas is best described as a change from one explanation for the tears to another; the speaker first blames physical pain and then cites emotional suffering as the cause of the tears.

57. Choice (C) is the correct answer. To harvest a fruit or vegetable is to gather or pick it—harvesting an apple means removing it from an apple tree. Onion bulbs grow underground and must be pulled up from the soil by their tops. The speaker says in lines 16–17 that "When the season ends," the onions will be "unplugged from their sleep." In other words, at the end of the growing season, the onions will be harvested. The phrase "unplugged from their sleep" refers to the physical act of harvesting, which somewhat resembles pulling a plug from a socket, and uses a metaphor to suggest that onions "sleep" underground until they are awakened, or harvested.

58. Choice (C) is the correct answer. The speaker remarks that "nothing will heal/ Under the rain's broken fingers." It can be inferred that the problems of the workers

(the long hours and hard work) are unlikely to heal or change soon. No solution is provided by the speaker; the poem merely offers a dramatic account of the problems. Likewise, the rift between "we" (those who are working in the fields) and "you" (those who are buying the produce) seems to be an ongoing struggle with no sign of ending: "We won't forget what you failed to see,/And nothing will heal." On the other hand, the tears shed by the "you" in the poem almost certainly will end quickly; the tears in "your eyes" are merely those caused by chopping onions—the onions that have been laboriously harvested by others. It is only the problems of the workers and the rift between "we" and "you" that will not "heal."

59. Choice (C) is the correct answer. Each stanza of the poem ends with an image that either metaphorically evokes or directly conveys the harshness of physical labor in challenging conditions: "the light ... rubs/The horizon until it catches fire"; "Waving off the dragonflies/That ladder the air"; "the salt blown/From one blister into another"; "The wind pressing us closer to the ground." The final statement, "And nothing will heal/Under the rain's broken fingers," fits the pattern, capturing the inescapable and relentless physical challenges (rain, broken fingers) of the work. The image of the "rain's broken fingers," like the other images, portrays the difficulty of the workers' situation.

60. Choice (E) is the correct answer. The images associated with the workers' labor are those of pain ("salt blown/From one blister into another"; "The wind pressing us closer to the ground"; "nothing will heal/Under the rain's broken fingers") and also of lack of gratitude from consumers ("tears the onions raise/Do not begin in your eyes but in ours"; "You will never waken to bear/The hour timed to a heart beat"; "We won't forget what you failed to see"). The workers' physical labor is characterized as both painful and unappreciated.

61. Choice (A) is the correct answer. The speaker characterizes the "you" in the poem as someone who either does not know or does not care about the plight of those who harvest the crops. This "you" is referred to three times. In lines 8–9, the speaker asserts that the "tears the onions raise/Do not begin in your eyes but in ours," suggesting that the consumer who is chopping onions purchased at the supermarket knows nothing about the demanding physical labor of harvesting onions. In lines 13–14, the speaker claims that "You will never waken to bear/The hour timed to a heart beat," implying that the consumer will never share the workers' experience. Finally, in line 18 the speaker refers directly to "what you failed to see." Throughout the poem the speaker suggests that the "you" being discussed is both ignorant and unseeing.

Chapter 2

United States History

Purpose

The emphasis of the Subject Test in United States History is on U.S. history from pre-Columbian times to the present, as well as basic social science concepts, methods, and generalizations as they are found in the study of history. It is not tied to any single textbook or instructional approach.

Format

This is a one-hour test with 90 multiple-choice questions. The questions cover political, economic, social, intellectual, and cultural history as well as foreign policy.

Content

The questions may require you to:

- recall basic information and require you to know facts, terms, concepts, and generalizations
- analyze and interpret material such as graphs, charts, paintings, text, cartoons, photographs, and maps
- understand important aspects of U.S. history
- relate ideas to given data
- evaluate data for a given purpose basing your judgment either on internal evidence, such as proof and logical consistency, or on external criteria, such as comparison with other works, established standards, and theories

Material Covered*	Approximate Percentage of Test
Political History	31–35%
Economic History	13–17%
Social History	20–24%
Intellectual and Cultural History	13–17%
Foreign Policy	13–17%
Periods Covered	
Pre-Columbian history to 1789	20%
1790 to 1898	40%
1899 to the present	40%

* Social science concepts, methods, and generalizations are incorporated in this material.

How to Prepare

The only essential preparation is a sound, one-year course in U.S. history at the college-preparatory level. Most of the test questions are based on material commonly taught in U.S. history courses in secondary schools, although some of the material may be covered in other social studies courses. Knowledge gained from social studies courses and from outside reading could be helpful. No one textbook or method of instruction is considered better than another. Familiarize yourself with the directions in advance. The directions in this book are identical to those that appear on the test.

Score

The total score is reported on the 200-to-800 scale.

Sample Questions

The types of questions used in the test and the abilities they measure are described below. Questions may be presented as separate items or in sets based on quotations, maps, pictures, graphs, or tables.

Directions: Each of the questions or incomplete statements below is followed by five suggested answers or completions. Select the one that is best in each case and then fill in the corresponding circle on the answer sheet.

Some questions require you to know facts, terms, concepts, and generalizations. They test your recall of basic information and your understanding of significant aspects of U.S. history and the social studies. Question 1 is a sample of this type.

1. Harriet Tubman was known as the "Moses" of her people because she
   (A) helped slaves escape from the South
   (B) was instrumental in bringing about suffrage reform
   (C) advocated emigration to Africa for Black people
   (D) organized mass civil rights demonstrations
   (E) traveled as a lay minister preaching the gospel

Choice (A) is the correct answer to question 1. To answer this question you need to know that Harriet Tubman was a notable African American abolitionist. As the use of the name "Moses" may help you to remember, Tubman led many slaves to freedom in the North along the route of the Underground Railroad as referred to in choice (A). The other choices only describe activities that Tubman did not pursue.

Some questions require you to analyze and interpret materials. Question 2, based on the chart below, illustrates a question that tests your ability to use these skills.

Popular Vote for Presidential Electors, Georgia, 1848 and 1852

	Democratic Electors	Whig Electors	Webster Electors
1848	44,809	47,538	—
1852	40,516	16,660	5,324

2. Using the table above, one might conclude that the most plausible explanation for the Georgia Democrats' victory in 1852, following their defeat in 1848, was that
   (A) many new voters increased the turnout in 1852, to the advantage of the Democrats
   (B) many voters abstained from voting in 1852, to the disadvantage of the Whigs
   (C) Webster, who had not run in 1848, drew sufficient votes from the Whigs to cost them the election of 1852
   (D) the Democrats, who had run a highly unpopular candidate in 1848, ran a highly popular candidate in 1852
   (E) the Democrats cast fraudulent ballots to increase their share of the votes in 1852

Choice (B) is the correct answer to question 2. To answer this question, you must analyze the electoral data given for 1848 and 1852, noting that the voter turnout dropped dramatically in 1852 and that the Whigs suffered a much larger decline in voter turnout than did the Democrats. As a consequence, the Whigs lost their majority position. Choices (A), (C), (D), and (E) are not logically consistent with this data. For example, choice (C) is incorrect because the table shows that the Democratic Electors received more votes than the Whig and Webster Electors combined. Choice (B) is the correct answer because it is the only plausible explanation for the change in the fortunes of the Georgia Democrats.

Other questions test your ability to analyze material as well as your ability to recall information related to the materials, or to make inferences and interpolations based on the material. Questions 3, 4, 5, and 6 are illustrations of questions that test a combination of interpretation and recall.

3. "What is man born for but to be a reformer, a remaker of what man has made; a renouncer of lies; a restorer of truth and good, imitating that great Nature which embosoms us all, and which sleeps no moment on an old past, but every hour repairs herself, yielding every morning a new day, and with every pulsation a new life?"

   These sentiments are most characteristic of

   (A) fundamentalism
   (B) Social Darwinism
   (C) pragmatism
   (D) neoorthodoxy
   (E) transcendentalism

Choice (E) is the correct answer to question 3. Several elements in the quotation suggest this as the correct answer. The emphasis that the quotation places on reform, on nature as a source of moral truth, and on the infinite possibilities open to people mark it as an example of the thought of the transcendentalist movement. This combination of elements is not pertinent to any of the other choices. Even if you do not know the source of the material, your understanding of the nature of transcendentalism should lead you to choice (E).

Questions 4–5 refer to the following map.

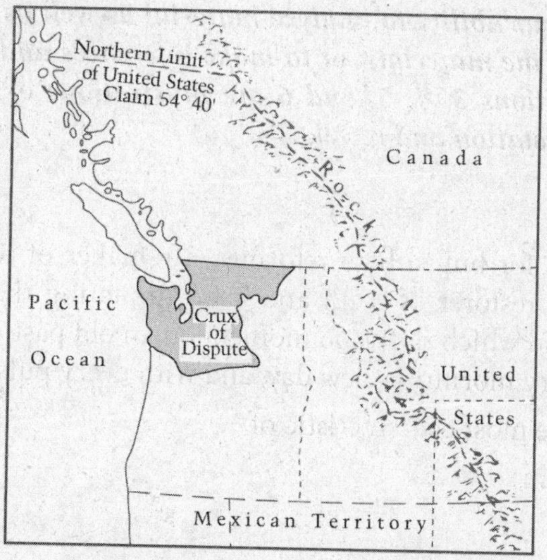

4. The controversy with Great Britain over control of the shaded section was settled during the presidency of
   (A) John Quincy Adams
   (B) James K. Polk
   (C) Franklin Pierce
   (D) James Buchanan
   (E) Andrew Johnson

Choice (B) is the correct answer to question 4. To answer this question, you must interpret the map and recognize the shaded section as part of the Oregon territory. The Oregon dispute with Great Britain was settled during the presidency of James K. Polk.

5. To the northwest of the area shown on the map is a continental territory purchased by Secretary of State William H. Seward from
   (A) Great Britain
   (B) Canada
   (C) Russia
   (D) France
   (E) Spain

Choice (C) is the correct answer to question 5. To answer this question, you must go beyond the content of the map in order to determine that the territory referred to in the question is Alaska. If you recall that Secretary of State Seward purchased the territory from Russia in 1867, you will choose the correct answer.

Courtesy of the New York Historical Society

6. The point of view expressed by this cartoon would probably have met with the approval of
   (A) Daniel Webster
   (B) James K. Polk
   (C) Martin Van Buren
   (D) Roger B. Taney
   (E) Stephen A. Douglas

Choice (A) is the correct answer to question 6. To answer this question, you must first note the anti-Jackson tone of the cartoon, which portrays King Andrew the First trampling the Constitution of the United States. You must then decide which of the choices given opposed Jackson's use of the veto to return important bills to Congress. Only the Whig Daniel Webster fits that description. The others were Democrats who either supported Andrew Jackson or were politically active at a later time.

Some questions require you to select or relate hypotheses, concepts, principles, or generalizations to given data. The questions may begin with concrete specifics and ask for the appropriate concept, or they may begin with a concept and apply it to particular problems or situations. Thus, you may need to use inductive and deductive reasoning. Questions 7 and 8 are examples of questions in this category.

7. From 1870 to 1930, the trend in industry was for hours to be generally reduced, while both money wages and real wages rose. What factor was primarily responsible for this trend?
   (A) A reduction in profit margins
   (B) Minimum wage laws
   (C) Restriction of the labor supply
   (D) Increased output per hour of work
   (E) Right-to-work legislation

Choice (D) is the correct answer to question 7. To arrive at this answer, you must be aware that the trend referred to in the question came about primarily because of technological advances that resulted in increased productivity. None of the other answer choices satisfactorily accounts for all the conditions described in the question.

8. Which of the following wars of the United States would fit the description of a war neither lost nor won?

   I. The War of 1812
   II. The Mexican War
   III. The Spanish-American War
   IV. The Second World War

(A) I only
(B) II only
(C) I and III only
(D) II and IV only
(E) III and IV only

Choice (A) is the correct answer to question 8. In answering this question, you must recognize that a war not won, though not necessarily lost, is one in which a country either fails to achieve clear victory on the battlefield or fails to sign a peace treaty that is definitive and fulfills its goals. Only the War of 1812 is an illustration of the kind of war defined by the question. That war was ended by The Treaty of Ghent, which provided for the *Status quo ante bellum*, or a return to things as they had been before the war.

Some questions require you to judge the value of data for a given purpose, either basing your judgment on internal evidence, such as accuracy and logical consistency, or on external criteria, such as accepted historical scholarship. Question 9 is an illustration of this kind of question.

9. Which of the following would most probably provide the widest range of information for a historian wishing to analyze the social composition of an American city in the 1880s?

(A) The minutes of the city council
(B) A debutante's diary
(C) A manuscript census tabulating the residence, ethnicity, occupation, and wealth of each city resident
(D) Precinct-level voting returns in a closely contested mayoral election held in a presidential election year
(E) A survey of slum housing conditions carried out by a Social Gospel minister in the year following several epidemics

Choice (C) is the correct answer to question 9. In answering this question, you must be able to eliminate from consideration choices that offer information about the city that is either irrelevant or less relevant than other options to understanding the social composition of the city, choices (A) and (D). You must also eliminate choices that offer relevant information but are limited to a particular section of the population of the city, choices (B) and (E). Choice (C) contains the widest range of information about the social composition of a city.

United States History Subject Test

Practice Helps

The test that follows is an actual, previously administered SAT Subject Test in United States History. To get an idea of what it's like to take this test, practice under conditions that are much like those of an actual test administration.

- Set aside an hour when you can take the test uninterrupted.
- Sit at a desk or table with no other books or papers. Dictionaries, other books, or notes are not allowed in the test room.
- Tear out an answer sheet from the back of this book and fill it in just as you would on the day of the test. One answer sheet can be used for up to three Subject Tests.
- Read the instructions that precede the practice test. During the actual administration you will be asked to read them before answering test questions.
- Time yourself by placing a clock or kitchen timer in front of you.
- After you finish the practice test, read the sections "How to Score the SAT Subject Test in United States History" and "How Did You Do on the Subject Test in United States History?"
- The appearance of the answer sheet in this book may differ from the answer sheet you see on test day.

UNITED STATES HISTORY TEST

The top portion of the page of the answer sheet that you will use to take the United States History Test must be filled in exactly as illustrated below. When your supervisor tells you to fill in the circle next to the name of the test you are about to take, mark your answer sheet as shown.

○ Literature	○ Mathematics Level 1	○ German	○ Chinese Listening	○ Japanese Listening
○ Biology E	○ Mathematics Level 2	○ Italian	○ French Listening	○ Korean Listening
○ Biology M	● U.S. History	○ Latin	○ German Listening	○ Spanish Listening
○ Chemistry	○ World History	○ Modern Hebrew		
○ Physics	○ French	○ Spanish	**Background Questions:** ① ② ③ ④ ⑤ ⑥ ⑦ ⑧ ⑨	

After filling in the circle next to the name of the test you are taking, locate the Background Questions section, which also appears at the top of your answer sheet (as shown above). This is where you will answer the following Background Questions on your answer sheet.

BACKGROUND QUESTIONS

Please answer the two questions below by filling in the appropriate circle in the Background Questions box on your answer sheet. <u>The information you provide is for statistical purposes only and will not affect your test score.</u>

<u>Question I</u>

How many semesters of United States History have you taken from grade 9 to the present? (If you are taking United States History this semester, count it as a full semester.) Fill in only <u>one</u> circle of circles 1-4.

- One semester or less —Fill in circle 1.
- Two semesters —Fill in circle 2.
- Three semesters —Fill in circle 3.
- Four or more semesters —Fill in circle 4.

<u>Question II</u>

Which, if any, of the following social studies courses have you taken from grade 9 to the present? (Fill in ALL circles that apply.)

- One or more semesters of government —Fill in circle 5.
- One or more semesters of economics —Fill in circle 6.
- One or more semesters of geography —Fill in circle 7.
- One or more semesters of psychology —Fill in circle 8.
- One or more semesters of sociology or anthropology —Fill in circle 9.

If you have taken none of these social studies courses, leave the circles 5 through 9 blank.

When the supervisor gives the signal, turn the page and begin the United States History Test. There are 100 numbered circles on the answer sheet and 90 questions in the United States History Test. Therefore, use only circles 1 to 90 for recording your answers.

UNITED STATES HISTORY TEST

Directions: Each of the questions or incomplete statements below is followed by five suggested answers or completions. Select the one that is best in each case and then fill in the corresponding circle on the answer sheet.

1. During the seventeenth and eighteenth centuries, the English colonial system was based most explicitly on the economic and political principles of

(A) mercantilism
(B) free trade
(C) salutary neglect
(D) enlightened despotism
(E) physiocracy

2. The concept of the separation of powers, as articulated by the framers of the Constitution, refers to the

(A) right of free speech
(B) right of freedom of assembly
(C) organization of the national government in three branches
(D) separation of church and state
(E) political rights of confederated states

3. The Trail of Tears refers to the

(A) movement of slaves from eastern states into the West after the 1820's
(B) relocation of Cherokee Indians from the Southeast to settlements in what is now Oklahoma
(C) difficult movement of settlers over the Oregon Trail
(D) Lewis and Clark's expedition during the Jefferson presidency
(E) movement of thousands of people across the Great Plains during the California gold rush

4. All of the following reformers are correctly paired with the reform issue with which they were most involved EXCEPT

(A) Elizabeth Cady Stanton . . suffrage
(B) Sojourner Truth . . antislavery
(C) Harriet Beecher Stowe . . prohibition
(D) Emma Willard . . women's education
(E) Dorothea Dix . . treatment of people with mental and emotional disabilities

GO ON TO THE NEXT PAGE

BLACK POPULATION IN THE UNITED STATES, 1820 – 1850
FREE AND SLAVE (in thousands)

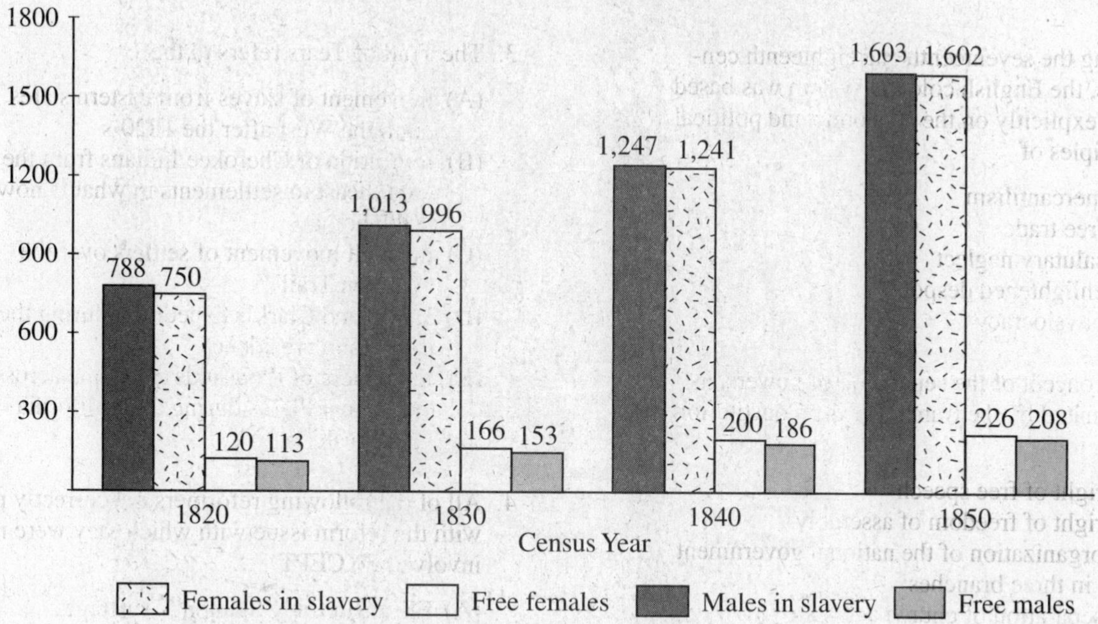

5. Which of the following statements about the period from 1820 to 1850 is supported by the diagram above?

   (A) The percentage of the Black population held in slavery declined.
   (B) The ratio of Black males to Black females remained fairly constant.
   (C) Black males were more likely than Black females to be free.
   (D) The number of Black females doubled every 20 years.
   (E) The total Black population in each census exceeded two million.

GO ON TO THE NEXT PAGE

Punch Ltd.

6. The cartoon above illustrates popular reaction to publication of a theory by

   (A) Malthus
   (B) Darwin
   (C) Marx
   (D) Einstein
   (E) Freud

---

7. In the early years of the twentieth century, the majority of female workers employed outside of the home were

   (A) widowed
   (B) divorced
   (C) married with young children
   (D) married with grown children
   (E) young and unmarried

8. President Franklin D. Roosevelt attempted to "pack" the Supreme Court in 1937 for which of the following reasons?

   (A) He wanted to make sure that New Deal laws would be found constitutional.
   (B) He believed that additional conservative justices would balance the Court.
   (C) He owed favors to many political friends who were trained lawyers.
   (D) He wanted to increase minority representation on the Court.
   (E) He wanted socialists and communists to be represented on the Court.

GO ON TO THE NEXT PAGE

By Permission of Chuck Asay and Creator's Syndicate, Inc.

9. The cartoon above makes which of the following points about federal aid policies in the years following the Second World War?

(A) The federal government has always been reluctant to offer financial aid to farmers.
(B) American farmers have never needed government support to maintain self-sufficiency.
(C) Much federal aid goes to individuals in forms other than welfare payments.
(D) Congress should cease paying both welfare and price supports.
(E) Price supports paid to farmers are not a significant percentage of the federal budget.

GO ON TO THE NEXT PAGE

10. The United States supported the Bay of Pigs invasion in 1961 in an attempt to overthrow

    (A) Nikita Khrushchev
    (B) Gamal Abdel Nasser
    (C) Fidel Castro
    (D) Chiang Kai-shek
    (E) Ngo Dinh Diem

11. Single women and widows in the eighteenth-century British North American colonies had the legal right to

    (A) hold political office
    (B) serve as Protestant ministers
    (C) vote
    (D) own property
    (E) serve on juries

12. Which of the following was most responsible for the repeal of the Stamp Act in 1766 ?

    (A) The dumping of the East India Company's tea into Boston Harbor
    (B) Petitions by the First Continental Congress to Parliament
    (C) The boycott of British imports
    (D) Acceptance by the Massachusetts colonists of alternate taxation
    (E) Pressure on Parliament by the king

13. *Marbury* v. *Madison* was a significant turning point in the interpretation of the United States Constitution because it

    (A) upheld the separation of church and state
    (B) validated the principle of the free press
    (C) established the practice of judicial review
    (D) abolished the slave trade
    (E) overturned the Alien and Sedition Acts

14. After the Civil War, sharecropping was an important element in the agricultural economy of which of the following regions?

    (A) The Middle Atlantic states
    (B) The South
    (C) The Great Plains
    (D) The West Coast
    (E) New England

15. "Texas has been absorbed into the Union in the inevitable fulfillment of the general law which is rolling our population westward. . . . It was disintegrated from Mexico in the natural course of events, by a process perfectly legitimate on its own part, blameless on ours. . . . [Its] incorporation into the Union was not only inevitable, but the most natural, right and proper thing in the world."

    The statement above is an expression of

    (A) Social Darwinism
    (B) antiabolitionism
    (C) federalism
    (D) Manifest Destiny
    (E) self-determination

GO ON TO THE NEXT PAGE

Reprinted by permission of the New York Historical Society

16. The nineteenth-century cartoon above supports which of the following conclusions about the United States economy?

    (A) The emergence of strong unions resulted in loss of productivity.
    (B) The emergence of big government resulted in loss of liberties.
    (C) Railroad corporations wielded tremendous power in American society.
    (D) Southern planters wielded tremendous power in the Senate.
    (E) Rapid urbanization led to unsanitary conditions in many cities.

GO ON TO THE NEXT PAGE

17. "There was never the least attention paid to what was cut up for sausage; there would come all the way back from Europe old sausage that had been rejected, and that was moldy and white—it would be dosed with borax and glycerine, and dumped into the hoppers, and made over again for home consumption. . . . There would be meat stored in great piles in rooms; and the water from leaky roofs would drip over it, and thousands of rats would race about on it."

The passage above is most likely excerpted from

(A) John Steinbeck's *The Grapes of Wrath*
(B) Theodore Dreiser's *An American Tragedy*
(C) Jane Addams' *Twenty Years at Hull-House*
(D) Lincoln Steffens' *The Shame of the Cities*
(E) Upton Sinclair's *The Jungle*

MAJOR HOUSEHOLD EXPENDITURES, 1900 and 1928

1900	
2 Bicycles	$ 70
Wringer and washboard	$ 5
Brushes and brooms	$ 5
Sewing machine (mechanical)	$ 25
Total	$ 105
1928	
Automobile	$ 700
Radio	$ 75
Phonograph	$ 50
Washing machine	$ 150
Vacuum cleaner	$ 50
Sewing machine (electric)	$ 60
Other electrical equipment	$ 25
Telephone (year)	$ 35
Total	$1,145

18. The chart above shows the major household expenditures of a middle-class American family in 1900 and a similar family in 1928. Which of the following is an accurate statement supported by the chart?

(A) Families needed more mechanical help with housework in 1928 than they did in 1900 because they had less domestic help.
(B) Inflation caused a significant increase in the prices of most household goods by 1928.
(C) Many families moved from rural to urban areas between 1900 and 1930 in search of employment opportunities.
(D) By 1928 more consumer goods were available to families than had been available in 1900.
(E) Increased consumer spending was a major cause of the stock market crash of 1929.

GO ON TO THE NEXT PAGE

19. "Rosie the Riveter" was a nickname given during the Second World War to

    (A) American women who did industrial work in the 1940's
    (B) American women who cared for soldiers wounded in battle
    (C) a machine that increased the speed of construction work
    (D) a woman who was a popular radio talk-show host of the 1940's
    (E) a woman who broadcast Japanese propaganda to American troops

GO ON TO THE NEXT PAGE

UPI/Corbis-Bettmann

20. The picture above illustrates efforts in the 1960's to organize a boycott that focused attention on the

(A) long hours of grocery clerks and stock clerks
(B) problems of Mississippi Valley fruit growers
(C) labor shortages in produce transport companies
(D) plight of migrant farmworkers
(E) problems of West Coast wineries

GO ON TO THE NEXT PAGE

21. Which of the following statements best describes the response of Native Americans to the continued settlement of Europeans in North America during the eighteenth century?
    (A) Native Americans traded with the French and the English as a means of maintaining their autonomy.
    (B) Native Americans in the southern part of New France negotiated treaties with the French that allowed the peaceful expansion of the European timber trade.
    (C) Some Native Americans created a horse-based nomadic culture in the Northeast.
    (D) Native Americans in the Great Plains assimilated with the European settlers.
    (E) The Iroquois did not adopt European firearms and metal tools, in an effort to maintain their own traditions.

22. In the seventeenth century, the British colonies in the Chesapeake Bay region became economically viable due to the
    (A) adoption of representative government
    (B) introduction of tobacco cultivation
    (C) flourishing trade with American Indians
    (D) export of dried cod and whale tallow
    (E) cultivation of cotton

23. All of the following were aspects of the Constitution that was submitted to the states for ratification in 1787 EXCEPT
    (A) the ability to levy taxes
    (B) congressional authority to declare war
    (C) a two-term limit for Presidents
    (D) provision for impeachment of the President
    (E) provision for presidential State of the Union messages

GO ON TO THE NEXT PAGE

The St. Louis Art Museum. Gift Bank of America

24. The painting above, which shows an antebellum election site, supports which of the following statements?

    (A) Women were equal participants in the voting process.
    (B) The sale and provision of liquor was prohibited on election day.
    (C) Party workers had to remain at least 50 yards away from the polling place.
    (D) There were no property restrictions for male voters.
    (E) Elections were a welcome social event as well as a political obligation.

---

25. The introduction of canals, railroads, and new factory technology in the mid-nineteenth century affected which of the following regions LEAST?

    (A) New England
    (B) New York and Pennsylvania
    (C) New Jersey and Delaware
    (D) The South
    (E) The Midwest

GO ON TO THE NEXT PAGE

Questions 26-27 are based on the passage below.

"Unsanitary housing, poisonous sewage, contaminated water, infant mortality, the spread of contagion, adulterated food, impure milk, smoke-laden air, ill-ventilated factories . . . unwholesome crowding, prostitution and drunkenness are the enemies which the modern cities must face and overcome, would they survive. Logically their electorate should be made up of those who . . . have at least attempted to care for children, to clean houses, to prepare foods, to isolate the family from moral dangers. . . . To test the elector's fitness to deal with this situation by his ability to bear arms is absurd. . . . City housekeeping has failed partly because women, the traditional housekeepers, have not been consulted as to its multiform activities. The men have been carelessly indifferent to much of this civic housekeeping, as they have been carelessly indifferent to the details of the household."

Jane Addams, 1906.

26. Which of the following best reflects the main argument of the passage?

(A) Men should spend less time away from home and participate more fully in domestic life.
(B) Women should be able to vote in order to apply their proven housekeeping abilities to the civic sphere.
(C) Military solutions to social problems are ineffective because they ignore moral issues.
(D) Solving the problems of cities mostly depends on providing for poor children.
(E) Modern cities have been saved from ruin only by the involvement of women in civic issues.

27. The passage above suggests that Jane Addams would probably have supported all of the following EXCEPT

(A) military preparedness
(B) woman suffrage
(C) prohibition
(D) settlement houses
(E) the Pure Food and Drug Act

GO ON TO THE NEXT PAGE

PITTSBURG: A CITY ASHAMED

McCLURE'S MAGAZINE

MAY

LINCOLN STEFFENS'S exposure of another type of municipal grafting; how Pittsburg differs from St. Louis and Minneapolis.

THE END OF THE WORLD, by Professor Newcomb. A powerful story, yet a scientific prediction; pictures by the famous French artist, Henri Lanos.

IDA M. TARBELL on the Standard tactics which brought on the famous oil crisis of 1878.

SIX SHORT STORIES

Culver Pictures, Inc.

28. The articles appearing in this 1905 issue of *McClure's Magazine* illustrate all of the following trends in the early twentieth-century United States EXCEPT:

(A) Popular magazines were beginning to turn their attention to issues of reform.
(B) Reform of municipal city governments was a growing concern.
(C) Exposure of monopolistic business practices was beginning to draw public attention.
(D) Scientific methods were increasingly called on to lend credibility to all sorts of theories.
(E) Reformers of both government and society enjoyed widespread support among leading industrialists.

GO ON TO THE NEXT PAGE

Questions 29-30 are based on the chart below.

IMMIGRATION TO THE UNITED STATES BY AREA OF ORIGIN

Year	All Countries	Europe	Asia	Americas	Africa	Australasia
1921	805,228	652,364	25,034	124,118	1,301	2,281
1922	309,556	216,385	14,263	77,448	520	915
1924	706,896	364,339	22,065	318,855	900	679
1925	294,314	148,366	3,578	141,496	412	462
1927	335,175	168,368	3,669	161,872	520	746
1928	307,255	158,513	3,380	144,281	475	606
1929	279,678	158,598	3,758	116,177	509	636

29. Which of the following areas of origin showed the greatest percentage decline in the number of immigrants to the United States between 1921 and 1929 ?

(A) Europe
(B) Asia
(C) The Americas
(D) Africa
(E) Australasia

30. Which of the following best accounts for the trend in immigration shown in the chart?

(A) Improved economic conditions in many areas of origin
(B) Warfare in several areas of the world during this period
(C) New United States immigration legislation
(D) Economic instability in the United States
(E) Increased immigration to other areas of North America

GO ON TO THE NEXT PAGE

31. In the seventeenth century, some Pueblo Indians of the desert Southwest adopted Christianity as

(A) an added dimension to their own religious culture, adding the Christian God as another deity
(B) evidence of an ancient European culture that they were willing to embrace
(C) a means of improving their agricultural practices
(D) as a means of establishing greater equality within their community
(E) a means of direct communication with the afterlife through the practice of Christian prayer

32. Of the following, who challenged the religious establishment in Puritan New England?

(A) Cotton Mather
(B) Thomas Hutchinson
(C) Anne Hutchinson
(D) John Winthrop
(E) Abigail Adams

33. Henry Clay's "American System" included which of the following?

(A) A protective tariff that would fund internal improvements
(B) Restriction on the use of federal money for national defense
(C) Restriction on immigration from Asian countries
(D) Elimination of the national bank
(E) Protection of the property rights of Native Americans

34. In 1860 a southern writer, D. R. Hundley, wrote: "Know, then, that the Poor Whites of the South constitute a separate class to themselves; the Southern Yeomen are as distinct from them as the Southern Gentleman is from the Cotton Snob."

Which of the following characterizations would Hundley probably accept as best describing the southern yeoman?

(A) A class of White plantation employees who oversaw slave labor
(B) A group of landowners who generally owned more than 100 slaves and who formed the elite of southern society
(C) A group of independent farmers who owned small plots and few, if any, slaves
(D) A small group of farmers who believed that there were few, if any, class distinctions in the South
(E) A class of people known for their poor manners and lack of education

35. The Exclusion Act of 1882 prohibited the immigration of which of the following groups?

(A) Irish
(B) Mexicans
(C) Eastern European Jews
(D) Japanese
(E) Chinese

GO ON TO THE NEXT PAGE

MONTHLY WAGES AND SEXUAL COMPOSITION OF THE WORKFORCE IN SELECTED TRADES IN NEW YORK CITY, 1850

Trade	Average Male Wage	Average Female Wage	Percent Male	Percent Female
Clothing and tailors	$ 9.75	$ 6.99	48.5	51.5
Hats and millinery	27.51	17.14	43.5	56.5
Shoes and boots	24.32	10.43	75.2	24.8
Printing	36.28	14.48	71.3	28.7

36. Which of the following statements about the trades listed above is supported by the data in the table?

(A) The majority of female workers were in the hats and millinery trade.
(B) Both men and women received wages that were inadequate to support their families.
(C) In trades where women were in the majority, the difference between men's and women's wages was less than in trades where women were in the minority.
(D) The trades in which women were most highly represented had the lowest wages in the economy.
(E) The most skilled female workers were paid less than unskilled male workers.

GO ON TO THE NEXT PAGE

37. All of the following statements about the American home front during the Second World War are correct EXCEPT:

(A) The government instituted direct price controls to halt inflation.
(B) The Supreme Court upheld the forced relocation of Japanese Americans on the West Coast.
(C) Black workers migrated in large numbers from the rural South to the industrial cities of the North and West.
(D) Unemployment continued at Depression-era levels.
(E) Business leaders served as heads of the federal war-mobilization programs.

38. Which of the following events of the civil rights movement best illustrates the concept of "non-violent civil disobedience"?

(A) The *Brown* v. *The Board of Education of Topeka* case of 1954
(B) The lunch-counter sit-ins of the early 1960's
(C) The March on Washington, D.C., in 1963
(D) The formation of the Black Panther party in 1966
(E) The desegregation of Little Rock, Arkansas, Central High School

39. In the 1950's John Kenneth Galbraith's *The Affluent Society* and W. H. Whyte's *The Organization Man* were significant because they

(A) criticized American conformity and the belief that economic growth would solve all problems
(B) challenged the American view that the Soviet Union was responsible for the Cold War
(C) advocated the nationalization of basic industries to increase production and profits
(D) were novels describing life among the "beat generation"
(E) urged a greater role for religion in American life and acceptance of Christian ethics by business executives

The Odd Couple

Reprinted by permission of Bill Mauldin and the Watkins/Loomis Agency.

40. Which of the following policies is the subject of the cartoon above?

(A) Vietnamization
(B) Containment
(C) Détente
(D) Interventionism
(E) Isolationism

41. The Halfway Covenant adopted by many Puritan congregations in the late seventeenth century did which of the following?

(A) Strengthened the Anglican church in New England.
(B) Undermined religious toleration in New England.
(C) Promoted Christianity among American Indians in New England.
(D) Eased the requirements for church membership.
(E) Encouraged belief in the doctrine of predestination.

GO ON TO THE NEXT PAGE

42. At the time of the American Revolution, the most valuable cash crop produced in the southern states was

(A) cotton
(B) corn
(C) sugar
(D) wheat
(E) tobacco

43. The War of 1812 resulted in

(A) an upsurge of nationalism in the United States
(B) the acquisition of territories from Great Britain
(C) the strengthening of Napoleon in Europe
(D) the large-scale emigration of Europeans to the United States
(E) the elimination of United States shipping from European waters

44. Which of the following provides the best evidence of Lincoln's talents as a political leader?

(A) His success in getting his Reconstruction policies passed by Congress
(B) His skill in getting the South to acknowledge responsibility for the outbreak of the Civil War
(C) His success in securing adoption of the Fifteenth Amendment
(D) His ability to keep his party relatively united despite its internal conflicts
(E) His success in winning public support for a military draft

45. All of the following situations contributed to agrarian discontent in the late nineteenth century EXCEPT:

(A) Cotton averaged 5.8 cents a pound between 1894 and 1898, whereas it had been 15.1 cents a pound between 1870 and 1873.
(B) Short-haul railroad rates rose 60 percent in the 1890's.
(C) Farmers borrowed more heavily from banks than they had before the Civil War.
(D) European countries raised duties on agricultural products in the 1880's.
(E) The wheat harvest in Europe declined 30 percent in 1897.

46. At the beginning of the twentieth century, critics labeled individuals who exploited workers, charged high prices, and bribed public officials as

(A) robber barons
(B) free silverites
(C) knights of labor
(D) captains of industry
(E) muckrakers

GO ON TO THE NEXT PAGE

DISTRIBUTION OF TOTAL PERSONAL INCOME AMONG THE UNITED STATES POPULATION, 1950–1970

Year	Poorest Fifth	Second Poorest Fifth	Middle Fifth	Second Wealthiest Fifth	Wealthiest Fifth
1950	3.1%	10.5%	17.3%	24.1%	45.0%
1960	3.2%	10.6%	17.6%	24.7%	44.0%
1970	3.6%	10.3%	17.2%	24.7%	44.1%

47. The chart above supports which of the following statements?

(A) Federal antipoverty programs in the 1960's had little impact on the national distribution of income.
(B) Between 1950 and 1970, children tended to remain in the same socioeconomic groups as their parents.
(C) The wealthiest people earned about the same amount of money in 1970 as they earned in 1960.
(D) The increased number of women in the labor force in the 1970's had little effect on the amount of total family income.
(E) The number of people in the "poorest fifth" remained about the same from 1950 to 1970.

GO ON TO THE NEXT PAGE

48. "One who breaks an unjust law must do so openly, lovingly, and with a willingness to accept the penalty. I submit that an individual who breaks the law that conscience tells him is unjust, and who willingly accepts the penalty of imprisonment in order to arouse the conscience of the community over its injustice, is in reality expressing the highest respect for the law."

The quotation above most clearly expresses the views of

(A) Malcolm X
(B) Phyllis Schlafly
(C) Martin Luther King, Jr.
(D) Douglas MacArthur
(E) Barry Goldwater

49. Rachel Carson's book *Silent Spring* was a

(A) forestry manual
(B) description of deaf people's perception of the changing seasons
(C) protest against noise pollution
(D) protest against overuse of chemical insecticides
(E) protest against the Vietnam War

50. Which of the following was a consequence of President Lyndon B. Johnson's Great Society program?

(A) An end to the urban population decline in the East and Midwest
(B) Full employment until the end of the 1960's
(C) The near elimination of urban and rural poverty
(D) A major redistribution of the income tax burden
(E) An increase in federal spending on social services

51. "For we must consider that we shall be as a city upon a hill, the eyes of all people are upon us. So that if we shall deal falsely with our God in this work we shall have undertaken, and so cause Him to withdraw His present help from us, we shall be made a story and a by-word through the world."

The statement above was made by

(A) Jonathan Edwards preaching to a congregation during the Great Awakening
(B) John Winthrop defining the purpose of the Puritan colony
(C) Thomas Jefferson on the adoption of the Declaration of Independence
(D) William Penn defining the purpose of the Pennsylvania colony
(E) Benjamin Franklin gathering support for the American Revolution

52. Which of the following best characterizes the Anti-Federalists?

(A) They wanted a strong executive branch.
(B) They were loyal supporters of the Crown.
(C) They drew support primarily from rural areas.
(D) They favored universal suffrage.
(E) They favored rapid industrial development.

53. The Missouri Compromise was, in part, an effort to maintain the balance between the number of northerners and southerners in which of the following United States institutions?

(A) The Senate
(B) The House of Representatives
(C) Congress
(D) The Supreme Court
(E) The electoral college

GO ON TO THE NEXT PAGE

54. Which of the following is true of the Black Codes of the Reconstruction era?

(A) They promised every adult male former slave "forty acres and a mule."
(B) They were Andrew Johnson's response to criticism that he was not doing enough for former slaves.
(C) They were the result of joint actions by scalawags and carpetbaggers in the southern states.
(D) They were passed by the Radical Republicans in Congress to ensure the rights of former slaves.
(E) They were passed by Southern state legislatures to restrict the rights of former slaves.

55. Advocates of a free silver policy argued that the free coinage of silver would

(A) increase the supply of money and end economic depressions
(B) facilitate free trade between countries
(C) limit the market power of farmers
(D) stabilize the value of gold in relation to silver
(E) increase the value of the dollar in relation to currencies of foreign countries

56. Skilled male workers felt threatened by all of the following changes that occurred in the United States economy between 1890 and 1920 EXCEPT the

(A) arrival of large numbers of immigrants from southern Europe, eastern Europe, and Mexico
(B) introduction of "scientific management" to increase factory production and lower labor costs
(C) growing power of major corporations
(D) increasingly widespread distribution of inexpensive consumer goods
(E) growing presence of women workers in industry

57. Which of the following was demonstrated by the outcome of the presidential election of 1928 ?

(A) The nation had become convinced of the futility of Prohibition.
(B) "Republican prosperity" was a persuasive campaign slogan.
(C) Ethnic and religious differences among Americans exerted little influence on their voting behavior.
(D) Great numbers of ethnic minority-group voters switched from the Democratic to the Republican Party.
(E) The Ku Klux Klan was the commanding force in United States politics during the 1920's.

58. "[The American] is intensely and cocksurely moral, but his morality and his self-interest are crudely identical. He is emotional and easy to scare, but his imagination cannot grasp an abstraction. He is a violent nationalist and patriot, but he admires rogues in office and always beats the tax-collector if he can. He is violently jealous of what he conceives to be his rights, but brutally disregardful of the other fellow's."

The author of the quotation above is the noted journalist and satirist

(A) Dorothy Thompson
(B) Lillian Hellman
(C) H. L. Mencken
(D) Will Rogers
(E) Pearl Buck

GO ON TO THE NEXT PAGE

59. Which of the following contributed most to ending the post-Second World War economic boom?

(A) Women leaving the workforce
(B) Development of the computer
(C) Consolidation of agriculture
(D) A shift in population to the Sunbelt
(E) The Arab oil embargo

60. The United States of the 1970's was characterized by an increase in all of the following EXCEPT

(A) computer technology and marketing
(B) an awareness of the rights of minorities
(C) the migration of Americans from the Frostbelt to the Sunbelt
(D) the strength of political party attachments
(E) the number of multinational corporations

61. Colonists in eighteenth-century South Carolina benefited from the knowledge of Africans about the cultivation of

(A) tobacco
(B) rice
(C) sugar
(D) cotton
(E) wheat

62. In the hundred years prior to 1776, which of the following had the LEAST influence on the emergence of the movement for independence in England's North American colonies?

(A) The control of money bills by colonial legislatures
(B) The long period of conflict between England and France
(C) The models provided by the autonomous governments of other English colonies
(D) The distance between England and its colonies
(E) Constitutional developments in England

63. "To maintain the existing relations between the two races, inhabiting that section of the Union, is indispensable to the peace and happiness of both. It cannot be subverted without drenching the country in blood, and extirpating one or the other of the races."

The statement above was most likely made by which of the following?

(A) John C. Calhoun to the United States Senate
(B) Frederick Douglass to the Anti-Slavery Society
(C) Daniel Webster to the South Carolina legislature
(D) John Brown at Harpers Ferry
(E) Abraham Lincoln in Springfield, Illinois

64. "In the late nineteenth century, the federal government followed a laissez-faire policy toward the economy."

A historian could argue against this thesis using all of the following pieces of evidence EXCEPT

(A) tariff laws protecting various industries from European competition
(B) laws granting land to the transcontinental railroad corporations
(C) government policy toward the unemployed during the depression of the 1890's
(D) the Bland-Allison Act of 1878 and the Sherman Silver Purchase Act of 1890
(E) the Interstate Commerce Act of 1887

65. Booker T. Washington encouraged Black people to pursue all of the following EXCEPT

(A) accommodation to White society
(B) racial solidarity
(C) industrial education
(D) economic self-help
(E) public political agitation

GO ON TO THE NEXT PAGE

66. "What we want to consider is, first, to make our employment more secure, and, secondly, to make wages more permanent. . . . I say the labor movement is a fixed fact. It has grown out of the necessities of the people, and, although some may desire to see it fail, still the labor movement will be found to have a strong lodgment in the hearts of the people, and we will go on until success has been achieved."

The quotation above best reflects the philosophy of which of the following organizations around 1900 ?

(A) Industrial Workers of the World
(B) National Labor Union
(C) American Federation of Labor
(D) Congress of Industrial Organizations
(E) Knights of Labor

67. Theodore Roosevelt issued his corollary to the Monroe Doctrine primarily because

(A) Japan's actions in Manchuria had violated the "open door"
(B) United States protection was needed by the colonies acquired in the Spanish-American War
(C) the Filipino people revolted against United States rule
(D) the financial difficulties of Caribbean nations threatened to bring about European intervention
(E) the declining toll revenue from the Panama Canal threatened Panamanian stability

68. "The problem lay buried, unspoken, for many years in the minds of American women. It was a strange stirring, a sense of dissatisfaction, a yearning that women suffered in the middle of the twentieth century in the United States. Each suburban wife struggled with it alone. As she made the beds, shopped for groceries, ate peanut butter sandwiches with her children, chauffeured Cub Scouts and Brownies, she was afraid to ask even of herself the silent question—'Is this all?'"

The passage above supports which of the following statements about women in the middle of the twentieth century?

(A) Women were no longer interested in political activities.
(B) Feminism tended to be a middle-class movement.
(C) Feminism renewed interest in religion among women.
(D) There were very few educational opportunities for women.
(E) Most women supported the feminist movement.

69. "Government is not the solution to our problems. Government is the problem."

The statement above was made by

(A) John F. Kennedy, asserting that the government did not do enough for the people
(B) Dwight D. Eisenhower, arguing that the government interfered with the military's operations
(C) Jimmy Carter, claiming that the government was inefficient and unfair
(D) Gerald Ford, charging that the government was corrupt
(E) Ronald Reagan, contending that the government had taken on functions properly belonging to the private sector

GO ON TO THE NEXT PAGE

From Herblock At Large (Pantheon, 1987)

70. Which of the following best summarizes the idea expressed in the 1987 cartoon above?

(A) In the 1980's, budget and trade deficits and scandal undermined the international standing of the United States.
(B) President Reagan expected that an international economic summit would enable the United States to solve its financial problems.
(C) In the 1980's, the United States could not look to its economic partners for help in solving its economic problems.
(D) The economic problems of the United States in the 1980's resulted from European economic policies.
(E) Had it not been for the Iran-Contra scandal, the United States could have solved its economic problems.

GO ON TO THE NEXT PAGE

71. "No man was a warmer wisher for reconciliation than myself, before the fatal nineteenth of April 1775, but the moment the event of that day was made known, I rejected the hardened, sullen tempered Pharaoh of England for ever; and disdain the wretch, that with the pretended title of FATHER OF HIS PEOPLE, can unfeelingly hear of their slaughter, and composedly sleep with their blood upon his soul."

The passage above comes from

(A) the Declaration of Independence
(B) *The Federalist* papers
(C) *Letters from a Farmer in Pennsylvania*
(D) the Virginia Resolves against the Stamp Act
(E) *Common Sense*

72. Alexander Hamilton's plan for stimulating economic growth in the United States included all of the following EXCEPT

(A) acquisition of additional territory
(B) a protective tariff
(C) expansion of manufacturing
(D) establishment of a national bank
(E) federal assumption of debts incurred by states during the Revolutionary War

73. The first American party system, which developed in the 1790's, maintained party discipline at the federal level primarily by means of

(A) caucuses
(B) nominating conventions
(C) rotation in office
(D) restrictive primaries
(E) "pork barrel" legislation

74. Which of the following was true of the Jacksonian Democrats in the 1830's?

(A) They were the minority party in the nation.
(B) They opposed a national bank.
(C) They supported South Carolina's nullification of the protective tariff.
(D) They were stronger in New England than in the West.
(E) They generally repudiated the ideas of the Jeffersonian Republicans.

75. "We hold these truths to be self-evident: that all men and women are created equal. . . . The history of mankind is a history of repeated injuries and usurpations on the part of man toward woman, having in direct object the establishment of an absolute tyranny over her."

The quotation above is excerpted from the

(A) Seneca Falls Declaration of Sentiments and Resolutions
(B) United States Declaration of Independence
(C) United States Constitution
(D) Declaration of Rights and Grievances
(E) Equal Rights Amendment (ERA)

76. Which of the following is true of the Pullman strike of 1894 ?

(A) It brought a substantial portion of American railroads to a standstill.
(B) It started when Pullman workers were fired after the Haymarket riot.
(C) It was caused by grievances about unsafe working conditions.
(D) It ended when the government forced management to settle with the union.
(E) It ended when the courts issued a blanket injunction against management.

GO ON TO THE NEXT PAGE

77. "We must be the great arsenal of democracy. For this is an emergency as serious as war itself. We must apply ourselves to our task with the same resolution, the same sense of urgency, the same spirit of patriotism, and sacrifice, as we would show were we at war."

The emergency to which the speaker refers was

(A) German U-boat attacks in 1917
(B) the Spanish Civil War in 1936
(C) German warfare against Britain in 1940
(D) the Berlin Blockade of 1948
(E) the Cuban missile crisis of 1962

78. The legislation passed between 1935 and 1937 dealing with the rôle of the United States in future wars seemed to reflect a belief that

(A) totalitarianism directly threatened the security of the United States
(B) the United States should quickly intervene in any future world wars
(C) the United States had made a mistake in not joining the League of Nations
(D) the United States should not have become involved in the First World War
(E) the United States should take a position of leadership in world affairs

79. Civil rights organizations in the 1950's and 1960's based their court suits primarily on the

(A) five freedoms of the First Amendment
(B) Fourteenth Amendment
(C) Thirteenth Amendment
(D) "necessary and proper" clause of the Constitution
(E) Preamble to the Constitution

80. The Nixon administration differed from previous administrations in adopting which of the following Vietnam War policies?

I. The bombing of North Vietnam
II. The use of American combat troops
III. The invasion of Cambodia
IV. The mining of North Vietnamese harbors

(A) I only
(B) I and III only
(C) II and III only
(D) II and IV only
(E) III and IV only

81. Which of the following political ideas or philosophies inspired the American revolutionaries of the eighteenth century?

(A) Progressivism
(B) Populism
(C) Manifest Destiny
(D) Republicanism
(E) The Social Gospel

82. The first major nineteenth-century political conflict over the issue of slavery was settled by the

(A) Alien and Sedition Acts
(B) Kentucky and Virginia Resolutions
(C) Missouri Compromise
(D) Kansas-Nebraska Act
(E) *Dred Scott* decision

GO ON TO THE NEXT PAGE

83. During the 1850's, Kansas became a significant issue for which of the following reasons?

(A) The territory was an important way station in the Underground Railroad.
(B) Northern and southern states vied to establish the first transcontinental railway through Kansas.
(C) Kansas served as a center for the Peoples (Populist) Party's agitation against railroads and banks.
(D) John Quincy Adams invoked the gag rule to prevent the discussion of slavery in the Senate.
(E) It led to a divisive debate over the expansion of slavery into the territories.

84. Which of the following was a significant movement in American literature during the late nineteenth century?

(A) Creationism
(B) Modernism
(C) Romanticism
(D) Classicism
(E) Realism

85. Edward Bellamy's *Looking Backward*, written in the 1880's, was a utopian reaction to which of the following?

(A) The disillusionment with an increasingly competitive and industrial society
(B) The plight of farmers who were driven off their land during the Great Depression
(C) The disillusionment of the planter aristocracy in the post-Civil War era
(D) The growing number of immigrants who regretted leaving their homes in Europe
(E) Increasing concerns over the growth and power of labor unions in the railroad industry

86. The Harlem Renaissance refers to

(A) Marcus Garvey's "back to Africa" crusade
(B) the reemergence of the Ku Klux Klan as a force in American politics
(C) writers and artists in New York who expressed pride in their African American culture
(D) American expatriate writers living in Paris who wrote critically of American society
(E) the political success of the Democratic Party in northern urban neighborhoods

87. The Federal Reserve Act of 1913 established a

(A) single central bank like the Bank of England
(B) method of insuring bank deposits against loss
(C) system to guarantee the continued existence of the gold standard
(D) system of local national banks
(E) system of district banks coordinated by a central board

88. The Korean War and the Vietnam War differed in that only one involved

(A) a formal declaration of war
(B) a communist-led government
(C) troops under United Nations auspices
(D) Soviet arms support to one of the belligerents
(E) United States air and ground forces

GO ON TO THE NEXT PAGE

From Herblock On All Fronts (New American Library, 1980)

89. Which of the following best summarizes the idea expressed in the cartoon above?

(A) Most people are too dependent on computers in their daily lives.
(B) The amount of information available via computers is so overwhelming that people are no longer able to use the information effectively.
(C) Individual privacy is being threatened by the computerization of personal information.
(D) Many industries in the United States are threatened with significant layoffs as computers replace workers.
(E) People in the United States have been more reluctant to begin using computers than have people in other parts of the world.

GO ON TO THE NEXT PAGE

90. Which of the following is an accurate statement about the Equal Rights Amendment to the Constitution proposed in the 1970's?

    (A) It was opposed primarily by those who feared a loss of political power.
    (B) It guaranteed equal opportunity for women in the workplace.
    (C) It became a part of the Constitution in 1978.
    (D) It represented the first effort to enfranchise women.
    (E) It failed to gain the necessary votes for ratification within the constitutional time limit.

STOP

IF YOU FINISH BEFORE TIME IS CALLED, YOU MAY CHECK YOUR WORK ON THIS TEST ONLY.
DO NOT TURN TO ANY OTHER TEST IN THIS BOOK.

How to Score the SAT Subject Test in United States History

When you take an actual SAT Subject Test in United States History, your answer sheet will be "read" by a scanning machine that will record your response to each question. Then a computer will compare your answers with the correct answers and produce your raw score. You get one point for each correct answer. For each wrong answer, you lose one-fourth of a point. Questions you omit (and any for which you mark more than one answer) are not counted. This raw score is converted to a scaled score that is reported to you and to the colleges you specify.

Worksheet 1. Finding Your Raw Test Score

STEP 1: Table A on the following page lists the correct answers for all the questions on the Subject Test in United States History that is reproduced in this book. It also serves as a worksheet for you to calculate your raw score.

- Compare your answers with those given in the table.
- Put a check in the column marked "Right" if your answer is correct.
- Put a check in the column marked "Wrong" if your answer is incorrect.
- Leave both columns blank if you omitted the question.

STEP 2: Count the number of right answers.

Enter the total here: ________________

STEP 3: Count the number of wrong answers.

Enter the total here: ________________

STEP 4: Multiply the number of wrong answers by .250.

Enter the product here: ______________

STEP 5: Subtract the result obtained in Step 4 from the total you obtained in Step 2.

Enter the result here: _______________

STEP 6: Round the number obtained in Step 5 to the nearest whole number.

Enter the result here: _______________

The number you obtained in Step 6 is your raw score.

Table A

Answers to the Subject Test in United States History and Percentage of Students Answering Each Question Correctly

Question Number	Correct Answer	Right	Wrong	Percentage of Students Answering the Question Correctly*	Question Number	Correct Answer	Right	Wrong	Percentage of Students Answering the Question Correctly*
1	A			71	33	A			43
2	C			85	34	C			38
3	B			89	35	E			42
4	C			64	36	C			46
5	B			92	37	D			64
6	B			80	38	B			64
7	E			62	39	A			32
8	A			77	40	C			29
9	C			74	41	D			37
10	C			77	42	E			54
11	D			72	43	A			52
12	C			61	44	D			37
13	C			61	45	E			33
14	B			77	46	A			57
15	D			80	47	A			32
16	C			74	48	C			48
17	E			69	49	D			30
18	D			83	50	E			57
19	A			69	51	B			39
20	D			53	52	C			47
21	A			41	53	A			28
22	B			55	54	E			63
23	C			71	55	A			49
24	E			90	56	D			39
25	D			56	57	B			32
26	B			53	58	C			19
27	A			83	59	E			27
28	E			36	60	D			29
29	B			57	61	B			15
30	C			60	62	C			23
31	A			31	63	A			18
32	C			43	64	C			25

Table A continued on next page

Table A continued from previous page

Question Number	Correct Answer	Right	Wrong	Percentage of Students Answering the Question Correctly*	Question Number	Correct Answer	Right	Wrong	Percentage of Students Answering the Question Correctly*
65	E			41	78	D			30
66	C			26	79	B			26
67	D			29	80	E			11
68	B			32	81	D			23
69	E			29	82	C			33
70	A			40	83	E			64
71	E			38	84	E			35
72	A			36	85	A			23
73	A			28	86	C			82
74	B			36	87	E			16
75	A			31	88	C			18
76	A			24	89	C			68
77	C			12	90	E			24

* These percentages are based on an analysis of the answer sheets of a representative sample of 8,509 students who took the original administration of this test and whose mean score was 534. They may be used as an indication of the relative difficulty of a particular question.

Answer explanations for the Subject Test in United States History can be found on page 115.

Finding Your Scaled Score

When you take SAT Subject Tests, the scores sent to the colleges you specify are reported on the College Board scale, which ranges from 200–800. You can convert your practice test score to a scaled score by using Table B. To find your scaled score, locate your raw score in the left-hand column of Table B; the corresponding score in the right-hand column is your scaled score. For example, a raw score of 39 on this particular edition of the Subject Test in United States History corresponds to a scaled score of 560.

Raw scores are converted to scaled scores to ensure that a score earned on any one edition of a particular Subject Test is comparable to the same scaled score earned on any other edition of the same Subject Test. Because some editions of the tests may be slightly easier or more difficult than others, College Board scaled scores are adjusted so that they indicate the same level of performance regardless of the edition of the test taken and the ability of the group that takes it. Thus, for example, a score of 400 on one edition of a test taken at a particular administration indicates the same level of achievement as a score of 400 on a different edition of the test taken at a different administration.

When you take the SAT Subject Tests during a national administration, your scores are likely to differ somewhat from the scores you obtain on the tests in this book. People perform at different levels at different times for reasons unrelated to the tests themselves. The precision of any test is also limited because it represents only a sample of all the possible questions that could be asked.

Table B

Raw Score	Scaled Score	Raw Score	Scaled Score	Raw Score	Scaled Score
90	800	52	630	14	430
89	800	51	630	13	430
88	800	50	620	12	420
87	800	49	620	11	420
86	800	48	610	10	410
85	800	47	610	9	410
84	800	46	600	8	400
83	800	45	600	7	400
82	800	44	590	6	390
81	800	43	590	5	390
80	800	42	580	4	380
79	800	41	580	3	380
78	790	40	570	2	370
77	780	39	560	1	370
76	780	38	560	0	360
75	770	37	550	-1	360
74	760	36	550	-2	350
73	750	35	540	-3	350
72	750	34	540	-4	340
71	740	33	530	-5	330
70	730	32	530	-6	330
69	730	31	520	-7	320
68	720	30	520	-8	310
67	710	29	510	-9	310
66	710	28	510	-10	300
65	700	27	500	-11	290
64	700	26	490	-12	290
63	690	25	490	-13	280
62	680	24	480	-14	270
61	680	23	480	-15	270
60	670	22	470	-16	260
59	670	21	470	-17	260
58	660	20	460	-18	250
57	660	19	460	-19	250
56	650	18	450	-20	240
55	650	17	450	-21	230
54	640	16	440	-22	230
53	640	15	440		

Scaled Score Conversion Table
Subject Test in United States History

How Did You Do on the Subject Test in United States History?

After you score your test and analyze your performance, think about the following questions:

Did you run out of time before reaching the end of the test?

If so, you may need to pace yourself better. For example, maybe you spent too much time on one or two hard questions. A better approach might be to skip the ones you can't answer right away and try answering all the questions that remain on the test. Then if there's time, go back to the questions you skipped.

Did you take a long time reading the directions?

You will save time when you take the test by learning the directions to the Subject Test in United States History ahead of time. Each minute you spend reading directions during the test is a minute that you could use to answer questions.

How did you handle questions you were unsure of?

If you were able to eliminate one or more of the answer choices as wrong and guess from the remaining ones, your approach probably worked to your advantage. On the other hand, making haphazard guesses or omitting questions without trying to eliminate choices could cost you valuable points.

How difficult were the questions for you compared with other students who took the test?

Table A shows you how difficult the multiple-choice questions were for the group of students who took this test during its national administration. The right-hand column gives the percentage of students that answered each question correctly.

A question answered correctly by almost everyone in the group is obviously an easier question. For example, 85 percent of the students answered question 2 correctly. But only 19 percent answered question 58 correctly.

Keep in mind that these percentages are based on just one group of students. They would probably be different with another group of students taking the test.

If you missed several easier questions, go back and try to find out why: Did the questions cover material you haven't yet reviewed? Did you misunderstand the directions?

Answer Explanations for the United States History Subject Test

1. Choice (A) is the correct answer. In the seventeenth and eighteenth centuries, the English colonial system was based largely on the principles of mercantilism, the theory that a nation's prosperity depends upon its supply of capital and the purpose of colonies is to enrich the home country. The English government implemented in its colonies such measures as the Navigation Acts, a series of acts intended to restrict England's carrying trade to English ships. Some of these acts enumerated colonial products, such as sugar, tobacco, indigo, rice, and molasses, that could only be shipped directly to England or to another English colony. These acts contributed to the unrest that led to the rebellion of the American colonies.

2. Choice (C) is the correct answer. The term "separation of powers" refers to the framers' division of governmental authority among the legislative, executive, and judicial branches of the government. This division of authority allows each branch to check the actions of the others, more or less balancing the powers of each branch.

3. Choice (B) is the correct answer. As a result of the enforcement of the Treaty of New Echota, Native American land in the East was exchanged for lands west of the Mississippi River. The Trail of Tears refers to the forced removal of the Cherokee tribe in 1838-39. Almost 17,000 tribe members were rounded up in camps and forced to relocate to the West. An estimated 4,000 Cherokees died during the relocation.

4. Choice (C) is the correct answer. Harriet Beecher Stowe, the author of *Uncle Tom's Cabin*, advocated the abolition of slavery. She was not involved with prohibition.

5. Choice (B) is the correct answer. The diagram indicates that the ratio of black males to black females remained fairly constant during the period from 1820 to 1850.

6. Choice (B) is the correct answer. The cartoon's caption ("Man Is But a Worm") and the portrayal of human figures alongside monkeys and other animals refer to Darwin's theory of evolutionary progress through natural selection.

7. Choice (E) is the correct answer. In the early twentieth century, young and unmarried women became more likely to work outside of the home. It was unusual for women who were married or had been married to work outside the home in the early years of the twentieth century.

8. Choice (A) is the correct answer. President Franklin D. Roosevelt initiated the New Deal programs in 1933 to provide economic relief during the Great Depression, but in the following year the Supreme Court began to find significant parts of the New Deal unconstitutional. In 1937, Roosevelt proposed the Judiciary Reorganization Bill, also known as the Court-packing Bill, which would allow him to increase the number of Supreme Court judges. He proposed this measure in order to appoint justices who would uphold the New Deal legislation.

9. Choice (C) is the correct answer. The cartoon depicts an individual portrayed as a farmer refusing welfare packets, while joyously accepting the same measures when they are called "price supports." This is a reference to the New Deal measures that guaranteed farmers a minimum price for their products in order to encourage the flow of production during the Great Depression.

10. Choice (C) is the correct answer. In 1959, Fidel Castro overthrew the regime of Fulgencio Batista and oversaw Cuba's transformation into a Communist state. In January 1961, President Dwight D. Eisenhower broke diplomatic ties with Cuba and, in April, newly inaugurated President John F. Kennedy approved and enacted an invasion of Cuba. The Bay of Pigs invasion was undertaken in an attempt to overthrow Castro.

11. Choice (D) is the correct answer. In colonial America, women could not hold political office, serve as clergy, vote, or serve as jurors, but single women and widows did have the right to own property.

12. Choice (C) is the correct answer. In 1765, the British Parliament passed the Stamp Act, an act that implemented direct taxation of legal documents, permits, commercial contracts, newspapers, pamphlets, and playing cards in the American colonies by requiring that they carry a tax stamp. The Stamp Act was protested by the colonists, who refused to use the stamps and boycotted imports from British merchants and manufacturers.

13. Choice (C) is the correct answer. The decision in *Marbury v. Madison* is significant because it asserted the principle of judicial review, or the power of the judiciary branch—in particular, the Supreme Court—to determine the constitutionality of legislation passed by Congress.

14. Choice (B) is the correct answer. Sharecropping was a system that evolved after the abolition of slavery in the South. Former slaves used their crops to pay for their rent, while planters provided cash advances to secure labor for their lands. It was a system that provided a source of labor for planters and a meager source of income for poor laborers.

15. Choice (D) is the correct answer. "Manifest Destiny," a term coined in the 1840s, refers to the belief that the United States has a destiny to expand its territorial borders and to spread its ideals of democracy and freedom. The quote discusses the annexation of Texas and expansion as a preordained ideal ("the most natural, right and proper thing in the world").

16. Choice (C) is the correct answer. The cartoon depicts the growing power of railroads, represented by the figure of a steam engine. People watch fearfully as the giant figure symbolizing the railroad walks through a ravaged area carrying a club labeled "CAPITAL." The cartoon suggests that the financial interests of the railroads were taking precedence over all other cultural values.

17. Choice (E) is the correct answer. *The Jungle*, a book written in 1906 by Upton Sinclair, was concerned with issues of food processing such as those listed in the passage. Sinclair, a socialist, wrote the book to elicit sympathy for workers but was ultimately successful in securing government legislation regarding food. The uproar caused by *The Jungle* aided the passage of the Meat Inspection Act and the Pure Food and Drug Act in 1906.

18. Choice (D) is the correct answer. The chart indicates that by 1928 many consumer goods not available to middle-class American families in 1900—including automobiles, radios, vacuum cleaners, and telephones—had become available.

19. Choice (A) is the correct answer. The nickname "Rosie the Riveter" referred to women who went to work in United States factories during the Second World War. Many women were employed by manufacturing plants to fill the positions left empty by men who were fighting in the war.

20. Choice (D) is the correct answer. The picture depicts striking migrant workers. The captions in the placards held by the workers refer to the NFWA, the National Farm Workers Association, which was founded by César Chávez in 1962. In 1965, Chávez and the NFWA led a strike by California grape pickers and a boycott of California grapes.

21. Choice (A) is the correct answer. In response to the continued settlement of Europeans in North America during the eighteenth century, Native Americans sought to establish trading relations with the French and the English.

22. Choice (B) is the correct answer. The Chesapeake Bay colonies began to thrive economically only after the cultivation of tobacco as a cash crop.

23. Choice (C) is the correct answer. The Twenty-second Amendment, proposed in 1947 and ratified in 1951, limits the president to two terms in office. The amendment was passed after President Franklin D. Roosevelt had been elected to a fourth term.

24. Choice (E) is the correct answer. The painting depicts men socializing at an election site in the mid-nineteenth century.

25. Choice (D) is the correct answer. New England, New York and Pennsylvania, New Jersey and Delaware, and the Midwest saw tremendous economic growth with the mid-nineteenth-century introduction of canals, railroads, and new factory technology. The South was the area that was least advanced in transportation and industry, and thus saw the least economic growth from the expansion in modes of transportation and industrial production.

26. Choice (B) is the correct answer. The quotation implies that women, who have proven their abilities in the domestic sphere ("those who . . . have at least attempted to care for children, to clean houses, to prepare foods"), should be allowed to vote in order to extend their helpful influence into the political sphere ("civic housekeeping").

27. Choice (A) is the correct answer. Jane Addams was a pacifist and the passage does not indicate her support for war. As her statement suggests ("To test the elector's fitness . . . by his ability to bear arms is absurd"), Addams thought society valued military prowess too highly. Moreover, choices (B), (C), (D), and (E) all describe reforms that Addams seems to think are necessary, given the information in the passage.

28. Choice (E) is the correct answer. The articles in this issue of *McClure's Magazine* illustrate the nature and some of the tactics of Progressive reform. Progressives sought to reform municipal governments ("exposure of another type of municipal grafting") and business practices of monopoly ("famous oil crisis of 1878"), and to emphasize scientific investigations ("A powerful story, yet a scientific prediction"). Progressives also attempted to regulate business and therefore were not always looked on favorably by industrialists, so it is incorrect to suggest that the reformers enjoyed widespread support among industrialists.

29. Choice (B) is the correct answer. Asia shows the sharpest drop in immigration during this period. The enforcement of the Chinese Exclusion Act coupled with the passage of the National Origins Act in 1924 resulted in a sharp decline in Asian immigration during this period.

30. Choice (C) is the correct answer. The chart shows declining immigration due to the passage of the National Origins Act, which restricted immigration in 1924 by establishing a system of national quotas. The Act, which strengthened legislation passed in 1921 and virtually barred immigration from Asia, severely limited immigration from southern and eastern Europe.

31. Choice (A) is the correct answer. Upon contact with Christianity, which had spread into South and Central America through the influence of the Spanish, some Pueblo Indians incorporated elements of Christianity into their own religious beliefs. This incorporation of Christian features into traditional belief systems occurred among native groups throughout the Americas.

32. Choice (C) is the correct answer. This question is about dissent in seventeenth-century Puritan New England. Anne Hutchinson challenged the authority of the clergy. Choices (A) and (D) are incorrect, as Cotton Mather and John Winthrop were leading members of the Puritan clergy. Choices (B) and (E) are incorrect, as both Thomas Hutchinson and Abigail Adams lived during a later time period.

33. Choice (A) is the correct answer. Henry Clay's "American System" was proposed during a period of heightened nationalism after the War of 1812. The American System was designed to promote national economic growth through high tariffs, internal improvements, western settlement, and reconciliation of regional differences. The other options were not aspects of Clay's system.

34. Choice (C) is the correct answer. The quotation suggests that "yeomen" are neither "Poor Whites" nor "Southern Gentlemen." Choices (A), (B), (D), and (E) do not describe southern yeomen.

35. Choice (E) is the correct answer. This question tests knowledge of immigration policy in the nineteenth century. The Exclusion Act of 1882 was passed as a reaction to Chinese immigration in the late nineteenth century. Many Chinese had come to the United States during the Gold Rush, and tended to work hard for low wages. When the United States economy suffered instability in the 1870s, Chinese immigrants were singled out.

36. Choice (C) is the correct answer. The chart indicates that the gap between the wages of men and women was far smaller in clothing, tailoring, hats, and millinery—jobs in which women were in the majority. None of the other statements are supported by the data in the table.

37. Choice (D) is the correct answer. Statement (D) is inaccurate. There was a sharp decrease in unemployment due to wartime industrial production. The need for workers was so great that thousands of women were employed in factories for the first time. All of the other statements are accurate.

38. Choice (B) is the correct answer. Nonviolent civil disobedience is the protest act of breaking laws in a peaceful manner and without any harm to others. The lunch-counter sit-ins were such an example, as African American students entered restaurants and cafes that were segregated and sat in areas marked for "Whites only," despite the fact that there were laws supporting segregation. Choice (A) is incorrect. This was a Supreme Court ruling that overturned school segregation and was not a protest. Choices (C) and (D) are incorrect. They refer to protests and events that were legal. Choice (E) is incorrect. This is a reference to a government initiative that was implemented through the use of military force.

39. Choice (A) is the correct answer. John Kenneth Galbraith and W. H. Whyte were two prominent social critics who criticized the American emphasis on materialism and conformity in the 1950s. The other choices do not describe Galbraith's and Whyte's books.

40. Choice (C) is the correct answer. Détente was a policy of peaceful coexistence of the United States and the Soviet Union. The cartoon depicts the American eagle and the Russian bear and symbolizes the two countries in harmony and united as a family. Choice (A) is incorrect. Vietnamization referred to the escalating conflict in Vietnam and the cartoon indicates harmony. Choice (B) is incorrect. Containment was a policy that sought to check the spread of communism pitting the United States against the Soviet Union. Choice (D) is incorrect. It refers to intervention in the internal affairs of another country. Choice (E) is incorrect. Isolationism did not mean harmony and cooperation, but rather an effort to exclude the outside world.

41. Choice (D) is the correct answer. The Halfway Covenant was adopted to address the problem of declining church membership in the late seventeenth century. Under this covenant, adults who had been baptized into the church as children but who had not yet experienced the conversion necessary for full membership could nonetheless have their children baptized. The other choices are incorrect.

42. Choice (E) is the correct answer. Tobacco was the most valuable export crop that was produced in the South on the eve of the Revolution in the 1770s. Cotton, choice (A), did not surpass tobacco as the South's chief crop until the 1800s. Choices (B), (C), and (D) are incorrect.

43. Choice (A) is the correct answer. The War of 1812 did lead to a rising spirit of nationalism. Choice (B) is incorrect. The war did not lead to the acquisition of territories. Choice (C) is incorrect. The war did not strengthen Napoleon. Choice (D) is incorrect. There was no large-scale emigration from Europe after the war. Choice (E) is incorrect. U.S. shipping and trade with Europe resumed after the war.

44. Choice (D) is the correct answer. Lincoln displayed remarkable political skills in holding the Republican Party together during the Civil War period, as radicals and moderates contended to shape policy. The other choices are incorrect.

45. Choice (E) is the correct answer. A declining wheat harvest in Europe did not contribute to agrarian discontent in the United States in the late nineteenth century. It helped to raise farm prices, relieving U.S. farmers. Each of the other choices did contribute to the economic depression suffered by American farmers in the 1890s.

46. Choice (A) is the correct answer. Critics called wealthy industrialists who engaged in exploitative practices "robber barons." Choice (D) was not a term of criticism that

was applied to these individuals, and choices (B), (C), and (E) are terms that applied to those who opposed the practices described in the question.

47. Choice (A) is the correct answer. The chart shows that despite the passage of Great Society programs in the 1960s, the distribution of income remained relatively unchanged in 1970. One possible explanation may be due to the difficulty of promoting political and economic change through federal initiatives. Another reason may be due to the fact that in the 1970s technological change and economic growth had raised everyone's standard of living, minimizing the potential for wealth to be redistributed. The other statements are not supported by the information in the chart.

48. Choice (C) is the correct answer. The quotation is an excerpt from the "Letter from a Birmingham Jail" by Martin Luther King, Jr., in which he expresses his philosophy of civil disobedience. The other choices are not correct.

49. Choice (D) is the correct answer. This question concerns Rachel Carson's work on environmental pollution and its effects. Rachel Carson's book documented the harmful effects of chemicals. The other choices are incorrect.

50. Choice (E) is the correct answer. This question asks about the effects of the Great Society programs. The programs, which included Head Start, Job Corps, and VISTA, did increase federal spending on social services. Choice (A) is incorrect. The Great Society programs did not lead to a decline in urban population. Choice (B) is incorrect. There was no full employment during this period. Choice (C) is incorrect. The Great Society programs did not eliminate poverty, although they made efforts to provide assistance to the poor. Choice (D) is incorrect. The programs did not change the income tax structure.

51. Choice (B) is the correct answer. The quotation is an excerpt of John Winthrop's address to his Puritan congregation. The idea of "a city upon a hill," or a community that is an example to others, has been invoked by politicians, including Ronald Reagan, to describe the nation as a whole. The other choices are incorrect.

52. Choice (C) is the correct answer. The Anti-Federalists, persons who opposed ratification of the U.S. Constitution in 1787-89, drew their support primarily from farmers in rural areas. Choice (A) is incorrect. The Anti-Federalists feared a strong central government. Choice (B) is incorrect. The Anti-Federalists were not supporters of the Crown. Choice (D) is incorrect. The Anti-Federalists did not favor universal suffrage.

Choice (E) is incorrect. The Anti-Federalists were opposed to industrial development and favored an agrarian economy.

53. Choice (A) is the correct answer. This question asks for an identification of one of the goals of the Missouri Compromise of 1820. The Compromise was an effort to maintain the balance between slave states and free states in the Senate, which in 1819 had senators from 11 free states and 11 slave states, by admitting Maine (free) and Missouri (slave) at the same time. Choices (B) and (C) are incorrect, as the Compromise did not change the House of Representatives. The other choices are incorrect, as the Compromise did not affect the balance in any of the other agencies of government.

54. Choice (E) is the correct answer. This question asks about the purpose of the Black Codes. The Black Codes were laws passed by Southerners to restrict the freedom of former slaves. Choices (A) and (B) are incorrect, as the Black Codes restricted the rights of former slaves. Choice (C) is incorrect, as Southerners, not carpetbaggers, passed the Codes. Choice (D) is incorrect, as the measures passed by Radical Republicans were intended to help former slaves (or freed slaves) and the Black Codes had the opposite effect.

55. Choice (A) is the correct answer. Advocates of free silver argued that the United States' tight domestic monetary policies were the cause of the economic depressions of the late nineteenth century. They believed that increasing the circulation of silver would help farmers by raising crop prices and allow farmers and others to pay their debts more easily. The other choices are incorrect.

56. Choice (D) is the correct answer. Although consumerism began in the 1870s with catalog buying, it did not become widespread until the mid-twentieth century. Skilled male workers were not threatened by consumerism during this period. Each of the other choices reflects a specific threat to skilled male workers around the turn of the century.

57. Choice (B) is the correct answer. In 1928, Republican Herbert Hoover, bolstered by years of economic prosperity under Republican administrations, defeated Alfred E. Smith, a Catholic who suffered from anti-Catholic prejudice.

58. Choice (C) is the correct answer. The quote is an excerpt from the work of H. L. Mencken, a satirist and critic of American social and cultural weaknesses. As

the quote suggests, Mencken was famous for exposing American pretensions and hypocrisy.

59. Choice (E) is the correct answer. The question asks about the primary reason for the end of the post–Second World War boom. The 1973 oil embargo led to a huge increase in oil prices, inflation, and the end of the economic boom. The other choices are incorrect.

60. Choice (D) is the correct answer. The election of 1972 was the first presidential election in which most of the Southern states broke ranks with the Democratic Party and voted Republican. This shift in allegiances contradicted traditional party affiliations and also changed Southern politics.

61. Choice (B) is the correct answer. Colonists in South Carolina gained knowledge of rice cultivation from slaves from the "Rice Coast," the traditional rice-growing region of West Africa.

62. Choice (C) is the correct answer. The colonists were not influenced by autonomous governments in other English colonies because there were no autonomous governments in other English colonies. All the other choices refer to factors that contributed to the emergence of an independence movement.

63. Choice (A) is the correct answer. This is an excerpt from an address by John C. Calhoun to the United States Senate. This speech reflects Calhoun's anti-abolitionist views.

64. Choice (C) is the correct answer. The government provided no support for the unemployed during the 1890s. All other choices refer to intervention by the government to help particular interests and therefore could be used to disprove the statement that the government followed a laissez-faire, or "hands off," policy.

65. Choice (E) is the correct answer. Booker T. Washington never advocated direct political activism for black people. Washington believed that black people would be best served by pursuing the goals listed in the other choices.

66. Choice (C) is the correct answer. The quote represents the position of the American Federation of Labor, the sole unifying agency of the American labor movement in the early twentieth century.

67. Choice (D) is the correct answer. Theodore Roosevelt responded to a crisis in the Caribbean, where the Dominican Republic stopped payments on its debts to various nations, by issuing a corollary to the Monroe Doctrine. This statement reasserted the intention of the United States to prevent European intervention in Latin America, as established by the Monroe Doctrine.

68. Choice (B) is the correct answer. The passage is a quote from Betty Friedan and describes the frustrations of suburban middle-class women in the 1950s who generated the modern feminist movement. The other choices are not supported by the passage.

69. Choice (E) is the correct answer. This statement expresses Ronald Reagan's policy of small government: cutting taxes, scaling back government intervention, and letting the market and the private sector attempt to solve domestic social problems. This attitude toward government is a hallmark of the Reagan Revolution.

70. Choice (A) is the correct answer. The cartoon depicts the United States, symbolized by Ronald Reagan and Uncle Sam, afflicted by debt and scandals and no longer able to command respect from other nations.

71. Choice (E) is the correct answer. This is an excerpt from Thomas Paine's *Common Sense*, a pamphlet published in January 1776 that sold 150,000 copies and helped inflame the American Revolution. Paine was referring to the day of fighting between colonists and British soldiers at Lexington and Concord, during which several colonists were killed.

72. Choice (A) is the correct answer. Hamilton did not consider territorial acquisition as a primary factor in developing the economy and was a strong proponent of developing the manufacturing and mercantile base. The other choices represent aspects of his plan.

73. Choice (A) is the correct answer. The caucus was the apparatus for selecting political candidates during this period. In every election from 1800 to 1824, members of Congress from each party met in a caucus to choose the party's candidates for president and vice president.

74. Choice (B) is the correct answer. Jacksonian Democrats were vehemently opposed to a national bank, which they viewed as an instrument of mercantile interests. The other choices are inaccurate statements about the Jacksonian Democrats.

75. Choice (A) is the correct answer. The quote is an excerpt from the Seneca Falls Declaration. This Declaration, which was drawn up at a meeting in Seneca Falls, New York, in 1848, uses the language and the logic of the Declaration of Independence to make the case for women's rights.

76. Choice (A) is the correct answer. The Pullman strike was a major strike begun by Pullman rail workers who were angry about reduced wages. When sympathetic railway workers agreed to boycott all trains carrying Pullman cars, rail service was disrupted nationwide. Federal troops ended the strike and arrested the organizers.

77. Choice (C) is the correct answer. This is a quote from Franklin D. Roosevelt's speech after Germany's attack on Britain in 1940, before the United States entered the Second World War. Roosevelt appealed to factory owners and workers to turn their efforts to weapons production to aid in the fight against Germany.

78. Choice (D) is the correct answer. The neutrality acts passed between 1935 and 1937 sought to keep the United States out of the coming Second World War and were based on the belief that the United States' involvement in the First World War was a mistake. The other choices are incorrect.

79. Choice (B) is the correct answer. Civil rights organizations used the "due process" and "equal protection" clause of the Fourteenth Amendment, which guarantees equal rights under the law to all Americans, to force changes in existing laws. In *Brown v. Board of Education of Topeka*, for example, the Supreme Court held that segregated schools were unconstitutional under the Fourteenth Amendment.

80. Choice (E) is the correct answer. The invasion of Cambodia and the mining of North Vietnamese harbors were policies that were initiated by the Nixon administration. Previous administrations had sent thousands of combat troops to Vietnam and engaged in bombing the North.

81. Choice (D) is the correct answer. The eighteenth-century revolutionaries were inspired by the principles of republicanism, which emphasized popular sovereignty, equality, and liberty. The other terms are all associated with later periods in American history.

82. Choice (C) is the correct answer. The Missouri Compromise of 1820, which admitted Maine into the Union as a free state and Missouri as a slave state (but with some restrictions), solved the first major political conflict over slavery in the nineteenth

century. The Missouri Compromise did not last; it was superceded by the Kansas-Nebraska Act of 1854. The other choices are incorrect.

83. Choice (E) is the correct answer. The Kansas-Nebraska Act of 1854 allowed people in the territories of Kansas and Nebraska to decide for themselves whether to allow slavery. Rival groups of settlers, some pro-slavery and some anti-slavery, moved into Kansas and fought with one another to determine the future of the state. After seven years of well-publicized bitter conflict, Kansas entered the Union as a free state in January 1861. The conflict in Kansas reverberated throughout the country and set the stage for the Civil War.

84. Choice (E) is the correct answer. This was a period when writers like William Dean Howells and Theodore Dreiser tried to portray the challenges posed by social and economic realities.

85. Choice (A) is the correct answer. Edward Bellamy's novel imagines a plan for repairing the problems of industrial society. The novel's main character awakes in the year 2000 after 113 years of sleep and is pleased to find himself living in an organized utopian society under wise government control.

86. Choice (C) is the correct answer. The term "Harlem Renaissance" refers to an outpouring of artistic and literary work by African American writers and artists centered in Harlem, in New York City, during the 1920s. The other choices are incorrect.

87. Choice (E) is the correct answer. The Federal Reserve Act created a network of regional Federal Reserve banks. The Federal Reserve System includes 12 Federal Reserve banks, a governing board, and several thousand member banks.

88. Choice (C) is the correct answer. The Korean War was supported by a United Nations resolution and involved United Nations troops. No U.N. troops participated in the Vietnam conflict. The other choices are incorrect.

89. Choice (C) is the correct answer. The cartoon depicts Americans living in a fishbowl, symbolizing the loss of privacy that comes with the storing of personal information on computers. The 1978 cartoon reflects early fears about the security of computer technology. The other choices are incorrect.

90. Choice (E) is the correct answer. The Equal Rights Amendment never gained sufficient votes for ratification. The amendment led to deep divisions within the feminist movement and was perceived by some opponents as a threat to family values.

Chapter 3

World History

Purpose

The Subject Test in World History measures your understanding of the development of major world cultures and your use of historical techniques, including the application and weighing of evidence and the ability to interpret and generalize. The test covers all historical fields:

- political and diplomatic
- intellectual and cultural
- social and economic

Format

This one-hour test consists of 95 multiple-choice questions. Many of the questions are global in nature, dealing with issues and trends that have significance throughout the modern world.

Content

The questions test your:

- knowledge of facts and terms commonly used in the social sciences
- understanding of cause-and-effect relationships
- knowledge of the history and geography necessary for understanding major historical developments
- understanding of concepts essential to historical analysis
- capacity to interpret artistic materials
- ability to assess quotations from speeches, documents, and other published materials
- ability to use historical knowledge in interpreting data based on maps, graphs, and charts

Material Covered	Approximate Percentage of Test
Global or Comparative	25%
Europe	25%
Africa	10%
Southwest Asia	10%
South and Southeast Asia	10%
East Asia	10%
The Americas	10%
Periods Covered	
Prehistory and Civilizations to 500 Common Era (C.E.)*	25%
500–1500 C.E.	20%
1500–1900 C.E.	25%
Post–1900 C.E.	20%
Cross-chronological	10%

* The SAT Subject Test in World History uses the chronological designations B.C.E. (before common era) and C.E. (common era). These labels correspond to B.C. (before Christ) and A.D. (anno Domini), which are used in some world history textbooks.

How to Prepare

You can prepare academically for the test by taking a one-year comprehensive course in world or global history at the college-preparatory level and through independent reading of materials on historical topics. Because secondary school programs differ, the Subject Test in World History is not tied to any one textbook or particular course of study. Familiarize yourself with the directions in advance. The directions in this book are identical to those that appear on the test.

Score

The total score is reported on the 200-to-800 scale.

Sample Questions

All questions on the Subject Test in World History are multiple-choice, requiring you to choose the BEST response from five choices. The following sample questions illustrate the types of questions on the test, their range of difficulty, and the abilities they measure. Questions may be presented as separate items or in sets based on quotations, maps, pictures, graphs, or tables.

Directions: Each of the questions or incomplete statements below is followed by five suggested answers or completions. Select the one that is best in each case and then fill in the corresponding circle on the answer sheet.

Note: The World History Test uses the chronological designation B.C.E. (before common era) and C.E. (common era). These labels correspond to B.C. (before Christ) and A.D. (anno Domini), which are used in some world history textbooks.

Some questions require you to know social science terms, factual cause-and-effect relationships, geography, and other data necessary for understanding major historical developments. Questions 1 and 2 fall into this category.

1. Which of the following was immediately responsible for precipitating the French Revolution?
   (A) The threat of national bankruptcy
   (B) An attack upon the privileges of the middle class
   (C) The desire of the nobility for a written constitution
   (D) The suffering of the peasantry
   (E) The king's attempt to restore feudalism

Choice (A) is the correct answer to question 1. To answer this question, you need to recall the circumstances that led in May 1789 to the first meeting of the French Estates-General in over a century and a half, an event that arrayed the Third Estate against the nobility and Louis XVI in the first stage of a political struggle that was to evolve into the French Revolution. With his debt-ridden government brought to a halt, the king, by mid-1788, was left with no other recourse than a promise to convene the Estates-General in the months ahead.

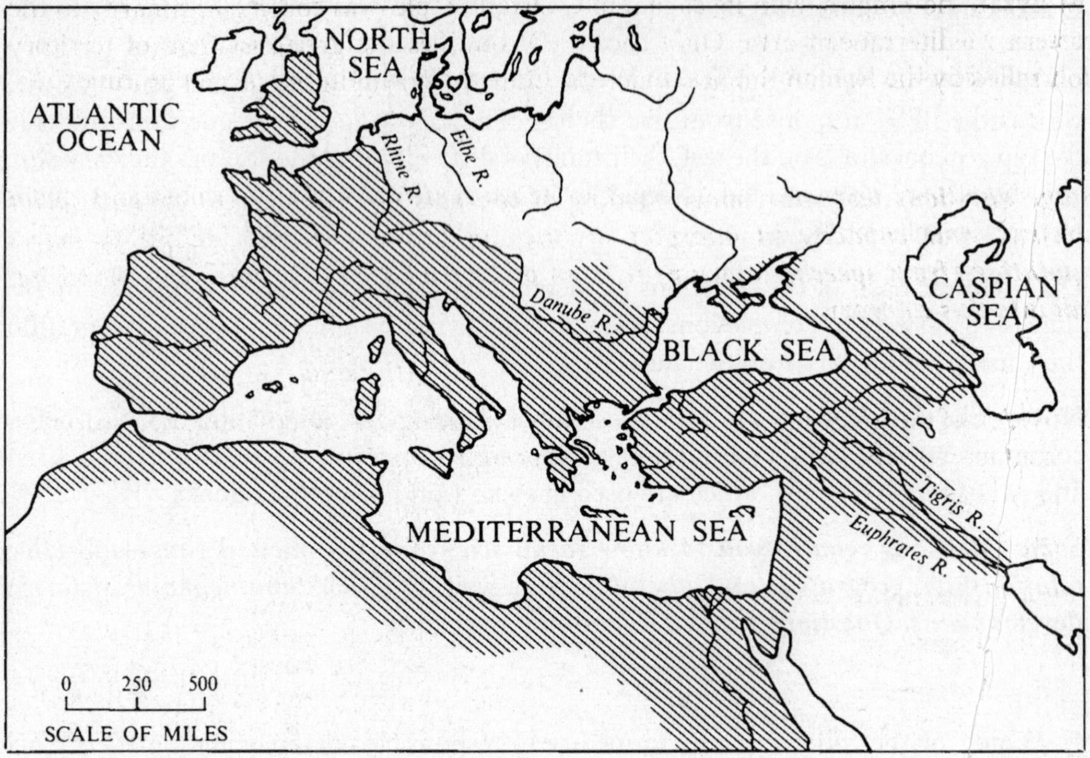

2. The shaded area in the map above shows the extent of which of the following?

(A) Irrigation agriculture in 1000 B.C.E.
(B) Greek colonization in 550 B.C.E.
(C) Alexander the Great's empire in 323 B.C.E.
(D) The Roman Empire in 117 C.E.
(E) The Byzantine Empire in 565 C.E.

Choice (D) is the correct answer to question 2. This question tests your knowledge of both history and geography. To answer it you must know something about the extent to which irrigated farming was practiced in Africa, Europe, and Southwest Asia three thousand years ago, and you need to have a general idea of the extent of the territory controlled by four major ancient civilizations at specific points in time. Choice (A) can be eliminated because irrigation in this early period would have been confined to the regions along the major rivers of the Middle East and Southwest Asia. Choice (B) can be eliminated because Greek colonization was confined primarily to the eastern Mediterranean and did not extend as far north in Europe as shown in the shaded areas of the map. Choice (C) can be eliminated because Alexander the Great's empire did not extend into either the western Mediterranean or northwestern Europe. Choice (E) can be eliminated because the Byzantine Empire, with its capital in Constantinople, was confined primarily to the eastern Mediterranean area. Only choice (D) outlines the greatest extent of territory controlled by the Roman Empire under the Emperor Trajan in the second century C.E.

Some questions test your understanding of concepts essential to history and social science, your capacity to interpret artistic materials, and your ability to assess quotations from speeches, documents, and other published materials. Questions 3–6 fall into this category.

3. Which of the following was introduced into the diet of Europeans only after European contact with the Americas in the fifteenth century?

   (A) Tea

   (B) Rice

   (C) Cinnamon

   (D) Sugar

   (E) Potatoes

Choice (E) is the correct answer to question 3. It is correct because the potato is native to the Peruvian-Bolivian Andes and, after its "discovery" by the Europeans in the fifteenth century, became a staple of the European diet. The potato is now a major food crop worldwide. To answer this question you need to have some basic information about what has come to be known as the "Columbian Exchange," i.e., the enormous biological transfer that occurred as a result of the fifteenth- and sixteenth-century European voyages of discovery. Choice (A) can be ruled out because tea comes from China, not from the Americas, and was not widely used in Europe until the mid-seventeenth century. Choice (B) can be eliminated because the origin of rice culture has been traced to India. Rice was introduced into southern Europe in medieval times. Choice (C) can be eliminated because the cinnamon tree is native to South Asia and, like rice, has been known in Europe since medieval times. Choice (D) can be eliminated because sugarcane originated in what is now known as New Guinea, followed human migration routes from Southeast Asia through Southwest Asia to Europe and, although rare and expensive, was known to the European aristocracy in medieval times.

4. The nineteenth-century wood block print above is associated with the culture of
   - (A) Japan
   - (B) India
   - (C) Iran
   - (D) Myanmar (Burma)
   - (E) Thailand

Choice (A) is the correct answer to question 4. The scene depicted in this dramatic picture is world-famous. Although the spatial arrangement and perspective are generally East Asian and the title at the upper left-hand corner is written in Chinese characters, there are a number of characteristics that identify the picture as Japanese. The dramatic subject matter, with Mount Fuji in the background, is Japanese. In addition, colorful wood-block prints depicting famous scenery, beautiful women, warriors, and well-known theater subjects were popular in Japan from the seventeenth to the nineteenth centuries because they were widely affordable. This work is by the nineteenth-century artist Hokusai.

Questions 5 and 6 refer to the following passage.

> *We have heard that in your country opium is prohibited with the utmost strictness and severity—this is a strong proof that you know full well how hurtful it is to humankind. Since then you do not permit it to injure your own country, you ought not to have the injurious drug transferred to another country, and above all others, how much less to the Middle Kingdom!*

5. The author of the diplomatic dispatch above lived in which of the following countries?
   (A) Ghana
   (B) The Netherlands
   (C) Iran
   (D) China
   (E) Germany

Choice (D) is the answer to question 5. The above discussion of the forced importation of opium suggests China's struggle against Great Britain, culminating in the Opium War of the mid-nineteenth century. The tone of the dispatch, expressing indignation at Great Britain's flaunting of Chinese law, is consistent with China's concern over growing opium addiction in China and with Chinese resistance to the British. From your study of China you will also remember that the Chinese used to refer to their country as the Middle Kingdom.

6. The country which went to war in the nineteenth century over the issue raised in the dispatch was
   (A) France
   (B) Egypt
   (C) Great Britain
   (D) India
   (E) Japan

Choice (C) is the correct answer to question 6. Great Britain was expanding its Asian trade and needed a product to exchange for Chinese goods. Opium from India was Great Britain's answer to this dilemma. The dispatch above was sent by a representative of the Chinese emperor to Queen Victoria shortly before the Opium War (1839–1842), in which China was defeated by the British and therefore was not able to enforce its prohibition against the importation of opium.

Questions posed in the negative, like question 7, account for at most 25 percent of the test questions. Variations of this question format employ the capitalized words NOT or LEAST, as in the following examples: "Which of the following is NOT true?" "Which of the following is LEAST likely to occur?"

7. All of the following are "Pillars of Islam" EXCEPT

   (A) giving alms for the support of society's poor

   (B) praying five times a day in the direction of Mecca

   (C) fasting for one month of the year

   (D) making a pilgrimage to Mecca at least once during a lifetime

   (E) attending mosque prayers daily

Choice (E) is the correct answer to question 7. This question asks you to identify the exception in a series of true statements. In other words, you are being asked to locate the false answer among the five options. To answer this question, you need to draw on your knowledge of Islam. Choices (A) through (D) are true because they refer to four of the five "Pillars of Islam." Choice (E) is false because Muslims are not required to attend mosque prayers daily. The fifth pillar actually is the "profession of faith."

Questions based on graphs, charts, or cartoons require you to use historical knowledge in interpreting data. Questions 8–10 fall into this category.

ANNUAL PRODUCTION OF STEEL
(in thousands of metric tons)

Year				
1865	225	13	97	41
1870	286	68	169	83
1875	723	396	370	258
1880	1,320	1,267	660	388
1885	2,020	1,739	1,202	533
1890	3,637	4,346	2,161	566
1895	3,444	6,212	3,941	899
1900	5,130	10,382	6,645	1,565
1905	5,983	20,354	10,066	2,110
1910	6,374	26,512	13,698	3,506

8. Read from left to right, the column headings for the table above should be
   - (A) Great Britain, United States, Germany, and France
   - (B) Italy, Great Britain, Russia, and Germany
   - (C) Germany, Great Britain, Russia, and France
   - (D) Great Britain, United States, France, and Germany
   - (E) Germany, Russia, Great Britain, and United States

Choice (A) is the correct answer to question 8. To answer this question, you need to know in which country the Industrial Revolution began and which other countries caught up early or late. Great Britain was industrialized by 1850, the United States and Germany were next, and France, Italy, and Russia followed later in the nineteenth century.

Questions containing charts and graphs require careful study and therefore may be more time-consuming than other types of questions. Remember to budget your time accordingly.

Questions 9 and 10 are based on the August 1914 *Punch* cartoon below.

BRAVO, BELGIUM!

9. The "No Thoroughfare" sign in the cartoon is a reference to
   (A) an international treaty guaranteeing the neutrality of Belgium
   (B) the heavy defensive fortifications built by Belgium in the preceding decade
   (C) a bilateral nonaggression pact between Belgium and Germany
   (D) an alliance between Belgium and France
   (E) the treacherous, swampy terrain on the Belgian-German border

Choice (A) is the correct answer to question 9. In this question set you are asked to interpret a British political cartoon published during the tense diplomatic period before the outbreak of the First World War. Choice (A) refers to treaties signed by the Great Powers in 1839 guaranteeing the neutrality of Belgium and Luxembourg in the event of war.

10. This cartoon is a comment on Germany's attempt to

(A) acquire valuable mineral resources in Belgium
(B) invade France through Belgium
(C) force Belgium to repeal tariffs on German goods
(D) intimidate Belgium into signing a military alliance with Germany
(E) pressure Belgium into withdrawing from the Triple Alliance

Choice (B) is the correct answer to question 10. This question focuses on Belgium's resistance to the more powerful Germany's threat of aggression if Belgium, situated between Germany and France, will not give transit to German troops.

Other types of questions rely on knowledge of historical methodology or a grasp of important issues still affecting the world today. Questions 11 and 12 fall into this category.

11. Which of the following statements would be most difficult for historians to prove true or false?

(A) There was little organized education in Europe during the Middle Ages.
(B) Greece contributed more to Western civilization than Rome.
(C) The invention of the steam engine influenced the way people lived.
(D) Russia is territorially the largest country in the world.
(E) The tourist industry in Europe increased markedly after the Second World War.

Choice (B) is the correct answer to question 11. The assertion that Greece's contribution to Western civilization was greater than Rome's requires the most justification. In a methodology question such as the one above, you must make the distinction between statements that are verifiable by fact and statements that are based on judgments. The latter are more difficult than the former to prove true or false because they are evaluations. In this question, choice (B) is the most opinionated of the statements and therefore the one most difficult to prove or disprove.

12. The term "green revolution" refers to

(A) protests against the placement of nuclear weapons in Europe

(B) ecological changes in the ocean because of algae growth

(C) increased agricultural output resulting from development of hybrid seeds and chemical fertilizers

(D) expanded irrigation farming made possible by the construction of large dams

(E) thinning of the atmospheric ozone layer resulting in changes in the growing season

Choice (C) is the correct answer to question 12. To answer this question, you need to know about modern scientific breakthroughs in agricultural research that have allowed countries like India, formerly subject to terrible famines, to become self-sufficient in grain production.

World History Subject Test

Practice Helps

The test that follows is an actual, previously administered SAT Subject Test in World History. To get an idea of what it's like to take this test, practice under conditions that are much like those of an actual test administration.

- Set aside an hour when you can take the test uninterrupted.
- Sit at a desk or table with no other books or papers. Dictionaries, other books, or notes are not allowed in the test room.
- Tear out an answer sheet from the back of this book and fill it in just as you would on the day of the test. One answer sheet can be used for up to three Subject Tests.
- Read the instructions that precede the practice test. During the actual administration you will be asked to read them before answering test questions.
- Time yourself by placing a clock or kitchen timer in front of you.
- After you finish the practice test, read the sections "How to Score the SAT Subject Test in World History" and "How Did You Do on the Subject Test in World History?"
- The appearance of the answer sheet in this book may differ from the answer sheet you see on test day.

WORLD HISTORY TEST

The top portion of the page of the answer sheet that you will use to take the World History Test must be filled in exactly as illustration below. When your supervisor tells you to fill in the circle next to the name of the test you are about to take, mark your answer sheet as shown.

○ Literature	○ Mathematics Level 1	○ German	○ Chinese Listening	○ Japanese Listening
○ Biology E	○ Mathematics Level 2	○ Italian	○ French Listening	○ Korean Listening
○ Biology M	○ U.S. History	○ Latin	○ German Listening	○ Spanish Listening
○ Chemistry	● World History	○ Modern Hebrew		
○ Physics	○ French	○ Spanish	**Background Questions:** ① ② ③ ④ ⑤ ⑥ ⑦ ⑧ ⑨	

After filling in the circle next to the name of the test you are taking, locate the Background Questions box on your answer sheet (as shown above). This is where you will answer the following Background Questions on your answer sheet.

BACKGROUND QUESTIONS

Please answer the two questions below by filling in the appropriate circle in the Background Questions box on your answer sheet. <u>The information you provide is for statistical purposes only and will not affect your test score.</u>

<u>Question I</u>

How many semesters of world history, world cultures, or European history have you taken from grade 9 to the present? (If you are taking a course this semester, count it as a full semester.) Fill in only <u>one</u> circle of circles 1- 4.

- One semester or less —Fill in circle 1.
- Two semesters —Fill in circle 2.
- Three semesters —Fill in circle 3.
- Four or more semesters —Fill in circle 4.

<u>Question II</u>

For the courses in world history, world cultures, or European history you have taken, which of the following geographical areas did you study? Fill in <u>all</u> of the circles that apply.

- Africa —Fill in circle 5.
- Asia —Fill in circle 6.
- Europe —Fill in circle 7.
- Latin America —Fill in circle 8.
- Middle East —Fill in circle 9.

When the supervisor gives the signal, turn the page and begin the World History Test. There are 100 numbered circles on the answer sheet and 95 questions in the World History Test. Therefore, use only circles 1 to 95 for recording your answers.

WORLD HISTORY TEST

Directions: Each of the questions or incomplete statements below is followed by five suggested answers or completions. Select the one that is best in each case and then fill in the corresponding circle on the answer sheet.

Note: The World History Test uses the chronological designations B.C.E. (before common era) and C.E. (common era). These labels correspond to B.C. (before Christ) and A.D. (anno Domini), which are used in some world history textbooks.

1. Which of the following was true of both Greece and China in the period around 500 B.C.E.?

   (A) Both fostered vibrant philosophical schools that debated the human condition.
   (B) Both were threatened by more powerful neighboring civilizations.
   (C) Both experienced economic revolutions brought on by the discovery of iron.
   (D) Both underwent social revolutions that led to the seclusion of women.
   (E) Both suffered from overpopulation that led to class warfare and massive emigration.

2. Which of the following is true of the epic poems the *Mahabharata*, the *Iliad*, and the *Tales of the Heike* ?

   (A) All three were influenced by Chinese literary forms.
   (B) All three stress the exploits of a warrior elite.
   (C) All three were written down at first and later transmitted orally.
   (D) All three stress humanity's independence from the influence of the gods.
   (E) Historians have conclusively identified the authors of the three works.

3. Which of the following statements about the effects of Muhammad's teaching is true?

   (A) Islam initially attracted many followers, but gradually became less popular.
   (B) Muhammad believed that social differences needed to be preserved, which encouraged divisions in society.
   (C) Islam affected every aspect of life and encouraged unity among converts with widely diverse backgrounds.
   (D) Muhammad believed that wealth should be renounced; thus Islam did not attempt to expand.
   (E) Muslims set up a complex priesthood that mediated the contact between Allah and individual believers.

4. The military campaigns of the Huns under Attila contributed to which of the following?

   (A) The introduction of the bubonic plague to Asia
   (B) The fall of the western Roman Empire
   (C) The division of Charlemagne's empire
   (D) The introduction of horse domestication into western Europe
   (E) The defeat of the Muslims in Spain

GO ON TO THE NEXT PAGE

5. After the fall of the Han dynasty, the nomadic peoples who invaded China did which of the following?
   (A) They attempted to restore the Han dynasty to power.
   (B) They tried unsuccessfully to convert the Chinese to Islam.
   (C) They outlawed the use of the Chinese language by governing officials.
   (D) They launched an invasion of Japan.
   (E) They adopted Chinese culture and customs.

6. Mahavira and Buddha were similar in that both
   (A) were successful military leaders who conquered most of India
   (B) resisted the spread of Islam in India
   (C) were theorists who pioneered new mathematical concepts
   (D) led religious movements that challenged the social order of Hinduism
   (E) were martyred for their beliefs

7. "Warfare in nineteenth-century southern Africa was revolutionized with the development of the short, stabbing spear, the body shield, and a tactical formation known as the ox's horns."

   The above describes innovations developed by the
   (A) Zulu
   (B) Xhosa
   (C) Sotho
   (D) Shona
   (E) Ibo

8. All of the following are central to the practice of Islam EXCEPT
   (A) Observation of Ramadan through fasting
   (B) Monotheism
   (C) Prayer five times a day facing Mecca
   (D) Making a pilgrimage to Mecca at least once
   (E) Realistic representations of people in art

9. Which of the following is a pair of neighboring countries both of which had acquired the capability of exploding nuclear weapons by the late 1990's?
   (A) Argentina and Chile
   (B) Mexico and the United States
   (C) The Czech Republic and Germany
   (D) India and Pakistan
   (E) North Korea and South Korea

10. Which of the following best describes the economic strategy of the Soviet Union under Stalin?
    (A) Development of a mixed economy
    (B) Creation of a landowning peasant class
    (C) Production for export
    (D) Centralized economic planning
    (E) Government encouragement of free enterprise

11. Historiography is
    (A) a single, accurate account of events in past time
    (B) the study of how historical accounts are produced
    (C) a chronological chart of historical events
    (D) a historical account based only on written records
    (E) the official record of past events, usually produced by a government

12. Which of the following describes the primary role of the scholar-gentry in imperial China?
    (A) The mainstay of the imperial bureaucracy
    (B) The development of political revolution
    (C) The education of China's peasantry
    (D) The dissemination of European culture in China
    (E) The advancement of engineering and agricultural science

GO ON TO THE NEXT PAGE

13. The Japanese victory in the Russo-Japanese War demonstrated to other non-Western peoples that
    (A) successful modernization was not a strictly Western phenomenon
    (B) countries that held traditional values could not defeat a European power
    (C) passive resistance could be effectively employed in the defeat of a European power
    (D) the distance between Asia and Europe would make Asian industrialization difficult
    (E) further expansion by Russia in Asia was inevitable

14. The defeat of the Umayyads by the Abbasids in 750 C.E. led to the relocation of the caliphate and of the primary center of Islamic culture from
    (A) Mecca to Medina
    (B) Jerusalem to Cairo
    (C) Damascus to Baghdad
    (D) Constantinople to Beirut
    (E) Córdoba to Alexandria

15. Which of the following is an example of an ancient megalithic structure?
    (A) Stonehenge
    (B) The Coliseum
    (C) Angkor Wat
    (D) The Acropolis
    (E) Great Zimbabwe

16. The Aztec viewed the Toltec as
    (A) barbarians who lacked culture
    (B) slaves, fit only for conquest
    (C) the givers of civilization
    (D) heretics who practiced a forbidden religion
    (E) the greatest rivals to the Aztec dominance of the valley of Mexico

17. The terms Indo-European and Bantu were created to describe
    (A) biological races
    (B) language groups
    (C) religious movements
    (D) artistic styles
    (E) ancient empires

18. According to one theory of state formation, large states first developed in river valleys because
    (A) coordination of large-scale irrigation projects created the need for more complex organizations
    (B) the healthier climates of river valleys allowed large populations to develop there
    (C) river valleys provided the best natural defensive barriers for growing states
    (D) river valleys were the only sources of drinking water large enough to support concentrated populations
    (E) river valleys were the best sources of metal ores for weapons and tools

19. In England in the late nineteenth century it was socially acceptable for young working-class women to take jobs as domestic servants because
    (A) many of their employers allowed them to do volunteer work among the urban poor on evenings and weekends
    (B) this work was believed to contribute to habits of hard work, cleanliness, and obedience, which were seen as good preparation for marriage
    (C) such jobs provided opportunities for them to meet and marry men from higher social classes
    (D) the training they received in household management provided them with skills needed for later careers in business
    (E) residence in middle- or upper-class homes contributed to their political education

20. In Chinese history, the phrase "Mandate of Heaven" refers to the
    (A) divine selection of China as the holiest place in the world
    (B) obligation of each individual to obey religious teachings
    (C) divine favor enjoyed by wise and benevolent rulers
    (D) Chinese version of the Ten Commandments
    (E) most important of the Confucian writings

GO ON TO THE NEXT PAGE

21. Which of the following is the commonly accepted meaning of the term *Homo sapiens* ?

(A) The southern apes
(B) The upright-walking humans
(C) The consciously thinking humans
(D) The animal with a large brain
(E) The missing link

22. In their original form, all of the following major religions focused on humanity's relationship to a god or gods EXCEPT

(A) Buddhism
(B) Christianity
(C) Hinduism
(D) Islam
(E) Judaism

23. Social Darwinism is most closely associated with the idea that

(A) government should provide support for disadvantaged members of society
(B) competition is natural to society
(C) revolution is inevitable
(D) imperialistic expansion will increase economic pressures on citizens
(E) technological development will decrease the gap between rich and poor

24. Which of the following led Great Britain and France to declare war on Germany in 1939 ?

(A) Hitler established a fascist dictatorship in Germany.
(B) Germany occupied France.
(C) Germany annexed Austria.
(D) Germany invaded Poland.
(E) Germany passed anti-Semitic laws.

25. The pyramids in ancient Egypt were built to function primarily as

(A) temples
(B) tombs
(C) watchtowers
(D) astronomical observatories
(E) sundials

26. In the Hindu caste system, members of the Brahman caste originally served as

(A) priests
(B) farmers
(C) warriors
(D) merchants
(E) herders

27. Which of the following is attributed to Alexander the Great?

(A) Three centuries of political stability in the Middle East
(B) The establishment of the basic political forms of the Roman Empire
(C) The concept of kingship limited by elected representatives
(D) The spread of Greek cultural forms into western Asia
(E) The extension of property and inheritance rights to women

28. Prior to the Roman conquests of Gaul, Spain, and Britain, these areas were inhabited primarily by

(A) Celts
(B) Goths
(C) Greeks
(D) Mongols
(E) Scythians

29. Which of the following major ancient civilizations did NOT originate along a river valley?

(A) Chinese
(B) Indian
(C) Egyptian
(D) Mesopotamian
(E) Greek

GO ON TO THE NEXT PAGE

30. Which of the following changes best characterizes the commercial revolution that accelerated during the 1400's and continued throughout the Age of Exploration?

    (A) The growth of capitalism as an economic system
    (B) The shift of the center of trading from the Mediterranean Sea to the Indian Ocean
    (C) The development and application of communism
    (D) The decline in the production of consumer goods
    (E) The loss of overseas empires by western European nations

31. The words "alchemy," "algebra," "assassin," "sugar," "zenith," and "zero" entered the English language as a result of the influence on Europe of which of the following cultures?

    (A) Arabic
    (B) Turkish
    (C) Indian
    (D) Aramaic
    (E) Hebrew

32. The principal development during the Neolithic Age was the

    (A) disappearance of the Neanderthals
    (B) invention of writing
    (C) beginning of metallurgy
    (D) domestication of animals and plants
    (E) appearance of craft specialization

33. Cultivation of which of the following crops most drastically changed the geographical distribution of human populations?

    (A) Sugar
    (B) Opium
    (C) Tobacco
    (D) Tea
    (E) Cotton

34. Which of the following crops originated in Mesoamerica and spread to South America and the present-day United States in the pre-Columbian period?

    (A) Maize
    (B) Oats
    (C) Peanuts
    (D) Potatoes
    (E) Wheat

35. The African kingdoms of Mali and Ghana acquired much of their wealth from

    (A) trade across the Sahara
    (B) trade with Portuguese ships along the Atlantic coast
    (C) trade across the Atlantic with the Maya and Aztecs
    (D) production of food for export to Europe
    (E) tribute from the Islamic states north of the Sahara

GO ON TO THE NEXT PAGE

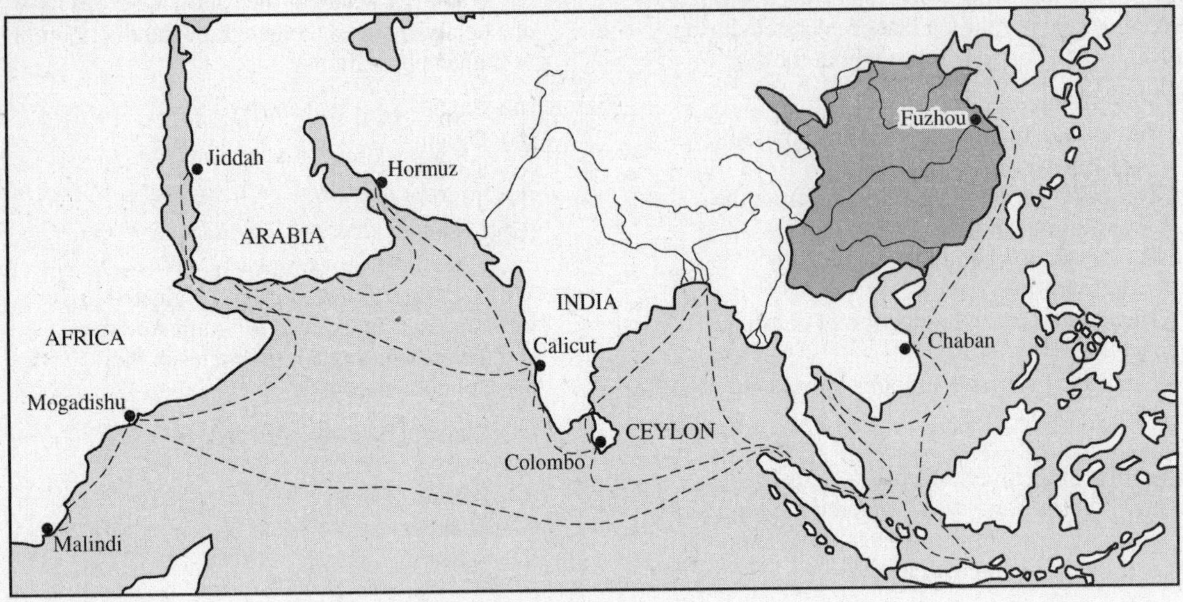

36. The map above shows the route of

(A) Marco Polo on his travels to the court of Kublai Khan
(B) Ibn Battutah on his travels through Dar al-Islam
(C) Zheng He in his seafaring voyages from China
(D) the Arab slave traders
(E) the Buddhist pilgrim Xuanzang

GO ON TO THE NEXT PAGE

37. Which of the following was NOT a Swahili city-state?

(A) Zimbabwe
(B) Mogadishu
(C) Kilwa
(D) Mombasa
(E) Sofala

38. The large earthen mounds built in North America between the tenth and the thirteenth centuries C.E., such as those at Cahokia, are most likely evidence for

(A) the use of communal dwellings
(B) the importance of trade and commerce
(C) a large-scale commitment to road-building
(D) the importance of religious ceremonies and rituals
(E) a democratic form of government

39. Following the First World War, the governments of many of the world's industrialized nations urged women to

(A) leave the paid workforce
(B) provide food and shelter for disabled veterans
(C) take advantage of new opportunities for higher education
(D) join the army to offset war losses
(E) volunteer their services in understaffed hospitals and rehabilitation centers

40. Which of the following Southeast Asian nations has an Islamic majority?

(A) Singapore
(B) Indonesia
(C) The Philippines
(D) Vietnam
(E) Thailand

GO ON TO THE NEXT PAGE

EURASIA, 1300 C.E.

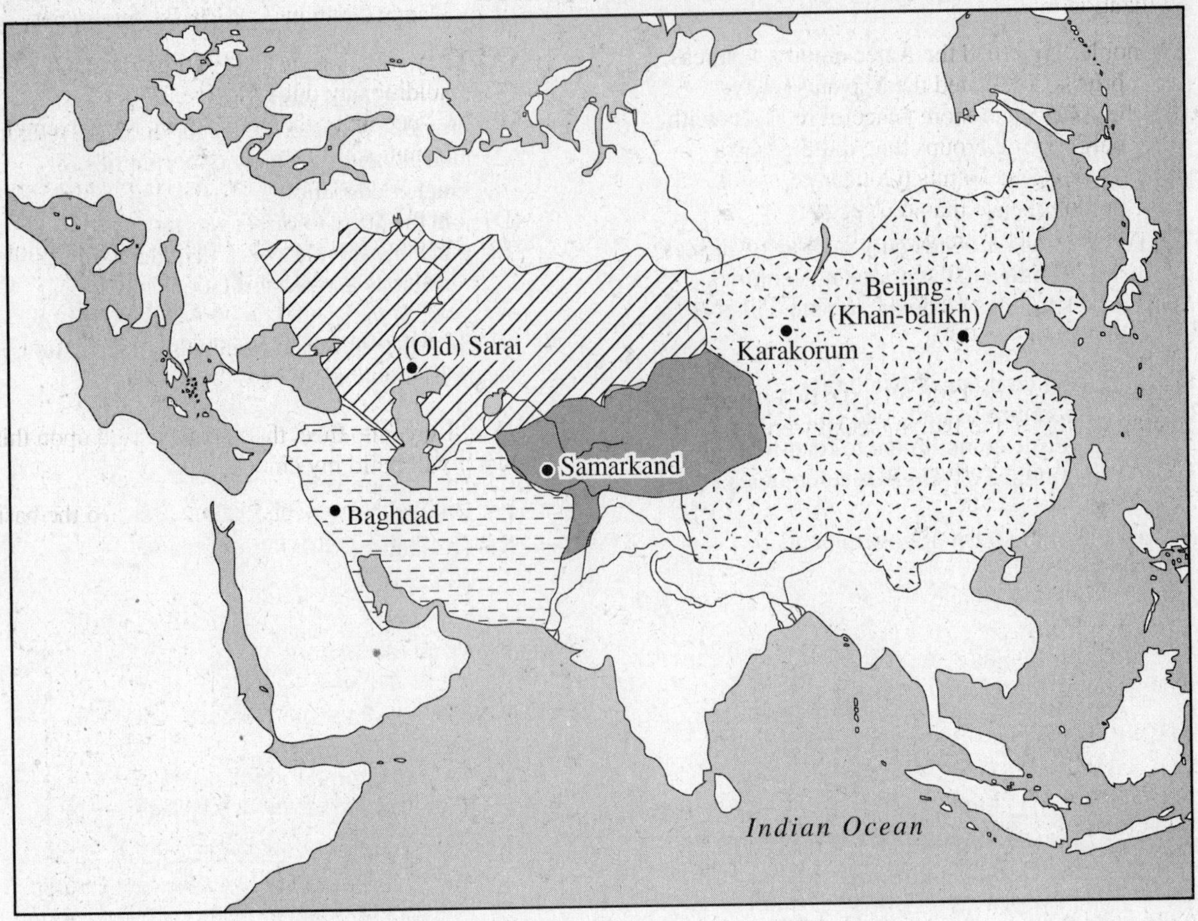

41. The four differently shaded land regions on the map above were collectively known as the

(A) Quadruple Alliance
(B) Hellenistic Kingdoms
(C) Mongol Khanates
(D) Mamluk Sultanates
(E) Tetrarchy

GO ON TO THE NEXT PAGE

42. Mayan civilization differed from Aztec civilization in that

(A) nobles governed the Aztec empire, whereas priests dominated the Mayan society
(B) the Aztecs had more peaceful relations with neighboring groups than did the Maya
(C) the Aztecs had a much longer period of predominance than did the Maya
(D) Mayan cities were generally independent, but Aztec cities were not
(E) Mayan society was much more expansionist than Aztec society

43. In the period before 1500 C.E., the two primary trading groups in the Indian Ocean were the

(A) Africans and Portuguese
(B) Arabs and Indians
(C) Arabs and Portuguese
(D) Chinese and Europeans
(E) Chinese and Indians

44. The first armed attempt to gain Mexican independence from Spain was led by

(A) Simón Bolívar
(B) Antonio López de Santa Anna
(C) Bernardo O'Higgins
(D) Father Miguel Hidalgo
(E) José de San Martín

45. The feudal periods in Japan and western Europe were similar in that both

(A) coincided with a period of growth in the money economy
(B) were characterized by frequent warfare
(C) saw the development of strong monarchies
(D) were marked by greater freedom for women than had existed previously
(E) were dominated by religious strife

46. Which of the following cities had the largest population in 1000 C.E.?

(A) Constantinople
(B) London
(C) Paris
(D) Rome
(E) Toledo

47. Which of the following is true of the legal status of Jews and Christians in early Islamic society?

(A) They were categorically forbidden from holding any public office.
(B) As "people of the book," they were exempt from taxation.
(C) They were required to serve in the army in place of Muslims.
(D) They were allowed to practice their religions with some restrictions.
(E) They were treated as equals of Muslim citizens and were accorded all the same rights and privileges as Muslims.

48. "And I say unto thee, thou art Peter and upon this rock I will build my church."

The Biblical passage cited above formed the basis in the early Catholic church for the

(A) authority of the pope
(B) emphasis on clerical celibacy
(C) seven sacraments
(D) construction of cathedrals
(E) location of the Vatican

49. What was the most significant impact of the period of the Mongol rule on Russia?

(A) The period of Mongol rule reinforced the isolation of Russia from western Europe.
(B) The Mongols aided the Russians in gaining political dominance over the peoples of the Central Asian steppes.
(C) The period of Mongol rule introduced many Muslims into the region of Russia.
(D) The Mongol domination resulted in the destruction of Eastern Orthodoxy and the rise of Nestorian Christianity.
(E) Russians' admiration of Mongol culture led them to abandon their Byzantine roots.

GO ON TO THE NEXT PAGE

50. Which of the following was an important characteristic of the Inca road system?

(A) It was well equipped for even the heaviest wheeled wagons.
(B) It was kept up by privately owned commercial companies.
(C) It required frequent repair because of the high tides and salt water of the Pacific.
(D) It facilitated transportation among the towns of the high Andes mountains.
(E) It linked independent city-states.

51. As a result of the defeats of China in the first Anglo-Chinese war (1839-1842) and in later conflicts with Westerners, the Chinese were forced to do all of the following EXCEPT

(A) allow Western missionaries to seek converts in China
(B) cede Hong Kong territory to the British
(C) open numerous port cities to foreign traders
(D) grant Westerners in China the privilege of extraterritoriality
(E) ban the import of opium into China

52. In 750 C.E., a major political difference between China and Europe was that, unlike Europe, China

(A) was a unified empire
(B) was a theocracy
(C) was controlled by rulers who came from outside its borders
(D) was under threat of invasion from all sides
(E) had a republican form of government

53. "When the personal life is cultivated, the family will be regulated; when the family is regulated, the state will be in order; and when the state is in order, there will be peace throughout the world."

The quotation above reflects a key tenet of which of the following teachings?

(A) Taoism
(B) Zen Buddhism
(C) Mahayana Buddhism
(D) Shinto
(E) Confucianism

54. Early Roman religious ritual was heavily influenced by the religious practices of the

(A) Scythians
(B) Gauls
(C) Etruscans
(D) Carthaginians
(E) Druids

55. After amassing the largest land empire ever known, most of the Mongols and Turks who invaded central and south Asia converted to

(A) Confucianism
(B) Christianity
(C) Buddhism
(D) Judaism
(E) Islam

56. In the seventeenth century, European maritime trade was dominated by the

(A) English
(B) Dutch
(C) French
(D) Swedes
(E) Spanish

57. The failure of Europe's potato crop in the late 1840's spurred mass emigration from

(A) Sweden
(B) Spain
(C) Ireland
(D) Italy
(E) Russia

58. Which of the following became important New World contributions to the world's food crops?

(A) Wheat and barley
(B) Rice and sugarcane
(C) Oats and millet
(D) Corn and potatoes
(E) Bananas and melons

GO ON TO THE NEXT PAGE

59. Alexander II emancipated the serfs and introduced government reforms following Russia's defeat in the

(A) Balkan Wars
(B) Crimean War
(C) First World War
(D) Russo-Turkish Wars
(E) Russo-Japanese War

60. After independence, India pursued a foreign policy that led to which of the following?

(A) Its membership in the Soviet-backed Warsaw Pact
(B) Its membership in the Southeast Asia Treaty Organization
(C) Its signing of a mutual defense pact with the People's Republic of China
(D) Its emergence as a leader of the Nonaligned Movement
(E) Its avoidance of armed conflict with its neighbors

61. Which of the following best characterizes the classical economic theory of Adam Smith?

(A) The demands of consumers are met most cheaply by competition among individual producers.
(B) Since land is the source of value, the whole economy will benefit if small holdings are consolidated into large estates.
(C) An increase in wages will increase the demand for manufactured goods, making the economy as a whole grow.
(D) Since the interests of businessmen and workers are necessarily in conflict, the interests of one can thrive only at the expense of the other.
(E) To encourage the growth of infant national industries, government should protect them from unfair foreign competition by imposing tariffs.

62. Which of the following countries are members of the Organization of Petroleum Exporting Countries (OPEC) ?

(A) Argentina, Mexico, and Turkey
(B) China, Egypt, and the United States
(C) Great Britain, Canada, and Morocco
(D) The Soviet Union, Syria, and Kenya
(E) Venezuela, Nigeria, and Iraq

63. The navigator James Cook was most famous for

(A) being the first to sail around the world
(B) charting a northwest passage
(C) exploring the Antarctic continent
(D) scientific observation on Caribbean islands
(E) charting the seas around Australia and New Zealand

64. In closing Japan to Europeans, the Tokugawa shogunate was motivated primarily by a desire to limit

(A) the influence of Westerners on Japanese government and society
(B) a large influx of European immigrants
(C) widespread intermarriage between Japanese and Europeans
(D) the despoiling of Japan's pristine natural environment by Europeans
(E) the spread of industrialization to Japan

65. Which of the following was a major consequence of the opening of large silver mines in Spanish colonies in the Americas during the 1500's?

(A) The production of goods in Spain for export to its colonies in America was greatly stimulated.
(B) The increased wealth circulating in Spain's colonies fueled a resurgence of Native American culture.
(C) The European economy experienced an extended period of price inflation.
(D) The Spanish colonies where the mines were located were successful in declaring their independence from Spain.
(E) Other European powers succeeded in capturing the mines from Spain.

GO ON TO THE NEXT PAGE

66. Which of the following societies was the LEAST dependent on livestock?

(A) Aztec society
(B) Chinese society
(C) Persian society
(D) Tartar society
(E) Roman society

67. Which of the following was called "the Sick Man of Europe" in the nineteenth century?

(A) Italy
(B) Spain
(C) The Netherlands
(D) The Ottoman Empire
(E) Russia

68. The eighteenth-century philosophy of Deism was strongly denounced by

(A) Voltaire and his followers
(B) the Roman Catholic church
(C) essayists in Diderot's *Encyclopèdie*
(D) Locke and his followers
(E) Frederick the Great of Prussia

69. Which of the following was one of the major effects of the spread of gunpowder technology in Europe in the 1400's and 1500's C.E.?

(A) The superior firepower of European armies led to the reconquest of most lands that had been lost to the Ottoman Turks.
(B) The widespread use of guns in hunting led to a virtual extermination of game animals and game birds in Europe.
(C) The high cost of equipping armies with guns led to a strengthening of some centralized monarchies at the expense of feudal lords.
(D) Fear of the new technology led to religious revivals in many areas of Europe.
(E) Many European countries sought to avoid conflicts with each other because gunpowder made wars more destructive.

70. Which of the following factors contributed to the success of independence movements in Latin America during the early 1800's?

(A) Military and economic aid from the United States
(B) An increase in the production of precious metals from Latin American mines
(C) The establishment of universities throughout Latin America
(D) The drain on Spain's resources caused by the Napoleonic Wars
(E) Intervention by professional revolutionaries from France

71. In the sixteenth and seventeenth centuries, the primary interest of the European powers in the East Indies was to

(A) buy rice and other food grains
(B) obtain wood for shipbuilding
(C) obtain spices for trading
(D) to seek markets for exports
(E) exploit silver mines in the area

72. The most characteristic feature of Enlightenment thought was

(A) opposition to slavery
(B) antimaterialism
(C) opposition to religious belief
(D) an emphasis on reason
(E) a belief in sexual equality

73. Mazzini, Cavour, and Garibaldi are most often associated with

(A) parliamentary democracy in Italy
(B) Italian unification
(C) the rebuilding of Rome
(D) Italian imperialism in Ethiopia
(E) Italian industrialization

GO ON TO THE NEXT PAGE

74. When Siddhartha Gautama (the Buddha) embarked on his spiritual quest in the sixth century B.C.E., his primary concern was

(A) whether there is one God or many
(B) whether there is life after death
(C) why humans suffer
(D) how to convert nonbelievers
(E) the relationship between religion and the state

75. Which of the following best explains ancient Egypt's ability to support a large population?

(A) Its strategic location on the Mediterranean Sea
(B) The approval its religious leaders gave to the concept of large families
(C) The yearly flooding of the Nile River
(D) The early introduction of technology from Mesopotamia
(E) The use of the three-field crop rotation system

76. Which of the following best characterizes demographic change in eighteenth century England?

(A) Destruction of the nuclear family during the Industrial Revolution caused the population to decline.
(B) Unhealthy conditions in crowded cities caused the population to decline.
(C) Pressures of the enclosure movement caused the population to decline.
(D) Dramatically rising birth rates caused the population to increase.
(E) Falling death rates caused the population to increase.

GO ON TO THE NEXT PAGE

77. The cartoon above shows President Gamal Abdel Nasser (1956-1970) encouraging Egyptians to see the advantages of

(A) maintaining equality in the workplace
(B) curbing population growth
(C) reducing consumption
(D) increasing savings
(E) legalizing unions

78. Of the following Southeast Asian countries, which is NOT matched with the colonial power that dominated it during the colonial period?

(A) Vietnam	France
(B) Burma	Germany
(C) Indonesia	the Netherlands
(D) Malaya	Great Britain
(E) The Philippines	the United States

79. The Boxer Rebellion was a revolt of

(A) Indian soldiers against British domination
(B) Vietnamese against French domination
(C) Arabs against the Ottoman Empire
(D) Chinese against Western imperialism
(E) Koreans against Japanese rule

Mansell Collection

80. The picture above, which depicts the symbolic crowning of a twelfth-century king of Sicily by Christ, reveals the cultural influence of

(A) Russia
(B) Scandinavia
(C) Spain
(D) Islam
(E) Byzantium

GO ON TO THE NEXT PAGE

81. The political and religious center at Great Zimbabwe, which reached its height in the fifteenth century, was characterized by all of the following EXCEPT

(A) long-distance trading
(B) gold mining
(C) significant population expansion
(D) a written epic tradition
(E) copper and bronze ornament making

82. Which of the following art forms originated in the United States?

(A) Impressionism
(B) Surrealist poetry
(C) Social realism
(D) Jazz
(E) Atonal music

83. The Provisional Government failed to keep the support of the Russian people in 1917 because it

(A) executed the entire royal family
(B) collectivized agriculture and industry
(C) allowed Nicholas II to rule as a constitutional monarch
(D) suffered a humiliating defeat by the Japanese
(E) continued Russia's participation in the First World War

84. Which of the following best describes the Indian National Congress?

(A) The first national political organization in India to challenge British rule
(B) The first all-Indian legislative body formed after independence in 1947
(C) An organization formed by Hindus that primarily preached tolerance of Indian Muslims
(D) An organization formed by Hindus and Muslims that sought social reform within India
(E) A conference of Muslim religious leaders that convened to discuss Indian statehood

85. Of all the dictatorial regimes established in Europe between the First and Second World Wars, the one that held power the longest was that of

(A) Hitler
(B) Stalin
(C) Mussolini
(D) Pilsudski
(E) Franco

86. One of the principal strengths of the Byzantine empire was its

(A) constitutional monarchy
(B) sound economic base
(C) preference for decentralized government
(D) close relationship with the Roman Catholic church
(E) orderly system of succession to the throne

87. The first significant test of the ability of the League of Nations to respond when a major nation acted as an aggressor occurred when

(A) Japan invaded Manchuria
(B) the Soviet Union invaded Poland
(C) Japan declared war on China
(D) Franco's rebels attacked Spanish loyalists
(E) Hitler incorporated Austria into the Third Reich

88. In the 1980's, which of the following Muslim countries most actively promoted Islamic fundamentalism?

(A) Morocco
(B) Iran
(C) Iraq
(D) Indonesia
(E) Turkey

89. Mao Zedong revolutionized Chinese Marxist doctrine in the 1920's by advocating that the

(A) Chinese Communist Party sever its ties with the Soviet Union to preserve its independence
(B) Chinese Communist Party allow its rival, the Kuomintang, to reform a separate government on the island of Taiwan
(C) Chinese Communist Party renounce the use of violence to achieve revolution
(D) rural peasants, not the urban proletariat, lead the revolution in China
(E) landlord and capitalist classes be allowed to survive even after the communists took power

GO ON TO THE NEXT PAGE

90. The economies of China, North Korea, and North Vietnam were relatively isolated from the world economy during much of the third quarter of the twentieth century primarily because of their

(A) adherence to a planned, Marxist economy
(B) inability to recover from the devastation of the Second World War
(C) subjection to a trade embargo enforced by the United Nations
(D) subjection to almost continual civil wars
(E) enduring extended droughts due to global climate change

91. The partition of Korea at the end of the Second World War in 1945 was primarily the result of

(A) rivalry between the United States and the Soviet Union
(B) Japanese dominance of important sectors of the Korean economy
(C) the emergence of China as a major world power
(D) the inability of the Koreans to agree on a form of government
(E) sharp cultural differences between northern and southern Korea

92. During the American occupation of Japan following the Second World War, authorities seeking to restructure Japanese society received the strongest support from which of the following Japanese groups?

(A) Socialist leaders
(B) Business leaders
(C) Military leaders
(D) Expatriates returning to Japan
(E) Members of the imperial court

93. Many historians believe that the end of the French Revolutionary era was the

(A) execution of King Louis XVI
(B) Reign of Terror
(C) storming of the Bastille prison
(D) defeat of Napoleon in Russia
(E) peace settlement at the Congress of Vienna

94. The nations that signed and confirmed the 1975 Helsinki Accords agreed to

(A) establish uniform prices for crude oil
(B) establish peace in the Middle East
(C) cooperate among themselves and respect human rights
(D) end the Vietnam conflict and withdraw all foreign troops
(E) end the Cold War

95. In the late twentieth century, experts began to question the value of building large dam projects in the developing world primarily because these projects tend to

(A) reduce the cost of electric power in the countries in which they are built
(B) displace people from their homes and disturb the ecology of the regions in which they are built
(C) encourage separatist movements in the areas in which they are built
(D) conflict with the development plans of the central governments of the countries in which they are built
(E) disrupt road and rail communications across the rivers on which the dams are built

STOP

If you finish before time is called, you may check your work on this test only. Do not turn to any other section in the test.

NO TEST MATERIAL ON THIS PAGE

How to Score the SAT Subject Test in World History

When you take an actual SAT Subject Test in World History, your answer sheet will be "read" by a scanning machine that will record your response to each question. Then a computer will compare your answers with the correct answers and produce your raw score. You get one point for each correct answer. For each wrong answer, you lose one-fourth of a point. Questions you omit (and any for which you mark more than one answer) are not counted. This raw score is converted to a scaled score that is reported to you and to the colleges you specify.

Worksheet 1. Finding Your Raw Test Score

STEP 1: Table A on the following page lists the correct answers for all the questions on the World History Test that is reproduced in this book. It also serves as a worksheet for you to calculate your raw score.

- Compare your answers with those given in the table.
- Put a check in the column marked "Right" if your answer is correct.
- Put a check in the column marked "Wrong" if your answer is incorrect.
- Leave both columns blank if you omitted the question.

STEP 2: Count the number of right answers.

Enter the total here: ________________

STEP 3: Count the number of wrong answers.

Enter the total here: ________________

STEP 4: Multiply the number of wrong answers by .250.

Enter the product here: ______________

STEP 5: Subtract the result obtained in Step 4 from the total you obtained in Step 2.

Enter the result here: ________________

STEP 6: Round the number obtained in Step 5 to the nearest whole number.

Enter the result here: ________________

The number you obtained in Step 6 is your raw score.

Table A

Answers to the Subject Test in World History and Percentage of Students Answering Each Question Correctly									
Question Number	Correct Answer	Right	Wrong	Percentage of Students Answering the Question Correctly*	Question Number	Correct Answer	Right	Wrong	Percentage of Students Answering the Question Correctly*
1	A			66	33	A			41
2	B			59	34	A			64
3	C			76	35	A			50
4	B			49	36	C			52
5	E			65	37	A			24
6	D			79	38	D			59
7	A			61	39	A			33
8	E			93	40	B			71
9	D			57	41	C			69
10	D			76	42	D			19
11	B			35	43	B			37
12	A			54	44	D			37
13	A			80	45	B			55
14	C			41	46	A			67
15	A			51	47	D			51
16	C			21	48	A			36
17	B			43	49	A			60
18	A			29	50	D			55
19	B			81	51	E			69
20	C			71	52	A			65
21	C			47	53	E			65
22	A			73	54	C			45
23	B			85	55	E			62
24	D			82	56	B			32
25	B			95	57	C			89
26	A			73	58	D			65
27	D			68	59	B			43
28	A			46	60	D			35
29	E			77	61	A			46
30	A			48	62	E			65
31	A			73	63	E			46
32	D			56	64	A			83

Table A continued on next page

Table A continued from previous page

Question Number	Correct Answer	Right	Wrong	Percentage of Students Answering the Question Correctly*	Question Number	Correct Answer	Right	Wrong	Percentage of Students Answering the Question Correctly*
65	C			53	81	D			49
66	A			27	82	D			88
67	D			63	83	E			52
68	B			50	84	A			41
69	C			36	85	E			12
70	D			52	86	B			31
71	C			71	87	A			41
72	D			82	88	B			53
73	B			60	89	D			56
74	C			77	90	A			55
75	C			65	91	A			47
76	E			20	92	B			54
77	B			80	93	E			38
78	B			39	94	C			26
79	D			74	95	B			77
80	E			67					

* These percentages are based on an analysis of the answer sheets of a representative sample of 9,745 students who took the original administration of this test and whose mean score was 611. They may be used as an indication of the relative difficulty of a particular question.

Answer explanations for the Subject Test in World History can be found on page 167.

Finding Your Scaled Score

When you take SAT Subject Tests, the scores sent to the colleges you specify are reported on the College Board scale, which ranges from 200 to 800. You can convert your practice test score to a scaled score by using Table B. To find your scaled score, locate your raw score in the left-hand column of Table B; the corresponding score in the right-hand column is your scaled score. For example, a raw score of 39 on this particular edition of the World History Test corresponds to a scaled score of 580.

Raw scores are converted to scaled scores to ensure that a score earned on any one edition of a particular Subject Test is comparable to the same scaled score earned on any other edition of the same Subject Test. Because some editions of the tests may be slightly easier or more difficult than others, College Board scaled scores are adjusted so that they indicate the same level of performance regardless of the edition of the test taken and the ability of the group that takes it. Thus, for example, a score of 400 on one edition of a test taken at a particular administration indicates the same level of achievement as a score of 400 on a different edition of the test taken at a different administration.

When you take the SAT Subject Tests during a national administration, your scores are likely to differ somewhat from the scores you obtain on the tests in this book. People perform at different levels at different times for reasons unrelated to the tests themselves. The precision of any test is also limited because it represents only a sample of all the possible questions that could be asked.

Table B

Scaled Score Conversion Table World History Test					
Raw Score	Scaled Score	Raw Score	Scaled Score	Raw Score	Scaled Score
95	800	55	670	15	440
94	800	54	660	14	440
93	800	53	660	13	430
92	800	52	650	12	420
91	800	51	640	11	420
90	800	50	640	10	410
89	800	49	630	9	410
88	800	48	630	8	400
87	800	47	620	7	400
86	800	46	620	6	390
85	800	45	610	5	380
84	800	44	610	4	380
83	800	43	600	3	370
82	800	42	590	2	370
81	800	41	590	1	360
80	800	40	580	0	360
79	800	39	580	-1	350
78	800	38	570	-2	350
77	790	37	570	-3	340
76	790	36	560	-4	340
75	780	35	560	-5	330
74	770	34	550	-6	330
73	770	33	550	-7	330
72	760	32	540	-8	320
71	760	31	530	-9	320
70	750	30	530	-10	310
69	750	29	520	-11	310
68	740	28	520	-12	300
67	740	27	510	-13	300
66	730	26	510	-14	300
65	720	25	500	-15	290
64	720	24	490	-16	280
63	710	23	490	-17	280
62	710	22	480	-18	270
61	700	21	480	-19	260
60	690	20	470	-20	250
59	690	19	470	-21	250
58	680	18	460	-22	240
57	680	17	450	-23	230
56	670	16	450	-24	220

How Did You Do on the Subject Test in World History?

After you score your test and analyze your performance, think about the following questions:

Did you run out of time before reaching the end of the test?

If so, you may need to pace yourself better. For example, maybe you spent too much time on one or two hard questions. A better approach might be to skip the ones you can't answer right away and try answering all the questions that remain on the test. Then if there's time, go back to the questions you skipped.

Did you take a long time reading the directions?

You will save time when you take the test by learning the directions to the World History Test ahead of time. Each minute you spend reading directions during the test is a minute that you could use to answer questions.

How did you handle questions you were unsure of?

If you were able to eliminate one or more of the answer choices as wrong and guess from the remaining ones, your approach probably worked to your advantage. On the other hand, making haphazard guesses or omitting questions without trying to eliminate choices could cost you valuable points.

How difficult were the questions for you compared with other students who took the test?

Table A shows you how difficult the multiple-choice questions were for the group of students who took this test during its national administration. The right-hand column gives the percentage of students that answered each question correctly.

A question answered correctly by almost everyone in the group is obviously an easier question. For example, 82 percent of the students answered question 24 correctly. But only 19 percent answered question 42 correctly.

Keep in mind that these percentages are based on just one group of students. They would probably be different with another group of students taking the test.

If you missed several easier questions, go back and try to find out why: Did the questions cover material you haven't yet reviewed? Did you misunderstand the directions?

Answer Explanations for the World History Subject Test

1. Choice (A) is the correct answer. Philosophical schools flourished in both Greece and China around 500 B.C.E. In Greece, during the sixth and fifth centuries B.C.E., many influential philosophers, including Pythagoras, Parmenides, Heraclitus, Socrates, and Plato debated the human condition. At the same time in China, Lao Tzu wrote *Tao Te Ching*, in which he outlined a new philosophical understanding and practice of human life, eventually known as Taoism. Also in China, the philosophy of Confucianism took shape at this time.

2. Choice (B) is the correct answer. The central characters of these three epic poems are all from the elite class of warriors of their respective civilizations. The *Mahabharata* recounts the battle between two branches of the same Indian warrior family, the Kauravas and the Pandavas. The *Iliad* focuses on the battle between the Trojan and the Achaean (or Greek) warriors. The *Tales of the Heike* is an account of the struggle between two Japanese samurai clans, the Taira and the Minamoto.

3. Choice (C) is the correct answer. Islam, founded on Muhammad's teaching, stresses the influence of Allah (God) on every aspect of human life. As such, Islam's teachings and decrees affected the entire life of its converts, thus establishing similarity and unity among followers of diverse backgrounds.

4. Choice (B) is the correct answer. Attila led his empire and armies of the Huns from 434 C.E. until his death in 453 C.E. Although he never gained full control over the area covered by the Western Roman Empire, in the 450s, Attila invaded and ravaged much of the Empire, entirely destroying several cities. This damage by Attila contributed to the deterioration of the Western Roman Empire and its eventual fall in 476.

5. Choice (E) is the correct answer. After the fall of the Han dynasty, northern China eventually came to be ruled by nomadic peoples. They were far fewer than the Chinese people they governed. As a result, they tended to assimilate or adopt the customs of the larger Chinese population.

6. Choice (D) is the correct answer. Both Mahavira and Buddha led religious movements in India sometime between the sixth and fourth centuries B.C.E. They both came from prominent families in Hindu society and developed religious systems that challenged that social order. Mahavira impoverished himself and spread teachings that became the basic tenets of Jainism. Buddha developed the religious system that has come to be known as Buddhism.

7. Choice (A) is the correct answer. In 1816, Shaka took over leadership of the Zulu. Shaka reorganized the Zulu army and instituted the use of short spears that forced close warfare. He also developed military tactics that utilized several groups of warriors, some of which encircled the foe from the sides like a set of ox's horns. Under Shaka, the Zulu were incredibly successful warriors who dominated southern Africa throughout the nineteenth century.

8. Choice (E) is the correct answer. Realistically representing people in art is not central to Islamic faith and is generally considered to go against the teachings of Muhammad. The five central pillars of Islam are fasting during Ramadan (A); professing faith in the one God, Allah (B); praying five times daily facing Mecca (C); making a pilgrimage to Mecca at least once (D); and giving alms to the poor.

9. Choice (D) is the correct answer. In the late 1990s, Pakistan acquired the capability of exploding nuclear weapons. India had acquired this capability in 1974. The two countries share their western and eastern borders, respectively, and historically have a strained relationship, especially with respect to the disputed territory of Kashmir, so the acquisition of nuclear weapons by both countries is a matter of global concern.

10. Choice (D) is the correct answer. The main tenet of Stalin's governing strategy was to centralize as much control of the Soviet Union as possible. A major strategy for achieving strong central control was to centralize economic planning. Soviet economic decisions under Stalin were made by a central State authority; companies were not allowed to make private economic decisions.

11. Choice (B) is the correct answer. Historiography is the study of different ways historical events are interpreted and recorded, not the study of the events themselves. Historiography is also the study of the methodology and practices used when writing history. Its elements include inquiry into the nature and credibility of the source, evolving views of history, and the specific perspective from which a particular history or historical narrative has been written.

12. Choice (A) is the correct answer. In imperial China, the scholar-gentry (sometimes referred to as scholar-officials or mandarins) composed the most important part of the official bureaucracy. The members of the scholar-gentry usually came from landowner families and were the imperial civil servants. They were well educated and, by the Tang dynasty (618–907 C.E.), had to pass civil service exams to receive a position. At this time, wealthy merchants paid to educate their sons so they could pass the exam and become imperial bureaucrats.

13. Choice (A) is the correct answer. Japan's defeat of Russia in the Russo-Japanese War (1904–1905) demonstrated that modernization was not limited to Western nations. Japan was able to defeat the massive Russian navy and much of the Russian army. By using its newly modernized forces, Japan's victory established it as a world power in the modern era and was a source of inspiration for anti-colonial movements throughout the world.

14. Choice (C) is the correct answer. After defeating the Umayyads at the Battle of the Zab River in 750 C.E., the Abbasids moved the caliphate from Damascus to Baghdad. The Umayyad caliphs had held power of the Islamic world at Damascus since 661 C.E. The Abbasids were more open to relationships with non-Arab peoples, and were helped by Persian converts to Islam in their defeat of the Umayyads.

15. Choice (A) is the correct answer. A megalithic structure is a structure made of large rocks that may be free-standing or may be connected without the use of cement or mortar. Stonehenge is the most famous megalithic structure. Located near Amesbury, England, Stonehenge is a circular arrangement of stone monuments that was constructed between 3100 B.C.E. and 2000 B.C.E.

16. Choice (C) is the correct answer. The Toltec were a Native American people who thrived in central Mexico between the tenth and twelfth century C.E. When the Aztec came to power in the fourteenth century, they claimed that they had descended from the Toltec, whom they regarded as the givers of civilization. The Aztec did, in fact, speak Nahuatl, the language of the Toltec, and the two peoples shared many customs and rituals.

17. Choice (B) is the correct answer. Indo-European and Bantu are both terms historians use to describe language groups. Indo-European refers to the large language group now found throughout much of Europe and Asia that includes many modern languages such as English, Persian (or Farsi), Russian, Spanish, and Hindi. The Bantu language family, which includes Zulu, Xhosa, Kongo, Swahili, and Sotho, is found throughout much of Sub-Saharan Africa.

18. Choice (A) is the correct answer. One historical theory proposes that the need for flood protection and irrigation in river valleys caused civilizations in these areas to develop large bureaucratic, impersonal, and often despotic governments. Agricultural-based civilizations relied on the irrigation of water and large-scale irrigation projects required a strong centralized government to be successful. These river-valley civilizations (called "hydraulic civilizations" by Karl Wittfogel) developed a complex social organization, usually with forced labor, a bureaucratic government, and a powerful emperor who was often identified with the gods.

19. Choice (B) is the correct answer. Working-class women in nineteenth-century England had limited social and employment opportunities. Many young working-class women were encouraged by their parents to take jobs as domestic servants in higher-class homes, not for future professional training (D) or with the hopes of marrying wealthier men (C), but primarily to make extra money for their families, while learning habits and skills they could apply later on as wives.

20. Choice (C) is the correct answer. Beginning in the Zhou dynasty, emperors of China used the concept of the Mandate of Heaven to justify their power. According to the Mandate of Heaven, as long as an emperor ruled wisely and justly, he enjoyed divine blessing. If he began to misuse his position, he would lose the Mandate. Throughout Chinese history, the Mandate of Heaven was used to justify the passing of power from one dynasty to the next. As one dynasty began to misuse its power, the next claimed the authority of the Mandate to avoid suffering any disasters or disturbances.

21. Choice (C) is the correct answer. It is commonly accepted that the term *Homo sapiens* classifies humans who can consciously think. In evolutionary theory, *Homo sapiens* (translated from Latin as "wise or thinking man") are distinguished from their closest ancestors or related species by the advanced form of conscious thinking that their large brain allows. Other related species, like *Homo erectus*, may have walked upright, but probably lacked the level of conscious thinking of *Homo sapiens*.

22. Choice (A) is the correct answer. Although some later branches of Buddhism include belief in a god, Buddhism, in its original form, is a religious system that focuses on humanity's correct path through life without making reference to any god or gods. Buddhism originated in the late sixth century B.C.E. in northeastern India as a belief system centered on the religious and philosophical teachings of the Buddha. The wider tradition of Hinduism includes belief in many different deities (C). Christianity (B), Islam (D), and Judaism (E) are all religions that are centered on the belief in one god.

23. Choice (B) is the correct answer. Social Darwinism applies Charles Darwin's theory of natural selection in plant and animal development to the development of human societies. According to Social Darwinism, social groups follow the same natural law of "survival of the fittest" as plants and animals. Social groups naturally compete for power and resources and the strongest, most fit societies will be the ones that survive. In the late nineteenth and early twentieth century C.E., the theory of Social Darwinism was used to justify the competition of laissez-faire capitalism and class stratification, arguing that it was in the best interest of human development for weaker societies and classes to be eliminated in favor of stronger, more fit humans.

24. Choice (D) is the correct answer. The Second World War officially started on September 3, 1939, when Great Britain and France declared war on Germany in response to the German invasion of Poland. Germany had invaded Poland on September 1. Six days earlier, on August 25, Great Britain had signed a treaty with Poland pledging assistance in the event of a German invasion.

25. Choice (B) is the correct answer. The pyramids of ancient Egypt were built primarily to be huge monumental tombs. The Pyramids of Giza, located on the west bank of the Nile River in northern Egypt, were built as tombs for three kings—Khufu, Khafre, and Menkaure—who reigned during the Fourth dynasty (circa 2575–2465 B.C.E.).

26. Choice (A) is the correct answer. The term "caste system," often used to describe Hindu society, is characterized as a rigid socially stratified society. While the term "caste" itself does not originate in Hinduism, Hindu society was traditionally divided into four levels. The Brahman enjoy the highest position in society and were originally the priests and teachers of the Hindu scriptures.

27. Choice (D) is the correct answer. From his ascent to the Macedonian throne in 336 B.C.E. until his death in 323 B.C.E., Alexander the Great led continuous successful military expeditions that expanded the Greek Empire beyond the Middle East and into Asia. In 333 B.C.E., he defeated the main Persian army, and eventually gained control over the Persian Empire throughout western Asia. As he took control of lands with different cultures, Alexander encouraged the intermingling of Greek and non-Greek peoples and customs. By the time of his death, he had spread Greek cultural forms from the Mediterranean to India, laying the foundation for the Hellenistic Age.

28. Choice (A) is the correct answer. The Celts are a group of ancient Indo-European peoples who inhabited the British Isles and western Europe from prehistory until their eventual absorption into the Roman Empire. In the first century B.C.E., Julius

Caesar led the Roman conquests over the Celts in Gaul. Britain was conquered by the Romans a century later, thus ending the history of Celtic political power in Europe.

29. Choice (E) is the correct answer. Greek civilization did not originate along a river valley, but around the Aegean Sea, a branch of the Mediterranean Sea. The other four civilizations all originated in river valleys: the Chinese (A), along the Huang He (Yellow) River; the Indian (B), along the Indus and Ganges rivers; the Egyptian (C), along the Nile River; and the Mesopotamian (D), between the Tigris and Euphrates rivers.

30. Choice (A) is the correct answer. Beginning in the 1400s C.E., European states underwent a commercial revolution in which the capitalistic trade of goods became more central to their economies. In the developing capitalistic economies, the European states competed for new trade routes, products, and partners. With the invention of larger and stronger ships capable of navigating the Atlantic Ocean, European explorers expanded the reach of these economies to the Americas and Africa, during what has come to be called the Age of Exploration.

31. Choice (A) is the correct answer. All of these English words are derivations of Arabic words and reflect the intermingling of Arab and European cultures.

32. Choice (D) is the correct answer. The term "Neolithic" refers to the period in human technological development characterized by the domestication of plants and animals. Originally associated with the end of the Old Stone Age in Europe, Asia, and Africa, "Neolithic" is now more commonly used to refer to the developmental period of any culture when plant and animal domestication occurs. Metallurgy, or the development of metal tools, marks the end of the Neolithic Age.

33. Choice (A) is the correct answer. The spread of sugar cultivation to the Americas was accompanied by a major shift in human population. Sugar cultivation was labor intensive, and the Europeans who established plantations on Caribbean islands and the mainland relied on enslaved Africans to do most of the work. Though exact numbers are unobtainable, millions of Africans were transported to the Americas during the sixteenth through nineteenth centuries. Probably more than three-quarters of them were sent to sugar plantations. Choice (B) is incorrect. Although the importation of opium into China caused major disruptions of Chinese society, cultivation of opium was not associated with large-scale population shifts. Choice (C) is incorrect. In the Americas, the number of slaves employed in the production of tobacco was much smaller than the number employed in sugar production. Choice (D) is incorrect. Although the cultivation of tea spread from China to South Asia and

other areas, it was not accompanied by population shifts of the size associated with the spread of sugar cultivation. Choice (E) is incorrect. In the Americas, the number of slaves employed in cotton production was smaller than the number employed in sugar production. Although cotton cultivation spread through the southern United States in the early nineteenth century, the numbers of slaves moved and the distances they traveled were still smaller than was the case for sugar cultivation.

34. Choice (A) is the correct answer. Domestic cultivation of maize, or corn, probably began to spread from the Oaxaca Valley of Mexico (part of Mesoamerica) around 3500 B.C.E. Maize spread widely during the pre-Columbian era, becoming a staple food in many pre-Columbian cultures throughout North and South America.

35. Choice (A) is the correct answer. The West African Muslim kingdoms of Ghana (eighth to thirteenth century C.E.) and Mali (fourteenth to sixteenth century C.E.) acquired vast amounts of wealth through the trans-Saharan trade routes to the North African cities along the Mediterranean Sea. The West African kingdoms desired the salt of the Mediterranean regions and, in return, provided gold and slaves.

36. Choice (C) is the correct answer. This map shows the routes of Zheng He's seafaring voyages from China across the Indian Ocean to Africa, Arabia, India, Ceylon, and Southeast Asia. Zheng He, a Chinese Muslim, commanded massive expeditions of up to 30,000 men on more than 300 ships for the Ming emperors during the fifteenth century C.E.

37. Choice (A) is the correct answer. Mogadishu, Kilwa, Mombasa, and Sofala were all Swahili city-states along the coast of East Africa. Starting around 1000 C.E., numerous Swahili city-states developed along Africa's eastern coast through successful trading with one another and with landlocked African regions like Zimbabwe. Although it interacted with the Swahili city-states, Zimbabwe was an interior empire, not a Swahili city-state.

38. Choice (D) is the correct answer. Between the tenth and thirteenth centuries C.E., mound-building cultures thrived in North America. These cultures built large earthen mounds that were most likely used as sites for religious ceremonies and burials. The largest of these mounds was built in the 1000s C.E. in the Native American city of Cahokia, in present-day Illinois.

39. Choice (A) is the correct answer. During the First World War, many women in Europe and the United States filled industrial jobs left vacant by the men who were

fighting. By including women, who were previously excluded, in the workforce, industrial nations were able to maintain and increase productivity during the war. When the men returned at the end of the war, many women were asked to leave their jobs to make room for the unemployed veterans.

40. Choice (B) is the correct answer. Islam is the dominant religion in Indonesia. Arab merchants brought Islam to Indonesia beginning around the twelfth century C.E. Indonesia is now the most populous Muslim nation in the world.

41. Choice (C) is the correct answer. The shaded areas on the map together comprise the extent of the Mongol Khanates. The Mongol Empire, began by Genghis Khan, spread throughout Europe and Asia during the thirteenth and fourteenth centuries. At its height, it was the largest empire in world history, stretching, as the map indicates, from the Pacific Ocean to the Middle East. After the reign of Kublai Khan, the empire was divided into four Khanates as shown.

42. Choice (D) is the correct answer. The Maya civilization, which originated in Mesoamerica around 1500 B.C.E., was characterized by large cities that were politically independent of one another. In contrast, the Aztecs, a Mesoamerican civilization during the fourteenth to sixteenth centuries C.E., were governed by powerful emperors who ruled from the capital city of Tenochtitlán.

43. Choice (B) is the correct answer. In the period before 1500 C.E., the Indian Ocean was used primarily by Indian and Arab merchants. After 1500 C.E., Europeans, including many successful Portuguese merchants, began to use the Indian Ocean for trade. Chinese admiral Zheng He had sailed throughout the Indian Ocean before 1500 C.E., but he was primarily interested in diplomacy and exploration rather than trade.

44. Choice (D) is the correct answer. On September 16, 1810, Father Miguel Hidalgo began Mexico's long war with Spain to gain independence. A parish priest from the town of Dolores, Hidalgo roused his parishioners to arms with the famous Grito de Dolores (Cry of Dolores). Hidalgo's armed group was able to capture some towns, but failed to take Mexico City. It was not until 1821, in part under the leadership of Antonio López de Santa Anna (B), that Mexico gained its independence from Spain. José de San Martín (E) was an Argentine revolutionary leader; Bernardo O'Higgins (C) was a Chilean revolutionary leader; and Simón Bolívar (A) was a South American revolutionary hero.

45. Choice (B) is the correct answer. The feudal periods in both Japan and western Europe were characterized by frequent warfare. In feudal Japan (eleventh to nineteenth centuries C.E.), feudal families were led by daimyo (warlords) who fought both among each other as well as with outside invaders like the Mongols. The feudal period in western Europe (fifth to sixteenth centuries C.E.) was also characterized by warfare among small feudal principalities. In both Japan and Europe, the frequent warfare hindered the development of a money economy and a centralized monarchy.

46. Choice (A) is the correct answer. In 1000 C.E., Constantinople, now the Turkish city of Istanbul, was the capital of the Eastern Roman, or Byzantine, Empire and the largest city in Europe. At that time, London, Paris, Rome, and Toledo, although important cities in their own right, were all smaller than Constantinople.

47. Choice (D) is the correct answer. In early Islamic society, Jews and Christians were allowed to practice their own religions but were subject to some restrictions within society. Jews and Christians were allowed to hold some public offices, but could not be rulers (A). They were exempt from the Muslim *zakat* tax, but were required to pay the poll tax, *jizya,* which was often higher (B). They were exempt from serving in the army (C) and were tolerated, but they were considered second-class citizens (E).

48. Choice (A) is the correct answer. This Biblical passage (Matthew 16:19) was used in the early Catholic Church to argue for the authority of the pope. As Bishop of Rome, the pope traces his authority back to Peter the Apostle, who was martyred and buried in Rome. According to the doctrine of "the apostolic primacy of Peter," the Bishops of Rome had authority over the other bishops who traced their authority to other apostles of Jesus. This passage, in which Jesus states that he will build his church on Peter, was used as the Biblical basis for that doctrine.

49. Choice (A) is the correct answer. The period of Mongol rule over Russia during the thirteenth century reinforced Russia's isolation from western Europe. Under Mongol rule, large sections of Russia were unified, but because the Mongol Empire did not extend into western Europe, the political and cultural lines dividing Russia and western Europe became more defined. The Mongols did not force most Russians to adopt Mongol culture or Islam. As a result, when Mongol rule ended, Eastern Christian Orthodoxy was still thriving.

50. Choice (D) is the correct answer. The Inca road system was a series of foot trails traversing the high Andes Mountains in Peru and linking the towns of the Inca Empire. Unfit for wheeled vehicles, the roads were used by travelers on foot to carry messages and goods between distant Incan towns.

51. Choice (E) is the correct answer. British merchants were able to continue importing harmful opium into China. After losing the first Anglo-Chinese War (also known as the First Opium War) to the United Kingdom, the Chinese signed the Treaty of Nanking in 1842. This treaty, along with settlements after other defeats, ceded Hong Kong to the British (B), opened numerous ports to foreign traders (C), allowed Western missionaries in China (A), and granted Westerners the privilege of extraterritoriality (D). Additionally, China lost the power to ban the import of opium into China.

52. Choice (A) is the correct answer. Unlike Europe, China was a unified empire in 750 C.E. At this time, China was unified under the Tang dynasty, which is often considered to be a high point in China's cultural history. In contrast, in 750 C.E., Europe was undergoing a period of political division. After the fall of the Western Roman Empire in the fifth century C.E., Europe was subject to continual invasion from various peoples such as the Goths and the Huns.

53. Choice (E) is the correct answer. This quotation reflects a key tenet of the Chinese philosophy of Confucianism. Confucianism, developed from the teachings of Chinese philosopher Confucius (551–479 B.C.E.), draws a connection between the private lives of individuals and wider political stability. Much of Confucius' teachings centered on cultivating a personal life in line with principles of righteousness. Confucianism holds that wider political order rests on the order achieved by individuals in their own families.

54. Choice (C) is the correct answer. Many early Roman religious rituals and beliefs were influenced by the religious practices of the Etruscans. The Etruscans, who inhabited ancient Italy before the rise of Roman civilization, believed that there were many gods who interacted intimately with humans. Religious rituals were used to persuade the gods to act favorably toward humans. The Romans adopted the same system, appeasing and consulting the gods in all important affairs through religious rituals.

55. Choice (E) is the correct answer. The Mongol and Turkish people who made up the armies of the Mongol Khans who invaded central and south Asia later converted to Islam. Securing control over these territories, the Mongols and Turks helped define and defend the Islamic world against European Christian crusaders.

56. Choice (B) is the correct answer. During the seventeenth century, the Dutch dominated European maritime trade. In 1602, the Dutch East India Company, promoting Dutch colonization and trade throughout Asia, was established. The company gained European monopolies, often violently, on the trade of many spices throughout modern-day Indonesia. The Dutch West India Company, which was

granted a charter in 1621, established colonies and trade in North America and in the Caribbean. The success of these Dutch trading companies broke the dominance of European trade that Spain had enjoyed throughout the sixteenth century.

57. Choice (C) is the correct answer. The Irish Potato Famine, which occurred from 1845 to 1849, spurred mass emigration of starving Irish families to Great Britain, the United States, Canada, and Australia. The famine resulted from the failure of the potato crop, a staple food for many Irish families. After a devastating potato fungus destroyed the potato crop, oppressive economic policies and incompetent farming methods created widespread hunger throughout Ireland. Hundreds of thousands of Irish died or emigrated as a direct result of the famine.

58. Choice (D) is the correct answer. Corn and potatoes originated in South America and spread throughout the world as a result of European colonization. Potatoes, first grown in the Andes Mountains, were brought to Spain in the sixteenth century and eventually became a major European staple. Likewise, corn, also called maize, originated in ancient Mesoamerica and was brought to the Old World by Europeans.

59. Choice (B) is the correct answer. In 1856, Tsar Alexander II of Russia signed the Treaty of Paris with the United Kingdom, France, and the Ottoman Empire to end the Crimean War. Following the war, Alexander II emancipated the serfs and instituted radical government reforms that reflected the progressive ideas of the educated classes. He hoped these measures would help to restore Russian power.

60. Choice (D) is the correct answer. After gaining independence from the United Kingdom in 1947, India pursued a foreign policy of nonalignment. Prime Minister Jawaharlal Nehru first outlined the principles of nonalignment in 1954 as a guide to India's relationship with China. The principles were: respect for territorial integrity; mutual nonaggression; mutual noninterference in domestic affairs; equality and mutual benefit; and peaceful coexistence. These principles eventually became the foundation for the international organization, Nonaligned Movement, established in 1961.

61. Choice (A) is the correct answer. In 1776, Scottish economist Adam Smith published his economic theory in *The Wealth of Nations*. The basic idea of his theory is that when producers compete to sell their goods to consumers in an unrestricted market, consumers will benefit by paying the cheapest sustainable prices. Consequently, governments should regulate trade and manufacturing as little as possible, allowing the natural forces of competition among producers to regulate the prices of products. This is known as laissez-faire economics.

62. Choice (E) is the correct answer. Venezuela, Nigeria, and Iraq are all members of OPEC. Founded in 1960 by Iran, Iraq, Kuwait, Saudi Arabia, and Venezuela, OPEC is an international association created to protect the interests of oil-producing countries. The organization was founded in response to price cuts of crude oil forced on these countries by European and U.S. oil companies. Since then, OPEC has worked to regulate and increase the profits of oil-producing countries. OPEC now has 13 members: Iran, Iraq, Kuwait, Saudi Arabia, Venezuela, Algeria, Indonesia, Libya, Qatar, United Arab Emirates, Nigeria, Ecuador, and Angola.

63. Choice (E) is the correct answer. Eighteenth-century British navigator James Cook charted the seas around Australia and New Zealand during his Pacific expeditions. A superior navigator and cartographer, Cook was the first European to discover the east coast of Australia and the Hawaiian Islands and to circumnavigate New Zealand.

64. Choice (A) is the correct answer. In the seventeenth century, the Tokugawa shogunate became increasingly hostile to the influence of Western culture on Japanese society. As a result of trade with European nations, Western cultural practices like Christianity were gaining ground in Japan. The Tokugawa enacted a number of anti-Western policies and eventually closed its trading seaports to all foreigners except China and the Dutch East India Company.

65. Choice (C) is the correct answer. During the 1500s, the Spanish colonies in the Americas, especially in Peru, opened large silver mines. The abundance of silver taken to European and world markets from these mines contributed to a huge price inflation in the European economy. As a result of the abundant mines and the increase in Spain's power, Spain strengthened its control over its colonies in the Americas. During this period, Spain was able to rebuff European attacks (E), suppress Native American culture (B), and quell political uprisings (D).

66. Choice (A) is the correct answer. The Aztec society relied primarily on agriculture for its subsistence. Most of their diet consisted of maize and beans. They did domesticate turkeys and dogs, but maintaining large animals as livestock was not a significant part of their society. The domestication of livestock was a significant part of Chinese (B), Persian (C), Tartar (D), and Roman (E) societies.

67. Choice (D) is the correct answer. In the nineteenth century, the Ottoman Empire was called "the Sick Man of Europe" by Nicholas I of Russia. The Ottoman Empire had been a major European power since the fifteenth century. By the nineteenth century, however, it had lost much of its territory in the Balkans and was economically

dominated by other European nations. Following the end of the First World War, the Ottoman Empire finally collapsed in 1922.

68. Choice (B) is the correct answer. The eighteenth-century philosophy of Deism, which based theology on rationality rather than church authority, was strongly denounced by the Roman Catholic Church. Enlightenment thinkers like Voltaire and Thomas Paine proposed Deism as a rational approach to religion, arguing that God set the universe on its course governed by natural laws and then ceased to intervene in its affairs. Religious ideas like miracles, divine intervention, and petitionary prayer were seen as irrational and false. The Catholic Church denounced Deism as heretical.

69. Choice (C) is the correct answer. The 1400s and 1500s saw the decline of power for European feudal families and the rise of strong central monarchies, sometimes called the "new monarchs." The development of gunpowder gave a significant advantage to armies who used firearms. The high costs of equipping troops with firearms were more easily met by a larger centralized government, ruled by a monarch who had access to large tax revenues. Thus, monarchs were successful in gaining and maintaining power at the expense of feudal lords.

70. Choice (D) is the correct answer. In the early 1800s, many of Spain's colonies in the Americas successfully revolted and declared independence. The success of these revolts was, in large part, due to the fact that Spain was unable to dedicate enough troops and resources to maintain control over the colonies. Spain had drained its resources battling Napoleon's forces. In 1807, Napoleon had invaded Spain, triggering a long and draining war. By 1813, Napoleon's forces had been driven out of Spain. These efforts, however, had seriously weakened Spanish power.

71. Choice (C) is the correct answer. During the sixteenth and seventeenth centuries, European powers colonized the East Indies (Southeast Asia) to obtain spices for trading. In 1513, the Portuguese were the first Europeans to establish trade in modern-day Indonesia, obtaining cloves from Ternate, one of the Spice Islands. The United Kingdom, France, and Spain also established spice trade in the East Indies, but it was the Netherlands, through the Dutch East India Company, that eventually gained the greatest economic and political power in the region.

72. Choice (D) is the correct answer. Enlightenment thought was characterized by reliance on reason, rather than religious or traditional authority, in the pursuit of truth. During the period of time historians call the Enlightenment, or the Age of Reason (seventeenth and eighteenth centuries), philosophers such as René Descartes, Jean-Jacques Rousseau, Voltaire, and John Locke applied reason and the scientific

method to the study of many aspects of human life. By shifting the study of philosophy, education, law, and politics away from tradition and religion and toward the use of rational methods of observation and argumentation, Enlightenment philosophers were profoundly influential.

73. Choice (B) is the correct answer. Giuseppe Mazzini, Count Camillo Benso di Cavour, and Giuseppe Garibaldi were all major contributors to the Italian unification (Il Risorgimento), the process of unifying the various countries on the Italian peninsula into one Italian state during the nineteenth century. All three men worked, in different capacities, for the modernization and unification of Italy.

74. Choice (C) is the correct answer. According to tradition, around 530 B.C.E., at age 29, Siddhartha Gautama (later called "the Buddha" or "the Enlightened One") left his life as a prince to travel as a monk in search of a way to relieve human suffering. After six years of extreme self-deprivation, Siddhartha achieved "enlightenment" and discovered "The Middle Way" between indulgence and deprivation to escape suffering. Siddhartha began to teach his idea that through correct thought and action, one could get rid of one's cravings, the source of human suffering. His teachings eventually developed into the major world religion known as Buddhism.

75. Choice (C) is the correct answer. The ancient Egyptian civilization flourished for years along the banks of the Nile River in northern Africa. The yearly flooding of the Nile watered and refertilized Egypt, allowing the land to sustain a large population. Without the yearly flooding, the region would remain too dry to grow large amounts of crops. Because it was so essential to the survival of the civilization, the yearly flooding of the Nile was prominent in Egyptian legend and society.

76. Choice (E) is the correct answer. In the eighteenth century, technological advances (particularly in agriculture and transportation) and industrialization began to change the lives of people in England. One benefit of the technological advances was a drop in death rates, which in turn led to population growth. Industrialization solidified gender roles and strengthened, not destroyed, the traditional nuclear family (A). Although unhealthy conditions in overcrowded cities contributed to a rising infant mortality rate (D), technological advances kept the death rate down (B), allowing the population to increase (C).

77. Choice (B) is the correct answer. President Gamal Abdel Nasser, second president of Egypt from 1956 to 1970, was extremely powerful and influential in stabilizing and modernizing Egypt. Nasser sought to influence as much of Egyptian society as possible. His attempts to raise the standard of living of Egyptians, however, were

partially thwarted by a high birth rate in the lower classes. This cartoon depicts Nasser showing Egyptians that lowering the birth rate would increase the available resources for Egyptian economic development.

78. Choice (B) is the correct answer. All of these Southeast Asian countries are correctly matched with the dominating colonial power except Burma. Burma, also known as Myanmar, was colonized by Great Britain, not Germany. Under British control for most of the nineteenth century, Burma gained its independence from Great Britain in 1948.

79. Choice (D) is the correct answer. The Boxer Rebellion was a revolt of the Chinese against Western imperialists in northern China from 1899 to 1901. The term "Boxers" referred to the "Righteous Uprising Society," a group of Chinese who rebelled against the economic and political exploitation of German, British, French, Belgian, Japanese, Russian, Dutch, and U.S. forces. Although the Boxers were eventually supported by the Chinese Imperial army, the Western powers were able to suppress the uprising.

80. Choice (E) is the correct answer. This picture of Christ crowning a twelfth-century king of Sicily reflects the Byzantine influence on Sicilian culture. Sicily had been part of the Byzantine Empire from 552 to 965 C.E. After a period under a religiously tolerant Arab rule, it was governed by the Normans during the eleventh and twelfth centuries. Byzantine Christianity was still prevalent in Sicilian culture at this time, as seen in this traditional Byzantine iconic depiction of Christ crowning the monarch.

81. Choice (D) is the correct answer. The site of Great Zimbabwe in southern Africa was a major center of African civilization, reaching its peak in the fifteenth century. The powerful civilization traded extensively with Arabs and the Swahili city-states (A); mined and smelted gold (B), copper, and bronze (E); and expanded its population into much of the Zimbabwean Plateau (C); but it did not record its history in a written epic.

82. Choice (D) is the correct answer. Jazz originated in United States in the late 1800s. It combined African rhythms, European harmonies, and U.S. instruments, and emphasized the improvisational interplay of the musicians. Impressionism (A) is a school of painting that originated in France during the late 1800s. Surrealist poetry (B) is a movement in literature founded in Paris, France, in the 1920s. Social realism (C) is an artistic and literary movement that flourished in several countries in the years between World Wars I and II. Atonal music (E) developed in Germany in the early 1900s.

83. Choice (E) is the correct answer. The Russian Provisional Government was created in 1917 when the Russian Empire finally collapsed and Tsar Nicholas II abdicated the throne. The Provisional Government continued Russia's involvement in the First World War. The Russian people, weary of fighting, rapidly became disillusioned with the government. The people's discontent and the Provisional Government's weakness eventually led to the Bolshevik Revolution (or October Revolution) and the rise to power of Vladimir Lenin.

84. Choice (A) is the correct answer. Founded in 1885 to advance the political aspirations of educated Indians, the Indian National Congress (INC) was the first Indian organization to challenge British rule. During India's struggle for independence in the 1940s, the INC grew to include a diverse representation of India's population, including both Hindus and Muslims. Although never an official member, Mahatma Gandhi was supported by and associated with the INC during his efforts to free India of British rule.

85. Choice (E) is the correct answer. Francisco Franco took control of the Spanish Nationalist Army in 1936, and later took control of all of Spain at the end of the Spanish Civil War in 1939. He ruled Spain for 36 years until his death in 1975. Hitler ruled Germany for 12 years, from 1933 to 1945 (A). Stalin ruled the Soviet Union for 29 years, from 1924 to 1953 (B). Mussolini ruled Italy for 21 years, from 1922 to 1943 (C). Pilsudski ruled Poland for 4 years, from 1918 to 1922 (D).

86. Choice (B) is the correct answer. The Byzantine Empire, also called the Eastern Roman Empire, began in the fourth century C.E. and flourished for over a thousand years until its final collapse in the fifteenth century. Reaching its peak from the ninth to the eleventh centuries, the empire's success came from a sound economic base fueled by high levels of production and trade. The Byzantine Empire was ruled by a centralized nonconstitutional monarchy—choices (A) and (C)—whose succession of power was not often clear (E). The Byzantine Empire also saw the separation of its Eastern Orthodox Christian church from the Roman Catholic Church (D).

87. Choice (A) is the correct answer. In 1919, the League of Nations was established at the Paris Peace Conference as a means of settling international disputes. The League received its first major test when Japan invaded the Chinese territory of Manchuria in 1931. The League of Nations eventually determined that Japan had acted unfairly and called for Japan to relinquish control of Manchuria. Japan withdrew their membership from the League and ignored the decree. Unable to garner military or diplomatic support from its members or the United States, the League of Nations failed in rebuffing the Japanese aggression.

88. Choice (B) is the correct answer. During the 1980s, Islamic fundamentalism flourished in the Islamic Republic of Iran. In 1979, Ayatollah Ruhollah Khomeini successfully led the Iranian Revolution, overthrowing the constitutional monarchy and establishing an Islamic theocratic republic under his control. During his rule, which lasted until his death in 1989, Khomeini enforced the Sharia law that governed Iranians' entire lives according to Islamic fundamentalist ideas.

89. Choice (D) is the correct answer. In the 1920s, Mao Zedong revolutionized Chinese Marxist thought by claiming that the Chinese peasantry needed to be mobilized for a communist revolution to succeed in China. Traditional Marxist doctrine focused on the exploitation of the urban working class and their eventual overthrow of their oppressors. Mao Zedong argued that because China was predominantly an agrarian society, the massive support needed for a revolution had to be found in the rural peasantry. Eventually, in 1949, the Chinese communist revolution succeeded and the People's Republic of China was established under the leadership of Mao Zedong.

90. Choice (A) is the correct answer. During much of the third quarter of the twentieth century, the economies of China, North Korea, and North Vietnam were isolated from the world economy because of their adherence to Marxist economic policies. In these economies, economic decisions regarding production and trade are all centrally planned and governed by the state. Fully governed by their states, these economies were isolated from the competition among private companies in the international markets.

91. Choice (A) is the correct answer. The division of Korea into North and South Korea was primarily the result of the political rivalry between the United States and the Soviet Union. Japan ruled Korea from 1910 until the end of the Second World War. At the close of the war, the United States and the Soviet Union agreed that Japanese soldiers north of the 38th parallel would surrender to the Soviets, and those south of the line would surrender to the United States. The two powers then proceeded to establish and back governments aligned with their political perspectives. North Korea developed a communist government, while South Korea eventually developed into a democracy.

92. Choice (B) is the correct answer. During the U.S. occupation of Japan following the Second World War from 1945 to 1952, U.S. and Japanese authorities were supported by Japanese business leaders. The U.S. occupiers had the task of maintaining control while reconstructing Japan's infrastructure and economy. Many Japanese business leaders benefited from the production and trade policies established by the U.S. occupiers and, as a result, they were generally supportive.

93. Choice (E) is the correct answer. Many historians use the peace settlement reached by the major European powers at the Congress of Vienna in 1815 to mark the end of the French Revolutionary era. The settlement redefined European boundaries after the Napoleonic Wars and reestablished prerevolution monarchies. The Congress coincided with the final defeat of French Revolutionary leader Napoleon Bonaparte at Waterloo.

94. Choice (C) is the correct answer. The signing of the Helsinki Accords in 1975 by the United States, Canada, the Soviet Union, and most European countries concluded the Conference on Security and Cooperation in Europe held in Helsinki, Finland. The Conference and the Helsinki Accords largely focused on establishing mutual cooperation and respect for the basic freedoms and rights of all humans, including racial minorities.

95. Choice (B) is the correct answer. Toward the end of the twentieth century, politicians and engineers began questioning the value of building big dams to produce hydroelectricity because of their effect on the people who live along the dammed rivers. Although the huge dams produce electricity and create jobs, they also alter the flow of the river, flooding land and displacing many families from their homes. Many political activists have protested on behalf of the communities most affected, arguing that the detrimental effects of the projects outweigh their benefits.

Chapter 4

Mathematics

Purpose

There are two one-hour Subject Tests in mathematics: Mathematics Level 1 and Mathematics Level 2. The purpose of these tests is to measure your knowledge of mathematics through the first three years of college-preparatory mathematics for Level 1 and through precalculus for Level 2.

Mathematics Level 1 Subject Test

Format

Mathematics Level 1 is a one-hour broad survey test that consists of 50 multiple-choice questions. The test has questions in the following areas:

- Number and Operations
- Algebra and Functions
- Geometry and Measurement (plane Euclidean, coordinate, three-dimensional, and trigonometry)
- Data Analysis, Statistics, and Probability

How to Prepare

The Mathematics Level 1 Subject Test is intended for students who have taken three years of college-preparatory mathematics, including two years of algebra and one year of geometry. You are not expected to have studied every topic on the test. Familiarize yourself with the test directions in advance. The directions in this book are identical to those that appear on the test.

Calculator Use

It is NOT necessary to use a calculator to solve every question on the Level 1 test, but it is important to know when and how to use one. **Students who take the test without a calculator will be at a disadvantage.** For about 50 to 60 percent of the questions, there is no advantage, perhaps even a disadvantage, to using a calculator. For about 40 to 50 percent of the questions, a calculator may be useful or necessary.

A graphing calculator may provide an advantage over a scientific calculator on some questions. However, you should bring the calculator with which you are most familiar. If you are comfortable with both a scientific calculator and a graphing calculator, you should bring the graphing calculator.

Mathematics Level 2 Subject Test

Format

Mathematics Level 2 is also a one-hour test that contains 50 multiple-choice questions that cover the following areas:

- Number and Operations
- Algebra and Functions
- Geometry and Measurement (coordinate geometry, three-dimensional geometry, and trigonometry)
- Data Analysis, Statistics, and Probability

How to Prepare

The Mathematics Level 2 Subject Test is intended for students who have taken college-preparatory mathematics for more than three years, including two years of algebra, one year of geometry, and elementary functions (precalculus) and/or trigonometry. You are not expected to have studied every topic on the test.

Choosing Between Mathematics Levels 1 and 2

If you have taken trigonometry and/or elementary functions (pre-calculus), received grades of B or better in these courses, and are comfortable knowing when and how to use a scientific or a graphing calculator, you should select the Level 2 test. If you are sufficiently prepared to take Level 2, but elect to take Level 1 in hopes of receiving a higher score, you may not do as well as you expect. You may want to consider taking the test that covers the topics you learned most recently, since the material will be fresh in your mind. You should also consider the requirements of the colleges and/or programs you are interested in.

Pages 189 and 190 explain in greater detail the similarities and differences between the two Mathematics tests. Take the time to review this information prior to deciding which Mathematics test to take. Seek advice from your high school math teacher if you are still unsure of which test to take. Keep in mind you can choose to take either test on test day, regardless of what test you registered for.

Calculator Use

It is NOT necessary to use a calculator to solve every question on the Level 2 test, but it is important to know when and how to use one. For about 35 to 45 percent of the questions, there is no advantage, and perhaps even a disadvantage, to using a calculator. For about 55 to 65 percent of the questions, a calculator may be useful or necessary.

As with the Level 1 test, a graphing calculator may provide an advantage over a scientific calculator on some questions. However, you should bring the calculator with which you are most familiar. If you are comfortable with both a scientific calculator and a graphing calculator, you should bring the graphing calculator.

Calculator Policy: You may NOT use a calculator on any Subject Test other than the Mathematics Level 1 and Level 2 Tests.

What Calculator to Bring

- Bring a calculator that you are used to using. If you're comfortable with both a scientific calculator and a graphing calculator, bring the graphing calculator.
- Before you take the test, make sure that your calculator is in good working order. You may bring batteries and a backup calculator to the test center.
- The test center will not have substitute calculators or batteries on hand. Students may not share calculators.
- If your calculator malfunctions during one of the Mathematics Level 1 or Level 2 Tests and you do not have a backup calculator, you must tell your test supervisor when the malfunction occurs. The supervisor will then cancel the scores on that test only, if you desire to do so.

What Is NOT Permitted

- calculators that have QWERTY keypads (e.g., TI-92 Plus, Voyage 200) or have pen-input, stylus,* or touch-screen capability (e.g., PDAs, Casio Class Pad)
- calculators that have wireless, Bluetooth, cellular, audio/video recording and playing, camera, or any other cell-phone type feature
- calculators that make noise or "talk," require an electrical outlet, or use paper tape
- calculators that can access the Internet
- laptops, portable handheld computers, electronic writing pads, or pocket organizers

* The use of the stylus with the Sharp EL-9600 calculator will not be permitted. The Sharp EL-9600 remains on the list of approved graphing calculators.

Additional information about calculator usage can be found on collegeboard.org.

Using Your Calculator

- Only some questions on these tests require the use of a calculator. First decide how you will solve a problem, then determine if you need a calculator. For many of the questions, there's more than one way to solve the problem. **Don't pick up a calculator if you don't need to**—you might waste time.
- **The answer choices are often rounded**, so the answer you get might not match the answer in the test book. Since the choices are rounded, plugging the choices into the problem might not produce an exact answer.
- **Don't round any intermediate calculations**. For example, if you get a result from your calculator for the first step of a solution, keep the result in the calculator and use it for the second step. If you round the result from the first step and the answer choices are close to each other, you might choose the wrong answer.
- **Read the question carefully** so that you know what you are being asked to do. Sometimes a result that you may get from your calculator is NOT the final answer. If an answer you get is not one of the choices in the question, it may be that you didn't answer the question being asked. You should read the question again. It may also be that you rounded at an intermediate step in solving the problem, and that's why your answer doesn't match any of the choices in the question.
- **Think about how you are going to solve the question** before picking up your calculator. It may be that you only need the calculator for the final step or two and can do the rest in your test book or in your head. Don't waste time by using the calculator more than necessary.
- If you are taking the **Level 1 test, make sure your calculator is in degree mode** ahead of time so you won't have to worry about it during the test. If you're taking the Level 2 test, make sure your calculator is in the correct mode (degree or radian) for the question being asked.
- For some questions on these tests, a **graphing calculator** may provide an advantage. If you use a graphing calculator, you should know how to perform calculations (e.g., exponents, roots, trigonometric values, logarithms), graph functions and analyze the graphs, find zeros of functions, find points of intersection of graphs of functions, find minima/maxima of functions, find numerical solutions to equations, generate a table of values for a function, and perform data analysis features, including finding a regression equation.
- **You will not be allowed to share calculators.** You will be dismissed and your scores canceled if you use your calculator to share information during the test, or to remove test questions or answers from the test room.

Comparing the Two Tests

Although there is some overlap between Mathematics Levels 1 and 2, the emphasis for Level 2 is on more advanced content. Here are the differences in the two tests.

Topics Covered*	Approximate Percentage of Test	
	Level 1	Level 2
Number and Operations	**10–14%**	**10–14%**
Operations, ratio and proportion, complex numbers, counting, elementary number theory, matrices, sequences, *series, vectors*		
Algebra and Functions	**38–42%**	**48–52%**
Expressions, equations, inequalities, representation and modeling, properties of functions (linear, polynomial, rational, exponential, *logarithmic, trigonometric, inverse trigonometric, periodic, piecewise, recursive, parametric*)		
Geometry and Measurement	**38–42%**	**28–32%**
Plane Euclidean/Measurement	18–22%	—
Coordinate	8–12%	10–14%
Lines, parabolas, circles, *ellipses, hyperbolas*, symmetry, transformations, *polar coordinates*		
Three-dimensional	4–6%	4–6%
Solids, surface area and volume (cylinders, cones, pyramids, spheres, prisms), *coordinates in three dimensions*		
Trigonometry	6–8%	12–16%
Right triangles, identities, *radian measure, law of cosines, law of sines, equations, double angle formulas*		
Data Analysis, Statistics, and Probability	**8–12%**	**8–12%**
Mean, median, mode, range, interquartile range, *standard deviation*, graphs and plots, least-squares regression (linear, *quadratic, exponential*), probability		

* Topics in italics are tested on Level 2 only. The content of Level 1 overlaps somewhat with that on Level 2, but the emphasis on 2 is on more advanced content. Plane Euclidean Geometry is not tested directly on Level 2.

Areas of Overlap

The content of Level 1 has some overlap with Level 2, especially in the following areas:

- elementary algebra
- three-dimensional geometry
- coordinate geometry
- statistics
- basic trigonometry

How Test Content Differs

Although some questions may be appropriate for both tests, the emphasis for Level 2 is on more advanced content. The tests differ significantly in the following areas:

Number and Operations. Level 1 measures a more basic understanding of the topics than Level 2. For example, Level 1 covers the *arithmetic of complex numbers*, but Level 2 also covers *graphical and other properties of complex numbers*. Level 2 also includes *series* and *vectors*.

Algebra and Functions. Level 1 contains mainly *algebraic* equations and functions, whereas Level 2 also contains more advanced equations and functions, such as *exponential*, *logarithmic*, and *trigonometric*.

Geometry and Measurement. A significant percentage of the questions on Level 1 is devoted to *plane Euclidean geometry and measurement*, which is not tested directly on Level 2. On Level 2, the concepts learned in plane geometry are applied in the questions on *coordinate geometry* and *three-dimensional geometry*.

The trigonometry questions on Level 1 are primarily limited to *right triangle trigonometry* (*sine, cosine, tangent*) and *the fundamental relationships among the trigonometric ratios*. Level 2 includes questions about *ellipses*, *hyperbolas*, *polar coordinates*, and *coordinates in three dimensions*. The trigonometry questions on Level 2 place more emphasis on *the properties and graphs of trigonometric functions*, *the inverse trigonometric functions*, *trigonometric equations and identities*, and *the laws of sines and cosines*.

Data Analysis, Statistics, and Probability. Both Level 1 and Level 2 include *mean, median, mode, range, interquartile range, data interpretation*, and *probability*. Level 2 also includes *standard deviation*. Both include *least-squares linear regression*, but Level 2 also includes *quadratic and exponential regression*.

Scores

The total score for each test is reported on the 200 to 800 point scale. Because the content measured by Level 1 and Level 2 differs considerably, you should not use your score on one test to predict your score on the other.

Note: Geometric Figures

Figures that accompany problems are intended to provide information useful in solving the problems. They are drawn as accurately as possible EXCEPT when it is stated in a particular problem that the figure is not drawn to scale. Even when figures are not drawn to scale, the relative positions of points and angles may be assumed to be in the order shown. Also, line segments that extend through points and appear to lie on the same line *may be assumed to be* on the same line.

When "Note: Figure not drawn to scale," appears below a figure in a question, it means that degree measures may not be accurately shown and specific lengths may not be drawn proportionately.

Mathematics Level 1

Sample Questions

All questions in the Mathematics Level 1 and Level 2 Tests are multiple-choice questions in which you must choose the BEST response from the five choices offered. The directions that follow are the same as those on the Mathematics Level 1 Test.

For each of the following problems, decide which is the BEST of the choices given. If the exact numerical value is not one of the choices, select the choice that best approximates this value. Then fill in the corresponding circle on the answer sheet.

Notes: (1) A scientific or graphing calculator will be necessary for answering some (but not all) of the questions in this test. For each question you will have to decide whether or not you should use a calculator.

(2) The only angle measure used on this test is degree measure. Make sure your calculator is in the degree mode.

(3) Figures that accompany problems in this test are intended to provide information useful in solving the problems. They are drawn as accurately as possible EXCEPT when it is stated in a specific problem that its figure is not drawn to scale. All figures lie in a plane unless otherwise indicated.

(4) Unless otherwise specified, the domain of any function f is assumed to be the set of all real numbers x for which $f(x)$ is a real number. The range of f is assumed to be the set of all real numbers $f(x)$, where x is in the domain of f.

(5) Reference information that may be useful in answering the questions in this test can be found on the page preceding Question 1.

Reference Information: The following information is for your reference in answering some of the questions in this test.

Volume of a right circular cone with radius r and height h: $V = \frac{1}{3}\pi r^2 h$

Volume of a sphere with radius r: $V = \frac{4}{3}\pi r^3$

Surface Area of a sphere with radius r: $S = 4\pi r^2$

Volume of a pyramid with base area B and height h: $V = \frac{1}{3}Bh$

Numbers and Operations

1. The 3rd term of an arithmetic sequence is 14 and the 17th term is 63. What is the sum of the first 10 terms of the sequence?

   (A) 227.5
   (B) 245
   (C) 262.5
   (D) 297.5
   (E) 385

Choice (A) is the correct answer to question 1. In an arithmetic sequence, the difference between consecutive terms is constant. Since the 3rd term of the sequence is 14 and the 17th term is 63, the common difference is $\frac{63-14}{17-3} = 3.5$.

If the 3rd term of the sequence is 14, the 2nd term is $14 - 3.5 = 10.5$, and the 1st term is 7. Likewise, the 10th term is equal to $7 + 9(3.5) = 38.5$. The sum of the first 10 terms of the sequence is given by $S_{10} = \frac{10(7+38.5)}{2} = 227.5$.

Algebra and Functions

2. From which of the following statements must it follow that $x > y$?
   (A) $x = 2y$
   (B) $2x = y$
   (C) $x + 2 = y$
   (D) $x - 2 = y$
   (E) $2 - x = y$

Choice (D) is the correct answer to question 2. If $x > y$, then $x = y + d$ where $d > 0$. In $x - 2 = y$, which is equivalent to $x = y + 2$ fitting the definition of "greater than."

Another way to solve this problem is to look at each of the choices to see if it implies that $x > y$ for all values of x and y.

First look at choice (A). Here x is not greater than y in the cases where both x and y are 0 or negative. For example, if $x = -2$ and $y = -1$, then $x = 2y$, but x is not greater than y.

Likewise, in choice (B) if $x = y = 0$, then $2x = y$, but x is not greater than y.

In choice (C), x is always 2 less than y, so it is not possible for $x > y$.

In choice (D), x is always 2 greater than y. Thus, the statement $x - 2 = y$ implies that $x > y$ for all values of x and y. The correct answer is choice (D).

In choice (E), when $x = y = 1$, it is true that $2 - x = y$, but x is not greater than y.

3. If $y = 2x^3 + 18x^2 - 20$ for $0 \leq x \leq 10$, the maximum value of y occurs when $x =$
   (A) 0
   (B) 1.13
   (C) 6
   (D) 8.87
   (E) 10

Choice (C) is the correct answer to question 3. You can use a graphing calculator to help you solve this problem. Graph the equation in an appropriate viewing window that allows you to see the maximum value of y. You can do this by setting the values of x from 0 to 10 and then selecting a zoom option that fits the y-values for the given x-values. Once you graph the equation, use the "maximum" feature of the calculator to find the maximum value of y on the interval $0 \leq x \leq 10$. You can see from the graph that the maximum value of y is 196, which occurs when $x = 6$. It is important to remember that the minimum or maximum values do not necessarily occur at the endpoints of the domain interval.

4. Money invested in an account paying interest at an annual percentage rate of 9 percent compounded annually doubles in value in approximately 8 years. At what annual percentage rate, compounded annually, would the same investment take 16 years to double?
   (A) 0.4%
   (B) 4.4%
   (C) 5%
   (D) 12.5%
   (E) 18%

Choice (B) is the correct answer to question 4. Let P represent the amount being invested. According to the question $P(1.09)^8$ is approximately equal to $2P$. To find the rate at which the investment will take 16 years to double, set up the equation $P(1+r)^{16}=2P$ or $(1+r)^{16}=2$ If you take the 16th root of both sides of the equation, you get $(1+r)=2^{\frac{1}{16}}$ or $1+r\approx 1.044$. Thus, the rate is 4.4%.

5. If $f(x)=x^2+x-6$, what are all values of a for which $f(a)=f(-a)$?
   (A) −3 and 2 only
   (B) −2 and 3 only
   (C) 0 only
   (D) 2 only
   (E) All real numbers

Choice (C) is the correct answer to question 5. If $f(a)=f(-a)$, then $a^2+a-6=(-a)^2-a-6$. This simplifies to $a=-a$. The only value of a for which this is true is 0.

You can also use a graphing calculator to examine the graphs of $y=f(x)$ and $y=f(-x)$. The only point of intersection of the two graphs is at $x=0$.

6. If $f(g(x)) = x$ and $f(x) = 3x + 1$, which of the following is $g(x)$?

(A) $g(x) = \frac{1}{3}x - \frac{1}{9}$

(B) $g(x) = \frac{1}{3}x - \frac{1}{3}$

(C) $g(x) = \frac{1}{3}x + 1$

(D) $g(x) = \frac{1}{3}x - 1$

(E) $g(x) = 3x - 1$

Choice (B) is the correct answer to question 6. If $f(g(x)) = x$ and $f(x) = 3x + 1$, then $f(g(x)) = 3g(x) + 1 = x$. Solving this equation for $g(x)$ yields $x - 1 = 3g(x)$ and $g(x) = \frac{x-1}{3}$ or $\frac{1}{3}x - \frac{1}{3}$.

Geometry and Measurement: Plane Geometry

7. Square $ABCD$ has sides of length 8. Square $MNOP$ is formed by connecting the midpoints of the sides of $ABCD$. Square $WXYZ$ is formed by connecting the midpoints of the sides of $MNOP$. What is the ratio of the area of $WXYZ$ to the area of $ABCD$?

(A) 1 to 8

(B) 1 to 4

(C) 1 to 2

(D) $\sqrt{2}$ to 4

(E) $\sqrt{2}$ to 2

It is helpful to draw a figure.

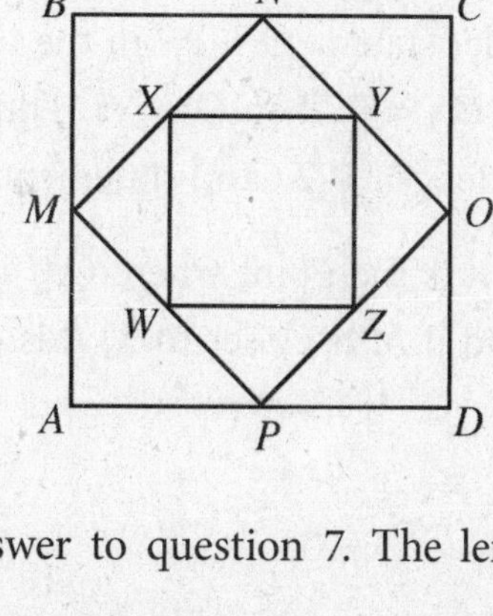

Choice (B) is the correct answer to question 7. The length of each of segments $\overline{AM}$ and $\overline{AP}$ is 4. Since $\triangle PAM$ is an isosceles right triangle, by the Pythagorean theorem, the length of segment $\overline{MP}$ is $\sqrt{4^2+4^2}=\sqrt{32}=4\sqrt{2}$. Thus, the length of each of segments $\overline{MW}$ and $\overline{MX}$ is $\frac{4\sqrt{2}}{2}=2\sqrt{2}$. Again, by the Pythagorean theorem, the length of $\overline{WX}$ is $\sqrt{(2\sqrt{2})^2+(2\sqrt{2})^2}=\sqrt{16}=4$. The area of square $WXYZ$ is $4^2=16$, and the area of square $ABCD$ is $8^2=64$. So the ratio of the area of $WXYZ$ to the area of $ABCD$ is 1 to 4.

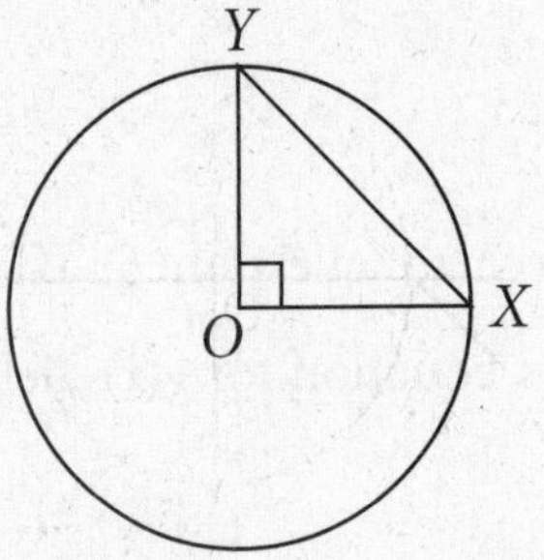

8. In the figure above, X and Y are points on the circle with center O. Point M (not shown) is a point on the minor arc $\overset{\frown}{XY}$ such that $\overline{OM}$ intersects $\overline{XY}$ at point R (not shown). If $OX = 5$, which of the following must be true?

   I. $XY = 5\sqrt{2}$

   II. $XR = RY$

   III. $OM = 5$

   (A) I only
   (B) II only
   (C) III only
   (D) I and II
   (E) I and III

Choice (E) is the correct answer to question 8. In this type of question, each of three statements, labeled I, II, and III, must be considered independently based on the information given. First, consider statement I. From the figure we know $\overline{OX} \perp \overline{OY}$. Since $\overline{OX}$ and $\overline{OY}$ are both radii and $OX = 5$, then $OY = 5$. Thus, $\overline{XY}$ is the hypotenuse of an isosceles right triangle and has length $5\sqrt{2}$, and statement I is true.

In statement II, we know that R is the point where $\overline{OM}$ intersects $\overline{XY}$. If M is closer to Y, then R is also closer to Y, and if M is closer to X, R is closer to X. Thus, it *cannot* be concluded that $XR = RY$.

In statement III, since we know the circle has radius 5 and that $\overline{OM}$ is a radius of the circle, statement III is true. Therefore, the correct answer is choice (E) because statements I and III *must* be true.

Geometry and Measurement: Coordinate Geometry

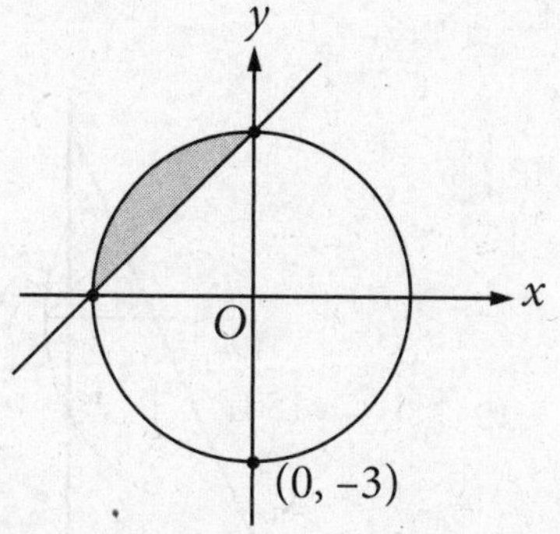

9. In the figure above, the origin O is the center of the circle. What is the area of the shaded region?
   (A) 0.21
   (B) 0.29
   (C) 2.57
   (D) 14.35
   (E) 19.27

Choice (C) is the correct answer to question 9. The figure shows a circle with radius 3. The area of the shaded region is equal to the area of a quarter circle minus the area of the right triangle shown. Thus, the area of the shaded region is $\frac{9\pi}{4} - \frac{1}{2}(3)(3)$, which is approximately equal to 2.5686.

Geometry and Measurement: Three-Dimensional Geometry

10. A cylindrical container with an inside height of 6 feet has an inside radius of 2 feet. If the container is $\frac{2}{3}$ full of water, what is the volume, in cubic feet, of the water in the container?
    (A) 25.1
    (B) 37.7
    (C) 50.3
    (D) 62.3
    (E) 75.4

Choice (C) is the correct answer to question 10. The volume V of a cylinder with radius r and height h is given by $V = \pi r^2 h$. Thus, the volume, in cubic feet, of the container is $\pi \cdot 2^2 \cdot 6 = 24\pi$. Since the container is $\frac{2}{3}$ full of water, the volume of the water in the container is $\frac{2}{3} \cdot 24\pi \approx 50.3$.

Geometry and Measurement: Trigonometry

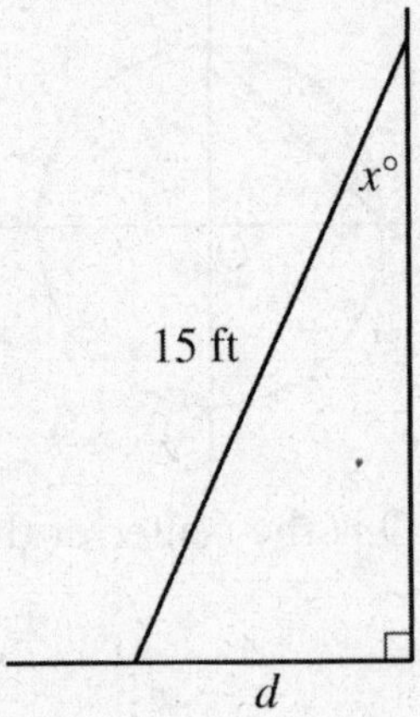

Note: Figure not drawn to scale.

11. In the figure above, a 15-foot ladder is leaning against a vertical wall so that the top of the ladder makes an angle of $x°$ with the wall. If $x = 16$, what is the ratio of the length of the ladder to d, the distance that the base of the ladder is from the base of the wall?

    (A) 0.28
    (B) 1.04
    (C) 3.48
    (D) 3.63
    (E) 4.13

Choice (D) is the correct answer to question 11. Use right triangle trigonometry to set up the equation $\sin 16° = \frac{d}{15}$. Thus, $d = 15 \sin 16°$. The ratio of the length of the ladder to d is $\frac{15}{15 \sin 16°} \approx 3.63$, since the length of the ladder is 15 feet.

You could also solve this problem by realizing that the ratio of d to 15 is equal to $\sin 16°$, so the ratio of 15 to d equals $\frac{1}{\sin 16°}$.

Data Analysis, Statistics, and Probability

12. A random number generator will randomly select an integer between 1 and 100, inclusive. What is the probability that the integer selected will be the product of two odd integers greater than 1?

(A) $\frac{25}{100}$

(B) $\frac{26}{100}$

(C) $\frac{28}{100}$

(D) $\frac{29}{100}$

(E) $\frac{30}{100}$

Choice (A) is the correct answer to question 12. An integer that satisfies the given conditions must be odd and not prime. There are 49 odd integers that are greater than 1 and less than 100. Of these, 24 are prime, which leaves 25 integers that meet the given conditions. The probability of choosing one of these integers is $\frac{25}{100}$.

Mathematics Level 1 Subject Test

Practice Helps

The test that follows is an actual, previously administered SAT Subject Test in Mathematics Level 1. To get an idea of what it's like to take this test, practice under conditions that are much like those of an actual test administration.

- Set aside an hour when you can take the test uninterrupted.
- Sit at a desk or table with no other books or papers. Dictionaries, other books, or notes are not allowed in the test room.
- Remember to have a scientific or graphing calculator with you.
- Tear out an answer sheet from the back of this book and fill it in just as you would on the day of the test. One answer sheet can be used for up to three Subject Tests.
- Read the instructions that precede the practice test. During the actual administration you will be asked to read them before answering test questions.
- Time yourself by placing a clock or kitchen timer in front of you.
- After you finish the practice test, read the sections "How to Score the SAT Subject Test in Mathematics Level 1" and "How Did You Do on the Subject Test in Mathematics Level 1?"
- The appearance of the answer sheet in this book may differ from the answer sheet you see on test day.

MATHEMATICS LEVEL 1 TEST

The top portion of the page of the answer sheet that you will use to take the Mathematics Level 1 Test must be filled in exactly as illustrated below. When your supervisor tells you to fill in the circle next to the name of the test you are about to take, mark your answer sheet as shown.

○ Literature	● Mathematics Level 1	○ German	○ Chinese Listening	○ Japanese Listening
○ Biology E	○ Mathematics Level 2	○ Italian	○ French Listening	○ Korean Listening
○ Biology M	○ U.S. History	○ Latin	○ German Listening	○ Spanish Listening
○ Chemistry	○ World History	○ Modern Hebrew		
○ Physics	○ French	○ Spanish	Background Questions: ①②③④⑤⑥⑦⑧⑨	

After filling in the circle next to the name of the test you are taking, locate the Background Questions section, which also appears at the top of your answer sheet (as shown above). This is where you will answer the following Background Questions on your answer sheet.

BACKGROUND QUESTIONS

Please answer Part I and Part II below by filling in the appropriate circle in the Background Questions box on your answer sheet. The information you provide is for statistical purposes only and will not affect your test score.

Part I. Which of the following describes a mathematics course you have taken or are currently taking? (FILL IN **ALL** CIRCLES THAT APPLY.)

- Algebra I or Elementary Algebra **OR** Course I of a college preparatory mathematics sequence —Fill in circle 1.
- Geometry **OR** Course II of a college preparatory mathematics sequence —Fill in circle 2.
- Algebra II or Intermediate Algebra **OR** Course III of a college preparatory mathematics sequence —Fill in circle 3.
- Elementary Functions (Precalculus) and/or Trigonometry **OR** beyond Course III of a college preparatory mathematics sequence —Fill in circle 4.
- Advanced Placement Mathematics (Calculus AB or Calculus BC) —Fill in circle 5.

Part II. What type of calculator did you bring to use for this test? (FILL IN THE **ONE** CIRCLE THAT APPLIES. If you did not bring a scientific or graphing calculator, do not fill in any of circles 6-9.)

- Scientific —Fill in circle 6.
- Graphing (Fill in the circle corresponding to the model you used.)

  Casio 9700, Casio 9750, Casio 9800, Casio 9850, Casio 9860, Casio FX 1.0, Casio CG-10, Sharp 9200, Sharp 9300, Sharp 9600, Sharp 9900, TI-82, TI-83, TI-83 Plus, TI-83 Plus Silver, TI-84 Plus, TI-84 Plus Silver, TI-85, TI-86, or TI-Nspire —Fill in circle 7.

  Casio 9970, Casio Algebra FX 2.0, HP 38G, HP 39 series, HP 40 series, HP 48 series, HP 49 series, HP 50 series, TI-89, TI-89 Titanium, or TI-Nspire CAS —Fill in circle 8.

  Some other graphing calculator —Fill in circle 9.

When the supervisor gives the signal, turn the page and begin the Mathematics Level 1 Test. There are 100 numbered circles on the answer sheet and 50 questions in the Mathematics Level 1 Test. Therefore, use only circles 1 to 50 for recording your answers.

MATHEMATICS LEVEL 1 TEST

REFERENCE INFORMATION

THE FOLLOWING INFORMATION IS FOR YOUR REFERENCE IN ANSWERING SOME OF THE QUESTIONS IN THIS TEST.

Volume of a right circular cone with radius r and height h: $V = \frac{1}{3}\pi r^2 h$

Volume of a sphere with radius r: $V = \frac{4}{3}\pi r^3$

Surface Area of a sphere with radius r: $S = 4\pi r^2$

Volume of a pyramid with base area B and height h: $V = \frac{1}{3}Bh$

DO NOT DETACH FROM BOOK.

GO ON TO THE NEXT PAGE

MATHEMATICS LEVEL 1 TEST

For each of the following problems, decide which is the BEST of the choices given. If the exact numerical value is not one of the choices, select the choice that best approximates this value. Then fill in the corresponding circle on the answer sheet.

Notes: (1) A scientific or graphing calculator will be necessary for answering some (but not all) of the questions in this test. For each question you will have to decide whether or not you should use a calculator.

(2) The only angle measure used on this test is degree measure. Make sure your calculator is in the degree mode.

(3) Figures that accompany problems in this test are intended to provide information useful in solving the problems. They are drawn as accurately as possible EXCEPT when it is stated in a specific problem that its figure is not drawn to scale. All figures lie in a plane unless otherwise indicated.

(4) Unless otherwise specified, the domain of any function f is assumed to be the set of all real numbers x for which $f(x)$ is a real number. The range of f is assumed to be the set of all real numbers $f(x)$, where x is in the domain of f.

(5) Reference information that may be useful in answering the questions in this test can be found on the page preceding Question 1.

USE THIS SPACE FOR SCRATCHWORK.

1. If $xy + 7y = 84$ and $x + 7 = 3$, what is the value of y?

(A) −4
(B) 4.9
(C) 8.4
(D) 12
(E) 28

GO ON TO THE NEXT PAGE

MATHEMATICS LEVEL 1 TEST—*Continued*

USE THIS SPACE FOR SCRATCHWORK.

2. When four given numbers are multiplied together, the product is negative. Which of the following could be true about the four numbers?

(A) One is negative, two are positive, and one is zero.
(B) Two are negative, one is positive, and one is zero.
(C) Two are negative and two are positive.
(D) Three are negative and one is positive.
(E) Four are negative.

3. If $x + y = 5$ and $x - y = 3$, then $x^2 - y^2 =$

(A) 9 (B) 15 (C) 16 (D) 25 (E) 34

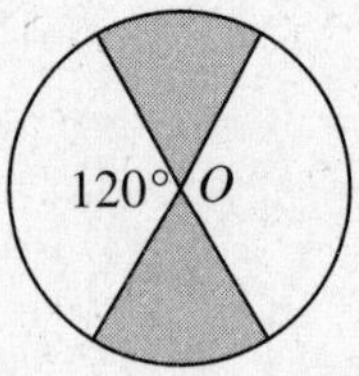

4. In the figure above, what fraction of the circular region with center O is shaded?

(A) $\frac{1}{6}$ (B) $\frac{1}{5}$ (C) $\frac{1}{4}$ (D) $\frac{1}{3}$ (E) $\frac{3}{5}$

GO ON TO THE NEXT PAGE

MATHEMATICS LEVEL 1 TEST—*Continued*

USE THIS SPACE FOR SCRATCHWORK.

5. Which of the following is the graph of a linear function with both a negative slope and a negative y-intercept?

(A)
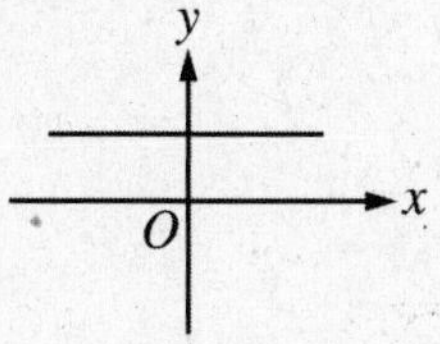

(B)
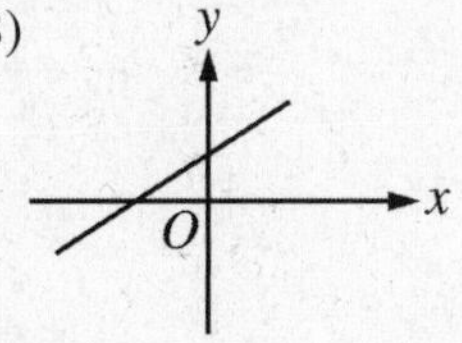

(C)
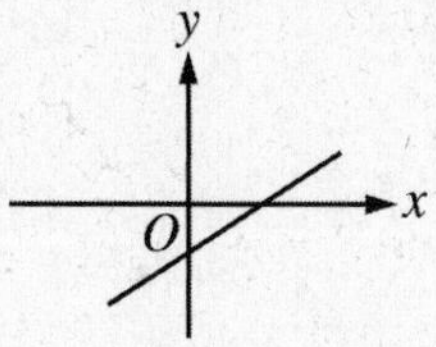

(D)
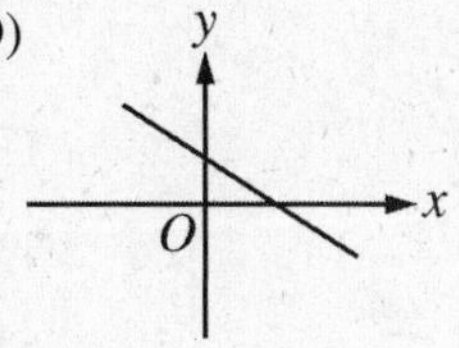

(E)
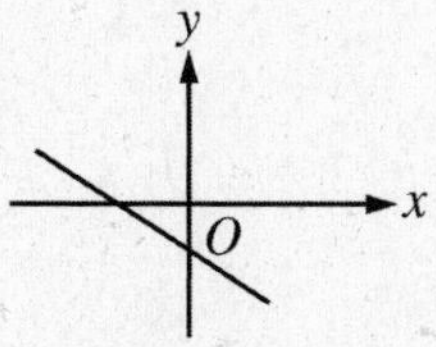

6. If $k^2 - 4 = 4 - k^2$, what are all possible values of k?

(A) 0 only
(B) 2 only
(C) 4 only
(D) −2 and 2 only
(E) −2, 0, and 2

7. If $b^{2x+1} = b^{3x-1}$ for all values of b, what is the value of x?

(A) 2 (B) $\frac{3}{2}$ (C) $\frac{2}{3}$ (D) −2 (E) −3

GO ON TO THE NEXT PAGE

USE THIS SPACE FOR SCRATCHWORK.

8. At North High School, the number of students taking French is decreasing by 20 students per year and the number of students taking Spanish is increasing by 10 students per year. This year 250 students are taking French, and 100 students are taking Spanish. Which of the following equations could be used to find the number of years n until the number of students is the same in both courses?

(A) $250 - 20n = 100 + 10n$
(B) $250 + 10n = 100 - 20n$
(C) $250 + 20n = 100 - 10n$
(D) $20n - 250 = 100 + 10n$
(E) $n(250 - 20) = n(100 + 10)$

9. If $y = x^3 - 1.5$, for what value of x is $y = 2$?

(A) 0.79
(B) 1.14
(C) 1.52
(D) 1.87
(E) 6.50

10. The length of a rectangle is four times its width. If the perimeter of the rectangle is 40 centimeters, what is its area?

(A) 4 cm^2
(B) 16 cm^2
(C) 20 cm^2
(D) 40 cm^2
(E) 64 cm^2

GO ON TO THE NEXT PAGE

MATHEMATICS LEVEL 1 TEST—*Continued*

USE THIS SPACE FOR SCRATCHWORK.

11. The function g, where $g(t) = 0.066t + 0.96$, can be used to represent the relation between grade point average $g(t)$ and the number of hours t spent studying each week. Based on this function, a student with a grade point average of 3.5 studied how many hours per week?

(A) 0.96
(B) 1.2
(C) 14.5
(D) 38.5
(E) 67.8

12. $x^2 - 2x + 3 = x^3 + 2x + x^2$ is equivalent to

(A) 0
(B) $2x^2 - 4x = 0$
(C) $-x^3 + 4x - 3 = 0$
(D) $x^3 - 2x^2 - 3 = 0$
(E) $x^3 + 4x - 3 = 0$

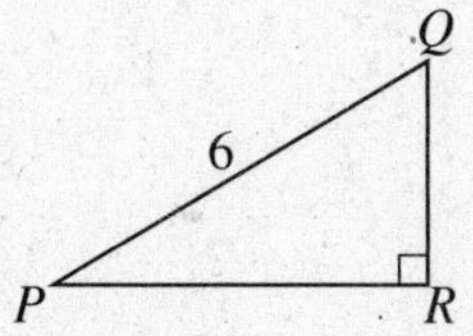

13. In right triangle PQR in the figure above, $\sin P = 0.5$. What is the length of side QR ?

(A) 2
(B) 3
(C) 5
(D) 6
(E) 12

GO ON TO THE NEXT PAGE

MATHEMATICS LEVEL 1 TEST—*Continued*

USE THIS SPACE FOR SCRATCHWORK.

14. Which of the following numbers is a COUNTEREXAMPLE to the statement "All odd numbers greater than 2 are prime numbers" ?

(A) 2 (B) 3 (C) 5 (D) 7 (E) 9

15. If $f(x) = \dfrac{2x - 1}{x^2}$, what is the value of $f(-0.1)$?

(A) −120
(B) −100
(C) 100
(D) 120
(E) 220

16. On a blueprint, 0.4 inch represents 6 feet. If the actual distance between two buildings is 76 feet, what would be the distance between the corresponding buildings on the blueprint?

(A) 3.2 in
(B) 5.1 in
(C) 12.7 in
(D) 30.4 in
(E) 31.7 in

GO ON TO THE NEXT PAGE

MATHEMATICS LEVEL 1 TEST—*Continued*

USE THIS SPACE FOR SCRATCHWORK.

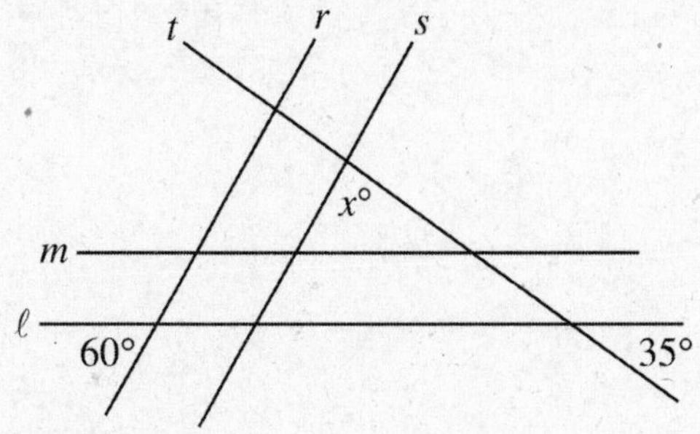

17. In the figure above, if $\ell \parallel m$ and $r \parallel s$, what is the value of x?

(A) 65
(B) 80
(C) 85
(D) 95
(E) 115

18. For what value of x is $\frac{2x}{3x-1}$ undefined?

(A) $-\frac{1}{3}$ (B) 0 (C) $\frac{1}{3}$ (D) $\frac{1}{2}$ (E) 1

19. A sales team sold an average (arithmetic mean) of 10.375 mobile phones per week during the first 8 weeks of the last quarter of the year. The members of the sales team will receive a bonus if they sell a total of 185 phones for the quarter. What must their average sales, in phones per week, be for the remaining 5 weeks of the quarter if they are to receive the bonus?

(A) 4.2
(B) 20.4
(C) 83
(D) 102
(E) 174.6

GO ON TO THE NEXT PAGE

MATHEMATICS LEVEL 1 TEST—*Continued*

USE THIS SPACE FOR SCRATCHWORK.

20. What is the y-coordinate of the point at which the line whose equation is $3x - 2y - 7 = 0$ crosses the y-axis?

(A) $-\frac{7}{2}$

(B) $-\frac{7}{3}$

(C) $\frac{7}{3}$

(D) $\frac{7}{2}$

(E) 7

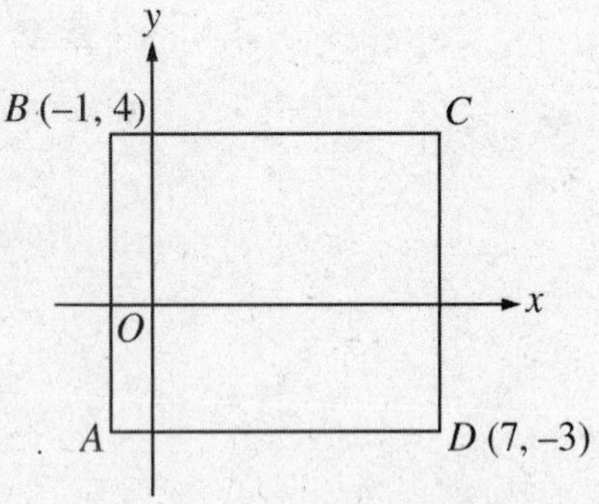

21. In the figure above, the sides of rectangle $ABCD$ are parallel to the axes. What is the distance between point A and point C?

(A) 6.07
(B) 7
(C) 10.1
(D) 10.6
(E) 15

GO ON TO THE NEXT PAGE

MATHEMATICS LEVEL 1 TEST—*Continued*

USE THIS SPACE FOR SCRATCHWORK.

22. Four signal flags — one red, one blue, one yellow, and one green — can be arranged from top to bottom on a signal pole. Every arrangement of the four flags is a different signal. How many different signals using all four flags have the red flag at the top?

(A) 3 (B) 4 (C) 6 (D) 16 (E) 24

23. Triangle FGH is similar to triangle JKL. The length of side GH is 2.1 meters, the length of corresponding side KL is 1.4 meters, and the perimeter of $\triangle JKL$ is 3.6 meters. What is the perimeter of $\triangle FGH$?

(A) 2.4 m
(B) 3.3 m
(C) 4.3 m
(D) 5.1 m
(E) 5.4 m

24. Which of the following is an equation of a line that is parallel to the line with equation $2x - y = 7$?

(A) $y = -2x - 7$

(B) $y = -2x + 7$

(C) $y = -\frac{1}{2}x - 7$

(D) $y = \frac{1}{2}x - 7$

(E) $y = 2x + 7$

GO ON TO THE NEXT PAGE

MATHEMATICS LEVEL 1 TEST—*Continued*

USE THIS SPACE FOR SCRATCHWORK.

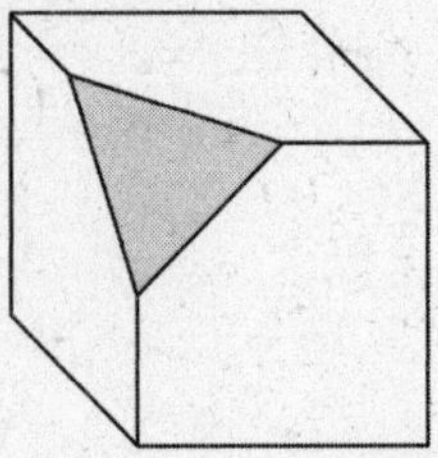

25. A tetrahedron was cut from the corner of the cube shown above, with three of its vertices at the midpoints of three edges of the cube. If tetrahedrons of the same size are cut from the remaining seven corners of the cube, how many faces will the resulting solid have?

(A) 6 (B) 8 (C) 12 (D) 14 (E) 16

26. The consecutive vertices of a certain parallelogram are A, B, C, and D. Which of the following are NOT necessarily congruent?

(A) $\angle A$ and $\angle C$
(B) $\angle B$ and $\angle D$
(C) $\overline{AC}$ and $\overline{BD}$
(D) $\overline{AB}$ and $\overline{CD}$
(E) $\overline{AD}$ and $\overline{BC}$

GO ON TO THE NEXT PAGE

MATHEMATICS LEVEL 1 TEST—*Continued*

USE THIS SPACE FOR SCRATCHWORK.

27. A car traveled 200 miles at an average speed of 45 miles per hour. Of the following, which is the closest approximation to the amount of time that could be saved on this 200-mile trip if the average speed had increased 20 percent?

(A) 1 hour

(B) $\frac{3}{4}$ hour

(C) $\frac{1}{2}$ hour

(D) $\frac{1}{4}$ hour

(E) $\frac{1}{5}$ hour

28. If c is a negative integer, for which of the following values of d is $|c - d|$ greatest?

(A) −10 (B) −4 (C) 0 (D) 4 (E) 10

29. In $\triangle PQR$, $\angle Q$ is a right angle. Which of the following is equal to $\cos P$?

(A) $\frac{PQ}{PR}$

(B) $\frac{PR}{PQ}$

(C) $\frac{PR}{QR}$

(D) $\frac{QR}{PQ}$

(E) $\frac{QR}{PR}$

GO ON TO THE NEXT PAGE

MATHEMATICS LEVEL 1 TEST—*Continued*

USE THIS SPACE FOR SCRATCHWORK.

30. The junior class is sponsoring a drama production to raise funds and plans to charge the same price for all admission tickets. The class has $700 in expenses for this production. If 300 tickets are sold, the class will make a profit of $1,100. What will be the profit for the class if 500 tickets are sold?

(A) $1,133
(B) $1,833
(C) $2,300
(D) $3,000
(E) $3,700

31. In the xy-plane, the point (6, 3) is the midpoint of the line segment with endpoints $(x, 5)$ and $(9, y)$. What is the value of $x + y$?

(A) 4 (B) 9 (C) 14 (D) 18 (E) 32

32. If $\frac{1}{2}$ is $\frac{3}{4}$ of $\frac{4}{5}$ of a certain number, what is that number?

(A) $\frac{3}{10}$

(B) $\frac{5}{6}$

(C) $\frac{11}{10}$

(D) $\frac{6}{5}$

(E) $\frac{10}{3}$

GO ON TO THE NEXT PAGE

MATHEMATICS LEVEL 1 TEST—*Continued*

USE THIS SPACE FOR SCRATCHWORK.

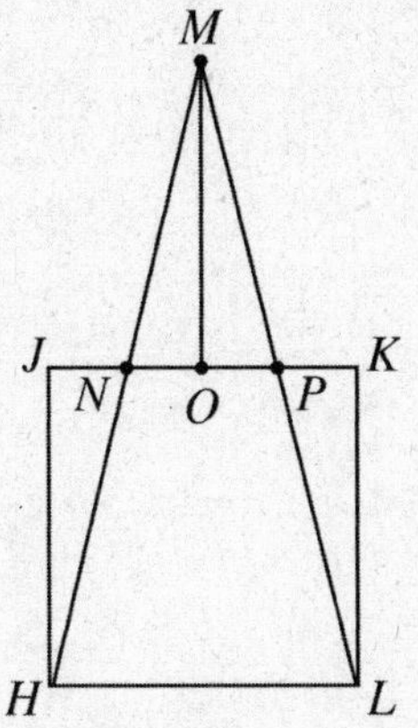

33. In the figure above, $HJKL$ is a square and $JN = NO = OP = PK$. What is the ratio of the area of $\triangle MNP$ to the area of square $HJKL$?

(A) $\frac{1}{8}$ (B) $\frac{1}{4}$ (C) $\frac{1}{3}$ (D) $\frac{3}{8}$ (E) $\frac{1}{2}$

34. Which of the following numbers is NOT contained in the domain of the function f if $f(x) = \frac{x+2}{x+3} - \frac{1}{x}$?

(A) -3 (B) -2 (C) 1 (D) $\sqrt{3}$ (E) 3

35. Which of the following is the graph of all values of x for which $1 \leq x^2 \leq 4$?

(A) 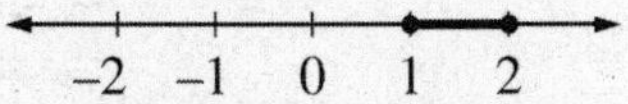

(B) 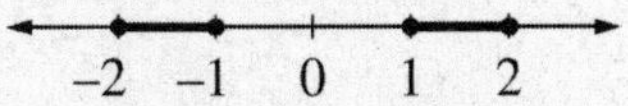

(C) 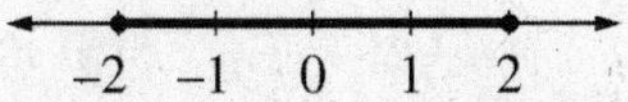

(D) 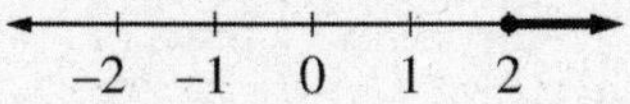

(E) 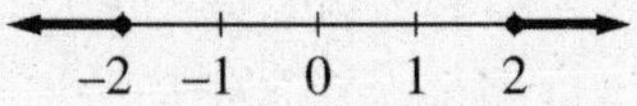

GO ON TO THE NEXT PAGE

MATHEMATICS LEVEL 1 TEST—*Continued*

USE THIS SPACE FOR SCRATCHWORK.

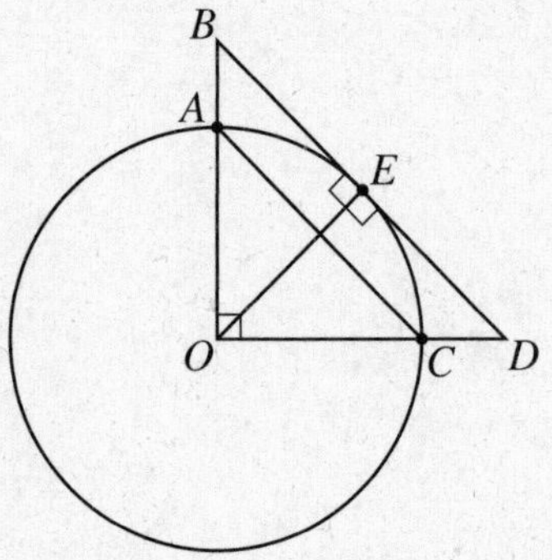

36. The circle in the figure above has center O and radius r. If $OB = OD$, how many of the line segments shown (with labeled endpoints) have length r ?

(A) Two
(B) Three
(C) Four
(D) Five
(E) Six

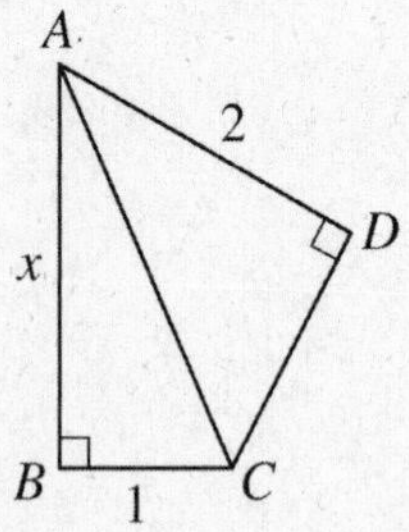

37. In the figure above, if $\triangle ABC$ and $\triangle ADC$ are right triangles, then $CD =$

(A) $\sqrt{x^2 - 3}$

(B) $\sqrt{x^2 + 1}$

(C) $\sqrt{x^2 + 1} + 2$

(D) $\sqrt{x^2 + 3}$

(E) $x^2 + 5$

GO ON TO THE NEXT PAGE

MATHEMATICS LEVEL 1 TEST—*Continued*

USE THIS SPACE FOR SCRATCHWORK.

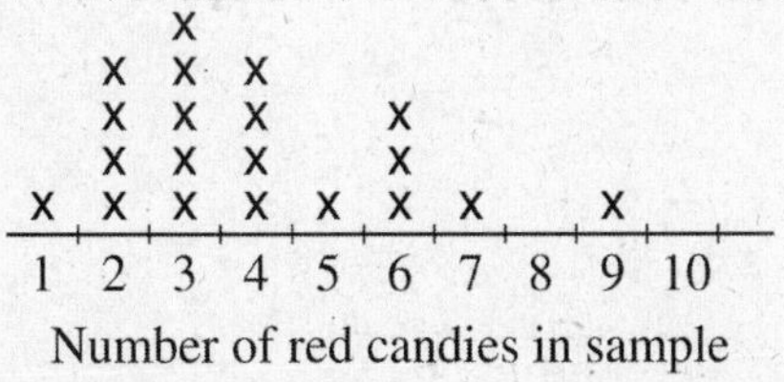

38. Each of 20 students in a class took a sample of 10 candies from a large bag and counted the number of red candies in the sample. The distribution of red candies in their samples is shown above. If one of the students were chosen at random, what is the probability that the student's sample would have at least 5 red candies?

(A) $\frac{3}{5}$

(B) $\frac{3}{10}$

(C) $\frac{1}{4}$

(D) $\frac{3}{20}$

(E) $\frac{1}{20}$

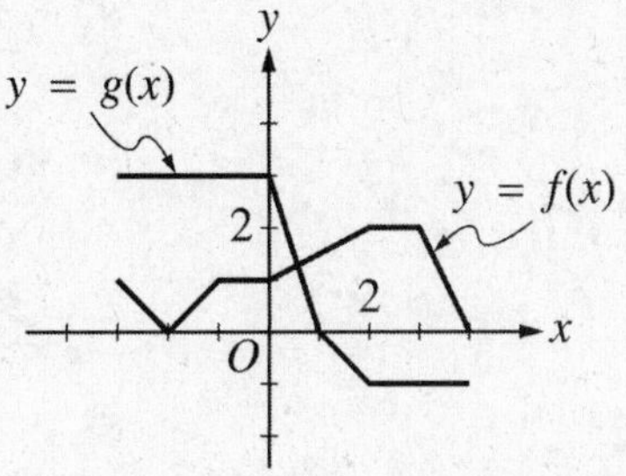

39. The figure above shows the graphs of functions f and g. What is the value of $f(g(3))$?

(A) –2 (B) –1 (C) 0 (D) 1 (E) 2

GO ON TO THE NEXT PAGE

MATHEMATICS LEVEL 1 TEST—*Continued*

USE THIS SPACE FOR SCRATCHWORK.

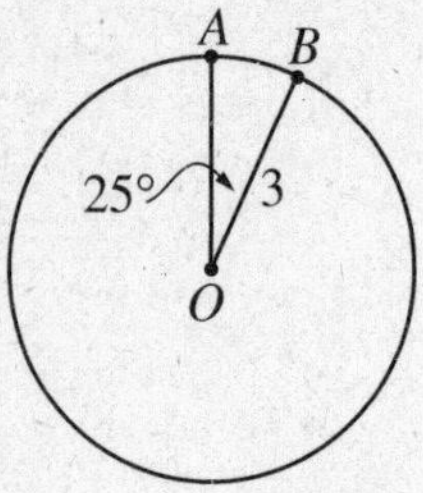

40. If O is the center of the circle in the figure above, what is the length of minor arc AB ?

(A) 0.65
(B) 1.27
(C) 1.31
(D) 1.40
(E) 1.96

41. In the xy-plane, which of the following are the points of intersection of the circles whose equations are $x^2 + y^2 = 4$ and $(x - 2)^2 + y^2 = 4$?

(A) $(-1, \sqrt{3}), (-1, -\sqrt{3})$
(B) $(1, \sqrt{3}), (1, -\sqrt{3})$
(C) $(1, \sqrt{3}), (-1, \sqrt{3})$
(D) $(1, 1), (-1, 1)$
(E) $(1, 1), (1, -2)$

GO ON TO THE NEXT PAGE

MATHEMATICS LEVEL 1 TEST—*Continued*

USE THIS SPACE FOR SCRATCHWORK.

42. The area of one face of a cube is x square meters. Which of the following gives an expression for the volume of this cube, in cubic meters?

(A) $x\sqrt{x}$

(B) $3\sqrt{x}$

(C) $x^2\sqrt{x}$

(D) x^3

(E) $3x^3$

43. For which of the following equations is it true that the sum of the roots equals the product of the roots?

(A) $x^2 - 4 = 0$
(B) $x^2 - 2x + 1 = 0$
(C) $x^2 - 4x + 4 = 0$
(D) $x^2 - 5x + 6 = 0$
(E) $x^2 + 4x + 4 = 0$

44. If the positive integers, starting with 1, are written consecutively, what will be the 90th digit written?

(A) 0 (B) 1 (C) 5 (D) 8 (E) 9

GO ON TO THE NEXT PAGE

MATHEMATICS LEVEL 1 TEST—*Continued*

USE THIS SPACE FOR SCRATCHWORK.

45. The function f is defined by
$f(x) = x^4 - 4x^2 + x + 1$ for $-5 \le x \le 5$.
In which of the following intervals does the minimum value of f occur?

(A) $-5 < x < -3$
(B) $-3 < x < -1$
(C) $-1 < x < 1$
(D) $1 < x < 3$
(E) $3 < x < 5$

46. In convex polygon P, the sum of the measures of the interior angles is 1,800°. How many sides does P have?

(A) 8 (B) 10 (C) 12 (D) 14 (E) 18

47. What is the least integer value of k such that $x^2(3k+1) - 6x + 2 = 0$ has no real roots?

(A) 5 (B) 2 (C) 1 (D) −1 (E) −2

48. If $\angle A$ is an acute angle and $\dfrac{\sin^2 A}{\cos^2 A} = 2.468$, what is the value of $\tan A$?

(A) 1.234
(B) 1.571
(C) 2.468
(D) 4.936
(E) 6.091

GO ON TO THE NEXT PAGE

MATHEMATICS LEVEL 1 TEST—*Continued*

USE THIS SPACE FOR SCRATCHWORK.

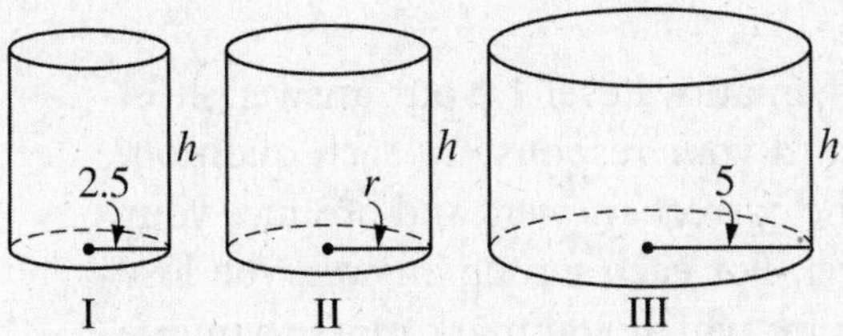

49. In the figure above, all of the right circular cylinders have height h. Cylinders I and III have a base radius of 2.5 and 5, respectively. If the volume of cylinder II is the mean of the volumes of cylinders I and III, what is the radius r of cylinder II?

(A) 1.98
(B) 3.75
(C) 3.95
(D) 4.00
(E) 15.63

50. If f and g are functions, where $f(x) = x^3 - 10x^2 + 27x - 18$ and $g(x) = x^3 - x^2 - 6x$, which of the following gives a relationship between f and g?

(A) $g(x) = 3f(x)$
(B) $g(x) = f(x) - 3$
(C) $g(x) = f(x) + 3$
(D) $g(x) = f(x - 3)$
(E) $g(x) = f(x + 3)$

STOP

IF YOU FINISH BEFORE TIME IS CALLED, YOU MAY CHECK YOUR WORK ON THIS TEST ONLY. DO NOT TURN TO ANY OTHER TEST IN THIS BOOK.

How to Score the SAT Subject Test in Mathematics Level 1

When you take an actual SAT Subject Test in Mathematics Level 1, your answer sheet will be "read" by a scanning machine that will record your response to each question. Then a computer will compare your answers with the correct answers and produce your raw score. You get one point for each correct answer. For each wrong answer, you lose one-fourth of a point. Questions you omit (and any for which you mark more than one answer) are not counted. This raw score is converted to a scaled score that is reported to you and to the colleges you specify.

Worksheet 1. Finding Your Raw Test Score

STEP 1: Table A on the following page lists the correct answers for all the questions on the Subject Test in Mathematics Level 1 that is reproduced in this book. It also serves as a worksheet for you to calculate your raw score.

- Compare your answers with those given in the table.
- Put a check in the column marked "Right" if your answer is correct.
- Put a check in the column marked "Wrong" if your answer is incorrect.
- Leave both columns blank if you omitted the question.

STEP 2: Count the number of right answers.

Enter the total here: ____________________

STEP 3: Count the number of wrong answers.

Enter the total here: ____________________

STEP 4: Multiply the number of wrong answers by .250.

Enter the product here: ________________

STEP 5: Subtract the result obtained in Step 4 from the total you obtained in Step 2.

Enter the result here: ________________

STEP 6: Round the number obtained in Step 5 to the nearest whole number.

Enter the result here: ________________

The number you obtained in Step 6 is your raw score.

Table A

Answers to the Subject Test in Mathematics Level 1 and Percentage of Students Answering Each Question Correctly									
Question Number	Correct Answer	Right	Wrong	Percentage of Students Answering the Question Correctly*	Question Number	Correct Answer	Right	Wrong	Percentage of Students Answering the Question Correctly*
1	E			92	26	C			64
2	D			95	27	B			68
3	B			83	28	E			59
4	D			91	29	A			71
5	E			91	30	C			53
6	D			83	31	A			59
7	A			90	32	B			56
8	A			83	33	B			53
9	C			88	34	A			66
10	E			85	35	B			45
11	D			84	36	D			49
12	E			84	37	A			41
13	B			81	38	B			49
14	E			89	39	D			41
15	A			70	40	C			42
16	B			87	41	B			36
17	C			89	42	A			33
18	C			81	43	C			29
19	B			78	44	C			29
20	A			75	45	B			30
21	D			77	46	C			28
22	C			63	47	B			18
23	E			75	48	B			46
24	E			78	49	C			37
25	D			70	50	E			41

* These percentages are based on an analysis of the answer sheets of a representative sample of 21,848 students who took the original administration of this test and whose mean score was 605. They may be used as an indication of the relative difficulty of a particular question.

Answer explanations for the Subject Test in Mathematics Level 1 can be found on page 229.

Finding Your Scaled Score

When you take SAT Subject Tests, the scores sent to the colleges you specify are reported on the College Board scale, which ranges from 200–800. You can convert your practice test score to a scaled score by using Table B. To find your scaled score, locate your raw score in the left-hand column of Table B; the corresponding score in the right-hand column is your scaled score. For example, a raw score of 28 on this particular edition of the Subject Test in Mathematics Level 1 corresponds to a scaled score of 600.

Raw scores are converted to scaled scores to ensure that a score earned on any one edition of a particular Subject Test is comparable to the same scaled score earned on any other edition of the same Subject Test. Because some editions of the tests may be slightly easier or more difficult than others, College Board scaled scores are adjusted so that they indicate the same level of performance regardless of the edition of the test taken and the ability of the group that takes it. Thus, for example, a score of 400 on one edition of a test taken at a particular administration indicates the same level of achievement as a score of 400 on a different edition of the test taken at a different administration.

When you take the SAT Subject Tests during a national administration, your scores are likely to differ somewhat from the scores you obtain on the tests in this book. People perform at different levels at different times for reasons unrelated to the tests themselves. The precision of any test is also limited because it represents only a sample of all the possible questions that could be asked.

Table B

Scaled Score Conversion Table Subject Test in Mathematics Level 1					
Raw Score	Scaled Score	Raw Score	Scaled Score	Raw Score	Scaled Score
50	800	28	600	6	390
49	800	27	580	5	390
48	790	26	570	4	380
47	780	25	560	3	370
46	770	24	550	2	360
45	760	23	540	1	360
44	750	22	530	0	350
43	740	21	520	-1	340
42	730	20	510	-2	330
41	720	19	500	-3	330
40	720	18	490	-4	320
39	710	17	490	-5	310
38	700	16	480	-6	300
37	690	15	470	-7	290
36	680	14	460	-8	280
35	670	13	450	-9	270
34	660	12	440	-10	260
33	650	11	440	-11	260
32	640	10	430	-12	250
31	630	9	420		
30	620	8	410		
29	610	7	400		

How Did You Do on the Subject Test in Mathematics Level 1?

After you score your test and analyze your performance, think about the following questions:

Did you run out of time before reaching the end of the test?

If so, you may need to pace yourself better. For example, maybe you spent too much time on one or two hard questions. A better approach might be to skip the ones you can't answer right away and try answering all the questions that remain on the test. Then if there's time, go back to the questions you skipped.

Did you take a long time reading the directions?

You will save time when you take the test by learning the directions to the Subject Test in Mathematics Level 1 ahead of time. Each minute you spend reading directions during the test is a minute that you could use to answer questions.

How did you handle questions you were unsure of?

If you were able to eliminate one or more of the answer choices as wrong and guess from the remaining ones, your approach probably worked to your advantage. On the other hand, making haphazard guesses or omitting questions without trying to eliminate choices could cost you valuable points.

How difficult were the questions for you compared with other students who took the test?

Table A shows you how difficult the multiple-choice questions were for the group of students who took this test during its national administration. The right-hand column gives the percentage of students that answered each question correctly.

A question answered correctly by almost everyone in the group is obviously an easier question. For example, 89 percent of the students answered question 14 correctly. But only 29 percent answered question 43 correctly.

Keep in mind that these percentages are based on just one group of students. They would probably be different with another group of students taking the test.

If you missed several easier questions, go back and try to find out why: Did the questions cover material you haven't yet reviewed? Did you misunderstand the directions?

Answer Explanations for the Mathematics Level 1 Subject Test

The solutions presented here provide one method for solving each of the problems on this test. Other mathematically correct approaches are possible.

1. Choice (E) is the correct answer. Since $x+7=3$, $x=-4$. Thus,

$$-4y+7y=84$$
$$3y=84$$
$$y=28$$

2. Choice (D) is the correct answer. For the product of the numbers to be negative, an odd number of them must be negative, and none of the numbers can be zero. This is true for choice (D) only.

3. Choice (B) is the correct answer. Since $x^2-y^2=(x+y)(x-y)$, $x^2-y^2=(5)(3)=15$.

4. Choice (D) is the correct answer. Two diameters of the circle are drawn. The central angle of each of the shaded sectors is 60°. Each shaded sector is $\frac{60}{360}$ or $\frac{1}{6}$ of the circular region. Therefore, $\frac{1}{3}$ of the circular region is shaded.

5. Choice (E) is the correct answer. A line with a negative slope slants downward from left to right, and a line with a negative y-intercept crosses the negative y-axis. Only choice (E) satisfies both of these conditions. Choice (A) is incorrect. The line is horizontal so its slope is 0, and the y-intercept is positive. Choice (B) is incorrect. The slope of the line is positive, and the y-intercept is positive. Choice (C) is incorrect. Although the y-intercept is negative, the slope of the line is positive. Choice (D) is incorrect. Although the slope of the line is negative, the y-intercept is positive.

6. Choice (D) is the correct answer. The left and right sides of the equation are opposites of each other. The only number equal to its opposite is 0, so you should find the values of k for which $k^2 - 4 = 0$. These are 2 and −2, which is choice (D). You could also solve the equation by combining like terms. If $k^2 - 4 = 4 - k^2$, then $2k^2 - 8 = 0$ or $k^2 = 4$.

7. Choice (A) is the correct answer. Since $b^{2x+1} = b^{3x-1}$, $2x + 1 = 3x - 1$ and $x = 2$.

8. Choice (A) is the correct answer. The number of students taking French is decreasing by 20 students per year. After n years, there will be $20n$ fewer students taking French. Currently, there are 250 students taking French. Thus, after n years, there will be $250 - 20n$ students taking French. The number of students taking Spanish is increasing by 10 students per year. After n years, there will be $10n$ more students taking Spanish. Currently, there are 100 students taking Spanish. Thus, after n years, there will be $100 + 10n$ students taking Spanish. To find when the number of students is the same in both courses, set the two expressions equal to each other; $250 - 20n = 100 + 10n$.

9. Choice (C) is the correct answer. To find the value of x when $y = 2$, you need to solve the equation $2 = x^3 - 1.5$, which is equivalent to $3.5 = x^3$. Taking the cube root of both sides of the equation yields $x \approx 1.52$.

10. Choice (E) is the correct answer. If the width of the rectangle is w, then the length of the rectangle is $4w$, and the perimeter is $w + 4w + w + 4w = 10w = 40$. Thus, the width of the rectangle is 4 centimeters, and the length is 16 centimeters. Therefore, the area is equal to $4 \cdot 16 = 64\ \text{cm}^2$. Choice (A) is incorrect. This is the width of the rectangle. Choice (B) is incorrect. This is the length of the rectangle. Choice (D) is incorrect. This is the perimeter of the rectangle.

11. Choice (D) is the correct answer. According to the function, if a student has a grade point average of 3.5, then $3.5 = 0.066t + 0.96$ and $2.54 = 0.066t$. Thus, $t \approx 38.48$, meaning that a student with a grade point average of 3.5 studied approximately 38.5 hours per week.

12. Choice (E) is the correct answer. Since x^2 is on both sides of the equation, the equation can be written as

$$-2x+3=x^3+2x$$
$$3=x^3+4x$$
$$0=x^3+4x-3$$

13. Choice (B) is the correct answer. In a right triangle, the sine of an angle is equal to the ratio of the length of the opposite side to the length of the hypotenuse. If $\sin P=0.5$, then $\frac{QR}{PQ}=\frac{1}{2}$. So, $\frac{QR}{6}=\frac{1}{2}$ and $QR=3$.

14. Choice (E) is the correct answer. A counterexample to the statement "All odd numbers greater than 2 are prime numbers" would be an odd number greater than 2 that is <u>not</u> a prime number. Choice (A) is not odd, so it cannot be a counterexample. Choices (B), (C), and (D) are odd numbers greater than 2, but they are prime numbers, so they are not counterexamples. Choice (E) is odd and it is greater than 2. However, since 9 is equal to 3×3, it is not a prime number. Therefore 9 is a counterexample to the statement.

15. Choice (A) is the correct answer. $f(-0.1)=\frac{2(-0.1)-1}{(-0.1)^2}=\frac{-0.2-1}{0.01}=-120.$

16. Choice (B) is the correct answer. To solve the problem, set up a proportion, where x represents the distance between the buildings on the blueprint.

$$\frac{0.4\text{ in}}{6\text{ ft}}=\frac{x\text{ in}}{76\text{ ft}}$$
$$\frac{76(0.4)}{6}=x$$
$$x=5.0\overline{6}\approx 5.1$$

17.

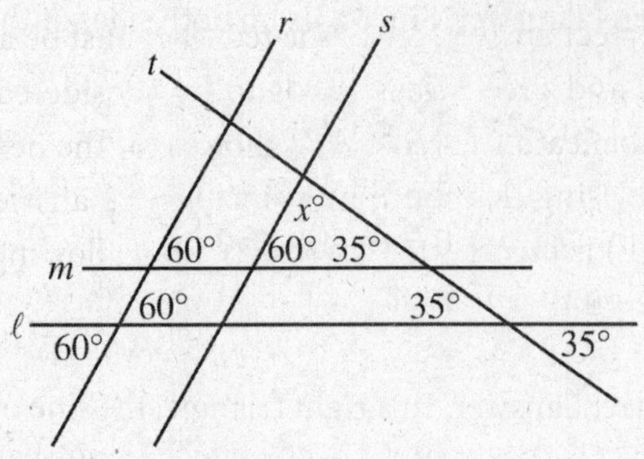

Choice (C) is the correct answer. Using the fact that vertical angles are congruent and corresponding angles are congruent, you can determine the measures of five additional angles as shown in the figure above. Since the sum of the degree measures of the interior angles in a triangle is 180, $x = 180 - (60 + 35) = 85$.

18. Choice (C) is the correct answer. The expression $\frac{2x}{3x-1}$ is undefined when $3x - 1$ is equal to 0. If $3x - 1 = 0$, then $x = \frac{1}{3}$.

19. Choice (B) is the correct answer. The total number of phones sold in the first 8 weeks of the last quarter is equal to $8 \cdot 10.375 = 83$. In order to sell 185 phones for the quarter, the team must sell 102 phones during the last five weeks, resulting in an average of 20.4 $[102 \div 5]$ phones to be sold per week for the last five weeks. Choice (C) is incorrect. This is the total number of phones sold in the first 8 weeks. Choice (D) is incorrect. This is the total number of phones the team needs to sell for the remaining 5 weeks.

20. Choice (A) is the correct answer. At the point where a line crosses the y-axis, the value of the x-coordinate will be 0. When 0 is substituted into the equation, the result is $-2y - 7 = 0$. Solving for y produces a value of $-\frac{7}{2}$ for the y-coordinate.

21. Choice (D) is the correct answer. Because $ABCD$ is a rectangle, it has congruent diagonals. The distance from A to C is the same as the distance from B to D. You can use the distance formula to get $BD = \sqrt{(-1-7)^2 + (4-(-3))^2} = \sqrt{64+49} = \sqrt{113} \approx 10.6$.

22. Choice (C) is the correct answer. Since the red flag must be at the top, only the order of the blue, yellow, and green flags needs to be considered. Thus, there are three choices for the flag beneath the red one, 2 choices for the next position, and 1 choice for the lowest spot. Using the counting principle, the answer is $3 \cdot 2 \cdot 1 = 6$, which is choice (C). Choice (E) is incorrect. This results from allowing any flag at the top and computing $4 \cdot 3 \cdot 2 \cdot 1 = 24$.

23. Choice (E) is the correct answer. Since the triangles are similar, the lengths of the sides and the perimeters are in proportion. If $\frac{GH}{KL} = \frac{2.1}{1.4} = 1.5$, then $\frac{\text{perimeter of } \triangle FGH}{\text{perimeter of } \triangle JKL} = 1.5$. Thus, $\frac{\text{perimeter of } \triangle FGH}{3.6} = 1.5$, so the perimeter of $\triangle FGH$ is $(3.6)(1.5) = 5.4$ meters, which is choice (E). Choice (A) is incorrect. This results from recognizing that KL is $\frac{2}{3}$ of GH and multiplying 3.6 by $\frac{2}{3}$ instead of $\frac{3}{2}$. Choice (C) is incorrect. This results from reasoning that since $GH - KL = 0.7$, the perimeter of $\triangle FGH$ is $3.6 + 0.7 = 4.3$.

24. Choice (E) is the correct answer. The line with equation $2x - y = 7$ can be written in $y = mx + b$ form as $y = 2x - 7$. The slope of the line is 2, and any line parallel to the line will also have a slope of 2.

25. Choice (D) is the correct answer. Since the original cube has 6 faces and 8 corners, placing a new face on each corner will add 8 faces to the resulting solid for a total of 14 faces.

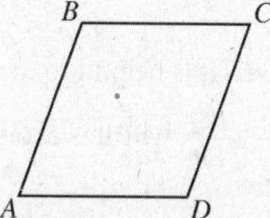

26.

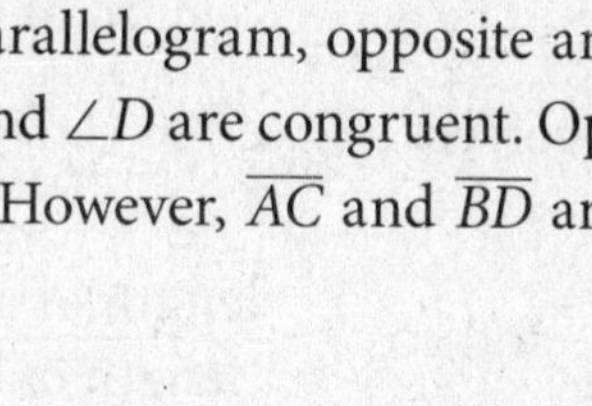

Choice (C) is the correct answer. It is helpful to draw and label a parallelogram to answer this question. In a parallelogram, opposite angles are congruent, so $\angle A$ and $\angle C$ are congruent, and $\angle B$ and $\angle D$ are congruent. Opposite sides are also congruent, so $\overline{AB} \cong \overline{CD}$ and $\overline{BC} \cong \overline{AD}$. However, $\overline{AC}$ and $\overline{BD}$ are not necessarily congruent, as shown in the figure.

27. Choice (B) is the correct answer. At a rate of 45 miles per hour, the time it takes to go 200 miles is $\frac{200}{45} \approx 4.44$ hours. If the speed increases by 20 percent, the new speed will be $45 \cdot 1.2 = 54$ miles per hour. At 54 miles per hour, it would take $\frac{200}{54} \approx 3.70$ hours to travel 200 miles. The time saved by going at the faster speed would be approximately $4.44 - 3.70 = 0.74$ hour, or approximately $\frac{3}{4}$ of an hour, which is choice (B). Choice (E) is incorrect. It results from assuming that an increase in speed of 20 percent yields a reduction in time of 20 percent of an hour.

28. Choice (E) is the correct answer. To solve the problem, it is helpful to think of the absolute value of the difference of two quantities as the distance between their corresponding points on the number line. Thus, you have to determine which of the five choices is furthest from c. Since c is negative, c is to the left of 0, 4, and 10 on the number line. Therefore, c is further from 10 than from either 0 or 4. To see that c is also further from 10 than -10 and -4, consider two cases. Case (1): c is between -10 and 0. Then, c is less than 10 units from -10 and -4. Since c is more than 10 units from 10, c is further from 10 than from either -10 or -4. Case (2): c is less than -10. Then, it is obvious that c is further from 10 than from either -10 or -4. Thus, in all cases, c is furthest from 10 than it is from -10, -4, 0, and 4.

29.

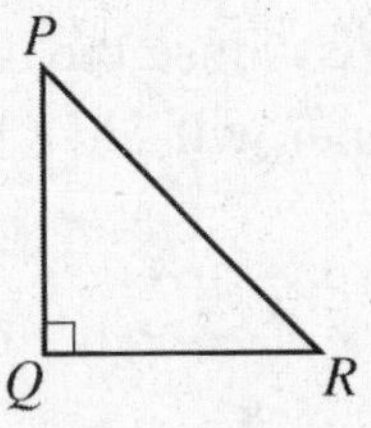

Choice (A) is the correct answer. It is helpful to draw and label $\triangle PQR$

$\cos P = \frac{\text{length of adjacent side}}{\text{length of hypotenuse}} = \frac{PQ}{PR}$, which is choice (A).

Choice (B) is incorrect.

$\frac{PR}{PQ} = \frac{\text{length of hypotenuse}}{\text{length of adjacent side}}$ and $\cos P = \frac{\text{length of adjacent side}}{\text{length of hypotenuse}}$.

This is the reciprocal of the correct answer, or sec P.

Choice (C) is incorrect.

$\frac{PR}{QR} = \frac{\text{length of hypotenuse}}{\text{length of opposite side}}$ and $\cos P = \frac{\text{length of adjacent side}}{\text{length of hypotenuse}}$. $\frac{PR}{QR} = \csc P$.

Choice (D) is incorrect.

$\frac{QR}{PQ} = \frac{\text{length of opposite side}}{\text{length of adjacent side}}$ and $\cos P = \frac{\text{length of adjacent side}}{\text{length of hypotenuse}}$. $\frac{QR}{PQ} = \tan P$.

Choice (E) is incorrect.

$\frac{QR}{PR} = \frac{\text{length of opposite side}}{\text{length of hypotenuse}}$ and $\cos P = \frac{\text{length of adjacent side}}{\text{length of hypotenuse}}$. $\frac{QR}{PR} = \sin P$.

30. Choice (C) is the correct answer. To answer this question, you must use the fact that profit is equal to revenue minus expenses. The class has \$700 in expenses. The problem gives the profit when 300 tickets are sold. If x represents the price per ticket, in dollars, the revenue for this sale is $300x$. Therefore, $\$1{,}100 = 300x - 700$, which implies that the price per ticket is \$6. If 500 tickets are sold at the same price, the revenue is $500 \cdot \$6 = \$3{,}000$. The profit on the sale of the 500 tickets would be $\$3{,}000 - \$700 = \$2{,}300$.

31. Choice (A) is the correct answer. The midpoint of the line segment that has endpoints $(x, 5)$ and $(9, y)$ is given by $\left(\frac{x+9}{2}, \frac{5+y}{2}\right)$. Thus, $\frac{x+9}{2} = 6$ yielding $x = 3$, and $\frac{5+y}{2} = 3$ yielding $y = 1$. The sum of x and y is 4.

32. Choice (B) is the correct answer. If $\frac{1}{2}$ is $\frac{3}{4}$ of $\frac{4}{5}$ of a number n, then $\frac{1}{2} = \frac{3}{4} \cdot \frac{4}{5} n$.

$$\frac{1}{2} = \frac{3}{5} n$$

$$\frac{5}{2} = 3n$$

$$\frac{5}{6} = n$$

33. Choice (B) is the correct answer. In $\triangle MHL$, $\overline{NP}$ is a midsegment because $\overline{NP} \parallel \overline{HL}$ and $NP = \frac{1}{2} HL$. Because $\overline{NP}$ is a midsegment of $\triangle MHL$, $HN = NM$. Since vertical angles are congruent, $\angle JNH \cong \angle ONM$. Together with the given information that $JN = NO$, you can conclude that $\triangle HJN \cong \triangle MON$ by side-angle-side congruence. Corresponding parts of congruent triangles are congruent, so $JH = MO$.

$$\text{Area of } \triangle MNP = \frac{1}{2}(NP)(MO)$$
$$= \frac{1}{2}\left(\frac{1}{2}HL\right)(JH)$$
$$= \left(\frac{1}{4}\right)(HL)(JH)$$
$$= \frac{1}{4}(\text{area of square } HJKL)$$

This shows that the area of $\triangle MNP$ is $\frac{1}{4}$ the area of square $HJKL$.

34. Choice (A) is the correct answer. The function f given by $f(x) = \frac{x+2}{x+3} - \frac{1}{x}$ is not defined for values of x that result in a denominator of 0. The value $x = -3$ results in a denominator of 0 in $\frac{x+2}{x+3}$, and the value $x = 0$ results in a denominator of 0 in $\frac{1}{x}$. The only choice given that is not contained in the domain of f is -3.

35. Choice (B) is the correct answer. If x^2 must be between 1 and 4, then the absolute value of x must be between 1 and 2. If x is positive, then $1 \le x \le 2$. If x is negative, then $-2 \le x \le -1$. Choice (B) shows the graph of all numbers x such that $-2 \le x \le -1$ or $1 \le x \le 2$.

36. Choice (D) is the correct answer. $\overline{OA}$, $\overline{OE}$, and $\overline{OC}$ are radii of the circle, so they all have length r. Since $OB = OD$, angles B and D are each 45°. Thus, $OE = ED$ and $OE = BE$. So, there are five labeled segments with length r: $\overline{OA}$, $\overline{OE}$, $\overline{OC}$, $\overline{BE}$, and $\overline{ED}$.

37. Choice (A) is the correct answer. To solve the problem, you will need to use the Pythagorean theorem twice. In right triangle ABC,

$$(AC)^2 = (AB)^2 + (BC)^2$$
$$(AC)^2 = x^2 + 1^2 = x^2 + 1$$
$$AC = \sqrt{x^2 + 1}$$

In right triangle ADC,

$$(AC)^2 = (AD)^2 + (CD)^2$$
$$\left(\sqrt{x^2 + 1}\right)^2 = 2^2 + (CD)^2$$

$$x^2+1=4+(CD)^2$$
$$x^2-3=(CD)^2$$
$$CD=\sqrt{x^2-3}$$

Choice (B) is incorrect. $\sqrt{x^2+1}=AC$, not CD. Choice (D) is incorrect. It results from using 3 instead of −3 in the solution. Choice (E) is incorrect. If you added 4 instead of subtracting 4 from both sides of the equation, and you also forgot to take the square root of both sides, you would have chosen choice (E).

38. Choice (B) is the correct answer. To answer this question, you need to determine the number of students that have at least 5 red candies. From the distribution, there are 6 students who each had at least 5 red candies. Therefore, the probability that the student's sample would have at least 5 red candies is equal to $\frac{6}{20}$ or $\frac{3}{10}$.

39. Choice (D) is the correct answer. From the graph, you can determine $g(3)=-1$. Thus, $f(g(3))=f(-1)$. From the graph, you can determine that $f(-1)$ is 1.

40. Choice (C) is the correct answer. The measure of $\angle AOB$ is 25°, which is $\frac{25}{360}$ of the circle, so the length of $\overset{\frown}{AB}$ is $\frac{25}{360}$ of the circumference of the circle. Since the radius of the circle is 3, the circumference of the circle is $2\pi r = 6\pi$. Thus, the length of $\overset{\frown}{AB}$ is $\frac{25}{360}(6\pi)\approx 1.31$.

41. Choice (B) is the correct answer. To find the points of intersection, you need to solve the system $\begin{cases} x^2+y^2=4 \\ (x-2)^2+y^2=4 \end{cases}$ for x and y. One way to solve the system is to subtract the second equation from the first and solve for x and y.

$$x^2+y^2=4$$
$$-\left[(x-2)^2+y^2=4\right]$$
$$x^2-(x-2)^2=0$$
$$x^2-(x^2-4x+4)=0$$
$$4x-4=0$$
$$x=1$$

If $x = 1$, then $1^2 + y^2 = 4$. Thus, $y^2 = 3$ and $y = \pm\sqrt{3}$. The points of intersection are $(1, \sqrt{3})$ and $(1, -\sqrt{3})$.

42. Choice (A) is the correct answer. If the area of one face of the cube is x, then the length of each edge of the cube is $\sqrt{x}$. Therefore, the volume of the cube is equal to $(\sqrt{x})^3 = x\sqrt{x}$.

43. Choice (C) is the correct answer. The quadratic equation $ax^2 + bx + c = 0$ with $a \neq 0$ has solutions $x = \dfrac{-b + \sqrt{b^2 - 4ac}}{2a}$ and $\dfrac{-b - \sqrt{b^2 - 4ac}}{2a}$, so the sum of the two roots is $-\dfrac{b}{a}$, and their product is $\dfrac{c}{a}$. Therefore, you need an equation in which $-\dfrac{b}{a} = \dfrac{c}{a}$, or $-b = c$. The only choice satisfying this condition is choice (C).
You could also solve this problem by finding the actual roots of each of the five given equations, either by factoring, using the quadratic formula, or using a graphing calculator. After you find the two roots of an equation, find their sum and product and compare them. Choice (A) is incorrect. The roots of the equation are -2 and 2. The sum of the roots is 0, and the product is -4. Choice (B) is incorrect. $x^2 - 2x + 1 = (x - 1)^2$, so there is a double root at $x = 1$. The sum of the roots is 2, and the product is 1. Choice (D) is incorrect. $x^2 - 5x + 6 = (x - 3)(x - 2)$, so the roots are 3 and 2. The sum of the roots is 5, and the product is 6. Choice (E) is incorrect. $x^2 + 4x + 4 = (x + 2)^2$, so there is a double root at $x = -2$. The sum of the roots is -4, and the product is 4.

44. Choice (C) is the correct answer. Of the 90 digits you need to write, the first 9 digits correspond to the integers 1–9, and the next 81 digits come from two-digit positive integers (10, 11, ...). Because each of these are two-digit positive integers, there will be 40 complete two-digit positive integers written, and the 90th digit will be the tens digit of the 41st two-digit positive integer. Since 10 is the first two-digit positive integer, 50 is the 41st two-digit positive integer. Thus, the 90th digit will be 5.

45. Choice (B) is the correct answer. In this question, it is helpful to use a graphing calculator to graph $y = x^4 - 4x^2 + x + 1$. Since the domain of the function is $-5 \leq x \leq 5$, set the viewing window to go from $x = -5$ to $x = 5$, and graph the function. The minimum value of the function occurs when $x \approx -1.473$, which is in the interval $-3 < x < -1$. Choice (A) is incorrect. The minimum value of the function is $y \approx -4.444$,

which is $f(-1.473)$. The question asks for the interval in which the minimum value of f occurs. Choice (A) results from confusing x with y, since the minimum value of the function is $y \approx -4.444$.

46. Choice (C) is the correct answer. The sum of the measures of the interior angles of a convex polygon with n sides is equal to $(n-2)180°$. Thus, $(n-2)180° = 1{,}800°$ and $n - 2 = 10$, so $n = 12$.

47. Choice (B) is the correct answer. The quadratic equation $ax^2 + bx + c = 0$ has no real roots if $b^2 - 4ac < 0$. Thus, the equation $x^2(3k+1) - 6x + 2 = 0$ has no real roots if $(-6)^2 - 4(3k+1)(2) < 0$. This simplifies to $28 - 24k < 0$. The least integer value of k that satisfies this inequality is 2.

48. Choice (B) is the correct answer. Since $\frac{\sin^2 A}{\cos^2 A} = \tan^2 A = 2.468$, $\tan A = \sqrt{2.468} \approx 1.571$.

49. Choice (C) is the correct answer. The volume of a cylinder with radius r and height h is equal to $\pi r^2 h$. Thus, the volume of cylinder I is $\pi(2.5)^2 h = 6.25\pi h$, and the volume of cylinder III is $25\pi h$. The volume of cylinder II is the mean of the volumes of cylinders I and III. Thus, $\pi r^2 h = \frac{6.25\pi h + 25\pi h}{2} = 15.625\pi h$ and $r^2 = 15.625$. The value of r is $\sqrt{15.625}$, which is approximately 3.95. Choice (B) is incorrect. This is the mean of the radii of cylinders I and III. Using this value for r will not give a volume for cylinder II that is the mean of the volumes of cylinders I and III. Choice (E) is incorrect. This is the value of r^2. You need to take the square root of this value to find the radius of cylinder II.

50. Choice (E) is the correct answer. A graphing calculator is helpful for this problem. If you graph functions f and g in a standard viewing window of $[-10, 10]$ by $[-10, 10]$, you can see that the graph of g is identical to the graph of f, but it is shifted 3 units to the left. Thus, $g(x) = f(x+3)$.

Mathematics Level 2

Sample Questions

All questions in the Mathematics Level 2 Test are multiple-choice questions in which you must choose the BEST response from the five choices offered. The directions that follow are the same as those that are in the Mathematics Level 2 test.

For each of the following problems, decide which is the BEST of the choices given. If the exact numerical value is not one of the choices, select the choice that best approximates this value. Then fill in the corresponding circle on the answer sheet.

Notes: (1) A scientific or graphing calculator will be necessary for answering some (but not all) of the questions in this test. For each question you will have to decide whether or not you should use a calculator.

(2) For some questions in this test you may have to decide whether your calculator should be in the radian mode or the degree mode.

(3) Figures that accompany problems in this test are intended to provide information useful in solving the problems. They are drawn as accurately as possible EXCEPT when it is stated in a specific problem that its figure is not drawn to scale. All figures lie in a plane unless otherwise indicated.

(4) Unless otherwise specified, the domain of any function f is assumed to be the set of all real numbers x for which $f(x)$ is a real number. The range of f is assumed to be the set of all real numbers $f(x)$, where x is in the domain of f.

(5) Reference information that may be useful in answering the questions in this test can be found on the page preceding Question 1.

Reference Information: The following information is for your reference in answering some of the questions in this test.

Volume of a right circular cone with radius r and height h: $V = \frac{1}{3}\pi r^2 h$

Volume of a sphere with radius r: $V = \frac{4}{3}\pi r^3$

Surface Area of a sphere with radius r: $S = 4\pi r^2$

Volume of a pyramid with base area B and height h: $V = \frac{1}{3}Bh$

Number and Operations

1. From a group of 6 juniors and 8 seniors on the student council, 2 juniors and 4 seniors will be chosen to make up a 6-person committee. How many different 6-person committees are possible?

(A) 84
(B) 85
(C) 1,050
(D) 1,710
(E) 1,890

Choice (C) is the correct answer to question 1. The 2 juniors on the committee can be chosen from the 6 juniors in $\binom{6}{2} = 15$ ways. The 4 seniors on the committee can be chosen from the 8 seniors in $\binom{8}{4} = 70$ ways. Therefore, there are $(15)(70) = 1{,}050$ possibilities for the 6-person committee.

Algebra and Functions

2. If $2^x = 3$, what does 3^x equal?

(A) 5.7
(B) 5.2
(C) 2.0
(D) 1.8
(E) 1.6

A calculator is useful for this problem. To solve for x, you can take the natural log of both sides of the equation.

$$\ln 2^x = \ln 3$$
$$x \ln 2 = \ln 3$$
$$x = \frac{\ln 3}{\ln 2} = \frac{1.0986}{0.6931} \approx 1.5850$$
$$3^x \approx 5.7045$$

Choice (A) is the correct answer to question 2. Since the directions to this test state, "If the exact numerical value is not one of the choices, select the choice that best approximates this value," the correct answer is choice (A).

You can also solve this problem by graphing $Y1 = 2^x$ and $Y2 = 3$ and finding the point of intersection of the two graphs in the standard viewing window. The two graphs intersect at the point with x-coordinate $\approx$ 1.5850. You can store this x-value and then evaluate 3^x, which gives 5.7045. Many graphing calculators retain the last calculation from the graph screen in memory. If you return to the home screen immediately after finding the point of intersection, you can use the x-coordinate (called "X" or "xc," depending on the calculator) to evaluate 3^x.

$$ax^5 + bx^4 + cx^3 + dx^2 + e = 0$$

3. Let a, b, c, d, and e represent nonzero real numbers in the equation above. If the equation has $2i$ as a root, which of the following statements must be true?
   (A) The only other nonreal root of the equation is $-2i$.
   (B) The equation has an odd number of nonreal roots.
   (C) The equation has exactly one real root.
   (D) The equation has an odd number of real roots.
   (E) All real roots of the equation are positive.

Choice (D) is the correct answer to question 3. Since $ax^5 + bx^4 + cx^3 + dx^2 + e = 0$ is a 5th-degree polynomial equation with real coefficients, the equation has exactly 5 roots in the complex number system. Because $2i$ is a root of the equation, $-2i$ is also a root. Complex roots always occur in conjugate pairs $a \pm bi$, where a and b are real numbers and $b \neq 0$.

There are two possibilities for the other 3 roots of the equation.
(1) 1 real root, 2 complex (nonreal) roots
(2) 3 real roots

Since the equation could have 4 nonreal roots, choice (A) does not have to be true. Since nonreal roots always occur in pairs, choice (B) cannot be true. Since the equation could have 3 real roots, choice (C) does not have to be true. We do not have enough information about the polynomial equation to determine the sign of the real roots. Therefore, choice

(E) does not have to be true. Since the equation could have 1 or 3 real roots, choice (D) must be true.

4. Two environmentalists have proposed two different function models for the survival rate of a particular endangered species.

$$f(t) = 100(0.7)^t$$

$$g(t) = 100(0.999993)^{t^5}$$

For the functions f and g above, $f(t)$ and $g(t)$ represent the percentage of the species that survive t years from a starting point $t = 0$. Which of the following statements about the models are true?

I. Both models give the same prediction at approximately $t = 15$ years.

II. Model g predicts that the population size will decrease most rapidly from $t = 0$ to $t = 5$ years.

III. The greatest difference in the two model predictions occurs at approximately $t = 6$ years.

(A) I only
(B) I and II only
(C) I and III only
(D) II and III only
(E) I, II, and III

Choice (C) is the correct answer to question 4 since statements I and III are true. You can use a graphing calculator to help you solve this problem. Enter functions f and g in the calculator as $Y1$ and $Y2$, respectively.

By examining the graphs of the two functions or a table of values for the two functions, you can determine that $f(t) = g(t)$ for a value between $t = 15$ and $t = 16$. Both models give the same prediction at approximately $t = 15.024$. Thus, statement I is true.

By examining the graph of g or a table of values for g on the interval from $t = 0$ to $t = 5$, you can see that the $g(t)$ values are fairly constant and show little decrease. The function values start to decrease after $t = 5$ years. Thus, statement II is not true.

You can look at the graph of $Y1 - Y2$ or a table of values for $Y1 - Y2$ to determine where the greatest difference between the two model predictions occurs. The greatest difference occurs at approximately $t = 5.976$. Thus, statement III is true.

5. If $f(x) = \frac{1-x}{x-1}$ for all $x \neq 1$, which of the following statements must be true?

I. $f(3) = f(2)$

II. $f(0) = f(2)$

III. $f(0) = f(4)$

(A) None

(B) I only

(C) II only

(D) II and III only

(E) I, II, and III

Choice (E) is the correct answer to question 5. Realizing that $\frac{1-x}{x-1} = -1$ for all $x \neq 1$ greatly simplifies this problem. Since $f(0)$, $f(2)$, $f(3)$, and $f(4)$ are all equal to -1, statements I, II, and III are all true. If you do not realize $f(x) = -1$, you can easily substitute the numbers in f. Using a calculator may actually be a disadvantage to you if you spend time substituting the numbers into an expression of this kind to find the answer. However, using a graphing calculator, you can graph $y = \frac{1-x}{x-1}$ and see that the graph is a horizontal line crossing the y-axis at -1. Therefore, $f(x) = -1$ for all values of x except 1.

6. Let h be the function defined by $h(t) = |5\cos\left(\frac{2}{3}t\right) - 2|$. What is the period of h ?

(A) $\frac{2}{3}$

(B) 3

(C) 5

(D) 2π

(E) 3π

Choice (E) is the correct answer to question 6. The period of h corresponds to the length of one cycle of the graph of h. The smallest positive real number k such that $h(x+k) = h(x)$ for every value of x in the domain of h is the period. By examining the graph of h on your graphing calculator, you can see that the values of $h(x)$ repeat every 3π units.

Alternately, note that the graph of h is obtained from the graph of $y = \cos t$ by applying several transformations. The vertical "stretch" by a factor of 5 units and the shift down 2 units do not affect the period of the function. The absolute value, in this case, also does not affect the period of the function. The horizontal "stretch" is a result of the $\frac{2}{3}$.

This affects the period. Since the period of $\cos t$ is 2π, the period of h can be found by $\frac{2\pi}{\left|\frac{2}{3}\right|} = 3\pi$.

7. If $f(x) = \frac{1}{x-5}$ and $g(x) = \sqrt{x+4}$, what is the domain of $f - g$?

   (A) All x such that $x \neq 5$ and $x \leq 4$

   (B) All x such that $x \neq -5$ and $x \leq 4$

   (C) All x such that $x \neq 5$ and $x \geq -4$

   (D) All x such that $x \neq -4$ and $x \geq -5$

   (E) All real numbers x

Choice (C) is the correct answer to question 7. The function $f - g$ will be defined at exactly those points where f and g are both defined. In other words, the domain of $f - g$ is the intersection of the domain of f and the domain of g. Since $f(x) = \frac{1}{x-5}$ is defined for all $x \neq 5$, and $g(x) = \sqrt{x+4}$ is defined for all $x \geq -4$, the domain of $f - g$ is all x such that $x \neq 5$ and $x \geq -4$.

You can also examine the graph of $f - g$. The graph is defined for all real numbers $x \geq -4$ except for $x = 5$, where the graph has a vertical asymptote.

Geometry and Measurement: Coordinate Geometry

8. A translation in the xy-plane moves the point with coordinates (x, y) to the point with coordinates $(x - 4, y + 7)$. If point A' is the image of point A under this translation, what is the distance between points A and A'?

   (A) 3.0

   (B) 5.7

   (C) 7.9

   (D) 8.1

   (E) 11.0

Choice (D) is the correct answer to question 8. Point A' is 4 units to the left and 7 units above point A in the xy-plane. Point A can be represented by coordinates (x, y) and point A' can be represented by coordinates $(x - 4, y + 7)$. You can use the distance formula to find the distance between the two points.

$$\begin{aligned} \text{distance} &= \sqrt{((x-4)-x)^2 + ((y+7)-y)^2} \\ &= \sqrt{16+49} = \sqrt{65} \approx 8.1 \end{aligned}$$

Geometry and Measurement: Three-Dimensional Geometry

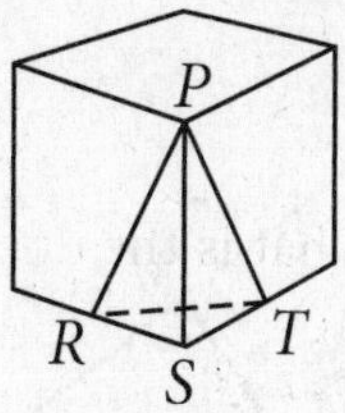

9. In the figure above, R and T are the midpoints of two adjacent edges of the cube. If the length of each edge of the cube is h, what is the volume of pyramid $PRST$?

(A) $\frac{h^3}{24}$

(B) $\frac{h^3}{12}$

(C) $\frac{h^3}{8}$

(D) $\frac{h^3}{6}$

(E) $\frac{h^3}{4}$

The formula for the volume of the pyramid and several other formulae are given in the reference information at the beginning of the test. The volume of a pyramid is $\frac{1}{3}Bh$, where B is the area of the base of the pyramid and h is its height. It may be helpful to mark the figure to indicate those parts whose lengths are given or that can be deduced.

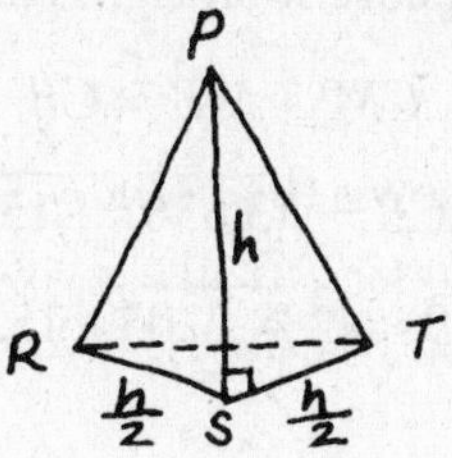

Choice (A) is the correct answer to question 9. Since $\overline{PS}$ is perpendicular to the triangular base RST, its length h is the height of the pyramid $PRST$. R and T are the midpoints of the two adjacent edges of the cube; therefore, $RS = ST = \frac{h}{2}$. Since $\triangle RST$ is a right triangle, its area is $\left(\frac{1}{2}\right)\left(\frac{h}{2}\right)\left(\frac{h}{2}\right) = \frac{h^2}{8}$. Thus, the volume of $PRST$ is $\left(\frac{1}{3}\right)\left(\frac{h^2}{8}\right)(h) = \frac{h^3}{24}$.

Geometry and Measurement: Trigonometry

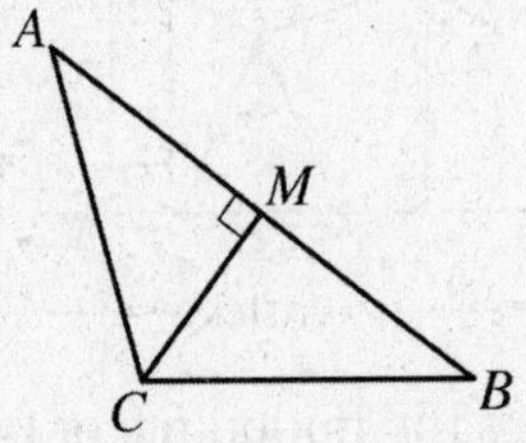

Note: Figure not drawn to scale.

10. In $\triangle ABC$ above, $\overline{CM} \perp \overline{AB}$ If $AM = 9$, $MB = 15$, and the measure of $\angle BAC$ is 22°, what is the length of $\overline{CB}$?
   (A) 3.64
   (B) 9.71
   (C) 15.43
   (D) 17.16
   (E) 17.49

Choice (C) is the correct answer to question 10. You can use right triangle *ACM* to find the length of $\overline{CM}$.

$$\tan 22° = \frac{CM}{9}; \text{ thus, } CM \approx 3.636.$$

Now you can use the Pythagorean theorem on right triangle *CMB* to find the length of $\overline{CB}$.

$$CM^2 + MB^2 = CB^2$$

$$CB = \sqrt{(3.636)^2 + 15^2}$$

$$CB \approx \sqrt{238.2205} \approx 15.43$$

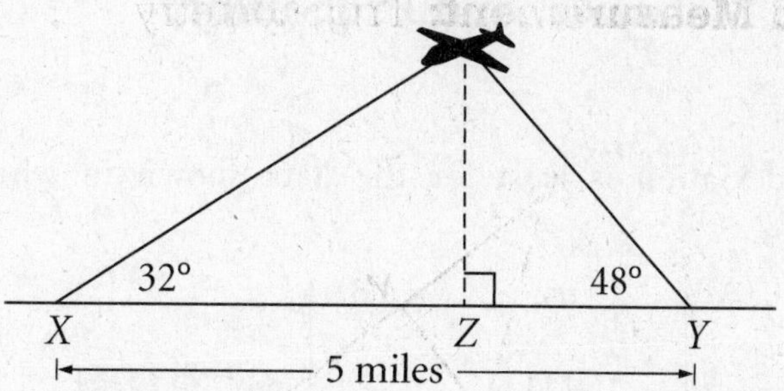

11. The airplane in the figure above is flying directly over point Z on a straight, level road. The angles of elevation for points X and Y are 32° and 48°, respectively. If points X and Y are 5 miles apart, what is the distance, in miles, from the airplane to point X?

(A) 1.60

(B) 2.40

(C) 2.69

(D) 3.77

(E) 7.01

Choice (D) is the correct answer to question 11. Label the location of the airplane as point W. Then in $\triangle XYW$, the measure of $\angle X$ is 32°, the measure of $\angle Y$ is 48°, and the measure of $\angle W$ is 100°. Let x, y, and w denote the lengths, in miles, of the sides of $\triangle XYW$ opposite $\angle X$, $\angle Y$, and $\angle W$, respectively. By the law of sines, $\frac{x}{\sin X} = \frac{y}{\sin Y} = \frac{w}{\sin W}$. Since $w = 5$ and the distance from the plane to point X is y, it follows that $\frac{5}{\sin 100°} = \frac{y}{\sin 48°}$. This gives $y \approx 3.77$ for the distance, in miles, from the plane to point X.

Data Analysis, Statistics, and Probability

12. The standard deviation is least for the data shown in which of the following histograms?

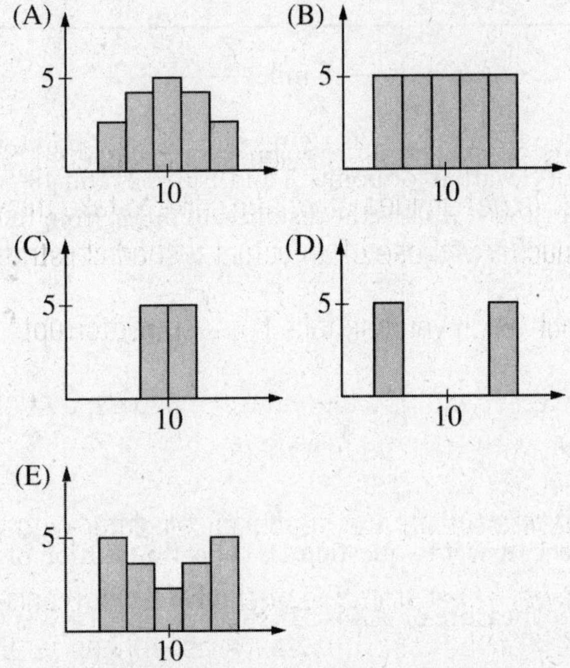

Choice (C) is the correct answer to question 12. The standard deviation is a measure of spread—how far the observations in a set of data are from their mean.

The data is closest to 10 in the histogram in choice (C), and thus has the least standard deviation. In each of the other choices, the data is further spread from 10.

Mathematics Level 2 Subject Test

Practice Helps

The test that follows is an actual, previously administered SAT Subject Test in Mathematics Level 2. To get an idea of what it's like to take this test, practice under conditions that are much like those of an actual test administration.

- Set aside an hour when you can take the test uninterrupted.
- Sit at a desk or table with no other books or papers. Dictionaries, other books, or notes are not allowed in the test room.
- Remember to have a scientific or graphing calculator with you.
- Tear out an answer sheet from the back of this book and fill it in just as you would on the day of the test. One answer sheet can be used for up to three Subject Tests.
- Read the instructions that precede the practice test. During the actual administration you will be asked to read them before answering test questions.
- Time yourself by placing a clock or kitchen timer in front of you.
- After you finish the practice test, read the sections "How to Score the SAT Subject Test in Mathematics Level 2" and "How Did You Do on the Subject Test in Mathematics Level 2?"
- The appearance of the answer sheet in this book may differ from the answer sheet you see on test day.

MATHEMATICS LEVEL 2 TEST

The top portion of the page of the answer sheet that you will use to take the Mathematics Level 2 Test must be filled in exactly as illustrated below. When your supervisor tells you to fill in the circle next to the name of the test you are about to take, mark your answer sheet as shown.

○ Literature	○ Mathematics Level 1	○ German	○ Chinese Listening	○ Japanese Listening
○ Biology E	● Mathematics Level 2	○ Italian	○ French Listening	○ Korean Listening
○ Biology M	○ U.S. History	○ Latin	○ German Listening	○ Spanish Listening
○ Chemistry	○ World History	○ Modern Hebrew		
○ Physics	○ French	○ Spanish	**Background Questions:** ① ② ③ ④ ⑤ ⑥ ⑦ ⑧ ⑨	

After filling in the circle next to the name of the test you are taking, locate the Background Questions section, which also appears at the top of your answer sheet (as shown above). This is where you will answer the following Background Questions on your answer sheet.

BACKGROUND QUESTIONS

Please answer Part I and Part II below by filling in the appropriate circle in the Background Questions box on your answer sheet. <u>The information you provide is for statistical purposes only and will not affect your test score.</u>

<u>Part I.</u> Which of the following describes a mathematics course you have taken or are currently taking? (FILL IN <u>**ALL**</u> CIRCLES THAT APPLY.)

- Algebra I or Elementary Algebra <u>**OR**</u> Course I of a college preparatory mathematics sequence —Fill in circle 1.
- Geometry <u>**OR**</u> Course II of a college preparatory mathematics sequence —Fill in circle 2.
- Algebra II or Intermediate Algebra <u>**OR**</u> Course III of a college preparatory mathematics sequence —Fill in circle 3.
- Elementary Functions (Precalculus) and/or Trigonometry <u>**OR**</u> beyond Course III of a college preparatory mathematics sequence —Fill in circle 4.
- Advanced Placement Mathematics (Calculus AB or Calculus BC) —Fill in circle 5.

<u>Part II.</u> What type of calculator did you bring to use for this test? (FILL IN THE <u>**ONE**</u> CIRCLE THAT APPLIES. If you did not bring a scientific or graphing calculator, do not fill in any of circles 6-9.)

- Scientific —Fill in circle 6.
- Graphing (Fill in the circle corresponding to the model you used.)

  Casio 9700, Casio 9750, Casio 9800, Casio 9850, Casio 9860, Casio FX 1.0, Casio CG-10, Sharp 9200, Sharp 9300, Sharp 9600, Sharp 9900, TI-82, TI-83, TI-83 Plus, TI-83 Plus Silver, TI-84 Plus, TI-84 Plus Silver, TI-85, TI-86, or TI-Nspire —Fill in circle 7.

  Casio 9970, Casio Algebra FX 2.0, HP 38G, HP 39 series, HP 40 series, HP 48 series, HP 49 series, HP 50 series, TI-89, TI-89 Titanium, or TI-Nspire CAS —Fill in circle 8.

  Some other graphing calculator —Fill in circle 9.

When the supervisor gives the signal, turn the page and begin the Mathematics Level 2 Test. There are 100 numbered circles on the answer sheet and 50 questions in the Mathematics Level 2 Test. Therefore, use only circles 1 to 50 for recording your answers.

MATHEMATICS LEVEL 2 TEST

REFERENCE INFORMATION

THE FOLLOWING INFORMATION IS FOR YOUR REFERENCE IN ANSWERING SOME OF THE QUESTIONS IN THIS TEST.

Volume of a right circular cone with radius r and height h: $V = \frac{1}{3}\pi r^2 h$

Volume of a sphere with radius r: $V = \frac{4}{3}\pi r^3$

Surface Area of a sphere with radius r: $S = 4\pi r^2$

Volume of a pyramid with base area B and height h: $V = \frac{1}{3}Bh$

DO NOT DETACH FROM BOOK.

GO ON TO THE NEXT PAGE

MATHEMATICS LEVEL 2 TEST

For each of the following problems, decide which is the BEST of the choices given. If the exact numerical value is not one of the choices, select the choice that best approximates this value. Then fill in the corresponding circle on the answer sheet.

Notes: (1) A scientific or graphing calculator will be necessary for answering some (but not all) of the questions in this test. For each question you will have to decide whether or not you should use a calculator.

(2) For some questions in this test you may have to decide whether your calculator should be in the radian mode or the degree mode.

(3) Figures that accompany problems in this test are intended to provide information useful in solving the problems. They are drawn as accurately as possible EXCEPT when it is stated in a specific problem that its figure is not drawn to scale. All figures lie in a plane unless otherwise indicated.

(4) Unless otherwise specified, the domain of any function f is assumed to be the set of all real numbers x for which $f(x)$ is a real number. The range of f is assumed to be the set of all real numbers $f(x)$, where x is in the domain of f.

(5) Reference information that may be useful in answering the questions in this test can be found on the page preceding Question 1.

USE THIS SPACE FOR SCRATCHWORK.

1. If $3x + 6 = \frac{k}{4}(x + 2)$ for all x, then $k =$

(A) $\frac{1}{4}$ (B) 3 (C) 4 (D) 12 (E) 24

GO ON TO THE NEXT PAGE

MATHEMATICS LEVEL 2 TEST—*Continued*

USE THIS SPACE FOR SCRATCHWORK.

2. The relationship between a reading C on the Celsius temperature scale and a reading F on the Fahrenheit temperature scale is $C = \frac{5}{9}(F - 32)$, and the relationship between a reading on the Celsius temperature scale and a reading K on the Kelvin temperature scale is $K = C + 273$. Which of the following expresses the relationship between readings on the Kelvin and Fahrenheit temperature scales?

(A) $K = \frac{5}{9}(F - 241)$

(B) $K = \frac{5}{9}(F + 305)$

(C) $K = \frac{5}{9}(F - 32) + 273$

(D) $K = \frac{5}{9}(F - 32) - 273$

(E) $K = \frac{5}{9}(F + 32) + 273$

3. What is the slope of the line containing the points (3, 11) and (−2, 5)?

(A) 0.17
(B) 0.83
(C) 1.14
(D) 1.20
(E) 6

4. If $x + y = 2$, $y + z = 5$, and $x + y + z = 10$, then $y =$

(A) −3

(B) $\frac{3}{17}$

(C) 1

(D) 3

(E) $\frac{17}{3}$

GO ON TO THE NEXT PAGE

MATHEMATICS LEVEL 2 TEST—*Continued*

USE THIS SPACE FOR SCRATCHWORK.

5. If $f(x) = 3\ln(x) - 1$ and $g(x) = e^x$, then $f(g(5)) =$

(A) 6.83
(B) 12
(C) 14
(D) 45.98
(E) 568.17

6. The intersection of a cube with a plane could be which of the following?

I. A square
II. A parallelogram
III. A triangle

(A) I only
(B) II only
(C) III only
(D) I and III only
(E) I, II, and III

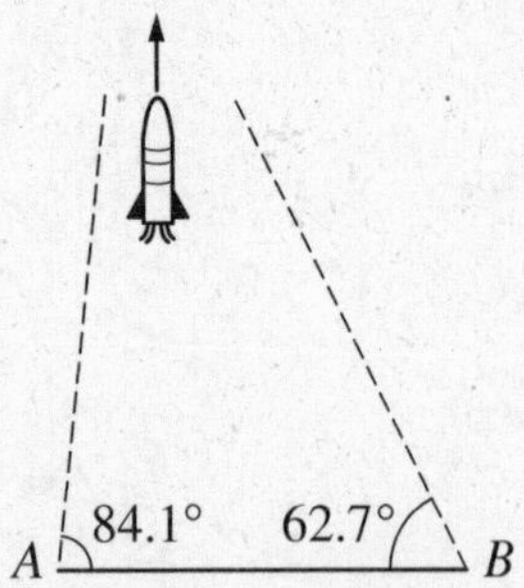

7. The figure above shows a rocket taking off vertically. When the rocket reaches a height of 12 kilometers, the angles of elevation from points A and B on level ground are 84.1° and 62.7°, respectively. What is the distance between points A and B?

(A) 0.97 km
(B) 6.36 km
(C) 7.43 km
(D) 22.60 km
(E) 139.37 km

GO ON TO THE NEXT PAGE

MATHEMATICS LEVEL 2 TEST—*Continued*

USE THIS SPACE FOR SCRATCHWORK.

8. What is the value of x^2 if $x = \sqrt{15^2 - 12^2}$?

(A) $\sqrt{3}$ (B) 3 (C) 9 (D) 81 (E) 81^2

9. The points in the rectangular coordinate plane are transformed in such a way that each point $P(x, y)$ is moved to the point $P'(2x, 2y)$. If the distance between a point P and the origin is d, then the distance between the point P' and the origin is

(A) $\frac{1}{d}$

(B) $\frac{d}{2}$

(C) d

(D) $2d$

(E) d^2

10. If $f(g(x)) = \dfrac{2\sqrt{x^2+1} - 1}{\sqrt{x^2+1} + 1}$ and $f(x) = \dfrac{2x - 1}{x + 1}$, then $g(x) =$

(A) $\sqrt{x}$

(B) $\sqrt{x^2+1}$

(C) x

(D) x^2

(E) $x^2 + 1$

GO ON TO THE NEXT PAGE

MATHEMATICS LEVEL 2 TEST—*Continued*

USE THIS SPACE FOR SCRATCHWORK.

11. If A is the degree measure of an acute angle and $\sin A = 0.8$, then $\cos(90° - A) =$

(A) 0.2
(B) 0.4
(C) 0.5
(D) 0.6
(E) 0.8

12. The set of points (x, y, z) such that $x^2 + y^2 + z^2 = 1$ is

(A) empty
(B) a point
(C) a sphere
(D) a circle
(E) a plane

13. The graph of the rational function f, where $f(x) = \dfrac{5}{x^2 - 8x + 16}$, has a vertical asymptote at $x =$

(A) 0 only
(B) 4 only
(C) 5 only
(D) 0 and 4 only
(E) 0, 4, and 5

GO ON TO THE NEXT PAGE

MATHEMATICS LEVEL 2 TEST—*Continued*

USE THIS SPACE FOR SCRATCHWORK.

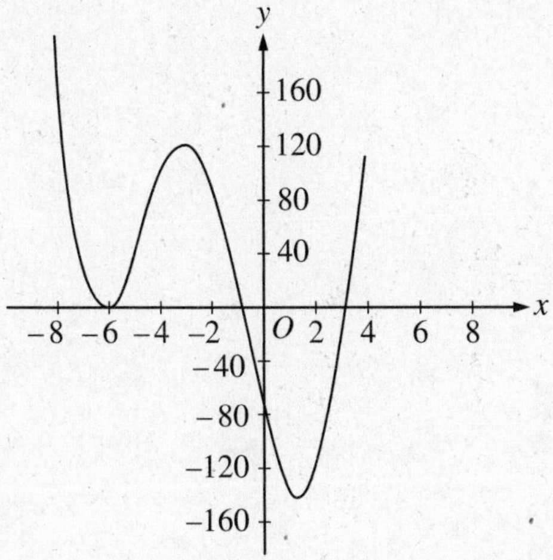

14. The graph of $y = x^4 + 10x^3 + 10x^2 - 96x + c$ is shown above. Which of the following could be the value of c ?

(A) 3,240
(B) 1,080
(C) 72
(D) −72
(E) −3,240

15. If $\cos x = 0.4697$, then $\sec x =$

(A) 2.1290
(B) 2.0452
(C) 1.0818
(D) 0.9243
(E) 0.4890

GO ON TO THE NEXT PAGE

MATHEMATICS LEVEL 2 TEST—*Continued*

USE THIS SPACE FOR SCRATCHWORK.

16. A club is planning a trip to a museum that has an admission price of \$7 per person. The club members going on the trip must share the \$200 cost of a bus and the admission price for 2 chaperones who will accompany them on the trip. Which of the following correctly expresses the cost, in dollars, for each club member as a function of n, the number of club members going on the trip?

(A) $c(n) = \dfrac{200 + 7n}{n}$

(B) $c(n) = \dfrac{214 + 7n}{n}$

(C) $c(n) = \dfrac{200 + 7n}{n + 2}$

(D) $c(n) = \dfrac{200 + 7n}{n - 2}$

(E) $c(n) = \dfrac{214 + 7n}{n - 2}$

17. Which of the following is an equation whose graph is the set of points equidistant from the points $(0, 0)$ and $(0, 4)$?

(A) $x = 2$
(B) $y = 2$
(C) $x = 2y$
(D) $y = 2x$
(E) $y = x + 2$

18. What is the sum of the infinite geometric series

$\frac{1}{4} + \frac{1}{8} + \frac{1}{16} + \frac{1}{32} + \ldots$?

(A) $\frac{1}{2}$ (B) 1 (C) $\frac{3}{2}$ (D) 2 (E) $\frac{5}{2}$

GO ON TO THE NEXT PAGE

USE THIS SPACE FOR SCRATCHWORK.

19. Which of the following is equivalent to $p + s > p - s$?

(A) $p > s$
(B) $p > 0$
(C) $s > p$
(D) $s > 0$
(E) $s < 0$

20. If a and b are in the domain of a function f and $f(a) < f(b)$, which of the following must be true?

(A) $a = 0$ or $b = 0$
(B) $a < b$
(C) $a > b$
(D) $a \neq b$
(E) $a = b$

21. In a recent survey, it was reported that 75 percent of the population of a certain state lived within ten miles of its largest city and that 40 percent of those who lived within ten miles of the largest city lived in single-family houses. If a resident of this state is selected at random, what is the probability that the person lives in a single-family house within ten miles of the largest city?

(A) 0.10
(B) 0.15
(C) 0.30
(D) 0.35
(E) 0.53

22. To the nearest degree, what is the measure of the smallest angle in a right triangle with sides of lengths 3, 4, and 5 ?

(A) 27°
(B) 30°
(C) 37°
(D) 45°
(E) 53°

GO ON TO THE NEXT PAGE

MATHEMATICS LEVEL 2 TEST—*Continued*

USE THIS SPACE FOR SCRATCHWORK.

23. Which of the following is an equation of a line perpendicular to $y = -2x + 3$?

(A) $y = 3x - 2$

(B) $y = 2x - 3$

(C) $y = \frac{1}{2}x + 4$

(D) $y = -\frac{1}{2}x + 3$

(E) $y = \frac{1}{-2x + 3}$

24. What is the range of the function f, where $f(x) = -4 + 3\sin(2x + 5\pi)$?

(A) $-7 \le f(x) \le 3$
(B) $-7 \le f(x) \le -1$
(C) $-3 \le f(x) \le 3$
(D) $-3 \le f(x) \le -1$
(E) $-1 \le f(x) \le 1$

25. Of the following lists of numbers, which has the smallest standard deviation?

(A) 1, 5, 9
(B) 3, 5, 8
(C) 4, 5, 8
(D) 7, 8, 9
(E) 8, 8, 8

GO ON TO THE NEXT PAGE

MATHEMATICS LEVEL 2 TEST—*Continued*

USE THIS SPACE FOR SCRATCHWORK.

26. The formula $A = Pe^{0.08t}$ gives the amount A that a savings account will be worth after an initial investment P is compounded continuously at an annual rate of 8 percent for t years. Under these conditions, how many years will it take an initial investment of \$1,000 to be worth approximately \$5,000 ?

(A) 4.1
(B) 5.0
(C) 8.7
(D) 20.1
(E) 23.0

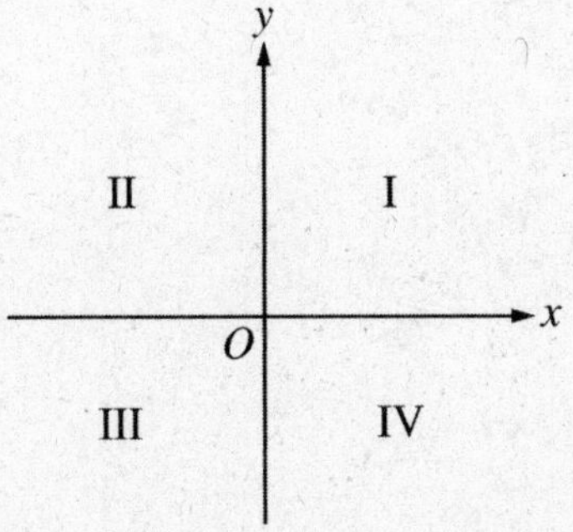

27. If $\sin\theta > 0$ and $\sin\theta\cos\theta < 0$, then θ must be in which quadrant in the figure above?

(A) I
(B) II
(C) III
(D) IV
(E) There is no quadrant in which both conditions are true.

GO ON TO THE NEXT PAGE

MATHEMATICS LEVEL 2 TEST—*Continued*

USE THIS SPACE FOR SCRATCHWORK.

28. If $f(-x) = f(x)$ for all real numbers x and if (3, 8) is a point on the graph of f, which of the following points must also be on the graph of f ?

(A) (−8, −3)
(B) (−3, −8)
(C) (−3, 8)
(D) (3, −8)
(E) (8, 3)

If $x = y$, then $x^2 = y^2$.

29. If x and y are real numbers, which of the following CANNOT be inferred from the statement above?

(A) In order for x^2 to be equal to y^2, it is sufficient that x be equal to y.
(B) A necessary condition for x to be equal to y is that x^2 be equal to y^2.
(C) x is equal to y implies that x^2 is equal to y^2.
(D) If x^2 is not equal to y^2, then x is not equal to y.
(E) If x^2 is equal to y^2, then x is equal to y.

30. In how many different orders can 9 students arrange themselves in a straight line?

(A) 9
(B) 81
(C) 181,440
(D) 362,880
(E) 387,420,489

GO ON TO THE NEXT PAGE

MATHEMATICS LEVEL 2 TEST—*Continued*

USE THIS SPACE FOR SCRATCHWORK.

31. What value does $\frac{\ln x}{x - 1}$ approach as x approaches 1 ?

(A) 0
(B) 0.43
(C) 1
(D) 2
(E) It does not approach a unique value.

32. If $f(x) = |5 - 3x|$, then $f(2) =$

(A) $f(-2)$

(B) $f(-1)$

(C) $f(1)$

(D) $f\left(\frac{4}{3}\right)$

(E) $f\left(\frac{7}{3}\right)$

33. What is the period of the graph of $y = 2\tan(3\pi x + 4)$?

(A) $\frac{2\pi}{3}$

(B) $\frac{2}{3}$

(C) 2

(D) $\frac{1}{3}$

(E) $\frac{\pi}{3}$

GO ON TO THE NEXT PAGE

MATHEMATICS LEVEL 2 TEST—*Continued*

USE THIS SPACE FOR SCRATCHWORK.

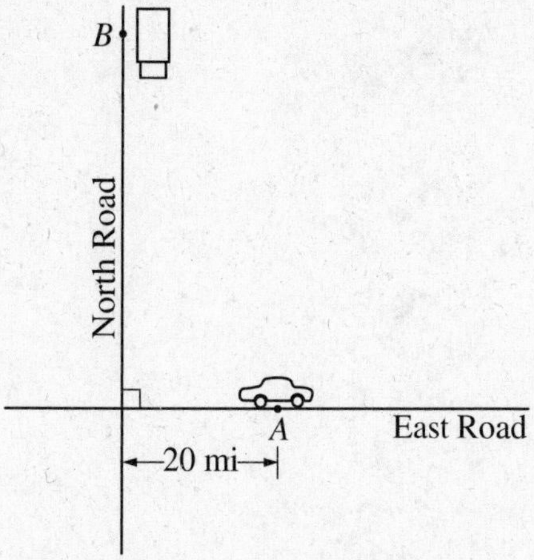

34. The figure above shows a car that has broken down on East Road. A tow truck leaves a garage on North Road at point *B*. The straight-line distance between points *A* and *B* is 50 miles. If the tow truck travels at an average speed of 45 miles per hour along North and East Roads, how long will it take the tow truck to get to the car?

(A) 27 minutes
(B) 1 hour and 7 minutes
(C) 1 hour and 28 minutes
(D) 1 hour and 33 minutes
(E) 1 hour and 46 minutes

GO ON TO THE NEXT PAGE

MATHEMATICS LEVEL 2 TEST—*Continued*

USE THIS SPACE FOR SCRATCHWORK.

x	$f(x)$
−1	0
0	1
1	−1
2	0

35. If f is a polynomial of degree 3, four of whose values are shown in the table above, then $f(x)$ could equal

(A) $\left(x+\frac{1}{2}\right)(x+1)(x+2)$

(B) $(x+1)(x-2)\left(x-\frac{1}{2}\right)$

(C) $(x+1)(x-2)(x-1)$

(D) $(x+2)\left(x-\frac{1}{2}\right)(x-1)$

(E) $(x+2)(x+1)(x-2)$

36. The only prime factors of a number n are 2, 5, 7, and 17. Which of the following could NOT be a factor of n ?

(A) 10 (B) 20 (C) 25 (D) 30 (E) 34

37. If $0 \leq x \leq \frac{\pi}{2}$ and $\sin x = 3\cos x$, what is the value of x ?

(A) 0.322
(B) 0.333
(C) 0.340
(D) 1.231
(E) 1.249

GO ON TO THE NEXT PAGE

MATHEMATICS LEVEL 2 TEST—*Continued*

USE THIS SPACE FOR SCRATCHWORK.

38. If $f(x) = 5\sqrt{2x}$, what is the value of $f^{-1}(10)$?

(A) 0.04
(B) 0.89
(C) 2.00
(D) 2.23
(E) 22.36

39. The Fibonacci sequence can be defined recursively as

$a_1 = 1$

$a_2 = 1$

$a_n = a_{n-1} + a_{n-2}$ for $n \geq 3$.

What is the 10th term of this sequence?

(A) 21
(B) 34
(C) 55
(D) 89
(E) 144

40. If $f(x) = x^3 - 4x^2 - 3x + 2$, which of the following statements are true?

I. The function f is increasing for $x \geq 3$.
II. The equation $f(x) = 0$ has two nonreal solutions.
III. $f(x) \geq -16$ for all $x \geq 0$.

(A) I only
(B) II only
(C) I and II
(D) I and III
(E) II and III

GO ON TO THE NEXT PAGE

MATHEMATICS LEVEL 2 TEST—*Continued*

USE THIS SPACE FOR SCRATCHWORK.

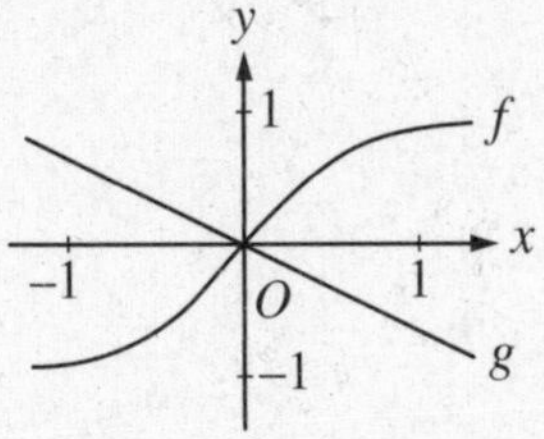

41. Portions of the graphs of f and g are shown above. Which of the following could be a portion of the graph of fg ?

(A)

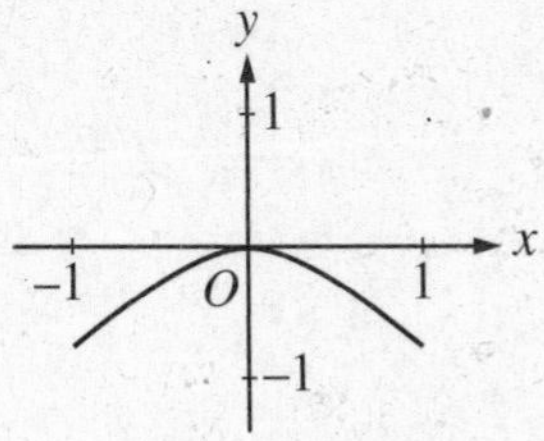

(B)

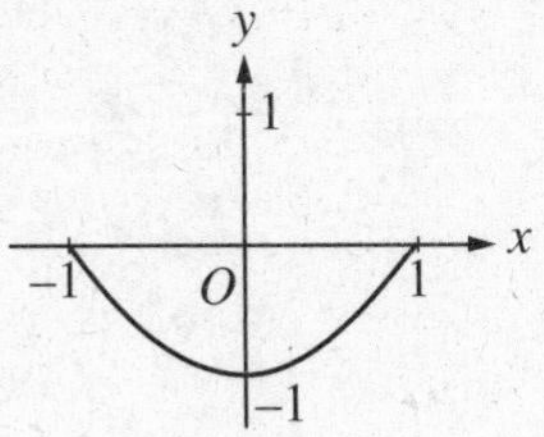

(C)

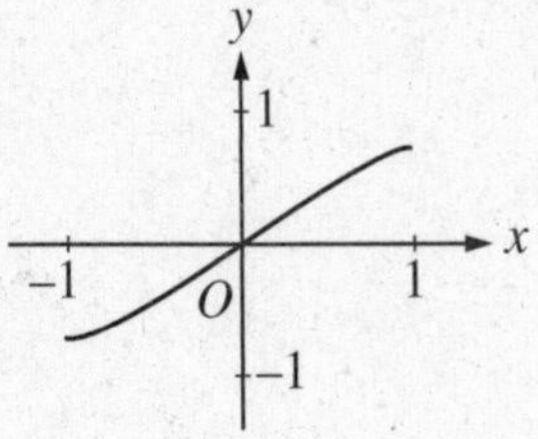

(D)

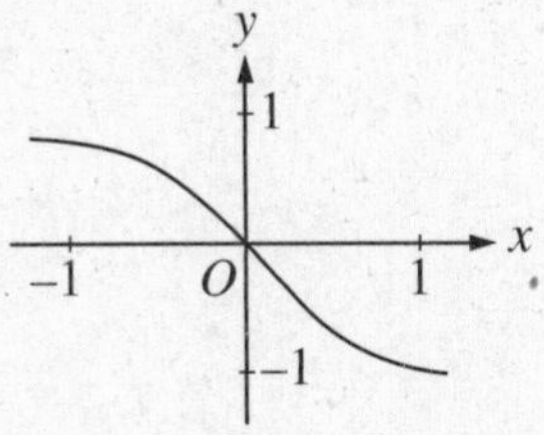

(E)

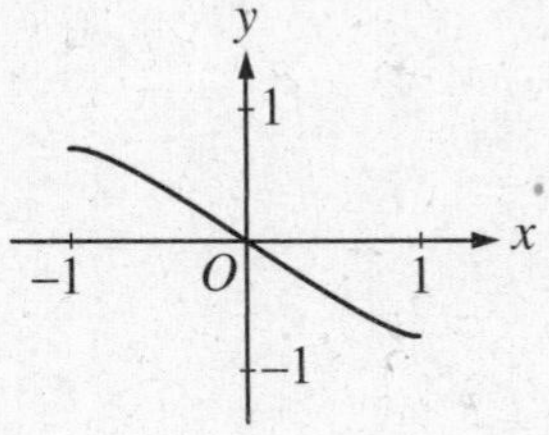

GO ON TO THE NEXT PAGE

MATHEMATICS LEVEL 2 TEST—*Continued*

USE THIS SPACE FOR SCRATCHWORK.

42. The set of all real numbers x such that $\sqrt{x^2} = -x$ consists of

(A) zero only
(B) nonpositive real numbers only
(C) positive real numbers only
(D) all real numbers
(E) no real numbers

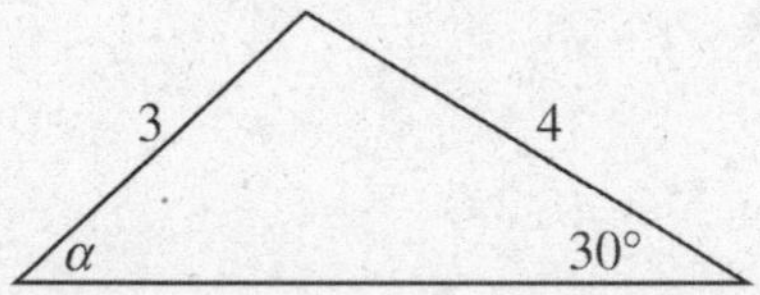

43. In the triangle shown above, $\sin \alpha =$

(A) $\frac{3}{8}$

(B) $\frac{1}{2}$

(C) $\frac{2}{3}$

(D) $\frac{3}{4}$

(E) $\frac{4}{5}$

44. The length, width, and height of a rectangular solid are 8, 4, and 1, respectively. What is the length of the longest line segment whose end points are two vertices of this solid?

(A) $4\sqrt{5}$
(B) 9
(C) $3\sqrt{10}$
(D) 10
(E) 12

GO ON TO THE NEXT PAGE

MATHEMATICS LEVEL 2 TEST—*Continued*

USE THIS SPACE FOR SCRATCHWORK.

45. If $\log_a 3 = x$ and $\log_a 5 = y$, then $\log_a 45 =$

(A) $2x + y$
(B) $x^2 + y$
(C) $x^2 y$
(D) $x + y$
(E) $9x + y$

46. If $\sin\theta = t$, then, for all θ in the interval $0 < \theta < \frac{\pi}{2}$, $\tan\theta =$

(A) $\frac{1}{\sqrt{1-t^2}}$
(B) $\frac{t}{\sqrt{1-t^2}}$
(C) $\frac{1}{1-t^2}$
(D) $\frac{t}{1-t^2}$
(E) 1

47. Which of the following shifts of the graph of $y = x^2$ would result in the graph of $y = x^2 - 2x + k$, where k is a constant greater than 2 ?

(A) Left 2 units and up k units
(B) Left 1 unit and up $k + 1$ units
(C) Right 1 unit and up $k + 1$ units
(D) Left 1 unit and up $k - 1$ units
(E) Right 1 unit and up $k - 1$ units

GO ON TO THE NEXT PAGE

MATHEMATICS LEVEL 2 TEST—*Continued*

USE THIS SPACE FOR SCRATCHWORK.

48. If the height of a right circular cone is decreased by 8 percent, by what percent must the radius of the base be decreased so that the volume of the cone is decreased by 15 percent?

(A) 4%
(B) 7%
(C) 8%
(D) 30%
(E) 45%

49. If matrix A has dimensions $m \times n$ and matrix B has dimensions $n \times p$, where m, n, and p are distinct positive integers, which of the following statements must be true?

I. The product BA does not exist.
II. The product AB exists and has dimensions $m \times p$.
III. The product AB exists and has dimensions $n \times n$.

(A) I only
(B) II only
(C) III only
(D) I and II
(E) I and III

GO ON TO THE NEXT PAGE

MATHEMATICS LEVEL 2 TEST—*Continued*

USE THIS SPACE FOR SCRATCHWORK.

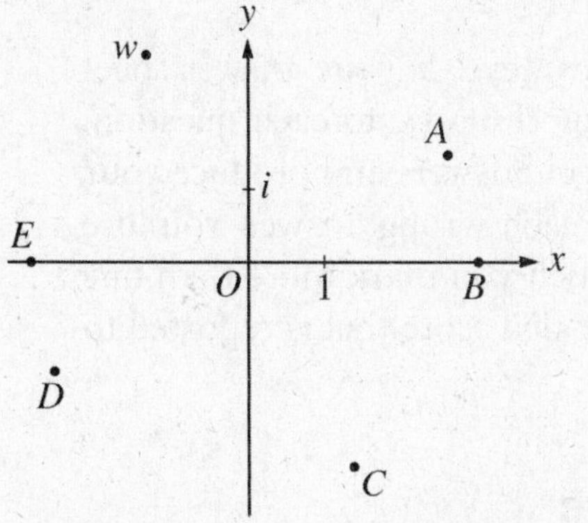

50. If w is the complex number shown in the figure above, which of the following points could be $-iw$?

(A) A (B) B (C) C (D) D (E) E

STOP

IF YOU FINISH BEFORE TIME IS CALLED, YOU MAY CHECK YOUR WORK ON THIS TEST ONLY.
DO NOT TURN TO ANY OTHER TEST IN THIS BOOK.

How to Score the SAT Subject Test in Mathematics Level 2

When you take an actual SAT Subject Test in Mathematics Level 2, your answer sheet will be "read" by a scanning machine that will record your response to each question. Then a computer will compare your answers with the correct answers and produce your raw score. You get one point for each correct answer. For each wrong answer, you lose one-fourth of a point. Questions you omit (and any for which you mark more than one answer) are not counted. This raw score is converted to a scaled score that is reported to you and to the colleges you specify.

Worksheet 1. Finding Your Raw Test Score

STEP 1: Table A on the following page lists the correct answers for all the questions on the Subject Test in Mathematics Level 2 that is reproduced in this book. It also serves as a worksheet for you to calculate your raw score.

- Compare your answers with those given in the table.
- Put a check in the column marked "Right" if your answer is correct.
- Put a check in the column marked "Wrong" if your answer is incorrect.
- Leave both columns blank if you omitted the question.

STEP 2: Count the number of right answers.

Enter the total here: ________________

STEP 3: Count the number of wrong answers.

Enter the total here: ________________

STEP 4: Multiply the number of wrong answers by .250.

Enter the product here: ________________

STEP 5: Subtract the result obtained in Step 4 from the total you obtained in Step 2.

Enter the result here: ________________

STEP 6: Round the number obtained in Step 5 to the nearest whole number.

Enter the result here: ________________

The number you obtained in Step 6 is your raw score.

Table A

Answers to the Subject Test in Mathematics Level 2 and Percentage of Students Answering Each Question Correctly									
Question Number	Correct Answer	Right	Wrong	Percentage of Students Answering the Question Correctly*	Question Number	Correct Answer	Right	Wrong	Percentage of Students Answering the Question Correctly*
1	D			88	26	D			85
2	C			91	27	B			70
3	D			90	28	C			65
4	A			87	29	E			47
5	C			90	30	D			73
6	E			54	31	C			54
7	C			62	32	D			72
8	D			93	33	D			23
9	D			85	34	C			62
10	B			89	35	B			57
11	E			84	36	D			51
12	C			54	37	E			63
13	B			87	38	C			52
14	D			75	39	C			52
15	A			88	40	D			48
16	B			67	41	A			42
17	B			62	42	B			33
18	A			70	43	C			63
19	D			76	44	B			54
20	D			72	45	A			46
21	C			82	46	B			46
22	C			67	47	E			44
23	C			70	48	A			35
24	B			66	49	D			25
25	E			60	50	A			26

* These percentages are based on an analysis of the answer sheets of a representative sample of 15,855 students who took the original administration of this test and whose mean score was 652. They may be used as an indication of the relative difficulty of a particular question.

Answer explanations for the Subject Test in Mathematics Level 2 can be found on page 279.

Finding Your Scaled Score

When you take SAT Subject Tests, the scores sent to the colleges you specify are reported on the College Board scale, which ranges from 200–800. You can convert your practice test score to a scaled score by using Table B. To find your scaled score, locate your raw score in the left-hand column of Table B; the corresponding score in the right-hand column is your scaled score. For example, a raw score of 26 on this particular edition of the Subject Test in Mathematics Level 2 corresponds to a scaled score of 620.

Raw scores are converted to scaled scores to ensure that a score earned on any one edition of a particular Subject Test is comparable to the same scaled score earned on any other edition of the same Subject Test. Because some editions of the tests may be slightly easier or more difficult than others, College Board scaled scores are adjusted so that they indicate the same level of performance regardless of the edition of the test taken and the ability of the group that takes it. Thus, for example, a score of 400 on one edition of a test taken at a particular administration indicates the same level of achievement as a score of 400 on a different edition of the test taken at a different administration.

When you take the SAT Subject Tests during a national administration, your scores are likely to differ somewhat from the scores you obtain on the tests in this book. People perform at different levels at different times for reasons unrelated to the tests themselves. The precision of any test is also limited because it represents only a sample of all the possible questions that could be asked.

Table B

Scaled Score Conversion Table Subject Test in Mathematics Level 2					
Raw Score	Scaled Score	Raw Score	Scaled Score	Raw Score	Scaled Score
50	800	28	630	6	470
49	800	27	630	5	460
48	800	26	620	4	450
47	800	25	610	3	440
46	800	24	600	2	430
45	800	23	600	1	420
44	800	22	590	0	410
43	790	21	580	-1	400
42	780	20	580	-2	390
41	770	19	570	-3	370
40	760	18	560	-4	360
39	750	17	560	-5	350
38	740	16	550	-6	340
37	730	15	540	-7	340
36	710	14	530	-8	330
35	700	13	530	-9	330
34	690	12	520	-10	320
33	680	11	510	-11	310
32	670	10	500	-12	300
31	660	9	490		
30	650	8	480		
29	640	7	480		

How Did You Do on the Subject Test in Mathematics Level 2?

After you score your test and analyze your performance, think about the following questions:

Did you run out of time before reaching the end of the test?

If so, you may need to pace yourself better. For example, maybe you spent too much time on one or two hard questions. A better approach might be to skip the ones you can't answer right away and try answering all the questions that remain on the test. Then if there's time, go back to the questions you skipped.

Did you take a long time reading the directions?

You will save time when you take the test by learning the directions to the Subject Test in Mathematics Level 2 ahead of time. Each minute you spend reading directions during the test is a minute that you could use to answer questions.

How did you handle questions you were unsure of?

If you were able to eliminate one or more of the answer choices as wrong and guess from the remaining ones, your approach probably worked to your advantage. On the other hand, making haphazard guesses or omitting questions without trying to eliminate choices could cost you valuable points.

How difficult were the questions for you compared with other students who took the test?

Table A shows you how difficult the multiple-choice questions were for the group of students who took this test during its national administration. The right-hand column gives the percentage of students that answered each question correctly.

A question answered correctly by almost everyone in the group is obviously an easier question. For example, 93 percent of the students answered question 8 correctly. But only 23 percent answered question 33 correctly.

Keep in mind that these percentages are based on just one group of students. They would probably be different with another group of students taking the test.

If you missed several easier questions, go back and try to find out why: Did the questions cover material you haven't yet reviewed? Did you misunderstand the directions?

Answer Explanations for the Mathematics Level 2 Subject Test

The solutions presented here provide one method for solving each of the problems on this test. Other mathematically correct approaches are possible.

1. Choice (D) is the correct answer. You need to solve the equation $3x+6=\frac{k}{4}(x+2)$ for k.

$$3x+6=\frac{k}{4}(x+2)$$
$$4(3x+6)=k(x+2)$$
$$12x+24=k(x+2)$$
$$12(x+2)=k(x+2)$$
$$12=k$$

2. Choice (C) is the correct answer. Since $C=\frac{5}{9}(F-32)$, you can substitute for C in the equation $K=C+273$. Thus, $K=\frac{5}{9}(F-32)+273$.

3. Choice (D) is the correct answer. The slope of the line is $\frac{11-5}{3-(-2)}=\frac{6}{5}=1.2$.

4. Choice (A) is the correct answer. One way to find the value of y is to notice that if $x+y=2$ and $y+z=5$, then $x+y+y+z=2+5=7$. Since $x+y+z=10$, you can conclude that $y=7-10=-3$.

5. Choice (C) is the correct answer. $g(5)=e^5$, and $f(e^5)=3\ln(e^5)-1=3\cdot 5-1=14$. Thus, $f(g(5))=14$.

6. Choice (E) is the correct answer. If a plane intersects a cube such that the plane is parallel to a face of the cube, the intersection will be a square, so I is possible. Since a square is a type of parallelogram, II is possible. If a plane intersects a cube so that

it slices through three adjacent faces at a corner of the cube, the intersection will be a triangle, so III is possible. Since I, II, and III are all possible.

7.

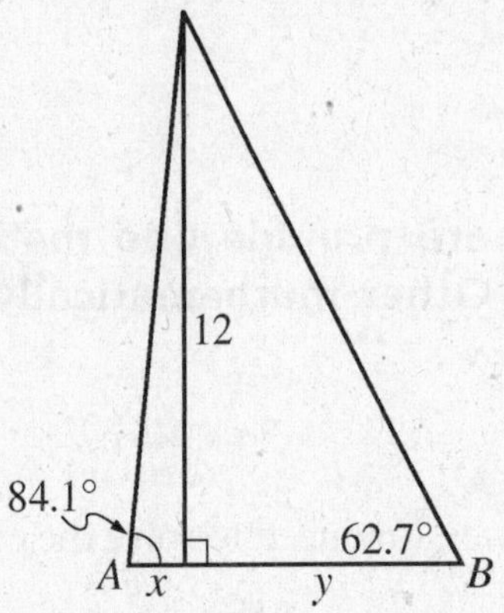

Choice (C) is the correct answer. It is helpful to draw a figure with the information given in the problem. The distance between A and B is $x + y$, so you need to find x and y. Since $\tan 84.1° = \frac{12}{x}$, $x = \frac{12}{\tan 84.1°}$, which is approximately 1.24. Since $\tan 62.7° = \frac{12}{y}$, $y = \frac{12}{\tan 62.7°}$, which is approximately 6.19. Thus, $AB = x + y \approx 1.24 + 6.19 = 7.43$ km.

Choice (A) is incorrect. $0.97 \approx \frac{\tan 84.1°}{12} + \frac{\tan 62.7°}{12}$. Choice (D) is incorrect. This results from using incorrect ratios.

$$\sin 84.1° = \frac{x}{12} \qquad \sin 62.7° = \frac{y}{12}$$

$$x = 12 \sin 84.1° \qquad y = 12 \sin 62.7°$$

$$\begin{aligned} AB &= x + y \\ &= 12 \sin 84.1° + 12 \sin 62.7° \\ &\approx 22.60 \end{aligned}$$

Choice (E) is incorrect. This results from using incorrect ratios.

$$\tan 84.1° = \frac{x}{12} \qquad \tan 62.7° = \frac{y}{12}$$

$$x = 12 \tan 84.1° \qquad y = 12 \tan 62.7°$$

$$\begin{aligned} AB &= x + y \\ &= 12 \tan 84.1° + 12 \tan 62.7° \\ &\approx 139.37 \end{aligned}$$

8. Choice (D) is the correct answer. If $x = \sqrt{15^2 - 12^2}$, then $x^2 = 15^2 - 12^2$, which is equal to $225 - 144 = 81$.

9. Choice (D) is the correct answer. The distance d from the origin to point $P(x, y)$ is equal to $\sqrt{x^2+y^2}$. The distance from the origin to point $P'(2x, 2y)$ is equal to $\sqrt{4x^2+4y^2}=\sqrt{4(x^2+y^2)}=2\sqrt{x^2+y^2}$, which is $2d$.

10. Choice (B) is the correct answer. You are looking for the input value that gives an output value of $\frac{2\sqrt{x^2+1}-1}{\sqrt{x^2+1}+1}$. In this case, $f\left(\sqrt{x^2+1}\right)=\frac{2\sqrt{x^2+1}-1}{\sqrt{x^2+1}+1}$. Thus, $g(x)=\sqrt{x^2+1}$.

11. Choice (E) is the correct answer. Since $\sin A=\cos(90°-A)$, it follows that if $\sin A=0.8$, then $\cos(90°-A)$ is also equal to 0.8.

12. Choice (C) is the correct answer. $x^2+y^2+z^2=r^2$ is the standard form for the equation of a sphere with center (0, 0, 0) and radius r. Thus, $x^2+y^2+z^2=1$ is a sphere with center (0, 0, 0) and radius 1.

13. Choice (B) is the correct answer. The graph of f has vertical asymptotes at x values for which $f(x)$ is undefined. This occurs when the denominator equals 0. Since $x^2-8x+16=(x-4)^2=0$ when $x=4$, the graph has a vertical asymptote at $x=4$ only. Choice (A) is incorrect. Since $f(0)$ is defined, $x=0$ is not a vertical asymptote. The graph of f has a horizontal asymptote at $y=0$. Choice (C) is incorrect. The numerator does not give information about vertical asymptotes. Since $f(5)$ is defined, $x=5$ is not a vertical asymptote.

14. Choice (D) is the correct answer. To answer this question, it is helpful to realize that finding c in the equation is equivalent to finding the y-intercept of the graph, since $y=c$ when $x=0$. From the figure shown, the graph appears to intersect the y-axis near −80. Only −72 is near −80. Since (−6, 0) is a point on the graph, you can verify that −72 is correct by substituting −6 for x in the equation $(-6)^4+10(-6)^3+10(-6)^2-96(-6)-72=0$.

15. Choice (A) is the correct answer. Since the secant of an angle is the reciprocal of the cosine, $\sec x=\frac{1}{\cos x}=\frac{1}{0.4697}\approx 2.1290$.

16. Choice (B) is the correct answer. The question asks for the cost for each club member to go on the trip. Each club member must pay the admission price of \$7. The n club members must share the \$200 cost of the bus, so each member must pay $\frac{200}{n}$ dollars. In addition, the n club members must share the \$14 for admission for the 2 chaperones. So each member must pay a total of $7+\frac{200}{n}+\frac{14}{n}$ dollars. This is equal to $7+\frac{214}{n}$ or $\frac{7n+214}{n}$ dollars. Choice (A) is incorrect. This answer does not include the \$14 for admission for the 2 chaperones. Each member must pay $\frac{14}{n}$ dollars of that amount.

17. Choice (B) is the correct answer. For any point (x, y) on the graph, the distance between (x, y) and (0, 0) should equal the distance between (x, y) and (0, 4). That is, $\sqrt{x^2+y^2}=\sqrt{x^2+(y-4)^2}$. Solving the equation gives $y=2$. Both of the given points lie on the y-axis. The set of points equidistant from these points is a horizontal line that goes through (0, 2). The equation of this line is $y=2$.

18. Choice (A) is the correct answer. The sum S of an infinite geometric series is given by $S=\frac{a}{1-r}$, where a is the first term and r is the common ratio. In this series, $a=\frac{1}{4}$ and $r=\frac{1}{2}$. Thus, the sum is $\frac{\frac{1}{4}}{1-\frac{1}{2}}=\frac{\frac{1}{4}}{\frac{1}{2}}=\frac{1}{2}$. Choice (D) is incorrect. This results from $\frac{1}{1-\frac{1}{2}}=2$ (forgetting to include the first term) or from thinking that $S=\frac{1-r}{a}=\frac{\frac{1}{2}}{\frac{1}{4}}=2$.

19. Choice (D) is the correct answer. The inequality $p+s > p-s$ is equivalent to $s>-s$, which is equivalent to $2s>0$. So, $s>0$.

20. Choice (D) is the correct answer. Since a and b are in the domain of the function f and $f(a)<f(b)$, it must be true that $f(a)\neq f(b)$. This implies that $a\neq b$. Note that a could be less than b if, for example, the function is increasing, and a could be greater than b if the function is decreasing.

21. Choice (C) is the correct answer. You need to recognize that the probability you seek corresponds to a compound event, since the person must live within 10 miles of the largest city *and* live in a single-family house. If P represents the entire state's population, then $0.75P$ residents live within 10 miles of the largest city. Of the $0.75P$ residents, 40% live in single-family houses. This is equal to $(0.40)(0.75P) = (0.30)P$. This tells you that 30% of the state's population live in single-family houses within 10 miles of the largest city. This means that the desired probability is 0.30. Choice (A) is incorrect. This results from taking 40% of the 25% of the population that do not live within ten miles of the largest city (0.40×0.25). Choice (B) is incorrect. This is equal to 0.60×0.25. Choice (D) is incorrect. This is equal to $0.75 - 0.40$.

22. Choice (C) is the correct answer. In the right triangle, the length of the hypotenuse is 5, and the length of the side opposite the smallest angle A in the triangle is 3. Thus, $\sin A = \frac{3}{5}$ and $\sin^{-1}\left(\frac{3}{5}\right) \approx 36.87°$. The measure of the smallest angle in the right triangle rounded to the nearest degree is 37°.

23. Choice (C) is the correct answer. The product of the slopes of two perpendicular lines is -1. Since the line $y = -2x + 3$ has a slope of -2, a line perpendicular to that line has a slope of $\frac{1}{2}$. Among the choices, only choice (C) gives the equation of a line that has a slope of $\frac{1}{2}$.

24. Choice (B) is the correct answer. The range of the function f depends on the range of $\sin(2x + 5\pi)$. Since $-1 \le \sin(2x + 5\pi) \le 1, -3 \le 3\sin(2x + 5\pi) \le 3$ and $-7 \le -4 + 3\sin(2x + 5\pi) \le -1$.

25. Choice (E) is the correct answer. The standard deviation of three numbers will be smallest for the numbers that are closest to each other. In choice (E), the three numbers all have the same value, so their standard deviation is 0. If all three numbers are not identical, then the standard deviation of the numbers, regardless of how small the numbers are, will always be greater than 0.

26. Choice (D) is the correct answer. According to the formula, $5{,}000 = 1{,}000e^{0.08t}$, which is equivalent to $5 = e^{0.08t}$. Taking the natural logarithm of both sides of the equation gives $\ln 5 = 0.08t$. Thus, $t = \dfrac{\ln 5}{0.08} \approx 20.1$.

27. Choice (B) is the correct answer. Since $\sin\theta > 0$, the product $\sin\theta\cos\theta$ will be negative only when $\cos\theta$ is negative. Since $\sin\theta$ is positive in the first and second quadrants, and $\cos\theta$ is negative in the second and third quadrants, θ must be in the second quadrant. Choice (A) is incorrect. In quadrant I, the second inequality fails. Choice (C) is incorrect. In quadrant III, $\sin\theta < 0$, so the first inequality fails.

28. Choice (C) is the correct answer. The graph of the function f is the set of points $(x, f(x))$. Since (3, 8) is on the graph, $f(3) = 8$. Since $f(-x) = f(x)$, $f(-3) = f(3) = 8$. This means that the point (–3, 8) is also on the graph of f.

29. Choice (E) is the correct answer. It is given that if $x = y$, then $x^2 = y^2$. You need to examine each choice to see if it can or cannot be inferred. Choice (A) can be inferred. If $x = y$, we know that x^2 must be equal to y^2 from the given statement. Choice (B) can be inferred. If $x^2 \neq y^2$, then it must be true that $x \neq y$. Choice (C) can be inferred. This is another way to state that if $x = y$, then $x^2 = y^2$. Choice (D) can be inferred. If $x^2 \neq y^2$, then it is not possible for x to equal y. Choice (E) cannot be inferred. If $x^2 = y^2$, then $x = y$ or $x = -y$.

30. Choice (D) is the correct answer. There are 9 choices for the first position, 8 choices for the second position, and so on. So, nine students can arrange themselves in a straight line in $9 \cdot 8 \cdot 7 \cdot 6 \cdot 5 \cdot 4 \cdot 3 \cdot 2 \cdot 1$ ways. The product is $9! = 362{,}880$.

31. Choice (C) is the correct answer. By using a graphing calculator, one can see that the value of the function $\dfrac{\ln x}{x-1}$ approaches 1 as x approaches 1 from both sides. You can examine the graph of the function or a table of values for the function as x approaches 1 from both sides. Thus, $\lim\limits_{x\to 1} \dfrac{\ln x}{x-1} = 1$.

32. Choice (D) is the correct answer. $f(2) = |5 - 3 \cdot 2| = |-1| = 1$. Since $|-1| = |1|$, $f(x) = |1|$ when $5 - 3x = 1$ or when $x = \dfrac{4}{3}$. Thus, $f(2) = f\left(\dfrac{4}{3}\right)$.

33. Choice (D) is the correct answer. The period of the graph of $y = 2\tan(3\pi x + 4)$ is the same as the period of the graph of $y = \tan(3\pi x)$. Since the period of the graph of $y = \tan x$ is π, the period of the graph of $y = \tan(3\pi x)$ is $\left(\frac{1}{3\pi}\right)\pi = \frac{1}{3}$.

34. Choice (C) is the correct answer. Let n represent the distance the truck travels along North Road. Then $n^2 + 20^2 = 50^2$, so $n = \sqrt{2{,}100}$ miles. Thus, the total distance traveled by the truck from point B to point A is $\sqrt{2{,}100} + 20$ miles. The time it takes the truck to get to the car is equal to $\frac{(\sqrt{2{,}100} + 20) \text{ miles}}{45 \text{ miles/hour}} \approx 1.46$ hours. The 0.46 hours is converted to minutes by multiplying 0.46 by 60, which gives 27.6 or 28 minutes. Choice (A) is incorrect. This is equal to the time it takes to travel from the intersection to A along East Road. Choice (B) is incorrect. This is equal to the time it takes to drive from B to A directly instead of along North and East Roads. Choice (D) is incorrect. This is obtained by adding the two given values, 50 miles and 20 miles, and computing the time to travel 70 miles. Choice (E) is incorrect. It takes the truck 1.46 hours to get to the car, and 0.46 hour is not the same as 46 minutes.

35. Choice (B) is the correct answer. Since $f(-1) = 0$, $(x + 1)$ is a factor of $f(x)$. Similarly, since $f(2) = 0$, $(x - 2)$ is a factor of $f(x)$. This means that $f(x)$ can be written as $f(x) = (x + 1)(x - 2)(x - a)$ for some real number a. Using $f(0) = 1$ gives $(0 + 1)(0 - 2)(0 - a) = 1$, which simplifies to $a = \frac{1}{2}$. Similarly, using $f(1) = -1$ gives $(1 + 1)(1 - 2)(1 - a) = -1$, which also simplifies to $a = \frac{1}{2}$. Thus, $f(x)$ could be equal to $f(x) = (x + 1)(x - 2)(x - \frac{1}{2})$.

36. Choice (D) is the correct answer. Since the only prime factors of the number n are 2, 5, 7, and 17, the only prime factors of any factor of n are 2, 5, 7, and 17. Hence the numbers $10 = 2 \times 5$, $20 = 2^2 \times 5$, $25 = 5^2$, and $34 = 2 \times 17$ are all possible factors of n, but $30 = 2 \times 3 \times 5$ could <u>not</u> be a factor of n, since 3 is not one of the prime factors of n.

37. Choice (E) is the correct answer. The equation $\sin x = 3 \cos x$ can be rewritten as $\tan x = 3$, when $x \neq \frac{\pi}{2}$. Solving for x yields $x = \tan^{-1}(3) \approx 1.249$.

38. Choice (C) is the correct answer. To find $f^{-1}(10)$, you need to find the value of x for which $10 = 5\sqrt{2x}$. This equation simplifies to $2 = \sqrt{2x}$ and so $x = 2$.

39. Choice (C) is the correct answer. In the sequence, a_n is equal to the sum of the previous two terms for $n \geq 3$. Thus, the first ten terms of the sequence are 1, 1, 2, 3, 5, 8, 13, 21, 34, 55. Choice (A) is incorrect. This is a_8. Choice (B) is incorrect. This is a_9. Choice (D) is incorrect. This is $a_{11} = a_{10} + a_9 = 89$. Choice (E) is incorrect. This is $a_{12} = a_{11} + a_{10} = 144$.

40. Choice (D) is the correct answer. Use a graphing calculator to draw the graph of the function f. The graph shows that f has three x-intercepts; therefore, the equation $f(x) = 0$ has three real solutions. Thus, statement II is false. The graph also shows that f has just two turning points: a local maximum at the point $\left(-\frac{1}{3}, \frac{68}{27}\right)$ and a local minimum at the point $(3, -16)$. Thus, f is increasing for $x \geq 3$ and $f(x) \geq -16$ for all $x \geq 0$. Statements I and III are true.

41. Choice (A) is the correct answer. For $x > 0$, $f(x) > 0$ and $g(x) < 0$, so $(fg)(x) = f(x)g(x) < 0$. For $x < 0$, $f(x) < 0$ and $g(x) > 0$, so $(fg)(x) = f(x)g(x) < 0$. Thus, $(fg)(x) < 0$ for all nonzero x shown and $(fg)(0) = f(0)g(0) = 0 \cdot 0 = 0$. Moreover, since $|(fg)(x)|$ increases as $|x|$ increases, fg is increasing for $x < 0$ and decreasing for $x > 0$.

42. Choice (B) is the correct answer. Every positive number n has two square roots, one positive and the other negative, but $\sqrt{n}$ denotes the positive number whose square is n. The square root of 0 is 0. In this case, this means that $\sqrt{x^2} \geq 0$, therefore $-x$ must be nonnegative and x must be nonpositive. Hence, the set of all real numbers x such that $\sqrt{x^2} = -x$ consists of nonpositive real numbers only.

43. Choice (C) is the correct answer. Using the law of sines, $\frac{4}{\sin \alpha} = \frac{3}{\sin 30°}$. Since $\sin 30° = \frac{1}{2}$ this becomes $\frac{4}{\sin \alpha} = 6$. Hence, $\sin \alpha = \frac{4}{6} = \frac{2}{3}$.

44. 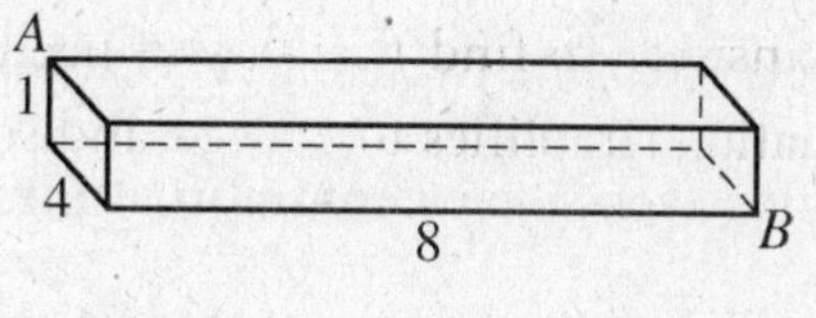

Choice (B) is the correct answer. To answer this question, it is helpful to draw a figure. The longest line segment shown in the figure is the segment between the points labeled A and B. $\overline{AB}$ is the hypotenuse of a right triangle in which one leg is the height of the rectangular solid and the second leg is the diagonal of the face with sides of length 4 and 8. By the Pythagorean theorem, the length of $\overline{AB}$ is $\sqrt{1^2+\left(\sqrt{4^2+8^2}\right)^2}=\sqrt{1+\left(\sqrt{80}\right)^2}=\sqrt{81}=9$. Choice (A) is incorrect. This is the length of the longest diagonal of any face of the solid. However, a segment joining opposite vertices is longer than a diagonal of a face.

45. Choice (A) is the correct answer.
Since $\log_a 45=\log_a(9\cdot 5)=\log_a 9+\log_a 5=\log_a 3^2+\log_a 5=2\log_a 3+\log_a 5=2x+y$, thus, $\log_a 45=2x+y$.

46. Choice (B) is the correct answer. Since $\sin^2\theta+\cos^2\theta=1$, $\cos^2\theta=1-\sin^2\theta$. Thus, $\cos^2\theta=1-t^2$, since $\sin\theta=t$; and $\cos\theta=\sqrt{1-t^2}$, since $0<\theta<\frac{\pi}{2}$. Hence, $\tan\theta=\frac{\sin\theta}{\cos\theta}=\frac{t}{\sqrt{1-t^2}}$.

47. Choice (E) is the correct answer. Completing the square yields $y=(x^2-2x+1)-1+k=(x-1)^2+(k-1)$. Hence, shifting the graph of $y=x^2$ right 1 unit and up $k-1$ units would result in the graph of $y=x^2-2x+k$.

48. Choice (A) is the correct answer. You can solve this problem by comparing the volumes of the original and new cones. If you use h and r for the height and radius, respectively, of the original cone, its volume is $V=\frac{1}{3}\pi r^2 h$. In the new cone, the height is $0.92h$ and the volume is $0.85V$. You need to determine the percent decrease in the radius, so you could represent the new radius length by kr, where $0<k<1$ and $(1-k)(100)$ is the percent you are looking for. This gives you the volume of the

new cone as $0.85V=\frac{1}{3}\pi(kr)^2(0.92h)$. By using $V=\frac{1}{3}\pi r^2h$, we have $0.85\left(\frac{1}{3}\pi r^2 h\right)=$ $\frac{1}{3}\pi(kr)^2(0.92h)$. If you divide each side by common terms, you get $0.85=k^2\cdot(0.92)$ so that $k^2\approx 0.9239$ or $k\approx 0.9612$. The percent decrease in the radius is $100(1-k)$, so the correct answer is 4%. Choice (C) is incorrect. If V is the volume of the original cone, the volume of the new cone is equal to $0.85V=\frac{1}{3}\pi(kr)^2(0.92h)$. If you use k instead of k^2, your answer will be 8%.

49. Choice (D) is the correct answer. For two matrices M and N, the product MN exists provided the number of columns of M equals the number of rows of N. The product MN has as many rows as M and as many columns as N. Since matrix B has p columns and matrix A has m rows, the product BA does not exist, so statement I is true. Since A has n columns and B has n rows, the product AB exists and has as many rows as A, which is m rows, and as many columns as B, which is p columns. Thus, statement II is true and statement III is false.

50. Choice (A) is the correct answer. The complex number w is equal to $a+bi$, where $a<0$ and $b>0$. Multiplying by $-i$ will give $-ai-bi^2=b-ai$. Thus, $b>0$ and $-a>0$. So $-iw$ is in quadrant I. The x-coordinate of $-iw$ equals b, and the y-coordinate equals $-a$. Choice (C) is incorrect. It results from not recognizing that a was originally negative and thus $-a$ is positive, which will give a point in quadrant IV. Choice (D) is incorrect. This corresponds to omitting the minus sign, and concluding that the point iw is in quadrant III. Choices (B) and (E) are incorrect. They both result from ignoring the a term in $a+bi$. This would mean that $w=bi$, so multiplying by i would produce a complex number with only a real part.

Chapter 5

Biology E/M

Purpose

The Subject Test in Biology E/M measures the knowledge students would be expected to have after successfully completing a college-preparatory course in high school. The test is designed to be independent of whichever textbook you used or the instructional approach of the biology course you have taken. The Biology E/M Test is for students taking a biology course that has placed particular emphasis on either ecological or molecular biology, with the understanding that evolution is inherent in both. The test lets you choose the area in biology for which you feel best prepared. If you are unsure of the emphasis in your biology course, consult your teacher.

Format

The Subject Test in Biology E/M with either ecological (Biology-E) or molecular (Biology-M) emphasis has a common core of 60 questions, followed by 20 questions in each specialized section (Biology-E or Biology-M). Each test-taker answers 80 questions.

Content

The content covered in the Subject Test in Biology E/M and descriptions of the topics are shown in the chart on page 290.

Biology E/M Test Topics Covered in Common Core	Approximate Percentage of E Test	Approximate Percentage of M Test
Cellular and Molecular Biology	15%	27%
Cell structure and organization, mitosis, photosynthesis, cellular respiration, enzymes, biosynthesis, biological chemistry		
Ecology	23%	13%
Energy flow, nutrient cycles, populations, communities, ecosystems, biomes, conservation biology, biodiversity, effects of human intervention		
Classical Genetics	15%	20%
Meiosis, Mendelian genetics, inheritance patterns, molecular genetics, population genetics		
Organismal Biology	25%	25%
Structure, function, and development of organisms (with emphasis on plants and animals), animal behavior		
Evolution and Diversity	22%	15%
Origin of life, evidence of evolution, natural selection, speciation, patterns of evolution, classification and diversity of organisms		

How to Prepare

Before you take the Biology E/M Test, you should have completed a one-year course not only in biology but also in algebra so that you can understand simple algebraic concepts (including ratios and direct and inverse proportions) and apply such concepts to solving word problems. Success in high school biology courses typically requires good reasoning and mathematical skills. Your preparation in biology should have enabled you to develop these and other skills that are important to the study of biology. Familiarize yourself with directions in advance. The directions in this book are identical to those that appear on the test.

Biology-E and Biology-M Skills Specifications	Approximate Percentage of Test
Knowledge of Fundamental Concepts:	30%
remembering specific facts; demonstrating straightforward knowledge of information and familiarity with terminology	
Application:	35%
understanding concepts and reformulating information into other equivalent forms; applying knowledge to unfamiliar and/or practical situations; solving problems using mathematical relationships	
Interpretation:	35%
inferring and deducing from qualitative and quantitative data and integrating information to form conclusions; recognizing unstated assumptions	

You should be able to recall and understand the major concepts of biology and to apply the principles you have learned to solve specific problems in biology. You should also be able to organize and interpret results obtained by observation and experimentation and to draw conclusions or make inferences from experimental data, including data presented in graphic and/or tabular form. Laboratory experience is a significant factor in developing reasoning and problem-solving skills. Although testing of laboratory skills in a multiple-choice test is necessarily limited, reasonable experience in the laboratory will help you prepare for the test.

Notes: (1) You will not be allowed to use a calculator during the Biology E/M Test.

(2) Numerical calculations are limited to simple arithmetic.

(3) The metric system is used in these tests.

How to Choose Biology-E or Biology-M

- Take Biology-E if you feel more comfortable answering questions pertaining to biological communities, populations, and energy flow.
- Take Biology-M if you feel more comfortable answering questions pertaining to biochemistry, cellular structure and processes, such as respiration and photosynthesis.
- Indicate choice of Biology-E or Biology-M on your answer sheet on test day.

You can decide whether you want to take Biology-E or Biology-M on the test day by gridding the appropriate code for the test you have chosen on your answer sheet. *Only questions pertaining to the test code that is gridded on your answer sheet will be scored.*

Note: Because there is a common core of questions, you are not allowed to take Biology-E and Biology-M on the same test date. You can take them on two different test dates.

Score

The total score for each test is reported on the 200-to-800 scale.

Sample Questions

Classification Questions

Each set of classification questions has five lettered choices in the heading that are used in answering all of the questions in the set. The choices may be statements that refer to concepts, principles, organisms, substances, or observable phenomena; or they may be graphs, pictures, equations, formulas, or experimental settings or situations.

Because the same five choices are applicable to several questions, classification questions usually require less reading than other types of multiple-choice questions. Answering a question correctly depends largely on the sophistication of the set of questions. One set may test recall; another may ask you to apply your knowledge to a specific situation or to translate information from one form to another (descriptive, graphical, mathematical). The directions for this type of question specifically state that you should not eliminate a choice simply because it is the correct answer to a previous question.

The following are directions for and an example of a classification set.

Core Section of Biology E/M

Directions: Each set of lettered choices below refers to the numbered statements immediately following it. Select the one lettered choice that best fits each statement and then fill in the corresponding circle on the answer sheet. A choice may be used once, more than once, or not at all in each set.

Questions 1–3 refer to the following pairs of organisms.

(A) Monerans and protists
(B) Angiosperms and gymnosperms
(C) Algae and fungi
(D) Ferns and mosses
(E) Monocots and dicots

1. Distinguished from each other by the presence or absence of a nuclear envelope

2. Distinguished from each other by the presence or absence of flowers

3. Distinguished from each other by the presence or absence of vascular tissue

The questions in this group are based on biological diversity and refer, in particular, to identification of distinguishing characteristics among certain groups of organisms that have arisen during evolutionary history.

Choice (A) is the correct answer to question 1. This question asks you to recognize that the absence of a nuclear envelope in cells separates prokaryotic cells from all other cells that do have a nuclear envelope, namely the eukaryotes. This characteristic is significant enough to place prokaryotes (including bacteria) in a separate taxonomic group.

Choice (B) is the correct answer to question 2. This question asks you to recognize that the presence or absence of flowers depends on whether seed plants produce seeds that are not enclosed in specialized structures or whether they are contained in specialized complex reproductive structures called ovaries. The former are called gymnosperms and appeared about 200 million years before the emergence of the flowering plants or angiosperms.

Choice (D) is the correct answer to question 3. This question is based on the recognition that the development of vascular tissue (phloem and xylem) was a major adaptation in the long evolution of photosynthetic organisms. Mosses were among the first autotrophs to display evolutionary adaptations to land existence, but they are usually less than 20 centimeters tall because they lack the woody tissue required to support tall plants on land. The evolutionary development of vascular tissue made possible the transporting of water and minerals and food between leaves and roots. Ferns are examples of vascular plants.

Five-Choice Questions

The five-choice question is written either as an incomplete statement or as a question. It is appropriate when: (1) the problem presented is clearly delineated by the wording of the question so that you are asked to choose not a universal solution but the best of the solutions offered; (2) the problem is such that you are required to evaluate the relevance of five plausible, or even scientifically accurate, options and to select the one most pertinent; (3) the problem has several pertinent solutions and you are required to select the one inappropriate solution that is presented. Such questions normally contain a word in capital letters such as NOT, LEAST, or EXCEPT.

A special type of five-choice question is used in some tests, including the SAT Subject Test in Biology E/M, to allow for the possibility of multiple correct answers. For these questions, you must evaluate each response independently of the others in order to select the most appropriate combination. In questions of this type several (usually three or four) statements labeled by Roman numerals are given with the question. One or more of these statements may correctly answer the question. You must select from among the five lettered choices that follow the one combination of statements that best answers the question. In the test, questions of this type are mixed in with the more standard five-choice questions. (Question 5 is an example of this type of question.)

In five-choice questions, you may be asked to convert the information given in a word problem into graphical form or to select and apply the mathematical relationship necessary to solve the scientific problem. Alternatively, you may be asked to interpret experimental data, graphical stimulus, or mathematical expressions.

When the experimental data or other scientific problems to be analyzed are comparatively extensive, it is often convenient to organize several five-choice questions into sets, that is, to direct each question in a set to the same material. This practice allows you to answer several questions based on the same material. In no case, however, is the answer to one question necessary for answering a subsequent question correctly. Each question in a set is independent of the others but refers to the same material given for the entire set.

The following are directions for and examples of five-choice questions.

Directions: Each of the questions or incomplete statements below is followed by five suggested answers or completions. Some questions pertain to a set that refers to a laboratory or experimental situation. For each question, select the one choice that is the best answer to the question and then fill in the corresponding circle on the answer sheet.

4. All of the following are population characteristics EXCEPT

    (A) number of individuals
    (B) phenotype
    (C) sex ratio
    (D) age distribution
    (E) death rate

Choice (B) is the correct answer to question 4. This question is a question on population ecology and asks you to consider what constitutes a population. An investigator necessarily has to define the limits of the population, but once those parameters are set, it is possible to study the variations in the time and space in the size and density of the population thus defined. A population can be characterized by the number of individuals present, the age distribution, the death rate within the population, and the sex ratio among the individuals. However, the phenotype is a characteristic of an organism and is observed at the level of the individual rather than at the level of a population.

5. ATP is produced during which of the following processes?

   I. Photosynthesis

   II. Aerobic respiration

   III. Fermentation

(A) I only
(B) II only
(C) I and III only
(D) II and III only
(E) I, II, and III

Choice (E) is the correct answer to question 5. This is a question on cellular and molecular biology that asks you to consider whether ATP is produced by more than one metabolic pathway. Each of the processes designated by a Roman numeral must be evaluated independently. In photosynthesis, solar energy captured by chlorophyll-containing plants creates a flow of electrons that results in the synthesis of ATP. Thus I is correct. Aerobic respiration, the process by which glucose is broken down to CO_2 and H_2O in the presence of O_2, is the most efficient mechanism by which cells produce the ATP they need to carry on their other metabolic activities. Thus II is also correct. Fermentation also involves the breakdown of glucose but without O_2. Under these conditions, substances such as lactic acid or ethyl alcohol and CO_2 are produced, together with limited quantities of ATP. Although the carbon-containing end products of fermentation still have much of the energy contained in the original glucose, fermentation permits a cell to produce some ATP under anaerobic conditions.

Questions 6–8

In a breeding experiment using gray and white mice of unknown genotypes, the following results were obtained.

	Parents			Offspring	
Cross	Female		Male	Gray	White
I	Gray	X	White	82	78
II	Gray	X	Gray	118	39
III	White	X	White	0	50
IV	Gray	X	White	74	0

6. Heterozygous gray female parents occur in

(A) cross I only
(B) cross II only
(C) cross IV only
(D) crosses I and II only
(E) crosses II and IV only

7. If two gray progeny of cross IV mate with each other, what is the probability that any individual offspring will be gray?
   (A) 100%
   (B) 75%
   (C) 50%
   (D) 25%
   (E) 0%

8. If the gray female from cross IV were mated with the gray male from cross II, then which of the following would most likely be true?
   (A) All of the offspring would be gray.
   (B) All of the offspring would be white.
   (C) Half of the offspring would be gray.
   (D) One-quarter of the offspring would be gray.
   (E) One-quarter of the offspring would be white.

Questions 6–8 are on heredity. They refer to the experiment described in the introductory material. You are asked to draw conclusions from the results of the experiment and to predict the results of further experimentation on the basis of the information obtained.

Choice (D) is the correct answer to question 6. This question asks you to determine which gray female parents were heterozygous. First you must realize from the ratio of offspring obtained in all the crosses that gray coat color is dominant over white in these mice. Next, you should note that no white offspring were obtained in cross IV. Thus, the gray female in this cross was homozygous gray. In cross I, approximately 50 percent of the offspring were gray. Therefore, the gray female, mated with a white male, must have been heterozygous. In cross II, a gray female was mated with a gray male, and a 3:1 ratio of gray to white offspring was obtained. Therefore, both gray female and gray male parents were heterozygous. Thus heterozygous females occurred only in crosses I and II.

Choice (B) is the correct answer to question 7. This question proposes a hypothetical mating between two gray progeny of cross IV. Since these progeny resulted from a cross between a gray female and a white male and no white offspring were produced, you can conclude that the female parent was homozygous gray and that all the offspring are heterozygous gray. Therefore, the mating of the gray progeny of cross IV will produce offspring in the ratio of 3 gray to 1 white. The probability, therefore, of an offspring of this cross being gray is 75 percent.

Choice (A) is the correct answer to question 8. This question asks you to predict the results of a cross between the gray female from cross IV and the gray male from cross II. From the data given, you can determine that the gray female in cross IV is homozygous, and the male in cross II is heterozygous. Thus you could expect that all of the offspring from such a mating would be gray.

Questions 9–11

Three students added equal volumes of pond water to each of four beakers (I–IV) and placed each in a different constant-temperature bath.

The baths were maintained at 5°C, 15°C, 25°C, and 35°C, respectively. The students then added 6 water fleas, *Daphnia pulex*, to each of the four beakers. After 1 hour, the students removed 3 *Daphnia pulex* from each beaker and each student immediately observed one *Daphnia pulex* under low-power magnification of a light microscope. (The transparent body of the *Daphnia pulex* can be seen easily under a light microscope.) Heart rates were recorded as beats per minute. The results of the experiment are summarized below.

Beaker	Temperature	Time Daphnia Added	Time Daphnia Removed	Heartbeats per Minute (average of 3 Daphnia)
I	5°C	2:00 p.m.	3:00 p.m.	41
II	15°C	2:10 p.m.	3:10 p.m.	119
III	25°C	2:20 p.m.	3:20 p.m.	202
IV	35°C	2:30 p.m.	3:30 p.m.	281

9. The independent variable in this experiment is the
   (A) amount of light
   (B) number of water fleas
   (C) pH of the water
   (D) temperature of the water
   (E) average heart rate

10. If a graph is constructed using the data given in the table, it will most closely resemble which of the following?

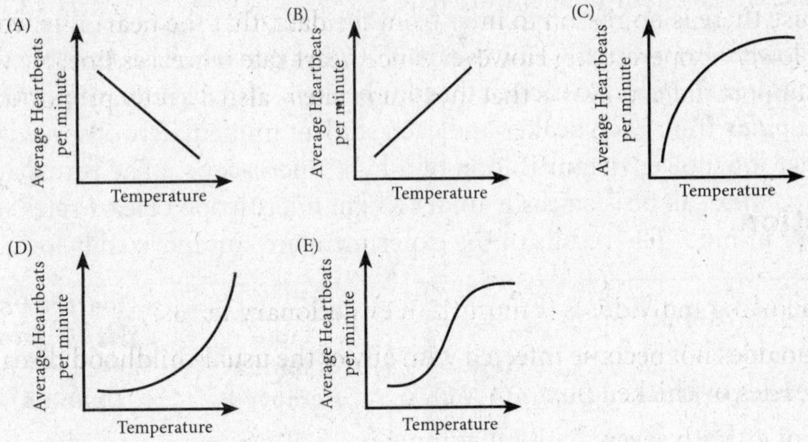

11. The data obtained in this experiment lend support to which of the following hypotheses?
    (A) At 45°C the heart rate of Daphnia would be 320 beats/minute.
    (B) Daphnia swim more slowly at high temperature.
    (C) Metabolic rate in Daphnia is directly proportional to water temperature.
    (D) Heart rate in Daphnia is inversely proportional to water temperature.
    (E) Between 0°C and 5°C, the heart rate of Daphnia would remain constant.

Questions 9–11 describe an experiment that seeks to determine how the metabolism of water fleas is affected by temperature. The experimental setup states that equal volumes of pond water were added to each of four beakers and the same number of fleas were added to each beaker.

Choice (D) is the correct answer to question 9. In this question, choices (B) and (C) are incorrect because both remained constant. Choice (A) is irrelevant in the case of water fleas, and choice (E) is the result the experiment seeks to measure. The only variable that changed during the course of the experiment was the temperature.

Choice (B) is the correct answer to question 10. This question requires examination of the data in the table. The results show that the average heartbeat per minute of these water fleas increased by about 80 heartbeats per every 10°C increase in temperature. This represents a linear increase of heartbeat with temperature, and only one of the five graphs given shows this.

Choice (C) is the correct answer to question 11. This question asks students to evaluate which of the five choices given is a hypothesis that is supported by the data. Choice (A) is incorrect because, although there are no data for the heart rate of the fleas at 45°C, a reasonable inference would be that the heart rate should increase about 80 heartbeats above that at 35°C, to about 360. Choice (B) is not a reasonable hypothesis since the water fleas are likely to move more rapidly at high temperatures when the heart rate is higher. Choice (D) is incorrect because it directly contradicts the data, and choice (E) is also incorrect because there is no reason to infer from the data, that the heart rate would remain constant at lower temperatures. However, since heart rate increases linearly with temperature, data support the hypothesis that metabolic rate is also directly proportional to heart rate.

Biology-E Section

12. Which of the following individuals is most fit in evolutionary terms?

(A) A child who does not become infected with any of the usual childhood diseases, such as measles or chicken pox

(B) A woman of 40 with seven adult offspring

(C) A woman of 80 who has one adult offspring

(D) A 100-year-old man with no offspring

(E) A childless man who can run a mile in less than five minutes

Choice (B) is the correct answer to question 12. For this question you must know the premises upon which Darwin based his explanation of evolutionary change in terms of natural selection. To be fit in evolutionary terms means not only that organisms possessing favorable variations will be able to survive better than those with less favorable variations, but also that the most fit organism will have a higher ability to leave more viable offspring in the next generation. Thus a child who is resistant to certain diseases has not yet demonstrated fitness. Therefore, choice (A) is not the answer to this question. Similarly a person with no offspring has not demonstrated fitness, whether or not she or he is actively exercising. Thus, choices (D) and (E) are incorrect. Finally a woman with numerous surviving offspring is more fit in the evolutionary sense than a woman with one surviving offspring, regardless of the life span of the woman. Thus choice (B) is a better answer than choice (C).

Questions 13–15

Known numbers of seeds from two species (*X* and *Y*) of annual plants are mixed together in different proportions and planted in five small plots of soil in the spring. The plants grow, flower, and produce seeds. It is found that the percentage of seeds of species *X* and species *Y* in the harvest is usually different from the proportion that was planted, although the total number of seeds produced is the same as the number of seeds planted. The data are plotted on the graph below.

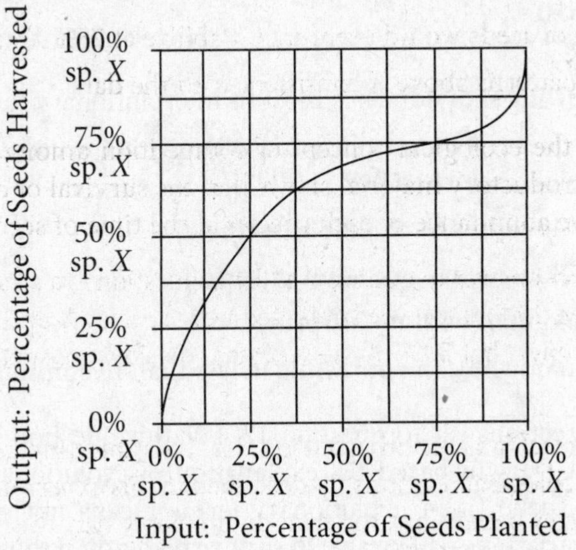

13. What mixture of seeds was harvested in the plot that was planted with 25 percent species *X* and 75 percent species *Y*?

	X	*Y*
(A)	25%	75%
(B)	40%	60%
(C)	50%	50%
(D)	60%	40%
(E)	75%	25%

14. What do the data indicate about the ecological relationship between species *X* and species *Y*?
    - (A) They are mutualistic for low percentages of *X* seeds.
    - (B) They are mutualistic for high percentages of *X* seeds.
    - (C) *X* and *Y* compete when both *X* and *Y* seeds are present.
    - (D) *Y* competes successfully against *X* at all percentages of *X* and *Y* seeds.
    - (E) *X* is parasite of *Y* when *Y* is rare.

15. If you started out with 25 percent species *X* seeds and 75 percent species *Y* seeds and replanted a plot year after year with the seeds produced each autumn, what pattern would you expect to see in the mixture of the two species over the years of the experiment?
   (A) Species *X* would increase to 100% while species *Y* would decrease to 0%.
   (B) Species *Y* would increase to 100% while species *X* would decrease to 0%.
   (C) One of the species would increase to 100% but which one depends on the initial mixture used to start the experiment.
   (D) The mixture of seeds would eventually stabilize at 75% *X* and 25% *Y*.
   (E) None of the patterns above is consistent with the data.

Questions 13–15 test the ecological concept of competition among species. The graph presented with the introductory material shows that the survival of either of two species depends on the relative abundance of each species at the time of seed planting.

Choice (C) is the correct answer to question 13. This question is a straightforward graph-reading question: when 25% of the seeds planted were species *X* and therefore 75% were species *Y*, the graph shows that 50% of the seeds harvested were species *X* and thus 50% were species *Y*.

Choice (C) is the correct answer to question 14. This question asks you to draw a conclusion about the ecological relationship described in this experiment. In a mutualistic relationship, both species benefit but the data do not show that this is true at either low or high percentages of species *X*. Thus choices (A) and (B) can be eliminated. There is no evidence for parasitism so choice (E) can be eliminated. Competition is occurring but not in a manner such that one species is successful over the other no matter what the percentage of seeds of each species planted. Thus choice (D) is incorrect.

Choice (D) is the correct answer to question 15. In this question, you are asked to predict the results of a proposed experiment. If you started by planting 25% species *X* seeds and 75% species *Y* seeds, you would recover 50% species *X* seeds and 50% species *Y* seeds at harvest time. If these seeds were replanted the following year, the graph shows about 70% species *X* and 30% species *Y* seeds would be harvested. Replanting these results year after year would increase the percentage of species *X* seeds harvested to 75% but there will be no further change in percentage of seeds planted and harvested. The percentage of seeds of each species would stabilize when 75% species *X* and 25% species *Y* are planted. Neither species would reach either 100% or 0% given the percentage of seeds from each species originally planted. Thus choices (A), (B), and (C) can be eliminated. Choice (E) can be eliminated because the pattern in choice (D) is consistent with the data.

Biology-M Section

16. Which of the following most accurately reveals common ancestry among many different species of organisms?
    (A) The amino acid sequence of their cytochrome C
    (B) Their ability to synthesize hemoglobin
    (C) The percentage of their body weight that is fat
    (D) The percentage of their body surface that is used in gas exchange
    (E) The mechanism of their mode of locomotion

Choice (A) is the correct answer to question 16. To assess common ancestry, or evolutionary relationship, among organisms, it is necessary to examine the similarities and differences among species for one or more structures that are homologous. For homologous structures—whether complex structures such as limbs or less complex structure such as a single gene product—the differences arise through the accumulation of mutations over time. Great similarity reflects a shorter time of divergence from a common ancestor. By this reasoning, only choice (A), examination of an enzyme of identical function in various organisms, represents a comparison of a homologous structure. Choice (B) can be ruled out because organisms either possess or lack the ability to synthesize hemoglobin; thus, this character allows one to sort organisms only into two groups, without providing information on relationships within those groups. Choice (C) can be ruled out because the amount of body fat is controlled physiologically, and varies within a single species. Choice (D) can be ruled out because gas exchange does not occur through the surface of some organisms that are only distantly related (e.g., mammals vs. insects) or occurs through the entire surface of many organisms that vary tremendously in relationship (e.g., all unicellular organisms). Choice (E) can be ruled out because many unrelated organisms do not move at all (e.g., plants vs. fungi), or derived their mode of locomotion independently (e.g., bats vs. birds vs. flying insects).

Questions 17–19

Thymine is used by animal cells primarily for the synthesis of DNA. A group of sea urchin eggs was fertilized in sea water containing radioactive thymine. Following fertilization samples of embryos were removed at regular intervals and the radioactivity in the embryos' nucleic acid was measured in counts per minute. The results obtained are shown in the figure below.

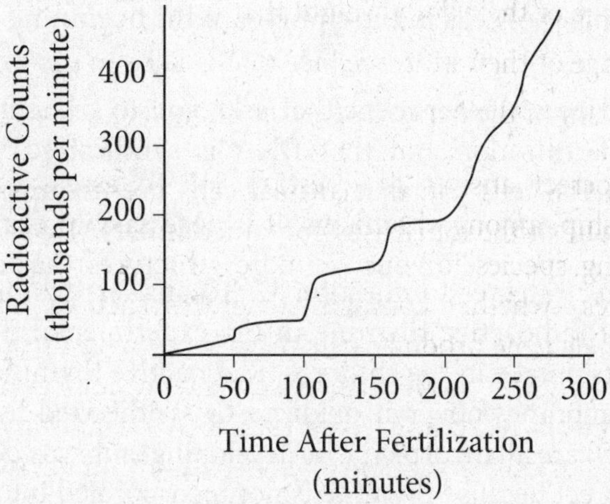

17. The increase in radioactivity of the embryos with time probably results from
    (A) synthesis of new proteins by the developing embryos
    (B) synthesis of radioactive thymine by the developing embryos
    (C) oxidation of radioactive thymine
    (D) incorporation of radioactive thymine in new cell membranes
    (E) incorporation of radioactive thymine in new DNA during replication

18. The time required for a complete cell division cycle in the sea urchin embryos studied in the experiment is approximately
    (A) 25 minutes
    (B) 50 minutes
    (C) 75 minutes
    (D) 100 minutes
    (E) 200 minutes

19. An appropriate control to show that this experiment measures DNA synthesis and not RNA synthesis would be to perform the same procedures but
    (A) not fertilize the eggs
    (B) sample the embryos at longer time intervals
    (C) add radioactive uracil instead of radioactive thymine
    (D) fertilize the eggs in sea water that does not contain radioactive thymine
    (E) count the number of cells in the embryos at the beginning and at the end of the experiment

Questions 17–19 describe an experiment that asks you to recognize that cell division occurs rapidly after fertilization and that DNA is synthesized when cells replicate. The introductory material tells you that animal cells use thymine primarily for DNA synthesis (thymine is one of the four bases contained in DNA).

Choice (E) is the correct answer to question 17. To answer this question, you need to realize that the use of radioactive thymine in the experimental design is needed as a means of measuring its uptake in the embryos. Radioactive thymine is not incorporated in embryonic cell membranes nor is it oxidized or synthesized by the embryos. Thus choices (B), (C), and (D) are all incorrect. The developing embryos do synthesize proteins but choice (A) is incorrect because thymine is not incorporated into proteins.

Choice (B) is the correct answer to question 18. To answer this question, you need to know that DNA is synthesized most rapidly during replication so that the largest increase in uptake of radioactive thymine would occur at that time. The graph indicates that the steepest jumps in radioactivity occur every 50 minutes so that would represent a complete cell division cycle.

Choice (C) is the correct answer to question 19. To answer this question, you need to know that uracil is contained in RNA but thymine is not. Thus using radioactive thymine measures DNA synthesis and not RNA synthesis. Use of radioactive uracil would yield data that measures RNA synthesis. Without the use of radioactive thymine in the sea water, the experimenter would have no mechanism for measuring any DNA synthesis at all, so choice (D) would not be an appropriate control. Collecting samples either at longer time intervals or only at the start and end of the experiment would provide less data and could not provide any appropriate control. Thus choices (B) and (E) are incorrect. Not fertilizing the eggs would provide no cell division whatsoever and so would provide no supporting evidence to show that the experiment measures DNA synthesis and not RNA synthesis. Thus choice (A) is also incorrect.

Biology E/M Subject Test

Practice Helps

The test that follows is an actual, previously administered SAT Subject Test in Biology E/M. To get an idea of what it's like to take this test, practice under conditions that are much like those of an actual test administration.

- Set aside an hour when you can take the test uninterrupted.
- Sit at a desk or table with no other books or papers. Dictionaries, other books, or notes are not allowed in the test room.
- Tear out an answer sheet from the back of this book and fill it in just as you would on the day of the test. One answer sheet can be used for up to three Subject Tests.
- Read the instructions that precede the practice test. During the actual administration you will be asked to read them before answering test questions.
- Time yourself by placing a clock or kitchen timer in front of you.
- After you finish the practice test, read the sections "How to Score the SAT Subject Test in Ecological Biology" or "How to Score the SAT Subject Test in Molecular Biology" and "How Did You Do on the Subject Test in Ecological Biology?" or "How Did You Do on the Subject Test in Molecular Biology?"
- The appearance of the answer sheet in this book may differ from the answer sheet you see on test day.

BIOLOGY–E TEST or BIOLOGY–M TEST

You must decide whether you want to take a Biology Test with Ecological Emphasis (BIOLOGY-E) or Molecular Emphasis (BIOLOGY-M) now, before the test begins. The top portion of the page of the answer sheet that you will use to take the Biology Test you have selected must be filled in exactly as illustrated below. When your supervisor tells you to fill in the circle next to the name of the test you are about to take, mark your answer sheet as shown.

For BIOLOGY-E

○ Literature	○ Mathematics Level 1	○ German	○ Chinese Listening	○ Japanese Listening
● Biology E	○ Mathematics Level 2	○ Italian	○ French Listening	○ Korean Listening
○ Biology M	○ U.S. History	○ Latin	○ German Listening	○ Spanish Listening
○ Chemistry	○ World History	○ Modern Hebrew		
○ Physics	○ French	○ Spanish	**Background Questions:** ①②③④⑤⑥⑦⑧⑨	

For BIOLOGY-M

○ Literature	○ Mathematics Level 1	○ German	○ Chinese Listening	○ Japanese Listening
○ Biology E	○ Mathematics Level 2	○ Italian	○ French Listening	○ Korean Listening
● Biology M	○ U.S. History	○ Latin	○ German Listening	○ Spanish Listening
○ Chemistry	○ World History	○ Modern Hebrew		
○ Physics	○ French	○ Spanish	**Background Questions:** ①②③④⑤⑥⑦⑧⑨	

After filling in the circle next to the name of the test you are taking, locate the Background Questions section, which also appears at the top of your answer sheet (as shown above). This is where you will answer the following Background Questions on your answer sheet.

BACKGROUND QUESTIONS

Please answer the four questions below by filling in the appropriate circle in the Background Questions box on your answer sheet. The information you provide is for statistical purposes only and will not affect your test score.

Question I — How many semesters of biology have you taken in high school? (If you are taking biology this semester, count it as a full semester.) Fill in only one circle of circles 1-3.

- One semester or less — Fill in circle 1.
- Two semesters — Fill in circle 2.
- Three semesters or more — Fill in circle 3.

Question II — Which of the following best describes your biology course? Fill in only one circle of circles 4-6.

- General Biology — Fill in circle 4.
- Biology with emphasis on ecology — Fill in circle 5.
- Biology with emphasis on molecular biology — Fill in circle 6.

Question III — Which of the following best describes your background in algebra? (If you are taking an algebra course this semester, count it as a full semester.) Fill in only one circle of circles 7-8.

- One semester or less — Fill in circle 7.
- Two semesters or more — Fill in circle 8.

Question IV — Have you had or are you currently taking Advanced Placement Biology? If you are, fill in circle 9.

When the supervisor gives the signal, turn the page and begin the Biology Test. There are 100 numbered circles on the answer sheet. There are 60 questions in the core Biology Test, 20 questions in the Biology-E section, and 20 questions in the Biology-M section. Therefore use ONLY circles 1-80 (for Biology-E) OR circles 1-60 plus 81-100 (for Biology-M) for recording your answers.

BIOLOGY E/M TEST

FOR BOTH BIOLOGY-E AND BIOLOGY-M, ANSWER QUESTIONS 1-60

Directions: Each set of lettered choices below refers to the numbered questions or statements immediately following it. Select the one lettered choice that best answers each question or best fits each statement and then fill in the corresponding circle on the answer sheet. A choice may be used once, more than once, or not at all in each set.

Questions 1-4 refer to the following plant cell types.

(A) Tracheids and vessel elements
(B) Guard cells
(C) Parenchyma cells
(D) Sieve tube members and companion cells
(E) Sclerenchyma cells

1. Chains of these nonliving cells form continuous tubes for the transport of water in vascular plants.

2. These cells take up potassium ions and water when sunlight and low concentrations of carbon dioxide are present, which causes them to become rigid.

3. These versatile cells serve as storage sites for sugars and starches in stems and roots.

4. These cells form a living tissue which transports sugar from one part of a vascular plant to another.

Questions 5-6 refer to the following.

(A) 2
(B) 4
(C) 16
(D) 25
(E) 50

5. The expected percentage of offspring with the recessive phenotype from a cross between two individuals heterozygous for a particular trait

6. The number of different phenotypes possible for the progeny of the cross $AaBb \times AaBb$, where A and B exhibit simple dominance

Questions 7-10

(A) Monera
(B) Protista
(C) Fungi
(D) Plantae
(E) Animalia

7. Contains all the protozoa and most of the algae

8. Contains multicellular heterotrophic organisms that reproduce asexually by spores

9. Contains organisms without membrane-bound organelles such as nuclei

10. Contains autotrophic organisms with cells that are organized into tissues and organs

GO ON TO THE NEXT PAGE

Questions 11-14 refer to the following illustration of protein synthesis in a mammalian cell.

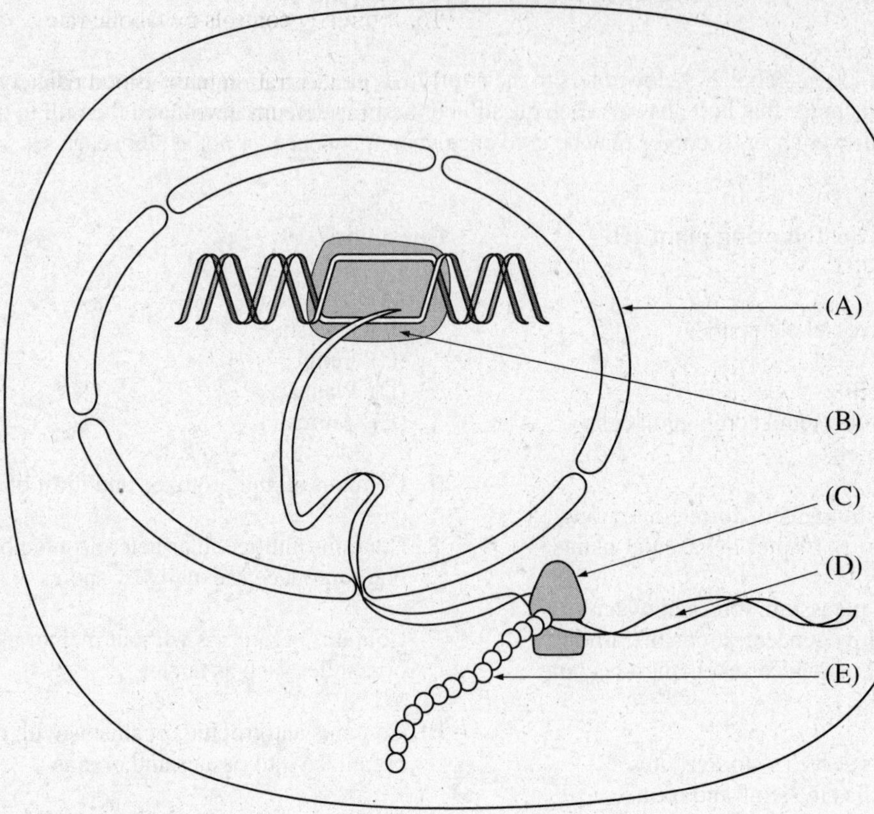

11. A strand of mRNA being translated

12. A polypeptide being synthesized

13. A barrier to diffusion of large proteins from nucleus to cytoplasm

14. A structure that contains a lipid bilayer

GO ON TO THE NEXT PAGE

Questions 15-17

(A) Insulin
(B) Growth hormone
(C) Progesterone
(D) Thyroxin
(E) Secretin

15. It is secreted by the pituitary gland.

16. It directly controls metabolic rate.

17. Its concentration in the blood rises when the corpus luteum develops.

GO ON TO THE NEXT PAGE

Directions: Each of the questions or incomplete statements below is followed by five suggested answers or completions. Some questions pertain to a set that refers to a laboratory or experimental situation. For each question, select the one choice that is the best answer to the question and then fill in the corresponding circle on the answer sheet.

18. The ribosomes of a cell are of primary importance for

(A) DNA replication
(B) transcription
(C) translation
(D) translocation
(E) repression

19. If a couple has two boys and one girl, what is the probability that the next child born to this couple will be a girl?

(A) $\frac{1}{4}$

(B) $\frac{1}{3}$

(C) $\frac{1}{2}$

(D) $\frac{2}{3}$

(E) $\frac{3}{4}$

20. Eggs fertilized by two sperm instead of one sometimes form a mitotic spindle with three poles. After mitosis the daughter cells will probably

(A) be indistinguishable from normal cells
(B) eliminate the chromosomes contributed by the second sperm
(C) eliminate the chromosomes contributed by the egg
(D) display an abnormal number of chromosomes
(E) stop protein synthesis immediately

21. In higher plant cells, a pigment important in the manufacture of carbohydrates from CO_2 and H_2O is contained in the

(A) nucleus
(B) vacuole
(C) cytoplasm
(D) chloroplast
(E) centrosome

GO ON TO THE NEXT PAGE

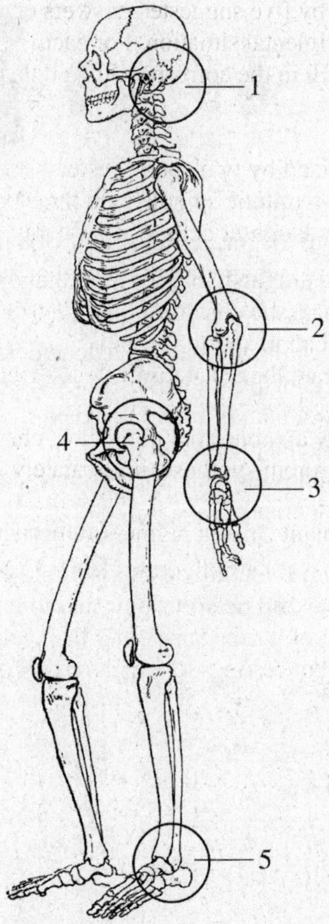

22. In the diagram of the human skeleton above, which of the following is a ball-and-socket joint?

(A) 1
(B) 2
(C) 3
(D) 4
(E) 5

23. Which of the following statements is true for red blood cells that have been added to a flask of saturated NaCl solution?

(A) The cells will undergo mitosis.
(B) The cells will increase in volume.
(C) The cells will lose water.
(D) The cells are hypertonic relative to the surrounding medium.
(E) The concentration of NaCl is lower outside the cells than inside.

24. Today's worldwide human population can best be described as

(A) oscillating
(B) declining
(C) fluctuating near equilibrium
(D) growing arithmetically
(E) growing exponentially

25. The base of the food web of the open ocean is provided by

(A) phytoplankton
(B) zooplankton
(C) kelp
(D) fish
(E) whales

26. Nitrogen fixation is the conversion of atmospheric nitrogen into

(A) ammonia
(B) protein
(C) urea
(D) carbon dioxide
(E) DNA

GO ON TO THE NEXT PAGE

27. In the fruit fly, the allele for normal wings (*W*) is dominant over the allele for vestigial wings (*w*). A cross of two normal-winged flies produced 76 normal-winged and 23 vestigial-winged offspring. It can be concluded that the genotypes of the two parent flies were which of the following?

(A) *WW* and *ww*
(B) *WW* and *Ww*
(C) *Ww* and *ww*
(D) *Ww* and *Ww*
(E) *WW* and *WW*

28. Factors that have been known to result in the elimination of a species in a particular area include which of the following?

I. Use of insecticides
II. Hunting of the species' prey
III. Habitat destruction

(A) I only
(B) II only
(C) I and III only
(D) II and III only
(E) I, II, and III

29. According to the partial karyotype of a mammal shown above, which of the following must be true?

(A) The organism has a single gene defect.
(B) The organism is a male.
(C) The organism is a homozygote.
(D) The organism is a human.
(E) The alleles on both chromosomes labeled 3 are identical.

30. An organism is examined and is found to be multicellular and heterotrophic and to have cell walls made of a substance other than cellulose. The organism belongs to which of the following kingdoms?

(A) Monera
(B) Protista
(C) Fungi
(D) Plantae
(E) Animalia

GO ON TO THE NEXT PAGE

31. Which of the following statements is correct?

(A) Heritable variation allows for evolution.
(B) Adaptive radiation allows for mutation.
(C) Crossing-over allows for mitosis.
(D) Translocation allows for DNA replication.
(E) Cellular differentiation allows for meiosis.

32. Behavior that remains unaffected by environmental changes is most likely

(A) territorial
(B) learned
(C) innate
(D) stereotyped
(E) conditioned

33. A man who has hemophilia and a woman who does not have hemophilia have a daughter who has hemophilia. Hemophilia is a recessive condition, and the gene is located on the X chromosome. Which of the following can be concluded?

(A) The mother is a carrier for hemophilia.
(B) Hemophilia is not a sex-linked trait.
(C) Crossing-over has occurred.
(D) All subsequent daughters of this couple will have hemophilia.
(E) All sons of this couple will have hemophilia.

34. All of the following are measures useful in describing a given population's growth rate EXCEPT

(A) fertility
(B) mortality
(C) survivorship
(D) age structure
(E) habitat

35. Which of the following is LEAST consistent with the fossil record?

(A) Bony fish evolved from amphibians.
(B) Mammals evolved from reptiles.
(C) Birds evolved from reptiles.
(D) Reptiles evolved from amphibians.
(E) Cartilaginous fish evolved from jawless fish.

36. Which of the following is NOT true of enzymes?

(A) Enzyme activity is affected by changes in temperature.
(B) Enzymes change the rate at which biochemical reactions proceed.
(C) Enzyme activity is affected by large shifts in pH.
(D) Enzymes often require the presence of cofactors or coenzymes to become active.
(E) Enzymes are assembled from vitamin subunits.

37. The gene for a particular trait that is passed only from fathers to sons is most likely

(A) autosomal recessive
(B) autosomal dominant
(C) codominant
(D) *Y*-linked
(E) *X*-linked

GO ON TO THE NEXT PAGE

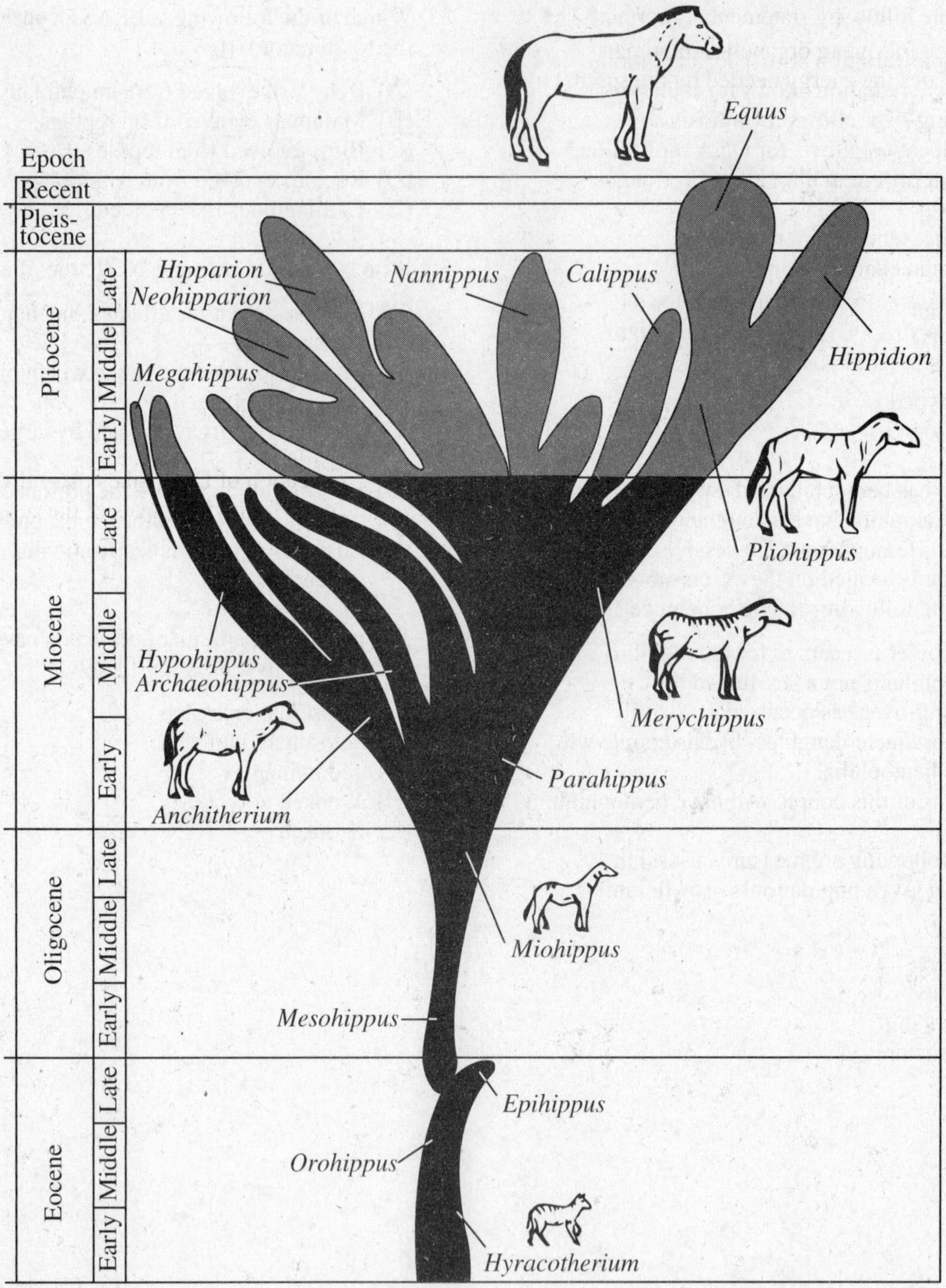

38. The diagram above illustrates a proposed phylogeny for horses. Which of the following genera is currently represented by live animals?

(A) *Epihippus*
(B) *Equus*
(C) *Hippidion*
(D) *Hyracotherium*
(E) *Nannippus*

GO ON TO THE NEXT PAGE

39. Which of the following organelles in human sperm provides the energy needed by the sperm?

(A) Flagellum
(B) Mitochondrion
(C) Y chromosome
(D) Centriole
(E) Nucleus

40. Which of the following organs secretes the hormone responsible for the "fight-or-flight" reaction in mammals?

(A) Liver
(B) Kidney
(C) Pancreas
(D) Cowper's gland
(E) Adrenal gland

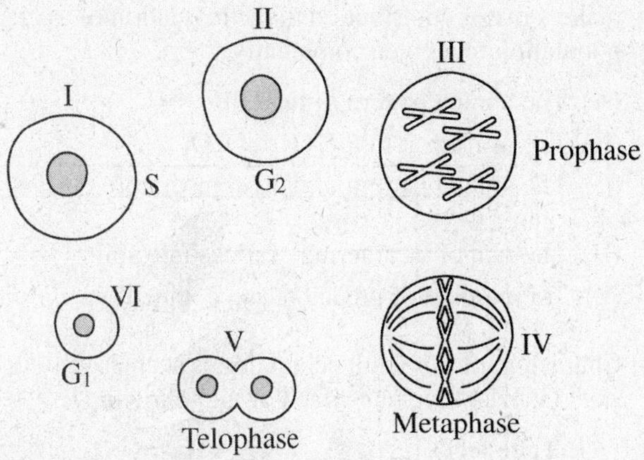

41. Most replication of DNA takes place during which of the following stages of the cell cycle?

(A) I
(B) II and III
(C) IV only
(D) IV and V
(E) VI

GO ON TO THE NEXT PAGE

42. Which of the following is a biotic factor that can make a major contribution to the regulation of a population in a given community?

(A) The annual pattern of rainfall
(B) The average ratio of O_2 to CO_2
(C) The annual pattern of daily temperature ranges
(D) The rate of weathering of rocks into soil
(E) The number of predators and competitors

43. Characteristics of adult echinoderms such as sea stars (starfish) include which of the following?

I. Tube feet
II. Bilateral symmetry
III. Water vascular system

(A) I only
(B) II only
(C) I and III only
(D) II and III only
(E) I, II, and III

44. If in an adult organism the genes *A* and *B* occur on one chromosome and their alleles *a* and *b* occur on its homologue, which of the following explains a combination of *Ab* or *aB* occurring in the gametes?

(A) Sex-linkage
(B) Lack of dominance
(C) Nondisjunction
(D) Crossing-over
(E) Blending

45. Which of the following is NOT a major function of the mammalian kidney?

(A) Elimination of urea and other nitrogenous wastes
(B) Maintenance of water balance
(C) Manufacture of antibodies
(D) Regulation of salt excretion
(E) Formation of urine from glomerular filtrate

46. An ecologically sound reason for conserving tropical rain forests is that they

(A) supply most of the oxygen that humans breathe
(B) occupy four-fifths of Earth's surface
(C) are the major producers of atmospheric nitrogen
(D) are crucial to migratory ungulates like bison and wildebeest
(E) are an important reservoir of biodiversity

GO ON TO THE NEXT PAGE

Questions 47-48

A population study of plants was done in an abandoned field. Each year for 3 years the vegetation was sampled. The chart below indicates the results of the study.

Year	Number of Plants per Acre				
	Sandspur	Ragweed	Timothy Grass	Goldenrod	Wire Grass
1	3,800	4,900	600	0	412
2	1,500	2,209	1,185	75	796
3	752	180	2,234	790	1,643

47. According to the data, which of the following are initially most successful in the succession taking place in the field described above?

(A) Sandspur and ragweed
(B) Sandspur and timothy grass
(C) Ragweed and timothy grass
(D) Ragweed and wire grass
(E) Sandspur and goldenrod

48. The data above suggest that

(A) fires cause the changes in the populations
(B) floods cause the changes in the populations
(C) the plants in the population have similar life spans
(D) plant populations are replacing one another
(E) the reproductive capacity of plants changes with time

GO ON TO THE NEXT PAGE

Questions 49-51

The figure below represents the increase in prevalence of both keratoses (thickened pigmented patches on the skin) and skin cancers in males of Irish descent in several geographic areas.

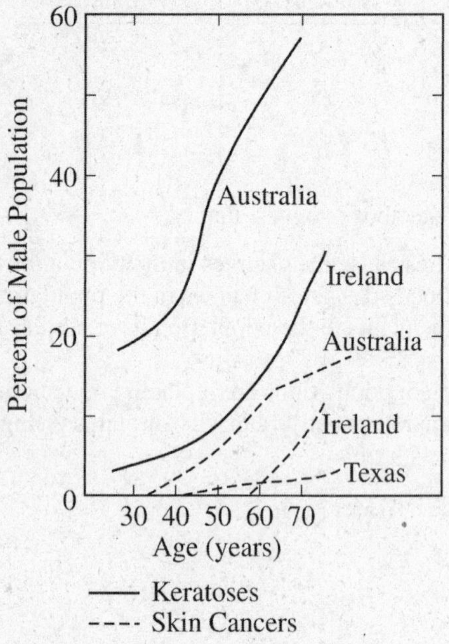

49. For which of the following groups can 20 percent of the male population be expected to have the indicated condition?

    (A) Skin cancers in Australia at age 50
    (B) Keratoses in Australia at age 30
    (C) Keratoses in Australia at age 70
    (D) Keratoses in Ireland at age 40
    (E) Keratoses in Ireland at age 80

50. Which of the following can be inferred from these data?

    (A) Skin cancers develop from keratoses.
    (B) Keratoses develop from skin cancers.
    (C) The majority of males with keratoses also have skin cancer.
    (D) The environment in Australia is more likely to cause keratoses than is the environment in Ireland.
    (E) The intensity of sunlight is the primary factor causing the development of skin cancers.

51. If the study were conducted as a function of the age of the female population in the same geographic areas, which of the following results would be most likely?

    (A) The data would show a higher percentage of females with the diseases at all ages.
    (B) The data would show a lower incidence of the diseases, because females have higher levels of estrogen.
    (C) The data would be the same as for males in Australia and Ireland, but no predictions can be made for Texas.
    (D) The data would be the same as for males with regard to keratoses but not for skin cancers.
    (E) No accurate predictions can be made from the data because the sample populations would be different.

GO ON TO THE NEXT PAGE

NO TEST MATERIAL ON THIS PAGE

Questions 52-55

Charles Darwin and his son Francis performed a series of experiments on phototropism (growth toward light) of the coleoptile (the cap that covers the first leaves of new seedlings of grass). The treatments they used are described below.

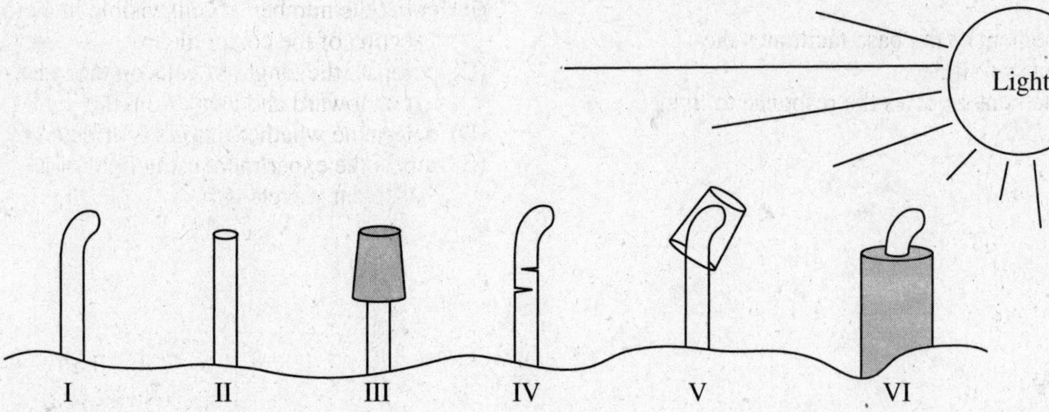

	Treatment	Growth Toward Light
I	Coleoptile untreated.	Allowed
II	Tip of coleoptile cut off.	Prevented
III	Opaque cap placed over coleoptile tip.	Prevented
IV	Coleoptile cut halfway through.	Allowed
V	Transparent cap placed over coleoptile tip.	Allowed
VI	Opaque sleeve placed over base of coleoptile.	Allowed

52. Comparison of treatments I and II shows which of the following?

(A) Growth is promoted by cutting off the tip.
(B) The tip is the site of sensing light.
(C) The tip is the site of auxin synthesis.
(D) The tip is necessary for the response to light.
(E) There is a range of response to a single treatment.

53. The fact that the effect of cutting off the tip (treatment II) is not simply due to wounding of the plant is demonstrated by comparison of which of the following treatments?

(A) IV and V
(B) I, II, and III
(C) I, II, and IV
(D) II, III, and IV
(E) IV, V, and VI

GO ON TO THE NEXT PAGE

54. Comparison of treatments III, V, and VI shows that

(A) the tip plays a role in sensing the light
(B) the base plays a role in sensing the light
(C) confinement of the tip inhibits the response to light
(D) confinement of the base facilitates the response to light
(E) confinement reverses the response to light

55. To test the hypothesis that the response to light involves differential cell elongation, an experimenter could

(A) measure the distance between marks made on the seedling after it has bent
(B) count the number of cells visible in a cross section of the coleoptile
(C) compare the length of cells on the sides of the stem toward and away from the light
(D) determine whether mitosis is affected by light
(E) repeat the experiment using light of a different wavelength

GO ON TO THE NEXT PAGE

Questions 56-60

During normal development of the sea urchin, the egg divides once to give two cells. Each of these cells divides again. The cells continue to divide and, eventually, a sea-urchin larva is formed. It is possible to separate the cells of a young sea-urchin embryo and allow them to develop independently. The results of several such experiments are shown below.

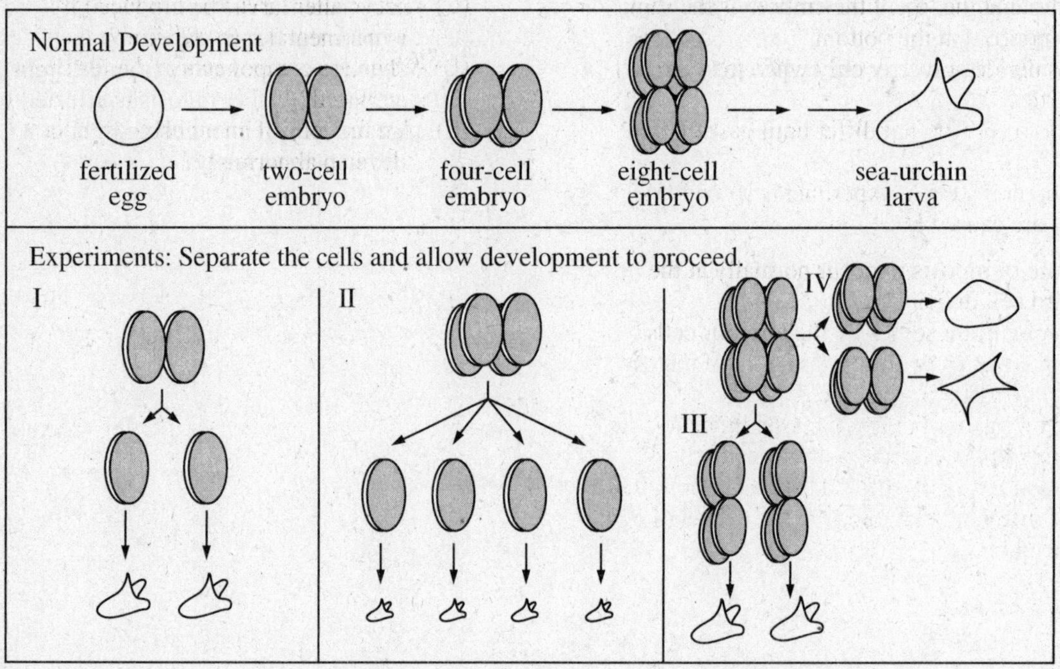

56. Experiment I suggests that

(A) sea urchins would be better adapted if they had smaller eggs
(B) embryo cells are committed to different developmental fates
(C) different cells of an embryo can have equal potential for development
(D) a particular cell of an embryo always develops into the same structure
(E) cell division ensures that both cells will develop identically

57. Experiments I and II suggest that

(A) sea-urchin embryos often grow to full-size adults
(B) larva size is determined by the amount of material in the embryo
(C) development must always occur the same way in every embryo
(D) embryo cells do not interact with each other
(E) natural selection favors the formation of small larvae

GO ON TO THE NEXT PAGE

58. Experiments III and IV together suggest that

(A) there is a difference between separating cells along the vertical axis and the horizontal axis of an eight-cell embryo
(B) embryo cells cannot be separated without damaging development
(C) material at the top of the embryo is the same as material at the bottom
(D) cells divide correctly only when they are vertical
(E) embryo cells do not differ until gastrulation

59. The different results in experiments III and IV probably are caused by

(A) failure of mitosis to occur normally at the third cell division
(B) loss of chromosomes by the top four cells
(C) fertilization of the top and bottom of the egg by two different sperm
(D) different genes being expressed in the top four cells than in the bottom four cells
(E) some genes in the left half of the embryo that are different from those in the right half of the embryo

60. Which of the following questions is NOT addressed by this series of experiments?

(A) When do the cells of an embryo become different from each other?
(B) Can cells of an embryo survive when separated from each other?
(C) Can smaller larvae be produced by experimental manipulation?
(D) When are components in the fertilized egg activated?
(E) Can the cells of an embryo be made to develop abnormally?

If you are taking the Biology-E test, continue with questions 61-80.
If you are taking the Biology-M test, go to question 81 now.

GO ON TO THE NEXT PAGE

BIOLOGY-E TEST

Directions: Each of the questions or incomplete statements below is followed by five suggested answers or completions. Some questions pertain to a set that refers to a laboratory or experimental situation. For each question, select the one choice that is the best answer to the question and then fill in the corresponding circle on the answer sheet.

61. Stream and river ecosystems differ from other aquatic ecosystems because streams and rivers

    (A) move continuously in one direction and have a nutrient content that is dependent on location
    (B) support a greater diversity of aquatic plants
    (C) have highly variable salinity
    (D) include the greatest biodiversity of all ecosystems because of the fluctuating water levels
    (E) support the largest stationary plankton communities

62. A trophic level within an ecosystem is best characterized by the

    (A) size of food eaten at that level
    (B) nutrient source of the organisms in each level
    (C) stages in ecological succession
    (D) habitats of the organisms within that level
    (E) elevation above sea level

63. According to most scientific theories of the origin of life, the first organisms were

    (A) eukaryotic
    (B) parasitic
    (C) symbiotic
    (D) anaerobic
    (E) pathogenic

64. The global cycles of nitrogen and phosphorus differ in that

    (A) nitrogen is recycled whereas phosphorus is not
    (B) animals get most of their nitrogen from the water they drink whereas they get their phosphorus from the food they eat
    (C) nitrogen occurs primarily in deep sediments whereas phosphorus occurs primarily in the atmosphere
    (D) nitrogen is lost to the oceans whereas phosphorus is not
    (E) nitrogen has a gaseous phase whereas phosphorus does not

GO ON TO THE NEXT PAGE

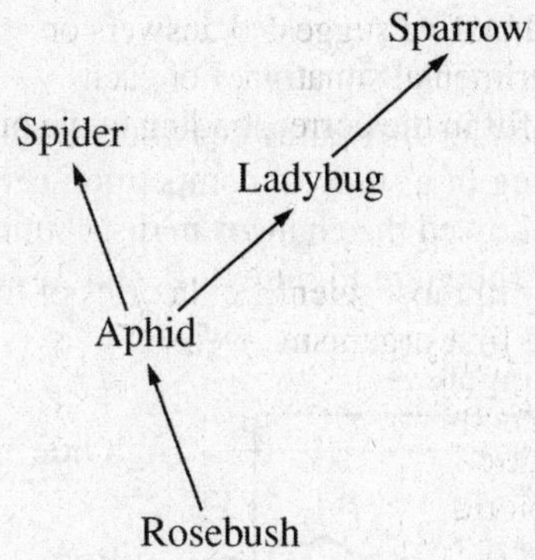

65. In the food web shown above, in which the arrows indicate the direction of energy flow, the ladybug is considered to be a

(A) herbivore
(B) primary consumer
(C) decomposer
(D) producer
(E) carnivore

66. A stream is free of pollutants within a few miles downstream of a point at which a small amount of sewage is being dumped into it. This is most likely the result of

(A) succession
(B) biological magnification
(C) evaporation
(D) photosynthesis
(E) decomposition

67. The term "adaptive radiation" refers to the

(A) ability of one species to adapt to only one niche
(B) ability of a species to adapt itself to rapidly changing conditions
(C) evolution from a single ancestral species into several species adapted to various environments
(D) ability of a species to adjust its temperature by radiating heat
(E) advantages of radial symmetry to a stationary species

68. Which of the following does NOT refer primarily to a relationship between members of different species?

(A) Mutualism
(B) Hibernation
(C) Parasitism
(D) Commensalism
(E) Predation

69. Plant seeds can be dispersed by which of the following?

I. Wind
II. Water
III. Birds

(A) I only
(B) III only
(C) I and II only
(D) I and III only
(E) I, II, and III

GO ON TO THE NEXT PAGE

Questions 70-72

Two types of barnacles, *Chthamalus* and *Balanus*, grow on rocks along the North Atlantic coastline. Both grow on rock surfaces exposed at low tide and covered at high tide. At the beginning of a study of competition between these barnacles, a researcher removed selected *Balanus* from a region and followed the changes in distribution of both species for 12 months. The distribution of *Chthamalus* and *Balanus* are shown in Figures 1, 2, and 3.

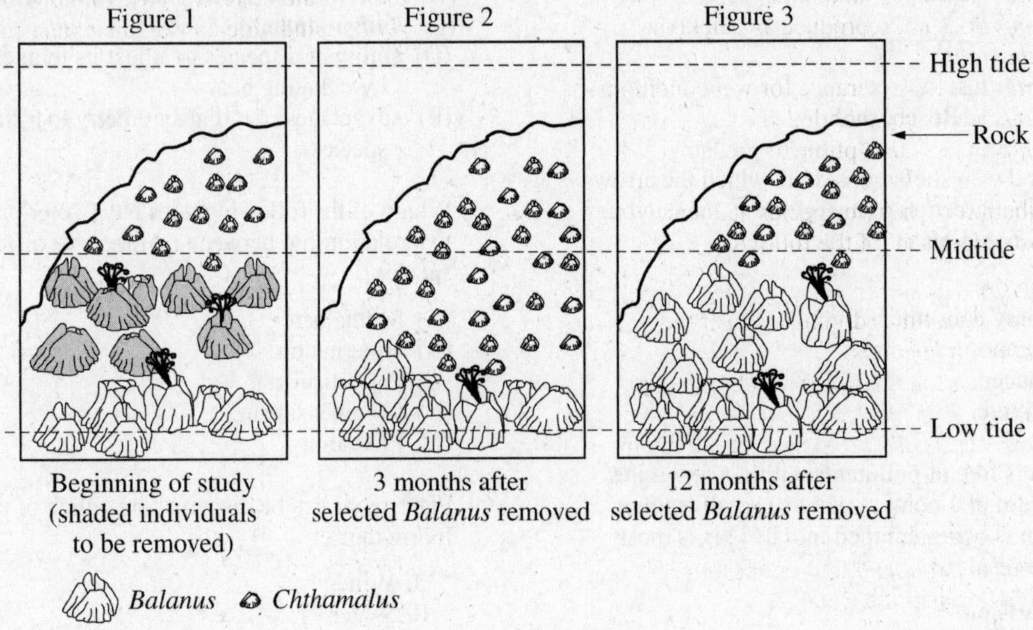

GO ON TO THE NEXT PAGE

70. Since both species of barnacles have free-swimming larvae that settle on hard surfaces, the change in the distribution of *Chthamalus* observed 3 months after removal of the larger *Balanus* individuals could best be explained by which of the following?

(A) *Balanus* feeds on *Chthamalus* larvae.
(B) *Balanus* does not reproduce as quickly as *Chthamalus*.
(C) *Balanus* has less tolerance for wet conditions.
(D) *Balanus* adults are mobile.
(E) *Balanus* is less susceptible to predators.

71. The distribution of the two species at 3 and 12 months suggests all of the following EXCEPT:

(A) *Balanus* sometimes dominates over the smaller *Chthamalus*.
(B) *Chthamalus* can tolerate more drying than *Balanus*.
(C) *Balanus* adults are swept away more often than *Chthamalus*.
(D) *Balanus* and *Chthamalus* larvae can settle in the same area.
(E) *Balanus* is larger and thus needs more feeding time in the water.

72. Based on this study, on rocks with tops below the midtide line, it can be predicted that

(A) more of the rock surface would be covered by *Chthamalus*
(B) the two barnacle populations would be equal
(C) there would be few, if any, *Balanus*
(D) there would be few, if any, *Chthamalus*
(E) *Balanus* individuals would become smaller

GO ON TO THE NEXT PAGE

Questions 73-75 refer to the following experiment in which an agar petri dish was prepared as shown below. Using aseptic techniques, an experimenter spread *E. coli* bacteria on the agar uniformly throughout the dish. The dish was then incubated at 37°C for 24 hours.

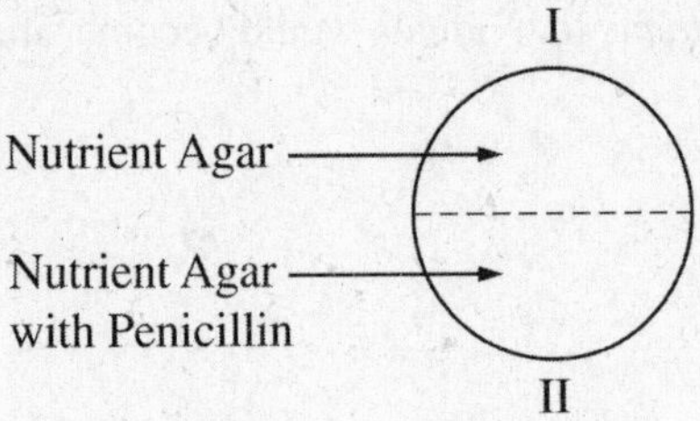

73. Which of the following distributions of bacterial colonies is most likely to be observed on completion of the experiment? (Dots represent bacterial colonies.)

(A)

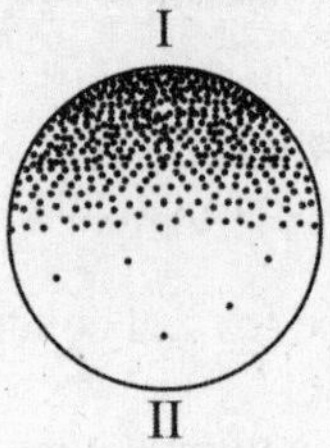

(B)

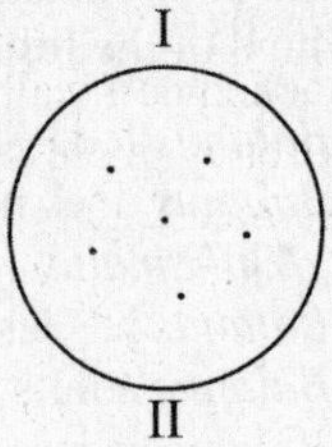

(C)

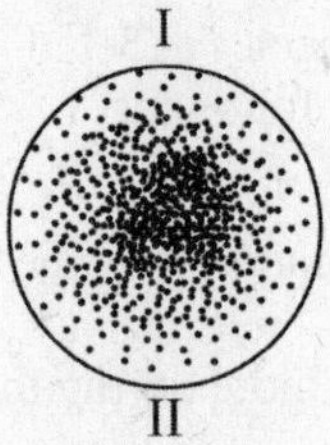

(D)

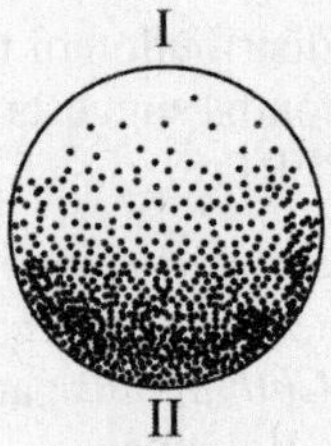

(E)

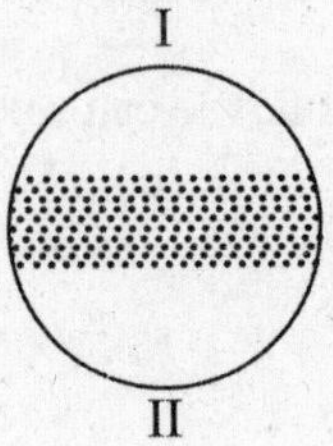

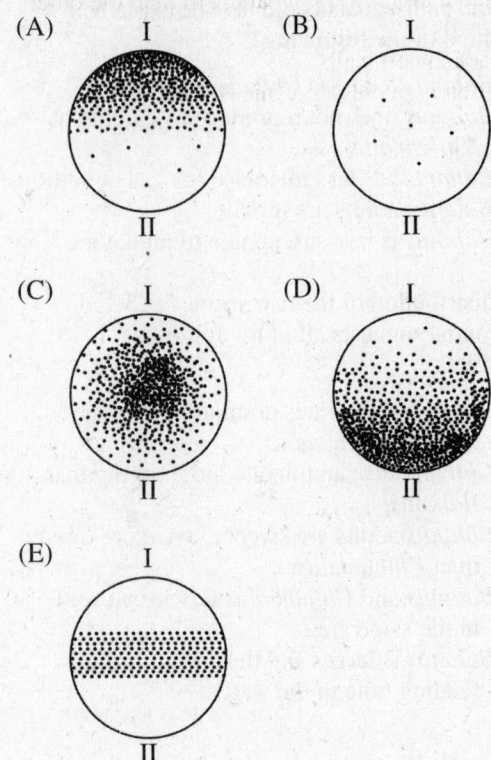

GO ON TO THE NEXT PAGE

74. The cells that survived exposure to penicillin were most likely able to do so because they

(A) mutated as a result of the exposure
(B) had a more rapid metabolism than the other cells
(C) lacked cell walls
(D) already possessed penicillin resistance
(E) formed spores

75. In the experiment, penicillin causes a stress that, in an ecosystem, would promote

(A) natural selection
(B) Lamarckian evolution
(C) competition
(D) mutation
(E) parasitism

GO ON TO THE NEXT PAGE

Questions 76-80

A scientist studied a field that had been burned in a brushfire ten years before. She identified seven different species and produced the table below.

Scientific Name	Gross Form	Microscopic Form	Stem Form	Color	Reproduction
Platismartia glauca	sheetlike	eukaryotic and prokaryotic filaments	not applicable	green on top white below	none evident
Funaria americana	cushionlike	eukaryotic multicellular	not applicable	green throughout	spore-producing structures on stalks
Dryopteris spinulosa	roots, under-ground stems, compound leaves	eukaryotic multicellular	fleshy	green leaves, white stem and roots	spores on underside of leaves
Picea rubens	roots, stems, needlelike leaves	eukaryotic multicellular	erect, woody	green leaves, brown stem and roots	cones
Smilax herbacea	roots, vine, broad leaves	eukaryotic multicellular	erect, herbaceous	green leaves and stem, white roots	flowers
Smilax rotundifolia	roots, woody vine, broad leaves	eukaryotic multicellular	erect	green leaves, brown stem and roots	none evident
Monotropa uniflora	roots, stems, broad leaves	eukaryotic multicellular	erect	white throughout	fruits

76. The organism that evolutionarily is most closely related to *Smilax herbacea* is

(A) *Platismatia glauca*
(B) *Dryopteris spinulosa*
(C) *Picea rubens*
(D) *Smilax rotundifolia*
(E) *Monotropa uniflora*

77. Symbiosis is best illustrated by which of the following organisms?

(A) *Platismatia glauca*
(B) *Dryopteris spinulosa*
(C) *Picea rubens*
(D) *Smilax herbacea*
(E) *Smilax rotundifolia*

GO ON TO THE NEXT PAGE

78. Which of the following shows the simplest level of physical organization?

(A) *Funaria americana*
(B) *Monotropa uniflora*
(C) *Dryopteris spinulosa*
(D) *Picea rubens*
(E) *Smilax rotundifolia*

79. Which of the following is most likely a flowering plant?

(A) *Platismatia glauca*
(B) *Funaria americana*
(C) *Dryopteris spinulosa*
(D) *Picea rubens*
(E) *Monotropa uniflora*

80. The appearance of these plants in the burned area is an example of what biological process?

(A) Evolution by natural selection
(B) Succession
(C) Mutation
(D) Eutrophication
(E) Recombination

STOP

IF YOU FINISH BEFORE TIME IS CALLED, YOU MAY CHECK YOUR WORK ON THE ENTIRE BIOLOGY-E TEST.

BIOLOGY-M SECTION

If you are taking the Biology-M test, continue with questions 81-100.
Be sure to start this section of the test by filling in circle 81 on your answer sheet.

Directions: Each of the questions or incomplete statements below is followed by five suggested answers or completions. Some questions pertain to a set that refers to a laboratory or experimental situation. For each question, select the one choice that is the best answer to the question and then fill in the corresponding circle on the answer sheet.

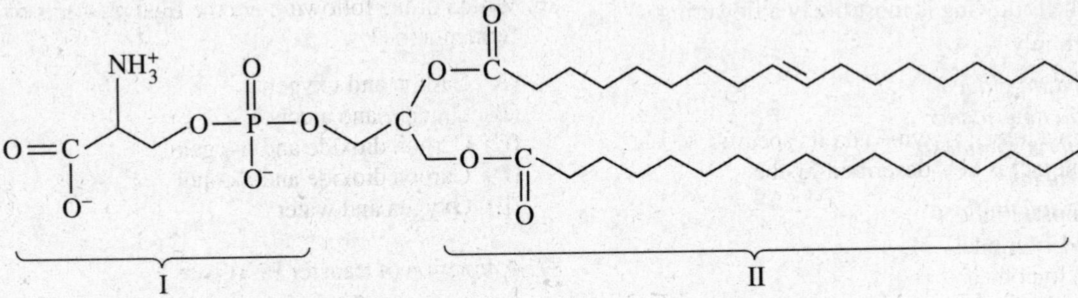

81. Which of the following is correct about the phospholipid shown above?

(A) Only I would be found in the middle of the lipid bilayer.
(B) Only II would be found in the middle of the lipid bilayer.
(C) Both I and II would be found in the middle of the lipid bilayer.
(D) II is hydrophilic.
(E) I and II are hydrophobic.

GO ON TO THE NEXT PAGE

82. Products of the light reactions of photosynthesis that later participate in the dark reactions of photosynthesis include which of the following?

I. Reduced NADP (NADPH)
II. ATP
III. O_2

(A) I only
(B) II only
(C) III only
(D) I and II only
(E) I, II, and III

83. The way in which an enzyme and its specific substrate interact is best described by the

(A) fluid-mosaic model
(B) induced-fit model
(C) Oparin hypothesis
(D) Lyon hypothesis
(E) competitive-exclusion principle

84. If a somatic cell in a diploid organism contains ten pairs of chromosomes, what is the total number of <u>chromatids</u> that are present in the cell after the DNA has replicated but before mitosis has taken place?

(A) 10
(B) 20
(C) 30
(D) 40
(E) 80

85. Which of the following atmospheric gases shows a net release during photosynthesis in plants?

(A) Carbon dioxide
(B) Oxygen
(C) Methane
(D) Hydrogen
(E) Nitrogen

86. Which of the following are the final products of fermentation?

(A) Carbon and oxygen
(B) Glucose and alcohol
(C) Carbon dioxide and oxygen
(D) Carbon dioxide and alcohol
(E) Oxygen and water

87. A function of transfer RNA is to

(A) receive the genetic information from nuclear DNA
(B) store the genetic information in the nucleus
(C) store RNA in the ribosomes
(D) transfer the genetic information from the nucleus to the cytoplasm
(E) position amino acids for protein synthesis by pairing with codons in messenger RNA

GO ON TO THE NEXT PAGE

88. Which of the following statements most accurately describes a basic difference between mitosis and meiosis?

(A) Homologous chromosomes form tetrads in mitosis but not in meiosis.
(B) Homologous chromosomes form tetrads in meiosis but not in mitosis.
(C) The nuclear membrane disappears in mitosis but not in meiosis.
(D) A spindle forms in mitosis but not in meiosis.
(E) A spindle forms in meiosis but not in mitosis.

89. The *Bt* protein produced in the bacterium, *Bacillus thuringiensis*, kills corn earworms that ingest the *Bacillus*. If the *Bt* gene were transferred to corn so that corn could express the *Bt* protein, which of the following would be expected to occur when corn earworms eat the corn?

I. Corn earworms that eat the *Bt* corn would be killed.
II. *Bacillus* bacteria that infect the *Bt* corn would be killed.
III. The corn earworms would incorporate the *Bt* gene into their chromosomes.

(A) I only
(B) II only
(C) III only
(D) I and III only
(E) II and III only

90. The wavelengths of light absorbed by chlorophyll are similar to the wavelengths of light that are associated with the greatest amount of oxygen release by plants. Based on these observations which of the following is a reasonable hypothesis about the function of chlorophyll?

(A) It plays a role in cell respiration.
(B) It plays a role in the light reactions of photosynthesis.
(C) It takes part in H_2O release.
(D) It takes part in CO_2 fixation.
(E) It generates energy.

91. Cellular respiration shares which of the following characteristics with the light-dependent reactions of photosynthesis?

(A) Production of ATP
(B) Production of AMP
(C) Production of GTP
(D) Production of oxygen
(E) Use of carbon dioxide in synthetic reactions

92. The position of a mutation in a gene and the location of an altered amino acid sequence in the corresponding protein are

(A) not related
(B) inversely related
(C) related in bacteria but not in mammals
(D) species-dependent
(E) in the same relative position

93. In order for an animal that was cloned from its mother to grow and develop normally, it must have received

(A) half of its mother's DNA sequences
(B) half of its father's RNA sequences
(C) all of its mother's RNA sequences
(D) all of its father's DNA sequences
(E) all of its mother's DNA sequences

GO ON TO THE NEXT PAGE

Questions 94-97

Bowls 1 and 7 — water only
Bowls 2 and 8 — water + 20 water plants
Bowls 3 and 9 — water + 40 water plants
Bowls 4 and 10 — water + 2 goldfish
Bowls 5 and 11 — water + 4 goldfish
Bowls 6 and 12 — water + 20 water plants + 2 goldfish

A biologist set up 12 bowls as described above. She exposed bowls 1 to 6 to light for 24 hours and placed bowls 7 to 12 in the dark for 24 hours. She determined the CO_2 content of the water in micromoles per liter for each bowl at the end of the 24 hours. The results are indicated below.

Experimental Results

Light		Dark	
Bowl #	$[CO_2]$	Bowl #	$[CO_2]$
1	10.0	7	10.2
2	4.3	8	13.7
3	2.1	9	16.9
4	14.9	10	14.1
5	18.3	11	17.9
6	10.2	12	19.2

94. The process responsible for the relatively low concentrations of CO_2 in bowls 2 and 3 is

(A) respiration
(B) fermentation
(C) photosynthesis
(D) photoperiodism
(E) transpiration

95. The main controls for bowl 4 are

(A) 1 and 3
(B) 1 and 6
(C) 1 and 10
(D) 2 and 5
(E) 2 and 8

96. The difference in CO_2 concentrations for bowls 2 and 6 can best be explained by

(A) photosynthesis carried out by water plants
(B) respiration carried out by water plants
(C) respiration carried out by goldfish
(D) competition between water plants and goldfish
(E) experimental error

97. Which of the following is the best explanation for the fact that the CO_2 concentration of bowl 4 is almost the same as that of bowl 10 and the CO_2 concentration of bowl 5 is almost the same as that of bowl 11 ?

(A) Photosynthesis does not occur in the light.
(B) Photosynthesis does not occur in the dark.
(C) Respiration and photosynthesis occur at the same rate in the light.
(D) Respiration is not affected by either light or dark.
(E) Goldfish are more active in the absence than in the presence of plants.

GO ON TO THE NEXT PAGE

Questions 98-100 refer to the following experimental procedure.

A protein is purified from a frog embryo. The protein sample is divided into five fractions. One fraction is not treated. The other fractions are partially digested by using enzymes that act on specific amino acid sequences. In every case, the digestions are carried out at the appropriate temperature and pH. The samples are then separated by electrophoresis as shown below.

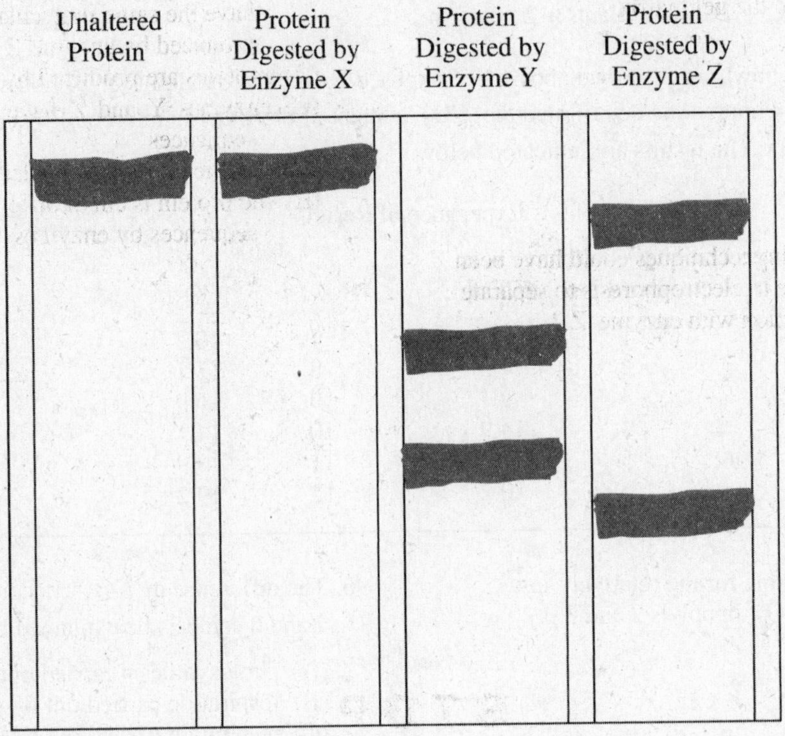

GO ON TO THE NEXT PAGE

98. In the electrophoresis experiment described, the distance moved by a fragment within the electric field is influenced by which of the following?

    I. The number of amino acids in the fragment
    II. The amount of electric current used in the apparatus
    III. The porosity of the gel matrix

    (A) I only
    (B) II only
    (C) I and II only
    (D) II and III only
    (E) I, II, and III

99. Which of the following techniques could have been used as an alternative to electrophoresis to separate the products of digestion with enzyme Z ?

    I. Translation
    II. Chromatography
    III. Serial dilution

    (A) I only
    (B) II only
    (C) III only
    (D) II and III only
    (E) I, II, and III

100. Of the two fragments resulting from the digestion of the protein with enzyme Z, one is larger and the other is smaller than either of the fragments resulting from the digestion with enzyme Y. The most logical explanation for this is that

    (A) the protein fragments produced by enzyme Y have the same molecular weights as those produced by enzyme Z
    (B) proteins are produced by ribosomes
    (C) enzymes Y and Z have different amino acid sequences
    (D) electric current is divided into discrete units
    (E) the protein is cut at different amino acid sequences by enzymes Y and Z

STOP

IF YOU FINISH BEFORE TIME IS CALLED, YOU MAY CHECK YOUR WORK ON THE ENTIRE BIOLOGY-M TEST.

How to Score the SAT Subject Test in Ecological Biology

When you take an actual SAT Subject Test in Ecological Biology, your answer sheet will be "read" by a scanning machine that will record your response to each question. Then a computer will compare your answers with the correct answers and produce your raw score. You get one point for each correct answer. For each wrong answer, you lose one-fourth of a point. Questions you omit (and any for which you mark more than one answer) are not counted. This raw score is converted to a scaled score that is reported to you and to the colleges you specify.

Worksheet 1. Finding Your Raw Test Score

STEP 1: Table A on the following page lists the correct answers for all the questions on the Subject Test in Ecological Biology that is reproduced in this book. It also serves as a worksheet for you to calculate your raw score.

- Compare your answers with those given in the table.
- Put a check in the column marked "Right" if your answer is correct.
- Put a check in the column marked "Wrong" if your answer is incorrect.
- Leave both columns blank if you omitted the question.

STEP 2: Count the number of right answers.

Enter the total here: ________________

STEP 3: Count the number of wrong answers.

Enter the total here: ________________

STEP 4: Multiply the number of wrong answers by .250.

Enter the product here: ________________

STEP 5: Subtract the result obtained in Step 4 from the total you obtained in Step 2.

Enter the result here: ________________

STEP 6: Round the number obtained in Step 5 to the nearest whole number.

Enter the result here: ________________

The number you obtained in Step 6 is your raw score.

Table A

Answers to the Subject Test in Ecological Biology and Percentage of Students Answering Each Question Correctly

Question Number	Correct Answer	Right	Wrong	Percentage of Students Answering the Question Correctly*	Question Number	Correct Answer	Right	Wrong	Percentage of Students Answering the Question Correctly*
1	A			45	33	A			75
2	B			48	34	E			53
3	C			32	35	A			47
4	D			37	36	E			65
5	D			79	37	D			78
6	B			45	38	B			89
7	B			68	39	B			64
8	C			72	40	E			80
9	A			68	41	A			37
10	D			55	42	E			80
11	D			64	43	C			34
12	E			74	44	D			69
13	A			78	45	C			80
14	A			57	46	E			54
15	B			54	47	A			78
16	D			44	48	D			69
17	C			49	49	B			83
18	C			47	50	D			77
19	C			76	51	E			78
20	D			54	52	D			59
21	D			85	53	C			32
22	D			78	54	A			77
23	C			60	55	C			60
24	E			70	56	C			47
25	A			76	57	B			58
26	A			60	58	A			72
27	D			76	59	D			55
28	E			73	60	D			59
29	B			71	61	A			85
30	C			44	62	B			57
31	A			55	63	D			63
32	C			64	64	E			46

Table A continued on next page

Table A continued from previous page

Question Number	Correct Answer	Right	Wrong	Percentage of Students Answering the Question Correctly*	Question Number	Correct Answer	Right	Wrong	Percentage of Students Answering the Question Correctly*
65	E			61	73	A			83
66	E			67	74	D			71
67	C			47	75	A			56
68	B			83	76	D			73
69	E			77	77	A			32
70	B			65	78	A			75
71	C			44	79	E			80
72	D			67	80	B			68

* These percentages are based on an analysis of the answer sheets of a representative sample of 3,130 students who took the original administration of this test and whose mean score was 601. They may be used as an indication of the relative difficulty of a particular question.

Answer explanations for the Subject Test in Ecological Biology can be found on page 350.

Finding Your Scaled Score

When you take SAT Subject Tests, the scores sent to the colleges you specify are reported on the College Board scale, which ranges from 200–800. You can convert your practice test score to a scaled score by using Table B. To find your scaled score, locate your raw score in the left-hand column of Table B; the corresponding score in the right-hand column is your scaled score. For example, a raw score of 21 on this particular edition of the Subject Test in Ecological Biology corresponds to a scaled score of 450.

Raw scores are converted to scaled scores to ensure that a score earned on any one edition of a particular Subject Test is comparable to the same scaled score earned on any other edition of the same Subject Test. Because some editions of the tests may be slightly easier or more difficult than others, College Board scaled scores are adjusted so that they indicate the same level of performance regardless of the edition of the test taken and the ability of the group that takes it. Thus, for example, a score of 400 on one edition of a test taken at a particular administration indicates the same level of achievement as a score of 400 on a different edition of the test taken at a different administration.

When you take the SAT Subject Tests during a national administration, your scores are likely to differ somewhat from the scores you obtain on the tests in this book. People perform at different levels at different times for reasons unrelated to the tests themselves. The precision of any test is also limited because it represents only a sample of all the possible questions that could be asked.

Table B

Scaled Score Conversion Table
Subject Test in Ecological Biology

Raw Score	Scaled Score	Raw Score	Scaled Score	Raw Score	Scaled Score
80	800	46	610	12	390
79	800	45	610	11	380
78	800	44	600	10	370
77	800	43	600	9	370
76	790	42	590	8	360
75	780	41	590	7	350
74	780	40	580	6	350
73	770	39	570	5	340
72	770	38	570	4	340
71	760	37	560	3	330
70	750	36	560	2	330
69	750	35	550	1	320
68	740	34	540	0	320
67	730	33	540	-1	310
66	730	32	530	-2	310
65	720	31	520	-3	300
64	720	30	520	-4	300
63	710	29	510	-5	290
62	710	28	500	-6	290
61	700	27	500	-7	280
60	690	26	490	-8	280
59	690	25	480	-9	270
58	680	24	480	-10	270
57	680	23	470	-11	270
56	670	22	460	-12	260
55	670	21	450	-13	260
54	660	20	450	-14	260
53	650	19	440	-15	250
52	650	18	430	-16	250
51	640	17	420	-17	240
50	640	16	420	-18	240
49	630	15	410	-19	230
48	630	14	400	-20	220
47	620	13	400		

How Did You Do on the Subject Test in Ecological Biology?

After you score your test and analyze your performance, think about the following questions:

Did you run out of time before reaching the end of the test?

If so, you may need to pace yourself better. For example, maybe you spent too much time on one or two hard questions. A better approach might be to skip the ones you can't answer right away and try answering all the questions that remain on the test. Then if there's time, go back to the questions you skipped.

Did you take a long time reading the directions?

You will save time when you take the test by learning the directions to the Subject Test in Ecological Biology ahead of time. Each minute you spend reading directions during the test is a minute that you could use to answer questions.

How did you handle questions you were unsure of?

If you were able to eliminate one or more of the answer choices as wrong and guess from the remaining ones, your approach probably worked to your advantage. On the other hand, making haphazard guesses or omitting questions without trying to eliminate choices could cost you valuable points.

How difficult were the questions for you compared with other students who took the test?

Table A shows you how difficult the multiple-choice questions were for the group of students who took this test during its national administration. The right-hand column gives the percentage of students that answered each question correctly.

A question answered correctly by almost everyone in the group is obviously an easier question. For example, 85 percent of the students answered question 21 correctly. But only 32 percent answered question 77 correctly.

Keep in mind that these percentages are based on just one group of students. They would probably be different with another group of students taking the test.

If you missed several easier questions, go back and try to find out why: Did the questions cover material you haven't yet reviewed? Did you misunderstand the directions?

How to Score the SAT Subject Test in Molecular Biology

When you take an actual SAT Subject Test in Molecular Biology, your answer sheet will be "read" by a scanning machine that will record your response to each question. Then a computer will compare your answers with the correct answers and produce your raw score. You get one point for each correct answer. For each wrong answer, you lose one-fourth of a point. Questions you omit (and any for which you mark more than one answer) are not counted. This raw score is converted to a scaled score that is reported to you and to the colleges you specify.

Worksheet 1. Finding Your Raw Test Score

STEP 1: Table A on the following page lists the correct answers for all the questions on the Subject Test in Molecular Biology that is reproduced in this book. It also serves as a worksheet for you to calculate your raw score.

- Compare your answers with those given in the table.
- Put a check in the column marked "Right" if your answer is correct.
- Put a check in the column marked "Wrong" if your answer is incorrect.
- Leave both columns blank if you omitted the question.

STEP 2: Count the number of right answers.

Enter the total here: ________________

STEP 3: Count the number of wrong answers.

Enter the total here: ________________

STEP 4: Multiply the number of wrong answers by .250.

Enter the product here: ________________

STEP 5: Subtract the result obtained in Step 4 from the total you obtained in Step 2.

Enter the result here: ________________

STEP 6: Round the number obtained in Step 5 to the nearest whole number.

Enter the result here: ________________

The number you obtained in Step 6 is your raw score.

Table A

Answers to the Subject Test in Molecular Biology and Percentage of Students Answering Each Question Correctly									
Question Number	Correct Answer	Right	Wrong	Percentage of Students Answering the Question Correctly*	Question Number	Correct Answer	Right	Wrong	Percentage of Students Answering the Question Correctly*
1	A			51	33	A			84
2	B			55	34	E			57
3	C			37	35	A			54
4	D			47	36	E			80
5	D			87	37	D			84
6	B			54	38	B			91
7	B			75	39	B			73
8	C			76	40	E			85
9	A			74	41	A			55
10	D			63	42	E			81
11	D			73	43	C			39
12	E			84	44	D			80
13	A			84	45	C			87
14	A			73	46	E			57
15	B			62	47	A			82
16	D			49	48	D			72
17	C			58	49	B			86
18	C			66	50	D			78
19	C			85	51	E			81
20	D			61	52	D			64
21	D			92	53	C			35
22	D			78	54	A			79
23	C			68	55	C			68
24	E			71	56	C			54
25	A			78	57	B			62
26	A			67	58	A			78
27	D			85	59	D			62
28	E			73	60	D			62
29	B			81	81	B			53
30	C			52	82	D			52
31	A			64	83	B			77
32	C			71	84	D			48

Table A continued on next page

Table A continued from previous page

Question Number	Correct Answer	Right	Wrong	Percentage of Students Answering the Question Correctly*	Question Number	Correct Answer	Right	Wrong	Percentage of Students Answering the Question Correctly*
85	B			86	93	E			79
86	D			65	94	C			82
87	E			69	95	C			64
88	B			67	96	C			79
89	A			67	97	D			86
90	B			77	98	E			43
91	A			77	99	B			35
92	E			60	100	E			76

* These percentages are based on an analysis of the answer sheets of a representative sample of 3,964 students who took the original administration of this test and whose mean score was 640. They may be used as an indication of the relative difficulty of a particular question.

Answer explanations for the Subject Test in Molecular Biology can be found on page 350.

Finding Your Scaled Score

When you take SAT Subject Tests, the scores sent to the colleges you specify are reported on the College Board scale, which ranges from 200–800. You can convert your practice test score to a scaled score by using Table B. To find your scaled score, locate your raw score in the left-hand column of Table B; the corresponding score in the right-hand column is your scaled score. For example, a raw score of 21 on this particular edition of the Subject Test in Molecular Biology corresponds to a scaled score of 470.

Raw scores are converted to scaled scores to ensure that a score earned on any one edition of a particular Subject Test is comparable to the same scaled score earned on any other edition of the same Subject Test. Because some editions of the tests may be slightly easier or more difficult than others, College Board scaled scores are adjusted so that they indicate the same level of performance regardless of the edition of the test taken and the ability of the group that takes it. Thus, for example, a score of 400 on one edition of a test taken at a particular administration indicates the same level of achievement as a score of 400 on a different edition of the test taken at a different administration.

When you take the SAT Subject Tests during a national administration, your scores are likely to differ somewhat from the scores you obtain on the tests in this book. People perform at different levels at different times for reasons unrelated to the tests themselves. The precision of any test is also limited because it represents only a sample of all the possible questions that could be asked.

Table B

Scaled Score Conversion Table Subject Test in Molecular Biology					
Raw Score	Scaled Score	Raw Score	Scaled Score	Raw Score	Scaled Score
80	800	46	620	12	400
79	800	45	620	11	390
78	800	44	610	10	390
77	800	43	610	9	380
76	790	42	600	8	370
75	790	41	590	7	370
74	780	40	590	6	360
73	780	39	580	5	350
72	770	38	580	4	350
71	760	37	570	3	340
70	760	36	560	2	340
69	750	35	560	1	330
68	750	34	550	0	330
67	740	33	550	-1	320
66	730	32	540	-2	320
65	730	31	530	-3	310
64	720	30	530	-4	310
63	720	29	520	-5	300
62	710	28	510	-6	300
61	710	27	510	-7	290
60	700	26	500	-8	290
59	690	25	490	-9	280
58	690	24	490	-10	280
57	680	23	480	-11	280
56	680	22	470	-12	270
55	670	21	470	-13	270
54	670	20	460	-14	270
53	660	19	450	-15	260
52	650	18	440	-16	260
51	650	17	440	-17	250
50	640	16	430	-18	250
49	640	15	420	-19	240
48	630	14	420	-20	240
47	630	13	410		

How Did You Do on the Subject Test in Molecular Biology?

After you score your test and analyze your performance, think about the following questions:

Did you run out of time before reaching the end of the test?

If so, you may need to pace yourself better. For example, maybe you spent too much time on one or two hard questions. A better approach might be to skip the ones you can't answer right away and try answering all the questions that remain on the test. Then if there's time, go back to the questions you skipped.

Did you take a long time reading the directions?

You will save time when you take the test by learning the directions to the Subject Test in Molecular Biology ahead of time. Each minute you spend reading directions during the test is a minute that you could use to answer questions.

How did you handle questions you were unsure of?

If you were able to eliminate one or more of the answer choices as wrong and guess from the remaining ones, your approach probably worked to your advantage. On the other hand, making haphazard guesses or omitting questions without trying to eliminate choices could cost you valuable points.

How difficult were the questions for you compared with other students who took the test?

Table A shows you how difficult the multiple-choice questions were for the group of students who took this test during its national administration. The right-hand column gives the percentage of students that answered each question correctly.

A question answered correctly by almost everyone in the group is obviously an easier question. For example, 87 percent of the students answered question 5 correctly. But only 35 percent answered question 53 correctly.

Keep in mind that these percentages are based on just one group of students. They would probably be different with another group of students taking the test.

If you missed several easier questions, go back and try to find out why: Did the questions cover material you haven't yet reviewed? Did you misunderstand the directions?

Answer Explanations for the Biology Subject Test (Both Ecological and Molecular)

1. Choice (A) is the correct answer. Since water transport is driven by the passive process of transpiration, no transport activity from the cell is required. Tracheids and vessel elements are the water-conducting cells of the xylem and die upon maturity. Trachieds are long, tapered cells with perforated walls and are composed of the hard substance lignin. Vessel elements have the same function but contain a cylindrical shape.

2. Choice (B) is the correct answer. When sunlight and low concentrations of carbon dioxide are available, the guard cells will take up potassium, causing water to enter the cells by osmosis. This results in the cells becoming turgid and opening the stoma, allowing the passage of gases and transpiration of water.

3. Choice (C) is the correct answer. Parenchyma cells are alive at maturity and are the most abundant type of plant tissue. These cells store sugars and starches in stems and roots and also perform photosynthesis and cellular respiration.

4. Choice (D) is the correct answer. Sieve-tube members and companion cells form a network of vessels that functions to transport glucose throughout the plant. The sieve-tube members of these living cells are composed of thin-walled tubes into which the glucose is loaded by the companion cells.

5. Choice (D) is the correct answer. This question requires knowledge of Mendelian genetics. Individuals who are heterozygous for a particular trait have both the dominant and the recessive allele for that trait. According to Mendel's Law of Segregation, each allele will separate and enter a separate gamete during meiosis. Upon fertilization, these alleles will combine randomly to form either a homozygous dominant (both dominant alleles), a homozygous recessive (both recessive alleles), or a heterozygous individual. The predicted genotype ratios resulting from a heterozygous cross are 1/4 homozygous dominant (or 25 percent), 2/4 heterozygous (or 50 percent), and 1/4 homozygous recessive (or 25 percent). An individual with both recessive alleles will express the phenotype for the recessive trait. Since this question asks you to predict the recessive phenotype from a heterozygous cross, the correct answer is 25 percent.

6. Choice (B) is the correct answer. This question requires the application of knowledge of Mendel's Law of Independent Assortment using the example of a dihybrid cross. Each individual is heterozygous for two traits, and each trait consists of either dominant or recessive alleles. During meiosis, each gamete will receive an independent combination of each allele. Therefore, each trait will be expressed separately. This indicates that the gametes can contain one of four possible genotype combinations: AB, Ab, aB, and ab. Since there are two alleles for trait A and two alleles for trait B and each follows simple rules of inheritance, there will be 4 possible phenotypical outcomes.

7. Choice (B) is the correct answer. This question asks which of the five kingdoms contain single-celled organisms of some complexity. Protozoans have animal characteristics, whereas algae are very similar to plants; this demonstrates the spectrum of diversity of the organisms within this kingdom. The kingdom Protista contains organisms with complex, specialized structures.

8. Choice (C) is the correct answer. This question involves the characteristics of the fungi. These organisms are large (with the exception of yeast) and are therefore multicellular. They have no chlorophyll, which indicates that they are heterotrophic and feed by absorption of organic matter. They are capable of reproducing sexually or asexually by forming spores.

9. Choice (A) is the correct answer. This question involves the distinction between prokaryotic and eukaryotic cell types. The kingdom Monera contains the oldest life forms on Earth, the bacteria, which have a simple prokaryotic cellular design. They contain DNA, which is not enclosed in a membrane and does not have other membrane-bound organelles such as mitochondria or chloroplasts. These organelles are found in eukaryotic cell types.

10. Choice (D) is the correct answer. Plants contain complex structures such as leaves, roots, and vascular systems, which indicates that they are complex, multicellular organisms. They contain chlorophyll within chloroplasts and are capable of manufacturing their own nutrients. These are all characteristics of organisms belonging to the kingdom Plantae.

11. Choice (D) is the correct answer. This question requires knowledge of both the processes of protein synthesis and where each process occurs within the cell. The diagram shows a ribbonlike structure seated within a round ribosome from which a "strand of beads" is emerging. These structures are located within the cytoplasm of the cell, where translation occurs. Part of the ribbon is also located within the

nucleus. This indicates that the ribbon must represent mRNA, since only mRNA can cross the nuclear membrane.

12. Choice (E) is the correct answer. In the diagram, the polypeptide is represented by a "strand of beads" and is seen emerging from the area where the gray ribosome meets the mRNA. This is the site where tRNA matches the anticodon to the correct codon of the mRNA information and assembles the amino acids in the proper sequence. As the mRNA is read, more amino acids are assembled, and these produce the polypeptide chain. This is the process of translation, and it occurs in the cytoplasm.

13. Choice (A) is the correct answer. The arrow for choice (A) indicates the structure surrounding the DNA and therefore must indicate the nuclear membrane. Several types of large proteins are contained within the nucleus, such as histones around which chromatin DNA is wound. Smaller molecules, such as mRNA, can leave the nucleus through pores in the membrane. This membrane also keeps the process of transcription within the nucleus.

14. Choice (A) is the correct answer. The membrane indicated by the arrow for choice (A) is surrounding the nucleus and consists of a lipid bilayer similar to that of the plasma membrane. This bilayer forms an extension that becomes the rough endoplasmic reticulum in which ribosomes are embedded. This is the area in which translation will begin.

15. Choice (B) is the correct answer. The question requires knowledge of the endocrine system and the hormones it secretes. The pituitary gland, located at the base of the brain, contains an anterior and a posterior lobe. The anterior lobe produces growth hormone as well as thyroid-stimulating hormone, adrenocorticotropic hormone, prolactin, follicle-stimulating hormone, leutinizing hormone, and melanocyte-stimulating hormone. Growth hormone targets organs and tissues to stimulate effects related to growth.

16. Choice (D) is the correct answer. Thyroxine is produced by the thyroid gland and released upon stimulus from the pituitary gland. It targets cells and causes them to increase cellular respiration, which results in increasing metabolic rate.

17. Choice (C) is the correct answer. Progesterone is produced by a structure that forms within an ovarian follicle after it releases a mature egg. This structure, called the corpus luteum, will continue to produce progesterone, which targets the lining of the uterus. The lining becomes thicker and more vascularized, preparing for implantation

by a fertilized egg. If there is no pregnancy, the corpus luteum disintegrates, the production of progesterone stops, and the lining of the uterus sheds, producing a menstrual flow.

18. Choice (C) is the correct answer. This question requires knowledge of cellular processes. Ribosomes are important for translation during protein synthesis. DNA replication occurs in the nucleus and requires specific enzymes; transcription occurs in the nucleus and requires only mRNA; and repression and translocation refer to genetic interactions occurring within the DNA itself.

19. Choice (C) is the correct answer. Although this couple has three children, each time the couple has a child it is considered a genetically separate event. In any pregnancy, the probability that the child will be a girl is ½, or 50 percent. Therefore, there is a 50 percent probability that the child will be a girl.

20. Choice (D) is the correct answer. A fertilized egg undergoes rapid mitotic divisions until a fluid-filled ball (blastula) is formed and the process of cell movement and cell differentiation (gastrulation) begins. During mitosis, mitotic spindles form two poles to guide the replicated chromosomes to opposite directions of the cell, preparing the cell for division into two daughter cells with the same number of chromosomes. If three poles are formed, chromosomes will be directed toward three positions within the cell. The resulting daughter cells would not have the same number of chromosomes.

21. Choice (D) is the correct answer. This question requires knowledge of cell structure. A chloroplast is a double-membraned structure that is located within plant cells and contains chlorophyll. Chlorophyll is a photosynthetic pigment that captures solar energy to convert CO_2 and H_2O into glucose and O_2. In plants, glucose is stored in large carbohydrate chains that form starch.

22. Choice (D) is the correct answer. The hip joint is a ball-and-socket joint. The round head of the femur is situated within a deep depression located within the hip. This arrangement allows for movement in three planes as well as rotation.

23. Choice (C) is the correct answer. This question requires knowledge of the principles of osmosis. Osmosis is the process of water diffusion across a cell membrane. The direction of water movement is determined by the difference in water concentration on each side of the membrane, and water will flow along its concentration gradient. There is very little water in a high solute concentration. If a cell is surrounded by a

high solute concentration such as NaCl, water will move across the cell membrane into the area where there is less water—in this case, into the saturated NaCl solution. The cells are hypotonic to the solution, and therefore lose water.

24. Choice (E) is the correct answer. The worldwide human population is increasing exponentially. An arithmetic increase would indicate an increase by the addition of a constant amount. However, human populations double whenever they have offspring. Each offspring in turn has children, and this doubles the population again in exponential form.

25. Choice (A) is the correct answer. Photosynthetic organisms are autotrophic and produce the source of energy required to sustain an ecosystem. In the open ocean, phytoplankton are the producers. They are small, photosynthetic protists that float on the surface of the water and provide the initial energy source that will be transferred directly or indirectly to the other organisms within the food web.

26. Choice (A) is the correct answer. Nitrogen fixation is the initial step in the conversion of nitrogen into nitrates and nitrites, which are absorbed by plant roots. This process converts nitrogen gas into a form that can be passed along and utilized by organisms. This conversion process is initiated by nitrogen-fixing bacteria, which are located deep within soil and within root nodules of plants such as clover, peanuts, and soybeans. This step is significant because it begins the process of converting free nitrogen into the chemical form ammonia, which can then be converted into nitrates and nitrites, which can be absorbed by plants and passed on to other organisms.

27. Choice (D) is the correct answer. A cross between two heterozygous individuals will produce a genotype ratio of 1:2:1. There is a probability that ¼ of the offspring will be homozygous dominant, ²⁄₄ will be heterozygous, and ¼ will be homozygous recessive. Since both homozygous dominant and heterozygous individuals will express the dominant phenotype for normal wings, the phenotypic ratio will be 3:1. Because 76 and 23 are close to this ratio, choices (A) and (C) are ruled out. Choices (B) and (E) will produce only offspring expressing the dominant phenotype.

28. Choice (E) is the correct answer. All of these factors will reduce the population of a species either directly (use of insecticides and habitat destruction) or indirectly over a longer period of time (hunting of the species' prey).

29. Choice (B) is the correct answer. The organism has an X and a Y chromosome, which indicates that the organism is a male; if the mammal were female, both chromosomes

would be X. Since a karyotype contains an individual's chromosome pairs only, we cannot determine any information about alleles or single-gene defects. And it is clear that the mammal is not a human, since the karyotype only contains four chromosome pairs.

30. Choice (C) is the correct answer. This question requires knowledge of the characteristics of each of the five kingdoms. The organism belongs to the kingdom Fungi. Since the organism is heterotrophic, we can eliminate autotrophic plants (D). The organism is multicellular, which eliminates Monera (A) and Protista (B). And animals (E) do not have cells surrounded by cell walls.

31. Choice (A) is the correct answer. Darwin's evolution theory states that in order for natural selection to occur, traits must be heritable, or capable of being passed to offspring. Choice (B) is incorrect because mutation occurs randomly. Crossing-over only occurs during the process of meiosis, so choice (C) is incorrect. Translocation is a repositioning of segments of DNA and has no effect on DNA replication, so choice (D) is incorrect. And choice (E) is incorrect because cellular differentiation occurs during zygote development.

32. Choice (C) is the correct answer. Innate behavior is most likely to remain unaffected by environmental changes. Choices (B), (D), and (E) are behaviors that are acquired from imitation of other individuals within their species; choice (A) is a behavior that occurs during sexual maturity and is mostly modulated by production of hormones.

33. Choice (A) is the correct answer. Hemophilia is a recessive trait that can only be present on the X chromosome; therefore, males who inherit this X chromosome will always express this recessive trait. Since women inherit two X chromosomes, it is possible for them to carry one recessive allele for hemophilia. The mother is a carrier for hemophilia. Choice (B) is incorrect because this inheritance pattern is inconsistent with that of a sex-linked trait. Crossing-over has no effect on this inheritance pattern, since one chromosome will still contain the hemophilia allele, so choice (C) can be ruled out. And choices (D) and (E) can be eliminated because the mother has one normal allele, so there is a 50 percent chance that her other sons and daughters will *not* inherit the allele for hemophilia.

34. Choice (E) is the correct answer. Population growth rate depends on the number of females of reproductive age (A), the death rate of the individuals within the population (B), the number of individuals surviving into adulthood (C), and the number of people within each age group (D). Habitat is not a useful measure in describing a population's growth rate.

35. Choice (A) is the correct answer. Through the evidence provided by similarities in structure and the time period in which the fossils were discovered, we know that bony fish were the oldest of the vertebrates. They were the first and oldest vertebrate fossils to be discovered, followed by fossils of amphibians. Choices (B), (C), (D), and (E) are all consistent with the fossil record: mammal and bird fossils appeared more recently than reptile fossils, reptile fossils were found later than amphibian fossils, and jawless fish fossils appeared prior to those of cartilaginous fish.

36. Choice (E) is the correct answer. Enzymes are not assembled from vitamin subunits. They are proteins that are specialized to facilitate reactions by binding to substrates to form products, so choice (B) is incorrect. Choices (A) and (C) can be eliminated because protein tertiary structure is affected by drastic changes in temperature and pH; these changes break the bonds that keep the enzyme in its specific conformation. And choice (D) is incorrect because enzymes often become more effective when bound to cofactors (which include metal ions) or other coenzymes (organic molecules including vitamins).

37. Choice (D) is the correct answer. Only sons inherit a Y chromosome, so the gene for a particular trait passed only from father to son is most likely Y-linked. Autosomal traits are not carried on the sex chromosomes and may appear in either sex, so choices (A) and (B) can be eliminated. Codominance is an inheritance pattern observed in both males and females in which both alleles are expressed, so choice (C) is incorrect. And choice (E) is incorrect because if this were a sex-linked trait appearing on the X chromosome, it would be possible for the trait to be passed on to the daughters.

38. Choice (B) is the correct answer. This question requires the ability to interpret a phylogenetic diagram. The y-axis represents epochs, with the oldest starting at the zero point. As the y-axis increases, the time periods become more recent. Equus is located at the uppermost branch of the tree, indicating that this species evolved most recently and is extant. *Hyracotherium* is the oldest species, since it is located near the x-axis. *Hyracotherium*, *Epihippus*, *Hippidion*, and *Nannippus* are all extinct; these species are located at branches of the tree, and termination of a branch indicates extinction of a species.

39. Choice (B) is the correct answer. Mitochondria provide energy in the form of ATP. The flagella is composed of proteins and will provide mostly motility, so choice (A) is incorrect. Sperm may be carrying an X or a Y chromosome, so choice (C) is incorrect. Choice (D) can be eliminated because the centriole acts as a basal body for the flagella. And choice (E) can be eliminated because the nucleus contains DNA.

40. Choice (E) is the correct answer. The "fight-or-flight" response results from the release of adrenalin (or epinephrine) from the adrenal glands, which are endocrine glands. The pancreas (C) does function as an endocrine gland, but only for blood glucose regulation. The liver (A), kidneys (B), and Cowper's glands (D) are not endocrine glands and do not secrete the hormone responsible for the fight-or-flight reaction.

41. Choice (A) is the correct answer. Synthesis occurs as a prelude to cell division; most replication of DNA takes place during stage S. G2 (step II), in which a second pair of centrioles is produced, occurs after S as a prelude for mitosis (step III). This eliminates choice (B). Choices (C) and (D) refer to specific stages of mitosis and are incorrect. Choice (E) is incorrect because it refers to G1 (step VI), in which nondividing cells perform functions essential for their survival, such as energy production and protein synthesis.

42. Choice (E) is the correct answer. The key here is to distinguish between biotic and abiotic factors: Biotic factors result from interactions with other individuals, most commonly predation and competition. Abiotic factors, such as rainfall and temperature, are nonliving factors that affect a population. Choices (A), (B), (C), and (D) are all abiotic factors.

43. Choice (C) is the correct answer. Tube feet and a water vascular system are both characteristics of the echinoderms. And echinoderms have radial symmetry, not bilateral symmetry.

44. Choice (D) is the correct answer. Since one homologue contains both recessive alleles and the other contains both dominant alleles, the only explanation for these results would be from crossing-over during Prophase I of meiosis. Since the chromosomes are homologues, sex-linkage (A) is incorrect. Lack of dominance heredity patterns (B) and blending (E) could only be determined by examining the phenotype. And each chromosome contains both alleles, so nondisjunction (C) hasn't occurred.

45. Choice (C) is the correct answer. The manufacture of antibodies occurs within the lymphocytes. The other options—elimination of nitrogenous wastes (A), water balance regulation (B), salt or electrolyte regulation (D), and formation of urine (E)—are all major functions of the mammalian kidney.

46. Choice (E) is the correct answer. Rain forests provide an environment in which many species have evolved and are the most biologically diverse ecosystems. Choice

(A) is incorrect; although rain forests do provide oxygen into the atmosphere, most of our oxygen supply is provided by phytoplankton in the ocean. Choice (B) can be eliminated because rain forests are located only in tropical areas where annual rainfall is greatest. Atmospheric nitrogen is produced by denitrifying bacteria, so choice (C) is incorrect, and migratory ungulates are located in grasslands or prairies where expanse is greatest, so choice (D) can be eliminated.

47. Choice (A) is the correct answer. To determine initial success of the species, you need to locate the greatest numbers in the Year 1 row. The largest numbers occur in the species columns for sandspur (3,800 plants per acre) and ragweed (4,900 plants per acre).

48. Choice (D) is the correct answer. The data suggest that plant populations are replacing one another. The species with the largest numbers in Year 1 (sandspur and ragweed) have the smallest numbers in Year 3, while the species with the smallest numbers in Year 1 (timothy grass, goldenrod, and wire grass) have the largest numbers in Year 3. There is no information provided about environmental conditions, so we cannot conclude that fires (A) or floods (B) have affected the populations. Choice (C) is incorrect because the number of plant species changes during the three-year span of the experiment. And there is insufficient information to evaluate reproductive capacity (E).

49. Choice (B) is the correct answer. The 20 percent mark on the y-axis intersects with keratoses in Australia at age 30 and keratoses in Ireland between ages 60 and 70; only "keratoses in Australia at age 30" is given as an answer choice. Skin cancer incidents in Australia do not reach 20 percent, so choice (A) is incorrect. Choice (C) is incorrect because this age group in Australia has incidents of keratoses well above 20 percent. Choice (D) is incorrect because this age group in Ireland has incidents of keratoses below 20 percent. There are insufficient data available to determine keratoses in Ireland at age 80, so choice (E) can be eliminated.

50. Choice (D) is the correct answer. The graph only provides information about the geographic distribution of these conditions within the male population (broken down into age categories), so we can only infer that the environment in Australia is more likely to cause keratoses than is the environment in Ireland. The given data do not indicate that skin cancers develop from keratoses (A), that keratoses develop from skin cancers (B), or that the majority of males with keratoses also have skin cancer (C). And no information about sunlight intensity (E) is given.

51. Choice (E) is the correct answer. No accurate predictions can be made from the data because the sample populations would be different; we have no information about the incidents of keratoses and skin cancer for female populations. This eliminates choices (A), (B), (C), and (D). Choice (B) is also incorrect because the age groups sampled would presumably include females of all ages, and estrogen levels fluctuate with age.

52. Choice (D) is the correct answer. The only difference between treatments I and II is the presence or absence of a coleoptile. Only the shoot with the intact coleoptile—treatment I—responded to light, indicating that the tip is necessary for the response to light.

53. Choice (C) is the correct answer. To determine these results, you need to compare the cut coleoptiles (treatments II and IV) to an uncut control (treatment I). Treatment IV demonstrates that a plant that is wounded but not completely cut can still grow toward light.

54. Choice (A) is the correct answer. When treatments III, V, and VI are compared, it is clear that the tip plays a role in sensing the light. In treatment III, where a light-blocking cap is placed over the coleoptile tip, growth toward light is prevented; however, in both treatment V, where the coleoptile tip is covered by a transparent cap, and treatment VI, where the coleoptile tip is uncovered, growth toward light is allowed.

55. Choice (C) is the correct answer. An experimenter could test the hypothesis that the response to light involves differential cell elongation by comparing the length of cells on the sides of the stem toward and away from the light. Choices (A) and (B) provide no information for elongated differentiated cells. Choice (D) is incorrect because mitosis would affect cell quantity without cell differentiation. And choice (E) is incorrect because it would introduce another variable into the experiment.

56. Choice (C) is the correct answer. Experiment I indicates that when the individual cells of a two-cell embryo are separated, each has the capacity to develop into a distinct larva. At this early stage, no cellular specialization has started to occur; each embryotic cell is totipotent. Each cell has the ability to become specialized. There is no information provided about adaptation, so choice (A) is incorrect. Experiment II disproves choice (B), which is incorrect. Choice (D) is shown to be incorrect by experiment IV, as is choice (E).

57. Choice (B) is the correct answer. When comparing Experiment I with Experiment II, we see that the only difference is in the size of the larva. In the early stages of cell division during animal development, the zygote undergoes a rapid series of mitotic cleavages. Each of these divisions results in an increased number of cells, but not in an increase of cytoplasm. This indicates that cells from a four-cell stage of development would contain less cytoplasm than the cells produced during the two-cell stage of development. This would result in the production of smaller larvae from the four-stage cells. There is no information provided about adult embryos, therefore choices (A) and (E) are incorrect. Choice (C) is eliminated by the results of experiment IV, while comparison of experiments III and IV eliminate choice (D).

58. Choice (A) is the correct answer. Experiments III and IV indicate that there is a distinct difference when separating an eight-cell embryo along a horizontal or vertical axis. This difference indicates that at the eight-cell stage the cells have started the process of differentiation and are no longer able to develop independently into fully functioning larva. Experiment IV disproves choices (C) and (E), while (B) is shown to be incorrect by the results of experiment III. Choice (D) is incorrect because only the eight-day stage of development was tested.

59. Choice (D) is the correct answer. When the results of Experiment III are compared to Experiment IV, it is clear that only a vertical separation of the embryonic cells produces intact larva. This indicates that individual cells are communicating, and that different chemical signals are directed toward specific cells. When the top four cells in Experiment IV are separated, they produce a different structure than that of the bottom four cells. This indicates that each group of cells is receiving different genetic information. Choice (A) can be eliminated because both experiments use an eight-cell embryo; therefore mitosis has been occurring normally. A loss of all chromosomes would prevent any type of development, which is not the case in experiment IV, so choice (B) is incorrect. Cell division is initiated by fertilization and would be halted at the two-cell stage if two different sperm were used, so choice (C) is incorrect. And choice (E) can be eliminated because the cells from the left half and the right half of the embryo developed normally.

60. Choice (D) is the correct answer. This series of experiments does not address the question of when components in the fertilized egg are activated; the experiments provide no information about the events occurring during fertilization. The results of experiments III and IV eliminate choice (A). The results of experiment II eliminate choices (B) and (C). And the results of experiment IV eliminate choice (E).

Ecological Biology Only (Questions 61–80)

61. Choice (A) is the correct answer. Unlike other aquatic ecosystems, streams and rivers flow continuously in one direction and have a nutrient content that is dependent on location. Nutrient availability varies in different locations. The ecosystems of streams and rivers incorporate mineral contributions from the surrounding terrestrial environment and nutrients from decomposition of organic matter. High water movement aerates the water, thus increasing content of gases such as nitrogen and oxygen. Since the rate of water movement is determined by the terrain, waters may move very rapidly or more slowly in some areas. This movement creates a gradient of temperature, nutrient availability, and oxygen content. Aquatic plants are most populous in ponds or lakes where there is little water disturbance, so choice (B) is incorrect. Choice (D) is incorrect because high-diversity aquatic ecosystems, such as estuaries, are located along coastlines where there is mixing of fresh and saline water. Choice (C) also describes estuaries, which have daily variations in salinity and water levels, so it can be eliminated. Choice (E) is incorrect because plankton float on the water surface and require stationary water for photosynthesis; moving water will disrupt them.

62. Choice (B) is the correct answer. Trophic levels describe how nutrient resources are distributed within an ecosystem and therefore describe the energy distribution within that ecosystem. Choice (A) is incorrect because the amount of resources consumed will not vary the trophic relationships among ecosystem inhabitants. Choices (C), (D), and (E) are incorrect because ecosystems are established according to resources available.

63. Choice (D) is the correct answer. Oxygen did not exist in the atmosphere of the early earth; therefore, the earliest organisms must have been small, anaerobic prokaryotes. Choices (A) and (C) are incorrect; eukaryotic organisms are believed to have developed later as a result of anaerobic symbiosis. Choices (B) and (E) are incorrect because both parasitic and pathogenic organisms require host organisms.

64. Choice (E) is the correct answer. Free nitrogen gas composes roughly 80 percent of our atmospheric air, while phosphorus does not exist in gaseous form within our atmosphere. Phosphorus exists in a solid form within our atmosphere and is cycled by weathering. Choices (B) and (C) can be eliminated because nitrogen is captured from the atmosphere and converted into a chemical form that can be absorbed by plants. Choices (A) and (D) are incorrect because phosphorus is recycled from the runoff of weathered rocks.

65. Choice (E) is the correct answer. The ladybug feeds on the aphid; it is a carnivore. Producers are always located at the base of the food web; the rosebush is the producer, so choice (D) is incorrect. Choices (A) and (B) are incorrect because they refer to animals that feed directly on producers; the ladybug does not feed directly on the rosebush. And choice (C) is incorrect because decomposers break down dead organisms; the ladybug is not a decomposer.

66. Choice (E) is the correct answer. Sewage is composed of organic waste products, which are broken down by decomposers; the stream is most likely free of pollutants because of decomposition. Succession refers to a process in which one species replaces another, which is not the case here, so choice (A) is incorrect. Choice (B) is incorrect; biological magnification refers to the consumption of toxic substances by organisms within a food chain. This results in a concentration of the toxin within the tissues of the top consumer. Choice (C) refers to conversion of liquid materials to vapor, whereas most sewage is solid, so this choice is incorrect. And plants are producers, which eliminates choice (D).

67. Choice (C) is the correct answer. This term refers to several species that developed minor physical differences to adapt to various environments. This suggests that they evolved from a common ancestor. This eliminates choices (A), (B), and (E). Choice (D) is incorrect because this behavior is an individual response to immediate changes in the environment.

68. Choice (B) is the correct answer. Mutualism, parasitism, commensalism, and predation all refer to relationships between two or more different species. Hibernation is a decrease in activity carried out by one individual.

69. Choice (E) is the correct answer. Plant seeds differ among plant species and have evolved to be scattered most effectively. Some are specialized to be distributed by wind, some are specialized to be distributed by water, and some are specialized to be distributed by birds.

70. Choice (B) is the correct answer. Figure 2, which shows the new distribution of *Chthamalus*, suggests that *Balanus* does not reproduce as quickly as *Chthamalus*; *Chthamalus* rapidly colonized the bare areas created by the removal of *Balanus*, while *Balanus* did not rapidly reproduce. Choices (A) and (E) can be eliminated; there is no way to determine from the figures that *Balanus* feeds on *Chthamalus* larvae or that *Balanus* is less susceptible to predators. Choice (C) is incorrect because *Balanus* is located over the low-tide mark. And choice (D) is incorrect because adult barnacles are stationary, whereas the larvae are free swimming.

71. Choice (C) is the correct answer. Figures 2 and 3 do not suggest that *Balanus* adults are swept away more often than *Chthamalus*; Figure 3 shows that the population of *Balanus* has actually increased, while the population of *Chthamalus* has decreased. The figures show that *Balanus* individuals have settled in areas formerly occupied by *Chthamalus*; this suggests both that *Balanus* sometimes dominates over the smaller *Chthamalus* (A) and that *Balanus* and *Chthamalus* larvae can settle in the same area (D). The figures also indicate that *Balanus* spends more time in the water, which suggests that *Chthamalus* can tolerate more drying than *Balanus* (B) and also that *Balanus*, the larger of the two types of barnacles, needs more feeding time in the water (E).

72. Choice (D) is the correct answer. From the figures, we see that *Chthamalus* populations are most abundant above the midtide water mark. This indicates that they spend a substantial portion of each day exposed to less water and have adapted to these environmental conditions. Further, although the *Chthamalus* population below the midtide water mark increased in the 3 months following the removal of selected *Balanus* from that region (Figure 2), Figure 3 shows that *Balanus* outnumbered *Chthamalus* below the midtide water mark after 12 months. This suggests that *Balanus* is a stronger competitor within this environment. Therefore, on rocks with tops below the midtide line, one would expect to find few, if any, *Chthamalus*. The predictions described in choices (A), (B), (C), and (E) are not supported by this study.

73. Choice (A) is the correct answer. The antibiotic Penicillin would be predicted to kill the bacteria. This is best represented by the distribution in choice (A).

74. Choice (D) is the correct answer. Dish A shows that many bacteria survived in the area containing agar and that a few survived in the lower area, which contained agar mixed with penicillin. It is most likely that the individuals that survived did so because they had acquired a gene for penicillin resistance. Choice (A) can be eliminated because mutation caused by exposure would show expression in future generations. There is no information provided about metabolism, so choice (B) can be eliminated. And choices (C) and (E) are incorrect because bacteria have cell walls and reproduce by budding.

75. Choice (A) is the correct answer. In this experiment, penicillin killed the *E. coli* individuals that did not have the gene for penicillin resistance. The individuals that survived the penicillin stressor will produce offspring that carry the gene for penicillin resistance, enabling them to survive in this new environment. In an ecosystem, when some members of a population develop a mutation that enhances their survival, they will produce more offspring than the individuals without the mutation. This is an example of natural selection.

76. Choice (D) is the correct answer. The table shows that *Smilax rotundifolia* evolutionarily is most closely related to *Smilax herbacea*. These species share the same genus and have the closest structural similarity.

77. Choice (A) is the correct answer. There were prokaryotic filaments located on this species, indicating that bacteria were present. This was not found in any other species; therefore, *Platismatia glauca* best illustrates symbiosis.

78. Choice (A) is the correct answer. *Funaria americana* has no vascular system and reproduces by spores, indicating that it is a primitive plant form. The other choices refer to plants that have stems, indicating that they have a well-developed vascular system.

79. Choice (E) is the correct answer. *Monotropa uniflora* produces fruit, indicating that it belongs to the flowering plant division, Anthophyta. Choices (A) and (B) are incorrect because they refer to species with no stems, which are characteristic of Anthophyta. Spores are present in *Dryopteris spinulosa* and cone reproductive structures are found in *Picea rubens*, so choices (C) and (D) are also incorrect.

80. Choice (B) is the correct answer. The appearance of these plants in a burned area is an example of secondary succession. Several different plant divisions are established here, indicating a pattern of establishment by several species. This follows the pattern of succession. The other choices are incorrect because there is no domination by one species.

Molecular Biology Only (Questions 81–100)

81. Choice (B) is the correct answer. The structure shown is a phospholipid, which has a hydrophilic head in area I and two hydrophobic fatty acid chains in area II. The long fatty acid chains do not interact with water and arrange themselves so that they are in direct contact with each other. This arrangement of fatty acid tails forms the inner layer of the membrane. Structure I represents the phosphate area of this molecule and is hydrophilic. This area of the molecule is directed toward water. This eliminates choices (A) and (C). The hydrophobic areas of adjoining phospholipids position themselves to avoid contact with water and would be located in the center of the membrane, the lipid bilayer; therefore, choices (D) and (E) are incorrect.

82. Choice (D) is the correct answer. Both reduced NADP (NADPH) and ATP are required for the dark reaction. Choices (A) and (B) are incorrect because they do not

include both I and II. Oxygen is only used during the light reaction of photosynthesis to produce ATP, so choices (C) and (E) are incorrect.

83. Choice (B) is the correct answer. Enzymes are proteins designed to facilitate specific reactions and have active sites designed specifically to bind to a substrate. Choice (A) is incorrect because the fluid-mosaic model applies to phospholipids. Choices (C) and (D) are incorrect because the Oparin hypothesis refers to the conditions that composed the early earth and the Lyon hypothesis refers to X-chromosome inactivation in females. And choice (E) is incorrect because it refers to competitive interacts among different species.

84. Choice (D) is the correct answer. When DNA replicates, each chromosome copies itself. These copies are joined at a centromere. After DNA synthesis, each chromosome now is composed of two chromatids. If an organism has ten chromosomes, they will now each contain two chromatids for a total of 40 chromatids.

85. Choice (B) is the correct answer. Oxygen is initially produced during photosynthesis and is used for cellular respiration. Choice (A) is incorrect because carbon dioxide is used to produce glucose during the dark reaction. Choices (C), (D), and (E) are also incorrect; these gases are not used by the plant during photosynthesis.

86. Choice (D) is the correct answer. Carbon dioxide and alcohol are final products of fermentation. Fermentation is an anaerobic process that occurs when oxygen availability is low or unavailable. In yeast and bacteria, fermentation produces both carbon dioxide and alcohol. Fermentation does not produce oxygen, so choices (A), (C), and (E) can be eliminated. Choice (B) is incorrect because fermentation does not produce glucose.

87. Choice (E) is the correct answer. Transfer RNA is located within the cytoplasm and helps with the translation process of protein synthesis. Choices (A) and (D) are incorrect because they refer to messenger RNA and the process of DNA transcription. Choice (B) can be eliminated because it describes the function of DNA. And choice (C) is incorrect because ribosomal RNA is stored in the ribosome.

88. Choice (B) is the correct answer. Tetrad formation and crossing-over occurs during Prophase I of meiosis. All of the other processes described occur in *both* mitosis and meiosis.

89. Choice (A) is the correct answer. If the *Bt* gene were incorporated into the DNA of the corn, the gene would be activated to express the *Bt* protein as it would in the bacteria, and the translation process would be carried out as would any corn protein. Therefore, the corn earworms that eat the *Bt* corn would be killed (I). The bacteria infecting the *Bt* corn would not be killed, and the process of the *Bt* gene being incorporated into the corn earworms' chromosomes could only occur by mutation or genetic manipulation of the earworms.

90. Choice (B) is the correct answer. The only information we are given is that oxygen release is correlated to specific wavelengths of visible light; this suggests that chlorophyll plays a role in the light reactions of photosynthesis. Since oxygen is not a product of cellular respiration, choice (A) is incorrect. Choice (C) can be eliminated because photosynthesis requires water. Choice (D) can be eliminated because carbon dioxide fixation does not require light. Choice (E) is incorrect because chlorophyll captures but does not generate energy.

91. Choice (A) is the correct answer. Both cellular respiration and the light-dependent reactions of photosynthesis produce ATP. AMP (B), GTP (C), and oxygen (D) are not produced during cellular respiration, and carbon dioxide use in synthetic reactions (E) only occurs during the light-independent reaction of photosynthesis, in which glucose is produced.

92. Choice (E) is the correct answer. Proteins consist of amino acids, which are transcribed from genes. During transcription, mRNA copies a section of DNA that contains bases that code for a series of amino acids. During translation, the copy of the bases will be matched to their corresponding amino acids. If a mutation occurs in a base, a different amino acid will be substituted in the same relative position in the corresponding protein. The direct relationship between the DNA base and the amino acid eliminates choices (A) and (B). Mutations occur randomly and can occur in any species, therefore choices (C) and (D) are incorrect.

93. Choice (E) is the correct answer. Cloning results from stimulating egg development through mitosis without fertilization. This initiates the process of embryonic development, in which a rapid series of mitotic divisions occurs, each resulting in identical daughter cells. Since this animal would be cloned from its mother, it would contain all of the mother's DNA sequences. This eliminates choices (B) and (D). Mitosis produces two identical daughter cells, so (A) is incorrect. And choice (C) is incorrect because RNA will be produced from the DNA of the animal cloned from its mother.

94. Choice (C) is the correct answer. Photosynthesis requires carbon dioxide and removes it from the water. Bowls 2 and 3 contain plants, with bowl 3 containing twice as many plants as bowl 2; this explains why the water in bowl 3 has half of the carbon dioxide content of bowl 2. Respiration (A) and fermentation (B) *produce* carbon dioxide; transpiration (D) refers to water transport in plants; and photoperiodism (E) refers to day length.

95. Choice (C) is the correct answer. Bowls 1 and 10 are the main controls for bowl 4. Bowl 1 is the primary control and contains no organisms; this provides the baseline carbon dioxide amount for comparison. And both bowl 4 and bowl 10 contain 2 goldfish. However, bowl 4 was exposed to light, while bowl 10 was kept in the dark. In this case we are only checking for production of carbon dioxide by 2 goldfish.

96. Choice (C) is the correct answer. Both bowl 2 and bowl 6 contain water + 20 plants and were exposed to light; the only difference between the two bowls is the addition of 2 goldfish to bowl 6. Therefore, the difference in carbon dioxide concentrations for bowls 2 and 6 must be due to respiration carried out by the goldfish in bowl 6.

97. Choice (D) is the correct answer. The process of cellular respiration occurs in all living organisms, including plants and goldfish. This process requires oxygen and glucose and produces carbon dioxide and water as its waste products. Bowls 4 and 10 contain only water and 2 goldfish; bowl 4 was exposed to light and bowl 10 was placed in the dark, but the bowls have almost the same carbon dioxide concentration. Likewise, bowls 5 and 11 contain only water and 4 goldfish, and even though bowl 5 was exposed to light while bowl 11 was placed in the dark, the bowls have almost the same carbon dioxide concentration. Because each pair of identical bowls had similar carbon dioxide concentrations even though one bowl was in the dark and one bowl was exposed to light, we can conclude that respiration is not affected by either light or dark.

98. Choice (E) is the correct answer. The number of amino acids in the fragment, the amount of electric current used in the apparatus, and the porosity of the gel matrix are all factors that influence the movement of protein fragments along the electrical gradient during electrophoresis.

99. Choice (B) is the correct answer. Chromatography separates proteins according to their affinity for solvents; this technique could have been used as an alternative to electrophoresis. Translation and serial dilution could not have been used; translation would not be effective because the proteins have already been assembled from DNA chromosome sequences, and serial dilution would decrease the amount of protein in a sample.

100. Choice (E) is the correct answer. Enzymes target very specific substrates—in this case, amino acids. Since there are 20 amino acids, proteins may contain varying lengths and combinations of these molecules. The digestive enzymes used for treating this protein target amino acids that form a specific sequence. Choice (A) is incorrect because the enzyme-treated samples all migrated to different points, indicating that they are all different molecular weights. All proteins are translated by ribosomes and the electrical current is distributed evenly along the gel; this eliminates choices (B) and (D). And choice (C) can be eliminated because we are not given any information about the enzyme.

Chapter 6

Chemistry

Purpose

The Subject Test in Chemistry measures the understanding of chemistry you would be expected to have after successfully completing a college-preparatory course in high school and is designed to be independent of the particular textbook or instructional approach used.

Format

This is a one-hour test with 85 multiple-choice questions.

Content

The test covers the topics listed in the chart on the next page. Different aspects of these topics are stressed from year to year. However, because high school courses differ, both in the amount of time devoted to each major topic and in the specific subtopics covered, it is likely that most students will encounter some questions on topics with which they are not familiar. Every edition of the test contains approximately five questions on equation balancing and/or predicting products of chemical reactions; these are distributed among the various content categories.

Topics Covered	Approximate Percentage of Test
I. Structure of Matter	25%
Atomic Structure, including experimental evidence of atomic structure, quantum numbers and energy levels (orbitals), electron configurations, periodic trends **Molecular Structure**, including Lewis structures, three-dimensional molecular shapes, polarity **Bonding**, including ionic, covalent, and metallic bonds; relationships of bonding to properties and structures; intermolecular forces such as hydrogen bonding, dipole-dipole forces, dispersion (London) forces	
II. States of Matter	16%
Gases, including the kinetic molecular theory, gas law relationships, molar volumes, density, stoichiometry **Liquids and Solids**, including intermolecular forces in liquids and solids, types of solids, phase changes and phase diagrams **Solutions**, including molarity and percent by mass concentrations; solution preparation and stoichiometry; factors affecting solubility of solids, liquids, and gases; qualitative aspects of colligative properties	
III. Reaction Types	14%
Acids and Bases, including Brønsted-Lowry theory, strong and weak acids and bases, pH, titrations, indicators **Oxidation-Reduction**, including recognition of oxidation-reduction reactions, combustion, oxidation numbers, use of acitvity series **Precipitation**, including basic solubility rules	
IV. Stoichiometry	14%
Mole Concept, including molar mass, Avogadro's number, empirical and molecular formulas **Chemical Equations**, including the balancing of equations, stoichiometric calculations, percent yield, limiting reactants	
V. Equilibrium and Reaction Rates	5%
Equilibrium Systems, including factors affecting position of equilibrium (LeChâtelier's principle) in gaseous and aqueous systems, equilibrium constants, equilibrium expressions **Rates of Reactions**, including factors affecting reaction rates, potential energy diagrams, activation energies	
VI. Thermochemistry	6%
Including conservation of energy, calorimetry and specific heats, enthalpy (heat) changes associated with phase changes and chemical reactions, heating and cooling curves, randomness (entropy)	
VII. Descriptive Chemistry	12%
Including common elements, nonmenclature of ions and compounds, periodic trends in chemical and physical properties of the elements, reactivity of elements and prediction of products of chemical reactions, examples of simple organic compounds and compounds of environmental concern	
VIII. Laboratory	8%
Including knowledge of laboratory equipment, measurements, procedures, observations, safety, calculations, data analysis, interpretation of graphical data, drawing conclusions from observations and data	

Skills Specifications	Approximate Percentage of Test
Recall of Knowledge	20%
Remembering fundamental concepts and specific information; demonstrating familiarity with terminology	
Application of Knowledge	45%
Applying a single principle to unfamiliar and/or practical situations to obtain a qualitative result or solve a quantitative problem	
Synthesis of Knowledge	35%
Inferring and deducing from qualitative data and/or quantitative data; integrating two or more relationships to draw conclusions or solve problems	

How to Prepare

- Take a one-year introductory chemistry course at the college-preparatory level.
- Laboratory experience is a significant factor in developing reasoning and problem-solving skills and should help in test preparation even though laboratory skills can be tested only in a limited way in a multiple-choice test.
- Mathematics preparation that enables handling simple algebraic relationships and applying these to solving word problems will help.
- Familiarize yourself with the concepts of ratio and direct and inverse proportions, exponents, and scientific notation.
- Familiarize yourself with directions in advance. The directions in this book are identical to those that appear on the test.

You should have the ability to

- recall and understand the major concepts of chemistry and to apply the principles to solve specific problems in chemistry.
- organize and interpret results obtained by observation and experimentation and to draw conclusions or make inferences from experimental data, including data presented in graphic and/or tabular form.

Notes: (1) A periodic table indicating the atomic numbers and masses of elements is provided for all test administrations.

(2) Calculators aren't allowed to be used during the test.

(3) Problem solving requires simple numerical calculations.

(4) The metric system of units is used.

Score

The total score is reported on the 200-to-800 scale.

Sample Questions

Three types of questions are used in the Chemistry Subject Test: classification questions, relationship analysis questions, and five-choice completion questions.

Note: For all questions involving solutions, assume that the solvent is water unless otherwise noted.

Classification Questions

Each set of classification questions has, in the heading, five lettered choices that you will use to answer all of the questions in the set. The choices may be statements that refer to concepts, principles, substances, or observable phenomena; or they may be graphs, pictures, equations, numbers, or experimental settings or situations.

Because the same five choices are applicable to several questions, the classification questions usually require less reading than other types of multiple-choice questions. Answering a question correctly depends on the sophistication of the set of questions. One set may test your ability to recall information; another set may ask you to apply information to a specific situation or to translate information from one form to another (descriptive, graphical, mathematical). The directions for this type of question specifically state that you should not eliminate a choice simply because it is the correct answer to a previous question.

Following are the directions for and an example of a classification set.

Directions: Each set of lettered choices below refers to the numbered statements immediately following it. Select the one lettered choice that best fits each statement or answers each question and then fill in the corresponding circle on the answer sheet. A choice may be used once, more than once, or not at all in each set.

Questions 1–3 refer to the following aqueous solutions:

(A) 0.1 *M* HCl

(B) 0.1 *M* NaCl

(C) 0.1 *M* $HC_2H_3O_2$

(D) 0.1 *M* CH_3OH

(E) 0.1 *M* KOH

1. Is weakly acidic

2. Has the highest pH

3. Reacts with an equal volume of 0.05 *M* $Ba(OH)_2$ to form a solution with pH = 7

These three questions belong to the topic category of acids and bases and require you to apply knowledge in this area to the particular solutions specified in the five choices.

Choice (C) is the correct answer to question 1. To answer the first question, you must recognize which of the choices above are acid solutions. Only choices (A) and (C) satisfy this requirement. Choice (B) refers to a neutral salt solution, choice (D) is a solution of an alcohol, and choice (E) is a basic solution. Both choices (A) and (C) are acidic solutions, but choice (A) is a strong acid that is completely ionized in aqueous solution, while choice (C) is only partially ionized in aqueous solution. Since the concentrations of all the solutions are the same, you do not need to consider this factor. The hydrogen ion concentration of a 0.1-molar acetic acid solution is considerably smaller than 0.1-molar. The hydrogen ion concentration in choice (A) is equal to 0.1-molar. Thus, choice (C) is a weakly acidic solution and is the correct answer.

Choice (E) is the correct answer to question 2. To answer the second question, you need to understand the pH scale, which is a measure of the hydrogen ion concentration in solution and is defined as $pH = -\log [H^+]$. The higher the pH, the lower the hydrogen ion concentration and the more basic the solution. Among the choices given above, choice (E) is the most basic solution.

Choice (A) is the correct answer to question 3. To answer the third question, you need to know that acids react with bases to form salts and water. Since the question refers to equal volumes of each solution, assume 1 liter of each solution is available. Barium hydroxide solution is a strong base, i.e., is completely ionized in water, and 1 liter of 0.05 *M* $Ba(OH)_2$ provides 0.1 mole of OH^- ions in solution. When 1 liter of this solution is added to 1 liter of either 0.1 *M* NaCl, 0.1 *M* CH_3OH, or 0.1 *M* KOH no reactions occur and the resulting solutions remain basic, i.e., the pH will be greater than 7 in each case. When 0.1 mole OH^- ions reacts with 0.1 mole of acetic acid, the resulting solution will also be basic and have a pH greater than 7 because acetic acid is a weak acid, i.e., is incompletely ionized in water. The acetic acid reacts with the OH^- ions as follows:

$$HC_2H_3O_2 + OH^- \rightleftarrows C_2H_3O_2^- + H_2O$$

The acetate salt formed hydrolyzes in water yielding a solution containing more OH^- ions than H^+ ions. When 1 liter of 0.05 *M* $Ba(OH)_2$ reacts with 1 liter of 0.1 *M* HCl, there is a reaction between 0.1 mole OH^- ions and 0.1 mole H^+ to form 0.1 mole H_2O. The resulting solution contains Ba^{2+} ions and Cl^- ions and equal concentrations of OH^- and H^+ ions. The solution formed is neutral and the pH is 7.

Relationship Analysis Questions

This type of question consists of a specific statement or assertion (Statement I) followed by an explanation of the assertion (Statement II). The question is answered by determining if the assertion and the explanation are each true statements and, if so, whether the explanation (or reason) provided does in fact properly explain the statement given in the assertion.

This type of question tests your ability to identify proper cause-and-effect relationships. It probes whether you can assess the correctness of the original assertion and then evaluate the truth of the "reason" proposed to justify it. The analysis required by this type of question provides you with an opportunity to demonstrate developed reasoning skills and the scope of your understanding of a particular topic.

On the actual Chemistry Test, the following type of question must be answered on a special section (labeled "Chemistry") at the lower left-hand corner of your answer sheet. These questions will be numbered beginning with 101 and must be answered according to the following directions.

SAMPLE ANSWER GRID

	I		II		CE*
101	(T)	(F)	(T)	(F)	( )

Directions: Each question below consists of two statements, I in the left-hand column and II in the right-hand column. For each question, determine whether statement I is true or false <u>and</u> whether statement II is true or false and fill in the corresponding T or F circles on your answer sheet. <u>Fill in circle CE only if statement II is a correct explanation of the true statement I.</u>

EXAMPLES:

I		II
EX 1. H_2SO_4 is a strong acid	BECAUSE	H_2SO_4 contains sulfur.
EX 2. An atom of oxygen is electrically neutral	BECAUSE	an oxygen atom contains an equal number of protons and electrons.

SAMPLE ANSWERS

	I		II		CE
EX 1	●	(F)	●	(F)	○
EX 2	●	(F)	●	(F)	●

	I		II
4.	The electrolysis of a concentrated solution of sodium chloride produces chlorine	BECAUSE	sodium chloride is a covalent compound.

The above question has several components. Statement I, the assertion, has to do with an oxidation-reduction reaction, more specifically, an electrochemical reaction. This statement is true because the electrolysis of a concentrated sodium chloride solution yields chlorine gas at the anode (oxidation) and hydrogen gas at the cathode (reduction). The electrolytic solution gradually becomes alkaline with the accumulation of hydroxide ions (i.e., OH^- ions) as the reaction proceeds.

Statement II, the reason, is false because the type of chemical bonding in sodium chloride is ionic. According to the directions for answering this question type, you should fill in the corresponding T and F circles on your answer sheet.

	I		II
5.	Atoms of different elements can have the same mass number	BECAUSE	atoms of each element have a characteristic number of protons in the nucleus.

This is a question on atomic structure. The sum of the number of protons plus the number of neutrons contained in the nucleus of an atom is the mass number. However, atoms of the same element may have different numbers of neutrons in their nuclei and thus have different masses. Such atoms, which have the same number of protons but different numbers of neutrons, are called isotopes of an element ($^{12}_{6}C$ and $^{14}_{6}C$, for example). The existence of isotopes makes it possible for atoms of different elements, that is, with different numbers of protons, to have the same total mass or mass number ($^{14}_{6}C$ and $^{14}_{7}N$, for example). Thus Statement I is true. Statement II is also true because the number of protons in the nucleus of an atom is a characteristic feature that identifies each element. But it is not the reason that explains the existence of isotopes and so does not properly explain Statement I. Thus, to answer this question, you should fill in both T circles for this question, but not the CE circle.

I		II
6. When the system $CO(g) + Cl_2(g) \rightleftarrows COCl_2(g)$ is at equilibrium and the pressure on the system is increased by decreasing the volume at constant temperature, more $COCl_2(g)$ will be produced	BECAUSE	an increase of pressure on a system will be relieved when the system shifts to a smaller total number of moles of gas.

Statement I is true because whenever stress is applied to a system at equilibrium the system will tend to shift to relieve the stress (Le Chatelier's principle). In the system described, the stress is caused by an increase in pressure resulting from a decrease in the volume and will be relieved by the reaction of some CO and Cl_2 to form more $COCl_2$. The new equilibrium that will be established will contain a smaller total number of moles of gas, thereby reducing the pressure stress. This is the explanation given in Statement II, which is not only true but also correctly explains the phenomenon described in Statement I. Thus, to answer this question correctly you should fill in both T circles as well as the CE circle.

Five-Choice Completion Questions

The five-choice completion question is written either as an incomplete statement or as a question. It is appropriate when: (1) the problem presented is clearly delineated by the wording of the question so that you are asked to choose not a universal solution but the best of the solutions offered; (2) the problem is such that you are required to evaluate the relevance of five plausible, or even scientifically accurate, options and to select the one most pertinent; (3) the problem has several pertinent solutions and you are required to select the one inappropriate solution that is presented. Such questions normally contain a word in capital letters such as NOT, LEAST, or EXCEPT.

A special type of five-choice completion question is used in some tests, including the SAT Subject Test in Chemistry, to allow for the possibility of multiple correct answers. For these questions, you must evaluate each response independently of the others in order to select the most appropriate combination. In questions of this type several (usually three or four) statements labeled by Roman numerals are given with the question. One or more of these statements may correctly answer the question. You must select, from among the five lettered choices that follow, the one combination of statements that best answers the question. In the test, questions of this type are intermixed among the more standard five-choice completion questions. (Question 8 is an example of this type of question.)

In five-choice completion questions, you may be asked to convert the information given in a word problem into graphical form or to select and apply the mathematical relationship necessary to solve the scientific problem. Alternatively, you may be asked to interpret experimental data, graphical stimuli, or mathematical expressions.

When the experimental data or other scientific problems to be analyzed are comparatively extensive, it is often convenient to organize several five-choice completion questions into sets, that is, direct each question in a set to the same material. This practice allows you to answer several questions based on the same material. In no case, however, is the answer to one question necessary for answering a subsequent question correctly. Each question in a set is independent of the others and refers only to the material given for the entire set.

Directions: Each of the questions or incomplete statements below is followed by five suggested answers or completions. Select the one that is best in each case and then fill in the corresponding circle on the answer sheet.

7. The hydrogen ion concentration of a solution prepared by diluting 50 milliliters of 0.100-molar HNO_3 with water to 500 milliliters of solution is

(A) 0.0010 *M*

(B) 0.0050 *M*

(C) 0.010 *M*

(D) 0.050 *M*

(E) 1.0 *M*

Choice (C) is the correct answer to question 7. This is a question that concerns solution concentrations. One way to solve the problem is through the use of ratios. In this question, a solution of nitric acid is diluted 10-fold; therefore, the concentration of the solution will decrease by a factor of 10, that is, from 0.100-molar to 0.010-molar. Alternatively, you could calculate the number of moles of H^+ ions present and divide this value by 0.50 liter: $(0.100 \times 0.050)/0.5 = M$ of the diluted solution.

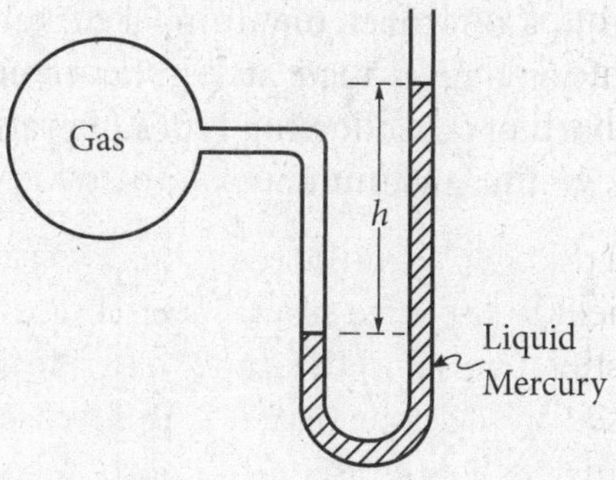

8. The bulb of the open-end manometer shown above contains a gas. True statements about this system include which of the following?

   I. Only atmospheric pressure is exerted on the exposed mercury surface in the right side of the tube.

   II. The gas pressure is greater than atmospheric pressure.

   III. The difference in the height, *h*, of mercury levels is equal to the pressure of the gas.

   (A) II only
   (B) III only
   (C) I and II only
   (D) I and III only
   (E) I, II, and III

Choice (C) is the correct answer to question 8. This is a laboratory-oriented question pertaining to the measurement of gas pressures. It demands higher-level analytical skills that involve drawing conclusions from results obtained in an experiment. To answer this question correctly, you must first understand that, in an open type of manometer, the air exerts pressure on the column of liquid in the open side of the U-tube and the gas being studied exerts pressure on the other side of the U-tube. It is clear then that Statement I is true since the data given show that the manometer is open-ended and its right side is exposed to the atmosphere. Statement II is also a true statement because the level of liquid mercury is higher in the right side, which is exposed to the atmosphere, than in the left side, which is exposed to the gas. Thus the gas pressure is greater than atmospheric pressure. Statement III is not a correct statement because the pressure of the gas in the bulb, expressed in millimeters of mercury, is equal to the difference in height, *h*, of the two mercury levels, plus the atmospheric pressure. Thus only Statements I and II are correct.

9. A thermometer is placed in a test tube containing a melted pure substance. As slow cooling occurs, the thermometer is read at regular intervals until well after the sample has solidified. Which of the following types of graphs is obtained by plotting temperature versus time for this experiment?

(A)
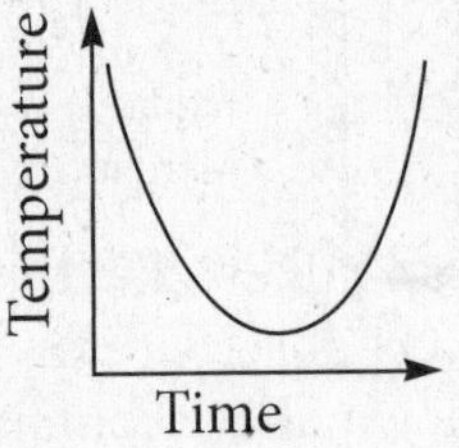

(B)
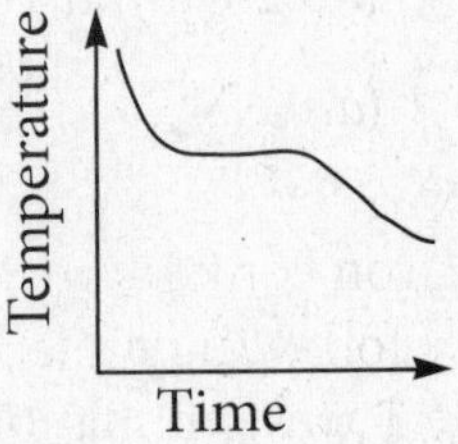

(C)
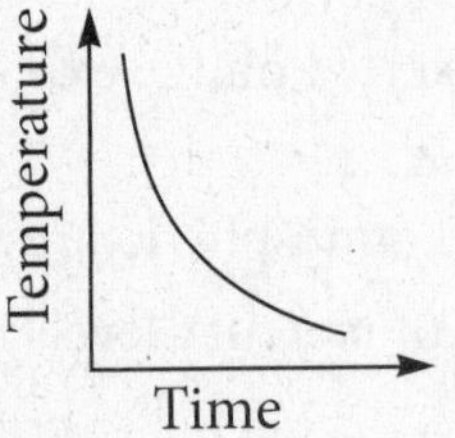

(D)
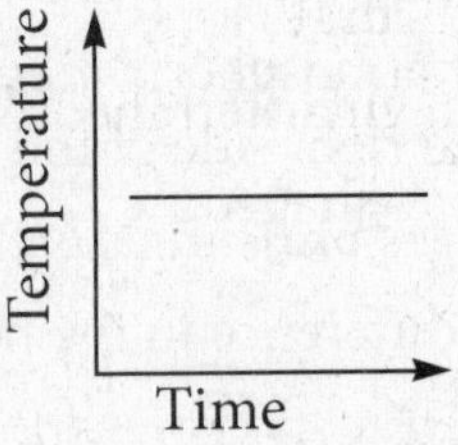

(E)
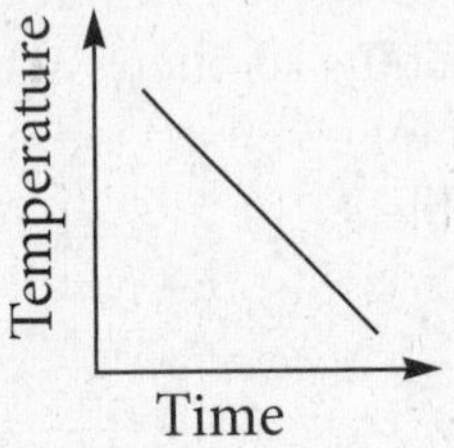

Choice (B) is the correct answer to question 9. This is a question on states of matter. You must convert the description of the physical phenomenon given in the question to graphical form. When a liquid is cooled slowly, its temperature will decrease with time. Thus the first portion of a graph depicting this phenomenon must show a decrease when temperature is plotted against time. When a pure liquid substance reaches its fusion (melting) point, continued cooling will release heat with time as the substance solidifies. During this period there is no drop in temperature. After the substance has completely solidified, further cooling will cause an additional drop in temperature. The only graph shown that accurately depicts the events described is (B), which is the answer.

$$\ldots Cu^{2+}(aq) + \ldots I^{-}(aq) \rightarrow \ldots CuI(s) + \ldots I_2(s)$$

10. When the equation above is balanced and all coefficients are reduced to lowest whole-number terms, the coefficient for I^{-} *(aq)* is

(A) 1
(B) 2
(C) 3
(D) 4
(E) 5

Choice (D) is the correct answer to question 10. This question pertains to the balancing of chemical equations. In order to answer this question correctly, you need to recognize that both mass and charge must be conserved in any chemical equation. With this in mind, the chemical equation is correctly written as

$$2\,Cu^{2+}(aq) + 4\,I^{-}(aq) \rightarrow 2\,CuI(s) + I_2(s)$$

The coefficient for $I^{-}(aq)$ is 4.

11. From their electron configurations, one can predict that the geometric configuration for which of the following molecules is NOT correct.
   (A) PF_3 trigonal planar
   (B) CF_4 tetrahedral
   (C) $CHCl_3$ irregular tetrahedron
   (D) OF_2 bent (v-shaped)
   (E) HF linear

Choice (A) is the correct answer to question 11. This is a question on chemical bonding and requires you to apply the principles of molecular bonding. Each of the molecules given is correctly paired with the term describing its molecular geometry except choice (A). The geometry of PF_3 is not trigonal planar, but trigonal pyramidal, because this geometry corresponds to a maximum possible separation of the electron pairs around the central atom, phosphorus, and therefore yields the most stable configuration; the central atom of the molecule is surrounded by three single bonds and one unshared electron pair. Thus, the correct answer is choice (A). Note that this is the type of question that asks you to identify the *one* solution to the problem that is *inappropriate*.

$$\ldots SO_2(g) + \ldots O_2(g) \rightarrow .?.$$

12. According to the reaction above, how many moles of $SO_2(g)$ are required to react completely with 1 mole of $O_2(g)$?
   (A) 0.5 mole
   (B) 1 mole
   (C) 2 moles
   (D) 3 moles
   (E) 4 moles

Choice (C) is the correct answer to question 12. This is a question on descriptive chemistry that also tests your ability to balance chemical equations. The correct answer to this question depends first on your knowing that the combustion of sulfur dioxide, $SO_2(g)$, produces sulfur trioxide, SO_3. The stoichiometry of the correctly balanced equation indicates that 2 moles of $SO_2(g)$ are needed to react completely with 1 mole of $O_2(g)$ to form 2 moles of SO_3.

13. Analysis by mass of a certain compound shows that it contains 14.4 percent hydrogen and 85.6 percent carbon. Which of the following is the most informative statement that can properly be made about the compound on the basis of these data?

(A) It is a hydrocarbon.

(B) Its empirical formula is CH_2.

(C) Its molecular formula is C_2H_4.

(D) Its molar mass is 28 grams.

(E) It contains a triple bond.

Choice (B) is the correct answer to question 13. This is a question on stoichiometry that tests the important skill of scientific reasoning based on experimental evidence. The question states that 100 percent of the composition of the compound analyzed can be accounted for with the elements hydrogen and carbon. Thus, this compound is a hydrocarbon and choice (A) is a correct statement. It is not the correct answer to the question, however, because you can deduce more specific conclusions about this compound from the information given. The relative percentage composition provides evidence that the atomic ratio of carbon to hydrogen in the compound must be 85.6/12.0 : 14.4/1.0 or 1:2. Therefore, you can conclude that the empirical formula for the compound is CH_2, a hydrocarbon. Thus choice (B) is a better answer than choice (A). Since you do not know the total number of moles of the compound used for analysis, you cannot calculate the molar mass or derive the molecular formula for this compound. Thus choices (C) and (D) cannot be determined from the information given and so they are not correct answers to the question. It is known, however, that a substance with an empirical formula of CH_2 cannot have a triple bond. Therefore, choice (E) is incorrect.

Chemistry Subject Test

Practice Helps

The test that follows is an actual, previously administered SAT Subject Test in Chemistry. To get an idea of what it's like to take this test, practice under conditions that are much like those of an actual test administration.

- Set aside an hour when you can take the test uninterrupted.
- Sit at a desk or table with no other books or papers. Dictionaries, other books, or notes are not allowed in the test room.
- Tear out an answer sheet from the back of this book and fill it in just as you would on the day of the test. One answer sheet can be used for up to three Subject Tests.
- Read the instructions that precede the practice test. During the actual administration you will be asked to read them before answering test questions.
- Time yourself by placing a clock or kitchen timer in front of you.
- After you finish the practice test, read the sections "How to Score the SAT Subject Test in Chemistry" and "How Did You Do on the Subject Test in Chemistry?"
- The appearance of the answer sheet in this book may differ from the answer sheet you see on test day.

CHEMISTRY TEST

The top portion of the page of the answer sheet that you will use to take the Chemistry Test must be filled in exactly as illustrated below. When your supervisor tells you to fill in the circle next to the name of the test you are about to take, mark your answer sheet as shown.

○ Literature	○ Mathematics Level 1	○ German	○ Chinese Listening	○ Japanese Listening
○ Biology E	○ Mathematics Level 2	○ Italian	○ French Listening	○ Korean Listening
○ Biology M	○ U.S. History	○ Latin	○ German Listening	○ Spanish Listening
● Chemistry	○ World History	○ Modern Hebrew		
○ Physics	○ French	○ Spanish	**Background Questions:** ①②③④⑤⑥⑦⑧⑨	

After filling in the circle next to the name of the test you are taking, locate the Background Questions section, which also appears at the top of your answer sheet (as shown above). This is where you will answer the following Background Questions on your answer sheet.

BACKGROUND QUESTIONS

Please answer the four questions below by filling in the appropriate circle in the Background Questions box on your answer sheet. <u>The information you provide is for statistical purposes only and will not affect your test score.</u>

<u>Question I</u>

How many semesters of chemistry have you taken in high school? (If you are taking chemistry this semester, count it as a full semester.) Fill in only <u>one</u> circle of circles 1-3.

- One semester or less —Fill in circle 1.
- Two semesters —Fill in circle 2.
- Three semesters or more —Fill in circle 3.

<u>Question II</u>

How recently have you studied chemistry?

- I am currently enrolled in or have just completed a chemistry course. —Fill in circle 4.
- I have not studied chemistry for 6 months or more. —Fill in circle 5.

<u>Question III</u>

Which of the following best describes your preparation in algebra? (If you are taking an algebra course this semester, count it as a full semester.) Fill in only <u>one</u> circle of circles 6-8.

- One semester or less —Fill in circle 6.
- Two semesters —Fill in circle 7.
- Three semesters or more —Fill in circle 8.

<u>Question IV</u>

Are you currently taking Advanced Placement Chemistry? If you are, fill in circle 9.

When the supervisor gives the signal, turn the page and begin the Chemistry Test. There is a total of 85 questions in the Chemistry Test (1-70 plus questions 101-115 that must be answered on the special section at the lower left-hand corner of the answer sheet).

CHEMISTRY TEST

MATERIAL IN THE FOLLOWING TABLE MAY BE USEFUL IN ANSWERING THE QUESTIONS IN THIS EXAMINATION.

DO NOT DETACH FROM BOOK.

PERIODIC TABLE OF THE ELEMENTS

1 **H** 1.0079																	2 **He** 4.0026
3 **Li** 6.941	4 **Be** 9.012											5 **B** 10.811	6 **C** 12.011	7 **N** 14.007	8 **O** 16.00	9 **F** 19.00	10 **Ne** 20.179
11 **Na** 22.99	12 **Mg** 24.30											13 **Al** 26.98	14 **Si** 28.09	15 **P** 30.974	16 **S** 32.06	17 **Cl** 35.453	18 **Ar** 39.948
19 **K** 39.10	20 **Ca** 40.08	21 **Sc** 44.96	22 **Ti** 47.90	23 **V** 50.94	24 **Cr** 52.00	25 **Mn** 54.938	26 **Fe** 55.85	27 **Co** 58.93	28 **Ni** 58.69	29 **Cu** 63.55	30 **Zn** 65.39	31 **Ga** 69.72	32 **Ge** 72.59	33 **As** 74.92	34 **Se** 78.96	35 **Br** 79.90	36 **Kr** 83.80
37 **Rb** 85.47	38 **Sr** 87.62	39 **Y** 88.91	40 **Zr** 91.22	41 **Nb** 92.91	42 **Mo** 95.94	43 **Tc** (98)	44 **Ru** 101.1	45 **Rh** 102.91	46 **Pd** 106.42	47 **Ag** 107.87	48 **Cd** 112.41	49 **In** 114.82	50 **Sn** 118.71	51 **Sb** 121.75	52 **Te** 127.60	53 **I** 126.91	54 **Xe** 131.29
55 **Cs** 132.91	56 **Ba** 137.33	57 ***La** 138.91	72 **Hf** 178.49	73 **Ta** 180.95	74 **W** 183.85	75 **Re** 186.21	76 **Os** 190.2	77 **Ir** 192.2	78 **Pt** 195.08	79 **Au** 196.97	80 **Hg** 200.59	81 **Tl** 204.38	82 **Pb** 207.2	83 **Bi** 208.98	84 **Po** (209)	85 **At** (210)	86 **Rn** (222)
87 **Fr** (223)	88 **Ra** 226.02	89 **†Ac** 227.03	104 **Rf** (261)	105 **Db** (262)	106 **Sg** (263)	107 **Bh** (262)	108 **Hs** (265)	109 **Mt** (266)	110 **§** (269)	111 **§** (272)	112 **§** (277)						

§Not yet named

*Lanthanide Series	58 **Ce** 140.12	59 **Pr** 140.91	60 **Nd** 144.24	61 **Pm** (145)	62 **Sm** 150.4	63 **Eu** 151.97	64 **Gd** 157.25	65 **Tb** 158.93	66 **Dy** 162.50	67 **Ho** 164.93	68 **Er** 167.26	69 **Tm** 168.93	70 **Yb** 173.04	71 **Lu** 174.97
†Actinide Series	90 **Th** 232.04	91 **Pa** 231.04	92 **U** 238.03	93 **Np** 237.05	94 **Pu** (244)	95 **Am** (243)	96 **Cm** (247)	97 **Bk** (247)	98 **Cf** (251)	99 **Es** (252)	100 **Fm** (257)	101 **Md** (258)	102 **No** (259)	103 **Lr** (260)

CHEMISTRY TEST

Note: For all questions involving solutions, assume that the solvent is water unless otherwise stated.

Throughout the test the following symbols have the definitions specified unless otherwise noted.

H	= enthalpy	atm	= atmosphere(s)
M	= molar	g	= gram(s)
n	= number of moles	J	= joule(s)
P	= pressure	kJ	= kilojoule(s)
R	= molar gas constant	L	= liter(s)
S	= entropy	mL	= milliliter(s)
T	= temperature	mm	= millimeter(s)
V	= volume	mol	= mole(s)
		V	= volt(s)

Part A

Directions: Each set of lettered choices below refers to the numbered statements or questions immediately following it. Select the one lettered choice that best fits each statement or answers each question and then fill in the corresponding circle on the answer sheet. A choice may be used once, more than once, or not at all in each set.

Questions 1-3 refer to the following pieces of laboratory equipment.

(A) Condenser
(B) Funnel
(C) Pipet
(D) Balance
(E) Barometer

1. Commonly used to transfer an exact volume of liquid from one container to another

2. Commonly used in a distillation setup

3. Commonly used in a filtration setup

Questions 4-6 refer to the following information.

Na_2CrO_4, a soluble yellow solid
$PbCrO_4$, an insoluble yellow solid
$NaNO_3$, a soluble white solid
$Pb(NO_3)_2$, a soluble white solid

(A) Yellow solid and colorless solution
(B) Yellow solid and yellow solution
(C) White solid and colorless solution
(D) No solid and yellow solution
(E) No solid and colorless solution

4. Observed when 1.0 mol of Na_2CrO_4 and 2.0 mol of $Pb(NO_3)_2$ are mixed with 1 L of water

5. Observed when 3.0 mol of Na_2CrO_4 and 1.0 mol of $Pb(NO_3)_2$ are mixed with 1 L of water

6. Observed when 1.0 mol of $NaNO_3$ and 1.0 mol of $Pb(NO_3)_2$ are mixed with 1 L of water

GO ON TO THE NEXT PAGE

Questions 7-9 refer to the following.

(A) Reduction potential
(B) Ionization energy (ionization potential)
(C) Electronegativity
(D) Heat of formation
(E) Activation energy

7. Is the energy change accompanying the synthesis of a compound from its elements in their standard states

8. Is the energy needed to remove an electron from a gaseous atom in its ground state

9. Is the minimum energy needed for molecules to react and form products

Questions 10-13 refer to the following pairs of substances.

(A) NH_3 and N_2H_4
(B) ^{16}O and ^{17}O
(C) NH_4Cl and NH_4NO_3
(D) CH_3OCH_3 and CH_3CH_2OH
(E) O_2 and O_3

10. Are isotopes

11. Have both ionic and covalent bonds

12. Are allotropes

13. Are strong electrolytes in aqueous solution

Questions 14-17 refer to the following subshells.

(A) 1*s*
(B) 2*s*
(C) 3*s*
(D) 3*p*
(E) 3*d*

14. Contains up to ten electrons

15. Contains one pair of electrons in the ground-state electron configuration of the lithium atom

16. Is exactly one-half filled in the ground-state electron configuration of the phosphorus atom

17. Contains the valence electrons in the ground-state electron configuration of the magnesium atom

Questions 18-20 refer to the following gases.

(A) O_3
(B) O_2
(C) CO
(D) Cl_2
(E) SO_2

18. Contributes to acid rain

19. In the stratosphere, screens out a large fraction of ultraviolet rays from the Sun

20. Is a product of the incomplete combustion of hydrocarbons

GO ON TO THE NEXT PAGE

Questions 21-24 refer to the lettered solutions in the laboratory schemes represented below.

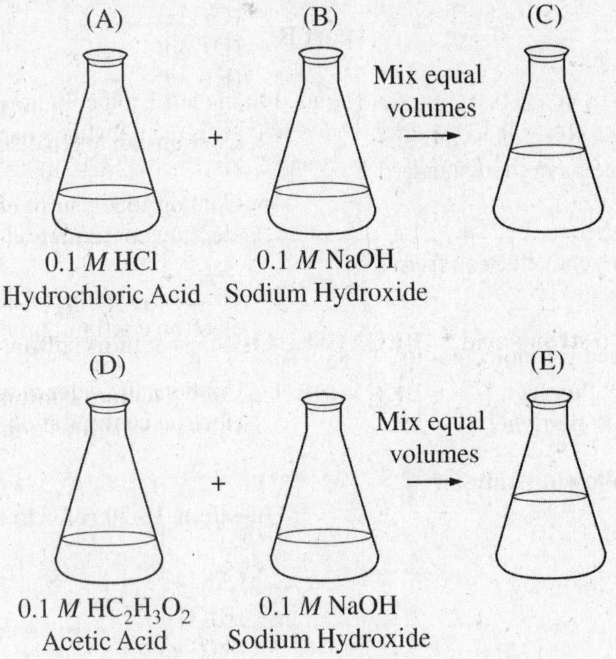

21. Has a hydroxide ion concentration of 10^{-7} *M* at 298 K

22. Has the highest pH at 298 K

23. Has a pH greater than 7, but less than 13 at 298 K

24. Has a pH greater than 2, but less than 7 at 298 K

GO ON TO THE NEXT PAGE

PLEASE GO TO THE SPECIAL SECTION LABELED CHEMISTRY AT THE LOWER LEFT-HAND CORNER OF THE PAGE OF THE ANSWER SHEET YOU ARE WORKING ON AND ANSWER QUESTIONS 101-115 ACCORDING TO THE FOLLOWING DIRECTIONS.

Part B

Directions: Each question below consists of two statements, I in the left-hand column and II in the right-hand column. For each question, determine whether statement I is true or false and whether statement II is true or false and fill in the corresponding T or F circles on your answer sheet. Fill in circle CE only if statement II is a correct explanation of the true statement I.

EXAMPLES:

	I		II
EX 1.	**H_2SO_4 is a strong acid**	**BECAUSE**	**H_2SO_4 contains sulfur.**
EX 2.	**An atom of oxygen is electrically neutral**	**BECAUSE**	**an oxygen atom contains an equal number of protons and electrons.**

SAMPLE ANSWERS

	I		II		CE*
EX1	●	Ⓕ	●	Ⓕ	○
EX2	●	Ⓕ	●	Ⓕ	●

	I		II
101.	C_2H_2 and C_6H_6 have the same chemical and physical properties	BECAUSE	C_2H_2 and C_6H_6 have the same percentages by mass of hydrogen.
102.	The melting of ice is an exothermic process	BECAUSE	water has a relatively high specific heat capacity.
103.	A 2 g sample of nitrogen and a 2 g sample of oxygen contain the same number of molecules	BECAUSE	equal masses of gaseous substances contain the same number of molecules.
104.	When an atom absorbs a photon of visible light, one of its electrons is promoted to a higher energy state	BECAUSE	an electron has a negative charge.
105.	The alkali metals are very good reducing agents	BECAUSE	the alkali metals are easily oxidized.
106.	A 1.0 g sample of calcium citrate, $Ca_3(C_6H_5O_7)_2$ (molar mass 498 g/mol), contains more Ca than a 1.0 g sample of calcium carbonate, $CaCO_3$ (molar mass 100 g/mol),	BECAUSE	there are more Ca atoms in 1.0 mol of calcium carbonate than in 1.0 mol of calcium citrate.
107.	The water molecule is polar	BECAUSE	the radius of an oxygen atom is greater than that of a hydrogen atom.

GO ON TO THE NEXT PAGE

	I		II
108.	All indicators are colorless in neutral solution	BECAUSE	indicators develop color only in the presence of a strong acid or a strong base.
109.	A 1 *M* sucrose solution and a 1 *M* NaCl solution have the same freezing point	BECAUSE	a 1 *M* sucrose solution and a 1 *M* NaCl solution contain the same number of solute particles per liter of solution.
110.	The average kinetic energy of gas molecules increases as the temperature increases	BECAUSE	the average speed of gas molecules decreases as the temperature increases.
111.	When a concentrated acid is diluted, the acid should be added slowly to the water	BECAUSE	if water is added to a concentrated acid, violent splattering might occur.
112.	Methane, CH_4, is very soluble in water	BECAUSE	water molecules form hydrogen bonds with methane molecules.
113.	A 1 mol sample of electrons is required to reduce 0.5 mol of chlorine gas to chloride ions	BECAUSE	chlorine molecules are diatomic and the charge on the chloride ion is −1.
114.	In 0.1 *M* acetic acid, $[H^+]$ is smaller than $[H^+]$ is in 0.1 *M* hydrochloric acid	BECAUSE	a molecule of acetic acid contains more atoms than does a molecule of hydrogen chloride.
115.	A fluoride ion, F^-, and an oxide ion, O^{2-}, have the same diameter	BECAUSE	the fluoride ion, F^-, and the oxide ion, O^{2-}, have the same number of electrons.

RETURN TO THE SECTION OF YOUR ANSWER SHEET YOU STARTED FOR **CHEMISTRY** AND ANSWER QUESTIONS 25-70.

GO ON TO THE NEXT PAGE

Part C

Directions: Each of the questions or incomplete statements below is followed by five suggested answers or completions. Select the one that is best in each case and then fill in the corresponding circle on the answer sheet.

$$\ldots H_2S(g) + \ldots O_2(g) \rightarrow \ldots H_2O(g) + \ldots SO_2(g)$$

25. When 2 mol of $H_2S(g)$ react with an excess of oxygen according to the equation above, how much $H_2O(g)$ is produced? (Equation is <u>not</u> balanced.)

(A) 1 mol
(B) 2 mol
(C) 3 mol
(D) 4 mol
(E) 6 mol

26. Increasing the temperature of a gas in a rigid closed container increases which of the following?

I. The pressure of the gas
II. The average speed of the gas molecules
III. The mass of the gas

(A) I only
(B) II only
(C) I and II only
(D) II and III only
(E) I, II, and III

27. The number of electrons in $^{118}_{50}Sn^{2+}$ is

(A) 2
(B) 48
(C) 50
(D) 52
(E) 68

28. When two colorless liquid reagents are mixed, which of the following observations would suggest that a chemical reaction has occurred?

I. Formation of a precipitate
II. A color change
III. Appearance of gas bubbles

(A) I only
(B) III only
(C) I and II only
(D) II and III only
(E) I, II, and III

29. Which of the following is the correct and complete Lewis electron-dot diagram for PF_3 ?

(A) 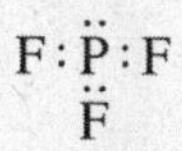

(B) 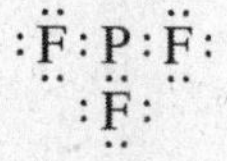

(C) 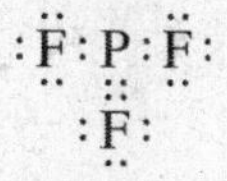

(D) 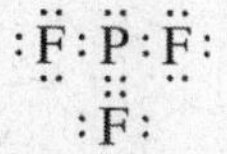

(E) 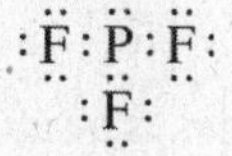

GO ON TO THE NEXT PAGE

30. Which of the following is a transition element?

(A) Iron
(B) Carbon
(C) Potassium
(D) Tin
(E) Radium

31. When 50. mL of 1.5 *M* $NaCl(aq)$ is diluted with pure water to a final volume of 150. mL, what is the molarity of the resulting solution?

(A) 0.10 *M*
(B) 0.50 *M*
(C) 1.5 *M*
(D) 4.5 *M*
(E) 5.0 *M*

32. A 40.0 g sample of a hydrated salt was heated until all the water was driven off. The mass of the solid remaining was 32.0 g. What was the percent of water by mass in the original sample?

(A) 13.0%
(B) 20.0%
(C) 25.0%
(D) 75.0%
(E) 80.0%

33. A solution that has pH of 6.0 is

(A) strongly basic
(B) slightly basic
(C) neutral
(D) slightly acidic
(E) strongly acidic

34. Which of the following molecules is a saturated hydrocarbon?

(A) C_3H_8
(B) C_2H_4
(C) CH_3Cl
(D) CCl_4
(E) CO_2

$$\ldots Fe_2O_3(s) + \ldots CO(g) \rightarrow \ldots Fe(s) + \ldots CO_2(g)$$

35. When the equation above is balanced and all the coefficients are reduced to lowest whole-number terms, what is the coefficient for $Fe_2O_3(s)$?

(A) 1
(B) 2
(C) 3
(D) 4
(E) 5

36. In which of the following compounds does nitrogen have an oxidation number of +5 ?

(A) HNO_3
(B) N_2
(C) NO_2
(D) N_2O
(E) NH_2OH

37. If both NaOH and KOH were the same price per kilogram, it would be cheaper to use NaOH to neutralize a quantity of acid because NaOH

(A) weighs less per mole than KOH
(B) weighs more per mole than KOH
(C) neutralizes more acid per mole than KOH
(D) neutralizes less acid per mole than KOH
(E) is less dense than KOH

38. When a given amount of $Ca(OH)_2$ is completely neutralized with H_2SO_4, which of the following is the mole ratio of $Ca(OH)_2$ to H_2SO_4 in this reaction?

(A) 1 : 4
(B) 1 : 2
(C) 1 : 1
(D) 2 : 1
(E) 4 : 1

GO ON TO THE NEXT PAGE

39. Factors that influence whether or not two colliding molecules will react include which of the following?

    I. The energy of the collision
    II. The orientation of the molecules
    III. The size difference between the reactant and product molecules

(A) I only
(B) III only
(C) I and II only
(D) I and III only
(E) I, II, and III

$$2\ SO_2(g) + O_2(g) \rightleftarrows 2\ SO_3(g)$$

40. What is the expression for the equilibrium constant, K_{eq}, for the reaction represented above?

(A) $K_{eq} = \dfrac{[SO_3]}{[SO_2][O_2]}$

(B) $K_{eq} = \dfrac{[SO_3]^2}{[SO_2]^2[O_2]}$

(C) $K_{eq} = \dfrac{[SO_2] + [O_2]}{[SO_3]}$

(D) $K_{eq} = \dfrac{[SO_2]^2 + [O_2]}{[SO_3]^2}$

(E) $K_{eq} = \dfrac{[SO_3]}{[SO_2] + [O_2]}$

41. A solution contains 1.00 mol of glucose, $C_6H_{12}O_6$, and 2.00 mol of urea, $(NH_2)_2CO$, in 7.00 mol of water. What is the mole fraction of glucose in the solution?

(A) 0.100
(B) 0.143
(C) 0.200
(D) 0.333
(E) 0.500

Temperature (°C)	Vapor Pressure of Ethyl Alcohol (mm Hg)
60	350
70	538
80	813
90	1,182
100	1,698

42. The barometric pressure on Pikes Peak (14,109 feet) in Colorado averages 455 mm Hg. From the table above, one can conclude that the boiling point of ethyl alcohol at this altitude would be

(A) 100°C
(B) between 90°C and 100°C
(C) between 80°C and 90°C
(D) between 70°C and 80°C
(E) between 60°C and 70°C

$$\ldots Zn(s) + \ldots H^+(aq) \rightarrow$$

43. When the equation for the reaction represented above is completed and balanced and all coefficients are reduced to lowest whole-number terms, the coefficient for $H^+(aq)$ is

(A) 2
(B) 3
(C) 4
(D) 5
(E) 6

44. Which of the following statements is true concerning a saturated solution of a salt at a constant temperature?

(A) The concentrations of salt and solvent are usually equal.
(B) The amount of dissolved salt is constant.
(C) Addition of solid salt shifts the equilibrium, which results in an increase in the amount of dissolved salt.
(D) The solution is unstable and sudden crystallization could occur.
(E) At the same temperature, a saturated solution of any other salt has the same concentration.

GO ON TO THE NEXT PAGE

$$2\,CO(g) + O_2(g) \rightarrow 2\,CO_2(g)$$

45. According to the reaction represented above, 1.00 mol of $CO(g)$ reacts at 0°C and 1 atm to consume how much $O_2(g)$?

(A) 32.0 g
(B) 11.2 L
(C) 22.4 L
(D) 1.00 mol
(E) 2.00 mol

46. Species that in water can either accept or donate protons include which of the following?

I. CH_4
II. HCO_3^-
III. HPO_4^{2-}

(A) I only
(B) II only
(C) III only
(D) II and III only
(E) I, II, and III

47. The ionization energies of Li and H are 520 kJ/mol and 1,312 kJ/mol, respectively. The ionization energy of He is

(A) 496 kJ/mol
(B) 656 kJ/mol
(C) 899 kJ/mol
(D) 1,086 kJ/mol
(E) 2,372 kJ/mol

48. An active ingredient in common household bleach solutions is most likely to be which of the following?

(A) NaCl
(B) NaClO
(C) $NaHCO_3$
(D) Na_2SO_4
(E) $HC_2H_3O_2$

$${}^{2}_{1}H + {}^{3}_{1}H \rightarrow {}^{1}_{0}n + \_\_\_\_$$

49. The missing product in the nuclear reaction represented above is

(A) ${}^{1}_{1}H$
(B) ${}^{3}_{2}He$
(C) ${}^{4}_{2}He$
(D) ${}^{4}_{3}Li$
(E) ${}^{5}_{3}Li$

$$HCl(g) + H_2O(l) \rightarrow H_3O^+(aq) + Cl^-(aq)$$

50. All of the following statements are correct for the reaction represented by the equation above EXCEPT:

(A) H_3O^+ is the conjugate acid of H_2O.
(B) Cl^- is the conjugate base of HCl.
(C) H_2O is behaving as a Brønsted-Lowry base.
(D) HCl is a weaker Brønsted-Lowry acid than H_2O.
(E) The reaction proceeds essentially to completion.

GO ON TO THE NEXT PAGE

P (atm)	2	1	0.5	0.4
V (L)	100	200	400	500
T (K)	200	200	200	200

51. The data given in the table above describe the behavior of a sample of gas. Which of the following empirical laws does the data illustrate? (k is a constant.)

(A) $P = kT$ at constant V

(B) $P_T = P_1 + P_2 + P_3 + \ldots$ at constant V and T

(C) $P = \dfrac{k}{V}$ at constant T

(D) $V = kT$ at constant P

(E) $P = kn$ (number of moles) at constant V and T

52. Of the following, which is an example of an oxidation-reduction reaction?

(A) $Fe(s) + Sn^{2+}(aq) \rightarrow Sn(s) + Fe^{2+}(aq)$
(B) $HCO_3^-(aq) + OH^-(aq) \rightarrow CO_3^{2-}(aq) + H_2O(l)$
(C) $Pb^{2+}(aq) + 2\,I^-(aq) \rightarrow PbI_2(s)$
(D) $HCl(g) + NH_3(g) \rightarrow NH_4Cl(s)$
(E) $Ba^{2+}(aq) + MnO_4^{2-}(aq) \rightarrow BaMnO_4(s)$

$$N_2(g) + 3\,H_2(g) \rightleftarrows 2\,NH_3(g) + \text{heat}$$

53. Which of the following statements about the reaction represented above is true?

(A) The forward reaction is endothermic.
(B) A 28 g sample of $N_2(g)$ reacts completely with a 3 g sample of $H_2(g)$.
(C) $NH_3(g)$ will dissociate into equal masses of $N_2(g)$ and $H_2(g)$.
(D) The reactants occupy a smaller volume than the products when measured at the same temperature and pressure.
(E) The equilibrium concentration of ammonia is affected by a change in temperature.

GO ON TO THE NEXT PAGE

54. The element carbon is the chief constituent of all of the following EXCEPT

(A) coal
(B) glass
(C) diamond
(D) charcoal
(E) graphite

55. At 0°C and 1.0 atm, the density of C_2H_4 gas is approximately

(A) 0.80 g/L
(B) 1.0 g/L
(C) 1.3 g/L
(D) 2.5 g/L
(E) 28 g/L

56. Which of the following contains a weak organic acid?

(A) Vinegar
(B) Hydrogen peroxide
(C) Baking soda
(D) Freon gas
(E) Ammonia

$$\ldots P_4O_{10}(s) + \ldots H_2O(l) \rightarrow \ldots H_3PO_4(aq)$$

57. When 1 mol of $P_4O_{10}(s)$ reacts completely with water to produce $H_3PO_4(aq)$ according to the reaction represented by the unbalanced equation above, the number of moles of $H_2O(l)$ consumed is

(A) 1 mol
(B) 3 mol
(C) 4 mol
(D) 6 mol
(E) 12 mol

58. Increased randomness results under which of the following conditions?

I. A 1 L sample of He(g) and a 1 L sample of Ne(g) are mixed in a 2 L flask.
II. Ice melts.
III. CaO(s) reacts with $CO_2(g)$ to form $CaCO_3(s)$.

(A) I only
(B) II only
(C) I and II only
(D) II and III only
(E) I, II, and III

$$C_5H_{12}(l) + 8\,O_2(g) \rightarrow 5\,CO_2(g) + 6\,H_2O(l)$$

59. According to the balanced equation above, when 4 mol of $O_2(g)$ react completely with $C_5H_{12}(l)$, which of the following is true?

(A) 1 mol of $C_5H_{12}(l)$ must react.
(B) 2 mol of $C_5H_{12}(l)$ must react.
(C) 3 mol of $H_2O(l)$ must be formed.
(D) 12 mol of $H_2O(l)$ must be formed.
(E) 5 mol of $CO_2(g)$ must be formed.

60. True statements about transition metals include which of the following?

I. Most can exhibit more than one stable oxidation state.
II. Their compounds are often colored.
III. Their ions have partially filled *p*-orbitals.

(A) I only
(B) III only
(C) I and II only
(D) II and III only
(E) I, II, and III

61. The molarity of solution X is to be determined by a titration procedure. To carry out this procedure, all of the following must be known EXCEPT the

(A) equation for the chemical reaction that occurs during the titration
(B) volume of solution X that is used
(C) mass of solution X that is used
(D) volume of the solution that reacts with X
(E) molarity of the solution that reacts with X

62. The primary intermolecular attraction that makes it possible to liquefy hydrogen gas is called

(A) London dispersion forces
(B) dipole-dipole attraction
(C) covalent bonding
(D) ionic bonding
(E) hydrogen bonding

GO ON TO THE NEXT PAGE

Questions 63-65

$$Mg(s) + 2\,H^+ \rightarrow Mg^{2+} + H_2(g)$$

A student performed an experiment to determine the amount of hydrogen gas released in a reaction. The student produced the hydrogen gas by reacting hydrochloric acid and a strip of magnesium metal according to the equation above. All of the magnesium metal was consumed and the hydrogen gas was collected by displacement of water in an inverted bottle. The student's data contain the following information.

Mass of Mg .... 0.024 g
Volume of gas collected over water......25.2 mL
Water temperature............................ 22.0°C
Room temperature............................. 22.0°C
Atmospheric pressure.........................749.8 mm Hg
Vapor pressure of water at 22°C......... 19.8 mm Hg

63. What number of moles of magnesium was used?

(A) 5.8×10^{-1} mol
(B) 3.0×10^{-2} mol
(C) 2.4×10^{-2} mol
(D) 1.4×10^{-3} mol
(E) 1.0×10^{-3} mol

64. Why is it essential to know the water temperature in this experiment?

I. To find the vapor pressure of the water
II. To control the rate of reaction
III. To make sure that the reaction goes to completion

(A) I only
(B) II only
(C) I and III only
(D) II and III only
(E) I, II, and III

65. The volume of the dry hydrogen gas at 1 atm and room temperature would be

(A) $\dfrac{(25.2)(749.8 + 19.8)}{760}$ mL

(B) $\dfrac{(25.2)(760 - 19.8)}{749.8}$ mL

(C) $\dfrac{(25.2)(749.8 - 19.8)}{760}$ mL

(D) $\dfrac{(749.8 - 19.8)}{(760)(25.2)}$ mL

(E) $\dfrac{(760 - 19.8)}{(749.8)(25.2)}$ mL

GO ON TO THE NEXT PAGE

$H_2(g) + F_2(g) \rightarrow 2\ HF(g) + 537.6\ kJ$

66. If 0.10 mol of $HF(g)$ is formed according to the reaction represented above, approximately how much heat is evolved?

(A) 13 kJ
(B) 27 kJ
(C) 54 kJ
(D) 110 kJ
(E) 220 kJ

67. A chemical reaction is used to separate a mixture into separate substances in which of the following situations?

(A) Pure water is obtained from ocean water by evaporating the water and condensing it.
(B) Iron filings are separated from sand by the use of a magnet.
(C) Iron metal is produced from ore containing iron(III) oxide.
(D) Plant pigments in a solution are separated by the use of paper chromatography.
(E) Sand is obtained from a sand-sugar mixture by adding water to dissolve the sugar.

68. If a compound has an empirical formula of CH_2 and a molar mass of 70 g/mol, which of the following is most likely to be its molecular formula?

(A) C_3H_6
(B) C_4H_4
(C) C_4H_8
(D) C_5H_5
(E) C_5H_{10}

$PCl_5(g) + \text{energy} \rightleftarrows PCl_3(g) + Cl_2(g)$

69. The system above is at equilibrium in a closed container. Which of the following would increase the amount of PCl_3 in the system?

(A) Decreasing the pressure of the system at constant temperature
(B) Lowering the temperature at constant pressure
(C) Adding a catalyst
(D) Adding some $Cl_2(g)$ to the reaction vessel
(E) Removing some $PCl_5(g)$ from the reaction vessel

70. Which of the following terms gives a qualitative rather than a quantitative description of the concentration of a solution?

(A) Molality
(B) Mass percentage
(C) Dilute
(D) Mole fraction
(E) Molarity

STOP

IF YOU FINISH BEFORE TIME IS CALLED, YOU MAY CHECK YOUR WORK ON THIS TEST ONLY.
DO NOT TURN TO ANY OTHER TEST IN THIS BOOK.

How to Score the SAT Subject Test in Chemistry

When you take an actual SAT Subject Test in Chemistry, your answer sheet will be "read" by a scanning machine that will record your response to each question. Then a computer will compare your answers with the correct answers and produce your raw score. You get one point for each correct answer. For each wrong answer, you lose one-fourth of a point. Questions you omit (and any for which you mark more than one answer) are not counted. This raw score is converted to a scaled score that is reported to you and to the colleges you specify.

Worksheet 1. Finding Your Raw Test Score

STEP 1: Table A on the following page lists the correct answers for all the questions on the Subject Test in Chemistry that is reproduced in this book. It also serves as a worksheet for you to calculate your raw score.

- Compare your answers with those given in the table.
- Put a check in the column marked "Right" if your answer is correct.
- Put a check in the column marked "Wrong" if your answer is incorrect.
- Leave both columns blank if you omitted the question.

STEP 2: Count the number of right answers.

Enter the total here: ____________________

STEP 3: Count the number of wrong answers.

Enter the total here: ____________________

STEP 4: Multiply the number of wrong answers by .250.

Enter the product here: ________________

STEP 5: Subtract the result obtained in Step 4 from the total you obtained in Step 2.

Enter the result here: __________________

STEP 6: Round the number obtained in Step 5 to the nearest whole number.

Enter the result here: __________________

The number you obtained in Step 6 is your raw score.

Table A

Answers to the Subject Test in Chemistry and Percentage of Students Answering Each Question Correctly									
Question Number	Correct Answer	Right	Wrong	Percentage of Students Answering the Question Correctly*	Question Number	Correct Answer	Right	Wrong	Percentage of Students Answering the Question Correctly*
1	C			77	33	D			80
2	A			71	34	A			58
3	B			75	35	A			60
4	A			35	36	A			61
5	B			31	37	A			54
6	E			59	38	C			63
7	D			60	39	C			55
8	B			69	40	B			66
9	E			77	41	A			60
10	B			79	42	E			73
11	C			52	43	A			56
12	E			39	44	B			44
13	C			48	45	B			50
14	E			68	46	D			55
15	A			51	47	E			42
16	D			71	48	B			33
17	C			69	49	C			66
18	E			66	50	D			53
19	A			73	51	C			74
20	C			78	52	A			53
21	C			48	53	E			48
22	B			48	54	B			71
23	E			40	55	C			32
24	D			51	56	A			63
25	B			85	57	D			70
26	C			84	58	C			24
27	B			71	59	C			76
28	E			78	60	C			41
29	E			66	61	C			45
30	A			66	62	A			25
31	B			64	63	E			52
32	B			78	64	A			37

Table A continued on next page

Table A continued from previous page

Question Number	Correct Answer	Right	Wrong	Percentage of Students Answering the Question Correctly*	Question Number	Correct Answer	Right	Wrong	Percentage of Students Answering the Question Correctly*
65	C			23	106	F,F			22
66	B			54	107	T,T			51
67	C			51	108	F,F			38
68	E			70	109	F,F			37
69	A			37	110	T,F			81
70	C			67	111	T,T,CE			62
101	F,T			40	112	F,F			43
102	F,T			47	113	T,T,CE			45
103	F,F			68	114	T,T			26
104	T,T			58	115	F,T			36
105	T,T,CE			67					

* These percentages are based on an analysis of the answer sheets of a representative sample of 5,571 students who took the original administration of this test and whose mean score was 593. They may be used as an indication of the relative difficulty of a particular question.

Answer explanations for the Subject Test in Chemistry can be found on page 403.

Finding Your Scaled Score

When you take SAT Subject Tests, the scores sent to the colleges you specify are reported on the College Board scale, which ranges from 200–800. You can convert your practice test score to a scaled score by using Table B. To find your scaled score, locate your raw score in the left-hand column of Table B; the corresponding score in the right-hand column is your scaled score. For example, a raw score of 39 on this particular edition of the Subject Test in Chemistry corresponds to a scaled score of 590.

Raw scores are converted to scaled scores to ensure that a score earned on any one edition of a particular Subject Test is comparable to the same scaled score earned on any other edition of the same Subject Test. Because some editions of the tests may be slightly easier or more difficult than others, College Board scaled scores are adjusted so that they indicate the same level of performance regardless of the edition of the test taken and the ability of the group that takes it. Thus, for example, a score of 400 on one edition of a test taken at a particular administration indicates the same level of achievement as a score of 400 on a different edition of the test taken at a different administration.

When you take the SAT Subject Tests during a national administration, your scores are likely to differ somewhat from the scores you obtain on the tests in this book. People perform at different levels at different times for reasons unrelated to the tests themselves. The precision of any test is also limited because it represents only a sample of all the possible questions that could be asked.

Table B

Scaled Score Conversion Table
Subject Test in Chemistry

Raw Score	Scaled Score	Raw Score	Scaled Score	Raw Score	Scaled Score
85	800	49	640	13	450
84	800	48	630	12	440
83	800	47	630	11	440
82	800	46	620	10	430
81	790	45	620	9	420
80	790	44	610	8	420
79	780	43	610	7	410
78	780	42	600	6	400
77	770	41	600	5	400
76	770	40	590	4	390
75	760	39	590	3	390
74	760	38	580	2	380
73	750	37	580	1	370
72	750	36	570	0	370
71	740	35	570	-1	360
70	740	34	560	-2	350
69	730	33	560	-3	350
68	730	32	550	-4	340
67	720	31	550	-5	340
66	720	30	540	-6	330
65	710	29	540	-7	320
64	710	28	530	-8	320
63	710	27	530	-9	310
62	700	26	520	-10	310
61	700	25	520	-11	300
60	690	24	510	-12	300
59	690	23	500	-13	300
58	680	22	500	-14	290
57	680	21	490	-15	290
56	670	20	490	-16	290
55	670	19	480	-17	280
54	660	18	480	-18	280
53	660	17	470	-19	280
52	650	16	470	-20	270
51	650	15	460	-21	270
50	640	14	450		

How Did You Do on the Subject Test in Chemistry?

After you score your test and analyze your performance, think about the following questions:

Did you run out of time before reaching the end of the test?

If so, you may need to pace yourself better. For example, maybe you spent too much time on one or two hard questions. A better approach might be to skip the ones you can't answer right away and try answering all the questions that remain on the test. Then if there's time, go back to the questions you skipped.

Did you take a long time reading the directions?

You will save time when you take the test by learning the directions to the Subject Test in Chemistry ahead of time. Each minute you spend reading directions during the test is a minute that you could use to answer questions.

How did you handle questions you were unsure of?

If you were able to eliminate one or more of the answer choices as wrong and guess from the remaining ones, your approach probably worked to your advantage. On the other hand, making haphazard guesses or omitting questions without trying to eliminate choices could cost you valuable points.

How difficult were the questions for you compared with other students who took the test?

Table A shows you how difficult the multiple-choice questions were for the group of students who took this test during its national administration. The right-hand column gives the percentage of students that answered each question correctly.

A question answered correctly by almost everyone in the group is obviously an easier question. For example, 79 percent of the students answered question 10 correctly. But only 40 percent answered question 23 correctly.

Keep in mind that these percentages are based on just one group of students. They would probably be different with another group of students taking the test.

If you missed several easier questions, go back and try to find out why: Did the questions cover material you haven't yet reviewed? Did you misunderstand the directions?

Answer Explanations for the Chemistry Subject Test

1. Choice (C) is the correct answer. Choice (C) is the only equipment listed that can be used to measure and transfer an accurate volume of liquid. A rubber bulb is often used with a pipet as a simple way of handling and transferring the liquid.

2. Choice (A) is the correct answer. Choice (A) is the only equipment listed that is necessary in a distillation setup. Distillation is the process in which a liquid is heated above its boiling point so it is transformed into a gaseous vapor; before the vapor is cooled, it is transformed back to a liquid, and collected as a liquid. A condenser is necessary to cool the hot gaseous vapors so they are transformed back to the liquid phase.

3. Choice (B) is the correct answer. Filtration is the process of removing solid particles from a liquid. This is achieved by passing a mixture of a solid and a liquid through a funnel containing a porous medium. There are various types of funnels designed for specific filtering applications. For example, Buchner and Hirsch funnels are used with filter paper to collect very fine particles.

4. Choice (A) is the correct answer.
   The reaction can be written as follows:
   $Na_2CrO_4 + 2\ Pb(NO_3)_2 \rightarrow 2\ NaNO_3 + PbCrO_4 + Pb(NO_3)_2$

   Both Na_2CrO_4 and $Pb(NO_3)_2$ are soluble ionic compounds. The cations (Na^+, Pb^{2+}) and anions (CrO_4^{2-}, NO_3^-) exchange partners to form $NaNO_3$ and $PbCrO_4$. The Na_2CrO_4 can be thought of as the limiting reagent, and $Pb(NO_3)_2$ as the excess reagent. This is why unreacted $Pb(NO_3)_2$ is present at the end of the reaction. The solution is colorless because $NaNO_3$ and $Pb(NO_3)_2$ are both soluble white solids. The precipitate, $PbCrO_4$, is yellow.

5. Choice (B) is the correct answer.

   The reaction can be written as follows:
   $3\ Na_2CrO_4 + Pb(NO_3)_2 \rightarrow 2\ NaNO_3 + PbCrO_4 + 2\ Na_2CrO_4$

   Both Na_2CrO_4 and $Pb(NO_3)_2$ are soluble ionic compounds. The cations (Na^+, Pb^{2+}) and anions (CrO_4^{2-}, NO_3^-) exchange partners to form $NaNO_3$ and $PbCrO_4$. The $Pb(NO_3)_2$ can be thought of as the limiting reagent, and Na_2CrO_4 as the excess reagent. This is why unreacted Na_2CrO_4 is present at the end of the reaction, making the solution yellow. The precipitate, $PbCrO_4$, is also yellow.

6. Choice (E) is the correct answer. When $NaNO_3$ and $Pb(NO_3)_2$ are mixed with water, no reaction occurs, as both compounds dissociate to release the same anion. The soluble white solids will remain in water as a colorless solution.

7. Choice (D) is the correct answer. When elements in their standard state react to form a compound, the heat of formation is the energy change that accounts for any difference in the initial and final energy of this system. If the internal energy of the products is greater than the reactants, the process is endothermic, and the system gains energy as heat from its surroundings. If the internal energy of the products is less than the reactants, the process is exothermic, and the system must lose energy as heat to its surroundings.

8. Choice (B) is the correct answer. The ionization energy is defined as the energy needed to remove an electron from the ground state of the isolated gaseous atom or ion atom. Elements have different ionization energies depending on their electron configuration. The greater the ionization energy, the more difficult it is to remove an electron. In addition, the ionization energy of an element increases as successive electrons are removed.

9. Choice (E) is the correct answer. The activation energy is defined as the minimum energy needed for molecules to react. This is true even if the reaction is an exothermic process.

10. Choice (B) is the correct answer. Isotopes are atoms of the same element that do not have the same number of neutrons. Because atoms of the same element always have the same number of protons, the isotope is specified by the mass number (superscript to the left of the chemical symbol), or the sum of protons and neutrons in the atom.

11. Choice (C) is the correct answer. Ionic bonding occurs between oppositely charged ions. In NH_4Cl the NH_4^+ is ionically bound to Cl^-, and in NH_4NO_3 the NH_4^+ is ionically bound to NO_3^-. In each cation and anion there are covalent bonds where the electrons are shared equally: in NH_4^+ there are 3 covalent bonds between the N atom and each of the three H atoms, and in NO_3^- there are 3 covalent bonds between the N atom and each of the three O atoms.

12. Choice (E) is the correct answer. Allotropes are different molecular forms of the same element in the same state. For example, O_2 and O_3 are allotropes that are both made of oxygen atoms, and are both in the gaseous state. However, they have different structures due to their different bond arrangements.

13. Choice (C) is the correct answer. A strong electrolyte will almost completely dissociate in aqueous solution. Almost all soluble ionic compounds are strong electrolytes. Ionic compounds can be roughly defined as compounds composed of metals and nonmetals, or compounds containing the ammonium cation (NH_4^+). Both NH_4Cl and NH_4NO_3 are ionic compounds that dissociate to release the ammonium cation and an anion (either Cl^- or NO_3^-).

14. Choice (E) is the correct answer. The 3*d* subshell has 5 orbitals, or 5 possible values of m_l (–2, –1, 0, 1, and 2). According to the Pauli exclusion principle, each orbital contains a maximum of 2 electrons with opposite spins. Therefore, the 3*d* subshell can contain up to 10 electrons (5 orbitals x 2 electrons per orbital).

15. Choice (A) is the correct answer. The ground state is the lowest energy, or most stable state of an atom. The lithium atom has 3 electrons, and in its most stable state the 1*s* subshell, or lowest energy orbital, contains a pair of electrons. According to the Pauli exclusion principle, an orbital can hold a maximum of 2 electrons with opposite spins, so the third electron resides in the 2*s* orbital.

16. Choice (D) is the correct answer. The ground state is the lowest energy, or most stable state of an atom. The phosphorus atom has 15 electrons, and in its most stable, low energy state the lowest energy subshells will be occupied. The electrons fill the orbitals of a subshell before coupling in electron spin pairs. For phosphorus, 12 electrons will fill the 1*s*, 2*s*, 2*px*, *y*, *z*, and 3*s* orbitals. The remaining 3 electrons will fill exactly one half of the 3*p* orbital, with all of the spins in the same direction.

17. Choice (C) is the correct answer. The ground-state valence electrons for elements in Group 2A of the periodic table are all in the *ns* subshell, where *n* is the row number. Since magnesium is in the third row of the periodic table, $n = 3$, and in its ground-state electron configuration its valence electrons reside in subshell 3*s*.

18. Choice (E) is the correct answer. Sulfur dioxide (SO_2) dissolves in H_2O to form sulfurous acid, according to the reaction: $SO_2(g) + H_2O(l) \rightarrow H_2SO_3$. This reaction, as well as the reaction of SO_3 with water to form sulfuric acid, are largely responsible for acid rain. In general, most nonmetal oxides combine with water to form oxyacids.

19. Choice (A) is the correct answer. The ozone (O_3) in the stratosphere absorbs ultraviolet rays from the sun. It is formed by the reaction $O(g) + O_2(g) \rightarrow O_3(g)$.

20. Choice (C) is the correct answer. When any compound containing C, H, and O is completely combusted, it reacts with the $O_2(g)$ in air to produce $CO_2(g)$ and $H_2O(g)$. However, incomplete combustion occurs when there is too little $O_2(g)$ present. In this case, CO is produced along with $CO_2(g)$. If there is a severe limitation of $O_2(g)$, then fine particles of C, or soot, are also produced.

21. Choice (C) is the correct answer. A neutral solution has a hydroxide ion concentration of 10^{-7} *M*. In other words, $[H^+] = [OH^-]$, since the product of $[H^+]$ and $[OH^-]$ must always be 10^{-14}. A neutralization reaction occurs between HCl, a strong acid, and NaOH, a strong base. Because strong acids and bases fully dissociate in aqueous solution, $0.1M\ HCl(aq) \rightarrow 0.1M\ H^+(aq) + 0.1M\ Cl^-(aq)$ and $0.1M\ NaOH(aq) \rightarrow 0.1M\ Na^+(aq) + 0.1M\ OH^-(aq)$. Therefore, $[H^+] = [OH^-]$. The products of the reaction are $H_2O(l)$ and table salt, NaCl. NaCl is a strong soluble electrolyte, but neither Na^+ nor Cl^- contribute to pH.

22. Choice (B) is the correct answer. Because $pH = -\log[H^+]$, a high pH value indicates a low concentration of H^+ ions. In aqueous solution, acids ionize to produce H^+ ions, and bases produce OH^- ions. Therefore, acidic solutions have low pH values, and basic solutions have high pH values. NaOH is one of the most common soluble strong bases, and it is the only lettered solution that is a base.

23. Choice (E) is the correct answer. A solution with a pH greater than 7 but less than 13 is basic. Because NaOH is a strong base, it is completely dissociated in aqueous solution ($NaOH(aq) \rightarrow Na^+(aq) + OH^-(aq)$). Therefore, a 0.1*M* solution of NaOH has a pH of 13 ($pH = 14 - pOH$; therefore $pH = 14 - (-\log 0.1) = 14 - 1 = 13$). A neutralization reaction occurs by mixing aqueous solutions of NaOH and $HC_2H_3O_2$. However, because $HC_2H_3O_2$ is a weak acid, it is only partially dissociated ($HC_2H_3O_2(aq) \leftrightarrow H^+(aq) + C_2H_3O_2^-(aq)$). Therefore, the solution is still basic, because $[H^+(aq)] < [OH^-(aq)]$.

24. Choice (D) is the correct answer. $HC_2H_3O_2$ is a weak acid, therefore it only partially ionizes in an aqueous solution: $HC_2H_3O_2(aq) \leftrightarrow H^+(aq) + C_2H_3O_2^-(aq)$. The H^+ ions make the solution acidic, but not as acidic as a strong acid. For this reason the pH of $HC_2H_3O_2$ must be less than 7, which is neutral, but greater than 2, which is the pH of a strong acid.

25. Choice (B) is the correct answer. The equation can be balanced as follows: $2H_2S + 3O_2 \rightarrow 2H_2O + 2SO_2$. Beginning with 2 mol of H_2S, there must be 2 mol of SO_2 to balance the S atoms, and 2 mol of H_2O to balance the O atoms. Therefore, there are 3 mol of O_2, or an excess of oxygen.

26. Choice (C) is the correct answer. Temperature determines how effective attractive forces between molecules are. Increasing the temperature can be thought of as adding energy in the form of heat, which can be used to overcome the mutual attractive force between molecules, allowing them to move faster. This increased movement also reduces the amount of free space in which the molecules can move, increasing the pressure of the system.

27. Choice (B) is the correct answer. This expression of tin contains information on the atomic number (lower left, number of protons), mass number (upper left, sum of protons and neutrons), and the charge on the atom (upper right). Because the

atomic number of tin is 50, a neutral tin atom contains 50 protons and 50 electrons. However, the charge of 2+ indicates that there are 2 fewer electrons than protons. Therefore, the atom contains 50 – 2 = 48 electrons.

28. Choice (E) is the correct answer. The formation of a precipitate, a color change, or the appearance of gas bubbles all suggest that a chemical reaction has occurred. A precipitate indicates that soluble reactants form an insoluble product. A color change suggests that the reactants have formed a product that interacts differently with visible light. The appearance of gas bubbles indicates the formation of gaseous products.

29. Choice (E) is the correct answer. Phosphorous (Group 5A) has 5 valence shell electrons, and fluorine (Group 7A) has 7. The total number of valence electrons is therefore 5 + (7*3) = 26. For a single covalent bond between the P and each F, there should be 2 electrons (2*3 = 6 valence electrons for covalent bonds). Next, electrons are placed around each F, as an atom is most stable with 8 valence electrons (6*3 = 18 electrons to complete F octets). Finally, the remaining 2 electrons are placed on the central P atom to complete its octet.

30. Choice (A) is the correct answer. A transition element is a metal with its outer electrons filling the *d* subshell, which is characteristic of Group 3 to Group 12 metals. Iron is a Group 8 metal, therefore it is a transition element.

31. Choice (B) is the correct answer. Molarity is a measure of solution concentration, defined as: *M* = moles of solute/volume of solution in liters. Therefore, a 1.5 *M* solution of NaCl = 1.5 moles/1L of solution. To perform this calculation, we must remember that there are 1000 mL/1L:

$$0.05\,\text{L} \times \frac{1.5\text{ mol Na}}{1\text{ L}} = 0.075\text{ mol Na} \quad \text{then} \quad \frac{0.075\text{ mol Na}}{0.150\text{ L}} = 0.50\text{ M}$$

32. Choice (B) is the correct answer. The hydrated salt had a mass of 40.0g. After the water was boiled off, the mass of the salt was 32.0g. This means that there were 8.0g of water in the original sample. 8.0g is one-fifth of 40.0g, so the percentage of water by mass in the original sample was 20 percent: 8.0g/40.0g = 0.20 = 20%.

33. Choice (D) is the correct answer. Water, which is neutral, has a pH of 7.0. A pH less than 7.0 is acidic, and a pH greater than 7.0 is basic. Strong acids have a pH closer to 1.0, and strong bases have a pH closer to 13.0. Therefore, a solution with a pH of 6.0 is slightly acidic.

34. Choice (A) is the correct answer. The simplest type of organic compound is a hydrocarbon, a compound that contains only carbon and hydrogen. Saturated hydrocarbons contain only single bonds of C-H and C-C, so their general formula is C_nH_{2n+2} (the maximum number of H atoms per C). Therefore, of the two hydrocarbons given as lettered answers, C_3H_8 is the only saturated hydrocarbon.

35. Choice (A) is the correct answer. The equation is balanced as follows so that there is the same number of each element on both sides of the equation: $Fe_2O_3 + 3CO \rightarrow 2Fe + 3CO_2$. Therefore, the coefficient of Fe_2O_3 is 1.

36. Choice (A) is the correct answer. The oxidation number of an atom is its actual charge if it is a monotomic ion; otherwise, it is a hypothetical number assigned using a set of rules. Knowing that (1) the sum of the oxidation numbers of all atoms in a neutral compound is zero, (2) the oxidation number of hydrogen is +1 when bonded to nonmetals, and (3) the oxidation number of oxygen is usually –2, we can see that the oxidation number of nitrogen in HNO_3 must be +5 in order for the sum of oxidation numbers to be zero.

37. Choice (A) is the correct answer. A solution in which $[H^+] > [OH^-]$ is acidic, and a solution in which $[H^+] = [OH^-]$ is neutral. Therefore, to neutralize an acid, additional OH^- ions must be added to the solution. Since NaOH and KOH are both strong bases, they completely dissociate in aqueous solution to produce OH^-(*aq*) ions. Therefore, they neutralize the same amount of acid per mole. However, the atomic weight of Na is less than that of K, so a lesser weight of NaOH can neutralize the same quantity of acid.

38. Choice (C) is the correct answer. A solution of $Ca(OH)_2$ is basic, therefore $[H^+] < [OH^-]$. In order to neutralize the solution, enough H_2SO_4 must be added such that $[H^+] = [OH^-]$. Because $Ca(OH)_2$ has two OH^- ions and H_2SO_4 has two H^+ ions, in order for $[H^+]$ to equal $[OH^-]$, the mole ratio of $Ca(OH)_2$ to H_2SO_4 must be 1 : 1. The complete chemical reaction can be written in a balanced equation as follows:

$Ca(OH)_2 + H_2SO_4 \rightarrow CaSO_4 + H_2O$.

39. Choice (C) is the correct answer. According to the collision model, molecules must collide in order to react. However, only a small fraction of those collisions actually lead to a reaction. In all reactions, molecules must possess a certain minimum amount of energy in order to react (activation energy). Also, the molecules must be oriented so the atoms are positioned to form new bonds. However, the size difference between reactant and product molecules does not affect whether or not a reaction will occur.

40. Choice (B) is the correct answer. For the general equilibrium equation $aA + bB \leftrightarrow cC + dD$, the equilibrium constant K_{eq} can be written as:

$K_{eq} = \frac{([C]^C[D]^D)}{([A]^A[B]^B)}$. In other words, the equilibrium constant is the product of the concentration of products (raised to the power of their molecular coefficient), divided by the product of the reactants (each raised to the power of their molecular coefficient). Therefore, the equilibrium constant for $2SO_2 + O_2 \leftrightarrow 2SO_3$ can be written as:

$$K_{eq} = \frac{\left([SO_3]^2\right)}{\left([SO_2]^2[O_2]\right)}.$$

41. Choice (A) is the correct answer. The total number of moles of solution is: 1.00 mol glucose + 2.00 mol urea + 7.00 mol water = 10.00 mol total. Therefore, the mole fraction of glucose in the solution is 1 mol glucose/10 mol total = 0.100.

42. Choice (E) is the correct answer. The boiling point of a substance occurs when its vapor pressure equals the atmospheric pressure of its environment. Therefore, the boiling point of ethyl alcohol on Pikes Peak will occur when its vapor pressure = 455 mm Hg. According to the table, the vapor pressure of ethyl alcohol is 455 mm Hg between 60°C and 70°C.

43. Choice (A) is the correct answer. The outermost electron subshell of zinc is 4*s*, and it contains 2 electrons that are easily lost to form a noble-gas electron configuration. Therefore, Zn often assumes a charge of +2 in an ionic compound, and this reaction can be written as $Zn(s) + 2H^+(aq) \rightarrow Zn^{2+}(aq) + H_2^+(aq)$, with a coefficient of 2 for H^+ to balance the equation.

44. Choice (B) is the correct answer. A saturated solution of a salt contains the maximum amount of dissolved salt that produces an equilibrium solution. Therefore, the solution is stable, and the amount of dissolved salt cannot be increased further without interrupting the equilibrium. The concentration of salt that produces a saturated solution depends on the solubility of the salt in question, and varies widely. Therefore, the only true statement is that at a constant temperature, the amount of salt will remain constant, due to the equilibrium established.

45. Choice (B) is the correct answer. According to the equation, the ratio of $CO:O_2$ is 2:1. Therefore, 1.00 mol of CO reacts with 0.50 mol of O_2 to produce CO_2. Avogadro's hypothesis states that 1 mole of any gas at constant temperature and pressure (taken as 0°C and 1 atm) has a volume of 22.4 L. Therefore, 1 mole of oxygen at 0°C and 1 atm has a volume of 22.4 L, so 0.50 mol of oxygen at 0°C and 1 atm must have a volume of 11.2 L.

46. Choice (D) is the correct answer. Both HCO_3^- and HPO_4^{2-} are amphoteric, meaning that they can act as an acid when combined with something more basic than themselves, or as a base when combined with something more acidic. CH_4, on the other hand, is not capable of acting as either a Brønsted acid/base (proton donor/acceptor) or Lewis acid/base (electron acceptor/donor).

47. Choice (E) is the correct answer. The ionization energy of an atom is the minimum amount of energy needed to remove one electron from the atom in its ground state. Both Li (Group I) and H (Group I) each have one valence electron. On the contrary, He (Group 8A) has a full valence shell with 8 electrons. Therefore, the ionization energy of He must be greater than that of either Li or H, since removing an electron from an atom with a full, stable outer shell will require more energy. Therefore, Choice (E) is the only possible choice.

48. Choice (B) is the correct answer. Bleach often works via oxidation, and often contains NaClO, which readily accepts electrons. This answer can be reached by process of elimination, as NaClO is the only oxidizer listed as an answer: NaCl is table salt, $NaHCO_3$ is baking soda and can act as a weak acid or a weak base, and Na_2SO_4 and $HC_2H_3O_2$ are both acids.

49. Choice (C) is the correct answer. In a nuclear equation, the mass numbers (superscript, sum of protons and neutrons) and atomic numbers (subscript, number of protons) must be balanced on both sides of the equation. The sum of the mass numbers for the reactants is 3+2 = 5, and the sum of the atomic numbers 1+1 = 2. Therefore, the mass number of the missing product must be 4 (5-1), and the atomic number 2 (2-0 = 2).

50. Choice (D) is the correct answer. Brønsted-Lowry acids are proton donors, and since HCl is a strong acid, it fully dissociates in H_2O, and is therefore capable of donating many more H^+ than H_2O, which can act as either a Brønsted-Lowry acid or base.

51. Choice (C) is the correct answer. According to the data, the temperature is the only parameter that is held constant. This eliminates all answer choices except choice (C). In addition, the data show an inverse relationship between volume and pressure, which is expressed as $P = k/V$ where k is constant.

52. Choice (A) is the correct answer. In an oxidation-reduction reaction, electrons are transferred from an oxidized substance (oxidation state increases) to a reduced substance (oxidation state decreases). The only answer where this occurs is with the transfer of electrons from Fe to Sn^{2+}.

53. Choice (E) is the correct answer. The reaction describes the production of ammonia, which is an exothermic process (releases heat). The coefficients of the reactants and products indicate that NH_3 will not dissociate into equal masses of N_2 and H_2 gas, that 28g of N_2 is not enough to completely react with H_2, and that the reactants do not occupy a smaller volume than the products. It is true that the equilibrium concentration of NH_3 is affected by a change in temperature, according to Le Chatelier's principle.

54. Choice (B) is the correct answer. Carbon has several allotropes. In other words, the element can bond in different structures, producing very physically different materials. Glass is the only substance listed that does not contain carbon. It is an amorphous, noncrystalline solid and can be made from many different materials.

55. Choice (C) is the correct answer. According to Avogadro's hypothesis, 1 mol of gas has a volume of 22.4 L at 0°C and 1 atm. The molar mass of C_2H_4 is the sum of the molar masses of each element: 2(12 g/mol) + 4 (1 g/mol) = 28 g/mol. The density of the gas is then found by dividing the molar mass by the volume of one mole of gas: (28 g/mol)/(22.4 L/mol) ≈ 1.3 g/L.

56. Choice (A) is the correct answer. Acetic acid (H_3C_2OOH) is the characteristic component of vinegar. It is a weak acid, only partially dissociating in aqueous solution. Hydrogen peroxide (H_2O_2) is best known as an oxidizer, baking soda ($NaHCO_3$) is an important source of carbon dioxide, freon gas is made of carbon, and ammonia (NH_3) is a strong Brønsted base.

57. Choice (D) is the correct answer. The equation can be balanced as follows: P_4O_{10} + $6H_2O \rightarrow 4H_3PO_4$. According to the balanced equation, the ratio of $P_4O_{10} : H_2O$ is 1 : 6. Therefore, 1 mol of P_4O_{10} reacts completely with 6 mol of H_2O.

58. Choice (C) is the correct answer. When a 1 L sample of He(*g*) and a 1 L sample of Ne(*g*) are mixed in a 2 L flask, disorder or randomness has increased, as there are two types of gas molecules distributed throughout a larger volume. When ice melts, disorder increases because the H_2O molecules that were stationary in a crystal lattice are free to move about with respect to one another. However, disorder decreases when CaO(*s*) reacts with CO_2(*g*) to form $CaCO_3$(*s*), as the molecules are confined to a more ordered position.

59. Choice (C) is the correct answer. According to the balanced equation, the ratio of the reactants $O_2 : C_5H_{12}$ is 8 : 1. Therefore, if half as much O_2 is available for reaction, half as much C_5H_{12} is needed. This eliminates choices (A) and (B). Furthermore, the ratio of O_2 reacting : H_2O produced is 8 : 6, or 4 : 3. Therefore, if 4 mol of O_2 reacts with 0.5 mol of C_5H_{12}, then the reaction must form 3 mol of H_2O.

60. Choice (C) is the correct answer. The transition metals reside in the d-block of the periodic table, or the 10 columns from Group 3–12. Two of their main characteristics are the existence of multiple stable oxidation states and colored compounds. These are both due to their partially filled *d* orbitals. They often form positive ions due to their low ionization energy. Because the transition metals would need to gain electrons in order to have partially filled *p* orbitals, this makes statement (III) false.

61. Choice (C) is the correct answer. During a titration, a specific volume of a solution with a known concentration is combined with a solution of unknown concentration.

An indicator is used to show the end point of the titration, where stoichiometric equivalent quantities of the solutions have been combined. It is then straightforward to calculate the unknown concentration (mol/L) from the volume of both solutions, and the stoichiometry of the chemical reaction occurring during the titration. Once the unknown concentration is determined, the quantity, or mass of solute in the unknown is calculated from the molar mass of the unknown (g/mol).

62. Choice (A) is the correct answer. Hydrogen is a nonpolar molecule with only 2 electrons, so the attractive forces between molecules are weak. London dispersion forces are the attractive forces caused by an induced dipole that can cause the molecules of hydrogen gas to become a liquid. This happens by choosing a temperature or pressure where these attractive forces are greater than the motional energies that create the relatively more mobile, disordered gaseous state of matter. While hydrogen can participate in the other intermolecular attractions listed, these do not apply to the case of liquefying hydrogen.

63. Choice (E) is the correct answer. In this experiment 0.024 g of Mg were used. This mass can be converted to moles using the molar mass of magnesium, which is about 24 g/mol. The mass of the Mg used divided by the molar mass of magnesium will yield the number of moles of Mg that were used: (0.024 g)/(24 g/mol) = 1.0×10^{-3} mol.

64. Choice (A) is the correct answer. The water temperature is not relevant to the rate or progress of the reaction, because it is not directly involved in the reaction between hydrochloric acid and magnesium metal. However, as water temperature increases, its vapor pressure increases exponentially, which affects the ability of the hydrogen gas to displace the water.

65. Choice (C) is the correct answer. Because the temperature has remained constant, but the atmospheric pressure has changed, Boyle's law may be used to calculate the new volume of the gas. From the student's data, V_1 = 25.2 mL and P_1= 749.8 mm Hg – 19.8 mm Hg. The vapor pressure of water must be subtracted from the atmospheric pressure, since it is an opposing force. From the information in the question, P_2 = 1 atm = 760 mm Hg. Therefore, to find V_2:

$$P_1V_1 = P_2V_2 \Rightarrow V_2 = \frac{P_1V_1}{P_2}$$

$$V_2 = (749.8 - 19.8)\frac{(25.2)}{760} = (25.2)\frac{(749.8 - 19.8)}{760}$$

66. Choice (B) is the correct answer. According to the stoichiometry of the reaction, the formation of 2 moles HF produces 537.6 kJ of heat. Therefore, if only 0.10 mol of HF is formed, then $\left(\frac{2}{537.6}\right) = \left(\frac{0.1}{x}\right)$, and x = 27 kJ of heat.

67. Choice (C) is the correct answer. Choice (C) is the only separation that involves a chemical reaction, as the production of iron metal from ore containing iron(III) oxide involves a change in oxidation states. The other process described in choices (A), (B), (D), and (E) are not chemical reactions, as the chemical properties of the substances do not change in the process.

68. Choice (E) is the correct answer. The empirical formula CH_2 corresponds to 14 g/mol, since the molar mass of C is about 12 g/mol, and that of H is about 1 g/mol. If the compound has a molar mass of 70 g/mol, this corresponds to 5 units with the empirical formula CH_2 $\left(\frac{70}{14} = 5\right)$. Therefore, the compound is most likely C_5H_{10} (5* $CH_2 = C_5H_{10}$).

69. Choice (A) is the correct answer. If the pressure of the system is decreased, this is equivalent to saying that the volume has increased, since pressure and volume are inversely related at constant *T*. According to Le Chatelier's principle, the equilibrium of the reaction will shift in the direction that produces more gas molecules, thereby increasing the amount of $PCl_3(g)$. A catalyst will increase the rate of reaction without affecting the overall equilibrium, and lowering the temperature at constant *P*, adding $Cl_2(g)$, or removing $PCl_5(g)$ would all decrease the amount of $PCl_3(g)$ in the system.

70. Choice (C) is the correct answer. The mass percentage, mole fraction, and molarity all are numerical values related to the molecular weight of the solute that give a quantitative description of the concentration of a solution. Quantitatively speaking, a more dilute solution has relatively fewer moles of solute in a given volume of solvent, where less dilute solution has relatively more moles of solute in a given volume of solvent.

101. Statement I is false, but statement II is true. Acetylene (C_2H_2: %H by mass = 2/26 = 7.69%) and benzene (C_6H_6: %H by mass = 6/78 = 7.69%) have the same percentage by mass of hydrogen. The ratio of carbon to hydrogen in each compound is 1 : 1. However, C_2H_2 is a gas, whereas C_6H_6 is a liquid. Also, C_2H_2 contains only two carbon atoms (each with an *s* and a *p* orbital) and degenerate *sp* orbitals, whereas C_6H_6 contains six carbon atoms that are arranged in a cyclic structure and that are all sp^2 hybridized.

102. Statement I is false, but statement II is true. The enthalpy of reaction ($\Delta H = H_{products} - H_{reactants}$) is negative for an exothermic process and positive for an endothermic process. The melting of ice ($H_2O(s) \rightarrow H_2O(l)$) is an endothermic process because it has a positive ΔH value. This means that the process absorbs heat, which is required for ice to melt. An interesting property of liquid H_2O (water) is its relatively high specific heat capacity, or the relatively large amount of heat it can absorb while maintaining its temperature. This is why the ocean is important for regulating

the temperature of the earth's climate and why water plays an important role in maintaining the temperature of our bodies.

103. Both statements I and II are false. A 2 g sample of nitrogen and a 2 g sample of oxygen do not contain the same number of molecules because they have different molecular weights (nitrogen = 14 $gmol^{-1}$; oxygen = 16 $gmol^{-1}$). A 2 g sample of nitrogen contains more molecules than a 2 g sample of oxygen because the molecular weight of nitrogen is less than the molecular weight of oxygen. Likewise, equal masses of gaseous substances do not contain the same number of molecules.

104. Both statements I and II are true. When an atom absorbs a photon of visible light, it gains energy from the photon (E = hv). This energy promotes an electron to a higher energy state. An electron is defined as a negatively charged subatomic particle. However, it is not the negative charge of the electron that allows it to be promoted to a higher energy state.

105. Both statements I and II are true, and statement II is true because of statement I. The alkali metals (group IA of the periodic table) are very good reducing agents because they readily give up electrons. This is because their valence shells contain one electron. Whereas reduction refers to gaining electrons, oxidation refers to the loss of electrons. Therefore, when a chemical acts as a reducing agent, it is oxidized because it loses electrons.

106. Both statements I and II are false. A 1 g sample of calcium citrate contains *less* Ca than does a 1 g sample of calcium carbonate. Although each mole of calcium citrate contains three times more Ca than each mole of calcium carbonate, its molecular weight is more than three times larger than that of calcium carbonate. The calculations are as follows:

$$1\,g\,Ca_3(C_6H_5O_7)_2 \times \left(\frac{1\,mol}{498\,g}\right) \times \left(\frac{3\,mol\,Ca}{1\,mol\,Ca_3(C_6H_5O_7)_2}\right) = 6.02 \times 10^{-3}\,mol\,Ca \text{ in } (C_6H_5O_7)_2$$

$$1\,g\,CaCO_3 \times \left(\frac{1\,mol}{100\,g}\right) \times \left(\frac{1\,mol\,Ca}{1\,mol\,Ca_3CO_3}\right) = 1.0 \times 10^{-2}\,mol\,Ca \text{ in } CaCO_3.$$

Likewise, there are *fewer* Ca atoms in 1 mole of calcium carbonate than there are in 1 mole of calcium citrate because each mole of calcium citrate contains three times more Ca than each mole of calcium carbonate:

$$1\,\text{mol}\,Ca_3(C_6H_5O_7)_2 \times \left(\frac{3\,\text{mol}\,Ca}{1\,\text{mol}\,Ca_3(C_6H_5O_7)_2}\right) = 3\,\text{mol}\,Ca$$

$$1\,\text{mol}\,CaCO_3 \times \left(\frac{1\,\text{mol}\,Ca}{1\,\text{mol}\,CaCO_3}\right) = 1\,\text{mol}\,Ca$$

107. Both statements I and II are true. The water molecule is polar because the molecular structure of water is an angle with the more electronegative oxygen molecule at the vertex and the two hydrogen atoms at the tips. This causes a separation of electric charge, where the molecule is slightly more negative at the oxygen-containing vertex than at the tips. The radius of an oxygen atom is greater than that of a hydrogen atom because the oxygen atom contains significantly more subatomic particles than the hydrogen atom. However, it is not the difference in radius of the oxygen and hydrogen atoms that makes water a polar molecule.

108. Both statements I and II are false. Not all indicators are colorless in a neutral solution. Indicators are chemicals that change color depending on the hydrogen ion concentration of a solution. They are used to visually determine the pH of a solution, and different indicators are selected depending on the pH range in which the indicator exhibits a color change.

109. Both statements I and II are false. A 1 *M* sucrose solution and a 1*M* NaCl solution do not have the same freezing point. Although the solutions have the same molar concentration, the chemical properties of the solutions are different because sucrose and NaCl have different chemical properties. Therefore, the freezing point of the solutions, or the temperature at which the solutions change from a liquid to a solid, are different. Another difference is the number of solute molecules when the molar concentrations are equal. Water separates NaCl into Na^+ and Cl^- ions because of its polar nature, whereas sucrose is not capable of separating into ionic components.

110. Statement I is true, and statement II is false. The average kinetic energy of gas molecules depends on the temperature of the system. The temperature and the average kinetic energy are directly related, so as the temperature increases, the energy also increases. According to the kinetic theory of gases, heating a gas causes the gas molecules to move faster and the temperature of the gas to increase. Therefore, statement II is false.

111. Both statements I and II are true, and statement I is true because of statement II. When a concentrated acid is diluted, the acid should be added slowly to the water because if water is added to a concentrated acid, violent splattering might occur. This is because the neutralization of a concentrated acid is an exothermic reaction, and if water is added to the concentrated acid, the strongly exothermic reaction will be maximized by the overwhelming amount of acid molecules compared with water

molecules. On the contrary, if the acid is added to the water, there is plenty of water to neutralize the acid, and the high specific heat capacity of water will prevent the solution from a high increase in temperature.

112. Both statements I and II are false. Methane is not very soluble in water because it is not a polar molecule. The principle of "like dissolves like" dictates what solutes are soluble in a particular solvent. Methane will be soluble in similarly apolar solvents. Likewise, water molecules will not form hydrogen bonds with methane molecules because hydrogen bonds are dipole-dipole interactions.

113. Both statements I and II are true, and statement II is true because of statement I. A 1 mol sample of electrons is required to reduce 0.5 mol of chlorine gas to chloride ions because chlorine gas is a diatomic molecule, whereas the chloride ion is a single ion with a corresponding charge of −1.

114. Both statements I and II are true. 0.1 *M* acetic acid contains a lower concentration of H^+ ions than does 0.1 *M* hydrochloric acid because HCl fully dissociates in solution, whereas acetic acid does not. It is also true that a molecule of acetic acid contains more atoms than a molecule of hydrogen chloride, but this is not related to its lack of dissociating fully in solution.

115. Statement I is false, and statement II is true. A fluoride ion and an oxide ion do not have the same diameter, but they do have the same number of electrons. Fluorine is to the right of oxygen on the periodic table and has one additional proton than oxygen. For this reason, the electromagnetic force between the protons and the electrons of the fluoride ion is stronger than that of the oxide ion. Therefore, the protons of the fluoride ion pull the electrons closer to the center of the atom, causing the fluoride ion to have a smaller radius than the oxide ion. While the fluoride ion is smaller than the oxide ion, they do have the same number of electrons. The oxide ion contains two extra electrons since its charge is negative 2, and the fluoride ion contains one extra electron since its charge is negative 1. Both ions have a total of 10 electrons.

Chapter 7

Physics

Purpose

The Subject Test in Physics measures the knowledge you would be expected to have after successfully completing a college-preparatory course in high school. The test is not based on any one textbook or instructional approach, but concentrates on the common core of material found in most texts.

Format

This one-hour test consists of 75 multiple-choice questions. Topics that are covered in most high school courses are emphasized. Because high school courses differ, both in percentage of time devoted to each major topic and in the specific subtopics covered, most students will find that there are some questions on topics with which they are not familiar.

Content

This test covers topics listed in the chart on the next page.

Topics Covered	Approximate Percentage of Test
I. Mechanics	36–42%
Kinematics, such as velocity, acceleration, motion in one dimension, motion of projectiles **Dynamics**, such as force, Newton's laws, statics, friction **Energy and Momentum**, such as potential and kinetic energy, work, power, impulse, conservation laws **Circular Motion**, such as uniform circular motion and centripetal force **Simple Harmonic Motion**, such as mass on a spring and the pendulum **Gravity**, such as the law of gravitation, orbits, Kepler's Laws	
II. Electricity and Magnetism	18–24%
Electric Fields, Forces, and Potentials, such as Coulomb's law, induced charge, field and potential of groups of point charges, charged particles in electric fields **Capacitance**, such as parallel-plate capacitors and transients **Circuit Elements and DC Circuits**, such as resistors, lightbulbs, series and parallel networks, Ohm's law, Joule's law **Magnetism**, such as permanent magnets, fields caused by currents, particles in magnetic fields, Faraday's law, Lenz's law	
III. Waves and Optics	15–19%
General Wave Properties, such as wave speed, frequency, wavelength, superposition, standing waves, Doppler effect **Reflection and Refraction**, such as Snell's law, changes in wavelength and speed **Ray Optics**, such as image formation using pinholes, mirrors, and lenses **Physical Optics**, such as single-slit diffraction, double-slit interference, polarization, color	
IV. Heat and Thermodynamics	6–11%
Thermal Properties, such as temperature, heat transfer, specific and latent heats, thermal expansion **Laws of Thermodynamics**, such as first and second laws, internal energy, entropy, heat engine efficiency	
V. Modern Physics	6–11%
Quantum Phenomena, such as photons, photoelectric effect **Atomic**, such as the Rutherford and Bohr models, atomic energy levels, atomic spectra **Nuclear and Particle Physics**, such as radioactivity, nuclear reactions, fundamental particles **Relativity**, such as time dilation, length contraction, mass-energy equivalence	
VI. Miscellaneous	4–9%
General, such as history of physics and general questions that overlap several major topics **Analytical Skills**, such as graphical analysis, measurement, math skills **Contemporary Physics**, such as astrophysics, superconductivity, chaos theory	

How to Prepare

The test is intended for students who have completed a one-year introductory physics course at the college-preparatory level. You should be able to:

- recall and understand the major concepts of physics and to apply these physical principles you have learned to solve specific problems
- understand simple algebraic, trigonometric, and graphical relationships, and the concepts of ratio and proportion and apply these to physics problems
- application of laboratory skills in the context of physics

Laboratory experience is a significant factor in developing reasoning and problem-solving skills. This multiple-choice test can measure laboratory skills only in a limited way, such as data analysis. Familiarize yourself with directions in advance. The directions in this book are identical to those that appear on the test.

Skills Specification	Approximate Percentage of Test
Recall	20–33%
Generally involves remembering and understanding concepts or information	
Single-Concept Problem	40–53%
Recall and use of a single physical relationship	
Multiple-Concept Problem	20–33%
Recall and integration of two or more physical relationships	
Laboratory Skills	
In each of the six major content topics, some questions may deal with laboratory skills in context	

Notes: (1) This test assumes that the direction of any current is the direction of flow of positive charge (conventional current).

(2) Calculator use is not allowed during the test.

(3) Numerical calculations are not emphasized and are limited to simple arithmetic.

(4) This test predominantly uses the metric system.

Score

The total score for each test is reported on the 200-to-800 scale.

Sample Questions

Two types of questions are used in the Subject Test in Physics and are shown in the following samples. All questions in the test are multiple-choice questions in which you must choose the BEST response from the five choices offered.

Classification Questions

Each set of classification questions includes five lettered choices that you will use to answer all of the questions in the set (see sample questions 1–4). These choices appear before the questions in the set. In addition, there may be descriptive material that is relevant in answering the questions in the set. The choices may take various forms, such as words, phrases, sentences, graphs, pictures, equations, or data. The numbered questions themselves may also take such forms, or they may be given in the question format directly. To answer each question, select the lettered choice that provides the most appropriate response. You should consider all of the lettered choices before answering a question. The directions for this type of question state specifically that a choice cannot be eliminated just because it is the correct answer to a previous question.

Because the same five choices are applicable to several questions, the classification questions usually require less reading than other types of multiple-choice questions. Therefore, classification questions provide a quick means, in terms of testing time, of determining how well you have mastered the topics represented. The set of questions may ask you to recall appropriate information, or the set may ask you to apply information to a specific situation or to translate information between different forms (descriptive, graphical, mathematical). Thus, different types of abilities can be tested by this type of question.

Directions: Each set of lettered choices below refers to the numbered questions immediately following it. Select the one lettered choice that best answers each question and then fill in the corresponding circle on the answer sheet. A choice may be used once, more than once, or not at all in each set.

Questions 1–2

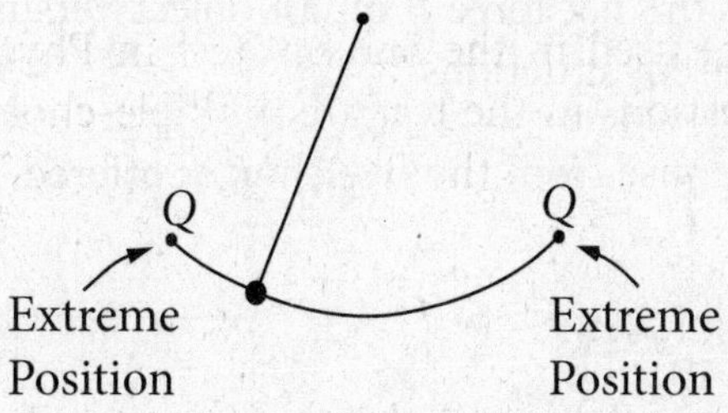

A small sphere attached to the end of a string swings as a simple pendulum. The sphere moves along the arc shown above. Consider the following properties of the sphere.

(A) Acceleration
(B) Kinetic energy
(C) Mass
(D) Potential energy
(E) Velocity

1. Which property remains constant throughout the motion of the sphere?

2. Which property goes to zero and changes direction at each extreme position Q?

Choice (C) is the correct answer to question 1. To answer this question, you may know that in classical mechanics mass is a fundamental property of an object that does not depend on the position or velocity of the object. Alternately, you may realize that, since a pendulum during its motion repeatedly speeds up, slows down, and changes direction, the sphere's velocity, kinetic energy, and acceleration must also change. Also, since the height of the sphere varies, so must its potential energy. Thus you can also obtain the answer by the process of elimination.

Choice (E) is the correct answer to question 2. To answer this question, you must know some specific details about the motion of the pendulum. At each extreme position Q, the velocity and the kinetic energy (which is proportional to the square of the speed) are both zero, but kinetic energy has magnitude only and thus no direction to change. Velocity does have direction, and in this case the velocity of the sphere is directed away from the center, or equilibrium position, just before the sphere reaches Q, but directed toward the center just after leaving Q. The velocity changes direction at each point Q. The only other choice that has direction is acceleration, but acceleration has its maximum magnitude at each point Q and is directed toward the center, both shortly before and shortly after the sphere is at Q.

Questions 3–4

The following graphs show the net force F on an object versus time t, for the object in straight-line motion in different situations.

(A)

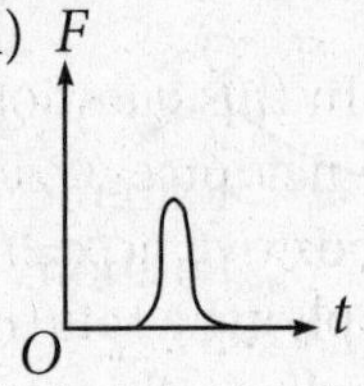

(B)

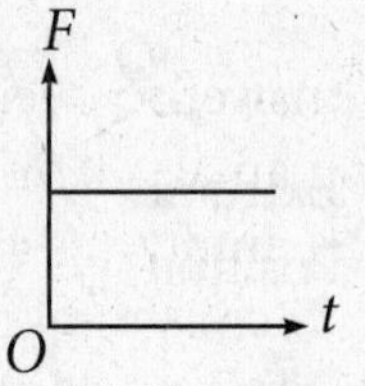

(C)

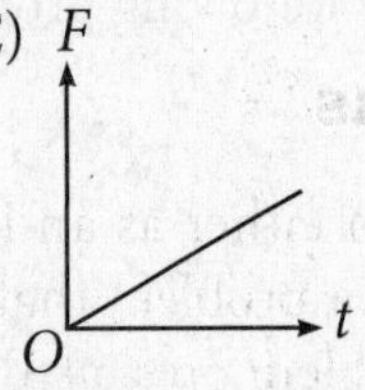

(D)

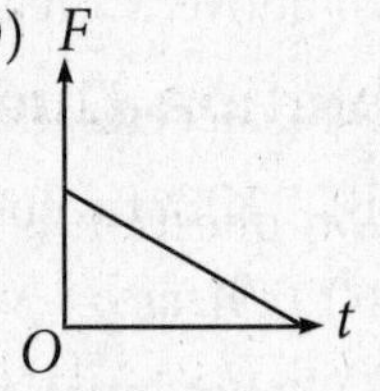

(E)

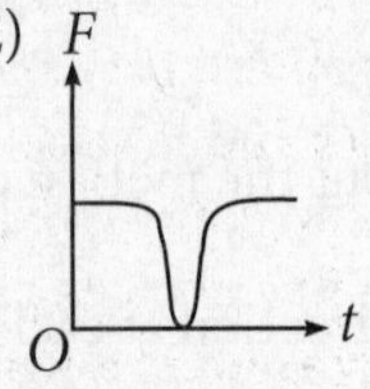

For each of the following speed v versus time t graphs for the object, choose the graph above with which it is consistent.

3.

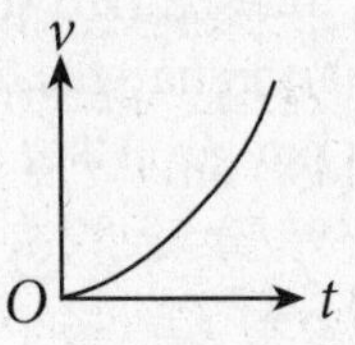

4.

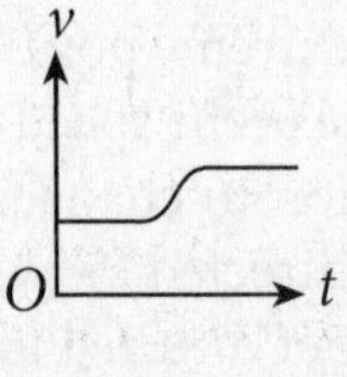

Questions 3 and 4 test the application of physical principles to information presented in graphical form. In each of these questions two concepts are involved. From Newton's second law we know that the net force on an object is equal to the object's acceleration multiplied by the object's mass, a constant. Thus graphs of acceleration versus time must have the same shape as the graphs of force versus time that are given in the options. We must also know that at a particular time the acceleration of an object in its direction of motion is equal to the rate of change of its speed, as determined by the slope of the speed v versus time t graph at that particular time.

Choice (C) is the answer to question 3. The slope of the graph continually increases with increasing t; therefore, the object's acceleration and consequently the net force on the object must also increase continually. The only graph that shows this relationship is graph (C).

Choice (A) is the correct answer to question 4. In this question, the graph initially shows a constant speed, implying an acceleration and net force of zero. Then the curve sharply increases for a brief time, implying a large positive acceleration and large net force. Finally the curve returns to constant speed, implying a return to a zero net force. Graph (A) is the only choice that shows a force that varies in this manner.

Five-Choice Completion Questions

The five-choice completion question is written either as an incomplete statement or as a question. In its simplest application, it poses a problem that intrinsically has a unique solution. It is also appropriate when: (1) the problem presented is clearly delineated by the wording of the question so that you choose not a universal solution but the best of the five offered solutions; (2) the problem is such that you are required to evaluate the relevance of five plausible, or scientifically accurate, choices and to select the one most pertinent; or (3) the problem has several pertinent solutions and you are required to select the one that is *inappropriate* or *not correct* from among the five choices presented. Questions of this latter type (see sample question 6) will normally contain a word in capital letters such as NOT, EXCEPT, or LEAST.

A special type of five-choice completion question is used in some tests to allow for the possibility of more than one correct answer. Unlike many quantitative problems that must by their nature have one unique solution, situations do arise in which there may be more than one correct answer. In such situations, you should evaluate each answer independently of the others in order to select the most appropriate combination (see sample question 7). In questions of this type, several (usually three) statements labeled by Roman numerals are given with the question. One or more of these statements may correctly answer the question. The statements are followed by five lettered choices, with each choice consisting of some combination of the Roman numerals that label the statements. You must select from among the five lettered choices the one that gives the combination of statements that best answers the question. In the test, questions of this type are intermixed among the more standard five-choice completion questions.

The five-choice completion question also tests problem-solving skills. With this type of question, you may be asked to convert the information given in a word problem into graphical forms or to select and apply the mathematical relationship necessary to solve the scientific problem. Alternatively, you may be asked to interpret experimental data, graphs, or mathematical expressions. Thus, the five-choice completion question can be adapted to test several kinds of abilities.

When the experimental data or other scientific problems to be analyzed are comparatively long, it is often convenient to organize several five-choice completion questions into sets, with each question in the set relating to the same common material that precedes the set (see sample questions 8–9). This practice allows you to answer several questions based on information that may otherwise take considerable testing time to read and comprehend. Such sets also test how thorough your understanding is of a particular situation. Although the questions in a set may be related, you do not have to know the answer to one question in a set to answer a subsequent question correctly. Each question in a set can be answered directly from the common material given for the entire set.

Directions: Each of the questions or incomplete statements below is followed by five suggested answers or completions. Select the one that is best in each case and then fill in the corresponding circle on the answer sheet.

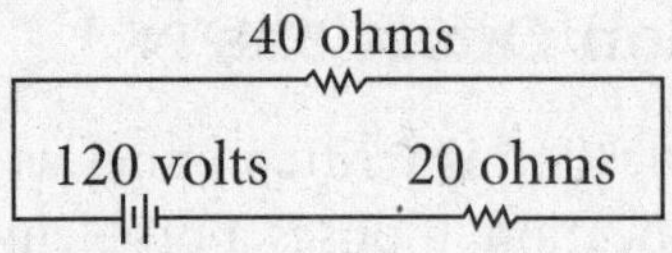

5. If the internal resistance of the 120-volt battery in the circuit shown above is negligible, the current in the wire is

   (A) 0 A
   (B) 2 A
   (C) 3 A
   (D) 6 A
   (E) 9 A

Choice (B) is the correct answer to question 5. In this question, you must apply two concepts to solve the problem. First, you must recognize that the two resistors are connected in series and thus are equivalent to a single resistor whose resistance is 60 ohms, the sum of the two component resistances. Next, applying Ohm's law, you will find that the current is given by the potential difference divided by this equivalent resistance. Thus, the answer is $\frac{120 \text{ volts}}{60 \text{ ohms}}$, which equals 2 amperes.

6. All of the following are vector quantities EXCEPT

   (A) force
   (B) velocity
   (C) acceleration
   (D) power
   (E) momentum

Choice (D) is the correct answer to question 6. This question is a straightforward question that tests your knowledge of vector and scalar quantities. A vector quantity is one that has both magnitude and direction. All five quantities have a magnitude associated with them, but only quantities (A), (B), (C), and (E) also have a direction. Power, a rate of change of energy, is not a vector quantity, so the correct answer is choice (D).

7. A ball is thrown upward. Air resistance is negligible. After leaving the hand, the acceleration of the ball is downward under which of the following conditions?

I. On the way up

II. On the way down

III. At the top of its rise

(A) I only

(B) III only

(C) I and II only

(D) II and III only

(E) I, II, and III

Choice (E) is the correct answer to question 7. In this question, one or several of the phrases represented by the Roman numerals may be correct answers to the question. One must evaluate each in turn. When the ball is on the way up, its speed is decreasing so the acceleration of the ball must be directed in the direction opposite to the ball's velocity. Since the velocity is upward, the acceleration must be downward, making I correct. When the ball is on the way down, its speed is increasing, so its acceleration must be directed in the same direction as its velocity, which is downward. So II is also correct. Finally, at the top of the rise, the ball has an instantaneous speed of zero, but its velocity is changing from upward to downward, implying a downward acceleration and making III correct also. A simpler analysis would be to realize that in all three cases, the ball is acted on by the downward force of gravity and no other forces. By Newton's second law, the acceleration must be in the direction of the net force, so it must be downward in all three cases. Since the phrases in I, II, and III are each correct answers to the question, the correct answer is choice (E).

Questions 8–9

In the following graph, the speed of a small object as it moves along a horizontal straight line is plotted against time.

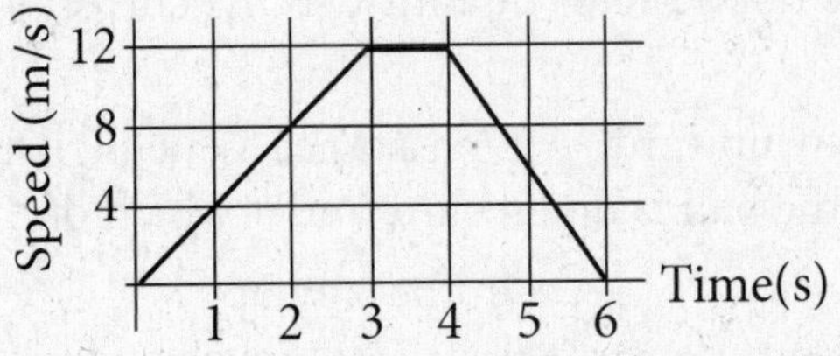

8. The magnitude of the acceleration of the object during the first 3 seconds is
   (A) 3 m/s^2
   (B) 4 m/s^2
   (C) 6 m/s^2
   (D) 12 m/s^2
   (E) 36 m/s^2

9. The average speed of the object during the first 4 seconds is
   (A) 1.9 m/s
   (B) 3.0 m/s
   (C) 4.0 m/s
   (D) 6.0 m/s
   (E) 7.5 m/s

Questions 8 and 9 are a set of questions, both based on the graph provided.

Choice (B) is the correct answer to question 8. To answer this question, you need to know that the magnitude of the acceleration is equal to the magnitude of the slope of a graph of speed versus time. In this situation, from time = 0 to time = 3 seconds, the graph has a constant slope of $\frac{12 \text{ m/s}}{3 \text{ s}} = 4 \text{ m/s}^2$, which is the magnitude of the acceleration. So the correct answer is choice (B).

Choice (E) is the correct answer to question 9. The average speed of an object during a certain time is equal to the total distance traveled by the object during that time divided by the time. In question 9, the total distance traveled by the object during the first 4 seconds is equal to the area under the graph from time = 0 to time = 4 seconds. This area is $\frac{1}{2}(3 \text{ s})(12 \text{ m/s}) + (1 \text{ s})(12 \text{ m/s}) = 18 \text{ m} + 12 \text{ m} = 30\text{m}$. The average speed is therefore $\frac{30 \text{ m}}{4 \text{ s}} = 7.5 \text{ m/s}$.

Physics Subject Test

Practice Helps

The test that follows is an actual, previously administered SAT Subject Test in Physics. To get an idea of what it's like to take this test, practice under conditions that are much like those of an actual test administration.

- Set aside an hour when you can take the test uninterrupted.
- Sit at a desk or table with no other books or papers. Dictionaries, other books, or notes are not allowed in the test room.
- Do not use a calculator. Calculators are not allowed for the Subject Test in Physics.
- Tear out an answer sheet from the back of this book and fill it in just as you would on the day of the test. One answer sheet can be used for up to three Subject Tests.
- Read the instructions that precede the practice test. During the actual administration you will be asked to read them before answering test questions.
- Time yourself by placing a clock or kitchen timer in front of you.
- After you finish the practice test, read the sections "How to Score the SAT Subject Test in Physics" and "How Did You Do on the Subject Test in Physics?"
- The appearance of the answer sheet in this book may differ from the answer sheet you see on test day.

PHYSICS TEST

The top portion of the page of the answer sheet that you will use in taking the Physics Test must be filled in exactly as illustrated below. When your supervisor tells you to fill in the circle next to the name of the test you are about to take, mark your answer sheet as shown.

○ Literature	○ Mathematics Level 1	○ German	○ Chinese Listening	○ Japanese Listening
○ Biology E	○ Mathematics Level 2	○ Italian	○ French Listening	○ Korean Listening
○ Biology M	○ U.S. History	○ Latin	○ German Listening	○ Spanish Listening
○ Chemistry	○ World History	○ Modern Hebrew		
● Physics	○ French	○ Spanish	**Background Questions:** ① ② ③ ④ ⑤ ⑥ ⑦ ⑧ ⑨	

After filling in the circle next to the name of the test you are taking, locate the Background Questions section, which also appears at the top of your answer sheet (as shown above). This is where you will answer the following Background Questions on your answer sheet.

BACKGROUND QUESTIONS

Please answer the three questions below by filling in the appropriate circle in the Background Questions box on your answer sheet. <u>The information you provide is for statistical purposes only and will not affect your test score.</u>

<u>Question 1</u>

How many semesters of physics have you taken in high school, including any semester in which you are currently enrolled? (Count as <u>two</u> semesters any case in which a full year's course is taught in a one-semester [half-year] compressed schedule.) Fill in only <u>one</u> circle of circles 1-3.

- One semester or less —Fill in circle 1.
- Two semesters —Fill in circle 2.
- Three semesters or more —Fill in circle 3.

<u>Question 2</u>

About how often did you do lab work in your first physics course? (Include any times when you may have watched a film or a demonstration by your teacher and then discussed or analyzed data.) Fill in only <u>one</u> circle of circles 4-7.

- Less than once a week —Fill in circle 4.
- About once a week —Fill in circle 5.
- A few times a week —Fill in circle 6.
- Almost every day —Fill in circle 7.

<u>Question 3</u>

If you have taken or are currently taking an Advanced Placement (AP) Physics course, which of the following describes the course? Fill in both circles if applicable. (If you have never had AP Physics, leave circles 8 and 9 blank.)

- A course that uses algebra and trigonometry but NOT calculus (Physics B) —Fill in circle 8.
- A course that uses calculus (Physics C) —Fill in circle 9.

When the supervisor gives the signal, turn the page and begin the Physics Test. There are 100 numbered circles on the answer sheet and 75 questions in the Physics Test. Therefore, use only circles 1 to 75 for recording your answers.

PHYSICS TEST

Note: To simplify calculations, you may use $g = 10\ \text{m/s}^2$ in all problems.

Part A

Directions: Each set of lettered choices below refers to the numbered questions immediately following it. Select the one lettered choice that best answers each question, and then fill in the corresponding circle on the answer sheet. A choice may be used once, more than once, or not at all in each set.

Questions 1-3

(A) Coefficient of linear expansion
(B) Latent heat of fusion
(C) Latent heat of vaporization
(D) Specific heat
(E) Coefficient of thermal conductivity

Select the quantity above that should be used in the calculation of each of the following.

1. The amount of heat required to change 100 grams of ice at 0° C into water at 0° C

2. The temperature at which a 0.5-centimeter gap between 1.0-meter concrete slabs in a sidewalk will close up completely

3. The time required for 100 joules of heat to pass through a copper rod of length 2 meters and cross-sectional area 0.5 square meter that connects two objects at different temperatures

Questions 4-5 relate to the following particles.

(A) Electron
(B) Neutron
(C) Proton
(D) Neutrino
(E) Photon

4. Which particle constitutes the nucleus of an ordinary hydrogen atom?

5. Which charged particle in the list is the least massive?

Questions 6-7

An automobile starts from rest and moves along a straight road. In the graph below, the distance x of the automobile from its starting point is given as a function of time t.

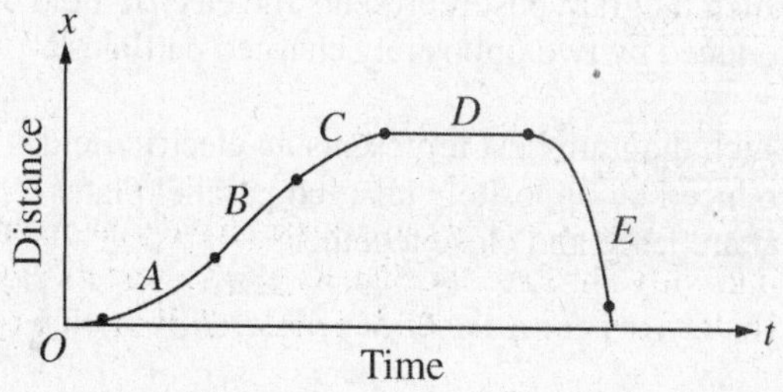

(A) Interval A
(B) Interval B
(C) Interval C
(D) Interval D
(E) Interval E

6. During which interval is the automobile stationary and farthest from its starting position?

7. During which interval does the speed of the automobile have its maximum value?

GO ON TO THE NEXT PAGE

Questions 8-9 relate to the field lines that are shown in the following diagrams.

(A)
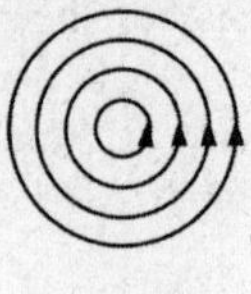

(B)
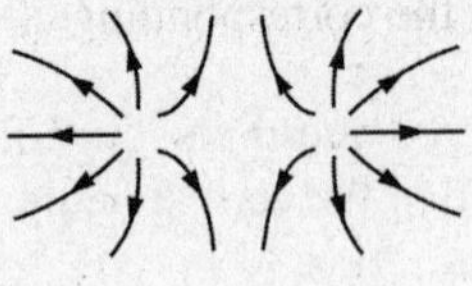

(C)

(D)
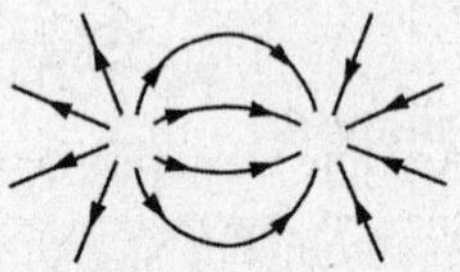

(E)

8. Which diagram best represents the electric field produced by two oppositely charged particles?

9. Which diagram best represents an electric field produced by oppositely charged parallel plates that are large and close together?

Questions 10-12 relate to calculations or explanations based on the following principles.

(A) Conservation of energy alone
(B) Conservation of momentum alone
(C) Conservation of both energy and momentum
(D) Conservation of charge
(E) Mechanical equivalence of heat

10. Used to calculate the velocity of two moving freight cars, after they couple and move together, given the initial masses and velocities of the freight cars

11. Used to calculate the speed of a lump of clay that hits and sticks to a block of wood suspended as a pendulum, given the height to which the block swings and the masses of the block and the clay

12. Used to calculate the speed of a pendulum bob at the bottom of its swing given the height from which the bob is released from rest

GO ON TO THE NEXT PAGE

Part B

Directions: Each of the questions or incomplete statements below is followed by five suggested answers or completions. Select the one that is best in each case and then fill in the corresponding circle on the answer sheet.

13. A skydiver has been in the air long enough to be falling at a constant terminal speed of 50 meters per second. How much farther will the skydiver fall in the next 2.00 seconds?

(A) 19.6 m
(B) 50 m
(C) 98 m
(D) 100 m
(E) 120 m

14. It takes about 1.0 second for an object to fall 5 meters vertically. If this same object is thrown horizontally with a speed of 30 meters per second from a roof-top 5 meters above ground, about how many meters from the base of the building will the object land?

(A) 30 m
(B) $30\sqrt{2}$ m
(C) $30\sqrt{3}$ m
(D) 60 m
(E) 90 m

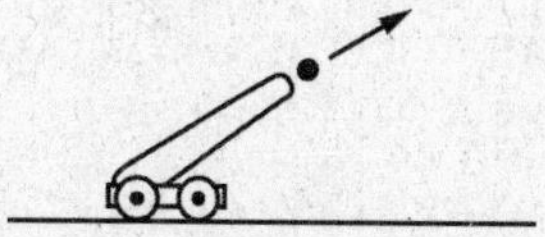

15. Assume that every projectile fired by the toy cannon shown above experiences a constant net force F along the entire length of the barrel. If a projectile of mass m leaves the barrel of the cannon with a speed v, at what speed will a projectile of mass $2m$ leave the barrel?

(A) $\frac{v}{2}$
(B) $\frac{v}{\sqrt{2}}$
(C) v
(D) $2v$
(E) $4v$

GO ON TO THE NEXT PAGE

Questions 16-17

The following diagram shows a permanent magnet and a coil of copper wire that is part of a closed circuit.

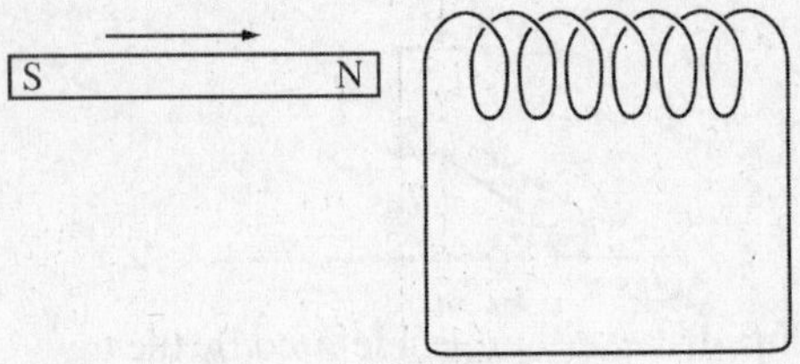

16. What happens as the north pole of the magnet is moved at constant speed into the coil?
  (A) The magnet gains potential energy.
  (B) The magnet attracts the coil.
  (C) The coil attracts the magnet.
  (D) A current flows in the coil, producing a magnetic field.
  (E) The magnet loses kinetic energy.

17. Which of the following would be different if the magnet were turned around so the south pole moved into the coil at the same speed as before?
  (A) The direction of the forces on the magnet
  (B) The direction of the energy transfer
  (C) The direction of the current in the coil
  (D) The magnitude of the current in the coil
  (E) The sign of the charges moving in the coil

18. An electric current in a copper wire is the result of the motion of which of the following?
  (A) Copper atoms
  (B) Copper oxide molecules
  (C) Protons
  (D) Electrons
  (E) Neutrons

19. Eyeglasses, magnifying glasses, and optical microscopes depend for their operation primarily on the phenomenon of
  (A) reflection
  (B) refraction
  (C) interference
  (D) dispersion
  (E) diffraction

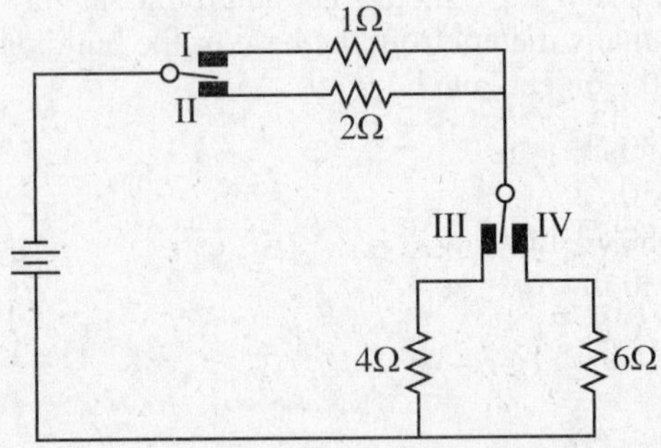

20. In the circuit shown above, the current through the battery will be greatest when the switches are in which of the following positions?
  (A) I and III
  (B) I and IV
  (C) II and III
  (D) II and IV
  (E) The current will be the same regardless of how the switches are positioned.

GO ON TO THE NEXT PAGE

Questions 21-23

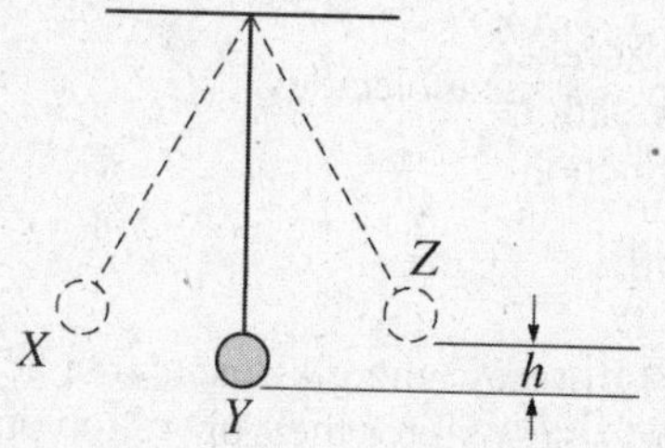

The diagram above shows a pendulum that swings to a maximum height h above its lowest point Y. The mass of the pendulum bob is 0.05 kilogram. At point Y, the bob has a speed of 3.0 meters per second.

21. The momentum of the pendulum bob as it passes through point Y is most nearly

(A) 0.05 kg·m/s
(B) 0.15 kg·m/s
(C) 0.23 kg·m/s
(D) 0.45 kg·m/s
(E) 0.50 kg·m/s

22. The height h is most nearly

(A) 0.15 m
(B) 0.30 m
(C) 0.45 m
(D) 0.60 m
(E) 0.90 m

23. If the potential energy of the pendulum bob is zero at point Y, the total energy (kinetic plus potential) of the pendulum bob is most nearly

(A) 0.05 J
(B) 0.15 J
(C) 0.23 J
(D) 0.45 J
(E) 0.50 J

Questions 24-25

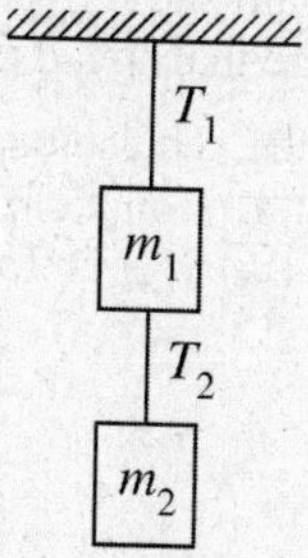

Two masses m_1 and m_2 are hung from the ceiling by two ropes as shown above. The tension in the upper rope is T_1 and the tension in the lower rope is T_2.

24. Which of the following is correct?

(A) T_1 is always greater than T_2.
(B) T_1 is always less than T_2.
(C) T_1 is always equal to T_2.
(D) T_1 is greater than T_2 only if m_1 is greater than m_2.
(E) T_1 is greater than T_2 only if m_2 is greater than m_1.

25. Which of the following best represents the forces acting on m_2?

(A)

(B)

(C)
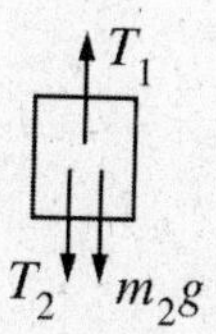

(D)
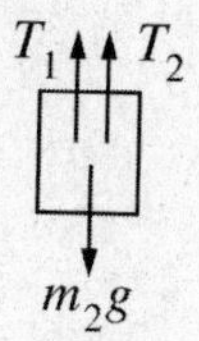

(E)
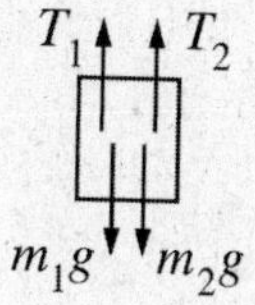

GO ON TO THE NEXT PAGE

26. A boat that can move at 5 kilometers per hour in still water is crossing a river whose current is 2 kilometers per hour. The problem is to steer the boat so that it will land directly across the river from where it started. The solution to the problem is best represented by which of the following sketches in which the river is flowing to the right?

(A) 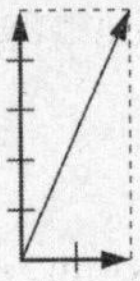

(B) 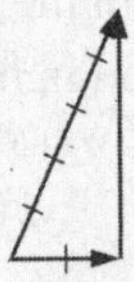

(C) 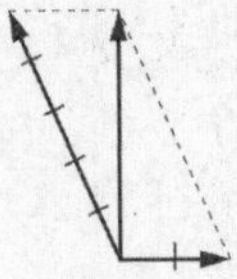

(D) 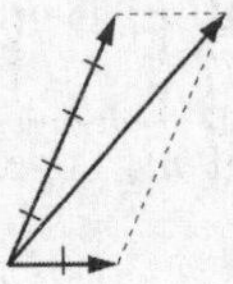

(E) 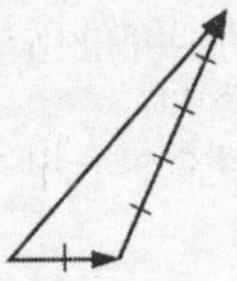

27. One harmonic of a note produced by a flute has a wavelength λ and an associated frequency f. If the wavelength of another harmonic of this note is 2λ, what is its associated frequency?

(A) $\frac{1}{4}f$

(B) $\frac{1}{2}f$

(C) f

(D) $2f$

(E) $4f$

28. Sound waves can exhibit which of the following wave properties?

I. Interference
II. Diffraction
III. Refraction

(A) I only
(B) II only
(C) I and III only
(D) II and III only
(E) I, II, and III

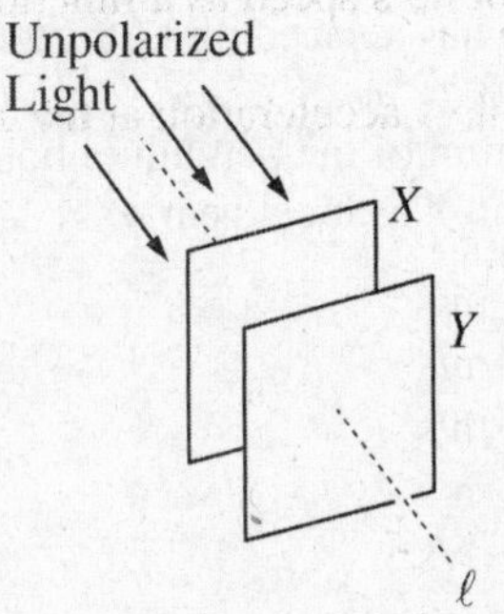

29. Polarizing sheets X and Y shown above are oriented so that none of the unpolarized light shining on X is transmitted through Y. Axis ℓ is perpendicular to both sheets. Which of the following will result in the transmission of light through Y?

(A) Rotation of Y by 90° about axis ℓ
(B) Rotation of Y by 180° about axis ℓ
(C) Rotation of Y by 360° about axis ℓ
(D) Placement of a third polarizer between X and Y, with its polarizing axis oriented the same way as X
(E) Placement of a third polarizer between X and Y, with its polarizing axis oriented the same way as Y

GO ON TO THE NEXT PAGE

Questions 30-32

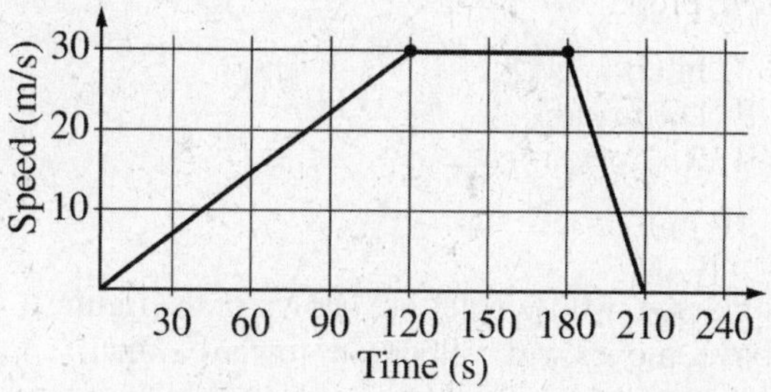

An automobile with a mass of 1.5×10^3 kilograms is traveling on a flat, level road. The above graph shows the automobile's speed as a function of time.

30. The automobile's acceleration at the end of 60 seconds is

(A) 0.25 m/s^2
(B) 2.5 m/s^2
(C) 4 m/s^2
(D) 15 m/s^2
(E) 60 m/s^2

31. The constant braking force applied to stop the car is

(A) 1.7 N
(B) 50 N
(C) 1.5×10^3 N
(D) 4.5×10^4 N
(E) 1.4×10^5 N

32. The speed of the automobile 10 seconds after the brakes are applied is

(A) 1 m/s
(B) 10 m/s
(C) 15 m/s
(D) 20 m/s
(E) 30 m/s

33. An object of mass m is attached to a vertically mounted spring that has spring constant k. The object is displaced from its equilibrium position and allowed to oscillate. Assume that air resistance and friction are negligible. To increase the frequency of the motion, one could

(A) increase the amplitude of the motion
(B) change to a spring with a greater spring constant
(C) mount the spring horizontally
(D) attach an object of greater mass
(E) attach an object of the same mass but greater density

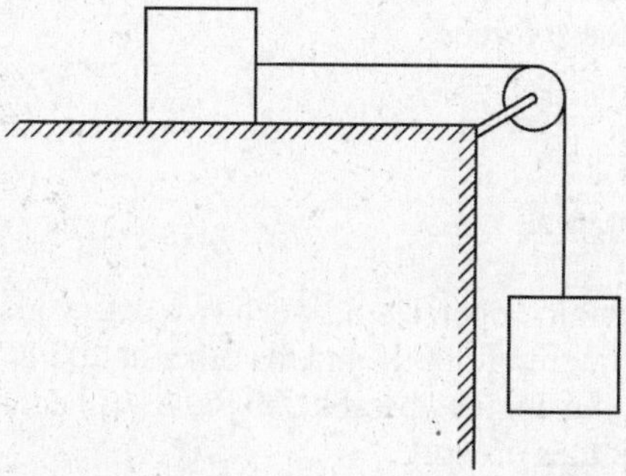

34. Two blocks of identical mass are connected by a light string as shown above. The surface is frictionless and the pulley is massless and frictionless. The acceleration of the two-block system is most nearly

(A) 20 m/s^2
(B) 15 m/s^2
(C) 10 m/s^2
(D) 5 m/s^2
(E) 2.5 m/s^2

GO ON TO THE NEXT PAGE

35. Consider the following four forces involving an object at rest on a tabletop.

    I. The gravitational force on the object due to the Earth
    II. The gravitational force on the Earth due to the object
    III. The force on the tabletop due to the object
    IV. The force on the object due to the tabletop

    Which, if any, of these forces are action-reaction pairs in accordance with Newton's third law?

    (A) Pair I and II only
    (B) Pair I and IV only
    (C) Pair I and II, and pair III and IV
    (D) Pair I and IV, and pair II and III
    (E) There are no action-reaction pairs among these forces.

Questions 36-37

A heat engine operates between two reservoirs, one at a temperature of 300 K and the other at 200 K. In one cycle, the engine absorbs 600 joules of heat and does 150 joules of work.

36. How much heat is exhausted by the engine in one cycle?

    (A) 150 J
    (B) 450 J
    (C) 550 J
    (D) 600 J
    (E) 750 J

37. The actual efficiency of the engine is most nearly

    (A) 75%
    (B) 67%
    (C) 50%
    (D) 33%
    (E) 25%

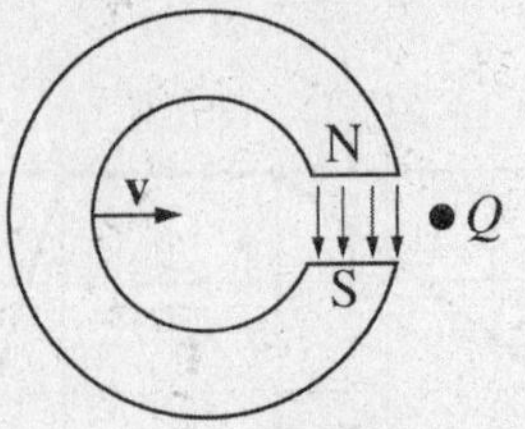

38. A magnet, whose poles are shown in the figure above, moves with velocity **v** toward a small object of charge Q initially at rest. Which of the following is a correct statement about the force on the object due to the magnet as the object initially encounters the field?

    (A) It is zero.
    (B) It is perpendicular to the page.
    (C) It is directed parallel to the magnetic field.
    (D) It is in the same direction as **v**.
    (E) It is in the direction opposite to **v**.

GO ON TO THE NEXT PAGE

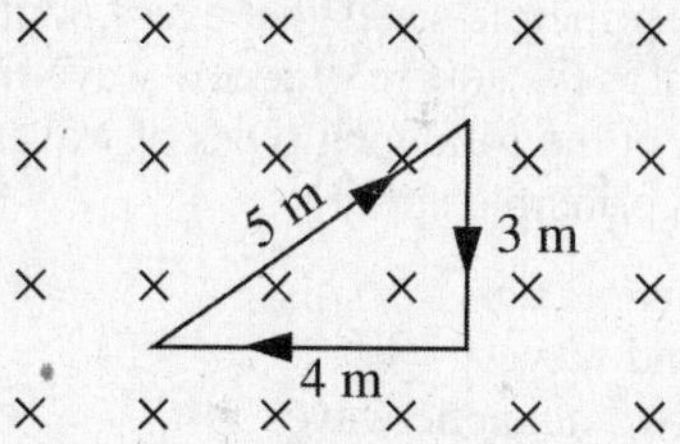

$B = 6$ teslas

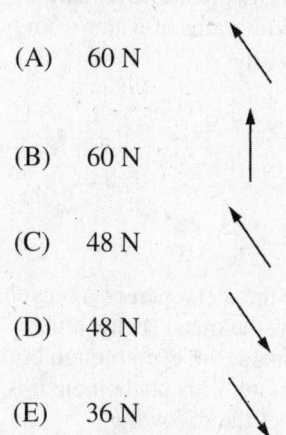

39. A loop of wire shaped into a triangle, shown above, carries a current of 2 amperes in a clockwise direction. A magnetic field of 6 teslas is directed into the paper. What are the magnitude and direction of the force applied by the magnetic field to the 5-meter edge of the triangle?

Magnitude	Direction
(A) 60 N	
(B) 60 N	
(C) 48 N	
(D) 48 N	
(E) 36 N	

40. If two electrically charged particles repel each other with forces of equal magnitude, then the charges must

(A) have different magnitudes
(B) have the same magnitude
(C) have different signs
(D) have the same sign
(E) be separated by unit distance

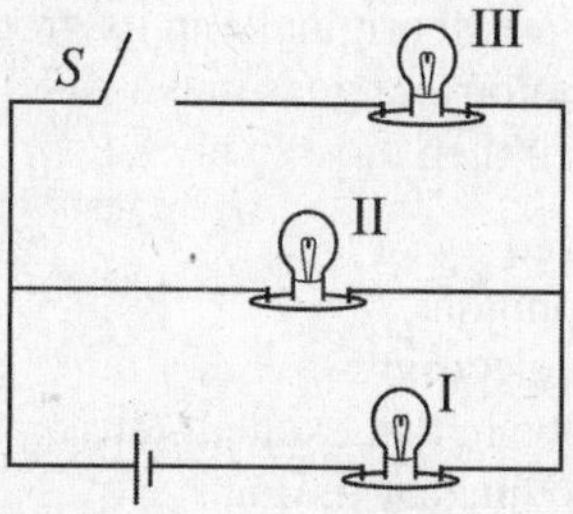

41. A battery and three identical lightbulbs are connected as shown in the figure above. With the switch S closed, the brightness of each lightbulb is noted. When switch S is opened, the brightness of which of the lightbulbs will change?

(A) I only
(B) III only
(C) I and II only
(D) II and III only
(E) I, II, and III

42. All of the following scientists made significant contributions to the field of nuclear physics EXCEPT

(A) Galileo
(B) Rutherford
(C) Becquerel
(D) Curie
(E) Fermi

43. Which of the following distinguishes an atom of one isotope of an element from an atom of a different isotope of the same element?

(A) The addition or loss of a beta particle
(B) The addition or loss of an alpha particle
(C) The amount of nuclear charge
(D) The number of orbital electrons
(E) The amount of nuclear mass

GO ON TO THE NEXT PAGE

44. A hydrogen atom, originally in its ground state, absorbs a photon and goes into an excited state. The atom will then most likely

(A) be ionized
(B) emit a photon
(C) emit an electron
(D) always be in that excited state
(E) undergo nuclear fission

45. A worker hits a metal pipe with a hammer. The ratio of the intensity of loudness as heard by people standing 100 meters away from the worker to the intensity as heard by people standing 200 meters away from the worker is

(A) 4:1
(B) 2:1
(C) 1:1
(D) 1:2
(E) 1:4

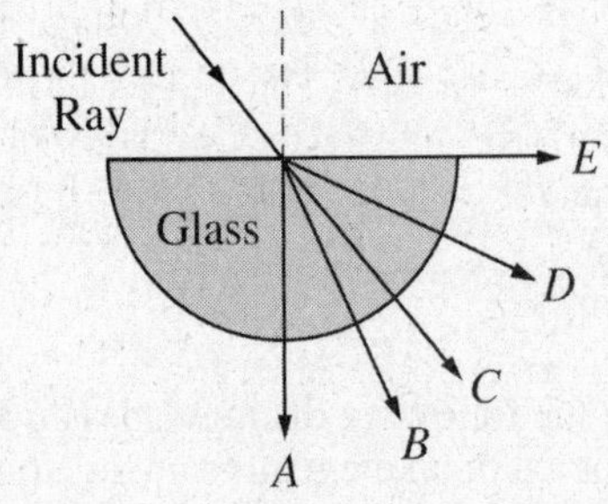

46. A light ray is incident from air upon a semicircular piece of glass as shown above. Which of the labeled rays best represents the subsequent path of the light?

(A) *A*
(B) *B*
(C) *C*
(D) *D*
(E) *E*

47. Huygens' principle states that every point on a wave front is the source of a new wave front. To which of the following types of waves does Huygens' principle apply?

I. Water waves
II. Sound waves
III. Electromagnetic waves

(A) I only
(B) II only
(C) III only
(D) II and III only
(E) I, II, and III

48. When coal burns, it produces heat in the amount of 2.5×10^4 joules per gram. About 4,000 joules of heat is required to raise the temperature of one kilogram of water by one degree. The amount of coal required to heat 5 kilograms of water from 10°C to 60°C is most nearly

(A) 10 grams
(B) 40 grams
(C) 100 grams
(D) 400 grams
(E) 1,600 grams

49. When a person touches the metal part of a bicycle handlebar on a cold day, the metal seems much colder than the plastic handgrip, even though both are at the same temperature. This phenomenon is due primarily to which of the following?

(A) The thermal conductivity of the metal is greater than that of the plastic.
(B) The thermal conductivity of the metal is less than that of the plastic.
(C) The density of the metal is greater than that of the plastic.
(D) The density of the metal is less than that of the plastic.
(E) The latent heat of fusion of the metal is greater than that of the plastic.

GO ON TO THE NEXT PAGE

50. An object of mass m rests on a horizontal frictionless surface. A force F making an angle θ with the horizontal is then applied to the object to move it along the surface. The acceleration of the object is

(A) $\frac{F}{m}$

(B) $\frac{F}{2m}$

(C) $\frac{F\cos\theta}{m}$

(D) $\frac{F\sin\theta}{m}$

(E) $\frac{F\tan\theta}{m}$

Questions 51-52

A person is standing on a scale that is located on a platform at the surface of Earth. The platform is supported by a machine that can move the platform up and down at various accelerations while keeping it level.

51. At what acceleration of the platform does the machine have to exert the LEAST force on the platform?

(A) Zero
(B) 4.9 m/s^2 down
(C) 9.8 m/s^2 up
(D) 9.8 m/s^2 down
(E) 19.6 m/s^2 up

52. If the person's weight has apparently doubled according to the reading on the scale, what is the acceleration of the platform?

(A) About 9.8 m/s^2 up
(B) About 9.8 m/s^2 down
(C) About 19.6 m/s^2 up
(D) About 19.6 m/s^2 down
(E) It cannot be determined without knowing the mass of the person.

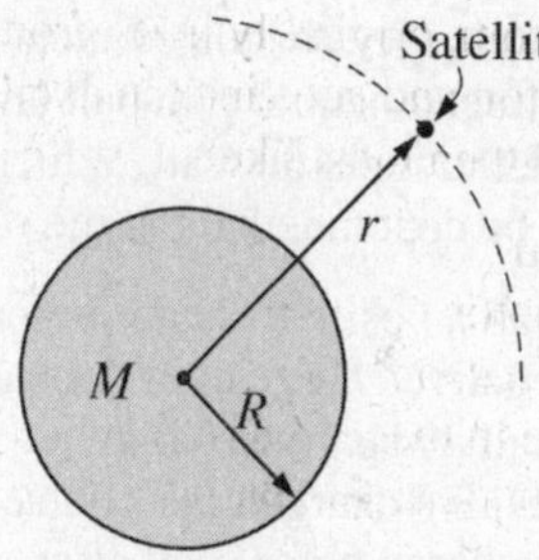

53. A satellite moves in a circular orbit of radius r around a planet of mass M and radius R, as shown above. The speed of the satellite would be greater if M and r were changed in which of the following ways?

	$\underline{M}$	$\underline{r}$
(A)	Decreased	No change
(B)	Decreased	Increased
(C)	No change	No change
(D)	No change	Increased
(E)	Increased	No change

54. A circuit consists of a battery of voltage V and a resistor of resistance R. The current through the circuit is I. If the battery is changed to one of voltage $2V$ and the resistor to one with resistance $4R$, the current through the circuit is

(A) $4I$
(B) $2I$
(C) I
(D) $\frac{I}{2}$
(E) $\frac{I}{4}$

GO ON TO THE NEXT PAGE

55. An electrically charged, insulated metal rod is observed to attract a neutral pith ball and, after contact is made, to repel the ball. Which of the following can be concluded about the rod?

(A) The rod had a positive charge before contact and a negative charge after contact.
(B) The rod had a negative charge before contact and a positive charge after contact.
(C) The rod's charge before and after contact had the same sign.
(D) The rod had a charge before contact, but no charge after contact.
(E) The rod had less charge before contact than after contact.

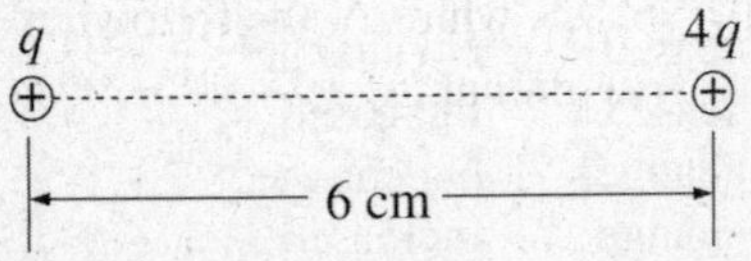

56. Two positive charges of magnitudes q and $4q$ are 6 centimeters apart, as shown above. If the electric field is zero at a point P (not shown) located on the line segment joining the charges, what is the distance of point P from the charge of magnitude q ?

(A) 1 cm
(B) 2 cm
(C) 3 cm
(D) 4 cm
(E) 5 cm

57. A beam of light traveling through the air strikes the surface of a material in which the speed of light is different from what it is in the air. Which of the following is true of the light as it passes into the new medium?

(A) The frequency changes but the wavelength stays the same.
(B) The wavelength changes but the frequency stays the same.
(C) Neither the frequency nor the wavelength change.
(D) Both the frequency and the wavelength change.
(E) Since the speed of light is a universal constant, the speed in the new material is the same as it was in air.

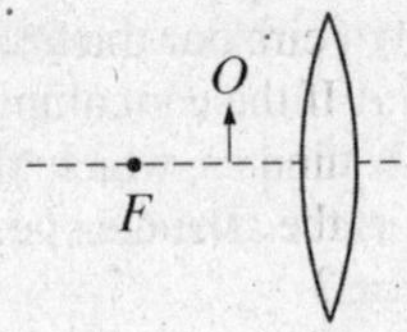

58. A convex lens is used as a magnifier when a real object O is placed inside the focus F, as shown above. The image produced is

(A) real and inverted
(B) real and upright
(C) virtual and inverted
(D) virtual and upright
(E) none of the above

59. The separation of white light into colors by a glass prism is a result of

(A) interference
(B) diffraction
(C) total internal reflection
(D) variation of absorption with wavelength
(E) variation of index of refraction with frequency

60. An object with a mass of 5 kilograms is placed at rest on an imaginary planet where the gravitational field is 4 newtons per kilogram. One can be certain that the object on this planet, as compared to the object when it is on Earth, will

(A) require a greater force to accelerate it on a horizontal surface at 1 m/s^2
(B) have less weight
(C) have less mass
(D) have greater mass
(E) have greater acceleration during free fall

GO ON TO THE NEXT PAGE

61. A car travels around a circular track that has a radius of 1 kilometer. If the car completes 3 trips around the track in 5 minutes, which of the following expressions gives the average speed of the car in kilometers per hour?

(A) $\dfrac{(3)(2\pi)(1)}{5(1/60)}$

(B) $\dfrac{(5)(60)(2\pi)(1)}{3}$

(C) $\dfrac{(3)(2\pi)(1)}{5(60)}$

(D) $\dfrac{(5)(2\pi)(1)}{(3)(60)}$

(E) $\dfrac{(3\pi)(1)}{5(1/60)}$

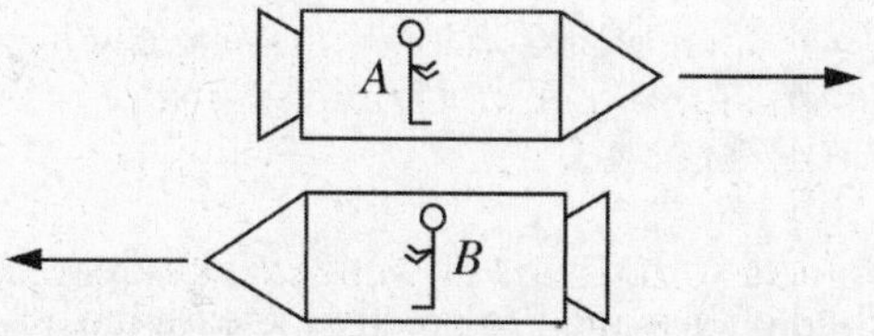

62. Two identical, human-looking robots are standing and facing forward in separate spaceships. Both ships are moving at $0.8c$ but are traveling in opposite directions, as shown above. If a person on the spaceship with robot *A* could make measurements on both robots, which of the following would the person observe to be different?

(A) The robots' heights
(B) The length of the robots' feet from toe to heel
(C) The width of the robots' faces
(D) The length of the robots' legs
(E) The width of the robots' shoulders

63. The experimental study of the photoelectric effect and its analysis by Einstein confirmed the assumption of the

(A) photon aspect of light
(B) crystal structure of materials
(C) discrete charge on the electron
(D) energy-mass relationship of special relativity
(E) uncertainty principle of position and momentum

64. The radius of the first Bohr orbit of an electron in a hydrogen atom is about 10^{-11} meter. The radius of the nucleus is about 10^{-15} meter. If a model of the hydrogen atom were built with the diameter of the electron orbit equal to the width of a classroom (about 10 meters), which of the following would most closely represent the size of the nucleus?

(A) The chair you are sitting in
(B) Your head
(C) The eraser on the end of a new pencil
(D) The point of a ball point pen
(E) A red blood cell

65. Which of the following is true of any material in a superconducting state that carries a current?

(A) It has a large internal magnetic field.
(B) It has no external magnetic field.
(C) It has no resistance.
(D) It has a temperature of absolute zero.
(E) It has a very high temperature.

GO ON TO THE NEXT PAGE

66. The graphs below represent velocity as a function of time t for five different particles, each moving along a straight line. Which particle experiences the greatest displacement between $t = 0$ and $t = 1$ second?

(A)
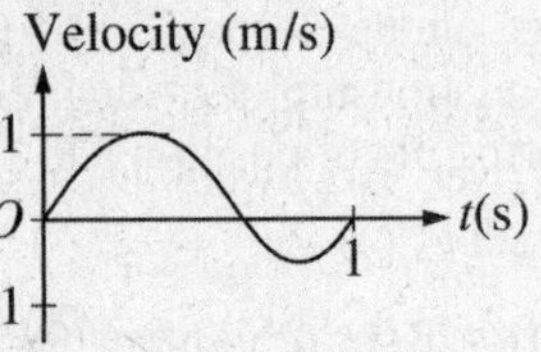

(B)
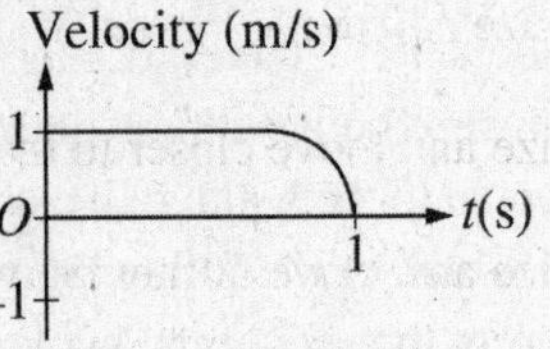

(C)
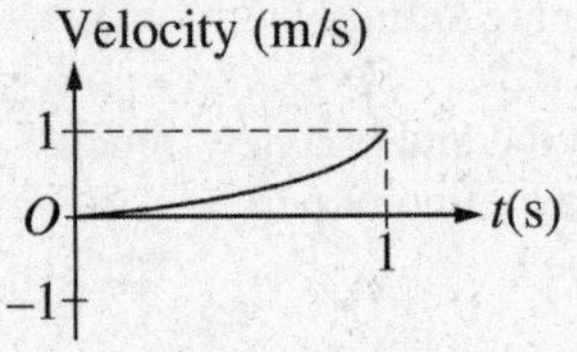

(D)
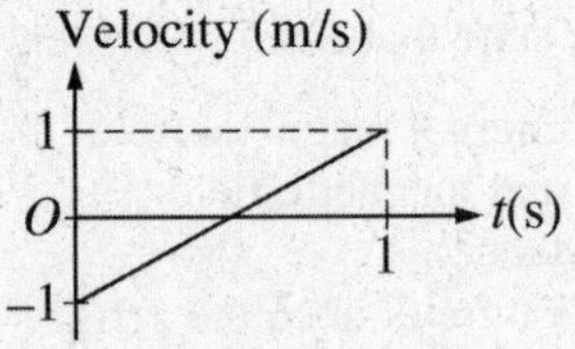

(E)
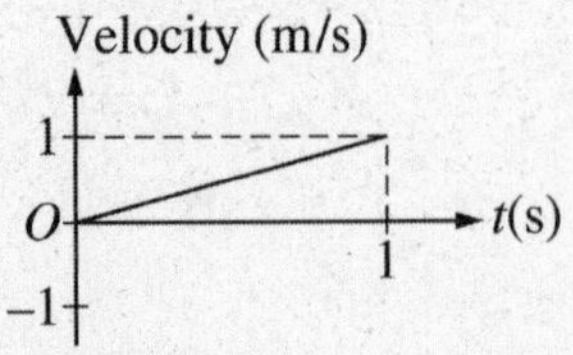

67. The density of a certain material is 3 grams per cubic centimeter. What is the density of the material expressed in kilograms per cubic meter?

(A) 0.3 kg/m^3
(B) 3 kg/m^3
(C) 30 kg/m^3
(D) 300 kg/m^3
(E) 3,000 kg/m^3

68. A system consists of two pucks moving without friction on a horizontal surface. If the pucks collide elastically, properties of the system that are the same before and after the collision include which of the following?

I. Momentum
II. Kinetic energy
III. Total energy

(A) I only
(B) III only
(C) I and II only
(D) II and III only
(E) I, II, and III

69. It takes an amount of work W to stretch a spring a distance x beyond its natural length. If the spring obeys Hooke's law, how much work is required to stretch the spring a distance $2x$ beyond its natural length?

(A) W
(B) $2W$
(C) $3W$
(D) $4W$
(E) $6W$

70. A child on a swing can greatly increase the amplitude of the swing's motion by "pumping" at the natural frequency of the swing. This is an example of which of the following?

(A) Conservation of momentum
(B) Newton's first law of motion
(C) Newton's third law of motion
(D) Resonance
(E) Interference

GO ON TO THE NEXT PAGE

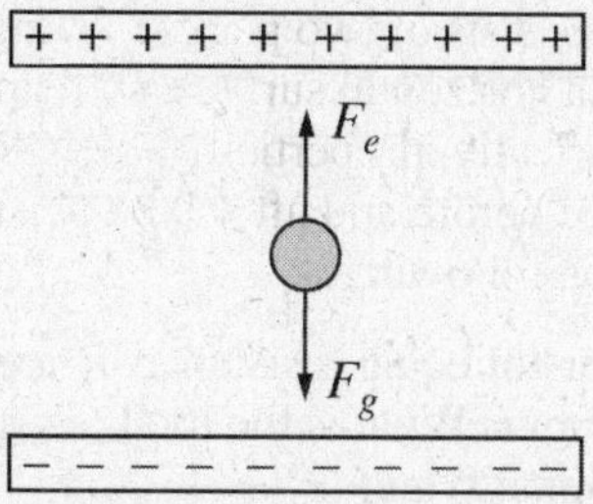

71. A negatively charged oil drop is maintained at rest between charged parallel plates, as shown above, by balancing the downward gravitational force F_g on the drop with an upward electric force F_e. If the mass of the oil drop is 1×10^{-6} kilogram and the electric field strength between the plates is 10 newtons per coulomb, then the charge on the oil drop is most nearly

(A) 1×10^{-3} C
(B) 1×10^{-4} C
(C) 1×10^{-5} C
(D) 1×10^{-6} C
(E) 1×10^{-19} C

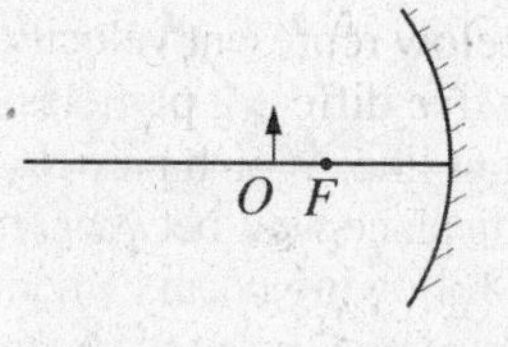

72. An object O is just outside the focal point F of a concave mirror, as shown in the diagram above. As the object is moved away from the mirror, the image will do which of the following?

(A) Decrease in size and move closer to the mirror.
(B) Decrease in size and move farther from the mirror.
(C) Increase in size and move closer to the mirror.
(D) Increase in size and move farther from the mirror.
(E) It cannot be determined without knowing the exact focal length.

GO ON TO THE NEXT PAGE

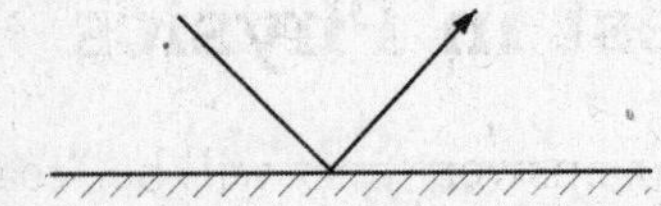

73. Which of the following occurs when light is reflected from a smooth flat glass surface, as shown above?

(A) The light is somewhat intensified.
(B) The light is somewhat polarized.
(C) The light is focused.
(D) The velocity of the light is reduced.
(E) The color of the light is shifted toward the blue end of the spectrum.

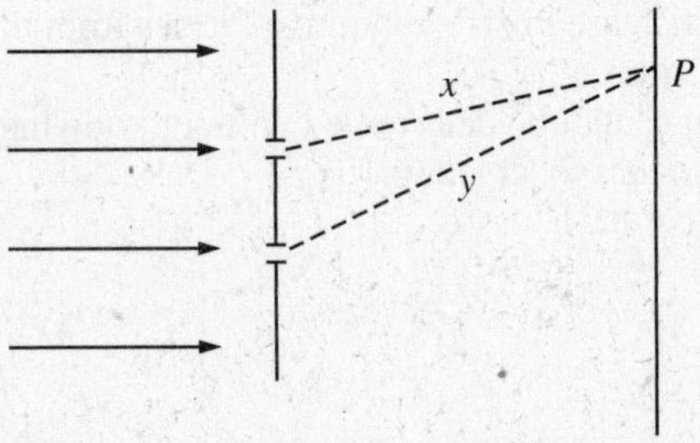

74. Light of wavelength λ is incident from the left on a pair of narrow slits, as shown above. If point P is a bright spot (maximum intensity) on a distant screen, one can be certain that the difference between distances x and y is

(A) zero

(B) $\lambda/2$

(C) $n\lambda$, where n is an integer

(D) $\left(n + \frac{1}{2}\right)\lambda$, where n is an integer

(E) $\left(n - \frac{1}{2}\right)\lambda$, where n is an integer

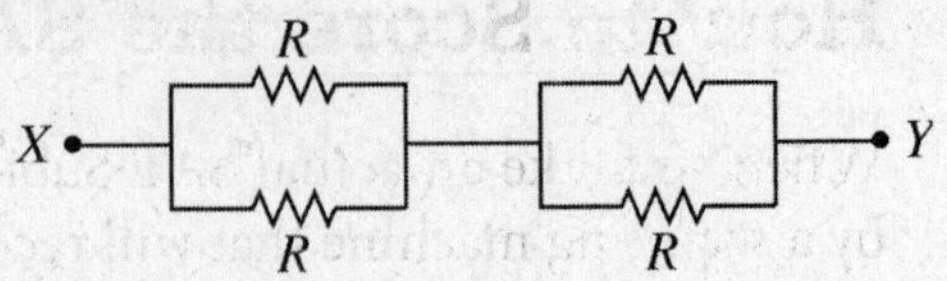

75. Four resistors of equal resistance R are connected as shown above. What is the total resistance between points X and Y?

(A) $\frac{R}{4}$

(B) $\frac{R}{2}$

(C) R

(D) $2R$

(E) $4R$

STOP

If you finish before time is called, you may check your work on this test only. Do not turn to any other test in this book.

How to Score the SAT Subject Test in Physics

When you take an actual SAT Subject Test in Physics, your answer sheet will be "read" by a scanning machine that will record your response to each question. Then a computer will compare your answers with the correct answers and produce your raw score. You get one point for each correct answer. For each wrong answer, you lose one-fourth of a point. Questions you omit (and any for which you mark more than one answer) are not counted. This raw score is converted to a scaled score that is reported to you and to the colleges you specify.

Worksheet 1. Finding Your Raw Test Score

STEP 1: Table A on the following page lists the correct answers for all the questions on the Subject Test in Physics that is reproduced in this book. It also serves as a worksheet for you to calculate your raw score.

- Compare your answers with those given in the table.
- Put a check in the column marked "Right" if your answer is correct.
- Put a check in the column marked "Wrong" if your answer is incorrect.
- Leave both columns blank if you omitted the question.

STEP 2: Count the number of right answers.

Enter the total here: ____________________

STEP 3: Count the number of wrong answers.

Enter the total here: ____________________

STEP 4: Multiply the number of wrong answers by .250.

Enter the product here: ________________

STEP 5: Subtract the result obtained in Step 4 from the total you obtained in Step 2.

Enter the result here: __________________

STEP 6: Round the number obtained in Step 5 to the nearest whole number.

Enter the result here: __________________

The number you obtained in Step 6 is your raw score.

Table A

Answers to the Subject Test in Physics and Percentage of Students Answering Each Question Correctly

Question Number	Correct Answer	Right	Wrong	Percentage of Students Answering the Question Correctly*	Question Number	Correct Answer	Right	Wrong	Percentage of Students Answering the Question Correctly*
1	B			54	33	B			57
2	A			76	34	D			28
3	E			80	35	C			66
4	C			72	36	B			59
5	A			63	37	E			61
6	D			89	38	B			38
7	E			55	39	A			30
8	D			76	40	D			65
9	E			60	41	E			40
10	B			70	42	A			64
11	C			65	43	E			56
12	A			69	44	B			33
13	D			83	45	A			40
14	A			67	46	B			58
15	B			14	47	E			38
16	D			80	48	B			49
17	C			69	49	A			77
18	D			87	50	C			71
19	B			71	51	D			65
20	A			61	52	A			46
21	B			87	53	E			57
22	C			49	54	D			69
23	C			58	55	C			35
24	A			76	56	B			39
25	A			61	57	B			37
26	C			60	58	D			37
27	B			62	59	E			32
28	E			44	60	B			65
29	A			42	61	A			48
30	A			78	62	B			34
31	C			66	63	A			41
32	D			74	64	D			29

Table A continued on next page

Table A continued from previous page

Question Number	Correct Answer	Right	Wrong	Percentage of Students Answering the Question Correctly*	Question Number	Correct Answer	Right	Wrong	Percentage of Students Answering the Question Correctly*
65	C			40	71	D			30
66	B			51	72	A			24
67	E			42	73	B			28
68	E			56	74	C			33
69	D			43	75	C			51
70	D			43					

* These percentages are based on an analysis of the answer sheets of a representative sample of 2,410 students who took this test and whose mean score was 628. They may be used as an indication of the relative difficulty of a particular question.

Answer explanations for the Subject Test in Physics can be found on page 451.

Finding Your Scaled Score

When you take SAT Subject Tests, the scores sent to the colleges you specify are reported on the College Board scale, which ranges from 200–800. You can convert your practice test score to a scaled score by using Table B. To find your scaled score, locate your raw score in the left-hand column of Table B; the corresponding score in the right-hand column is your scaled score. For example, a raw score of 41 on this particular edition of the Subject Test in Physics corresponds to a scaled score of 670.

Raw scores are converted to scaled scores to ensure that a score earned on any one edition of a particular Subject Test is comparable to the same scaled score earned on any other edition of the same Subject Test. Because some editions of the tests may be slightly easier or more difficult than others, College Board scaled scores are adjusted so that they indicate the same level of performance regardless of the edition of the test taken and the ability of the group that takes it. Thus, for example, a score of 400 on one edition of a test taken at a particular administration indicates the same level of achievement as a score of 400 on a different edition of the test taken at a different administration.

When you take the SAT Subject Tests during a national administration, your scores are likely to differ somewhat from the scores you obtain on the tests in this book. People perform at different levels at different times for reasons unrelated to the tests themselves. The precision of any test is also limited because it represents only a sample of all the possible questions that could be asked.

Table B

Scaled Score Conversion Table
Subject Test in Physics

Raw Score	Scaled Score	Raw Score	Scaled Score	Raw Score	Scaled Score
75	800	39	660	3	410
74	800	38	650	2	400
73	800	37	640	1	400
72	800	36	640	0	390
71	800	35	630	-1	380
70	800	34	620	-2	380
69	800	33	620	-3	370
68	800	32	610	-4	360
67	800	31	600	-5	360
66	800	30	600	-6	350
65	800	29	590	-7	340
64	800	28	580	-8	330
63	800	27	580	-9	330
62	800	26	570	-10	320
61	800	25	560	-11	310
60	800	24	560	-12	310
59	800	23	550	-13	300
58	790	22	540	-14	290
57	780	21	530	-15	290
56	780	20	530	-16	280
55	770	19	520	-17	280
54	760	18	510	-18	270
53	750	17	510	-19	270
52	750	16	500		
51	740	15	490		
50	730	14	490		
49	730	13	480		
48	720	12	470		
47	710	11	470		
46	710	10	460		
45	700	9	450		
44	690	8	450		
43	690	7	440		
42	680	6	430		
41	670	5	420		
40	670	4	420		

How Did You Do on the Subject Test in Physics?

After you score your test and analyze your performance, think about the following questions:

Did you run out of time before reaching the end of the test?

If so, you may need to pace yourself better. For example, maybe you spent too much time on one or two hard questions. A better approach might be to skip the ones you can't answer right away and try answering all the questions that remain on the test. Then if there's time, go back to the questions you skipped.

Did you take a long time reading the directions?

You will save time when you take the test by learning the directions to the Subject Test in Physics ahead of time. Each minute you spend reading directions during the test is a minute that you could use to answer questions.

How did you handle questions you were unsure of?

If you were able to eliminate one or more of the answer choices as wrong and guess from the remaining ones, your approach probably worked to your advantage. On the other hand, making haphazard guesses or omitting questions without trying to eliminate choices could cost you valuable points.

How difficult were the questions for you compared with other students who took the test?

Table A shows you how difficult the multiple-choice questions were for the group of students who took this test during its national administration. The right-hand column gives the percentage of students that answered each question correctly.

A question answered correctly by almost everyone in the group is obviously an easier question. For example, 89 percent of the students answered question 6 correctly. But only 14 percent answered question 15 correctly.

Keep in mind that these percentages are based on just one group of students. They would probably be different with another group of students taking the test.

If you missed several easier questions, go back and try to find out why: Did the questions cover material you haven't yet reviewed? Did you misunderstand the directions?

Answer Explanations for the Physics Subject Test

1. Choice (B) is the correct answer. Latent heat is the energy required to change the phase of a substance, and fusion describes the phase change from solid to liquid. In the case of changing ice into water, a certain amount of heat is needed to change the phase from solid (ice) to liquid (water). The amount of heat needed is called the latent heat of fusion. The energy of the latent heat of fusion causes the molecules to move from the stiff arrangement of a solid to the more loose arrangement of a liquid. The latent heat only changes the phase, as opposed to the temperature, of the substance.

2. Choice (A) is the correct answer. The coefficient of linear expansion depends on the material; the higher the coefficient of linear expansion, the more the material expands when heated. To determine what temperature would close the gap between two concrete slabs, the coefficient of linear expansion of concrete is needed. This coefficient indicates to what degree the concrete expands when heated, which is a property of the concrete.

3. Choice (E) is the correct answer. The coefficient of thermal conductivity depends on the material; the higher the coefficient of thermal conductivity, the faster heat travels through a material. For example, metals have high coefficients of thermal conductivity because heat travels quickly through them. This is why a spoon in hot tea becomes hot very quickly. However, plastics have lower coefficients of thermal conductivity because heat does not travel quickly through them. This is why coolers and other insulators are often made of foam.

4. Choice (C) is the correct answer. The atomic number of hydrogen is 1, which means there is one proton in a hydrogen atom. The atomic mass of hydrogen is approximately 1 atomic mass unit (amu). Because the mass of a proton and the mass of a neutron are both 1 amu, this means the ordinary hydrogen atom has only one proton and no neutrons. Protons and neutrons are located in the center, or the nucleus, of an atom. Since there are no neutrons in an ordinary hydrogen atom, the nucleus of the atom is composed of one proton.

5. Choice (A) is the correct answer. The only charged particles in the list are the electron, with a negative charge, and the proton, with a positive charge. The mass of a proton is 1 amu, and a proton is about 1,000 times more massive than an electron. Therefore, the electron is the least massive charged particle in the list.

6. Choice (D) is the correct answer. The automobile remains in the same position throughout the time interval *D*. This is why the line is flat here; for any time during the interval *D*, the corresponding distance is the same. This is also when the automobile is farthest from its starting point. The distance *x* during interval *D* is greater than the distance during any other interval.

7. Choice (E) is the correct answer. The speed is greatest during interval *E* because a greater distance (almost the entire distance) is traveled in about the same amount of time as the other intervals. This means that the automobile must have been moving faster, or with a greater speed, in interval *E*. Speed can be calculated by dividing the distance traveled by the time it took to travel that distance. This is represented in the formula $s = \frac{\Delta d}{\Delta t}$. On a distance vs. time graph, this is the same as the slope of the graph. The slope of the graph is most steep during interval *E*, and the speed has its maximum value where the slope is the very steepest.

8. Choice (D) is the correct answer. Field lines point away from positively charged particles and toward negatively charged particles. Therefore diagram *D* is a diagram of the field lines of a positively charged particle on the left, and a negatively charged particle on the right.

9. Choice (E) is the correct answer. Field lines point away from positively charged particles and toward negatively charged particles. Therefore diagram *E* is a diagram of the field lines between a positively charged plate at the bottom and a negatively charged plate above it. The field produced between two large and close together parallel plates has the same strength anywhere between the plates, which is why the field lines are evenly spaced in the diagram.

10. Choice (B) is the correct answer. Momentum is conserved in all collisions. Therefore the initial momentum of the freight cars before the collision is equal to the final momentum of the freight cars after the collision. The final velocity of the freight cars after the collision can be calculated by setting the final momentum equal to the initial momentum. The initial momentum can be calculated using the initial velocities and the masses, and the final mass is the sum of the two masses together. Conservation of energy cannot be used here because kinetic energy is not conserved

during the collision. Some of the initial kinetic energy converts to other forms of energy such as heat and internal energy as a result of the friction between the cars during the collision.

11. Choice (C) is the correct answer. Momentum is conserved in the collision of the clay into the block, but kinetic energy is not conserved. For this reason, conservation of momentum must be used to relate the initial velocity of the clay to the final velocity of the clay and block after the collision, as shown in the equation:

    $m_{clay} v_{clay} = (m_{clay} + m_{block}) v_f$.

    We can approximate that the mechanical energy (or sum of the gravitational potential energy and the kinetic energy) is conserved from just after the collision to the highest point reached by the clay and block pendulum. If we assume the lowest point of the pendulum to be h = 0, then just after the collision, all of the energy in the system is kinetic. At the highest point reached by the pendulum, all of the energy in the system is gravitational potential. Therefore, the principle of conservation of energy can be applied as shown:

    $\frac{1}{2}(m_{clay} + m_{block}) v_f^{\,2} = (m_{clay} + m_{block}) gh.$

    Using these two equations from the principles of conservation of momentum and conservation of energy, the initial velocity of the clay could be determined.

12. Choice (A) is the correct answer. The initial energy of the pendulum when held at rest is all gravitational potential. If we assume the lowest point of the pendulum to be h=0, then the energy of the pendulum at the bottom of the swing is all kinetic. The principal of conservation of energy can be applied as shown to determine the speed of the bob at the bottom of the swing:

$$E_i = E_f$$

$$E_{potential} = E_{kinetic}$$

$$mgh = \frac{1}{2}mv^2 \Rightarrow v = \sqrt{(2gh)}.$$

13. Choice (D) is the correct answer. The skydiver reached terminal velocity, so the skydiver is no longer accelerating. The speed of the skydiver is now constant and falling at a rate of 50 meters per second. Therefore, in 2 seconds the skydiver will fall 100 m.

14. Choice (A) is the correct answer. If we neglect air resistance, the velocity of the object in the horizontal direction is constant; every second, the object travels 30 meters horizontally. However, the object is falling in the vertical direction, and it takes about 1 second for the object to fall 5 meters. Since the object is thrown from 5 meters above the ground, it will take 1 second for the object to hit the ground. In 1 second, the object will have traveled 30 meters horizontally. Therefore, the object will land 30 m from the base of the building.

15. Choice (B) is the correct answer. The cannon is doing work on the projectile throughout the length of the barrel. The work applied is energy entering the system, and this energy converts to the kinetic energy of the projectile. This is shown using the work-energy theorem: $W = \Delta E$.

Since the cannon experiences a constant net force along the length of the barrel, the work done can be written as $W = Fd$, and the change in energy of the projectile is the kinetic energy gained. Substituting the equations for work and kinetic energy, the equation becomes:

$$Fd = \frac{1}{2}mv^2.$$

When rewritten, we find that $W = Fd$

If the mass is doubled, then the final velocity becomes:

$$\frac{\sqrt{(2Fd)}}{\sqrt{(2m)}} = \frac{1}{\sqrt{2}}\left(\frac{\sqrt{(2Fd)}}{\sqrt{(m)}}\right) = \frac{1}{\sqrt{2}}v = \frac{v}{\sqrt{2}}.$$

Therefore, if the mass is doubled, the velocity of the projectile as it leaves the barrel will be $\frac{v}{\sqrt{2}}$.

16. Choice (D) is the correct answer. When the magnetic field passing through a loop or coil is changing, a current is induced in the loop to produce a magnetic field opposing that change. This is called Faraday's law of induction, and the direction of the induced current is determined by Lenz's law.

17. Choice (C) is the correct answer. According to Lenz's law, the induced current has a direction such that the magnetic field due to the current opposes the change in the magnetic field passing through the loop or coil. The magnetic fields of the north and south poles point in opposite directions. Therefore, when moved into the coil, the magnetic poles will induce currents pointing in opposite directions.

18. Choice (D) is the correct answer. Current is the flow of electrons. Unlike protons and neutrons, electrons are located on the outside of the nucleus and bound to the atom by the electromagnetic force. However, when a potential difference is applied across a copper wire, the electromagnetic force caused by the potential difference pulls the electrons toward lower potential, thereby creating a current. The electrons move, but the atoms, protons, and neutrons do not.

19. Choice (B) is the correct answer. When a light ray hits a medium such as glass at an angle, the light ray bends depending on the index of refraction of the medium. This phenomenon is called refraction. Eyeglasses, magnifying glasses, and optical microscopes are all made of glass lenses. The surfaces of these lenses are shaped convex or concave so that oncoming light rays will hit at different angles and then bend due to refraction. This causes the light rays to converge or diverge, changing the location, size, or orientation of the formed image. Eyeglasses assist the lenses in the eye by focusing light rays on the retina. Magnifying glasses and optical microscopes enlarge images, making small objects visible.

20. Choice (A) is the correct answer. Ohm's law ($V = IR$) shows the inverse relationship between current and resistance. In a circuit connected to a constant voltage source, a lower resistance will result in a higher current. Therefore, the current through the battery will be greatest in the circuit with least resistance. The switches connect the resistors in series, therefore the equivalent resistance can be found by adding the resistance of the resistors. If the switches are in positions I and III, the current will flow through the 1Ω and the 4Ω resistors. This combination yields the smallest equivalent resistance, and so the current will be greatest when the switches are in these positions.

21. Choice (B) is the correct answer. The momentum of an object can be calculated using the formula $\rho = mv$, where ρ is the momentum, m is the mass, and v is the velocity. The momentum of the bob at point Y is then $(0.05\text{kg})(3.0\text{m/s}) = 0.15\text{kg} \cdot \text{m/s}$.

22. Choice (C) is the correct answer. We can assume air resistance to be negligible, so the mechanical energy of the bob is conserved throughout the swing. Therefore, the total energy of the bob at point Y is equal to the total energy of the bob at point Z. If we set $h = 0$ at point Y, then the energy of the bob at point Y is all kinetic because it is in motion. The energy of the bob at point Z is all gravitational potential because it is at a height h above zero and the bob has no velocity at that instant. From conservation of energy, the height h can be determined:

$$E_y = E_z$$

$$\frac{1}{2}mv^2 = mgh$$

Mass cancels, leaving:

$$\frac{1}{2}v^2 = gh \Rightarrow \frac{\left(\frac{1}{2}v^2\right)}{g} = h = \frac{\left(\frac{1}{2}(3m/s)^2\right)}{10m/s^2} = .45m.$$

23. Choice (C) is the correct answer. Air resistance is negligible, therefore the total energy of the bob will remain the same throughout the swing. For this reason, the total energy could be calculated at any point during the swing. Since we are given the velocity and potential energy of the bob at point *Y*, it will be easiest to calculate the total energy of the bob at that point. At point *Y*, all of the energy of the bob is kinetic. Using the formula for kinetic energy, the kinetic energy of the bob at point *Y*, and therefore the total energy of the bob, can be calculated:

$$E_{kinetic} = \frac{1}{2}mv^2 = \frac{1}{2}(0.05kg)(3.0m/s)^2 = 0.23J.$$

24. Choice (A) is the correct answer. T_1 must equal the weight of m_1 plus the weight of m_2, whereas T_2 is equal to the weight of m_2 only. Since the combined weight of both of the masses is greater than the weight of just one mass, T_1 must always be greater than T_2.

25. Choice (A) is the correct answer. The weight of the mass is acting downward, and the only object in contact with the mass is the rope. Therefore, the only other force that can be acting on the mass is T_2. This force pulls upward on the mass and is equal in magnitude to the weight of the mass because the mass is in equilibrium. T_1 and m_1 cannot be applying a force on m_2 because they are not in contact with m_2.

26. Choice (C) is the correct answer. Because the river is flowing toward the right, the boat must angle to the left so that it can land directly across from where it started. The river current can be represented as a velocity vector two units long pointing horizontally toward the right. The velocity of the boat relative to the river can be represented by a vector five units long angled to the left. The addition of these vectors yields the velocity of the boat relative to an observer on the land. This vector points vertically across the river. The vector addition shown in the diagram can also be written as an equation:

$$V_{\text{river relative to the land}} + V_{\text{boat relative to the river}} = V_{\text{boat relative to the land}}$$

The addition of these vectors forms a right triangle.

27. Choice (B) is the correct answer. The velocity of a wave is given by the formula $v = \lambda f$, where λ is the length of the wave and f is the frequency of the wave. The velocity of sound depends on the medium the sound is traveling through. In this example, the sound waves are traveling through air, so the velocity of the sound wave will be the same regardless of the note played. Therefore, if the wavelength were to increase, the frequency must decrease for the velocity of the sound wave to remain the same. According to the formula $v = \lambda f$, if the wavelength were to increase by a factor of two, the frequency would be half as much.

28. Choice (E) is the correct answer. Sound waves exhibit interference when waves combine constructively or destructively. Diffraction of sound waves occurs when sound waves encounter small physical obstacles. Refraction of sound waves occurs when a sound wave passes from one medium to another. This is because the speed of sound depends on the medium through which it is traveling. If a sound wave passes from one medium to another at an angle, the wave will bend due to the different speed of the wave.

29. Choice (A) is the correct answer. If no light can pass through *X* and *Y*, then the direction of polarization of *Y* must be perpendicular to the direction of polarization of *X*. For example, if *X* were polarized in the horizontal direction, this would allow horizontally polarized waves to pass through *X*. If *Y* were polarized in the vertical direction, then the horizontally polarized waves from *X* would not be able to pass through *Y*, and no light would be transmitted. To allow for the transmission of light through *Y*, *Y* must be rotated. If *Y* were rotated 90°, the polarizing direction of *Y* would then be the same as the polarizing direction of *X*. In the case of the example above, they would both be polarized in the horizontal direction. This would allow for horizontally polarized waves to pass through both *X* and *Y*, and therefore result in the transmission of light through *Y*.

30. Choice (A) is the correct answer. The acceleration of the automobile is constant from 0 to 120 seconds. In other words, the automobile increases in speed at a constant rate. In 120s, the speed of the automobile increased by 30m/s. Using the equation for acceleration, the acceleration of the automobile can be found:

$$a = \frac{\Delta v}{\Delta t} = \frac{(30\text{m/s})}{120\text{s}} = .25\text{m/s}^2.$$

Because the acceleration is constant in the time interval 0-120s, the acceleration is also $.25\text{m/s}^2$ at the end of 60s.

31. Choice (C) is the correct answer. The automobile's speed decreases at a constant rate from 180s-210s. During this time interval the automobile must be braking. The

acceleration of the automobile, while braking, can be found by dividing the change in velocity by the change in time:

$$a = \frac{\Delta v}{\Delta t} = \frac{(30\text{m/s})}{30\text{s}} = 1\text{m/s}^2.$$

So, Newton's second law can be used to calculate the braking force:

$$F = ma = \left(1.5\times10^3\ \text{kg}\right)\left(1\text{m/s}^2\right) = 1.5\times10^3\ \text{kg}\bullet\text{m/s}^2 = 1.5\times10^3\ \text{N}.$$

32. Choice (D) is the correct answer. The brakes are first applied at 180s. This is when the speed of the automobile starts to decrease. The acceleration of the automobile, while braking, can be found by dividing the change in velocity by the change in time:

$$a = \frac{\Delta v}{\Delta t} = \frac{(30\text{m/s})}{30\text{s}} = 1\text{m/s}^2.$$

So at 190s, ten seconds later, $\Delta v = a\Delta t = 1\text{m/s}^2 \bullet 10\text{s} = 10\text{m/s}$. Since the change in velocity is 10m/s and the brakes were first applied when the speed of the automobile was 30m/s, the speed of the automobile at 190s (10 seconds after the brakes are applied) is 30m/s – 10m/s = 20m/s.

33. Choice (B) is the correct answer. The frequency of an oscillating spring is given by the formula $\omega = \sqrt{(k/m)}$, where ω is the frequency, *k* is the spring constant of the spring, and *m* is the mass attached to the spring. According to this formula, if *k* is increased, ω will increase. Conceptually, this means that a stiff spring, or spring with a high spring constant, will oscillate faster than a loose spring, or spring with a low spring constant.

34. Choice (D) is the correct answer. Newton's second law can be applied to both blocks. For the block on the table, the only force acting on the block is tension. Therefore, the tension must equal the mass of the block multiplied by the acceleration of the block:

$$F_{net} = ma \Rightarrow T = ma.$$

For the hanging block, there are two forces acting on the block: the tension pulling up on the block and the weight pulling down on the block. The weight of the block is greater than the tension because the block is falling. One can apply Newton's second law, and write the following equation:

$$F_{net} = ma \Rightarrow mg - T = ma.$$

The masses of the two blocks are equal, and their accelerations are equal as well because they are moving together. For this reason, the first equation can be substituted into the second equation, and the equation can be rearranged to find the acceleration:

$$mg - (ma) = ma \Rightarrow mg = 2ma \Rightarrow g = 2a \Rightarrow a = \frac{g}{2} = \frac{\left(10\text{m/s}^2\right)}{2} = 5\text{m/s}^2.$$

35. Choice (C) is the correct answer. Newton's third law says that for every force, there is a reaction force that is equal in magnitude and opposite in direction. These force pairs of interacting bodies are called action-reaction pairs. In the case of the object on the table, if the gravitational force due to the Earth pulls down on the object, then the object must also pull up on the Earth. This can be written as an equation, where the negative sign indicates the opposite direction:

$$F_{\text{Earth on the object}} = -F_{\text{object on the Earth}}$$

The object also exerts a downward force on the tabletop. According to Newton's third law, if the object pushes down on the table, the table must push up on the object. This can also be written in the form of an equation:

$$F_{\text{object on the table}} = -F_{\text{table on the object}}$$

36. Choice (B) is the correct answer. Heat is a kind of energy, and can therefore be converted to other types of energy. A heat engine works to convert heat into mechanical energy, which is more useful than heat. In this example, the engine absorbs 600 J of heat. This can be seen as energy entering the system. It then does 150 J of work, which can be seen as energy leaving the system. The remainder 450 J of energy is exhausted by the engine during the conversion process.

37. Choice (E) is the correct answer. The efficiency of the engine is given by the ratio of the output energy (or the work done by the engine) to the energy put into the system:

$$\text{efficiency} = \text{output energy/input energy} = 150\text{ J}/600\text{ J} = 25\%.$$

This ratio shows what percentage of the input energy was used productively. In this case, only 25 percent of the input energy was used to do work. The remaining energy was exhausted by the engine in the form of less useful energy, such as internal energy or heat.

38. Choice (B) is the correct answer. Though the magnet is moving and the charge is not, the situation is analogous to a charge moving through a magnetic field. Relative to the magnet, the charge is moving through its magnetic field with velocity v headed toward the magnet. For this reason, the equation for the force exerted on a charge moving through a magnetic field can be used: $F = qv \times B$. To find the direction

of the force, the cross product of v × B must be considered. The resultant vector points perpendicular to both the velocity vector and the magnetic field. Since the direction of v is horizontal and B is vertical, the cross product of v × B must point perpendicular to the page. This is the direction of the force exerted on the charge.

39. Choice (A) is the correct answer. The force exerted by a magnetic field onto a current carrying wire is given by the formula F = i L × B, where i is the current, L is the length of the wire, and B is the magnetic field. The cross product of L × B gives the direction of the force, where the direction of L is the direction of the current. The direction of the force must be perpendicular to L and B because that is the nature of the cross product. In this problem, the direction of the magnetic field is into the page and the direction of L is up and to the right for the 5-meter edge of the triangle. Therefore, the direction perpendicular to both B and L is up and to the left. This is the direction of the force, leaving answer choices (A) and (C) as the only possible solutions. To determine the magnitude of the force, we can plug into the equation:

$$F = i(L \times B) \Rightarrow F = i(|L||B|\sin\theta).$$

Because L and B are perpendicular in this problem, θ equals 90° and so $\sin\theta$ equals 1:

$$F = i(|L||B|\sin\theta) = i|L||B| = (2A)(5m)(6T) = 60N.$$

40. Choice (D) is the correct answer. Opposite charges attract, and like charges repel. Therefore, if two electrically charged particles repel each other, then they must have the same sign. Choice (A) cannot be correct because the magnitude of the forces will always be equal, even if the magnitude of one charge is big and the other is small. This is because of Newton's third law, which states that action-reaction pairs exert forces of equal magnitude.

41. Choice (E) is the correct answer. The brightness of bulb III will change because when the switch is closed the bulb will be lit, and when the switch is open the bulb will be off because no current will flow through it. To determine the changes in brightness of bulbs I and II, one must consider the current flowing through these bulbs. The resistance of the bulbs and potential drop across the bulbs will remain the same regardless if the switch is open or closed. However, the current flowing through the bulbs will change. The current impacts the brightness of the bulb, where a larger current yields a brighter bulb. For this reason, the brightness of bulb II will change when the switch is opened because the total current will flow through bulb II, rather than split between bulb II and bulb III. Therefore, bulb II will be brighter when the switch is opened. The brightness of bulb I will also change. This is because the equivalent resistance of the circuit is different when the switch is closed or open.

When the switch is closed, the equivalent resistance is less than when the switch is opened. Therefore, bulb I will be dimmer when the switch is opened.

42. Choice (A) is the correct answer. Galileo lived from 1564 to 1642, and nuclear physics did not become a field of study until the late 1800s. Galileo's biggest contributions to science include his work on the telescope and his support of the heliocentric view of the universe. His view that the sun rather than the Earth was the center of the universe was controversial at that time.

43. Choice (E) is the correct answer. Atoms of the same element have the same number of protons, but they can have different numbers of electrons and neutrons. The number of neutrons in an atom of a certain element is what characterizes the isotopes of that element. In other words, the number of neutrons in an atom is what distinguishes one isotope of an element from another isotope of the same element. In addition, the number of neutrons impacts the nuclear mass of the atom because one neutron has a mass of 1 amu. For this reason, choice (E) is the correct answer.

44. Choice (B) is the correct answer. Atoms and molecules absorb only photons with the exact amount of energy needed to cause an electron to jump to a higher energy level. The absorption of a photon causes the atom to move from ground state to an excited state. Once in the excited state, the atom quickly undergoes spontaneous emission, and emits a photon with the same wavelength as the one it had absorbed. This causes the electron to jump back to a lower energy level, and returns the atom to ground state. If the atom were to absorb a photon with a large enough energy, it could cause an electron to break out of its orbit and leave the atom. This process is called ionization. However, most often the absorption of a photon results in the emission of a photon.

45. Choice (A) is the correct answer. The intensity of sound is inversely proportional to the square of the distance from the sound source: $I \propto \frac{1}{r^2}$. Therefore, if the distance r were to double, then the sound intensity would decrease by a factor of four. If the distance r were to triple, then the intensity would decrease by a factor of nine, and so on.

46 Choice (B) is the correct answer. According to Snell's law, when a light ray is incident at an angle on the surface of a medium different from the medium through which it is traveling, the light ray will bend. The direction and degree of the bend depends on the index of refraction of the two mediums. If the index of refraction of the second

medium is greater than that of the first medium, then the light ray bends toward the normal of the surface, and vice versa.

This phenomenon occurs because the speed of light is different in different mediums. The speed of light in a vacuum is *c*, but the speed of light is slower in air, and even slower through more dense material such as glass. Therefore, when a light ray traveling through air is incident on glass at an angle, the light ray bends toward the normal of the surface of the glass.

47. Choice (E) is the correct answer. Huygens' principle allows you to determine where a wave front will be after time t given its initial position. To determine the future location of a wave front, Huygens' treats every point on the wave front as the source of a new spherical wave. This theory was developed as a wave theory for light, but it applies to all waves including sound and water waves. Though these waves are different, the nature of the wave as having a moving wave front remains the same.

48. Choice (B) is the correct answer. If it takes 4,000 J to raise the temperature of 1 kg of water by 1°, then it must take five times the amount of energy, or 20,000 J, to raise the temperature of 5 kg of water by 1°. To raise this amount of water by 50°, the amount of heat must then be multiplied by 50. The result is that it takes 1,000,000 J to raise the temperature of 5 kg of water by 50°. When coal burns, it produces 4,000 J/g. Since 1,000,000 J are needed, then 40g of coal must be burned:

$$1{,}000{,}000 \div 25{,}000 \text{ J/g} = 40\text{g}.$$

49. Choice (A) is the correct answer. Metal conducts heat better than plastic. When you touch metal on a cold day, heat from your hand travels to the metal. The loss of heat in your hand makes your hand feel cold. When you touch plastic, heat is not as readily drawn because the thermal conductivity of plastic is less than that of metal. For this reason the metal feels colder than the plastic, though they are the same temperature.

50. Choice (C) is the correct answer. Because the object is on a horizontal surface, the object will accelerate in the horizontal direction, unless it is lifted off the table. We can write Newton's second law for the horizontal direction:

$$\Sigma F_X = ma_X.$$

Because the surface is frictionless, the only force acting in the horizontal direction is the x-component of the applied force, which equals $F_{\cos\theta}$. The equation then becomes:

$$F_{\cos\theta} = ma_X.$$

The total acceleration of the object will be in the x-direction because it is being pulled across a horizontal surface. Therefore we can substitute a for a_x and solve for the acceleration:

$$F_{\cos\theta} = ma \Rightarrow a = F_{\cos\theta} / m.$$

51. Choice (D) is the correct answer. In the absence of the machine, the platform would accelerate at a rate of 9.8m/s^2 downward due to the gravitational force acting on the platform. Therefore, the machine would not have to exert any force on the platform in order for it to accelerate at a rate of 9.8m/s^2 downward. If the platform had zero acceleration, the machine would have to exert a force equal to the combined weight of the platform, scale, and person. If the platform were accelerating upward, the machine would have to exert a force greater than the combined weight of the platform, scale, and person.

52. Choice (A) is the correct answer. Newton's second law can be applied to the person on the scale. There are two forces acting on the person standing on the scale: the normal force applied by the scale and the force due to gravity. The acceleration of the person is equal to the acceleration of the platform:

$$F_{net} = ma$$

$$N - F_g = ma$$

If we rearrange for the normal force and plug in mg for F_g, we have:

$$N = ma + mg.$$

The reading on the scale is equal to the magnitude of the normal force. If the acceleration of the platform is zero, then the normal force equals the weight of the person. If the platform is accelerating upward, then the normal force will be greater than the weight of the person. In this case the reading on the scale is doubled, so the platform must be accelerating upward. The reading on the scale was originally the weight of the person, or mg, so the new reading must be 2mg. In order for the reading on the scale to be 2mg, the acceleration must equal g, or 9.8m/s^2. This can be shown using the equation derived above:

$N = mg$, if the platform is not accelerating.

$N = ma + mg$, if the platform is accelerating.

The reading on the scale doubled, so $N = 2mg$.

If $N = 2mg$, then a must equal g:

$$N = ma + mg = mg + mg = 2mg.$$

Therefore, a = g = 9.8m/s^2 up.

53. Choice (E) is the correct answer. Newton's second law can be applied to the satellite in the centripetal direction:

$$F_c = ma_c$$

$$F_c = \frac{mv^2}{r}.$$

The centripetal force acting on the satellite is the force due to gravity caused by the planet. This force keeps the satellite circling the planet rather than heading into outer space. The magnitude of the force can be determined using Newton's law of gravitation: $F_g = \frac{GMm}{r^2}$, where *G* is the gravitational constant, *M* is the mass of the planet, *m* is the mass of the satellite, and *r* is the distance from the center of the planet to the center of the satellite. If we set the equation for centripetal force equal to the equation of the force due to gravity, we have:

$$F_c = F_g$$

$$\frac{mv^2}{r} = \frac{GMm}{r^2}.$$

Canceling like terms, this simplifies to:

$$v^2 = \frac{GM}{r}.$$

From this expression, it is apparent that increasing *M* or decreasing *r* would result in a greater speed of the satellite. Because decreasing *r* is not an answer choice, choice (E) is the correct answer.

54. Choice (D) is the correct answer. Ohm's law states that V = IR, so if the voltage of the battery is V and the resistance of the resistor is R, then the current must be $\frac{V}{R}$. If the voltage is increased to 2V and the resistance increased to 4R, then the new current would be $\frac{2V}{4R}$, which simplifies to $\frac{V}{2R}$ or $\frac{1}{2}\left(\frac{V}{R}\right)$. This is half of the original current. Therefore, if the original current was I, then the new current must be $\frac{I}{2}$.

55. Choice (C) is the correct answer. The electrically charged rod attracts the pith ball because of polarization. When brought near the electrically charged rod, the molecules in the pith ball stretch so that the charges of the opposite sign are closest

to the charged rod. The charged rod attracts the opposite charges in the pith ball, and so pulls the ball close until the rod and the ball touch. When the pith ball touches the rod, some of the excess charge on the rod goes to the pith ball. This gives the pith ball a net charge the same sign as the rod, and so the ball repels the rod.

56 Choice (B) is the correct answer. The electric field will be zero where the electric fields of each charge cancel each other, or where the magnitude of the electric field of the charge on the left equals the magnitude of the electric field of the charge on the right. Because the charge on the right is four times greater than the charge on the left, point *P* must be closer to the charge on the left than the charge on the right. This eliminates answer choices (C), (D), and (E). To find the exact distance, we must consider the formula for the magnitude of an electric field: $E = \frac{kq}{r^2}$.

According to this formula, if the charge on the right is 4 times greater, then the distance must be 2 times further for the electric fields to be equal. Therefore, point *P* must be 2 cm from the charge on the left, and 4 cm from the charge on the right.

57. Choice (B) is the correct answer. The speed of light *in a vacuum* is a universal constant, however light travels at a slower speed through different mediums. The velocity of a wave is given by the formula $v = \lambda f$, where λ is the wavelength and f is the frequency. According to this formula, if the speed of a light beam changes, then the wavelength or the frequency must change as well. When a light beam traveling through air hits glass, the light beam slows down, causing the waves to bunch together. This decreases the wavelength of the light, however the frequency remains the same. Therefore, the answer is choice (B).

58. Choice (D) is the correct answer. Two rays can be drawn from object *O* to determine the location and orientation of the image. A ray drawn parallel to the central axis will bend at the lens and pass through the focal point on the other side of the lens. A ray drawn through the center of the lens will have no change in direction. These two rays diverge, so to find the image the rays must be extended on the left side of the lens. The image forms where the rays converge. This ray diagram reveals that the image is virtual (located on the left side of the lens), upright, and enlarged.

59. Choice (E) is the correct answer. The index of refraction of a medium depends on the frequency of the light passing through it. For example, blue light bends more than red light when incident on a glass surface. When white light traveling through air encounters a medium such as glass, the colors that make up the white light refract at different angles. This causes the separation of white light into rainbow colors.

60. Choice (B) is the correct answer. The gravitational field of a planet is equal to the acceleration due to gravity on that planet. For example, if the gravitational field is 4N/kg, then the acceleration due to gravity is $4 m/s^2$. In fact, the unit N/kg is the same as the unit $4 m/s^2$ because $1N = 1kg \times (m/s^2)$. Using the strength of the gravitational field, the weight of the object on the imaginary planet can be calculated:

$$4\ N/kg \times 5kg = 20N$$

The weight of the object on Earth can also be calculated:

$$9.8\ m/s^2 \times 5kg \cong 50\ m/s^2 \times kg \text{ or } 50N.$$

The weight of the object on the imaginary planet is less than the weight of the object on Earth because the gravitational field is weaker. However, the mass of the object remains the same.

61. Choice (A) is the correct answer. The average speed can be calculated using the formula $s = \frac{\Delta d}{\Delta t}$. The distance traveled by the car is equal to three times the circumference of the track with a radius of 1km:

$$\Delta d = (3)(2\pi r) = (3)(2\pi)(1km).$$

The time is equal to 5 minutes, which must be converted to hours. Because 60 minutes equals 1 hour, 1 minute equals $\frac{1}{60}$ hours. The time can be found by multiplying 5 by $\frac{1}{60}$ hours:

$$\Delta t = 5\,\text{min} = 5\ \frac{1}{60}\text{hour}.$$

If we plug the distance and time into the equation for speed, we have:

$$s = \frac{\Delta d}{\Delta t} = \frac{(3)(2\pi)(1)}{5\ \frac{1}{60}} \text{ kilometers per hour.}$$

62. Choice (B) is the correct answer. The high speed of the spaceships causes length contraction in the direction parallel to the spaceships' velocity. Because the spaceships are moving in the horizontal direction, only horizontal dimensions will be contracted. The height of the robots will not appear to be different because height is a vertical dimension. The width of the robots' shoulders will not appear to be

different because that dimension is perpendicular to the direction of travel. The only dimension listed that is parallel to the spaceships' velocity is the length of the robot's feet from toe to heel. The feet of the robot in spaceship *B* will appear to be shorter.

63. Choice (A) is the correct answer. The photoelectric effect demonstrates that when light of a certain frequency is shone on a piece of metal, the metal emits electrons. Einstein's study of this phenomenon supported the photon aspect of light. Before this study, light was considered a wave, and the energy of a light wave was thought to be proportional to the light's intensity. For example, the waves in a bright red light were thought to have more energy than those in a dim red light. However, in his study of the photoelectric effect, Einstein found that an increase in the intensity of light increased the rate of emitted electrons, but did not change the amount of energy with which they were emitted. Furthermore, frequencies of light below the threshold frequency of a given metal did not emit any electrons, regardless of the intensity of the light. To explain these results, Einstein proposed that light was made up of photons, and that the quantized energy of these photons was proportional to the frequency of the light, not the intensity. This explained why dim light of a high frequency would cause the emission of electrons, while bright light of a lower frequency would not.

64. Choice (D) is the correct answer. The radius of the electron orbit is 10,000 times bigger than the radius of the nucleus $\left(\frac{10^{-11}}{10^{-15}} = 10{,}000\right)$. If the width of the classroom represents the diameter of the electron orbit, then the object representing the nucleus should be 10,000 times smaller than the width of the classroom. The width of the classroom is about 10m, so the width of the object should be about 0.001m, or 1mm. Of the answer choices, the diameter of the point of a ballpoint pen is closest to 1mm.

65. Choice (C) is the correct answer. Superconductors have absolutely no resistance, which means that once a current is started in a superconductor, it will keep going without a battery being present. Very low temperatures of just a few Kelvin are required to achieve this effect, but the temperature is not absolute zero.

66. Choice (B) is the correct answer. The displacement of an object is equal to the area under a velocity versus time curve. The displacement of particle (D) is zero because the negative area cancels the positive area. The greatest displacement is that of particle (B) because it has the largest area under the curve. This can be explained conceptually as well. Particle (B) started with a velocity of 1m/s and maintained that velocity for most of the time interval. Particles (C) and (E) started with zero velocity and worked their way up to a velocity of 1m/s. So, it makes sense that particle (B) had a greater displacement than (C) or (E) because it traveled at a faster speed.

67. Choice (E) is the correct answer. Units may be converted through multiplying by conversion factors. The conversion factors needed for this example are $100^3\ cm^3 = 1\ m^3$ and 1kg = 1000g. Therefore:

$$\frac{3g}{cm^3} \times \left(\frac{100^3 cm^3}{1m^3}\right) \times \left(\frac{1kg}{1000g}\right) = 3{,}000\frac{kg}{m^3}.$$

68. Choice (E) is the correct answer. Momentum is conserved in all collisions. Kinetic energy is conserved in this collision because it is an *elastic* collision. Elastic collisions imply that no kinetic energy is lost. The total energy is also conserved because no energy left the system. The initial energy of the pucks is all kinetic, and the final energy of the pucks is also kinetic.

69. Choice (D) is the correct answer. The work done on a spring can be calculated using the formula $W = \frac{1}{2}kx^2$. Because work is proportional to the square of the distance stretched, if the distance increases by a factor of two, the work must increase by a factor of four. This can be shown mathematically as well:
$W = \frac{1}{2}kx^2$, where W is the amount of work needed to stretch the spring a distance x

If the distance doubles, we have:

$$\frac{1}{2}k(2x)^2 = \frac{1}{2}k(4)x^2 = 4\left(\frac{1}{2}kx^2\right) = 4W.$$

70. Choice (D) is the correct answer. Resonance occurs when the natural frequency of a system equals the frequency of the external driving force. The natural frequency is the frequency a system would have if it were left to oscillate freely. In this case, it would be the frequency of the swing if the child did not "pump." The driving frequency is the frequency of the driving force. In this case, the driving force is the child pumping. When the natural and the driving frequencies are in phase, the amplitude of the oscillations is increased. The greatest amplitude occurs when the natural frequency is equal to the driving frequency, a condition called resonance. However, if the frequencies are out of phase, the oscillations may be dampened. For this reason, a child on a swing pumps at a certain time and rate so that amplitude of the swing is increased.

71. Choice (D) is the correct answer. The oil drop is in equilibrium, therefore the electric force must be equal in magnitude to the gravitational force:

$$F_e = F_g.$$

If we substitute the equations for these forces, we have:

$$qE = mg.$$

This can be rearranged to solve for q, and then the values can be plugged in:

$$q = \frac{mg}{E} = \left(1\times10^{-6}\,\text{kg}\right)\left(10\,\text{m/s}^2\right)\left(\frac{10\,\text{N}}{\text{C}}\right) = 1\times10^{-6}\,\text{C}.$$

72. Choice (A) is the correct answer. If two rays are drawn from the tip of object O, say one ray parallel to the central axis and another that crosses through the focal point, the place at which the rays converge is where the image is formed. If the object O is moved further from the mirror and these two rays are drawn again, it will be apparent that the image has decreased in size and moved closer to the mirror. The change in location of the image can also be shown mathematically. The following equation relates the focal point, *f*, of a mirror to the position of the object, *p*, and the location of the image, *i*, as measured from the center of the mirror:

$$\frac{1}{p} + \frac{1}{i} = \frac{1}{F}.$$

The focal point of the mirror does not change. Therefore if the object distance *p* were to increase, the image distance *i* must decrease. For this reason, as the object moves further from the mirror, the image moves closer to the mirror.

73. Choice (B) is the correct answer. The incident light ray is unpolarized, therefore the E-field vectors oscillate in all directions perpendicular to the direction of travel. When the light ray hits the glass surface, some of the light is reflected (as shown) and some of the light is refracted into the glass. The E-field vectors of the light are reflected and refracted accordingly: the E-field vectors perpendicular to the plane of incidence are mostly reflected, and the E-field vectors parallel to the plane of incidence are mostly refracted. This means that the E-field vectors of the reflected light oscillate mostly in one direction, and therefore the light is somewhat polarized.

74. Choice (C) is the correct answer. If P is a bright spot, then the waves from the two slits must interfere constructively at point P. This means that the two waves must be in phase at point P, even though the wave from the lower slit must travel an additional distance ΔL. If ΔL equals a certain number of wavelengths exactly (i.e., $n\lambda$ where n is an integer), then the waves will interfere fully constructively at point P. This is because the peaks and troughs of the waves will match completely.

75. Choice (C) is the correct answer. The two pairs of resistors are connected in parallel. The equivalent resistance of each pair can be found by using the following equation:

$$\frac{1}{R_{eq}} = \frac{1}{R_1} + \frac{1}{R_2} = \frac{1}{R} + \frac{1}{R} = \frac{2}{R}.$$

If we take the reciprocal, we find that $R_{eq} = \frac{R}{2}$.

The equivalent resistance of the two pairs are now connected in series. The equivalent resistance can be found using the following equation:

$$R_{eq} = R_1 + R_2 = \frac{R}{2} + \frac{R}{2} = \frac{2R}{2} = R.$$

Therefore, the equivalent resistance between X and Y is equal to R.

Chapter 8

Chinese with Listening

Purpose

The Subject Test in Chinese with Listening measures your understanding of Mandarin Chinese in the context of contemporary Chinese culture. The questions on the test are written to reflect general trends in high school curricula and are independent of particular textbooks or methods of instruction.

Format

This is a one-hour test with about 20 minutes of listening comprehension and 40 minutes of usage and reading comprehension. There are 85 multiple-choice questions in three sections.

Content

Listening comprehension questions test the ability to understand the spoken language and are based on short, spoken dialogues and narratives primarily about everyday topics. There are two different kinds of listening comprehension questions: (A) a spoken statement, question, or exchange, followed by a choice of three possible responses (also spoken); (B) a spoken dialogue or monologue with a printed question or questions (in English) about what was said.

Usage questions ask you to select the answer that best completes a Chinese sentence in a way that is structurally and logically correct. Questions are written to reflect instructional practices of the curriculum. This section of the test is therefore presented in four columns across two pages of the test book to allow each question and its answer choices to be shown in four different ways of representing Chinese: traditional and simplified Chinese characters on the left page, and phonetic transcriptions in Pinyin romanization and the Chinese phonetic alphabet (Bopomofo) on the right page. You should choose the writing form you are most familiar with and read only from that column.

Reading comprehension questions test your understanding of such points as main and supporting ideas, themes, and the setting of passages. Some of the passages are based on real-life materials such as timetables, forms, advertisements, notes, letters, diaries, and newspaper articles. All passages are printed in both traditional and simplified Chinese characters. While most questions deal with understanding of literal meaning, some inference questions may also be included. All reading comprehension questions are in English.

Chinese with Listening	
Skills Measured	Approximate Percentage of Test
Listening Comprehension	33%
Usage	33%
Reading Comprehension	33%

CD Players

Using CD Players for Language Tests with Listening

Take an acceptable CD player to the test center. Your CD player must be in good working order, so insert fresh batteries on the day before the test. You may bring additional batteries and a backup player to the test center. CD players cannot be shared with other test-takers.

Test center staff won't have batteries, CD players, or earphones for your use, so your CD player must be:

- equipped with earphones
- portable (hand-held)
- battery operated

You are not allowed to use a CD player with recording or duplicating capabilities.

Note

If the volume on your CD player disturbs other test-takers, the test center supervisor may ask you to move to another seat.

What to do if your CD player malfunctions:

- Raise your hand and tell the test supervisor.
- Switch to backup equipment if you have it and continue the test. If you don't have backup equipment, your score on the Chinese with Listening Test will be canceled. However, scores on other Subject Tests you take that day will still be counted.

What if you receive a defective CD on test day? Raise your hand and ask the supervisor for a replacement.

How to Prepare

The best preparation is gradual development of competence in Chinese over a period of years. The test is appropriate for students who have studied Mandarin Chinese as a second or foreign language for two to four years in high school, or the equivalent. A practice audio CD for the full-length practice test is included with this book. A practice CD with different sample questions can be obtained, along with a copy of the *Getting Ready for the SAT Subject Tests* booklet, from your school counselor, or you can access the listening files at www.collegeboard.org. If your counselor does not have the CD or booklet, he or she can order them from the College Board. Familiarize yourself with the test directions in advance. The directions in this book are identical to those that appear on the test.

Note

The SAT Subject Test in Chinese with Listening is offered only at designated test centers on designated test dates. **To take the test, you MUST bring an acceptable CD player with earphones to the test center.**

Scores

The total score is reported on the 200-to-800 scale. Listening, usage, and reading subscores are reported on the 20-to-80 scale.

Sample Questions

Following are some samples for each section of the SAT Subject Test in Chinese with Listening. All questions are multiple choice. You must choose the best response from the three or four choices offered for each question.

In an actual test administration, all spoken Chinese will be presented as recorded audio. Text that appears in this section in brackets ([ ]) will be recorded in an actual test and it will not be printed in your test book. Spoken text appears in printed form here because a recorded version is not available.

Sample Listening Questions

Please note that the CD does not start here. Begin using the CD when you start the actual practice test on page 483.

Part A

Directions: In this part of the test, you will hear short questions, statements, or commands in Mandarin Chinese followed by three responses in Mandarin Chinese designated (A), (B), and (C). You will hear the questions or statements, as well as the responses, just one time, and they are not printed in your test book. Therefore, you must listen very carefully. Select the best choice and fill in the corresponding circle on your answer sheet.

Question 1

(Narrator) [Number 1

(Woman) 請問圖書館在哪兒?

(Man) (A) 圖書館九點開門。

(B) 圖書館裏書很多。

(C) 圖書館就在前面。] (5 seconds)

Choice (C) is the correct answer because it responds to the question "where is the library?" Choice (A) is incorrect because it tells when the library opens, and choice (B) is incorrect because it tells what's inside the library.

Question 2

(Narrator) [Number 2

(Man) 這本書貴不貴?

(Woman) 不貴，也不便宜。

(Man) (A) 多久了?

(B) 多少錢?

(C) 多不多?] (5 seconds)

Choice (B) is the correct answer because it asks how much the book costs. The conversation concerns the price of a book. The man asks if the book is expensive, and the woman replies that it is neither expensive nor cheap. Choice (A) is incorrect because it asks about length of time. Choice (C) is incorrect because it asks if there are many.

Part B

Directions: You will now hear a series of short selections. You will hear them only once, and they are not printed in your test book. After each selection, you will be asked to answer one or more questions about what you have just heard. These questions, each with four possible answers, are printed in your test book. Select the best answer to each question from among the four choices printed and fill in the corresponding circle on your answer sheet. You will have fifteen seconds to answer each question.

Questions 3–4

(Narrator) [Questions 3 and 4. Listen to find out what the woman will do next summer.

(Woman) 你去過香港嗎?

(Man) 沒去過，可是我明年夏天從日本到中國去的時候會經過香港。

(Woman) 明年夏天我得留在美國上暑期班，哪兒都不能去。

(Narrator) Now answer questions 3 and 4.] (30 seconds)

3. Where will the woman spend the summer next year?
   (A) In China
   (B) In Japan
   (C) In Hong Kong
   (D) In the United States

Choice (D) is the correct answer because the woman states in the conversation that she will stay in the United States next summer. Choices (A), (B), and (C) are the places where the man will go next summer.

4. What will the woman do?
   (A) Visit friends
   (B) Go to school
   (C) Look for a job
   (D) Travel abroad

Choice (B) is the correct answer because the woman states in the conversation that she will go to summer school. None of the other answer choices are mentioned by the woman in the conversation.

Sample Usage Questions

Directions: This section consists of a number of incomplete sentences, each of which has four possible completions. Select the word or phrase that best completes the sentence structurally and logically and fill in the corresponding circle on your answer sheet.

This section of the test is presented in four columns to allow each question to be shown in four different ways of representing Chinese: traditional characters, simplified characters, Pinyin romanization, and the Chinese phonetic alphabet (Bopomofo). TO SAVE TIME, IT IS RECOMMENDED THAT YOU CHOOSE THE WRITING FORM WITH WHICH YOU ARE MOST FAMILIAR AND **READ ONLY FROM THAT COLUMN** AS YOU WORK THROUGH THIS SECTION OF THE TEST.

Question 5

5. 我很喜歡這部電影。
你 ____ ?

(A) 阿
(B) 嗎
(C) 吧
(D) 呢

5. 我很喜欢这部电影。
你 ____ ?

(A) 阿
(B) 吗
(C) 吧
(D) 呢

5. Wǒ hěn xǐhuan zhèi bù diànyǐng.
Nǐ ____ ?

(A) a
(B) ma
(C) ba
(D) ne

5. ㄨㄛˇ ㄏㄣˇ ㄒㄧˇ ㄏㄨㄢ ㄓㄟˋ ㄅㄨˋ ㄉㄧㄢˋ ㄧㄥˇ。
ㄋㄧˇ ____?

(A) ˙ㄚ
(B) ˙ㄇㄚ
(C) ˙ㄅㄚ
(D) ˙ㄋㄜ

This question tests the use of sentence-final particles.

Choice (D) is the correct answer to question 5. Of the four answer choices, only choice (D) *ne* following the second-person singular pronoun *ni* conveys the intended meaning "How about you?" as a question appended to the preceding statement, "I really like this movie."

Question 6

6. 他____生氣____臉紅。

(A) 連 ..... 都
(B) 一 ..... 就
(C) 不跟 ..... 一樣
(D) 雖然 ..... 可是

6. 他____生气____脸红。

(A) 连 ..... 都
(B) 一 ..... 就
(C) 不跟 ..... 一样
(D) 虽然 ..... 可是

6. Tā ____ shēngqì ____ liǎnhóng.

(A) lián ..... dōu
(B) yì ..... jiù
(C) bù gēn ..... yíyàng
(D) suīrán ..... kěshì

6. ㄊㄚ ____ ㄕㄥ ㄑㄧˋ ____ ㄌㄧㄢˇ ㄏㄨㄥˊ。

(A) ㄌㄧㄢˊ ..... ㄉㄡ
(B) ㄧˋ ..... ㄐㄧㄡˋ
(C) ㄅㄨˋ ㄍㄣ ..... ㄧˊ ㄧㄤˋ
(D) ㄙㄨㄟ ㄖㄢˊ ..... ㄎㄜˇ ㄕˋ

This question tests the use of sentence-linking constructions.

Choice (B) is the correct answer to question 6 because the nonmovable forwarding-linking adverb *yi* is paired with *jiu* to convey the meaning “as soon as … then.” None of the other answer choices are structurally or logically correct in this context.

Sample Reading Questions

Directions: Read the following texts carefully for comprehension. Each is followed by one or more questions or incomplete statements. Select the answer or completion that is best according to the text and fill in the corresponding circle on the answer sheet.

This section of the test is presented in two writing systems: traditional characters and simplified characters. IT IS RECOMMENDED THAT YOU CHOOSE THE WRITING SYSTEM WITH WHICH YOU ARE MORE FAMILIAR AND **READ ONLY THAT VERSION** AS YOU WORK THROUGH THIS SECTION OF THE TEST.

Questions 7–8

國立台灣師範大學音樂系

張鳴欣
教授　作曲家

國立台灣師範大學
台北市和平東路一段162號

電話: 公(02)321-8400

国立台湾师范大学音乐系

张鸣欣
教授　作曲家

国立台湾师范大学
台北市和平东路一段162号

电话: 公(02)321-8400

7. What is this?
   (A) A business card
   (B) A thank-you note
   (C) A return envelope
   (D) A concert ticket

Choice (A) is the correct answer to question 7. The text contains a person's name, workplace, profession, office address, and telephone number, all arranged in the standard format for an individual's business card.

8. The person named is a
   - (A) professor
   - (B) singer
   - (C) conductor
   - (D) journalist

Choice (A) is the correct answer to question 8. The text of the business card shows that the person works in the music department of a university and gives the person's professional title as "professor and composer."

Chinese with Listening Subject Test

Practice Helps

The test that follows is an actual, previously administered SAT Subject Test in Chinese with Listening. To get an idea of what it's like to take this test, practice under conditions that are much like those of an actual test administration.

- Set aside an hour when you can take the test uninterrupted.
- Sit at a desk or table with no other books or papers. Dictionaries, other books, or notes are not allowed in the test room.
- Tear out an answer sheet from the back of this book and fill it in just as you would on the day of the test. One answer sheet can be used for up to three Subject Tests.
- Read the instructions that precede the practice test. During the actual administration you will be asked to read them before answering test questions.
- Time yourself by placing a clock or kitchen timer in front of you.
- After you finish the practice test, read the sections "How to Score the SAT Subject Test in Chinese with Listening" and "How Did You Do on the Subject Test in Chinese with Listening?"
- The appearance of the answer sheet in this book may differ from the answer sheet you see on test day.

NO TEST MATERIAL ON THIS PAGE

CHINESE TEST WITH LISTENING

The top portion of the page of the answer sheet that you will use to take the Chinese Test with Listening must be filled in exactly as illustrated below. When your supervisor tells you to fill in the circle next to the name of the test you are about to take, mark your answer sheet as shown.

○ Literature	○ Mathematics Level 1	○ German	● Chinese Listening	○ Japanese Listening
○ Biology E	○ Mathematics Level 2	○ Italian	○ French Listening	○ Korean Listening
○ Biology M	○ U.S. History	○ Latin	○ German Listening	○ Spanish Listening
○ Chemistry	○ World History	○ Modern Hebrew		
○ Physics	○ French	○ Spanish	Background Questions: ①②③④⑤⑥⑦⑧⑨	

After filling in the circle next to the name of the test you are taking, locate the Background Questions box on your answer sheet (as shown above). This is where you will answer the following Background Questions on your answer sheet.

BACKGROUND QUESTIONS

Please answer Part I and Part II below by filling in the appropriate circle in the Background Question box on your answer sheet. <u>The information you provide is for statistical purposes only and will not affect your test score.</u>

PART I Which of the following is the **primary** source of your knowledge of the Chinese language? (**CHOOSE ONLY ONE**.)

—Circle 1 — Living in a place and/or a home in which Mandarin Chinese is used

—Circle 2 — Living in a place and/or a home in which Chinese other than Mandarin is used

—Circle 3 — Studying Chinese in an extracurricular (after-school, weekend, summer, and/or study-abroad) program (e.g., Chinese language school)

—Circle 4 — Studying Chinese in classes at your regular elementary and/or middle school (grades K through 8)

—Circle 5 — Studying Chinese in classes at your regular high school (grades 9 through 12)

PART II How long have you studied Chinese in your regular high school (grades 9 through 12)? (**CHOOSE ONLY ONE**.)

—Circle 6 — 0 (zero) to 1½ years

—Circle 7 — 2 to 2½ years

—Circle 8 — 3 to 3½ years

—Circle 9 — 4 years

When the supervisor tells you to do so, turn the page and begin the Chinese Test with Listening. There are 100 numbered circles on your answer sheet. Use only circles 1 to 85 to record your answers to the 85 questions in the Chinese Test with Listening.

CHINESE TEST WITH LISTENING

PLEASE NOTE THAT YOUR ANSWER SHEET HAS FIVE ANSWER POSITIONS, MARKED A, B, C, D, AND E, WHILE THE QUESTIONS THROUGHOUT THIS TEST CONTAIN EITHER THREE OR FOUR ANSWER CHOICES. BE SURE NOT TO MAKE ANY MARKS IN COLUMN E, AND DO NOT MAKE ANY MARKS IN COLUMN D IF THERE ARE ONLY THREE CHOICES GIVEN.

SECTION I
LISTENING
Approximate time—20 minutes
Questions 1-30

Part A

Directions: In this part of the test, you will hear short questions, statements, or commands in Mandarin Chinese, followed by three responses in Mandarin Chinese, designated (A), (B), and (C). You will hear the questions or statements, as well as the responses, just one time, and they are not printed in your test booklet. Therefore, you must listen very carefully. Select the best response and fill in the corresponding circle on your answer sheet. Now listen to the following example, but do not mark the answer on your answer sheet.

You will hear:

You will also hear:

The answer that most logically responds to the question is (C). Therefore, you should choose answer (C).

Now listen to the first exchange.

1. Mark your answer on your answer sheet.
2. Mark your answer on your answer sheet.
3. Mark your answer on your answer sheet.
4. Mark your answer on your answer sheet.
5. Mark your answer on your answer sheet.
6. Mark your answer on your answer sheet.
7. Mark your answer on your answer sheet.
8. Mark your answer on your answer sheet.
9. Mark your answer on your answer sheet.
10. Mark your answer on your answer sheet.
11. Mark your answer on your answer sheet.
12. Mark your answer on your answer sheet.
13. Mark your answer on your answer sheet.
14. Mark your answer on your answer sheet.
15. Mark your answer on your answer sheet.
16. Mark your answer on your answer sheet.
17. Mark your answer on your answer sheet.
18. Mark your answer on your answer sheet.
19. Mark your answer on your answer sheet.

END OF PART A.
GO ON TO PART B.

GO ON TO THE NEXT PAGE

Part B

Directions: You will now hear a series of short selections. You will hear them only once, and they are not printed in your test booklet. After each selection, you will be asked to answer one or more questions about what you have just heard. These questions, each with four possible answers, are printed in your test booklet. Select the best answer to each question from among the four choices printed and fill in the corresponding circle on your answer sheet. You will have fifteen seconds to answer each question.

Now listen to the following example, but do not mark the answer on your answer sheet.

You will hear:

You will see:

What are the two people talking about?

(A) Food
(B) Homework
(C) History
(D) Language

The best answer to the question is (D), "Language." Therefore, you should choose answer (D).

Now listen to the first selection.

Questions 20-21

20. What is the man's native language?

(A) French
(B) Chinese
(C) English
(D) German

21. How did the man's son learn German?

(A) His father taught him.
(B) He took lessons from the woman.
(C) He studied it in college.
(D) He grew up in Germany.

Question 22

22. What is the speaker's problem?

(A) He spent too long debating an issue.
(B) He got up too late for work.
(C) His sleeping pills are all gone.
(D) He has a headache and can't concentrate.

Question 23

23. Which of the following activities is NOT mentioned by the speaker?

(A) Watching television
(B) Singing songs
(C) Riding bicycles
(D) Playing tennis

Question 24

24. What happened to the man?

(A) He forgot to return all the books.
(B) He missed the train.
(C) He lost his football tickets.
(D) He took the wrong bus.

GO ON TO THE NEXT PAGE

Questions 25-26

25. What color shoes did Xiaohua originally want?

(A) White
(B) Yellow
(C) Brown
(D) Black

26. What does Xiaohua dislike about the pair of brown shoes?

(A) The price
(B) The size
(C) The style
(D) The quality

Question 27

27. What information is provided in the announcement?

(A) A change of location
(B) Additional show times
(C) A revision to the program
(D) The deadline for purchasing tickets

Questions 28-29

28. On which day of the week is the event being held?

(A) Monday
(B) Wednesday
(C) Saturday
(D) Sunday

29. Which of the following statements about the male speaker is true?

(A) He is living in a dormitory.
(B) He is the woman's classmate.
(C) He is a Chinese history major.
(D) He is the organizer of the event.

Question 30

30. Which of the following items is the man NOT required to bring?

(A) Photos
(B) Transcript
(C) Medical report
(D) ID card

END OF SECTION I.
DO NOT GO ON TO SECTION II UNTIL YOU ARE TOLD TO DO SO.

TIME FOR SECTIONS II AND III - 40 minutes

SECTION II
USAGE

Suggested time—15 minutes

Questions 31-55

Directions: This section consists of a number of incomplete statements, each of which has four possible completions. Select the word or phrase that best completes the sentence structurally and logically and fill in the corresponding circle on your answer sheet.

This section of the test is presented in four columns across two pages to allow each question to be shown in four different ways of representing Chinese: traditional characters, simplified characters, Pinyin romanization, and the Chinese phonetic alphabet (Bopomofo). TO SAVE TIME, IT IS RECOMMENDED THAT YOU CHOOSE THE WRITING FORM WITH WHICH YOU ARE MOST FAMILIAR AND **READ ONLY FROM THAT COLUMN** AS YOU WORK THROUGH THIS SECTION OF THE TEST.

Example:

他____有空____喜歡看書。	他____有空____喜欢看书。	Tā____yǒu kòng____xǐhuan kànshū.	ㄊㄚ____ㄧㄡˇ ㄎㄨㄥˋ____ㄒㄧˇ ㄏㄨㄢ ㄎㄢˋ ㄕㄨ。
(A) 連 ..... 都	(A) 连 ..... 都	(A) lián ..... dōu	(A) ㄌㄧㄢˊ ..... ㄉㄡ
(B) 一 ..... 就	(B) 一 ..... 就	(B) yī ..... jiù	(B) ㄧ ..... ㄐㄧㄡˋ
(C) 從 ..... 到	(C) 从 ..... 到	(C) cóng ..... dào	(C) ㄘㄨㄥˊ ..... ㄉㄠˋ
(D) 是 ..... 的	(D) 是 ..... 的	(D) shì ..... de	(D) ㄕˋ ..... ˙ㄉㄜ

The best completion is answer (B). Therefore, you should choose answer (B) and fill in the corresponding circle on your answer sheet. **Remember to work with one column only** and start by filling in one of the circles next to number 31 on your answer sheet.

GO ON TO THE NEXT PAGE

31. 校長說的話，你都 _____ 嗎？
(A) 看得到
(B) 拿不出
(C) 聽懂了
(D) 放下去

31. 校长说的话，你都 _____ 吗？
(A) 看得到
(B) 拿不出
(C) 听懂了
(D) 放下去

32. 今天上午他 _____ 。
(A) 很得晚起來
(B) 起來得很晚
(C) 來得晚起很
(D) 晚得起很來

32. 今天上午他 _____ 。
(A) 很得晚起来
(B) 起来得很晚
(C) 来得晚起很
(D) 晚得起很来

33. 做了一天的事， _____ 。
(A) 大家了都累也
(B) 也累了都大家
(C) 累了大家也都
(D) 大家也都累了

33. 做了一天的事， _____ 。
(A) 大家了都累也
(B) 也累了都大家
(C) 累了大家也都
(D) 大家也都累了

34. 他的車子壞了， _____ 要我去接他。
(A) 所以
(B) 以外
(C) 不論
(D) 如此

34. 他的车子坏了， _____ 要我去接他。
(A) 所以
(B) 以外
(C) 不论
(D) 如此

35. 她唱歌唱得比我 _____ 好。
(A) 再
(B) 就
(C) 更
(D) 並

35. 她唱歌唱得比我 _____ 好。
(A) 再
(B) 就
(C) 更
(D) 并

GO ON TO THE NEXT PAGE

31. Xiàozhǎng shuō de huà, nǐ dōu _____ ma?
    (A) kàn de dào
    (B) ná bu chū
    (C) tīngdǒngle
    (D) fàng xiaqu

31. ㄒㄧㄠˋ ㄓㄤˇ ㄕㄨㄛ ˙ㄉㄜ ㄏㄨㄚˋ，ㄋㄧˇ ㄉㄡ _____ ˙ㄇㄚ？
    (A) ㄎㄢˋ ˙ㄉㄜ ㄉㄠˋ
    (B) ㄋㄚˊ ˙ㄅㄨ ㄔㄨ
    (C) ㄊㄧㄥ ㄉㄨㄥˇ ˙ㄌㄜ
    (D) ㄈㄤˋ ㄒㄧㄚˋ ˙ㄑㄩ

32. Jīntiān shàngwǔ tā _____ .
    (A) hěn de wǎn qǐlai
    (B) qǐlai de hěn wǎn
    (C) lái de wǎn qǐ hěn
    (D) wǎn de qǐ hěn lái

32. ㄐㄧㄣ ㄊㄧㄢ ㄕㄤˋ ㄨˇ ㄊㄚ _____。
    (A) ㄏㄣˇ ˙ㄉㄜ ㄨㄢˇ ㄑㄧˇ ˙ㄌㄞ
    (B) ㄑㄧˇ ˙ㄌㄞ ˙ㄉㄜ ㄏㄣˇ ㄨㄢˇ
    (C) ㄌㄞˊ ˙ㄉㄜ ㄨㄢˇ ㄑㄧˇ ㄏㄣˇ
    (D) ㄨㄢˇ ˙ㄉㄜ ㄑㄧˇ ㄏㄣˇ ㄌㄞˊ

33. Zuòle yì tiān de shì, _____ .
    (A) dàjiā le dōu lèi yě
    (B) yě lèile dōu dàjiā
    (C) lèile dàjiā yě dōu
    (D) dàjiā yě dōu lèi le

33. ㄗㄨㄛˋ ˙ㄌㄜ ㄧˋ ㄊㄧㄢ ˙ㄉㄜ ㄕˋ，_____。
    (A) ㄉㄚˋ ㄐㄧㄚ ˙ㄌㄜ ㄉㄡ ㄌㄟˋ ㄧㄝˇ
    (B) ㄧㄝˇ ㄌㄟˋ ˙ㄌㄜ ㄉㄡ ㄉㄚˋ ㄐㄧㄚ
    (C) ㄌㄟˋ ˙ㄌㄜ ㄉㄚˋ ㄐㄧㄚ ㄧㄝˇ ㄉㄡ
    (D) ㄉㄚˋ ㄐㄧㄚ ㄧㄝˇ ㄉㄡ ㄌㄟˋ ˙ㄌㄜ

34. Tā de chēzi huài le, _____ yào wǒ qù jiē tā.
    (A) suǒyǐ
    (B) yǐwài
    (C) búlùn
    (D) rúcǐ

34. ㄊㄚ ˙ㄉㄜ ㄔㄜ ˙ㄗ ㄏㄨㄞˋ ˙ㄌㄜ，_____ ㄧㄠˋ ㄨㄛˇ ㄑㄩˋ ㄐㄧㄝ ㄊㄚ。
    (A) ㄙㄨㄛˇ ㄧˇ
    (B) ㄧˇ ㄨㄞˋ
    (C) ㄅㄨˊ ㄌㄨㄣˋ
    (D) ㄖㄨˊ ㄘˇ

35. Tā chànggē chàng de bǐ wǒ _____ hǎo.
    (A) zài
    (B) jiù
    (C) gèng
    (D) bìng

35. ㄊㄚ ㄔㄤˋ ㄍㄜ ㄔㄤˋ ˙ㄉㄜ ㄅㄧˇ ㄨㄛˇ _____ ㄏㄠˇ。
    (A) ㄗㄞˋ
    (B) ㄐㄧㄡˋ
    (C) ㄍㄥˋ
    (D) ㄅㄧㄥˋ

GO ON TO THE NEXT PAGE

36. 我們可不可以 _____ 休息一會兒？
(A) 唱起來
(B) 坐下來
(C) 聽出來
(D) 看上來

37. 他 _____ 去了。
(A) 到公園孩子帶已經
(B) 孩子帶公園已經到
(C) 公園已經帶到孩子
(D) 已經帶孩子到公園

38. 我上班的地方 _____。
(A) 不遠太離我家
(B) 太不遠我家離
(C) 我家離不遠太
(D) 離我家不太遠

39. 雖然他在英國住過，_____ 他不太會說英文。
(A) 然後
(B) 但是
(C) 而且
(D) 於是

40. 我去他家的時候，他 _____ 睡覺。
(A) 正在
(B) 剛才
(C) 從來
(D) 然後

36. 我们可不可以 _____ 休息一会儿？
(A) 唱起来
(B) 坐下来
(C) 听出来
(D) 看上来

37. 他 _____ 去了。
(A) 到公园孩子带已经
(B) 孩子带公园已经到
(C) 公园已经带到孩子
(D) 已经带孩子到公园

38. 我上班的地方 _____。
(A) 不远太离我家
(B) 太不远我家离
(C) 我家离不远太
(D) 离我家不太远

39. 虽然他在英国住过，_____ 他不太会说英文。
(A) 然后
(B) 但是
(C) 而且
(D) 于是

40. 我去他家的时候，他 _____ 睡觉。
(A) 正在
(B) 刚才
(C) 从来
(D) 然后

GO ON TO THE NEXT PAGE

36. Wǒmen kě bù kěyǐ _____ xiūxi yíhuìr?

(A) chàng qilai

(B) zuò xialai

(C) tīng chulai

(D) kàn shanglai

36. ㄨㄛˇ ˙ㄇㄣ ㄎㄜˇ ㄅㄨˋ ㄎㄜˇ ㄧˇ _____ ㄒㄧㄡ ㄒㄧˊ ㄧˋ ㄏㄨㄟˇ ˙ㄦ?

(A) ㄔㄤˋ ㄑㄧˇ ˙ㄌㄞ

(B) ㄗㄨㄛˋ ㄒㄧㄚˋ ˙ㄌㄞ

(C) ㄊㄧㄥ ㄔㄨ ˙ㄌㄞ

(D) ㄎㄢˋ ㄕㄤˋ ˙ㄌㄞ

37. Tā _____ qù le.

(A) dào gōngyuán háizi dài yǐjīng

(B) háizi dài gōngyuán yǐjīng dào

(C) gōngyuán yǐjīng dài dào háizi

(D) yǐjīng dài háizi dào gōngyuán

37. ㄊㄚ _____ ㄑㄩˋ ˙ㄌㄜ。

(A) ㄉㄠˋ ㄍㄨㄥ ㄩㄢˊ ㄏㄞˊ ˙ㄗ ㄉㄞˋ ㄧˇ ㄐㄧㄥ

(B) ㄏㄞˊ ˙ㄗ ㄉㄞˋ ㄍㄨㄥ ㄩㄢˊ ㄧˇ ㄐㄧㄥ ㄉㄠˋ

(C) ㄍㄨㄥ ㄩㄢˊ ㄧˇ ㄐㄧㄥ ㄉㄞˋ ㄉㄠˋ ㄏㄞˊ ˙ㄗ

(D) ㄧˇ ㄐㄧㄥ ㄉㄞˋ ㄏㄞˊ ˙ㄗ ㄉㄠˋ ㄍㄨㄥ ㄩㄢˊ

38. Wǒ shàngbān de dìfang _____ .

(A) bù yuǎn tài lí wǒ jiā

(B) tài bù yuǎn wǒ jiā lí

(C) wǒ jiā lí bù yuǎn tài

(D) lí wǒ jiā bú tài yuǎn

38. ㄨㄛˇ ㄕㄤˋ ㄅㄢ ˙ㄉㄜ ㄉㄧˋ ㄈㄤ _____ 。

(A) ㄅㄨˋ ㄩㄢˇ ㄊㄞˋ ㄌㄧˊ ㄨㄛˇ ㄐㄧㄚ

(B) ㄊㄞˋ ㄅㄨˋ ㄩㄢˇ ㄨㄛˇ ㄐㄧㄚ ㄌㄧˊ

(C) ㄨㄛˇ ㄐㄧㄚ ㄌㄧˊ ㄅㄨˋ ㄩㄢˇ ㄊㄞˋ

(D) ㄌㄧˊ ㄨㄛˇ ㄐㄧㄚ ㄅㄨˊ ㄊㄞˋ ㄩㄢˇ

39. Suīrán tā zài Yīngguó zhùguo, _____ tā bú tài huì shuō Yīngwén.

(A) ránhòu

(B) dànshì

(C) érqiě

(D) yúshì

39. ㄙㄨㄟ ㄖㄢˊ ㄊㄚ ㄗㄞˋ ㄧㄥ ㄍㄨㄛˊ ㄓㄨˋ ˙ㄍㄨㄛ，_____ ㄊㄚ ㄅㄨˊ ㄊㄞˋ ㄏㄨㄟˋ ㄕㄨㄛ ㄧㄥ ㄨㄣˊ。

(A) ㄖㄢˊ ㄏㄡˋ

(B) ㄉㄢˋ ㄕˋ

(C) ㄦˊ ㄑㄧㄝˇ

(D) ㄩˊ ㄕˋ

40. Wǒ qù tā jiā de shíhou, tā _____ shuìjiào.

(A) zhèngzài

(B) gāngcái

(C) cónglái

(D) ránhòu

40. ㄨㄛˇ ㄑㄩˋ ㄊㄚ ㄐㄧㄚ ˙ㄉㄜ ㄕˊ ˙ㄏㄡ，ㄊㄚ _____ ㄕㄨㄟˋ ㄐㄧㄠˋ。

(A) ㄓㄥˋ ㄗㄞˋ

(B) ㄍㄤ ㄘㄞˊ

(C) ㄘㄨㄥˊ ㄌㄞˊ

(D) ㄖㄢˊ ㄏㄡˋ

GO ON TO THE NEXT PAGE

41. _____ 火車站走路 _____ 宿舍要多久？
(A) 向 ..... 在
(B) 從 ..... 到
(C) 往 ..... 同
(D) 由 ..... 沿

41. _____ 火车站走路 _____ 宿舍要多久？
(A) 向 ..... 在
(B) 从 ..... 到
(C) 往 ..... 同
(D) 由 ..... 沿

42. 晚上我們 _____ 去看個朋友。
(A) 向
(B) 從
(C) 更
(D) 得

42. 晚上我们 _____ 去看个朋友。
(A) 向
(B) 从
(C) 更
(D) 得

43. 去年他 _____ 寫了三封信給我。
(A) 曾
(B) 沒
(C) 送
(D) 會

43. 去年他 _____ 写了三封信给我。
(A) 曾
(B) 没
(C) 送
(D) 会

44. 這間房間是 _____ 為你預備的。
(A) 特別
(B) 比較
(C) 相當
(D) 非常

44. 这间房间是 _____ 为你预备的。
(A) 特别
(B) 比较
(C) 相当
(D) 非常

45. 那份報告 _____ 去了。
(A) 給叫借同事
(B) 叫同事給借
(C) 借同事叫給
(D) 同事借給叫

45. 那份报告 _____ 去了。
(A) 给叫借同事
(B) 叫同事给借
(C) 借同事叫给
(D) 同事借给叫

GO ON TO THE NEXT PAGE

41. _____ huǒchēzhàn zǒulù _____ sùshè yào duō jiǔ?
   (A) Xiàng ..... zài
   (B) Cóng ..... dào
   (C) Wàng ..... tóng
   (D) Yóu ..... yán

42. Wǎnshang wǒmen _____ qù kàn ge péngyǒu.
   (A) xiàng
   (B) cóng
   (C) gèng
   (D) děi

43. Qùnián tā _____ xiěle sān fēng xìn gěi wǒ.
   (A) céng
   (B) méi
   (C) sòng
   (D) huì

44. Zhèi jiān fángjiān shì _____ wèi nǐ yùbèi de.
   (A) tèbié
   (B) bǐjiào
   (C) xiāngdāng
   (D) fēicháng

45. Nèi fèn bàogào _____ qù le.
   (A) gěi jiào jiè tóngshì
   (B) jiào tóngshì gěi jiè
   (C) jiè tóngshì jiào gěi
   (D) tóngshì jiè gěi jiào

41. _____ ㄏㄨㄛˇ ㄔㄜ ㄓㄢˋ ㄗㄡˇ ㄌㄨˋ _____ ㄙㄨˋ ㄕㄜˋ ㄧㄠˋ ㄉㄨㄛ ㄐㄧㄡˇ ?
   (A) ㄒㄧㄤˋ ..... ㄗㄞˋ
   (B) ㄘㄨㄥˊ ..... ㄉㄠˋ
   (C) ㄨㄤˋ ..... ㄊㄨㄥˊ
   (D) ㄧㄡˊ ..... ㄧㄢˊ

42. ㄨㄢˇ ˙ㄕㄤ ㄨㄛˇ ˙ㄇㄣ _____ ㄑㄩˋ ㄎㄢˋ ㄍㄜˋ ㄆㄥˊ ㄧㄡˇ。
   (A) ㄒㄧㄤˋ
   (B) ㄘㄨㄥˊ
   (C) ㄍㄥˋ
   (D) ㄉㄟˇ

43. ㄑㄩˋ ㄋㄧㄢˊ ㄊㄚ _____ ㄒㄧㄝˇ ˙ㄌㄜ ㄙㄢ ㄈㄥ ㄒㄧㄣˋ ㄍㄟˇ ㄨㄛˇ。
   (A) ㄘㄥˊ
   (B) ㄇㄟˊ
   (C) ㄙㄨㄥˋ
   (D) ㄏㄨㄟˋ

44. ㄓㄟˋ ㄐㄧㄢ ㄈㄤˊ ㄐㄧㄢ ㄕˋ _____ ㄨㄟˋ ㄋㄧˇ ㄩˋ ㄅㄟˋ ˙ㄉㄜ。
   (A) ㄊㄜˋ ㄅㄧㄝˊ
   (B) ㄅㄧˇ ㄐㄧㄠˇ
   (C) ㄒㄧㄤ ㄉㄤ
   (D) ㄈㄟ ㄔㄤˊ

45. ㄋㄟˋ ㄈㄣˋ ㄅㄠˋ ㄍㄠˋ _____ ㄑㄩˋ ˙ㄌㄜ。
   (A) ㄍㄟˇ ㄐㄧㄠˋ ㄐㄧㄝˋ ㄊㄨㄥˊ ㄕˋ
   (B) ㄐㄧㄠˋ ㄊㄨㄥˊ ㄕˋ ㄍㄟˇ ㄐㄧㄝˋ
   (C) ㄐㄧㄝˋ ㄊㄨㄥˊ ㄕˋ ㄐㄧㄠˋ ㄍㄟˇ
   (D) ㄊㄨㄥˊ ㄕˋ ㄐㄧㄝˋ ㄍㄟˇ ㄐㄧㄠˋ

GO ON TO THE NEXT PAGE

46. 學費大概要三千塊錢，可是吃跟住並不包括 _____ 。
(A) 另外
(B) 在內
(C) 以上
(D) 其中

47. 他最喜歡 _____ 別人的毛病。
(A) 拿
(B) 放
(C) 做
(D) 挑

48. 雖然你不想去，可是 _____ 得去。
(A) 已
(B) 剛
(C) 也
(D) 連

49. 他想讀幾本 _____ 中國歷史的書。
(A) 對於
(B) 關於
(C) 由於
(D) 至於

50. 前天他剛從英國回美國來，明天 _____ 要去英國了。
(A) 還
(B) 再
(C) 才
(D) 又

46. 学费大概要三千块钱，可是吃跟住并不包括 _____ 。
(A) 另外
(B) 在内
(C) 以上
(D) 其中

47. 他最喜欢 _____ 别人的毛病。
(A) 拿
(B) 放
(C) 做
(D) 挑

48. 虽然你不想去，可是 _____ 得去。
(A) 已
(B) 刚
(C) 也
(D) 连

49. 他想读几本 _____ 中国历史的书。
(A) 对于
(B) 关于
(C) 由于
(D) 至于

50. 前天他刚从英国回美国来，明天 _____ 要去英国了。
(A) 还
(B) 再
(C) 才
(D) 又

GO ON TO THE NEXT PAGE

46. Xuéfèi dàgài yào sānqiān kuài qián, kěshì chī gēn zhù bìng bù bāokuò _____ .

(A) lìngwài

(B) zài nèi

(C) yǐshàng

(D) qízhōng

46. ㄒㄩㄝˊ ㄈㄟˋ ㄉㄚˋ ㄍㄞˋ ㄧㄠˋ ㄙㄢ ㄑㄧㄢ ㄎㄨㄞˋ ㄑㄧㄢˊ，ㄎㄜˇ ㄕˋ ㄔ ㄍㄣ ㄓㄨˋ ㄅㄧㄥˋ ㄅㄨˋ ㄅㄠ ㄎㄨㄛˋ _____ 。

(A) ㄌㄧㄥˋ ㄨㄞˋ

(B) ㄗㄞˋ ㄋㄟˋ

(C) ㄧˇ ㄕㄤˋ

(D) ㄑㄧˊ ㄓㄨㄥ

47. Tā zuì xǐhuan _____ biéren de máobing.

(A) ná

(B) fàng

(C) zuò

(D) tiāo

47. ㄊㄚ ㄗㄨㄟˋ ㄒㄧˇ ㄏㄨㄢ _____ ㄅㄧㄝˊ ㄖㄣˊ ˙ㄉㄜ ㄇㄠˊ ˙ㄅㄧㄥ。

(A) ㄋㄚˊ

(B) ㄈㄤˋ

(C) ㄗㄨㄛˋ

(D) ㄊㄧㄠ

48. Suīrán nǐ bù xiǎng qù, kěshì _____ děi qù.

(A) yǐ

(B) gāng

(C) yě

(D) lián

48. ㄙㄨㄟ ㄖㄢˊ ㄋㄧˇ ㄅㄨˋ ㄒㄧㄤˇ ㄑㄩˋ，ㄎㄜˇ ㄕˋ _____ ㄉㄟˇ ㄑㄩˋ。

(A) ㄧˇ

(B) ㄍㄤ

(C) ㄧㄝˇ

(D) ㄌㄧㄢˊ

49. Tā xiǎng dú jǐ běn _____ Zhōngguó lìshǐ de shū.

(A) duìyú

(B) guānyú

(C) yóuyú

(D) zhìyú

49. ㄊㄚ ㄒㄧㄤˇ ㄉㄨˊ ㄐㄧˇ ㄅㄣˇ _____ ㄓㄨㄥ ㄍㄨㄛˊ ㄌㄧˋ ㄕˇ ˙ㄉㄜ ㄕㄨ。

(A) ㄉㄨㄟˋ ㄩˊ

(B) ㄍㄨㄢ ㄩˊ

(C) ㄧㄡˊ ㄩˊ

(D) ㄓˋ ㄩˊ

50. Qiántiān tā gāng cóng Yīngguó huí Měiguó lái, míngtiān _____ yào qù Yīngguó le.

(A) hái

(B) zài

(C) cái

(D) yòu

50. ㄑㄧㄢˊ ㄊㄧㄢ ㄊㄚ ㄍㄤ ㄘㄨㄥˊ ㄧㄥ ㄍㄨㄛˊ ㄏㄨㄟˊ ㄇㄟˇ ㄍㄨㄛˊ ㄌㄞˊ，ㄇㄧㄥˊ ㄊㄧㄢ _____ ㄧㄠˋ ㄑㄩˋ ㄧㄥ ㄍㄨㄛˊ ˙ㄌㄜ。

(A) ㄏㄞˊ

(B) ㄗㄞˋ

(C) ㄘㄞˊ

(D) ㄧㄡˋ

GO ON TO THE NEXT PAGE

51. 報紙 _____ 風 _____ 吹到
地上去了。
(A) 讓 ..... 給
(B) 為 ..... 都
(C) 把 ..... 也
(D) 連 ..... 還

52. 林老師 _____ 放春假的機會，
帶學生去了趟中國。
(A) 藉著
(B) 靠著
(C) 按著
(D) 顧著

53. 今天你過生日，我們
應該 _____ 吃一頓！
(A) 好
(B) 大
(C) 更
(D) 很

54. 你是不是去年到英國去 _____ ？
(A) 嗎
(B) 吧
(C) 的
(D) 著

55. 你 _____ 給他寫信，
不如給他打電話。
(A) 關於
(B) 因而
(C) 與其
(D) 無論

51. 报纸 _____ 风 _____ 吹到
地上去了。
(A) 让 ..... 给
(B) 为 ..... 都
(C) 把 ..... 也
(D) 连 ..... 还

52. 林老师 _____ 放春假的机会，
带学生去了趟中国。
(A) 借着
(B) 靠着
(C) 按着
(D) 顾着

53. 今天你过生日，我们
应该 _____ 吃一顿！
(A) 好
(B) 大
(C) 更
(D) 很

54. 你是不是去年到英国去 _____ ？
(A) 吗
(B) 吧
(C) 的
(D) 着

55. 你 _____ 给他写信，
不如给他打电话。
(A) 关于
(B) 因而
(C) 与其
(D) 无论

GO ON TO THE NEXT PAGE

51. Bàozhǐ _____ fēng _____ chuī dào dìshang qù le.

(A) ràng ..... gěi

(B) wèi ..... dōu

(C) bǎ ..... yě

(D) lián ..... hái

51. ㄅㄠˋ ㄓˇ _____ ㄈㄥ _____ ㄔㄨㄟ ㄉㄠˋ ㄉㄧˋ ˙ㄕㄤ ㄑㄩˋ ˙ㄌㄜ。

(A) ㄖㄤˋ ..... ㄍㄟˇ

(B) ㄨㄟˋ ..... ㄉㄡ

(C) ㄅㄚˇ ..... ㄧㄝˇ

(D) ㄌㄧㄢˊ ..... ㄏㄞˊ

52. Lín lǎoshī _____ fàng chūnjià de jīhuì, dài xuésheng qù le tàng Zhōngguó.

(A) jièzhe

(B) kàozhe

(C) ànzhe

(D) gùzhe

52. ㄌㄧㄣˊ ㄌㄠˇ ㄕ _____ ㄈㄤˋ ㄔㄨㄣ ㄐㄧㄚˋ ˙ㄉㄜ ㄐㄧ ㄏㄨㄟˋ，ㄉㄞˋ ㄒㄩㄝˊ ㄕㄥ ㄑㄩˋ ˙ㄌㄜ ㄊㄤˋ ㄓㄨㄥ ㄍㄨㄛˊ。

(A) ㄐㄧㄝˋ ˙ㄓㄜ

(B) ㄎㄠˋ ˙ㄓㄜ

(C) ㄢˋ ˙ㄓㄜ

(D) ㄍㄨˋ ˙ㄓㄜ

53. Jīntiān nǐ guò shēngri, wǒmen yīnggāi _____ chī yí dùn!

(A) hǎo

(B) dà

(C) gèng

(D) hěn

53. ㄐㄧㄣ ㄊㄧㄢ ㄋㄧˇ ㄍㄨㄛˋ ㄕㄥ ㄖˋ，ㄨㄛˇ ˙ㄇㄣ ㄧㄥ ㄍㄞ _____ ㄔ ㄧˊ ㄉㄨㄣˋ！

(A) ㄏㄠˇ

(B) ㄉㄚˋ

(C) ㄍㄥˋ

(D) ㄏㄣˇ

54. Nǐ shì bú shì qùnián dào Yīngguó qù _____ ?

(A) ma

(B) ba

(C) de

(D) zhe

54. ㄋㄧˇ ㄕˋ ㄅㄨˊ ㄕˋ ㄑㄩˋ ㄋㄧㄢˊ ㄉㄠˋ ㄧㄥ ㄍㄨㄛˊ ㄑㄩˋ _____ ?

(A) ˙ㄇㄚ

(B) ˙ㄅㄚ

(C) ˙ㄉㄜ

(D) ˙ㄓㄜ

55. Nǐ _____ gěi tā xiě xìn, bùrú gěi tā dǎ diànhuà.

(A) guānyú

(B) yīn'ér

(C) yǔqí

(D) wúlùn

55. ㄋㄧˇ _____ ㄍㄟˇ ㄊㄚ ㄒㄧㄝˇ ㄒㄧㄣˋ，ㄅㄨˋ ㄖㄨˊ ㄍㄟˇ ㄊㄚ ㄉㄚˇ ㄉㄧㄢˋ ㄏㄨㄚˋ。

(A) ㄍㄨㄢ ㄩˊ

(B) ㄧㄣ ㄦˊ

(C) ㄩˇ ㄑㄧˊ

(D) ㄨˊ ㄌㄨㄣˋ

END OF SECTION II.
GO ON TO SECTION III.

SECTION III
READING COMPREHENSION

Suggested time—25 minutes

Questions 56-85

WHEN YOU BEGIN THIS SECTION, BE SURE THAT YOU MARK YOUR ANSWER TO THE FIRST QUESTION BY FILLING IN ONE OF THE CIRCLES NEXT TO <u>NUMBER 56</u> ON YOUR ANSWER SHEET.

Directions: Read the following texts carefully for comprehension. Each is followed by one or more questions or incomplete statements. Select the answer or completion that is best according to the text and fill in the corresponding circle on your answer sheet. There is no example for this section.

This section of the test is presented in two writing systems: traditional characters and simplified characters. IT IS RECOMMENDED THAT YOU CHOOSE THE WRITING SYSTEM WITH WHICH YOU ARE MORE FAMILIAR AND **<u>READ ONLY THAT VERSION</u>** AS YOU WORK THROUGH THIS SECTION OF THE TEST.

Question 56

大華電影院　購票須知

十二歲以下兒童，
必須由家長陪同入場。
凡超過二十人以上的團體，
必須以電話預訂門票。

大华电影院　购票须知

十二岁以下儿童，
必须由家长陪同入场。
凡超过二十人以上的团体，
必须以电话预订门票。

56. What information is given?

(A) Title of the movie being shown
(B) Date and time of the show
(C) Procedure for requesting a refund
(D) Procedure for purchasing group tickets

GO ON TO THE NEXT PAGE

Question 57

食品 八折優待 星期一、二、三、四	食品 八折优待 星期一、二、三、四

57. On what day can the coupon be used?

(A) Tuesday
(B) Friday
(C) Saturday
(D) Sunday

Questions 58-59

愛用者請注意 (一) 本品藥效可維持十二小時，一天只須服用兩次，每次三粒。 (二) 只有六粒盒裝，盒上印有康明400感冒藥，才是眞品。	爱用者请注意 (一) 本品药效可维持十二小时，一天只须服用两次，每次三粒。 (二) 只有六粒盒装，盒上印有康明400感冒药，才是真品。

58. Where would this message most likely be found?

(A) On a bulletin board
(B) On a medicine label
(C) In an appliance manual
(D) In a cookbook

59. How often should this product be used?

(A) Twice each month
(B) Every three weeks
(C) Once a day
(D) Every twelve hours

GO ON TO THE NEXT PAGE

Questions 60-61

黄教授喜歡自己一個人住在山上。他寫信告訴我他住的地方不但風景好而且空氣新鮮。家裏有電話也有電視，只是交通不太方便。每天早上他坐六點半的公共汽車到山腳下的學校去上班。下午下班以後，再走四十分鐘的路回家。因爲山上沒有河也沒有湖，所以喝的水都得從山下運上去，因此他每個月最大的開支就是水費。

黄教授喜欢自己一个人住在山上。他写信告诉我他住的地方不但风景好而且空气新鲜。家里有电话也有电视，只是交通不太方便。每天早上他坐六点半的公共汽车到山脚下的学校去上班。下午下班以后，再走四十分钟的路回家。因为山上没有河也没有湖，所以喝的水都得从山下运上去，因此他每个月最大的开支就是水费。

60. What does Professor Huang like about the place where he lives?

(A) Fresh air
(B) Convenient location
(C) Lake-front view
(D) Friendly neighbors

61. According to the passage, which of the following is true about Professor Huang?

(A) He lives with his family.
(B) He takes the bus to work every day.
(C) He likes to go swimming in the lake.
(D) He walks to school in the morning.

Question 62

【本報專訊】 今年感恩節前後出入機場的旅客特別多，停車位更是難找。市政府特別提醒市民，不要開車去機場。最好的方式是坐地鐵到體育館，然後在體育館前面乘公共汽車前往。

【本报专讯】 今年感恩节前后出入机场的旅客特别多，停车位更是难找。市政府特别提醒市民，不要开车去机场。最好的方式是坐地铁到体育馆，然后在体育馆前面乘公共汽车前往。

62. The passage recommends boarding a bus in front of the

(A) sports arena
(B) city hall
(C) hotel parking lot
(D) airport

GO ON TO THE NEXT PAGE

Question 63

金 園

新 張 營 業

菜式任點，附湯、水果

金 园

新 张 营 业

菜式任点，附汤、水果

63. What is this advertisement about?

(A) A grand opening
(B) A special rate
(C) A new location
(D) An end-of-season sale

Questions 64-66

盛暑之下，天氣炎熱，不宜大魚大肉。在此介紹一道簡易涼拌黃瓜。這道小菜不但味美，而且消暑。

材料：　小黃瓜四條，切薄片加鹽。約半小時後倒去所出汁水。

調味料：加入白沙糖和醋，拌匀即成。

盛暑之下，天气炎热，不宜大鱼大肉。在此介绍一道简易凉拌黄瓜。这道小菜不但味美，而且消暑。

材料：　小黄瓜四条，切薄片加盐。约半小时后倒去所出汁水。

调味料：加入白沙糖和醋，拌匀即成。

64. This excerpt is most likely from a

(A) fast-food advertisement
(B) restaurant review
(C) newspaper food column
(D) room-service menu

65. The featured item is a

(A) beverage
(B) vegetable dish
(C) main course
(D) dessert

66. Which of the following is true of the item described in the excerpt?

(A) It contains various herbs and spices.
(B) It is quite expensive.
(C) It tastes best when served hot.
(D) It is a simple, easily prepared dish.

GO ON TO THE NEXT PAGE

Question 67

一律八折　　　　一律八折

67. What information is given in the sign?

(A) An exchange rate
(B) A dosage
(C) A discount
(D) A time period

Question 68

北京新街口外大街二十五號

王鐵群先生收

上海南京路六十三號　李寄

北京新街口外大街二十五号

王铁群先生收

上海南京路六十三号　李寄

68. Who sent this letter?

(A) A student
(B) A manager
(C) A resident of Shanghai
(D) A resident of Beijing

GO ON TO THE NEXT PAGE

Questions 69-71

紅紅是我的小學同學也是鄰居。她的父親開了一家照相館，離我父親的理髮店不遠。小時候我們常常去找她父親給我們照相。紅紅有個當老師的哥哥，他喜歡到處拍風景照，可是技術不太好。照出來的照片，不是距離不對，就是光線太暗。紅紅常說她哥哥沒有她跟她父親那麼有藝術眼光。

红红是我的小学同学也是邻居。她的父亲开了一家照相馆，离我父亲的理发店不远。小时候我们常常去找她父亲给我们照相。红红有个当老师的哥哥，他喜欢到处拍风景照，可是技术不太好。照出来的照片，不是距离不对，就是光线太暗。红红常说她哥哥没有她跟她父亲那么有艺术眼光。

69. What does Honghong's brother like to do?

(A) Take pictures of scenery
(B) Design new hairstyles
(C) Teach Honghong to read
(D) Repair neighbors' appliances

70. What is the occupation of Honghong's father?

(A) Hairdresser
(B) Photographer
(C) Technician
(D) Teacher

71. What can be concluded about Honghong?

(A) She very much enjoys nature photography.
(B) She wants to become a hair designer.
(C) She does not consider her brother an artist.
(D) She does not like to have her picture taken.

Question 72

文化學院留學生聯誼會，為歡迎一九九五年春季漢語進修班的外國學生，特訂於一月三十日晚上六時在廣信大樓七號大廳舉行招待會。

邀請本學院各系教職員工，

踴躍出席。

文化学院留学生联谊会，为欢迎一九九五年春季汉语进修班的外国学生，特订于一月三十日晚上六时在广信大楼七号大厅举行招待会。

邀请本学院各系教职员工，

踊跃出席。

72. This is an invitation to a

(A) spring festival
(B) welcoming reception
(C) class reunion
(D) student orientation

GO ON TO THE NEXT PAGE

Question 73

自然博物館	自然博物馆
開放時間： 星期二至星期日 上午九點至下午七點 午飯時間照常開放	开放时间： 星期二至星期日 上午九点至下午七点 午饭时间照常开放
短片放映時間：週六下午三點至四點	短片放映时间：周六下午三点至四点

73. When is this place closed?

(A) Saturday afternoon
(B) Every Monday
(C) During lunchtime
(D) From 3 P.M. to 4 P.M.

Questions 74-75

《黃河大合唱》是許多中國人所喜愛的一首歌曲。一九三八年十一月，有一位姓張的詩人，搭船經過黃河。他看到黃河的滾滾流水和船夫們跟黃河急流的搏鬥，得到了啓發。後來他和一位作曲家談起黃河的壯觀景象，作曲家也非常感動。兩個人用了五、六天的時間，合作寫出了《黃河大合唱》這首歌。

《黄河大合唱》是许多中国人所喜爱的一首歌曲。一九三八年十一月，有一位姓张的诗人，搭船经过黄河。他看到黄河的滚滚流水和船夫们跟黄河急流的搏斗，得到了启发。后来他和一位作曲家谈起黄河的壮观景象，作曲家也非常感动。两个人用了五、六天的时间，合作写出了《黄河大合唱》这首歌。

74. What inspired Mr. Zhang?

(A) Watching a traditional Chinese dance
(B) Hearing a famous singer
(C) Seeing the view from a boat
(D) Reading a work by a young poet

75. How long did the two people take to complete their work?

(A) Three to four hours
(B) Five to six days
(C) Two to three weeks
(D) One to two months

GO ON TO THE NEXT PAGE

Questions 76-77

日本餐館
本州中部請有經驗營業經理
週六日有休假並提供宿舍
有意者請電 555-7729

日本餐馆
本州中部请有经验营业经理
周六日有休假并提供宿舍
有意者请电 555-7729

76. What position is being advertised?
    (A) Salesperson
    (B) Research librarian
    (C) Restaurant manager
    (D) Dietitian

77. Which of the following is required of the applicant?
    (A) Be a college graduate
    (B) Be experienced
    (C) Be willing to work long hours
    (D) Be fluent in Japanese

Questions 78-79

劉立最喜歡他的爺爺。因爲小時候爸爸媽媽白天去上班，只有爺爺在家照顧他。每天早上爺爺都在後院打太極拳。劉立以爲爺爺在跳舞，所以就一邊唱歌，一邊跟爺爺學。可是爺爺打拳的時候，總是不理他，也不跟他說話。劉立長大以後才明白，原來打太極拳的時候，非得集中精神不可。劉立還記得爺爺下午午睡起來以後，一定先喝杯熱茶，然後看報紙。有時候晚上爺爺也跟劉立一起看電視上的體育節目。

刘立最喜欢他的爷爷。因为小时候爸爸妈妈白天去上班，只有爷爷在家照顾他。每天早上爷爷都在后院打太极拳。刘立以为爷爷在跳舞，所以就一边唱歌，一边跟爷爷学。可是爷爷打拳的时候，总是不理他，也不跟他说话。刘立长大以后才明白，原来打太极拳的时候，非得集中精神不可。刘立还记得爷爷下午午睡起来以后，一定先喝杯热茶，然后看报纸。有时候晚上爷爷也跟刘立一起看电视上的体育节目。

78. Why is Liu Li especially fond of his grandfather?
    (A) He taught Liu Li how to read.
    (B) He was a kung fu master.
    (C) He knew many folk songs.
    (D) He took care of Liu Li as a child.

79. What did Liu Li's grandfather usually do in the afternoon?
    (A) Watch television
    (B) Read the newspaper
    (C) Do stretching exercises
    (D) Go for a walk

GO ON TO THE NEXT PAGE

Question 80

有人說可以根據以下情況來預測天氣：	有人说可以根据以下情况来预测天气：
一．冬天吹東風時會下雨，吹西風時是好天。	一．冬天吹东风时会下雨，吹西风时是好天。
二．下雪的第二天會是好天。	二．下雪的第二天会是好天。
三．山看起來很近的時候，第二天會下雨。	三．山看起来很近的时候，第二天会下雨。
四．煙一直往上飄時，會是好天。	四．烟一直往上飘时，会是好天。

80. According to the passage, which of the following is supposed to predict fair weather?

(A) A west wind blowing in the summer
(B) Smoke rising straight up into the sky
(C) Snow melting when it touches the ground
(D) Mountains appearing to be closer than they really are

Questions 81-82

實用中級英語會話	实用中级英语会话
□ 全套九卷錄音帶包括：發音練習專輯、生字詞匯表和會話朗讀。	□ 全套九卷录音带包括：发音练习专辑、生字词汇表和会话朗读。
□ 介紹口語語法及基本句型。	□ 介绍口语语法及基本句型。
□ 中級會話十課包括：家庭、職業、天氣、打電話、上餐館、去銀行、買東西、看醫生、邀請朋友和找工作。	□ 中级会话十课包括：家庭、职业、天气、打电话、上餐馆、去银行、买东西、看医生、邀请朋友和找工作。

81. What does this flyer advertise?

(A) A class in business English
(B) A new method for teaching conversational English
(C) A video for beginning English learners
(D) An audiocassette series for learning English

82. Which of the following is NOT included?

(A) Pronunciation drills
(B) Sentence patterns
(C) Writing exercises
(D) A vocabulary list

GO ON TO THE NEXT PAGE

Questions 83-85

人人書局與您共渡中秋節

電腦書籍、禮品八折優待

文具半價

優待時間：本月十九日至二十一日

人人书局与您共渡中秋节

电脑书籍、礼品八折优待

文具半价

优待时间：本月十九日至二十一日

83. For which of the following is the largest discount offered?

(A) Books
(B) Gift items
(C) Computers
(D) Stationery

84. What is the occasion for the sale?

(A) A grand opening
(B) An anniversary
(C) A holiday
(D) A closeout

85. How long does the sale last?

(A) One day
(B) Three days
(C) A week
(D) A month

END OF SECTION III.

STOP

IF YOU FINISH BEFORE TIME IS CALLED, YOU MAY CHECK YOUR WORK ON SECTIONS II AND III.
DO NOT TURN TO ANY OTHER TEST IN THIS BOOK.

How to Score the SAT Subject Test in Chinese with Listening

When you take an actual SAT Subject Test in Chinese with Listening, you receive an overall composite score as well as three subscores: one for the listening section, one for the reading section, and one for the usage section.

The listening, reading, and usage scores are reported on the College Board's 20–80 scale. However the composite score, which is the most significant of the scores reported to the colleges you specify, is in the form of the College Board's 200–800 scale.

Worksheet 1. Finding Your Raw Listening Subscore

STEP 1: Table A on page 513 lists the correct answers for all the questions on the Subject Test in Chinese with Listening that is reproduced in this book. It also serves as a worksheet for you to calculate your raw Listening subscore.

- Compare your answers with those given in the table.
- Put a check in the column marked "Right" if your answer is correct.
- Put a check in the column marked "Wrong" if your answer is incorrect.
- Leave both columns blank if you omitted the question.

STEP 2: Count the number of right answers for questions 1–19.

Enter the total here: ____________________

STEP 3: Count the number of wrong answers for questions 1–19.

Enter the total here: ____________________

STEP 4: Multiply the number of wrong answers from Step 3 by .500.

Enter the product here: ________________

STEP 5: Subtract the result obtained in Step 4 from the total you obtained in Step 2.

Enter the result here: __________________

STEP 6: Count the number of right answers for questions 20–30.

Enter the total here: ____________________

STEP 7: Count the number of wrong answers for questions 20–30.

Enter the total here: ____________________

STEP 8: Multiply the number of wrong answers from Step 7 by .333.

Enter the product here: ________________

STEP 9: Subtract the result obtained in Step 8 from the total you obtained in Step 6.

Enter the result here: __________________

STEP 10: Add the result obtained in Step 5 to the result obtained in Step 9.

Enter the sum here: ______________

STEP 11: Round the number obtained in Step 10 to the nearest whole number.

Enter the result here: ______________

The number you obtained in Step 11 is your raw Listening subscore.

Worksheet 2. Finding Your Raw Reading Subscore

STEP 1: Table A lists the correct answers for all the questions on the Subject Test in Chinese with Listening that is reproduced in this book. It also serves as a worksheet for you to calculate your raw Reading subscore.

STEP 2: Count the number of right answers for questions 56–85.

Enter the total here: ____________________

STEP 3: Count the number of wrong answers for questions 56–85.

Enter the total here: ____________________

STEP 4: Multiply the number of wrong answers by .333.

Enter the product here: ________________

STEP 5: Subtract the result obtained in Step 4 from the total you obtained in Step 2.

Enter the result here: ___________________

STEP 6: Round the number obtained in Step 5 to the nearest whole number.

Enter the result here: ___________________

The number you obtained in Step 6 is your raw Reading subscore.

Worksheet 3. Finding Your Raw Usage Subscore

STEP 1: Table A lists the correct answers for all the questions on the Subject Test in Chinese with Listening that is reproduced in this book. It also serves as a worksheet for you to calculate your raw Usage subscore.

STEP 2: Count the number of right answers for questions 31–55.

Enter the total here: ____________________

STEP 3: Count the number of wrong answers for questions 31–55.

Enter the total here: ____________________

STEP 4: Multiply the number of wrong answers by .333.

Enter the product here: ________________

STEP 5: Subtract the result obtained in Step 4 from the total you obtained in Step 2.

Enter the result here: __________________

STEP 6: Round the number obtained in Step 5 to the nearest whole number.

Enter the result here: __________________

The number you obtained in Step 6 is your raw Usage subscore.

Worksheet 4. Finding Your Raw Composite Score

STEP 1: Enter your unrounded raw Listening subscore from Step 10 of Worksheet 1.

Enter the result here: ________________

STEP 2: Enter your unrounded raw Reading subscore from Step 5 of Worksheet 2.

Enter the result here: ________________

STEP 3: Enter your unrounded raw Usage subscore from Step 5 of Worksheet 3.

Enter the result here: ________________

STEP 4: Add the results obtained in Steps 1, 2, and 3.

Enter the sum here: ________________

STEP 5: Round the number obtained in Step 4 to the nearest whole number.

Enter the result here: ________________

The number you obtained in Step 5 is your raw composite score.

Table A

Answers to the Subject Test in Chinese with Listening and Percentage of Students Answering Each Question Correctly									
Question Number	Correct Answer	Right	Wrong	Percentage of Students Answering the Question Correctly*	Question Number	Correct Answer	Right	Wrong	Percentage of Students Answering the Question Correctly*
1	B			99	33	D			98
2	C			98	34	A			98
3	C			99	35	C			96
4	C			98	36	B			97
5	A			98	37	D			98
6	C			93	38	D			97
7	A			85	39	B			94
8	C			90	40	A			91
9	C			94	41	B			95
10	C			98	42	D			79
11	A			98	43	A			69
12	B			99	44	A			82
13	A			98	45	B			60
14	C			97	46	B			69
15	C			94	47	D			70
16	A			98	48	C			78
17	B			96	49	B			78
18	A			67	50	D			79
19	A			93	51	A			72
20	B			82	52	A			42
21	D			95	53	B			70
22	D			97	54	C			65
23	C			99	55	C			37
24	D			98	56	D			92
25	A			98	57	A			97
26	C			97	58	B			92
27	B			69	59	D			91
28	C			69	60	A			91
29	A			64	61	B			94
30	D			79	62	A			67
31	C			98	63	A			80
32	B			96	64	C			67

Table A continued on next page

Table A continued from previous page

Question Number	Correct Answer	Right	Wrong	Percentage of Students Answering the Question Correctly*	Question Number	Correct Answer	Right	Wrong	Percentage of Students Answering the Question Correctly*
65	B			75	76	C			79
66	D			71	77	B			71
67	C			70	78	D			83
68	C			64	79	B			79
69	A			92	80	B			70
70	B			82	81	D			55
71	C			68	82	C			68
72	B			45	83	D			59
73	B			70	84	C			83
74	C			78	85	B			94
75	B			90					

* These percentages are based on an analysis of the answer sheets of a representative sample of 1,363 students who took the original administration of this test and whose mean composite score was 723. They may be used as an indication of the relative difficulty of a particular question.

Answer explanations for the Subject Test in Chinese with Listening can be found on page 521.

Finding Your Scaled Score

When you take SAT Subject Tests, the scores sent to the colleges you specify are reported on the College Board scale, which ranges from 200–800. Subscores are reported on a scale which ranges from 20–80. You can convert your practice test scores to scaled scores by using Tables B, C, D and E on the following pages. To find your scaled score, locate your raw score in the left-hand column of the table; the corresponding score in the right-hand column is your scaled score. For example, a raw score of 59 on this particular edition of the Subject Test in Chinese with Listening corresponds to a scaled composite score of 690.

Raw scores are converted to scaled scores to ensure that a score earned on any one edition of a particular Subject Test is comparable to the same scaled score earned on any other edition of the same Subject Test. Because some editions of the tests may be slightly easier or more difficult than others, College Board scaled scores are adjusted so that they indicate the same level of performance regardless of the edition of the test taken and the ability of the group that takes it. Thus, for example, a score of 400 on one edition of a test taken at a particular administration indicates the same level of achievement as a score of 400 on a different edition of the test taken at a different administration.

When you take the SAT Subject Tests during a national administration, your scores are likely to differ somewhat from the scores you obtain on the tests in this book. People perform at different levels at different times for reasons unrelated to the tests themselves. The precision of any test is also limited because it represents only a sample of all the possible questions that could be asked.

Your scaled composite score from Table B is ______________________.

Your scaled listening score from Table C is ______________________.

Your scaled reading score from Table D is ______________________.

Your scaled usage score from Table E is ______________________.

Table B

Scaled Score Conversion Table
Subject Test in Chinese with Listening Composite Score

Raw Score	Scaled Score	Raw Score	Scaled Score	Raw Score	Scaled Score
85	800	47	630	9	430
84	800	46	620	8	420
83	800	45	620	7	420
82	800	44	610	6	410
81	800	43	610	5	410
80	800	42	600	4	400
79	790	41	590	3	400
78	790	40	590	2	390
77	780	39	580	1	390
76	780	38	580	0	380
75	770	37	570	-1	380
74	770	36	570	-2	370
73	760	35	560	-3	370
72	750	34	560	-4	360
71	750	33	550	-5	360
70	740	32	550	-6	350
69	740	31	540	-7	350
68	730	30	540	-8	340
67	730	29	530	-9	340
66	720	28	530	-10	330
65	720	27	520	-11	330
64	710	26	520	-12	320
63	710	25	510	-13	320
62	700	24	510	-14	310
61	700	23	500	-15	310
60	690	22	500	-16	300
59	690	21	490	-17	290
58	680	20	490	-18	290
57	680	19	480	-19	280
56	670	18	480	-20	280
55	670	17	470	-21	270
54	660	16	470	-22	270
53	660	15	460	-23	260
52	650	14	460	-24	260
51	650	13	450	-25	250
50	640	12	440	-26	250
49	640	11	440	-27	240
48	630	10	430	-28	240
				-29	230
				-30	230
				-31	220

Table C

Scaled Score Conversion Table Subject Test in Chinese with Listening Listening Subscore					
Raw Score	Scaled Score	Raw Score	Scaled Score	Raw Score	Scaled Score
30	80	15	54	0	42
29	78	14	53	-1	41
28	74	13	53	-2	40
27	71	12	52	-3	39
26	69	11	51	-4	38
25	66	10	51	-5	37
24	64	9	50	-6	35
23	63	8	49	-7	34
22	61	7	49	-8	33
21	60	6	48	-9	32
20	59	5	47	-10	31
19	58	4	46	-11	30
18	57	3	45	-12	29
17	56	2	44	-13	28
16	55	1	43		

Table D

Scaled Score Conversion Table Subject Test in Chinese with Listening Reading Subscore					
Raw Score	Scaled Score	Raw Score	Scaled Score	Raw Score	Scaled Score
30	80	16	68	2	50
29	80	15	68	1	47
28	79	14	67	0	45
27	78	13	66	-1	44
26	77	12	65	-2	42
25	76	11	64	-3	41
24	75	10	63	-4	41
23	75	9	62	-5	40
22	74	8	61	-6	40
21	73	7	59	-7	40
20	72	6	58	-8	39
19	71	5	56	-9	39
18	70	4	54	-10	38
17	69	3	52		

Table E

Scaled Score Conversion Table
Subject Test in Chinese with Listening
Usage Subscore

Raw Score	Scaled Score	Raw Score	Scaled Score	Raw Score	Scaled Score
25	80	14	65	3	49
24	80	13	64	2	47
23	79	12	62	1	46
22	77	11	61	0	44
21	76	10	59	-1	43
20	74	9	58	-2	41
19	73	8	56	-3	40
18	71	7	55	-4	38
17	70	6	53	-5	37
16	68	5	52	-6	35
15	67	4	50	-7	34
				-8	32

How Did You Do on the Subject Test in Chinese with Listening?

After you score your test and analyze your performance, think about the following questions:

Did you run out of time before reaching the end of the test?

If so, you may need to pace yourself better. For example, maybe you spent too much time on one or two hard questions. A better approach might be to skip the ones you can't answer right away and try answering all the questions that remain on the test. Then if there's time, go back to the questions you skipped.

Did you take a long time reading the directions?

You will save time when you take the test by learning the directions to the Subject Test in Chinese with Listening ahead of time. Each minute you spend reading directions during the test is a minute that you could use to answer questions.

How did you handle questions you were unsure of?

If you were able to eliminate one or more of the answer choices as wrong and guess from the remaining ones, your approach probably worked to your advantage. On the other hand, making haphazard guesses or omitting questions without trying to eliminate choices could cost you valuable points.

How difficult were the questions for you compared with other students who took the test?

Table A shows you how difficult the multiple-choice questions were for the group of students who took this test during its national administration. The right-hand column gives the percentage of students that answered each question correctly.

A question answered correctly by almost everyone in the group is obviously an easier question. For example, 98 percent of the students answered question 4 correctly. But only 37 percent answered question 55 correctly.

Keep in mind that these percentages are based on just one group of students. They would probably be different with another group of students taking the test.

If you missed several easier questions, go back and try to find out why: Did the questions cover material you haven't yet reviewed? Did you misunderstand the directions?

Answer Explanations for the Chinese with Listening Subject Test

1. Choice (B) is the correct answer. The woman admires the man's tie and asks him where he bought it. He responds that it was a gift from his girlfriend. The other two choices, choice (A) "You know this is the wrong way," and choice (C) "You want me to bring him here too?" do not make sense in this context.

2. Choice (C) is the correct answer. The woman asks, "What kind of sports (involving a ball) do you like to play?" and the man responds, "I only play tennis." The other two choices, choice (A) "I like talking on the phone," and choice (B) "I want to buy a pair of athletic shoes," do not make sense in this context.

3. Choice (C) is the correct answer. The man asks, "What time does your plane depart?" and the woman responds, "At about 2:30." The other two choices, choice (A) "We'll pick you up at the airport," and choice (B) "He's free anytime," do not make sense in this context.

4. Choice (C) is the correct answer. The man asks, "Can you speak a foreign language?" and the woman responds, "Only Japanese. How about you?" The other two choices, choice (A) "I hear it will rain tomorrow evening," and choice (B) "Don't say any more, he's already angry," do not make sense in this context.

5. Choice (A) is the correct answer. The young man says, "Auntie Zhang, this is my sister Xiao Hong," to which the woman responds, "The two of you look a lot alike." The other two choices, choice (B) "No problem, I'll come right away," and choice (C) "This table does not belong to your little sister," do not make sense in this context.

6. Choice (C) is the correct answer. The man says, "Your calligraphy is quite good!" to which the woman responds, "Compared to yours, I've got a long way to go." The other two choices, choice (A) "If you make a mistake, fix it right away!" and choice (B) "Your sweater is so pretty. Who gave it to you?" do not make sense in this context.

7. Choice (A) is the correct answer. The woman says, "Let me introduce you to Professor Lu," to which the man responds, "I've been looking forward to meeting you." The other two choices, "Take it easy," and "You flatter me," are inappropriate responses in this context.

8. Choice (C) is the correct answer. The woman asks, "Is there a gas station nearby?" and the man responds, "Just keep going straight ahead; it will be right there." The other two choices, choice (A) "My home is near the post office," and choice (B) "Please stand up right now," do not make sense in this context.

9. Choice (C) is the correct answer. The woman exclaims, "It's snowing hard outside!" and the man responds, "Yes! It's really cold." The other two choices, choice (A) "Oh, it's so hot!" and choice (B) "That's right! The refrigerator is too small," are inappropriate responses in this context.

10. Choice (C) is the correct answer. The woman says, "My brother has gone out. He's not home right now." The man then asks, "When will he be back?" She replies, "I don't know. He didn't tell me." The other two choices, choice (A) "No need, he knows how to do it now," and choice (B) "Hard to say, he might not go," do not make sense in this context.

11. Choice (A) is the correct answer. The man asks, "Where shall we go now?" and the woman responds, "Let's go for a walk in the park!" To this, he responds by saying, "That would be great." The other two choices, choice (B) "It tastes terrible," and choice (C) "[He's] very rich," do not make sense in this context.

12. Choice (B) is the correct answer. The man asks, "Have you been to Taipei?" and the woman responds, "No, but I'd like to go. What about you?" He replies, "I go often." The other two choices, choice (A) "He's here," and choice (C) "You've been here before," do not make sense in this context.

13. Choice (A) is the correct answer. The girl asks her brother, "Let's go to the movies later, okay?" He says, "Oh no, I can't. I have to go to class." Her response is, "Then let's go tonight." The other two choices, choice (B) "Then you'd better go to the doctor right away," and choice (C) "That's the book he uses in class," do not make sense in this context.

14. Choice (C) is the correct answer. The man says, "I really don't like the weather here." The woman asks why, and he responds, "Because it rains too much." The other two choices, choice (A) "It's not good to get angry too often," and choice (B) "He's coming here today," do not make sense in this context.

15. Choice (C) is the correct answer. The woman asks, "What you are going to do after you graduate?" The man answers, "I haven't decided yet. Have you?" to which the woman replies, "I'd like to be an elementary school teacher." The other two choices, choice (A) "I've already arrived in the U.S.," and choice (B) "I just got back after eating," do not make sense in this context.

16. Choice (A) is the correct answer. The woman asks, "Let's go swimming together, okay?" The man responds, "That's a good idea, but I can't swim. What shall we do?" She says, "Don't worry, I can teach you." The other two choices, choice (B) "There's no other way, he insists on going," and choice (C) "Please don't be polite, go ahead and use it," do not make sense in this context.

17. Choice (B) is the correct answer. The woman caller asks, "Is Manager Hu there?" The man responds, "I'm sorry, he's in a meeting right now and can't come to the phone." The woman says, "Please tell him Xiao Lin wants to talk to him about something." The other two choices, choice (A) "Please wait a moment. I'll go call for him," and choice (C) "Please come see him as soon as you are finished with your meeting," do not make sense here.

18. Choice (A) is the correct answer. The man asks, "Can you come over to my house tomorrow?" The woman responds, "I can in the morning." The man says, "Then let's have breakfast together!" The other two choices, choice (B) "Then you can take the noon bus," and choice (C) "Then I'll wait for you to come tomorrow evening," do not make sense in this context.

19. Choice (A) is the correct answer. The man asks, "How was the basketball game last night?" The woman replies, "It was great! How come we didn't see you there?" The man answers, "I got there late so I couldn't get a ticket." The other two choices, choice (B) "There are too many people, you won't be able to find him," and choice (C) "There's no need, I saw him yesterday," do not make sense in this context.

20. Choice (B) is the correct answer. The man's native language is Chinese. In the dialogue, the man and the woman are discussing the man's son who speaks very good German. The man and his son lived in Germany for many years and only moved

to the U.S. recently. When asked which language—English or German—was easier, he said, "Chinese," to which the woman said, "You're Chinese; of course you find Chinese easy!" There is no mention of French in the dialogue.

21. Choice (D) is the correct answer. The woman complimented the man's son on his fluency in German and asked whether he had learned it in college. The man replied that the boy grew up in Germany.

22. Choice (D) is the correct answer. The speaker says he cannot discuss the issue at hand now because he went to bed late the night before and woke up with a headache, which has persisted even though he took some pills.

23. Choice (C) is the correct answer. There was no mention of riding bicycles. At the party at Lao Chen's house, people sang, watched TV, played tennis, and danced.

24. Choice (D) is the correct answer. He boarded the wrong bus—#203 is bound for the train station, but he needed #302, which would have taken him to the sports arena. Now he needs to get off at the next stop, the library, and change buses.

25. Choice (A) is the correct answer. He originally wanted white shoes, but couldn't find any suitable ones. There was a pair of brown shoes in his size, but he didn't like the style. So he eventually bought black shoes. The passage does not mention yellow shoes.

26. Choice (C) is the correct answer. The brown shoes fit him, but he didn't like the way they looked. The passage does not mention their price or quality.

27. Choice (B) is the correct answer. The announcement states that shows are being added on two days—the 15th and the 18th. It gives the prices and urges listeners to reserve their tickets as soon as possible. There is no mention of a revision to the program, the location of the performances, or a deadline to buy tickets.

28. Choice (C) is the correct answer. This Saturday, the girl is having a dance party for her classmate Zhang Li, whose birthday is next Wednesday. She invites her brother, but he has a paper due on Monday and so is unable to attend. They do not mention Sunday in their conversation.

29. Choice (A) is the correct answer. The male speaker says that he must stay in the dormitory to study over the weekend, rather than attend the party his sister is planning, so it is logical to assume that he lives in a dormitory. The party is for Zhang Li, who is his sister's classmate in the history department.

30. Choice (D) is the correct answer. The male speaker is instructed to bring two photographs, his transcript, his medical report, and 20 yuan to register. There is no mention of an ID card.

31. Choice (C) is the correct answer. The prompt refers to "what the principal said"; the question therefore must ask whether you heard and/or understood what was said. The completed question asks, "Did you *understand* (by hearing) everything that the principal said?" It does not make sense to ask if you, choice (A) "can see," choice (B) "cannot take out," or choice (D) "set down," what the principal said.

32. Choice (B) is the correct answer. It completes the sentence, "This morning he *got up very late*," and is the only choice that presents the words "got up very late" in a grammatical order.

33. Choice (D) is the correct answer. It completes the sentence, "After working all day, *everyone was tired*," and is the only choice that presents the words "everyone was tired" in a grammatical order.

34. Choice (A) is the correct answer. It provides the appropriate conjunction, "so," or "therefore," to complete the sentence, "His car broke down, <u>so</u> he wants me to pick him up." The other choices are choice (B) "other than," choice (C) "no matter," and choice (D) "in this fashion," which do not make sense in this context.

35. Choice (C) is the correct answer. It means "even more so," and completes the sentence, "She sings *even* better than I do." The other choices mean approximately, choice (A) "once more," choice (B) "right away," and choice (D) "furthermore," and do not make sense in this context.

36. Choice (B) is the correct answer. It means "sit down," and completes the sentence, "Is it okay if we *sit down* and rest a while?" The other choices mean, choice (A) "begin singing," choice (C) "discern by listening," and choice (D) "seem by appearance," and do not make sense in this context.

37. Choice (D) is the correct answer. It completes the sentence, "He *already took the children to the park*," and is the only choice that presents the words "already took the children to the park" in a grammatical order.

38. Choice (D) is the correct answer. It completes the sentence, "Where I work *is not too far from my home*," and is the only choice that presents the words "is not too far from my home" in a grammatical order.

39. Choice (B) is the correct answer. It completes the sentence, "Although he's lived in England, [but] he can't really speak English." *Dànshì* means "but," and *suīrán* .... *dànshì* ("although ... but") is a set pattern in Chinese. The other choices mean, choice (A) "then," choice (C) "furthermore," and choice (D) "thereupon," and do not make sense in this context.

40. Choice (A) is the correct answer. It means "was (in the middle of) doing something," and completes the sentence, "When I went to his house, he *was sleeping*." The other choices mean, choice (B) "a moment ago," choice (C) "all along," and choice (D) "then," and do not make sense in this context.

41. Choice (B) is the correct answer. It means "from ... to," and completes the sentence, "How long does it take to walk *from* the train station *to* the dormitory?" The other choices mean, choice (A) "toward ... at," choice (C) "in the direction of ... with," and choice (D) "starting from ... along," and do not make sense in this context.

42. Choice (D) is the correct answer. It means "must" or "have to," and completes the sentence, "Tonight we *have to* go see a friend." The other choices mean, choice (A) "toward," choice (B) "from," and choice (C) "even more," and do not make sense in this context.

43. Choice (A) is the correct answer. *Céng* works with the particle *le* to indicate an event that happened in the past, and completes the sentence, "Last year he wrote me three letters." The other choices are not grammatical in this context. Choice (B) *Méi*, indicates an action that did not happen and is not used with *le*; choice (C) *sòng*, means "to give" and does not make sense here; and choice (D) *huì*, indicates an action that will occur in the future, which does not fit here because the sentence indicates "last year."

44. Choice (A) is the correct answer. It means "specially," and completes the sentence, "This room was *specially* prepared for you." The other choices mean, choice (B) "comparatively," choice (C) "quite," and choice (D) "extremely," and do not make sense in this context.

45 Choice (B) is the correct answer. It completes the sentence, "*That report was borrowed by a colleague*," and is the only choice that presents the words "was borrowed by a colleague" in a grammatical order.

46. Choice (B) is the correct answer. It means "within," and completes the sentence, "Tuition is approximately three thousand dollars, but room and board is not included *within* (that sum)." The other choices mean approximately, choice (A) "in addition," choice (C) "the above," and choice (D) "among these," and are not appropriate responses in this context.

47. Choice (D) is the correct answer. It means "pick (on)," and completes the sentence, "He always likes to *pick on* other peoples' shortcomings." The other choices mean, choice (A) "take," choice (B) "let loose," and choice (C) "make," and do not make sense in this context.

48. Choice (C) is the correct answer. In this context, it means something like "and still, but still," and completes the sentence, "Although you don't want to go, you *still* have to go." The other choices mean choice (A) "already," choice (B) "just now," and choice (D) "even," and do not make sense in this context.

49. Choice (B) is the correct answer. It means "about," and completes the sentence, "He would like to read a few books *about* Chinese history." The other choices mean, choice (A) "as for," choice (C) "because of," and choice (D) "as to," and do not make sense in this context.

50. Choice (D) is the correct answer. It is paired with the particle *le* and means "again," and completes the sentence, "He just got back to the U.S. from England the day before yesterday. Tomorrow he's going to England *again* (*already*)." Choice (A) can mean "in addition," or "still," and choice (C) means "not until"; they do not work in this context. Choice (B) also means "again," but word order and the presence of the particle *le* makes it inappropriate here. *Yòu* … *le* indicates a sense of disbelief at the shortness of time between event 1 (returning home) and event 2 (leaving again).

51. Choice (A) is the correct answer. It indicates the passive voice, and completes the sequence, "The newspaper was blown to the floor by the wind." The other choices mean approximately, choice (B) "for the sake of ... still," choice (C) "take (it) and ...," and choice (D) "even ... still," and are not appropriate in this context.

52. Choice (A) is the correct answer. It completes the expression, "take advantage of an opportunity," in the sentence, "*Taking advantage* of the opportunity provided by spring break, Teacher Lin took the students to China." The other choices mean, choice (B) "relying on," choice (C) "according to," and choice (D) "taking into consideration," and do not combine meaningfully with the term "opportunity" in the sentence.

53. Choice (B) is the correct answer. This is idiomatic usage; the sentence states, "Today is your birthday; we should have a feast!" The Chinese way of saying this is to "big eat"; not to "choice (A) good eat," or to "choice (C) even more eat," or to "choice (D) very eat."

54. Choice (C) is the correct answer. The particle *de* forms part of the *shì* ... *de* pattern that is used when discussing details, such as when or with whom an event is known to have occurred. In this case, it completes the sentence, "Was it last year that you went to England?" The other particles indicate, choice (A) a question (inappropriate because the sentence is already a question), choice (B) a suggestion (inappropriate because the sentence is a question), and choice (D) ongoing action (inappropriate because the action is set in the past).

55. Choice (C) is the correct answer. It means "rather than," and completes the sentence, "*Rather than* writing him, it would be better to call him on the phone." The other choices mean, choice (A) "concerning," choice (B) "therefore," and choice (D) "no matter," and are not appropriate in this context.

56. Choice (D) is the correct answer. The notice states that children under 12 must be accompanied by a parent or guardian, and that parties of more than 20 people must reserve tickets by telephone.

57. Choice (A) is the correct answer. The notice states that the coupon can be used to receive a 20 percent discount on Monday, Tuesday, Wednesday, or Thursday. Choice (A) is Tuesday.

58. Choice (B) is the correct answer. The notice indicates frequency of use and proper dosage, and also states that only packages properly imprinted with the name of the cold medicine are genuine.

59. Choice (D) is the correct answer. The notice states that the medication is effective for 12 hours and need only be taken twice a day, three pills each time.

60. Choice (A) is the correct answer. In Professor Huang's letter, he said he liked the view and the fresh air. Choice (B) is incorrect: He lives on top of a mountain, which is not convenient. Choice (C) is incorrect: There is no lake on the mountain. Choice (D) is incorrect: He has no neighbors.

61. Choice (B) is the correct answer: Professor Huang takes the 6:30 a.m. bus to school every day. Choice (A) is incorrect: He lives alone on the mountain. Choice (C) is incorrect: There is no lake on the mountain in which to swim. Choice (D) is incorrect: He walks home after work, not in the morning.

62. Choice (A) is the correct answer: People bound for the airport are advised to take the subway to the sports arena and board a bus for the airport there. Choice (B) is incorrect: The city government is making the suggestion; however, buses for the airport do not depart from city hall. Choice (C) is incorrect: There is no mention of a hotel parking lot. Choice (D) is incorrect: The airport is the final destination.

63. Choice (A) is the correct answer. The advertisement states, "Golden Garden/newly opened for business/select the dishes you please, complimentary soup and fruit."

64. Choice (C) is the correct answer. [A] newspaper food column would likely provide the recipe for a light summer cucumber dish, which is shown here.

65. Choice (B) is the correct answer. The recipe is for a lightly dressed cucumber dish, which is generally served as an appetizer or a side dish. It is not a, choice (A) beverage, choice (C) main course, or choice (D) dessert.

66. Choice (D) is the correct answer. The cucumber slices should be lightly salted and then dressed with vinegar and sugar. The dish, choice (A) contains no herbs or spices, choice (B) is inexpensive, and choice (C) should be served cold.

67. Choice (C) is the correct answer. The sign states, "All items 20% off" ("All items are 80% of their original price"). It refers to a sale, not, choice (A) an exchange rate, choice (B) a dosage, or choice (D) a time period.

68. Choice (C) is the correct answer. As indicated by the text in the bottom right-hand corner, the letter was sent by someone named Li, residing in Shanghai, not choice (D) Beijing. There is no indication that the sender is, choice (A) a student, or choice (B) a manager.

69. Choice (A) is the correct answer. The passage indicates that Honghong's brother likes to take pictures. There is no mention of any of the other choices.

70. Choice (B) is the correct answer. Honghong's father is a photographer and runs his own studio. The author's father is choice (A) the hairdresser. Honghong's brother is choice (D) the teacher, and his technique in photography is not good. There is no mention of choice (C) a technician.

71. Choice (C) is the correct answer. The passage states that Honghong often said her brother did not have the "artistic eye" that she and her father had: His pictures were always either out of focus or too dark. The author mentions that she and Honghong often sought out Honghong's father to take their pictures, making it unlikely that she, choice (D) does not like to have her picture taken. The passage makes no mention of Honghong, choice (A) enjoying nature photography (her brother is the nature photographer), or choice (B) wanting to become a hair designer (the author's father is the hairdresser).

72. Choice (B) is the correct answer. The invitation is to a welcoming reception for foreign students learning Chinese, in the spring semester of 1995, in the Cultural Institute. The reception is to be held at 6 p.m., on January 30, in the Guangxin Building, Hall #7. The event is not a, choice (A) spring festival, choice (C) class reunion, or choice (D) student orientation.

73. Choice (B) is the correct answer. The operating hours of the Museum of Natural History are Tuesday through Sunday, 9 a.m. to 7 p.m., including during lunch. On Saturday afternoons from 3 to 4 p.m., a short film is shown. The museum is closed every Monday, and open all the times named in the other choices.

74. Choice (C) is the correct answer. The poet Mr. Zhang was inspired when riding on a boat going down the Yellow River. The passage does not mention choice (A) a dance, choice (B) a famous singer, or choice (D) reading the work of a young poet.

75. Choice (B) is the correct answer. The poet and the songwriter worked for five to six days to write the "Yellow River Chorus," as stated in the last sentence of the passage. There is no mention of the other choices.

76. Choice (C) is the correct answer. The Japanese restaurant is looking for an experienced manager, not a, choice (A) salesperson, choice (B) librarian, or choice (D) dietitian.

77. Choice (B) is the correct answer. The ad specifies that the candidate be experienced as a manager; not that he or she be, choice (A) a college graduate, choice (C) willing to work long hours (the ad specifies that the position includes weekends off), or choice (D) fluent in Japanese.

78. Choice (D) is the correct answer. Liu Li's grandfather took care of him as a child while his parents were at work. The passage indicates that he practiced Tai Chi daily, not that he was a, choice (B) kung fu master. Liu Li liked to sing songs, but there is no mention of his grandfather, choice (C) knowing many folk songs; and while his grandfather liked to read the paper after his nap, there is no mention of his, choice (A) having taught Liu Li to read.

79. Choice (B) is the correct answer. Liu Li's grandfather liked to read newspapers in the afternoon, after getting up from his nap. He, choice (A) watched TV in the evening. There is no mention in the passage of his doing, choice (C) stretching exercises, or choice (D) going for a walk.

80. Choice (B) is the correct answer. The passage states that smoke rising straight up predicts good weather, as does a west wind blowing in the wintertime (not choice (A) summer). The second day after a snowfall is good weather—there is no mention of, choice (C) snow melting upon touching the ground. When the, choice (D) mountains appear closer than they are, rainfall (not good weather) is predicted for the second day.

81. Choice (D) is the correct answer. The flyer advertises a set of nine cassettes of practical, intermediate level, conversational English lessons. The ad does not mention, choice

(A) business English, choice (B) a new method for teaching conversational English, or choice (C) a video for beginning learners.

82. Choice (C) is the correct answer. The ad explicitly states that, in the order in which they appear in the flyer, choice (A) pronunciation drills, choice (D) a vocabulary list, and choice (B) sentence patterns are included. It does not list writing exercises among the features.

83. Choice (D) is the correct answer. Stationery is half off. All other items, including, as they appear sequentially in the sign, choice (C) computers, choice (A) books, and choice (B) gift items, are 20 percent off.

84. Choice (C) is the correct answer. The sale commemorates the Mid-Autumn Festival holiday, not choice (A) a grand opening, choice (B) an anniversary, or choice (D) a closeout.

85. Choice (B) is the correct answer. The sale lasts three days—from the 19th to the 21st of the present month.

Chapter 9
French

Purpose

There are two Subject Tests in French: French and French with Listening. Both tests evaluate your reading skills through precision of vocabulary, structure use, and comprehension of a variety of texts. The Subject Test in French with Listening measures your ability to understand spoken as well as written French.

Format

- The Subject Test in French takes one hour and includes 85 multiple-choice questions.
- The Subject Test in French with Listening also takes one hour, with about 20 minutes for listening questions and 40 minutes for reading questions. There are 85 to 90 multiple-choice listening and reading questions.

Content

Both tests evaluate your reading ability in three areas through a variety of questions requiring a wide-ranging knowledge of French:

Precision of vocabulary questions test knowledge of words representing different parts of speech and some basic idioms within culturally authentic contexts.

Structure questions measure your ability to select an appropriate word or expression that is grammatically correct within a sentence. One part of the test contains vocabulary and structure questions embedded in longer paragraphs.

Reading comprehension questions test your understanding of such points as main and supporting ideas, themes, and setting of a passage. Selections are drawn from fiction, essays, historical works, newspaper and magazine articles, or everyday materials such as advertisements, timetables, forms, and tickets.

French	
Skills Measured	Approximate Percentage of Test
Vocabulary in Context	30%
Structure	30–40%
Reading Comprehension	30–40%

In addition to these reading questions, the Subject Test in French with Listening also measures your ability to understand the spoken language with three types of *listening questions*:

Type one asks you to identify the sentence that most accurately describes what is presented in a picture or a photograph or what someone in the picture or photograph might say.

Type two tests your ability to answer general content questions based on short dialogues or monologues.

Type three requires you to answer more specific questions based on longer dialogues or monologues.

French with Listening		
Types of Questions		Approximate Percentage of Test
Listening Section	(20 Minutes)	35%
Pictures:	8–12 questions	
Short dialogues:	6–12 questions	
Long dialogues:	10–15 questions	
Reading Section	(40 minutes)	65%
Vocabulary:	16–20 questions	
Structure:	16–20 questions	
Reading Comprehension:	20–25 questions	

How to Prepare

Both tests are written to reflect general trends in high school curricula and are independent of particular textbooks or methods of instruction. The French Tests are appropriate for you if you have studied the language for three or four years in high school, or the equivalent; however, if you have two years of strong preparation in French, you are also encouraged to take the tests. Your best preparation for the tests is a gradual development of competence in French over a period of years. Familiarize yourself with the directions in advance. The directions in this book are identical to those that appear on the test.

French with Listening

A practice audio CD for the full-length practice test is included with this book. A practice CD with different sample questions can be obtained, along with a copy of the *Getting*

Ready for the SAT Subject Tests booklet, from your school counselor, or you can access the listening files at www.collegeboard.org. If your counselor does not have the CD or booklet, he or she can order them from the College Board.

CD Players

Using CD Players for Language Tests with Listening

Take an acceptable CD player to the test center. Your CD player must be in good working order, so insert fresh batteries on the day before the test. You may bring additional batteries and a backup player to the test center. CD players cannot be shared with other test-takers.

Test center staff won't have batteries, CD players, or earphones for your use, so your CD player must be:

- equipped with earphones
- portable (hand-held)
- battery operated

You are not allowed to use a CD player with recording or duplicating capabilities.

Note

If the volume on your CD player disturbs other test-takers, the test center supervisor may ask you to move to another seat.

What to do if your CD player malfunctions:

- Raise your hand and tell the test supervisor.
- Switch to backup equipment if you have it and continue the test. If you don't have backup equipment, your score on the Subject Test in French with Listening will be canceled. But scores on other Subject Tests you take that day will still be counted.

What if you receive a defective CD on test day? Raise your hand and ask the supervisor for a replacement.

Scores

For both tests, the total score is reported on the 200-to-800 scale. For the listening test, listening and reading subscores are reported on the 20-to-80 scale.

Sample Reading Questions

Four types of reading questions are used in the French Tests. All questions in the tests are multiple-choice questions in which you must choose the BEST response from the four choices offered.

Your answer sheet has five answer positions marked A, B, C, D, and E, while the questions throughout this test contain only four choices. Be sure NOT to make any marks in column E.

Part A

Directions: This part consists of a number of incomplete statements, each having four suggested completions. Select the most appropriate completion and fill in the corresponding circle on the answer sheet.

1. J'ai perdu mon argent parce qu'il y avait un trou dans la ... de mon pantalon.
   (A) manche
   (B) jambe
   (C) poche
   (D) ceinture

Choice (C) is the correct answer because pants have pockets in which people keep money. This question tests vocabulary. You are asked to choose the appropriate noun from the four answer choices. Choices (A) and (D) are not normally used to carry money, and choice (B) refers to a part of the body.

2. Charles avait tant mangé qu'il ne pouvait plus ... une bouchée.
   (A) soutenir
   (B) emporter
   (C) avaler
   (D) évaluer

Choice (C) is the correct answer to question 2. In this question, you are asked to find the appropriate verb from the four answer choices. The verb *avaler* is the only option that can be used correctly in connection with *une bouchée.* Choices (A), (B), and (D) are incorrect.

Part B

Directions: Each of the following sentences contains a blank. From the four choices given, select the one that can be inserted in the blank to form a grammatically correct sentence and fill in the corresponding circle on the answer sheet. Choice (A) may consist of dashes that indicate that no insertion is required to form a grammatically correct sentence.

3. Dans sa cuisine, il fallait toujours que tout_____impeccable et reluisant.

   (A) est

   (B) soit

   (C) était

   (D) serait

Choice (B) is the correct answer to question 3 because from the four answer choices *soit* is the correct form of the verb *être.* You need to know that *il fallait que* in the sentence is the past tense of *il faut que*, an impersonal expression that is followed by a verb in the subjunctive. Choices (A), (C), and (D) are forms of *être* in the indicative and are therefore incorrect.

4. _____ est le meilleur joueur de cette équipe?

   (A) Qu'

   (B) Quelle

   (C) Qu'est-ce qu'

   (D) Qui

Choice (D) is the correct answer to question 4. In this question you are asked to choose the appropriate pronoun from the four answer choices. The question mark tells you that the missing pronoun is interrogative and the verb *est* tells you that it is the subject of the sentence. *Qui* is an interrogative pronoun and the subject. Choices (A), (B), and (C) are incorrect because choice (A) cannot be used as a subject, choice (B) is an interrogative adjective, and choice (C) is an interrogative pronoun used as a direct object.

Part C

Directions: The paragraphs below contain blank spaces indicating omissions in the text. For some blanks it is necessary to choose the completion that is most appropriate to the meaning of the passage; for other blanks, to choose the one completion that forms a grammatically correct sentence. In some instances, choice (A) may consist of dashes that indicate that no insertion is required to form a grammatically correct sentence. In each case, indicate your answer by filling in the corresponding circle on the answer sheet. Be sure to read the paragraph completely before answering the questions related to it.

Dès que vous __5__ le temps de prendre contact avec elle, donnez- __6__ un coup de téléphone. Il faut l'avertir que tout soit arrangé et que j'arriverai __7__ vingt.

5. (A) auriez
   (B) ayez
   (C) aurez
   (D) aviez

6. (A) lui
   (B) elle
   (C) vous
   (D) la

7. (A) le
   (B) au
   (C) sur le
   (D) dans le

5. Choice (D) is the correct answer to question 5; *aurez* is the future tense of the verb *avoir.* Expressions such as *quand* and *dès que* are followed by the future in French when the verb in the main clause is in the present tense, as it is here with the present imperative *donnez.* Choice (A) *auriez* is the conditional, choice (B) *ayez* is the present subjunctive, and choice (D) *aviez* is the imperfect.

6. Choice (A) is the correct answer to question 6. What is missing in this part of the sentence is an indirect object pronoun that refers back to *elle* (in *avec elle*). The indirect object indicates the person to whom the *coup de téléphone* should be given. The correct pronoun form in question 6 is *lui.* Choice (B) *elle* is not correct because it is used for the subject of a sentence or after a preposition, choice (C) *vous* is incorrect because something should be given to the woman designated by *elle*, not the person spoken to, and choice (D) *la* is incorrect because it is the direct object pronoun, not the indirect object pronoun.

7. Choice (A) is the correct answer to question 7. When giving arrival and departure dates in French (the sentence here provides an arrival date), the date is preceded by *le* without a preposition. The other suggested answers contain prepositions and are therefore incorrect.

Part D

Directions: Read the following selections carefully for comprehension. Each selection is followed by a number of questions or incomplete statements. Select the completion or answer that is BEST according to the selection and fill in the corresponding circle on the answer sheet.

Ligne

«Image Center» est l'histoire d'une passion. Hésitant entre l'art et la science, Sylvie Magnus, 24 ans, passe deux ans à l'Ecole des Beaux Arts et complète sa formation à Londres, où elle apprend les applications de l'informatique sur l'image. Et c'est le déclic, peindre avec la lumière, créer des décors magiques pour des défilés de mode, ou des effets spéciaux pour le cinéma, tout la fascine. Une étude de marché lui apprend qu'il n'existe pas d'agence spécialisée dans la conception de ces images. Sylvie décide donc de combler l'espace: elle crée, grâce à un prêt de famille et à des subventions, la première agence européenne conseil en image de synthèse: «Image Center».

8. Qu'est-ce que Sylvie Magnus a étudié après ses deux ans à l'Ecole des Beaux Arts?
   (A) Les arts décoratifs
   (B) La cinématographie
   (C) Les nouvelles technologies
   (D) La médicine

Choice (C) is the correct answer to qustion 8. The text tells you that Sylvie Magnus studied computer graphics after finishing her fine arts education *(Sylvie Magnus passe deux ans à l'Ecole des Beaux Arts et complète sa formation à Londres, où elle apprend les applications de l'informatique sur l'image*, lines 2–5). The other choices are incorrect.

9. A la ligne 10, «combler l'espace» veut dire
   (A) répondre à un besoin
   (B) louer un bureau
   (C) faire des recherches scientifiques
   (D) faire des subventions

Choice (A) is the correct answer to question 9. The text states that Sylvie Magnus has learned that there was no agency that specialized in computer graphics and decided to create one. The expression does not mean that she rented an office (B), did scientific research (C), or subsidized anything (D). On the contrary, she received a subsidy (line 11).

10. Comment est-ce que Sylvie Magnus a trouvé l'argent pour lancer «Image Center»?
   (A) Elle a travaillé dans un hôpital.
   (B) Elle en a gagné pendant la révolution.
   (C) Elle a organisé des défilés de mode.
   (D) Elle en a emprunté à ses parents.

Choice (D) is the correct answer to question 10. The text tells you that *grâce à un prêt de famille* (lines 10–11) Sylvie Magnus was able to create her agency. She did not obtain the money by working in a hospital (A), earning it during a revolution (B), or organizing fashion shows (C).

Sondage

Vous, amateurs de télé—

Question 1

Utilisez-vous personnellement une télécommande?

Question 2

Vous-même, quand vous utilisez cette télécommande, vous vous en servez pour: couper le son et faire autre chose? changer de chaîne dès que le programme ne vous plaît pas? suivre plusieurs émissions en même temps? chercher une émission particulière? éviter la publicité? rechercher la publicité?

Résultats:	en %
Proportion des Français âgés de 15 ans et plus	
Question 1: qui utilisent personnellement une télécommande	**46**
Question 2: qui s'en servent pour	
—couper le son pour faire autre chose	26
—changer de chaîne dès que le programme ne leur plaît pas	43
—suivre plusieurs émissions en même temps	12
—chercher une émission particulière	31
—éviter la publicité	23
—rechercher la publicité	2

11. Qu'est-ce qu'une télécommande?
    (A) Une sorte de téléviseur
    (B) Une émission de télévision
    (C) Une sorte de publicité
    (D) Un appareil électronique

Choice (D) is the correct answer to question 11. What a *télécommande* is must be inferred because it is not stated directly in the survey. The text tells you that, among other things, a *télécommande* can be used to change television channels and to cut the sound of a program. It is a remote control. It is not a kind of television set (A), nor a television program (B), nor publicity (C).

12. Selon ce sondage, on se sert le plus souvent d'une télécommande pour
    (A) acheter quelque chose
    (B) trouver une émission plus intéressante
    (C) pouvoir regarder deux émissions à la fois
    (D) vérifier le bon fonctionnement de son téléviseur

Choice (B) is the correct answer to question 12. This question asks you what the remote control is most frequently used for, according to the survey results. You must select the use in the chart that was selected by the most respondents and has the highest percentage. This use is *changer de chaîne dès que le programme ne leur plaît pas*, or "change the channel as soon as they no longer like the program." The other choices were selected by a lower percentage of respondents.

French Subject Test

Practice Helps

The test that follows is an actual, previously administered SAT Subject Test in French. To get an idea of what it's like to take this test, practice under conditions that are much like those of an actual test administration.

- Set aside an hour when you can take the test uninterrupted.
- Sit at a desk or table with no other books or papers. Dictionaries, other books, or notes are not allowed in the test room.
- Tear out an answer sheet from the back of this book and fill it in just as you would on the day of the test. One answer sheet can be used for up to three Subject Tests.
- Read the instructions that precede the practice test. During the actual administration you will be asked to read them before answering test questions.
- Time yourself by placing a clock or kitchen timer in front of you.
- After you finish the practice test, read the sections "How to Score the SAT Subject Test in French" and "How Did You Do on the Subject Test in French?"
- The appearance of the answer sheet in this book may differ from the answer sheet you see on test day.

FRENCH TEST

The top portion of the page of the answer sheet that you will use to take the French Test must be filled in exactly as illustrated below. When your supervisor tells you to fill in the circle next to the name of the test you are about to take, mark your answer sheet as shown.

○ Literature	○ Mathematics Level 1	○ German	○ Chinese Listening	○ Japanese Listening
○ Biology E	○ Mathematics Level 2	○ Italian	○ French Listening	○ Korean Listening
○ Biology M	○ U.S. History	○ Latin	○ German Listening	○ Spanish Listening
○ Chemistry	○ World History	○ Modern Hebrew		
○ Physics	● French	○ Spanish	**Background Questions:** ① ② ③ ④ ⑤ ⑥ ⑦ ⑧ ⑨	

After filling in the circle next to the name of the test you are taking, locate the Background Questions section, which also appears at the top of your answer sheet (as shown above). This is where you will answer the following Background Questions on your answer sheet.

BACKGROUND QUESTIONS

Please answer either Part I or Part II below by filling in the appropriate circle in the Background Questions box on your answer sheet. Fill in ONLY ONE circle, as described below, to indicate how you obtained your knowledge of French. <u>The information you provide is for statistical purposes only and will not affect your test score.</u>

Part I — If your knowledge of French comes primarily from any of the following: living in a home where French is the main spoken language, living for six months or longer in a French-speaking country that included significant experience in the French language, courses taken at a college, or special study of French, fill in <u>circle 9</u> and leave the remaining circles blank, regardless of how long you studied the subject in school.

Part II — If your knowledge of French comes primarily from courses taken in secondary school, fill in the circle that indicates the level of the French course in which you are currently enrolled. If you are not now enrolled in a French course, fill in the circle that indicates the level of the most advanced course in French that you have completed.

- First year: first or second half —Fill in circle 1.
- Second year: first half —Fill in circle 2.
  second half —Fill in circle 3.
- Third year: first half —Fill in circle 4.
  second half —Fill in circle 5.
- Fourth year: first half —Fill in circle 6.
  second half —Fill in circle 7.
- Advanced Placement course or a course at a level higher than fourth year, second half
  or
  high school course work plus a minimum of four weeks of study abroad —Fill in circle 8.

When the supervisor gives the signal, turn the page and begin the French Test. There are 100 numbered circles on the answer sheet and 85 questions in the French Test. Therefore, use only circles 1 to 85 for recording your answers.

FRENCH TEST

PLEASE NOTE THAT YOUR ANSWER SHEET HAS FIVE ANSWER POSITIONS MARKED A, B, C, D, and E, WHILE THE QUESTIONS THROUGHOUT THIS TEST CONTAIN ONLY FOUR CHOICES. BE SURE NOT TO MAKE ANY MARKS IN COLUMN E.

Part A

Directions: This part consists of a number of incomplete statements, each having four suggested completions. Select the most appropriate completion and fill in the corresponding circle on the answer sheet.

1. Elle ne peut pas se le payer. C'est beaucoup trop ------- pour elle.

(A) cher
(B) fort
(C) gentil
(D) plein

2. Ce matin je n'ai pas eu le temps de lire le -------.

(A) paquet
(B) nouveau
(C) journal
(D) magasin

3. Le chef du personnel a ordonné que toutes les portes des bureaux soient ------- à cinq heures.

(A) serrées
(B) fumées
(C) levées
(D) fermées

4. Tu as vraiment mauvaise mémoire; tu ------- toujours mon anniversaire!

(A) oublies
(B) obliges
(C) perds
(D) poses

5. Attendez! Je ne peux pas vous comprendre si vous parlez tous -------.

(A) à la fois
(B) à l'heure
(C) à l'occasion
(D) à la prochaine

6. Nous sommes en retard. Il faut nous -------.

(A) endormir
(B) dépêcher
(C) promener
(D) moucher

7. Suzanne est punie parce qu'elle a ------- une gifle à sa soeur.

(A) pris
(B) donné
(C) prêté
(D) volé

8. Il pourra quitter l'hôpital dès qu'il n'aura plus de -------.

(A) coffre
(B) fièvre
(C) drogue
(D) confort

9. Claudette s'est servie d'une ------- pour s'essuyer les mains.

(A) assiette
(B) fourchette
(C) allumette
(D) serviette

10. Denise a été ------- affectée par le vol de sa voiture.

(A) brillamment
(B) cordialement
(C) sagement
(D) fortement

GO ON TO THE NEXT PAGE

11. Quel temps magnifique! Il n'y a pas un seul -------.

(A) nuage
(B) champ
(C) ciel
(D) moment

12. Dans cet immeuble il y a un ------- qui s'arrête au quinzième étage.

(A) ascenseur
(B) éleveur
(C) trottoir
(D) aspirateur

13. Je voudrais recoudre un bouton à ce veston. As-tu -------?

(A) une épingle
(B) une aiguille
(C) un clou
(D) une boutonnière

14. L'herbe était toute ------- parce qu'il n'avait pas plu depuis des semaines.

(A) molle
(B) forte
(C) vide
(D) sèche

15. Pour faire du bateau à -------, il faut du vent.

(A) voiles
(B) vapeur
(C) rames
(D) réaction

16. Mon chien m'adore et il me suit comme mon -------.

(A) idole
(B) souffle
(C) idéal
(D) ombre

17. Plus de télé ce soir! L'électricité est -------.

(A) en désordre
(B) en haut
(C) en vente
(D) en panne

18. Qu'on est bien près du feu à écouter les ------- crépiter dans la cheminée!

(A) bûches
(B) coupures
(C) bâtons
(D) allumettes

19. Elle a planté toute une variété d'arbres fruitiers dans son -------.

(A) fermier
(B) berger
(C) prunier
(D) verger

20. Vous n'aurez pas de peine à la faire parler. Elle est très -------.

(A) économe
(B) réservée
(C) bavarde
(D) généreuse

21. Il faut se faire ------- pour voter aux élections présidentielles.

(A) raccorder
(B) afficher
(C) écrire
(D) inscrire

22. Le Père Noël a ------- le fond de son sac pour trouver encore des cadeaux.

(A) aperçu
(B) gardé
(C) surveillé
(D) fouillé

GO ON TO THE NEXT PAGE

Part B

Directions: Each of the following sentences contains a blank. From the four choices given, select the one that can be inserted in the blank to form a grammatically correct sentence and fill in the corresponding circle on the answer sheet. Choice (A) may consist of dashes that indicate that no insertion is required to form a grammatically correct sentence.

23. On me demande toujours ------- je vais faire de ma vie. Je n'en sais rien!

(A) ce dont
(B) quoi
(C) ce que
(D) qu'est-ce qui

24. Je vois que vous aimez les livres. Vous ------- avez beaucoup dans votre bibliothèque.

(A) lui
(B) leur
(C) en
(D) y

25. David et Daniel sont sortis de la maison en -------.

(A) courant
(B) ayant couru
(C) courir
(D) avoir couru

26. Il est important de ------- soigner, Madame. Prenez un cachet d'aspirine et téléphonez au médecin.

(A) vous
(B) toi
(C) lui
(D) te

27. Je ------- qu'il devait me téléphoner.

(A) regrette
(B) pense
(C) doutais
(D) craignais

28. Après l'accident, on a transporté Sandrine au ------- hôpital de la ville.

(A) nouvel
(B) neuf
(C) beau
(D) moderne

29. Les agents ont suggéré que tu t'addresses à ------- pour te renseigner.

(A) leur
(B) eux
(C) soi
(D) ceux

30. Je préfère cette voiture à la -------.

(A) sienne
(B) autre
(C) leurs
(D) bleu

31. Il me semble que la Tour d'Argent est un des ------- restaurants de France; la cuisine y est excellente.

(A) meilleurs
(B) mieux
(C) supérieurs
(D) bien

32. J'ai rendu visite à Philippe en -------.

(A) juillet
(B) Paris
(C) printemps
(D) dimanche

GO ON TO THE NEXT PAGE

33. Heureusement, le roman n'était pas ------- ennuyeux que le film.

(A) assez
(B) tant
(C) peu
(D) aussi

34. Nous invitons ------- amis.

(A) plusieurs
(B) beaucoup
(C) un peu
(D) un peu d'

35. Même si tu n'as pas beaucoup de temps pour visiter la ville, va ------- voir le musée.

(A) moins
(B) moins de
(C) le moindre
(D) au moins

36. D'un seul geste, elles ont toutes ------- la main.

(A) levé
(B) levés
(C) levée
(D) levées

37. Quelle peinture préférez-vous, cette peinture-ci ou ------- qui est là-bas?

(A) laquelle
(B) l'une
(C) cette
(D) celle

38. A ma grande surprise, ce film ------- a beaucoup plu.

(A) lui
(B) l'
(C) en
(D) les

39. Cette année, les cerises coûtent douze francs ------- kilo.

(A) par
(B) un
(C) le
(D) pour

GO ON TO THE NEXT PAGE

Part C

Directions: The paragraphs below contain blank spaces indicating omissions in the text. For some blanks, it is necessary to choose the completion that is most appropriate to the meaning of the passage; for other blanks, to choose the one completion that forms a grammatically correct sentence. In some instances, choice (A) may consist of dashes that indicate that no insertion is required to form a grammatically correct sentence. In each case, indicate your answer by filling in the corresponding circle on the answer sheet. Be sure to read the paragraph completely before answering the questions related to it.

C'était en général __(40)__ la fin de l'après-midi que __(41)__ à la porte de l'immeuble. Je montais vite jusqu'à l'appartement. Jacques m'accueillait avec un sourire empressé. «Je ne __(42)__ dérange pas?» «Tu ne me déranges __(43)__ .» «Comment ça va?» «Ça va toujours très bien __(44)__ je te vois.» Sa gentillesse me touchait et me __(45)__ le coeur.

40. (A) vers
    (B) par
    (C) autour de
    (D) à travers

41. (A) je sonnais
    (B) j'ouvrais
    (C) je sortais
    (D) je quittais

42. (A) lui
    (B) les
    (C) me
    (D) te

43. (A) jamais
    (B) rien
    (C) aucun
    (D) personne

44. (A) quand
    (B) mais
    (C) donc
    (D) pourtant

45. (A) réchauffait
    (B) battait
    (C) lançait
    (D) rendait

GO ON TO THE NEXT PAGE

Le juge d'instruction pensait au début qu'il __(46)__ arriver à une décision la semaine suivante. Pourtant, __(47)__ entendu __(48)__ disaient les témoins, il a changé __(49)__.

46. (A) a pu
    (B) pourrait
    (C) pourra
    (D) puisse

47. (A) après
    (B) bien
    (C) ayant
    (D) sans

48. (A) ce qui
    (B) ce que
    (C) quoi
    (D) à quoi

49. (A) d'avis
    (B) l'opinion
    (C) sa mémoire
    (D) de l'esprit

GO ON TO THE NEXT PAGE

Sophie et Michel pensent déjà __(50)__ leurs vacances de l'été __(51)__. Ils ont l'intention de traverser __(52)__ Europe à bicyclette et en train avec des amis __(53)__ ont déjà fait ce voyage. Chacun n'emportera __(54)__ un sac à dos pour __(55)__ les excédents de bagage. Leur itinéraire sera établi d'avance et le club sportif qui organise __(56)__ a prévu de nombreuses __(57)__ afin que les cyclistes se reposent et fassent un peu de tourisme.

50. (A) de
(B) pour
(C) à
(D) sur

51. (A) passé
(B) prochain
(C) futur
(D) présent

52. (A) ---
(B) en
(C) l'
(D) dans

53. (A) quels
(B) qui
(C) qu'
(D) dont

54. (A) d'
(B) qu'
(C) ni
(D) pas

55. (A) payer
(B) créer
(C) éviter
(D) traîner

56. (A) ce match
(B) ce chemin
(C) cette course
(D) cette randonnée

57. (A) averses
(B) escalades
(C) démarches
(D) étapes

GO ON TO THE NEXT PAGE

Part D

Directions: Read the following texts carefully for comprehension. Each is followed by a number of questions or incomplete statements. Select the answer or completion that is best according to the text and fill in the corresponding circle on the answer sheet.

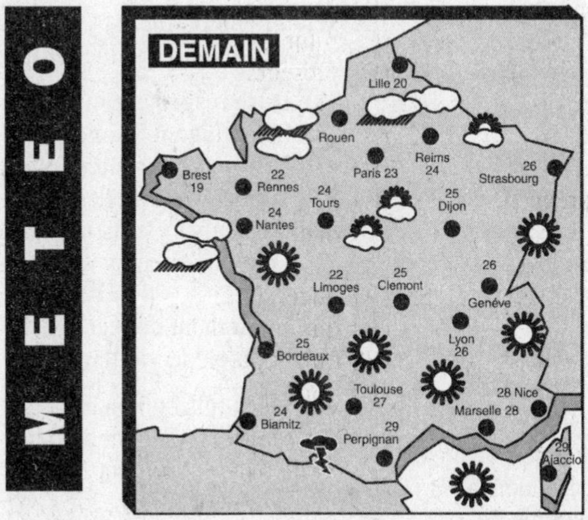

Orages en fuite, chaleur à la baisse, vents d'ouest et nuages arrivent.

58. Demain il y aura moins de

(A) chaleur
(B) vent
(C) nuages
(D) fraîcheur

59. Quel temps fera-t-il demain à Lyon?

(A) Il pleuvra.
(B) Il fera beau.
(C) Il neigera.
(D) Il y aura des orages.

GO ON TO THE NEXT PAGE

Peter Schulz avait soixante-quinze ans. Il était de santé délicate, et l'âge ne l'avait pas épargné. Sa vie avait été pauvre en événements. Il était seul depuis des années. Sa femme était morte. Il en conservait un souvenir attendri. Il y avait vingt-cinq ans qu'il l'avait perdue: et, pas un soir depuis, il ne s'était endormi, sans un petit entretien mental, triste et tendre, avec elle; il l'associait à chacune de ses journées. Il n'avait pas eu d'enfants: c'était le grand regret de sa vie. Il avait reporté son besoin d'affection sur ses élèves, auxquels il était attaché, comme un père à ses fils. Il avait trouvé peu de retour. Un vieux coeur peut se sentir très près d'un jeune coeur, et presque du même âge: il sait combien sont brèves les années qui l'en séparent. Mais le jeune homme ne s'en doute point: le vieillard est pour lui un homme d'une autre époque.

Le vieux Schulz avait rencontré parfois quelque reconnaissance chez des élèves, touchés par l'intérêt vif et frais qu'il prenait à tout ce qui leur arrivait d'heureux ou de malheureux: ils venaient le voir de temps en temps; ils lui écrivaient, pour le remercier, quand ils quittaient l'université; certains lui écrivaient encore, une ou deux fois, les années suivantes. Puis, le vieux Schulz n'entendait plus parler d'eux, sinon par les journaux, qui lui faisaient connaître l'avancement de tel ou tel: et il se réjouissait de leurs succès, comme si c'étaient les siens. Il ne leur en voulait pas de leur silence: il y trouvait mille excuses; il ne doutait point de leur affection, et prêtait aux plus égoïstes les sentiments qu'il avait pour eux.

60. Le grand regret de la vie de Schulz était

(A) d'avoir perdu sa femme
(B) d'avoir des élèves ingrats
(C) d'être sans enfants
(D) de ne pas avoir une bonne santé

61. Qu'est-ce qui décrit <u>le mieux</u> l'attitude de Schulz envers ses anciens élèves?

(A) Il s'intéresse beaucoup à leurs vies.
(B) Il les trouve égoïstes.
(C) Il est jaloux de leur succès.
(D) Il ne les trouve pas du tout reconnaissants.

62. Quelle a été la profession de Peter Schulz?

(A) Médecin
(B) Professeur
(C) Journaliste
(D) Psychologue

63. Selon l'auteur, qu'est-ce qui décrit <u>le mieux</u> les rapports entre les jeunes et les vieux?

(A) Ils se respectent mutuellement.
(B) Ils partagent les mêmes idées.
(C) Les vieux se sentent plus proches des jeunes que les jeunes des vieux.
(D) Les jeunes estiment plus les vieux quand ils ont eux-mêmes vieilli.

64. A quel moment de leur vie les jeunes ont-ils le plus apprécié le vieillard?

(A) Quand ils étaient enfants
(B) Quand ils étaient heureux
(C) Quand ils avaient fini leurs études universitaires
(D) Quand ils avaient trouvé du travail

65. Comment Schulz apprend-il les nouvelles de ses anciens élèves?

(A) Ses anciens élèves lui écrivent souvent.
(B) Il leur écrit pour demander des nouvelles.
(C) Il lit les journaux.
(D) L'université lui envoie des nouvelles.

66. Selon l'auteur, Peter Schulz a eu une vie

(A) très malheureuse
(B) active et mouvementée
(C) bien appréciée et respectée
(D) consacrée au succès des autres

GO ON TO THE NEXT PAGE

Cela devient malheureusement une banalité que de constater le déclin de la natalité dans notre pays et, plus particulièrement, dans les grandes villes.

Pour des parents, avoir des enfants et les élever représente, en milieu urbain, des contraintes beaucoup plus fortes qu'ailleurs, notamment lorsque le père et la mère travaillent.

Une contrainte se situe souvent au niveau du logement. Il est cher et, dans les logements neufs, les dimensions des pièces sont souvent réduites au minimum, les plans sont mal conçus pour des familles nombreuses. La venue d'un enfant supplémentaire conduit bien souvent à un changement d'appartement, ce qui pose des problèmes financiers difficiles.

67. Le sujet principal que traite l'auteur est

(A) la population des grandes villes
(B) le manque de logements en milieu urbain
(C) le nombre croissant de familles nombreuses
(D) la baisse du nombre de naissances

68. L'auteur exprime son point de vue sur les faits qu'il présente surtout par le mot

(A) malheureusement (ligne 1)
(B) notamment (ligne 6)
(C) logement (ligne 9)
(D) minimum (ligne 11)

69. Le "changement d'appartement" (ligne 13) est causé par

(A) l'arrivée d'un nouveau-né
(B) une femme qui travaille
(C) des problèmes financiers
(D) la peur des grandes villes

GO ON TO THE NEXT PAGE

Bonjour, voisin.

Dans la grande communauté humaine, nous sommes tous voisins. Et être un bon voisin, c'est aussi apprendre à s'intégrer dans la texture locale de la communauté.

Chez Komatsu, nous produisons des machines industrielles et des engins de construction tels que: excavateurs, robots, lasers et machines–outils. C'est–à–dire des instruments permettant d'obtenir une meilleure qualité de vie. De même, nous nous efforçons d'oeuvrer pour le bien de la communauté, en développant la collaboration locale dans le monde des affaires, des entreprises alliées, des échanges commerciaux et des services. En un mot, à coopérer pour un monde meilleur.

Ensemble pour un monde meilleur

KOMATSU

Siege social 2-3-6 Akasaka Minato-ku Tokyo 107 Japon
Telephone (03) 5561-2617 Telecopieur (03) 505-9662

70. Cette publicité a pour titre "Bonjour, voisin" pour suggérer qu'on

(A) doit dire "bonjour" aux voisins
(B) veut vendre des tentures aux voisins
(C) habite tous la terre
(D) veut tous se rencontrer

71. Komatsu est une compagnie qui fabrique des machines pour

(A) l'industrie d'équipements
(B) les petits commerces
(C) les besoins ménagers
(D) l'aérospatiale

72. Selon cette publicité, la philosophie de Komatsu est

(A) de construire des machines moins chères
(B) de créer un monde plus harmonieux
(C) d'encourager l'artisanat
(D) de prévoir le monde à venir

GO ON TO THE NEXT PAGE

La rue était maintenant déserte et silencieuse. Les lampadaires s'étaient allumés depuis un instant seulement. Le ciel demeurait rougeâtre à l'horizon. Un imperceptible souffle de vent passa. Un chat noir aussi.

Le mendiant, assis dos au mur d'un immeuble sombre et vétuste, s'étira et bâilla. D'un regard circulaire, il embrassa la rue étroite et maintenant calme du marché. Il tira à lui la petite cuvette de bois et compta les pièces de monnaie qui s'y trouvaient; puis il fourra sa main dans une poche de son boubou qui avait dû être blanc, et en sortit d'autres pièces de monnaie qu'il compta aussi avant de tout mettre dans un minuscule sac de toile. Il resta ainsi un moment, pensif. Il sortit d'une autre poche une pièce de monnaie et la contempla un long moment; c'était une pièce que lui avait donnée la dame au foulard. Elle lui en donnait tous les matins en ressortant du marché, et c'était son seul bon moment de la journée. Quand il la voyait surgir d'entre deux rangées d'étalages puis traverser la ruelle et s'avancer vers lui, il était heureux. Il la regardait s'avancer de sa démarche calme et régulière, quelque peu nonchalante, avec son éternel foulard blanc noué autour du cou. Arrivée devant lui, elle s'arrêtait et le regardait; lui aussi la regardait. Puis elle lui tendait une pièce; il la prenait et elle s'en allait. Tous les matins, il guettait sa venue. Tous les matins, sauf le dimanche. Elle ne venait jamais le dimanche; c'est pour cela que le mendiant n'aimait pas le dimanche, même si les gens lui donnaient beaucoup plus d'argent ce jour-là.

Et justement demain c'est dimanche.

Il remit la pièce dans la poche d'où il l'avait prise.

Demain dimanche.

Il inclina tristement la tête.

73. D'après le début du texte, à quel moment de la journée la scène se passe-t-elle?

(A) A l'aube
(B) Dans l'après-midi
(C) Au crépuscule
(D) En pleine nuit

74. Le mendiant met la pièce que la dame au foulard lui donne dans une autre poche parce que cette pièce

(A) a une grande valeur monétaire
(B) a une grande valeur affective
(C) est une pièce de collection
(D) est contrefaite

75. Quand la dame au foulard s'avançait vers le mendiant, comment marchait-elle?

(A) Avec hésitation
(B) A pas rapides
(C) Sans regarder où elle allait
(D) Sans se presser

76. La dame au foulard rend le mendiant heureux parce qu'elle

(A) jette une pièce dans sa cuvette
(B) le guette tous les matins
(C) communique silencieusement avec lui
(D) contemple la pièce

77. A la fin de l'histoire le mendiant est triste parce que, le dimanche, la dame au foulard

(A) lui manque
(B) le chasse
(C) lui donne peu d'argent
(D) lui remet une vieille pièce

GO ON TO THE NEXT PAGE

Les Routes ROI RENÉ

Les Routes Roi René, qui furent aussi celles des **Plantagenêts,** regroupent, notamment, l'essentiel des châteaux de l'Anjou ouverts au public; pour la plupart habités par leurs propriétaires, ils offrent une image vivante du patrimoine historique et architectural angevin.
Elles permettent également de découvrir de nombreux sites et monuments et de comprendre l'âme du "pays": l'Art de vivre en Anjou se perpétue et fait du Maine–et–Loire d'aujourd'hui une terre privilégiée de la Vallée de la Loire.
Le Roi René, cousin du Roi de France, fut l'instigateur de la vie artistique et littéraire de l'Anjou. Quel plus bel emblème pour ces itinéraires?
Les Routes Roi René font partie des **Routes de Beauté.**

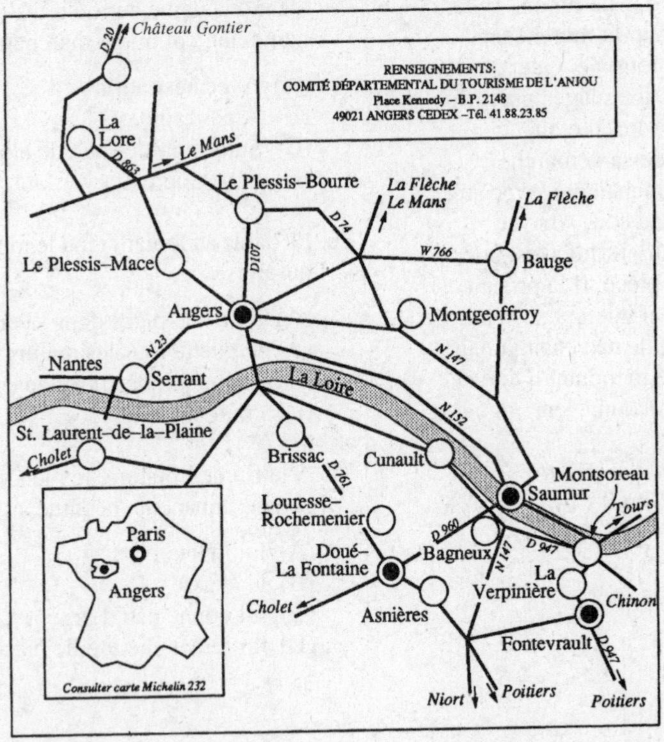

78. Le Comité du Tourisme a choisi ces châteaux parce qu'ils
    (A) intéressent les spécialistes
    (B) appartiennent tous à l'Etat
    (C) sont ouverts au public de temps en temps
    (D) sont un bel exemple de l'architecture angevine

79. Parmi les "Routes de Beauté", on a nommé ce segment les "Routes Roi René" parce
    (A) qu'il parcourt une région où le déplacement est pratique
    (B) qu'on y trouve des monuments de toute époque
    (C) qu'il honore un protecteur des lettres et des arts
    (D) qu'il est l'emblème des Rois de France

GO ON TO THE NEXT PAGE

C'était dans l'hiver de 1792. La disette régnait à Strasbourg. La maison de Dietrich, le maire, était pauvre, la table frugale, mais hospitalière pour Rouget de Lisle.

Accablé d'une inspiration sublime, le jeune officier s'endormit la tête sur son clavecin et ne s'éveilla qu'au jour. Les chants de la nuit, impressions d'un rêve, lui remontèrent avec peine dans la mémoire. Il les écrivit, les nota, et courut chez Dietrich. La femme et les filles du vieux patriote n'étaient pas encore levées. Dietrich les éveilla, il appela quelques amis, tous passionnés comme lui pour la musique.

Sa fille ainée accompagna, Rouget chanta. A la première strophe les visages pâlirent; à la seconde, les larmes coulèrent; aux dernières, le délire de l'enthousiasme éclata. L'hymne de la patrie était trouvé!

Le nouveau chant, exécuté quelques jours après à Strasbourg, vola de ville en ville sur tous les orchestres populaires. Marseille l'adopta pour être chanté au commencement et à la fin des séances de ses clubs. Les Marseillais le répandirent en France, en le chantant sur leur route. De là lui vint le nom de "Marseillaise".

80. Où est-ce que la "Marseillaise" a été composée?

(A) A Marseille
(B) A Strasbourg
(C) A Lille
(D) Sur la route

81. L'inspiration pour la musique est née

(A) d'un rêve
(B) d'un poème
(C) d'un repas
(D) d'une bataille

82. Quelle profession Rouget de Lisle exerçait-il à ce moment-là?

(A) Troubadour
(B) Maire
(C) Chef d'orchestre
(D) Soldat

83. Qui a interprété la "Marseillaise" pour la première fois?

(A) Le maire et sa femme
(B) Rouget de Lisle et la femme du maire
(C) Rouget de Lisle et la fille du maire
(D) Le maire et sa fille

84. D'après le texte, quel a été le destin du nouveau chant?

(A) On ne l'a plus joué.
(B) Les autres villes l'ont volé.
(C) On l'a beaucoup modifié.
(D) On l'a chanté un peu partout.

85. Pourquoi l'hymne national français s'appelle-t-il la "Marseillaise"?

(A) Un Marseillais l'a composé.
(B) Les Marseillais l'ont rendu populaire.
(C) Les Marseillais étaient les plus patriotiques.
(D) Les Marseillais étaient les meilleurs chanteurs.

STOP

IF YOU FINISH BEFORE TIME IS CALLED, YOU MAY CHECK YOUR WORK ON THIS TEST ONLY. DO NOT TURN TO ANY OTHER TEST IN THIS BOOK.

How to Score the SAT Subject Test in French

When you take an actual SAT Subject Test in French, your answer sheet will be "read" by a scanning machine that will record your response to each question. Then a computer will compare your answers with the correct answers and produce your raw score. You get one point for each correct answer. For each wrong answer, you lose one-third of a point. Questions you omit (and any for which you mark more than one answer) are not counted. This raw score is converted to a scaled score that is reported to you and to the colleges you specify.

Worksheet 1. Finding Your Raw Test Score

STEP 1: Table A on the following page lists the correct answers for all the questions on the Subject Test in French that is reproduced in this book. It also serves as a worksheet for you to calculate your raw score.

- Compare your answers with those given in the table.
- Put a check in the column marked "Right" if your answer is correct.
- Put a check in the column marked "Wrong" if your answer is incorrect.
- Leave both columns blank if you omitted the question.

STEP 2: Count the number of right answers.

Enter the total here: ____________________

STEP 3: Count the number of wrong answers.

Enter the total here: ____________________

STEP 4: Multiply the number of wrong answers by .333.

Enter the product here: ________________

STEP 5: Subtract the result obtained in Step 4 from the total you obtained in Step 2.

Enter the result here: __________________

STEP 6: Round the number obtained in Step 5 to the nearest whole number.

Enter the result here: __________________

The number you obtained in Step 6 is your raw score.

Table A

Answers to the Subject Test in French and Percentage of Students Answering Each Question Correctly									
Question Number	Correct Answer	Right	Wrong	Percentage of Students Answering the Question Correctly*	Question Number	Correct Answer	Right	Wrong	Percentage of Students Answering the Question Correctly*
1	A			92	33	D			45
2	C			92	34	A			51
3	D			88	35	D			58
4	A			95	36	A			51
5	A			74	37	D			49
6	B			85	38	A			25
7	B			70	39	C			23
8	B			81	40	A			57
9	D			78	41	A			31
10	D			74	42	D			86
11	A			83	43	A			79
12	A			66	44	A			92
13	B			36	45	A			39
14	D			75	46	B			53
15	A			83	47	C			35
16	D			54	48	B			39
17	D			43	49	A			49
18	A			22	50	C			47
19	D			22	51	B			84
20	C			52	52	C			49
21	D			35	53	B			77
22	D			21	54	B			48
23	C			67	55	C			66
24	C			75	56	D			16
25	A			74	57	D			13
26	A			88	58	A			39
27	B			60	59	B			89
28	A			71	60	C			93
29	B			68	61	A			79
30	A			66	62	B			88
31	A			70	63	C			53
32	A			61	64	C			61

Table A continued on next page

Table A continued from previous page

Question Number	Correct Answer	Right	Wrong	Percentage of Students Answering the Question Correctly*	Question Number	Correct Answer	Right	Wrong	Percentage of Students Answering the Question Correctly*
65	C			56	76	C			44
66	D			45	77	A			61
67	D			34	78	D			76
68	A			69	79	C			49
69	A			63	80	B			83
70	C			30	81	A			81
71	A			83	82	D			65
72	B			85	83	C			60
73	C			38	84	D			39
74	B			61	85	B			70
75	D			57					

* These percentages are based on an analysis of the answer sheets of a representative sample of 3,607 students who took the original administration of this test and whose mean score was 600. They may be used as an indication of the relative difficulty of a particular question.

Answer explanations for the Subject Test in French can be found on page 564.

Finding Your Scaled Score

When you take SAT Subject Tests, the scores sent to the colleges you specify are reported on the College Board scale, which ranges from 200–800. You can convert your practice test score to a scaled score by using Table B. To find your scaled score, locate your raw score in the left-hand column of Table B; the corresponding score in the right-hand column is your scaled score. For example, a raw score of 37 on this particular edition of the Subject Test in French corresponds to a scaled score of 570.

Raw scores are converted to scaled scores to ensure that a score earned on any one edition of a particular Subject Test is comparable to the same scaled score earned on any other edition of the same Subject Test. Because some editions of the tests may be slightly easier or more difficult than others, College Board scaled scores are adjusted so that they indicate the same level of performance regardless of the edition of the test taken and the ability of the group that takes it. Thus, for example, a score of 400 on one edition of a test taken at a particular administration indicates the same level of achievement as a score of 400 on a different edition of the test taken at a different administration.

When you take the SAT Subject Tests during a national administration, your scores are likely to differ somewhat from the scores you obtain on the tests in this book. People perform at different levels at different times for reasons unrelated to the tests themselves. The precision of any test is also limited because it represents only a sample of all the possible questions that could be asked.

Table B

Scaled Score Conversion Table Subject Test in French					
Raw Score	Scaled Score	Raw Score	Scaled Score	Raw Score	Scaled Score
85	800	47	630	9	420
84	800	46	620	8	420
83	800	45	610	7	410
82	800	44	610	6	410
81	800	43	600	5	400
80	800	42	600	4	400
79	800	41	590	3	390
78	800	40	590	2	390
77	800	39	580	1	380
76	800	38	580	0	380
75	800	37	570	-1	370
74	790	36	570	-2	370
73	790	35	560	-3	370
72	780	34	560	-4	360
71	770	33	550	-5	360
70	770	32	550	-6	350
69	760	31	540	-7	350
68	750	30	530	-8	350
67	750	29	530	-9	340
66	740	28	520	-10	340
65	730	27	520	-11	330
64	730	26	510	-12	330
63	720	25	510	-13	330
62	710	24	500	-14	320
61	710	23	500	-15	320
60	700	22	490	-16	310
59	700	21	490	-17	310
58	690	20	480	-18	300
57	680	19	470	-19	300
56	680	18	470	-20	290
55	670	17	460	-21	290
54	660	16	460	-22	280
53	660	15	450	-23	280
52	650	14	450	-24	270
51	650	13	440	-25	260
50	640	12	440	-26	250
49	640	11	430	-27	240
48	630	10	430	-28	230

How Did You Do on the Subject Test in French?

After you score your test and analyze your performance, think about the following questions:

Did you run out of time before reaching the end of the test?

If so, you may need to pace yourself better. For example, maybe you spent too much time on one or two hard questions. A better approach might be to skip the ones you can't answer right away and try answering all the questions that remain on the test. Then if there's time, go back to the questions you skipped.

Did you take a long time reading the directions?

You will save time when you take the test by learning the directions to the Subject Test in French ahead of time. Each minute you spend reading directions during the test is a minute that you could use to answer questions.

How did you handle questions you were unsure of?

If you were able to eliminate one or more of the answer choices as wrong and guess from the remaining ones, your approach probably worked to your advantage. On the other hand, making haphazard guesses or omitting questions without trying to eliminate choices could cost you valuable points.

How difficult were the questions for you compared with other students who took the test?

Table A shows you how difficult the multiple-choice questions were for the group of students who took this test during its national administration. The right-hand column gives the percentage of students that answered each question correctly.

A question answered correctly by almost everyone in the group is obviously an easier question. For example, 95 percent of the students answered question 4 correctly. But only 22 percent answered question 19 correctly.

Keep in mind that these percentages are based on just one group of students. They would probably be different with another group of students taking the test.

If you missed several easier questions, go back and try to find out why: Did the questions cover material you haven't yet reviewed? Did you misunderstand the directions?

Answer Explanations for the French Subject Test

1. Choice (A) is the correct answer. Because the first sentence indicates that she cannot afford something, that thing must be too *expensive* for her, not too *strong* (B), *kind* (C), or *full* (D).

2. Choice (C) is the correct answer. The speaker is saying that he or she did not have time this morning to read the *newspaper.* It does not make sense to say that he or she did not have time to read the *package* (A), the *new thing* (B), or the *department store* (D).

3. Choice (D) is the correct answer. The chief of staff ordered all the office doors to be *closed* at 5 o'clock. It does not make sense to say that he or she ordered the doors to be *smoked* (B) or *raised* (C), and it is not clear how one could order doors to be *tight* (A) at a certain time.

4. Choice (A) is the correct answer. The speaker first accuses the listener of having a bad memory and then explains that the listener always *forgets* the speaker's birthday. It does not make sense to say that the listener always *obliges* (B), *loses* (C), or *puts* (D) the speaker's birthday.

5. Choice (A) is the correct answer. The speaker is indicating that he or she cannot understand the listeners if they all talk *at once*. It does not make sense to say that the listeners cannot be understood if they all talk *on time* (B), *on occasion* (C), or *the next time* (D).

6. Choice (B) is the correct answer. The speaker is saying that he or she and some others are late and that they must *hurry.* It does not make sense to say that people who are late for something must *fall asleep* (A), *take a walk* (C), or *blow their noses* (D).

7. Choice (B) is the correct answer. *Donner* ("give") is the correct verb to use with the object *gifle* ("slap to the face"). Suzanne is being punished because she *gave* her sister a slap in the face. It does not make sense to say that she *took* (A), *lent* (C), or *stole* (D) the slap.

8. Choice (B) is the correct answer. He will be able to leave the hospital as soon as he no longer has any *fever.* It does not make sense to say that he must wait until he no longer has any *chest* (A), *drug* (C), or *comfort* (D).

9. Choice (D) is the correct answer. Claudette used a *napkin* to wipe her hands. It does not make sense to say she used a *plate* (A), *fork* (B), or *match* (C) to do this.

10. Choice (D) is the correct answer. Denise was *strongly* affected by the theft of her car. It does not make sense to say that she was *brilliantly* (A), *cordially* (B), or *wisely* (C) affected by a negative event.

11. Choice (A) is the correct answer. The speaker remarks that the weather is magnificent and adds that there is not a single *cloud.* It does not make sense in this context to say that there is not a single *field* (B), *sky* (C), or *moment* (D).

12. Choice (A) is the correct answer. The speaker indicates that in this apartment building there is an *elevator* that stops on the 15th floor. It does not make sense to say that there is a *breeder* (B), *sidewalk* (C), or *vacuum cleaner* (D) that stops on a certain floor.

13. Choice (B) is the correct answer. Because the speaker would like to sew a button on a jacket, he or she asks for a *needle.* A *pin* (A) can hold fabric together, but it is not used to sew. And it does not make sense to say that the speaker would ask for a *nail* (C) or a *buttonhole* (D) in order to sew a button on a jacket.

14. Choice (D) is the correct answer. The grass was completely *dry* because it hadn't rained in weeks. It does not make sense in this context to say that the grass was *soft* (A), *strong* (B), or *empty* (C).

15. Choice (A) is the correct answer. You need wind in order to go *sailboating.* The missing word completes the phrase that describes the type of boating that requires wind. *Bateau à voiles* (A) is *sailboating. Bateau à vapeur* (B) is *steamboating*, *bateau à rames* (C) is *rowboating*, and *bateau à réaction* (D) is *jet boating*; these types of boating do not require wind.

16. Choice (D) is the correct answer. The speaker says that his or her dog adores the speaker and follows the speaker like his or her *shadow.* It does not make sense to say

that the dog follows the speaker like his or her *idol* (A), *breath* (B), or *ideal* (C); these are not things that physically follow someone, as a shadow does.

17. Choice (D) is the correct answer. The speaker says that there is no more television tonight because the electricity is *out*. It does not make sense to say that the electricity is *in disorder* (A), *at the top* (B), or *for sale* (C).

18. Choice (A) is the correct answer. The speaker remarks how nice it is near the fire, listening to the *logs* crackle in the fireplace. It does not make sense to say that *cuts* (B) crackle in the fireplace. And a fire burning in a fireplace is much more likely to contain logs than *sticks* (C) or *matches* (D), though both sticks and matches might be used when starting a fire.

19. Choice (D) is the correct choice. She has planted a whole variety of fruit trees in her *orchard*. It does not make sense to say that the fruit trees were planted in her *farmer* (A), *shepherd* (B), or *plum tree* (C).

20. Choice (C) is the correct answer. In order to assure the listener that he or she will not have any difficulty getting an unnamed female to talk, the speaker says that the unnamed female is very *talkative*. There is no reason to say that she is *economical* (A) or *generous* (D), because these qualities do not have to do with talking. And if she is *reserved* (B), it might in fact be difficult to get her to talk.

21. Choice (D) is the correct answer. In order to vote in presidential elections, it is necessary to get oneself *registered*. One does not have to get *connected* (A), *displayed* (B), or *written* (C) in order to vote.

22. Choice (D) is the correct answer. Father Christmas *searched* the bottom of his bag to find more presents. It does not make sense to say that he *noticed* (A), *kept* (B), or *monitored* (C) the bottom of the bag to find the presents.

23. Choice (C) is the correct answer. People are always asking the speaker *what* he or she is going to do with his or her life. *Ce que* ("what") is the appropriate indefinite relative pronoun to follow the verb *demander* ("ask") and serve as the direct object of *faire* ("to do"). Choice (A), *ce dont* ("that of which"), cannot serve as the direct object of a verb; it can be used only to replace phrases that would otherwise begin with *de*. Choice (B), *quoi* ("what"), can be used as a relative pronoun only if it is preceded by a preposition; it cannot follow *demander* or serve as the direct object of *faire*. Choice

(D), *qu'est-ce qui* ("who"), is not a relative pronoun but an interrogative pronoun, so it cannot follow *demander*; further, it is in the subject form and cannot serve as the object of *faire*.

24. Choice (C) is the correct answer. The speaker remarks that the listener must like books because he or she has so many *of them* in his or her library. The speaker could have said *Vous avez beaucoup de livres dans votre bibliothèque* but avoids a repetition by replacing *de livres* with the pronoun *en*. Choices (A), *lui* ("to him/her/it"); (B), *leur* ("to them"); and (D), *y* ("there"), cannot replace an object introduced by *de*.

25 Choice (A) is the correct answer. The only form of a verb allowed after *en* is the present participle—in this case, *courant* ("running"). Choice (B), *ayant couru* ("having run"), is a present perfect participle; choice (C), *courir* ("to run"), is in the infinitive present tense; and choice (D), *avoir couru* ("to have run"), is in the perfect infinitive tense.

26. Choice (A) is the correct answer. The speaker tells a woman that it is important that she take care of herself and advises her to take an aspirin and call a doctor. The missing pronoun is the direct object of the verb *soigner* ("to take care of"). Because the speaker is speaking directly to the woman and calls her *Madame*, the formal second person object pronoun *vous* is used. Choice (B), *toi*, is informal and the wrong form of the pronoun to use before a verb. Choice (C), *lui*, is a third person indirect object pronoun with no referent in these sentences. And choice (D), *te*, is informal and should not be used with *Madame*.

27. Choice (B) is the correct answer. The speaker *thinks* that an unnamed male was supposed to call him or her. *Penser* ("to think") is compatible with the use of the indicative *devais* in the subordinate clause. The verbs in choices (A), *regretter* ("to regret"); (C), *douter* ("to doubt"); and (D), *craindre* ("to fear"), all require the use of the subjunctive in the clause that depends on them.

28. Choice (A) is the correct answer. After the accident, they took Sandrine to the town's *new* hospital. *Nouvel* is the only adjective that can be placed before the noun and whose form accommodates *hôpital*, which starts with a vowel sound. The adjectives in choices (B), *neuf* ("new"), and (D), *moderne* ("modern"), cannot ordinarily be placed before the noun they modify. And choice (C), *beau* ("beautiful"), would have to take the form of *bel* before *hôpital*.

29. Choice (B) is the correct answer. The officers have suggested that the listener speak to *them* to get information. *Eux* ("them") is the only pronoun among the choices that can be used after the preposition *à* and also make sense in the sentence. Choice (A), *leur* ("to them"), cannot be used after a preposition. Choice (C), *soi* ("oneself"), would refer to an indeterminate third person singular such as *on*. And choice (D), *ceux* ("those"), can only be used in conjunction with a relative pronoun (*qui* or *que*) or with *-ci* or *-là*.

30. Choice (A) is the correct answer. The speaker prefers this car to *his* or *her* [another person's] car. The article *la* indicates that the missing word must start with a consonant and be singular and feminine. *Sienne* is the only choice that fits grammatically in the sentence. Choice (B), *autre* ("other one"), starts with a vowel; choice (C), *leurs* ("theirs"), is plural; and choice (D), *bleu* ("blue"), is masculine.

31. Choice (A) is the correct answer. The speaker remarks that la Tour d'Argent is one of the *best* restaurants in France, noting that the cuisine is excellent. The missing word must be an adjective that can be put before a noun and that is masculine and plural to modify *restaurants.* Choice (B), *mieux* ("better"), and choice (D), *bien* ("well"), are adverbs. And choice (C), *supérieurs* ("superior"), is an adjective not ordinarily found before a noun.

32. Choice (A) is the correct answer. The speaker says that he or she visited Philippe in *July. Juillet* is the only noun among the choices that can follow the preposition *en.* Choice (B), *Paris,* would be preceded by the preposition *à.* Choice (C), *printemps* ("spring"), would be preceded by the preposition *au.* And choice (D), *dimanche* ("Sunday"), would not be preceded by any preposition at all.

33. Choice (D) is the correct answer. Luckily, the novel wasn't *as* boring as the film. The missing word is an adverb that modifies the adjective *ennuyeux* ("boring") and completes the comparative construction with *que.* Choices (A), *assez* ("enough"), (B) *tant* ("so"), and (C) *peu* ("hardly"), cannot be used in conjunction with *que.*

34. Choice (A) is the correct answer. The speaker states that his or her group invites *several* friends. *Plusieurs* ("several") is the only choice that fits grammatically in the blank. Choice (B), *beaucoup* ("a lot"), must be followed by *de.* Choice (C), *un peu* ("a little"), also must be followed by *de.* Both choice (C), *un peu,* and choice (D), *un peu d',* mean "a little" and can only be used to modify mass nouns, not nouns you can count.

35. Choice (D) is the correct answer. The speaker tells the listener that even if he or she does not have a lot of time to visit the city, he or she should go *at least* to see the museum. It does not make sense to tell someone to go *less* (A), *less than* (B), or *the least* (C) to see the museum. Further, choice (B), *moins de*, must be followed by a number or a noun, not an infinitive such as *voir.*

36. Choice (A) is correct. With a single gesture, all the unnamed females *raised* their hands. The missing word is the past participle of *lever.* Since this verb is conjugated with *avoir,* its past participle needs to agree with the direct object if and only if that object comes before the verb. In this sentence, *la main* is the object and it follows rather than precedes the verb; therefore, there should not be agreement. In choices (B), (C), and (D), the past participle is unduly modified.

37. Choice (D) is the correct answer. The speaker asks which painting the listener prefers: this painting or *the one* that is over there? The missing word must be a demonstrative pronoun replacing *cette peinture* (*qui est là-bas*). Choice (A), *laquelle* ("which"), is a relative or interrogative pronoun, which cannot be modified by a relative clause (*qui est là-bas*). Choice (B), *l'une* ("the one"), is not a demonstrative pronoun; it is used in constructions that contrast *l'un(e)* with *l'autre.* And choice (C), *cette* ("this/that"), is not a pronoun but an adjective that must be followed by a noun.

38. Choice (A) is the correct answer. The speaker indicates great surprise that an unnamed person was pleased with that film very much. The verb *plaire* ("to please") is usually complemented by an indirect object introduced by the preposition *à*; the missing word must be a pronoun that would indicate the person who finds something pleasing or, literally, "to whom" something is pleasing. Choices (B), *l'* ("him/her"), and (D), *les* ("them"), are pronouns that only stand in for direct objects. Choice (C), *en*, is a pronoun that only stands in for an indirect object introduced by the preposition *de*, and that is usually a thing, not a person.

39. Choice (C) is the correct answer. This year, cherries cost 12 francs *per* pound. When expressing the price of something per unit in French, the definite article is used, so *le* is the correct choice. Choices (A), (B), and (D) are unidiomatic.

40. Choice (A) is the correct answer. *Vers* is the only preposition that is idiomatically correct in conjunction with *la fin de l'après-midi*, meaning "toward the end of the afternoon."

41. Choice (A) is the correct answer. The verb *sonner* ("to ring") is the only verb among the choices that can be used without being complemented by an object. Choice (B), *j'ouvrais* ("I would open"), and choice (D), *je quittais* ("I would leave"), both require a direct object to complement them. And in this context, choice (C), *je sortais* ("I would go out"), would require an indirect object introduced by the preposition *de*.

42. Choice (D) is the correct answer. The author is speaking directly to Jacques and asks if he or she is disturbing him. The missing pronoun is therefore the second person direct object form *te*. *Déranger* constructs its complement as a direct object, and *lui* (A) is an indirect object pronoun. Choice (B), *les*, is a third person plural that has no referent in the passage. And choice (C), *me*, is incorrect because the author can only be disturbing the addressee of the question (Jacques), not himself or herself.

43. Choice (A) is the correct answer. *Jamais* is the only choice that fits grammatically in the sentence. Jacques tells the author that he *never* disturbs him. The verb *déranger* already has a direct object (*me*), so neither choice (B), *rien* ("nothing"), nor choice (D), *personne* ("no one"), which are also direct objects, is possible. Choice (C), *aucun* ("no"), must be followed by a noun, which would then be the object of the verb *déranger*, so it is not possible either.

44. Choice (A) is the correct answer. The missing word must connect the two clauses *Ça va toujours très bien* ("Everything is always very good") and *je te vois* ("I see you"). *Quand* ("when") is the best choice: "Everything is always very good *when* I see you." It does not make much sense to say "Everything is always very good *but* I see you" (B), "Everything is always very good *therefore* I see you" (C), or "Everything is always very good *nevertheless* I see you" (D), especially when the next sentence refers to the kindness of what has been said. Further, choice (D), *pourtant*, is an adverb, not a conjunction, and should not be used to join two clauses in this way.

45. Choice (A) is the correct answer. Jacques' kindness touched the author and *warmed* his or her heart. It does not make sense to say that the kindness *beat* (B), *launched* (C), or *gave back* or *rendered* (D) the author's heart.

46. Choice (B) is the correct answer. The magistrate thought that he *would be able* to reach a decision the following week. Since the clause is referring to an action that was still in the future ("*la semaine suivante*") at a point in the past, the conditional form of the verb is used. The present perfect or *passé composé* (A), future (C), and subjunctive (D) forms of the verb are incorrect in this context.

47. Choice (C) is the correct answer. The present participle, *ayant*, is the only choice that fits grammatically and logically in the sentence: "*Having* heard ...., he changed ... ." Choice (A), *après* ("after"), and choice (D), *sans* ("without"), would have to be followed by the perfect infinitive ("*avoir entendu*"), not just the past participle ("*entendu*"). Choice (B), *bien entendu*, means "of course," but this phrase makes no sense in the sentence.

48. Choice (B) is the correct answer. In the second clause of this sentence, the subject *les témoins* ("the witnesses") and the verb *disaient* ("were saying") are inverted, so what is missing is the direct object. *Ce que* ("what") is the appropriate indefinite relative pronoun to follow the verb *entendre* ("hear") and serve as the direct object of *disaient*: "Having heard *what* the witnesses were saying, he changed ... ." Choice (A), *ce qui* ("what"), is a subject form and cannot be used as the direct object of *disaient*. Choice (C), *quoi* ("what"), can be used as a relative pronoun only if it is preceded by a preposition and cannot directly follow *entendu* or serve as the direct object of *disaient*. Choice (D), *à quoi* ("to which"), can be used as a relative pronoun only when preceded by *ce* and cannot serve as the direct object of *disaient*.

49. Choice (A) is the correct answer. After hearing what the witnesses were saying, he changed *his mind* ("changer d'avis"). To be grammatical, choice (B) would have to be *d'opinion*, not *l'opinion*. It does not make sense to say that he changed *his memory* (C), and it is not idiomatically acceptable to say that he changed *the mind* (D).

50. Choice (C) is the correct answer. The correct preposition to use after the verb *penser* is *à*. Sophie and Michel are already thinking *about* something. Choice (A), *de* ("of"); choice (B), *pour* ("for"); and choice (D), *sur* ("on"), are unidiomatic.

51. Choice (B) is the correct answer. *Prochain* ("next") is the only choice that fits logically in the blank. The missing word describes which summer vacation Sophie and Michel are already thinking about. The word *déjà* ("already") implies that it is still early for them to be thinking about this, and the rest of the paragraph describes future plans, so the summer must still be in the future. Therefore, choice (A), *passé* ("past"), and choice (D), *présent* ("present"), are incorrect. Because there are many future summers, not just one, choice (C), the phrase *été futur* ("future summer"), cannot be used with the definite article *l'*.

52. Choice (C) is the correct answer. They plan to cross Europe by bicycle and train. *Europe* is the direct object of the verb *traverser* ("cross"), and in this position, it is preceded by the definite article *l'*. Omitting the article, as in choice (A), is incorrect.

Traverser is not followed by a preposition, so choices (B), *en*, and (D), *dans*, are also incorrect.

53. Choice (B) is the correct answer. The missing word is a relative pronoun that refers to *des amis* ("friends") and is the subject of the clause that follows it. They plan to travel with friends *who* have already made the trip. Choice (A), *quels* ("which"), cannot be used as a relative pronoun in this position. Neither choice (C), the object relative pronoun *qu'* ("that"), nor choice (D), *dont* ("whose" or "of which"), can be used as the subject of the relative clause.

54. Choice (B) is the correct answer. The missing word completes the negative construction beginning with *ne*. *Ne ... que/qu'* means "only" or "merely" and grammatically and logically fits in the sentence: Each of them will bring *only* one backpack. Choice (A), *d'*, cannot grammatically complete the negative construction beginning with *ne*. Choice (C), *ni* ("neither"), can be used with *ne*, but it must be followed by another *ni*. And choice (D) is incorrect because it is unidiomatic to say that "Each of them will *not* bring a backpack."

55. Choice (C) is the correct answer. Each of them will bring only one backpack to *avoid* excess baggage. It does not make sense to say that they will bring only backpacks in order to *pay* (A), *create* (B), or *drag* (D) excess baggage.

56. Choice (D) is the correct answer. Their route will be established in advance, and the sports club that organizes *this excursion* has provided for something. This paragraph is about travel plans, so it does not make sense to say that the sports club organizes *this match* (A), *this way* (B), or *this race* (C).

57. Choice (D) is the correct answer. The sports club has provided for numerous *stopping points* so that the cyclists can rest and do a little tourism. It does not make sense to say that the club has provided for *downpours* (A), *climbs* (B), or *steps* (C), for these reasons.

58. Choice (A) is the correct answer. The phrase *chaleur à la baisse* indicates that temperatures will drop tomorrow, and there will therefore be less heat. Choices (B) and (C) are incorrect because winds and clouds will actually be arriving. Choice (D) is incorrect because there will be more, not less, cool weather tomorrow.

59. Choice (B) is the correct answer. The sun icons near Lyon on the map indicate that the weather will be nice (*il fera beau*), not that *it will rain* (A), that *it will snow* (C), or that *there will be storms* (D).

60. Choice (C) is the correct answer. In lines 8–9, the sentence *Il n'avait pas eu d'enfants: c'était le grand regret de sa vie* explicitly states that being without children is the great regret of Schulz's life. Choice (A) is incorrect: Schulz is sad about the loss of his wife, but there is no indication that this is his great regret. Choice (B) is incorrect: Although Schulz no longer hears from his former students, they were not ungrateful, and he still holds them in high esteem. Choice (D) is also incorrect: Schulz's delicate health is mentioned in line 2, but there is no indication that this is a great regret of his.

61. Choice (A) is the correct answer. Lines 17–20 state explicitly that Schulz has a most lively interest ("*il prenait un intérêt vif et frais*") in anything that happens to his students, be it good things or bad things ("*à tout ce qui leur arrivait d'heureux ou de malheureux*"). Schulz does not consider his students *selfish* (B); he attributes to the most selfish ones the good feelings he had for them (lines 29–30). He is not *jealous of their success* (C); in fact, he rejoices in their successes (line 26). And Schulz is sure of his students' affection (lines 28–29) and does not consider them *ungrateful* (D).

62. Choice (B) is the correct answer. Schulz was a teacher. Lines 9–11 and the second paragraph talk about his relationship with his former students ("*élèves*"). There is no indication that Schulz was a *doctor* (A), a *journalist* (C), or a *psychologist* (D).

63. Choice (C) is the correct answer. According to the author, the old feel closer to the young than the young do to the old. Lines 12–16 ("*Un vieux coeur ... d'une autre époque*") explain this point of view: "An old heart can feel very close to a young heart and nearly the same age: it knows how short the years that separate them are. But the young man has no doubt: the old man is for him a man from a different era." The author does not say that the young and the old *respect each other* (A) or *share the same ideas* (B), or that *the young value the old more when they have themselves aged* (D).

64. Choice (C) is the correct answer. The young people most appreciated the old man when they had finished their university studies: "They would write to him to thank him when they left the university" ("*ils lui écrivaient ... l'université*"). The author does not mention a time when the young people *were children* (A), *were happy* (B), or *had found work* (D).

65. Choice (C) is the correct answer. Schulz learns about his former students by reading about them in the newspapers ("*par les journaux ... tel*"). Some of his students write to him when they graduate and one or two times in the following years (lines 22–23), but they do not *write to him often* (A). Schulz *does not write to them asking for news* (B), nor does *the university send him news* (D).

66. Choice (D) is the correct answer. According to the author, Peter Schulz's life has been dedicated to the success of others, as evidenced in the fatherly affection he has developed for his students ("*Il avait reporté ... fils*") and the joy he takes in their successes ("*et il se réjouissait ... siens*"). The author does not say that Schulz has had a *very sad* life (A); he seems to have loved his wife (lines 4–5), and he does take joy in his former students' successes (lines 26–27). His life was not *active and thrilling* (B); in fact, his life has been uneventful ("*Sa vie ... événements*"). Although many of his students have shown him some gratitude (lines 17–23), they seem not to have fully *appreciated and respected him* (C), and he has found little in return for the affection he gave them (line 12).

67. Choice (D) is the correct answer. The main subject of the reading is the decrease in the number of births. The author writes only indirectly about *the population in big cities* (A) by mentioning the declining birthrates there (line 3). The author talks in the third paragraph about the problems of housing for large families in urban settings, but not about *a lack of housing* (B). The author talks in the second and third paragraphs about the financial and logistical problems of large families in cities, which encourage a lower birthrate; he or she does not discuss *the growing number of large families* (C).

68. Choice (A) is the correct answer. The word *malheureusement* ("unfortunately") in the first sentence sets the tone for the passage and makes it clear that the author does not consider the declining birthrate to be a good thing. The use of *notamment* ("notably") in line 6 (B) applies only to the specific situation in which both parents work, not to the entire passage. *Logement* ("housing") in line 9 (C) is simply a noun and does not express the author's point of view at all. *Minimum* ("minimum") in line 11 (D) refers to one characteristic of urban housing and does not apply to all the facts in the passage.

69. Choice (A) is the correct answer. Lines 12–13 say that a change of apartment is frequently caused by the arrival of a newborn, or of a "supplemental child" ("*un enfant supplémentaire*"). The mention of a mother who works (line 6), and thus a *woman who works* (B), is unrelated to changing apartments. The *financial problems* (C) are a result of changing apartments, not the cause (line 14). There is no discussion of the *fear of big cities* (D).

70. Choice (C) is the correct answer. The first sentence says that we are all neighbors in the great human community, and the final sentence calls for cooperation for a better world; the title of the ad, *"Hello, neighbor,"* is used to suggest that we all live on the earth and are therefore neighbors. The word *voisin* ("neighbor") is used metaphorically, and there is no direction to *say hello* to our actual neighbors (A). The man in the picture is holding a tapestry to suggest that being a good neighbor means learning to integrate into the texture of the local community (lines 2–3); however, there is no discussion of *selling tapestries to neighbors* — or anyone else — in the ad (B). The ad suggests that we should all work together for a better world, but not that we all *want to meet each other* (D).

71. Choice (A) is the correct answer. The first sentence of the second paragraph says that Komatsu produces industrial machines and construction engines, or machines for *the equipment industry.* These machines are not appropriate for *small businesses* (B), *household needs* (C), or *aerospace* (D).

72. Choice (B) is the correct answer. The ad talks about Komatsu's philosophy of producing instruments that permit a better quality of life ("*C'est-à-dire ... vie*") and working for the good of the community through collaboration (*De même ... services*) — in other words, Komatsu's philosophy of *creating a more harmonious world.* It does not talk about *building less expensive machines* (A), *encouraging the craftsman* (C), or *foreseeing the world to come* (D).

73. Choice (C) is the correct answer. The first paragraph indicates that the streetlamps had come on just a moment before and that the sky remained reddish at the horizon, implying that it was light before and is just getting dark — that is *dusk*. It is not *dawn* (A), because it is getting dark, not light. It is not *afternoon* (B), because it is dark and the streets are empty. And it is not *the middle of the night* (D), because the sky is still reddish and the streetlamps have only just come on.

74. Choice (B) is the correct answer. Every day (except Sunday), the lady with the scarf gives the beggar a coin, and it is the only good moment of his day ("*Elle lui en donnait ... journée*"); this indicates that the coin *has a great emotional value.* There is nothing that indicates that this coin *has a greater monetary value* than do the other coins (A), that *it is part of a collection* (C), or that *it is counterfeit* (D).

75. Choice (D) is the correct answer. When the lady approaches the beggar, her steps are calm and regular, a little nonchalant ("*Il la regardait ... nonchalante*"); it is clear she is not rushing. The way she walks does not indicate that she approaches *with hesitation*

(A) or *with rapid steps* (B). Nothing indicates that she *does not watch where she is going* (C); in fact, she seems to approach the beggar quite deliberately.

76. Choice (C) is the correct answer. When the lady with the scarf arrives in front of the beggar, she looks at him and he looks at her before she hands him a coin and goes away ("*Arrivée ... elle s'en allait*"). The reader can infer that as they look at each other, the lady communicates silently with the beggar, which makes him happy. She does not *toss the coin in his bowl* (A); rather, she holds it out to him and he takes it. She does more than *watch him every morning* (B); she approaches him deliberately and walks away. There is nothing that indicates that she *contemplates the coin* (D) before or after she gives it to him.

77. Choice (A) is the correct answer. Sunday is the one day that the lady with the scarf does not come, which is why the beggar does not like Sunday ("*Elle venait jamais le dimanche: c'est pour cela que le mendiant n'aimait pas le dimanche*"); the beggar is sad because tomorrow is Sunday and he will miss the lady. He never sees the lady at all on Sunday, so she does not *chase him* (B), *give him little money* (C), or *give him back an old coin* (D) on that day of the week.

78. Choice (D) is the correct answer. The end of the first sentence ("*ils offrent ...*") states that these chateaux offer a living image of the historic and architectural heritage of Anjou, so the chateaux must have been chosen because they are a beautiful example of the architecture of Anjou. There is no indication that these chateaux would interest only *specialists* (A). Most of the chosen chateaux are occupied by their owners ("*pour la plupart habités par leurs propriétaires*"), so they do not *belong to the state* (B). These chateaux are open to the public ("*ouverts au public*") presumably all the time, not just *from time to time* (C).

79. Choice (C) is the correct answer. Les Routes Roi René are named to honor le Roi René, instigator of the artistic and literary life of Anjou ("*instigateur ... l'Anjou*")—in other words, a *protector of letters and arts*. The name has nothing to do with *the routes crossing a region where travel is convenient* (A), or *the presence there of monuments from all eras* (B). Le Roi René was a cousin of the King of France, not king himself; there is no reason to believe this segment of the scenic routes would be named Le Roi René as an *emblem of the Kings of France* (D).

80. Choice (B) is the correct answer. The first paragraph lays out the setting for the story that follows, and the second sentence indicates that famine reigned in Strasbourg ("*La disette régnait à Strasbourg*"); this implies that *La Marseillaise* was composed in Strasbourg. Marseille (A) adopted the anthem after it was composed, and Lille (C) is

not mentioned at all. The song was composed after Rouget de Lisle slept at home with his head on his harpsichord ("*Accablé ... nota*"), not while he was *on the road* (D).

81. Choice (A) is the correct answer. The sublime inspiration for Rouget de Lisle's composition was the songs of the night, impressions of a dream which rose with difficulty in his memory after he awoke ("*Accablé d'une inspiration sublime ... mémoire*"). The passage does not indicate that Rouget de Lisle was inspired by a *poem* (B), a *meal* (C), or a *battle* (D).

82. Choice (D) is correct. The fact that Rouget de Lisle is referred to as the young officer ("*le jeune officier*") indicates that he was at the time a *soldier*, not a *troubadour* (A), *mayor* (B), or *orchestra director* (C). Dietrich, not de Lisle, was the mayor of Strasbourg.

83. Choice (C) is the correct answer. After Mayor Dietrich awakened his family, his oldest daughter accompanied Rouget de Lisle as he sang ("*Sa fille ... chanta*"); they were the first to perform *La Marseillaise*. Although Dietrich's family was in attendance, the song was not performed by *the mayor and his wife* (A), *Rouget de Lisle and the mayor's wife* (B), or *the mayor and his daughter* (D).

84. Choice (D) is the correct answer. According to the passage, the new song flew from town to town ("*Le nouveau chant ... populaires*") and was spread by citizens of Marseille ("*Les Marseillais ... route*"), so the new song was sung *everywhere*. It is not true that the song *was not played again* (A), or that *other towns stole it* (B)—in the passage, the verb *vola* means "flew," not "stole." There is nothing to indicate that the song *was greatly modified* (C).

85. Choice (B) is the correct answer. The citizens of Marseille adopted the song to be sung at the beginning of their club meetings and then spread it through France while singing it on their route, making it popular, so the French national anthem is now called *La Marseillaise* ("*Marseille l'adopta ... 'Marseillaise'*"). The anthem was not *composed by someone from Marseille* (A); Rouget de Lisle was from Strasbourg. There is no indication that *the citizens of Marseille were the most patriotic* (C), and there is no discussion of whether *the citizens of Marseille were the best singers* (D).

French with Listening

The Subject Test in French with Listening is offered once a year only at designated test centers. **To take the test you MUST bring an acceptable CD player with earphones to the test center.**

Sample Listening Questions

The following three types of questions appear on the Subject Test in French with Listening. All questions in this section of the test are multiple-choice questions in which you must choose the BEST response from three or four choices offered. Text in brackets [ ] is recorded on the CD only; it will not appear in your test book. Please note that the CD does not start here. Begin using the CD when you start the actual practice test on page 587.

Part A

Your answer sheet has five answer positions marked A, B, C, D, and E, while the questions throughout this part contain only four choices. Be sure NOT to make any marks in column E.

Directions: For each item in this part, you will hear four sentences designated (A), (B), (C), and (D). They will not be printed in your test book. As you listen, look at the picture in your test book and select the choice that best reflects what you see in the picture or what someone in the picture might say. Then fill in the corresponding circle on the answer sheet. You will hear the choices only once. Now look at the following example.

You see:

You hear:

[(A) Quelle joie d'être seul!
(B) Que c'est agréable de faire du vélo!
(C) Le moteur fait trop de bruit!
(D) Nous adorons la course à pied.]

Choice (B) is the correct answer. Statement (B), "Que c'est agréable de faire du vélo!" best reflects what you see in the picture or what someone in the picture might say.

1. You see:

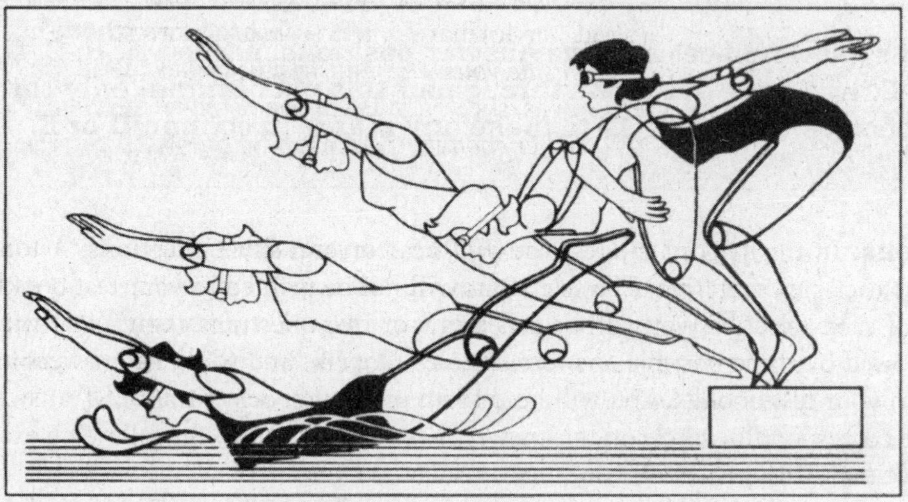

You hear:

[Numéro 1

(Woman) (A) Elle porte toujours un bonnet de bain.

(B) Elle a toujours peur de l'eau.

(C) Le ski nautique lui plaît beaucoup.

(D) Elle est en train de plonger dans l'eau.]

(7 seconds)

Choice (D) is the correct answer to question 1. In this question you see a drawing that shows a slow motion scene of a girl diving into a pool. Choice (D) best reflects what can be seen in the picture. Choices (A), (B), and (C) are incorrect because the girl in the picture is not wearing a cap, does not seem to be afraid of water, and is not shown on water skis.

Part B

Your answer sheet has five answer positions marked A, B, C, D, and E, while the questions throughout this part contain only three choices. Be sure NOT to make any marks in column D or E.

Directions: In this part of the test you will hear several short selections. A tone will announce each new selection. The selections will not be printed in your test booklet. At the end of each selection, you will be asked one or two questions about what was said, each followed by three possible answers, choices (A), (B), and (C). The answers are not printed in your test booklet. You will hear them only *once*. Select the BEST answer and fill in the corresponding circle on the answer sheet. Now listen to the following example, but do not mark the answer on your answer sheet.

You hear:

[(Tone)

(Man B) Papa, ta voiture est chez le garagiste.
(Man A) Mais pourquoi? Elle a toujours bien marché.
(Man B) Euh, en réalité, j'ai eu un accident.
(Man A) Quoi? Tu plaisantes, n'est-ce pas?

(5 seconds)

(Woman A) Qu'est-ce qu'on peut dire de la voiture en question?

(A) Elle est en réparation.
(B) Elle est sur la route.
(C) Elle est chez un ami.]

(7 seconds)

Choice (A) is the correct answer. The best answer to the question, "Qu'est-ce qu'on peut dire de la voiture en question?" is choice (A), "Elle est en réparation" because we heard it got into an accident and that it is at the mechanic.

Questions 2–3

You hear:

[(Tone)
(Man) Votre passeport, madame.
(Woman) Voilà.
(Man) Et qu'est-ce que vous ferez au Canada?
(Woman) Je vais passer les vacances avec ma famille.
(Man) Très bien, madame. Je vous souhaite un bon séjour.]
(5 seconds)

2. [Numéro 2
(Man) Qui parle à cette femme?
(A) Un professeur.
(B) Un douanier.
(C) Un chauffeur.]
(7 seconds)

Choice (B) is the correct answer to question 2, *Un douanier,* because the woman is crossing the border into Canada. In this question, you choose the person who is talking to the woman in the dialogue. *Un professeur* or *un chauffeur* would not ask to see the woman's passport. Therefore, choices (A) and (C) are incorrect.

3. [Numéro 3
(Man) Qu'est-ce que la femme va faire?
(A) Obtenir un passeport.
(B) Chercher sa famille.
(C) Entrer au Canada.]
(7 seconds)

Choice (C) is the correct answer to question 3. This question asks what the woman is about to do. Choice (C) is the only logical answer according to the dialogue. After crossing the border, the woman will enter Canada. Choice (A) is incorrect because she already has a passport, and choice (B) is incorrect because she is vacationing with her family, not looking for them.

Part C

Your answer sheet has five answer positions marked A, B, C, D, and E, while the questions throughout this part contain only four choices. Be sure NOT to make any marks in column E.

Directions: You will now hear some extended dialogues or monologues. You will hear each only once. After each dialogue or monologue, you will be asked several questions about what you have just heard. These questions are also printed in your test book. Select the best answer to each question from among the four choices printed in your test book and fill in the corresponding circle on the answer sheet. There is no sample question for this part.

Questions 4–6

(Man) [Dialogue numéro 1. Marie-Hélène et son amie Maude parlent de cinéma et de littérature.

(Woman A) Tiens, Marie-Hélène, tu as acheté *Danse avec les loups* en anglais?

(Woman B) Oui, j'ai acheté ce livre à Boston. Je me suis dit que c'était, euh, d'abord je n'avais pas vu le film et avant de voir le film j'avais vraiment envie de lire le livre; c'est tout. Et puis, tu sais, Maude, finalement je n'ai pas pu le lire, je n'ai pas eu le temps.

(Woman A) Il faudra te dépêcher de le lire parce que le film est encore sur les écrans mais je ne sais pas combien de temps il va y rester. Il a beaucoup de succès, le film; le livre, je ne le connais pas. Il paraît qu'il est très très bien, le film, mais un peu long; moi, je compte aller le voir la semaine prochaine.]

4. (Man) [Qu'est-ce que Marie-Hélène déclare?]

(12 seconds)

Qu'est-ce que Marie-Hélène déclare?

(A) Avoir vu un film.
(B) Avoir l'intention de lire un livre.
(C) Avoir lu un livre.
(D) Avoir l'intention d'aller à Boston.

Choice (B) is the correct answer to question 4. Marie-Hélène states in the dialogue that she bought the book *Dances with Wolves* in Boston so that she could read it before seeing the movie. She also states *je n'ai pas pu le lire, je n'ai pas eu le temps*, which means that she has not yet read the book. Choice (C) is therefore incorrect. Choices (A) and (D) are incorrect because she did not see the movie (A) and does not mention that she intends to go to Boston (D).

5. (Man) [Qu'est-ce que Maude avoue à son amie?]
(12 seconds)
Qu'est-ce que Maude avoue à son amie?

(A) Elle a lu le livre.
(B) Elle n'a pas encore vu le film.
(C) Elle n'a pas compris la critique.
(D) Elle a écouté la cassette.

Choice (B) is the correct answer to question 5. When Maude answers her friend, she tells her at the end: *Il paraît qu'il est très très bien, le film ... je compte aller le voir la semaine prochaine.* Choice (A) is incorrect because Maude states the opposite (*le livre, je ne le connais pas*). According to the dialogue, Maude admits neither choice (C) nor choice (D); both choices are therefore incorrect.

6. (Man) [Dans cette discussion, qu'est-ce qu'on peut dire des deux amies?]
(12 seconds)
Dans cette discussion, qu'est-ce qu'on peut dire des deux amies?

(A) Elles se font des compliments.
(B) Elles s'ignorent.
(C) Elles s'inquiètent.
(D) Elles partagent les mêmes goûts.

Choice (D) is the correct answer to question 6. It can be inferred from the dialogue that the two friends share the same interests, at least with regard to movies. Choices (A), (B), and (C) cannot be said about the two friends. They do not exchange compliments (A), do know each other (B), and do not become anxious or upset (C).

French with Listening Subject Test

Practice Helps

The test that follows is an actual, previously administered SAT Subject Test in French with Listening. To get an idea of what it's like to take this test, practice under conditions that are much like those of an actual test administration.

- Set aside an hour when you can take the test uninterrupted.
- Sit at a desk or table with no other books or papers. Dictionaries, other books, or notes are not allowed in the test room.
- Tear out an answer sheet from the back of this book and fill it in just as you would on the day of the test. One answer sheet can be used for up to three Subject Tests.
- Read the instructions that precede the practice test. During the actual administration you will be asked to read them before answering test questions.
- Time yourself by placing a clock or kitchen timer in front of you.
- After you finish the practice test, read the sections "How to Score the SAT Subject Test in French with Listening" and "How Did You Do on the Subject Test in French with Listening?"
- The appearance of the answer sheet in this book may differ from the answer sheet you see on test day.

FRENCH TEST WITH LISTENING

The top portion of the page of the answer sheet that you will use to take the French Test with Listening must be filled in exactly as illustrated below. When your supervisor tells you to fill in the circle next to the name of the test you are about to take, mark your answer sheet as shown.

○ Literature	○ Mathematics Level 1	○ German	○ Chinese Listening	○ Japanese Listening
○ Biology E	○ Mathematics Level 2	○ Italian	● French Listening	○ Korean Listening
○ Biology M	○ U.S. History	○ Latin	○ German Listening	○ Spanish Listening
○ Chemistry	○ World History	○ Modern Hebrew		
○ Physics	○ French	○ Spanish	Background Questions: ①②③④⑤⑥⑦⑧⑨	

After filling in the circle next to the name of the test you are taking, locate the Background Questions box on your answer sheet (as shown above). This is where you will answer the following Background Questions on your answer sheet.

BACKGROUND QUESTIONS

Please answer either Part I or Part II below by filling in the appropriate circle in the Background Questions box on your answer sheet. Fill in ONLY ONE circle, as described below, to indicate how you obtained your knowledge of French. <u>The information you provide is for statistical purposes only and will not affect your test score.</u>

Part I — If your knowledge of French comes primarily from any of the following: living in a home where French is the main spoken language, living for six months or longer in a French-speaking country that included significant experience in French language, courses taken at a college, or special study of French, fill in <u>circle 9</u> and leave the remaining circles blank, regardless of how long you studied the subject in school.

Part II — If your knowledge of French comes primarily from courses taken in secondary school, fill in the circle that indicates the level of the French course in which you are currently enrolled. If you are not now enrolled in a French course, fill in the circle that indicates the level of the most advanced course in French that you have completed.

• First year:	first or second half	—Fill in circle 1.
• Second year:	first half	—Fill in circle 2.
	second half	—Fill in circle 3.
• Third year:	first half	—Fill in circle 4.
	second half	—Fill in circle 5.
• Fourth year:	first half	—Fill in circle 6.
	second half	—Fill in circle 7.
• Advanced Placement course or a course at a level higher than fourth year, second half or high school course work plus a minimum of four weeks of study abroad		—Fill in circle 8.

When the supervisor gives the signal, turn the page and begin the French Test with Listening. There are 100 numbered circles on the answer sheet and 86 questions in the French Test with Listening. Therefore, use only circles 1 to 86 for recording your answers.

FRENCH TEST WITH LISTENING

SECTION I

LISTENING

Approximate time—20 minutes

Questions 1-27

PLEASE NOTE THAT YOUR ANSWER SHEET HAS FIVE ANSWER POSITIONS, MARKED A, B, C, D, AND E, WHILE THE QUESTIONS THROUGHOUT THIS PART CONTAIN ONLY FOUR CHOICES. BE SURE NOT TO MAKE ANY MARKS IN COLUMN E.

Part A

Directions: For each question in this part, you will hear four sentences, designated (A), (B), (C), and (D). They will not be printed in your test booklet. As you listen, look at the picture in your test booklet and select the choice that best reflects what you see in the picture or what someone in the picture might say. Then fill in the corresponding circle on the answer sheet. You will hear the choices only once. Now look at the following example.

You see:

You hear:

Statement (B), "Que c'est agréable de faire du vélo," best reflects what you see in the picture or what someone in the picture might say. Therefore, you should choose answer (B).

GO ON TO THE NEXT PAGE

1.

2.

GO ON TO THE NEXT PAGE

3.

4.

GO ON TO THE NEXT PAGE

5.

6.

GO ON TO THE NEXT PAGE

7.

8.

GO ON TO THE NEXT PAGE

PLEASE NOTE THAT YOUR ANSWER SHEET HAS FIVE ANSWER POSITIONS, MARKED A, B, C, D AND E, WHILE THE QUESTIONS THROUGHOUT PART B CONTAIN ONLY THREE CHOICES. BE SURE NOT TO MAKE ANY MARKS IN COLUMN D OR E.

Part B

Directions: In this part of the test you will hear several short selections. A tone will announce each new selection. The selections will not be printed in your test booklet and will be heard only once. At the end of each selection, you will be asked one or two questions about what was said, each followed by three possible answers, (A), (B), and (C). The answers will not be printed in your test booklet. You will hear them only once. Select the best answer and fill in the corresponding circle on the answer sheet. Now listen to the following example, but do not mark the answer on your answer sheet.

You hear:

The best answer to the question "Qu'est-ce qu'on peut dire de la voiture en question?" is (A), "Elle est en réparation." Therefore, you should choose answer (A).

9. Mark your answer on your answer sheet.
10. Mark your answer on your answer sheet.

11. Mark your answer on your answer sheet.
12. Mark your answer on your answer sheet.

13. Mark your answer on your answer sheet.
14. Mark your answer on your answer sheet.

15. Mark your answer on your answer sheet.
16. Mark your answer on your answer sheet.

GO ON TO THE NEXT PAGE

PLEASE NOTE THAT YOUR ANSWER SHEET HAS FIVE ANSWER POSITIONS, MARKED A, B, C, D, AND E, WHILE THE QUESTIONS THROUGHOUT THIS PART CONTAIN ONLY FOUR CHOICES. BE SURE NOT TO MAKE ANY MARKS IN COLUMN E.

Part C

Directions: You will now hear some extended dialogues or monologues. You will hear each only once. After each dialogue or monologue, you will be asked several questions about what you have just heard. These questions are also printed in your test booklet. Select the best answer to each question from among the four choices printed in your test booklet and fill in the corresponding circle on the answer sheet. There is no sample question for this part.

Dialogue numéro 1

17. Quel genre de film vont-ils voir?

(A) Une histoire de pirates.
(B) Un film d'aventures.
(C) Un film d'espionnage.
(D) Un sujet d'actualité.

18. Qu'est-ce que Bernard et Sophie doivent faire à la fin de leur discussion?

(A) Ils doivent se séparer.
(B) Ils doivent se dépêcher.
(C) Ils doivent rentrer chez eux.
(D) Ils doivent aller dîner.

19. Quelle impression donne le garçon?

(A) Il est conciliant.
(B) Il n'a pas d'opinions.
(C) Il est entêté.
(D) Il est comique.

20. Pourquoi ont-ils choisi ce film?

(A) Parce que la jeune fille n'aime pas rire.
(B) Parce que le garçon en a entendu parler.
(C) Parce que la jeune fille s'intéresse aux problèmes sociaux.
(D) Parce que le garçon a envie de s'amuser ce soir-là.

Dialogue numéro 2

21. Quel est l'un des jours où Philippe va à l'école seulement le matin?

(A) Le samedi.
(B) Le lundi.
(C) Le mardi.
(D) Le jeudi.

22. Que fait Philippe dès qu'il rentre chez lui?

(A) Il prend un goûter.
(B) Il regarde la télé.
(C) Il téléphone à ses amis.
(D) Il lit un roman.

23. A part le tennis, quelle autre activité sportive Philippe préfère-t-il?

(A) Le foot.
(B) La course.
(C) La marche.
(D) Le vélo.

GO ON TO THE NEXT PAGE

Dialogue Numéro 3

24. Qu'est-ce qu'on peut dire du travail de Marie-France?

    (A) Il n'est pas exigeant.
    (B) C'est un emploi temporaire.
    (C) Il oblige Marie-France à se déplacer.
    (D) Il n'intéresse pas Marie-France.

25. Qu'est-ce que Marie-France pense des ordinateurs portatifs?

    (A) Elle les trouve intimidants.
    (B) Elle croit qu'ils déshumanisent la vie.
    (C) Elle trouve qu'ils coûtent trop cher.
    (D) Elle ne s'en occupe pas.

26. Qu'est-ce que Marie-France craint?

    (A) Que ses enfants ne se servent trop de son ordinateur portatif.
    (B) Qu'elle n'efface des lignes importantes dans un dossier.
    (C) Que l'ordinateur portatif ne provoque des disputes.
    (D) Que l'ordinateur portatif n'apporte la vie du travail à la maison.

27. Comment peut-on caractériser l'attitude de Caroline sur l'emploi des ordinateurs portatifs?

    (A) Elle est neutre.
    (B) Elle est désintéressée.
    (C) Elle est sarcastique.
    (D) Elle est encourageante.

END OF SECTION I.
DO NOT GO ON TO SECTION II UNTIL YOU ARE TOLD TO DO SO.

SECTION II

READING

Time—40 minutes

Questions 28-86

WHEN YOU BEGIN THE READING SECTION, BE SURE THAT YOU MARK YOUR ANSWER TO THE FIRST READING QUESTIONS BY FILLING IN ONE OF THE CIRCLES NEXT TO NUMBER 28 ON THE ANSWER SHEET.

Part A

Directions: This part consists of a number of incomplete statements, each having four suggested completions. Select the most appropriate completion and fill in the corresponding circle on the answer sheet.

28. Pour trouver la meilleure route de Paris à Tours, il faut consulter la -------.

(A) ville
(B) plaine
(C) carte
(D) campagne

29. Arrêtez cette radio! Ce ------- me fatigue.

(A) bain
(B) brouillard
(C) bouchon
(D) bruit

30. Les deux candidats voulaient se faire élire, donc chacun a ------- beaucoup d'améliorations au public.

(A) promis
(B) demandé
(C) refusé
(D) repris

31. Il faut attendre le feu vert avant ------- la rue.

(A) de croiser
(B) de traverser
(C) d'éteindre
(D) de réparer

32. Le cinéma ne me passionne pas trop. J'y vais seulement -------.

(A) à tort et à travers
(B) comme-ci, comme-ça
(C) de temps en temps
(D) à plusieurs reprises

33. Yves parle toujours à voix basse; donc personne ne l' -------.

(A) emporte
(B) apprend
(C) entend
(D) attire

34. La soif le tourmentait et il passait sa langue sur ses ------- sèches.

(A) lèvres
(B) joues
(C) mâchoires
(D) paupières

35. Ces murs sont très sales; il faudrait les -------.

(A) retourner
(B) rejoindre
(C) repeindre
(D) remonter

GO ON TO THE NEXT PAGE

36. J'ai tellement mal au ------- que je ne peux pas jouer au tennis.

    (A) coude
    (B) coup
    (C) jambon
    (D) droit

37. On voyait son grand âge à ses joues pleines de -------.

    (A) lignes
    (B) traits
    (C) rides
    (D) traces

38. Dominique, ferme le robinet! Sinon, tu vas faire ------- la baignoire.

    (A) dérober
    (B) déborder
    (C) dégoûter
    (D) dérouter

39. Le bébé a fait ses premiers ------- tout seul et toute la famille a applaudi.

    (A) pas
    (B) mots
    (C) pieds
    (D) pleurs

GO ON TO THE NEXT PAGE

Part B

Directions: Each of the following sentences contains a blank. From the four choices given, select the one that can be inserted in the blank to form a grammatically correct sentence and fill in the corresponding circle on the answer sheet. Choice (A) may consist of dashes that indicate that no insertion is required to form a grammatically correct sentence.

40. D'un commun accord, elles se sont toutes -------.

(A) levé
(B) levée
(C) levés
(D) levées

41. L'été prochain je voudrais voyager ------- Mexique.

(A) dans
(B) en
(C) à la
(D) au

42. Les jeunes mariés se sont installés dans leur ------- appartement.

(A) grande
(B) beau
(C) propre
(D) moderne

43. On voudrait bien savoir ------- a volé ces beaux tableaux.

(A) qu'
(B) auquel
(C) qui
(D) quel

44. Fermez la porte, afin que la pièce ------- rester fraîche.

(A) peut
(B) pouvait
(C) pouvez
(D) puisse

45. On partira ------- vous serez prêts.

(A) si
(B) dès que
(C) sans que
(D) avant que

46. Je voudrais y aller avec -------.

(A) elles
(B) tu
(C) leur
(D) ils

47. Croyant qu'Henri serait là, Jeannette ne s'est ------- fait de souci.

(A) souvent
(B) encore
(C) nul
(D) guère

48. Ils ------- à Montréal depuis trois ans et ils s'y plaisent.

(A) seraient
(B) ont été
(C) étaient
(D) sont

49. C'est un événement ------- je me souviendrai toujours.

(A) que
(B) qui
(C) auquel
(D) dont

50. Mon avocat s'occupe bien ------- mes affaires.

(A) des
(B) de
(C) à
(D) en

GO ON TO THE NEXT PAGE

Part C

Directions: The paragraphs below contain blank spaces indicating omissions in the text. For some blanks, it is necessary to choose the completion that is most appropriate to the meaning of the passage; for other blanks, to choose the one completion that forms a grammatically correct sentence. In some instances, choice (A) may consist of dashes that indicate that no insertion is required to form a grammatically correct sentence. In each case, indicate your answer by filling in the corresponding circle on the answer sheet. Be sure to read the paragraph completely before answering the questions related to it.

Hier soir, comme nous n' _(51)_ rien de mieux à faire, nous nous sommes promenés dans le parc pendant deux heures et _(52)_ avant de rentrer nous coucher. Mon copain, _(53)_ rien ne gêne, s'est tout de suite endormi _(54)_ que moi, je n'ai pas pu fermer _(55)_. J'avais toujours devant moi _(56)_ de ce pauvre homme _(57)_ que nous avions vu assis sur _(58)_ près de la porte d'entrée du parc.

51. (A) avons
    (B) avions
    (C) aurions
    (D) ayons

52. (A) midi
    (B) trente
    (C) demie
    (D) le quart

53. (A) que
    (B) quel
    (C) celui
    (D) quelqu'un

54. (A) tandis
    (B) de sorte
    (C) sans
    (D) autant

55. (A) l'oreiller
    (B) le lit
    (C) l'oeil
    (D) la couverture

56. (A) le site
    (B) l'image
    (C) la copie
    (D) le signe

57. (A) filé
    (B) fumé
    (C) enterré
    (D) affamé

58. (A) une banlieue
    (B) un banc
    (C) un banquet
    (D) une banque

GO ON TO THE NEXT PAGE

Hier, nous avons fait une balade en montagne. Nous sommes partis très tôt __(59)__, et c'est mon père __(60)__ a conduit. Il __(61)__ encore très frais, mais le soleil brillait. Et, bien sûr, tout le monde était __(62)__ ! Quand nous sommes arrivés dans __(63)__ magnifique, nous avons décidé __(64)__ marcher, en nous __(65)__ de temps en temps pour __(66)__ reposer. Vers midi nous avons pique-niqué __(67)__ d'un torrent. Nous avions tous très faim, et les sandwichs ont vite disparu.

59. (A) le matin
(B) matin
(C) du matin
(D) dans le matin

60. (A) ---
(B) il
(C) qui
(D) qu'

61. (A) faisait
(B) avait
(C) montait
(D) était

62. (A) à la rigueur
(B) de bonne heure
(C) dans le vent
(D) de bonne humeur

63. (A) un endroit
(B) un lac
(C) une place
(D) une altitude

64. (A) ---
(B) pour
(C) de
(D) à

65. (A) arrêtons
(B) arrêter
(C) arrêtés
(D) arrêtant

66. (A) ---
(B) se
(C) me
(D) nous

67. (A) au bord
(B) à bord
(C) autour
(D) au fond

GO ON TO THE NEXT PAGE

Part D

Directions: Read the following texts carefully for comprehension. Each is followed by a number of questions or incomplete statements. Select the answer or completion that is best according to the text and fill in the corresponding circle on the answer sheet.

(Ce passage a été écrit en 1856.)

Que faites-vous, Gaston? Quand viendrez-vous? Vous aviez pourtant promis de nous rejoindre. Comment avez-vous pu rester dix grands jours sans me voir? Quand nous étions ensemble dans notre cher Arlange, vous ne saviez pas me quitter pour une heure. Dieu! que les heures sont longues à Paris! Maman me parle à chaque instant contre vous, mais à votre nom seul il se fait dans mon coeur un tapage qui m'empêche d'entendre. Elle me dit que vous m'avez abandonnée: vous devinez que je n'en crois rien.

Vous n'êtes pas homme à fermer un si bon livre à la première page. Moi, depuis que je ne vous ai plus, je suis tout hébétée et toute languissante. Imaginez-vous que par moments je crois que je ne suis pas votre femme, et que cette belle cérémonie de l'église, et ce bal où nous étions si heureux, sont un rêve qui a trop tôt fini. Vous n'imaginerez jamais combien vous me manquez. Quand je sors avec maman, je vous cherche dans les rues: tout ce que j'ai vu à Paris jusqu'à présent, c'est que vous n'y êtes pas. Le soir, j'embrouille régulièrement votre nom dans mes prières; le matin, en m'éveillant, je regarde si vous n'êtes point autour de moi. Est-il possible que je pense tant à vous et que vous m'ayez oubliée? Peut-être m'en voulez-vous de vous avoir quitté si brusquement et sans vous dire adieu. Si vous saviez! Ce n'est pas moi qui suis partie; c'est maman qui m'a enlevée.

68. De quoi la narratrice de ce passage se plaint-elle?
    (A) De l'absence de Gaston
    (B) Du bruit de la ville
    (C) De la mère de Gaston
    (D) De sa maladie récente

69. Où la narratrice de ce passage se trouve-t-elle?
    (A) A la campagne
    (B) Près de la mer
    (C) Dans son village natal
    (D) Dans une grande ville

70. Quelle est l'attitude de la mère de la narratrice envers Gaston?
    (A) Elle le trouve assez sympathique.
    (B) Elle éprouve de l'indifférence envers lui.
    (C) Elle montre une certaine hostilité à son égard.
    (D) Elle l'aime presqu'autant que sa fille.

71. A qui la narratrice écrit-elle?
    (A) A son frère
    (B) A son amant
    (C) A son fiancé
    (D) A son mari

72. La phrase, "Vous n'êtes pas homme à fermer un si bon livre à la première page" (lignes 11-12) laisse entendre que
    (A) la narratrice a épousé Gaston récemment
    (B) la narratrice est bibliothécaire
    (C) Gaston se méfie de la narratrice
    (D) Gaston n'aime pas les livres courts

73. D'après le texte, que fait la narratrice quand elle se promène avec sa mère?
    (A) Elle fait des prières pour Gaston.
    (B) Elle achète des cadeaux pour Gaston.
    (C) Elle cherche Gaston partout.
    (D) Elle parle de Gaston à sa mère.

74. Selon la narratrice, quel pourrait être l'état d'esprit de Gaston?
    (A) Il a peur de lui dire adieu.
    (B) Il est triste quand il y a du brouillard.
    (C) Il est plutôt religieux.
    (D) Il est en colère contre elle.

75. La narratrice a quitté Gaston parce qu'elle
    (A) préfère Paris à la campagne
    (B) a été obligée de le faire
    (C) a besoin de soins médicaux
    (D) veut se faire religieuse

GO ON TO THE NEXT PAGE

LA CARTE INTEGRALE
(carte orange annuelle)

La carte Intégrale, c'est :

Un coupon unique, valable toute l'année pour tous vos déplacements en Ile de France.

Un abonnement personnel et permanent, utilisable à volonté sur les RER, Bus, Métros et trains d'Ile de France, en fonction des zones choisies (mêmes zones au choix que la carte orange).

Ses avantages :

"Chaque mois, elle vous simplifie la vie !",

une seule démarche lors du premier abonnement.

–Vous n'avez plus de file d'attente en fin de mois.

–Vous n'avez même plus besoin d'y penser.

Vous avez déjà votre coupon.

"Vous choisissez, vous changez d'avis, votre abonnement c'est comme vous en avez envie !"

76. La carte Intégrale vous permettra

(A) de louer une voiture à tarif réduit
(B) d'utiliser tous les transports publics
(C) de régler toutes vos factures mensuelles à la fois
(D) d'obtenir les hebdomadaires les plus récents

77. Le coupon est valide pendant

(A) toute la vie
(B) un mois
(C) les vacances
(D) douze mois

GO ON TO THE NEXT PAGE

Oh! ces journées de neige, quelle transformation subite elles opéraient en nous, autour de nous dès les premiers flocons! La lumière se retirait. Tout devenait terne: le plâtre des façades prenait une couleur grise, fanée, les arbres paraissaient plus noirs. Dehors, quand nous levions la tête, c'était presque une ivresse de recevoir sur la figure, sans savoir où elles se poseraient, ces mille petites abeilles blanches dont le froid nous piquait le visage, avec une si furtive, une si délicate précision qu'elles semblaient avoir choisi, tout en tourbillonnant, la place où elles nous atteindraient. Le ciel n'était plus gris; il était roux, opaque. Et peu à peu, les grilles du collège, les branches, les bancs, les toits, devenaient d'autres grilles, d'autres branches, d'autres bancs, d'autres toits.

Mais le vent cessait. Alors elle tombait plus vite et recouvrait tout, uniformément, de sa blancheur duveteuse comme si elle avait profité de ce moment d'inattention pour s'installer, en dominatrice, pour s'infiltrer jusqu'entre les fentes des persiennes, sous les tuiles, et même dans les recoins du grenier en passant par un carreau cassé.

78. Les enfants semblent accueillir la neige avec

(A) plaisir
(B) dégoût
(C) tristesse
(D) crainte

79. Les flocons de neige sont comparés à des

(A) fleurs
(B) pierres
(C) oiseaux
(D) insectes

80. Quel effet la neige a-t-elle pour l'auteur?

(A) Elle détruit le monde qui l'entoure.
(B) Elle crée un nouveau décor.
(C) Elle attriste l'observateur.
(D) Elle enlaidit le paysage.

81. Dans le deuxième paragraphe, la neige envahit

(A) une maison
(B) un jardin
(C) une place
(D) une ville

82. Dans ce passage, la neige est

(A) cultivée
(B) balayée
(C) personnifiée
(D) enlevée

83. L'auteur attribue à la neige un pouvoir

(A) fortifiant
(B) magique
(C) chimique
(D) exotique

GO ON TO THE NEXT PAGE

84. Qu'est-ce que cette publicité veut encourager?

(A) La course à pied
(B) La recherche médicale
(C) Des dons d'argent
(D) Des dons d'organes

85. Qui va participer à l'événement annoncé?

(A) Des médecins
(B) Des malades
(C) Des sportifs
(D) Des chercheurs

86. Qu'est-ce qui doit être amélioré?

(A) L'entraînement des jeunes sportifs
(B) L'éducation des futurs médecins
(C) Les techniques médicales
(D) Les chances de survie

END OF SECTION II

STOP

IF YOU FINISH BEFORE TIME IS CALLED, YOU MAY CHECK YOUR WORK ON SECTION II OF THIS TEST.

DO NOT TURN TO ANY OTHER TEST IN THIS BOOK.

How to Score the SAT Subject Test in French with Listening

When you take an actual SAT Subject Test in French with Listening, you receive an overall composite score as well as two subscores: one for the reading section, one for the listening section.

The reading and listening scores are reported on the College Board's 20–80 scale. However the composite score, which is the most significant of the scores reported to the colleges you specify, is in the form of the College Board's 200–800 scale.

The worksheets to calculate your scores are on the following pages.

Worksheet 1. Finding Your Raw Listening Subscore

STEP 1: Table A on page 609 lists the correct answers for all the questions on the Subject Test in French with Listening that is reproduced in this book. It also serves as a worksheet for you to calculate your raw Listening subscore.

- Compare your answers with those given in the table.
- Put a check in the column marked "Right" if your answer is correct.
- Put a check in the column marked "Wrong" if your answer is incorrect.
- Leave both columns blank if you omitted the question.

STEP 2: Count the number of right answers for questions 1–8 and 17–27.

Enter the total here: ________________

STEP 3: Count the number of wrong answers for questions 1–8 and 17–27.

Enter the total here: ________________

STEP 4: Multiply the number of wrong answers by .333.

Enter the product here: ________________

STEP 5: Subtract the result obtained in Step 4 from the total you obtained in Step 2.

Enter the result here: ________________

STEP 6: Count the number of right answers for questions 9–16.

Enter the total here: ________________

STEP 7: Count the number of wrong answers for questions 9–16.

Enter the total here: ________________

STEP 8: Multiply the number of wrong answers for step 7 by .500.

Enter the product here: ________________

STEP 9: Subtract the result obtained in Step 8 from the total you obtained in Step 6.

Enter the result here: ________________

STEP 10: Add the result obtained in Step 5 to the result obtained in Step 9.

Enter the result here: ________________

STEP 11: Round the number obtained in Step 10 to the nearest whole number.

Enter the result here: ________________

The number you obtained in Step 11 is your raw Listening subscore.

Worksheet 2. Finding Your Raw Reading Subscore

STEP 1: Table A lists the correct answers for all the questions on the Subject Test in French with Listening that is reproduced in this book. It also serves as a worksheet for you to calculate your raw Reading subscore.

STEP 2: Count the number of right answers for questions 28–86.

Enter the total here: ____________________

STEP 3: Count the number of wrong answers for questions 28–86.

Enter the total here: ____________________

STEP 4: Multiply the number of wrong answers by .333.

Enter the product here: ____________________

STEP 5: Subtract the result obtained in Step 4 from the total you obtained in Step 2.

Enter the result here: ____________________

STEP 6: Round the number obtained in Step 5 to the nearest whole number.

Enter the result here: ____________________

The number you obtained in Step 6 is your raw Reading subscore.

Worksheet 3. Finding Your Raw Composite Score

STEP 1: Enter your unrounded raw Reading subscore from Step 5 of Worksheet 2.

Enter the result here: ________________

STEP 2: Enter your unrounded raw Listening subscore from Step 10 of Worksheet 1.

Enter the result here: ________________

STEP 3: Add the result obtained in Step 1 to the result obtained in Step 2.

Enter the result here: ________________

STEP 4: Round the number obtained in Step 3 to the nearest whole number.

Enter the result here: ________________

The number you obtained in Step 4 is your raw composite score.

Table A

Answers to the Subject Test in French with Listening and Percentage of Students Answering Each Question Correctly									
Question Number	Correct Answer	Right	Wrong	Percentage of Students Answering the Question Correctly*	Question Number	Correct Answer	Right	Wrong	Percentage of Students Answering the Question Correctly*
1	B			94	33	C			87
2	B			56	34	A			63
3	A			90	35	C			76
4	B			70	36	A			43
5	B			36	37	C			26
6	C			49	38	B			33
7	C			75	39	A			38
8	D			55	40	D			97
9	B			94	41	D			59
10	B			82	42	C			37
11	C			51	43	C			88
12	A			82	44	D			45
13	C			95	45	B			44
14	C			62	46	A			55
15	C			30	47	D			22
16	B			27	48	D			35
17	D			92	49	D			36
18	B			69	50	B			60
19	A			51	51	B			72
20	C			84	52	C			85
21	A			55	53	A			38
22	A			61	54	A			45
23	D			73	55	C			73
24	C			55	56	B			93
25	B			26	57	D			42
26	D			50	58	B			44
27	D			75	59	A			26
28	C			92	60	C			87
29	D			86	61	A			69
30	A			90	62	D			77
31	B			87	63	A			55
32	C			92	64	C			60

Table A continued on next page

Table A continued from previous page

Question Number	Correct Answer	Right	Wrong	Percentage of Students Answering the Question Correctly*	Question Number	Correct Answer	Right	Wrong	Percentage of Students Answering the Question Correctly*
65	D			41	76	B			98
66	D			63	77	D			68
67	A			56	78	A			61
68	A			95	79	D			34
69	D			83	80	B			50
70	C			85	81	A			28
71	D			73	82	C			80
72	A			64	83	B			54
73	C			80	84	D			31
74	D			39	85	C			63
75	B			83	86	D			72

* These percentages are based on an analysis of the answer sheets of a representative sample of 1,519 students who took the original administration of this test and whose mean composite score was 602. They may be used as an indication of the relative difficulty of a particular question.

Answer explanations for the Subject Test in French with Listening can be found on page 616.

Finding Your Scaled Score

When you take SAT Subject Tests, the scores sent to the colleges you specify are reported on the College Board scale, which ranges from 200–800. Subscores are reported on a scale which ranges from 20–80. You can convert your practice test scores to scaled scores by using Tables B, C, and D on the following pages. To find your scaled score, locate your raw score in the left-hand column of the table; the corresponding score in the right-hand column is your scaled score. For example, a raw score of 47 on this particular edition of the Subject Test in French with Listening corresponds to a scaled composite score of 610.

Raw scores are converted to scaled scores to ensure that a score earned on any one edition of a particular Subject Test is comparable to the same scaled score earned on any other edition of the same Subject Test. Because some editions of the tests may be slightly easier or more difficult than others, College Board scaled scores are adjusted so that they indicate the same level of performance regardless of the edition of the test taken and the ability of the group that takes it. Thus, for example, a score of 400 on one edition of a test taken at a particular administration indicates the same level of achievement as a score of 400 on a different edition of the test taken at a different administration.

When you take the SAT Subject Tests during a national administration, your scores are likely to differ somewhat from the scores you obtain on the tests in this book. People perform at different levels at different times for reasons unrelated to the tests themselves. The precision of any test is also limited because it represents only a sample of all the possible questions that could be asked.

Your scaled composite score from Table B is ____________________.

Your scaled listening score from Table C is ____________________.

Your scaled reading score from Table D is ____________________.

Table B

Scaled Score Conversion Table Subject Test in French with Listening Composite Score					
Raw Score	Scaled Score	Raw Score	Scaled Score	Raw Score	Scaled Score
86	800	48	620	10	400
85	800	47	610	9	390
84	800	46	600	8	390
83	800	45	600	7	380
82	800	44	590	6	370
81	800	43	590	5	370
80	800	42	580	4	360
79	800	41	580	3	350
78	800	40	570	2	340
77	800	39	560	1	340
76	800	38	560	0	330
75	800	37	550	-1	320
74	790	36	550	-2	320
73	780	35	540	-3	310
72	770	34	540	-4	300
71	770	33	530	-5	290
70	760	32	530	-6	290
69	750	31	520	-7	280
68	750	30	520	-8	280
67	740	29	510	-9	270
66	730	28	510	-10	270
65	730	27	500	-11	260
64	720	26	490	-12	260
63	710	25	490	-13	260
62	710	24	480	-14	260
61	700	23	480	-15	250
60	690	22	470	-16	240
59	690	21	470	-17	230
58	680	20	460	-18	230
57	670	19	460	-19	220
56	670	18	450	-20	220
55	660	17	440	-21	220
54	650	16	440	-22	220
53	650	15	430	-23	210
52	640	14	430	-24	210
51	640	13	420	-25	210
50	630	12	410	-26	210
49	620	11	410	-27	200
				-28	200
				-29	200
				-30	200

Table C

Scaled Score Conversion Table Subject Test in French with Listening Listening Subscore					
Raw Score	Scaled Score	Raw Score	Scaled Score	Raw Score	Scaled Score
27	80	12	56	-3	30
26	80	11	54	-4	28
25	80	10	53	-5	27
24	79	9	51	-6	26
23	76	8	50	-7	25
22	74	7	48	-8	24
21	72	6	47	-9	23
20	70	5	45	-10	22
19	68	4	43		
18	66	3	42		
17	64	2	40		
16	62	1	38		
15	60	0	36		
14	59	-1	34		
13	57	-2	32		

Table D

Scaled Score Conversion Table Subject Test in French with Listening Reading Subscore					
Raw Score	Scaled Score	Raw Score	Scaled Score	Raw Score	Scaled Score
59	80	32	61	5	40
58	80	31	60	4	39
57	80	30	59	3	38
56	80	29	59	2	37
55	80	28	58	1	36
54	80	27	57	0	35
53	80	26	56	-1	33
52	79	25	55	-2	32
51	78	24	55	-3	31
50	77	23	54	-4	30
49	76	22	53	-5	29
48	76	21	52	-6	28
47	75	20	52	-7	28
46	74	19	51	-8	27
45	73	18	50	-9	26
44	72	17	49	-10	26
43	71	16	49	-11	25
42	70	15	48	-12	24
41	69	14	47	-13	23
40	68	13	46	-14	22
39	67	12	46	-15	22
38	67	11	45	-16	21
37	66	10	44	-17	21
36	65	9	43	-18	20
35	64	8	42	-19	20
34	63	7	41	-20	20
33	62	6	40		

How Did You Do on the Subject Test in French with Listening?

After you score your test and analyze your performance, think about the following questions:

Did you run out of time before reaching the end of the test?

If so, you may need to pace yourself better. For example, maybe you spent too much time on one or two hard questions. A better approach might be to skip the ones you can't answer right away and try answering all the questions that remain on the test. Then if there's time, go back to the questions you skipped.

Did you take a long time reading the directions?

You will save time when you take the test by learning the directions to the Subject Test in French with Listening ahead of time. Each minute you spend reading directions during the test is a minute that you could use to answer questions.

How did you handle questions you were unsure of?

If you were able to eliminate one or more of the answer choices as wrong and guess from the remaining ones, your approach probably worked to your advantage. On the other hand, making haphazard guesses or omitting questions without trying to eliminate choices could cost you valuable points.

How difficult were the questions for you compared with other students who took the test?

Table A shows you how difficult the multiple-choice questions were for the group of students who took this test during its national administration. The right-hand column gives the percentage of students that answered each question correctly.

A question answered correctly by almost everyone in the group is obviously an easier question. For example, 95 percent of the students answered question 13 correctly. But only 22 percent answered question 47 correctly.

Keep in mind that these percentages are based on just one group of students. They would probably be different with another group of students taking the test.

If you missed several easier questions, go back and try to find out why: Did the questions cover material you haven't yet reviewed? Did you misunderstand the directions?

Answer Explanations for the French with Listening Subject Test

1. Choice (B) is the correct answer. The picture shows a cheese stall at an outdoor market, so the statement "The cheese is sold at a market outdoors" best reflects what you see in the picture. Choice (A), "The people are shopping in a department store," is incorrect because the picture is of an outdoor market, not a department store. Choice (C), "The saleswoman has few things to offer," is incorrect because the saleswoman has many cheeses to choose from. Choice (D), "The woman is buying fruits and vegetables," is incorrect because the woman is buying cheese.

2. Choice (B) is the correct answer. The picture shows two men at a table eating, and one man appears to be cutting something on his plate; the statement "This meat is difficult to cut" best reflects what one of the men in the picture might say. Choice (A), "How many guests there are around this table!" is not the best choice because there are only two people at the table. Choice (C), "I like to drink coffee with meals," is incorrect because no one is drinking coffee and there are no coffee cups on the table. Choice (D), "You shouldn't wear the cap at the table!" is incorrect because no one is wearing a cap.

3. Choice (A) is the correct answer. The picture shows a chalet on a wooded, snow-covered hill; the statement "The ski slopes must be very close to the chalet" best reflects what someone in the picture might say. Choice (B), "It's too bad there's no vegetation," is incorrect because there are trees in the picture. Choice (C), "The beach is very close to the chalet," is incorrect because it is unlikely that a beach would be near this snowy, mountainous scene. Choice (D), "We live in a small house with a flat roof," is incorrect because the picture shows a large, three-story chalet with a pitched roof.

4. Choice (B) is the correct answer. The picture shows two people looking at a painting on a wall, so the statement "In my opinion, it is a great work of art," best reflects what someone in the picture might say. Choice (A), "This sculpture doesn't impress me at all," is incorrect because the people are looking at a painting, not a sculpture. Choice (C), "It's difficult for me to decipher these writings," is incorrect because they are not looking at writings. Choice (D), "It's rather a masterpiece of modern architecture," is incorrect because the painting does not depict a modern building.

5. Choice (B) is the correct answer. The picture shows a tiny island with a desk, a computer, and a man waving a flag that he has made out of his shirt; the statement "He is calling for help" best reflects what you see in the picture. Choice (A), "He is doing the laundry," is incorrect because the man is not washing any clothing. Choice (C), "He is using his computer is incorrect," because he is not looking at the computer in the picture. Choice (D), "He is learning to swim," is incorrect because he is not in the water or trying to swim.

6. Choice (C) is the correct answer. The picture shows a smiling performer before a group of eight men, seven of whom are laughing very hard and one of whom looks serious or frightened; the statement "Only one man is not laughing" best reflects what you see in the picture. Choice (A), "They're talking a lot among themselves," is incorrect because the men are laughing, not talking. Choice (B), "They're all enjoying themselves wildly," is incorrect because one of the men in the audience does not appear to be having a good time. Choice (D), "It's difficult to hear," is incorrect because the men in the audience all seem to hear what the performer is saying.

7. Choice (C) is the correct answer. The picture shows a smiling woman in shorts riding a bicycle through the countryside, so the statement "The weather is great for discovering the region" best reflects what the woman in the picture might say. Choice (A), "It's too bad that the weather is cold!" is not the best choice because the woman's clothing indicates that it is quite warm. Choice (B), "How many people there are around me!" is incorrect because the woman is alone. Choice (D), "Traffic is very intense here," is incorrect because there is no traffic and the woman is not even on a paved road.

8. Choice (D) is the correct answer. The picture shows a woman at a sale holding a teacup in front of a table of cups and saucers; the statement, "These cups are a bargain!" best reflects what the woman in the picture might say. Choice (A), "I love going for walks," is incorrect because the woman is shopping, not walking. Choice (B), "I hate doing the dishes," is incorrect because she is not washing the cups and saucers. Choice (C), "Exactly, I needed napkins!" is incorrect because there are no napkins in the picture.

9. Choice (B) is the correct answer. This question asks what Pierre wants to do on Monday. Pierre wants to have fun with his friends. When his father asks him what he wants to do for his birthday on Monday, Pierre says that he is not sure what he wants to do, but rather than have a party, as little kids do, he will perhaps invite two or three friends to dinner and then go to the movies. Although his father suggests going to the park (A), that is not what Pierre says he wants to do. And although Pierre requests a

piece of software as a gift, he does not say that he wants to read a computer manual (C).

10. Choice (B) is the correct answer. This question asks what the father would like to do. He would like to offer his son a gift. After asking Pierre what he would like to do and listening to his thoughts, the father then asks Pierre what he would like as a present. The father does not indicate that he would like to invite his son to dinner in town (A) or to talk to his son's friends (C).

11. Choice (C) is the correct answer. This question asks what Marie's cousin is like. He is thin with long hair. He is not short with short hair (A); in fact, he is rather tall with long hair. He is not heavy with a beard (B) either; he does have a beard, but he is thin (*mince*), not heavy.

12. Choice (A) is the correct answer. This question asks how Marie's cousin will be dressed. Marie says her cousin will be wearing jeans without a doubt; he will be wearing pants, not shorts (B), or a suit (C).

13. Choice (C) is the correct answer. This question asks why Aurélie hasn't seen her friend. She hasn't seen him because she was away on vacation. She went camping in the mountains one week and then spent a week at her sister's; she wasn't on the coast (B) or visiting her mother (A).

14. Choice (C) is the correct answer. This question asks which activity Aurélie usually prefers. Aurélie says that she loves swimming, water-skiing, and the sea, and that she rarely goes camping, so it is clear that she prefers trips to the seaside. She does not mention her grandparents at all, so it cannot be said that she prefers visits to her grandparents (A). Although she enjoyed camping in the mountains (B) and found it a nice change, it is clear that Aurélie's preference is for the sea.

15. Choice (C) is the correct answer. This question asks what the recording advises doing. The recording says, "As a result of congestion, your request cannot succeed. Please call again later (*ultérieurement*)." In other words, the recording says to call later, not to redial the number (A) or check the number (B).

16. Choice (B) is the correct answer. This question asks why the call cannot go through. It is because of congestion (*encombrements*) caused by too many people using the

telephone. It is not because the phone is out of order (A) or because no one answers (C).

17. Choice (D) is the correct answer. This question asks what type of movie the boy and girl are going to see. They are going to see a documentary on unemployment in some other country ("*Un film documentaire ... sur le chômage dans je ne sais plus quel pays*") — in other words, a topical issue. They are not going to see *a pirate story* (A), *an adventure film* (B), or *a spy film* (C).

18. Choice (B) is the correct answer. This question asks what Bernard and Sophie must do at the end of their discussion. *They must hurry* because the movie starts in ten minutes ("*La prochaine séance commence dans dix minutes*"). They do not have to *separate* (A), *go home* (C), or *go to dinner* (D).

19. Choice (A) is the correct answer. This question asks what impression the boy gives. *He is conciliatory*; he agrees to go to the documentary, but only to make Sophie happy ("*Bon, bon, mais c'est vraiment pour te faire plaisir*"). It is not true that the boy *doesn't have any opinions* (B), that *he is stubborn* (C), or that *he is funny* (D).

20. Choice (C) is the correct answer. This question asks why they chose this film. They chose it *because the girl is interested in social problems*, as shown by her comments about serious films making one think about current problems ("*Et puis, les films sérieux font réfléchir aux problèmes actuels. Le chômage, les gens sans travail, il y en a partout, même chez nous*"). They did not choose it *because the girl doesn't like to laugh* (A). They did not choose it *because the boy heard about it* (B) — it is the girl who heard about it. And they did not choose it *because the boy wants to have fun this evening* (D) — the boy would like to have fun, but he would prefer a comedy to a serious documentary.

21. Choice (A) is the correct answer. This question asks which is one of the days that Philippe goes to school only in the morning. Philippe says that he has classes from Monday to Saturday, but on Wednesdays and Saturdays he only "works" (that is, takes classes) in the morning from 8:00 to 12:30 ("*J'ai ... le mercredi et le samedi je ne travaille que le matin. ... heures.*"). *Saturday* is the correct answer, not *Monday* (B), *Tuesday* (C), or *Thursday* (D).

22. Choice (A) is the correct answer. This question asks what Philippe does as soon as he gets home. Philippe says that when he gets home, *he has a snack* ("*Quand je rentre*

chez moi, je prends un petit goûter") before he does other things. He does not *watch television* (B), *call his friends* (C), or *read a novel* (D).

23. Choice (D) is the correct answer. This question asks aside from tennis what other sports activity Philippe prefers. Philippe says he really likes to ride a bike ("... *j'aime bien faire de la bicyclette aussi*"), so the correct answer is *cycling*, not *soccer* (A), *running* (B), or *walking* (C).

24. Choice (C) is the correct answer. This question asks what can be said about Marie-France's work. Marie-France talks about not liking the idea of dragging her work laptop computer into hotels and on to planes ("... *je n'aime pas l'idée de traîner ces machines dans les hôtels, les avions*"), so presumably her work *obliges her to travel*. It cannot be said, based on the dialogue, that her work *is not demanding* (A), that *it is a temporary job* (B), or that *it does not interest Marie-France* (D).

25. Choice (B) is the correct answer. This question asks what Marie-France thinks of laptop computers. Marie-France says that dragging her laptop everywhere deprives her of all intimacy ("... *l'idée de traîner ces machines dans les hôtels, les avions, ou dans ma chambre chez moi. Ça me prive de toute intimité!*"), thus *dehumanizing life*. She does not find laptops *intimidating* (A), nor does *she not deal with them* (D) — she has been using computers for years ("*Ça fait des années que je me sers d'ordinateurs*"). And she does not *think they cost too much* (C) — she does not mention price.

26. Choice (D) is the correct answer. This question asks what Marie-France fears. Marie-France says she likes the boundaries between her professional and personal life and is afraid this computer will erase them ("... *j'aime bien les frontières entre ma vie professionnelle et ma vie personnelle. J'ai un peu peur que cet ordinateur les efface*"); in other words, she fears *that the laptop computer will bring her work life home*. She does not fear *that her children will use the laptop too much* (A), *that she will erase important lines in a report* (B), or *that the computer will cause disputes* (C) — in fact, Caroline suggests a laptop will mean less arguing between Marie-France and her children over computer use. In all the choices the word *ne* is not a negative but rather a grammatical form that appears in clauses following the verb *craindre* ("to fear").

27. Choice (D) is the correct answer. This question asks how one can characterize Caroline's attitude toward the use of laptop computers. Caroline lists the advantages of the laptop and says that everything will work out and the laptop will simplify things ("*Tout se passera bien et cet ordinateur portatif va simplifier les choses!*"). Caroline is *encouraging*, not *neutral* (A), *uninterested* (B), or *sarcastic* (C).

28. Choice (C) is the correct answer. To find the best route from Paris to Tours, one must consult the *map*, not the *city* (A), the *plain* (B), or the *countryside* (D).

29. Choice (D) is the correct answer. The speaker says to turn off the radio because that *noise* is annoying him or her. It does not make sense to say that that *bath* (A), *fog* (B), or *cork* (C) is annoying him or her.

30. Choice (A) is the correct answer. The two candidates wanted to get elected, so each *promised* a lot of improvements to the public. It does not make sense to say that they *asked for* (B), *refused* (C), or *took back* (D) these improvements.

31. Choice (B) is the correct answer. It is necessary to wait for the green light before *crossing* the street. The verb *traverser* means to cross from one side of something to the other. The verb *croiser* (A) can also be translated as "cross," but in the sense of intersecting, so it does not make sense in this context. It does not make sense to say that one must wait for the green light before *extinguishing* (C) or *repairing* (D) the street.

32. Choice (C) is the correct answer. The speaker says that movies don't really excite him or her that much; he or she goes there just *from time to time* (*de temps en temps*). Choices (A), *randomly*, (B), *so-so*, and (D), *repeatedly*, do not make sense in this context.

33. Choice (C) is the correct answer. Yves always speaks in a low voice; therefore, no one *hears* him. It does not make sense to say that no one *carries* (A), *learns* (B), or *attracts* (D) him for this reason.

34. Choice (A) is the correct answer. Thirst tormented him and he passed his tongue over his dry *lips*. It does not make sense to say that he passed his tongue over his dry *cheeks* (B), *jaws* (C), or *eyelids* (D) due to thirst.

35. Choice (C) is the correct answer. These walls are very dirty; they should be *repainted*. It does not make sense to say that the walls should be *returned* (A), *joined* (B), or *climbed back up* (D).

36. Choice (A) is the correct answer. The speaker says he or she has such a sore *elbow* that he or she can hardly play tennis. It does not make sense to say that he or she has a sore *blow* (B), *ham* (C), or *right* (D).

37. Choice (C) is the correct answer. One saw his or her great age in his or her cheeks [which were] full of *wrinkles*. Choice (A), *lignes* ("lines"), refers to lines that are drawn or to rows of things, so it does not make sense in this context. Similarly, choice (B), *traits* ("marks" or "lines"), refers to lines that are made by something such as a pen and does not logically complete the sentence. Choice (D), *traces* ("traces" or "tracks"), also does not logically complete the sentence.

38. Choice (B) is the correct answer. The speaker tells Dominique to turn off the faucet. Otherwise, she is going to cause the bathtub to *overflow*. It does not make sense to say that she is going to *steal* (A), *disgust* (C), or *divert* (D) the bathtub.

39. Choice (A) is the correct answer. The baby took its first *steps* all alone and the whole family applauded. As the object of *a fait*, *pas* completes the idiomatic expression *faire ... pas* ("take ... steps"). The other choices — *words* (B), *feet* (C), and *tears* (D) — do not fit idiomatically or logically in the sentence.

40. Choice (D) is the correct answer. By mutual agreement, they all stood up. The subject of the sentence (*elles*) is feminine and plural and the verb is reflexive and therefore conjugated with *être*, so the past participle must agree with the subject; the past participle *levées* has the feminine *-e* and the plural *–s* endings. The other choices are ungrammatical: Choice (A), *levé*, is masculine singular; choice (B), *levee*, is feminine singular; and choice (C), *levés*, is masculine plural.

41. Choice (D) is the correct answer. The speaker says that next summer he or she would like to travel *to* Mexico. After the verb *voyager* ("travel") and before a masculine place name such as *Mexique*, the idiomatic combination of preposition and article to use is *au*. Choice (B), *en*, is used before feminine place names. Choices (A), *dans*, and (C), *à la*, are not idiomatic after *voyager*.

42. Choice (C) is the correct answer. The newlyweds moved into their *own* apartment. *Propre* ("own") is the only choice that fits grammatically before the masculine noun *appartement* ("apartment"). Choices (A), *grande* ("large"), and (D), *moderne* ("modern"), are both feminine and cannot be used to modify *appartement*; further, *moderne* must follow the noun it modifies, not precede it. Choice (B), *beau* ("beautiful"), is masculine, but it is not the correct form to use before a noun that begins with a vowel; before *appartement*, the form *bel* would have to be used.

43. Choice (C) is the correct answer. The missing pronoun is the subject of the verb *a volé* ("stole") in the second clause, and because only people can steal, the pronoun

must refer to a person: "We would really like to know *who* (*qui*) stole those beautiful paintings." Choice (A), *qu'* ("that"), is incorrect because it is an object pronoun, not a subject pronoun. Likewise, choice (B), *auquel* ("to which" or "to whom"), is incorrect because it cannot serve as the subject of the second clause. Choice (D), *quel* ("which"), is incorrect, because as a subject pronoun it can only refer to things, not to people.

44. Choice (D) is the correct answer. The speaker tells someone to close the door so that the room *can* (*puisse*) stay cool. After the conjunction *afin que* ("so that"), the subjunctive form of the verb is used. All the other choices are indicative forms and therefore ungrammatical. Additionally, choice (C), *pouvez* ("can"), is the second person plural form and therefore cannot be used with the third person singular subject of the second clause, *la pièce* ("the room").

45. Choice (B) is the correct answer. Because the verb in the second clause *serez* ("will be") is in the future tense, the only conjunction among the choices that can be used to join the two clauses is *dès que* ("as soon as"): "We will leave *as soon as* you are [literally, *will be*] ready." Choice (A), *si* ("if"), is incorrect because in a sentence with one verb in the future tense, such as *partira* ("will leave"), the verb after *si* would have to be in the present tense (*êtes*). Choices (C), *sans que* ("without"), and (D), *avant que* ("before"), are incorrect, because they must be followed by the subjunctive (*soyez*), not the indicative.

46. Choice (A) is the correct answer. *Elles* ("them") is the only pronoun among the choices that can grammatically follow a preposition, such as *avec* ("with"). The writer says he or she would like to go there with *them* (*elles*). Choices (B), *tu* ("you"), and (D), *ils* ("they"), are subject pronouns and cannot follow a preposition. As an indirect object pronoun, choice (C), *leur* ("to them"), can only be used before a verb, not after a preposition. As a possessive adjective, *leur* ("their") must be followed by a noun; as a possessive pronoun, *leur* ("theirs") must be preceded by a definite article *le* or *la*. So *leur* is also ungrammatical.

47. Choice (D) is the correct answer. *Guère* ("hardly") is the only choice that can grammatically complete the negative construction *ne ... [?]* around the verb in this sentence: "Believing that Henri would be there, Jeanne *hardly* worried. Choices (A), *souvent* ("often"), and (B), *encore* ("again"), are incorrect because they cannot complete a negative construction beginning with *ne*. Choice (C), *nul* ("no"), is incorrect because although it can form a negative construction with *ne*, it must be immediately followed by a noun, which it modifies.

48. Choice (D) is the correct answer. They *have been* (*sont*) in Montreal for three years and they like it there. The phrase *depuis trois ans* ("for three years") indicates that they are still living in Montreal. In French, unlike in English, when describing a situation that began in the past and continues to the present, the present tense (here, *sont*) is used. The tenses in the other choices are ungrammatical.

49. Choice (D) is the correct answer. The missing word is a relative pronoun that refers to *événement* ("event") and grammatically completes the second clause *je me souviendrai toujours* ("I will always remember"). Because the verb *se souvenir* ("remember") does not take a direct object but is instead followed by a phrase beginning with *de*, the correct choice is *dont* ("of which"): the speaker says that this is an event *that* [literally, *of which*] he or she will always remember. Choice (A), *que* ("that"), is incorrect because it is a direct object pronoun, but *se souvenir* does not take a direct object. Choice (B), *qui* ("that"), is incorrect because it is a subject pronoun, but *se souvenir* already has a subject, *je*. Choice (C), *auquel* ("to which"), is incorrect because *se souvenir* is followed by the preposition *de*, not *à*.

50. Choice (B) is the correct answer. The speaker says that his or her lawyer handles his or her affairs well. *De* is the preposition that idiomatically follows the verb *s'occuper* ("to handle"). Choice (A), *des*, formed from *de* + *les*, cannot grammatically occur before the possessive adjective *mes*. And choices (C), *á*, and (D), *en*, are not idiomatic.

51. Choice (B) is the correct answer. Because the situation described was in the past, specifically last night (*hier soir*), the verb must be in the past tense. The imperfect tense *avions* is the only choice in a past tense: "Last night as we *had* nothing better to do ..." The other choices do not logically complete the sentence: *avons* (A) is the present tense, *aurions* (C) is the conditional, and *ayons* (D) is the imperative.

52. Choice (C) is the correct answer: "... we walked in the park for two and a *half* hours ..." *Demie* ("half") is used to refer to a half hour when talking about a period of time. Choice (A), *midi* ("noon"), does not make sense in this context. Choices (B), *trente* ("thirty"), and (D), *le quart* ("a quarter"), are used in expressions for telling time, but not to describe periods of time.

53. Choice (A) is the correct answer. The missing word is a relative pronoun that refers to *mon copain* ("my friend") and serves as the direct object of *gêne* ("bothers"), which has the subject *rien* ("nothing"): "My friend, *whom* (*que*) nothing bothers, fell asleep right away ..." *Que* is the only choice that is a direct object relative pronoun. Choices (B), *quell* ("which" or "what"), (C), *celui* ("that one"), and (D), *quelqu'un* ("someone"), are not relative pronouns and do not fit grammatically in the sentence.

54. Choice (A) is the correct answer. *Tandis [que]* ("whereas") is the only choice that fits logically and grammatically in the sentence: "My friend ... fell asleep right away, *whereas* I could not close [...]" Choices (B), *de sorte [que]* ("so that"), and (D), *autant [que]* ("so much that"), do not fit logically in the sentence. Choice (C) is ungrammatical: *Sans [que]* ("without") must be followed by a subjunctive verb, but the verb here *ai* is in the indicative.

55. Choice (C) is the correct answer. *L'oeil* ("eye") idiomatically completes the expression *ne pas fermer l'oeil* ("not sleep a wink"): "My friend ... fell asleep right away, whereas I could not sleep a wink [literally, *close the eye*]." Choices (A), *l'oreiller* ("the pillow"), (B), *le lit* ("the bed"), and (D), *la couverture* ("the blanket"), do not fit idiomatically or logically in the sentence.

56. Choice (B) is the correct answer. The writer says that he or she still had before him or her *the image* (*l'image*) of that poor man ... Choices (A), *le site* ("the site"), (C), *la copie* ("the copy"), and (D), *le signe* ("the sign"), do not fit logically in the sentence.

57. Choice (D) is the correct answer. The writer describes the poor *hungry* (*affamé*) man that they saw sitting at the entrance of the park. Choices (A), *file* ("spun"), (B), *fume* ("smoked"), and (C), *enterré* ("buried"), do not fit logically in the sentence.

58. Choice (B) is the correct answer. The poor hungry man was seated on *a bench* (*un banc*). It does not make sense to suggest that he was seated on *a suburb* (A), *a banquet* (C), or *a bank* (D).

59. Choice (A) is the correct answer. *Tôt le matin* is the idiomatic way to express "early in the morning." The other choices—*Tôt matin* (B), *Tôt du matin* (C), and *Tôt dans le matin* (D)—are not idiomatic.

60. Choice (C) is the correct answer. The missing word is a relative pronoun that refers to *mon père* ("my father") and serves as the subject of *a conduit* ("drove"): "It was my father *who* (*qui*) drove." Choice (A) is ungrammatical; *a conduit* requires a subject, and *mon père* is already the complement of *est* ("is"), so it cannot also be the subject of *a conduit*. Choice (B), *il* ("he"), is not a relative pronoun and cannot join the two clauses. Choice (D), *qu'* ("that"), is an object pronoun and cannot serve as the subject of *a conduit*.

61. Choice (A) is the correct answer. When speaking about the weather, *faire* is the idiomatic verb to use with *frais* ("cool"): "It [the weather] *was* (*faisait*) still very cool, but the sun was shining." The other choices are not idiomatic.

62. Choice (D) is the correct answer. "And of course, everyone was *in a good mood* (*de bonne humeur*)." It does not make sense to say that everyone was *if absolutely necessary* (A), *early* (B), or *in the wind* (C) in this context.

63. Choice (A) is the correct answer. The writer says, "When we arrived in a magnificent *place* (*endroit*) ..." It does not make sense to say that they arrived in a magnificent *lake* (B) or *altitude* (D). *Une place* (C) can be translated as "a place," but in the sense of a town plaza, a space, or a seat, since the family was going for a hike in the mountains, it does not make sense here.

64. Choice (C) is the correct answer. *De* is the idiomatic preposition to use after the verb *avons décidé* ("decided") before an infinitive (here, *marcher* "walk"). The other choices are not idiomatic. The preposition *à* (D) is used after the reflexive verb *se décider*, but here the verb is not reflexive.

65. Choice (D) is the correct answer. Because the clause begins with the preposition *en*, the following verb must be the present participle *arrêtant*; the *nous* before the verb is not the subject "we," but the reflexive object "ourselves": "... we decided to walk, *stopping* [ourselves] from time to time ..." The other choices are ungrammatical.

66. Choice (D) is the correct answer. The verb *reposer* requires a reflexive object, and *nous* ("ourselves") is the correct reflexive object for the subject *nous* ("we"): "... we decided to walk, stopping from time to time to rest [*ourselves*]." Choice (A) lacks an object for *reposer.* Choices (B), *se* ("oneself"), and (C), *me* ("myself"), do not match the subject *nous*, so they are ungrammatical.

67. Choice (A) is the correct answer. The writer says, "Around noon we picnicked *along* (*au bord d'*) a mountain stream. Choices (B), *à bord d'* ("on board"), (C), *autour d'* ("around"), and (D), *au fond d'* ("at the bottom of"), do not fit logically in the sentence.

68. Choice (A) is the correct answer. This question asks what the narrator of the passage is complaining about. She is complaining about the absence of Gaston, her husband. She asks when he will come, reminds him that he promised to join her and her mother, and wonders how he could have gone ten long days without seeing her

(*Quand viendrez-vous? ... sans me voir*). She does not complain about *the noise of the city* (B), Gaston's mother (C) — she writes only of her own mother — or *her recent illness* (D) — she mentions no illness at all, other than being listless (*languissante*) without him.

69. Choice (D) is the correct answer. This question asks where the narrator of the passage finds herself. She writes of how long the hours are in Paris (*Dieu! Que les heures sont longues à Paris*) and of looking for Gaston in the streets of Paris when she goes out with her mother (*Quand je sors ... vous n'y êtes pas*), so it is clear she is *in a large city* (Paris). She is not *in the countryside* (A), *near the sea* (B), or *in her home village* (C).

70. Choice (C) is the correct answer. This question asks what the attitude of the narrator's mother toward Gaston is. The narrator says that her mother does nothing but speak badly of Gaston (*Maman me parle à chaque instant contre vous*), so she shows a certain hostility toward him. She does not *find him nice* (A), she does not *feel indifference toward him* (B), nor does she *love him nearly as much as her daughter* (D).

71. Choice (D) is the correct answer. This question asks to whom the narrator is writing. She says that at moments she believes she is not the wife of the man she is writing to and that the beautiful ceremony at the church — their wedding — was a dream that ended too soon (*Imaginez-vous que ... a trop tôt fini*). Thus, the man is *her husband*, not *her brother* (A), *her lover* (B), or *her fiancé* (C).

72. Choice (A) is the correct answer. This question asks what the phrase "You are not a man who would close a good book on the first page" implies. Because the narrator talks of her wedding to Gaston (lines 15-16) and her mother's claim that he has now abandoned her, which she does not herself believe (lines 9-10), we can understand that *the narrator recently married Gaston* and does not believe that he would end things so prematurely. The phrase does not imply that *the narrator is a librarian* (B), that *Gaston distrusts the narrator* (C), or that *Gaston does not like short books* (D).

73. Choice (C) is the correct answer. This question asks what the text indicates the narrator does when she goes for walks with her mother. The narrator writes that when she goes out with her mother, she looks for Gaston in the streets (*Quand je sors ... dans les rues*, lines 18-19); in other words, *she looks for Gaston everywhere*. She does not talk about *saying prayers for Gaston* (A), *buying presents for Gaston* (B), or *talking about Gaston to her mother* (D).

74. Choice (D) is the correct answer. This question asks what the narrator suggests Gaston's state of mind might be. The narrator suggests that Gaston might be annoyed at her for having left so brusquely without saying goodbye (*Peut-être m'en voulez-vous de vous avoir quitté si brusquement et sans vous dire adieu*, lines 25-26); in other words, she suggests Gaston *is angry with her.* She does not suggest that *he is afraid to tell her goodbye* (A), that *he is sad when it is foggy* (B), or that *he is rather religious* (C).

75. Choice (B) is the correct answer. This question asks why the narrator left Gaston. The narrator says that it was not she who left; it was her mother who took her away (*Ce n'est pas moi ... qui m'a enlevée*); in other words, she *was obliged to leave him*. She does not say that she *prefers Paris to the countryside* (A), that she *needs medical treatment* (C), or that she *wants to become a nun* (D).

76. Choice (B) is the correct answer. This question asks what *la carte Intégrale* allows you to do. The text says that the card is a personal, permanent subscription that can be used at will on the commuter trains, buses, and subways in Ile de France (*Un abonnement personnel ... d'Ile de France*). Thus, it allows you *to use all public transportation*. It does not allow you *to rent a car at a reduced rate* (A), *to manage all your monthly expenses at once* (C), or *to get the most recent weekly publications* (D).

77. Choice (D) is the correct answer. This question asks for what period the card is valid. The title of the ad calls it an annual orange card (*carte orange annuelle*) and the second sentence says the card is valid the whole year (*valable toute l'année*), so it is valid for *twelve months*. Although it is referred to as a permanent subscription (*abonnement ... permanent*), it is not valid for *a lifetime* (A), nor is it valid for only *a month* (B), or just during *vacation* (C).

78. Choice (A) is the correct answer. This question asks what emotion the children seem to welcome the snow with. The use of exclamation points in the first two sentences indicate an excitement about the sudden changes the snow makes, and the author speaks of a near intoxication of feeling the snowflakes on their faces (*Dehors, quand nous ... c'était presque une ivresse ... visage*). The children greeted the snow with *pleasure*, not *disgust* (B), *sadness* (C), or *fear* (D).

79. Choice (D) is the correct answer. This question asks what the snowflakes are compared to. The writer speaks of the snowflakes as thousands of small white bees whose coldness stung their faces (... *ces milles petites abeilles blanches* ...); he or she is comparing the snowflakes to *insects*, not to *flowers* (A), *stones* (B), or *birds* (C).

80. Choice (B) is the correct answer. This question asks what effect the snow has for the author. The author talks about the sudden transformation the snow causes around them (... *quelle transformation subite* ...), and how the snow changes the gates of the college, branches, and roofs into different gates, benches, and roofs (*Et peu à peu ... toits*). Clearly, the author feels that the snow *creates a new scenery*, not that *it destroys the world around him or her* (A), that *it saddens the observer* (C), or that *it spoils the landscape* (D).

81. Choice (A) is the correct answer. This question asks what, in the second paragraph, the snow invades. The writer talks about the snow infiltrating the corners of the attic (*grenier*) through a broken rooftile (*carreau cassé*), so the snow is invading *a house*, not *a garden* (B), *a plaza* (C), or *a town* (D).

82. Choice (C) is the correct answer. This question asks how the snow is treated in the passage. To describe the snow's actions, the author uses verbs such as *choisir* ("choose"), *profiter de* ("take advantage of"), *s'installer* ("settle in"), and *s'infiltrer* ("infiltrate"), which normally describe actions performed by people. The snow is *personified*; it is not *cultivated* (A), *swept* (B), or *removed* (D) in the passage.

83. Choice (B) is the correct answer. This question asks what type of power the author attributes to the snow. Since the author talks about the transformation caused by the snow (... *quelle transformation subite* ...) and the way it changes everything into something different (*Et peu à peu ... toits*), the best word to describe the snow's power is *magical*, not *invigorating* (A), *chemical* (C), or *exotic* (D).

84. Choice (D) is the correct answer. This question asks what the announcement aims to encourage. The ad says that 6,000 sick people are waiting for a transplant (*greffe*) that will save their lives and then says what they are *not* waiting for: progress in medical treatment (*progrès dans le traitement*) or available medical teams (*qu'une équipe médicale soit disponible*). What the people want is the kidney, heart, lung, liver that is irreparably lost (*le rein ... perdus*). The ad then calls on readers to pass on life (*Faites passer la vie*). Although the ad announces a relay race before the Paris marathon, the aim of the ad and of the relay is to encourage *organ donation*, not *a race* (A), *medical research* (B), or *monetary donations* (C).

85. Choice (C) is the correct answer. This question asks who is going to participate in the announced event. Because it is a relay race (*relais*), the participants will be *athletes*, not *doctors* (A), *patients* (B), or *researchers* (D).

86. Choice (D) is the correct answer. This question asks what should be improved. Currently 6,000 people need organ transplants, so their *chances of survival* should be improved. The ad makes no mention of *the training of young athletes* (A) or *the education of future doctors* (B). The announcement says that *the medical techniques* (C) are fully developed (*parfaitment à point*), so they do not need to be improved.

Chapter 10
German

Purpose

There are two Subject Tests in German: German and German with Listening. The reading-only test measures your ability to understand written German. German with Listening measures your ability to understand spoken and written German.

Format

- The Subject Test in German takes one hour and includes 85 multiple-choice questions.
- The Subject Test in German with Listening also takes one hour and includes 90 multiple-choice listening and reading questions. Listening questions require answers to questions based on shorter and longer listening selections.
- Both tests evaluate your reading ability through a variety of questions requiring a wide-ranging knowledge of German.

Content

Both tests comply with the German spelling reform (Rechtschreibreform) as much as possible. They evaluate reading ability in these areas:

Sentence completion and paragraph completion questions test vocabulary and grammar requiring you to know the meaning of words and idiomatic expressions in context and to identify usage that is structurally correct and appropriate. For each omission, you must select the choice that BEST fits each sentence.

Reading comprehension questions test your understanding of the content of various materials taken from sources such as advertisements, timetables, street signs, forms, and tickets. They also examine your ability to read passages representative of various styles and levels of difficulty. Each test edition has several prose passages followed by questions that test your understanding of the passage. The passages, mostly adapted from literary sources and newspapers or magazines, are generally one or two paragraphs in length and test whether you can identify the main idea or comprehend facts or details in the text.

The Subject Test in German with Listening also measures the ability to understand spoken language with two types of listening questions:

Type One contains short dialogues/monologues with one or two multiple-choice questions. Dialogues/monologues, questions, and answer choices are recorded. The test questions are also printed in the test book.

Type Two contains longer dialogues and monologues with several multiple-choice questions. Dialogues/monologues and questions are only recorded and not printed in the test book. Answer choices are not recorded; they appear only in the test book.

German	
Skills Measured	Approximate Percentage of Test
Vocabulary in Context and Structure in Context (grammar)	50%
Reading Comprehension (authentic stimulus materials and passages)	50%

German with Listening	
Test Sections	Approximate Percentage of Test
Listening Section (20 minutes)	35%
Short dialogues/monologues Long dialogues/monologues	
Reading Section (40 minutes)	65%
Vocabulary in Context Structure in Context (grammar) Reading Comprehension—(authentic stimulus materials and passages)	

How to Prepare

Both tests assume differences in language preparation; neither is tied to a specific textbook or method of instruction. The German tests are appropriate for students who have completed two, three, or four years of German language study in high school or the equivalent. Your best preparation for these tests is a gradual development of competence in German over a period of years. Familiarize yourself with directions in advance. The directions in this book are identical to those that appear on the test.

German with Listening

A practice audio CD for the full-length practice test is included with this book. A practice CD with different sample questions can be obtained, along with a copy of the *Getting Ready for the SAT Subject Tests* booklet, from your school counselor, or you can access the files at www.collegeboard.org. If your counselor does not have the CD or booklet, he or she can order these from the College Board.

CD Players

Using CD Players for Language Tests with Listening

Take an acceptable CD player to the test center. Your CD player must be in good working order, so insert fresh batteries on the day before the test. You may bring additional batteries and a backup player to the test center. CD players cannot be shared with other test-takers.

Test center staff won't have batteries, CD players, or earphones for your use, so your CD player must be:

- equipped with earphones
- portable (hand-held)
- battery operated

You are not allowed to use a CD player with recording or duplicating capabilities.

Note

If the volume on your CD player disturbs other test-takers, the test center supervisor may ask you to move to another seat.

What to do if your CD player malfunctions:

- Raise your hand and tell the test supervisor.
- Switch to backup equipment if you have it and continue the test. If you don't have backup equipment, your score on the Subject Test in German with Listening will be canceled. But scores on other Subject Tests you take that day will still be counted.

What if you receive a defective CD on test day? Raise your hand and ask the supervisor for a replacement.

Scores

For both tests, the total score is reported on the 200-to-800 scale. For the listening test, listening and reading subscores are reported on the 20-to-80 scale.

Sample Reading Questions

Your answer sheet has five answer positions marked A, B, C, D, and E, while the questions throughout this test contain only four choices. Be sure NOT to make any marks in column E.

Part A

Directions: This part consists of a number of incomplete statements, each having four suggested completions. Select the most appropriate completion and fill in the corresponding circle on the answer sheet.

1. Ich glaube, er kommt schon........Mittwoch zurück.
   (A) nächstem
   (B) nächster
   (C) nächstes
   (D) nächsten

Choice (D) is the correct answer to question 1. This question tests your knowledge of the correct weak adjective ending following a presupposed dative-preposition that would answer to the question "when" ("wann"). You need to know that the gender of "Mittwoch" is masculine and that the correct preposition (eliminated here) would be "an." The entire prepositional phrase would be: an dem (am) nächsten Mittwoch; however, "am" or "an dem" is eliminated, an ellipsis very commonly used in temporal phrases. Choices (A), (B), and (C) cannot structurally be preceded by "am" or "an dem."

2. Diesen Sommer konnten die Touristen in Europa gar nicht über das Wetter........
   (A) sagen
   (B) kennen
   (C) klagen
   (D) denken

Choice (C) is the correct answer to question 2. This question tests your knowledge of verbs in combination with a negation and a preposition. You are asked to choose the verb that fits best. Given the context (tourists could not complain about the weather in Europe this year), "klagen" is the only possible option that not only fits contextually but also structurally.

3. Annie ist die jüngste Tochter der Familie, bei........wir diesen Sommer gewohnt haben.
   (A) dem
   (B) denen
   (C) der
   (D) die

Choice (C) is the correct answer to question 3. This question asks you to choose the correct form of the relative pronoun "die" following the preposition "bei." You should know that "bei" asks for the dative and that the gender of "Familie," to which the relative pronoun refers, is feminine. Choice (C) is therefore the only possible answer, since "der" is the dative form of "die."

Part B

Directions: In each of the following paragraphs, there are numbered blanks indicating that words or phrases have been omitted. For each numbered blank, four completions are provided. First read through the entire paragraph. Then, for each numbered blank, choose the completion that is most appropriate and fill in the corresponding circle on the answer sheet.

Ich verabschiede mich jetzt, weil ich morgen ____________________.

4. (A) gern
   (B) früh
   (C) schon
   (D) langsam

aufstehen muss, um __________ Berlin zu einer wichtigen

5. (A) auf
   (B) an
   (C) nach
   (D) zu

Konferenz __________

6. (A) fährt
   (B) fahren
   (C) gefahren
   (D) zu fahren

Choice (B) is the correct answer to question 4. This question is a vocabulary question that tests your knowledge of adverbs. You are asked to choose the adverb that fits best. Given the context (the person has to go on a business trip), "früh" is the most appropriate of the four choices to complement the verb "aufstehen."

Choice (C) is the correct answer to question 5. In this question, you are asked to choose the correct preposition, which, here is part of an idiomatic expression. You need to know that of the four choices only the preposition "nach" is appropriate in connection with a motion verb (fahren) and the name of a city (Berlin).

Choice (D) is the correct answer to question 6. In this question, you are asked to choose the correct form of the verb "fahren." The infinitive form of "fahren" with "zu" is required because the clause is introduced by "um." The other choices—(A) third person singular present tense, (B) infinitive without "zu," (C) past participle—are therefore not appropriate to form a grammatically correct sentence.

Part C

Directions: Read the following texts carefully for comprehension. Each is followed by a number of questions or incomplete statements. Select the answer or completion that is best according to the text and fill in the corresponding circle on the answer sheet.

Betreten der Baustelle verboten

Eltern haften für ihre Kinder!

7. Wo findet man dieses Schild?
   (A) Auf einem Kinderspielplatz
   (B) An einem Gefängnis
   (C) Vor einer Baumschule
   (D) Auf einem Bauplatz

Choice (D) is the correct answer to question 7. This question asks you where you would see such a sign. This sign tells you that you are not to enter the construction site. It continues that parents are responsible for their children's actions. "Bauplatz" in choice (D) is a synonym for "Baustelle." Both nouns, translated into English, mean construction site. Choice (A) refers to a playground (*Kinderspielplatz*), choice (B) to a prison (*Gefängnis*), and choice (C) to a nursery (*Baumschule*).

Der Frankfurter Sinkkasten ist ein Verein, der von drei jungen Leuten—Aina, Wolfgang und Werner—in einem Kellergewölbe am Main gegründet wurde, nachdem sie sich eines Tages entschlossen hatten, ihren Feierabend nicht weiter in Kneipen zu verbringen.

Der Sinkkasten verlangt einen Mitgliedsbeitrag von drei Euro monatlich, obgleich es ihm gar nicht um Gewinne geht. Hier können aber endlich jeden Abend Jugendliche zusammenkommen und fröhlich sein. Im Sinkkasten treten außerdem viele prominente Musiker und Gruppen auf. Dazu kommen dann noch interessante Theateraufführungen. Oft werden den Gästen auch sehr gute Filme gezeigt. Junge Maler können hier ihre ersten Werke ausstellen, und regelmäßig dürfen die jungen Gäste selbst auch mal Künstler spielen: sie können beim freien Malen ihre bisher verborgenen Talente entdecken. Die schönsten Werke werden anschließend ausgestellt.

Das Programm ersetzt den Jugendlichen Theater, Kino und Kneipe zugleich. Deshalb kommen sie auch in Scharen! Längst hat es sich herumgesprochen, dass man im Sinkkasten ganz nette Leute kennenlernen kann. Die Stadtverwaltung von Frankfurt am Main hat inzwischen den Sinkkasten schätzen gelernt: seit Anfang 1995 wird der Klub vom Kulturamt mit Geld unterstützt.

8. Was können die Gäste in diesem Klub tun?
   - (A) Ihre eigenen Schöpfungen ausstellen
   - (B) Endlich ihre Kochkunst zeigen
   - (C) Ohne monatlichen Beitrag alles mitmachen
   - (D) Die täglichen Hausaufgaben erledigen

Choice (A) is the correct answer to question 8. In this question, you are asked what club members and guests can do when visiting the "Sinkkasten." To answer this question, you have to read the second and third paragraphs carefully. Nothing is mentioned with respect to choices (B) "Kochkunst" and (D) "Hausaufgaben." "Monatlicher Beitrag" in choice (C) is mentioned in the second paragraph ("Mitgliedsbeitrag … monatlich"), but it is stated here that each member of the "Sinkkasten" has to contribute 3,-E per month, while choice (C) describes exactly the opposite. Choice (A) *Ihre eigenen Schöpfungen ausstellen* is the only correct answer to the question and is supported by "regelmäßig dürfen die jungen Gäste selbst auch mal Künstler spielen:" … up to … "Die schönsten Werke werden anschließend ausgestellt."

9. Was kann man im allgemeinen über den Klub sagen?
   (A) Er ist das Kulturzentrum der Stadt Frankfurt.
   (B) Er ist finanzieller Mittelpunkt für die Stadtväter.
   (C) Er ist Anziehungspunkt für viele junge Leute.
   (D) Er ist als kultureller Treffpunkt nicht erfolgreich.

Choice (C) is the correct answer to question 9. This question asks what can be said in general about this club ("Der Sinkkasten"). The entire reading passage includes information about how and where young people used to spend their free time and how "der Sinkkasten" has changed their habits and what the club means to them. Choice (C) *Er ist Anziehungspunkt für viele junge Leute* summarizes in one sentence this passage and is therefore the only correct answer. Choice (A) describes the club as the cultural center ("Kulturzentrum") of the city of Frankfurt, which is obviously never mentioned in the text. Choice (B) refers wrongly to the club as a financial center for representatives of the city government, and choice (D) claims erroneously that the club is unsuccessful as a cultural meeting place.

German Subject Test

Practice Helps

The test that follows is an actual, previously administered SAT Subject Test in German. To get an idea of what it's like to take this test, practice under conditions that are much like those of an actual test administration.

- Set aside an hour when you can take the test uninterrupted.
- Sit at a desk or table with no other books or papers. Dictionaries, other books, or notes are not allowed in the test room.
- Tear out an answer sheet from the back of this book and fill it in just as you would on the day of the test. One answer sheet can be used for up to three Subject Tests.
- Read the instructions that precede the practice test. During the actual administration you will be asked to read them before answering test questions.
- Time yourself by placing a clock or kitchen timer in front of you.
- After you finish the practice test, read the sections "How to Score the SAT Subject Test in German" and "How Did You Do on the Subject Test in German?"
- The appearance of the answer sheet in this book may differ from the answer sheet you see on test day.

GERMAN TEST

The top portion of the page of the answer sheet that you will use to take the German Test must be filled in exactly as illustrated below. When your supervisor tells you to fill in the circle next to the name of the test you are about to take, mark your answer sheet as shown.

○ Literature	○ Mathematics Level 1	● German	○ Chinese Listening	○ Japanese Listening
○ Biology E	○ Mathematics Level 2	○ Italian	○ French Listening	○ Korean Listening
○ Biology M	○ U.S. History	○ Latin	○ German Listening	○ Spanish Listening
○ Chemistry	○ World History	○ Modern Hebrew		
○ Physics	○ French	○ Spanish	**Background Questions:** ① ② ③ ④ ⑤ ⑥ ⑦ ⑧ ⑨	

After filling in the circle next to the name of the test you are taking, locate the Background Questions box on your answer sheet (as shown above). This is where you will answer the following Background Questions on your answer sheet.

BACKGROUND QUESTIONS

Please answer either Part I or Part II below by filling in the appropriate circle in the Background Questions box on your answer sheet. Fill in ONLY ONE circle, as described below, to indicate how you obtained your knowledge of German. The information you provide is for statistical purposes only and will not affect your test score.

Part I — If your knowledge of German comes primarily from any of the following: living in a home where German is the main spoken language, living for six months or longer in a German-speaking country that included significant experience in German language, courses taken at a college, or special study of German, fill in circle 9 and leave the remaining circles blank, regardless of how long you studied the subject in school.

Part II — If your knowledge of German comes primarily from courses taken in secondary school, fill in the circle that indicates the level of the German course in which you are currently enrolled. If you are not now enrolled in a German course, fill in the circle that indicates the level of the most advanced course in German that you have completed.

• First year:	first or second half	—Fill in circle 1.
• Second year:	first half	—Fill in circle 2.
	second half	—Fill in circle 3.
• Third year:	first half	—Fill in circle 4.
	second half	—Fill in circle 5.
• Fourth year:	first half	—Fill in circle 6.
	second half	—Fill in circle 7.
• Advanced Placement course or a course at a level higher than fourth year, second half or high school course work plus a minimum of four weeks of study abroad		—Fill in circle 8.

When the supervisor gives the signal, turn the page and begin the German Test. There are 100 numbered circles on the answer sheet and 85 questions in the German Test. Therefore, use only circles 1 to 85 for recording your answers.

GERMAN TEST

PLEASE NOTE THAT YOUR ANSWER SHEET HAS FIVE ANSWER POSITIONS, MARKED A, B, C, D, E, WHILE THE QUESTIONS THROUGHOUT THIS TEST CONTAIN ONLY FOUR CHOICES. BE SURE NOT TO MAKE ANY MARKS IN COLUMN E.

PART A

Directions: This part consists of a number of incomplete statements, each having four suggested completions. Select the most appropriate completion and fill in the corresponding circle on the answer sheet.

1. ------- ist die neue Schülerin in unserer Klasse.

(A) Er
(B) Sie
(C) Wir
(D) Ihr

2. Ich möchte mir den Film ansehen. Gehen wir ------- Kino.

(A) ans
(B) ins
(C) aufs
(D) zum

3. Brigitte, bitte ------- mir nicht böse!

(A) seien
(B) sei
(C) sein
(D) seist

4. Sie isst viel Gemüse und Obst, ------- es gesund ist.

(A) weil
(B) ob
(C) bevor
(D) nachdem

5. Ich mache dir eine Skizze, denn mein Haus ist nicht leicht -------.

(A) zu finden
(B) finden
(C) findend
(D) gefunden

6. Das hier ist doch dein Buch. Siehst du irgendwo -------?

(A) meine
(B) meins
(C) mein
(D) meinen

7. Warum fragst du mich das schon wieder? Hast du denn nicht -------?

(A) aufgepasst
(B) angehört
(C) wiederholt
(D) vergessen

8. Deine Bemerkung beim Essen war doch etwas -------.

(A) richtig
(B) frühzeitig
(C) gut
(D) eigenartig

9. Heike ist arbeitslos. Sie möchte sich bei uns ------- eine Stelle bewerben.

(A) in
(B) um
(C) an
(D) über

GO ON TO THE NEXT PAGE

10. Bei mir zu Hause musste man ------- immer vor dem Essen die Hände waschen.

(A) wir
(B) dich
(C) sie
(D) sich

11. Es ist ------- sehr spät und ich gehe schlafen.

(A) fast
(B) schon
(C) erst
(D) schön

12. Wir sind nicht -------, so viel Geld für ein neues Auto auszugeben.

(A) zufrieden
(B) fertig
(C) vollständig
(D) imstande

13. Franz ist in der Küche und will ------- Hühnchen braten.

(A) einen
(B) eine
(C) ein
(D) eines

14. Wir sind alle zu ihrem Geburtstag eingeladen -------.

(A) worden
(B) wurden
(C) werden
(D) geworden

15. Wie spät ist es? Meine ------- ist stehen geblieben.

(A) Uhr
(B) Zeit
(C) Stunde
(D) Seite

16. Nach ------- Krankheit ist ihr Vater endlich wieder gesund.

(A) lange
(B) langer
(C) langes
(D) langem

17. Ich sage dir nicht, was dieses Wort -------!

(A) versteht
(B) kennt
(C) kann
(D) bedeutet

18. Gib mir bitte noch ein Stück -------!

(A) Brot
(B) von Brot
(C) Brote
(D) dem Brot

GO ON TO THE NEXT PAGE

PART B

Directions: In each of the following paragraphs, there are numbered blanks indicating that words or phrases have been omitted. For each numbered blank, four completions are provided. First read through the entire paragraph. Then, for each numbered blank, choose the completion that is most appropriate and fill in the corresponding circle on the answer sheet.

Mark geht einkaufen

Mark wurde in die Stadt geschickt, um einige Besorgungen (19) . Zuerst ging er (20) Markt, wo er Gemüse (21) wollte. Er fand die (22) preiswert und ließ sich ein Kilogramm abwiegen. Dann (23) er auch noch zum Bäcker gehen.

19. (A) machen
(B) macht
(C) zu machen
(D) gemacht

20. (A) zum
(B) nach
(C) beim
(D) im

21. (A) kaufe
(B) kauft
(C) kaufen
(D) kaufst

22. (A) Tasche
(B) Bohnen
(C) Blumen
(D) Torte

23. (A) musst
(B) müssten
(C) müsst
(D) musste

GO ON TO THE NEXT PAGE

Ein Theaterbesuch

Liebe Hilde,

Gestern Abend haben Anne und ___(24)___ im Theater die „Dreigroschenoper" gesehen. Du kannst dir nicht ___(25)___, wie toll das war. Der Mann, ___(26)___ die Hauptrolle gespielt hat, ist nicht nur ein guter Sänger, ___(27)___ auch ein großartiger Schauspieler. Als er ___(28)___ Tochter von Peachum das Liebeslied sang, wäre ich ___(29)___ aufgestanden, um sie vor ihm zu warnen. Die ___(30)___ Schauspieler waren aber auch gut. Nächste Woche, wenn du zu uns kommst, solltest du unbedingt die Vorstellung sehen. ___(31)___ mir Bescheid, wenn ich dir eine Karte besorgen soll.

Alles Gute,

Gunter

24. (A) er
    (B) ich
    (C) sie
    (D) ihr

25. (A) vorstellen
    (B) ansehen
    (C) vornehmen
    (D) einbilden

26. (A) was
    (B) wer
    (C) das
    (D) der

27. (A) aber
    (B) wie
    (C) sondern
    (D) obwohl

28. (A) die
    (B) der
    (C) dem
    (D) den

29. (A) täglich
    (B) morgens
    (C) beinahe
    (D) immer

30. (A) andere
    (B) anderer
    (C) anderen
    (D) anderes

31. (A) Gib
    (B) Gibt
    (C) Gebe
    (D) Gibst

GO ON TO THE NEXT PAGE

Ein neues Geschäft

Gestern habe ich noch schnell Blumen für meine Freundin __(32)__, denn sie hat heute ihre neue Boutique __(33)__. Auf dieses Geschäft ist sie sehr __(34)__, und ich bin auch begeistert davon. Schließlich war es meine __(35)__ gewesen so etwas anzufangen.

32. (A) gesehen
    (B) bestellt
    (C) besucht
    (D) gewachsen

33. (A) erschöpft
    (B) erwacht
    (C) eröffnet
    (D) erwartet

34. (A) stolz
    (B) steif
    (C) spät
    (D) starr

35. (A) Zeit
    (B) Sorge
    (C) Idee
    (D) Kunst

GO ON TO THE NEXT PAGE

Berufswahl

Sabine kann sehr gut zeichnen. Wegen dieser __(36)__ überlegt sie sich, ob sie sich vielleicht __(37)__ die Werbung interessieren sollte. Dort kann __(38)__ sicher besser verdienen __(39)__ in den anderen Berufen, von __(40)__ sie schon einmal geträumt hat. Sie wird jedenfalls __(41)__ das Abitur machen und sich dann um __(42)__ Studienplatz an einer Fachhochschule __(43)__.

36. (A) Begabung
(B) Beratung
(C) Bezeichnung
(D) Besetzung

37. (A) in
(B) über
(C) auf
(D) für

38. (A) wer
(B) es
(C) man
(D) etwas

39. (A) wie
(B) als
(C) so
(D) dann

40. (A) denen
(B) dem
(C) der
(D) den

41. (A) oft
(B) neulich
(C) zuerst
(D) meistens

42. (A) einen
(B) einem
(C) eine
(D) ein

43. (A) beworben
(B) bewirbt
(C) bewerben
(D) zu bewerben

GO ON TO THE NEXT PAGE

PART C

Directions: Read the following texts carefully for comprehension. Each is followed by a number of questions or incomplete statements. Select the answer or completion that is best according to the text and fill in the corresponding circle on your answer sheet.

DIESE WOCHE

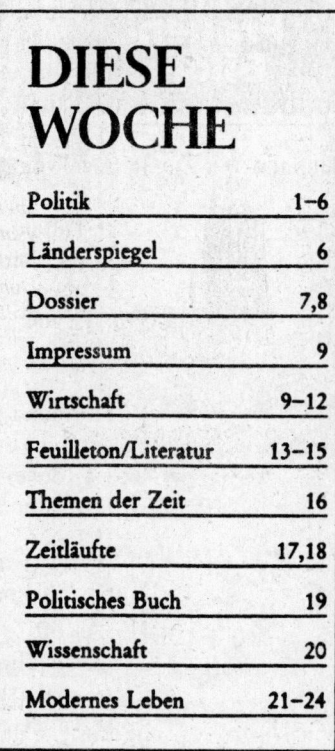

Politik	**1–6**
Länderspiegel	**6**
Dossier	**7,8**
Impressum	**9**
Wirtschaft	**9–12**
Feuilleton/Literatur	**13–15**
Themen der Zeit	**16**
Zeitläufte	**17,18**
Politisches Buch	**19**
Wissenschaft	**20**
Modernes Leben	**21–24**

44. Dieses Verzeichnis informiert über den Inhalt
    (A) eines Romans
    (B) einer Zeitung
    (C) eines Pakets
    (D) einer Tasche

GO ON TO THE NEXT PAGE

MARKEN&MOTIVE

Berühmte Frauen porträtiert die Deutsche Bundespost in einer Sondermarken-Dauerserie. Die beiden neuesten Marken sind der Hirnforscherin Cécile Vogt und der

Komponistin Fanny Hensel gewidmet. Cécile Vogt (1864–1962), von Geburt Französin, forschte viele Jahrzehnte gemeinsam mit ihrem Mann, dem Neurologen Oskar Vogt. Unter anderem gelang den beiden erstmals eine Zuordnug von Reizeffekten zu architektonisch definierten Feldern der Hirnrinde. Die Komponistin Fanny Hensel (1805–1847) hingegen stammte aus einer berühmten Bankiers- und Philosophenfamilie. Sie aber

zog es ebenso wie ihren Bruder, Felix Mendelssohn-Bartholdy, zur Musik; unter dem Namen des Bruders veröffentlichte sie ihre ersten Kunstlieder, später trat sie

aber unter ihrem eigenen Namen auf. Zum 750-jährigen Bestehen des Frankfurter Doms und für die wichtige Rolle, die Kinder in der Gesellschaft spielen, haben Professor Ernst Kößlinger und die Berliner Grafikerin Lilo Fromm zwei weitere neue Briefmarken entworfen.

45. Woher stammte die Hirnforscherin Cécile Vogt ursprünglich?

(A) Aus Berlin
(B) Aus Frankfurt
(C) Aus Deutschland
(D) Aus Frankreich

46. Was war Fanny Hensels Bruder wohl von Beruf?

(A) Bankier
(B) Philosoph
(C) Komponist
(D) Kunstschmied

47. Weshalb sind Ernst Kößlinger und Lilo Fromm hier genannt?

(A) Sie haben ein neues Spielzeug erfunden.
(B) Sie haben den Frankfurter Dom gebaut.
(C) Sie haben ein neues Kinderzentrum eröffnet.
(D) Sie haben für die Bundespost Marken gestaltet.

48. Als die Marken herauskamen, bezahlte man am wenigsten für die Briefmarke, die

(A) den Frankfurter Dom zeigt
(B) die Hirnforscherin Cécile Vogt darstellt
(C) ein Porträt der Fanny Hensel abbildet
(D) den Kindern gewidmet ist

GO ON TO THE NEXT PAGE

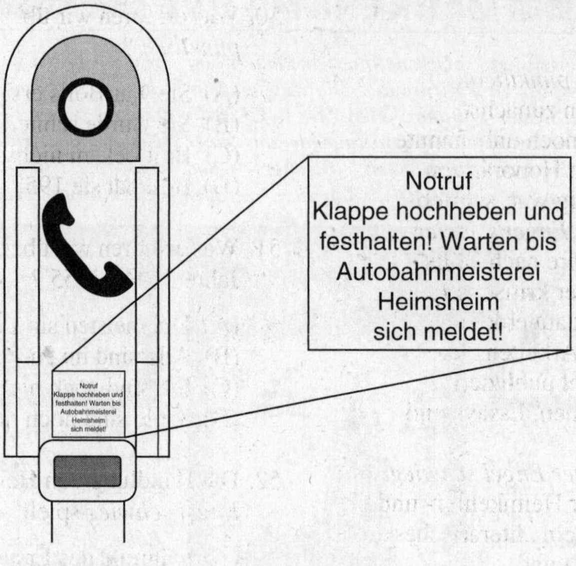
Notruf
Klappe hochheben und festhalten! Warten bis Autobahnmeisterei Heimsheim sich meldet!

49. Wann würde man diesen Apparat benutzen?

(A) Bei einem Kinobesuch
(B) Nur spät abends
(C) Bei einem Unfall
(D) Nur früh morgens

GO ON TO THE NEXT PAGE

Der Engel schwieg

Von der Erzählung *Der Zug war pünktlich*, Heinrich Bölls erstem Buch, wurden zunächst etwa 145 Exemplare verkauft. Der noch unbekannte Autor erhielt dafür im Juni 1950 ein Honorar von nur 58 Mark. Obwohl das sehr wenig war, schrieb Böll weiter. Sein erster Roman *Der Engel schwieg* wurde im Jahr 1992, also sieben Jahre nach Bölls Tod, aufgearbeitet und soll Teil einer kritischen Böll-Gesamtausgabe werden. Es ist außerdem bekannt, dass weit über 100 seiner Arbeiten aus den Jahren 1946 bis 1955 noch nicht publiziert sind. Darunter sind Hörspiele, Dramen, Essays und Erzählungen.

Ein Kritiker nennt den Roman *Der Engel schwieg* ein „charakteristisches Exempel der Heimkehrer- und Trümmerliteratur". Der Roman sei ein „literarisches ‚Dokument' über deutsche Zustände und Befindlichkeiten im Mai 1945".

Am Tage der Kapitulation kehrt der Soldat Hans Schnitzler in seine zerbombte Heimatstadt Köln, die auch Bölls Heimatstadt war, zurück. Dieser Roman enthält viel Autobiographisches. Schnitzler hat, wie Böll, Buchhändler gelernt, beide kehren ohne gültige Papiere heim, beide sind sie Moralisten. Eindrucksvoll schildert Böll die Stunde Null, den Hunger, den Gestank, die seelische Verwüstung und natürlich die große Liebe.

50. Was erfahren wir über die Erzählung *Der Zug war pünktlich* ?

(A) Sie war Bölls erster Roman.
(B) Sie wurde schnell und gut verkauft.
(C) Böll bekam nicht viel Geld dafür.
(D) Böll hat sie 1958 geschrieben.

51. Was erfahren wir über Bölls Werke aus den Jahren 1946-1955 ?

(A) Die meisten sind verloren gegangen.
(B) Alle sind im Juni 1950 erschienen.
(C) Sie sind noch nicht interpretiert worden.
(D) Viele sind noch nicht veröffentlicht worden.

52. Die Handlung von Heinrich Bölls Roman *Der Engel schwieg* spielt

(A) während des Ersten Weltkriegs
(B) am Ende des Zweiten Weltkriegs
(C) in den zwanziger Jahren
(D) in den sechziger Jahren

53. Wovon handelt der Roman *Der Engel schwieg* ?

(A) Von einer Zugfahrt
(B) Von einem kranken Kind
(C) Von einem wichtigen Dokument
(D) Von einem Heimkehrer

54. Wie sieht ein Kritiker den Roman *Der Engel schwieg* ?

(A) Als Beschreibung des Lebens in Deutschland unmittelbar nach Kriegsende
(B) Als ein typisches Beispiel der deutschen klassischen Literatur
(C) Als Kapitulation vor den Problemen des Lebens
(D) Als Beschreibung der zerbombten Städte nach dem Krieg

GO ON TO THE NEXT PAGE

Restaurant »Mühlenbach«

Familie W. Marx

Feine und bürgerliche Küche

Wir empfehlen unsere Räume für Familienfeiern, Hochzeiten etc. bis 40 Personen.

Parkplätze vorhanden. Montag Ruhetag.

5166 Kreuzau-Untermaubach • Rurstraße • Telefon 0 24 22 / 41 58

55. Wofür macht das Restaurant besonders Reklame?

(A) Für Parkanlagen
(B) Für günstige Preise
(C) Für die Betriebsstunden
(D) Für Partyräume

GO ON TO THE NEXT PAGE

Der Waldkauz

Hu, Huuu, Huuuuh, seufzt der Waldkauz durch die laue Frühlingsnacht. Er lässt sich von einem Ast fallen, breitet seine ein Meter großen Flügel aus und segelt lautlos über den Waldboden. Es ist stockdunkel, aber der Kauz weicht elegant jedem Hindernis aus, als hätte er eine Infrarot-Brille auf. Hu, Huuu! Wer nachts den Ruf des Waldkauzes hört, denkt an das Jammern schrecklicher Gespenster. Dabei ist sein Ruf nichts anderes als eine Liebeserklärung. Das Huu, Huuu bedeutet: „Hallo, Waldkäuzin, wo bist du? Ich liebe dich!“

Warum findet sich der Waldkauz in der Nacht so gut zurecht? Er hat besonders lichtempfindliche Augen und sieht deshalb nachts zehnmal besser als wir Menschen. Er sieht zwar nicht in Farbe, kann aber bei ein bisschen Mondlicht alles erkennen.

Noch viel wichtiger ist sein Gehör. Der Waldkauz hat ein großes Trommelfell, hört im Umkreis von zehn Metern auch das kleinste Geräusch und weiß sofort, ob es nur ein Windhauch oder eine Maus war. Durch sein gutes Gehör kann er zentimetergenau feststellen, wo eine Maus gerade läuft. Lautlos fliegt er über sein Opfer, ergreift es und verspeist es auf einer Lichtung.

Waldkäuze sind Eulen. Sie leben in Wäldern und Parks und werden bis zu 38 cm groß und 10 Jahre alt. Das „Familienleben“ des Waldkauzes ist bekannt. Mit seinem Hu-Huuu-Rufen lockt er ein Weibchen in sein bis zu 20 Hektar großes Revier und verjagt damit gleichzeitig andere Männchen. Seiner Partnerin bleibt er ein Leben lang treu und füttert sie auch, während sie die Eier in einer Baumhöhle ausbrütet.

56. Welche Wirkung hat das Rufen des Waldkauzes?

(A) Es verjagt Gespenster.
(B) Es erschreckt Rehe.
(C) Es lockt Weibchen an.
(D) Es weckt Männchen auf.

57. Was erfahren wir über das Gehör des Waldkauzes?

(A) Es ist sehr gut entwickelt.
(B) Es funktioniert nicht bei Dunkelheit.
(C) Es wird mit zunehmendem Alter besser.
(D) Es nimmt keine Tierlaute wahr.

58. Warum kann der Waldkauz nachts so gut sehen?

(A) Seine Augen sind größer als die von Menschen.
(B) Seine Augen sind sehr dunkel.
(C) Seine Augen reagieren auf das geringste Licht.
(D) Seine Augen leuchten in der Nacht auf.

59. Was frisst der Waldkauz wohl?

(A) Beeren
(B) Kleintiere
(C) Vogeleier
(D) Blätter

60. Was erfahren wir über das Verhältnis des Waldkauzes zu einer Partnerin?

(A) Er verbringt sein Leben mit nur einer Partnerin.
(B) Er lebt nur im Sommer mit einer Partnerin.
(C) Er hat mehrere Partnerinnen gleichzeitig.
(D) Er teilt eine Partnerin mit anderen Männchen.

GO ON TO THE NEXT PAGE

FÜR DIE GLÜCKWÜNSCHE, BLUMEN UND GESCHENKE ANLÄSSLICH UNSERER HOCHZEIT SAGEN WIR GANZ HERZLICH:

»DANKE SCHÖN«

ROLF UND ANGELIKA NEUMEYER

61. Was lesen wir hier?

(A) Eine Hochzeitsanzeige
(B) Eine Danksagung
(C) Eine Glückwunschkarte
(D) Eine Einladung

GO ON TO THE NEXT PAGE

62. Was für eine Karte ist das?

    (A) Eine Eintrittskarte
    (B) Eine Platzkarte
    (C) Eine Telefonkarte
    (D) Eine Postkarte

63. Was bedeutet „Freie Platzwahl"?

    (A) Der Eintritt ist frei.
    (B) Die Plätze sind nicht reserviert.
    (C) Man kann umsonst mit dem Bus fahren.
    (D) Man bekommt einen freien Parkplatz.

GO ON TO THE NEXT PAGE

Peter Wiegand aus Tegernsee

So viel ist wohl noch kein Bayer in der Welt herumgekommen: Peter Wiegand aus Tegernsee ist seit 27 Jahren auf allen Meeren unterwegs. Jetzt konnte der Seemann in Sydney (Australien) ein tolles Jubiläum feiern: 30-mal die Welt umrundet, 3 000 000 Kilometer. Es gibt kaum ein Plätzchen dieser Erde, das der 47-Jährige nicht kennt: Ob Alaska oder Grönland, ob die Bora Bora – oder Fidschi-Inseln, ob Leningrad oder New York – er ist mit allen Wassern gewaschen.

Dabei hatte Wiegand eine Bilderbuchkarriere: Als 20-Jähriger begann er als Steward auf dem Luxusschiff Berlin. Damals waren Kreuzfahrten noch weitgehend unbekannt. Seit Jahren ist der „Weltenbummler" Hoteldirektor auf Deutschlands Luxusliner Nummer eins, der MS Europa. Dort ist er nach dem Kapitän der zweite Mann und Chef von 220 Mitarbeitern. Wenn das Schiff – meist morgens – in einen Hafen einläuft, dann ist Wiegand mit dem Proviantmeister auf den Märkten dieser Welt unterwegs, um Frischwaren zu kaufen.

Neun Monate pro Jahr dampft der Seebär durch die Welt, freie Tage gibt's nicht, dafür aber drei Monate durchgehend Urlaub. Den verbringt Wiegand am liebsten im Sommer auf seiner Terrasse mit herrlichem Blick über den Tegernsee. In der Freizeit verreist der „Kilometer-Millionär" kaum, geht höchstens spazieren und steht als Hobbykoch mit „Vorliebe für exotisches Essen" hinter dem Herd.

64. Wiegand war in Australien, weil

(A) er dort seinen Urlaub verbrachte
(B) sein Schiff dort im Hafen lag
(C) er Sydneys 30. Jubiläum feiern wollte
(D) er das Land kennen lernen wollte

65. Warum hat Wiegand den Titel „Hoteldirektor"?

(A) In jeder Hafenstadt muss er Zimmer für die Passagiere finden.
(B) Er bucht nur Zimmer für seine Mitarbeiter.
(C) Ein großes Luxusschiff ist eigentlich wie ein Hotel.
(D) Er wird lieber „Hoteldirektor" als „Weltenbummler" genannt.

66. Auf welchem Schiff arbeitet Wiegand jetzt?

(A) Auf der Berlin
(B) Auf der Sydney
(C) Auf der Tegernsee
(D) Auf der Europa

67. In der Freizeit hat Wiegand keine Lust,

(A) auf der Terrasse seines Hauses zu sitzen
(B) Zeit in der Küche zu verbringen
(C) ausgedehnte Reisen zu machen
(D) den Tegernsee zu besuchen

GO ON TO THE NEXT PAGE

Mosel - Saar - Ruwer
„Ferien nach Herzenslust"

Natur und Gastlichkeit im Landkreis Trier-Saarburg – viele Sehenswürdigkeiten, Burgen, malerische Städte und Dörfer laden ein.

Der neue Ferienkatalog mit vielen interessanten Angeboten wartet auf Ihre Anforderung.

Zu erhalten über: Kreisverwaltung Trier-Saarburg
Mustorstraße 12, 5500 Trier
Telefon (06 51) 71 53 74

197

68. Was will man mit dieser Anzeige?

(A) Ein Urlaubsziel bekannt machen
(B) Zu einer Malklasse einladen
(C) Leute zum Einkaufen anregen
(D) Burgen zum Verkauf anbieten

69. „Ferien nach Herzenslust" bedeutet hier wohl, das zu machen, was

(A) gut für den Kreislauf ist
(B) man anfordern muss
(C) man besonders gerne macht
(D) die Kreisverwaltung vorschlägt

GO ON TO THE NEXT PAGE

Rettung für Halbaffen?

Sie sind so groß wie Katzen, ihre Ohren sehen aus wie die von Fledermäusen, und sie haben Schnauzen wie Ratten. Besonders auffällig ist ihr extrem langer Mittelfinger. Die Fingertiere sind die Primaten, die am ehesten vom Aussterben bedroht sind. Fingertiere gehören zu den 30 Lemurenarten, die noch auf der ostafrikanischen Insel Madagaskar leben.

Im Primatenzentrum der Duke University (US-Staat North Carolina) ist nun vor wenigen Wochen erstmals ein Fingertier, das man auf Madagaskar „Aye-Aye" nennt, in Gefangenschaft geboren worden. Die Primatologen haben bereits insgesamt 400 Tiere aus 15 verschiedenen Lemurenarten in den Wäldern von North Carolina aufgezogen. Sie wollen die ausgewachsenen Halbaffen später einmal in besonderen Reservaten auf Madagaskar aussetzen.

Leider werden die seltenen Lemuren vor allem durch die Zerstörung der tropischen Wälder auf der ostafrikanischen Insel bedroht. Rund 85 Prozent der Bäume sind bereits abgeholzt oder abgebrannt. Außerdem sehen viele, die auf Madagaskar leben, die „Aye-Ayes" als Unglücksbringer; sie verfolgen und töten sie.

70. Warum werden die Lemuren in North Carolina aufgezogen?

(A) Sie sollen vor dem Aussterben gerettet werden.
(B) Sie sollen dort eine neue Heimat finden.
(C) Die Primatologen dürfen in Madagaskar nicht arbeiten.
(D) Es gibt dort keine Unglücksbringer.

71. Welche Gefahr herrscht für die Halbaffen in ihrer ursprünglichen Heimat?

(A) Die Inseln werden bevölkert.
(B) Die Wälder werden zerstört.
(C) Sie werden von Ratten bedroht.
(D) Es gibt dort nicht genug Primatologen.

72. Was haben die US-Wissenschaftler erreicht?

(A) Sie haben den Aberglauben der Leute auf Madagaskar bekämpft.
(B) Sie haben den seltsamen Mittelfinger dieser Tiere entwickelt.
(C) Sie haben die Halbaffen außerhalb ihrer Heimat gezüchtet.
(D) Sie haben den Namen der „Aye-Aye" bekannt gemacht.

73. Was wollen die US-Primatologen eines Tages mit den Halbaffen tun?

(A) Sie nach Madagaskar zurückbringen
(B) Sie den Eingeborenen schenken
(C) Sie in North Carolina aussetzen
(D) Sie in einem Primatenzentrum behalten

74. Wie sehen viele Einwohner Madagaskars die Halbaffen?

(A) Sie halten sie für hässlich.
(B) Sie finden sie uninteressant.
(C) Sie finden sie besonders delikat.
(D) Sie fühlen sich von ihnen bedroht.

GO ON TO THE NEXT PAGE

75. Was kann man mit dieser Karte machen?

(A) In den Zoo gehen
(B) Im Europa-Center arbeiten
(C) Eine Vorstellung besuchen
(D) Eine Berlinrundfahrt buchen

GO ON TO THE NEXT PAGE

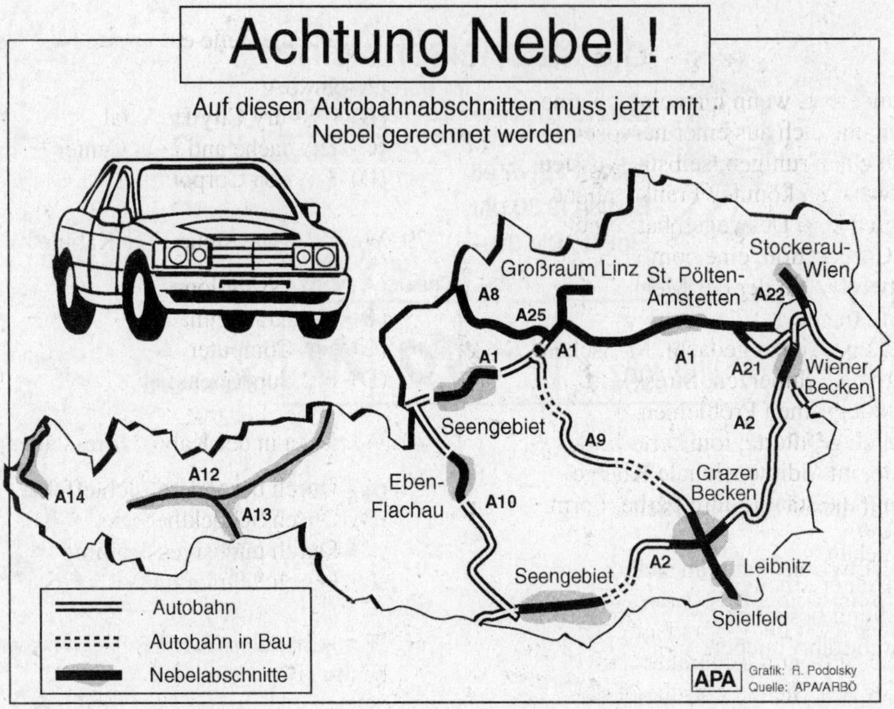

76. Worauf macht diese Anzeige den Autofahrer aufmerksam?

(A) Eine Wetterlage
(B) Entfernungen
(C) Eine Umleitung
(D) Bauarbeiten

77. Weshalb ist diese Anzeige für Autofahrer so wichtig?

(A) Sie beschreibt Umleitungen.
(B) Sie gibt Entfernungen an.
(C) Sie weist auf Tankstellen hin.
(D) Sie warnt vor schlechter Sicht.

GO ON TO THE NEXT PAGE

Seelendusche

Wäre es nicht wunderbar, wenn man einfach eine Telefonzelle betreten und sich aus einer nervösen, unsicheren Person in einen ruhigen, selbstbewussten Supermenschen verwandeln könnte? Frank Italiane glaubt an diese Möglichkeit. Deswegen hat seine Firma, die Environ Corporation, eine computergelenkte Kabine entworfen, in der der Mensch eine stressfreie Umgebung findet.

Der „Environ" Raum ist dazu gedacht, Menschen bei der Bewältigung von Schmerzen, Stress und verschiedenen psychologischen Problemen zu helfen: und zwar durch gefilterte, ionisierte Luft, wohl riechende Düfte, multidimensionale Klänge und eine Beleuchtung, die ständig ihre Farbe, Form und Intensität wechselt.

Beim Design des „Environ" hat man sich die anthropometrische Technologie der NASA zunutze gemacht. Anthropometrie ist die Erforschung der Größen-, Gestalt- und Bewegungscharakteristika des menschlichen Körpers. Sie hat entscheidende Bedeutung beim Design von Kleidung, Ausrüstung und Arbeitsplätzen in den Flugkörpern der NASA.

Die am Century City Hospital in Los Angeles und im Headache and Pain Center in Beverly Hills getestete Kabine ist 2,30 m hoch, 1,80 m lang und 1,20 m breit. Die erste Generation des „Environ" wird an Krankenhäuser, Stiftungen und andere medizinische Betriebe verkauft werden, aber bis zum Jahre 2010 sollen billigere Modelle für den Hausgebrauch auf dem Markt sein.

78. Wer hat die Zelle entworfen?
    - (A) NASA
    - (B) Century City Hospital
    - (C) Headache and Pain Center
    - (D) Environ Corporation

79. Wer oder was steuert die Kabine?
    - (A) Ein Psychologe
    - (B) Ein Krankenhaus
    - (C) Ein Computer
    - (D) Ein Supermensch

80. Wie kann in der Kabine Stress abgebaut werden?
    - (A) Durch besondere Lichteffekte
    - (B) Durch Schocktherapie
    - (C) Durch intensives Training
    - (D) Durch Schmerzmittel

81. Wer sollte den „Environ" Raum hauptsächlich benutzen?
    - (A) Verschiedene Psychologen
    - (B) Leidende Menschen
    - (C) Supermenschen
    - (D) Computerspezialisten

82. Welche Wirkung soll die Kabine haben?
    - (A) Sie soll Menschen helfen.
    - (B) Sie soll die Welt verändern.
    - (C) Sie soll Telekommunikation verbessern.
    - (D) Sie soll zur Abrüstung beitragen.

83. Wo sollen diese neuen Kabinen zuerst eingesetzt werden?
    - (A) In Privatwohnungen
    - (B) In Kasernen
    - (C) In Kaufhäusern
    - (D) In Krankenhäusern

GO ON TO THE NEXT PAGE

. . . da bleibt noch Zeit für mich
Wenn Sie bei uns als
• Sekretärin
• Sachbearbeiterin
mit EDV-Kenntnissen und Englisch auf Zeit arbeiten.
Den Wunsch nach einer abwechslungsreichen Tätigkeit sollten Sie schon mitbringen.
'TeamWork'
Personal per Sofort
Tel. 089/33 30 41
Leopoldstraße 28a
8000 München 40

84. Wofür ist diese Annonce?

(A) Eine Arbeitsstelle
(B) Ein Hotel in den Alpen
(C) Einen Skiurlaub
(D) Freizeitkleidung

85. Wenn man bei „TeamWork“ angestellt ist,

(A) bekommt man EDV-Kenntnisse
(B) lernt man Englisch
(C) hat man seinen eigenen Telefonanschluss
(D) hat man ausreichende Freizeit

STOP

IF YOU FINISH BEFORE TIME IS CALLED, YOU MAY CHECK YOUR WORK ON THIS TEST ONLY. DO NOT TURN TO ANY OTHER TEST IN THIS BOOK.

How to Score the SAT Subject Test in German

When you take an actual SAT Subject Test in German, your answer sheet will be "read" by a scanning machine that will record your response to each question. Then a computer will compare your answers with the correct answers and produce your raw score. You get one point for each correct answer. For each wrong answer, you lose one-third of a point. Questions you omit (and any for which you mark more than one answer) are not counted. This raw score is converted to a scaled score that is reported to you and to the colleges you specify.

Worksheet 1. Finding Your Raw Test Score

STEP 1: Table A on the following page lists the correct answers for all the questions on the SAT Subject Test in German that is reproduced in this book. It also serves as a worksheet for you to calculate your raw score.

- Compare your answers with those given in the table.
- Put a check in the column marked "Right" if your answer is correct.
- Put a check in the column marked "Wrong" if your answer is incorrect.
- Leave both columns blank if you omitted the question.

STEP 2: Count the number of right answers.

Enter the total here: ________________

STEP 3: Count the number of wrong answers.

Enter the total here: ________________

STEP 4: Multiply the number of wrong answers by .333.

Enter the product here: ________________

STEP 5: Subtract the result obtained in Step 4 from the total you obtained in Step 2.

Enter the result here: ________________

STEP 6: Round the number obtained in Step 5 to the nearest whole number.

Enter the result here: ________________

The number you obtained in Step 6 is your raw score.

Table A

Answers to the Subject Test in German and Percentage of Students Answering Each Question Correctly									
Question Number	Correct Answer	Right	Wrong	Percentage of Students Answering the Question Correctly*	Question Number	Correct Answer	Right	Wrong	Percentage of Students Answering the Question Correctly*
1	B			94	33	C			76
2	B			95	34	A			67
3	B			74	35	C			79
4	A			92	36	A			19
5	A			84	37	D			48
6	B			29	38	C			88
7	A			37	39	B			70
8	D			22	40	A			34
9	B			21	41	C			72
10	D			93	42	A			55
11	B			83	43	C			59
12	D			10	44	B			80
13	C			46	45	D			76
14	A			40	46	C			78
15	A			89	47	D			63
16	B			50	48	A			64
17	D			88	49	C			85
18	A			88	50	C			59
19	C			64	51	D			62
20	A			67	52	B			78
21	C			87	53	D			64
22	B			77	54	A			49
23	D			59	55	D			86
24	B			97	56	C			37
25	A			60	57	A			64
26	D			69	58	C			65
27	C			36	59	B			75
28	B			35	60	A			71
29	C			42	61	B			86
30	C			39	62	A			73
31	A			72	63	B			72
32	B			63	64	B			30

Table A continued on next page

Table A continued from previous page

Question Number	Correct Answer	Right	Wrong	Percentage of Students Answering the Question Correctly*	Question Number	Correct Answer	Right	Wrong	Percentage of Students Answering the Question Correctly*
65	C			63	76	A			32
66	D			51	77	D			40
67	C			45	78	D			70
68	A			66	79	C			51
69	C			69	80	A			46
70	A			42	81	B			47
71	B			52	82	A			60
72	C			38	83	D			64
73	A			61	84	A			83
74	D			39	85	D			57
75	C			69					

* These percentages are based on an analysis of the answer sheets of a representative sample of 629 students who took the original administration of this test and whose mean score was 543. They may be used as an indication of the relative difficulty of a particular question.

Answer explanations for the Subject Test in German can be found on page 669.

Finding Your Scaled Score

When you take SAT Subject Tests, the scores sent to the colleges you specify are reported on the College Board scale, which ranges from 200–800. You can convert your practice test score to a scaled score by using Table B. To find your scaled score, locate your raw score in the left-hand column of Table B; the corresponding score in the right-hand column is your scaled score. For example, a raw score of 37 on this particular edition of the Subject Test in German corresponds to a scaled score of 490.

Raw scores are converted to scaled scores to ensure that a score earned on any one edition of a particular Subject Test is comparable to the same scaled score earned on any other edition of the same Subject Test. Because some editions of the tests may be slightly easier or more difficult than others, College Board scaled scores are adjusted so that they indicate the same level of performance regardless of the edition of the test taken and the ability of the group that takes it. Thus, for example, a score of 400 on one edition of a test taken at a particular administration indicates the same level of achievement as a score of 400 on a different edition of the test taken at a different administration.

When you take the SAT Subject Tests during a national administration, your scores are likely to differ somewhat from the scores you obtain on the tests in this book. People perform at different levels at different times for reasons unrelated to the tests themselves. The precision of any test is also limited because it represents only a sample of all the possible questions that could be asked.

Table B

Scaled Score Conversion Table
Subject Test in German

Raw Score	Scaled Score	Raw Score	Scaled Score	Raw Score	Scaled Score
85	800	47	550	9	350
84	800	46	550	8	350
83	800	45	540	7	340
82	790	44	530	6	340
81	790	43	530	5	330
80	780	42	520	4	330
79	770	41	520	3	320
78	770	40	510	2	320
77	760	39	500	1	310
76	760	38	500	0	310
75	750	37	490	-1	300
74	740	36	490	-2	300
73	740	35	480	-3	300
72	730	34	470	-4	290
71	720	33	470	-5	290
70	720	32	460	-6	280
69	710	31	460	-7	280
68	700	30	450	-8	270
67	690	29	450	-9	270
66	690	28	440	-10	260
65	680	27	440	-11	260
64	670	26	430	-12	250
63	660	25	430	-13	250
62	660	24	420	-14	240
61	650	23	420	-15	240
60	640	22	410	-16	240
59	630	21	410	-17	230
58	630	20	400	-18	230
57	620	19	400	-19	220
56	610	18	390	-20	220
55	610	17	390	-21	210
54	600	16	380	-22	200
53	590	15	380	-23	200
52	580	14	370	-24	200
51	580	13	370	-25	200
50	570	12	360	-26	200
49	560	11	360	-27	200
48	560	10	360	-28	200

How Did You Do on the Subject Test in German?

After you score your test and analyze your performance, think about the following questions:

Did you run out of time before reaching the end of the test?

If so, you may need to pace yourself better. For example, maybe you spent too much time on one or two hard questions. A better approach might be to skip the ones you can't answer right away and try answering all the questions that remain on the test. Then if there's time, go back to the questions you skipped.

Did you take a long time reading the directions?

You will save time when you take the test by learning the directions to the Subject Test in German ahead of time. Each minute you spend reading directions during the test is a minute that you could use to answer questions.

How did you handle questions you were unsure of?

If you were able to eliminate one or more of the answer choices as wrong and guess from the remaining ones, your approach probably worked to your advantage. On the other hand, making haphazard guesses or omitting questions without trying to eliminate choices could cost you valuable points.

How difficult were the questions for you compared with other students who took the test?

Table A shows you how difficult the multiple-choice questions were for the group of students who took this test during its national administration. The right-hand column gives the percentage of students that answered each question correctly.

A question answered correctly by almost everyone in the group is obviously an easier question. For example, 92 percent of the students answered question 4 correctly. But only 19 percent answered question 36 correctly.

Keep in mind that these percentages are based on just one group of students. They would probably be different with another group of students taking the test.

If you missed several easier questions, go back and try to find out why: Did the questions cover material you haven't yet reviewed? Did you misunderstand the directions?

Answer Explanations for the German Subject Test

1. Choice (B) is the correct answer. *She* is the new female student in our class. The missing subject must be third person singular to match the third person singular verb *ist* ("is") and feminine to match the feminine complement *Schülerin* ("female student"). Choice (B), *Sie*, is third person singular and feminine. Choices (A), *Er* ("he"), (C), *Wir* ("we"), and (D), *ihr* ("you"), are ungrammatical in this sentence.

2. Choice (B) is the correct answer. The speaker says, "I'd like to see that movie. Let's go *into the* movie theater." *In* ("in"), indicating motion into or towards a location, is the idiomatic preposition to use after *gehen* ("go") and before *Kino* ("movie theater"); *ins* is the contraction of *in* and the definite article *das*. It does not make sense to suggest going *up to the* movie theater (A) or *on the* movie theater (C). Although choice (D), *zum*, literally translates to "to the" in English, it is unidiomatic in this context in German.

3. Choice (B) is the correct answer. The speaker is telling Brigitte not to be angry, so the second person singular imperative (*sei*) is used: "Brigitte, please don't *be* angry!" Choice (A), *seien*, can be used as a formal imperative, but it must then be followed by *Sie*; further, the use of Brigitte's first name indicates this is an informal situation. Choices (C), the infinitive *sein*, and (D), the subjunctive *seist*, are ungrammatical here.

4. Choice (A) is the correct answer. She eats a lot of vegetables and fruit *because* it is healthy. It does not make sense to say that she eats vegetables and fruits *whether* it is healthy (B), *before* it is healthy (C), or *after* it is healthy (D).

5. Choice (A) is the correct answer. The speaker says, "I'll make you a sketch because my house is not easy *to find*." After an adjective, such as *leicht* ("easy"), an infinitive form of a verb with *zu* is used. Choice (B), *finden*, is an infinitive but lacks the necessary *zu*. Choice (C) is the present participle *findend* and choice (D) is the past participle *gefunden*; both choices are ungrammatical here.

6. Choice (B) is the correct answer. The speaker says, "This is your book. Do you see *mine* anywhere?" The missing pronoun must refer to a singular neuter *Buch* ("book"), so the singular neuter *meins* ("mine") is used. The other choices are ungrammatical. Choice (A), *meine*, is feminine or plural. Choice (C), *mein*, cannot be used as a pronoun on its own; it must be used before a noun. And choice (D), *meinen*, is masculine accusative or plural dative.

7. Choice (A) is the correct answer. The speaker asks, "Why are you asking me that again? Haven't you *paid attention*?" Choice (B), *angehört* ("heard" or "listened to"), requires a direct object; since there is no direct object in the second question, this choice is ungrammatical here. And in this context, it does not make sense for the speaker to ask "Haven't you *repeated*?" (C) or "Haven't you *forgotten*?" (D).

8. Choice (D) is the correct answer. The writer says, "Your comment during the meal was somewhat *peculiar*." Choice (A), *richtig* ("right"), is an absolute — something is either right or it is not — and therefore, it cannot be modified by a word like *etwas* ("somewhat"). Similarly, it is unidiomatic to use an adverb such as *etwas*, which limits the quality of an adjective, to modify *gut* ("good"), as in choice (C). Choice (B), *frühzeitig* ("early"), does not make sense; it is not clear why a comment would be considered "somewhat early."

9. Choice (B) is the correct answer. The speaker says, "Heike is unemployed. She would like to apply *for* a job with us." *Um* is the idiomatic preposition to use with *sich bewerben* ("apply"). Choice (A), *in* ("in"), (C), *an* ("at"), and (D), *über* (" about"), are unidiomatic.

10. Choice (D) is the correct answer. The speaker says, "At my house one had to wash one's hands before eating." This sentence already has a subject, *man* ("one"), and a direct object, *die Hände* ("the hands"), so the missing pronoun must be an indirect object. Further, the idiomatic way to express in German the washing of a body part is with a reflexive verb, so the missing pronoun must be the reflexive indirect object *sich* ("oneself"), which corresponds with the third person singular subject *man*. Choices (A), *wir* ("we"), (B) *dich* ("you"), and (C), *sie* ("she" or "they"), cannot grammatically correspond with the subject *man* ("one").

11. Choice (B) is the correct answer. The speaker says, "It is *already* very late and I'm going to sleep." It does not make sense to say that it is *first* very late (C) or that it is *beautifully* very late (D). And it is more likely that someone would be going to sleep because it is *already* very late than because it is *almost* very late (A).

12. Choice (D) is the correct answer. The speaker says, "We are not *able* to spend so much money on a new car." It does not make sense to say that they are not *satisfied* (A), *finished* (B), or *complete* (C) to spend so much money on a car.

13. Choice (C) is the correct answer. Franz is in the kitchen and wants to roast *a* chicken. The missing indefinite article must be the neuter accusative form because it modifies *Hühnchen* ("chicken"), which is neuter (like other nouns that end in *-chen*), and is the direct object of *braten* ("to roast"). The other choices are ungrammatical. Choice (A), *einen*, is masculine accusative. Choice (B), *eine*, is feminine nominative or accusative. And choice (D), *eines*, is masculine or neuter genitive.

14. Choice (A) is the correct answer. The speaker says, "We have all *been* invited to her birthday." The German verb *werden* ("become") is used much like the English "be" to form passive sentences. Because the sentence already contains the conjugated helping verb *sind*, the missing word is the past participle of *werden*, not the conjugated past tense *wurden* (B) or the infinitive *werden* (C). Normally, the past participle of *werden* is *geworden* (D); however, when it is used in the passive with another past participle (here, *eingeladen*), the correct form of the past participle is *worden*.

15. Choice (A) is the correct answer. The speaker asks, "How late is it? My *watch* has stopped." It does not make sense to say that the speaker's *time* (B), *hour* (C), or *page* or *side* (D) has stopped.

16. Choice (B) is the correct answer. After a *long* illness, her father is finally well again. The missing adjective is the feminine dative *langer* because it modifies the noun *Krankheit* ("illness"), which is feminine (like other nouns that end in *–heit*), and follows the preposition *nach*, which takes a dative object. The other choices are ungrammatical. Choice (A), *lange*, is feminine or plural nominative or accusative, choice (C), *langes*, is neuter nominative or accusative, and choice (D), *langem*, is masculine or neuter dative.

17. Choice (D) is the correct answer. The speaker says, "I'm not telling you what this word *means*." It does not make sense to say that the speaker will not tell the listener what the word *understands* (A), *is acquainted with* (B), or *can* (C).

18. Choice (A) is the correct answer. The speaker says, "Please give me another piece *of bread*." In German, nouns of quantity such as *Stück* ("piece") are followed immediately by the name of the substance, such as *Brot* ("bread"), without an intervening preposition or article. Choices (B), *von Brot*, and (D), *dem Brot*, contain

an intervening preposition or article. Choice (C), the plural *Brote*, does not make sense in this sentence.

19. Choice (C) is the correct answer. Mark was sent into town *to run* a few errands. To show the purpose of an action (here, why Mark was sent to town), *um* ("in order to") is used, followed by *zu* + an infinitive (here, *zu machen*). Choice (A), the infinitive *machen* without a preceding *zu*, choice (B), the present tense *macht*, and choice (D), the past participle *gemacht*, are all incorrect because they cannot be used in this clause beginning with *um*.

20. Choice (A) is the correct answer. First, he went *to the* market . . . *Zu* ("to") is an idiomatic preposition to use after *ging* ("went") and before *Markt* ("market"). *Zu* takes a dative object, so *zum*, the contraction of the preposition and the dative definite article *dem*, is correct. Choice (B), *nach*, can also mean "to," but is not idiomatic here; further, it is not followed by the necessary article. Choice (C), *beim* ("at the" or "near the"), does not make sense in this sentence. Choice (D), *im* ("in the"), does not make sense in this sentence either. *Im* is a contraction of *in* ("in") and the dative definite article *dem*; however, in this sentence, because the verb *ging* indicates motion from outside to inside the market, *in* would have to be followed by the accusative article *den*, not *dem*.

21. Choice (C) is the correct answer. First, he went to the market, where he wanted *to buy* vegetables. The missing verb must be the infinitive *kaufen* because the clause already contains the conjugated verb *wollte* ("wanted"). Choices (A), (B), and (D) are all conjugated present tense forms of *kaufen* and cannot be used grammatically in the clause with *wollte*. In any event, the first person *kaufe* (A) and second person *kaufst* (D) cannot be used with the third person subject *er* ("he").

22. Choice (B) is the correct answer. He found the *beans* inexpensive and had a kilogram weighed out. Because Mark wanted to buy vegetables, it does not make sense to say that he found the *bag* (A), the *flowers* (C), or the *cake* (D) inexpensive. Further, bags, flowers, and cakes are not usually priced by the kilogram.

23. Choice (D) is the correct answer. Then he also *had to* go to the baker's. Because the rest of the story is in the past tense, the verb in this sentence must be in the past tense as well. Choices (A), *musst*, and (C), *müsst*, are in the present tense. Choice (B), *müssten*, is in the subjunctive tense. Further, only choice (D) is a singular third person form; it is the only choice that can be used with the singular third person subject *er* ("he").

24. Choice (B) is the correct answer. Gunter writes, "Last night Anne and *I* saw 'Threepenny Opera' in the theater." Because Gunter is writing the letter and so far has mentioned no other person but Anne, it only makes sense that he would be talking about what he himself did with Anne. The description later in the letter makes it clear that Gunter was at the theater. Choices (A), *er* ("he"), and (C), *sie* ("she" or "they"), are not appropriate because there is no referent for these pronouns. Choice (D), *ihr* ("you all"), is illogical because it does not make sense for Gunter to send a letter to Hilde telling her what she and others did and describing how it was.

25. Choice (A) is the correct answer. Gunter tells Hilde that she cannot *imagine* how great it ["Threepenny Opera"] was. The missing verb is reflexive, as shown in the sentence by the pronoun *dir*. The reflexive meanings of choices (B), *ansehen* ("take a look at"), and (C), *vornehmen* ("intend"), do not logically complete the sentence. Choice (D), *einbilden*, like *vorstellen*, can be translated as "imagine," but in the sense of being under an illusion that something is true rather than picturing something for yourself. Therefore, *vorstellen*, not *einbilden*, is the correct choice.

26. Choice (D) is the correct answer. The missing word is a relative pronoun that refers to *der Mann* ("the man") and is the subject of the verb *gespielt hat* ("played"). Gunter writes, "The man *who* played the leading role is ..." Choices (A), *was* ("what"), and (C), *das* ("that"), are neuter and cannot be used to refer to the masculine *Mann*. Choice (B), *wer* ("who" or "whoever"), cannot be used as relative pronoun to refer back to a specific individual.

27. Choice (C) is the correct answer. Gunter writes, "The man ... is not only a good singer, *but* also a great actor." *Sondern* correctly completes the structure *nicht nur ... sondern auch* ("not only ... but also"). The other choices are unidiomatic.

28. Choice (B) is the correct answer. Gunter writes, "When he sang the love song *to the* daughter of Peachum ..." The clause beginning with *als* has a subject *er* ("he") and a direct object *Liebeslied* ("love song"), so the singular feminine noun *Tochter* ("daughter") must be an indirect object. The article preceding *Tochter* must thus be feminine and dative. The other choices are ungrammatical. Choice (A), *die*, is feminine but nominative or accusative. Choice (C), *dem*, is dative, but masculine or neuter. And choice (D), *den*, can be dative, but then it must be plural.

29. Choice (C) is the correct answer. Gunter writes, "When he sang the love song ... I *nearly* stood up to warn her against him." It does not make sense to say that Gunter *daily* (A), *in the mornings* (B), or *always* (D) stood up during the show he saw last night.

30. Choice (C) is the correct answer. Gunter writes that the other (*anderen*) actors were also good. *Schauspieler* ("actors") is the plural subject of the sentence and is therefore preceded by the nominative plural definite article *die*. The correct ending for an adjective between this *die* and a plural noun is *-en*. The other choices are ungrammatical.

31. Choice (A) is the correct answer. Gunter tells Hilde to let him know when he should buy her a ticket, so the verb must be the second person singular imperative *gib* ("give"). Choice (B), *gibt*, is a second person imperative, but it is plural and not appropriate for speaking to one person (Hilde). Choice (C), *gebe*, is the first person present indicative and choice (D), *gibst*, is the second person present indicative; both of these choices are ungrammatical in this sentence.

32. Choice (B) is the correct answer. The writer states that yesterday he or she *ordered* flowers for his or her girlfriend. There is no reason to suggest that the writer is indicating that he or she *saw* (A), *visited* (C), or *grew* (D) the flowers yesterday. Furthermore, *wachsen* ("grow") is an intransitive verb and cannot be used here with the direct object *Blumen* ("flowers").

33. Choice (C) is the correct answer. The writer states that he or she ordered the flowers "because she [the girlfriend] *opened* her new boutique today." It does not make sense to say that she *exhausted* (A), *woke* (B), or *expected* (D) her new boutique today.

34. Choice (A) is the correct answer. The writer states that the girlfriend is very *proud* of the business. It does not make sense to say that she is *stiff* (B), *late* (C), or *rigid* (D) of the business. Further, *stolz* is the only choice that is used idiomatically with the preposition *auf* ("of").

35. Choice (C) is the correct answer. The writer states, "After all, it was my *idea* to start something like this." It does not make sense to say it was his or her *time* (A), *worry* (B), or *art* (D) to start something like this, especially since it is the girlfriend who opened the boutique, not the writer.

36. Choice (A) is the correct answer. Sabine can draw very well, and because of this *talent* she is considering something. It does not make sense to refer to Sabine's drawing ability as *advice* (B) or as a *designation* or *title* (C). And the writer is clearly referring to Sabine's skill, not indicating that drawing is Sabine's *occupation* (D).

37. Choice (D) is the correct answer. Because of her talent, Sabine is considering whether she should take an interest *in* advertising. *Für* is the idiomatic preposition to use with the reflexive verb *sich interessieren* ("to take an interest"). Choices (A), *in*, (B), *über*, and (C), *auf*, are unidiomatic.

38. Choice (C) is the correct answer. The missing word is the subject of the verb phrase *kann sicher besser verdienen* ("can certainly earn more"), so it must be a person. The writer states, "There [in advertising], *one* can certainly earn more ..." Choice (A), *wer* ("whoever"), does not make sense in this sentence. Choices (B), *es* ("it"), and (D), *etwas* ("something"), refer to things, not people; they cannot be the subject of the verb *verdienen* in this context.

39. Choice (B) is the correct answer. The writer states that in advertising "one can certainly earn more *than* in other careers." *Als* ("than") correctly completes the comparative structure [comparative adjective/adverb] + *als*. The other choices do not grammatically complete the comparative structure and do not make sense in the sentence.

40. Choice (A) is the correct answer. The writer refers to "other careers, of *which* she [Sabine] once dreamt." The missing word is a relative pronoun that refers to the plural noun *Berufen* ("careers") and is the object of preposition *von* ("of"), which takes a dative object, so the pronoun must be the plural dative *denen*. Choice (B), *dem*, is dative, but it is masculine or neuter singular. Choice (C), *der*, can be dative, but it is then feminine singular. And choice (D), *den*, is masculine singular accusative.

41. Choice (C) is the correct answer. *Abitur machen* refers to taking one's final high school exams in order to graduate. The writer says that Sabine will first graduate high school before moving on to something else. It does not make sense to say that Sabine will *often* graduate high school (A), *recently* graduate high school (B), or *mostly* graduate high school (D) before doing something else.

42. Choice (A) is the correct answer. The missing indefinite article modifies the masculine noun *Studienplatz*, the object of the preposition *um*, which takes an accusative object. The article must therefore be the masculine accusative *einen*. Choice (B), *einem*, can be masculine, but it is dative. Choice (C), *eine*, is feminine or plural. And choice (D), *ein*, can be masculine, but it is then nominative; it can also be accusative, but it is then neuter.

43. Choice (C) is the correct answer. The writer says, "She will ... then *apply* for a place at a technical college." Because the missing verb follows the verb *wird* ("will"), the infinitive form *bewerben* is used. Choice (A), the past participle *beworben*, is ungrammatical and does not make sense. Choice (B), the present tense third person *bewirbt*, and choice (D), the infinitive with an extraneous *zu*, are ungrammatical and do not make sense in this sentence either.

44. Choice (B) is the correct answer. The question asks which thing this directory gives information about the content of. The main heading, *This Week* ("Diese Woche"), and the section headings, including *Politics* ("Politik"), *Economy* ("Wirtschaft"), *Themes of the Day* ("Themen der Zeit"), and *Modern Living* ("Modernes Leben"), are typical of what you would find in the index for *a newspaper*, not *a novel* (A), *a package* (C), or *a bag* (D).

45. Choice (D) is the correct answer. The question asks where the brain researcher Cécile Vogt originally came from. The passage says that Vogt was a *Frenchwoman by birth* ("von Geburt Französin"), so she was from *France*, not from the country *Germany* (C) or the German cities *Berlin* (A) or *Frankfurt* (B).

46. Choice (C) is the correct answer. The question asks what Fanny Hensel's brother's profession probably was. The passage says that Fanny was from a famous family of bankers and philosophers but was drawn to music, like her brother, and published her first compositions under his name ("*Die Komponistin Fanny Hensel ... ihren ersten Kunstlieder*"). It is clear that Fanny's brother was a *composer*, not a *banker* (A), a *philosopher* (B) or a *metal worker* (D).

47. Choice (D) is the correct answer. The question asks why Ernst Kößlinger and Lilo Fromm are named here. The passage says that for the 750-year existence of the Frankfurt cathedral and the important role children play in society, Professor Ernst Kößlinger and the Berlin graphic designer Lilo Fromm have designed two more new stamps ("*Zum 750- jährigen Bestehen ... entworfen*"). Kößlinger and Fromm are named here because *they have created stamps for the post office*, not because *they have invented a new toy* (A), because *they built the Frankfurt cathedral* (B), or because *they opened a new children's center* (C).

48. Choice (A) is the correct answer. The question asks which stamp one paid the least for when the stamps came out. The passage shows pictures of the stamps, and each has a number representing its value: Cécile Vogt (140), Fanny Hensel (300), the Frankfurt cathedral (60), and children at play (100). The least costly was the stamp that shows *the Frankfurt cathedral*, not the stamp that features *brain researcher Cécile Vogt* (B),

the stamp that depicts *a portrait of Fanny Hensel* (C), or the stamp that is *dedicated to the children* (D).

49. Choice (C) is the correct answer. The question asks when this device would be used. The sign begins with *emergency call* ("Notruf") and tells the user to wait until the highway control center of Heimsheim responds ("*Warten bis ...sich meldet*"). It is clear that this device is used *in case of an accident*, not *during a trip to the movies* (A), *only late at night* (B), or *only early in the morning* (D).

50. Choice (C) is the correct answer. The question asks what we learn about the story *The Train Was on Time*. The first paragraph says that Böll, the yet unknown author, obtained a fee of only 58 marks for the story in June 1950 ("*Der noch unbekannte Autor ... 58 Mark*"); that is, *Böll did not receive much money for it*. The story was not Böll's *first novel* (A); it was his first book ("*Heinrich Bölls erstem Buch*"), but *The Silent Angel* was his first novel ("*Sein erster Roman* Der Engel schwieg ..."). The book did not *sell quickly and well* (B); at first it sold only about 145 copies ("*Von der Erzählung ... wurden etwa145 Exemplare verkauft*"). And Böll did not *write the story in 1958* (D); he was paid for the story in June 1950, so presumably he wrote it before then.

51. Choice (D) is the correct answer. The question asks what we learn about Böll's works from the years 1946-1955. The passage says that it is known that well over 100 of Böll's works from the years 1946 to 1955 are not yet published ("*Es ist außerdem bekannt ... publiziert sind*"); in other words, *many have not yet been published*. The passage does not indicate that *most have been lost* (A); that *all appeared in June 1950* (B), the date Böll was paid for his first book; or that *they have not yet been interpreted* (or *analyzed*) (C).

52. Choice (B) is the correct answer. The question asks when the plot of Heinrich Böll's novel *The Silent Angel* takes place. The novel is described as a literary document of German conditions and sensitivities in May 1945 ("*Der Roman sei ... Mai 1945*"), so it is set a*t the end of the Second World War*. It does not take place *during the First World War* (A); World War I happened long before 1945. Further, the passage states that the action takes place on the day of surrender ("*Am Tage der Kapitulation*"), so it is clear that the novel is set at the end of a war rather than during one. It is also clear that the novel is not set in *the 1920s* (C) or *the 1960s* (D).

53. Choice (D) is the correct answer. The question asks what the novel *The Silent Angel* is about. The passage talks about the soldier Hans Schnitzler returning to his bombed-out hometown, Cologne, on the day of surrender ("*Am Tage der Kapitulation*

... *Heimatstadt Köln*"). The novel clearly is about a person returning home, or a *returnee*, not *a train trip* (A) or *a sick child* (B). Although the novel itself is referred to as a literary document ("*ein literarisches , Dokument*'"), it is not about *an important document* (C).

54. Choice (A) is the correct answer. The question asks how a critic views the novel *The Silent Angel*. The passage says a critic referred to the novel as a literary document of German conditions and sensitivities in May 1945 (*Ein Kritiker ... Der Roman sei ein „literarisches,Dokument' über deutsche Zustände und Befindlichkeiten im Mai 1945*"). The use of *sei* rather than *ist* in the second sentence indicates that the author is reporting the critic's words; it is the critic that sees the novel as *a description of life in Germany immediately after the end of World War II*. The critic calls the novel "a characteristic example" of so-called homecoming and rubble literature ("*Ein Kritiker ... Trümmerliteratur*") but does not see it *as a typical example of classical German literature* (B). The novel takes place on the day of surrender at the end of the war ("*Am Tage der Kapitulation*"), but it is not described *as the surrender to life's problems* (C). And although the novel is set in the bombed-out city of Cologne ("*zerbombte ... Köln*"), it is not seen *as a description of the bombed-out cities after the war* (D).

55. Choice (D) is the correct answer. The question asks what the restaurant advertises especially. The advertisement reads, "We recommend our rooms for family parties, weddings, etc. up to 40 people" ("*Wir empfehlen ... Personen*"); the restaurant is touting its *party rooms*. The advertisement mentions that parking spaces are available ("*Parkplätze vorhanden*"), but it does not advertise its *grounds* (A). The ad does not say that the restaurant has *low prices* (B) or extol the restaurant's *business hours* (C).

56. Choice (C) is the correct answer. The question asks what effect the wood owl's call has. The passage says that the owl's call is nothing other than a declaration of love, and that the "hoo, hooo" ("*Huu, Huuu*") means, "Hello, female wood owl, where are you? I love you" ("*Dabei ist sein Ruf ... Ich liebe dich*"). In other words, the call *attracts females*. Although the call makes one think of the wailing of terrible ghosts ("*Wer nachts den Ruf ... schrecklicher Gespenster*"), it does not *chase ghosts away* (A). The passage does not say that the call *startles deer* (B). The passage does say that the call chases other males away ("*Mit seinem Hu-Huuuu-Rufen ... verjagt damit gleichzeitig andere Männchen*"), but not that it *wakes up males* (D).

57. Choice (A) is the correct answer. The question asks what we learn about the hearing of the wood owl. The passage says that the wood owl has a large ear drum and can hear even the slightest noise within a radius of 10 meters and know immediately whether it is a breeze or a mouse ("*Der Waldkauz hat ein großes ... eine Maus war*"). Clearly, the wood owl's hearing *is very well developed*. The passage says that the owl

sees ten times better at night than people do ("*Er hat besonders ... Menschen*"), not that its hearing *does not function in the dark* (B). There is no indication that the owl's hearing *gets better with increasing age* (C). And the owl clearly perceives mice, so it is not true that it *perceives no animal sounds* (D).

58. Choice (C) is the correct answer. The question asks why the wood owl can see so well at night. The passage says that the owl has especially light-sensitive eyes and that by a little moonlight it can recognize everything ("*Er hat besonders lichtempfindliche Augen ... alles erkennen*"). In other words, the owl's *eyes react to the slightest light*. The passage does not say that the owl's *eyes are bigger than people's* (A), that its *eyes are very dark* (B), or that its *eyes light up at night* (D).

59. Choice (B) is the correct answer. The question asks what the wood owl probably eats. The passage tells of the owl predicting a mouse's next move, flying over its prey, capturing it, and eating it in a clearing ("*Durch sein gutes Gehör ... auf einer Lichtung*"); it is clear that the owl eats *small animals*, not *berries* (A), *birds' eggs* (C), or *leaves* (D).

60. Choice (A) is the correct answer. The question asks what we learn about the relationship of a wood owl to his mate. The passage says that the owl remains true to his mate his whole life ("*Seiner Partnerin bleibt er ein Leben lang treu*"); that is, *he spends his life with only one mate*. The passage does not say that *he lives with his mate only in the summer* (B), that *he has many mates at the same time* (C), or that *he shares his mate with other males* (D).

61. Choice (B) is the correct answer. The message from Rolf and Angelika Neumeyer reads, "For the congratulations, flowers and gifts on the occasion of our wedding we say: 'thank you very much.'" The note expresses *thanks*. It is not *a wedding announcement* (A), *a greeting card* (C), or *an invitation* (D).

62. Choice (A) is the correct answer. The question asks what kind of card this is. The card mentions a concert hall ("*Konzerthaus*"), the Vienna Chamber Orchestra ("*Wiener Kammerorchester*"), and a price ("*70,00*"), along with a day, date, and time ("*Freitag, 5.November 93, 19.30 Uhr*"), so it is clear that the card is an *admissions ticket*, not *a telephone card* (C) or *a postcard* (D). The announcement of open seating ("*Freie Platzwahl*") makes it clear that this is not *a seat reservation* (B).

63. Choice (B) is the correct answer. The question asks what "Freie Platzwahl" (literally, *free seat selection*) means. This announcement of open seating means that *the seats*

are not reserved, not that *entrance is free* (A), that *one can ride the bus for free* (C), or that *one will receive a free parking place* (D).

64. Choice (B) is the correct answer. The question asks why Wiegand was in Australia. The passage says that Peter Wiegand has been sailing all the oceans for 27 years and was able to celebrate a great anniversary in Sydney: having circumnavigated the world 30 times and traveled 3 million kilometers ("*Peter Wiegand aus Tegernsee ist seit 27 ... Kilometer*"). Because most of the passage is about Wiegand's work on ships and the last paragraph says that Wiegand prefers not to travel during his time off, it can be inferred that Wiegand was in Sydney for his job. It follows, then, that *his ship was in the harbor there.* There is nothing to indicate that Wiegand *took a vacation there* (A), that *he wanted to celebrate Sydney's 30th jubilee* (C), or that *he wanted to get to know the country* (D).

65. Choice (C) is the correct answer. The question asks why Wiegand has the title "hotel director." The passage says that for years the "globetrotter" has been the hotel director of Germany's number one luxury liner, the MS Europa ("*Seit Jahren ist ... der MS Europa*"). This implies that *a big luxury liner is actually like a hotel.* The passage does not indicate that Wiegand *has to find rooms for passengers in each port city* (A); he goes with the quartermaster to buy fresh produce in the markets ("*Wenn das Schiff ... Frischwaren zu kaufen*"). Wiegand is the second man and boss of 220 employees ("*... der zweite Mann und Chef von 220 Mitarbeitern*"), but the passage does not indicate that *he only books rooms for his coworkers* (B). And nothing in the passage indicates that *he would rather be called "hotel director" than "globetrotter"* (D).

66. Choice (D) is the correct answer. The question asks which ship Wiegand now works on. The passage says that for years he has been hotel director of Germany's number one luxury liner, the MS Europa (*Seit Jahren ist ... der MS Europa*), so he now works *on the Europa.* As a 20-year-old, he started as a steward on the luxury liner Berlin ("*Als 20-Jähriger ... Berlin*"), but he does not work *on the Berlin* (A) now. *Sydney* (B) is the name of the city Wiegand was in, not the ship he currently works on. Nor is *Tegernsee* (C) a ship — it is the name of a lake and the town that Wiegand is from.

67. Choice (C) is the correct answer. The question asks what Wiegand has no desire to do in his free time. The passage says that Wiegand likes to pass the summer on his terrace with a magnificent view of Lake Tegern. In his free time, the "kilometer millionaire" hardly travels, goes walking at most and stands over the stove as a hobby chef, with a "preference for exotic food" ("*Den verbringt Wiegand ... hinter dem Herd*"). In his free time, Wiegand has no desire *to take extended trips.* But he does like *to sit on the terrace of his house* (A), *spend time in the kitchen* (B), and *visit Lake Tegern* (D).

68. Choice (A) is the correct answer. The purpose of the ad is to *introduce a vacation destination.* The ad describes the region Mosel-Saar-Ruwer in the county of Trier-Saarburg with the tagline "Vacation to Your Heart's Content" ("*Ferien nach Herzenslust*"). It mentions the many sights, castles, and picturesque towns and villages that beckon ("*viele Sehenswürdigkeiten ... laden ein*"). The ad is not intended to *extend an invitation to a painting class* (B), *encourage people to shop* (C), or *offer castles for sale* (D).

69. Choice (C) is the correct answer. The question asks what *Ferien nach Herzenslust* ("Vacation to Your Heart's Content") means one should do. As in the English translation, it means one should do what one *particularly likes to do*, not what *is good for circulation* (A) or what *the district administration proposes* (D). It does not make sense to say that one should do what one *must request* (B).

70. Choice (A) is the correct answer. The question asks why the lemurs are raised in North Carolina. The passage says that the "Aye-Ayes" are the primates most threatened by extinction ("*Die Fingertiere sind ... bedroht sind*") and explains that primatologists are raising different kinds of lemurs at Duke University in North Carolina and want to release them on a special preserve in Madagascar after they are grown ("*Die Primatologen haben ... auf Madagaskar aussetzen*"). The passage indicates that the lemurs are raised in North Carolina *in order to be saved from extinction*, not *because they are supposed to find a new home there* (B), *because the primatologists are not allowed to work in Madagascar* (C), or *because there are no things that bring bad luck there* (D).

71. Choice (B) is the correct answer. The question asks what danger predominates ("*herrscht*") for the prosimians ("*Halbaffen*," literally "semi-apes") in their original home. The passage says that the rare lemurs are threatened above all by the destruction of the tropical forests on the East African island ("*Leider werden die seltenen ... bedroht*"). So the prevailing danger, as emphasized by the phrase *vor allem* ("above all"), is that *the forests are being destroyed*. People follow and kill the "Aye-Ayes" ("*sie verfolgen und töten sie*"), but the greatest danger is not that *the islands are becoming populated* (A) — in fact, there is no indication that the population is growing. The lemurs have snouts like rats ("*Schnauzen wie Ratten*"), but they are not *threatened by rats* (C). And there is no indication that the main danger is that *there are not enough primatologists* (D).

72. Choice (C) is the correct answer. The question asks what the U.S. scientists have accomplished. The passage says that a few weeks ago at the primate center of Duke University, for the first time an "Aye-Aye" was born in captivity ("*Im Primatenzentrum ... geboren worden*"); in other words, the scientists *have bred the prosimians outside of*

their native home. The last sentence of the passage discusses the superstitious belief of many people on Madagascar that "Aye-Ayes" bring bad luck, but the passage does not say that the scientists *have combated the superstition of the people of Madagascar* (A). The long middle finger of the "Aye-Aye" occurs naturally; scientists did not *develop the unusual middle finger of these animals* (B). The name "Aye-Aye" is enclosed in quotation marks and treated as a foreign word in the passage, and the detailed description in the first paragraph implies that the animal is still relatively unknown, so it would not be correct to say that the scientists *have made the name of the Aye-Aye known* (D).

73. Choice (A) is the correct answer. The question asks what the U.S. primatologists want to do one day with the lemurs. The passage says that that primatologists want to release the lemurs on a special preserve in Madagascar after they are grown ("*Sie wollen die aufgewachsenen Halbaffen ... auf Madagaskar aussetzen*"); they want to *take them back to Madagascar*. They do not want to *give them to the indigenous people* (B), *release them in North Carolina* (C), or *keep them in a primate center* (D).

74. Choice (D) is the correct answer. The question asks how a lot of the inhabitants of Madagascar view the half-apes ("*Halbaffen*"). The passage says that many of Madagascar's inhabitants see the "Aye-Ayes" as bringers of bad luck ("*sehen viele, die auf Madagaskar leben, die „Aye-Ayes" als Unglücksbringer*"); the inhabitants *feel threatened by them*. The passage does not indicate that the inhabitants *consider them ugly* (A), *find them uninteresting* (B), or *find them especially delicate* (C).

75. Choice (C) is the correct answer. The question asks what one can do with this ticket. The ticket is for "the porcupines" ("*die stachelschweine*") in the Europa-Center, under the auspices of the Berlin Literary Cabaret ("*Berliner Literarisches Kabarett*"). There is a beginning time and an entry ("*Eintritt*") price, as well as row ("*Reihe*") and seat ("*Platz*") numbers. This ticket clearly allows one *to go to a show*, not *to go to the zoo* (A), to *work in the Europa-Center* (B), or *to book a round-trip to Berlin* (D).

76. Choice (A) is the correct answer. The announcement calls drivers' attention to *a weather condition*. The phrase at the top announces, "Caution: Fog!" ("*Achtung Nebel!*"), making it clear that drivers are being told about a weather condition, not *distances* (B), *a detour* (C) or *construction work* (D).

77. Choice (D) is the correct answer. The question asks why this announcement is so important for drivers. The announcement shows the stretches of highway where fog must be reckoned with ("*Auf diesen Autobahnabschnitten muss jetzt mit Nebel gerechnet werden*"). The announcement is important because *it warns about poor*

visibility; it does not *describe detours* (A), *give distances* (B), or *point out gas stations* (C).

78. Choice (D) is the correct answer. The question asks who developed the booth. The passage says that Frank Italiane's company, Environ Corporation, developed a computer-controlled booth in which one can experience a stress-free environment ("*... hat seine Firma, die Environ Corporation, eine ... Kabine entworfen ...*"). The booth was not developed by NASA (A), whose anthropometric technology Environ used ("*Beim Design des „Environ" hat ... zunutze gemacht*"), by Century City Hospital (B), or by Headache and Pain Center (C), where the booth was tested ("*Die am Century City Hospital ... und im Headache and Pain Center ... getestete Kabine ...*").

79. Choice (C) is the correct answer. The question asks who or what regulates the booth. The passage describes the booth as computer-controlled ("*computer-gelenkte*"), so it is *a computer* that regulates the booth. The passage mentions various psychological problems ("*verschiedene psychologischen Problemen*"), but *a psychologist* (A) does not regulate the booth. The booth was tested in a hospital, and the last paragraph indicates that the first generation of the booth will be sold to hospitals, but *a hospital* (B) does not regulate the booth. The first sentence suggests that people might use the booth like Superman to transform from nervous, insecure people to calm, self-confident ones, but *a superman* (D) does not regulate the booth.

80. Choice (A) is the correct answer. The question asks how stress can be reduced in the booth. Among other methods designed to help users, the passage discusses lighting that constantly changes color, shape, and intensity ("*... eine Beleuchtung, die ständig ihre Farbe, Form und Intensität wechselt*"). *Special light effects* are mentioned, but *shock therapy* (B), *intensive training* (C), and *painkillers* (D) are not.

81. Choice (B) is the correct answer. The question asks who primarily should use the "Environ" room. The passage says that the room is designed to help people cope with pain, stress, and various psychological problems ("*Der „Environ" Raum ist dazu gedacht ... zu*"). Therefore, the room should be used primarily by *people who are suffering*, not by *various psychologists* (A), *supermen* (C), or *computer specialists* (D).

82. Choice (A) is the correct answer. The question asks what effect the booth is supposed to have. The passage says that the room is designed to help people cope with pain, stress, and various psychological problems ("*Der „Environ" Raum ist dazu gedacht ... zu*"). It is clear that the room is supposed to *help people*, not *change the world* (B), *improve telecommunication* (C), or *contribute to disarmament* (D).

83. Choice (D) is the correct answer. The question asks where the new booths are supposed to be introduced at first. The passage says that the first generation of the "Environ" will be sold to hospitals, foundations, and other medical companies (*"Die erste Generation des „Environ" wird an Krankenhäuser ... verkauft warden"*). The booths will be introduced *in hospitals*, not *in private homes* (A), *in barracks* (B), or *in stores* (C).

84. Choice (A) is the correct answer. The announcement indicates that "If you work for us part-time as a secretary or clerk with data processing and English skills," you will have time for yourself (*"... da bleibt noch Zeit ...auf Zeit arbeiten"*). It then gives contact information. It is clear that this is an announcement for *a job* (A). The picture of the woman skiing is to illustrate how one might spend his or her free time with this job; this is not an ad for *a hotel in the Alps* (B), *a ski vacation* (C), or *leisurewear* (D).

85. Choice (D) is the correct answer. The question asks what happens when one is employed by "TeamWork." The slogan at the top says, "... there is still time for me," and the ad continues by explaining that this happens when you take a job with TeamWork. In other words, when you work at TeamWork, *you have sufficient free time*. TeamWork is looking for employees with data processing skills and who know English (*"mit EDV-Kenntnissen und Englisch"*); there is no indication that employees will *develop data processing skills* (A) or *learn English* (B). And there is nothing to indicate that each employee has his or her *own telephone line* (C).

German with Listening

The Subject Test in German with Listening is offered once a year only at designated test centers. **To take the test you MUST bring an acceptable CD player with earphones to the test center.**

Sample Listening Questions

The text in brackets [ ] is *only* recorded; it will not appear in your test book. The questions in Part A, however, will be recorded and printed in your test book. Please note that the CD does not start here. Begin using the CD when you start the actual practice test on page 690.

Your answer sheet has five answer positions marked A, B, C, D, and E. Because the questions throughout this test contain only three or four choices, do NOT make any marks in column E, and do not make any marks in column D if there are only three choices given.

Part A

Directions: In this part of the test you will hear several selections. They will not be printed in your test book. You will hear them <u>only once</u>. Therefore, you must listen very carefully. In your test book you will read one or two short questions about what was said. Another speaker will read the questions for you. Each question will be followed by <u>four</u> choices marked (A), (B), (C), and (D). The choices are <u>not</u> printed in your test book. You will hear them <u>once</u>. Select the best answer and fill in the corresponding circle on your answer sheet.

(Narrator) [Questions 1 and 2 refer to the following exchange.]

(Woman) [Könnten Sie mir bitte dieses Kleid heute noch reinigen.

(Man) Das ist leider unmöglich. Wir machen in einer Stunde, um neunzehn Uhr, Feierabend.

(Woman) Aber bitte, ich muss dieses Kleid unbedingt heute zum Konzert tragen!]

1. (Man) [Wo findet dieser Dialog wohl statt?]
Wo findet dieser Dialog wohl statt?

(Woman) [(A) In einer Reinigung.
(B) In einem Konzertsaal.
(C) In einer Boutique.
(D) Auf einem Ball.]

(5 seconds)

Choice (A) is the correct answer to question 1. In this question, you are asked to choose from the four answer choices where the short dialogue you just heard takes place. You have to understand the verb "reinigen" and make the connection between "reinigen" mentioned in the dialogue and the noun "Reinigung" in one of the answer choices. Choices (B), (C), and (D) do not apply to "reinigen" and are therefore incorrect.

2. (Man) [Welche Tageszeit ist est?]
Welche Tageszeit ist est?

(Woman) [(A) Morgen.
(B) Mittag.
(C) Abend.
(D) Nachtmittag.]

(5 seconds)

Choice (C) is the correct answer to question 2. In this question, you are asked to select from the four choices at which time of day the dialogue is taking place. The man in the dialogue says that they "machen Feierabend" in an hour, at 7 p.m. Even if the German 24-hour clock is not known, the use of the word "Feierabend" can also lead to the correct answer. Choices (A), (B), and (D) are incorrect because there is no reference to morning, noon, or afternoon in the dialogue.

Part B

Directions: You will now listen to some extended dialogues or monologues. You will hear each only once. After each dialogue or monologue, you will be asked several questions about what you have just heard. These questions are not printed in your test book. From the four printed choices, select the best answer to each question and fill in the corresponding circle on the answer sheet. There is no sample question for this part.

Questions 3–5

(Narrator) [Two students talk about Chris's year abroad.]

(Woman) [Du, Chris, stimmt es? Du wirst das nächste Schuljahr in Amerika verbringen?

(Man) Ja, ich soll bei einer Familie Lazarro in Los Angeles wohnen und mit ihrem Sohn Miguel zur Schule gehen.

(Woman) Welche Fächer wirst du denn da haben?

(Man) Weiß ich noch nicht, aber ich werde mit Miguel die 11. Klasse besuchen.

(Woman) In amerikanischen Highschools wird auch viel Sport getrieben, nicht?

(Man) Ja, Miguel soll sogar ein recht guter Schwimmer sein. Er hat schon einige Medaillen gewonnen.

(Woman) Das ist ja was für dich! Du schwimmst doch auch so gern!

(Man) Ja, aber jetzt muss ich zuerst noch fleißig Englisch üben. Ich will doch so viel wie möglich im Unterricht verstehen und mich natürlich auch mit meiner neuen Familie unterhalten können.

3. (Man) [Was für eine Schule wird Chris in Amerika besuchen?]
(12 seconds)

(A) Eine Kunstakademie.

(B) Eine Universität.

(C) Eine Oberschule.

(D) Eine Sportschule.

Choice (C) is the correct answer to question 3. In this question, you are asked to answer the question about what kind of school Chris will be going to in America. "Oberschule" is the German equivalent to high school mentioned in the dialogue. It is also mentioned that he will be in eleventh grade, thus referring to "Oberschule" but not to the schools in (A), (B), and (D). These choices are therefore incorrect.

4. (Man) [Warum glaubt Chris, dass Miguel ein guter Schwimmer ist?]
(12 seconds)

(A) Er besucht die Highschool.
(B) Er hat Auszeichnungen gewonnen.
(C) Er wohnt in Kalifornien.
(D) Er ist im Fernsehen erschienen.

Choice (B) is the correct answer to question 4. This question asks why Chris thinks that Miguel is a good swimmer. Chris states in the dialogue that Miguel has won several medals. The use of "Medaillen" (medals) is a more specific way to describe "Auszeichnungen," which is a more general term. It cannot be inferred from choices (A) and (C) that Miguel is a good swimmer, and choice (D) is not at all mentioned in the dialogue.

5. (Man) [Was will Chris noch vor seiner Reise tun?]
(12 seconds)

(A) Studienfächer auswählen.
(B) Medaillen gewinnen.
(C) Englisch lernen.
(D) Viel schwimmen.

Choice (C) is the correct answer to question 5. This question asks what Chris wants to do before he goes on his trip. At the end of the dialogue, Chris says that he needs to practice English in order to understand as much as possible in class and to be able to talk with his new family. Since the activities in the other answer choices are not mentioned as something he wants to do before leaving, choices (A), (B), and (D) are incorrect.

German with Listening Subject Test

Practice Helps

The test that follows is an actual, previously administered SAT Subject Test in German with Listening. To get an idea of what it's like to take this test, practice under conditions that are much like those of an actual test administration.

- Set aside an hour when you can take the test uninterrupted.
- Sit at a desk or table with no other books or papers. Dictionaries, other books, or notes are not allowed in the test room.
- Tear out an answer sheet from the back of this book and fill it in just as you would on the day of the test. One answer sheet can be used for up to three Subject Tests.
- Read the instructions that precede the practice test. During the actual administration you will be asked to read them before answering test questions.
- Time yourself by placing a clock or kitchen timer in front of you.
- After you finish the practice test, read the sections "How to Score the SAT Subject Test in German with Listening" and "How Did You Do on the Subject Test in German with Listening?"
- The appearance of the answer sheet in this book may differ form the answer sheet you see on test day.

GERMAN TEST WITH LISTENING

The top portion of the page of the answer sheet that you will use to take the German Test with Listening must be filled in exactly as illustrated below. When your supervisor tells you to fill in the circle next to the name of the test you are about to take, mark your answer sheet as shown.

○ Literature	○ Mathematics Level 1	○ German	○ Chinese Listening	○ Japanese Listening
○ Biology E	○ Mathematics Level 2	○ Italian	○ French Listening	○ Korean Listening
○ Biology M	○ U.S. History	○ Latin	● German Listening	○ Spanish Listening
○ Chemistry	○ World History	○ Modern Hebrew		
○ Physics	○ French	○ Spanish	**Background Questions:** ① ② ③ ④ ⑤ ⑥ ⑦ ⑧ ⑨	

After filling in the circle next to the name of the test you are taking, locate the Background Questions box on your answer sheet (as shown above). This is where you will answer the following Background Questions on your answer sheet.

BACKGROUND QUESTIONS

Please answer either Part I or Part II below by filling in the appropriate circle in the Background Questions box on your answer sheet. Fill in ONLY ONE circle, as described below, to indicate how you obtained your knowledge of German. The information you provide is for statistical purposes only and will not affect your test score.

Part I — If your knowledge of German comes primarily from any of the following: living in a home where German is the main spoken language, living for six months or longer in a German-speaking country that included significant experience in German language, courses taken at a college, or special study of German, fill in circle 9 and leave the remaining circles blank, regardless of how long you studied the subject in school.

Part II — If your knowledge of German comes primarily from courses taken in secondary school, fill in the circle that indicates the level of the German course in which you are currently enrolled. If you are not now enrolled in a German course, fill in the circle that indicates the level of the most advanced course in German that you have completed.

- First year: first or second half —Fill in circle 1.
- Second year: first half —Fill in circle 2.
  second half —Fill in circle 3.
- Third year: first half —Fill in circle 4.
  second half —Fill in circle 5.
- Fourth year: first half —Fill in circle 6.
  second half —Fill in circle 7.
- Advanced Placement course or a course at a level higher than fourth year, second half
  or
  high school course work plus a minimum of four weeks of study abroad —Fill in circle 8.

When the supervisor gives the signal, turn the page and begin the German Test with Listening. There are 100 numbered circles on the answer sheet and 87 questions in the German Test with Listening. Therefore, use only circles 1 to 87 for recording your answers.

GERMAN TEST WITH LISTENING

PLEASE NOTE THAT YOUR ANSWER SHEET HAS FIVE ANSWER POSITIONS MARKED A, B, C, D, and E, WHILE THE QUESTIONS THROUGHOUT THIS TEST CONTAIN ONLY FOUR CHOICES. BE SURE NOT TO MAKE ANY MARKS IN COLUMN E.

SECTION I

LISTENING

Approximate time—20 minutes

Question 1-27

PART A

Directions: In this part of the test you will hear several selections. They will not be printed in your test book. You will hear them only once. Therefore, you must listen very carefully. In your test book you will read one or two short questions about what was said. Another speaker will read the questions for you. Each question will be followed by four choices marked (A), (B), (C), and (D). The choices are not printed in your test book. You will hear them once. Select the best answer and fill in the corresponding circle on your answer sheet.

Listen to the following example.

You will hear:

You will hear and read: Was schenkt der Mann Lisa zum Geburtstag?

You will hear: Ⓐ ● Ⓒ Ⓓ

The best answer to the question „Was schenkt der Mann Lisa zum Geburtstag?“ is (B), „Ein Buch.“ Therefore you should choose option (B).

Now listen to the first selection.

1. Wie sind Christa und Julia mit Anna verwandt?

   Mark your answer on your answer sheet.

2. Warum gehen die beiden ins Altersheim?

   Mark your answer on your answer sheet.

3. Wo spielt sich diese Szene ab?

   Mark your answer on your answer sheet.

4. Was will die Frau nicht?

   Mark your answer on your answer sheet.

GO ON TO THE NEXT PAGE

5. Worüber sprechen die beiden?

   Mark your answer on your answer sheet.

6. Was bemerkt Erich am Anfang?

   Mark your answer on your answer sheet.

---

7. Was macht Tante Mia, als der Telefonanruf kommt?

   Mark your answer on your answer sheet.

8. Warum ruft Sonja ihre Tante an?

   Mark your answer on your answer sheet.

9. Was will dieser Mann?

   Mark your answer on your answer sheet.

10. Warum wird der Mann seinen Zug nicht verpassen?

    Mark your answer on your answer sheet.

---

11. Was hat der Mann nicht verstanden?

    Mark your answer on your answer sheet.

12. Was soll es in der folgenden Woche wieder geben?

    Mark your answer on your answer sheet.

GO ON TO THE NEXT PAGE

PART B

Directions: You will now listen to some extended dialogues or monologues. You will hear each only once. After each dialogue or monologue, you will be asked several questions about what you have just heard. These questions are not printed in your test book. From the four printed choices, select the best answer to each question and fill in the corresponding circle on the answer sheet. There is no sample question for this part.

Selection number 1

13. (A) Handtücher auf dem Boden.
    (B) Handtücher auf der Heizung.
    (C) Handtücher auf dem Regal.
    (D) Handtücher auf dem Halter.

14. (A) Sie beklagen sich über die Aktion.
    (B) Sie kennen die Hausregel nicht.
    (C) Sie boykottieren die Hotelkette.
    (D) Sie befürworten die Aktion.

15. (A) Handtücher zu erneuern.
    (B) Die Hotelkette auszubauen.
    (C) Abfallstoffe zu produzieren.
    (D) Die Umwelt zu schützen.

Selection number 2

16. (A) Am Bau.
    (B) In der Türkei.
    (C) In Frankfurt.
    (D) In Deutschland.

17. (A) Er ist Elektriker.
    (B) Er ist Verkäufer.
    (C) Er ist Baumeister.
    (D) Er ist Hilfsarbeiter.

18. (A) Er hatte kein eigenes Zimmer.
    (B) Er hat bei Fatimas Familie gewohnt.
    (C) Er hatte ein kleines Haus in Kreuzberg.
    (D) Er hatte keine Elektrizität.

19. (A) Sie haben keine Familien.
    (B) Es geht ihnen nicht so gut.
    (C) Sie haben Heimweh.
    (D) Sie arbeiten viel.

GO ON TO THE NEXT PAGE

Selection number 3

20. (A) In England.
    (B) In Paris.
    (C) In Deutschland.
    (D) In Indien.

21. (A) Weil er so schnell verkauft wurde.
    (B) Weil seine Farbe außergewöhnlich ist.
    (C) Weil er nach Indien geschickt wurde.
    (D) Weil er außergewöhnlich groß ist.

22. (A) Er ist weiß.
    (B) Er ist grün.
    (C) Er ist rot.
    (D) Er ist gelb.

23. (A) Er will den Diamanten verkaufen.
    (B) Er will den Diamanten seinem Vater zeigen.
    (C) Er will öfter nach Indien reisen.
    (D) Er will eine englischsprachige Zeitung finden.

Selection number 4

24. (A) Ein Jahr in den USA reisen.
    (B) In England studieren.
    (C) In den USA studieren.
    (D) Englisch unterrichten.

25. (A) Fremdsprachen sind dafür nicht nötig.
    (B) Informatik ist in den USA fortgeschritten.
    (C) Für ihr Fach braucht man Auslandserfahrung.
    (D) Sie will Fernsehansagerin werden.

26. (A) Sie möchte sich persönlich ein Bild vom amerikanischen Leben machen.
    (B) Sie möchte mehr Gelegenheit haben, amerikanisches Fernsehen zu sehen.
    (C) Sie möchte Amerikanern ein anderes Image der Deutschen vermitteln.
    (D) Sie möchte, dass man in Deutschland mehr amerikanische Programme zeigt.

27. (A) Sie weiß, wie gut ihr Image ist.
    (B) Sie hat Reisefieber.
    (C) Sie will einfach von Deutschland weg.
    (D) Sie weiß, was sie will.

END OF SECTION I

DO NOT GO ON TO SECTION II UNTIL YOU ARE TOLD TO DO SO.

SECTION II

READING

Time—40 minutes

Question 28-87

WHEN YOU BEGIN THE READING SECTION, BE SURE THAT YOU MARK YOUR ANSWER TO THE FIRST READING QUESTION BY FILLING IN ONE OF THE CIRCLES NEXT TO NUMBER 28 ON THE ANSWER SHEET.

PART A

Directions: This part consists of a number of incomplete statements, each having four suggested completions. Select the most appropriate completion and fill in the corresponding circle on the answer sheet.

In der Schule

28. Man schreibt mit ------- an die Tafel.

(A) Tusche
(B) Bleistift
(C) Kugelschreiber
(D) Kreide

29. Unsere Lehrerin ------- fünf Fremdsprachen.

(A) kann
(B) weiß
(C) zeigt
(D) bekennt

30. Solche Aufgaben ------- mir keine Schwierigkeiten.

(A) haben
(B) machen
(C) tun
(D) sind

Konversation auf einer Party

31. Ich meine, der Film hat zu lange -------.

(A) gedauert
(B) genommen
(C) geleistet
(D) gesehen

32. Sabine besucht ihre Tante sehr oft, ------- sie wohnt gleich nebenan.

(A) sondern
(B) obwohl
(C) oder
(D) denn

33. ------- ich viel Geld hätte, würde ich eine lange Reise machen.

(A) Ob
(B) Dann
(C) Wenn
(D) Obwohl

34. Was ------- Sie von moderner Musik?

(A) fühlen
(B) betrachten
(C) halten
(D) gefallen

35. Wenn ich das Buch zuerst gelesen hätte, hätte ich den Film sicher besser -------.

(A) verstehen
(B) verstanden
(C) verstände
(D) verstehe

GO ON TO THE NEXT PAGE

Auf der Reise

36. Du bist schon wieder da? Du musst aber schnell gelaufen -------!

(A) sein
(B) gewesen
(C) sei
(D) warst

37. Morgen müssen wir ------- aufstehen, denn wir fahren um 6 Uhr ab.

(A) früh
(B) spät
(C) bald
(D) langsam

Zu Hause

38. Warum sprichst du nicht einmal mit deinem Lehrer -------?

(A) darüber
(B) damit
(C) darin
(D) dafür

39. ------- zwei Wochen wohne ich bei meiner Großmutter.

(A) Vor
(B) Seit
(C) Bis
(D) Um

40. Ich weiß nicht, ------- sie mit uns ins Restaurant kommt.

(A) ob
(B) dass
(C) als
(D) wenn

41. Ich war mit meinen Hausaufgaben heute schnell fertig, denn sie waren sehr -------.

(A) freundlich
(B) einzig
(C) einfach
(D) pünktlich

42. Es ist hier kalt. Ist ------- Heizung an?

(A) der
(B) das
(C) den
(D) die

43. Ich hatte diese politische Lage falsch gesehen und musste meine Meinung -------.

(A) nehmen
(B) umdrehen
(C) ändern
(D) ausprobieren

GO ON TO THE NEXT PAGE

PART B

Directions: In each of the following paragraphs, there are numbered blanks indicating that words or phrases have been omitted. For each numbered blank, four completions are provided. First read through the entire paragraph. Then, for each numbered blank, choose the completion that is most appropriate and fill in the corresponding circle on the answer sheet.

Ein guter Arbeitsplatz

Je länger ich _(44)_ der Firma Meyer bin, _(45)_ besser gefällt es mir dort. Die Firma Meyer ist eine Druckerei, die Einladungen und Glückwunschkarten _(46)_. Ich sitze aber nicht nur im _(47)_, sondern besuche auch Kunden. Meine Kollegen, _(48)_ Arbeit ich weniger interessant finde, sind alle älter als ich. Aber es ist leicht, mit ihnen _(49)_.

44. (A) bei
    (B) vor
    (C) zu
    (D) an

45. (A) denn
    (B) so
    (C) desto
    (D) dann

46. (A) kann
    (B) herstellt
    (C) verbraucht
    (D) legt

47. (A) Auto
    (B) Aufzug
    (C) Büro
    (D) Bahnhof

48. (A) die
    (B) deren
    (C) dessen
    (D) der

49. (A) auszukommen
    (B) auskommen
    (C) ausgekommen
    (D) auskommt

GO ON TO THE NEXT PAGE

Vergessen

Herr Hoffmann wollte gerade das Haus __(50)__, um den Frühzug zu __(51)__, als seine Frau ihm einen __(52)__ in die Hand drückte. „Vergiss bitte nicht, ihn einzuwerfen, __(53)__ du ins Büro gehst, damit __(54)__ Freundin ihn morgen noch bekommt! Er ist sehr wichtig!“ Aber __(55)__ Mann vergaß doch, ihn einzuwerfen. __(56)__ er am Abend wieder nach Hause kam, hatte er den Brief immer noch in der Tasche.

50. (A) gehen
    (B) vergehen
    (C) verlassen
    (D) lassen

51. (A) erwerben
    (B) sehen
    (C) hören
    (D) erreichen

52. (A) Schreiben
    (B) Brief
    (C) Telegramm
    (D) Paket

53. (A) bevor
    (B) nachdem
    (C) seitdem
    (D) wonach

54. (A) meiner
    (B) meine
    (C) meines
    (D) mein

55. (A) ihr
    (B) ihre
    (C) ihrer
    (D) ihren

56. (A) Wenn
    (B) Wann
    (C) Als
    (D) Ob

GO ON TO THE NEXT PAGE

Anne-Maries Wunsch

Anne-Marie möchte einen __(57)__ CD-Player, hat aber noch nicht genug __(58)__ dafür gespart. Ihre Eltern sind __(59)__ Meinung, sie solle jobben. Ihr wäre es natürlich lieber, __(60)__ ihr die Eltern einen CD-Player zum Geburtstag __(61)__ würden.

57. (A) neu
(B) neue
(C) neuen
(D) neues

58. (A) Geduld
(B) Mark
(C) Zeit
(D) Geld

59. (A) die
(B) der
(C) dem
(D) das

60. (A) weil
(B) damit
(C) nachdem
(D) wenn

61. (A) belohnen
(B) schenken
(C) beibringen
(D) spielen

GO ON TO THE NEXT PAGE

PART C

Directions: Read the following texts carefully for comprehension. Each is followed by a number of questions or incomplete statements. Select the answer or completion that is best according to the text and fill in the corresponding circle on your answer sheet.

Herzlichen Dank

allen, die uns durch Wort, Schrift, Kranz- und Blumenspenden ihre Anteilnahme an unserer Trauer erwiesen haben.

Im Namen der Angehörigen:
Karl Steinke

Frankfurt am Main, im August 1990

62. Was ist das?

(A) Eine Todesanzeige
(B) Eine Entschuldigung
(C) Eine Hochzeitsanzeige
(D) Eine Danksagung

63. Diese Anzeige ist an Leute gerichtet, die

(A) ihr Beileid ausgedrückt haben
(B) Geschenke verschickt haben
(C) Geld verteilt haben
(D) ihre Angehörigen benachrichtigt haben

GO ON TO THE NEXT PAGE

Pittsburghs Wandlung

Wo man heute in eleganten Boutiquen einkauft und in Feinschmeckerrestaurants speist, rauchten früher die Kamine der Eisen- und Stahlindustrie. Der größte Arbeitgeber in der Stadt ist jetzt die „University of Pittsburgh". Dazu kommen anspruchsvolle Jobs in 170 Forschungsinstitutionen und 700 Hochtechnologiefirmen.

Nach einem kurzen Spaziergang durch Pittsburghs „Downtown", die nach europäischen Maßstäben sauber und sicher ist, erreicht man das William Penn Hotel in der Grant Street. Der Pittsburgher Kohle-König Henry Clay Frick ließ es 1916 bauen, weil er unbedingt das größte und schönste Hotel zwischen Chicago und New York besitzen wollte. Heute gilt das liebevoll restaurierte Haus mit 595 Zimmern als einziges „Grand Hotel" in Pittsburgh. Wenn man die Hotelhalle betritt, fühlt man sich wie in einem Schlosssaal mit hohen Fensterbögen, Stuckdecken, Kristallleuchtern und vielen Zimmerpalmen. Zum „Afternoon-Tea" klimpert ein Klavierspieler heitere Melodien.

Vom „Golden Triangle", der geschäftigen Innenstadt Pittsburghs, lohnt sich ein kleiner Abstecher zum Station Square. Über die Smithfield Street Bridge, die den Monongahela-Fluss überspannt, kommt man zum „Pittsburgh & Lake Erie Railroad"– Bahnhof. Er wurde 1901 fertig gestellt. Ende der sechziger Jahre rollte der letzte Passagierzug aus dem Gebäude. Einige Zeit später baute Charles Muir aus Detroit die unteren Etagen in ein feines Restaurant um: Das Grand Concourse. In der großen Wartehalle richtete er den Speisesaal für 500 Gäste ein.

Doch nicht nur wegen ihrer Sehenswürdigkeiten, sondern auch wegen der Universitäten, des Museumskomplexes und der weltberühmten Krankenhäuser ist die Stadt Pittsburgh für Reisende aus Deutschland interessant; und auf dem Flughafen geht es so schnell und einfach, wie man es sich in den Warteschlangen auf den Airports in New York und Los Angeles immer wünscht.

64. Wofür war Pittsburgh früher bekannt?

(A) Für elegante Boutiquen
(B) Für viele Schulen
(C) Für große Krankenhäuser
(D) Für Schwerindustrie

65. Wo sind die meisten Einwohner von Pittsburgh heute angestellt?

(A) Auf dem Flughafen
(B) An der Universität
(C) Im William Penn Hotel
(D) Im Grand Concourse Restaurant

66. Wer war Henry Clay Frick?

(A) Ein bekannter Architekt
(B) Ein Bürgermeister von Pittsburgh
(C) Ein Industriemagnat
(D) Ein Restaurantbesitzer

67. Wozu wird heute der ehemalige Pittsburgher Bahnhof benutzt?

(A) Als Anschlussbahnhof
(B) Als Lagerhalle für Kohle
(C) Als Kongresshalle
(D) Als gutes Lokal

68. Was war Charles Muir wohl von Beruf?

(A) Lokomotivführer
(B) Museumsdirektor
(C) Baumeister
(D) Reiseführer

69. Warum lohnt es sich, Pittsburgh zu besuchen?

(A) Die Stadt hat viel zu bieten.
(B) Pittsburgh hat ein berühmtes Schloss.
(C) Die Leute sind freundlich.
(D) Die Hotels sind dort sehr billig.

GO ON TO THE NEXT PAGE

Fachbuchhandlung für Geisteswissenschaften

Sämtliche Semesterliteratur haben wir vorrätig, oder wir bemühen uns, diese sofort zu beschaffen. Bestellservice auch telefonisch.

BesTellBuch 8324051

Nahe der Rostlaube, neben der Mensa, Eingang Brümmerstraße, an der U-Bahnlinie zwischen Thielplatz und Dahlem-Dorf. Ein starkes wissenschaftliches Sortiment unterstützt Ihr Studium:

kompetent, freundlich, schnell.

Tell

Thielallee 34, **Mo. bis Fr. 9-18, Sa. 10-13 Uhr**

70. Was für Bücher kauft man bei Tell?

(A) Kinderbücher
(B) Reisebücher
(C) Lehrbücher
(D) Kochbücher

71. Welchen Service bietet die Fachbuchhandlung an?

(A) Bücher können ins Haus geliefert werden.
(B) Bücher können billiger beschafft werden.
(C) Bücher können ausgeliehen werden.
(D) Bücher können telefonisch bestellt werden.

GO ON TO THE NEXT PAGE

Der Kranführer Hans Magnussen sah auf die Uhr: zehn Minuten nach drei. „Bald Feierabend“, dachte er. Als Magnussen die Baggerschaufel noch einmal herunterließ, glaubte er, auf etwas Hartes zu stoßen. Er stellte den Bagger* ab und kletterte aus dem Kran, um zu sehen, was es sein könnte. Magnussen holte einen Spaten und begann zu graben. Da fand er eine relativ große Kiste, die – wie sich herausstellte – 23 200 Gold- und Silbermünzen aus dem 14. und 15. Jahrhundert enthielt. Es war der bedeutendste Fund in der Geschichte der deutschen Münzen.

Wem gehörte nun dieser Gold- und Silberschatz? Das Land, auf dem Magnussen die Kiste entdeckt hatte, gehörte dem Land Schleswig-Holstein, und Schleswig-Holstein hatte auch die Demolierung des Gebäudes in der Stadt Lübeck angeordnet, unter dem der Schatz verborgen lag. Nicht nur das Land Schleswig-Holstein, auch die Baggerfirma wollte den ganzen Fund für sich beanspruchen und behauptete, dass ja der Kranführer nur in ihrem Auftrag gehandelt habe.

Das deutsche Gesetz aber bestimmte Folgendes: Wenn etwas entdeckt wird, was schon so lange unter der Erde liegt, dass man den ursprünglichen Eigentümer nicht mehr feststellen kann, dann muss der Fund zwischen dem „Entdecker“ und dem Landeigentümer geteilt werden. Und so entschied auch das Bundesgericht. Das Land Schleswig-Holstein will jetzt den kulturell und historisch wertvollen Fund behalten und wird dem Kranführer Magnussen für seinen Anteil 700 000 Mark zahlen.

* *Bagger*: excavator

72. Wann entdeckte der Kranführer Magnussen den Fund?

(A) Kurz vor Arbeitsschluss
(B) Um die Mittagszeit
(C) Am frühen Morgen
(D) Mitten in der Nacht

73. Warum stellte Magnussen den Kran ab?

(A) Er dachte, es sei schon Feierabend.
(B) Der Bagger funktionierte nicht richtig.
(C) Der Schutt war zu schwer für die Schaufel.
(D) Er wollte wissen, was unter der Erde war.

74. Das Land Schleswig-Holstein wollte den ganzen Fund behalten, weil

(A) ihm das Land gehörte
(B) Magnussen in Lübeck wohnte
(C) Magnussen das Gebäude zerstörte
(D) der Eigentümer im Bundesgericht arbeitete

75. Wie alt waren die Münzen?

(A) Fast hundert Jahre
(B) Etwas über tausend Jahre
(C) Genau fünfzig Jahre
(D) Mehrere hundert Jahre

76. Das Bundesgericht entschied, dass

(A) die Baggerfirma die Münzen behalten durfte
(B) Schleswig-Holstein und Magnussen den Fund teilen sollten
(C) der Eigentümer des Fundes gesucht werden sollte
(D) die Demolierungsarbeiten abgebrochen werden sollten

77. Wer bekam am Ende den Schatz?

(A) Die Stadt Lübeck
(B) Die Baggerfirma
(C) Das Land Schleswig-Holstein
(D) Der ursprüngliche Eigentümer

GO ON TO THE NEXT PAGE

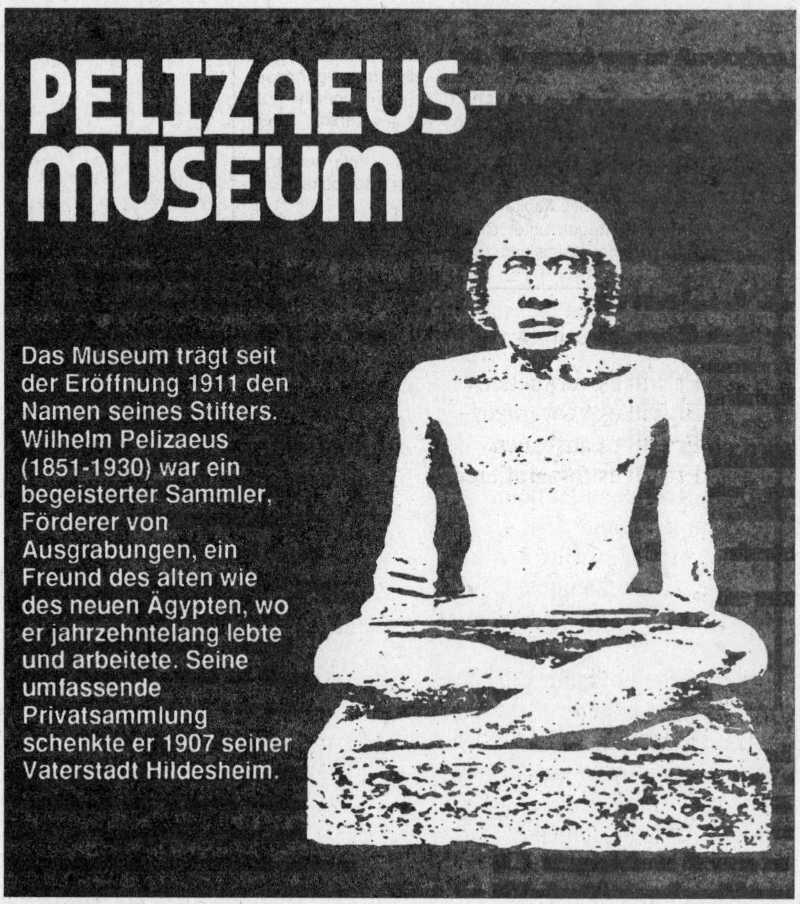
PELIZAEUS-
MUSEUM
Das Museum trägt seit der Eröffnung 1911 den Namen seines Stifters. Wilhelm Pelizaeus (1851-1930) war ein begeisterter Sammler, Förderer von Ausgrabungen, ein Freund des alten wie des neuen Ägypten, wo er jahrzehntelang lebte und arbeitete. Seine umfassende Privatsammlung schenkte er 1907 seiner Vaterstadt Hildesheim.

78. Aus dem Text geht hervor, dass Wilhelm Pelizaeus

(A) 1907 in Ägypten gestorben ist
(B) ein Museum in Ägypten gestiftet hat
(C) 1851 in Hildesheim geboren wurde
(D) Ausgrabungen in Hildesheim gemacht hat

79. Was wird im Pelizaeus-Museum hauptsächlich ausgestellt?

(A) Fotos von Wilhelm Pelizaeus
(B) Bilder einer Vaterstadt
(C) Büsten bekannter Sammler
(D) Funde aus dem alten Ägypten

GO ON TO THE NEXT PAGE

Miami/USA

Aus Altersgründen **zu verkaufen** gut gehendes, solides **Fotogeschäft** für professionelle Fotografen und Öffentlichkeit mit 4 versch. Zweigstellen an günstigen Lokalitäten (total ca. 15 000 sq. feet–1350 m²). International tätig, weiterausbau- und entwicklungsfähig. 40 Mitarbeiter. Erforderliches Kapital: 6 Mio. US-$.

Anfragen unter Chiffre X 240 673 F, NZZ, Inseratenabteilung, Postfach, 8021 Zürich.

VKX240 673F

80. Was will der Besitzer mit dem Geschäft machen?

(A) Er will es vermieten.
(B) Er will es loswerden.
(C) Er will es ausbauen.
(D) Er will es fotografieren.

GO ON TO THE NEXT PAGE

München hat mit dem Englischen Garten ein Rückzugsparadies, in dem man sich auch an den heißesten Sommertagen so wohl fühlt wie sonst nur an den exotischsten Urlaubszielen. Mal ist der Englische Garten ganz spannender Urwald, wo man einsam und allein auf Entdeckungstouren gehen kann, dann wieder die elegante Sonnenterrasse einer ganzen Stadt. Und wer Abkühlung sucht, findet sie im Eisbach und im See.

Wo sich heute Familien, Punks und Hippies sowie Studenten aus der nahen Uni aufhalten, wurden früher Wildschweine und andere Tiere gejagt. Die Idee, aus dem privaten Jagdrevier des Kurfürsten Carl Theodor einen Volksgarten zu machen, stammt eigentlich von Benjamin Thompson aus Massachusetts. Denn der schlug dem Kurfürsten vor, seine Soldaten sollten in ihrer Freizeit die Wildnis in Nutzgärten umwandeln. In den Anfängen des Englischen Gartens waren also Soldaten damit beschäftigt, mit Hacke und Spaten Kartoffeln anzupflanzen, die Thompson aus Amerika mitgebracht hatte. Entsprechend dem neuen Geist der Zeit nach der Französischen Revolution wurde 1792 der neu angelegte Garten den Bürgern übergeben.

Später hat der Landschaftsgärtner Friedrich Ludwig von Skell das grüne Idyll verschönert. Wie in den englischen Landschaftsgärten sollte in dem neuen Park die Natur so gestaltet werden, dass sie „möglichst echt" aussah. So bekam der See seine drei Inseln, und es wurden neue Bäche, Wasserfälle und harmonisch angeordnete Baumgruppen angelegt. Heute würde man nie ahnen, dass der Englische Garten über 200 Jahre lang eine Großbaustelle war.

81. Welche der folgenden Überschriften passt am besten zu diesem Text?

(A) Die Entstehung des Englischen Gartens
(B) Ein exotisches Reiseziel
(C) Ein Jagdparadies in München
(D) Das Leben des Kurfürsten Carl Theodor

82. Was haben die Soldaten auf diesem Land gemacht?

(A) Sie haben es verteidigt.
(B) Sie haben Gemüsegärten angelegt.
(C) Sie haben dort exerziert.
(D) Sie haben Bäume gepflanzt.

83. Benjamin Thompson schlug dem Kurfürsten vor,

(A) nach Amerika auszuwandern
(B) eine Universität zu gründen
(C) das Land anders zu verwenden
(D) Ludwig von Skell anzustellen

84. Wozu benutzt man heute den Englischen Garten?

(A) Um neue Kartoffelsorten zu entwickeln
(B) Um sich weiterzubilden
(C) Um exotische Tiere anzuschauen
(D) Um sich zu entspannen

85. Der Kurfürst Carl Theodor benutzte das Land des heutigen Englischen Gartens, um

(A) darin zu wandern
(B) einen See anzulegen
(C) dort zu jagen
(D) Soldaten auszubilden

GO ON TO THE NEXT PAGE

Nordamerika rückt ein Drittel näher :

- Haben Sie Geschäftspartner, Freunde oder Angehörige in Nordamerika?
- Telefonieren Sie oft in die Vereinigten Staaten oder nach Kanada?

Wenn Sie eine dieser Fragen mit ja beantworten können, dann haben Sie einen Grund zur Freude:

Seit 1. Mai telefonieren Sie 37% günstiger von Deutschland in die USA und nach Kanada.

86. Was will man mit dieser Anzeige mitteilen?

(A) Man soll sich Freunde in Amerika suchen.
(B) Deutsche reisen öfter nach Nordamerika.
(C) Man soll viel mehr in der ganzen Welt telefonieren.
(D) Anrufe nach Nordamerika sind jetzt billiger.

GO ON TO THE NEXT PAGE

Menschen '99

"Ich wollte schon immer meinen Weg allein gehen. Ich habe Abitur und danach eine Lehre gemacht. Anschließend habe ich 2 Jahre in einer Galerie in London gearbeitet. Heute weiß ich, was meine Ausbildung wert ist. Sie gibt mir Sicherheit, auch finanziell. Ich verdiene gut und kann sogar für die Zukunft vorsorgen. Wie, das diskutiere ich gerade mit der Deutschen Bank."

87. Warum ist diese Person froh über ihre Ausbildung?

(A) Sie kann ausreichend für sich sorgen.
(B) Sie kann bei der Deutschen Bank arbeiten.
(C) Sie bekommt dadurch viel Prestige.
(D) Sie kann damit ihr Abitur nachmachen.

END OF SECTION II

STOP

IF YOU FINISH BEFORE TIME IS CALLED, YOU MAY CHECK YOUR WORK ON SECTION II OF THIS TEST.
DO NO TURN TO ANY OTHER TEST IN THIS BOOK.

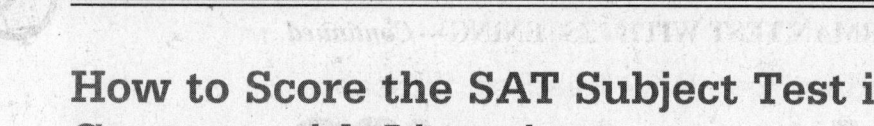

How to Score the SAT Subject Test in German with Listening

When you take an actual SAT Subject Test in German with Listening, you receive an overall composite score as well as two subscores: one for the reading section, one for the listening section.

The reading and listening scores are reported on the College Board's 20–80 scale. However the composite score, which is the most significant of the scores reported to the colleges you specify, is in the form of the College Board's 200–800 scale.

Worksheet 1. Finding Your Raw Listening Subscore

STEP 1: Table A on page 712 lists the correct answers for all the questions on the SAT Subject Test in German with Listening that is reproduced in this book. It also serves as a worksheet for you to calculate your raw Listening subscore.

- Compare your answers with those given in the table.
- Put a check in the column marked "Right" if your answer is correct.
- Put a check in the column marked "Wrong" if your answer is incorrect.
- Leave both columns blank if you omitted the question.

STEP 2: Count the number of right answers for questions 1–27.

Enter the total here: ________________

STEP 3: Count the number of wrong answers for questions 1–27.

Enter the total here: ________________

STEP 4: Multiply the number of wrong answers by .333.

Enter the product here: ________________

STEP 5: Subtract the result obtained in Step 4 from the total you obtained in Step 2.

Enter the result here: ________________

STEP 6: Round the number obtained in Step 5 to the nearest whole number.

Enter the result here: ________________

The number you obtained in Step 6 is your raw Listening subscore.

Worksheet 2. Finding Your Raw Reading Subscore

STEP 1: Table A lists the correct answers for all the questions on the SAT Subject Test in German with Listening that is reproduced in this book. It also serves as a worksheet for you to calculate your raw Reading subscore.

STEP 2: Count the number of right answers for questions 28–87.

Enter the total here: ________________

STEP 3: Count the number of wrong answers for questions 28–87.

Enter the total here: ________________

STEP 4: Multiply the number of wrong answers by .333.

Enter the product here: ________________

STEP 5: Subtract the result obtained in Step 4 from the total you obtained in Step 2.

Enter the result here: ________________

STEP 6: Round the number obtained in Step 5 to the nearest whole number.

Enter the result here: ________________

The number you obtained in Step 6 is your raw Reading subscore.

Worksheet 3. Finding Your Raw Composite Score

STEP 1: Enter your unrounded raw Reading subscore from Step 5 of Worksheet 2.

Enter the result here: ________________

STEP 2: Enter your unrounded raw Listening subscore from Step 5 of Worksheet 1.

Enter the result here: ________________

STEP 3: Add the result obtained in Step 1 to the result obtained in Step 2.

Enter the result here: ________________

STEP 4: Round the number obtained in Step 3 to the nearest whole number.

Enter the result here: ________________

The number you obtained in Step 4 is your raw composite score.

Table A

Answers to the Subject Test in German with Listening and Percentage of Students Answering Each Question Correctly

Question Number	Correct Answer	Right	Wrong	Percentage of Students Answering the Question Correctly*	Question Number	Correct Answer	Right	Wrong	Percentage of Students Answering the Question Correctly*
1	A			54	33	C			87
2	D			90	34	C			38
3	A			90	35	B			80
4	B			89	36	A			64
5	C			82	37	A			95
6	A			75	38	A			82
7	B			57	39	B			62
8	D			80	40	A			71
9	A			55	41	C			82
10	B			78	42	D			64
11	B			84	43	C			61
12	D			41	44	A			86
13	A			51	45	C			41
14	D			37	46	B			56
15	D			52	47	C			88
16	D			86	48	B			45
17	A			86	49	A			68
18	A			38	50	C			49
19	B			82	51	D			52
20	D			67	52	B			88
21	B			80	53	A			80
22	C			78	54	B			61
23	A			53	55	A			46
24	C			74	56	C			55
25	B			67	57	C			75
26	A			34	58	D			99
27	D			60	59	B			33
28	D			72	60	D			64
29	A			45	61	B			95
30	B			52	62	D			76
31	A			81	63	A			32
32	D			71	64	D			71

Table A continued on next page

Table A continued from previous page

Question Number	Correct Answer	Right	Wrong	Percentage of Students Answering the Question Correctly*	Question Number	Correct Answer	Right	Wrong	Percentage of Students Answering the Question Correctly*
65	B			66	77	C			67
66	C			50	78	C			54
67	D			46	79	D			73
68	C			73	80	B			27
69	A			90	81	A			66
70	C			85	82	B			56
71	D			85	83	C			54
72	A			47	84	D			52
73	D			55	85	C			31
74	A			57	86	D			87
75	D			68	87	A			50
76	B			59					

* These percentages are based on an analysis of the answer sheets of a representative sample of 483 students who took the original administration of this test and whose mean composite score was 589. They may be used as an indication of the relative difficulty of a particular question.

Answer explanations for the Subject Test in German with Listening can be found on page 719.

Finding Your Scaled Score

When you take SAT Subject Tests, the scores sent to the colleges you specify are reported on the College Board scale, which ranges from 200–800. Subscores are reported on a scale which ranges from 20–80. You can convert your practice test scores to scaled scores by using Tables B, C, and D on the following pages. To find your scaled score, locate your raw score in the left-hand column of the table; the corresponding score in the right-hand column is your scaled score. For example, a raw score of 47 on this particular edition of the Subject Test in German with Listening corresponds to a scaled composite score of 570.

Raw scores are converted to scaled scores to ensure that a score earned on any one edition of a particular Subject Test is comparable to the same scaled score earned on any other edition of the same Subject Test. Because some editions of the tests may be slightly easier or more difficult than others, College Board scaled scores are adjusted so that they indicate the same level of performance regardless of the edition of the test taken and the ability of the group that takes it. Thus, for example, a score of 400 on one edition of a test taken at a particular administration indicates the same level of achievement as a score of 400 on a different edition of the test taken at a different administration.

When you take the SAT Subject Tests during a national administration, your scores are likely to differ somewhat from the scores you obtain on the tests in this book. People perform at different levels at different times for reasons unrelated to the tests themselves. The precision of any test is also limited because it represents only a sample of all the possible questions that could be asked.

Your scaled composite score from Table B is ________________ .

Your scaled listening score from Table C is ________________ .

Your scaled reading score from Table D is ________________ .

Table B

Scaled Score Conversion Table
Subject Test in German with Listening
Composite Score

Raw Score	Scaled Score	Raw Score	Scaled Score	Raw Score	Scaled Score
87	800	49	580	11	390
86	780	48	580	10	390
85	770	47	570	9	380
84	770	46	570	8	370
83	760	45	570	7	370
82	760	44	560	6	360
81	750	43	560	5	360
80	750	42	550	4	350
79	740	41	550	3	350
78	740	40	540	2	340
77	740	39	540	1	340
76	730	38	540	0	330
75	730	37	530	-1	330
74	720	36	530	-2	330
73	720	35	520	-3	320
72	710	34	520	-4	320
71	710	33	510	-5	320
70	700	32	510	-6	310
69	700	31	500	-7	310
68	690	30	500	-8	310
67	690	29	490	-9	310
66	680	28	490	-10	300
65	680	27	480	-11	300
64	670	26	480	-12	300
63	660	25	470	-13	300
62	660	24	470	-14	300
61	650	23	460	-15	300
60	650	22	460	-16	300
59	640	21	450	-17	300
58	630	20	450	-18	290
57	630	19	440	-19	290
56	620	18	430	-20	290
55	620	17	430	-21	290
54	610	16	420	-22	290
53	600	15	420	-23	290
52	600	14	410	-24	290
51	590	13	400	-25	290
50	590	12	400	-26	290
				-27	280
				-28	280
				-29	270

Table C

Scaled Score Conversion Table
Subject Test in German with Listening
Listening Subscore

Raw Score	Scaled Score	Raw Score	Scaled Score	Raw Score	Scaled Score
27	78	13	54	-1	35
26	76	12	53	-2	34
25	74	11	51	-3	33
24	73	10	50	-4	32
23	71	9	49	-5	31
22	69	8	47	-6	31
21	67	7	46	-7	30
20	65	6	45	-8	29
19	63	5	43	-9	28
18	61	4	41		
17	60	3	40		
16	58	2	38		
15	57	1	37		
14	55	0	36		

Table D

Scaled Score Conversion Table Subject Test in German with Listening Reading Subscore					
Raw Score	Scaled Score	Raw Score	Scaled Score	Raw Score	Scaled Score
60	79	33	58	6	39
59	78	32	58	5	38
58	77	31	57	4	37
57	76	30	56	3	37
56	75	29	56	2	36
55	75	28	55	1	35
54	74	27	55	0	34
53	74	26	54	-1	34
52	73	25	53	-2	33
51	72	24	53	-3	33
50	72	23	52	-4	32
49	71	22	51	-5	32
48	70	21	51	-6	31
47	70	20	50	-7	31
46	69	19	49	-8	31
45	68	18	49	-9	30
44	67	17	48	-10	30
43	66	16	47	-11	30
42	66	15	46	-12	30
41	65	14	46	-13	30
40	64	13	45	-14	29
39	63	12	44	-15	29
38	62	11	43	-16	29
37	61	10	42	-17	29
36	60	9	42	-18	29
35	60	8	41	-19	29
34	59	7	40	-20	29

How Did You Do on the Subject Test in German with Listening?

After you score your test and analyze your performance, think about the following questions:

Did you run out of time before reaching the end of the test?

If so, you may need to pace yourself better. For example, maybe you spent too much time on one or two hard questions. A better approach might be to skip the ones you can't answer right away and try answering all the questions that remain on the test. Then if there's time, go back to the questions you skipped.

Did you take a long time reading the directions?

You will save time when you take the test by learning the directions to the Subject Test in German with Listening ahead of time. Each minute you spend reading directions during the test is a minute that you could use to answer questions.

How did you handle questions you were unsure of?

If you were able to eliminate one or more of the answer choices as wrong and guess from the remaining ones, your approach probably worked to your advantage. On the other hand, making haphazard guesses or omitting questions without trying to eliminate choices could cost you valuable points.

How difficult were the questions for you compared with other students who took the test?

Table A shows you how difficult the multiple-choice questions were for the group of students who took this test during its national administration. The right-hand column gives the percentage of students that answered each question correctly.

A question answered correctly by almost everyone in the group is obviously an easier question. For example, 95 percent of the students answered question 37 correctly. But only 27 percent answered question 80 correctly.

Keep in mind that these percentages are based on just one group of students. They would probably be different with another group of students taking the test.

If you missed several easier questions, go back and try to find out why: Did the questions cover material you haven't yet reviewed? Did you misunderstand the directions?

Answer Explanations for the German with Listening Subject Test

1. Choice (A) is the correct answer. Christa refers to Julia as "dear sister" (*Schwesterherz*) and talks about their Aunt Anna. Therefore, Christa and Julia are Anna's nieces, not Anna's sisters (B), cousins (C), or granddaughters (D).

2. Choice (D) is the correct answer. The sisters are going to the retirement home because they want to visit their aunt. Christa will bring a fruitcake, but the sisters will not necessarily bake it (A). Julia will bring flowers, but the sisters will not necessarily pick them (B). It would not be necessary to go to the retirement home if they wanted to make a telephone call (C).

3. Choice (A) is the correct answer. The scene begins with an announcement about the next train to Hamburg leaving in a minute and a warning to be careful on the platform. Based on what is happening in the scene, it is logical to say that it takes place in a train station. The man and woman are not on a train (B) since they are discussing whether or not they will make the train if they run. It does not make sense to suggest that the scene take place in a store (C) or a park (D).

4. Choice (B) is the correct answer. The woman does <u>not</u> want to wait two hours for another train. She actually suggests that they run (A) to catch the train, so it does not make sense to suggest that she does not want to run. Since she is already speaking, it is unlikely that she does not want to speak (C). Further, she does not mention not wanting to drive (D) at all.

5. Choice (C) is the correct answer. Anna and Erich are talking about Anna's ski vacation. They are not talking about the events of her day (A), Erich's ski trip (B), or his appearance (D).

6. Choice (A) is the correct answer. Erich remarks at the beginning of the conversation that Anna has a nice tan. By making this comment, he implies that she looks good. He does not talk about going on a trip himself (B), only that he has dreamed of a trip like Anna's. Anna says that it was sunny every day during the trip, but Erich does

not talk about the sun shining every day (C). Erich does not mention that he has too much work (D) either; in fact, he does not mention work at all.

7. Choice (B) is the correct answer. When the phone rings, Aunt Mia is watching television, specifically the news. She has already finished dinner, so she is not making it (A) or eating (C). Her niece is calling her; she is not calling her niece (D).

8. Choice (D) is the correct answer. Sonja is calling her aunt to invite her to her wedding next July in Saarbrücken. She does not want to visit her aunt (A), congratulate her (B), or hear news from her (C).

9. Choice (A) is the correct answer. The man wants a picee of information — he wants to know how to get to the train station. He does not ask for a ticket (B), a program (C), or an address (D).

10. Choice (B) is the correct answer. The man will not miss his train because the train station is nearby; his train leaves in 15 minutes and the woman tells him the station is only five minutes away. It is clear that the man is walking because the woman instructs him to walk (*gehen*) not drive, so he does not have a car (A). He does not know his way around (C) because he had to ask for directions to the station. Neither the man nor the woman mentions that the train has been delayed (D).

11. Choice (B) is the correct answer. The man did not understand the Swiss dialect of the saleswoman. The woman understood a few words (A), but the man understood absolutely nothing ("*absolut nichts*"). Nothing is said of the saleswoman's opinion (C), so it does not make sense to say that the man did not understand it. Further, although the man and woman are in Zurich, they do not say anything about life there (D).

12. Choice (D) is the correct answer. According to what the woman believes the saleswoman said, there should be similar pictures (*Bilder*) for sale again next week. No one says that there will be salespeople (A), Swiss people (B), or visitors (C) again next week.

13. Choice (A) is the correct answer. Only towels that are left on the floor are changed. Conversely, towels left on the radiator (*Heizung* or *Heizkörper*) (B) or on the towel bar (*Halter*) (D) are left for hotel guests to use again. Presumably, towels left on the shelf (*Regal*) (C) are not changed either.

14. Choice (D) is the correct answer. Hotel guests support the hotel's rule (". . . *die Gäste unterstützen diese Aktion*"). They do not complain about it (A) or boycott the hotel chain (C), nor are they unaware of the rule (B).

15. Choice (D) is the correct answer. The hotel chain hopes to protect the environment through its actions ("*Die Hotelkette hofft . . . die Umwelt zu schonen*"). It is not hoping to replace towels (A), expand the hotel chain (B), or produce waste (C); on the contrary, it hopes to reduce its use of detergent.

16. Choice (D) is the correct answer. Fatima was born in Germany, specifically in Kreuzberg ("*Ich bin in Deutschland geboren, hier in Kreuzberg*"). She was not born on a construction site (A), in Turkey (B), or in Frankfurt (C).

17. Choice (A) is the correct answer. Fatima's father went to night school to become an electrician (". . . *dann hat er in Abendkursen Elektriker gelernt*") and is now presumably an electrician. Her mother was a sales clerk (B), but her father was not. Fatima's father is not a building contractor (C), either. When he first came to Germany, he was a laborer (D) on a construction site, but that is no longer his job.

18. Choice (A) is the correct answer. At first, Fatima's father did not have his own room; he had to share his room with three others (". . . *hat sein Zimmer mit drei anderen teilen müssen*"). Fatima was not yet born nor did her father know her mother, so he did not live with Fatima's family (B). He did not have a small house in Kreuzberg (C), and there is no mention of whether he had electricity or not (D).

19. Choice (B) is the correct answer. Fatima says that her father's friends are not doing so well (". . . *den meisten von Vaters alten Freunden geht's noch nicht so gut*"). She does not mention whether or not they have families (A), are homesick (C), or work a lot (D).

20. Choice (D) is the correct answer. The diamond dealer Ronald Winston bought the stone in India ("*Der Diamantenhändler Ronald Winston, der den Stein in Indien gekauft hat*"). An article about the diamond appeared in a newspaper published in Paris (B), but the diamond was not purchased there. There is no mention of England (A) or Germany (C) in the news item.

21. Choice (B) is the correct answer. This diamond is in the news because it has an unusual color; only five diamonds are known to have this color ("*Soweit wissen wir*

nur von 5 Diamanten, die diese außergewöhnliche Farbe haben"). The diamond dealer is still waiting for a buyer, so it is not logical to say that it was sold very quickly (A). The dealer bought the diamond in India, but it was not necessarily sent there from somewhere else (C). There is no mention of the diamond's size, so it is probably not unusually large (D).

22. Choice (C) is the correct answer. The diamond is red; in sunlight it is cardinal red and in the shade it is deep purple ("*Im Sonnenlicht . . . tiefpurpur*"). It is not white (A), green (B), or yellow (D).

23. Choice (A) is the correct answer. Ronald Winston is waiting for a buyer, so he must want to sell the diamond ("*Der Diamantenhändler Ronald Winston, der . . . nun auf einen Käufer wartet*"). The verb tense Mr. Wilson uses to talk about his father ("*hatte nie . . . gesehen*") indicates that his father has already died, so it does not make sense to say that he wants to show the diamond to his father (B). He does not talk about traveling to India more frequently (C) or the desire to find an English-language newspaper (D).

24. Choice (C) is the correct answer. As noted by the interviewer, Anja would like to study for a year in the United States ("*Sie möchten ein Jahr lang in den USA studieren*"). She wants to study there, not travel around the country for a year (A). She has spent four weeks in England, which was not enough to become fluent in English, but she is not considering studying there (B) again. She wants to learn English, not teach it (D).

25. Choice (B) is the correct answer. Anja's plans are important for her studies because her chosen field, computer science, is more advanced in the United States ("*Außerdem studiere ich Informatik, und da sind die Amerikaner uns doch weit voraus*") and studying there will help her professionally. Anja thinks that mastering a foreign language is important; she does not say foreign languages are not necessary for her studies (A). There is no mention that her subject requires experience abroad (C). Though she talks about getting away from the image of Americans shown on television, she does not say that she wants to become a television announcer (D).

26. Choice (A) is the correct answer. Anja's last reason for her decision is that she would like to develop her own personal image of American life and get away from the image of Americans shown on television programs ("*. . . es mich einfach lockt, länger unter Amerikanern zu leben, um einmal von dem Image der Fernsehprogramme wegzukommen*"). She does not speak about a desire to have more opportunities to watch American television (B), to give Americans another image of Germans (C), or to have more American television programs shown in Germany (D).

27. Choice (D) is the correct answer. The impression that one gets of Anja is that she knows what she wants; she has carefully thought about her decision to study in the United States, and she clearly articulates her reasons for her desire to do so. She does not seem arrogant; in other words, she does not seem to know how good her image is (A). Her reasons for studying abroad involve learning about language, computer science, and the American people. Therefore, it does not make sense to say that she has travel fever (B). She also does not say anything negative about Germany, so it is unlikely that she just wants to get away from Germany (C).

28. Choice (D) is the correct answer. One writes with chalk (*Kreide*) on the blackboard, not with ink (A), pencil (B), or ballpoint pen (C).

29. Choice (A) is the correct answer. Our teacher can speak five foreign languages. The verb *kann* is used to show the ability to speak a language. Choice (B), *weiß* ("knows"), cannot be used with regard to knowing a language. Choices (C), *zeigt* ("shows"), and (D), *bekennt* ("admits"), do not make sense in this context.

30. Choice (B) is the correct answer. *Machen* completes the expression *machen jemandem Schwierigkeiten* ("cause or give someone trouble"); here the speaker says, "Such tasks give me no trouble." Choices (A), *haben* ("have"), (C), *tun* ("do"), and (D), *sind* ("are"), are unidiomatic in this sentence.

31. Choice (A) is the correct answer. The speaker says, "In my opinion, the movie lasted (*gedauert*) too long." Choices (B), *genommen* ("taken"), (C), *geleistet* ("achieved"), and (D), *gesehen* ("seen"), do not make sense in this context. Although "take too long" makes sense in English, it cannot be translated into German with the verb *nehmen* as in Choice (B). Further, the incorrect choices are all past participles of transitive verbs and do not fit grammatically in this sentence with no direct object.

32. Choice (D) is the correct answer. Sabine visits her aunt very often because (*denn*) she lives right next door. Choices (A), *sondern* ("but"), (B), *obwohl* ("although"), and (C), *oder* ("or"), do not make sense in this sentence.

33. Choice (C) is the correct answer. The speaker says, "If (*Wenn*) I had a lot of money, I would take a long trip." The missing word must be a subordinating conjunction because the verb *hätte* comes at the end of the first clause rather than after the subject. Choices (A), *ob* ("whether"), and (D), *obwohl* ("although"), are subordinating conjunctions, but they do not make sense in this sentence. Choice (B), *dann* ("then"),

is not a subordinating conjunction, so it does not fit grammatically or logically in this sentence.

34. Choice (C) is the correct answer. The speaker asks, "What do you think of modern music?" *Halten* is the only choice that can be followed by the preposition *von* and that makes sense in the sentence. Choices (A), *fühlen* ("feel"), (B), *betrachten* ("consider"), and (D), *gefallen* ("please"), do not fit grammatically or logically in this sentence.

35. Choice (B) is the correct answer. The speaker says, "If I had read the book first, I would have understood the movie better." The missing word must be a past participle because the clause already contains the conjugated verb *hätte. Verstanden* is the only choice that is a past participle.

36. Choice (A) is the correct answer. The speaker says, "You're here already? You must have run fast!" The missing word must be an infinitive because it follows the conjugated verb *musst* and completes the perfect infinitive *gelaufen sein* ("have run"). *Sein* is the only choice that is an infinitive.

37. Choice (A) is the correct answer. The speaker says, "Tomorrow we have to get up early (*früh*) because we are leaving at 6:00." Choices (B), *spät* ("late"), (C), *bald* ("soon"), and (D), *langsam* ("slowly"), do not fit logically in the sentence.

38. Choice (A) is the correct answer. The speaker asks, "Why don't you speak with your teacher about it (*darüber*)?" *Über* is the preposition that would normally follow the verb *sprechen* ("to speak") in this context, but because the object of the preposition is not explicitly expressed, the related adverb *darüber* is used in place of the prepositional phrase.

39. Choice (B) is the correct answer. The speaker says, "I have been staying with my grandmother for (*seit*) two weeks." The preposition *seit* is used with the present tense and before a period of time to indicate that an action or state began in the past and continues until now. Choice (A), *vor* ("before"), cannot be used here with the present tense. Choice (C), *bis* ("until"), must be followed by a specific point in time rather than a period of time. Choice (D), *um* ("toward" or "around"), does not fit idiomatically in this sentence.

40. Choice (A) is the correct answer. The speaker says, "I don't know whether (*ob*) she is coming with us to the restaurant." Choices (B), *dass* ("that"), (C), *als* ("when [at a

specific time in the past]"), and (D), *wenn* ("if [to introduce a condition]"), do not fit logically in this sentence.

41. Choice (C) is the correct answer. The speaker says that he or she finished his or her homework very quickly today because it was very easy (*einfach*), not because it was friendly (A), unique (B), or punctual (D). Choice (C) is the only answer that logically completes the sentence.

42. Choice (D) is the correct answer. The speaker says, "It is cold here. Is the heat on?" *Heizung* ("heat") is the singular subject of the question and, like other German words that end in *–ung*, is feminine; therefore, the missing definite article must be the singular feminine nominative *die*. Choice (A) is masculine nominative or feminine genitive or dative, Choice (B) is neuter, and Choice (C) is masculine accusative or plural dative.

43. Choice (C) is the correct answer. The speaker says, "I had misunderstood this political position and had to change (*ändern*) my opinion." *Ändern* ("change") is the idiomatic verb that should be used with the object *Meinung* ("opinion"). Choices (A), *nehmen* ("take"), (B), *umdrehen* ("turn over"), and (D), *ausprobieren* ("try out"), do not fit logically or idiomatically in the sentence.

44. Choice (A) is the correct answer. *Bei* ("with") is the only preposition that fits logically and idiomatically in the sentence: "The longer I am with the company . . . " Choices (B), *vor* ("before"), (C), *zu* ("to"), and (D), *an* ("on" or "by"), do not make sense here.

45. Choice (C) is the correct answer. The speaker says that the longer (*je länger)* he or she works at the company, the better (*desto besser*) he or she enjoys it. *Desto* correctly completes the construction *je [mehr] . . . desto [mehr]* ("the more ... the more"). The other choices are not grammatically correct.

46. Choice (B) is the correct answer. The sentence states, "The Meyer Company is a printer that produces (*herstellt*) invitations and greeting cards." Choices (A), *kann* ("can"), (C), *verbraucht* ("consumes"), and (D), *legt* ("lays"), do not fit logically in the sentence.

47. Choice (C) is the correct answer. Regarding his or her job, the speaker says, "I don't just sit in the office (*Büro*), I also visit clients." Choices (A), *Auto* ("car"), (B), *Aufzug* ("elevator"), and (D), *Bahnhof* ("train station"), do not fit logically in the sentence.

48. Choice (B) is the correct answer. The missing word is a relative pronoun that refers to the plural *meine Kollegen* ("my colleagues"). Because the relative clause has a subject *ich* ("I") and an object *Arbeit* ("work"), the missing pronoun must modify *Arbeit* and therefore be the plural genitive *deren* ("whose"). The speaker says, "My colleagues, whose (*deren*) work I find less interesting, are . . ." The other choices do not fit grammatically in the sentence: *die* (A) is either nominative or accusative; *dessen* (C) is genitive, but it is masculine, not plural; and *der* (D) is either masculine nominative or feminine dative.

49. Choice (A) is the correct answer. The speaker says that it is easy to get along (*auszukommen*) with them. After an adjective such as *leicht* ("easy"), an infinitive form of a verb is used with *zu*. In a verb with a separable prefix, such as *auskommen*, the *zu* is placed between the prefix and the rest of the verb. *Auskommen* (B) is an infinitive but lacks the necessary *zu*. *Ausgekommen* (C) is a past participle and *auskommt* (D) is a present tense form of the verb, so these choices cannot be used in this sentence.

50. Choice (C) is the correct answer. Mr. Hoffmann was just about to leave (*verlassen*) the house. Choices (A), *gehen* ("go"), (B), *vergehen* ("pass"), and (D), *lassen* ("let"), do not fit logically in the sentence. Further, *gehen* and *vergehen* are intransitive verbs and cannot be used with the object *Haus* ("house").

51. Choice (D) is the correct answer. Mr. Hoffmann was just about to leave the house in order to catch (*erreichen*) the early train. Choices (A), *erwerben* ("win"), (B), *sehen* ("see"), and (C), *hören* ("hear"), do not fit logically in the sentence.

52. Choice (B) is the correct answer. Mr. Hoffmann's wife put a letter (*Brief*) in his hand and told him not to forget to mail it. The missing word must be a masculine noun because it is preceded by the masculine accusative indefinite article *einen*. *Brief* ("letter") is the only masculine choice. Choices (A), *Schreiben* ("letter"), (C), *Telegramm* ("telegram"), and (D), *Paket* ("package"), are all neuter and therefore do not fit grammatically in the sentence. Further, the reader eventually learns that Mr. Hoffmann returns home with a letter still in his pocket ("*...hatte er den Brief immer noch in der Tasche*").

53. Choice (A) is the correct answer. Mr. Hoffman's wife asks him to mail the important letter before (*bevor*) he goes to the office so that her friend will receive it the next day. Choices (B), *nachdem* ("after"), (C), *seitdem* ("since"), and (D), *wonach* ("after which"), do not fit logically in the sentence.

54. Choice (B) is the correct answer. The missing possessive pronoun modifies the singular feminine noun *Freundin* ("friend"), which is the subject of the verb *bekommt* ("will receive"). The correct choice is the feminine nominative *meine* ("my"). The other choices are not grammatically correct: *meiner* (A) is feminine genitive or dative or plural genitive; *meines* (C) is masculine or neuter genitive; and *mein* (D) is masculine or neuter nominative.

55. Choice (A) is the correct answer. The missing possessive pronoun modifies the singular masculine noun *Mann* ("husband"), which is the subject of the verb *vergaß* ("forgot"). The correct choice is the masculine nominative *ihr* ("her"). The other choices are not grammatically correct: *ihre* (B) is feminine or plural nominative or accusative; *ihrer* (C) is feminine genitive or dative or plural genitive; and *ihren* (D) is masculine accusative or plural dative.

56. Choice (C) is the correct answer. The sentence states, "When (*Als*) Mr. Hoffmann came home in the evening, he still had the letter in his pocket." The missing word is a subordinating conjunction that connects the two clauses. *Als* ("when") is used to talk about the time when something happened in the past. Choices (A) and (D) are both subordinating conjunctions, but *wenn* ("if" or "when") cannot be used to talk about real events in the past and *ob* ("whether") does not fit logically in the sentence. Choice (B), *wann* ("when"), is used as a question and not as a conjunction, so it does not fit grammatically in the sentence.

57. Choice (C) is the correct answer. Adjectives that come between the accusative indefinite article *einen* and a singular masculine noun (in this instance, "CD player") take the ending *-en*, so *neuen* ("new") is correct. The other choices are not grammatically correct.

58. Choice (D) is the correct answer. Anne-Marie had not yet saved enough money (*Geld*) to buy a new CD player. It does not make sense to say she had not saved enough patience (A) or time (C) to do this. Although the mark (B) is the former currency of Germany, it is unidiomatic to say that she did not have "enough marks" saved for the purchase.

59. Choice (B) is the correct answer. According to the sentence, her parents are of the (*der*) opinion that she should get a job. The feminine genitive definite article *der* precedes the feminine noun *Meinung* to correctly complete the idiomatic expression *sind der Meinung* ("are of the opinion"). The other choices are unidiomatic or not grammatically correct.

60. Choice (D) is the correct answer. The use of the subjunctive *wäre* in the first clause and the conditional *würden* in the second clause indicates that this is a conditional sentence properly joined by *wenn* ("if"). She would naturally prefer it if (*wenn*) her parents were to give her a CD player for her birthday. Choices (A), *weil* ("because"), (B), *damit* ("thereby"), and (C), *nachdem* ("after"), do not fit grammatically or logically in the sentence.

61. Choice (B) is the correct answer. According to the sentence, she would naturally prefer it if her parents were to give (*schenken*) her a CD player for her birthday. Choices (A), *belohnen* ("reward"), (C), *beibringen* ("teach"), and (D), *spielen* ("play"), do not fit logically in the sentence.

62. Choice (D) is the correct answer. The announcement starts with *Herzlichen Dank* ("heartfelt thanks"), indicating that this is an expression of thanks from the family of the deceased Karl Steinke to people who have expressed their condolences. It is not a death announcement (A), an apology (B), or a wedding announcement (C).

63. Choice (A) is the correct answer. The announcement is directed to the people who have expressed their condolences, specifically to the people who have acknowledged the grief of the writers through [spoken] word, writing, wreaths and flowers ("*allen, die . . . haben*"). Although wreaths and flowers are mentioned, the announcement does not make reference to people who have sent gifts (B) or shared money (C). The announcement is from the immediate family of Karl Steinke, but it is not directed to people who notified their immediate families (D).

64. Choice (D) is the correct answer. Pittsburgh was once known for its heavy industry, specifically its iron and steel industries ("*Eisen- und Stahlindustrie*"). The first sentence mentions the city's elegant boutiques (A) and the last paragraph talks about its big hospitals (C), but those are features of Pittsburgh today, not of Pittsburgh in the past. Although the article talks about the University of Pittsburgh, no mention is made of Pittsburgh having many schools (B).

65. Choice (B) is the correct answer. The majority of Pittsburgh's residents are employed at the university ("*Der größte Arbeitgeber in der Stadt ist jetzt die 'University of Pittsburgh'*"). While the airport (A), the William Penn Hotel (C), and the Grand Concourse Restaurant (D) are all mentioned, the number of employees at each of these locations is not discussed at all.

66. Choice (C) is the correct answer. In the article, Henry Clay Frick is referred to as "The Pittsburgh Coal King" ("*Der Pittsburgher Kohle- König*"), so he was an industry magnate. Although he had a hotel built, he was not a well-known architect (A). He was not one of Pittsburgh's mayors (B). Further, Frick was a hotel owner, not a restaurant owner (D).

67. Choice (D) is the correct answer. The former Pittsburgh train station is used today as a good restaurant ("*ein feines Restaurant*"), namely The Grand Concourse. It is not used as a connecting train station (A), a coal warehouse (B), or a convention hall (C).

68. Choice (C) is the correct answer. Charles Muir was probably an architect or a building contractor because he converted the lower floors of the Pittsburgh train station into a restaurant ("*Einige Zeit später baute Charles Muir aus Detroit die unteren Etagen in ein feines Restaurant um*"). There is nothing to indicate that he might have been a railroad engineer (A), a museum director (B), or a tour guide (D).

69. Choice (A) is the correct answer. According to the article, it is worth visiting Pittsburgh because the city has a lot to offer: a beautiful hotel, a busy downtown, an impressive restaurant, universities, museum complexes, and world-renowned hospitals. ("*Doch nicht nur wegen ihrer Sehenswürdigkeiten . . . interessant*"). There is nothing that says that Pittsburgh has a famous castle (B), that the people are friendly (C), or that the hotels there are cheap (D).

70. Choice (C) is the correct answer. One can buy textbooks at Tell, as indicated by the first two lines of the advertisement that say it is a specialist bookstore for arts and humanities ("*Fachbuchhandlung für Geisteswissenschaften*"). There is nothing to suggest that the store sells children's books (A), travel books (B), or cookbooks (D).

71. Choice (D) is the correct answer. According to the advertisement, the bookstore also offers customers the service of being able to order books by phone, as indicated by the phrase "*Bestellservice auch telefonisch.*" Nothing in the advertisement says that books can be home delivered (A), provided more cheaply (B), or loaned out (C).

72. Choice (A) is the correct answer. At the beginning of the story, just before he discovered the coins, crane operator Hans Magnussen looked at his watch and noted that it was "almost quitting time" ("*Der Kranführer Hans Magnussen sah auf die Uhr: zehn Minuten nach drei. "Bald Feierabend", dachte er*"). So, he made the discovery shortly before the end of work. It was 3:10 in the afternoon, not around noon (B), early in the morning (C), or in the middle of the night (D).

73. Choice (D) is the correct answer. Magnussen had hit something hard with the excavator, so he turned the crane off because he wanted to know what was under the ground ("*Als Magnussen . . . was es sein könnte*"). He did not think that it was already quitting time (A); he had just noted that it was almost quitting time. The excavator was not functioning incorrectly (B) when he turned it off. There is no mention of rubble or that it was too heavy for the shovel (C), only that Magnussen had hit something unknown and hard.

74. Choice (A) is the correct answer. The province of Schleswig-Holstein wanted to keep the entire discovery because the land where it was found belonged to the province ("*Das Land . . . gehörte dem Land Schleswig-Holstein . . . unter dem der Schatz verborgen lag*"). The demolition was taking place in Lübeck, but there is no mention that Magnussen lived there (B). It was Magnussen's job to demolish the buildings, so the province was not claiming the discovery because he had destroyed the buildings (C). The province was the owner of the land, so the owner did not work in the federal court (D).

75. Choice (D) is the correct answer. The coins were from the fourteenth and fifteenth centuries ("*Gold- und Silbermünzen aus dem 14. und 15. Jahrhundert*"), so they were several hundred years old. They were not almost 100 years old (A); they were much older. They were not a little over a thousand years old (B); they were much newer. Nor were they exactly 50 years old (C).

76. Choice (B) is the correct answer. The federal court decided that Schleswig-Holstein and Magnussen should share the discovery because German law states that when something is discovered that has been buried so long that the original owner is unknown, the discovery must be shared between the discoverer and the landowner ("*Das deutsche Gesetz . . . geteilt werden*"). The court did not decide that the excavation company should keep the coins (A), that the owner of the discovery should be sought (C), or that the demolition work should be halted (D).

77. Choice (C) is the correct answer. In the end, the province of Schleswig-Holstein received the treasure after paying Magnussen for his share ("*Das Land Schleswig-Holstein will jetzt den kulturell und historisch wertvollen Fund behalten . . . zahlen*"). Neither the city of Lübeck (A), the excavation company (B), nor the original owner (D) received the treasure.

78. Choice (C) is the correct answer. Based on the text, it is logical to say that Wilhelm Pelizaeus was born in Hildesheim in 1851: the years of his life are given as 1851–1930 and Hildesheim is referred to as Pelizaeus's hometown ("*Vaterstadt*"). He did not die

in 1907 in Egypt (A); he died in 1930 in a location that is not mentioned in the text. The museum he established is in his hometown of Hildesheim, not in Egypt (B). Further, his excavations were done in Egypt, not in Hildesheim (D).

79. Choice (D) is the correct answer. The museum contains Pelizaeus's extensive private collection ("*Seine umfassende Privatsammlung*"), and the majority of the text talks about life and work in Egypt ("*begeisterter Sammler . . . arbeitete*). The picture also shows an Egyptian statue. Therefore, it can be inferred that the main things displayed in the Pelizaeus Museum are archeological finds from ancient Egypt, not photographs of Wilhelm Pelizaeus (A), pictures of a hometown (B), or busts of well-known collectors (C).

80. Choice (B) is the correct answer. The advertisement says that for age-related reasons, the prosperous, solid photography business is for sale ("*zu verkaufen*"). In other words, the owner of the business wants to get rid of it. The owner does not want to rent it out (A), expand it (C), or photograph it (D).

81. Choice (A) is the correct answer. The heading that best matches this text is "The Making of the English Gardens." The first paragraph describes the current English Gardens in Munich. In the second paragraph, the early history of the Gardens is described, from their inception until they were turned over to the citizens in 1792. Finally, the last paragraph discusses later improvements to the park. The other choices do not match well. While the first paragraph compares the well-being one experiences in the Gardens to what one might feel in the most exotic vacation destination ("*. . . so wohl fühlt wie sonst nur an den exotischsten Urlaubszielen*"), the heading "An Exotic Travel Destination" (B) does not cover all of the information provided in the passage. The first paragraph does refer to the Gardens as a retreat paradise ("*Rückzugsparadies*") and the second paragraph says that the Elector used to hunt wild animals there, but the heading "A Hunting Paradise in Munich" (C) does not accurately reflect the current use of the Gardens. Finally, although the Elector Carl Theodor was the original owner of the Gardens, the passage talks about him only with regard to his relationship to the park; therefore, the heading "The Life of the Elector Carl Theodor" (D) is not appropriate.

82. Choice (B) is the correct answer. The soldiers worked with hoes and spades to plant potatoes ("*. . . Soldaten [waren] damit beschäftigt, mit Hacke und Spaten Kartoffeln anzupflanzen*"); thus, they created vegetable gardens. They did not defend the land (A), drill there (C), or plant trees there (D).

83. Choice (C) is the correct answer. Benjamin Thompson suggested to the Elector that he use the land differently: he proposed that in their free time the Elector's soldiers should transform the wilderness into vegetable gardens ("*Denn der schlug dem Kurfürsten vor, seine Soldaten sollten in ihrer Freizeit die Wildnis in Nutzgärten umwandeln*"). Thompson did not suggest that the Elector emigrate to America (A), found a university (B), or hire Ludwig von Skell (D). In fact, Ludwig von Skell worked on the Gardens only after the Elector had turned the park over to the citizens.

84. Choice (D) is the correct answer. The first paragraph calls the English Gardens a "retreat paradise" ("*Rückzugsparadies*") that one can enjoy on the hottest summer days. The Gardens are further described as an exciting jungle ("*spannender Urwald*") where one can take a walk, and as a sun terrace ("*Sonnenterrasse*") with a refreshing brook and lake ("*Eisbach*" and "*See*"). In short, people today go to the English Gardens to relax. Potatoes were planted there in the past, but the Gardens are not used today to develop new types of potatoes (A). One does not use the Gardens to further educate oneself (B). Additionally, though this area originally contained wild boar and other animals ("*Wildschweine und andere Tiere*"), there is no mention of animals there today. Therefore, the Gardens are not a place where one can look at exotic animals (C).

85. Choice (C) is the correct answer. The second paragraph says that wild boar and other animals were hunted there ("*. . . Wildschweine und andere Tiere [wurden früher] gejagt*") and then refers to the area as the private hunting ground of the Elector Carl Theodor ("*. . . dem privaten Jagdrevier des Kurfürsten Carl Theodor*"). Therefore, it is logical to suggest that the Elector Carl Theodor used the land of the present-day English Gardens to hunt. The passage does not indicate that he used the land to hike (A), to create a lake (B), or to train soldiers (D). Soldiers worked there to plant potatoes, but they were not trained there.

86. Choice (D) is the correct answer. The purpose of this advertisement is to tell customers that calls to North America are now cheaper. The advertisement asks whether or not customers have friends or family in North America and how often they call the United States or Canada. It then gives customers a reason to be happy: as of May 1, phone calls from Germany to the United States and Canada are 37% more inexpensive (*günstiger*). The advertisement does not say that one should look for friends in America (A), that Germans travel more often to North America (B), or that one should make more calls all around the world (C).

87. Choice (A) is the correct answer. This person is happy with his or her education because he or she can adequately provide for himself or herself. The person says that he or she knows what his or her education is worth. It provides security, particularly

financial security. He or she is well paid and can even make provisions for the future ("*Heute . . . vorsorgen*"). The person does not work for Deutsche Bank (B); he or she is merely going to discuss future plans with someone at the bank. The person does not talk about getting a lot of prestige through education (C). Further, the person has already completed high school and an apprenticeship ("*Ich habe Abitur und danach eine Lehre gemacht*", so there is no need for him or her to go back to finish high school (D).

Chapter 11
Italian

Purpose

The Subject Test in Italian measures your ability to understand written Italian. The test allows for variation in language preparation and is independent of particular textbooks or methods of instruction. The test measures reading proficiency based on communicative materials authentic to the Italian culture.

Format

This is a one-hour test with 80 to 85 multiple-choice questions. Test questions are written to reflect current trends in high school curricula and to test reading skills and familiarity with the language structure.

Content

Questions range in difficulty from elementary through advanced, although most questions are at the intermediate level. The test measures reading proficiency through a variety of questions requiring a broad knowledge of the language.

The test covers commonly taught grammatical constructions, and all questions reflect current standard Italian.

The test includes three parts:

Passage completion questions test your knowledge of high-frequency vocabulary, appropriate idiomatic expressions and language structure in the context of paragraphs.

Sentence completion questions test your familiarity with grammatical structure and vocabulary.

Reading comprehension questions test your understanding of the content of various selections taken from sources such as newspaper and magazine articles, fiction, historical works, advertisements, tickets, brochures, forms, and schedules.

Italian	
Skills Measured	**Approximate Percentage of Test**
Vocabulary	30%
Structure	30%
Reading Comprehension	40%

How to Prepare

The Subject Test in Italian allows for variation in language preparation. You should develop competence in Italian over a period of years by taking two to four years of Italian language study in high school or the equivalent. Familiarize yourself with the directions in advance. The directions in this book are identical to those that appear on the test.

Score

The total score is reported on the 200-to-800 scale.

Sample Questions

Your answer sheet has five answer positions marked A, B, C, D, and E, while the questions throughout this test contain only four choices. Be sure NOT to make any marks in column E.

Part A

Directions: In each of the following passages there are numbered blanks indicating that words or phrases have been omitted. For each numbered blank, four completions are provided. First read through the entire passage. Then, for each numbered blank, choose the completion that is most appropriate given the context of the entire passage and fill in the corresponding circle on the answer sheet.

Un piccolo villaggio siciliano

Baria Dorica è il nome di un piccolo villaggio estivo situato sulla costa siciliana. Tutte le __1__ del villaggio danno sulla piazzetta, dove si trova l'unico locale pubblico: il bar, che fa anche da panineria, pizzeria e panetteria.

La piazzetta è un luogo ___2___ riservato solamente ai pedoni e i bambini vi possono correre e giocare liberamente. La sera, i ragazzini formano dei gruppetti sparsi qua e là e ___3___ animatamente degli eventi della giornata. Fino a tarda sera tutto è animato e risuona di voci.

1. (A) macchine
   (B) strade
   (C) luci
   (D) corriere

2. (A) silenzioso
   (B) solitario
   (C) sicuro
   (D) privato

3. (A) cantano
   (B) leggono
   (C) parlano
   (D) pensano

Choice (B) is the correct answer to question 1. In this question, you have to choose the appropriate noun from the four answer choices. Only *strade* can be used in connection with *danno sulla piazzetta* to form a meaningful sentence.

Choice (C) is the correct answer to question 2. In this question, you have to choose the adjective that fits best according to the context. The place in question can be considered *un luogo sicuro* since it is *riservato ai pedoni,* which means that there is no car traffic. Choices (A), (B), and (D) are incorrect because they are contradictory to what is said in the passage.

Choice (C) is the correct answer to question 3. In this question, you have to choose the appropriate verb from the four answer choices. The verb *parlare* is the only verb that fits logically. The other choices are not appropriate in this context even if choices (B) and (D) are verbs that could be used in connection with *eventi della giornata.*

Part B

Directions: In each sentence or dialogue below you will find a blank space indicating that a word or phrase has been omitted. Following each sentence are four completions. Of the four choices, select the one that best completes the sentence structurally and logically and fill in the corresponding circle on the answer sheet. In some instances, choice (A) may consist of dashes; by choosing this option, you are indicating that no insertion is required to form a grammatically correct sentence.

4. Molte turiste preferiscono comprare ____________ regali nei negozi del centro.
   (A) il loro
   (B) il suo
   (C) i loro
   (D) i suoi

Choice (C) is the correct answer to question 4. In this question, you are asked to choose the correct possessive adjective from the four answer choices. The possessive adjective *i loro* is used when the subject is third person, plural (*Molte turiste*), and the object is masculine, plural (*regali*). Choice (A) is incorrect because *il* refers to an object in the singular; choice (B) is incorrect because *il suo* refers to a third person, singular subject, and an object in the singular; choice (D) is incorrect because it refers to a third person, singular subject.

5. Dopo ____________ le camicie, il cliente saluta e esce.
   (A) aver comprato
   (B) comprava
   (C) abbia comprato
   (D) comprerà

Choice (A) is the correct answer to question 5. In this question, you have to choose from the four answer choices the form of the verb *comprare* that fits in the sentence grammatically. The verb *comprare* is in a subordinate clause introduced by *Dopo*. You need to know that *dopo* is used with a verb in the past infinitive. The other choices are incorrect because the verb *comprare* is (B) in the imperfect, (C) in the past subjunctive, and (D) in the future tense.

Part C

Directions: Read the following texts carefully for comprehension. Each text is followed by a number of questions or incomplete statements. Select the answer or completion that is best according to the text and fill in the corresponding circle on the answer sheet.

Questions 6–7

QUEL FANTASTICO VENERDI' DI REPUBBLICA.

"Il Venerdì", tutte le settimane con Repubblica, vi porta attualità, grandi re-portages, viaggi, inchieste e interviste: centotrentadue pagine a colori tutte per voi. "Il Venerdì" è in edicola ogni venerdì insieme a Repubblica e Affari & Finanza. Il tutto, per solo un euro.

la Repubblica

6. In quest' annuncio, che cos' è "Il Venerdì"?
   (A) Un libro
   (B) Un settimanale
   (C) Un notiziario
   (D) Un' inchiesta

7. Come si ottiene "Il Venerdì"?
   (A) Si deve andare in un negozio.
   (B) Si deve comprare *la Repubblica.*
   (C) Si devono spendere due euro.
   (D) Si deve aspettare la fine del mese.

Choice (B) is the correct answer to question 6. This question asks what *"Il Venerdì"* is. The text mentions *tutte le settimane* and also *"Il Venerdì" è in edicola ogni venerdì.* Choices (A), (C), and (D) are incorrect within the context of the ad.

Choice (B) is the correct answer to question 7. This question asks about how you obtain *"Il Venerdì."* The text mentions *"Il Venerdì" (...) con Repubblica,* and also *(...) insieme a Repubblica.* Choices (A), (C), and (D) are incorrect within the context of the ad.

Questions 8–10

È "Ferragosto", festa nazionale, e se ne sono andati tutti. Restano solo alcune auto, abbandonate lo scorso inverno, ancora più solitarie sotto il sole d'agosto.

E incredibile, poter attraversare Milano in un quarto d'ora, da un capo all'altro. E poi fermarsi e parcheggiare dove si vuole. Bellissimo, ma per fare che cosa, se è tutto chiuso da una settimana? ...

Vado all'edicola e la trovo sprangata. Il tabaccaio più vicino adesso si trova a un chilometro di distanza, e non ha più francobolli. Se in questo momento si fulmina una lampadina di casa sono perduto, non saprei dove comprarne una. Fortuna che per cibi e bevande mi ero fatto una scorta. L'assedio durerà fino al giorno 20, e occorre resistere.

Del resto non mi è mai piaciuto lo spettacolo di questo fuggi fuggi, di questo esodo di massa, come se a Milano fosse scoppiata un'epidemia di peste.

8. L'autore del brano si lamenta perchè
   (A) la città è affollata
   (B) è difficile attraversare la città
   (C) gli abitanti se ne vanno
   (D) c'è la peste

9. Secondo il brano durante il "Ferragosto" è probabile che chi ha una macchina possa
   (A) comprare la benzina a buon mercato
   (B) avere difficoltà nel parcheggiare
   (C) muoversi facilmente in auto per la città
   (D) stare in coda per un'ora per arrivare in centro

10. L'autore non morirà di fame perchè
   (A) sua moglie gli ha lasciato cibi e bevande
   (B) suo cognato ha un ristorante
   (C) ha deciso di non fare più la dieta
   (D) ha già comprato provviste sufficienti

Choice (C) is the correct answer to question 8. This question tests literal comprehension and refers to the reason for the author's complaint. The first line of the passage states … *se ne sono andati tutti*, so the correct answer is choice (C) *gli abitanti se ne vanno.* Choices (A), (B), and (D) are incorrect within the context of this passage.

Choice (C) is the correct answer to question 9. This question tests literal comprehension and refers to an important detail mentioned in the text. In the second paragraph, the author states …*È incredibile, poter attraversare Milano in un quarto d'ora,* (…) and also (…) *parcheggiare dove si vuole.* Choices (A), (B), and (D) are incorrect within the context of the passage.

Choice (D) is the correct answer to question 10. This question tests literal comprehension and refers to another important detail mentioned in the text. In the third paragraph, the author states *per cibi e bevande mi ero fatto una scorta,* so the correct answer is choice (D) *ha già comprato provviste sufficienti.* Choices (A), (B), and (C) are incorrect within the context of the passage.

Italian Subject Test

Practice Helps

The test that follows is an actual, previously administered SAT Subject Test in Italian. To get an idea of what it's like to take this test, practice under conditions that are much like those of an actual test administration.

- Set aside an hour when you can take the test uninterrupted.
- Sit at a desk or table with no other books or papers. Dictionaries, other books, or notes are not allowed in the test room.
- Tear out an answer sheet from the back of this book and fill it in just as you would on the day of the test. One answer sheet can be used for up to three Subject Tests.
- Read the instructions that precede the practice test. During the actual administration you will be asked to read them before answering test questions.
- Time yourself by placing a clock or kitchen timer in front of you.
- After you finish the practice test, read the sections "How to Score the SAT Subject Test in Italian" and "How Did You Do on the Subject Test in Italian?"
- The appearance of the answer sheet in this book may differ from the answer sheet you see on test day.

ITALIAN TEST

The top portion of the page of the answer sheet that you will use to take the Italian Test must be filled in exactly as illustrated below. When your supervisor tells you to fill in the circle next to the name of the test you are about take, mark your answer sheet as shown.

○ Literature	○ Mathematics Level 1	○ German	○ Chinese Listening	○ Japanese Listening
○ Biology E	○ Mathematics Level 2	● Italian	○ French Listening	○ Korean Listening
○ Biology M	○ U.S. History	○ Latin	○ German Listening	○ Spanish Listening
○ Chemistry	○ World History	○ Modern Hebrew		
○ Physics	○ French	○ Spanish	Background Questions: ① ② ③ ④ ⑤ ⑥ ⑦ ⑧ ⑨	

After filling in the circle next to the name of the test you are taking, locate the Background Questions box on your answer sheet (as shown above). This is where you will answer the following Background Questions on your answer sheet.

BACKGROUND QUESTIONS

Please answer either Part I or Part II below by filling in the appropriate circle in the Background Questions box on your answer sheet. Fill in ONLY ONE circle, as described below, to indicate how you obtained your knowledge of Italian. The information you provide is for statistical purposes only and will not affect your test score.

Part I If your knowledge of Italian comes primarily from any of the following: living in a home where Italian is the main spoken language, living for six months or longer in an Italian-speaking country that included significant experience in Italian language, courses taken at a college, or special study of Italian, fill in circle 9 and leave the remaining circles blank, regardless of how long you studied the subject in school.

Part II If your knowledge of Italian comes primarily from courses taken in grades 9 - 12, fill in the circle that indicates the level of the Italian course in which you are currently enrolled, or, if you are not now enrolled in an Italian course, fill in the circle that indicates the level of the most advanced course in Italian that you have completed.

- First year: first or second half —Fill in circle 1.
- Second year: first half —Fill in circle 2.
  second half —Fill in circle 3.
- Third year: first half —Fill in circle 4.
  second half —Fill in circle 5.
- Fourth year: first half —Fill in circle 6.
  second half —Fill in circle 7.
- A course at a level higher than fourth year, second half
  or
  high school course work plus a minimum of four weeks of study abroad —Fill in circle 8.

When the supervisor gives the signal, turn the page and begin the Italian Test. There are 100 numbered circles on the answer sheet and 82 questions in the Italian Test. Therefore, use only circles 1 to 82 for recording your answers.

ITALIAN TEST

Part A

Directions: In each of the following passages there are numbered blanks indicating that words or phrases have been omitted. For each numbered blank, four completions are provided. First read through the entire passage. Then, for each numbered blank, choose the completion that is most appropriate given the context of the entire passage and fill in the corresponding circle on the answer sheet.

Vita in un nuovo paese

La situazione degli immigranti che vengono a __(1)__ in un nuovo paese è qualche volta molto __(2)__. All'inizio si sentono __(3)__. Ci sono spesso molte differenze fra la loro vecchia cultura e quella nuova. Sono obbligati ad assumere una nuova identità ed ad imparare una nuova lingua. I bambini __(4)__ abbastanza velocemente la lingua del paese, ma gli adulti continuano __(5)__ a parlare il dialetto del loro paese.

1. (A) visitare
   (B) partire
   (C) abitare
   (D) accogliere

2. (A) saggia
   (B) difficile
   (C) disabitata
   (D) irresponsabile

3. (A) svegli
   (B) isolati
   (C) indipendenti
   (D) congeniali

4. (A) vivono
   (B) imparano
   (C) discutono
   (D) consigliano

5. (A) già
   (B) dopo
   (C) molto
   (D) spesso

GO ON TO THE NEXT PAGE

Grado

Grado, bella __(6)__ non lontana da Venezia, Trieste ed Aquileia, fu in origine un villaggio di pescatori. È formata da due isole ed è __(7)__ alla terraferma da un ponte di sabbia. Ha uno stabilimento balneare, un porto per __(8)__, e una marina dove approdano candidi yacht. Nella suggestiva basilica si eseguono, soprattutto d'estate, importanti manifestazioni __(9)__. Le valli intorno alla laguna di Grado sono romantiche e verdi, ordinate e ricche, e vi si __(10)__ vini sontuosi.

6. (A) società
   (B) spiaggia
   (C) cittadina
   (D) strada

7. (A) unita
   (B) messa
   (C) portata
   (D) sollevata

8. (A) barche da pesca
   (B) cavalli da corsa
   (C) automobili eleganti
   (D) biciclette di marca

9. (A) commerciali
   (B) industriali
   (C) musicali
   (D) sportive

10. (A) mettono
    (B) producono
    (C) compongono
    (D) costruiscono

GO ON TO THE NEXT PAGE

Trasporti

Posti in aereo non se ne trovano più? Volete __(11)__ al minimo la spesa delle vostre vacanze in una capitale europea? Ecco la soluzione ai due __(12)__: viaggiare in autobus.

Da Milano e da Roma, ma anche da Bologna, Firenze e Genova __(13)__ ogni giorno molti pullman granturismo che collegano le principali città d'Europa.

Rispetto all'aereo, il biglietto costa meno __(14)__. Il viaggio dura diverse ore più __(15)__, certo. In ogni caso, gli autobus viaggiano quasi sempre in __(16)__, e il tragitto è diretto, senza __(17)__.

Il biglietto rimane valido per sei mesi. Ogni passeggero può portare con sè una valigia e un bagaglio a __(18)__.

11. (A) includere
    (B) dare
    (C) ridurre
    (D) giungere

12. (A) soggetti
    (B) lavori
    (C) mezzi
    (D) problemi

13. (A) pagano
    (B) partono
    (C) stendono
    (D) toccano

14. (A) dell'energia
    (B) dell'economia
    (C) della gita
    (D) della metà

15. (A) del velo
    (B) del volo
    (C) della vela
    (D) della volta

16. (A) stazione
    (B) autostrada
    (C) silenzio
    (D) compagnia

17. (A) direzione
    (B) deviazioni
    (C) destinazioni
    (D) pazienza

18. (A) mano
    (B) piedi
    (C) terra
    (D) voce

GO ON TO THE NEXT PAGE

L'animatore turistico

Fare l'animatore in un villaggio turistico è il lavoro __(19)__ per eccellenza e sicuramente anche il più ambito durante l'estate. Significa infatti passare tre o quattro mesi in una __(20)__ di mare, preferibilmente all'estero, occupandosi di far divertire gli altri, organizzare __(21)__ e feste per bambini, __(22)__ tennis, windsurf, yoga o aerobica. L'animatore deve per prima cosa riuscire a trattare con i __(23)__, e con tutti, anche i più difficili, essere allegro e coinvolgente, senza mai __(24)__ la vita privata dei turisti.

19. (A) stagionale
    (B) mensile
    (C) giornaliero
    (D) annuale

20. (A) palestra
    (B) discoteca
    (C) pizzeria
    (D) località

21. (A) lavori
    (B) giochi
    (C) servizi
    (D) compiti

22. (A) insegnare
    (B) imparare
    (C) dare
    (D) frequentare

23. (A) pittori
    (B) clienti
    (C) passeggeri
    (D) commercianti

24. (A) cambiare
    (B) spiegare
    (C) invadere
    (D) occupare

GO ON TO THE NEXT PAGE

Part B

Directions: In each sentence or dialogue below you will find a blank space indicating that a word or phrase has been omitted. Following each sentence are four completions. Of the four choices, select the one that best completes the sentence structurally and logically and fill in the corresponding circle on the answer sheet. In some instances, choice (A) consists of dashes; by choosing this option, you are indicating that no insertion is required to form a grammatically correct sentence.

25. Luisa, qui fuori ci sono anche cartoline e giornali -------!

(A) illustrata
(B) illustrati
(C) illustrato
(D) illustrate

26. Buon giorno signora. ------- qualche rivista americana?

(A) È
(B) Ha
(C) Sia
(D) Abbia

27. Posso -------, se vuole.

(A) aiutarmi
(B) aiutarci
(C) aiutarLa
(D) aiutarsi

28. A quest'ora domani ------- già a Venezia.

(A) sia
(B) saremo
(C) eravamo
(D) fossimo

29. Ci sarà anche mio cugino. Sono cinque anni che non ------- vediamo.

(A) si
(B) ne
(C) mi
(D) ci

30. A che ora mi consigli di ------- da casa?

(A) parto
(B) parti
(C) partire
(D) partito

31. La ragazza ha viaggiato in aereo con ------- amici.

(A) dei
(B) nessuno
(C) alcuni
(D) tutti

32. Sei sicura di avere chiuso ------- la porta a chiave?

(A) bene
(B) buona
(C) migliore
(D) buonissima

33. Mi piace il colore ------- tue valigie.

(A) delle
(B) dalle
(C) nelle
(D) sulle

GO ON TO THE NEXT PAGE

34. Il telefono è il mio strumento di lavoro e lo uso ------- tutto il giorno.

    (A) ---
    (B) da
    (C) su
    (D) in

35. Cosa ------- fare lui per telefonare all'estero?

    (A) dovrai
    (B) dovrà
    (C) dovrò
    (D) dovranno

36. Oggi in Italia lo stress non risparmia -------.

    (A) qualcuno
    (B) nessuno
    (C) chiunque
    (D) ognuno

37. Accettò e rispose che avrebbe finito di lavorare entro ------- minuti.

    (A) qualche
    (B) troppo
    (C) pochi
    (D) un

38. Quando lui riceverà il mio telegramma, mi ------- subito.

    (A) risponde
    (B) risponderà
    (C) rispondeva
    (D) risponderebbe

39. ------- recenti studi delle Nazioni Unite, le donne italiane lavorano moltissimo.

    (A) Su
    (B) Fra
    (C) Sotto
    (D) Secondo

40. Gli italiani amano il mare. Molti ------- vanno durante le vacanze estive.

    (A) ci
    (B) gli
    (C) ne
    (D) lo

41. Sulla spiaggia è comodo affittare un ombrellone; io voglio ------- verde.

    (A) prenderlo
    (B) prenderci
    (C) prenderne
    (D) prendervi

42. Questo è l'albero più alto ------- io abbia mai visto.

    (A) quale
    (B) chi
    (C) che
    (D) cui

43. I nostri vicini preferiscono ------- guardare la televisione.

    (A) ---
    (B) di
    (C) a
    (D) da

GO ON TO THE NEXT PAGE

44. Vorrei ------- registrazioni di musica popolare moderna.

(A) di
(B) un po'
(C) niente
(D) alcune

45. Scusi, i biglietti per il concerto allo stadio ------- possono comprare qui?

(A) vi
(B) me
(C) si
(D) ti

46. Lo sai Anna, ------- piacciono i complessi italiani che suonano ad alto volume.

(A) mi
(B) me
(C) lo
(D) la

47. Quel pianista è bravissimo. L'ho sentito ------- alla Scala.

(A) suonato
(B) suonava
(C) suonare
(D) suonò

48. Al cinema Rex danno ------- ultimo film con Massimo Troisi.

(A) il
(B) l'
(C) lo
(D) la

49. Laura, ------- piace la pittura moderna?

(A) li
(B) lei
(C) ti
(D) si

50. Nel museo ci sono cataloghi splendidi! Li -------, se non costassero troppo.

(A) comprerei
(B) comprerò
(C) comprai
(D) compro

GO ON TO THE NEXT PAGE

Part C

<u>Directions:</u> Read the following texts carefully for comprehension. Each text is followed by a number of questions or incomplete statements. Select the answer or completion that is best according to the text and fill in the corresponding circle on the answer sheet.

<u>Questions 51-52</u>

> Per una gita diversa
> lontana dallo stress, in pieno relax
> a due passi da voi
>
> CAMPING
> **CITTÀ DI ANGERA**
>
> *ristorante tipico con cucina internazionale e piatti tipici locali, ampi saloni per banchetti, piscine, tennis, campi bocce, pallavolo, ping-pong, darsena, pontili d'attracco e spiagge*
>
> ANGERA (VA)
>
> Via Bruschera — Tel. (0331) 930.736

51. Angera è un luogo adatto per

    (A) sposarsi
    (B) riposarsi
    (C) sciare
    (D) lavorare

52. Il ristorante offre piatti

    (A) di ogni paese
    (B) solamente locali
    (C) rustici
    (D) dietetici

GO ON TO THE NEXT PAGE

Questions 53-57

C'era una festa a casa di Rolly Marchi ed io ci andai. Entrai e vidi un quadro ad olio ben illuminato, al centro di una parete del salotto. Riconobbi subito il segno di Guttuso. Ammiravo la sua arte, compravo tutti i disegni che trovavo in giro, ma non ne avevo mai incontrato l'autore. "È un Guttuso, no?", chiesi. "Sì, si chiama I naufraghi", mi rispose il padrone di casa. Il quadro continuava ad affascinarmi. Quando Rolly Marchi, per essere gentile, mi disse delle solite stupidaggini del tipo: "Che cosa posso offrirti?"; io puntai il dito sul Guttuso. "Quello", dissi. Rolly Marchi ci restò malissimo: "Ma come, quello l'ho appena comprato, non posso proprio dartelo". "Ma io te lo ricompro", insistevo io. E lui a dire di no, che semmai me lo avrebbe regalato, un quadro di Guttuso, però non quello. Sentii una voce dietro di me: una voce siciliana, profonda, vellutata. "Daglielo Rolly, te ne farò un altro". Mi girai: "Allora è lei Renato Guttuso? Io sono una sua grande ammiratrice". "Dal prossimo minuto io sarò un suo grande ammiratore", replicò. Tornai a casa felice con il mio quadro, e Renato Guttuso non lo vidi più per molti anni.

53. Chi era Guttuso?

(A) Un pittore
(B) Un attore
(C) Uno scrittore
(D) Uno scultore

54. Come è intitolata l'opera d'arte?

(A) Il padrone
(B) Rolly Marchi
(C) La festa
(D) I naufraghi

55. Che cosa affascinò la signora?

(A) Un dipinto
(B) Un colore
(C) L'accento
(D) La gente

56. Chi aveva una voce vellutata?

(A) Il naufrago
(B) Rolly Marchi
(C) Guttuso
(D) La signora

57. Che cosa ricevette in regalo la signora?

(A) Un'opera d'arte
(B) Un complimento
(C) Una casa
(D) Un ammiratore

GO ON TO THE NEXT PAGE

Questions 58-59

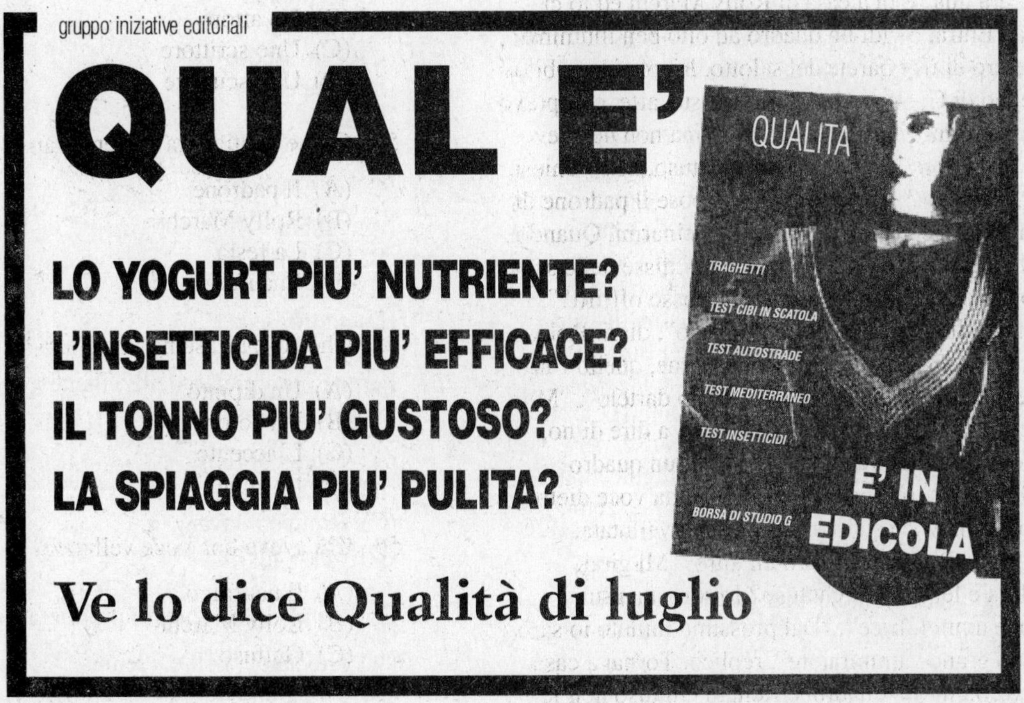
gruppo iniziative editoriali
QUAL E'
LO YOGURT PIU' NUTRIENTE?
L'INSETTICIDA PIU' EFFICACE?
IL TONNO PIU' GUSTOSO?
LA SPIAGGIA PIU' PULITA?
Ve lo dice Qualità di luglio
QUALITA
TRAGHETTI
TEST CIBI IN SCATOLA
TEST AUTOSTRADE
TEST MEDITERRANEO
TEST INSETTICIDI
BORSA DI STUDIO G
E' IN EDICOLA

58. Cosa è *Qualità*?

(A) Un giornale
(B) Una rubrica
(C) Un libro divertente
(D) Un periodico mensile

59. *Qualità* ci insegna soprattutto quale delle seguenti attività?

(A) A cucinare all'italiana
(B) A fare scelte informate
(C) A superare gli esami
(D) A nuotare con stile

GO ON TO THE NEXT PAGE

Questions 60-64

Da pochi mesi abito ad Arenzano (Genova), in quella che quarant'anni fa doveva essere una stupenda foresta. Oggi vi sono ancora dei pini, tra il campo da golf, quelli da tennis, il supermarket e la piazzetta tipo Porto Cervo, ma il mare è sporco. Una mattina, dalla finestra della stanza da letto, ho visto uno scoiattolo che sgranocchiava pinoli. Da quel giorno le sue evoluzioni e la sua lunga coda rendono i miei risvegli più sereni. Però ha un difetto: curiosa tra i vasi ed ogni tanto ne rovescia qualcuno; poi, ha fame, proprio come noi uomini che abbiamo distrutto la "sua" pineta, ed allora mangia persino i fiori colorati posti sui davanzali. I proprietari delle villette accanto, travolti dall'ondata ecologica, hanno pensato di cospargere il territorio di trappole velenose, per risolvere l'annoso problema dei fiori smangiucchiati! E poi discutono, seduti sulle panche della piazzetta, sul futuro della foresta amazzonica.

60. Secondo l'autore, molti anni fa la foresta era

(A) senza pini
(B) sporca
(C) piena di scoiattoli
(D) meravigliosa

61. Com'è il mare?

(A) Inquinato
(B) Sereno
(C) Burrascoso
(D) Stupendo

62. Quando osserva lo scoiattolo l'autore prova un sentimento di

(A) rabbia
(B) noia
(C) tranquillità
(D) indifferenza

63. Perchè i proprietari delle villette vogliono avvelenare lo scoiattolo?

(A) Mangia i fiori.
(B) Rovina i pini.
(C) Rompe i davanzali.
(D) Sporca il mare.

64. Come passano il tempo i proprietari delle villette?

(A) Giocano a golf e a tennis.
(B) Preparano trappole velenose.
(C) Coltivano i fiori.
(D) Discutono di problemi ecologici.

GO ON TO THE NEXT PAGE

Questions 65-67

L'INFORMATICA A TUA
IMMAGINE E SOMIGLIANZA.
Siamo la sola società di servizi informatici che offre una consulenza globale e un servizio completo per ogni problema informatico: dall'istruzione qualificata del personale alla pianificazione dell'ambiente di lavoro.
Siamo in grado di assicurare un servizio qualificato e tempestivo grazie alle nostre trenta filiali, capillarmente operative su tutto il territorio nazionale (indirizzi sulle pagine gialle alla voce "informatica").
IBIMAINT®

65. La Ibimaint non dà solo assistenza tecnica ma offre anche

    (A) corsi di manutenzione
    (B) consulenza e aiuto specifico
    (C) di rendere il computer simile al suo padrone
    (D) consulenza solo nel settore della programmazione

66. Cosa vende la Ibimaint?

    (A) Trenta filiali
    (B) Ambienti di lavoro
    (C) Servizi informatici
    (D) Spazio sulle pagine gialle

67. Secondo la pubblicità, cosa ha la Ibimaint?

    (A) Filiali da trent'anni
    (B) Una filiale solo a Milano
    (C) Filiali solo nell'Italia settentrionale
    (D) Filiali in tutto il paese

GO ON TO THE NEXT PAGE

Questions 68-72

In Italia incombe la paura di gigantesche catastrofi naturali. Acqua, terra e fuoco colpiscono il Belpaese con tragica regolarità e straordinaria forza. La prima minaccia sono i vulcani. Tre sono fra i più pericolosi: Vesuvio, Campi Flegrei e Vulcano.

Il secondo incubo sono i terremoti. In realtà quasi tutte le regioni italiane sono a rischio. Di edifici antisismici, che resistono ai terremoti, però, ne sono stati costruiti davvero pochi.

Un'altra minaccia sono le industrie. In Italia ci sono quattrocento fabbriche a grave rischio ambientale: stabilimenti chimici, farmaceutici, raffinerie rischiano di trasformarsi in bombe tossiche.

Ma non basta. Ogni anno c'è un appuntamento fisso: l'emergenza incendi che ogni estate divora una gran quantità di vegetazione. Negli ultimi quindici anni in Sardegna, in Liguria e in Piemonte intere foreste sono andate in fumo in poche ore.

68. Secondo il brano, gli italiani temono

(A) le esplosioni
(B) l'incubo
(C) i disastri
(D) il fumo

69. Cosa intende l'autore con la parola "Belpaese"?

(A) Una regione
(B) L'Italia
(C) Un vulcano
(D) La campagna

70. Gli edifici antisismici servono a

(A) prevenire i terremoti
(B) proteggere l'ambiente
(C) segnalare il pericolo
(D) ridurre i danni

71. L'articolo sostiene che l'industria italiana

(A) dà l'allarme
(B) costruisce le centrali nucleari
(C) propone un referendum
(D) intossica l'ambiente

72. Secondo l'articolo, gli incendi distruggono

(A) le isole
(B) le spiagge
(C) i boschi
(D) i villaggi

GO ON TO THE NEXT PAGE

Questions 73-74

BASILICA DI SAN MARCO - VENEZIA

in occasione della

VISITA ALLA Pala d'Oro

INTERO DIURNO
ha versato l'offerta di **Lire 3.000**

BIGLIETTI DI CONTROLLO (DA CONSERVARE)

Serie S Nº 41828

Offerta per il culto e per il decoro della Basilica. GRAZIE

73. Questo biglietto serve per

(A) pregare nella Basilica
(B) vedere la Pala d'Oro
(C) controllare le offerte
(D) visitare Venezia

74. I soldi pagati per questo biglietto sono usati per

(A) acquistare libri sulla Basilica
(B) conservare i gioielli
(C) decorare la Basilica
(D) ringraziare i turisti

GO ON TO THE NEXT PAGE

Questions 75-78

Dapprincipio non ho fatto caso al rumore. Veniva dal pianerottolo ed era come un lievissimo rosicchiare di topo, mescolato ai tanti cigolii, ronzii, tonfi condominiali, al basso continuo del traffico cinque piani più sotto.

Uno di quei suoni piccoli, insinuanti, mi si è infilato nelle orecchie senza che me ne accorgessi. Quel suono era troppo leggero; per la precisione era furtivo.

Ho messo l'occhio allo spioncino e ho visto il mio illustre ex marito che trafficava attorno alla porta di casa. Ho spalancato; mi è quasi caduto tra le braccia. Teneva in mano un minuscolo cacciavite.

"Riccardo, che fai?" Speravo che gli venisse la faccia del ladro sorpreso a rubare. Niente.

"Oh, ciao," ha detto. "Prendevo la targa."

Aveva già finito di staccare la placca circlee con il nome: Riccardo Prini. Sono rimasta a guardarlo, senza fiatare.

75. Dove si trova la narratrice?

(A) Allo zoo
(B) Al cinema
(C) In strada
(D) In casa

76. Quando si rende conto del rumore?

(A) Quando arriva il marito
(B) A poco a poco
(C) Verso le cinque
(D) Prima di andare a dormire

77. Che stava facendo l'ex marito?

(A) Faceva riparazioni in casa.
(B) Regolava il traffico.
(C) Lucidava la porta.
(D) Toglieva la targa.

78. Come reagisce la narratrice alla situazione?

(A) Tace per la sorpresa.
(B) Chiama immediatamente la polizia.
(C) Finisce il lavoro.
(D) Stacca la placca.

GO ON TO THE NEXT PAGE

Questions 79-81

Tè Star all'Arancia, freddo.
Il segreto della sua bontà è custodito nella sua bustina.
*Per vincere la sete, provate freddo Tè Star all'Arancia. Protetto dalle esclusive **Bustine Salvaroma**, il Tè Star mantiene intatta tutta la sua qualità. Preparatelo utilizzando 3 filtri per ogni litro, zuccheratelo a piacere e, se preferite, per esaltarne il profumo, aggiungete un po' di limone, così potrete assaporare tutta la sua bontà.*
STAR TEA
tè alla Arancia
STAR

79. Secondo la pubblicità, è meglio bere il tè Star

(A) freddo
(B) tiepido
(C) a temperatura ambiente
(D) con le arancie

80. La parola "Salvaroma" allude a

(A) una salvaguardia
(B) un elogio a Roma
(C) un'esortazione a salvare Roma
(D) una garanzia di fragranza

81. Secondo la pubblicità, per un maggiore aroma è possibile aggiungere

(A) ghiaccio
(B) limone
(C) latte
(D) zucchero

GO ON TO THE NEXT PAGE

Question 82

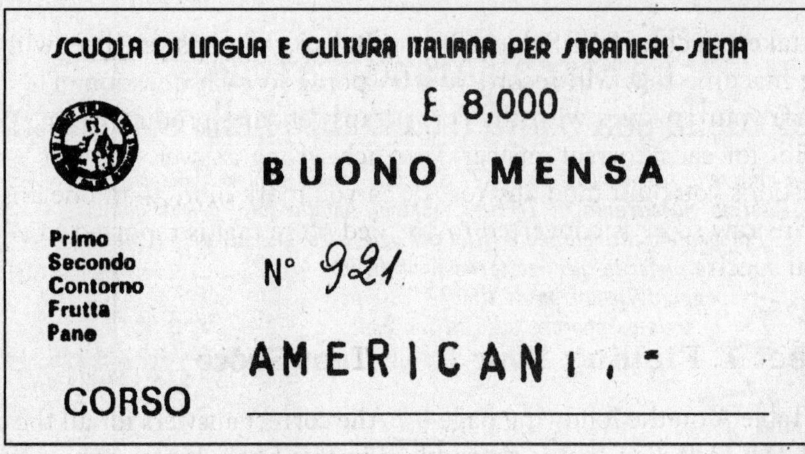
SCUOLA DI LINGUA E CULTURA ITALIANA PER STRANIERI - SIENA

£ 8,000

BUONO MENSA

Primo
Secondo
Contorno
Frutta
Pane

N° 921

AMERICANI. -

CORSO

82. Per quali delle seguenti attività è valido questo biglietto?

(A) Un corso alla scuola per stranieri a Siena
(B) Una gita sul motoscafo “Mensa”
(C) Un viaggio in treno a Siena
(D) Un pasto completo

STOP

IF YOU FINISH BEFORE TIME IS CALLED, YOU MAY CHECK YOUR WORK ON THIS TEST ONLY.
DO NOT TURN TO ANY OTHER TEST IN THIS BOOK.

How to Score the SAT Subject Test in Italian

When you take an actual SAT Subject Test in Italian, your answer sheet will be "read" by a scanning machine that will record your response to each question. Then a computer will compare your answers with the correct answers and produce your raw score. You get one point for each correct answer. For each wrong answer, you lose one-third of a point. Questions you omit (and any for which you mark more than one answer) are not counted. This raw score is converted to a scaled score that is reported to you and to the colleges you specify.

Worksheet 1. Finding Your Raw Test Score

STEP 1: Table A on the following page lists the correct answers for all the questions on the Subject Test in Italian that is reproduced in this book. It also serves as a worksheet for you to calculate your raw score.

- Compare your answers with those given in the table.
- Put a check in the column marked "Right" if your answer is correct.
- Put a check in the column marked "Wrong" if your answer is incorrect.
- Leave both columns blank if you omitted the question.

STEP 2: Count the number of right answers.

Enter the total here: ______________

STEP 3: Count the number of wrong answers.

Enter the total here: ______________

STEP 4: Multiply the number of wrong answers by .333.

Enter the product here: ______________

STEP 5: Subtract the result obtained in Step 4 from the total you obtained in Step 2.

Enter the result here: ______________

STEP 6: Round the number obtained in Step 5 to the nearest whole number.

Enter the result here: ______________

The number you obtained in Step 6 is your raw score.

Table A

Answers to the Subject Test in Italian and Percentage of Students Answering Each Question Correctly

Question Number	Correct Answer	Right	Wrong	Percentage of Students Answering the Question Correctly*	Question Number	Correct Answer	Right	Wrong	Percentage of Students Answering the Question Correctly*
1	C			94	33	A			84
2	B			94	34	A			84
3	B			84	35	B			76
4	B			93	36	B			67
5	D			68	37	C			74
6	C			67	38	B			73
7	A			76	39	D			64
8	A			87	40	A			34
9	C			22	41	A			78
10	B			69	42	C			84
11	C			23	43	A			51
12	D			92	44	D			49
13	B			78	45	C			80
14	D			30	46	A			76
15	B			48	47	C			76
16	B			62	48	B			92
17	B			66	49	C			85
18	A			82	50	A			45
19	A			47	51	B			86
20	D			75	52	A			76
21	B			83	53	A			76
22	A			61	54	D			63
23	B			69	55	A			49
24	C			71	56	C			54
25	B			92	57	A			50
26	B			64	58	D			54
27	C			58	59	B			74
28	B			78	60	D			66
29	D			71	61	A			31
30	C			74	62	C			57
31	C			60	63	A			40
32	A			60	64	D			51

Table A continued on next page

Table A continued from previous page

Question Number	Correct Answer	Right	Wrong	Percentage of Students Answering the Question Correctly*	Question Number	Correct Answer	Right	Wrong	Percentage of Students Answering the Question Correctly*
65	B			70	74	C			75
66	C			74	75	D			47
67	D			63	76	B			25
68	C			80	77	D			33
69	B			60	78	A			30
70	D			17	79	A			90
71	D			50	80	D			60
72	C			49	81	B			90
73	B			76	82	D			35

* These percentages are based on an analysis of the answer sheets of a representative sample of 255 students who took the original administration of this test and whose mean score was 594. They may be used as an indication of the relative difficulty of a particular question.

Answer explanations for the Subject Test in Italian can be found on page 767.

Finding Your Scaled Score

When you take SAT Subject Tests, the scores sent to the colleges you specify are reported on the College Board scale, which ranges from 200–800. You can convert your practice test score to a scaled score by using Table B. To find your scaled score, locate your raw score in the left-hand column of Table B; the corresponding score in the right-hand column is your scaled score. For example, a raw score of 55 on this particular edition of the Subject Test in Italian corresponds to a scaled score of 660.

Raw scores are converted to scaled scores to ensure that a score earned on any one edition of a particular Subject Test is comparable to the same scaled score earned on any other edition of the same Subject Test. Because some editions of the tests may be slightly easier or more difficult than others, College Board scaled scores are adjusted so that they indicate the same level of performance regardless of the edition of the test taken and the ability of the group that takes it. Thus, for example, a score of 400 on one edition of a test taken at a particular administration indicates the same level of achievement as a score of 400 on a different edition of the test taken at a different administration.

When you take the SAT Subject Tests during a national administration, your scores are likely to differ somewhat from the scores you obtain on the tests in this book. People perform at different levels at different times for reasons unrelated to the tests themselves. The precision of any test is also limited because it represents only a sample of all the possible questions that could be asked.

Table B

Scaled Score Conversion Table Subject Test in Italian					
Raw Score	Scaled Score	Raw Score	Scaled Score	Raw Score	Scaled Score
82	800	45	600	8	350
81	800	44	600	7	350
80	800	43	590	6	340
79	800	42	580	5	330
78	800	41	580	4	330
77	790	40	570	3	320
76	780	39	560	2	310
75	770	38	560	1	310
74	760	37	550	0	300
73	760	36	540	-1	290
72	750	35	540	-2	290
71	740	34	530	-3	280
70	740	33	520	-4	270
69	730	32	520	-5	270
68	720	31	510	-6	260
67	720	30	500	-7	250
66	710	29	490	-8	250
65	710	28	490	-9	240
64	700	27	480	-10	230
63	690	26	470	-11	230
62	690	25	460	-12	220
61	680	24	460	-13	220
60	680	23	450	-14	210
59	670	22	440	-15	210
58	670	21	440	-16	200
57	660	20	430	-17	200
56	660	19	430	-18	200
55	660	18	420	-19	200
54	650	17	410	-20	200
53	640	16	410	-21	200
52	640	15	400	-22	200
51	630	14	390	-23	200
50	630	13	390	-24	200
49	620	12	380	-25	200
48	620	11	370	-26	200
47	610	10	370	-27	200
46	610	9	360		

How Did You Do on the Subject Test in Italian?

After you score your test and analyze your performance, think about the following questions:

Did you run out of time before reaching the end of the test?

If so, you may need to pace yourself better. For example, maybe you spent too much time on one or two hard questions. A better approach might be to skip the ones you can't answer right away and try answering all the questions that remain on the test. Then if there's time, go back to the questions you skipped.

Did you take a long time reading the directions?

You will save time when you take the test by learning the directions to the Subject Test in Italian ahead of time. Each minute you spend reading directions during the test is a minute that you could use to answer questions.

How did you handle questions you were unsure of?

If you were able to eliminate one or more of the answer choices as wrong and guess from the remaining ones, your approach probably worked to your advantage. On the other hand, making haphazard guesses or omitting questions without trying to eliminate choices could cost you valuable points.

How difficult were the questions for you compared with other students who took the test?

Table A shows you how difficult the multiple-choice questions were for the group of students who took this test during its national administration. The right-hand column gives the percentage of students that answered each question correctly.

A question answered correctly by almost everyone in the group is obviously an easier question. For example, 94 percent of the students answered question 2 correctly. But only 17 percent answered question 70 correctly.

Keep in mind that these percentages are based on just one group of students. They would probably be different with another group of students taking the test.

If you missed several easier questions, go back and try to find out why: Did the questions cover material you haven't yet reviewed? Did you misunderstand the directions?

Answer Explanations for the Italian Subject Test

1. Choice (C) is the correct answer. The writer is talking about immigrants who come to live (*abitare*) in a new country. Since these people are called immigrants (*immigranti*) and the title of the passage is "Life in a New Country" (*Vita in un nuovo paese*), it does not make sense to say that these people come to visit (*visitare*) in a new country. It also does not make sense to say that they come to leave (*partire*) or to welcome (*accogliere*) in a new country either. Furthermore, *abitare* is the only choice that can be idiomatically or grammatically followed by the preposition *in* ("in").

2. Choice (B) is the correct answer. The sentence is describing what life is like for immigrants in a new country. It is logical to suggest that their situation is sometimes very difficult (*difficile*). It does not make sense to say that their situation is often wise (*saggia*), uninhabited (*disabitata*), or irresponsible (*irresponsabile*).

3. Choice (B) is the correct answer. This sentence is describing how the immigrants first feel in their new country. It is logical to say that they feel isolated (*isolati*). It does not make sense to say that they feel awake (*svegli*) or congenial (*congeniali*). Further, because the previous sentence says that life is sometimes very difficult for them, it does not make sense to say that they feel independent (*indipendenti*).

4. Choice (B) is the correct answer. According to the sentence, the children do something with the language of the country rather quickly. It is logical to say that they learn (*imparano*) the language quite quickly. It does not make sense to say that they live (*vivono*), discuss (*discutono*), or recommend (*consigliano*) the language quickly.

5. Choice (D) is the correct answer. The missing word in this sentence is an adverb describing how the adults continue to speak the dialect of their country. The adverb *spesso* ("often") best completes the sentence. It is not idiomatic and does not make sense to say that they continue to speak the dialect already (*già*), afterwards (*dopo*), or very much (*molto*).

6. Choice (C) is the correct answer. According to the sentence, Grado was originally a village of fishermen. The missing word should be another way of describing Grado. Because Grado used to be a fishing village, it is logical to describe it as a beautiful

small town (*cittadina*). It does not make sense to say that it is now a society or company (*società*), a beach (*spiaggia*), or a street or road (*strada*).

7. Choice (A) is the correct answer. According to the sentence, Grado is made up of two islands (*due isole*). The missing word must indicate how this island town is connected to the mainland by a sand bridge (*è . . . alla terraferma da un ponte di sabbia*). *Unita* ("joined") best completes the sentence. It does not make sense to say that Grado is put (*messa*), carried (*portata*), or raised (*sollevata*) to the mainland by a sand bridge.

8. Choice (A) is the correct answer. According to the sentence, Grado has a port for something. The missing word should indicate an item that uses a port. It is logical to say that there would be a port for *barche da pesca* ("fishing boats"). It does not make sense to say that the port is for racehorses (*cavalli da corsa*), stylish cars (*automobile eleganti*), or brand-name bicycles (*biciclette di marca*).

9. Choice (C) is the correct answer. According to the sentence, important events are carried out in the enchanting basilica, especially in the summer. The missing word should describe a type of event that would likely take place in such an elegant location. It is logical to suggest that musical (*musicali*) events are performed in the basilica. It is unlikely that commercial (*commerciali*), industrial (*industriali*), or sports (*sportive*) events would be carried out in a basilica.

10. Choice (B) is the correct answer. This sentence describes the marshes around Grado's lagoon and mentions a relationship between the marshes and sumptuous wines (*vini sontuosi*). The missing word should indicate the connection between the marshes and the wine. The reflexive *si* is used in this sentence to effectively make the meaning of the missing verb passive. It is logical to say that sumptuous wines are produced (*si producono*) there. It does not make sense to say that the wines are put (*si mettono*), composed (*si compongono*), or constructed (*si construiscono*) there.

11. Choice (C) is the correct answer. The writer asks readers if they want to do something to the expense of their vacation in a European capital so that it is minimized. It is logical to say that the writer's question would ask readers if they want to reduce (*ridurre*) the expense to a minimum. It does not make sense to ask if they want to include (*includere*), give (*dare*), or reach (*giungere*) the expense to a minimum.

12. Choice (D) is the correct answer. In this sentence, the writer is offering a solution (*soluzione*) to two things. *Problemi* ("problems") best completes the sentence. It does not make sense to say that the writer would be offering a solution to subjects

(*soggetti*), jobs (*lavori*), or means (*mezzi*) because these things do not typically have solutions.

13. Choice (B) is the correct answer. This sentence describes what many large tourist buses do from (*da*) the cities of Milan, Rome, Bologna, Florence, and Genoa. The missing word must be a verb that tells what the buses do from these locations. *Partono* ("depart") best completes the sentence. It does make sense to say that these buses pay (*pagano*), extend (*stendono*), or touch (*toccano*) from these cities. Further, *pagare, stendere,* and *toccare* are not idiomatically used with the preposition *da* ("from"), and *stendere* and *toccare* are generally transitive and do not fit grammatically in this sentence that has no direct object.

14. Choice (D) is the correct answer. This sentence is comparing the cost of a plane ticket and the cost of a bus ticket. *Della metà* ("than half") best completes the sentence; in other words, the bus ticket costs less (*meno*) than half the cost of the plane ticket. It does not make sense to say that the ticket costs less than the energy (*dell'energia*), than the economy or savings (*dell'economia*), or than the trip (*della gita*).

15. Choice (B) is the correct answer. This sentence is comparing the length of the bus trip with the duration of something else, saying that the bus trip lasts several hours longer. *Del volo* ("than the flight") best completes the sentence. Not only was there a comparison made in the previous sentence to a plane, but it also does not make sense to say that the bus trip lasts longer than the veil (*del velo*), than the sail (*dell vela*), or than the occasion (*della volta*).

16. Choice (B) is the correct answer. The sentence indicates that the buses almost always travel a certain way. *Autostrada* ("highway") best completes the sentence. Here, the preposition *in* cannot be translated literally as "in"; it is part of the idiomatic expression *in autostrada* ("by highway" or "on the highway"). It does not make sense to say that the buses travel in station (*stazione*), silence (*silenzio*), or company (*compagnia*).

17. Choice (B) is the correct answer. According to the sentence, the journey by bus is direct (*diretto*), without something in particular. It is logical to say that a direct trip would not have detours (*deviazioni*). It does not make sense to say that the journey is without direction (*direzione*), destinations (*destinazioni*), or patience (*pazienza*).

18. Choice (A) is the correct answer. According to the sentence, every passenger can bring with him or her a suitcase and a piece of hand (*mano*) luggage. Here, *mano*

forms part of the term *bagaglio a mano* ("hand luggage"). It does not make sense to speak of feet (*piedi*), earth (*terra*), or voice (*voce*) luggage.

19. Choice (A) is the correct answer. According to the sentence, working as an animator in a tourist village is the most sought-after job during the summer. The missing word must be an adjective to describe the job; the fact that this work is most popular during the summer implies that it is seasonal (*stagionale*), not monthly (*mensile*), daily (*giornaliero*), or annual (*annuale*). The next sentence confirms this by saying that it involves three or four months of work.

20. Choice (D) is the correct answer. According to the sentence, the job means actually passing three or four months in a place modified by the phrase *di mare* ("relating to the sea"). *Località* ("resort") best completes the sentence. It does not make sense to suggest that the job takes place at a sea gym (*palestra*), discotheque (*discoteca*), or pizzeria (*pizzeria*).

21. Choice (B) is the correct answer. This sentence explains the responsibilities of being an animator: among other things, keeping busy entertaining others and organizing parties and other things for children. The missing word indicates something that an animator would organize for children, in addition to parties. Because the job of an animator is to entertain others, *giochi* ("games") best completes the sentence. It does not make sense for an animator to organize jobs (*lavori*) or tasks (*compiti*) for children. Further, organizing services or toilet facilities (*servizi*) and parties is a far less likely combination than games and parties.

22. Choice (A) is the correct answer. According to the sentence, one of the duties of an animator is doing something related to tennis, windsurfing, yoga, or aerobics. It is logical to say that an animator would teach (*insegnare*) these things. It does not make sense to suggest that the job would entail learning (*imparare*), giving (*dare*), or attending (*frequentare*) these activities.

23. Choice (B) is the correct answer. This sentence tells the type of people that an animator must manage to deal with. An animator works in villages and resorts keeping people entertained, so his or her first priority is dealing with the clients (*clienti*), not the painters (*pittori*), passengers (*passeggeri*), or shopkeepers (*commercianti*).

24. Choice (C) is the correct answer. This sentence describes how an animator must interact with everyone, even the most difficult: be cheerful and engaging . . . without ever doing something with regard to the private lives of the tourists. It is logical to

say that an animator should not invade (*invadere*) the private lives of the tourists. It does not make sense to say that an animator must not change (*cambiare*), explain (*spiegare*), or occupy (*occupare*) the tourists' private lives.

25. Choice (B) is the correct answer. According to the sentence, there are also postcards (*cartoline*) and newspapers (*giornali*) outside. The missing adjective modifies either the masculine plural *giornali* ("newspapers") alone or the feminine plural *cartoline* ("postcards") and *giornali* together. In either case, to agree in gender and number, the adjective must be the masculine plural *illustrati* ("illustrated") because any group with even one masculine item is treated as masculine. *Illustrata* (A) is feminine singular, *illlustrato* (C) is masculine singular, and *illustrate* (D) is feminine plural.

26. Choice (B) is the correct answer. In this sentence, the speaker asks the woman if she has any American magazines. *Ha* ("Do you have") best completes the sentence. *È* ("Are you") does not make sense. Further, the subjunctive forms *sia* ("be") and *abbia* ("have") are not grammatically correct in this sentence.

27. Choice (C) is the correct answer. In this sentence, the speaker offers to help the listener if he or she wants. Because the third person verb *vuole* ("want") is used in the second clause to formally address the listener, the direct object pronoun added to the end of *aiutare* ("help") must be the formal *La* ("you"). *Auitarmi* ("help me"), *aiutarci* ("help us"), and *aiutarsi* ("help oneself") do not make sense in the sentence.

28. Choice (B) is the correct answer. In this sentence, the speaker is saying that something will likely occur "at this time tomorrow" (*A quest'ora domani*). Because the writer is talking about a likely condition tomorrow (*domani*), the future tense is used. Therefore, *saremo* ("we will be") best completes the sentence. Choice (A), *sia* ("he/she/ it be"), is the third person present subjunctive and choice (D), *fossimo* ("we were"), is the imperfect subjunctive. These are not used to talk about facts or likelihoods such as what will happen tomorrow. Further, choice (C), the imperfect *eravamo* ("we were"), is used to talk about past conditions, not future conditions.

29. Choice (D) is the correct answer. According to the sentence, the speaker says that it has been five years since he or she and his or her cousin have seen each other. Because the understood subject of the verb *vediamo* ("see") is *noi* ("we"), the correct reciprocal pronoun to use with it is *ci* ("ourselves," or in this instance, "each other"). *Si* ("oneself"), *ne* ("of him/her/it/them"), and *mi* ("me") do not make sense in this context.

30. Choice (C) is the correct answer. In this sentence, the speaker is asking what time he or she should leave the house. The infinitive form of the verb "to leave" (*partire*) must be used after the phrase *consigli* ("advise") *di. Parto* ("I go") and *parti* ("you go") are in the present tense; *partito* ("gone") is the past participle. Therefore, Choice (C) is the only choice that grammatically fits the sentence.

31. Choice (C) is the correct answer. According to the sentence, the girl traveled in the plane with friends (*amici*). *Alcuni* ("a few") is the only choice that can be used directly before the word *amici. Dei* ("some") can only be used before words beginning with a consonant sound; the word *degli* would have to be used before *amici. Nessuno* ("no") is singular and cannot be used before the plural noun *amici. Tutti* ("all") cannot immediately precede a noun; it must be followed first by a definite article (such as *gli*) or determiner (such as *questi*).

32. Choice (A) is the correct answer. In this sentence, the speaker is asking if the listener is sure that she locked the door a certain way. The missing word must be an adverb describing the verb *avere chiuso* ("to have closed"). *Bene* ("well") is the only adverb provided as a choice. All of the other choices — *buona* ("good"), *migliore* ("better"), and *buonissima* ("very good") — are adjectives and cannot modify verbs. The missing word is also in the wrong position for an adjective modifying the nouns *porta* ("door") or *chiave* ("key").

33. Choice (A) is the correct answer. According to the sentence, the speaker likes the color of the listener's suitcases. Because possessive adjectives such as *tue* ("your") are generally preceded by a definite article, all of the choices are actually combinations of prepositions and the definite article *le. Delle* ("of") is the only choice that logically and grammatically fits the sentence. *Dalle* ("from"), *nelle* ("in"), and *sulle* ("on") do not make sense in this context.

34. Choice (A) is the correct answer. According to the sentence, the speaker uses the telephone all day. The expression *tutto il giorno* ("all day") is used without any preceding prepositions. The other choices are not grammatically correct.

35. Choice (B) is the correct answer. In this sentence, the use of the third person subject pronoun *lui* ("he") after the verb *fare* ("to do") indicates that the conjugated verb must also be in the third person. *Dovrà* ("he will have [to]") is the only choice that grammatically fits the sentence. *Dovrai* ("you will have [to]"), *dovrò* ("I will have [to]"), and *dovranno* ("they will have [to]") are grammatically incorrect.

36. Choice (B) is the correct answer. According to the sentence, today in Italy stress spares no one (*nessuno*). *Nessuno* is the only choice that can be used as the object of a verb preceded by *non* ("not"). In Italian, many negative expressions are what would be considered incorrect double negatives if translated literally into English, for example *non . . . nessuno* ("not . . . no one"). However, in Italian the use of double negatives is correct. *Qualcuno* ("someone"), *chiunque* ("whoever" or "anyone"), and *ognuno* ("everyone") are not negative words and therefore cannot be used as the object of a verb preceded by *non*.

37. Choice (C) is the correct answer. According to the sentence, he or she accepted and replied that he or she would be finished with work within a particular amount of minutes (*minuti*). *Pochi* ("a few") is the only choice that can modify the plural noun *minuti*. *Qualche* ("some"), *troppo* ("too much"), and *un* ("one") are all singular and cannot grammatically modify *minuti*.

38. Choice (B) is the correct answer. The speaker in this sentence says that when an unnamed male receives his or her telegram, he will not reply to him or her immediately. In this sentence, two clauses are joined by *quando* ("when"). The use of the future tense verb *riceverà* ("will receive") in the first clause indicates that the future tense should also be used in the second clause. *Risponderà* ("will reply") is the only choice that is in the future tense. *Risponde* ("replies") is in the present tense; *rispondeva* ("was replying") is in the imperfect tense; and *risponderebbe* ("would respond") is in the conditional. Therefore, none of the other choices are grammatically correct.

39. Choice (D) is the correct answer. The sentence indicates a relationship between recent studies by the United Nations and the fact that Italian women work a lot. In other words, according to (*secondo*) these studies, Italian women work a lot. All of the other choices — *su* ("on"), *fra* ("between"), and *sotto* ("under") — do not make sense in this context.

40. Choice (A) is the correct answer. According to the sentences, Italians love the sea and many go during summer vacation. The missing word should refer back to "the sea" (*il mare*). *Ci* ("there") best completes the sentence. The other choices — *gli* ("to him/it/them"), *ne* ("of it/him/her/them"), and *lo* ("it/him") — do not have referents and are not grammatically correct. Although *gli* can be translated as "to it," this is only in its use as an indirect object not in the sense of moving toward a thing or a place.

41. Choice (A) is the correct answer. According to the sentence, it is convenient to rent a beach umbrella. Additionally, the speaker says that he or she wants to get it in green. The transitive verb *prendere* ("to take/get") requires a direct object, and *prenderlo*

("to get it") is the only choice with a logical direct object. This grammatical structure is also an idiomatic way to express the selection of a color for a particular item. Although *ci* in Choice (B) and *vi* in Choice (D) could be translated as direct object pronouns "us" and "you" respectively, this interpretation would make no sense at all. It is more logical to translate both *prenderci* (B) and *prendervi* (D) as "to take here/there." In that case, *prendere* would have no direct objet because *verde* ("green") alone cannot serve as a direct object, and the choices are not grammatically correct. *Prenderne* ("to get of it/them") also lacks a direct object and is not grammatically correct; to be grammatically correct, this choice would require *uno* ("one") before *verde*: *io voglio prenderne uno verde* ("I want to get a green one").

42. Choice (C) is the correct answer. In this sentence, the speaker says that this tree is the tallest that he or she has ever seen. The missing word is a relative pronoun that refers to *albero* ("tree") and serves as the direct object of *abbia visto* ("have seen"), so it must be the direct object relative pronoun *che* ("that"). *Quale* ("which/what"), as a relative pronoun, serves as the object of a preposition, not as a direct object. *Chi* ("that/who"), as a relative pronoun, serves as a subject, not as a direct object. *Cui* ("to which" or "which"), as a relative pronoun, serves as an indirect object or the object of a preposition, but not as a direct object.

43. Choice (A) is the correct answer. According to the sentence, the speaker's neighbors prefer to watch television. After the verb *preferire* ("to prefer"), no preposition is used before a subsequent infinitive such as *guardare* ("to watch"). The other choices are not grammatically correct.

44. Choice (D) is the correct answer. According to the sentence, the speaker would like recordings of modern popular music. The missing word is describing the plural noun *registrazioni* ("recordings"). *Alcune* ("some") is the only choice that can immediately precede and modify this plural noun. *Di* ("some") must be followed by the definite article *le* (that is, *delle*) in this position to be grammatically correct. *Un po'* ("a few") must be followed by *di* before a noun in order to be grammatically correct. To use *niente* ("no") in this position, the verb *vorrei* ("I would like") would have to be preceded by *non* ("not") to make it negative.

45. Choice (C) is the correct answer. In this sentence, the speaker is asking if the tickets for the concert at the stadium can be bought here. The third person reflexive pronoun *si* can be used in Italian to effectively make a verb passive; for example, in this instance, *si possono comprare* would be translated literally as "can buy themselves" but means "can be bought." *Vi* ("you" or "there") and *ti* ("you") do not make sense in this context and would be translated as "Can the tickets buy you here?" or "Can the

tickets buy there here?" Choice (B), *me* ("me"), cannot be used before a verb and is therefore entirely ungrammatical.

46. Choice (A) is the correct answer. According to the sentence, the speaker likes Italian bands that play loud. The concept of the English verb "like" is expressed in Italian by the verb *piacere* ("to please" or "to be pleasing"), which requires an indirect object. *Mi* ("to me") is the only choice that is an indirect object pronoun. *Me* ("me") is an object pronoun that must follow a verb or preposition; it cannot precede the verb or serve as an indirect object on its own. *Lo* ("him/it") and *la* ("her/it") are direct object pronouns and cannot be used with *piacciono* ("are pleasing") either.

47. Choice (C) is the correct answer. According to the sentence, the speaker believes that the pianist is very good and has heard him play. The verb *sentire* ("to hear") is used with a direct object and an infinitive, such as *suonare* ("to play"), to express the concept of hearing someone or something do something. The past participle *suonato* ("played"), the imperfect tense *suonava* ("was playing"), and the remote past tense *suonò* ("played") are not grammatically correct.

48. Choice (B) is the correct answer. According to the sentence, the Rex Cinema is showing the last movie of Massimo Troisi. The missing article refers to the masculine noun *film* ("movie"), so it must be masculine. The correct form of a definite article that comes before a word beginning with a vowel, such as *ultimo* ("last"), is *l'*. The forms of the definite article in the other choices are incorrect: *il* (A) is used before masculine nouns when followed by a word beginning with most consonants; *lo* (C) is used before masculine nouns when followed by a word beginning with *z* or *s* + a consonant; and *la* (D) is used before feminine nouns when followed by a word beginning with a consonant.

49. Choice (C) is the correct answer. The speaker in this sentence is asking if Laura likes modern painting. The concept of the English verb "like" is expressed in Italian by the verb *piacere* ("to please" or "to be pleasing"), which requires an indirect object. *Ti* ("to you") is the only choice that is grammatical and makes sense in the sentence. *Li* ("them") is a direct object pronoun and is therefore not grammatically correct. *Lei* ("she") is a subject or object pronoun, and it cannot be used as an indirect object without a preceding preposition. If *si* ("to oneself") were used in the sentence, it would translate as ". . . does modern painting like itself?" In other words, *si* does not make sense in this sentence.

50. Choice (A) is the correct answer. According to the sentence, the speaker says there are splendid catalogs in the museum. The speaker then goes on to say, "I would buy

(*comprerei*) them if they didn't cost too much." The use of the imperfect subjunctive *costassero* ("cost") in the clause beginning with *se* ("if") shows that the speaker is discussing a condition that does not truly exist: the speaker imagines that the catalogs did not cost too much, but in fact they do cost too much. Because this condition is not true, the conditional *comprerei* ("I would buy") is used in the first clause. None of the other choices — the future tense *comprerò* ("I will buy"), the remote past tense *comprai* ("I bought"), or the present tense *compro* ("I buy") — make sense in this sentence.

51. Choice (B) is the correct answer. According to the advertisement, Angera is the place to go "[f]or a different trip far from stress, in full relaxation at your doorstep" ("*Per una gita diversa lontana dallo stress, in pieno relax a due passi da voi*"). Therefore, Angera is a suitable place to rest up (*riposarsi*); it is not a suitable place to get married (*sposarsi*), to ski (*sciare*), or to work (*lavorare*).

52. Choice (A) is the correct answer. The advertisement describes a "typical restaurant with international cuisine and typical local dishes" ("*ristorante tipico . . . locali*"). In other words, the restaurant offers dishes from every country (*di ogni paese*), not dishes that are only local (*solamente locali*), rustic (*rustici*), or dietetic (*dietetici*).

53. Choice (A) is the correct answer. In lines 2–4, the author of the passage says that when she entered and saw a well-lit oil painting, she immediately recognized Guttuso's signature. She also mentions that she admired his art (*Entrai e vidi . . . la sua arte*). It is logical then to say that Guttuso is a painter (*un pittore*), not an actor (*un attore*), a writer (*uno scrittore*), or a sculptor (*uno scultore*).

54. Choice (D) is the correct answer. In lines 6–8, the author looks at the painting and asks if it is done by Guttuso. The owner of the house responds and tells the author the title of the painting ("'*È un Guttuso, no?' . . . mi rispose il padrone di casa*"). The owner clearly states that the title of the painting is *I naufraghi* ("The Castaways"). None of the other choices correctly identify the title of the painting.

55. Choice (A) is the correct answer. In line 8, the author of the passage says that the painting fascinated her ("*Il quadro continuava ad affascinarmi*"). Therefore, *un dipinto* ("a painting") is the most appropriate choice. The author does not suggest that a color (*un colore*), an accent (*l'accento*), or the people (*la gente*) fascinated her.

56. Choice (C) is the correct answer. In lines 16–19, the author of the passage says, "I heard a voice behind me: a Sicilian voice, deep, velvety . . . I turned: 'So are you

Renato Guttuso?'" ("*Sentii una voce . . . Renato Guttuso?'*"). Therefore, it is logical to suggest that the velvety voice belonged to Guttuso. It does not make sense to say the voice belonged to the castaway (*il naufrago*), one of the people in the painting; Rolly Marchi, the owner of the house and the painting; or the lady (*la signora*), the narrator of the story.

57. Choice (A) is the correct answer. In line 18, Guttuso tells Rolly to give the painting to the lady ("*Daglielo Rolly . . . altro*"). Then, in lines 21–22, the lady happily goes home with her painting ("*Tornai a casa felice con il mio quadro*"). It is logical to say that the lady received a work of art (*un'opera d'arte*). Although Guttoso tells the lady, "From the next minute I will be your great admirer" ("*Dal prossimo minute . . . ammiratore*"), she did not receive this compliment (*un complimento*) or an admirer (*un ammiratore*) as a gift. She also did not receive a house (*una casa*).

58. Choice (D) is the correct answer. The advertisement lists four different questions and says that the July *Qualità* will tell readers the answers ("*Ve lo dice Qualità di luglio*"); it also says that *Qualità* is in newstand[s] ("*È in edicola*"). It is logical to suggest that *Qualità* is a monthly magazine (*un periodica mensile*), not a newspaper (*un giornale*), a column (*una rubrica*), or an amusing book (*un libro divertente*).

59. Choice (B) is the correct answer. According to the advertisement, the July issue of *Qualità* promises to answer the following questions: "Which yogurt is most nutritious?" ("*Qual è lo yogurt più nutriente?*"); "Which insecticide is the most effective?" (*Qual è l'insetticida più efficace?*"); "Which tuna tastes the best?" (*Qual è il tonno più gustoso?*"); and "Which beach is the cleanest?" ("*Qual è la spiaggia più pulita?*"). It is logical to suggest that *Qualità* teaches readers how to make informed decisions (*a fare scelte informate*). The advertisement does not indicate that the magazine teaches readers how to cook Italian food (*a cucinare all'italiana*), pass exams (*a superare gli esami*), or swim with style (*a nuotare con stile*).

60. Choice (D) is the correct answer. In lines 1–3, the author starts by saying that for a few months he has lived in Arenzano, in what is supposed to have been a stupendous forest (*stupenda foresta*) 40 years ago. Therefore, according to the author, many years ago the forest was marvelous (*meravigliosa*), not without pines (*senza pini*), dirty (*sporca*), or full of squirrels (*piena di scoiattoli*).

61. Choice (A) is the correct answer. In line 5, the author says the sea is dirty (. . . *il mare è sporco*). Therefore, according to the passage, the sea is polluted (*inquinato*), not calm (*sereno*), stormy (*burrascoso*), or stupendous (*stupendo*).

62. Choice (C) is the correct answer. In lines 7–9, the author says that from the day that he first saw the squirrel, its developments and long tail made his awakenings more serene ("*Da quel giorno . . . sereni*). It is logical to suggest that the author felt tranquility (*tranquillità*) when watching the squirrel. The author does not indicate that he felt anger (*rabbia*), boredom (*noia*), or indifference (*indifferenza*).

63. Choice (A) is the correct answer. In lines 13–16, the author says that the owners of the nearby houses are overwhelmed by the ecological wave and have thought about scattering the area with poisonous traps to resolve the longstanding problem of the nibbled flowers ("*I proprietari . . . smangiucchiati!*"). In other words, they want to poison the squirrel because it eats the flowers (*mangia i fiori*), not because it damages the pines (*rovina i pini*), breaks the window sills (*rompe i davanzali*), or dirties the sea (*sporca il mare*).

64. Choice (D) is the correct answer. In lines 17–18, the author says that the owners, seated on benches in the town square, discuss the future of the Amazon rain forest ("*E poi discutono . . . foresta amazzonica*"). In other words, they discuss ecological problems (*discutono di problemi ecologici*). Nothing in the passage suggests that they play golf and tennis (*giocano a golf e a tennis*) or actually prepare poisonous traps (*preparano trappole velenose*). While the author says in lines 12–13 that the squirrel even eats the colored flowers placed on the window sills (. . . *ed allora mangia . . . davanzali*), he does not say that the homeowners spend their time growing the flowers (*coltivano i fiori*).

65. Choice (B) is the correct answer. According to the advertisement, Ibimaint is the only information services company that offers a global consulting service and a complete service for every information problem ("*Siamo la sola . . . problema informatico*"). In other words, it offers consulting and helps with specific information problems (*consulenza e aiuto specifico*). The advertisement says that the company provides qualified instruction of personnel ("*istruzione qualificata del personale*"), but not that it offers courses in maintenance (*corsi di manutenzione*). The tagline is "Information Science in Your Own Image" ("*L'informatica a tua immagine e somiglianza*"), but the company does not offer to make the computer similar to its owner (*di rendere il computer simile al suo padrone*). The company offers a wide range of services from qualified instruction to planning of the work environment (". . . *dall'istruzione . . . alla pianificazione dell'ambiente di lavoro*"), so it does not offer consulting only in the area of programming (*consulenza solo nel settore della programmazione*).

66. Choice (C) is the correct answer. According to the advertisement, Ibimaint is an information services company ("*società di servizi informatici*"), so it sells information services (*servizi informatici*). It has 30 branches ("*nostre trenta filiali*"), but it does not

sell 30 branches (*trenta filiali*). It consults on the planning of the work environment ("*pianificazione dell'ambiente di lavoro*"), but it does not sell work environments (*ambienti di lavoro*). The advertisement suggests looking in the yellow pages under "information science" ("*indirizzi sulle pagine gialle alla voce 'informatica'*"), but it does not sell space in the yellow pages (*spazio sulle pagine gialle*).

67. Choice (D) is the correct answer. According to the advertisement, Ibimaint's 30 branches are operative in the entire national territory ("*nostre trenta filiali . . . nazionale*"). In other words, Ibimaint has branches in the whole country (*filiali in tutto il paese*). Nothing in the advertisement indicates that it has had branches for 30 years (*filiali da trent'anni*) or that it has only one branch in Milan (*una filiale solo a Milano*). Further, since there are branches throughout the country, it is not logical to suggest that Ibimaint has branches only in northern Italy (*filiali solo nell'Italia settentrionale*).

68. Choice (C) is the correct answer. The first sentence of the passage says that the fear of gigantic natural catastrophes looms in Italy ("*In Italia incombe la paura di gigantesche catastrofi naturali*"). In other words, Italians fear disasters (*i disastri*). In lines 10–13, the passage talks about factories potentially being transformed into toxic bombs ("*In Italia . . . bombe tossiche*"), but it does not indicate that Italians fear explosions (*le esplosioni*). In line 6, earthquakes are described as a second nightmare ("*Il secondo incubo sono i terremoti*"), but there is no indication that Italians fear "the nightmare" (*l'incubo*). The passage also talks about entire forests going up in smoke ("*andate in fumo*"), but not about Italians fearing smoke (*il fumo*).

69. Choice (B) is the correct answer. The first sentence of the passage says that in Italy (*In Italia*) there looms the fear of gigantic natural catastrophes. The second sentence then refers back to this by specifying the catastrophes that strike *il Belpaese* ("the beautiful country"). The author is using *Belpaese* as another way of describing Italy (*l'Italia*), not a region (*una regione*), a volcano (*un vulcano*), or the countryside (*la campagna*).

70. Choice (D) is the correct answer. In lines 7–9, the passage says that very few anti-seismic buildings, which resist earthquakes, have actually been constructed ("*Di edifici antisismici . . . davvero pochi*"). The purpose of these buildings is to resist earthquakes and thus reduce damage (*ridurre i danni*), not to prevent earthquakes (*prevenire i terremoti*), to protect the environment (*proteggere l'ambiente*), or to signal danger (*segnalare il pericolo*).

71. Choice (D) is the correct answer. The passage says in lines 10–13 that there are 400 factories with serious environmental risk: chemical, pharmaceutical, and refinery

establishments that risk being transformed into toxic bombs ("*In Italia . . . bombe tossiche*"). Therefore, the passage argues that Italian industry is poisoning the environment (*intossica l'ambiente*). Nothing in the passage indicates that Italian industry is sounding the alarm (*dà l'allarme*), constructing nuclear centers (*costruisce le centrali nucleari*), or proposing a referendum (*propone un referendum*).

72. Choice (C) is the correct answer. According to lines 15–16 of the passage, every summer the fires devour a great quantity of vegetation (". . . *ogni estate . . . vegetazione*"). The author goes on to say in lines 17–18 that entire forests have gone up in smoke in a few hours (". . . *intere foreste . . . poche ore*"). Therefore, according to the passage, the fires destroy the woods (*i boschi*). There is nothing in the passage that indicates that the fires destroy the islands (*le isole*), the beaches (*le spiagge*), or the villages (*i villagi*).

73. Choice (B) is the correct answer. The ticket says it is for a visit to the golden altarpiece ("*in occasione della visita alla Pala d'Oro*") at the Basilica of St. Mark in Venice ("*Basilica di San Marco — Venezia*"). The ticket clearly states that it is used to see the golden altarpiece (*vedere la Pala d'Oro*), not to pray in the basilica (*pregare nella Basilica*), to check the donations (*controllare le offerte*), or to visit Venice (*visitare Venezia*).

74. Choice (C) is the correct answer. According to the ticket, the person who purchased the ticket has made a donation of 3,000 lire ("*ha versato l'offerta di Lire 3.000*"), and the donation is for the religion and for the decoration of the basilica ("*Offerta per il culto . . . Basilica*"). This statement is followed by "thank you" (*GRAZIE*). Therefore, the money is used to decorate the basilica (*decorare la Basilica*), not to acquire books about the basilica (*acquistare libri sulla Basilica*), to preserve the jewels (*conservare i gioielli*), or to thank the tourists (*ringraziare i turisti*).

75. Choice (D) is the correct answer. In lines 2–3, the narrator talks about a noise coming from the landing ("*Veniva dal pianerottolo*"). In line 10, she talks about putting her eye to the peephole ("*Ho messo l'occhio all spioncino*"). Finally, in lines 11–12, she mentions seeing her husband at the door of the house ("*ho visto . . . porta di casa*"). It makes sense to say that the narrator is at home (*in casa*). The other choices — at the zoo (*allo zoo*), at the movies (*al cinema*), and on the street (*in strada*) — do not make sense.

76. Choice (B) is the correct answer. In line 1, the narrator says she did not notice the noise at first ("*Dapprincipio non ho fatto caso al rumore*"). She later says in lines 6–7 that one of those small insinuating sounds slipped into her ear without her noticing

it ("*Uno di quei . . . accorgessi*"). In other words, she becomes aware of the sound gradually, or little by little (*a poco a poco*). She does not notice the sound at a specific point in time, such as those suggested in the other choices: when her husband arrives (*quando arriva il marito*), around 5 o'clock (*verso le cinque*), or before going to bed (*prima di andare a dormire*).

77. Choice (D) is the correct answer. When the narrator asks her ex-husband what he is doing, he says, "I was taking the nameplate" ("*Prendevo la targa*"), so he was removing the nameplate (*toglieva la targa*). Although line 13 says he had a tiny screwdriver in his hand ("*Teneva in mano un miniuscolo cacciavite*"), he was not making repairs in the house (*faceva riparazioni in casa*). The narrator uses the verb *trafficare* to say that her ex-husband was fiddling around outside the door of the house (". . . *trafficava attorno alla porta di casa*"), but he was not directing traffic (*regolava il traffico*). There is also nothing that indicates he was polishing the door (*lucidava la porta*).

78. Choice (A) is the correct answer. In lines 18–19, the narrator says she stood looking at her ex-husband without a murmur ("*Sono rimasta . . . senza fiatare*"). In other words, she is silent with surprise (*tace per la sorpresa*). Nothing in the passage indicates that she calls the police immediately (*chiama immediatamente la polizia*), finishes the work (*finisce il lavoro*), or peels off the nameplate (*stacca la placca*).

79. Choice (A) is the correct answer. The first line of the advertisement says "Star Tea with Orange, cold" ("*Tè Star all'Arancia, freddo*"), and the first line of text says, "To beat thirst, try Star Tea with Orange cold" ("*Per vincere . . . all'Arancia*"). Therefore, the advertisement suggests drinking it cold (*freddo*), not lukewarm (*tiepido*) or at room temperature (*a temperature ambiente*). It does suggest adding a little lemon ("*aggiungere un po' di limone*") to the orange-flavored tea, but it does not suggest drinking it with oranges (*con le arancie*).

80. Choice (D) is the correct answer. The word *Salvaroma* is made up of the words *salvare* ("to save") and *aroma* ("aroma"). It is used to describe the aroma-saving teabags ("*bustine salvaroma*"). It is logical to suggest that the word alludes to a guarantee of fragrance (*una garanzia di fraganza*). The other choices — a safeguard (*una salvaguardia*), a tribute to Rome (*un elogio a Roma*), and an exhortation to save Rome (*un'esortazione a salvare Roma*) — do not make sense.

81. Choice (B) is the correct answer. The advertisement suggests that to enhance the aroma readers can add a little lemon (". . . *per esaltarne il profumo . . . limone*"), not ice (*ghiaccio*), milk (*latte*), or sugar (*zucchero*).

82. Choice (D) is the correct answer. The large words near the center of this ticket are "Dining Hall Voucher" ("*Buono Mensa*"). To the left, various meal courses are listed: first course ("*Primo*"), main dish ("*Secondo*"), side dish ("*Contorno*"), fruit ("*Frutta*"), and bread ("*Pane*"). It is logical, then, to suggest that this ticket is for a complete meal (*un pasto completo*). The dining hall is at the School of Italian Culture and Language for Foreigners in Siena ("*Scuola di Lingua e Cultura Italiana Per Stranieri — Siena*"), but the ticket does not enable someone to take a course at the school for foreigners in Siena (*un corso all scuola per stranieri a Siena*). It is not for a ride on the motorboat "Mensa" (*una gita sul motoscafo "Mensa"*) — on this ticket, *mensa* means "dining hall"; it is not the name of a boat. The ticket is also not for a train trip to Siena (*un viaggio in treno a Siena*).

Chapter 12

Japanese with Listening

Purpose

The SAT Subject Test in Japanese with Listening measures your ability to communicate in Japanese in a culturally appropriate way.

Format

This is a one-hour test with about 20 minutes of listening and 40 minutes of usage and reading. There are 80 to 85 multiple-choice listening, reading, and usage questions written with high school curricula in mind. Questions represent situations you might readily encounter and reflect realistic and commonplace communication. Questions range in difficulty from elementary through advanced, although most are in the intermediate level.

Content

The test has a variety of questions requiring a wide-ranging knowledge of the Japanese language.

Listening comprehension questions are based on short, spoken dialogues and narratives primarily about everyday topics. A brief explanation about each selection and the question(s) are given in English. Explanations are also printed in your test book.

Usage questions require you to complete Japanese sentences in a way that is appropriate in terms of structure (grammar), vocabulary and context. Usage questions are printed in two different ways of representing Japanese. In the left column, the Japanese is written in the most common type of romanization (*rōmaji*), a modified Hepburn system. In the right column, the Japanese is presented in standard Japanese script with *furigana* for all *kanji*. You should choose the writing system you are familiar with and read only from that column on the test.

Reading comprehension questions are in English and test your understanding of such points as main and supporting ideas. The selections in this section are taken from materials you might encounter in everyday situations, such as notes, menus, newspaper articles, advertisements, and letters. The text is written in *katakana*, *hiragana*, and *kanji* without *furigana*.

Japanese with Listening	
Skills Measured	**Approximate Percentage of Test**
Listening Comprehension	35%
Usage	30%
Reading Comprehension	35%

How to Prepare

The best preparation is gradual development of competence in Japanese over a period of years. The test is appropriate for students who have studied Japanese as a second or foreign language for two, three, or four years in high school or the equivalent. You are more likely to perform successfully if you have completed at least two full years of Japanese language study. A practice audio CD for the full-length practice test is included with this book. A practice CD with different sample questions can be obtained, along with a copy of the *Getting Ready for the SAT Subject Tests* booklet, from your school counselor, or you can access the listening files at www.collegeboard.org. If your counselor does not have the CD or booklet, he or she can order them from the College Board. Familiarize yourself with the test directions in advance. The directions in this book are identical to those that appear on the test.

CD Players

Using CD Players for Language Tests with Listening

Take an acceptable CD player to the test center. Your CD player must be in good working order, so insert fresh batteries on the day before the test. You may bring additional batteries and a backup player to the test center. CD players cannot be shared with other test-takers.

Test center staff won't have batteries, CD players, or earphones for your use, so your CD player must be:

- equipped with earphones
- portable (hand-held)
- battery operated

You are not allowed to use a CD player with recording or duplicating capabilities.

Note

If the volume on your CD player disturbs other test-takers, the test center supervisor may ask you to move to another seat.

What to do if your CD player malfunctions:

- Raise your hand and tell the test supervisor.
- Switch to backup equipment if you have it and continue the test. If you don't have backup equipment, your score on the Japanese with Listening Test will be canceled. But scores on other Subject Tests you take that day will still be counted.

What if you receive a defective CD on test day? Raise your hand and ask the supervisor for a replacement.

Note

The Subject Test in Japanese with Listening is offered once a year only at designated tests centers. **To take the test you MUST bring an acceptable CD player with earphones to the test center.**

Scores

The total score is reported on the 200-to-800 scale. Listening, usage, and reading subscores are reported on the 20-to-80 scale.

Sample Questions

Your answer sheet has five answer positions marked A, B, C, D, and E, while the questions throughout this test contain only four choices. Be sure NOT to make any marks in column E.

Sample Listening Question

The text in brackets [ ] is *only* recorded; it is not printed in your test booklet. Please note that the CD does not start here. Begin using the CD when you start the actual practice test on page 790.

Directions: In this section of the test you will hear short dialogues and monologues. You will hear them only once, and they are not printed in your test booklet. At the end of each selection, you will be asked questions about what was said. Now listen to the following example.

(Narrator) [Listen to the following conversation in an office.

(Man) 明日(あした)家(うち)に電話してくださいませんか。

(Woman) ええ、いいですよ。　電話番号は？

(Man) あ、書きましょう。

(Narrator) Question 1. What does the man ask the woman to do?]

(16 seconds)

1. (A) Tell him her phone number.
   (B) Call him at home.
   (C) Check with him tomorrow at work.
   (D) Write down her phone number.

Choice (B) is the correct answer to question 1. This question tests students' knowledge of request forms. Choice (B) is the correct answer because this indicates the man's request. Choices (A), (C), and (D) are incorrect because they are not stated by the man.

Sample Usage Question

Directions: This section consists of a number of incomplete statements, each of which has four suggested completions. In some instances, choice (A) may consist of dashes that indicate that no insertion is required to form a correct sentence. Select the choice that best completes the sentence structurally and logically and fill in the corresponding circle on the answer sheet.

This section of the test is presented in two columns that provide identical information. Look at the example below and choose the one column of writing with which you are most familiar in order to answer this question. **DO NOT WASTE TIME BY SWITCHING FROM COLUMN TO COLUMN IN THIS SECTION.**

2. Sore wa totemo kirei ----- hana desu ne.

(A) -----
(B) no
(C) ni
(D) na

2. それはとてもきれい-----花ですねえ。

(A) -----
(B) の
(C) に
(D) な

Choice (D) is the correct answer to question 2. This question tests the proper usage of *kirei*. Choice (D) is the correct answer because *na* is always used to connect *kirei* with the noun that it modifies (in this case *hana*). Choices (A), (B), and (C) are incorrect because they do not follow this rule.

Sample Reading Question

Directions: Read the following texts carefully for comprehension. Each text is followed by one or more questions or incomplete statements based on its content. Select the answer or completion that is best according to the text and fill in the corresponding circle on the answer sheet.

This is a note to Akio from his mother.

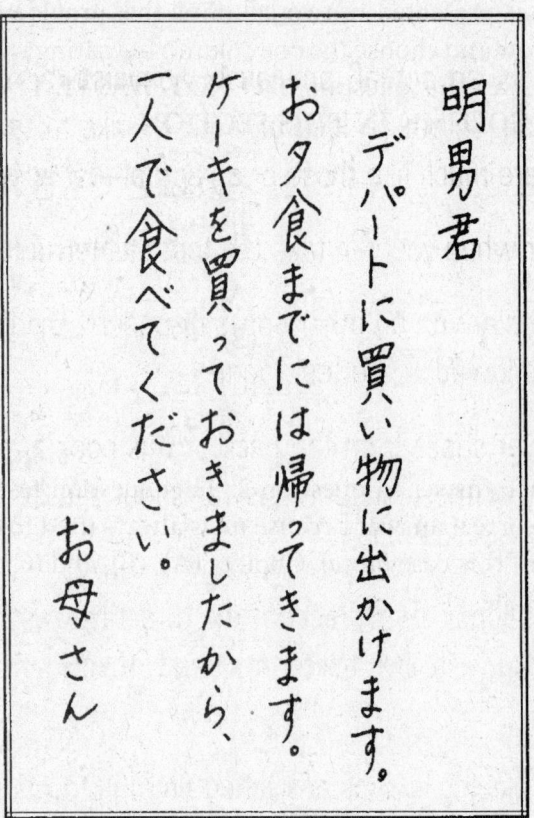

明男君
デパートに買い物に出かけます。
お夕食までには帰ってきます。
ケーキを買っておきましたから、
一人で食べてください。
お母さん

3. What does Akio's mother tell him to do?
   (A) Come home by dinner time
   (B) Eat the cake she bought
   (C) Buy some cake
   (D) Have dinner by himself

Choice (B) is the correct answer to question 3. To answer this question, students must know the content of the request, including the identity of the object about which the request is made. This is a request to eat the cake the writer bought. Choice (B) is the correct answer because it explicitly reflects the content of the written request. Choices (A), (C), and (D) are all incorrect because the note does not request Akio to come home by dinner time, buy cake, or have dinner by himself.

Japanese with Listening Subject Test

Practice Helps

The test that follows is an actual, previously administered SAT Subject Test in Japanese with Listening. To get an idea of what it's like to take this test, practice under conditions that are much like those of an actual test administration.

- Set aside an hour when you can take the test uninterrupted.
- Sit at a desk or table with no other books or papers. Dictionaries, other books, or notes are not allowed in the test room.
- Tear out an answer sheet from the back of this book and fill it in just as you would on the day of the test. One answer sheet can be used for up to three Subject Tests.
- Read the instructions that precede the practice test. During the actual administration you will be asked to read them before answering test questions.
- Time yourself by placing a clock or kitchen timer in front of you.
- After you finish the practice test, read the sections "How to Score the SAT Subject Test in Japanese with Listening" and "How Did You Do on the Subject Test in Japanese with Listening?"
- The appearance of the answer sheet in this book may differ from the answer sheet you see on test day.

JAPANESE TEST WITH LISTENING

The top portion of the page of the answer sheet that you will use to take the Japanese Test with Listening must be filled in exactly as illustrated below. When your supervisor tells you to fill in the circle next to the name of the test you are about to take, mark your answer sheet as shown.

○ Literature	○ Mathematics Level 1	○ German	○ Chinese Listening	● Japanese Listening
○ Biology E	○ Mathematics Level 2	○ Italian	○ French Listening	○ Korean Listening
○ Biology M	○ U.S. History	○ Latin	○ German Listening	○ Spanish Listening
○ Chemistry	○ World History	○ Modern Hebrew		
○ Physics	○ French	○ Spanish	**Background Questions:** ① ② ③ ④ ⑤ ⑥ ⑦ ⑧ ⑨	

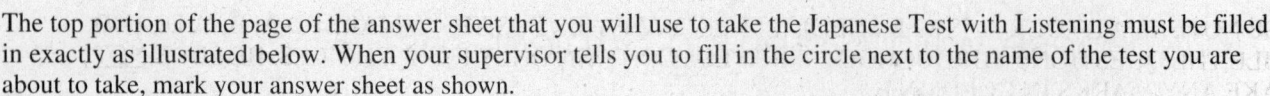

After filling in the circle next to the name of the test you are taking, locate the Background Questions box on your answer sheet (as shown above). This is where you will answer the following Background Questions on your answer sheet.

BACKGROUND QUESTIONS

Please answer the questions below by filling in the appropriate circle in the Background Questions box on your answer sheet. The information you provide is for statistical purposes only and will not affect your test score. Fill in only the circles that apply.

I If your knowledge of Japanese comes primarily from either of the following, fill in circle 9:

- Living in a home in which Japanese is the principal language spoken
- Residence in Japan after age ten for one year or more

II If your knowledge of Japanese comes primarily from living in a home where at least one family member speaks to you in Japanese, fill in circle 8.

III If your knowledge of Japanese comes primarily from courses taken in grades nine through twelve, fill in the circle that represents the total number of years you have studied Japanese.

Please respond to only one option for question III.

- Fewer than 2 years —Fill in circle 1.
- 2 years or more but fewer than 3 years —Fill in circle 2.
- 3 years or more but fewer than 4 years —Fill in circle 3.
- 4 years or more —Fill in circle 4.

IV If you have studied Japanese in a *nihongo gakkō* (supplementary program) and continued studying Japanese for two or more years beyond the eighth grade, fill in circle 5.

V If you have taken, or if you are currently taking, the Advanced Placement (AP) Japanese course, fill in circle 6.

VI If you have taken, or if you are currently taking, Japanese course(s) in college, fill in circle 7.

When the supervisor gives the signal, turn the page and begin the Japanese Test with Listening. There are 100 numbered circles on the answer sheet and 80 questions in the Japanese Test with Listening. Therefore, use only circles 1 to 80 for recording your answers.

JAPANESE TEST WITH LISTENING

PLEASE NOTE THAT YOUR ANSWER SHEET HAS FIVE ANSWER POSITIONS MARKED A, B, C, D, AND E, WHILE THE QUESTIONS THROUGHOUT THIS TEST CONTAIN ONLY FOUR CHOICES. BE SURE NOT TO MAKE ANY MARKS IN COLUMN E.

Directions: In this section of the test you will hear short dialogues and monologues. You will hear them only once, and they are not printed in your test booklet. At the end of each selection, you will be asked questions about what was said. Now listen to the following example, but do not mark the answer on your answer sheet.

You will hear:

Listen to this short conversation between two acquaintances.

How did the woman travel today?

(A) By bus.
(B) By car.
(C) By train.
(D) On foot.

The best answer to the question is (A), "By bus." Therefore, you would select choice (A) and fill in the corresponding circle on the answer sheet. Now listen to the first selection.

Listen to a conversation between two friends.

1. How does the man describe his weekend?

(A) Tiring.
(B) Restful.
(C) Boring.
(D) Fun.

Listen to a conversation during a flight to the United States.

2. What is the purpose of the man's trip?

(A) Sightseeing.
(B) Study.
(C) Business.
(D) Visiting friends.

3. How long does the man plan to stay in the United States?

(A) One month.
(B) Two months.
(C) Three months.
(D) Four months.

Listen to Kenta's mother talking to him.

4. What did Kenta do to upset his mother?

(A) He forgot to do his homework.
(B) He kept bothering Aki.
(C) He failed to clean his room.
(D) He came home late.

5. Why is Kenta's mother worried?

(A) Because Kenta's teacher called.
(B) Because Kenta's grandmother is coming.
(C) Because Aki complained.
(D) Because Aki is waiting.

GO ON TO THE NEXT PAGE

Listen to André introduce himself.

6. André is a citizen of what country?

   (A) France.
   (B) United States.
   (C) Russia.
   (D) Japan.

7. What does André say about Tokyo?

   (A) He was born there.
   (B) His parents live there.
   (C) He studied Japanese there.
   (D) He is visiting there for the first time.

Listen to this conversation in a classroom.

8. How is the window best described?

   (A) It is tinted.
   (B) It is closed.
   (C) It is broken.
   (D) It is covered.

9. What is the woman worried about?

   (A) Noise.
   (B) Heat.
   (C) Drafts.
   (D) Sunlight.

Two friends are talking on the street.

10. What type of place is under discussion?

    (A) A restaurant.
    (B) A ticket counter.
    (C) A hotel lobby.
    (D) A convenience store.

11. On what basis do the two friends make their decision?

    (A) Price.
    (B) Cleanliness.
    (C) Quality of service.
    (D) Number of customers.

Listen to the following exchange between a couple.

12. When was the baby born to the Yamashitas?

    (A) On the second of last month.
    (B) On the twentieth of last month.
    (C) On the second of this month.
    (D) On the twentieth of this month.

13. What does the man say about the baby?

    (A) That he has already heard about the baby.
    (B) That the baby's name sounds like a girl's.
    (C) That the Yamashitas wanted a girl this time.
    (D) That he wants to see the baby.

This is an announcement in a department store.

14. Why is the customer being paged?

    (A) They located her lost child.
    (B) She had an emergency telephone call.
    (C) She left something behind in the store.
    (D) The person she was to meet is looking for her.

Listen to this short conversation about the weather.

15. What was yesterday's weather probably like?

    (A) Rainy.
    (B) Cloudy.
    (C) Clear.
    (D) Snowy.

16. What will tomorrow's weather probably be like?

    (A) Rainy.
    (B) Cloudy.
    (C) Clear.
    (D) Snowy.

GO ON TO THE NEXT PAGE

Listen to the following conversation in a post office.

17. What is the woman trying to send?

    (A) A postcard.
    (B) A certified letter.
    (C) A money order.
    (D) A small package.

18. How long will the delivery take?

    (A) One day.
    (B) A few days.
    (C) One week.
    (D) Two weeks.

Listen to a man shouting.

19. What is the man shouting not to do?

    (A) Stand in the doorway.
    (B) Close the door.
    (C) Knock on the door.
    (D) Go in through the door.

This is a conversation between Kayoko and Satoshi at a party.

20. Why is Kayoko impressed?

    (A) All the pizza was eaten.
    (B) The pizza is easy to make.
    (C) Satoshi taught cooking.
    (D) Satoshi made pizza.

21. What is planned for Saturday?

    (A) Satoshi will visit Kayoko.
    (B) Kayoko will visit Satoshi.
    (C) Satoshi and Kayoko will have pizza at Kayoko's house.
    (D) Satoshi and Kayoko will go out for pizza.

Listen to a conversation at a hospital.

22. Who is Yuko's visitor?

    (A) Her classmate.
    (B) Her colleague.
    (C) Her teacher.
    (D) Her father.

23. Where is Yuko's hospital room located?

    (A) By a nurses' station.
    (B) On the eighth floor.
    (C) Near a gift shop.
    (D) Across from the elevator.

Listen to the following call to a radio station.

24. What does the caller want?

    (A) To voice his opinion.
    (B) To give away a puppy.
    (C) To order an item.
    (D) To get advice.

25. What does the woman in the studio learn about the caller?

    (A) He is moving to another city.
    (B) He does not like his college.
    (C) He cannot sleep well.
    (D) He is planning a party.

26. What does the caller say about the dog he mentions?

    (A) It is annoying.
    (B) It is cute.
    (C) It is housebroken.
    (D) It is too big.

GO ON TO THE NEXT PAGE

Listen to the following exchange between a customer and a bookstore clerk.

27. What does the customer learn about the book?

    (A) It is not yet available in bookstores.
    (B) It is coming in that afternoon.
    (C) It is sold out.
    (D) It is out of print.

28. What does the customer decide to do?

    (A) Go to another store.
    (B) Place a special order.
    (C) Call the publisher.
    (D) Come back in a few days.

Listen to a conversation at the entrance to a house.

29. Why has Mr. Tanaka stopped at the woman's house?

    (A) To lend her something.
    (B) To get out of the rain.
    (C) To borrow something.
    (D) To return something.

Listen to Mr. Yoshida and his daughter talking.

30. What does Mr. Yoshida urge his daughter to do?

    (A) Leave soon.
    (B) Come home early.
    (C) Eat her breakfast.
    (D) Call home.

END OF SECTION I.
DO NOT GO ON TO SECTION II UNTIL YOU ARE TOLD TO DO SO.

TIME FOR SECTIONS II AND III - 40 minutes

SECTION II

Usage

WHEN YOU BEGIN SECTION II, BE SURE THAT YOU MARK YOUR ANSWER TO THE FIRST USAGE QUESTION BY FILLING IN ONE OF THE CIRCLES NEXT TO NUMBER 31 ON THE ANSWER SHEET.

Directions: This section consists of a number of incomplete statements, each of which has four suggested completions. In some instances, choice (A) may consist of dashes that indicate that no insertion is required to form a correct sentence. Select the choice that best completes the sentence structurally and logically and fill in the corresponding circle on the answer sheet.

THIS SECTION OF THE TEST IS PRESENTED IN TWO COLUMNS THAT PROVIDE IDENTICAL INFORMATION. LOOK AT THE EXAMPLE BELOW AND CHOOSE THE ONE COLUMN OF WRITING WITH WHICH YOU ARE MOST FAMILIAR IN ORDER TO ANSWER THE QUESTION. DO NOT WASTE TIME BY SWITCHING FROM COLUMN TO COLUMN IN THIS SECTION.

Example:

Tōkyō wa ----- arimasu.	東京(とうきょう)は ----- あります。
(A) Doitsu de	(A) ドイツで
(B) Mekishiko o	(B) メキシコを
(C) Furansu e	(C) フランスへ
(D) Nihon ni	(D) 日本(にほん)に

The best completion is choice (D). Therefore, you would select choice (D) and fill in the corresponding circle on the answer sheet.

GO ON TO THE NEXT PAGE

31. Gakkō e -----.

(A) benkyō-shimashita

(B) ikimashita

(C) mimashita

(D) yasumimashita

31. 学校(がっこう)へ ----- 。

(A) 勉強(べんきょう)しました

(B) 行(い)きました

(C) 見(み)ました

(D) 休(やす)みました

32. Kirei ----- heya desu ne.

(A) -----

(B) ni

(C) da

(D) na

32. きれい ----- 部屋(へや)ですね。

(A) -----

(B) に

(C) だ

(D) な

33. Kyō wa asa kara ban ----- terebi o mite imashita.

(A) ni mo

(B) ni wa

(C) made

(D) e mo

33. 今日(きょう)は朝(あさ)から晩(ばん) ----- テレビを見(み)ていました。

(A) にも

(B) には

(C) まで

(D) へも

GO ON TO THE NEXT PAGE

34. Yūmei ----- desu ne.

(A) -----

(B) na

(C) da

(D) ni

35. Hayaku genki -----

natte kudasai.

(A) -----

(B) na

(C) ni

(D) no

36. Nōto o -----.

(A) mimashita

(B) arimashita

(C) dekimashita

(D) wakarimashita

34. 有名(ゆうめい) ----- ですね。

(A) -----

(B) な

(C) だ

(D) に

35. 早(はや)く元気(げんき) -----

なってください。

(A) -----

(B) な

(C) に

(D) の

36. ノートを ----- 。

(A) 見(み)ました

(B) ありました

(C) できました

(D) わかりました

GO ON TO THE NEXT PAGE

37. Kodomo ga hitori ----- imasu.

(A) -----

(B) ga

(C) mo

(D) ni

37. 子供(こども)が一人(ひとり)----- います。

(A) -----

(B) が

(C) も

(D) に

38. Ashita wa ame ga furu -----.

(A) deshō

(B) desu

(C) deshita

(D) omoimasu

38. あしたは雨(あめ)が降(ふ)る ----- 。

(A) でしょう

(B) です

(C) でした

(D) 思(おも)います

39. Taihen ----- ga kakarimasu ne.

(A) jikan

(B) go-jikan

(C) en

(D) go man-en

39. 大変(たいへん) ----- が かかりますね。

(A) 時間(じかん)

(B) 五時間(ごじかん)

(C) 円(えん)

(D) 五万円(ごまんえん)

GO ON TO THE NEXT PAGE

40. Atama ga itai ----- kaerimasu.

(A) de

(B) no de

(C) na no de

(D) da kara

40. 頭(あたま)が痛(いた)い ----- 帰(かえ)ります。

(A) で

(B) ので

(C) なので

(D) だから

41. Ichi-ban ----- wa dore?

(A) omoshiroi

(B) omoshiroku

(C) omoshirokute

(D) omoshiroi no

41. 一番(いちばん) ----- はどれ？

(A) おもしろい

(B) おもしろく

(C) おもしろくて

(D) おもしろいの

42. Motto ----- dekimasen ka.

(A) sukunaku

(B) sukunai

(C) sukoshi

(D) shōshō

42. もっと -----できませんか。

(A) 少(すく)なく

(B) 少(すく)ない

(C) 少(すこ)し

(D) 少々(しょうしょう)

GO ON TO THE NEXT PAGE

43. Chichi wa haha ----- jōzu desu.

(A) kara

(B) hodo

(C) made

(D) yori

43. 父(ちち)は母(はは) ----- 上手(じょうず)です。

(A) から

(B) ほど

(C) まで

(D) より

44. Ato ----- futatsu kudasai.

(A) shika

(B) dake

(C) yori

(D) mō

44. あと ----- 二(ふた)つください。

(A) しか

(B) だけ

(C) より

(D) もう

45. Osoku ----- dōmo sumimasen.

(A) naru

(B) natte

(C) natta

(D) natta kara

45. 遅(おそ)く ----- どうも すみません。

(A) なる

(B) なって

(C) なった

(D) なったから

GO ON TO THE NEXT PAGE

46. ----- ni kite kudasai.

(A) Ashita

(B) Kayōbi

(C) Mata

(D) Kesa

46. ----- に来(き)てください。

(A) 明日(あした)

(B) 火曜日(かようび)

(C) また

(D) 今朝(けさ)

47. ----- kedo wakarimasen.

(A) Mimashō

(B) Mimashita

(C) Mite

(D) Mitara

47. ----- けどわかりません。

(A) 見(み)ましょう

(B) 見(み)ました

(C) 見(み)て

(D) 見(み)たら

48. Ashita iku -----
kyō wa ie ni imasu.

(A) to

(B) kara

(C) demo

(D) desu ga

48. あした行(い)く -----
今日(きょう)は家(いえ)にいます。

(A) と

(B) から

(C) でも

(D) ですが

GO ON TO THE NEXT PAGE

49. ----- ikenai.

(A) Tsukau

(B) Tsukatta

(C) Tsukawanaku

(D) Tsukatte wa

49. ----- いけない。

(A) 使(つか)う

(B) 使(つか)った

(C) 使(つか)わなく

(D) 使(つか)っては

50. Iya ----- omotte yamemashita.

(A) -----

(B) da to

(C) ni natte

(D) de

50. いや ----- 思(おも)って やめました。

(A) -----

(B) だと

(C) になって

(D) で

51. Chotto ----- shite kudasai.

(A) yasuku

(B) benri na

(C) chiisai

(D) shizuka

51. ちょっと ----- してください。

(A) 安(やす)く

(B) 便利(べんり)な

(C) 小(ちい)さい

(D) 静(しず)か

GO ON TO THE NEXT PAGE

52. ----- ga shimashō.

(A) Watashi

(B) Anata

(C) Ano hito

(D) Imōto

53. Gakusei ----- no?

(A) na

(B) da

(C) darō

(D) ni

52. ----- がしましょう。

(A) 私(わたし)

(B) あなた

(C) あの人(ひと)

(D) 妹(いもうと)

53. 学生(がくせい) ----- の？

(A) な

(B) だ

(C) だろう

(D) に

END OF SECTION II.
GO ON TO SECTION III.

SECTION III

Reading

Directions: Read the following texts carefully for comprehension. Each text is followed by one or more questions or incomplete statements based on its content. Select the answer or completion that is best according to the text and fill in the corresponding circle on the answer sheet. There is no example for this section.

This is a message Lisa received.

> リサさん
> 高木さんから電話がありました。
> 山下さんが二時十五分に駅に着くから、
> 迎えに行ってくださいとのことです。
>
> 川村

54. This message relays

    (A) an apology
    (B) a complaint
    (C) an invitation
    (D) a request

55. What is Lisa expected to do after reading the note?

    (A) Contact Takagi
    (B) Call Kawamura
    (C) Wait for Takagi
    (D) Meet Yamashita

GO ON TO THE NEXT PAGE

Yuri sent the following e-mail message to Saori.

さおり

あさってうちでバーベキューするんだけど来ない？
こうすけもよしも来るって！
それからわるいけど、クッキー持って来てくれる？
来られるかどうか今日中に教えてね。

ゆり

56. What is the reader expected to bring to the barbecue?

(A) Cookies
(B) A cake
(C) A fruit salad
(D) Barbecue sauce

57. Who will host a barbecue?

(A) Saori
(B) Kosuke
(C) Yoshi
(D) Yuri

GO ON TO THE NEXT PAGE

This is part of a restaurant menu.

きょうのスペシャル

（サラダ又はスープ付き）

バーベキュー・リブ ¥1,700
（やわらかいリブを特製マリネにつけ込んでグリル）

シーフード・ミックスグリル ¥1,800
（新鮮な海の幸をバターソースでさっとグリル）

ベジタリアン・ミックスグリル ¥1,500
（ボリュームいっぱい。でも低カロリーのヘルシーチョイス）

58. The most expensive item uses

(A) a mixture of spices
(B) butter sauce
(C) imported ingredients
(D) fresh fruit

59. The least expensive dish is described as having

(A) few calories
(B) low cholesterol
(C) a small volume
(D) a special sauce

GO ON TO THE NEXT PAGE

The following is part of Mrs. Iwata's calendar for the coming week.

日	1:00 けんた 水泳大会（スイミングクラブ）
月	9:30 エアロビクス 2:00 メガネをとりにいく
火	7:00 マリ ピアノ
水	
木	マリのバースデーケーキ 4:00 パーティー（6人）
金	2:00 けんたの父母会
土	5:00 お父さん ゴルフ

60. Mrs. Iwata will pick up her eyeglasses on

(A) Sunday
(B) Monday
(C) Tuesday
(D) Saturday

61. Mrs. Iwata's activities this week include

(A) visiting Kenta's school
(B) competing in a swim meet
(C) playing golf with friends
(D) taking a piano lesson

62. Mrs. Iwata will host a birthday party for

(A) herself
(B) her husband
(C) her daughter
(D) her son

GO ON TO THE NEXT PAGE

This advertisement was placed in a newspaper.

大川駅前通りに新しくオープン！

カフェアルプス

モーニングサービスは７００円！
今週のスペシャルはフレンチトースト

忙しいあなたの朝に便利です！

63. The advertisement is for a

(A) take-out shop
(B) coffee shop
(C) French bakery
(D) natural food store

64. What does the advertisement say about the special?

(A) It is organic.
(B) It is tasty.
(C) It is featured for a week.
(D) It is available only in the afternoon.

65. What does the advertisement say about the establishment?

(A) It is located near the station.
(B) It provides friendly service.
(C) It offers numerous discounts.
(D) It will open next week.

GO ON TO THE NEXT PAGE

This is an excerpt from a newspaper column.

ボディーランゲージ

「若いカップルが手をつないで歩いている」というのはもう古いそうである。ではこのごろの若いカップルはどうしてカップルだとわかるのだろうか。町に出て見てみた。腕を組んだり、肩を組んだり、ちょっと新しいのはシャツのそでを結んでいる二人。

66. What is the topic of this passage?

(A) Body language
(B) New fashions
(C) Health issues
(D) Travel information

67. Why did the writer go into town?

(A) To do some window-shopping
(B) To make some observations
(C) To interview some couples
(D) To collect some new products

GO ON TO THE NEXT PAGE

This is a comment a math teacher wrote on Mamoru's homework paper.

二番だけ もう一度考えてごらん。
それ以外は よくできたね。
次の問題に 進んでよろしい。

68. How can the teacher's comment be characterized?

(A) Apologetic
(B) Humorous
(C) Ambiguous
(D) Encouraging

69. What does the teacher say about Mamoru's answer to the second problem?

(A) He should rethink it.
(B) He should rewrite it.
(C) He should compare it to the correct answer.
(D) He should share the solution with others.

GO ON TO THE NEXT PAGE

This is the beginning of a letter from Mr. Takamatsu to Ms. Sekine.

　お手紙ありがとう。先月久しぶりに会えて、とっても楽しかったです。先週からのかぜでまだ声がよく出ません。９月のリサイタルまでに直るかどうか心配です。
　送ってもらったテープ、さっそく聞いてみました。コロンビアのギター音楽は、ベネズエラのとゼンゼン違うんですね。いただいたのは軽くて明るいと思いました。

70. The last time Mr. Takamatsu saw Ms. Sekine was

(A) the previous day
(B) the previous month
(C) nine weeks before
(D) nine months before

71. What does Mr. Takamatsu plan to do soon?

(A) See Ms. Sekine.
(B) Give a recital.
(C) Send Ms. Sekine a ticket.
(D) Buy a guitar.

72. What does Mr. Takamatsu say about the cassette tape he just received?

(A) It is different from Colombian music.
(B) It is the same cassette tape he already owns.
(C) It is a collection of Venezuelan guitar music.
(D) It is light and cheerful.

GO ON TO THE NEXT PAGE

This is an e-mail message from Ms. Hayashi.

> 先日お話しした洋画友の会を九月十日にすることになりました。
> 私も当日は出席しますので、よろしかったら、ご一緒にいかがでしょうか。
> 若い人中心の楽しい会です。
>
> 林　由紀子

73. What does Ms. Hayashi say about the meeting?

    (A) It attracts young people.
    (B) Her friend organized it.
    (C) There will be fun games.
    (D) It is a good place to make friends.

GO ON TO THE NEXT PAGE

The following is a set of guidelines for foreign students in a homestay program in Japan.

(1) なるべく日本語でホストファミリーと話しましょう。分からない時は、辞書を調べながら話しましょう。

(2) 決められた時間には帰るようにしてください。ホストファミリーの人が心配しますから、遅くなる時は、電話をしてください。

(3) ホストファミリーの電話はなるべく使わないようにしてください。

(4) できるだけそうじや食事の手伝いをするようにしましょう。

(5) エネルギーをむだ使いしないようにしましょう。

74. What are the students encouraged to do?

(A) Return home by midnight
(B) Help with meals
(C) Ask questions about Japanese culture
(D) Do their own laundry

75. Students are asked not to

(A) let friends stay over at the house
(B) waste electricity and gas
(C) stay in their rooms all the time
(D) take food without asking

GO ON TO THE NEXT PAGE

Ms. Smith found the following note from her friend Akira Nishimura.

> スミスさん
>
> 約束の時間にビデオを取りに来たのですが、いらっしゃらないので、お借りしていきます。明日の英語のクラスの前にお返しします。
>
> 西村晃

76. Akira went to Ms. Smith's room because he wanted to

    (A) borrow something from Ms. Smith
    (B) make some plans with Ms. Smith
    (C) return something to Ms. Smith
    (D) give Ms. Smith a gift

77. What does Akira say he will do the next day?

    (A) Record a video.
    (B) Rent a video.
    (C) Show a video.
    (D) Return a video.

GO ON TO THE NEXT PAGE

This is a part of an advertisement.

スポーツの夏がやって来ました！
ショート・ヘアーはスポーツのあとのお手入れも簡単。
コンピューター・シミュレーションでいろいろなスタイル
を見て、お選びいただけます。

78. What is being advertised?

(A) Sporting goods
(B) Computer classes
(C) A hair salon
(D) A driving school

GO ON TO THE NEXT PAGE

This message is printed on an envelope from a local bank.

あなたのひまわり銀行

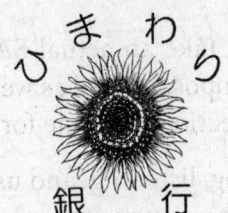

ひまわり銀行

ニューイヤーギフト

1月中にひまわりの住宅ローン「フューチャー」に申し込んで、
ゲームソフトをもらおう！！

79. As an incentive to customers, the bank offers
    (A) additional ATM locations
    (B) reduced service fees
    (C) financial counseling
    (D) attractive gifts

80. The purpose of this message is for the bank to promote
    (A) computerized banking
    (B) extended business hours
    (C) mortgage loans
    (D) new investment opportunities

STOP

IF YOU FINISH BEFORE TIME IS CALLED, YOU MAY CHECK YOUR WORK ON THIS TEST ONLY. DO NOT TURN TO ANY OTHER TEST IN THIS BOOK.

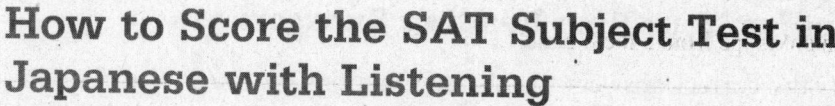

How to Score the SAT Subject Test in Japanese with Listening

When you take an actual SAT Subject Test in Japanese with Listening, you receive an overall composite score as well as three subscores: one for the reading section, one for the listening section, and one for the usage section.

The reading, listening, and usage scores are reported on the College Board's 20–80 scale. However the composite score, which is the most significant of the scores reported to the colleges you specify, is in the form of the College Board's 200–800 scale.

Worksheet 1. Finding Your Raw Listening Subscore

STEP 1: Table A on page 821 lists the correct answers for all the questions on the Subject Test in Japanese with Listening that is reproduced in this book. It also serves as a worksheet for you to calculate your raw Listening subscore.

- Compare your answers with those given in the table.
- Put a check in the column marked "Right" if your answer is correct.
- Put a check in the column marked "Wrong" if your answer is incorrect.
- Leave both columns blank if you omitted the question.

STEP 2: Count the number of right answers for questions 1–30.

Enter the total here: ________________

STEP 3: Count the number of wrong answers for questions 1–30.

Enter the total here: ________________

STEP 4: Multiply the number of wrong answers from Step 3 by .333.

Enter the product here: ________________

STEP 5: Subtract the result obtained in Step 4 from the total you obtained in Step 2.

Enter the result here: ________________

STEP 6: Round the number obtained in Step 5 to the nearest whole number.

Enter the result here: ________________

The number you obtained in Step 6 is your raw Listening subscore.

Worksheet 2. Finding Your Raw Reading Subscore

STEP 1: Table A lists the correct answers for all the questions on the Subject Test in Japanese with Listening that is reproduced in this book. It also serves as a worksheet for you to calculate your raw Reading subscore.

STEP 2: Count the number of right answers for questions 54-80.

Enter the total here: ____________________

STEP 3: Count the number of wrong answers for questions 54-80.

Enter the total here: ____________________

STEP 4: Multiply the number of wrong answers by .333.

Enter the product here: ____________________

STEP 5: Subtract the result obtained in Step 4 from the total you obtained in Step 2.

Enter the result here: ____________________

STEP 6: Round the number obtained in Step 5 to the nearest whole number.

Enter the result here: ____________________

The number you obtained in Step 6 is your raw Reading subscore.

Worksheet 3. Finding Your Raw Usage Subscore

STEP 1: Table A lists the correct answers for all the questions on the Subject Test in Japanese with Listening that is reproduced in this book. It also serves as a worksheet for you to calculate your raw Usage subscore.

STEP 2: Count the number of right answers for questions 31–53.

Enter the total here: ____________________

STEP 3: Count the number of wrong answers for questions 31–53.

Enter the total here: ____________________

STEP 4: Multiply the number of wrong answers by .333.

Enter the product here: ________________

STEP 5: Subtract the result obtained in Step 4 from the total you obtained in Step 2.

Enter the result here: ___________________

STEP 6: Round the number obtained in Step 5 to the nearest whole number.

Enter the result here: ___________________

The number you obtained in Step 6 is your raw Usage subscore.

Worksheet 4. Finding Your Raw Composite Score

STEP 1: Enter your unrounded raw Reading subscore from Step 5 of Worksheet 2.

Enter the result here: ____________________

STEP 2: Enter your unrounded raw Listening subscore from Step 5 of Worksheet 1.

Enter the result here: ____________________

STEP 3: Enter your unrounded raw Usage subscore from Step 5 of Worksheet 3.

Enter the result here: ____________________

STEP 4: Add the results obtained in Steps 1, 2 and 3.

Enter the sum here: ____________________

STEP 5: Round the number obtained in Step 4 to the nearest whole number.

Enter the result here: ____________________

The number you obtained in Step 5 is your raw composite score.

Table A

Answers to the Subject Test in Japanese with Listening and Percentage of Students Answering Each Question Correctly

Question Number	Correct Answer	Right	Wrong	Percentage of Students Answering the Question Correctly*	Question Number	Correct Answer	Right	Wrong	Percentage of Students Answering the Question Correctly*
1	D			96	33	C			90
2	B			82	34	A			78
3	C			88	35	C			88
4	C			96	36	A			83
5	B			92	37	A			59
6	B			92	38	A			75
7	D			73	39	A			55
8	B			79	40	B			51
9	A			91	41	D			59
10	A			89	42	A			29
11	D			43	43	D			83
12	B			65	44	D			60
13	B			55	45	B			52
14	C			62	46	B			72
15	A			86	47	B			61
16	C			86	48	B			44
17	D			39	49	D			75
18	B			70	50	B			64
19	D			81	51	A			49
20	D			84	52	A			40
21	B			49	53	A			46
22	D			55	54	D			74
23	B			69	55	D			83
24	D			47	56	A			87
25	C			67	57	D			89
26	A			72	58	B			87
27	C			63	59	A			85
28	A			50	60	B			96
29	D			61	61	A			55
30	A			50	62	C			87
31	B			90	63	B			59
32	D			92	64	C			83

Table A continued on next page

Table A continued from previous page

Question Number	Correct Answer	Right	Wrong	Percentage of Students Answering the Question Correctly*	Question Number	Correct Answer	Right	Wrong	Percentage of Students Answering the Question Correctly*
65	A			71	73	A			41
66	A			88	74	B			55
67	B			59	75	B			75
68	D			87	76	A			67
69	A			61	77	D			64
70	B			81	78	C			48
71	B			71	79	D			84
72	D			44	80	C			69

* These percentages are based on an analysis of the answer sheets of a representative sample of 371 students who took the original administration of this test and whose mean composite score was 566. They may be used as an indication of the relative difficulty of a particular question.

Answer explanations for the Subject Test in Japanese with Listening can be found on page 828.

Finding Your Scaled Score

When you take SAT Subject Tests, the scores sent to the colleges you specify are reported on the College Board scale, which ranges from 200–800. Subscores are reported on a scale which ranges from 20–80. You can convert your practice test scores to scaled scores by using Tables B, C, D, and E on the following pages. To find your scaled score, locate your raw score in the left-hand column of the table; the corresponding score in the right-hand column is your scaled score. For example, a raw score of 59 on this particular edition of the Subject Test in Japanese with Listening corresponds to a scaled composite score of 640.

Raw scores are converted to scaled scores to ensure that a score earned on any one edition of a particular Subject Test is comparable to the same scaled score earned on any other edition of the same Subject Test. Because some editions of the tests may be slightly easier or more difficult than others, College Board scaled scores are adjusted so that they indicate the same level of performance regardless of the edition of the test taken and the ability of the group that takes it. Thus, for example, a score of 400 on one edition of a test taken at a particular administration indicates the same level of achievement as a score of 400 on a different edition of the test taken at a different administration.

When you take the SAT Subject Tests during a national administration, your scores are likely to differ somewhat from the scores you obtain on the tests in this book. People perform at different levels at different times for reasons unrelated to the tests themselves. The precision of any test is also limited because it represents only a sample of all the possible questions that could be asked.

Your scaled composite score from Table B is ________________ .

Your scaled listening score from Table C is ________________ .

Your scaled reading score from Table D is ________________ .

Your scaled usage score from Table E is ________________ .

Table B

Scaled Score Conversion Table Subject Test in Japanese with Listening Composite Score					
Raw Score	Scaled Score	Raw Score	Scaled Score	Raw Score	Scaled Score
80	800	44	520	8	290
79	800	43	510	7	290
78	800	42	510	6	280
77	790	41	500	5	270
76	780	40	490	4	270
75	770	39	490	3	260
74	770	38	480	2	250
73	760	37	480	1	250
72	750	36	470	0	240
71	740	35	460	-1	230
70	730	34	460	-2	230
69	720	33	450	-3	220
68	710	32	440	-4	220
67	710	31	440	-5	210
66	700	30	430	-6	200
65	690	29	430	-7	200
64	680	28	420	-8	200
63	670	27	410	-9	200
62	660	26	410	-10	200
61	650	25	400	-11	200
60	640	24	390	-12	200
59	640	23	390	-13	200
58	630	22	380	-14	200
57	620	21	370	-15	200
56	610	20	370	-16	200
55	600	19	360	-17	200
54	590	18	360	-18	200
53	580	17	350	-19	200
52	580	16	340	-20	200
51	570	15	340	-21	200
50	560	14	330	-22	200
49	550	13	320	-23	200
48	550	12	320	-24	200
47	540	11	310	-25	200
46	530	10	300	-26	200
45	530	9	300	-27	200

Table C

Scaled Score Conversion Table Subject Test in Japanese with Listening Listening Subscore					
Raw Score	Scaled Score	Raw Score	Scaled Score	Raw Score	Scaled Score
30	80	16	50	2	29
29	77	15	48	1	27
28	75	14	47	0	26
27	72	13	45	-1	25
26	70	12	44	-2	23
25	68	11	42	-3	22
24	66	10	40	-4	21
23	64	9	39	-5	20
22	62	8	37	-6	20
21	59	7	36	-7	20
20	57	6	34	-8	20
19	55	5	33	-9	20
18	54	4	32	-10	20
17	52	3	30		

Table D

Scaled Score Conversion Table Subject Test in Japanese with Listening Reading Subscore					
Raw Score	Scaled Score	Raw Score	Scaled Score	Raw Score	Scaled Score
27	80	15	51	3	32
26	77	14	49	2	30
25	74	13	47	1	29
24	71	12	45	0	28
23	69	11	44	-1	27
22	67	10	42	-2	26
21	64	9	40	-3	24
20	62	8	39	-4	23
19	60	7	37	-5	22
18	57	6	36	-6	21
17	55	5	34	-7	20
16	53	4	33	-8	20
				-9	20

Table E

Scaled Score Conversion Table Subject Test in Japanese with Listening Usage Subscore					
Raw Score	Scaled Score	Raw Score	Scaled Score	Raw Score	Scaled Score
23	80	12	54	1	33
22	78	11	52	0	32
21	75	10	50	-1	30
20	73	9	48	-2	28
19	70	8	46	-3	26
18	68	7	44	-4	24
17	65	6	43	-5	22
16	63	5	41	-6	21
15	60	4	39	-7	20
14	58	3	37	-8	20
13	56	2	35		

How Did You Do on the Subject Test in Japanese with Listening?

After you score your test and analyze your performance, think about the following questions:

Did you run out of time before reaching the end of the test?

If so, you may need to pace yourself better. For example, maybe you spent too much time on one or two hard questions. A better approach might be to skip the ones you can't answer right away and try answering all the questions that remain on the test. Then if there's time, go back to the questions you skipped.

Did you take a long time reading the directions?

You will save time when you take the test by learning the directions to the Subject Test in Japanese with Listening ahead of time. Each minute you spend reading directions during the test is a minute that you could use to answer questions.

How did you handle questions you were unsure of?

If you were able to eliminate one or more of the answer choices as wrong and guess from the remaining ones, your approach probably worked to your advantage. On the other hand, making haphazard guesses or omitting questions without trying to eliminate choices could cost you valuable points.

How difficult were the questions for you compared with other students who took the test?

Table A shows you how difficult the multiple-choice questions were for the group of students who took this test during its national administration. The right-hand column gives the percentage of students that answered each question correctly.

A question answered correctly by almost everyone in the group is obviously an easier question. For example, 96 percent of the students answered question 4 correctly. But only 29 percent answered question 42 correctly.

Keep in mind that these percentages are based on just one group of students. They would probably be different with another group of students taking the test.

If you missed several easier questions, go back and try to find out why: Did the questions cover material you haven't yet reviewed? Did you misunderstand the directions?

Answer Explanations for the Japanese with Listening Subject Test

Note: Explanations use the Hepburn style of romanization.

1. Choice (D) is the correct answer. In response to the woman's question about the man's weekend, the man replies that "it was fun" (*tanoshikatta*) because he "played tennis" (*tenisu shite-itanda*) all day. The man does not indicate that his weekend was tiring (A), restful (B), or boring (C).

2. Choice (B) is the correct answer. When the woman wonders why the man is traveling to the United States, he replies that he is going to "study abroad" (*ryūgaku*). He does not say that the purpose of his trip is sightseeing (A), business (C), or visiting friends (D).

3. Choice (C) is the correct answer. The woman asks if the man will be spending a year abroad, and he tells her that he's staying for only "three months" (*san-ka-getsu*). Although the quantity *one* is mentioned in the conversation, it is one year, not one month (A). Neither two months (B) nor four months (D) is mentioned.

4. Choice (C) is the correct answer. In the first part of this conversation, Kenta's mother asks him why he hasn't "cleaned up his room yet" (*mada oheya katazukanai no*), noting that Aki's room is already clean. She doesn't suggest that Kenta forgot to do his homework (A), kept bothering Aki (B), or came home late (D).

5. Choice (B) is the correct answer. In the second part of the conversation, Kenta's mother tells Kenta to clean his room right away because his "grandmother is coming soon" (*obāchan mōsugu irassharu wayo*). Kenta's teacher (A) is not mentioned. Choices (C) and (D) are incorrect because the only mention of Aki is that her room is already clean.

6. Choice (B) is the correct answer. When André introduces himself, he notes that he is from the United States. Although his parents are French, he was born in California

and so "is an American citizen" (*boku wa Amerika-jin desu*), not a citizen of France (A), Russia (C), or Japan (D).

7. Choice (D) is the correct answer. André states that he is "visiting Tokyo for the first time" (*Tokyo wa hajimete desu*), so he intends to try to see various places. Although his birthplace is mentioned, it is California, not Tokyo (A), and his parents do not live in Tokyo (B). André explains that he is studying Japanese culture in school, not Japanese language (C).

8. Choice (B) is the correct answer. In this conversation, the man notes that because it's such a hot day, the woman should "open a window in the classroom" (*dōshite mado o akenai no*). Thus listeners can infer that the window is closed (B), not that it is tinted (A), broken (C), or covered (D).

9. Choice (A) is the correct answer. In response to the man's request, the woman states that it's very "noisy outside" (*soto ga urusai kara*) so it's better to keep the window closed so they can hear the teacher's voice. Unlike the man, the woman isn't concerned about the heat (B), nor does she mention drafts (C) or sunlight (D).

10. Choice (A) is the correct answer. In this lengthy conversation, the two friends agree that they're hungry and look around for somewhere to eat. The friends are discussing a restaurant; the woman asks about one restaurant, but the man replies that it's "too crowded" (*konde iru*) and suggests the place next door instead because it looks clean. The woman convinces him to eat at the first restaurant by noting that it has a lot of customers, which indicates that the food must be delicious. The friends do not talk about a ticket counter (B), a hotel lobby (C), or a convenience store (D).

11. Choice (D) is the correct answer. The friends make their final decision based on the "number of customers" (*okyakusan no ōi omise no hō ga kitto oishii*) in the first restaurant; the woman says that because the first restaurant has a lot of customers, the food must be delicious. The man likes the second restaurant because of its cleanliness (B), but the woman convinces him to eat at the first one. The conversation does not include anything about price (A) or quality of service (C).

12. Choice (B) is the correct answer. The couple is discussing the Yamashita family's new baby boy, who the woman says was born on the twentieth of last month. The question requires careful attention to the number (*hatsuka*) and the time word for "last month" (*sengetsu*) to avoid confusion. The baby was born on the twentieth of

last month, not on the second of last month (A), the second of this month (C), or the twentieth of this month (D).

13. Choice (B) is the correct answer. The woman tells the man that the new baby's name is Misaki, which the man says "sounds like a girl's name" (*onnano ko mitaina namae*). Choice (A) is incorrect; the man's first response, "Wow, when?" makes it clear that he hadn't heard about the baby previously. The Yamashitas are mentioned, but there is no indication that they wanted a girl this time (C). And the man doesn't say that he wants to see the baby (D).

14. Choice (C) is the correct answer. This department store announcement concerns an item that a customer has apparently "left behind" (*owasure mono*) while shopping. The customer, Nishitani Akiko, is asked to come to the ground floor information center to retrieve the item. There is no mention of a lost child (A), an emergency telephone call (B), or a person looking for her (D).

15. Choice (A) is the correct answer. The key to this short conversation is the word *mata* ("also," or "again"). The man states that it's "rainy again today" (*kyō mo mata ame desu ne*), from which we can infer that it was rainy yesterday as well. The man's statement does not indicate that it was cloudy (B), clear (C), or snowy (D) yesterday.

16. Choice (C) is the correct answer. The woman says she's heard that "tomorrow will be clear" (*ashita wa hareru sō desu yo*), not that tomorrow will be rainy (A), cloudy (B), or snowy (D).

17. Choice (D) is the correct answer. In this conversation, the woman, a customer, starts off by saying she would like to send something via air mail. After discussing how long it will take, the man asks whether there's a letter inside; the woman confirms that it's just a "magazine" (*zasshi*). It is illogical to suggest that a *postcard* (A), *a certified letter* (B), or *a money order* (C) would have either a letter or a magazine inside it; further, none of these items is mentioned in the conversation. It is logical, however, to assume that a magazine — a small item — would be sent to someone in a *small package*. The conversation suggests that the woman is trying to send someone a small package.

18. Choice (B) is the correct answer. In their exchange about how long the package will take to arrive at its destination, the woman asks whether it will be one week, but the man assures her that it will take just "two or three days" (*ni-san-nichi*); in other words, it will take *a few days*. The man does not say that the package will take one day (A), one week (C), or two weeks (D) to arrive at its destination.

19. Choice (D) is the correct answer. You hear the man shouting, "You can't enter through that door!" The key phrase here is *haitte wa ikenai yo*, with *nai* indicating the negative form. All of the choices refer to the door, but it is clear that the man is shouting about not going in through the door. He doesn't mention standing in the door (A), closing the door (B), or knocking on the door (C).

20. Choice (D) is the correct answer. Kayoko and Satoshi are chatting at a party. Kayoko compliments Satoshi on the pizza, saying it's "great" (*sugoi*) that he made it. Satoshi responds that it's *very easy—anyone can make it*, but Kayoko is clearly impressed that Satoshi was able to do so. Kayoko is not impressed by the fact that the pizza is easy to make (B), and the conversation does not indicate that all the pizza was eaten (A) or that Satoshi taught cooking (C).

21. Choice (B) is the correct answer. Satoshi offers to teach Kayoko how to make pizza, and they arrange for Kayoko to visit Satoshi at Satoshi's house the next Saturday about 4 p.m. Kayoko is going to Satoshi's house; Satoshi is not going to visit Kayoko (A), have pizza at Kayoko's house (C), or go out for pizza with Kayoko (D).

22. Choice (D) is the correct answer. At the hospital, the man, a Kinoshita "family member" (*kazuku no mono*), asks the woman where Yuko's room is. Since the only family member listed in the choices is father (D), that is the only correct choice. Classmate (A), colleague (B), and teacher (C) are all inappropriate in context.

23. Choice (B) is the correct answer. The man is directed to room 865, which he confirms is on the eighth floor (*hachi-kai desu ne*). The woman tells him to take the elevator near the gift shop (C); the elevator, not room 865, is near the gift shop. The conversation does not indicate that Yuko's room is by a nurse's station (A) or across from the elevator (D).

24. Choice (D) is the correct answer. In this dialogue, the woman announces the radio program, "Noontime Hotline" (*Hiru no sōdan-shitsu*). The caller to the hotline is a 21-year-old college student who is looking for advice. The student is not voicing his opinion (A) or ordering an item (C). The student mentions a dog (B), but it's not his so he can't give it away.

25. Choice (C) is the correct answer. The caller says that he moved into his apartment last month but cannot sleep well (*nemurenai*), as indicated by the negative *nai* in the phrase *nere naide komateiru*. He's going to college but doesn't say whether he likes it (B), and he's neither moving to another city (A) nor planning a party (D).

26. Choice (A) is the correct answer. The student is calling the hotline because the dog (*inu*) next door is so "noisy" (*urusakete*), which implies that the dog is annoying. The student does not say that the dog is cute (B), housebroken (C), or too big (D).

27. Choice (C) is the correct answer. The bookstore customer is seeking a book called *Japanese Ryokan*, published by Japan Times. After asking the customer to wait while he checks for the book, the clerk tells her that it is "sold out" (*urikire*), which means that it's already available in bookstores (A) and not out of print (D). If the customer orders the book today, it will take a week, not an afternoon (B), to come in.

28. Choice (A) is the correct answer. The customer thanks the clerk for his help but decides to "try another store" (*hoka ni itte mimasu*) instead of placing a special order (B), calling the publisher (C), or returning in a few days (D).

29. Choice (D) is the correct answer. A man (Mr. Tanaka) and a woman stand at the entrance to the woman's house. Mr. Tanaka greets the woman and then returns the "umbrella" (*kasa*) he "borrowed" (*oka rishita*) last time. The woman thanks him for coming out of his way, and the man replies that the umbrella was very helpful because the rain was so hard that day. The man is returning the umbrella rather than lending it (A) or borrowing it (C). It is clear that the rain happened on a different day, not today, so the man is not trying to get out of the rain (B).

30. Choice (A) is the correct answer. In this conversation, Mr. Yoshida urges his daughter to "leave soon" (*soro soro itta ra*). She asks what time it is, and when he replies that it's past 7, she agrees that she really has to rush. Mr. Yoshida asks his daughter what time she will be back tonight, to which she replies that it will probably be 6 p.m. The daughter offers to call home (D) if it will be later, but Mr. Yoshida doesn't urge her to do so; nor does he urge her to come home early (B) or eat her breakfast (C).

31. Choice (B) is the correct answer. The particle *e*, "to, toward," is usually used with a predicate of motion. Of all the choices, *ikimasu* is the only verb that indicates movement to a certain place. The complete sentence reads, "(I) *went* to school."

32. Choice (D) is the correct answer. *Kirei* belongs to *na*-adjective (or *na*-nominal), and it requires *na* when used to modify the following noun, *heya*, or "room." The complete sentence reads, "(It) is a beautiful/clean room, isn't it."

33. Choice (C) is the correct answer. The particle *made* ("until") is used together with another particle, *kara* ("from"), to indicate "from ... to ... ." The complete sentence reads, "(I) was watching TV today, from morning *until* night."

34. Choice (A) is the correct answer. What precedes the blank, *Yuumei*, belongs to *na*-adjective (or *na*-nominal). However, as other nouns, it is combined with *desu* without any particles in between to form a predicate. The complete sentence reads, "(It) is famous, isn't it."

35. Choice (C) is the correct answer. The verb *naru*, when combined with the *–ku* form of an adjective or noun plus the particle *ni*, indicates a change of state. Since *genki* is a noun, it requires *ni* before *naru*. The complete sentence reads, "Please get [literally, become] well soon."

36. Choice (A) is the correct answer. The particle *o* is used with action verbs. Of all the choices, *mimasu* is the only action verb. The complete sentence reads, "(I) *looked* at the note(book)."

37. Choice (A) is the correct answer. Quantity expressions such as *hitori*, "one person," usually occur without a following particle. The complete sentence reads, "(There) is a child," or "(I) have one child."

38. Choice (A) is the correct answer. The term *deshō*, a tentative form of *desu*, can be combined with the citation form of verbs to indicate a conjecture. Choice (D), *omoimasu*, requires the particle *to* after the citation form. The complete sentence reads, "(It) *will probably* rain tomorrow."

39. Choice (A) is the correct answer. The verb *kakaru*, or "(something) cost," can refer to both money (as in *[o]kane ga kakaru*) and time. Quantity expressions, such as *go-jikan* ("five hours") and *go-man'en* ("50,000 yen") usually occur without a following particle. The complete sentence reads, "(It) takes an awful lot of *time*, doesn't it."

40. Choice (B) is the correct answer. All the choices, when combined with the correct form, can indicate a reason for going home. *Itai*, which immediately precedes the blank, is an adjective. Choice (B) is the only choice that can be connected directly with *itai*; all of the other choices require a preceding noun. The complete sentence reads, "(I) will go home *because* (my) head hurts."

41. Choice (D) is the correct answer. In the */A wa B desu/* structure, *A* is usually a noun or noun phrase. Choice (D) is the only choice that includes the nominal *no* (making it a noun phrase). The complete sentence reads, "Which is the most *interesting* (*one*)?"

42. Choice (A) is the correct answer. The *–ku* form of adjectives can be linked with a following verb to describe manner. Choices (B), (C), and (D) are not *ku* form and do not fit with the sentence structure. The complete sentence reads, "Can't (it) be much *fewer/less*?"

43. Choice (D) is the correct answer. The */A wa B yori/* structure, with an affirmative predicate, expresses comparison. Choice (B), *hodo*, is usually used with a negative predicate. The complete sentence reads, "My father is more skilled *than* my mother."

44. Choice (D) is the correct answer. *Futatsu*, "two pieces," is a quantity expression. Of all the choices, (D), *mō*, is the only one that can precede a quantity expression. The complete sentence reads, "Please give (me) two *more* (pieces)."

45. Choice (B) is the correct answer. *Dōmo sumimasen* is an expression of apology. When providing a reason for an apology, the *–te* form (not *kara*) is usually used. The complete sentence reads, "(I am) sorry for *being* late."

46. Choice (B) is the correct answer. Relative time expressions, such as choices (A), *ashita* ("tomorrow"), and (D), *kesa* ("this morning"), usually do not require the particle *ni* to indicate time. Choice (C), *mata* ("again"), also does not require *ni*. Therefore, the correct answer is (B), *Kayōbi*. The complete sentence reads, "Please come on *Tuesday*."

47. Choice (B) is the correct answer. The particle *kedo*, "but," follows a predicate (a form that can be at the end of major sentences). Choices (A), (C), and (D) do not make sense when connected with the rest of the sentence. The complete sentence reads, "(I) *looked* at (it), but (I) don't understand."

48. Choice (B) is the correct answer. Choice (A), *to* ("and"), is usually not used to connect two sentences, and choice (C), *de mo* ("but"), usually occurs at the sentence's initial position. Choice (D) cannot follow a citation form of a verb (*iku*). The complete sentence reads, "*Since* (I)'ll go tomorrow, (I) will be at home today."

49. Choice (D) is the correct answer. *Ikenai* is typically used in two sequences: */–te wa ikenai/*, expressing a prohibition, and */–nakute wa ikenai/*, expressing obligation. In

this case, it is the former sequence, prohibition. The complete sentence reads, "(You) cannot *use* (it)."

50. Choice (B) is the correct answer. The verb *omou* ("think") usually requires the particle *to*. The complete sentence reads, "(I) quit, thinking that (it) is annoying."

51. Choice (A) is the correct answer. The verb *suru*, when combined with the adjectival *-ku* form or a noun plus the particle *ni*, indicates an intentional change of state. Choices (B) and (D) are nouns and would require *ni* (not *na*) to be combined with *suru*. Choice (C) is the adjectival *i*-form and thus is incorrect. The complete sentence reads, "Please make (it) a little *cheaper*."

52. Choice (A) is the correct answer. The predicate *shimashō* is a form of the verb *shimasu* ("do") indicating suggestions and intentions including the speaker. The complete sentence reads, "*I* shall/will do it."

53. Choice (A) is the correct answer. The ending *no* is a casual form of *n desu ka*. The *n desu* structure requires *na* when combined with the noun *gakusei* ("student"). Therefore, (A), *na*, is correct. The complete sentence reads, "Is it the case that (he) is a student?"

54. Choice (D) is the correct answer. The message Lisa received concerns a call from Takagi, who says that Yamashita will be arriving at the station at 2:15 and wants "Lisa to pick him up" (迎えに行ってください). The message is a request (D), not an apology (A), a complaint (B), or an invitation (C).

55. Choice (D) is the correct answer. After reading the note, Lisa should meet Yamashita. Although the names Takagi and Kamakura are both mentioned in the note, the request concerns Yamashita.

56. Choice (A) is the correct answer. In this e-mail message, Yuri invites Saori to a barbecue that will take place tomorrow at Yuri's house and asks Saori to "bring cookies" (クッキー持って来てくれる?). Cake (B), fruit salad (C), and barbecue sauce (D) are not mentioned.

57. Choice (D) is the correct answer. Yuri says he heard that Kosuke is also coming to the barbecue, but the message to Saori makes clear that the event will take place at Yuri's

house (うちで, "my house"). The barbecue will not be hosted by Saori (A), Kosuke (B), or Yoshi (C).

58. Choice (B) is the correct answer. The top two lines of this menu announce, "Today's Special (includes salad or soup)." The first item listed is barbecue, at 1,700 yen; the second is seafood mixed grill, at 1,800 yen; and the third is vegetarian mixed grill, at 1,500 yen. The description of the seafood mixed grill, the most expensive item, notes that the dish includes fresh seafood grilled with butter sauce (バターソース). Its ingredients do not include a mixture of spices (A), imported ingredients (C), or fresh fruit (D).

59. Choice (A) is the correct answer. The vegetarian mixed grill, the least expensive dish at 1,500 yen, is described as having 低カロリー, "low calories" or "few calories." The menu doesn't list low cholesterol (B), a small volume (C), or a special sauce (D) for this item.

60. Choice (B) is the correct answer. Mrs. Iwata's calendar lists activities for every day except Wednesday. On Monday at 2 o'clock, Mrs. Iwata needs to "pick up" (とりにいく) her "eyeglasses" (メガネ). The calendar does not indicate that Mrs. Iwata will pick up her eyeglasses on Sunday (A), Tuesday (C), or Saturday (D).

61. Choice (A) is the correct answer. On Sunday, the first day listed, Kenta—not Mrs. Iwata—has a swimming competition (B) at 1 o'clock, and on Tuesday there is Mari's piano lesson (D). Friday is the parents meeting (父母会, "meet parents") at Kenta's school, meaning that Mrs. Iwata will be visiting Kenta's school this week. There is no mention of golf with friends (C).

62. Choice (C) is the correct answer. On Thursday, the calendar has a reminder about "Mari's birthday cake" (マリのバースデーケーキ), implying that Mrs. Iwata will host a birthday party for her daughter, not for herself (A), her husband (B), or her son Kenta (D).

63. Choice (B) is the correct answer. The second line of the advertisement identifies the business as "Café Alps" (カフェアルプス), and the special of the week is listed as French toast. The ad makes it clear that the business is not a take-out shop (A) or a natural food store (D), and a café serving French toast is more likely to be a coffee shop than a French bakery (C).

64. Choice (C) is the correct answer. The French toast special is available in the coffee shop "this week" (今週のスペシャル). The advertisement doesn't mention that the French toast is organic (A), tasty (B), or available only in the afternoon (D).

65. Choice (A) is the correct answer. The first line of the advertisement lets customers know that the coffee shop has been newly opened "in front of the station" (大川駅前通り); in other words, the coffee shop is located near the station. The advertisement does not say that the establishment provides friendly service (B) or offers numerous discounts (C). And it is clear that the coffee shop has already opened; not that it will open next week (D).

66. Choice (A) is the correct answer. The title of this newspaper article, written from top to bottom and right to left, is "Body Language" (ボディーランゲージ), so that is clearly the topic of the passage. The columnist starts by saying that young couples holding hands is old-fashioned. The columnist then asks, how else can we tell that someone is a couple? The writer reports seeing arm-in-arm couples, arm-over-shoulder couples, and the newest style, couples with sleeves tied together. The article mentions a new style, not new fashions (B). The article is not concerned with health issues (C) or travel information (D).

67. Choice (B) is the correct answer. The columnist went to town to observe the new style of couple behavior (町に出て見てみた). The columnist did not do any window-shopping (A), interview couples (C), or collect new products (D).

68. Choice (D) is the correct answer. On Mamoru's paper the teacher writes, "Why don't you rethink number 2 (二番だけもう一度考えてごらん)? You did well on the rest (それ以外はよくできたね). You should go on to the next question." The tone of the comments is encouraging, not apologetic (A), humorous (B), or ambiguous (C).

69. Choice (A) is the correct answer. The teacher wants Mamoru to rethink his answer to the second problem, not rewrite it (B), compare it (C), or share it (D).

70. Choice (B) is the correct answer. The second sentence provides the answer to this question: Mr. Takamatsu last saw Ms. Sekine "the previous month" (先月), not the previous day (A). Since then he's caught a cold and worries about getting better by September's recital. The "9" (9月) in the fourth sentence stands for September, the ninth month, not nine weeks (C) or nine months (D).

71. Choice (B) is the correct answer. Mr. Takamatsu plans to "give a recital in September" (9月のリサイタル). Although the letter mentions seeing Ms. Sekine (A), the reference is to the past, not the future. There is no mention of sending a ticket (C), and the letter talks about guitar music but not about buying a guitar (D).

72. Choice (D) is the correct answer. In the second paragraph, Mr. Takamatsu notes that he received the cassette tape and that guitar music from Colombia is light and cheerful. Mr. Takamatsu notes that guitar music from Colombia is quite different from Venezuelan music, not the other way around, so choice (A) is incorrect. And the letter does not say that Mr. Takamatsu already owned the cassette tape (B) or that the tape is a collection of Venezuelan guitar music (C).

73. Choice (A) is the correct answer. Ms. Hayashi is e-mailing her friend about a Western movie gathering that will take place on September 10. In the final line of the message (before the signature line), she says that the gathering "will be mostly young people" (若い人中心). She does not say that her friend organized the gathering (B), that there will be fun games (C), or that it's a good place to make friends (D).

74. Choice (B) is the correct answer. The five guidelines listed for students in the homestay program include advice about communicating with the host family and obeying their rules. The fourth guideline tells students to "help with meals" (そうじや食事の手伝いをするようにしましょう). Although the second guideline addresses returning home (A), it only says that students should be home by the time the host family says they should and to call if they are going to be late; the guideline does not encourage students to return home by midnight. There is no mention of asking questions about Japanese culture (C) or of students doing their own laundry (D).

75. Choice (B) is the correct answer. The fifth guideline advises students to "not waste energy" (エネルギーをむだ使いしないようにしましょう). None of the guidelines addresses students letting friends stay over (A), staying in their rooms (C), or taking food without asking (D).

76. Choice (A) is the correct answer. In his note, Akira tells Ms. Smith that he came to pick up a video, but she wasn't there, so he "borrowed it" (お借りしていきます). He went to Ms. Smith's room to borrow something, not to make plans (B), to return something (C), or to give a gift (D).

77. Choice (D) is the correct answer. Akira promises to "return the video to Ms. Smith before English class tomorrow" (明日の英語のクラスの前にお返しします). He doesn't plan to record (A), rent (B), or show (C) the video.

78. Choice (C) is the correct answer. The top line of the advertisement announces that the summer sports season has come. Readers are told that "short hair is easy to take care of after sports" (ショートヘアーはスポーツのあとのお手入れも簡単), and that at the salon they can choose any hairstyle using a computer simulation. The ad is for a hair salon. Although the advertisement mentions sports and computers, it doesn't offer sporting goods (A) or computer classes (B). There is no mention of driving or of a driving school (D).

79. Choice (D) is the correct answer. The bank is offering its customers "game software" as an incentive (ゲームソフトをもらおう); in other words, the bank is offering attractive gifts as an incentive to customers. The message on the envelope does not mention additional ATM locations (choice A), reduced service fees (B), or financial counseling (C).

80. Choice (C) is the correct answer. The gift offer is made to customers to promote the bank's "mortgage loans" (住宅ローン). The bank is not offering computerized banking (A), extended business hours (B), or new investment opportunities (D).

Chapter 13

Korean with Listening

Purpose

The Subject Test in Korean with Listening measures your understanding of Korean and your ability to engage in purposeful communication in the context of contemporary Korean culture.

Format

This is a one-hour test with about 20 minutes of listening and 40 minutes of usage and reading. There are 80 to 85 multiple-choice questions.

Content

Listening comprehension questions test your ability to understand the spoken language. They are based on short, spoken Korean dialogues and narratives primarily about everyday topics. All listening questions and possible answers are in English. The questions will be spoken on a CD. They will also be printed in the test book.

Usage questions are written entirely in *Hangŭl* and require you to complete Korean sentences or phrases so that they are structurally and logically correct. Areas covered include vocabulary, honorifics, and various aspects of structure.

Reading comprehension questions test your understanding of such points as main and supporting ideas. All the passages in this section are written in *Hangŭl* and all the questions are in English. Most questions deal with understanding literal meaning, although some inference questions may be included. The Korean selections are drawn from authentic materials, such as notes, diaries, menus, newspaper articles, advertisements, letters, and literary texts.

Korean with Listening	
Skills Measured	Approximate Percentage of Test
Listening Comprehension	35%
Usage	30%
Reading Comprehension	35%

How to Prepare

This test is appropriate for students who have studied Korean as a second or foreign language for two to four years in high school, or the equivalent.

The best preparation is gradual development of competence in Korean over a period of years. A practice audio CD for the full-length practice test is included with this book. A practice CD with different sample questions can be obtained, along with a copy of the *Getting Ready for the SAT Subject Tests* booklet, from your school counselor, or you can access the listening files at www.collegeboard.org. If your counselor does not have the CD or booklet, he or she can order them from the College Board. Familiarize yourself with the directions in advance. The directions in this book are identical to those that appear on the test.

CD Players

Using CD Players for Language Tests with Listening

Take an acceptable CD player to the test center. Your CD player must be in good working order, so insert fresh batteries on the day before the test. You may bring additional batteries and a backup player to the test center. CD players cannot be shared with other test-takers.

Test center staff won't have batteries, CD players, or earphones for your use, so your CD player must be:

- equipped with earphones
- portable (hand-held)
- battery operated

You are not allowed to use a CD player with recording or duplicating capabilities.

Note

If the volume on your CD player disturbs other test-takers, the test center supervisor may ask you to move to another seat.

What to do if your CD player malfunctions:

- Raise your hand and tell the test supervisor.

- Switch to backup equipment if you have it and continue the test. If you don't have backup equipment, your score on the Korean with Listening Test will be canceled. But scores on other Subject Tests you take that day will not be canceled.

What if you receive a defective CD on test day? Raise your hand and ask the supervisor for a replacement.

Note

The Subject Test in Korean with Listening is offered only once a year at designated test centers. Check the current year *SAT Registration Booklet* for dates. **To take the test, you MUST bring an acceptable CD player with earphones to the test center.**

Scores

The total score is reported on the 200-to-800 scale. Listening, usage, and reading subscores are reported on the 20-to-80 scale.

Sample Listening Questions

The text in brackets [ ] is *only* recorded; it is not printed in your test book. Please note that the CD does not start here. Begin using the CD when you start the actual practice test on page 847.

Please note that your answer sheet has five answer positions marked A, B, C, D, and E, while the questions throughout this test contain only four choices. Be sure not to make any marks in column E.

Directions: In this part of the test you will hear several spoken selections. They will not be printed in your test book. You will hear them only once. After each selection you will be asked one or more questions about what you have just heard. These questions, with four possible answers, are printed in your test book. Select the best answer to each question from among the four choices printed and fill in the corresponding circle on your answer sheet. Now listen to the first selection.

(Narrator) [Listen to this short exchange between friends. Then answer Question 1.
(Man) 이번 방학에 뭐 해요?
(Woman) 방학에요? 일하려고 해요.
(Man) 그럼 일자리는 구했어요?
(Woman) 지금 찾는 중이에요.
일자리 있으면 소개해 주세요.
(Man) 요새는 일자리 구하기가
어려운데.

(Narrator) Question 1. What is the woman doing now?] (16 seconds)

1. (A) Looking for work.
(B) Looking for an apartment.
(C) Writing a paper.
(D) Preparing for summer school.

Choice (A) is the correct answer to question 1. This question requires the students' knowledge of vocabulary and expressions such as "-는 중이다," which conveys an action currently taking place.

Sample Usage Questions

Directions: This section consists of a number of incomplete statements, each of which has four suggested completions. Select the word or words that best complete the sentence structurally and logically and fill in the corresponding circle on the answer sheet.

2. 영수: 철수 일어났어요?
철수 누나: 아니오.
_____ 안 일어났어요.

(A) 방금
(B) 금방
(C) 아직
(D) 먼저

Choice (C) is the correct answer to question 2. To answer this question, students need to understand the usage of the adverb "아직," which best completes the sentence in the given context.

Sample Reading Questions

Directions: Read the following selections carefully for comprehension. Each selection is followed by one or more questions or incomplete statements based on its content. Choose the answer or completion that is best according to the selection and fill in the corresponding circle on the answer sheet.

Questions 3–4

행사 : 수미의 첫돌 잔치
장소 : 서울시 종로구 신영동
신영 아파트 234호
날짜 : 오월 삼십일 토요일
시간 : 저녁 여섯시 반

3. What is the occasion?
   (A) Baby shower
   (B) Baby's one hundredth day
   (C) Baby's first birthday
   (D) Nursery school graduation

4. The event will start at
   (A) 5:00 P.M.
   (B) 5:30 P.M.
   (C) 6:00 P.M.
   (D) 6:30 P.M.

Choice (C) is the correct answer to question 3. Choice (D) is the correct answer to question 4. The questions test the students' comprehension of vocabulary and time-related expressions.

Korean with Listening Subject Test

Practice Helps

The test that follows is an actual, previously administered SAT Subject Test in Korean with Listening. To get an idea of what it's like to take this test, practice under conditions that are much like those of an actual test administration.

- Set aside 60 minutes when you can take the test uninterrupted.
- Sit at a desk or table with no other books or papers. Dictionaries, other books, or notes are not allowed in the test room.
- Tear out an answer sheet from the back of this book and fill it in just as you would on the day of the test. One answer sheet can be used for up to three Subject Tests.
- Read the instructions that precede the practice test. During the actual administration you will be asked to read them before answering test questions.
- Time yourself by placing a clock or kitchen timer in front of you.
- After you finish the practice test, read the sections "How to Score the SAT Subject Test in Korean with Listening" and "How Did You Do on the SAT Subject Test in Korean with Listening?"
- The appearance of the answer sheet in this book may differ from the answer sheet you see on test day.

KOREAN TEST WITH LISTENING

The top portion of the page of the answer sheet that you will use to take the Korean Test with Listening must be filled in exactly as illustrated below. When your supervisor tells you to fill in the circle next to the name of the test you are about to take, mark your answer sheet as shown.

○ Literature	○ Mathematics Level 1	○ German	○ Chinese Listening	○ Japanese Listening
○ Biology E	○ Mathematics Level 2	○ Italian	○ French Listening	● Korean Listening
○ Biology M	○ U.S. History	○ Latin	○ German Listening	○ Spanish Listening
○ Chemistry	○ World History	○ Modern Hebrew		
○ Physics	○ French	○ Spanish	**Background Questions:** ①②③④⑤⑥⑦⑧⑨	

After filling in the circle next to the name of the test you are taking, locate the Background Questions box on your answer sheet (as shown above). This is where you will answer the following Background Questions on your answer sheet.

BACKGROUND QUESTIONS

Please answer all questions that apply by filling in the appropriate circle in the Background Questions box on your answer sheet. Fill in the circles, as described below, to indicate how you obtained your knowledge of Korean. The information you provide is for statistical purposes only and will not affect your test score.

I. Where have you learned Korean? (Fill in ALL circles that apply.)

- If you have learned Korean at home, —Fill in circle 1.
- If you have studied Korean in a U.S. high school, —Fill in circle 2.
- If you have studied Korean in a Korean Language School while attending grades K-8, —Fill in circle 3.
- If you have studied Korean in a Korean Language School while attending grades 9-12, —Fill in circle 4.
- If you have lived in Korea longer than one year after age ten, —Fill in circle 5.

II. How long did you study Korean while in grades 9-12 ? (Fill in the ONE circle that applies.)

- Less than 2 years —Fill in circle 6.
- 2 to 2-1/2 years —Fill in circle 7.
- 3 to 3-1/2 years —Fill in circle 8.
- More than 3-1/2 years —Fill in circle 9.

When the supervisor gives the signal, turn the page and begin the Korean Test with Listening. There are 100 numbered circles on the answer sheet and 80 questions in the Korean Test with Listening. Therefore, use only circles 1 to 80 for recording your answers.

KOREAN TEST WITH LISTENING

PLEASE NOTE THAT YOUR ANSWER SHEET HAS FIVE ANSWER POSITIONS MARKED A, B, C, D, AND E, WHILE THE QUESTIONS THROUGHOUT THIS TEST CONTAIN ONLY FOUR CHOICES. BE SURE NOT TO MAKE ANY MARKS IN COLUMN E.

SECTION I

LISTENING

Approximate time — 20 minutes

Questions 1-28

Directions: In this part of the test you will hear several spoken selections. They will not be printed in your test book. You will hear them only once. After each selection you will be asked one or more questions about what you have just heard. These questions, with four possible answers, are printed in your test book. Select the best answer to each question from among the four choices printed and fill in the corresponding circle on your answer sheet.

Now listen to the following example, but do not mark the answer on your answer sheet.

You will hear:

You will hear and see: What is the woman going to do during the vacation?

Sample Answer

Ⓐ ● Ⓒ Ⓓ

You will see:

(A) Stay home.
(B) Go to Korea.
(C) Go to school.
(D) Study Korean.

The best answer to the question is (B) "Go to Korea." Therefore, you should select choice (B) and fill in the corresponding circle on the answer sheet. Now listen to the first selection.

1. What is the father looking for?

(A) A letter from his daughter's school.
(B) A letter from the bank.
(C) His new checkbook.
(D) A receipt for a new desk.

2. Where is the item the father is looking for?

(A) Inside his briefcase.
(B) On the bookshelf.
(C) In the desk drawer.
(D) On the dining table.

GO ON TO THE NEXT PAGE

3. Why does the student have to reschedule the lesson?
   (A) His teacher's schedule has changed.
   (B) His concert is scheduled on the same day.
   (C) His teacher is going out of town.
   (D) His orchestra rehearsal was canceled.

4. What does the teacher suggest to him?
   (A) Move the lesson to Sunday.
   (B) Skip this week's lesson.
   (C) Change the lesson to a different time of the day.
   (D) Reschedule the lesson for the day after tomorrow.

---

5. What does the student want to know?
   (A) The school orientation date.
   (B) The after-school sports schedule.
   (C) His grade from last semester.
   (D) His upcoming class schedule.

6. What level did the student take last semester?
   (A) Beginning.
   (B) Intermediate.
   (C) Advanced.
   (D) Honors.

---

7. What does the woman ask the man to do?
   (A) Help her move tomorrow.
   (B) Look for a roommate.
   (C) Play basketball with her.
   (D) Help her with her homework.

8. What does the man say?
   (A) He will play basketball with the woman.
   (B) He will introduce his friends to the woman.
   (C) He will find someone to help the woman.
   (D) He will call the woman back with an answer.

9. What problem did the man have?
   (A) He fell ill.
   (B) He overslept.
   (C) He missed the train.
   (D) He lost his briefcase.

10. Why does the man feel fortunate?
   (A) He barely made it on time.
   (B) His proposal was accepted.
   (C) The meeting was postponed.
   (D) The woman attended in his place.

---

11. Why did the woman intend to call the man?
   (A) To ask for help.
   (B) To borrow some printer paper.
   (C) To invite him over.
   (D) To say hello.

12. What seems to be the man's reaction?
   (A) Disturbed.
   (B) Impressed.
   (C) Hesitant.
   (D) Enthusiastic.

GO ON TO THE NEXT PAGE

13. Where is the man trying to go?
    (A) The American embassy.
    (B) A gas station.
    (C) A glass shop.
    (D) The foreign exchange bank.

14. To reach his destination, where should the man turn left after crossing the street?
    (A) At the bank.
    (B) At the glass shop.
    (C) At the gas station.
    (D) At the embassy.

15. How is the building described?
    (A) New and made of brick.
    (B) New and made of glass.
    (C) Tall and made of glass.
    (D) Tall and made of brick.

---

16. Why is the woman interested in Dr. Oh?
    (A) She wants to choose him as her doctor.
    (B) She wants to take his class at her college.
    (C) She plans to review his book.
    (D) She plans to write an article about him.

17. What does Mr. Kim say about Dr. Oh?
    (A) He is a lung specialist.
    (B) He lectures at universities.
    (C) He does a lot of charity work.
    (D) He writes articles for the newspapers.

18. What is the recording?
    (A) Information on an area code change.
    (B) Information on a company's telephone menu.
    (C) Introduction of a new long-distance system.
    (D) Instructions on how to record a message.

---

19. Where is this conversation most likely taking place?
    (A) A park.
    (B) A plant nursery.
    (C) Sumi's backyard.
    (D) Sangjin's office.

20. What is Sangjin most likely going to do?
    (A) Visit his friend.
    (B) Go to Sumi's housewarming party.
    (C) Look for a bigger office.
    (D) Plant a tree.

21. What has Sangjin heard about Sumi?
    (A) Sumi has a flower garden.
    (B) Sumi has moved.
    (C) Sumi found a new job.
    (D) Sumi likes him.

GO ON TO THE NEXT PAGE

22. What kind of party is this?
    (A) A birthday party.
    (B) A wedding reception.
    (C) A wedding anniversary.
    (D) A family reunion.

23. Who is the speaker?
    (A) A professional singer.
    (B) One of the children.
    (C) A minister from the church.
    (D) An honoree of the celebration.

---

24. Who made the reservation?
    (A) The man himself.
    (B) The man's wife.
    (C) The man's secretary.
    (D) A travel agent.

25. What does the man claim?
    (A) He has a confirmation number.
    (B) He always gets a corporate discount rate.
    (C) The room was guaranteed with a credit card.
    (D) The reservation was made a week ago.

26. What is the son's plan for the summer?
    (A) To attend summer school.
    (B) To get a job.
    (C) To volunteer at a senior home.
    (D) To study abroad.

27. What does the mother request that the son do?
    (A) Visit home soon.
    (B) Call home often.
    (C) Help his father with his business.
    (D) Write to the grandparents.

28. What would the grandparents like to do for the grandson?
    (A) Take him out to dinner.
    (B) Find him a job.
    (C) Pay for the airfare.
    (D) Pay for his tuition.

END OF SECTION I.
DO NOT GO ON TO SECTION II UNTIL YOU ARE TOLD TO DO SO.

SECTION II

USAGE

Time — 40 minutes for Sections II and III

Questions 29-51

WHEN YOU BEGIN THE USAGE SECTION, BE SURE THAT YOU MARK YOUR ANSWER TO THE FIRST USAGE QUESTION BY FILLING IN ONE OF THE CIRCLES NEXT TO NUMBER 29 ON THE ANSWER SHEET.

Part A

Directions: This section consists of a number of incomplete statements, each of which has four suggested completions. Select the word or words that best complete the sentence structurally and logically and fill in the corresponding circle on the answer sheet.

29. 너무나 음식을 많이 만들어서 _____ 남았어요.

(A) 음식이
(B) 음식을
(C) 음식에
(D) 음식과

30. 영선: 지난여름 휴가에는 캐나다에 갔었어요.
승진: 그 때 거기 날씨가 _____?

(A) 어떨까요
(B) 어떤지요
(C) 어땠어요
(D) 어떻게요

31. 어제 우리 집에 누가 밤늦게 전화를 해서 받았는데, 전화를 받자마자 그 쪽에서 딱 끊어 _____.

(A) 두었다
(B) 말았다
(C) 놓았다
(D) 버렸다

32. 한 시간 전에 _____ 지금쯤은 틀림없이 도착했을 텐데요.

(A) 떠났으니까
(B) 떠날 테니까
(C) 떠나려니까
(D) 떠난다니까

GO ON TO THE NEXT PAGE

33. 우리 언니는 _____ 2년 됐어요.

(A) 결혼했던지
(B) 결혼하는지
(C) 결혼할지
(D) 결혼한 지

34. 할머니_____ 낮잠을 _____.

(A) 께.....주무십니다
(B) 께서.....주무십니다
(C) 께는.....잡니다
(D) 께로.....잡니다

35. 제가 어제 무슨 일이 생겨서
집에 늦게 _____
모두 기다리고 있었어요.

(A) 들어가다가
(B) 들어가더니
(C) 들어갔더니
(D) 들어갔다가

36. 머리가 _____ 여자가 제
여동생이에요.

(A) 길
(B) 긴
(C) 기른
(D) 기는

37. 내가 아기를 보는 동안 아기가
웬일인지 자꾸 _____.
그러니까 어머니는 나한테
왜 아기를 _____고 꾸중을 하셨다.

(A) 울렸다.....울리느냐
(B) 울었다.....울리느냐
(C) 울었다.....우느냐
(D) 울렸다.....우느냐

38. 현승: 주말에 보통 뭐 하세요?
민정: 영화 보_____ 운동해요.

(A) 기도
(B) 기만
(C) 거든
(D) 거나

39. 어제 우리 언니는
저희 할머님을 _____
시골집에 다녀왔습니다.

(A) 데리고
(B) 모시고
(C) 지니고
(D) 가지고

GO ON TO THE NEXT PAGE

40. 장미꽃 다섯 _____를 주세요.

(A) 켤레
(B) 자루
(C) 마리
(D) 송이

41. 제발 내가 늘 가는 서점에 이런 책이 _____ 바란다.

(A) 있다고
(B) 있기를
(C) 있으니
(D) 있을까

42. 같이 있었을 때 동생을 좀 더 잘 도와 _____ 이제 와서 내가 뉘우치지 않을걸.

(A) 줬더라면
(B) 주느라고
(C) 줬는데
(D) 줬으니

43. 오늘은 저녁을 하지 않고 중국 음식을 _____ 먹었습니다.

(A) 샀다가
(B) 사다가
(C) 샀고
(D) 사고

44. 경석: 하와이에 갔다 왔다면서요?
승진: 네, 간 _____에 관광도 많이 하고 수영도 많이 했어요.

(A) 김
(B) 일
(C) 중
(D) 새

45. 일이 너무 많이 _____ 내일까지 해주세요.

(A) 해야 하니까
(B) 밀렸으니까
(C) 만드니까
(D) 보니까

46. 할아버지께 언제 _____ 여쭤 보아라.

(A) 오시느냐고
(B) 오시느라고
(C) 오신다고
(D) 오시려고

GO ON TO THE NEXT PAGE

Part B

Directions: In each of the following paragraphs there are numbered blanks indicating that words or phrases have been omitted. For each numbered blank, four completions are provided. First read through the entire paragraph. Then, for each numbered blank, choose the completion that is most appropriate and fill in the corresponding circle on the answer sheet.

어느 날 공중전화에서 집 _____(47) 전화를 거는데, 동전 10전짜리 두 개와 5전짜리를 넣는 대로 _____(48) 도로 나왔다. 그래서 나는 전화통이 고장이 났나 해서 몇 번이고 다시 해 _____(49) 다른 전화통에도 가서 해 보았지만 _____(50) 마찬가지로 전화는 안 되고 동전이 도로 나왔다. 나는 왜 전화통마다 이 모양인가 하면서 투덜댔지만 아무 소용이 없었다. 나중에 알고 보니 공중 전화요금이 _____(51) 35전이 됐다는 것이었다.

47. (A) 을
    (B) 은
    (C) 에다
    (D) 에서

48. (A) 방글방글
    (B) 주르르
    (C) 반짝반짝
    (D) 따르릉

49. (A) 보면
    (B) 봐도
    (C) 보다가
    (D) 보니까

50. (A) 역시
    (B) 절대
    (C) 겨우
    (D) 별로

51. (A) 올라서
    (B) 몰라서
    (C) 걸어서
    (D) 나와서

END OF SECTION II.
GO ON TO SECTION III.

SECTION III

READING COMPREHENSION

Questions 52-80

Directions: Read the following selections carefully for comprehension. Each selection is followed by one or more questions or incomplete statements based on its content. Choose the answer or completion that is best according to the selection and fill in the corresponding circle on the answer sheet.

Questions 52-53

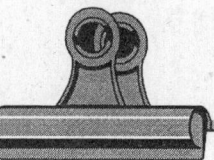

엄마,

오늘 늦으시네요. 엄마 오시면 뵙고 나가려고 했는데요, 오늘 꼭 부쳐야 하는 소포가 있어서 우체국에 다녀와야겠어요. 5시면 문을 닫잖아요? 참! 좀 전에 아빠가 전화하셨는데 오늘 회의가 있어서 늦으신대요. 우리끼리 그냥 저녁 먹으라고 하셨어요.

그럼 저 금방 다녀올게요.

제인

52. The main purpose of the note is to tell the mother that Jane
    (A) will be home late
    (B) is going to her father's office
    (C) has to go mail a package
    (D) is having dinner with her friend

53. What was the message from Jane's father?
    (A) He is bringing home a guest.
    (B) He wants Jane to pick him up.
    (C) He will be attending a meeting.
    (D) He wants to take the family out to dinner.

GO ON TO THE NEXT PAGE

Questions 54-55

제일 정비소

정비부: 나사 하나라도 소홀히 하지 않습니다.
오일 교환부터 엔진 수리까지
완벽을 추구합니다.

바디부: 99.99% 원형 복구를 추구합니다.
무료 토잉과 무료 견적 서비스합니다.

예약 필요 없습니다. 즉석에서 해 드립니다.

(510)123-4567

54. What is the ad about?
    (A) An automobile dealership
    (B) An automobile repair shop
    (C) A gasoline station
    (D) An auto parts store

55. The ad promises
    (A) free window washing
    (B) free air pumps
    (C) no need for appointment
    (D) no need for advance payment

GO ON TO THE NEXT PAGE

Questions 56-57

세계 운송 회사

이삿짐 전문 업체

* 무료 상담
* 약속한 날짜에 도착 책임짐
* 안전한 포장
* 선박 또는 항공 2주 특별 서비스
* 학생 반액 할인

이삿짐 문의: 1-800-123-2424

56. What is advertised?

(A) Express mail
(B) A travel agency
(C) Office supplies
(D) A moving company

57. What is offered?

(A) A student discount
(B) Free delivery
(C) Free assembly
(D) Flight insurance

GO ON TO THE NEXT PAGE

Question 58

안내 광고 게재 신청서

신청자 이름 ____________ 전화 __________
주소 ______________________________________
게재란 _____________ 게재 기간 __________
광고비 금액 __________
광고 내용
____

58. What is the form above?

(A) A form for advertisement
(B) A form for registered mail
(C) A library card application
(D) A job application

GO ON TO THE NEXT PAGE

Questions 59-60

옛날에 한 가난한 농부가 살았다. 이 농부는 가난했지만 열심히 일해서 좋은 포도밭을 가지게 되었다. 이 농부가 병이 나서 더 이상 일을 할 수 없게 되었다. 농부의 아들들은 게을러서 일을 하지 않았다. 그래서 밭에는 풀이 나고 포도는 열리지 않았다. 농부는 죽으면서 아들들에게 말했다. "포도밭을 파면 보물이 나올 것이다." 아들들은 포도밭으로 달려가서 포도밭을 파헤쳐 보았지만 아무것도 나오지 않았다. 그 해에 탐스러운 포도가 다시 주렁주렁 달렸다. 아들들은 그 때서야 아버지의 보물이 무엇인지 깨달았다.

59. Why did the sons dig in the field?

(A) To find a treasure
(B) To kill weeds
(C) To have more fruit
(D) To help their father

60. Which sentence best describes the story?

(A) The farmer sold his treasure.
(B) The farmer's sons were very diligent.
(C) The farmer died in an accident.
(D) The farmer was a wise, hardworking man.

GO ON TO THE NEXT PAGE

Question 61

> 저울질할 수 없는 당신의 건강!
> 어떻게 관리하고 계십니까?
> 여러분의 소중한 건강을 위하여
> 성실하고 세심한 의료 서비스를 제공하는
> **한미 종합병원**

61. What is being advertised?

    (A) A nursing home
    (B) A fitness center
    (C) A pharmacy
    (D) A medical center

GO ON TO THE NEXT PAGE

Question 62

독방 세 놓음
쾌적하고 조용한 지역
가족적인 분위기
학생 환영
(216) 310-4421

62. What is the purpose of this notice?

(A) To find a tutor.
(B) To lease a house.
(C) To rent a room.
(D) To get a roommate.

GO ON TO THE NEXT PAGE

Questions 63-64

3월 7일 흐렸다가 맑아짐

오늘은 아주 바쁜 날이다. 일 주일만 있으면 봄 방학이 시작되기 때문에 그 전에 마쳐야 할 일이 많다. 방학을 기다리기가 아주 힘들다. 방학이 되면 친구들이랑 보스턴으로 놀러 가기로 했다. 이 방학이 내가 대학을 졸업하기 전에 있는 마지막 방학이다. 그래서 친구끼리 놀러 가기로 했다. 다섯 명이서 갈까 했는데 한 명은 무슨 일이 생겨서 못 간다고 했다. 거기 가면 배도 타고 말도 타고 하면서 실컷 놀 계획이다.

63. The writer is a
    - (A) freshman
    - (B) sophomore
    - (C) junior
    - (D) senior

64. How many people are going on vacation together?
    - (A) Three
    - (B) Four
    - (C) Five
    - (D) Six

GO ON TO THE NEXT PAGE

Questions 65-66

독자 여러분의 원고를 모읍니다.
여러분의 경험담, 체험담, 감상문, 그리고
일터에서의 보람 등 흥미있는 이야기가 있으면
보내 주십시오.
보낼 곳은 서울 중앙 사서함 201호 편집부입니다.
채택된 원고에 대해선 기념품을 드리며
원고는 돌려 드리지 않습니다.
주소, 성명, 나이, 성별, 전화 번호를 명기하십시오.

65. What is the most appropriate form of writing requested here?

(A) Essays
(B) Poems
(C) Novels
(D) Dramas

66. What does the announcement say?

(A) Manuscripts will not be returned.
(B) Stories written by children will not be considered.
(C) Cash prizes will be awarded.
(D) Full-length novels will be considered.

GO ON TO THE NEXT PAGE

Questions 67-69

할머님께

그 동안 안녕하셨어요? 요즘 서울은 날씨가 어때요? 할머니께서 다녀가신 후 여기는 갑자기 태풍이 와서 온 동네가 물바다가 된 곳도 있고, 전기가 다 끊어진 곳도 많고 하지만 많은 사람들이 자기 집을 떠나 다른 곳으로 피신해서 다친 사람은 없습니다. 그런데 집, 가게, 빌딩들은 물이 들어와서 많이 버렸어요. 저희 집은 뒷마당에 있는 조그만 나무 하나가 쓰러졌지만 그것은 아무것도 아니지요.

할머니, 할머니께서 떠나신 지 열흘밖에 안 됐지만 아주 오래된 것 같아요. 겨울 방학 하면 할머니 뵈러 갈게요. 큰이모부랑 큰이모도 안녕하시지요? 안부 전해 주세요.
그럼 다시 뵐 때까지 안녕히 계십시오.

용진 올림

67. Yongjin tells his grandmother about

(A) the monsoon in Seoul
(B) a hurricane in his town
(C) an earthquake in his town
(D) an extended heat wave in Seoul

68. What information is given in Yongjin's letter?

(A) Most people did not leave town.
(B) Buildings were not damaged.
(C) People did not lose electricity.
(D) People were not injured.

69. What is Yongjin's plan?

(A) To plant more trees
(B) To buy additional insurance
(C) To visit his grandmother
(D) To help clean up the neighborhood

GO ON TO THE NEXT PAGE

Questions 70-71

국립 민속박물관은 1998년에 새로 문을 열었다. 대중 교육을 통하여 방문객에게 역사 지식을 넣어 주고 우리 문화에 대한 친밀감을 키우는 데에 목적을 두고 교육 활동을 하고 있다.

<u>대중 교육 활동 내용</u>

* 할머니 - 손녀 공예 교실
* 청소년 민속 강좌
* 외국인을 위한 민속 교실
* 각종 공연 및 학술 발표회

70. What institution is offering the service?

(A) The local school district
(B) The local public library
(C) The National Folk Museum
(D) The Ministry of Education

71. What is the stated objective of this institution?

(A) To introduce Korean history and culture
(B) To teach the Korean language to adults
(C) To demonstrate Korean song and dance
(D) To disseminate literature on Korea

GO ON TO THE NEXT PAGE

Questions 72-74

요즘에는 사람들이 무엇이든지 겉모양을 더 중요하게 생각하고 그 안에 든 내용물은 무시하는 것 같다. 그러다 보니 사람을 평가할 때에도 인격을 알기 전에 용모에 따라 판단해 버린다. 얼마 전, 가까운 친구들과 이에 관련된 이야기를 나눌 기회가 있었는데 우리가 얻은 결론은 사람의 겉모습이 인생에서 가장 중요한 것이 될 수 없다는 것이었다. 물론 부드러운 첫인상이 도움이 될 수도 있고 또, 누구나 텔레비전이나 잡지에서 예쁜 얼굴을 보기 원하는 것은 사실이지만, 시간이 흐르면 사람의 겉모습은 변하게 마련이다. 그러므로 먼저 훌륭한 인격을 갖추도록 노력하는 것이 더욱 중요한 일일 것이다.

72. According to the passage, people put too much emphasis on
    (A) money
    (B) career
    (C) maturity
    (D) looks

73. How did the writer arrive at the conclusion?
    (A) By watching television
    (B) By reading magazine articles
    (C) By talking to friends
    (D) By interviewing experts

74. What does the writer recommend?
    (A) Developing good character
    (B) Pursuing higher education
    (C) Having a goal in life
    (D) Exercising regularly

GO ON TO THE NEXT PAGE

Questions 75-76

사람은 누구도 이 세상을 혼자서 살아갈 수는 없다. 우리는 수많은 사람들과 만나고 관계를 맺으며 살아간다. 이처럼 여러 사람들이 공동체를 이루고 살아나가는 데는 반드시 지켜야 할 예절이 있게 마련이다. 예절은 인간만이 가지고 있는 아름다운 삶의 모습이다. 사람들끼리 만나서 인사를 주고받으며 친절한 말씨를 쓸 때, 우리가 사는 세상은 따뜻하고 사랑스러운 곳이 될 것이다.

75. What is the writer's main point?

(A) People should plan ahead.
(B) Smiling is a universal language.
(C) People tend to be more assertive nowadays.
(D) Every society has etiquette to observe.

76. The writer suggests that people should be

(A) patient
(B) polite
(C) diligent
(D) organized

GO ON TO THE NEXT PAGE

Questions 77-80

대학 졸업반이라 바쁘다고 하며 여기저기 뛰어 다니던 상호의 모습을 본 지가 엊그제 같은데, 상호가 벌써 애를 둘이나 둔 아버지가 되었다. 상호는 매년 여름 휴가 때면 식구들과 같이 2주일 동안 놀러 간다. 때로는 캠핑을 하면서 낚시질도 하고 뱃놀이도 한다. 좀 먼 곳이라도 상호는 가능하면 비행기를 안 타고 자동차로 여행하고 호텔에는 묵지 않는다. 그 이유는 비행기 여행은 요금이 많이 들고 또 호텔에 묵으면 식사로 비용이 거의 다 나가기 때문이다. 최소의 금액으로 최대의 효과를 내자는 것이다. 휴가는 건강에도 좋고 정신적으로도 마음의 안정을 주는 큰 힘과 약이 된다는 것을 휴가를 갈 때마다 상호는 절실히 느낀다고 한다.

77. What is still vivid in the writer's memory?
    (A) Sangho's graduation
    (B) Sangho's wedding
    (C) Sangho's senior year
    (D) Sangho's childhood

78. What does Sangho do for family vacations?
    (A) He usually stays in hotels.
    (B) He usually travels off-season.
    (C) He avoids traveling by car as much as possible.
    (D) He avoids traveling by airplane as much as possible.

79. Which word best characterizes Sangho's attitude toward money?
    (A) Generous
    (B) Frugal
    (C) Greedy
    (D) Careless

80. What does Sangho think about vacations?
    (A) They are difficult to plan.
    (B) They are over before you know it.
    (C) They bring tranquility.
    (D) They require lots of energy.

END OF SECTION III.

STOP

IF YOU FINISH BEFORE TIME IS CALLED, YOU MAY CHECK YOUR WORK ON THIS TEST ONLY. DO NOT TURN TO ANY OTHER TEST IN THIS BOOK.

How to Score the SAT Subject Test in Korean with Listening

When you take an actual SAT Subject Test in Korean with Listening, you receive an overall composite score as well as three subscores: one for the reading section, one for the listening section, and one for the usage section.

The reading, listening, and usage scores are reported on the College Board's 20–80 scale. However the composite score, which is the most significant of the scores reported to the colleges you specify, is in the form of the College Board's 200–800 scale.

Worksheet 1. Finding Your Raw Listening Subscore

STEP 1: Table A on page 874 lists the correct answers for all the questions on the Subject Test in Korean with Listening that is reproduced in this book. It also serves as a worksheet for you to calculate your raw Listening subscore.

- Compare your answers with those given in the table.
- Put a check in the column marked "Right" if your answer is correct.
- Put a check in the column marked "Wrong" if your answer is incorrect.
- Leave both columns blank if you omitted the question.

STEP 2: Count the number of right answers for questions 1–28.

Enter the total here: ____________

STEP 3: Count the number of wrong answers for questions 1–28.

Enter the total here: ____________

STEP 4: Multiply the number of wrong answers from Step 3 by .333.

Enter the product here: ____________

STEP 5: Subtract the result obtained in Step 4 from the total you obtained in Step 2.

Enter the result here: ____________

STEP 6: Round the number obtained in Step 5 to the nearest whole number.

Enter the result here: ____________

The number you obtained in Step 6 is your raw Listening subscore.

Worksheet 2. Finding Your Raw Reading Subscore

STEP 1: Table A lists the correct answers for all the questions on the Subject Test in Korean with Listening that is reproduced in this book. It also serves as a worksheet for you to calculate your raw Reading subscore.

STEP 2: Count the number of right answers for questions 52–80.

Enter the total here: ____________________

STEP 3: Count the number of wrong answers for questions 52–80.

Enter the total here: ____________________

STEP 4: Multiply the number of wrong answers by .333.

Enter the product here: ____________________

STEP 5: Subtract the result obtained in Step 4 from the total you obtained in Step 2.

Enter the result here: ____________________

STEP 6: Round the number obtained in Step 5 to the nearest whole number.

Enter the result here: ____________________

The number you obtained in Step 6 is your raw Reading subscore.

Worksheet 3. Finding Your Raw Usage Subscore

STEP 1: Table A lists the correct answers for all the questions on the Subject Test in Korean with Listening that is reproduced in this book. It also serves as a worksheet for you to calculate your raw Usage subscore.

STEP 2: Count the number of right answers for questions 29–51.

Enter the total here: ____________________

STEP 3: Count the number of wrong answers for questions 29–51.

Enter the total here: ____________________

STEP 4: Multiply the number of wrong answers by .333.

Enter the product here: ________________

STEP 5: Subtract the result obtained in Step 4 from the total you obtained in Step 2.

Enter the result here: __________________

STEP 6: Round the number obtained in Step 5 to the nearest whole number.

Enter the result here: __________________

The number you obtained in Step 6 is your raw Usage subscore.

Worksheet 4. Finding Your Raw Composite Score

STEP 1: Enter your unrounded raw Reading subscore from Step 5 of Worksheet 2.

Enter the result here: ____________________

STEP 2: Enter your unrounded raw Listening subscore from Step 5 of Worksheet 1.

Enter the result here: ____________________

STEP 3: Enter your unrounded raw Usage subscore from Step 5 of Worksheet 3.

Enter the result here: ____________________

STEP 4: Add the results obtained in Steps 1, 2 and 3.

Enter the sum here: ____________________

STEP 5: Round the number obtained in Step 4 to the nearest whole number.

Enter the result here: ____________________

The number you obtained in Step 5 is your raw composite score.

Table A

Answers to the Subject Test in Korean with Listening and Percentage of Students Answering Each Question Correctly

Question Number	Correct Answer	Right	Wrong	Percentage of Students Answering the Question Correctly*	Question Number	Correct Answer	Right	Wrong	Percentage of Students Answering the Question Correctly*
1	B			99	33	D			90
2	C			98	34	B			83
3	B			96	35	C			86
4	A			80	36	B			77
5	D			83	37	B			81
6	B			53	38	D			85
7	A			100	39	B			93
8	D			97	40	D			83
9	B			100	41	B			82
10	C			98	42	A			74
11	A			93	43	B			63
12	D			89	44	A			62
13	D			99	45	B			77
14	C			59	46	A			68
15	B			95	47	C			80
16	D			90	48	B			69
17	B			81	49	C			75
18	B			81	50	A			58
19	B			93	51	A			87
20	A			85	52	C			89
21	B			84	53	C			97
22	A			80	54	B			87
23	B			90	55	C			88
24	C			52	56	D			77
25	C			61	57	A			87
26	B			82	58	A			70
27	A			94	59	A			86
28	C			95	60	D			88
29	A			94	61	D			83
30	C			97	62	C			56
31	D			85	63	D			80
32	A			89	64	B			76

Table A continued on next page

Table A continued from previous page

Question Number	Correct Answer	Right	Wrong	Percentage of Students Answering the Question Correctly*	Question Number	Correct Answer	Right	Wrong	Percentage of Students Answering the Question Correctly*
65	A			51	73	C			81
66	A			80	74	A			82
67	B			76	75	D			56
68	D			85	76	B			89
69	C			93	77	C			54
70	C			65	78	D			84
71	A			79	79	B			81
72	D			92	80	C			84

* These percentages are based on an analysis of the answer sheets of a representative sample of 952 students who took the original administration of this test and whose mean composite score was 691. They may be used as an indication of the relative difficulty of a particular question.

Answer explanations for the Subject Test in Korean with Listening can be found on page 881.

Finding Your Scaled Score

When you take SAT Subject Tests, the scores sent to the colleges you specify are reported on the College Board scale, which ranges from 200–800. Subscores are reported on a scale which ranges from 20–80. You can convert your practice test scores to scaled scores by using Tables B, C, D and E on the following pages. To find your scaled score, locate your raw score in the left-hand column of the table; the corresponding score in the right-hand column is your scaled score. For example, a raw score of 59 on this particular edition of the Subject Test in Korean with Listening corresponds to a scaled composite score of 680.

Raw scores are converted to scaled scores to ensure that a score earned on any one edition of a particular Subject Test is comparable to the same scaled score earned on any other edition of the same Subject Test. Because some editions of the tests may be slightly easier or more difficult than others, College Board scaled scores are adjusted so that they indicate the same level of performance regardless of the edition of the test taken and the ability of the group that takes it. Thus, for example, a score of 400 on one edition of a test taken at a particular administration indicates the same level of achievement as a score of 400 on a different edition of the test taken at a different administration.

When you take the SAT Subject Tests during a national administration, your scores are likely to differ somewhat from the scores you obtain on the tests in this book. People perform at different levels at different times for reasons unrelated to the tests themselves. The precision of any test is also limited because it represents only a sample of all the possible questions that could be asked.

Your scaled composite score from Table B is ______________ .

Your scaled listening score from Table C is ______________ .

Your scaled reading score from Table D is ______________ .

Your scaled usage score from Table E is ______________ .

Table B

Scaled Score Conversion Table Subject Test in Korean with Listening Composite Score					
Raw Score	Scaled Score	Raw Score	Scaled Score	Raw Score	Scaled Score
80	800	44	590	8	370
79	800	43	590	7	370
78	800	42	580	6	360
77	790	41	570	5	350
76	790	40	570	4	350
75	780	39	560	3	340
74	780	38	560	2	340
73	770	37	550	1	330
72	760	36	540	0	320
71	760	35	540	-1	320
70	750	34	530	-2	310
69	750	33	520	-3	300
68	740	32	520	-4	300
67	730	31	510	-5	290
66	730	30	510	-6	290
65	720	29	500	-7	280
64	710	28	490	-8	270
63	710	27	490	-9	270
62	700	26	480	-10	260
61	700	25	480	-11	260
60	690	24	470	-12	250
59	680	23	460	-13	240
58	680	22	460	-14	240
57	670	21	450	-15	230
56	670	20	450	-16	220
55	660	19	440	-17	220
54	650	18	430	-18	210
53	650	17	430	-19	210
52	640	16	420	-20	200
51	640	15	410	-21	200
50	630	14	410	-22	200
49	620	13	400	-23	200
48	620	12	400	-24	200
47	610	11	390	-25	200
46	600	10	380	-26	200
45	600	9	380	-27	200

Table C

Scaled Score Conversion Table
Subject Test in Korean with Listening
Listening Subscore

Raw Score	Scaled Score	Raw Score	Scaled Score	Raw Score	Scaled Score
28	80	15	52	2	37
27	79	14	50	1	36
26	77	13	48	0	35
25	75	12	47	-1	34
24	73	11	46	-2	33
23	70	10	45	-3	33
22	67	9	43	-4	32
21	64	8	42	-5	31
20	62	7	41	-6	30
19	59	6	40	-7	29
18	57	5	39	-8	28
17	55	4	38	-9	26
16	53	3	38		

Table D

Scaled Score Conversion Table
Subject Test in Korean with Listening
Reading Subscore

Raw Score	Scaled Score	Raw Score	Scaled Score	Raw Score	Scaled Score
29	80	16	63	3	47
28	79	15	62	2	45
27	78	14	61	1	44
26	76	13	60	0	43
25	75	12	58	-1	41
24	74	11	57	-2	40
23	73	10	56	-3	39
22	71	9	54	-4	38
21	70	8	53	-5	36
20	69	7	52	-6	35
19	67	6	51	-7	34
18	66	5	49	-8	32
17	65	4	48	-9	31
				-10	30

Table E

Scaled Score Conversion Table Subject Test in Korean with Listening Usage Subscore					
Raw Score	Scaled Score	Raw Score	Scaled Score	Raw Score	Scaled Score
23	79	12	61	1	44
22	77	11	60	0	43
21	75	10	58	-1	41
20	74	9	57	-2	40
19	72	8	55	-3	38
18	71	7	54	-4	37
17	69	6	52	-5	35
16	68	5	51	-6	33
15	66	4	49	-7	32
14	65	3	47	-8	30
13	63	2	46		

How Did You Do on the Subject Test in Korean with Listening?

After you score your test and analyze your performance, think about the following questions:

Did you run out of time before reaching the end of the test?

If so, you may need to pace yourself better. For example, maybe you spent too much time on one or two hard questions. A better approach might be to skip the ones you can't answer right away and try answering all the questions that remain on the test. Then if there's time, go back to the questions you skipped.

Did you take a long time reading the directions?

You will save time when you take the test by learning the directions to the Subject Test in Korean with Listening ahead of time. Each minute you spend reading directions during the test is a minute that you could use to answer questions.

How did you handle questions you were unsure of?

If you were able to eliminate one or more of the answer choices as wrong and guess from the remaining ones, your approach probably worked to your advantage. On the other hand, making haphazard guesses or omitting questions without trying to eliminate choices could cost you valuable points.

How difficult were the questions for you compared with other students who took the test?

Table A shows you how difficult the multiple-choice questions were for the group of students who took this test during its national administration. The right-hand column gives the percentage of students that answered each question correctly.

A question answered correctly by almost everyone in the group is obviously an easier question. For example, 96 percent of the students answered question 3 correctly. But only 54 percent answered question 77 correctly.

Keep in mind that these percentages are based on just one group of students. They would probably be different with another group of students taking the test.

If you missed several easier questions, go back and try to find out why: Did the questions cover material you haven't yet reviewed? Did you misunderstand the directions?

Answer Explanations for the Korean with Listening Subject Test

1. Choice (B) is the correct answer. In this conversation between father and daughter, the father does not remember where he put a letter from the bank and is searching everywhere, including a bag and a dining table. The key vocabulary to answer this question correctly is “은행” (*bank*) and “편지” (*letter*).

2. Choice (C) is the correct answer. The daughter tells her father that she thinks he put the letter in the desk drawer. “책상 서랍” (*desk drawer*) is the key word to know to answer this question correctly.

3. Choice (B) is the correct answer. The student called his teacher to reschedule his lesson because his concert is scheduled on the same day. The key vocabulary to answer this question correctly is “연주회” (*concert*).

4. Choice (A) is the correct answer. The student wants to reschedule his lesson and asks about the day after tomorrow (“모레”). His teacher says that she is fully booked the day after tomorrow and suggests three days from today (“글피”), which is Sunday. The teacher does not suggest that they skip the lesson, move the lesson to a different time of the day, or reschedule the lesson for the day after tomorrow.

5. Choice (D) is the correct answer. The student is asking about his upcoming class schedule. He is calling his teacher to find out when the advanced level Korean class starts this semester and also wants to know the class hour (“수업 시간”) and classroom (“교실”).

6. Choice (B) is the correct answer. Insoo replies to the teacher’s question of who is calling, answering that he is a student from her Intermediate class last semester. The key vocabulary to answer this question correctly is “중급반” (*Intermediate class*).

7. Choice (A) is the correct answer. The woman is calling the man to see if he can help her move her belongings because she knows he has a truck. “이사” (*moving*) and

"짐을 나르다" (*move/carry luggage*) are the key words that indicate what the woman wants from the man.

8. Choice (D) is the correct answer. The man asks if the woman can move the day after tomorrow because he has promised to play basketball with his friend. Since the woman says that she'd have to move tomorrow in order to avoid paying another month's rent, the man agrees to call her back with an answer after finding out if he can change the appointment.

9. Choice (B) is the correct answer. The man answers the woman's question of why he was late by saying that he overslept. "늦잠을 자다" (*to oversleep*) is the key phrase to know to answer this question correctly.

10. Choice (C) is the correct answer. When the man says that he was unable to attend a meeting in the morning because he overslept, the woman says that the meeting has been postponed. This made the man feel fortunate. "회의가 연기되다" (*the meeting is postponed*) is the key phrase to know to answer this question correctly.

11. Choice (A) is the correct answer. The woman intended to call the man because she needed help with her broken computer. "도움이 필요하다" (*help is needed*) is the key phrase to know to answer this question correctly.

12. Choice (D) is the correct answer. At the woman's hesitant request for help, the man replies, "Just tell me anything. If there is something that I can do, I'll do it." ("뭐든지 말씀만 하세요. 제가 할 수만 있으면 해 드리지요"). This reaction is enthusiastic. The man is not disturbed or impressed. And although the woman is hesitant, the man is not hesitant.

13. Choice (D) is the correct answer. The man wants to go to the foreign exchange bank. "외환은행" (*foreign exchange bank*), in the very first line spoken by the man, is the key word to know to answer this question correctly.

14. Choice (C) is the correct answer. The woman instructs the man to first cross the street, and then turn to the left at the gas station. The bank is right behind the gas station. "주유소" (*gas station*) is the key word to know to answer this question correctly.

15. Choice (B) is the correct answer. To the man's question of how to get to the foreign exchange bank, the woman gives directions and describes what the building looks like. "새로 지은 유리로 된 건물" (*the new building made of glass*) is the key phrase to know to answer this question correctly.

16. Choice (D) is the correct answer. The woman asks the man about Dr. Oh in order to write an article for the school newspaper. The expression "기사를 싣다," which literally means *load an article* and can be used to mean *publish an article*, is the key expression to know to answer this question correctly.

17. Choice (B) is the correct answer. The man tells the woman that Dr. Oh is a famous dentist who has written three books and also lectures at universities. "강의 나가다" (*to go out to lecture*) is the key expression to know to answer the question correctly.

18. Choice (B) is the correct answer. The recording tells the caller to press the number of the person the caller wants to connect to, to press #1 for Korean service, or to press #2 for English service. The recorded message provides information on a company's telephone menu. It does not provide information about an area code change, a new long-distance system, or how to record a message.

19. Choice (B) is the correct answer. The conversation most likely takes place in a plant nursery. The key words that indicate the location are "화분" (*plant*) and "꽃" (*flower*). Sangjin is there to purchase a plant, so it is unlikely that Sumi and Sangjin are in a park, in Sumi's backyard, or at Sangjin's office.

20. Choice (A) is the correct answer. Sumi asks Sangjin what he is doing there. Sangjin answers that he stopped by the place because he is thinking of buying a plant for his friend, who has moved to a bigger office. Based on what he says, one can infer that Sangjin is going to visit his friend.

21. Choice (B) is the correct answer. The man says to the woman that he had heard about the woman's move to a new house. "이사 가셨다고 들었는데" (*I have heard that you moved*) is the key expression to know to answer this question correctly.

22. Choice (A) is the correct answer. The party is a birthday party. "칠순," which means *70 years of age*, is the key word to know to answer this question correctly. "잔치" means *banquet* or *party*. Thus, one can infer that this is a birthday party.

23. Choice (B) is the correct answer. "저희 어머님의," which means *our mother's*, is the main clue to this question. "저희 5 남매," which means *our five siblings*, also suggests that the speaker is one of the children.

24. Choice (C) is the correct answer. When the woman receptionist says that she can't find the man's reservation, the man insists that his secretary made the reservation. "비서" (*secretary*) is the key word to know to answer this question.

25. Choice (C) is the correct answer. The man claims that his secretary paid for the room (in advance) with a credit card when she made the reservation: "우리 비서가 신용카드로 선불까지 했다고 하던데요." The man does not claim that he has a confirmation number (A), or that he always gets a corporate discount (B). And the man claims the reservation was made two weeks ago ("이 주 전에 했는데요"), not one week ago (D).

26. Choice (B) is the correct answer. The son tells his mother that his exam is over and that he is in the middle of finding summer work. "일자리를 알아보다" (*find out about job*) is the key expression to know to answer this question correctly.

27. Choice (A) is the correct answer. The woman asks her son to visit home soon. The expression "한번 집에 들르지 않을래?" literally means *Won't you come by home once?* and is the key expression to know to answer this question.

28. Choice (C) is the correct answer. The woman tells her son that his grandparents miss him and will buy a plane ticket and send it to him if he comes home. "비행기 표는 사 보내 주신대" is the key expression to know to answer this question correctly.

29. Choice (A) is the correct answer. The speaker says that since he or she cooked too much food, something is left; it makes sense to say that food remains. *Food* is the subject of the second clause, and the verb *to remain* ("남다") is a verb that does not require an object. It would be incorrect to use the object particle "을" (B), the place or time particle "에" (C), or the noun connection particle "과" (D).

30. Choice (C) is the correct answer. The first speaker says she went to Canada on her vacation *last summer* ("지난 여름") and the second speaker asks what the weather was like then. Because they are discussing a summer that has already taken place, the second speaker would not ask *what the weather will be like* (A) or *what the weather is like* (B); and choice (D), *how*, simply does not make sense in the context.

31. Choice (D) is the correct answer. Somebody called the speaker's house last night and as soon as the speaker picked up the phone, the caller (*the other side,* literally) *hung up swiftly.* "~아/어 버리다" is the pattern that should be used, as it carries the meaning *to do something completely* or *to do it all in a swift manner.* Both choice (A) "~아/어 두다" and choice (C) "~아/어 놓다" are used to refer to one taking an action and leave something the way it is, as in "엄마가 불고기를 만들어 두었어요/놓았어요." Choice (B) is ungrammatical because "말다" should be used as "~고 말다," not "~아/어 말다."

32. Choice (A) is the correct answer. The speaker assumes that the person must have arrived by now since he or she *had left* an hour ago. It does not make sense to say that the person *is going to leave* (B), *intends to leave* (C), or *said to leave* (D).

33. Choice (D) is the correct answer. The pattern denoting that it has been a certain amount of time since something happened is "___(으)ㄴ 지 [time word] 되다." "___았/었는지," "___는지," or "_____(으)ㄹ 지" would typically be combined with "알아요/몰라요," not a time word and '되다.' Thus, choices (B) and (C) are incorrect. Similarly, choice (A), "~았/었던지," is incorrect because it can't be followed by the time word *two years* ("2년") in the sentence.

34. Choice (B) is the correct answer. This question involves the correct usage of honorifics. A *grandmother* is one of those respected people, and she is the subject of the sentence, so not only the honorific subject particle "께서" but also the honorific verb form of "자다," which is "주무시다," should be used. Choice (A), "께," is the honorific particle of "에게/한테" (*to*).

35. Choice (C) is the correct answer. The speaker says, "I recall that everyone was waiting for me when I went home late because something came up." The speaker recalls a situation in his or her past experience that resulted from or was in reaction to another situation (going home late and finding everyone waiting). Choice (A) "들어가다가" (*while I was going in*) does not make sense because it describes an interrupted action by the same subject. Choice (B) "들어가더니" is incorrect because one cannot recall one's present action. Choice (D) is incorrect because the "~았/었다가" pattern denotes the reversal or nullification of an action, or indicates a shift in action that takes place after the earlier action has been completed. Further, the subject of both clauses should be the same person, so it is incorrect to have "제가" in the first clause and "모두" in the second clause.

36. Choice (B) is the correct answer. *To be long* ("길다"), as in *the woman with long hair,* is a "ㄹ" irregular verb. "ㄹ" gets dropped before "ㄴ," "ㅂ," and "ㅅ," and this verb

is used in a noun modifying form ("[adjective stem] + (으)ㄴ N"). Since the subject particle "가" is added to *hair* ("머리"), not the object particle "를," choice (C) is incorrect.

37. Choice (B) is the correct answer. The first sentence indicates that *the baby cried* for no reason while the speaker was taking care of it. "울었다," a past tense form of the verb *cry* ("울다"), should be used; this rules out choices (A) and (D). Then, the second sentence indicates that the speaker's mother scolded the speaker when he or she *made the baby cry*. The causative form of "울다," which is "울리다," should be used. This rules out choice (C).

38. Choice (D) is the correct answer. When 현승 asks 민정 what she usually does on the weekend, 민정 answers that she either watches a movie or exercises, choosing one or the other. The correct pattern for "[verb] or [verb]" indicating a disjunctive choice is "거나."

39. Choice (B) is the correct answer. The speaker says that his or her older sister took their grandmother and visited (and came back from) their country home. Since *grandmother* is the object of *being taken*, an honorific form should be used. Choice (A), "데리고," the neutral form, is incorrect. Choices (C), "지니고," and (D), "가지고," are both used for things, not people.

40. Choice (D) is the correct answer. The correct noun-counter for a flower ("장미," or *rose*, in this sentence) is "송이." Choice (A), "켤레," is used for pairs such as socks, gloves, or shoes. Choice (B), "자루," is used for writing tools such as pencils or ballpoint pens. And choice (C), "마리," is used for counting animals.

41. Choice (B) is the correct answer. This sentence involves the usage of the pattern "~기(를) 바란다," which is commonly used to express one's wishes or hopes. The speaker *hopes that* there will be a book like this at the bookstore he or she always goes to.

42. Choice (A) is the correct answer. The speaker regrets that he or she did not help his or her younger sibling while they were still together. In order to make sense, the sentence must be subjunctive: "~았/었더라면," or *Had I helped … I wouldn't regret ....* Thus, choices (B), "주느라고" (*while I was helping*), (C), "줬는데" (*I helped him or her, but*), and (D), "줬으니" (*because I helped him or her*), are incorrect.

43. Choice (B) is the correct answer. The speaker did not cook dinner today and instead bought and ate *takeout*. "사다가" implies a change of place; that is, the place of buying and the place of eating are two different places. Choice (A) "샀다가" is incorrect because it is used to describe the reversal or nullification of an action (as in "샀다가 팔았어요") or to indicate a shift in action that takes place after the earlier action has been completed (as in "어제 버스를 탔다가 고등학교때 친구를 만났어요"). Choices (C), "샀고" (*bought and*), and (D), "사고" (*buy and*), are incorrect because they simply link two different actions. In order to describe closely connected actions such as "bought and ate" without implying two different locations, "사서," not "사고" or "샀고," should be used.

44. Choice (A) is the correct answer. 경석 says, "I've heard that you went to (and came back from) Hawaii, is that true?" 승진 replies, "Yes, *as long as I was there* I did lots of sightseeing and swimming as well." "___(으)ㄴ 김에" is a pattern that expresses the notion that one uses the opportunity presented in a given situation. Choices (B), "간 일에," (C), "간 중에," and (D), "간 새에," are simply not authentic Korean expressions.

45. Choice (B) is the correct answer. The speaker says, "Since work is really *backed up*, please get them done by tomorrow." *Work* ("일") is added by the subject particle "이," so the verb should be the passive verb "밀리다" (*backed up*). The verbs in choices (A) (*do*; "하다"), (C) (*make*; "만들다"), and (D) (*see*; "보다") are grammatically incorrect because they all require an object.

46. Choice (A) is the correct answer. This sentence is an indirect quotation; the speaker tells the listener to ask the listener's grandfather when he is coming. Since the verb "여쭤 보아라" means *try to ask*, the sentence should have an indirect quotation question form; thus choice (A), "오시느냐고," is correct. Choice (B), "느라고," is used when one could not complete his or her task as a result of doing something else (as in "숙제하느라고 잠을 못 잤어요"). Choice (C), "오신다고," is an indirect quotation form for a statement. And choice (D), "오시려고," denotes a speaker's or listener's intention.

47. Choice (C) is the correct answer. "집", or *home*, is the destination the phone call is directed to, so a directional particle "에다" or "에" should be used. Choice (A), "을," is an object particle. Choice (B), "은," is a topic marker. And choice (D), "에서," is a place particle, denoting the place where an activity takes place.

48. Choice (B) is the correct answer. The sentence requires a mimetic word that describes the manner of the coins rolling down the coin return slot of the public phone. Choice

(B), "주르르," is the word that describes the manner of something rolling down. Similarly, "주르르," is used to describe the manner of tears flowing, as in "눈물이 주르르 흘러내리다." Choice (A), "방글방글," is used to describe a manner of smile, typically a baby's smile. Choice (C), "반짝반짝," is used to describe the manner of something that twinkles, glitters, or sparkles, such as stars. And choice (D), "따르릉," is an onomatopoetic word that describes the sound of a telephone ringing.

49. Choice (C) is the correct answer. The writer was unable to complete a call. He or she kept trying to call again and went to other phones and tried, but the call didn't go through and the coins got returned. "보다가" (*while trying*) indicates that one action is superseded by another before the earlier action has been completed; *keep trying* is superseded by *go to other phones and try again*. Thus, the pattern in choice (C) is the correct pattern to use. Choice (A), "해 보면" (*if I try*), does not make sense because the writer already knows the result. Choices (B), "해 봐도" (*even though I tried*), and (D), "해 보니까" (*when I tried and found out*), are incorrect because they could be used only if the clause were not followed by "다른 전화통에도 가서 해 보았지만."

50. Choice (A) is the correct answer. The writer says that he or she tried to call many times, but the call did not go through and the coins got returned *as expected* ("역시"). The paragraph suggests that the writer did get the coins back, so choice (B), *never*, is incorrect. And it does not make sense to say that the coins got returned *barely* (C) or *not particularly* (D).

51. Choice (A) is the correct answer. The writer says that it turned out that because the fee for the pay phone *has gone up* ("올라서"), the fee became 35 cents. *I didn't know* (B), *walk* (C), and *come out* (D) do not logically complete the sentence.

52. Choice (C) is the correct answer. The note indicates that Jane is going to the post office to send a package that she must mail today. "소포," *package*, is the key word to know to answer this question correctly.

53. Choice (C) is the correct answer. Jane's father's message is that his family should eat dinner without him, as he will come home late because he has to attend a meeting. "회의가 있어서 늦으신대요" *(he said he would be late because he had a meeting)* is the key phrase to know to answer this question.

54. Choice (B) is the correct answer. The ad is about an automobile repair shop. "정비소," (*repair shop*) is the key word that indicates what this ad is about.

55. Choice (C) is the correct answer. The ad promises no need for an appointment. The last line of the ad says, *No need for advance reservation/appointment. Service provided on the spot.*

56. Choice (D) is the correct answer. A moving company is advertised. Words such as "운송" (*transportation* or *shipment*) and "이삿짐" (*moving load/luggage*) indicate what this ad is about.

57. Choice (A) is the correct answer. The ad mentions a *half-price discount for students* ("학생 반액 할인"). The ad also mentions a *free consultation, guaranteed delivery on appointed date, safe packaging,* and *two-week special service by sea mail or air mail.* There is no mention of free delivery, free assembly, or flight insurance.

58. Choice (A) is the correct answer. The form is an application form for placing an advertisement request. *Advertisement* ("광고") is the key word to know to answer this question correctly. The applicant should fill out this form if he or she wants to advertise something.

59. Choice (A) is the correct answer. The son's dug in the field because when their father was dying, he told his sons that *a treasure* ("보물") would come out if they dug the grape field.

60. Choice (D) is the correct answer. By having his sons dig in the field, the father made his sons realize that the treasure that the father mentioned was a result of hard work. The father, a farmer, clearly was a wise, hardworking man who taught his sons a lesson (they get what they work for) when they did not work.

61. Choice (D) is the correct answer. The advertisement is for *Hanmi General Hospital,* which provides *medical service* ("의료 서비스"). "건강" (*health*) and "병원" (*hospital*) are the key words to know to answer this question.

62. Choice (C) is the correct answer. The purpose of the notice is to rent a *single room* ("독방"). The notice says, *Renting a single room. Pleasant and quiet area. Family-like atmosphere. Student welcome.*

63. Choice (D) is the correct answer. The writer is a senior. This is made clear when he or she writes, "대학을 졸업하기 전에 있는 마지막 방학," or *This vacation is the last vacation before I graduate from college.*

64. Choice (B) is the correct answer. Four people are going on vacation together. Five were going to go together originally, but one could not make it because something came up ("한 명은 무슨 일이 생겨서 못 간다고 했다"). "한 명" (*one person*) and "무슨 일이 생겨서" (*something came up*) indicate that the group ended up with four people instead of five.

65. Choice (A) is the correct answer. The announcement requests *personal stories of experience* ("경험담, 체험담") and *observation/impression reports* ("감상문"). These are types of essays, not poems, novels, or dramas.

66. Choice (A) is the correct answer. The announcement says that essays are wanted and should be sent to Seoul Central Box 201, Editorial Department. It also says that *manuscripts will not be returned* ("원고는 돌려 드리지 않습니다").

67. Choice (B) is the correct answer. Yongjin tells his grandmother about a sudden weather change—a hurricane—that took place in his town after she visited him. "태풍," *hurricane*, is the key word to know to answer this question. And the weather change took place in Yongjin's town, not in Seoul, where his grandmother lives.

68. Choice (D) is the correct answer. Yongjin describes the damage caused by the hurricane: Some neighbors are completed flooded, the power is out in many places, and many houses, stores and buildings have damage caused by water. But Yongjin also says that because many people left their homes to escape ("피신하다"), nobody was hurt ("많은 사람들이 피신해서 다친 사람은 없습니다")—people were not injured.

69. Choice (C) is the correct answer. Yongjin indicates that his plan is to visit his grandmother. He says, *When the winter vacation starts, I will come see you* ("겨울 방학 하면 할머니 뵈러 갈게요").

70. Choice (C) is the correct answer. The institution offering the advertised service is "국립민속박물관," *The National Folk Museum*. This is mentioned in the first sentence.

71. Choice (A) is the correct answer. The stated objective of The National Folk Museum is to introduce Korean history and culture. "역사" (*history*) and "문화" (*culture*) are the key words to know to understand the institution's objective.

72. Choice (D) is the correct answer. The key words in the passage are "겉모양" and "용모," which mean *looks*. The writer claims that people these days think looks are more important than what is inside a person; clearly, he or she thinks people put too much emphasis on looks or appearances.

73. Choice (C) is the correct answer. The writer indicates that he or she arrived at the conclusion by talking to friends. In the third sentence, the writer states that he or she had a chance to talk about something related to this topic with his or her close friends ("가까운 친구들과 이야기를 나눌 기회가 있었는데"). "가까운 친구들," *close friends*, is the key phrase to know to answer this question.

74. Choice (A) is the correct answer. The writer recommends that people make an effort *to develop good character* ("훌륭한 인격을 갖추다") because looks are bound to change with the passage of time. The writer does not suggest that people should pursue higher education, have a goal in life, or exercise regularly.

75. Choice (D) is the correct answer. The writer's main point is that every society has etiquette to observe. He or she explicitly states, *There must be etiquettes to be observed for people to form a community and live* ("사람들이 공동체를 이루고 살아나가는 데는 반드시 지켜야 할 예절이 있게 마련이다").

76. Choice (B) is the correct answer. The writer suggests that people should be polite. The idea that people should *greet each other* ("인사를 주고 받으며") and *use kind language* ("친절한 말씨를 쓸 때") implies that it is important to be polite, not that it is important to be patient, diligent or organized.

77. Choice (C) is the correct answer. Sangho's senior year of college is still vivid in the writer's memory. In the very beginning of the passage, the writer states, *It feels like only yesterday that I saw Sangho, who was busy running around because he was in his college graduating class.* "대학 졸업반," *college graduating class*, is the same expression as "대학 사학년," *senior in college*.

78. Choice (D) is the correct answer. The writer indicates that Sangho avoids traveling by airplane as much as possible. The key sentence to understand is "상호는 가능하면 비행기를 안 타고 자동차로 여행하고 호텔에는 묵지 않는다," or *Sangho does not take planes but travels by car as much as possible, and does not stay at hotels.*

79. Choice (B) is the correct answer. The writer indicates that Sangho maximizes the effect with the minimum amount of money that he spends; in other words Sangho is frugal, or avoids wasting his money. "최소의 금액," *minimum amount of money*, and "최대의 효과," *maximum effect*, are the key phrases to know to answer this question correctly.

80. Choice (C) is the correct answer. "건강에 좋고," *good to health*, and "마음의 안정," *stability of heart*, are the key phrases that describe Sangho's view of vacations. It is clear that Sangho thinks vacations bring tranquility (which can be expressed by the phrase "stability of heart").

Chapter 14

Latin

Purpose

The Subject Test in Latin measures a wide-ranging knowledge of Latin. It is written to reflect general trends in high school curricula and is independent of particular textbooks or methods of instruction.

Format

This one-hour test includes 70 to 75 multiple-choice questions.

Content

The reading comprehension part has 30 to 37 questions based on three to five reading passages and one or two poetry passages. A set of questions following a poetry passage always includes one question requiring you to scan the first four feet of a line of dactylic hexameter verse or to determine the number of elisions in a line.

- **Forms**—select appropriate grammatical forms of Latin words
- **Derivatives**—choose Latin words from which English words are derived
- **Translation**—translate from Latin to English
- **Sentence completion**—complete Latin sentences
- **Substitution**—choose alternate ways of expressing the same thought in Latin
- **Reading comprehension**—answer a variety of questions based on short passages of prose or poetry

Latin	
Skills Measured	Approximate Percentage of Test
Grammar and Syntax	30%
Derivatives	5%
Translation and Reading Comprehension	65%

How to Prepare

The test is intended for students who have studied Latin for two to four years in high school (the equivalent of two to four semesters in college). The best way to prepare is by gradually developing competence in sight-reading Latin over a period of years. You may also prepare for the Subject Test in Latin as you would for any comprehensive test that requires knowledge of facts and concepts and the ability to apply them, thereby acquiring the equivalent of two to four years of classroom preparation. Familiarize yourself with the directions in advance. The directions in this book are identical to those that appear on the test.

Score

The total score is reported on the 200-to-800 scale.

Sample Questions

Please note: Your answer sheet has five circles marked A, B, C, D, and E, while the questions throughout this test contain only four choices. Be sure not to make any marks in column E.

Forms

This type of question asks you to select a specific grammatical form of a Latin word. Any form of a noun, pronoun, adjective, adverb, or verb can be asked for.

Directions: In the statement below, you are asked to give a specific form of the underlined word. Select the correct form from the choices given. Then fill in the corresponding circle on the answer sheet.

1. The future indicative of <u>potest</u> is

   (A) <u>potuerat</u>

   (B) <u>poterat</u>

   (C) <u>potuerit</u>

   (D) <u>poterit</u>

Choice (D) is the correct answer to question 1. In this question, you are asked to identify the future indicative of a very common irregular verb. Choice (A) is the pluperfect tense, choice (B) the imperfect, and choice (C) the future perfect.

Derivatives

In this type of question, you are given an English sentence with one word underlined. You must choose the Latin word from which the underlined English word is derived.

Directions: The English sentence below contains a word that is underlined. From among the choices, select the Latin word to which the underlined word is related by derivation. Then fill in the corresponding circle on the answer sheet.

2. The goalkeeper was out of position.
   (A) populus
   (B) pons
   (C) possum
   (D) pono

Choice (D) is the correct answer to question 2. The English word "position" is derived from *positus*, the past participle of the Latin verb *pōnō*, "to put or place." *Position* is not derived from the nouns *populus* and *pons*, which mean "people" and "bridge," nor from the verb *possum*, which means "to be able." Note that you will need to know the various forms of different Latin verbs to answer these questions.

Translation

You must choose the correct translation of the underlined Latin word or words. This type of question is more complex than the previous types, as it is based on the syntax of a complete Latin sentence.

Directions: In this section, part or all of the sentence is underlined. From among the choices, select the best translation for the underlined word or words. Then fill in the corresponding circle on the answer sheet.

3. Dux dīxit sē mīlitēs laudātūrum esse.
   (A) that they would praise the soldiers
   (B) that the soldiers had praised him
   (C) that he would praise the soldiers
   (D) that the soldiers should be praised

Choice (C) is the correct answer to question 3. To answer this question correctly, you must know that the underlined part of the sentence is testing an indirect statement that depends on the verb *dīxit*. The singular form of the future participle, *laudātūrum*, tells you that *sē* (he) is the subject of the indirect statement; therefore *mīlitēs* must be the direct object. The past tense of *dīxit* tells you that "would praise" is the correct translation of *laudātūrum esse.* None of the incorrect choices (A), (B), and (D) have both the correct subject of the indirect statement and the correct translation of the verb.

Sentence Completion

This type of question contains a Latin sentence in which a word or phrase has been omitted. You must select the Latin word or phrase that best fits grammatically into the sentence.

Directions: The sentence below contains a blank space indicating that a word or phrase has been omitted. For each blank, four completions are provided. Choose the word or phrase that best completes the sentence and fill in the corresponding circle on the answer sheet.

4. Ē castrīs ... nōluit.
   (A) ēgressus est
   (B) ēgredere
   (C) ut ēgrediātur
   (D) ēgredī

Choice (D) is the correct answer to question 4. To answer this question correctly, you must be able to translate the words *Ē castrīs ... nōluit* ("He did not wish ... from the camp") and then select the only choice that can be added to these two words to make a complete, grammatical Latin sentence. Here the correct answer is choice (D) *ēgredī*, the infinitive, since *nōlō* takes the infinitive. Choice (A) is incorrect because it is the present perfect form, choice (B) because it is the imperative, and choice (C) because *nōlō* does not take *ut* and the subjunctive. Note that *ēgredior* is a deponent verb.

Substitution

This type of question contains a complete Latin sentence, part or all of which is underlined. You are asked to select the substitution that is closest in meaning to the underlined words.

Directions: In the sentence below, part or all of the sentence is underlined. Select from the choices the expression that, when substituted for the underlined portion of the sentence, changes the meaning of the sentence LEAST. Then fill in the corresponding circle on the answer sheet.

5. Vēnit Rōmam ad <u>mātrem videndam</u>.
   (A) <u>cum mātrem vīdisset</u>
   (B) <u>mātre vīsā</u>
   (C) <u>qui mātrem vīdit</u>
   (D) <u>mātris videndae causā</u>

Choice (D) is the correct answer to question 5. In this example, the underlined portion is translated: "to see his/her mother." You must select the answer choice whose translation is closest in meaning to this underlined part: choice (D), *mātris videndae causā*, which also expresses purpose or intention. None of the other choices does so.

Reading Comprehension

This type of question presents you with a series of short passages of prose or poetry followed by several questions. These questions test either grammatical points (9 below), translation of a phrase or clause, grammatical reference (6), or summary/comprehension (7, 8, and 10). In addition, poetry passages always have one question on the scansion of the first four feet of a line of dactylic hexameter verse.

Note: The passages have titles, include definitions of uncommon words that appear in the text, and are adapted from Latin authors. There are approximately three to five passages with a total of 32 to 37 questions on the test. At least one (and no more than two) poetry passage appears on the test.

Directions: Read the following text carefully for comprehension. The text is followed by a number of questions or incomplete statements. Select the answer or completion that is best according to the text and fill in the corresponding circle on the answer sheet.

An enemy attack

Sabīnī multi, ut ad moenia Rōmae venīrent, illōs in agrīs vīventēs oppugnābant. Agrī dēlēbantur; terror urbī iniectus (injectus) est. Tum plēbs benignē arma cēpit ad Sabīnōs repellendos. Recūsantibus[1] frūstrā senātōribus, duo tamen exercitūs magnī cōnscriptī sunt.

[1] recūsō, recūsāre: oppose

6. The word vīventēs (line 1) refers to
   (A) Sabīnī (line 1)
   (B) moenia (line 1)
   (C) illōs (line 1)
   (D) agrīs (line 1)

Choice (C) is the correct answer to question 6. The word *vīventēs* refers to *illōs*. Choice (B) cannot be the correct answer because *moenia* is neuter plural, and choice (D) *agrīs* is incorrect because the fields cannot be living somewhere. The sense of the sentence tells you that choice (A) *Sabīnī* is incorrect and that the words *illōs in agrīs vīventēs* belong together.

7. The sentence Sabīnī … oppugnābant (line 1) tells us that the
   (A) Sabines wanted to get to the city walls
   (B) Sabines were the people living in the fields
   (C) Romans wanted to go nearer to the city walls
   (D) Romans wanted to attack the people living in the fields

Choice (A) is the correct answer to question 7. To answer this question correctly, you must know that *Sabīnī* is the subject of the sentence and that *illōs in agrīs vīventēs* is the object. You must also understand the purpose clause *ut ad moenia Rōmae venīrent* in line 1. The Sabines are therefore not the people living in the fields (B), nor is it the Romans who want to get nearer to the city walls (C) or to attack the people living in the fields (D).

8. The sentence <u>Agrī</u> ... <u>iniectus (injectus) est</u> (lines 1–2) tells us that the
   (A) Sabines were destroyed in the fields
   (B) Sabines were frightened of the city
   (C) fearful city was destroyed
   (D) city was filled with fear

Choice (D) is the correct answer to question 8. The sentence tells us that the fields were destroyed and that fear was "thrown into" the city.

9. The subject of <u>cēpit</u> (line 2) is
   (A) <u>terror</u> (line 2)
   (B) <u>plēbs</u> (line 2)
   (C) <u>arma</u> (line 2)
   (D) he (understood)

Choice (B) is the correct answer to question 9 because *plēbs* is in the nominative case and the subject of the sentence. Choice (A) *terror* is the subject of the previous clause and choice (C) *arma* is the object of *cēpit.* Choice (D) "he (understood)" is not the subject of this sentence, since there is an expressed subject.

10. The sentence <u>Recūsantibus</u> ... <u>cōnscriptī sunt</u> (lines 3–4) tells us that
   (A) armies were raised for the senators
   (B) armies were raised in vain
   (C) the senators prevented the raising of armies
   (D) the senators did not want armies to be raised

Choice (D) is the correct answer to question 10. The ablative absolute *Recūsantibus frūstra senātōribus* tells us that the armies were raised with the senators resisting in vain.

Latin Subject Test

Practice Helps

The test that follows is an actual, previously administered SAT Subject Test in Latin. To get an idea of what it's like to take this test, practice under conditions that are much like those of an actual test administration.

- Set aside an hour when you can take the test uninterrupted.
- Sit at a desk or table with no other books or papers. Dictionaries, other books, or notes are not allowed in the test room.
- Tear out an answer sheet from the back of this book and fill it in just as you would on the day of the test. One answer sheet can be used for up to three Subject Tests.
- Read the instructions that precede the practice test. During the actual administration you will be asked to read them before answering test questions.
- Time yourself by placing a clock or kitchen timer in front of you.
- After you finish the practice test, read the sections "How to Score the SAT Subject Test in Latin" and "How Did You Do on the Subject Test in Latin?"
- The appearance of the answer sheet in this book may differ from the answer sheet you see on test day.

LATIN TEST

The top portion of the page of the answer sheet that you will use to take the Latin Test must be filled in exactly as illustrated below. When your supervisor tells you to fill in the circle next to the name of the test you are about to take, mark your answer sheet as shown.

○ Literature	○ Mathematics Level 1	○ German	○ Chinese Listening	○ Japanese Listening
○ Biology E	○ Mathematics Level 2	○ Italian	○ French Listening	○ Korean Listening
○ Biology M	○ U.S. History	● Latin	○ German Listening	○ Spanish Listening
○ Chemistry	○ World History	○ Modern Hebrew		
○ Physics	○ French	○ Spanish	**Background Questions:** ① ② ③ ④ ⑤ ⑥ ⑦ ⑧ ⑨	

After filling in the circle next to the name of the test you are taking, locate the Background Questions box on your answer sheet (as shown above). This is where you will answer the following Background Questions on your answer sheet.

BACKGROUND QUESTIONS

Please answer either Part I or Part II below by filling in the appropriate circle in the Background Questions box on your answer sheet. Fill in ONLY ONE circle, as described below, to indicate how you obtained your knowledge of Latin. The information you provide is for statistical purposes only and will not affect your test score.

Part I If your knowledge of Latin does not come primarily from courses taken in grades 9 through 12, fill in circle 9 and leave the remaining circles blank, regardless of how long you studied the subject in school. For example, you are to fill in circle 9 if your knowledge of Latin comes primarily from any of the following sources: study prior to the ninth grade, courses taken at a college, or special study.

Part II If your knowledge of Latin does come primarily from courses taken in grades 9 through 12, fill in the circle that indicates the level of the Latin course in which you are currently enrolled. If you are not now enrolled in a Latin course, fill in the circle that indicates the level of the most advanced course in Latin that you have completed.

- First level: first or second half —Fill in circle 1.
- Second level: first half —Fill in circle 2.
  second half —Fill in circle 3.
- Third level: first half —Fill in circle 4.
  second half —Fill in circle 5.
- Fourth level: first half —Fill in circle 6.
  second half —Fill in circle 7.
- Advanced Placement course or a course beyond fourth level, second half —Fill in circle 8.

When the supervisor gives the signal, turn the page and begin the Latin Test. There are 100 numbered circles on the answer sheet and 74 questions in the Latin Test. Therefore, use only circles 1 to 74 for recording your answers.

LATIN TEST

PLEASE NOTE: Your answer sheet has five circles, marked A, B, C, D and E, while the questions throughout this test have only four choices. Be sure not to make any marks in column E.

Note: In some questions in this test, variations of Latin terms will appear in parentheses.

Part A

Directions: In each statement below, you are asked to give a specific form of the underlined word. Select the correct form from the choices given. Then fill in the corresponding circle on the answer sheet.

1. The accusative plural masculine of ācrior is

   (A) ācriōra
   (B) ācriōre
   (C) ācriōribus
   (D) ācriōrēs

2. The genitive singular of is is

   (A) eum
   (B) eius (ejus)
   (C) eī
   (D) eō

3. The present imperative plural of ferō is

   (A) ferātis
   (B) ferte
   (C) ferēs
   (D) fer

4. The imperfect indicative of dūcunt is

   (A) dūxērunt
   (B) dūcerent
   (C) dūxerint
   (D) dūcēbant

5. The accusative plural of hoc is

   (A) hōs
   (B) hās
   (C) hīs
   (D) haec

6. The perfect passive infinitive of dīligō is

   (A) dīligī
   (B) dīlectum esse
   (C) dīlexī
   (D) dīlexisse

7. The future of sequitur is

   (A) sequētur
   (B) sequātur
   (C) sequerētur
   (D) sequēbātur

8. The subjunctive of amāvī is

   (A) amārem
   (B) amāvissem
   (C) amāverim
   (D) amāverō

GO ON TO THE NEXT PAGE

Part B

Directions: Each of the following English sentences contains a word that is underlined. From among the choices, select the Latin word to which the underlined word is related by derivation. Then fill in the corresponding circle on the answer sheet.

9. Claudia showed great fortitude in her troubles.

(A) forum
(B) fore
(C) fortūna
(D) fortis

10. The volcano erupted violently.

(A) ēripiō
(B) errō
(C) ērumpō
(D) ērigō

11. He committed suicide.

(A) cadō
(B) caedō
(C) cēdō
(D) censeō

12. The congressional caucus intrigued the visiting reporters.

(A) conqueror
(B) congredior
(C) congruō
(D) congerō

GO ON TO THE NEXT PAGE

Part C

Directions: In each of the sentences below, part or all of the sentence is underlined. From among the choices, select the best translation for the underlined word or words. Then fill in the corresponding circle on the answer sheet.

13. Ubi eōs in cīvitātem adduxerō, concordia inter cīvēs omnēs erit.

(A) When I will draw them against the state
(B) When I might have induced them into the state
(C) When I will have led them into the state
(D) When I will have prompted them in the state

14. Trēs annōs rex aequē rexit.

(A) For the third year
(B) In the third year
(C) In three years
(D) For three years

15. Timeō nē amīcās meās nōn videam hodiē.

(A) that I may see my friends
(B) that I may not see my friends
(C) not to see my friends
(D) that my friends will not see

16. Quod dōnum Claudiae ā suīs amīcīs datum est?

(A) Because
(B) Since
(C) Who
(D) Which

17. Ab omnibus cīvibus īdem dux laudātus est.

(A) this
(B) himself
(C) a certain
(D) the same

18. Sī hoc dīcat, eum laudēmus.

(A) says
(B) should say
(C) has said
(D) will say

19. Lēgēs omnibus cīvibus defendendae sunt.

(A) from all citizens
(B) of all citizens
(C) to all citizens
(D) by all citizens

20. Amīcīs vīsīs, Anna ad oppidum currēbat.

(A) As her friends watched
(B) After her friends had been seen
(C) With the friends she had seen
(D) Since she was going to see her friends

21. Mercātor māne Rōmā profectus est.

(A) in Rome
(B) to Rome
(C) from Rome
(D) near Rome

22. Litterās coniugis (conjugis) legens, sibi putāvit: "Utinam nunc adessēs!"

(A) "So that you might be here now!"
(B) "As you are here now!"
(C) "Indeed you are here now!"
(D) "Would that you were here now!"

GO ON TO THE NEXT PAGE

23. Māter rēgis fīliō suō verba gravia locūtūra est.
    (A) will speak
    (B) is spoken
    (C) was spoken
    (D) has been spoken

24. Num hoc templum vīdistī?
    (A) Have you never seen this temple?
    (B) Did you see this temple?
    (C) You haven't seen this temple, have you?
    (D) You did see this temple, didn't you?

25. Anna līberōs ad hortum mīsit quī fructūs carperent.
    (A) who picked fruit
    (B) to pick fruit
    (C) who had picked fruit
    (D) who will pick fruit

26. Parvus puer clāmantem timet.
    (A) The little boy shouting is frightened.
    (B) The little boy is afraid of the person shouting.
    (C) The little boy fears the shouting.
    (D) The little boy is afraid to shout.

GO ON TO THE NEXT PAGE

Part D

Directions: Each of the sentences below contains a blank space indicating that a word or phrase has been omitted. For each blank, four completions are provided. Choose the option that best completes the sentence and fill in the corresponding circle on the answer sheet.

27. Peditēs in Galliam cum equitibus . . . imperātor.

(A) eīs
(B) ā Caesare
(C) mīsit
(D) et

28. . . . signum dedit.

(A) Ā tubā
(B) Tubam
(C) Tubās
(D) Tubā

29. Iūlia (Jūlia) dīxit . . . ad oppidum ventūram esse.

(A) eum
(B) illa
(C) suās
(D) sē

30. Marcus multa dōna . . . fīliae dedit.

(A) suō
(B) suae
(C) sē
(D) suus

31. Rēgīna, fēmina . . ., multa sacrificia fēcit.

(A) ad magnam pietātem
(B) magnae pietātis
(C) magnā cum pietāte
(D) magnam pietātem

32. Poēta . . . nocuit.

(A) eī
(B) eum
(C) eō
(D) eae

33. Crās . . . ab omnibus cīvibus.

(A) audiēminī
(B) audītis
(C) audīminī
(D) audiēbāminī

GO ON TO THE NEXT PAGE

Part E

Directions: In each of the sentences below, part or all of the sentence is underlined. Select from the choices the expression that, when substituted for the underlined portion of the sentence, changes the meaning of the sentence LEAST. Then fill in the corresponding circle on the answer sheet.

34. Est mihi canis bonus et magnus.

(A) Canem bonum et magnum habeō.
(B) Canem bonum habeō ut magnus sim.
(C) Canis, quī erat magnus, erat bonus.
(D) Canem, quī bonus et magnus erat, habēbam.

35. Sī Marcus imperātor erit, Rōma servābitur.

(A) Sī Marcus imperātor esset
(B) Marcō imperātōre
(C) Sī Marcus imperātor fuisset
(D) Marcum imperātōrem

36. Hae lēgēs magis idōneae quam illae sunt.

(A) illīs
(B) illī
(C) illae
(D) illā

37. Marcus nuntium mīsit ut ducem monēret.

(A) dum
(B) quī
(C) quae
(D) quod

38. Historia mihi legenda est.

(A) Mea historia lecta est.
(B) Placet mihi historiam legī.
(C) Ego historiam lēgī.
(D) Dēbeō historiam legere.

GO ON TO THE NEXT PAGE

Part F

Directions: Read the following texts carefully for comprehension. Each is followed by a number of questions or incomplete statements. Select the answer or completion that is best according to the text and fill in the corresponding circle on the answer sheet.

Rome then and now

Simplicitās rudis[1] ante fuit: nunc aurea Rōma est.
Et domitī[2] magnās possidet orbis opēs.
Aspice[3] quae nunc sunt Capitōlia, quaeque fuērunt:
alterius dīcēs illa fuisse Iovis (Jovis).
Prīsca[4] iuvent (juvent) aliōs:[5] ego mē nunc dēnique nātum
grātulor: haec aetās mōribus apta meīs.

[1] rudis, rude, adj.: plain
[2] domitī = victī
[3] Aspice = Spectā
[4] Prīsca = antīqua
[5] iuvent (juvent) aliōs = placeant aliīs

39. The case and number of aurea (line 1) are
(A) nominative singular
(B) nominative plural
(C) accusative plural
(D) ablative singular

40. How many elisions occur in line 1 ?
(A) One
(B) Two
(C) Three
(D) Four

41. In line 2, magnās modifies
(A) Simplicitās (line 1)
(B) rudis (line 1)
(C) orbis (line 2)
(D) opēs (line 2)

42. The understood subject of possidet (line 2) refers to
(A) Simplicitās (line 1)
(B) Rōma (line 1)
(C) orbis (line 2)
(D) opēs (line 2)

43. The words domitī . . . opēs (line 2) are translated
(A) the conquerors possess great wealth
(B) it possesses the great wealth of the conquered world
(C) great wealth conquers the possessors
(D) the world possesses great resources

44. Aspice (line 3) is translated
(A) to look at
(B) they look at
(C) look at
(D) he looks at

GO ON TO THE NEXT PAGE

45. The case and number of <u>Capitōlia</u> (line 3) are

(A) nominative singular
(B) nominative plural
(C) accusative singular
(D) ablative singular

46. The case and number of <u>illa</u> (line 4) are

(A) nominative singular
(B) nominative plural
(C) accusative plural
(D) ablative singular

47. In line 4, <u>fuisse</u> is translated

(A) are
(B) were
(C) will be
(D) will have been

48. Which of the following is the most accurate translation of the words <u>Prīsca iuvent (juvent)</u> (line 5) ?

(A) Let ancient times please
(B) If ancient times pleased
(C) Ancient times please
(D) Ancient times will please

49. The case and number of <u>mōribus</u> (line 6) are

(A) genitive plural
(B) dative plural
(C) accusative plural
(D) ablative plural

50. In line 6, the words <u>haec</u> . . . <u>meīs</u> are translated

(A) these ways are suitable to me
(B) my age makes me inclined to delay
(C) this age is fitting for my ways
(D) this time delays me

51. In the passage, the poet praises the

(A) former leaders of Rome
(B) wealth and power of Rome
(C) simplicity of Roman life
(D) good old ways

GO ON TO THE NEXT PAGE

A Roman dictator opposes Hannibal.

Dictātōrem populus creāvit et huic negōtium ab senātū datum, ut mūrōs turrēsque urbis firmāret, et pontēs flūminis dēlēret. Prō urbe ac penātibus[1] eī pugnandum erat, cum Italia dēfendī nōn posset.

Hannibal[2] rectō itinere vēnit. Vastātō agrō, urbem oppugnāre incēpit. Repulsus magnā caede suōrum, in agrum iter āvertit.

[1]penātēs, penātium, m.: Penates, household gods
[2]Hannibal, Hannibālis, m.: Hannibal, a Carthaginian general

52. The words huic negōtium ab senātū datum (lines 1-2) are translated

(A) he assigned this task to the senate
(B) the task was given to him by the senate
(C) this task was dedicated to the senate
(D) the senate handed over this task

53. The subject of firmāret (line 2) is

(A) dictātor (understood)
(B) Hannibal (understood)
(C) populus (line 1)
(D) negōtium (line 1)

54. The case of the word pontēs (line 3) is

(A) nominative
(B) genitive
(C) dative
(D) accusative

55. The words eī pugnandum erat (lines 3-4) are translated

(A) it is fought for him
(B) it should be fought for him
(C) he had to fight
(D) they had to fight

56. The word cum (line 4) is translated

(A) with
(B) so that
(C) therefore
(D) since

57. We learn in the first paragraph that one task of the dictator is to

(A) build bridges
(B) strengthen the city's walls
(C) negotiate for the senate
(D) conquer Italy

GO ON TO THE NEXT PAGE

58. Repulsus (line 6) modifies

(A) Hannibal (understood)
(B) caede (line 6)
(C) agrum (line 7)
(D) iter (line 7)

59. The words in agrum (lines 6-7) are translated

(A) in the countryside
(B) through the countryside
(C) into the countryside
(D) around the countryside

60. In the second paragraph, we learn which of the following about Hannibal's attack on the city?

(A) He attacked after destroying the countryside.
(B) He attacked before the city could be fortified.
(C) He intended to complete his conquest of Italy.
(D) He intended to slaughter the entire population.

GO ON TO THE NEXT PAGE

A multilingual monarch

Quintus Ennius tria corda habēre sēsē dīcēbat, quod loquī Graecē et Oscē et Latīnē scīret. Mithridātēs autem, Pontī atque Bīthȳniae rex clārus, quī ā Pompēiō bellō superātus est, quinque et vīgintī gentium quās sub diciōne[1] habuit linguās scīvit eārumque omnium gentium virīs numquam per interpretem conlocūtus est. Sed ut quisque ā rēge appellātus est, statim linguā et ōrātiōne ipsīus nōn minus scītē[2] quam sī gentīlis[3] eius (ejus) esset locūtus est.

[1] diciō, diciōnis, f.: power, sovereignty
[2] scītē: skillfully
[3] gentīlis, gentīlis, m.: fellow countryman

61. The case and number of corda (line 1) are

(A) nominative singular
(B) accusative plural
(C) ablative singular
(D) nominative plural

62. In line 1, habēre is translated

(A) have
(B) had
(C) having
(D) has

63. In line 1, sēsē is translated

(A) it
(B) they
(C) he
(D) his

64. Graecē, Oscē, and Latīnē in line 2 are

(A) adjectives
(B) nouns
(C) pronouns
(D) adverbs

65. The first sentence (lines 1-2) tells us that Quintus Ennius

(A) wanted to learn the Oscan language
(B) was able to speak several languages
(C) knew the Greek, Oscan, and Latin peoples
(D) had only the Latin language in his heart

66. In line 3, quī refers to

(A) Mithridates
(B) Pontus
(C) Ennius
(D) Bithynia

67. In line 4, bellō is translated

(A) war
(B) for war
(C) from war
(D) in war

68. The subject of habuit (line 5) is

(A) Ennius (line 1)
(B) Mithridātēs (line 2)
(C) Bīthȳniae (line 3)
(D) Pompēiō (line 3)

GO ON TO THE NEXT PAGE

69. In lines 4-5, quinque et . . . scīvit tells us that Mithridates knew

(A) 20 people who spoke 5 languages
(B) 25 people who spoke regional languages
(C) many nations where 25 languages were spoken
(D) the languages of 25 peoples in his realm

70. In line 7, ut is translated

(A) in order that
(B) as
(C) because
(D) lest

71. The word rēge (line 7) refers to

(A) Ennius (line 1)
(B) Mithridātēs (line 2)
(C) Pontī (line 3)
(D) Pompēiō (line 3)

72. In line 8, quam is translated

(A) which
(B) whom
(C) than
(D) who

73. In line 9, esset is translated

(A) he were
(B) he had been
(C) he would be
(D) he will be

74. In lines 7-9, statim linguā . . . locūtus est tells us that

(A) he spoke the language as well as a native of that country
(B) his language was as impressive as his oration
(C) his countrymen appreciated his skillful attempt
(D) he had never spoken the language of his countrymen

STOP

IF YOU FINISH BEFORE TIME IS CALLED, YOU MAY CHECK YOUR WORK ON THIS TEST ONLY. DO NOT TURN TO ANY OTHER TEST IN THIS BOOK.

How to Score the SAT Subject Test in Latin

When you take an actual SAT Subject Test in Latin, your answer sheet will be "read" by a scanning machine that will record your response to each question. Then a computer will compare your answers with the correct answers and produce your raw score. You get one point for each correct answer. For each wrong answer, you lose one-third of a point. Questions you omit (and any for which you mark more than one answer) are not counted. This raw score is converted to a scaled score that is reported to you and to the colleges you specify.

Worksheet 1. Finding Your Raw Test Score

STEP 1: Table A on the following page lists the correct answers for all the questions on the Subject Test in Latin that is reproduced in this book. It also serves as a worksheet for you to calculate your raw score.

- Compare your answers with those given in the table.
- Put a check in the column marked "Right" if your answer is correct.
- Put a check in the column marked "Wrong" if your answer is incorrect.
- Leave both columns blank if you omitted the question.

STEP 2: Count the number of right answers.

Enter the total here: ________________

STEP 3: Count the number of wrong answers.

Enter the total here: ________________

STEP 4: Multiply the number of wrong answers by .333.

Enter the product here: ________________

STEP 5: Subtract the result obtained in Step 4 from the total you obtained in Step 2.

Enter the result here: ________________

STEP 6: Round the number obtained in Step 5 to the nearest whole number.

Enter the result here: ________________

The number you obtained in Step 6 is your raw score.

Table A

Answers to the Subject Test in Latin and Percentage of Students Answering Each Question Correctly

Question Number	Correct Answer	Right	Wrong	Percentage of Students Answering the Question Correctly*	Question Number	Correct Answer	Right	Wrong	Percentage of Students Answering the Question Correctly*
1	D			91	33	A			56
2	B			74	34	A			80
3	B			72	35	B			35
4	D			88	36	A			34
5	D			51	37	B			44
6	B			71	38	D			30
7	A			70	39	A			81
8	C			43	40	A			63
9	D			94	41	D			87
10	C			48	42	B			83
11	B			53	43	B			80
12	B			65	44	C			86
13	C			86	45	B			45
14	D			88	46	C			28
15	B			83	47	B			50
16	D			79	48	A			53
17	D			55	49	B			61
18	B			52	50	C			63
19	D			74	51	B			55
20	B			57	52	B			83
21	C			39	53	A			70
22	D			43	54	D			77
23	A			53	55	C			54
24	C			38	56	D			75
25	B			31	57	B			74
26	B			16	58	A			74
27	C			70	59	C			77
28	D			58	60	A			68
29	D			54	61	B			70
30	B			68	62	B			34
31	B			49	63	C			56
32	A			22	64	D			11

Table A continued on next page

Table A continued from previous page

Question Number	Correct Answer	Right	Wrong	Percentage of Students Answering the Question Correctly*	Question Number	Correct Answer	Right	Wrong	Percentage of Students Answering the Question Correctly*
65	B			85	70	B			36
66	A			70	71	B			48
67	D			70	72	C			67
68	B			67	73	A			35
69	D			68	74	A			74

* These percentages are based on an analysis of the answer sheets of a representative sample of 802 students who took the original administration of this test and whose mean score was 593. They may be used as an indication of the relative difficulty of a particular question.

Answer explanations for the Subject Test in Latin can be found on page 920.

Finding Your Scaled Score

When you take SAT Subject Tests, the scores sent to the colleges you specify are reported on the College Board scale, which ranges from 200–800. You can convert your practice test score to a scaled score by using Table B. To find your scaled score, locate your raw score in the left-hand column of Table B; the corresponding score in the right-hand column is your scaled score. For example, a raw score of 36 on this particular edition of the Subject Test in Latin corresponds to a scaled score of 580.

Raw scores are converted to scaled scores to ensure that a score earned on any one edition of a particular Subject Test is comparable to the same scaled score earned on any other edition of the same Subject Test. Because some editions of the tests may be slightly easier or more difficult than others, College Board scaled scores are adjusted so that they indicate the same level of performance regardless of the edition of the test taken and the ability of the group that takes it. Thus, for example, a score of 400 on one edition of a test taken at a particular administration indicates the same level of achievement as a score of 400 on a different edition of the test taken at a different administration.

When you take the SAT Subject Tests during a national administration, your scores are likely to differ somewhat from the scores you obtain on the tests in this book. People perform at different levels at different times for reasons unrelated to the tests themselves. The precision of any test is also limited because it represents only a sample of all the possible questions that could be asked.

Table B

Scaled Score Conversion Table Subject Test in Latin					
Raw Score	Scaled Score	Raw Score	Scaled Score	Raw Score	Scaled Score
74	800	40	610	6	410
73	800	39	600	5	410
72	800	38	600	4	400
71	800	37	590	3	400
70	800	36	580	2	400
69	800	35	580	1	390
68	800	34	570	0	390
67	800	33	560	-1	380
66	800	32	560	-2	380
65	790	31	550	-3	370
64	780	30	540	-4	370
63	770	29	540	-5	360
62	770	28	530	-6	360
61	760	27	520	-7	350
60	750	26	520	-8	350
59	740	25	510	-9	340
58	740	24	510	-10	340
57	730	23	500	-11	330
56	720	22	490	-12	330
55	720	21	490	-13	320
54	710	20	480	-14	320
53	700	19	480	-15	320
52	700	18	470	-16	310
51	690	17	470	-17	310
50	680	16	460	-18	300
49	670	15	460	-19	300
48	670	14	450	-20	290
47	660	13	450	-21	290
46	650	12	440	-22	290
45	650	11	440	-23	280
44	640	10	430	-24	280
43	630	9	430	-25	270
42	620	8	420		
41	620	7	420		

How Did You Do on the Subject Test in Latin?

After you score your test and analyze your performance, think about the following questions:

Did you run out of time before reaching the end of the test?

If so, you may need to pace yourself better. For example, maybe you spent too much time on one or two hard questions. A better approach might be to skip the ones you can't answer right away and try answering all the questions that remain on the test. Then if there's time, go back to the questions you skipped.

Did you take a long time reading the directions?

You will save time when you take the test by learning the directions to the Subject Test in Latin ahead of time. Each minute you spend reading directions during the test is a minute that you could use to answer questions.

How did you handle questions you were unsure of?

If you were able to eliminate one or more of the answer choices as wrong and guess from the remaining ones, your approach probably worked to your advantage. On the other hand, making haphazard guesses or omitting questions without trying to eliminate choices could cost you valuable points.

How difficult were the questions for you compared with other students who took the test?

Table A shows you how difficult the multiple-choice questions were for the group of students who took this test during its national administration. The right-hand column gives the percentage of students that answered each question correctly.

A question answered correctly by almost everyone in the group is obviously an easier question. For example, 88 percent of the students answered question 4 correctly. But only 16 percent answered question 26 correctly.

Keep in mind that these percentages are based on just one group of students. They would probably be different with another group of students taking the test.

If you missed several easier questions, go back and try to find out why: Did the questions cover material you haven't yet reviewed? Did you misunderstand the directions?

Answer Explanations for the Latin Subject Test

1. Choice (D) is the correct answer. The word *ācrior* is the comparative form of the adjective *ācer* and means "more eager, braver"; the accusative masculine plural ending is *-ēs*. The accusative masculine plural form is created by adding the *-ēs* ending to the stem *ācrior-*. Therefore, the correct answer is *ācriōrēs*. Choice (A), *ācriōra*, is the nominative and accusative plural neuter form. Choice (B), *ācriōre*, is the ablative singular masculine, feminine, and neuter form. Choice (C), *ācriōribus*, is the dative and ablative plural masculine, feminine, and neuter form.

2. Choice (B) is the correct answer. The word *is* is the masculine demonstrative pronoun, meaning "he" or "this/that one (man)." The genitive singular is *eius* (*ejus*). Choice (A), *eum*, is accusative singular, choice (C), *eī*, is dative singular, and choice (D), *eō*, is ablative singular.

3. Choice (B) is the correct answer. The plural imperative form of *ferō* is *ferte*. Choice (A), *ferātis*, is the present subjunctive second person plural. Choice (C), *ferēs*, is the future indicative second person singular. Choice (D), *fer*, is the singular imperative.

4. Choice (D) is the correct answer. The verb *dūcō* belongs to the third conjugation. For that conjugation the third person plural imperfect form is created by adding the ending *-ēbant* to the stem *dūc-*, which results in *dūcēbant*. Choice (A) *dūxērunt* is the perfect indicative form, and choice (B) *dūcerent* is the imperfect subjunctive. Choice (C) *dūxerint* may be either future perfect indicative or perfect subjunctive.

5. Choice (D) is the correct answer. *Hoc* is a neuter singular demonstrative pronoun or adjective, meaning "it" or "this (thing)." The accusative plural of this neuter form is *haec*. Choice (A), *hōs*, is the accusative plural masculine, choice (B), *hās*, is the accusative plural feminine, and choice (C), *hīs*, is the dative or ablative plural masculine, feminine, or neuter.

6. Choice (B) is the correct answer. The perfect passive infinitive is formed by combining the infinitive *esse* and the fourth principal part of the verb. The fourth principal part of *dīligō* ("I love/esteem") is *dīlectum*; the perfect passive infinitive is therefore *dīlectum esse*. Choice (A), *dīligī*, is the present passive infinitive, choice (C),

dīlexī, is the first person singular perfect active indicative, and choice (D), *dīlexisse*, is the perfect active infinitive.

7. Choice (A) is the correct answer. *Sequor* is a third conjugation deponent verb. The third person singular form of the future tense is formed by adding *-ētur* to the stem *sequ-*, which results in *sequētur.* Choice (B), *sequātur,* is the present subjunctive, while choice (C), *sequerētur,* is the imperfect subjunctive. Choice (D), *sequēbātur,* is the imperfect indicative.

8. Choice (C) is the correct answer. *Amāvī* is the first person singular of the perfect indicative. The first person singular perfect subjunctive is formed by adding *-erim* to the stem of the third principal part. The stem of the third principal part of *amō* is *amāv-*; therefore the first person singular perfect subjunctive form is *amāverim.* Choice (A), *amārem,* is imperfect subjunctive. Choice (B), *amāvissem,* is pluperfect subjunctive. Choice (D), *amāverō,* is the future perfect indicative.

9. Choice (D) is the correct answer. The English word "fortitude" (meaning "courage, bravery") is derived from the Latin adjective *fortis* (meaning "brave"). It is not related by derivation or in meaning to *forum* ("public place, market"), *fore* (the future infinitive of the verb *sum*), or *fortuna* ("fortune, chance, luck").

10. Choice (C) is the correct answer. The English word "erupted" (meaning "burst forth by emitting lava") is derived from *ēruptum,* the fourth principal part of the Latin verb *ērumpō* ("break open, burst out"). "Erupted" is not related by derivation or in meaning to *ēripiō* ("tear away, pull away"), *errō* ("wander, lose one's way"), or *erigō* ("raise up, erect").

11. Choice (B) is the correct answer. The English word "suicide" (meaning "killing oneself") is derived from *cecīdī,* the third principal part of the Latin verb *caedō,* (meaning "kill"). It is not related by derivation or in meaning to *cadō* ("fall, die"), *cedō* ("yield"), or *censeō* ("assess, rate, think").

12. Choice (B) is the correct answer. The English word "congressional" is related by derivation to the Latin verb *congredior, congrēdī, congressus* ("meet") and most directly to its third principal part *congressus.* It is not derived from *conqueror* ("complain bitterly"), *congruō* ("coincide, correspond"), or *congerō* ("collect, build").

13. Choice (C) is the correct answer. The Latin preposition *in* is followed by a noun in the accusative case (*cīvitātem*) and should therefore be translated "into." It should not be translated "in," as in choice (D). The verb *adduxerō* is first person singular future perfect active indicative of *adducere* (meaning "to lead") and should therefore be translated "I will have led." It should not be translated by the simple future construction "I will draw," as in choice (A), or by the modal past perfect construction "I might have induced," as in choice (B). The entire sentence may be translated "When I will have led them into the state, there will be concord among all the citizens."

14. Choice (D) is the correct answer. The noun phrase *Trēs annōs* functions as an accusative of extent, indicating duration of time, and should therefore be translated "For three years." It should not be translated "For the third year" (indicating recurrence in time), as in choice (A); "In the third year" (indicating time within which), as in choice (B); or "In three years" (indicating future time), as in choice (C). The entire sentence may be translated "For three years the king ruled equitably."

15. Choice (B) is the correct answer. The conjunction *nē* introduces a clause of fearing and should therefore be translated "that." Within the clause of fearing, the verb *videam* is first person singular present subjunctive and is negated by *nōn*; it should therefore be translated "I may not see." It should not be translated by the unnegated "I may see," as in choice (A), or by the infinitive "not to see," as in choice (C). In choice (D), the accusative noun phrase *amīcās meās* is incorrectly translated as the subject rather than the direct object of the verb. The entire sentence may be translated "I fear that I may not see my friends today."

16. Choice (D) is the correct answer. In this sentence, *Quod* is an interrogative adjective modifying the noun *dōnum* and should therefore be translated "Which." It should not be translated by the conjunction "Because" or "Since," as in choices (A) and (B), or by the relative pronoun "Who," as in choice (C). The entire sentence may be translated "Which gift was given to Claudia by her friends?"

17. Choice (D) is the correct answer. In this sentence, *īdem* is the nominative masculine singular form of the adjective *īdem, eadem, īdem* (meaning "the same," "identical"), and it modifies the noun *dux*. The adjective *īdem* never means "this," as in choice (A), or "himself," as in choice (B), or "a certain," as in choice (C). The entire sentence may be translated "The same leader was praised by all the citizens."

18. Choice (B) is the correct answer. This sentence presents a future less vivid condition, with present subjunctive verbs in both the conditional clause and the main clause. The verb in the conditional clause, *dīcat*, should therefore be translated by the modal

construction "should say." A future less vivid conditional should not be translated without the modal verb "should," as in choices (A), (C), and (D). The entire sentence may be translated "If he should say this, we would praise him."

19. Choice (D) is the correct answer. The noun phrase *omnibus cīvibus* functions as dative of agent with the passive periphrastic verb *defendendae sunt.* It should therefore be translated with the preposition "by" (indicating agency) placed before the noun phrase "all citizens." It should not be translated with the preposition "from" (indicating separation), as in choice (A), with "of" (indicating possession), as in choice (B), or with "to" (indicating an indirect object), as in choice (C). The entire sentence may be translated "The laws must be defended by all citizens."

20. Choice (B) is the correct answer. *Amīcīs vīsīs* is an ablative absolute phrase. The perfect passive participle *vīsīs* (from *vidēre,* meaning "to see") indicates an action completed before the action of the main verb *currēbat,* which is in the imperfect tense. The phrase should therefore be translated as a subordinate clause introduced by "After" and containing the past perfect verb construction "had been seen." It should not be translated "As her friends watched" (indicating simultaneous action), as in choice (A), "With the friends she had seen" (indicating accompaniment), as in choice (C), or "Since she was going to see her friends" (indicating future action), as in choice (D). The entire sentence may be translated "After her friends had been seen, Anna was running toward the town."

21. Choice (C) is the correct answer. The noun *Rōmā* is in the ablative case and should therefore be translated "from Rome" (indicating separation). It should not be translated "in Rome" (indicating static location), as in choice (A), "to Rome" (indicating motion towards), as in choice (B), or "near Rome" (indicating proximity), as in choice (D).The entire sentence may be translated "The trader set forth from Rome in the morning."

22. Choice (D) is the correct answer. *Utinam* followed by an imperfect subjunctive verb such as *adessēs* expresses a wish that is unfulfilled in present time. It is appropriately translated into English by the archaic exclamatory expression "Would that" followed by the conditional "were." Choices (A), (B), and (C) are incorrect because they do not express an unfulfilled wish. Rather, they express purpose ("So that you might be"), comparison or cause ("As you are"), and factuality ("Indeed you are"), respectively. The entire sentence may be translated "Reading his wife's letter, he thought to himself 'Would that you were here now!'"

23. Choice (A) is the correct answer. The phrase *locūtūra est* is a third person singular active periphrastic form of the verb *loqui* ("to speak"), compounded of a future active participle and a present tense form of *esse*. As a periphrasis, it expresses in a roundabout way what might be more succinctly expressed by the third person singular future verb *loquētur*. It is therefore appropriately translated "will speak." Choices (B), (C), and (D) are incorrect because they all render the verb as passive ("is spoken," "was spoken," "has been spoken") rather than active. The entire sentence may be translated "The mother of the king will speak serious words to her son."

24. Choice (C) is the correct answer. The accusative noun phrase *hoc templum* ("this temple") is the direct object of the second person singular perfect active indicative verb *vīdistī* ("you have seen"), and the interrogative particle *Num* anticipates a negative answer, so the sentence is appropriately translated "You haven't seen this temple, have you?" The translations in choices (A), (B), and (D) each fail to indicate that a negative answer is anticipated. Choice (D), in fact, anticipates a positive answer.

25. Choice (B) is the correct answer. The use of the imperfect subjunctive form *carperent* indicates that *quī fructūs carperent* is a relative clause of purpose. It should therefore be translated "to pick fruit," with an infinitive indicating the mandated action. It should not be translated by a relative clause indicating a past action, as in choices (A) and (C), or a future action, as in choice (D). The entire sentence may be translated "Anna sent the children to the garden to pick fruit."

26. Choice (B) is the correct answer. The noun phrase *Parvus puer* ("The little boy") is in the nominative case and should therefore be translated as the subject of the verb *timet* ("fears," "is afraid of"). The present participle *clāmantem* (from *clāmāre*, meaning "to shout") does not modify any noun in the sentence and should therefore be translated as a substantive: "The little boy is afraid of the person shouting." The participle should not be translated as a modifier of the subject ("The little boy shouting"), as in choice (A), as a gerund ("the shouting"), as in choice (C), or as an infinitive ("to shout"), as in choice (D).

27. Choice (C) is the correct answer. The singular verb *mīsit* appropriately completes the sentence, agreeing with the sentence's singular subject, *imperator*, and taking the accusative noun *Peditēs* as its direct object. Choices (A), (B), and (D) fail to provide a verb of any kind, leaving the sentence grammatically incomplete. The correctly completed sentence may be translated "The commander sent foot soldiers into Gaul with the knights."

28. Choice (D) is the correct answer. The noun *Tubā* appropriately completes the sentence, providing an ablative of means to indicate the instrument by which the signal was given. The sentence is not meaningfully completed by an ablative of agent, as in option (A), or by a singular or plural accusative noun, as in options (B) and (C). The correctly completed sentence may be translated "He gave a signal by means of a trumpet."

29. Choice (D) is the correct answer. The reflexive pronoun *sē* appropriately completes the sentence, functioning as the accusative subject of the future infinitive verb *ventūram esse* in indirect statement. Choice (A) is incorrect because the masculine pronoun *eum* does not agree with the feminine participle *ventūram*. Choice (B) is incorrect because *illa* is nominative and cannot serve as the subject of the infinitive. Choice (C) is incorrect because the plural substantive *suās* does not agree with the singular participle *ventūram*. The completed sentence may be translated "Julia said that she was about to come to the town."

30. Choice (B) is the correct answer. The feminine dative singular possessive adjective *suae* (from *suus, sua, suum,* meaning "one's own") appropriately completes the sentence, serving as a modifier of the feminine dative singular noun *fīliae*. Neither the masculine dative adjective *suō* in choice (A) nor the masculine nominative adjective *suus* in choice (D) can modify the feminine dative noun *fīliae* because of gender and/or case disagreement. The accusative reflexive pronoun *sē* in choice (C) cannot be meaningfully inserted into a sentence that already has as its direct object the noun phrase *multa dōna*. The correctly completed sentence may be translated "Marcus gave many gifts to his own daughter."

31. Choice (B) is the correct answer. The noun phrase *magnae pietātis* appropriately modifies the noun *fēmina,* functioning as a genitive of characteristic. The prepositional phrases *ad magnam pietātem* in choice (A) and *magna cum pietāte* in choice (C) are adverbial in nature and therefore inappropriate modifiers of the noun *fēmina*. Because it is in the accusative case, the noun phrase *magnam pietātem* in choice (D) cannot function as a modifier of *fēmina*. The correctly completed sentence may be translated "The queen, a woman of great devotion, made many sacrifices."

32. Choice (A) is the correct answer. The dative singular pronoun *eī* (from *is*, *ea*, or *id*) functions as the object of *nocuit*, the third person singular perfect indicative form of the verb *nocēre*, which governs an object in the dative case. The verb *nocuit* does not permit an object in the accusative case (*eum*) as in choice (B), in the ablative case (*eō*) as in choice (C), or in the nominative case (*eae*) as in choice (D). The correctly completed sentence may be translated "The poet harmed her."

33. Choice (A) is the correct answer. As a future verb, *audiēminī* ("you will be heard") fits with the adverb *Crās* ("tomorrow"), and, as a passive verb, it fits with the ablative of personal agent construction *ab omnibus cīvibus* ("by all the citizens"). The present active verb *audītis* ("you hear") in choice (B) fits with neither *Crās* nor *ab omnibus cīvibus*. The present passive verb *audīminī* ("you are heard") in choice (C) and the imperfect passive verb *audiēbāminī* ("you were being heard") in choice (D) both fit with *ab omnibus cīvibus* but not with *Crās*. The correctly completed sentence may be translated "Tomorrrow you will be heard by all the citizens."

34. Choice (A) is the correct answer. It substitutes the transitive construction *Canem habeō* for the dative of possession construction *Est mihi canis*. The revised sentence and the original sentence both mean "I have a good and large dog." The other choices all have meanings different from the original. Choice (B) means "I have a good dog so that I may be large." Choice (C) means "The dog, which was large, was good." Choice (D) means "I used to have a dog that was good and large."

35. Choice (B) is the correct answer. It substitutes the ablative absolute construction *Marcō imperātōre* for the future conditional clause *Sī Marcus imperātor erit*. The revised sentence and the original sentence both mean "If in the future Marcus is commander, Rome will be saved." Choices (A) and (C) are incorrect because they provide present and past contrary-to-fact conditional clauses that differ in meaning from the future conditional clause of the original. Choice (D) is incorrect because it provides an accusative noun phrase that yields an ungrammatical sentence.

36. Choice (A) is the correct answer. It substitutes the plural ablative of comparison *illīs* for the comparative clause *quam illae*. The revised sentence and the original sentence both mean "These laws are more appropriate than those." The pronoun *illī* in choice (B) is an inappropriate substitute because it is masculine rather than feminine, singular rather than plural, and in the dative case, which cannot express comparison. The pronoun *illae* in choice (C) is an inappropriate substitute because, as a nominative, it cannot express comparison unless preceded by *quam*. The pronoun *illā* in choice (D) is an inappropriate substitute because it is singular rather than plural.

37. Choice (B) is the correct answer. It substitutes the relative pronoun *quī* (referring to *nuntium*) for the conjunction *ut*, changing an ordinary purpose clause into a relative clause of purpose. The revised sentence and the original sentence both mean "Marcus sent a messenger to warn the leader." The conjunctions *dum* and *quod* in choices (A) and (D) are inappropriate substitutes because they introduce a conditional clause and a causal clause, respectively, rather than a clause of purpose. The feminine nominative plural relative pronoun *quae* in choice (C) is an inappropriate substitute

because it does not agree in number or gender with its masculine singular antecedent *nuntium*.

38. Choice (D) is the correct answer. It substitutes an active construction with complementary infinitive (*Dēbēō historiam legere*) for a passive periphrastic construction with dative of agent (*Historia mihi legenda est*) to express an unfulfilled obligation. The revised sentence and the original sentence both mean "I must read the story." Choices (A) and (C) are inappropriate substitutes because they each express a completed action ("My story has been read"; "I have read a story") rather than an unfulfilled obligation. Choice (B) is an inappropriate substitute because it expresses pleasure at an action ("I am pleased that a story is being read") rather than an unfulfilled obligation.

39. Choice (A) is the correct answer. Out of context, *aurea* (from *aureus*, *-a*, *-um*, meaning "golden") may be either feminine nominative singular, neuter nominative plural, or neuter accusative plural. However, in line 1 *aurea* functions as a subject complement to *Rōma*, the feminine nominative singular subject of the sentence, and so must itself be nominative singular. Choices (B) and (C) are incorrect because, as a subject complement to a singular noun, *aurea* cannot be plural. Choice (D) is incorrect because *aurea* (with short final *-a*) is not ablative in form. The clause in which *aurea* occurs may be translated "now Rome is golden."

40. Choice (A) is the correct answer. Line 1 is a dactylic hexameter and is scanned as follows:

— ∪∪|— ∪∪ |— ∪∪|— — |—∪∪| — —

Simplicitās rudis ante fuit: nunc aurea Rōma _ est.

Only one elision occurs in this line. The elision occurs in the sixth foot, where the final vowel (*-a*) of *Rōma* is elided before the initial vowel (*e-*) of *est*.

41. Choice (D) is the correct answer. The feminine accusative plural adjective *magnās* (from *magnus*, *-a*, *-um*, meaning "large, great") modifies the feminine accusative plural noun *opēs*. An accusative plural adjective cannot modify a nominative noun (*Simplicitās*) as in choice (A), a nominative adjective (*rudis*), as in choice (B), or a genitive noun (*orbis*), as in choice (C). The sentence in which *magnās* occurs may be translated "And it possesses the great wealth of the conquered world."

42. Choice (B) is the correct answer. The nominative singular noun *Rōma* in line 1 is understood to be the subject of the singular verb *possidet* in line 2. It makes sense that the city of Rome, described as golden in line 1, would in line 2 be said to possess the great wealth of the conquered world. Choices (A), (C), and (D) are incorrect because it does not make sense to say that simplicity (*Simplicitās*), the world (*orbis*), or wealth (*opēs*) possesses the great wealth of the conquered world.

43. Choice (B) is the correct answer. The noun phrase *domitī orbis* ("of the conquered world") is in the genitive case, modifying the noun phrase *magnās opēs* ("great wealth"), which is in the accusative case and functions as the direct object of the third-person singular verb *possidet* ("it possesses"). The whole clause is therefore appropriately translated "it possesses the great wealth of the conquered world." Choice (A) is incorrect because it misconstrues the genitive singular participle *domitī* as a plural noun: "the conquerers." Choice (C) is incorrect because it misconstrues the plural accusative noun phrase *magnās opēs* as the subject and the participle *domitī* as a finite verb: "great wealth conquers." Choice (D) is incorrect because it misconstrues the genitive noun *orbis* as the subject of the verb *possidet*: "the world possesses."

44. Choice (C) is the correct answer. *Aspice* is the second person singular present active imperative form of the verb *aspicere* ("to look at") and should therefore be translated by the imperative form "Look at." The imperative verb is misconstrued as infinitive ("to look at") in choice (A) and as declarative ("they look at," "he looks at") in choices (B) and (D). The clause in which *Aspice* occurs may be translated "Look at what the Capitoline temple buildings are now."

45. Choice (B) is the correct answer. The word *Capitōlia* serves as the subject of the plural verb *sunt* and must therefore be the nominative plural form of the second-declension neuter noun *Capitōlium*, which in both its singular and plural forms refers to the temple of Jupiter in Rome. Choices (A), (C), and (D) are incorrect because the noun *Capitōlia* is not singular in form and could not serve as the subject of the plural verb *sunt* if it were.

46. Choice (C) is the correct answer. Out of context, *illa* might be a nominative singular feminine pronoun, a nominative plural neuter pronoun, or an accusative plural neuter pronoun. However, in line 4 *illa* serves as the subject of the infinitive *fuisse* in indirect statement and must therefore be accusative. It is the accusative plural form of the neuter demonstrative pronoun *illud* and refers to the neuter plural noun *Capitōlia* in line 3. It therefore cannot be nominative singular as in choice (A), nominative plural as in choice (B), or ablative singular as in choice (D). The clause in which *illa* occurs may be translated "you will say that they were of another Jupiter."

47. Choice (B) is the correct answer. In indirect statement a perfect infinitive denotes a time prior to that denoted by the main verb. When the main verb is in a past tense, the perfect infinitive should be translated by a past perfect construction ("had been"), and when the main verb is in a present or future tense, the perfect infinitive should be translated by a simple past construction ("was" or "were"). In this case the main verb, *dīcēs,* is in the future tense, so the perfect infinitive *fuisse* should be translated by a simple past construction: "were." Instead of a simple past construction, choice (A) provides a simple present construction ("are"), choice (C) provides a future construction ("will be"), and choice (D) provides a future perfect construction ("will have been").

48. Choice (A) is the correct answer. The neuter nominative plural *Prīsca* ("ancient times") is the subject of *iuvent*, the third person plural present active subjunctive form of the verb *iuvere* ("to please"). Here *iuvent* functions as a jussive subjunctive, mandating that an action be performed by the referent of the subject. The words should therefore be translated "Let ancient times please." Instead of a clause of command, choice (B) presents a past conditional clause ("If ancient times pleased"), choice (C) presents a present declarative clause ("Ancient times please"), and choice (D) presents a future declarative clause ("Ancient times will please").

49. Choice (B) is the correct answer. Out of context, *mōribus* may be either the dative plural or the ablative plural form of the noun *mōs* ("custom," "way"). But because the adjective *apta* ("suited," "fitting") takes only a dative as complement, *mōribus* must be construed as dative. Choices (A) and (C) are incorrect because *mōribus* is neither genitive nor accusative in form. Choice (D) is incorrect because the adjective *apta* cannot take an ablative as complement.

50. Choice (C) is the correct answer. The feminine singular noun phrase *haec aetās* ("this age") is nominative and must therefore be the subject of the understood verb *est* ("is"). The feminine nominative singular adjective *apta* ("fitting") functions as subject complement and is itself complemented by the dative plural noun phrase *mōribus meīs* ("for my ways"). The whole clause should therefore be translated "this age [is] fitting for my ways." Choice (A) is incorrect because it misconstrues the dative noun *mōribus* as a subject and the plural adjective *meīs* as a singular pronoun: "these ways are suitable to me." Choice (B) is incorrect because it misconstrues the dative plural adjective *meīs* as modifying the nominative singular noun *aetās* and confuses the noun *mōribus* ("ways") with a form of the verb *morārī* ("to delay"): "my age makes me inclined to delay." Choice (D) is incorrect because it confuses the noun *mōribus* with a form of the verb *morārī* ("to delay") and misconstrues the dative plural adjective *meīs* as a singular direct object: "this time delays me."

51. Choice (B) is the correct answer. In lines 5-6 the poet says that he enjoys living in Rome at the present time, a city that he describes in line 2 as having become wealthy through conquest. This clearly implies praise for the wealth and power of Rome. Choice (A) is incorrect because no former leaders of Rome are mentioned in the passage. Choice (C) is incorrect because the simplicity of Roman life, mentioned in line 1, is associated with former times (*ante*), times that the poet in lines 5-6 says he is content to have missed. This implies not praise but criticism of the simple life. Choice (D) is incorrect because in lines 5-6 the poet implies that the good old ways (*Prīsca*) may be pleasing—and therefore praiseworthy—to others but not to himself.

52. Choice (B) is the correct answer. It is important to understand that, as frequently happens in Latin, *est* has been omitted from the clause *huic negōtium ab senātū datum*. The main verb is *datum est* ("was given"), the perfect passive of the verb *dō*. The word *negōtium* ("the task") therefore cannot be accusative and must be the nominative subject of *datum est*. The word *huic* is the dative singular of *hic, haec, hoc* ("he, she, it") and indicates the person to whom the task was given. The prepositional phrase *ab senātū* is translated "by the senate." Thus a correct translation of the entire clause is "the task was given to him by the senate." None of the other options represents a correct translation of these words.

53. Choice (A) is the correct answer. Lines 1–2 tell us that the people created a dictator (*Dictātōrem populus creāvit*) and that a task was given to him by the senate (*huic negōtium ab senātū datum*). The purpose for which the dictator was created is expressed by *ut mūrōs turrēsque urbis firmāret* ("that he should strengthen the walls and towers of the city"). The understood subject of the verb *firmāret* thus refers to *Dictātōrem* in the first line, not to *Hannibal* as in choice (B), *populus* as in choice (C), or *negōtium* as in choice (D).

54. Choice (D) is the correct answer. The third declension plural form *pontēs* ("bridges") can be either nominative or accusative. Because in this case the verb *dēlēret* is singular, the plural *pontēs* cannot be its nominative subject and therefore must be its accusative object. The clause *et pontēs flūminis dēlēret* means "and that he should destroy the river's bridges." The word *pontēs* is not nominative as in choice (A), genitive as in choice (B), or dative as in choice (C).

55. Choice (C) is the correct answer. The words *eī pugnandum erat* are part of a passive periphrastic construction in Latin, expressing obligation or necessity. The verb is *pugnandum erat* (literally "it had to be fought"); the pronoun *eī* is a dative of agent, expressing by whom it had to be fought ("by him"). The literal translation "it had to be fought by him" is more idiomatically expressed in English by "he had to fight." None of the other options correctly translates this clause.

56. Choice (D) is the correct answer. The clause *cum Italia dēfendī nōn posset* expresses the circumstances under which the fighting had to take place ("since Italy could not be defended"). In this case *cum* cannot mean "with," as in choice (A), because there is no ablative object of the preposition. Choice (B), "so that," and choice (C), "therefore," are not possible meanings of *cum*.

57. Choice (B) is the correct answer. It is stated in the passage that one of the reasons the dictator was elected was that he strengthen the walls and towers of the city (*ut mūrōs turrēsque urbis firmāret*). He was elected to destroy bridges, not to build them, as stated in choice (A), and was given a task by the senate but not asked to negotiate on its behalf, as indicated in choice (C). Choice (D) is incorrect because the dictator is trying to defend Italy, not to conquer it; Hannibal is the one seeking to conquer the country.

58. Choice (A) is the correct answer. The masculine singular noun *Hannibal* is the subject of the singular verb *vēnit* in the first sentence of the paragraph and the understood subject of the singular verb *incēpit* in the second sentence of the paragraph. It follows that *Hannibal* is likewise the understood subject of the singular verb *āvertit* in the third sentence of the paragraph and therefore modified by the masculine singular nominative participle *Repulsus* ("Having been driven back, repulsed"). The sentence tells us that Hannibal was driven back before he changed his course. Because it is masculine nominative, *Repulsus* cannot modify the feminine ablative *caede* in choice (B), the accusative *agrum* in choice (C), or the neuter accusative *iter* in choice (D).

59. Choice (C) is the correct answer. The preposition *in* with the accusative expresses motion toward, or "into." The prepositional phrase *in agrum* is therefore correctly translated "into the countryside." Choice (A) is incorrect because "in the countryside" is rendered in Latin by *in* plus the ablative, not the accusative. Choices (B) and (D) are incorrect because *in* cannot mean "through" or "around."

60. Choice (A) is the correct answer. In the second paragraph we learn from the ablative absolute *Vastātō agrō* ("The countryside having been destroyed") that Hannibal had destroyed the countryside before he attacked the city (*urbem oppugnāre incēpit*). Although the fortification of the city is mentioned in the first paragraph (*ut mūrōs turrēsque urbis firmāret*), we do not learn that Hannibal attacked before the city could be fortified (B). Likewise, we do not learn that he intended to complete his conquest of Italy (C), although the first paragraph mentions that Italy could not be defended (*cum Italia dēfendī nōn posset*). The second paragraph does not tell us that Hannibal intended to slaughter the entire population (D), but rather that Hannibal was pushed back by the great slaughter of his men (*Repulsus magnā caede suōrum*).

61. Choice (B) is the correct answer. *Corda* can be either the nominative or accusative plural form of the third declension neuter noun *cor, cordis* ("heart"). In this case, it must be the accusative object of the infinitive *habēre* in the indirect statement *Quintus Ennius tria corda habēre sēsē dīcēbat* ("Quintus Ennius said that he had three hearts"). Choices (A) and (C) are incorrect because *corda* is plural, not singular. Choice (D) is incorrect because *dīcēbat* requires a nominative singular subject and *corda* is plural.

62. Choice (B) is the correct answer. A present infinitive in indirect statement refers to the same time as that to which the main verb refers, and its translation must reflect this. In this case, the main verb is the imperfect *dicēbat* ("used to say, was saying, said"), referring to past time, so the present infinitive *habēre* likewise refers to past time and must therefore be translated by the past tense verb "had": "Quintus Ennius used to say that he had three hearts." It cannot be correctly translated by a present tense, as in choices (A) and (D). Choice (C) is incorrect because it is the translation of a participle and not of an infinitive in indirect statement.

63. Choice (C) is the correct answer. The reflexive pronoun *sēsē* refers to the subject of the sentence, *Quintus Ennius*, which is the name of a man. It must therefore be translated "he." It cannot be correctly translated by the neuter "it," as in choice (A), because Quintus Ennius was a male human. It cannot be correctly translated by the plural "they," as in choice (B), because Quintus Ennius was just one person. And it cannot be correctly translated by the possessive adjective "his," as in choice (D), because the translation requires a substantive (noun or pronoun) rather than an adjective.

64. Choice (D) is the correct answer. The long -*ē* ending of *Graecē*, *Oscē*, and *Latinē* is an adverbial ending. *Graecē*, *Oscē*, and *Latinē* are not possible adjective (A), noun (B), or pronoun (C) forms in Latin.

65. Choice (B) is the correct answer. The first sentence may be translated "Quintus Ennius said that he had three hearts, because he knew (how) to speak in Greek, Oscan, and Latin." This makes it clear that Quintus Ennius was able to speak several languages. Choice (A) is incorrect; because Quintus Ennius already spoke Oscan, it is incorrect to state that he "wanted to learn the Oscan language." Choice (C) is incorrect because according to the Latin it is the languages he knows, not the peoples. Choice (D) is incorrect because he actually stated that he had three hearts (which implies one for each language he spoke), not that he "had only the Latin language in his heart."

66. Choice (A) is the correct answer. The subject of the second sentence is *Mithridātēs*, which is modified by the appositive phrase *Pontī atque Bīthȳniae rex clārus* ("the

famous king of Pontus and Bithynia"). This appositive phrase is followed by the relative pronoun *quī* ("who"), which in this context can refer only to the king Mithridates, not to Pontus (B), Ennius (C), or Bithynia (D).

67. Choice (D) is the correct answer. The form *bellō* can be either dative or ablative singular; the verb *superātus est* ("was conquered") indicates that in this context *bellō* is ablative and describes the circumstances under which Mithridates was conquered: "in war." Choice (A), "war," is incorrect because it cannot modify a verb at all. Choices (B), "for war," and (C), "from war," are incorrect because they do not make sense as modifiers of the verb "was conquered."

68. Choice (B) is the correct answer. *Mithridātēs* is the subject of the main verb *scīvit* and the understood subject of the verb in the relative clause *quās sub diciōne habuit* ("which he had under [his] power"). Choice (A), *Ennius,* is a possible grammatical subject of *habuit* but can be eliminated by the context because Ennius is not mentioned after the first line; after mentioning Ennius, the paragraph goes on to discuss Mithridates. Choices (C), *Bīthȳniae,* and (D), *Pompēiō,* cannot grammatically be the subject of *habuit* because they are not nominative singular forms.

69. Choice (D) is the correct answer. A translation of *quinque et vīgintī gentium quās sub diciōne habuit linguās scīvit* is "knew the languages of 25 peoples whom he had under (his) power." The direct object of *scīvit* ("knew") is *linguās* ("languages"). Lines 4–5 tell us that what Mithridates knew were languages, as in choice (D), not people, as in choices (A) and (B), or nations, as in choice (C).

70. Choice (B) is the correct answer. Choices (A) and (B) are both possible meanings of *ut.* The important thing to notice here is that the verb in the *ut* clause, *appellātus est,* is in the indicative. Therefore, in this case *ut* cannot mean "in order that," as in choice (A), because it would have to be followed by a subjunctive verb. Choices (C), "because," and (D), "lest," are not possible meanings of *ut.*

71. Choice (B) is the correct answer. The clearest clue that choice (B) is the correct answer is that Mithridates is the only person mentioned in the passage who is described as a king (*rex,* line 3). *Ennius* (A) is not the name of a person who is described in this way, nor is choice *Pompēiō* (D). Choice (C), *Pontī,* is the name of a place, not a person, and therefore cannot be correct.

72. Choice (C) is the correct answer. In this context *quam* is to be taken as a conjunction in the comparative expression *nōn minus scītē quam* ("not less skillfully than"). It is not a relative pronoun meaning "which" (A), "whom" (B), or "who" (D).

73. Choice (A) is the correct answer. The clause *sī gentīlis eius (ejus) esset* may be translated "if he were his fellow countryman." Since *esset* is the imperfect subjunctive form, it cannot be translated "he had been," as in choice (B), which would require a pluperfect Latin verb. Choice (D), "he will be," would require a Latin verb in the future tense. The context "not less skillfully than if he were" (*nōn minus scītē quam sī . . . esset*) rules out choice (C), "he would be."

74. Choice (A) is the correct answer. The Latin cited in the question may be translated "immediately he spoke in the language and speech of that man not less skillfully than if he were his fellow countryman." Here Mithridates' skill in speaking a foreign language is being compared to that of a native of the country whose language Mithridates is speaking. Mithridates' language and oration are not being compared (B). The Latin does not state that Mithridates' "countrymen appreciated his skillful attempt" (C), but that Mithridates speaks as well as a native speaker of the language. Likewise, the Latin does not state that Mithridates "had never spoken the language of his countrymen" (D).

Chapter 15

Modern Hebrew

Purpose

The Subject Test in Modern Hebrew measures competence in Modern Hebrew and allows for variation in language preparation.

Format

This one-hour test consists of 85 multiple-choice questions. The test evaluates your mastery of vocabulary, structure, and reading comprehension through questions that require a wide-ranging knowledge of the language.

Content

The test evaluates reading ability in three areas:

Vocabulary questions test knowledge of words representing different parts of speech and some basic idioms within culturally authentic contexts.

Structure questions test grammar, including parts of speech, and your ability to recognize appropriate language patterns.

Reading comprehension questions test your understanding of passages of varying levels of difficulty. These passages, most of which are vocalized, are generally adapted from literary sources and newspaper or magazine articles. Authentic material such as advertisements have been added to the test. (A sample advertisement appears in the Sample Questions below.) While some passages have biblical references, no material in the test is written in biblical Hebrew.

Modern Hebrew	
Skills Measured	Approximate Percentage of Test
Vocabulary in Context	30%
Structure in Context (grammar)	30%
Reading Comprehension	40%

How to Prepare

The Subject Test in Modern Hebrew allows for variation in language preparation. It does not depend on any particular textbooks or methods of instruction. You should develop competence in Modern Hebrew over a period of years by taking two to four years of Modern Hebrew language study in high school or the equivalent. Familiarize yourself with the directions in advance. The directions in this book are identical to those that appear on the test.

Score

The total score is reported on the 200-to-800 scale.

Sample Questions

The three types of multiple-choice questions used in the test are:

- sentence completion questions
- paragraph completion questions
- questions based on a series of passages that test your understanding of those passages

Please note that your answer sheet has five answer positions, marked A, B, C, D, and E, while the questions throughout this test contain only four choices. Be sure not to make any marks in column E.

Part A—Sentence Completion

This type of question tests vocabulary mastery and requires the student to know the meaning of words and idiomatic expressions in context. Other sentence completion questions test mastery of structure and require students to identify usage that is structurally correct.

Directions: This part consists of a number of incomplete statements, each having four suggested completions. Select the most appropriate completion and fill in the corresponding circle on the answer sheet.

1. הוא בָּא מֵאֵירוֹפָּה וְקָשֶׁה לוֹ ______ לַחֹם בְּיִשְׂרָאֵל.

(A) לְהִתְרַגֵּל

(B) לְהִתְבַּיֵּשׁ

(C) לְהִשְׁתַּזֵּף

(D) לְהִתְיַבֵּשׁ

2. הַמִּשְׁפָּחָה שֶׁלָּנוּ ______ בִּכְפָר קָטָן.

(A) גָּרִים

(B) גָּרוֹת

(C) גָּרָה

(D) לָגוּר

Choice (A) is correct answer to question 1. This question tests how well you have mastered vocabulary. All four choices are verbs, but choice (A) is the only one which expresses idiomatically that it is difficult for the person to *get used* to the hot weather in Israel. The other choices are inappropriate verbs in this particular context.

Choice (C) is the correct answer to question 2. This question tests command of structure. To answer correctly you need to recognize correct noun-verb agreement. The noun *family* is feminine singular, and choice (C) is the feminine singular verb. The other options are verbs of the same root but do not agree with the noun.

Part B—Paragraph Completion

In paragraph completion questions, you are presented with a paragraph(s) from which words have been omitted. You must select the option that is most appropriate to the context. The main difference between sentence completion and paragraph completion is that the paragraph enables you to answer correctly based on the content of the entire passage rather than a single sentence.

Directions: In each of the following paragraphs there are numbered blanks indicating that words or phrases have been omitted. For each numbered blank, four completions are provided; only one is correct. First read through the entire passage. Then for each numbered blank, choose the completion that is most appropriate and fill in the corresponding circle on the answer sheet.

בְּלֵיל הַסֵּדֶר יָשַׁב סַבָּא בְּרֹאשׁ הַשֻּׁלְחָן
(3) ________כָּל בְּנֵי הַמִּשְׁפָּחָה.
אֲנַחְנוּ, הַנְּכָדִים הַצְּעִירִים, יָשַׁבְנוּ קָרוֹב
(4) ________, וְכָל אֶחָד מֵאִתָּנוּ
(5) ________ בְּיָדוֹ הַגָּדָה מְצֻיֶּרֶת.
כְּשֶׁסַּבָּא (6) ________ שֶׁכָּל אֶחָד
מֵהַיְלָדִים יִקְרָא שׁוּרוֹת (7) ________
מִן הַהַגָּדָה, (8) ________ לִפְתֹּחַ אֶת
הַסֵּפֶר שֶׁלִּי, וְקָרָאתִי בּוֹ בְּשֶׁקֶט לְעַצְמִי,
כְּדֵי שֶׁלֹּא (9) ________ כְּשֶׁיַּגִּיעַ תּוֹרִי.

3. (A) כְּשֶׁסְּבִיבוֹ
(B) כְּשֶׁעָלָיו
(C) כְּשֶׁבְּתוֹכוֹ
(D) כְּשֶׁבִּשְׁבִילוֹ

4. (A) מִמֶּנּוּ
(B) אֵלָיו
(C) שֶׁלּוֹ
(D) אוֹתוֹ

5. (A) הִשְׁמִיעַ
(B) הִבִּיט
(C) הִקְשִׁיב
(D) הֶחֱזִיק

6. (A) כִּבֵּד
(B) דִּבֵּר
(C) בִּקֵּשׁ
(D) סִפֵּר

7. (A) מְעַט
(B) אֲחָדוֹת
(C) קְצָת
(D) עֲשָׂרוֹת

8. (A) הִפְסַקְתִּי
(B) שָׁכַחְתִּי
(C) הִשְׁאַרְתִּי
(D) מִהַרְתִּי

9. (A) אֶטְעֶה
(B) טוֹעָה
(C) יִטְעֶה
(D) טָעִיתִי

Choice (A) is the correct answer to question 3. You must find the correct preposition among the four prepositions that appear with the masculine singular. Choice (A), meaning *around him,* is the only choice that fits in this context.

Choice (B) is the correct answer to question 4. This question tests another preposition. The children sat close to *him*.

Choice (D) is the answer to question 5. This is a vocabulary question, and you are to choose the answer that means *held.*

Choice (C) is the correct answer to question 6. It is the only verb that fits idiomatically in the sentence, "Grandfather *asked.*"

Choice (B) is the correct answer to question 7. In this question, you are to choose the correct adjective to describe the noun *lines*, which is feminine plural. Choice (B) meaning *several or a few* is the correct answer.

Choice (D) is the correct answer to question 8. This question tests vocabulary. You are to find the appropriate verb. The verb *I hurried* is the only option that can be used correctly in this context.

Choice (A) is the correct answer to question 9. In this question, you are to choose the right tense of the verb *to make a mistake, to err.* Choice (A) is future tense for first person singular.

Part C—Reading Comprehension

This part examines your ability to read passages representative of various styles and levels of difficulty. Each SAT Subject Test in Modern Hebrew has several prose passages followed by questions that test understanding. Some are short newspaper items and/or ads; some are textual passages, one of which is unvocalized. The passages are generally adapted from literary sources. Most of the questions focus on main and supporting ideas. These questions test whether you comprehend the main idea and some facts and details contained in the text. The ad and the passage that follow are samples of the material that appears in the test.

Directions: Read the following passages carefully for comprehension. Each is followed by a number of questions or incomplete statements. Select the completion or answer that is best according to the passage and fill in the corresponding circle on the answer sheet.

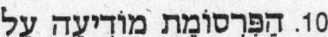

דרושים מורים למתמטיקה ולמדע לכיתות ה-ו,
לחצי משרה או למשרה מלאה.
דרישות: תואר ראשון בתחום מתאים,
ותעודת הוראה.
בית ספר תומר, רח׳ בן יהודה.
טלפון: 556677.

10. הַפִּרְסוֹמֶת מוֹדִיעָה עַל
(A) מוֹרִים שֶׁמְּחַפְּשִׂים עֲבוֹדָה
(B) מְקוֹמוֹת עֲבוֹדָה לְמוֹרִים
(C) סִפְרֵי לִמּוּד לְמָתֶמָטִיקָה וּמַדָּע
(D) תְּעוּדוֹת לְמוֹרִים

11. לְפִי הַפִּרְסוֹמֶת דְּרוּשִׁים
(A) מוֹרִים בְּאַרְצוֹת-הַבְּרִית
(B) כִּתּוֹת גְּדוֹלוֹת
(C) סִפְרֵי לִמּוּד
(D) בַּעֲלֵי תּוֹאַר רִאשׁוֹן

12. 556677 הוּא מִסְפַּר הַטֶּלֶפוֹן שֶׁל
(A) הַמּוֹרָה
(B) בֵּית סֵפֶר תּוֹמֶר
(C) בֶּן יְהוּדָה
(D) הַכִּתָּה

Questions 10–12 ask details about the advertisement.

Choice (B) is the correct answer to question 10. To answer this question, you need to know what is advertised in the ad. The correct answer is the school is looking for teachers.

Choice (D) is the correct answer to question 11. This question asks what are the requirements. Teachers holding a B.A. in Hebrew, their first academic degree, is correctly expressed in choice (D).

Choice (B) is the correct answer to question 12. This question checks if the reader understood whose phone number is given.

לְאַחֲרוֹנָה, הִתְחִילָה הַטֶּלֶוִיזְיָה הַיִּשְׂרְאֵלִית לְשַׁדֵּר כָּל יוֹם חֲדָשׁוֹת בַּשָּׂפָה הָאַנְגְּלִית. הַתָּכְנִית מְשֻׁדֶּרֶת בְּשָׁעָה שְׁמוֹנֶה בָּעֶרֶב וְהִיא נִמְשֶׁכֶת חֲמֵשׁ-עֶשְׂרֵה דַּקּוֹת. תָּכְנִית הַחֲדָשׁוֹת בְּאַנְגְּלִית זָכְתָה לְהַצְלָחָה גְּדוֹלָה מִשּׁוּם שֶׁהִיא מְשַׁדֶּרֶת אֶת הַחֲדָשׁוֹת בְּסִגְנוֹן אֲמֶרִיקָנִי וְיֵשׁ בָּהּ לְפָחוֹת עֲשָׂרָה נוֹשְׂאִים שׁוֹנִים.

קַרְיָנֵי-הַחֲדָשׁוֹת הֵם אֲנָשִׁים נְעִימִים עִם חִיּוּךְ עַל הַפָּנִים. בִּמְיֻחָד מָצְאָה-חֵן בְּעֵינֵי הַיִּשְׂרְאֵלִים הַקַּרְיָנִית סוּזָאן, יְלִידַת בּוֹסְטוֹן, בִּגְלַל סִגְנוֹנָהּ הַמְּיוּחָד. סוּזָאן שֶׁלָּמְדָה עִבְרִית בְּאַרְצוֹת-הַבְּרִית, בָּאָה לְיִשְׂרָאֵל לִשְׁנַת לִמּוּדִים וְהֶחְלִיטָה לְהִשָּׁאֵר. לְאַחַר שֶׁעָלְתָה לָאָרֶץ הִיא לָמְדָה תִּקְשֹׁרֶת בָּאוּנִיבֶרְסִיטָה הָעִבְרִית בִּירוּשָׁלַיִם.

13. אֵיךְ קִבְּלוּ הַיִּשְׂרְאֵלִים אֶת הַתָּכְנִית?

(A) הֵם הִתְנַגְּדוּ לִשְׂפַת-הַחֲדָשׁוֹת

(B) הֵם הִתְפַּלְּאוּ עַל שְׁעַת-הַחֲדָשׁוֹת

(C) הֵם בִּטְּלוּ אֶת הַתָּכְנִית

(D) הֵם קִבְּלוּ אוֹתָהּ בְּהִתְלַהֲבוּת

14. הַתָּכְנִית הִצְלִיחָה כִּי

(A) הָיְתָה עֲשִׁירָה וּמְעַנְיֶנֶת

(B) שֻׁדְּרָה פַּעֲמַיִם בְּיוֹם

(C) נֶעֶרְכָה עַל-יְדֵי הָאוּנִיבֶרְסִיטָה

(D) הַתִּקְשֹׁרֶת הָיְתָה טוֹבָה

15. מַדּוּעַ הִצְלִיחָה סוּזָאן כְּקַרְיָנִית?

(A) כִּי הִיא לָמְדָה עִבְרִית בְּאַרְצוֹת-הַבְּרִית

(B) כִּי הִיא הֶחְלִיטָה לַעֲלוֹת לְיִשְׂרָאֵל

(C) כִּי הִיא נוֹלְדָה בְּבוֹסְטוֹן

(D) כִּי הִגִּישָׁה יְדִיעוֹת בְּאֹפֶן מְעַנְיֵן

Questions 13–15 refer to the passage on the Israeli television's recently initiated news broadcast.

Choice (D) is the correct answer to question 13. This question asks how the Israelis accepted the new program. The passage describes the new program as having *gained much success*, thus choice (D) *they received it with enthusiasm* is the correct answer. The remaining three choices do not answer the question correctly.

Choice (A) is the correct answer to question 14. This question asks the reason for its success. *It was rich and interesting.* The passage describes the reason as: *It deals with at least ten different topics*. The other three choices are not the reasons for the program's success.

Choice (D) is the correct answer to question 15. This question asks the reason for the success of the broadcast's announcer. The correct answer is *She delivered the news in an interesting manner.* The passage talks about *her special style*. The other choices give additional details about her but are not the reason for her success.

Modern Hebrew Subject Test

Practice Helps

The test that follows is an actual, previously administered SAT Subject Test in Modern Hebrew. To get an idea of what it's like to take this test, practice under conditions that are much like those of an actual test administration.

- Set aside an hour when you can take the test uninterrupted.
- Sit at a desk or table with no other books or papers. Dictionaries, other books, or notes are not allowed in the test room.
- Tear out an answer sheet from the back of this book and fill it in just as you would on the day of the test. One answer sheet can be used for up to three Subject Tests.
- Read the instructions that precede the practice test. During the actual administration you will be asked to read them. before answering test questions.
- Time yourself by placing a clock or kitchen timer in front of you.
- After you finish the practice test, read the sections "How to Score the SAT Subject Test in Modern Hebrew" and "How Did You Do on the Subject Test in Modern Hebrew?"
- The appearance of the answer sheet in this book may differ from the answer sheet you see on test day.

MODERN HEBREW TEST

The top portion of the page of the answer sheet that you will use to take the Modern Hebrew Test must be filled in exactly as illustration below. When your supervisor tells you to fill in the circle next to the name of the test you are about to take, mark your answer sheet as shown.

○ Literature	○ Mathematics Level 1	○ German	○ Chinese Listening	○ Japanese Listening
○ Biology E	○ Mathematics Level 2	○ Italian	○ French Listening	○ Korean Listening
○ Biology M	○ U.S. History	○ Latin	○ German Listening	○ Spanish Listening
○ Chemistry	○ World History	● Modern Hebrew		
○ Physics	○ French	○ Spanish	**Background Questions:** ①②③④⑤⑥⑦⑧⑨	

After filling in the circle next to the name of the test you are taking, locate the Background Questions box on your answer sheet (as shown above). This is where you will answer the following Background Questions on your answer sheet.

BACKGROUND QUESTIONS

Please answer either Part I or Part II below by filling in the appropriate circle in the Background Questions box on your answer sheet. Fill in ONLY ONE circle, as described below, to indicate how you obtained your knowledge of Hebrew. The information you provide is for statistical purposes only and will not affect your test score.

Part I — If your knowledge of Hebrew comes primarily from any of the following: living in a home where Hebrew is the main spoken language, living for six months or longer in a Hebrew-speaking country that included significant experience in Hebrew language, courses taken at a college, or special study of Hebrew, fill in circle 9 and leave the remaining circles blank, regardless of how long you studied the subject in school.

Part II — If your knowledge of Hebrew comes primarily from courses taken in grades 9 through 12, fill in the circle that represents the total number of years you have studied Hebrew. Fill in only one of circles 1-7. (Leave circle 8 blank).

- Less than 2 years —Fill in circle 4.
- 2 to 2-1/2 years —Fill in circle 5.
- 3 to 3-1/2 years —Fill in circle 6.
- 4 years —Fill in circle 7.
- If you have studied Hebrew in a Jewish/Hebrew Day School up to the 8th grade only, —Fill in circle 1.
- If you have studied Hebrew in a Jewish/Hebrew Day School and less than 2 years in high school, —Fill in circle 2.
- If you have studied Hebrew in a Jewish/Hebrew Day School and 2 or more years of study beyond 8th grade, —Fill in circle 3.

When the supervisor gives the signal, turn the page and begin the Modern Hebrew Test. There are 100 numbered circles on the answer sheet and 85 questions in the Modern Hebrew Test. Therefore, use only circles 1 to 85 for recording your answers.

MODERN HEBREW TEST

PLEASE NOTE THAT YOUR ANSWER SHEET HAS FIVE ANSWER POSITIONS, MARKED A, B, C, D, AND E, WHILE THE QUESTIONS THROUGHOUT THIS TEST CONTAIN ONLY FOUR CHOICES. BE SURE NOT TO MAKE ANY MARKS IN COLUMN E.

Be sure to note that the questions are numbered on the RIGHT side of each column and begin on the RIGHT side of the page.

Part A

Directions: This part consists of a number of incomplete statements, each having four suggested completions. Select the most appropriate completion and fill in the corresponding circle on the answer sheet.

1. כַּאֲשֶׁר מְטַיְּלִים בִּירוּשָׁלַיִם ______ לְבַקֵּר גַּם בַּכְּנֶסֶת.

(A) יָכוֹל
(B) כְּדֵי
(C) כְּדַאי
(D) רוֹצֶה

2. חֲבֶרְתִּי הָאַרְכֵאוֹלוֹגִית ______ תַּפְקִיד חָשׁוּב בְּמַחְלֶקֶת הָעַתִּיקוֹת.

(A) הִתְקַבְּלָה
(B) מִתְקַבֶּלֶת
(C) קִבְּלָה
(D) מְקַבֶּלֶת

3. כַּאֲשֶׁר נוֹסְעִים בְּאוֹטוֹבּוּס מִתֵּל-אָבִיב לִירוּשָׁלַיִם, ______ בָּעִיר רַמְלָה.

(A) אוֹסְפִים
(B) עוֹבְרִים
(C) בּוֹדְקִים
(D) שׁוֹמְרִים

4. כָּל הַסְּפָרִים עַל הַנּוֹשֵׂא הַזֶּה ______ מֵהַסִּפְרִיָּה.

(A) נֶעֶלְמוּ
(B) נִכְנְסוּ
(C) נִקְרְעוּ
(D) נִרְשְׁמוּ

5. כַּאֲשֶׁר הִסְתַּיְּמָה הַמִּלְחָמָה, חָתְמוּ שְׁתֵּי הַמְּדִינוֹת עַל ______ שָׁלוֹם.

(A) עִתּוֹן
(B) הֶסְכֵּם
(C) הֶסְבֵּר
(D) סִפּוּר

6. אִם אַף אֶחָד לֹא רוֹצֶה לִקְרֹא אֶת הַסֵּפֶר הַזֶּה, אֲנִי ______ אוֹתוֹ לַסִּפְרִיָּה.

(A) הֶחְזַרְתִּי
(B) חוֹזֵר
(C) אֶחְזוֹר
(D) אַחְזִיר

GO ON TO THE NEXT PAGE

7. דִּינָה וְדַלְיָה הֶחְלִיטוּ ______ בְּכָל יוֹם שֵׁנִי.

(A) לִפְגֹּשׁ
(B) לְהִפָּגֵשׁ
(C) נִפְגְּשׁוּ
(D) פָּגְשׁוּ

8. אֲנָשִׁים רַבִּים חוֹשְׁבִים שֶׁלַּמֶּמְשָׁלָה אֵין זְכוּת ______ בְּעִנְיְנֵי הַפְּרָט.

(A) לְהִתְעָרֵב
(B) לְהִתְפַּלֵּא
(C) לְהִתְקַשֵּׁר
(D) לְהִתְעַשֵּׁר

9. הָרַעַשׁ בַּחוּץ הִפְרִיעַ לָנוּ ______ בַּלִּמּוּדִים.

(A) לִלְמֹד
(B) לִקְרֹא
(C) לְהִתְרַכֵּז
(D) לְהִתְגַּבֵּר

10. אֲנִי אֲנַסֶּה לְהַגִּיעַ לַמּוּזֵאוֹן מֻקְדָּם כְּדֵי לִקְנוֹת כַּרְטִיסֵי ______.

(A) שְׁמִירָה
(B) כְּנִיסָה
(C) סְגִירָה
(D) בְּחִירָה

11. נְשִׂיא מְדִינַת יִשְׂרָאֵל יְקַבֵּל בְּבֵיתוֹ ______ מִכָּל עֵדָה בְּיִשְׂרָאֵל לִכְבוֹד הַשָּׁנָה הַחֲדָשָׁה.

(A) נָצִיג
(B) נָבִיא
(C) שׁוֹפֵט
(D) שַׁלִּיט

12. הַאִם יֵשׁ ______ שֶׁתָּבוֹאִי לַמְּסִבָּה הָעֶרֶב ?

(A) שִׁנּוּי
(B) סִכּוּי
(C) חֵשֶׁק
(D) נִסָּיוֹן

13. דָּן נִרְאֶה הַיּוֹם בְּדִיּוּק כְּמוֹ שֶׁהָיָה נִרְאֶה לִפְנֵי עֶשְׂרִים שָׁנָה. הוּא בִּכְלָל לֹא ______.

(A) יִשְׁתַּנֶּה
(B) מְשַׁנֶּה
(C) שִׁנָּה
(D) הִשְׁתַּנָּה

14. בִּזְמַן חוּפְשַׁת הַקַּיִץ מַגִּיעִים לְנְיוּ-יוֹרְק תַּיָּרִים מֵאֲרָצוֹת ______.

(A) אַחֲרוֹנוֹת
(B) קוֹדְמוֹת
(C) רִאשׁוֹנוֹת
(D) שׁוֹנוֹת

GO ON TO THE NEXT PAGE

15. בְּכָל יוֹם הַמַּדְּעָנִים ______ מֵידָע חָדָשׁ בַּמֶּחְקָרִים שֶׁלָּהֶם.

(A) מְצַוִּים

(B) מְצַפִּים

(C) מְקַיְּמִים

(D) מְגַלִּים

16. יְרוּשָׁלַיִם הִיא עִיר מְפוּרְסֶמֶת בַּמְּקוֹמוֹת ______ שֶׁבָּהּ.

(A) הַקְּדוֹשׁוֹת

(B) קְדוֹשׁוֹת

(C) קְדוֹשִׁים

(D) הַקְּדוֹשִׁים

17. דִּינָה קָנְתָה אֶת הַסֵּפֶר, כִּי הִיא שָׁמְעָה ______ הַרְבֵּה דְּבָרִים טוֹבִים.

(A) מִמֶּנּוּ

(B) אֵלָיו

(C) אוֹתוֹ

(D) עָלָיו

18. בַּזְּמַן הָאַחֲרוֹן ______ הַמַּחְשֵׁב לִכְלִי חָשׁוּב וְשִׁמּוּשִׁי.

(A) לַהֲפוֹךְ

(B) הָפַךְ

(C) מִתְהַפֵּךְ

(D) יִתְהַפֵּךְ

19. הָעִיר ______ מְאֹד כִּי בָּאוּ לְשָׁם הַרְבֵּה תּוֹשָׁבִים חֲדָשִׁים.

(A) פִּתְּחָה

(B) הִתְפַּתְּחָה

(C) נִפְתְּחָה

(D) פָּתְחָה

20. הִיא הוֹדִיעָה לוֹ שֶׁאֵין לָהּ ______ לָצֵאת אִתּוֹ.

(A) תְּנַאי

(B) פְּנַאי

(C) עִתִּים

(D) זְמַנִּים

21. הָאוּנִיבֶרְסִיטָה הָעִבְרִית בִּירוּשָׁלַיִם ______ בִּשְׁנַת 1925 .

(A) נוֹלְדָה

(B) נוֹסְדָה

(C) נוֹסְפָה

(D) נוֹעֲדָה

22. ______ שֶׁיָּרְדוּ גְּשָׁמִים רַבִּים בַּשָּׁבוּעוֹת הָאַחֲרוֹנִים, עֲדַיִן קַיָּם מַחְסוֹר חָמוּר בְּמַיִם בְּרֹב חֶלְקֵי הָאָרֶץ.

(A) בִּגְלַל

(B) מִפְּנֵי

(C) לְעֻמַּת

(D) אַף-עַל-פִּי

GO ON TO THE NEXT PAGE

23. שָׂרָה ______ בְּסַבּוֹן מְיֻחָד, כִּי עוֹרָהּ רָגִישׁ.

(A) שִׁמְשָׁה

(B) לְהִשְׁתַּמֵּשׁ

(C) מִשְׁתַּמֶּשֶׁת

(D) מְשַׁמֶּשֶׁת

24. יוֹפִי הָאָרֶץ ______ אֵלֶיהָ מְבַקְּרִים רַבִּים.

(A) מוֹשֵׁךְ

(B) מַמְשִׁיךְ

(C) מוֹשֶׁכֶת

(D) מַמְשִׁיכָה

25. בַּבְּחִירוֹת הִצְבַּעְתִּי ______ הַנָּשִׂיא הֶחָדָשׁ.

(A) עַל

(B) אֶל

(C) בִּגְלַל

(D) בְּעַד

GO ON TO THE NEXT PAGE

Part B

Directions: In each of the following passages, there are numbered blanks indicating that words or phrases have been omitted. For each numbered blank, four completions are provided, of which only one is correct. First read through the entire passage. Then for each numbered blank, choose the completion that is most appropriate and fill in the corresponding circle on the answer sheet.

שְׁלוֹשָׁה אַחִים, רְאוּבֵן שִׁמְעוֹן וְדָנִי, בָּאוּ לְנְיוּ-יוֹרְק (26)______ בָּעִיר הַגְּדוֹלָה. הֵם שָׂכְרוּ חֶדֶר בַּקּוֹמָה הַשִּׁשִּׁים שֶׁל (27)______ גָּדוֹל. רְאוּבֵן נָתַן אֶת הַמַּפְתֵּחַ לְדָנִי וְאָמַר לוֹ (28) ______ הֵיטֵב עַל הַמַּפְתֵּחַ. אַחֲרֵי כֵן הֵם יָרְדוּ בַּמַּעֲלִית וְיָצְאוּ לְטַיֵּל בָּעִיר. הֵם טִיְּלוּ כָּל הַיּוֹם, וּכְשֶׁחָזְרוּ רָאוּ שֶׁהַמַּעֲלִית לֹא (29)______. הֵם הִתְחִילוּ לַעֲלוֹת בָּרֶגֶל לַקּוֹמָה הַשִּׁשִּׁים. רְאוּבֵן אָמַר: "יֵשׁ לִי (30)______ טוֹב. עַד הַקּוֹמָה הָעֶשְׂרִים אֲנִי אָשִׁיר שִׁירִים יָפִים. עַד הַקּוֹמָה הָאַרְבָּעִים שִׁמְעוֹן יְסַפֵּר (31) _____ מַצְחִיקִים, וְעַד הַקּוֹמָה הַשִּׁשִּׁים דָּנִי יְתָאֵר מִקְרִים עֲצוּבִים", וְכֻלָּם הִסְכִּימוּ. אֲבָל כְּשֶׁהִגִּיעַ תּוֹרוֹ שֶׁל דָּנִי הוּא אָמַר: "רַק דָּבָר עָצוּב אֶחָד קָרָה, (32) ______אֶת הַמַּפְתֵּחַ לְמַטָּה".

26. (A) לְבַקֵּר
(B) לִרְאוֹת
(C) לְחַפֵּשׂ
(D) לְהִסְתַּכֵּל

27. (A) מָלוֹן
(B) מָכוֹן
(C) בִּנְיָן
(D) מָדוֹר

28. (A) לִשְׁבֹּר
(B) לִזְרֹק
(C) לִכְתֹּב
(D) לִשְׁמֹר

29. (A) פּוֹעֶלֶת
(B) עוֹמֶדֶת
(C) נִקְשֶׁרֶת
(D) נִכְנֶסֶת

30. (A) הִגָּיוֹן
(B) חֲלוֹם
(C) רַעְיוֹן
(D) חֶשְׁבּוֹן

31. (A) חִבּוּרִים
(B) שִׁעוּרִים
(C) לִמּוּדִים
(D) סִפּוּרִים

32. (A) סָגַרְתִּי
(B) שָׁכַחְתִּי
(C) חָזַרְתִּי
(D) גָּמַרְתִּי

GO ON TO THE NEXT PAGE

בְּאֵיזוֹ שָׂפָה יְדַבְּרוּ ?

לִפְנֵי שָׁנָה טַנְיָה (33) ______ לָאָרֶץ מֵרוּסְיָה וְאָלֶכְּס בָּא מֵאַנְגְּלִיָּה. הֵם (34) ______ בְּיִשְׂרָאֵל וְהִתְחַתְּנוּ, וְעַכְשָׁו (35) ______ לָהֶם בַּת נֶחְמָדָה. בְּאֵיזוֹ שָׂפָה יְדַבְּרוּ אֶל הַתִּינֹקֶת ? דּוֹדָה אַחַת אוֹמֶרֶת שֶׁיְּדַבְּרוּ בְּאַנְגְּלִית כִּי זֹאת שָׂפָה חֲשׁוּבָה בָּעוֹלָם. דּוֹדָה אַחֶרֶת אוֹמֶרֶת שֶׁיְּדַבְּרוּ בְּרוּסִית, הֲרֵי (36) ______ מְאֹד שֶׁאִמָּא תְּדַבֵּר אֶל הַיַּלְדָּה בַּשָּׂפָה שֶׁלָּהּ. הִיא צְרִיכָה לָשִׁיר לָהּ שִׁירִים (37) ______ אוֹתָהּ אֶת הַמִּלִּים הָרִאשׁוֹנוֹת. הַדֶּרֶךְ הַטּוֹבָה בְּיוֹתֵר הִיא בַּשָּׂפָה הַטִּבְעִית שֶׁל הָאֵם. אֲבָל הֵם הֶחְלִיטוּ לֹא לְדַבֵּר בְּרוּסִית וְלֹא לְדַבֵּר בְּאַנְגְּלִית. הֵם עַכְשָׁו בְּיִשְׂרָאֵל וְהַיַּלְדָּה צְרִיכָה לִשְׁמֹעַ עִבְרִית מִן הַיּוֹם הָרִאשׁוֹן.

33. (A) עוֹלָה
(B) עָלְתָה
(C) עֲלִיָּה
(D) תַּעֲלֶה

34. (A) פָּגְשׁוּ
(B) יִפְגְּשׁוּ
(C) נִפְגְּשׁוּ
(D) יִפָּגְשׁוּ

35. (A) יָלְדָה
(B) הוֹלִידָה
(C) נוֹלֶדֶת
(D) נוֹלְדָה

36. (A) חָשׁוּב
(B) חָשְׁבוּ
(C) נֶחְשָׁב
(D) חֲשׁוּבָה

37. (A) וּלְלַמֵּד
(B) וְלִלְמֹד
(C) וְלִמְדָה
(D) וְלַמֵּד

GO ON TO THE NEXT PAGE

דִּינָה הִיא רַק בַּת עֶשֶׂר וְהִיא כְּבָר (38) ______ בָּאוּנִיבֶרְסִיטָה. בִּגְלַל גִּילָהּ הַצָּעִיר הִיא (39) ______ לַלִּמּוּדִים כָּל יוֹם כְּשֶׁאִמָּהּ (40)______ אוֹתָהּ.

לֹא כָּל הַסְּטוּדֶנְטִים הַמְּבֻגָּרִים (41)______ מִכָּךְ שֶׁיַּלְדָּה כָּל כָּךְ (42) ______לוֹמֶדֶת בְּאוֹתָהּ כִּתָּה אִתָּם. "אִם הִיא (43) ______ צִיּוּנִים יוֹתֵר טוֹבִים מִמֶּנִּי אֲנִי עוֹזֶבֶת אֶת הָאוּנִיבֶרְסִיטָה", אָמְרָה אַחַת הַסְּטוּדֶנְטִיּוֹת. "קָשֶׁה לִי (44)______ שֶׁיַּלְדָּה בַּת עֶשֶׂר לוֹמֶדֶת אִתִּי בְּאוֹתָהּ כִּתָּה וַאֲנִי בַּת עֶשְׂרִים", הִיא הוֹסִיפָה.

וְדִינָה אוֹמֶרֶת: "אֲנִי רוֹצָה (45)______ אֵלַי כְּמוֹ אֶל סְטוּדֶנְטִית רְגִילָה".

38. (A) לוֹמֶדֶת
(B) חוֹשֶׁבֶת
(C) לַמְדָנִית
(D) יַדְעָנִית

39. (A) מַצִּיעָה
(B) מַגִּיעָה
(C) מַבִּיעָה
(D) מוֹדִיעָה

40. (A) מְבִיאָה
(B) מַגִּישָׁה
(C) מַשְׁפִּיעָה
(D) מַחְלִיפָה

41. (A) רוֹצִים
(B) מְרוּצִים
(C) יִרְצוּ
(D) רָצוּ

42. (A) עֲשִׁירָה
(B) מְהִירָה
(C) צְעִירָה
(D) בְּהִירָה

43. (A) תְּקַבֵּל
(B) תְּסַפֵּר
(C) תְּחַבֵּר
(D) תְּתָאֵר

44. (A) לְהַחְלִיט
(B) לְהַזְמִין
(C) לְהַאֲמִין
(D) לְהַגְבִּיר

45. (A) שֶׁיִּשְׁמְעוּ
(B) שֶׁיִּתְיַחֲסוּ
(C) שֶׁיִּשְׁאֲלוּ
(D) שֶׁיִּתְבַּקְּשׁוּ

GO ON TO THE NEXT PAGE

הָעִיר רוֹמָא הָיְתָה (46) ______ בַּחֲכָמֶיהָ. אֶחָד מֵהֶם בָּא לִירוּשָׁלַיִם וְרָצָה לִבְחֹן אֶת חָכְמָתָם (47) ______ יַלְדֵי יְרוּשָׁלַיִם. הָלַךְ הָאִישׁ וּפָגַשׁ (48)______ יֶלֶד קָטָן. נָתַן לוֹ שְׁקָלִים אֲחָדִים וּבִקֵּשׁ (49)______ לִקְנוֹת בֵּיצִים וּגְבִינוֹת. קָנָה הַיֶּלֶד גְּבִינוֹת (50) ______ בֵּיצִים וְנָתַן לָאִישׁ. שָׁאַל אוֹתוֹ הָאִישׁ: ״הֲתוּכַל לְהַכִּיר אֵיזוֹ גְּבִינָה הִיא מֵעֵז לְבָנָה וְאֵיזוֹ מֵעֵז שְׁחוֹרָה?״ עָנָה לוֹ הַיֶּלֶד: ״אַתָּה (51)______ מִמֶּנִּי בְּשָׁנִים וּבְחָכְמָה; הַרְאֵה נָא לִי (52) ______ אֵיזוֹ בֵּיצָה הִיא שֶׁל תַּרְנְגֹלֶת לְבָנָה וְאֵיזוֹ שֶׁל שְׁחוֹרָה״.

46. (A) מְפַרְנֶסֶת
(B) מְפוּזֶּרֶת
(C) מְפַרְסֶמֶת
(D) מְפוּרְסֶמֶת

47. (A) שֶׁל
(B) עִם
(C) אֵצֶל
(D) אֶל

48. (A) בְּמַקְלוֹ
(B) בְּדַלְתּוֹ
(C) בִּדְבָרוֹ
(D) בְּדַרְכּוֹ

49. (A) לוֹ
(B) מִמֶּנּוּ
(C) אֵלָיו
(D) אֶצְלוֹ

50. (A) וּשְׁנֵי
(B) וּשְׁנַיִם
(C) וּשְׁתַּיִם
(D) וּשְׁתֵּי

51. (A) גָּדוֹל
(B) אָרֹךְ
(C) יָשָׁן
(D) עַתִּיק

52. (A) אֵיפֹה
(B) קוֹדֶם
(C) אֵיךְ
(D) לִפְנֵי

GO ON TO THE NEXT PAGE

אֲנַחְנוּ כָּל כָּךְ (53) ______ לִשְׁמוֹת הֶחֳדָשִׁים
בַּלּוּחַ הָעִבְרִי --תִּשְׁרֵי, חֶשְׁוָן, כִּסְלֵו, עַד שֶׁלִּפְעָמִים
אָנוּ (54) ______ שֶׁאֵלֶּה אֵינָם שֵׁמוֹת עִבְרִיִּים
(55)______ שֵׁמוֹת בַּבְלִיִּים (56) ______
לַלּוּחַ הָעִבְרִי בִּזְמַן שֶׁהָעָם יָשַׁב בַּגָּלוּת. בַּתַּנַ"ךְ
(57)______ שֵׁמוֹת אֲחֵרִים כְּמוֹ "יֶרַח זִיו" אוֹ
"הַחֹדֶשׁ הַשְּׁבִיעִי". נִשְׁאֶלֶת הַשְּׁאֵלָה אִם הָיָה
קַיָּם לוּחַ שָׁנָה קָדוּם.
בַּחֲפִירוֹת הָעִיר גֶּזֶר שֶׁבְּהָרֵי יְהוּדָה נִתְגַּלְּתָה
בִּשְׁנַת 1908 אֶבֶן (58) ______ חֲרוּטִים שֵׁמוֹת
שֶׁל שְׁמוֹנָה חֳדָשִׁים, וְזֶהוּ כַּנִּרְאֶה לוּחַ שָׁנָה עַתִּיק.
הַלּוּחַ הוּא מִתְּקוּפַת דָּוִד וּשְׁלֹמֹה. הַכְּתָב שֶׁבּוֹ
הִשְׁתַּמְּשׁוּ אָז בְּאֶרֶץ-יִשְׂרָאֵל הָיָה (59)______
לָעִבְרִים, לַכְּנַעֲנִים, לַמּוֹאָבִים וְלָאֲדוֹמִים.
הַלּוּחַ נִמְצָא כַּיּוֹם בְּמוּזֵאוֹן בְּטוּרְקִיָּה.

53. (A) רְגִילִים
(B) מְרֻגָּלִים
(C) מַרְגִּילִים
(D) מִתְרַגְּלִים

54. (A) שׁוֹמְרִים
(B) שׁוֹכְחִים
(C) שׁוֹפְטִים
(D) שׁוֹאֲלִים

55. (A) אֵלֶּה
(B) אִלּוּ
(C) אֶל
(D) אֶלָּא

56. (A) שֶׁהִתְכַּנְּסוּ
(B) שֶׁנִּכְנְסוּ
(C) שֶׁכִּנְּסוּ
(D) שֶׁנִּכְנָסִים

57. (A) נִזְכָּרִים
(B) נִזְכָּרוֹת
(C) מַזְכִּירוֹת
(D) זוֹכְרִים

58. (A) שֶׁאֵלֶיהָ
(B) שֶׁאֶצְלָהּ
(C) שֶׁעָלֶיהָ
(D) שֶׁבִּגְלָלָהּ

59. (A) מִשְׁתַּתֵּף
(B) שׁוּתָף
(C) מְשֻׁתָּף
(D) הִשְׁתַּתֵּף

GO ON TO THE NEXT PAGE

Part C

Directions: Read the following passages carefully for comprehension. Each passage is followed by a number of questions or incomplete statements. Select the answer or completion that is best according to the passage and fill in the corresponding circle on the answer sheet.

הַמַּשְׁקֶה הָאֲמֶרִיקָאִי קוֹקָה-קוֹלָה מוּכָּר בְּכָל הָעוֹלָם, מוּכָּר כִּמְעַט יוֹתֵר מֵאֲמֶרִיקָה עַצְמָהּ. אֲבָל לֹא יָדוּעַ שֶׁהֵכִינוּ וּמָכְרוּ אֶת הַכּוֹס הָרִאשׁוֹנָה שֶׁל קוֹקָה-קוֹלָה בְּבֵית הַמִּרְקַחַת שֶׁל יְהוּדִי אֲמֶרִיקָאִי בְּשֵׁם יוֹסֵף גֵ׳ייקוֹבְּס (Jacobs). אֶת הַמַּשְׁקֶה הִמְצִיא רוֹקֵחַ בְּשֵׁם פֶּמְבֶּרְטוֹן (Pemberton), אֲבָל לֹא הָיָה לוֹ כֶּסֶף אוֹ מָקוֹם לְיַצֵּר אוֹתוֹ. גֵ׳ייקוֹבְּס הִצְטָרֵף אֵלָיו וְהֵם הִתְחִילוּ לְיַצֵּר קוֹקָה-קוֹלָה בַּמַּרְתֵּף שֶׁל בֵּית הַמִּרְקַחַת שֶׁל גֵ׳ייקוֹבְּס.

כְּדַאי לְצַיֵּן שֶׁבַּיָּמִים הָהֵם נָהֲגוּ לִמְכֹּר בְּבָתֵּי מִרְקַחַת לֹא רַק תְּרוּפוֹת אֶלָּא גַּם אוֹכֶל קַל וּשְׁתִיָּה. בַּהַתְחָלָה הַטַּעַם שֶׁל הַמַּשְׁקֶה הָיָה מַר וְלֹא צִפּוּ לְהַצְלָחָתוֹ. לָכֵן מָכַר מַר גֵ׳ייקוֹבְּס אֶת חֶלְקוֹ בָּעֵסֶק. לְעֻמַּת זֹאת מַר פֶּמְבֶּרְטוֹן הִמְשִׁיךְ לְפַתֵּחַ אֶת הָעֵסֶק. הוּא הוֹסִיף סֻכָּר וְאָרַז אֶת הַמַּשְׁקֶה בְּבַקְבּוּק מְיֻחָד, וְעַד מְהֵרָה כָּבְשָׁה הַקּוֹקָה-קוֹלָה אֶת הָעוֹלָם וְהִיא נִמְכֶּרֶת בְּהַצְלָחָה רַבָּה עַד הַיּוֹם הַזֶּה.

60. לְפִי הַקֶּטַע, בְּבֵית מִרְקַחַת אֲמֶרִיקָאִי אִי אֶפְשָׁר הָיָה לִקְנוֹת

(A) תְּרוּפוֹת

(B) דִּבְרֵי אוֹכֶל

(C) מַשְׁקָאוֹת קַלִּים

(D) צַעֲצוּעִים

61. מַדּוּעַ לֹא זָכָה הַמַּשְׁקֶה לְהַצְלָחָה בַּהַתְחָלָה?

(A) לֹא הָיְתָה פִּרְסֹמֶת טוֹבָה

(B) הָיָה מָתוֹק מִדַּי

(C) הוּא לֹא הָיָה טָעִים

(D) הוּא נִמְכַּר בְּבֵית מִרְקַחַת

62. יוֹסֵף גֵ׳ייקוֹבְּס הִפְסִיד אֶת הַהִזְדַּמְּנוּת

(A) לְהַצְלִיחַ בַּעֲסָקִים

(B) לְטַיֵּל בָּעוֹלָם

(C) לַעֲבֹד בְּבֵית מִרְקַחַת

(D) לִמְכֹּר מַשְׁקָאוֹת

GO ON TO THE NEXT PAGE

מַרְטִין לוּתֶר קִינְג הַשְּׁלִישִׁי, בְּנוֹ שֶׁל הַמַּנְהִיג הַשָּׁחוֹר הַמְּפֻרְסָם, בִּקֵּר לָאַחֲרוֹנָה בְּיִשְׂרָאֵל, כְּדֵי לְהַכִּיר אֶת הַמַּצָּב בָּאָרֶץ. הַבִּקּוּר נֶעֱרַךְ בְּהַזְמָנַת אִרְגּוּן "בְּנֵי בְּרִית".

הוּא טִיֵּל בָּאָרֶץ בְּמֶשֶׁךְ שְׁמוֹנָה יָמִים וְנִפְגַּשׁ עִם שָׁמִיר, פֶּרֶס וּפְעִילִים לְמַעַן זְכֻיּוֹת הָאֶזְרָח שֶׁל יְהוּדֵי רוּסְיָה. הוּא נָטַע עֵץ בַּיַּעַר הַנּוֹשֵׂא אֶת שֵׁם אָבִיו, בְּאֵזוֹר הַגָּלִיל.

"עֵץ זֶה", אָמַר הַבֵּן, "מְסַמֵּל אֶת הֶמְשֵׁךְ מִפְעָלוֹ שֶׁל אָבִי".

63. לְפִי הַקֶּטַע, מַרְטִין לוּתֶר קִינְג הַשְּׁלִישִׁי בָּא לְיִשְׂרָאֵל כְּדֵי

(A) לְקַיֵּם אֶת הַבְטָחָתוֹ לְאָבִיו
(B) לְבַקֵּר בְּהָרֵי הַגָּלִיל
(C) לִפְגֹּשׁ מַנְהִיגִים יִשְׂרְאֵלִיִּים
(D) לִלְמֹד עַל הַחַיִּים בְּיִשְׂרָאֵל

64. הוּא נָטַע עֵץ בְּיַעַר

(A) "מִפְעַל הַגָּלִיל"
(B) "מַרְטִין לוּתֶר קִינְג"
(C) "בְּנֵי בְּרִית"
(D) "יַהֲדוּת רוּסְיָה

65. מַה מְסַמֵּל הָעֵץ שֶׁהוּא נָטַע ?

(A) אֶת מְדִינַת יִשְׂרָאֵל
(B) אֶת חֲלוֹמוֹ שֶׁל אָבִיו
(C) אֶת יְהוּדֵי אַרְצוֹת הַבְּרִית
(D) אֶת עֲבוֹדַת "בְּנֵי בְּרִית"

GO ON TO THE NEXT PAGE

משה ושרה כהן
מודיעים בשמחה על הולדת התאומים
אחים לרחל
הברית תתקיים ביום ג׳, 12 בספטמבר 1995
בשעה 10 לפנה״צ בביתנו
ברחוב קפלן 5, קרית שמונה
נשמח לראותכם

66. על מה המודעה ?

(A) על חגיגת יום הולדת
(B) על הולדת שני בנים
(C) על חגיגת אירוסין
(D) על חגיגה לרחל

67. לאן מוזמנים האורחים ?

(A) לבית משפחת כהן
(B) לבית משפחת קפלן
(C) לבית החולים
(D) לבית של רחל

GO ON TO THE NEXT PAGE

TA TEL-AVIV

שרות מוניות תל-אביב

הראשון, הגדול והפעיל ביותר בניו-יורק

מחפש נהגים מקצועיים, זהירים ומנומסים,

בעלי רכב חדיש.

* שעות עבודה - **24** שעות ביממה
* קהל לקוחות גדול
* הנהלה בעלת נסיון וידע מקצועי
* הכנסה גבוהה

בדבר פרטים נא לפנות ישירות לכתובתנו:

139 1st Ave (bet. 8-9 St)

לבקש את יונתן או חגית.

68. מי מתבקש לענות למודעה ?

(A) שירות מוניות
(B) נוסעים לתל-אביב
(C) נהגים
(D) לקוחות

69. מה מבטיחה המודעה ?

(A) משכורת טובה
(B) מכוניות חדשות
(C) נסיון מעניין
(D) עבודה קלה

GO ON TO THE NEXT PAGE

האם המחשב שלך דובר עברית?

עכשיו יוכלו ילדיך ללמוד עברית בקלות ובכיף

אליעזר בן יהודה (הנכד) מלמד בעזרת המחשב כיצד לדבר, לקרוא ולכתוב עברית.
התוכנה צבעונית ומעניינת ומתאימה את עצמה לקצב האישי של התלמיד.

אין צורך בקלטות, ספרים או וידיאו. המחשב עושה הכל עבור $99.95

אפשר לרכוש דיסק ללימוד לבר-מצווה

התקשר 1-800-555-4242
24 שעות ביממה

(24 Hours)

ILV SOFTWARE

70. מה מציעה המודעה?
(A) קלטות בעברית
(B) וידיאו בעברית
(C) תוכנה שמלמדת עברית
(D) מחשב שמלמד לבר-מצוה

71. לפי המודעה, כדי להשתמש בתוכנה צריך
(A) לקרוא ספרים
(B) מכשיר וידיאו
(C) רק מחשב
(D) להכיר את בן יהודה

GO ON TO THE NEXT PAGE

זְקֵנָה אַחַת, מִזְּקֵנוֹת הָעִיר צְפַת, נִפְטְרָה לִפְנֵי כַּמָּה יָמִים. הִיא בִּקְּשָׁה לְהִקָּבֵר בְּבֵית-הַקְּבָרוֹת הַיָּשָׁן שֶׁל צְפַת, לְיַד קֶבֶר בִּתָּהּ, שֶׁמֵּתָה לִפְנֵי שְׁלוֹשִׁים וְשֵׁשׁ שָׁנִים.

אַנְשֵׁי "חֶבְרָה קַדִּישָׁא" לֹא הִסְכִּימוּ לִקְבֹּר שָׁם אֶת הָאִשָּׁה, מִפְּנֵי שֶׁלֹּא קוֹבְרִים יוֹתֵר בְּבֵית-הַקְּבָרוֹת הַיָּשָׁן.

בְּנֵי מִשְׁפַּחְתָּהּ שֶׁל הַזְּקֵנָה אָמְרוּ, שֶׁהִיא קָנְתָה אֶת חֶלְקַת הַקֶּבֶר לִפְנֵי שְׁלוֹשִׁים שָׁנָה, וּבִקְּשָׁה מֵהֶם לִקְבֹּר אוֹתָהּ רַק שָׁם. לֹא הָיוּ לָהֶם הוֹכָחוֹת בִּכְתָב, אַךְ הָיְתָה לָהֶם הוֹכָחָה אַחֶרֶת: כַּאֲשֶׁר קָנְתָה הָאִשָּׁה אֶת הַקֶּבֶר, הִיא הֶחְבִּיאָה בְּתוֹכוֹ בַּקְבּוּק שֶׁמֶן כְּסִימָן שֶׁזֶּה הַקֶּבֶר שֶׁקָּנְתָה.

אַנְשֵׁי "חֶבְרָה קַדִּישָׁא" שָׁמְעוּ אֶת הַדְּבָרִים וְאָמְרוּ שֶׁיְּחַפְּשׂוּ אֶת הַבַּקְבּוּק. אִם הֵם יִמְצְאוּ אֶת הַבַּקְבּוּק בַּקֶּבֶר יִהְיֶה זֶה סִימָן שֶׁהַקֶּבֶר שַׁיָּךְ לַזְּקֵנָה וְהִיא תִּקָּבֵר בַּחֶלְקָה. לְאַחַר חִפּוּשִׂים הֵם מָצְאוּ אֶת הַבַּקְבּוּק. הָאִשָּׁה נִקְבְּרָה כְּפִי שֶׁבִּקְּשָׁה, לְיַד קֶבֶר בִּתָּהּ, וּבְנֵי הַמִּשְׁפָּחָה לָקְחוּ אִתָּם אֶת בַּקְבּוּק הַשֶּׁמֶן כִּסְגֻלָּה לְרִפּוּי מַחֲלוֹת.

72. מַדּוּעַ רָצְתָה הַזְּקֵנָה לְהִקָּבֵר דַּוְקָא בְּאוֹתוֹ מָקוֹם ?

(A) כִּי בַּעְלָהּ נִקְבַּר בְּבֵית הַקְּבָרוֹת הַיָּשָׁן

(B) בִּגְלַל הַקִּרְבָה לְקֶבֶר אֶחָד מִיְּלָדֶיהָ

(C) בִּגְלַל הַקִּרְבָה לְבֵיתָהּ בִּצְפַת

(D) כִּי הִיא אָהֲבָה אֶת בֵּית הַקְּבָרוֹת הַיָּשָׁן

73. מַדּוּעַ הָיוּ לַמִּשְׁפָּחָה קְשָׁיִים ?

(A) כִּי עַכְשָׁו קוֹבְרִים בְּבֵית הַקְּבָרוֹת הֶחָדָשׁ

(B) כִּי לֹא הָיָה לָהֶם כֶּסֶף לִקְבוּרָה

(C) כִּי בַּקְבּוּק הַשֶּׁמֶן אָבַד

(D) כִּי לֹא מָצְאוּ אֶת קִבְרָהּ שֶׁל הַבַּת

74. מָה עָשְׂתָה הַזְּקֵנָה בְּבַקְבּוּק הַשֶּׁמֶן ?

(A) הִיא הִשְׁתַּמְּשָׁה בּוֹ כְּדֵי לְרַפֵּא אֶת בִּתָּהּ.

(B) הִיא שָׁמְרָה אוֹתוֹ כְּדֵי שֶׁיִּקְבְּרוּ אוֹתוֹ.

(C) הִיא קָבְרָה אוֹתוֹ בַּחֲצַר בֵּיתָהּ.

(D) הִיא שָׂמָה אוֹתוֹ בְּתוֹךְ הַקֶּבֶר.

75. הַשֵּׁם הַמַּתְאִים בְּיוֹתֵר לַסִּפּוּר הוּא

(A) הַהִיסְטוֹרְיָה שֶׁל צְפַת

(B) בִּקּוּר קְרוֹבֵי הַמִּשְׁפָּחָה

(C) תְּמוּנַת בַּקְבּוּק הַשֶּׁמֶן

(D) הַסִּימָן שֶׁעָזַר

GO ON TO THE NEXT PAGE

הַזַּמֶּרֶת שׁוּלִי נָתָן

שְׁמָהּ הָיָה פַּעַם שׁוּלָה בָּאוּרְפְרוֹיְנְד. כְּשֶׁהָיְתָה לְזַמֶּרֶת בִּקְּשׁוּ מִמֶּנָּה לְהַחְלִיף אֶת שְׁמָהּ לְשֵׁם עִבְרִי פָּשׁוּט, וְאָז הִיא בָּחֲרָה בַּשֵּׁם נָתָן, שֶׁהוּא שֵׁם הַמִּשְׁפָּחָה שֶׁל אִמָּהּ, חַוָּה נָתָן.

הַשִּׁיר שֶׁבִּזְכוּתוֹ הָפְכָה שׁוּלִי נָתָן לְזַמֶּרֶת מְפֻרְסֶמֶת אַחֲרֵי מִלְחֶמֶת שֵׁשֶׁת הַיָּמִים, הוּא "יְרוּשָׁלַיִם שֶׁל זָהָב", אוּלַי הַשִּׁיר הַמְּפֻרְסָם בְּיוֹתֵר אַחֲרֵי "הַתִּקְוָה". הָיוּ אֲפִילוּ כָּאֵלֶּה שֶׁהִצִּיעוּ לַהֲפֹךְ אוֹתוֹ לַהִמְנוֹן הַלְּאֻמִּי בִּמְקוֹם "הַתִּקְוָה". בַּשָּׁנִים הָאַחֲרוֹנוֹת לֹא שָׁמַעְנוּ מִמֶּנָּה שִׁירִים חֲדָשִׁים. אֲבָל לָאַחֲרוֹנָה הִיא הִתְחִילָה שׁוּב לְהוֹפִיעַ עַל בָּמוֹת קְטַנּוֹת וְגַם קִבְּלָה הַזְמָנוֹת לְהוֹפִיעַ בְּחוּץ לָאָרֶץ. הִיא הוֹצִיאָה לֹא מִזְּמַן שְׁתֵּי קַלָּטוֹת וּבָהֶן שִׁירִים חֲדָשִׁים וּמְחֻדָּשִׁים.

שׁוּלִי חַיָּה עִם בַּעֲלָהּ וַחֲמֵשֶׁת יַלְדֵיהֶם. שׁוּלִי מַסְבִּירָה: "בְּמֶשֶׁךְ שְׁמוֹנֶה שָׁנִים גִּדַּלְתִּי אֶת יְלָדַי וְהָיִיתִי כָּל כָּךְ מְאֻשֶּׁרֶת שֶׁהַשִּׁירָה וְהַהוֹפָעוֹת כְּאִלּוּ נִשְׁכְּחוּ מִמֶּנִּי. אֲבָל לִפְנֵי שְׁנָתַיִם, בַּיּוֹם שֶׁלָּקַחְתִּי אֶת בְּנִי בֶּן הַשְּׁנָתַיִם לְגַן הַיְּלָדִים, חָזַרְתִּי הַבַּיְתָה וּבְלִי לְהַרְגִּישׁ הוֹצֵאתִי אֶת הַגִּיטָרָה מֵחֲדַר הַשֵּׁנָה וְהִתְחַלְתִּי לָשִׁיר".

מַה דַּעְתָּהּ שֶׁל שׁוּלִי עַל הַצְלָחַת הַשִּׁיר "יְרוּשָׁלַיִם שֶׁל זָהָב"? תְּשׁוּבָתָהּ: "עַד הַיּוֹם לֹא נוֹתְנִים לִי לָרֶדֶת מִשּׁוּם בָּמָה, בָּאָרֶץ אוֹ בְּחוּץ לָאָרֶץ, בְּלִי לָשִׁיר גַּם אֶת "יְרוּשָׁלַיִם שֶׁל זָהָב". זֶה לִפְעָמִים מַפְרִיעַ לִי, וַאֲנִי רוֹצָה לוֹמַר לָאֲנָשִׁים: - יֵשׁ לִי עוֹד שִׁירִים - עִם זֹאת כָּל כָּךְ הַרְבֵּה דְּלָתוֹת נִפְתְּחוּ בִּפְנֵי הוֹדוֹת לַשִּׁיר הַזֶּה, שֶׁאֲנִי מַרְגִּישָׁה אֶת עַצְמִי מְבֹרֶכֶת".

"הַאִם אַתְּ מְחַכָּה לְעוֹד אֵיזֶה "יְרוּשָׁלַיִם שֶׁל זָהָב"?

"בִּכְלָל לֹא" עוֹנָה שׁוּלִי.

76. לָמָּה שׁוּלִי שִׁנְּתָה אֶת שֵׁם מִשְׁפַּחְתָּהּ?

(A) כִּי הוּא הָיָה שֵׁם נְעוּרִים

(B) כִּי הִיא לֹא אָהֲבָה אוֹתוֹ

(C) כִּי אִמָּהּ בִּקְּשָׁה מִמֶּנָּה לְשַׁנּוֹת אוֹתוֹ

(D) כִּי שֵׁם קַל וְקָצָר חָשׁוּב לְפִרְסוּם

77. הַשִּׁיר "יְרוּשָׁלַיִם שֶׁל זָהָב" הָפַךְ

(A) לְהִמְנוֹן שֶׁל מְדִינַת יִשְׂרָאֵל

(B) לְשִׁיר יוֹתֵר מְפֻרְסָם מֵ"הַתִּקְוָה"

(C) לְשִׁיר מְפֻרְסָם כִּמְעַט כְּמוֹ "הַתִּקְוָה"

(D) לְשִׁיר מְפֻרְסָם רַק בְּחוּץ לָאָרֶץ

78. שׁוּלִי הִפְסִיקָה לָשִׁיר בְּמֶשֶׁךְ מִסְפַּר שָׁנִים כִּי

(A) הָיְתָה עֲסוּקָה בְּטִפּוּל בִּילָדֶיהָ

(B) הָיְתָה בְּחוּץ לָאָרֶץ וְלֹא הָיָה לָהּ זְמַן

(C) כֻּלָּם הִכִּירוּ אֶת הַשִּׁיר "יְרוּשָׁלַיִם שֶׁל זָהָב"

(D) הַקָּהָל לֹא אָהַב אֶת הַשִּׁירִים שֶׁלָּהּ

79. מָתַי חָזְרָה שׁוּלִי לָשִׁיר?

(A) אַחֲרֵי שֶׁהָיוּ לָהּ שְׁנֵי יְלָדִים

(B) אַחֲרֵי שֶׁשִּׁנְּתָה אֶת שְׁמָהּ

(C) כְּשֶׁבַּעֲלָהּ בִּקֵּשׁ מִמֶּנָּה

(D) כְּשֶׁבְּנָהּ הַצָּעִיר הָלַךְ לְגַן יְלָדִים

80. אֵיךְ הִשְׁפִּיעַ הַשִּׁיר "יְרוּשָׁלַיִם שֶׁל זָהָב" עַל שׁוּלִי?

(A) עָזַר לָהּ לְהִתְפַּרְסֵם

(B) גָּרַם לָהּ לְהַפְסִיק לָשִׁיר

(C) גָּרַם לָהּ לְחַכּוֹת לְשִׁירִים דּוֹמִים

(D) עָזַר לָהּ בְּגִדּוּל יְלָדֶיהָ

GO ON TO THE NEXT PAGE

אורן ואילן היו חברים טובים. הם למדו יחד ועזרו זה לזה בהכנת השיעורים. הם גם שיחקו ביחד בשכונה. בגלל החבירות שביניהם גם ההורים התידדו ובילו ביחד בחגים ובשמחות. יום אחד אורן ואילן רבו, וכשהלכו הביתה סיפרו להוריהם על הריב שהיה ביניהם. גם ההורים הצטרפו למריבה ולא דיברו ביניהם.

עבר זמן, הילדים השלימו והמשיכו להיות חברים טובים, אך ההורים היו עדיין ברוגז. השכנים התפלאו שההורים עדיין כעסו גם אחרי שהילדים השלימו ביניהם. כל משפחה חיכתה שהשנייה תעשה את הצעד הראשון להשלים.

לפני ראש השנה, כשכל אדם עושה את חשבון הנפש שלו, חשבו ההורים על הריב שהיה ביניהם וחיפשו דרך לחדש את יחסי החבירות. בערב יום הכיפורים, בדיוק באותו זמן, יצאו ההורים מביתם לכיוון בית חבריהם. באמצע הדרך ניפגשו שתי המשפחות, התחבקו בשמחה ואיחלו זו לזו שנה טובה, שנת אושר ושלום. הילדים שהיו בדרכם לבית הכנסת, שמעו את הברכות וענו "אמן".

81. איך נוצר הקשר בין המשפחות ?

(A) האימהות היו אחיות

(B) הן גרו באותה עיר

(C) היו להן אותם שכנים

(D) הבנים היו ידידים

82. שתי המשפחות

(A) עבדו באותו בית

(B) חגגו ביחד

(C) נסעו יחד לחופשה

(D) רבו בזמן החג

83. המשפחות רבו ביניהן כי

(A) כל אחת רצתה אותו תפקיד

(B) שני הבנים רצו את המתנה

(C) היה ריב בין שני הבנים

(D) השכנים כעסו על הבנים

84. מדוע לא השלימו שתי המשפחות ביניהן ?

(A) אף אחת לא רצתה לוותר

(B) אף אחת לא רצתה בשלום

(C) כי הבנים עדיין כעסו

(D) כי זה לא היה חשוב

85. מה אפשר ללמוד מהסיפור הזה ?

(A) שצריך להתערב בחיי הילדים

(B) שלא צריך לוותר לשכנים

(C) שצריך להיות עקשן

(D) שצריך לסלוח זה לזה

STOP

IF YOU FINISH BEFORE TIME IS CALLED, YOU MAY CHECK YOUR WORK ON THIS TEST ONLY. DO NOT TURN TO ANY OTHER TEST IN THIS BOOK.

How to Score the SAT Subject Test in Modern Hebrew

When you take an actual SAT Subject Test in Modern Hebrew, your answer sheet will be "read" by a scanning machine that will record your response to each question. Then a computer will compare your answers with the correct answers and produce your raw score. You get one point for each correct answer. For each wrong answer, you lose one-third of a point. Questions you omit (and any for which you mark more than one answer) are not counted. This raw score is converted to a scaled score that is reported to you and to the colleges you specify.

Worksheet 1. Finding Your Raw Test Score

STEP 1: Table A on the following page lists the correct answers for all the questions on the Subject Test in Modern Hebrew that is reproduced in this book. It also serves as a worksheet for you to calculate your raw score.

- Compare your answers with those given in the table.
- Put a check in the column marked "Right" if your answer is correct.
- Put a check in the column marked "Wrong" if your answer is incorrect.
- Leave both columns blank if you omitted the question.

STEP 2: Count the number of right answers.

Enter the total here: ______________

STEP 3: Count the number of wrong answers.

Enter the total here: ______________

STEP 4: Multiply the number of wrong answers by .333.

Enter the product here: ______________

STEP 5: Subtract the result obtained in Step 4 from the total you obtained in Step 2.

Enter the result here: ______________

STEP 6: Round the number obtained in Step 5 to the nearest whole number.

Enter the result here: ______________

The number you obtained in Step 6 is your raw score.

Table A

Answers to the Subject Test in Modern Hebrew and Percentage of Students Answering Each Question Correctly

Question Number	Correct Answer	Right	Wrong	Percentage of Students Answering the Question Correctly*	Question Number	Correct Answer	Right	Wrong	Percentage of Students Answering the Question Correctly*
1	C			72	33	B			91
2	C			89	34	C			27
3	B			90	35	D			71
4	A			73	36	A			74
5	B			93	37	A			85
6	D			57	38	A			97
7	B			38	39	B			82
8	A			55	40	A			85
9	C			52	41	B			41
10	B			91	42	C			97
11	A			50	43	A			98
12	B			48	44	C			95
13	D			52	45	B			83
14	D			85	46	D			83
15	D			46	47	A			71
16	D			60	48	D			94
17	D			90	49	B			78
18	B			81	50	D			70
19	B			38	51	A			82
20	B			33	52	B			82
21	B			39	53	A			59
22	D			72	54	B			84
23	C			90	55	D			72
24	A			23	56	B			63
25	D			57	57	A			66
26	A			82	58	C			83
27	A			74	59	C			76
28	D			97	60	D			71
29	A			84	61	C			82
30	C			98	62	A			69
31	D			96	63	D			73
32	B			97	64	B			65

Table A continued on next page

Table A continued from previous page

Question Number	Correct Answer	Right	Wrong	Percentage of Students Answering the Question Correctly*	Question Number	Correct Answer	Right	Wrong	Percentage of Students Answering the Question Correctly*
65	B			89	76	D			89
66	B			92	77	C			80
67	A			93	78	A			84
68	C			86	79	D			91
69	A			52	80	A			79
70	C			90	81	D			92
71	C			95	82	B			90
72	B			84	83	C			98
73	A			87	84	A			88
74	D			90	85	D			97
75	D			82					

* These percentages are based on an analysis of the answer sheets of a representative sample of 564 students who took the original administration of this test and whose mean score was 573. They may be used as an indication of the relative difficulty of a particular question.

Answer explanations for the Subject Test in Modern Hebrew can be found on page 969.

Finding Your Scaled Score

When you take SAT Subject Tests, the scores sent to the colleges you specify are reported on the College Board scale, which ranges from 200–800. You can convert your practice test score to a scaled score by using Table B. To find your scaled score, locate your raw score in the left-hand column of Table B; the corresponding score in the right-hand column is your scaled score. For example, a raw score of 55 on this particular edition of the Subject Test in Modern Hebrew corresponds to a scaled score of 530.

Raw scores are converted to scaled scores to ensure that a score earned on any one edition of a particular Subject Test is comparable to the same scaled score earned on any other edition of the same Subject Test. Because some editions of the tests may be slightly easier or more difficult than others, College Board scaled scores are adjusted so that they indicate the same level of performance regardless of the edition of the test taken and the ability of the group that takes it. Thus, for example, a score of 400 on one edition of a test taken at a particular administration indicates the same level of achievement as a score of 400 on a different edition of the test taken at a different administration.

When you take the SAT Subject Tests during a national administration, your scores are likely to differ somewhat from the scores you obtain on the tests in this book. People perform at different levels at different times for reasons unrelated to the tests themselves. The precision of any test is also limited because it represents only a sample of all the possible questions that could be asked.

Table B

Scaled Score Conversion Table
Subject Test in Modern Hebrew

Raw Score	Scaled Score	Raw Score	Scaled Score	Raw Score	Scaled Score
85	800	47	490	9	340
84	800	46	480	8	340
83	800	45	480	7	330
82	800	44	470	6	330
81	800	43	470	5	320
80	770	42	460	4	320
79	750	41	460	3	310
78	740	40	460	2	310
77	720	39	450	1	300
76	710	38	450	0	290
75	700	37	440	-1	290
74	680	36	440	-2	280
73	670	35	440	-3	280
72	660	34	430	-4	270
71	650	33	430	-5	260
70	640	32	430	-6	250
69	630	31	420	-7	250
68	620	30	420	-8	240
67	610	29	420	-9	230
66	610	28	410	-10	220
65	600	27	410	-11	210
64	590	26	410	-12	200
63	580	25	400	-13	200
62	580	24	400	-14	200
61	570	23	400	-15	200
60	560	22	390	-16	200
59	550	21	390	-17	200
58	550	20	390	-18	200
57	540	19	380	-19	200
56	530	18	380	-20	200
55	530	17	380	-21	200
54	520	16	370	-22	200
53	520	15	370	-23	200
52	510	14	360	-24	200
51	510	13	360	-25	200
50	500	12	360	-26	200
49	500	11	350	-27	200
48	490	10	350	-28	200

How Did You Do on the Subject Test in Modern Hebrew?

After you score your test and analyze your performance, think about the following questions:

Did you run out of time before reaching the end of the test?

If so, you may need to pace yourself better. For example, maybe you spent too much time on one or two hard questions. A better approach might be to skip the ones you can't answer right away and try answering all the questions that remain on the test. Then if there's time, go back to the questions you skipped.

Did you take a long time reading the directions?

You will save time when you take the test by learning the directions to the Subject Test in Modern Hebrew ahead of time. Each minute you spend reading directions during the test is a minute that you could use to answer questions.

How did you handle questions you were unsure of?

If you were able to eliminate one or more of the answer choices as wrong and guess from the remaining ones, your approach probably worked to your advantage. On the other hand, making haphazard guesses or omitting questions without trying to eliminate choices could cost you valuable points.

How difficult were the questions for you compared with other students who took the test?

Table A shows you how difficult the multiple-choice questions were for the group of students who took this test during its national administration. The right-hand column gives the percentage of students that answered each question correctly.

A question answered correctly by almost everyone in the group is obviously an easier question. For example, 93 percent of the students answered question 5 correctly. But only 23 percent answered question 24 correctly.

Keep in mind that these percentages are based on just one group of students. They would probably be different with another group of students taking the test.

If you missed several easier questions, go back and try to find out why: Did the questions cover material you haven't yet reviewed? Did you misunderstand the directions?

Answer Explanations for the Modern Hebrew Subject Test

1. Choice (C) is the correct answer. It is *worthwhile* to visit the *Knesset* (Parliament) when touring Jerusalem. It is illogical and ungrammatical to say that it *can (A)* to visit the Knesset, that it is *in order to* (B) to visit the Knesset, or that it *wants* (D) to visit the Knesset.

2. Choice (C) is the correct answer. My friend the archeologist *received* an important position with the Department of Antiquities. The noun is feminine singular and choice (C) *received* is the correct verb form to use with "an important position." It does not make sense to say that she *was accepted* (A), *is accepted* (B), or *is well accepted* (D) an important position.

3. Choice (B) is the correct answer. When traveling by bus from Tel-Aviv to Jerusalem *you pass* the town of Ramle. It does not make sense to say *you collect* (A), *you examine* (C), or *you guard* (D) the town of Ramle.

4. Choice (A) is the correct answer. The books on the subject *disappeared* from the library. It does not make sense to say that the books *did not enter* (B), *were not torn* (C), or *were not registered* (D) from the library.

5. Choice (B) is the correct answer. The countries signed a peace *agreement*. It does not make sense to say that they signed *a newspaper* (A), *an explanation* (C), *or a story* (D).

6. Choice (D) is the correct answer. This is a conditional sentence, which in Hebrew uses the future tense. The speaker says, "If no one wants to read this book, *I will return* it to the library." Choices (A), *I returned*, and (B), *I go back*, are not in the future tense. And in this context it does not make much sense to say (C), "*I will come back* to the library."

7. Choice (B) is the correct answer. Dinah and Daliah decided to *meet* every Monday. Although all choices are verbs of the same root, only choice B to *meet* (reflexive) is the

grammatically correct form. Choice (A), *to meet,* is the infinitive form. Choice (C), *they met,* is the past passive form, and choice (D), *they met,* is the simple past form.

8. Choice (A) is the correct answer. Many people think that the government has no right *to interfere* in the life of the individual. It does not make sense to say *to wonder* (B), *to contact* (C), or *to get rich* (D) in the life of the individual.

9. Choice (C) is the correct answer. The noise outside did not allow us *to concentrate* on our studies. It does not make sense to say *to learn* (A), *to read* (B), or *to overcome* (D) in our studies.

10. Choice (B) is the correct answer. I'll try to get to the museum early to buy *entry* tickets. It does not make sense to say *guarding* tickets (A), *closing* tickets (C), or *choice* tickets (D).

11. Choice (A) is the correct answer. The president of Israel will receive at his home *a representative* from every community in honor of the New Year. It does not make sense to say *a prophet* (B), *a judge* (C), or *a ruler* (D) of every community, since the occasion calls for a representative and not any other position.

12. Choice (B) is the correct answer. The speaker asks: is there *a chance* that you could come to the party this evening? It does not make sense to say *a change* (A), *a desire* (C), or *an experience* (D) that you could come to the party.

13. Choice (D) is the correct answer. Dan looks today the same as he looked twenty years ago; he *did not change* at all. All of the answer choices include verbs of the same root, but only choice (D) is grammatically correct in the sentence. In context it does not make sense to say Dan *will change* at all (A), *is changing* at all (B), or *changed* at all (C). Choice (D) is the reflexive form of the verb and is appropriate in this case.

14. Choice (D) is the correct answer. During the summer vacation tourists from *different* countries arrive in New York. It does not make sense to say that tourists from *last* (A), or *first* (C) countries arrive in New York. There is no reason to believe that the sentence is focusing on tourists from countries that no longer exist, so there is no reason to say that tourists from *former* (B) countries arrive.

15. Choice (D) is the correct answer. Every day scientists *discover* new information in their research. It does not make sense to say *order* (A), *expect* (B), or *fulfill* (C) new information on a daily basis in their research.

16. Choice (D) is the correct answer. Jerusalem is famous for *the holy* sites in the city. The adjective *holy* has to agree with the noun (*sites*) which is a definite article and masculine plural. Only choice (D), *holy*, is the grammatically correct form to use with the noun *sites*. Choice (A) is a definite article and feminine plural. Choice (B) is indefinite feminine plural, and choice (C) is indefinite masculine plural.

17. Choice (D) is the correct answer. Dinah bought the book because she heard good things *about it*. It does not make sense to say *from it* (A), *to it* (B), or *it* (C). Each choice is a preposition but only (D) is grammatically correct.

18. Choice (B) is the correct answer. Recently the computer *turned out* to be an important and useful instrument. The sentence refers to something that happened recently; that is, something that already happened. Therefore, a past-tense verb is required. Choices (A), *to turn*, (C), *is turning*, and (D), *will be turning*, are grammatically incorrect in this sentence.

19. Choice (B) is the correct answer. The city *has developed* since many new residents settled there. All of the answer choices are verbs of the same root, but only choice (B) is in the reflexive form *has developed*, is grammatically correct in the sentence. The same root in a different grammatical form can mean either develop or open. Choice (A), *developed*, is in the simple past tense; choice (C), *was opened*, is in the passive past tense; and choice (D), *opened*, is in the simple past tense.

20. Choice (B) is the correct answer. She notified him that she does not have *free time* to go out with him. It does not make sense to say *condition* (A), *periods* (C), or *times* (D) to go out with him.

21. Choice (B) is the correct answer. The Hebrew University in Jerusalem *was founded* in 1925. It does not make sense to say that the Hebrew University *was born* (A), or *was destined* (D) in 1925, and there is no indication that the university *was added* (C), to something else at that time.

22. Choice (D) is the correct answer. *Although* it rained heavily in recent weeks, there is still a serious shortage of water in many parts of the country. It is illogical to say there

is a shortage of water *because* (A) it rained heavily. Choices (B), *on account of,* and (C), *in contrast to,* are ungrammatical and do not make sense in this sentence.

23. Choice (C) is the correct answer. Sarah *is using* a special soap because of her sensitive skin. All of the answer choices are verbs of the same root, but only choice (C), *is using,* is grammatically correct in the sentence. The same root in a different grammatical form can mean either *to use* or *to serve.* Choice (A), *served,* is in the simple past tense; choice (B), *to use,* is an infinitive; and choice (D), *serves,* is in the present tense.

24. Choice (A) is the correct answer. This question tests subject-verb agreement. The beauty of the country *attracts* many visitors. The term "beauty of the country" is masculine, so choice (A) is grammatically correct. Choice (C) is incorrect because it is the feminine form of *attracts.* Choices (B) and (D) both mean *continues;* it does not make sense to say that the beauty of the county *continues* many visitors. Further, choice (D) is the feminine form of *continues.*

25. Choice (D) is the correct answer. In the elections I voted for the new president. Choice (D), *for,* is the proper preposition to use in this context. Choices (A), *on,* and (B), *to,* are unidiomatic. It does not make sense to say that one voted *because* (C) the new president.

The passage for the following questions (26–59) tells about three brothers that came to visit New York City. They rented a room on the sixtieth floor of a hotel. Reuven gave the key to Danny and asked him to guard it well. They all went out to town, and when they returned to the hotel they discovered that the elevator was out of order. They started to climb the stairs all the way to the sixtieth floor. Reuven suggested that up to the twentieth floor he would sing nice songs; up to the fortieth floor Shimon would tell funny stories, and up to the sixtieth floor Danny would tell sad stories. When it was Danny's turn, he said: "only one sad thing happened, I left the key downstairs."

26. Choice (A) is the correct answer. The passage is about three brothers who came to New York *to visit* in the big city. There is no reason to suggest that the brothers came *to search* in the big city (C); the passage does not indicate that they were searching for something. And it does not make sense to say that the brothers came *to see* (B) or *to observe* (D) in the big city.

27. Choice (A) is the correct answer. They rented a room on the sixtieth floor of a big *hotel.* There is no reason to suggest that people visiting a city would rent a room in an

institution (B). It does not make sense to say that they rented a room in a *construction* (C) or in a *section* (D); it is not clear what the construction of the section would be.

28. Choice (D) is the correct answer. Reuven gave the key to Danny and told him to *guard* it well. It does not make sense to say that Reuven told Danny to *break* (A), *throw* (B), or *write* (C) the key.

29. Choice (A) is the correct answer. When they returned to the hotel they saw that the elevator *was not working.* It does not make sense to say the elevator *was standing* (B), *was being tied* (C), or *was entering* (D).

30. Choice (C) is the correct answer. The brothers started to go up on foot to the sixtieth floor. Reuven said, "I have a good *idea.* On the way up to the twentieth floor, I'll sing nice songs." In context it is clear that Reuven was not indicating that he had a good *logic* (A), a good *dream* (B), or a good *account* (D).

31. Choice (D) is the correct answer. On the way up to the fortieth floor, Shimon will tell funny *stories.* It does not make sense to say he will tell funny *lessons* (B) or *studies* (C), and *compositions* (A) are usually written rather than told aloud.

32. Choice (B) is the correct answer. On the way up to the sixtieth floor, Danny will tell sad stories. When the brothers arrived, Danny said, "Only one sad thing happened, *I forgot* the key downstairs." It would not make sense for Danny to say "*I closed* the key downstairs" (A), "*I came back* the key downstairs" (C), or "*I finished* the key downstairs" (D).

33. Choice (B) is the correct answer. A year ago Tania *immigrated* to Israel from Russia, and Alex came from England. This question tests subject–verb agreement, and the correct form of the verb is feminine singular in the past tense. Choices (A), *immigrates,* (C), *immigration,* and (D), *will immigrate,* are ungrammatical in this sentence.

34. Choice (C) is the correct answer. They *met* and got married. The sentence requires a verb in the reflexive mode. All of the answer choices are verbs of the same root, but only choice (C), the reflexive form *met,* is grammatically correct in the sentence.

35. Choice (D) is the correct answer. A cute baby girl *was born.* All of the answer choices are verbs of the same root, but only choice (D), *was born,* which is in the past tense of

the reflexive-passive mode, is grammatically correct in the sentence. Choice (A), *gave birth,* is in the simple past tense; choice (B), another form of *gave birth,* is unidiomatic in this context. And choice (C), *is being born,* is in the present passive tense.

36. Choice (A) is the correct answer. One aunt is saying that they talk to the baby in Russian, since it is very *important* that a mother talks to the baby in her own language. All of the answer choices are words of the same root, but only choice (A) is grammatically correct. Choice (B), *they thought,* is in the simple past tense; choice (C), *it is thought,* is in the past passive tense, and choice (D), *important,* is in the feminine form.

37. Choice (A) is the correct answer. Another aunt says that the mother should sing to the baby *and teach* her first words. All of the answer choices are verbs of the same root, but only choice (A), *teach,* is grammatically correct in the sentence. Choices (B), *and to learn,* (C), *and she taught,* and (D), *and he taught,* are incorrect.

38. Choice (A) is the correct answer. Dinah is only ten years old and already she *is studying* in the university. It does not make sense to say she *is thinking* (B), *is learned (C),* or *is erudite* (D) in the university.

39. Choice (B) is the correct answer. She *arrives* to her studies every day. It does not make sense to say that Dinah *suggests* to her studies (A), *expresses* to her studies (C), or *informs* to her studies (D).

40. Choice (A) is the correct answer. Owing to her young age, her mother *brings* her. It does not make sense to say that Dinah arrives when her mother *serves* her (B), *influences* her (C), or *changes* her (D).

41. Choice (B) is the correct answer. Not all the adult students *are satisfied* with something. It does not make sense to say the students *want* (A), *will want* (C), or *wanted* (D) with something.

42. Choice (C) is the correct answer. The adult students are not satisfied that such a *young* girl studies in the same class as them. The passage focuses on the girl's age, there is no reason to say that the adult students were dissatisfied that she was a *rich* girl (A), a *quick* girl (B), or a *clear* girl (D).

43. Choice (A) is the correct answer. One student says, "If she *will receive* better grades than me, I will leave the university." It does not make sense to say that the student will leave the university if Dinah *will tell* better grades (B), *will add* better grades (C), or *will describe* better grades (D).

44. Choice (C) is the correct answer. Another student says, "It is difficult for me *to believe* that a ten-year-old girl studies with me in the same class." It does not make sense to say it is difficult for the student *to decide* (A), *to invite* (B), or *to increase* (D) that a ten-year-old girl is in the same class.

45. Choice (B) is the correct answer. Dinah says, "I hope that they *will treat* me like a regular student." It does not make sense that Dinah hopes that they *will hear* her (A), *will ask* her (C), or *will be asked* her (D) like a regular student.

46. Choice (D) is the correct answer. The city of Rome was *famous* for its wise men. It does not make sense to say that Rome was *maintained* (A), *scattered* (B), or *advertised* (C) for its wise men.

47. Choice (A) is the correct answer. One wise man came to Jerusalem and wanted to check the wisdom *of* the children. All of the answer choices are prepositions, but only choice (A), *of,* is grammatically correct. It is unidiomatic to use the preposition *with* (B), *at* (C), or *to* (D) in this context.

48. Choice (D) is the correct answer. The man went and met a young child *on his way.* It does not make sense to say he met a child *with his cane* (A), *with his door* (B), or *with his matter* (C).

49. Choice (B) is the correct answer. The man gave the child a few shekels and asked *him* [literally, *from him*] to buy eggs and cheeses. All of the answer choices are prepositions, but only choice (B), *from him,* is grammatically correct. Choices (A), *to him,* (C), *at him,* or (D), *close to him,* are unidiomatic.

50. Choice (D) is the correct answer. The boy bought cheeses and *two* eggs. This question involves the correct use of the number two, and only choice (D) is grammatically correct. *Egg* is a feminine noun in Hebrew. Choice (D) refers to *two* eggs in the feminine form in declination of number two. Choice (A) is the number *two* in the masculine form in declination, choice (B) is *two* in the simple masculine form, and choice (C) is *two* in the simple feminine form.

51. Choice (A) is the correct answer. The man asked the boy if he could tell which cheese was from a white goat and which was from a black one. The child said, "You are *greater* in years and wisdom than I am. It does not make sense to say, you are *long* in years and wisdom than I am" (B), "You are *ancient* in years and wisdom than I am" (C), or "You are *antiquated* in years and wisdom than I am" (D).

52. Choice (B) is the correct answer. After saying that the man is older, the child continues: "Show me *first* which egg is from a white hen and which is from a black one." It does not make sense to say that the child would ask the man to show him *where* (A), *how* (C), or *before* (D) which egg comes from which chicken.

53. Choice (A) is the correct answer. We *are used* to the months' names in the Hebrew calendar. Although all of the answer choices use the same root (r-g-l), they have different meanings. It does not make sense to say *we spy* the months' names (B) or that *we train* the months' names (C). It is clear that *we are used* to the months' names, already, not that *we are getting used* to the months' names (D).

54. Choice (B) is the correct answer. The passage notes that we are so *used* to the names of the months in the Hebrew calendar that we *forget* that they are not Hebrew names. It does not make sense to say that sometimes we *watch* (A), *judge* (C), or *ask* (D) that these are not Hebrew names.

55. Choice (D) is the correct answer. The names of the months in the Hebrew calendar are not Hebrew names *but* Babylonian names. Choice (D), the conjunction *but*, grammatically completes the sentence. Choices (A), *these*, (B), *if*, and (C), *to*, are ungrammatical and unidiomatic.

56. Choice (B) is the correct answer. These names are Babylonian names *that were entered* into the Hebrew calendar. Only choice (B), *that were entered*, makes sense and is in the necessary form. It does not make sense in this context to refer to the names *that were gathered* (A) or the names *that gathered* (C). Choice (D), *that are gathered*, is incorrect because it is clear that the names have already been entered.

57. Choice (A) is the correct answer. In the Bible different names *are mentioned*. Although all of the answer choices are verbs of the same root, only choice (A), *are mentioned*, is grammatically correct. Choice (B) does mean *are mentioned*, but it is in the feminine form. And it does not make sense to say that different names *remind* (C) or *remember* (D) in the Bible.

58. Choice (C) is the correct answer. In 1908 a stone was discovered, and *on it* were engraved names of eight months. All choices include prepositions, but only choice (C), *on it,* is grammatically correct. Choices (A), *to it,* (B), *at,* and (D), *because of it,* are ungrammatical and do not make sense in the sentence.

59. Choice (C) is the correct answer. The writing that was used at the time was *common* to the Hebrews, Canaanites, Moabites and Edomites. Although all of the answer choices have the same root, only choice (C), *common,* is grammatically correct. It is ungrammatical and does not make sense to say that the writing *participates* (A), *partner* (B), or *participated* (D) to these group.

60. Choice (D) is the correct answer. The passage indicates that American pharmacies used to sell *medicines* (A) as well as *food items* (B) and *soft drinks* (C). The passage makes no mention of *toys* (D).

61. Choice (C) is the correct answer. The question asks, "Why was the drink not successful in the beginning?" The passage mentions that in the beginning Coca Cola tasted bitter, and it was not expected that it would be successful. In other words, the drink was unsuccessful at first because *it was not tasty,* not because *there was not good advertisement* (A), because *it was too sweet* (B), or because *it was sold in a pharmacy* (D).

62. Choice (A) is the correct answer. According to the passage, Mr. Jacobs sold his share in the invention of Coca Cola. As a result, Joseph Jacobs lost his chance *to succeed in business* (A). There is no indication that he lost his chance *to travel in the world* (B), *to work in a pharmacy* (C), or *to sell drinks* (D).

63. Choice (D) is the correct answer. The article mentions that Martin Luther King III visited Israel in order to get acquainted with the situation in the land. In other words, he visited *to learn about life in Israel* (D). The passage does not indicate that he came to Israel *to fulfill his promise to his father* (A), *to tour the Galilee mountains* (B), or *to meet Israeli leaders* (C).

64. Choice (B) is the correct answer. The passage indicates that Martin Luther King III planted a tree in *Martin Luther King* Forest. The passage does not indicate that he planted a tree in *the Galilee Project* Forest (A), *B'nai Brith* Forest (C), or *Russian Jewry* Forest (D).

65. Choice (B) is the correct answer. The question asks what the tree symbolized. The son said, "This tree symbolizes the continuation of my father's work." That is, the tree symbolized the *father's dream* (B). The tree did not symbolize *the State of Israel* (A), *United States Jewry* (C), or *the work of B'nai Brith* (D).

66. Choice (B) is the correct answer. The ad announces the birth of twin boys; the ad is about *the birth of two brothers*. The ad is not about *a birthday party* (A), *an engagement party* (C), or *a party for Rachel* (D).

67. Choice (A) is the correct answer. The announcement indicates that guests invited *to the Cohen family home*, not *to the Kaplan's family home* (B), *to the hospital* (C), or *to Rachel's home* (D).

68. Choice (C) is the correct answer. This is an advertisement for a taxi company. The people who are asked to reply to the ad are experienced *drivers* (C), not *car service* (A), *passengers to Tel-Aviv* (B), or *clients* (D).

69. Choice (A) is the correct answer. The ad promises *a good salary*. It does not promise *new cars* (B), *an interesting experience* (C), or *an easy job* (D).

70. Choice (C) is the correct answer. This ad offers *software that teaches Hebrew* (C). It does not offer *Hebrew audio discs* (A), *Hebrew video* (B) or *a computer that prepares for Bar-Mitzvah* (D).

71. Choice (C) is the correct answer. Using the software requires *only a computer* (C). The software does not require one *to read books* (A) or *to know Ben Yehuda* (D), and it does not require *a video appliance* (B).

72. Choice (B) is the correct answer. The passage indicates that the woman wished to be buried in that place *because of the proximity to a grave of one of her children* (B). There is no indication that she wished to be buried there *because her husband was buried in the old cemetery* (A), *because of the proximity to her home in Safad* (C), or *because she liked the old cemetery* (D).

73. Choice (A) is the correct answer. The family wanted the old woman to be buried in the old cemetery, but burials were no longer being done there; the family had difficulties *because now they were burying in the new cemetery* (A). The passage does

not indicate that *the family* had difficulties *because they did not have money for burial* (B), *because the bottle of oil was lost* (C), or *because they could not find the daughter's grave* (D).

74. Choice (D) is the correct answer. The passage says that the old woman took the bottle of oil and *put it inside the grave* (D), not that she *used it to heal her daughter* (A), *kept it to be buried* (B), or *buried it in her yard* (C).

75. Choice (D) is the correct answer. The old woman had put the bottle of oil in the grave as a sign, or marker, that she bought the plot for her future grave; when the burial company people found the bottle, they finally agreed to bury the woman in the old cemetery. The most suitable name for this story is *The Marker That Helped* (D). The names *The History of Safad* (A), *The Visit of Family Members* (B), and *The Picture of the Bottle of Oil* (C) are not appropriate for the story.

76. Choice (D) is the correct answer. The passage indicates that Shuli changed her family name *because an easy and short name is important for publicity* (D), not *because it was her maiden name* (A), *because she did not like it* (B), or *because her mother asked her to change it* (C).

77. Choice (C) is the correct answer. The passage indicates that the song "Jerusalem of Gold" became *almost as famous a song as "Hatikvah"* (C). It does not indicate that the song became *the national anthem of Israel* (A), that it became *more famous than Hatikvah* (B), or that it became *a famous song only out of the country* (D).

78. Choice (A) is the correct answer. The passage indicates that Shuli stopped singing for a few years because *she was busy raising her children*, not because *she was abroad and did not have time* (B), because *everyone recognized the song "Jerusalem of Gold"* (C), or because *the crowd did not like her songs* (D).

79. Choice (D) is the correct answer. The passage indicates that Shuli returned to sing *when her youngest son went to kindergarten* (D). It does not indicate that she returned to singing *after she had two children* (A), *after she changed her name* (B), or *when her husband asked her* (C).

80. Choice (A) is the correct answer. The passage indicates that the influence of the song "Jerusalem of Gold" on Shuli was that *it helped her to become famous*, not that

it caused her to stop singing (B), that *it made her wait for similar songs* (C), or that *it helped her in raising her children* (D).

81. Choice (D) is the correct answer. The passage indicates that the relationship between the families was created because *the sons were good friends* (D), not because *the mothers were sisters* (A), *they lived in the same city* (B), or *they had the same neighbors* (C).

82. Choice (B) is the correct answer. The passage indicates that the two families *celebrated together.* There is no indication that they *worked in the same house* (A), *went together for vacation* (C), or *quarreled during the holiday* (D).

83. Choice (C) is the correct answer. The passage indicates that the families had a fight because *there was a fight between the two sons.* The families did not fight because *each one wanted the same role* (A), because the *two sons wanted the gift* (B), or because *the neighbors were angry with the sons* (D).

84. Choice (A) is the correct answer. The two families did not make peace because *no one wanted to yield* (A), not because *no one wanted peace* (B), because *the sons were still angry* (C), or because *it was not important* (D).

85. Choice (D) is the correct answer. From this tale people can learn *that they should forgive each other* (D). The lesson is not *that one should interfere in the life of the children* (A), *that one should not give in to neighbors* (B), or *that one should be stubborn* (C).

Chapter 16

Spanish

Purpose

There are two Subject Tests in Spanish: Spanish and Spanish with Listening. The reading-only test measures your ability to understand written Spanish. The Subject Test in Spanish with Listening measures your ability to understand spoken and written Spanish.

Format

- The Subject Test in Spanish takes one hour and includes 85 multiple-choice questions.
- The Subject Test in Spanish with Listening also takes one hour, with about 20 minutes for listening questions and 40 minutes for the reading section; it includes 85 multiple-choice listening and reading questions.
- Both tests evaluate your reading skills through precision of vocabulary, structure use, and comprehension of a variety of texts.

Content

In the reading section, the questions implicitly test vocabulary throughout the test, but some questions specifically test word meaning in the context of a sentence that reflects spoken or written language. Understanding of various parts of speech (nouns, verbs, adjectives, adverbs, etc.) and idiomatic expressions is tested. The reading section also asks structure and reading questions.

Vocabulary and structure questions ask you to identify usage that is both structurally correct and contextually appropriate. Other reading questions test vocabulary and grammatical usage in longer paragraphs.

Reading questions are based on selections from prose fiction, historical works, newspaper and magazine articles, as well as advertisements, flyers, and letters. They test points such as main and supporting ideas, themes, style, tone, and the spatial and temporal settings of a passage.

In addition to the reading questions, the Subject Test in Spanish with Listening also measures your ability to understand the spoken language with three parts of listening questions:

Part A questions ask you to identify the sentence that most accurately describes what is presented in a photograph or what someone in the photograph might say.

Part B questions test your ability to identify a plausible continuation of a short conversation.

Part C requires that you answer comprehension questions based on more extensive listening selections.

Spanish	
Skills Measured	Approximate Percentage of Test
Vocabulary and Structure	33%
Paragraph Completion	33%
Reading Comprehension	33%

Spanish with Listening	
Types of Questions	Approximate Percentage of Test
Listening Section (about 20 minutes) (approximately 30 questions)	40%
Pictures Rejoinders Selections	
Reading Section (40 minutes) (approximately 55 questions)	60%
Vocabulary and Structure Paragraph Completion Reading Comprehension	

How to Prepare

Both tests are written to reflect general trends in high school curricula and are independent of particular textbooks or methods of instruction. The Spanish tests are appropriate for you if you have studied the language for three to four years in high school or the equivalent; however, if you have two years of strong preparation in Spanish, you are also encouraged to take the tests. Your best preparation for the tests is a gradual development of competence in Spanish over a period of years. Familiarize yourself with the directions in advance. The directions in this book are identical to those that appear on the test.

Spanish with Listening

A practice audio CD for the full-length practice test is included with this book. A practice CD with different sample questions can be obtained, along with a copy of the *Getting Ready for the SAT Subject Tests* booklet, from your school counselor, or you can access the listening files at www.collegeboard.org. If your counselor does not have the CD or booklet, he or she can order them from the College Board. Familiarize yourself with the directions in advance. The directions in this book are identical to those that appear on the test.

CD Players

Using CD Players for Language Tests with Listening

Take an acceptable CD player to the test center. Your CD player must be in good working order, so insert fresh batteries on the day before the test. You may bring additional batteries and a backup player to the test center. CD players cannot be shared with other test-takers.

Test center staff won't have batteries, CD players, or earphones for your use, so your CD player must be:

- equipped with earphones
- portable (hand-held)
- battery operated

You are not allowed to use a CD player with recording or duplicating capabilities.

Note

If the volume on your CD player disturbs other test-takers, the test center supervisor may ask you to move to another seat.

What to do if your CD player malfunctions:

- Raise your hand and tell the test supervisor.
- Switch to backup equipment if you have it and continue the test. If you don't have backup equipment, your score on the Spanish with Listening Test will be canceled. But scores on other Subject Tests you take that day will still be counted.

What if you receive a defective CD on test day? Raise your hand and ask the supervisor for a replacement.

Scores

For both tests, the total score is reported on the 200-to-800 scale. For the listening test, listening and reading subscores are reported on the 20-to-80 scale.

Sample Reading Questions

Your answer sheet has five answer positions marked A, B, C, D, and E, while the questions throughout this test contain only four choices. Be sure NOT to make any marks in column E.

Part A

Directions: This part consists of a number of incomplete statements, each having four suggested completions. Select the most appropriate completion and fill in the corresponding circle on the answer sheet.

1. Juan Pablo tuvo que esperar unos minutos antes de tomar la sopa porque estaba demasiado
   (A) caliente
   (B) calurosa
   (C) mojada
   (D) perfumada

2. Me gustó tanto la novela de Isabel Allende que ____________ voy a recomendar a mis amigos.
   (A) le
   (B) lo
   (C) me la
   (D) se la

Choice (A) is the correct answer to question 1. This question tests how well you have mastered vocabulary. To answer correctly, you need to know that the only adjective that fits the context of the sentence is (A) *caliente*. The wrong choices, (B), (C), and (D), are inappropriate adjectives for describing soup in this context.

Choice (D) is the correct answer to question 2. This question tests command of structure. To answer correctly, you need to know the correct object pronoun usage and choose an indirect object with a singular, feminine direct object pronoun in the correct sequence. Choices (A), (B), and (C) have either an indirect object pronoun that would not agree with the plural indirect object, *mis amigos*, or a direct object pronoun that would not agree with the singular, feminine direct object, *la novela*.

Part B

Directions: In each of the following paragraphs, there are numbered blanks indicating that words or phrases have been omitted. For each numbered blank, four completions are provided. First, read through the entire paragraph. Then, for each numbered blank, choose the completion that is most appropriate given the context of the entire paragraph and fill in the corresponding circle on the answer sheet.

El mural más polémico del siempre volcánico Diego Rivera, *Sueño de una tarde dominical en la Alameda Central*, ya está por fin __3__ de todos. Considerada una de las __4__ más logradas de la corriente nacionalista mexicana, este mural __5__ encendidas controversias desde su creación en 1948.

3. (A) en vez
   (B) al lado
   (C) a la vista
   (D) a mediados

4. (A) manifestaciones
   (B) cuadras
   (C) artes
   (D) paredes

5. (A) despertó
   (B) despertará
   (C) despertando
   (D) despierte

Choice (C) is the correct answer to question 3. This question tests how well you have mastered vocabulary. To answer correctly, you need to know that the only phrase that fits the context of the passage is choice (C) *a la vista*. Choices (A), (B), and (D) are inappropriate for describing the state of the mural in this context.

Choice (A) is the correct answer to question 4. This question tests how well you have mastered vocabulary. To answer correctly, you need to know that the only noun that fits the context of the passage is choice (A) *manifestaciones*. The wrong choices, (B), (C), and (D), are inappropriate in this phrase describing the mural's significance as they do not apply to a mural.

Choice (A) is the correct answer to question 5. This question tests command of structure. To answer correctly, you need to know the correct preterite verb tense. The wrong choices, (B) *despertará*, (C) *despertando*, and (D) *despierte*, are different forms of the verb despertar that do not fit the syntax and context of the passage.

Part C

Directions: Read the following texts carefully for comprehension. Each is followed by a number of questions or incomplete statements. Select the answer or completion that is best according to the text and fill in the corresponding circle on the answer sheet.

Question 6

ENCICLOPEDIA
el Periódico
UNIVERSAL

Complete su
Enciclopedia Universal
El Periódico

Para conseguir los tomos que le falten de la ***Enciclopedia Universal El Periódico****, sólo tiene que rellenar el cupón de pedido—adjuntando 75. euro cents en sellos por cada tomo que solicite, más 45. euro cents en sellos por gastos de envío—y remitirlo a la siguiente dirección:*

El Periódico de Catalunya
Departamento de Distribución
C/. Comte d'Urgell, n.º 100
08011 Barcelona

6. ¿Para qué hay que mandar 45 euro cents?
   (A) Para pagar el costo de correos
   (B) Para recibir cupones de pedido
   (C) Para comprar un periódico catalán
   (D) Para pagar un anuncio ilustrado

Choice (A) is the correct answer to question 6. This question asks about a specific detail mentioned in the ad: the reason for sending 45 euro cents. In the text, *más 45 euro cents en sellos por gastos de envío* refers to shipping charges, so the correct answer is choice (A). Choices (B), (C), and (D) are incorrect within the context of the ad.

Questions 7–9

Un aire marino, pesado y fresco, entró en mis pulmones con la primera sensación confusa de la ciudad; una masa de casas dormidas; de establecimientos cerrados, de faroles como centinelas borrachos de soledad. Una respiración grande, dificultosa, venía con el cuchicheo de la madrugada. Muy cerca, a mi espalda, enfrente de las callejuelas misteriosas que conducen al Borne, sobre mi corazón excitado, estaba el mar.

El olor especial, el gran rumor de la gente, la luces siempre tristes de la estación de tren, tenían para mí un gran encanto, ya que envolvían todas mis impresiones en la maravilla de haber llegado por fin a una ciudad grande, adorada en mis ensueños por desconocida.

7. ¿Cómo se siente la narradora al llegar a la ciudad?
   (A) Perdida
   (B) Encantada
   (C) Cansada
   (D) Tranquila

8. ¿Qué efecto producen en la narradora las luces de la estación?
   (A) Le agradan mucho.
   (B) Le dan vergüenza.
   (C) La desorientan.
   (D) La adormecen.

9. ¿Dónde está la ciudad a la que llega la narradora?
   (A) En la costa
   (B) En una cordillera
   (C) Al lado de un río
   (D) Cerca de un lago

Choice (B) is the correct answer to question 7. This question tests literal comprehension, and refers to how the protagonist feels upon her arrival in the city. In the second paragraph, she describes her impressions of the city using words such as *especial*, *encanto*, and *maravilla*. Later in the same paragraph, she also refers to *haber llegado por fin a una ciudad grande, adorada en mis ensueños* (...), so the correct answer is choice (B) *Encantada*. Choices (A), (C), and (D) are incorrect within the context of the passage.

Choice (A) is the correct answer to question 8. This question tests literal comprehension and refers to the effect that the lights of the station have on the protagonist. In the second paragraph, she specifically mentions them, saying *tenían un gran encanto*. Thus, the correct answer is choice (A) *Le agradan mucho*. Choices (B), (C), and (D) are incorrect within the context of the passage.

Choice (A) is the correct answer to question 9. This question tests literal comprehension and asks about the setting of the narrative. In the first paragraph, both the first line, *Un aire marino* (...) and the last sentence, *Muy cerca (...) estaba el mar*, refer to being close to the sea. The correct answer is choice (A) *En la costa*. Choices (B), (C), and (D) are incorrect within the context of the passage.

Spanish Subject Test

Practice Helps

The test that follows is an actual, previously administered SAT Subject Test in Spanish. To get an idea of what it's like to take this test, practice under conditions that are much like those of an actual test administration.

- Set aside an hour when you can take the test uninterrupted.
- Sit at a desk or table with no other books or papers. Dictionaries, other books, or notes are not allowed in the test room.
- Tear out an answer sheet from the back of this book and fill it in just as you would on the day of the test. One answer sheet can be used for up to three Subject Tests.
- Read the instructions that precede the practice test. During the actual administration you will be asked to read them before answering the test questions.
- Time yourself by placing a clock or kitchen timer in front of you.
- After you finish the practice test, read the sections "How to Score the SAT Subject Test in Spanish" and "How Did You Do on the Subject Test in Spanish?"
- The appearance of the answer sheet in this book may differ from the answer sheet you see on test day.

SPANISH TEST

The top portion of the page of the answer sheet that you will use to take the Spanish Test must be filled in exactly as illustrated below. When your supervisor tells you to fill in the circle next to the name of the test you are about to take, mark your answer sheet as shown.

○ Literature	○ Mathematics Level 1	○ German	○ Chinese Listening	○ Japanese Listening
○ Biology E	○ Mathematics Level 2	○ Italian	○ French Listening	○ Korean Listening
○ Biology M	○ U.S. History	○ Latin	○ German Listening	○ Spanish Listening
○ Chemistry	○ World History	○ Modern Hebrew		
○ Physics	○ French	● Spanish	**Background Questions:** ① ② ③ ④ ⑤ ⑥ ⑦ ⑧ ⑨	

After filling in the circle next to the name of the test you are taking, locate the Background Questions section, which also appears at the top of your answer sheet (as shown above). This is where you will answer the following Background Questions on your answer sheet.

BACKGROUND QUESTIONS

Please answer either Part I or Part II below by filling in the appropriate circle in the Background Questions box on your answer sheet. Fill in ONLY ONE circle, as described below, to indicate how you obtained your knowledge of Spanish. The information you provide is for statistical purposes only and will not affect your test score.

Part I If your knowledge of Spanish comes primarily from any of the following: living in a home where Spanish is the main spoken language, or living for six months or longer in a Spanish-speaking country that included significant experience in the Spanish language, courses taken at a college, or special study of Spanish, fill in circle 9 and leave the remaining circles blank, regardless of how long you studied the subject in school.

Part II If your knowledge of Spanish comes primarily from courses taken in secondary school, fill in the circle that indicates the level of the Spanish course in which you are currently enrolled. If you are not now enrolled in a Spanish course, fill in the circle that indicates the level of the most advanced course in Spanish that you have completed.

- First year: first or second half —Fill in circle 1.
- Second year: first half —Fill in circle 2.
  second half —Fill in circle 3.
- Third year: first half —Fill in circle 4.
  second half —Fill in circle 5.
- Fourth year: first half —Fill in circle 6.
  second half —Fill in circle 7.
- Advanced Placement course or a course at a level higher than fourth year, second half
  or
  high school course work plus a minimum of four weeks of study abroad —Fill in circle 8.

When the supervisor gives the signal, turn the page and begin the Spanish Test. There are 100 numbered circles on the answer sheet and 85 questions in the Spanish Test. Therefore, use only circles 1 to 85 for recording your answers.

SPANISH TEST

PLEASE NOTE THAT YOUR ANSWER SHEET HAS FIVE ANSWER POSITIONS, MARKED A, B, C, D, E, WHILE THE QUESTIONS THROUGHOUT THIS TEST CONTAIN ONLY FOUR CHOICES. BE SURE NOT TO MAKE ANY MARKS IN COLUMN E.

Part A

Directions: This part consists of a number of incomplete statements, each having four suggested completions. Select the most appropriate completion and fill in the corresponding circle on the answer sheet.

1. Si quieren mandar hoy esta carta a Lucía, ------- un buzón en la esquina.

(A) haya
(B) han
(C) hay
(D) ha

2. ¡Elena, ya son las ocho! ¿Estás ------- para salir?

(A) lista
(B) lenta
(C) ligera
(D) larga

3. Mi ------- favorito es el pastel de manzana.

(A) camino
(B) comedor
(C) helado
(D) postre

4. Pepe es el mejor alumno ------- la clase.

(A) a
(B) de
(C) desde
(D) hasta

5. La casa de techo rojo es -------.

(A) el mío
(B) la nuestra
(C) el tuyo
(D) las suyas

6. Hacía un mes que queríamos ver esa película de Raúl Juliá y por fin ------- vimos la semana pasada.

(A) le
(B) lo
(C) la
(D) se

7. Cuando yo era pequeña, todos los años ------- el mes de agosto en la Playa de Luquillo.

(A) pasamos
(B) pasábamos
(C) hemos pasado
(D) pasaremos

8. Se me olvidó el bolígrafo. ¿Puedes ------- el tuyo?

(A) recordarme
(B) devolverme
(C) prestarme
(D) enseñarme

9. Me dijo que tenía muchas ganas de ------- a su pueblo en Paraguay.

(A) volver
(B) volviendo
(C) volverá
(D) volvería

10. Cuando va al supermercado, Roberto ------- demasiado dinero.

(A) extiende
(B) gasta
(C) busca
(D) cuesta

GO ON TO THE NEXT PAGE

11. Lola, ¿qué ------- te dieron en la clase de química?

    (A) señal
    (B) nota
    (C) tierra
    (D) saco

12. Los incas eran los ------- progresistas políticamente de todas las culturas indígenas.

    (A) mucho
    (B) muy
    (C) muchos
    (D) más

13. ------- gente se acercó para oír la discusión.

    (A) Este
    (B) El
    (C) La
    (D) Toda

14. El enorme tamaño de los murales mexicanos es ------- me gusta más.

    (A) los que
    (B) el que
    (C) lo que
    (D) las que

15. Me visitaron de -------; no los esperaba hasta el sábado.

    (A) orgullo
    (B) sospecha
    (C) pereza
    (D) sorpresa

16. Como ------- me fastidia, hago gimnasia para mantenerme en forma.

    (A) corro
    (B) él corre
    (C) corriendo
    (D) el correr

17. Quiero coser este botón; dame el ------- blanco y una aguja.

    (A) hielo
    (B) nivel
    (C) nido
    (D) hilo

18. Como Angela nunca lleva reloj, siempre me pregunta -------.

    (A) el tiempo
    (B) la hora
    (C) la vez
    (D) el lugar

19. ------- la una de la tarde.

    (A) Está
    (B) Es
    (C) Están
    (D) Son

20. Como la clase ya había empezado, entró ------- para que no lo viera el profesor.

    (A) alegremente
    (B) amargamente
    (C) disimuladamente
    (D) superficialmente

21. Después de hacer tanto ejercicio, los niños ------- muy cansados.

    (A) estaban
    (B) eran
    (C) tenían
    (D) hacían

22. Fernando siempre cumple ------- haber prometido algo.

    (A) sin que
    (B) después de
    (C) cuando
    (D) sobre

23. Mi hermana Cristina es aficionada a los ------- históricos de la Edad Media.

    (A) materias
    (B) temas
    (C) obras
    (D) ideas

24. Carlos, si quieres llegar al aeropuerto antes de las cinco, ------- ahora mismo para evitar el tráfico.

    (A) sale
    (B) salga
    (C) salgas
    (D) sal

GO ON TO THE NEXT PAGE

25. La abogada renunció a su ------- porque decidió jubilarse.

(A) dimensión
(B) pereza
(C) artículo
(D) puesto

26. Los turistas dijeron que ------- habían visto nada tan impresionante como los murales de Diego Rivera.

(A) todavía
(B) también
(C) nunca
(D) además

27. El lago Titicaca es tan profundo que no se puede ver -------.

(A) el fondo
(B) el inferior
(C) la base
(D) la orilla

GO ON TO THE NEXT PAGE

Part B

Directions: In each of the following paragraphs, there are numbered blanks indicating that words or phrases have been omitted. For each numbered blank, four completions are provided. First read through the entire paragraph. Then, for each numbered blank, choose the completion that is most appropriate given the context of the entire paragraph and fill in the corresponding circle on the answer sheet.

Soy oriunda de Bolivia, residente en Ottawa __(28)__ 1982, y me __(29)__ vuelto una lectora asidua de su __(30)__, que es una de las pocas publicaciones en idioma español que __(31)__ a Canadá. He leído con __(32)__ interés los artículos que publican, especialmente el dedicado a la "Historia Viva" de los carnavales, en __(33)__ mencionaban los de Venecia, Santiago de Cuba, Río de Janeiro . . . y en el cual se omite el carnaval de Oruro que __(34)__ en Bolivia todos los años y es único en su __(35)__: es el único carnaval folclórico en el cual participan miles y miles de danzarines y en donde el __(36)__ favorito es la Diablada de Oruro.

28. (A) donde
(B) desde
(C) hacia
(D) entre

29. (A) hubiera
(B) habré
(C) haya
(D) he

30. (A) revista
(B) lectura
(C) noticiero
(D) anuncio

31. (A) lleguen
(B) llegan
(C) llegaran
(D) llegarían

32. (A) mucha
(B) muchas
(C) mucho
(D) muchos

33. (A) quien
(B) lo cual
(C) el que
(D) cuyo

34. (A) se lleva a cabo
(B) viene a ser
(C) al parecer
(D) se da cuenta

35. (A) geranio
(B) género
(C) cansancio
(D) cariño

36. (A) conjunto
(B) camino
(C) freno
(D) monte

GO ON TO THE NEXT PAGE

María Fernández y su hijo Ángel son los únicos habitantes, __(37)__ más de quince años, de Foncebadón, una localidad de la provincia de León, que __(38)__ parte del Camino de Santiago. Madre e hijo se dedican a la ganadería. En sus establos, __(39)__ casas de otros vecinos, duermen ahora ovejas, cabras y vacas. Y __(40)__ más fieles compañeros son una gran multitud de perros que dormitan __(41)__ por todo el pueblo.

María es una mujer con una fortaleza de carácter __(42)__. Cuando se quedó sola en Foncebadón, su hijo __(43)__ tenía doce años. Y desde entonces, siempre ha luchado con __(44)__ por conservar lo poco que queda en pie de su pueblo y __(45)__ ello hace lo imposible.

37. (A) sin embargo
(B) supuesto
(C) desde hace
(D) a pesar de

38. (A) hace
(B) debe
(C) sueña
(D) forma

39. (A) antiguo
(B) antigüedad
(C) antiquísimo
(D) antiguamente

40. (A) su
(B) sus
(C) suyo
(D) suyos

41. (A) perezosos
(B) frenéticos
(C) despegados
(D) entusiasmados

42. (A) por lo general
(B) fuera de lo común
(C) a fin de cuentas
(D) de buenas a primeras

43. (A) poco
(B) nunca
(C) apenas
(D) aunque

44. (A) jabón y toalla
(B) pan y vino
(C) cuchara y tenedor
(D) uñas y dientes

45. (A) para
(B) sin
(C) como
(D) aun

GO ON TO THE NEXT PAGE

Investigaciones recientes realizadas sobre __(46)__ la vida en la especie humana parecen demostrar que el hombre está programado __(47)__ vivir 200 años, pero las circunstancias que lo rodean __(48)__ esa posibilidad. Al menos eso es __(49)__ asegura un profesor de la Universidad Complutense de Madrid.

El ocio y los vicios acortan la vida. Las personas __(50)__ trabajo requiere actividad física al aire libre y llevan una vida sencilla, tienen más posibilidades __(51)__ a viejos.

Un hecho que se ha observado repetidamente es que en __(52)__ la gente vive mucho __(53)__ en el continente. La dieta __(54)__ parece influir y así se ha visto que casi todas las personas que sobrepasan los __(55)__ años se han alimentado a base de vegetales, leche, yogur, quesos sin grasa, pan, carnes y frutas.

46. (A) el éxito en
(B) la duración de
(C) la dieta en
(D) el auxilio de

47. (A) para
(B) por
(C) de
(D) en

48. (A) ayudan
(B) representan
(C) realizan
(D) disminuyen

49. (A) lo que
(B) que
(C) como
(D) cual

50. (A) cuyas
(B) cuyo
(C) de quien
(D) de quienes

51. (A) para matar
(B) de morir
(C) de llegar
(D) a pasar

52. (A) las islas
(B) los hospitales
(C) las nubes
(D) los hogares

53. (A) no más que
(B) más de que
(C) más de
(D) más que

54. (A) ninguna
(B) nunca
(C) también
(D) tal vez

55. (A) cien
(B) ciento
(C) cientos
(D) centenares

GO ON TO THE NEXT PAGE

Part C

Directions: Read the following texts carefully for comprehension. Each text is followed by a number of questions or incomplete statements. Select the answer or completion that is best according to the text and fill in the corresponding circle on the answer sheet.

La América del Sur

La característica más notable del continente suramericano es la variedad de sus bellezas geográficas naturales, y la enorme extensión de los territorios donde éstas se encuentran. El sur de la Argentina, conocido como Tierra del Fuego, es una zona fría y desértica, que contrasta con las selvas amazónicas del Perú, el Ecuador y el Brasil. Las montañas que atraviesan el continente de norte a sur, y que conocemos como la cordillera de los Andes, recorren el oeste de las inmensas pampas argentinas —terrenos llanos de gran riqueza agrícola y ganadera—y llegan a los no menos extensos llanos de Venezuela, ricos también en ganadería. Las hermosas playas del Uruguay y del Brasil, bañadas por el Atlántico, o las de Colombia, que se extienden por los océanos Atlántico y Pacífico, contrastan con la aridez del desierto de Atacama, en Chile, rico en minas de hierro y cobre, pero donde pasan años sin que caiga una gota de lluvia. Las cataratas del Iguazú, frontera entre el Brasil y la Argentina, son 21 metros más altas que las cataratas del Niágara, en América del Norte, y su volumen de agua es muchas veces mayor. No obstante, una bellísima catarata en Venezuela, conocida como el Salto del Ángel, es la más alta del mundo; sus aguas caen desde más de 900 metros de altura.

56. Este texto probablemente se podría leer en
    - (A) una leyenda infantil
    - (B) un editorial político
    - (C) una revista deportiva
    - (D) un folleto turístico

57. Según el artículo, el sur de la Argentina es conocido por
    - (A) tener un clima cálido
    - (B) ser un área fría
    - (C) sus playas
    - (D) sus cataratas

GO ON TO THE NEXT PAGE

58. Las pampas son una zona geográfica muy ______.
    (A) fértil
    (B) montañosa
    (C) desértica
    (D) poblada

59. Según el pasaje, hay minas de hierro y cobre en
    (A) las playas de Colombia
    (B) los llanos de Venezuela
    (C) el desierto de Chile
    (D) las selvas del Brasil

60. ¿Porqué se distingue la catarata del Salto del Ángel?
    (A) Por su altura
    (B) Por el color del agua
    (C) Por sus plantas hidroeléctricas
    (D) Por ser la única catarata del continente

61. Según el artículo, se puede concluir que lo más destacado de la geografía suramericana es la
    (A) diversidad de sus paisajes
    (B) variedad de animales y plantas
    (C) selva amazónica
    (D) riqueza agrícola

Un fascinante viaje a través de 15.000 años para descubrir las obras de arte más bellas creadas por la humanidad.

Ahora el Club Internacional del Libro ha editado la colección *Tesoros Artísticos del Mundo*, en colaboración con los más prestigiosos Catedráticos y Profesores universitarios y especialistas en la historia del arte. Todo ello en 10 espectaculares volúmenes con más de 1.500 páginas ilustradas a todo color.

Realice la reserva de la colección antes de 15 días y consiga

GRATIS

Una colección de 10 vídeos de Grandes Épocas del Arte.

GO ON TO THE NEXT PAGE

62. ¿Cuántos años de arte incluye la colección de *Tesoros artísticos del mundo* ?

(A) Quince mil
(B) Quinientos
(C) Mil quinientos
(D) Quince

63. Según el anuncio, ¿quiénes han trabajado en esta colección?

(A) Artistas famosos
(B) Expertos en arte
(C) Estudiantes universitarios
(D) Los socios de un club

64. Para obtener esta colección con el regalo, es necesario

(A) hacer un viaje fascinante
(B) asistir a una universidad
(C) hacer una reserva lo antes posible
(D) llamar al museo de arte

65. Según el anuncio, ¿cómo se puede pagar por esta colección?

(A) A vuelta de correo
(B) Con tarjeta de crédito
(C) En efectivo
(D) A plazos mensuales

GO ON TO THE NEXT PAGE

Mi caballo, Cachito

Cuando era jovencita, me encantaba montar a caballo y siempre competía con las demás amazonas para atraer la atención de nuestra instructora, la Sra. Gómez. Yo creía ser una de las mejores amazonas puesto que nunca tenía miedo de saltar obstáculos por altos que fueran. Desafortunadamente mi caballo Cachito no tenía las mismas aspiraciones que yo.

A Cachito le encantaba comer y, al pasar de los años, había engordado a tal punto que se le dificultaban los obstáculos altos y empezó a rehusarlos. Esto tuvo un gran efecto en nuestra participación en las competencias. Después de una mala temporada de concursos, la Sra. Gómez puso a dieta a Cachito para que pudiera recuperar su habilidad en la pista. Esto no le gustó nada a Cachito, quien empezó a glotonear en cuanto se le presentaba la oportunidad. Cachito desarrolló varias nuevas costumbres, una de las cuales le disgustaba mucho a su cuidador, Manuel. Cachito lograba escapar de Manuel y, al soltarse, corría dos kilómetros al extremo del club hípico y comía pasto. Cachito permitía que Manuel se le acercara lo suficiente para tocarlo, pero en cuanto trataba de agarrar su cuerda corría al otro extremo del club donde repetía sus acciones. Al fracasar el plan de poner en forma a Cachito, la Sra. Gómez me dio un nuevo caballo, el Macadú, con el que volví a ganar competencias. Empezaron a usar a Cachito para enseñar a los novatos del club. Como éstos sólo saltaban obstáculos bajos, este trabajo no le disgustaba a Cachito.

66. ¿Cuál era uno de los placeres de Cachito?

(A) Dormir en el campo
(B) Pasear con Manuel
(C) Comer cuanto pudiera
(D) Volver al establo

67. ¿Por qué pensaba la narradora que montaba bien a caballo?

(A) Porque siempre ganaba
(B) Porque era muy rápida en las carreras
(C) Porque no le temía a los obstáculos difíciles
(D) Porque montaba sin silla

68. ¿Qué afectó negativamente la habilidad de Cachito?

(A) La tierra
(B) El peso
(C) La estatura
(D) El clima

69. ¿Por qué se enojaba el cuidador con Cachito?

(A) Porque se peleaba con otros caballos
(B) Porque no le permitía bañarlo
(C) Porque lo pateaba y mordía
(D) Porque se le escapaba constantemente

70. ¿Qué le ocurrió a la narradora como resultado de los problemas de Cachito?

(A) Dejó de montar.
(B) Nunca llegó a ganar una competencia.
(C) Recibió otro caballo.
(D) Cambió de club.

71. ¿Qué hicieron con el Cachito?

(A) Lo usaron para entrenar.
(B) Lo mandaron a otro rancho.
(C) Lo vendieron a una familia.
(D) Lo usaron para la agricultura.

72. Esta narración probablemente proviene de

(A) una autobiografía
(B) una novela de aventuras
(C) un artículo científico
(D) una enciclopedia

GO ON TO THE NEXT PAGE

De Miami a Nueva York
$49*
Todos los asientos se convierten en camas
Sale de Miami: martes • jueves • sábado
*Mes de enero
"Duerma en primera clase mientras viaja"
888-555-0022
"EL BUS CÓMODO"

73. Según este anuncio, una de las ventajas de este servicio es que

(A) los conductores son de primera clase
(B) se puede descansar durante el viaje
(C) se sirven bebidas durante el viaje
(D) el viaje dura tres días

GO ON TO THE NEXT PAGE

Ahora mi mamá me observa. He pasado anoche un susto terrible. Mis hermanos jugaban después de comer, corriendo en el patio, y yo los miraba desde el corredor, pensando en Angélica, cuando oí que mi mamá le decía a mi abuela: —¿Estará enfermo?—Y entonces me imaginé que estaban hablando de mí. No me atreví a mirarlas, pero sentía que ellas me miraban a mí. Y así era, de mí hablaban, porque mi mamá volvió a decir: —Hace muchas noches que no juega—. Y mi abuela le dijo que me dejara, que yo era así, apagado y tristón y no vivo como mis hermanos; pero mi mamá me llamó. Yo estaba como una estatua; ni voz tenía del susto . . . La pura verdad, yo creo que me estoy enfermando de amor, porque ya es mucho lo nervioso que me he puesto pensando en Angélica . . . —¿Por qué no corres tú también un poco?—me preguntó mi mamá, y yo le contesté que tenía sueño, y ella me tocaba la frente, creyendo que estaría con fiebre; pero yo le aseguré que no tenía nada, y me puse a reír, a la fuerza, eso sí, y porque sólo de pensar que, me creyeran enfermo, temblé. Mi abuela me encontró la frente fresca. Mi abuela opina siempre antes de examinar; así es que antes de haberme tocado ya tenía resuelto hallarme fresco. Algo bueno había de tener, la pobre. Si mi mamá tuviera ese carácter, yo sería muy independiente y más feliz. Pero me cuida demasiado. Porque me quiere será . . . y a mí me gusta que me quiera . . . pero es fastidioso que se fijen tanto en uno . . . y no le dejen vivir su vida privada y sus fantasías.

74. Se puede deducir del cuento que el narrador no participaba en los juegos de sus hermanos porque

(A) tenía un poco de fiebre
(B) su madre no se lo permitía
(C) estaba terriblemente asustado
(D) pensaba en una chica

75. Lo que el narrador del cuento desea es que

(A) su familia lo deje tranquilo
(B) sus hermanos lo traten bien
(C) su abuela lo quiera más
(D) Angélica piense en él

76. La madre estaba preocupada porque creía que el niño

(A) tenía problemas de salud
(B) estaba muy nervioso
(C) era demasiado travieso
(D) era un poco descuidado

77. Según el narrador, su abuela se caracteriza por

(A) su personalidad dominante
(B) su carácter analítico
(C) sus decisiones prematuras
(D) su naturaleza delicada

78. ¿Cómo reacciona el narrador ante las preguntas de su madre?

(A) Le confiesa sus preocupaciones.
(B) Se niega a contestarlas.
(C) Trata de engañarla.
(D) Se pone a llorar.

79. La abuela opina que el narrador es de temperamento

(A) melancólico
(B) hostil
(C) inestable
(D) vivo

80. ¿Qué le molesta al narrador?

(A) No poder entender a su mamá.
(B) Que no le den suficiente independencia.
(C) Que sus hermanos se rían de él.
(D) Sentir la soledad de la noche.

GO ON TO THE NEXT PAGE

SI VIENE A CONOCER ESPAÑA, NO PUEDE IRSE SIN VISITAR EL CORTE INGLÉS.

EN ESTE VIAJE, DESCUBRA LA PRIMERA CADENA EUROPEA DE GRANDES ALMACENES. UN NÚMERO UNO EN MODA, HOGAR, REGALOS, PRIMERAS MARCAS, EXCLUSIVIDAD Y EN OFRECER GARANTÍA Y SERVICIO.

ADEMÁS, PODRÁ HABLAR EN SU IDIOMA, COMPRAR UN RECUERDO, ALMORZAR CÓMODAMENTE EN EL RESTAURANTE, DARSE UN CORTE DE PELO, LLAMAR POR TELÉFONO A SU PAÍS, REVELAR LAS FOTOS EN UNA HORA, ENVIAR PAQUETES A CUALQUIER PARTE DEL MUNDO.

EN ESTE VIAJE A ESPAÑA, DESCUBRA LA PRIMERA CADENA EUROPEA DE GRANDES ALMACENES.

El Corte Inglés

GRANDES ALMACENES

UN LUGAR PARA COMPRAR. UN LUGAR PARA SOÑAR.

81. Según el anuncio, ¿qué se puede encontrar en El Corte Inglés?

(A) Un banco
(B) Una agencia de viajes
(C) Un hotel de lujo
(D) Una peluquería

82. Según el anuncio, El Corte Inglés ofrece el servicio de

(A) envíos a otros países
(B) enseñanza de idiomas
(C) fotocopiado gratis
(D) cuidado de niños

83. ¿A quién se dirige este anuncio principalmente?

(A) Turistas extranjeros
(B) Españoles que viajan fuera del país
(C) Profesores españoles
(D) Estudiantes de la escuela primaria

GO ON TO THE NEXT PAGE

¡PARTICIPA Y GANA!

¡PARTICIPA EN EL SORTEO DE 3 VIAJES A EURODISNEY!

Pensando en ti, sorteamos 3 fantásticos viajes a Eurodisney en París para 4 personas cada uno. Para que disfrutes, con tu familia y amigos, del maravilloso reino de Disney donde creatividad y magia se mezclan en un sueño que nunca olvidarás.
Y para que la estancia sea totalmente feliz, cada ganador recibirá además, una "bolsa de viaje" de 1.000 euros, como agradable complemento para todos sus gastos.

Por cualquier compra que realices de productos de catálogo YVES ROCHER, entrarás en el sorteo. Uno de estos viajes puede ser tuyo.

El sorteo se realizará ante notario el día 25 de enero.

84. ¿Qué se puede ganar en este sorteo?

(A) Un papel en una película
(B) Un viaje a París y dinero
(C) Un producto de un catálogo
(D) Un curso de magia

85. ¿Cómo se puede participar en este sorteo?

(A) Viajando frecuentemente
(B) Comprando billetes de lotería
(C) Adquiriendo un producto
(D) Siendo creativo

STOP

IF YOU FINISH BEFORE TIME IS CALLED, YOU MAY CHECK YOUR WORK ON THIS TEST ONLY.

DO NOT TURN TO ANY OTHER TEST IN THIS BOOK.

How to Score the SAT Subject Test in Spanish

When you take an actual SAT Subject Test in Spanish, your answer sheet will be "read" by a scanning machine that will record your response to each question. Then a computer will compare your answers with the correct answers and produce your raw score. You get one point for each correct answer. For each wrong answer, you lose one-third of a point. Questions you omit (and any for which you mark more than one answer) are not counted. This raw score is converted to a scaled score that is reported to you and to the colleges you specify.

Worksheet 1. Finding Your Raw Test Score

STEP 1: Table A on the following page lists the correct answers for all the questions on the Subject Test in Spanish that is reproduced in this book. It also serves as a worksheet for you to calculate your raw score.

- Compare your answers with those given in the table.
- Put a check in the column marked "Right" if your answer is correct.
- Put a check in the column marked "Wrong" if your answer is incorrect.
- Leave both columns blank if you omitted the question.

STEP 2: Count the number of right answers.

Enter the total here: ________________

STEP 3: Count the number of wrong answers.

Enter the total here: ________________

STEP 4: Multiply the number of wrong answers by .333.

Enter the product here: ________________

STEP 5: Subtract the result obtained in Step 4 from the total you obtained in Step 2.

Enter the result here: ________________

STEP 6: Round the number obtained in Step 5 to the nearest whole number.

Enter the result here: ________________

The number you obtained in Step 6 is your raw score.

Table A

Answers to the Subject Test in Spanish and Percentage of Students Answering Each Question Correctly									
Question Number	Correct Answer	Right	Wrong	Percentage of Students Answering the Question Correctly*	Question Number	Correct Answer	Right	Wrong	Percentage of Students Answering the Question Correctly*
1	C			77	33	C			33
2	A			92	34	A			34
3	D			88	35	B			51
4	B			98	36	A			27
5	B			66	37	C			68
6	C			75	38	D			80
7	B			83	39	D			28
8	C			75	40	B			80
9	A			76	41	A			36
10	B			72	42	B			41
11	B			92	43	C			48
12	D			87	44	D			40
13	C			85	45	A			39
14	C			80	46	B			82
15	D			77	47	A			78
16	D			29	48	D			67
17	D			41	49	A			62
18	B			75	50	B			20
19	B			87	51	C			43
20	C			47	52	A			79
21	A			83	53	D			61
22	B			47	54	C			76
23	B			45	55	A			55
24	D			46	56	D			93
25	D			41	57	B			85
26	C			82	58	A			72
27	A			41	59	C			89
28	B			83	60	A			90
29	D			63	61	A			84
30	A			69	62	A			83
31	B			63	63	B			79
32	C			60	64	C			94

Table A continued on next page

Table A continued from previous page

Question Number	Correct Answer	Right	Wrong	Percentage of Students Answering the Question Correctly*	Question Number	Correct Answer	Right	Wrong	Percentage of Students Answering the Question Correctly*
65	D			51	76	A			74
66	C			79	77	C			33
67	C			72	78	C			33
68	B			55	79	A			46
69	D			79	80	B			61
70	C			76	81	D			49
71	A			80	82	A			67
72	A			76	83	A			84
73	B			81	84	B			89
74	D			68	85	C			87
75	A			40					

* These percentages are based on an analysis of the answer sheets of a representative sample of 3,750 students who took the original administration of this test and whose mean score was 566. They may be used as an indication of the relative difficulty of a particular question.

Answer explanations for the Subject Test in Spanish can be found on page 1011.

Finding Your Scaled Score

When you take SAT Subject Tests, the scores sent to the colleges you specify are reported on the College Board scale, which ranges from 200–800. You can convert your practice test score to a scaled score by using Table B. To find your scaled score, locate your raw score in the left-hand column of Table B; the corresponding score in the right-hand column is your scaled score. For example, a raw score of 37 on this particular edition of the Subject Test in Spanish corresponds to a scaled score of 480.

Raw scores are converted to scaled scores to ensure that a score earned on any one edition of a particular Subject Test is comparable to the same scaled score earned on any other edition of the same Subject Test. Because some editions of the tests may be slightly easier or more difficult than others, College Board scaled scores are adjusted so that they indicate the same level of performance regardless of the edition of the test taken and the ability of the group that takes it. Thus, for example, a score of 400 on one edition of a test taken at a particular administration indicates the same level of achievement as a score of 400 on a different edition of the test taken at a different administration.

When you take the SAT Subject Tests during a national administration, your scores are likely to differ somewhat from the scores you obtain on the tests in this book. People perform at different levels at different times for reasons unrelated to the tests themselves. The precision of any test is also limited because it represents only a sample of all the possible questions that could be asked.

Table B

Scaled Score Conversion Table
Subject Test in Spanish

Raw Score	Scaled Score	Raw Score	Scaled Score	Raw Score	Scaled Score
85	800	47	540	9	350
84	800	46	540	8	350
83	800	45	530	7	340
82	790	44	520	6	340
81	790	43	520	5	340
80	780	42	510	4	330
79	780	41	510	3	330
78	770	40	500	2	320
77	760	39	500	1	320
76	760	38	490	0	310
75	750	37	480	-1	310
74	750	36	480	-2	300
73	740	35	470	-3	300
72	740	34	470	-4	290
71	730	33	460	-5	290
70	720	32	460	-6	280
69	710	31	450	-7	280
68	700	30	450	-8	270
67	700	29	440	-9	270
66	690	28	440	-10	260
65	680	27	430	-11	250
64	670	26	430	-12	250
63	660	25	420	-13	240
62	650	24	420	-14	230
61	640	23	420	-15	230
60	640	22	410	-16	230
59	630	21	410	-17	220
58	620	20	400	-18	220
57	610	19	400	-19	210
56	610	18	390	-20	210
55	600	17	390	-21	200
54	590	16	380	-22	200
53	580	15	380	-23	200
52	570	14	380	-24	200
51	570	13	370	-25	200
50	560	12	370	-26	200
49	550	11	360	-27	200
48	550	10	360	-28	200

How Did You Do on the Subject Test in Spanish?

After you score your test and analyze your performance, think about the following questions:

Did you run out of time before reaching the end of the test?

If so, you may need to pace yourself better. For example, maybe you spent too much time on one or two hard questions. A better approach might be to skip the ones you can't answer right away and try answering all the questions that remain on the test. Then if there's time, go back to the questions you skipped.

Did you take a long time reading the directions?

You will save time when you take the test by learning the directions to the Subject Test in Spanish ahead of time. Each minute you spend reading directions during the test is a minute that you could use to answer questions.

How did you handle questions you were unsure of?

If you were able to eliminate one or more of the answer choices as wrong and guess from the remaining ones, your approach probably worked to your advantage. On the other hand, making haphazard guesses or omitting questions without trying to eliminate choices could cost you valuable points.

How difficult were the questions for you compared with other students who took the test?

Table A shows you how difficult the multiple-choice questions were for the group of students who took this test during its national administration. The right-hand column gives the percentage of students that answered each question correctly.

A question answered correctly by almost everyone in the group is obviously an easier question. For example, 87 percent of the students answered question 12 correctly. But only 27 percent answered question 36 correctly.

Keep in mind that these percentages are based on just one group of students. They would probably be different with another group of students taking the test.

If you missed several easier questions, go back and try to find out why: Did the questions cover material you haven't yet reviewed? Did you misunderstand the directions?

Answer Explanations for the Spanish Subject Test

1. Choice (C) is the correct answer. This sentence requires knowledge of vocabulary in context. The word *hay* roughly translates to the English phrase "there is…" or "there are…" Further, the verb *haber* has two uses: as the auxiliary verb "have" used with past participles, and as *hay*, meaning "there is/there are." According to the sentence, *hay un buzón* ("there is a mailbox") if they would like to send this letter to Lucia today.

2. Choice (A) is the correct answer. These sentences require knowledge of vocabulary in context. The speaker first tells Elena that it is 8 o'clock. Then the speaker asks if Elena is ready to leave. The only adjective that fits into this context is (A) *lista* ("ready"). This choice is supported by the adverb *ya*, showing that the speaker is in a hurry.

3. Choice (D) is the correct answer. This sentence requires knowledge of vocabulary related to food. The only logical choice is *postre*, the category meaning "dessert." In order to answer correctly, one must recognize that *pastel de manzana* is a *postre*, or a kind of dessert.

4. Choice (B) is the correct answer. This sentence requires knowledge of parts of speech. The preposition *de*, which in this context translates to "of," is the only preposition that logically and grammatically fits the sentence. The other choices are inappropriate prepositions for this sentence.

5. Choice (B) is the correct answer. This sentence requires command of structure and agreement. Because *la casa* is feminine in gender and singular in number, the pronoun and its modifying possessive pronoun that appear later in the sentence must also be feminine and singular. *La nuestra* (B) is the only choice that has feminine singular pronouns.

6. Choice (C) is the correct answer. This sentence requires command of structure and agreement. The missing word must be a direct object pronoun referring to *esa*

pelicula. Because *esa pelicula* is feminine in gender, the direct object pronoun must also be feminine. Choice (C), *la*, is the feminine singular direct object pronoun.

7. Choice (B) is the correct answer. This sentence requires command of verb tense. Because the author is recounting something that was a recurring practice in the past, signified by *era* ("was") and *todos los años* ("every year"), the correct verb tense is the imperfect indicative: *pasábamos*.

8. Choice (C) is the correct answer. These sentences require knowledge of vocabulary in context. According to the sentence, the speaker has forgotten his pen and would like someone to lend him one. *Prestarme* ("to lend") is the only choice that logically completes the sentence because the possessive adjective *tuyo* eliminates the possibility of having his own pen returned (B).

9. Choice (A) is the correct answer. This sentence requires understanding of verbs that take a preposition when followed by an infinitive. In expressions using prepositions such as *de* followed by a verb, the verb must be in the infinitive tense. *Tener ganas de* is one of these expressions, and *volver* (A) is the only choice in the infinitive form.

10. Choice (B) is the correct answer. This sentence requires knowledge of vocabulary in context. According to the sentence, Roberto does something with too much money when he goes to the supermarket. The word *gasta* ("spends") is the only choice that logically completes the sentence.

11. Choice (B) is the correct answer. This sentence requires knowledge of vocabulary in context. According to the sentence, Lola was given something in chemistry class. A *nota* ("grade") is the choice that most logically completes the sentence.

12. Choice (D) is the correct answer. This sentence requires command of the superlative comparison structure *más . . . de*. In this sentence, *los incas* are being compared favorably to *todas las culturas indígenas* with respect to their progressive politics. *Más* is the only choice that correctly constructs the superlative comparison.

13. Choice (C) is the correct answer. This sentence requires command of noun gender and selection of definite articles. In this context, a definite article is needed, and it must be feminine because *gente* is a feminine noun. *La* is the feminine definite article.

14. Choice (C) is the correct answer. This sentence requires command of structure and pronouns. The neutral pronoun is used when referring to abstract qualities that are not expressed in definitive numbers. In this sentence, the missing pronoun refers to the quality *tamaño* ("size") that is generally associated with Mexican murals. Therefore, the neutral pronoun *lo que* must be used. The other choices are pronouns that have a gender.

15. Choice (D) is the correct answer. This sentence requires knowledge of vocabulary in context. According to the sentence, their visit caused a certain reaction because it was not expected until Saturday. *Sorpresa* ("surprise") logically completes the sentence.

16. Choice (D) is the correct answer. This sentence requires command of verb form. When action verbs such as *correr* ("to run") are used as nouns, they must be in the infinitive form preceded by the definite article. Choice (D) is the only choice that has this combination.

17. Choice (D) is the correct answer. This sentence requires knowledge of vocabulary in context. According to the sentence, the speaker wants to sew a button and asks for a needle (*aguja*) and something else that is white (*blanco*). In order to sew a button, one needs *hilo* ("thread") to use with a needle. The other choices do not make sense in this context.

18. Choice (B) is the correct answer. This sentence requires knowledge of vocabulary in context. According to the sentence, Angela never wears a watch (*reloj*) so she always asks what the time is. In Spanish, the current time is referred to as *la hora* (B), not *el tiempo* (A) or *la vez* (C). Choice (D), *el lugar* ("place"), does not make sense in this context.

19. Choice (B) is the correct answer. This sentence requires the ability to distinguish between the use of the verb *ser* and the use of the verb *estar*. *Ser* is used when referring to the precise time of day. One o'clock is singular because it is just one hour. *Es* (B) is the singular form of *ser*, so it is the only choice that logically and grammatically completes the sentence.

20. Choice (C) is the correct answer. This sentence requires knowledge of vocabulary in context. According to the sentence, the class had already begun, so he entered in a way so that the professor would not see him. The adverb *disimuladamente* ("reservedly") best completes the sentence; someone who enters a room in this manner is trying not to bring attention to himself. The other choices do not make sense in this context.

21. Choice (A) is the correct answer. This sentence requires knowledge of vocabulary in context. It also requires the ability to distinguish among the uses of the verbs *ser, estar, tener,* and *hacer,* which could all be translated as "to be" in the appropriate context. *Estar* is used when referring to conditions such as being tired because of exercise. The other choices are verbs that do not make sense in this context.

22. Choice (B) is the correct answer. This sentence requires knowledge of prepositional phrases. According to the sentence, Fernando always comes through [after] he has promised something. The prepositional phrase *despues de* ("after") best completes the sentence. The other choices are prepositional phrases that do not make sense in this context.

23. Choice (B) is the correct answer. This sentence requires command of gender agreement and knowledge of vocabulary in context. Because the missing word is preceded by *los*, it must be masculine. *Temas* (B) is the only choice that is masculine in gender.

24. Choice (D) is the correct answer. This sentence requires command of verb tense. According to the sentence, the speaker is telling Carlos to leave right now in order to avoid traffic and arrive at the airport before 5 o'clock. The command form of *salir* is needed here because the speaker is telling Carlos what he should do. *Sal* is the second person singular form of *salir* that completes the affirmative familiar command correctly. The other choices are incorrect conjugations of *salir* for an affirmative command.

25. Choice (D) is the correct answer. This sentence requires knowledge of vocabulary in context. According to the sentence, the lawyer resigned because she decided to retire. It makes sense to say that the lawyer resigned from her p*uesto* ("position"). The other choices do not make sense in this context.

26. Choice (C) is the correct answer. This sentence requires command of the use of negative expressions. According to the sentence, the tourists said they have never seen anything as impressive as Diego Rivera's murals. The negative words *nunca* and *nada* are used together in contexts such as that which appears in this sentence. In English, one negative word is used to complete a negative expression (i.e., ". . . they have <u>never</u> seen anything as . . ." or ". . . they have seen <u>nothing</u> as . . ."). In Spanish, however, two negative words are necessary to complete a negative expression. *Nunca* is the only choice that correctly completes the negative expression.

27. Choice (A) is the correct answer. This sentence requires knowledge of vocabulary in context. According to the sentence, Lake Titicaca is so deep that something cannot be seen. *El fondo* ("bottom") logically completes the sentence. The other choices do not make sense in this context.

28. Choice (B) is the correct answer. This sentence requires knowledge of vocabulary in context. The speaker is telling the reader that he or she lives in Ottawa. The missing word links the significance of 1982 and his or her living in Ottawa. The only word that logically completes the sentence is *desde* ("since"). The other choices do not make sense in this context.

29. Choice (D) is the correct answer. This sentence requires command of verb tense. The missing word must be in the present perfect indicative tense, which combines the perfect participle (*vuelto*) with the present tense form of the helping verb *haber. He* is the correct present tense form of *haber.* The other choices are not in the tense that is required to construct the present perfect indicative.

30. Choice (A) is the correct answer. This sentence requires knowledge of vocabulary in context and gender agreement. According to the sentence, the missing word is described as one of the few Spanish language publications that has arrived in Canada. The only word that fits the context of the sentence is *revista* ("magazine"). The other choices do not fit in this context.

31. Choice (B) is the correct answer. This sentence requires command of verb tense. To be consistent with the rest of the paragraph and the existence of the magazine, the missing word must be *llegan*, the present tense of the verb *llegar.* The other choices do not reflect the reality expressed by the present tense form.

32. Choice (C) is the correct answer. This sentence requires command of the use of adjectives. The missing adjective describes the noun *interés*, which is singular and masculine. The gender and number of the adjective must match that of the noun it modifies. *Mucho* is the only choice in the singular masculine form.

33. Choice (C) is the correct answer. This sentence requires command of relative pronouns. The missing pronoun refers to a specific part of an article referred to as *el dedicado*, which is a masculine item. *El que* is the only choice that grammatically fits the sentence. The other choices would be used to refer to people or when the antecedent is not mentioned.

34. Choice (A) is the correct answer. This sentence requires knowledge of idiomatic expressions. The missing expression indicated that *el carnaval de Oruro* takes place in Bolivia. *Se lleva a cabo* best completes the sentence and correctly forms the idiomatic expression. The other choices are inappropriate for describing the idea that something happens somewhere.

35. Choice (B) is the correct answer. This sentence requires knowledge of vocabulary in context. According to the sentence, the carnival is *único* ("unique"). The only word that fits the context of the passage is *género* ("genre"/"type"). The other choices are inappropriate for describing the characteristic that makes the *el carnaval de Osuro* unique.

36. Choice (A) is the correct answer. This sentence requires knowledge of vocabulary in context. According to the sentence, thousands of folk dancers participate in the carnival. The missing word refers to a particular dance group (*conjunto*) that is the favorite, the *Diablada de Oruro*. The other choices — a road, a brake, or a mountain — are inappropriate for referring to the *Diablada de Oruro*.

37. Choice (C) is the correct answer. This sentence requires knowledge of expressions of duration. According to the sentence, María Fernandez and her son have been the only inhabitants of *Foncebadón* for more than fifteen years. The only phrase that fits the context of the sentence is *desde hace*. The other choices are inappropriate for describing the connection between María Fernandez and her son to the phrase *más de quince años*.

38. Choice (D) is the correct answer. This sentence requires knowledge of vocabulary in context. According to the sentence, *Foncebadón* is a town in the province of León, and the missing word shows the relationship between *Foncebadón* and *parte del Camino de Santiago*. The only word that logically completes the sentence is *forma* ("makes up part of"). The other choices are inappropriate for indicating that *Foncebadón* makes up part of the *Camino de Santiago*.

39. Choice (D) is the correct answer. This sentence requires understanding of parts of speech in context. The missing word, selecting from words derived from the common stem *antiguo*, must be an adverb that modifies what the stables were before they were houses. The stables, formerly houses of *otros vecinos* ("other neighbors"), now serve as a place for the sheep, goats, and cows to sleep. *Antiguamente* is the only choice in the adverb form.

40. Choice (B) is the correct answer. This sentence requires command of the use of possessive adjectives. The missing word must be a possessive adjective in the plural form because it modifies the plural noun *compañeros*. *Sus* is the only choice that is a possessive adjective in the plural form.

41. Choice (A) is the correct answer. This sentence requires knowledge of vocabulary in context. According to the sentence, there are many dogs that nap all over the abandoned town. The only word that fits the context of the sentence is *perezosos* ("lazy"). The other choices (frantic, detached, and excited) are inappropriate for describing the dogs that are dozing all over town.

42. Choice (B) is the correct answer. This sentence requires knowledge of vocabulary in context. According to the sentence, María is a woman with strength of character. It makes sense to describe this quality as *fuera de común* ("uncommon"). The other choices are inappropriate for describing the strength of María's character.

43. Choice (C) is the correct answer. This sentence requires knowledge of vocabulary in context. According to the sentence, María's son was 12 years old when she was left alone in *Foncebadón*. It makes sense to describe her son's young age with the word *apenas* ("barely"). The other choices are inappropriate for emphasizing the young age of María's son.

44. Choice (D) is the correct answer. This sentence requires knowledge of idiomatic expressions. According to the sentence, María had to fight to conserve what was left of her town. The only idiomatic expression that fits the context of the sentence is *uñas y dientes* ("tooth and nail"). The other choices (soap and towel, bread and wine, and spoon and fork) do not appropriately emphasize how hard María fought.

45. Choice (A) is the correct answer. This sentence requires command of prepositions. The missing preposition must connect the phrase *ello hace lo imposible* to María's fight. The only preposition that fits in this context is *para*. The other choices do not appropriately connect these two parts of the sentence.

46. Choice (B) is the correct answer. This sentence requires reading comprehension. The missing phrase must connect recent research about human life to living 200 years. The only phrase that fits the context of the sentence is *la duración de* ("the duration of"). The other choices (success, diet, and assistance) do not provide an appropriate connection.

47. Choice (A) is the correct answer. This sentence requires command of prepositions. The missing preposition must connect the phrase *vivir 200 anos* to *el hombre esta programado.* The only preposition that fits in this context is *para*, meaning "in order to." The other choices do not appropriately make the required connection.

48. Choice (D) is the correct answer. This sentence requires knowledge of vocabulary in context. The missing word must describe the negative effects that environmental circumstances have on the potential life span of humans. The only word that fits the context of the sentence is *disminuyen* ("diminish/reduce"). The other choices do not provide an appropriate description.

49. Choice (A) is the correct answer. This sentence requires command of pronouns. In this sentence, the missing pronoun refers to the whole idea of the professor's argument about the human life span. This abstract idea has no number or gender. Therefore, *lo que* is the proper way to construct the neutral relative pronoun referring to the whole idea, rather than to a specific noun.

50. Choice (B) is the correct answer. This sentence requires command of adjective agreement. The missing adjective must not only express possession of *trabajo*, but also agree with its number and gender. Therefore, *cuyo* is the only relative possessive adjective that fulfills both requirements.

51. Choice (C) is the correct answer. This sentence requires knowledge of vocabulary in context. According to the sentence, some have possibilities of reaching old age. The only phrase that fits in this context is *de llegar.* The other choices do not express this idea.

52. Choice (A) is the correct answer. This sentence requires knowledge of vocabulary in context. In this sentence, a comparison is being made between people who live in two different places: *en el continente* ("on the continent") and somewhere else. The missing phrase must indicate another location. It is logical to compare people who live on the continent with people who live on the islands (*las islas*). The other choices do not establish a logical comparison with *el continente.*

53. Choice (D) is the correct answer. This sentence requires command of comparisons. The comparison in this context follows the structure of *más* or *menos* and the word *que*, as in *más que.* The other choices do not construct the comparison properly.

54. Choice (C) is the correct answer. This sentence requires knowledge of vocabulary in context. The missing word must express a relationship that *la dieta* has with ideas contained earlier in the passage. The only word that fits in this context is *también* ("also"). The other choices do not express this relationship.

55. Choice (A) is the correct answer. This sentence requires command of adjectives that drop the final syllable. The form for one hundred would be shortened to modify the noun *años*. *Ciento* always shortens to *cien* (A) before any masculine or feminine noun. It would remain *ciento* (B) if it were in front of a number smaller than itself, and it would not be shortened if it were used in multiples of one hundred, such as *doscientos* (C). *Centenares* (D) is a noun; therefore it does not fit the context of the sentence.

56. Choice (D) is the correct answer. This item requires the ability to determine the main idea of the article. The article provides information related to natural attractions in South America. The language is too sophisticated to be part of a legend for children (A). Further, the article does not express opinions of a political nature (B) or provide information of interest in a sports magazine (C). Therefore, the only appropriate response is *un folleto turístico* since beautiful sights are of interest to tourists.

57. Choice (B) is the correct answer. This item requires literal comprehension of a specific detail found in the text. The text states: "*El sur dela Argentina, conocidocomo Tierra del Fuego, es una zona fría y desértica*," clearly indicating that southern Argentina is a cold area. The other answer choices describe other regions mentioned in the article, but not *el sur de la Argentina*.

58. Choice (A) is the correct answer. This item requires literal comprehension and asks about the geographic region of *las pampas* ("the plains"). According to the passage, the plains are of rich agriculture and livestock ("*llanos de gran riqueza agrícola y ganadera*"). Thus, it would be logical to describe the zone as *fértil*. The other choices do not appropriately describe *las pampas*.

59. Choice (C) is the correct answer. This item requires literal comprehension and asks where the iron and copper mines are located in South America. The passage describes the "*desierto de Atacama*" in Chile as "*rico en minas de hierro y cobre*." In other words, this desert in Chile is rich in iron and copper mines. Therefore, *el desierto de Chile* is the correct answer. The passage does not mention any of the other choices as having these kinds of mines.

60. Choice (A) is the correct answer. This item requires literal comprehension and asks what distinguishes *la catarata del Salto del Ángel.* According to the passage, this Venezuelan waterfall is "*la más alta del mundo*" ("the tallest in the world"). Therefore, it makes sense that it would be distinguished *por su altura* ("for its height"). The other choices do not correctly describe the waterfall.

61. Choice (A) is the correct answer. This item requires the ability to draw conclusions based on information given throughout the passage. The passage begins by stating that the most notable characteristic of South America is "*la variedad de sus bellezas geográficas naturales*" ("the variety of its natural geographic beauty"). The passage goes on to list very diverse geographic locations throughout the region, including *una zona fria y desertica* ("a cold and desert-like zone"), *selvas amazonicas* ("Amazon jungles"), *la cordillera de los Andes* ("the Andes mountain range"), *las immensas pampas argentinas* ("the immense Argentinian plains"), and *cataratas* ("waterfalls"). Based on this information, it is logical to conclude that what stands out most about South American geography is the *diversidad de sus paisajes* ("the diversity of its landscapes").

62. Choice (A) is the correct answer. This item requires literal comprehension and knowledge of numbers. The first line of the advertisement announces a "*viaje a través de 15.000 años.*" Fifteen thousand would be written as *quince mil.*

63. Choice (B) is the correct answer. This item requires literal comprehension. The advertisement states that the collection of books was edited in collaboration "*con los más prestigiosos Catedráticos y Profesores universitarios y especialistas en la historia de arte.*" In other words, the most prestigious university professors and art historians helped to edit the collection. These people would certainly be considered *expertos en arte* ("art experts"). The advertisement does not mention any of the other choices as having helped with the collection.

64. Choice (C) is the correct answer. This item requires literal comprehension. The advertisement offers "*una colección de 10 videos*" for those who "*realice la reserva de colección antes de 15 dias.*" In other words, to receive the collection of ten videos, customers must *hacer una reserve lo antes possible* ("make their reservation as soon as possible"). The advertisement does not mention any of the other choices as options for receiving the video collection.

65. Choice (D) is the correct answer. This item requires literal comprehension. The advertisement states that one can receive the collection of books at their home "*por sólo 500 pesos al mes.*" The phrase *al mes* indicates that customers can pay for the

books for only 500 pesos per month. Therefore, *a plazos mensuales* ("in monthly installments") best describes how customers can pay for the book collection. The other choices are not mentioned in the advertisement as methods of payment.

66. Choice (C) is the correct answer. This item requires literal comprehension. The passage states that Cachito "*le encantaba comer*" ("loves to eat"). It also recounts that he "*había engordado*" ("became fat") and that, after being put on a diet, he "*empezó a glotonear en cuanto se le presentaba la oportunidad.*" In other words, he began to indulge himself as soon as the opportunity presented itself to him. Therefore, one of Cachito's pleasures was clearly *comer cuanto pudiera* ("to eat as much as he could").

67. Choice (C) is the correct answer. This item requires literal comprehension. In the first paragraph, the passage states that the narrator "*creia ser una de las mejores amazonas puesto que nunca tenía miedo de saltar obstáculos por altos que fueran.*" Once Cachito became overweight, he could no longer cooperate with the narrator's fearlessness of jumping high obstacles. When the narrator was given a new horse that could jump high obstacles, she won competitions again ("*volví a ganar competencias*"). Thus, the narrator thought she was a good rider because she was not afraid of the difficult obstacles (*porque no le temía a los obstaculos difíciles*).

68. Choice (B) is the correct answer. This item requires literal comprehension. In the second paragraph, the passage states that Cachito became fat to the point where he began to turn away from the tall, difficult obstacles ("*había engordado a tal punto que se le dificultaban los obstáculos altos y empezó a rehusarlos*"). Thus, it was *el peso* ("the weight") that negatively affected Cachito's ability.

69. Choice (D) is the correct answer. This item requires literal comprehension. In the second paragraph, the narrator tells the story of how Cachito would escape from Manuel, his *cuidador* ("trainer") and run to the other side of the club to eat grass. When Manuel would reach him, Cachito would run to the other side to eat more grass. According to the narrator, Cachito's habit upset Manuel ("*le disgustaba a su cuidador, Manuel*"). Thus, Manuel would get annoyed with Cachito because he constantly escaped (*porque se le escapaba constantemente*).

70. Choice (C) is the correct answer. This item requires literal comprehension. The narrator recounts that after Cachito became too fat to jump high obstacles, the club instructor Sra. Gomez put him on a diet. When Cachito proved he could not lose weight, the narrator says, "*la Sra. Gómez me dio un nuevo caballo*" ("Mrs. Gómez gave me a new horse"). With this new horse, she returned to winning competitions

("*volví a ganar competencias*"). Thus, the narrator received another horse (*recibió otro caballo*) because of Cachito's problems.

71. Choice (A) is the correct answer. This item requires literal comprehension. At the end of the passage, the narrator states that once she had received another horse they began to use Cachito to teach the novices, or beginners, at the club ("*empezaron a usar a Cachito para eñsenar a los novatos del club*"). Cachito kept working at the club; however, he no longer competed, but was used for training (*lo usaron para entrenar*).

72. Choice (A) is the correct answer. This item requires the ability to determine the general purpose of texts. The nature of Cachito's story and the details that are included suggest that the passage is more personal than academic (C) and (D). The story is funny and cute, but not particularly adventurous (B). Additionally, the passage is written in the first person. Therefore, the passage would best fit as part of *una autobiografia* ("an autobiography").

73. Choice (B) is the correct answer. This item requires literal comprehension. The advertisement provides several pieces of information emphasizing that passengers can rest on the bus. It claims that passengers can sleep in first class while they travel ("*duerma en primera clase mientras viaja*"); that all the seats convert to beds ("*todos los asientos se convierten en camas*"); and that the bus is called the comfortable bus ("*el bus cómodo*"). All of this information indicates that one of the advantages of their service is being able to rest during the trip (*se puede descansar durante el viaje*). Although the other choices are possibly true, they are not mentioned in the advertisement.

74. Choice (D) is the correct answer. This item requires literal comprehension. The narrator mentions several times throughout the passage that the reason why he is not playing with his siblings is not because he is sick, but rather because he is distracted by thoughts of Angélica. When the reader first meets the narrator, he says that he was thinking about Angélica ("*pensando en Angélica*"). He later restates how nervous he has gotten while thinking about Angélica ("*lo nervioso que me he puesto pensando en Angélica*").

75. Choice (A) is the correct answer. This item requires literal comprehension. Throughout the passage, the narrator gives the reader the sense that he would rather be left alone with his thoughts of Angélica. He then states that if his mother had his grandmother's character, he would be happier and very independent ("*Si mama tuviera ese carácter, yo sería muy independiente y más feliz*"). But, the narrator goes on to say, his mother takes care of him too much ("*Pero me cuida demasiado*"). Finally,

he closes the passage by simply stating that his family does not allow him to live his own life and fantasies ("*no le dejen vivir su vida privada y sus fantasías*"). In other words, he wishes that his family would leave him alone (*su familia lo deje tranquilo*).

76. Choice (A) is the correct answer. This item requires literal comprehension. The central idea of the passage is that the narrator's mother thinks he is sick, while in fact, the boy is simply thinking about a girl. He overhears his mother ask *¿Estará enfermo?* ("Is he sick?"). Later, he states that his mother felt his forehead, thinking that he had a fever ("*me tocaba la frente, creyendo que estaría con fiebre*").

77. Choice (C) is the correct answer. This item requires literal comprehension. Toward the end of the passage, the narrator compares his mother and his grandmother, wishing that his mother were more like his grandmother. He characterizes his grandmother as someone who always gives her opinion before she examines something or someone ("*opina siempre antes de examinar*"). In other words, he thinks his grandmother makes decisions prematurely, or too quickly (*sus decisiones prematuras*).

78. Choice (C) is the correct answer. This item requires literal comprehension and the ability to synthesize information throughout a passage. The narrator tells the reader that despite what his mother thinks, he is not sick, but rather simply thinking of Angelica. His mother suggests that he run a little as well ("*¿Por qué no corres tú también un poco?*"). In response, he misleads her, replying that he is tired ("*tenía sueño*"). When she thinks he is sick, he forces himself to laugh, not wanting them to think that he is sick ("*yo le aseguré que no tenía nada, y me puse a reír, a la fuerza*"). Rather than confess the truth, he tries to deceive, or trick, her (*trata de engañarla*).

79. Choice (A) is the correct answer. This item requires literal comprehension. When the narrator's mother complains to his grandmother, saying that there are many nights when he does not play ("*hace muchas noches que no juega*"), the grandmother replies that the narrator is quiet and sad ("*era así, apagado y tristón*"). *Apagado y tristón* describes a melancholy temperament (*melancólico*).

80. Choice (B) is the correct answer. This item requires literal comprehension. At the end of the passage, the narrator complains several times that his mother is overprotective. He says that she takes care of him too much ("*me cuida demasiado*") and that if his mother were more like his grandmother, he would be happier and very independent ("*yo sería muy independiente y más feliz*"). He concludes the passage by complaining that his family pays too much attention to him and they do not let him live his own life ("*se fijen tanto en uno. . . y no le dejen vivir su vida privada*"). He is clearly

annoyed because they do not give him enough independence (*que no le den suficiente independencia*).

81. Choice (D) is the correct answer. This item requires literal comprehension. In the second paragraph, the advertisement states that guests of *El Corte Inglés* could get a haircut ("*podrá . . . dares un corte de pelo*"). Thus, there must be *una peluqueria* ("a hair salon/barber") on site. The advertisement does not mention any of the other choices as things you can find in *El Corte Inglés*.

82. Choice (A) is the correct answer. This item requires literal comprehension. In the second paragraph, the advertisement states that guests of *El Corte Inglés* could send packages to any part of the world ("*podrá . . . enviar paquetes a cualquier parte del mundo*"). Therefore, guests can send items to other countries (*envíos a otros países*). The advertisement does not mention any of the other choices as services offered by *El Corte Inglés*.

83. Choice (A) is the correct answer. This item requires the ability to determine the general purpose and intended audience of texts. There are many elements throughout the advertisement that indicate that it is directed at *turistas extranjeros* ("foreign tourists"). First, the name itself suggests that the place caters to an international clientele. Additionally, the advertisement addresses those who come to visit and get to know Spain ("*viene a conocer España*"). It also describes various services that cater to tourists, such as "*hablar en su idioma*" ("to speak in your language"), "*comprar un recuerdo*" ("to buy a souvenir"), and "*llamar por teléfono a su país*" ("to make a telephone call to your country").

84. Choice (B) is the correct answer. This item requires literal comprehension. There are several statements throughout the announcement indicating that the winners of the raffle for three trips to EuroDisney ("*El Sorteo de 3 Viajes a EuroDisney*") will receive money and a trip to Paris (*un viaje a París y dinero*). The text of the announcement states that EuroDisney is in Paris and that, in addition to the trip, the winners will receive a bag of 1,000 euros ("*una 'bolsa de viaje' de 1.000 euros*").

85. Choice (C) is the correct answer. This item requires literal comprehension. Toward the end of the announcement, it states that anyone who buys products from a certain catalog will be entered in the raffle ("*Por cualquier compra que realices de productos . . . entarás en el sorteo*"). In other words, by purchasing a product (*adquiriendo un producto*), one is automatically entered in the raffle. The announcement does not indicate any of the other choices as ways that one can enter the contest.

Spanish with Listening

The SAT Subject Test in Spanish with Listening is offered once a year only at designated test centers. **To take the test you MUST bring an acceptable CD player with earphones to the test center.**

Sample Listening Questions

The text in brackets [ ] is *only* recorded; it is not printed in your test book. Please note that the CD does not start here. Begin using the CD when you start the actual practice test on page 1032.

Please note your answer sheet has five answer positions marked A, B, C, D, and E, while the questions throughout this test contain only four choices. Be sure not to make any marks in column E.

Part A

Directions: For each question in this part, you will hear four sentences, designated (A), (B), (C), and (D). They will not be printed in your test booklet. As you listen, look at the picture in your test booklet and select the choice that best reflects what you see in the picture or what someone in the picture might say. Then fill in the corresponding circle on the answer sheet. You will hear the choices only once. Now look at the following example.

You see:

You hear:

(Woman) [(A) Siento darles tan mala noticia.

(B) Tiene quince días para pagar la multa.

(C) Y aquí les mando la foto más reciente.

(D) Es preciso que se presente ante el juez.]

(7 seconds)

Choice (C) is the correct answer. *Y aquí les mando la foto más reciente* best reflects what you see in the picture or what someone in the picture might say.

Now we will begin. Look at the first picture and listen to the four choices.

1. (Narrator) [Número 1]

(Man) [(A) ¡Otro micrófono, por favor!
(B) La guitarra no tiene cuerdas.
(C) Adiós, ya estoy aburrido.
(D) ¡Cantemos todos juntos!]

(7 seconds)

Choice (D) is the correct answer to question 1. This question tests listening comprehension. To answer correctly, you need to recognize that (D) best reflects what the person in the photograph might say. The wrong choices, (A), (B), and (C), do not reflect what the singer might say in this instance.

Part B

Directions: In this part of the test you will hear several short conversations, or parts of conversations, followed by four choices designated (A), (B), (C), and (D). After you hear the four choices, choose the one that most logically continues or completes the conversation and mark your answer on your answer sheet. What you see in brackets ([ ]) will not be printed in your test booklet. Now listen to the following example.

You will hear:

(Man) [Yo creo que leer es muy importante.]

You will also hear:

(Woman) [(A) Pues no leas tanto.
(B) Estoy totalmente de acuerdo.
(C) No te acuerdas de nada.
(D) No me importan esas leyes.]

(7 seconds)

Choice (B) is the correct answer. It is the choice that most logically continues the conversation.

Now listen to the first conversation.

2. (Narrator) [Número 2]
(Woman) [Llegaste tarde; ¡ya no quedan entradas para esa obra!]
(Man) [(A) ¡Qué entradas tan caras!
(B) Hay otra puerta por aquí.
(C) Perdona, se atrasó el autobús.
(D) A la izquierda está la entrada.]

(7 seconds)

Choice (C) is the correct answer to question 2. This question tests listening comprehension. Choice (C) *Perdona, se atrasó el autobús* is the correct choice. To answer correctly, you need to recognize that choice (C) is the most appropriate response to the woman's statement. The wrong choices, (A), (B), and (D), are inappropriate responses to the woman's statement that there are no tickets left for the performance.

Part C

Directions: You will now hear a series of selections. For each selection, you will see printed in your test booklet one or more questions with four possible answers. They will not be spoken. Select the best answer to each question from among the four choices and fill in the corresponding circle on your answer sheet. You will have 12 seconds to answer each question. There will be no example for this part. Now listen to the first selection.

(Narrator)	[Selección Número 1. Escuchen esta conversación en la recepción del Hotel California.]
(Man)	[Hola, buenas tardes, señorita. ¿Tiene Ud. una reservación a nombre de Escalante?
(Woman)	Déjeme ver. Mmm. . . No la veo, señor. ¿La hizo directamente con nosotros?
(Man)	Sí, con ustedes. Aquí tengo la confirmación
(Woman)	Pues, señor, el problema es que el hotel está lleno y no quedan habitaciones
(Man)	Pero, ¿qué hago yo? He pagado un depósito.
(Woman)	Un momento, por favor. Llamaré al gerente para solucionar el problema.]
(Narrator)	[Ahora contesten las preguntas 3 y 4.]

(24 seconds)

3. ¿Qué problema tiene el Sr. Escalante?
   (A) Perdió su confirmación.
   (B) No quiere alojarse en el Hotel California.
   (C) El hotel no tiene su reservación.
   (D) Olvidó pagar el depósito.

4. ¿Cómo trata la recepcionista al Sr. Escalante?
   (A) Bruscamente
   (B) Respetuosamente
   (C) Insolentemente
   (D) Alegremente

Choice (C) *El hotel no tiene su reservación* is the correct answer to question 3. This question tests listening comprehension. To answer correctly, you need to recognize that Sr. Escalante's problem is that the hotel does not have his reservation. He made a reservation, paid a deposit, and received a confirmation from the hotel; therefore choices (A), (B), and (D) are incorrect.

Choice (B) *Respetuosamente* is the correct answer to question 4. This question tests listening comprehension. To answer correctly, you need to recognize that the receptionist treats Sr. Escalante respectfully in trying to help him. The wrong choices, (A), (C), and (D), do not accurately describe her manner towards him during the conversation.

Spanish with Listening Subject Test

Practice Helps

The test that follows is an actual, previously administered SAT Subject Test in Spanish with Listening. To get an idea of what it's like to take this test, practice under conditions that are much like those of an actual test administration.

- Set aside an hour when you can take the test uninterrupted.
- Sit at a desk or table with no other books or papers. Dictionaries, other books, or notes are not allowed in the test room.
- Tear out an answer sheet from the back of this book and fill it in just as you would on the day of the test. One answer sheet can be used for up to three Subject Tests.
- Read the instructions that precede the practice test. During the actual administration you will be asked to read them before answering test questions.
- Time yourself by placing a clock or kitchen timer in front of you.
- After you finish the practice test, read the sections "How to Score the SAT Subject Test in Spanish with Listening" and "How Did You Do on the Subject Test in Spanish with Listening?"
- The appearance of the answer sheet in this book may differ from the answer sheet you see on test day.

SPANISH TEST WITH LISTENING

The top portion of the page of the answer sheet that you will use to take the Spanish Test with Listening must be filled in exactly as illustrated below. When your supervisor tells you to fill in the circle next to the name of the test you are about to take, mark your answer sheet as shown.

○ Literature	○ Mathematics Level 1	○ German	○ Chinese Listening	○ Japanese Listening
○ Biology E	○ Mathematics Level 2	○ Italian	○ French Listening	○ Korean Listening
○ Biology M	○ U.S. History	○ Latin	○ German Listening	● Spanish Listening
○ Chemistry	○ World History	○ Modern Hebrew		
○ Physics	○ French	○ Spanish	**Background Questions:** ①②③④⑤⑥⑦⑧⑨	

After filling in the circle next to the name of the test you are taking, locate the Background Questions box on your answer sheet (as shown above). This is where you will answer the following Background Questions on your answer sheet.

BACKGROUND QUESTIONS

Please answer either Part I or Part II below by filling in the appropriate circle in the Background Questions box on your answer sheet. Fill in ONLY ONE circle, as described below, to indicate how you obtained your knowledge of Spanish. The information you provide is for statistical purposes only and will not affect your test score.

Part I If your knowledge of Spanish comes primarily from any of the following: living in a home where Spanish is the main spoken language, living for six months or longer in a Spanish-speaking country that included significant experience in Spanish language, courses taken at a college, or special study of Spanish, fill in circle 9 and leave the remaining circles blank, regardless of how long you studied the subject in school.

Part II If your knowledge of Spanish comes primarily from courses taken in secondary school, fill in the circle that indicates the level of the Spanish course in which you are currently enrolled. If you are not now enrolled in a Spanish course, fill in the circle that indicates the level of the most advanced course in Spanish that you have completed.

- First year: first or second half —Fill in circle 1.
- Second year: first half —Fill in circle 2.
  second half —Fill in circle 3.
- Third year: first half —Fill in circle 4.
  second half —Fill in circle 5.
- Fourth year: first half —Fill in circle 6.
  second half —Fill in circle 7.
- Advanced Placement course or a course at a level higher than fourth year, second half
  or
  high school course work plus a minimum of four weeks of study abroad. —Fill in circle 8.

When the supervisor gives the signal, turn the page and begin the Spanish Test with Listening. There are 100 numbered circles on the answer sheet and 85 questions in the Spanish Test with Listening. Therefore, use only circles 1 to 85 for recording your answers.

SPANISH TEST WITH LISTENING

PLEASE NOTE THAT YOUR ANSWER SHEET HAS FIVE ANSWER POSITIONS, MARKED A, B, C, D, AND E, WHILE THE QUESTIONS THROUGHOUT THIS TEST CONTAIN ONLY FOUR CHOICES. BE SURE NOT TO MAKE ANY MARKS IN COLUMN E.

SECTION I

LISTENING

Approximate time—20 minutes

Questions 1-30

Part A

Directions: For each question in this part, you will hear four sentences, designated (A), (B), (C), and (D). They will not be printed in your test booklet. As you listen, look at the picture in your test booklet and select the choice that best reflects what you see in the picture or what someone in the picture might say. Then fill in the corresponding circle on the answer sheet. You will hear the choices only once. Now look at the following example.

You see:

You hear:

Statement (C), "Y aquí les mando la foto más reciente," best reflects what you see in the picture or what someone in the picture might say. Therefore, you would choose answer (C). Now we will begin. Look at the first picture and listen to the four choices.

GO ON TO THE NEXT PAGE

1.

2.

GO ON TO THE NEXT PAGE

3.

4.

GO ON TO THE NEXT PAGE

5.

©Elyse Lewin / The Image Bank

6.

UPI/Bettmann

GO ON TO THE NEXT PAGE

7.

8.

Unauthorized copying or reuse of any part of this page is illegal.

GO ON TO THE NEXT PAGE

9.

GO ON TO THE NEXT PAGE

Part B

Directions: In this part of the test you will hear several short conversations or parts of conversations, followed by four choices, designated (A), (B), (C), and (D). After you hear the four choices, choose the one that most logically continues or completes the conversation and mark your answer on your answer sheet. Neither the conversations nor the choices will be printed in your test booklet. Now listen to the following example.

You will hear:

You will also hear:

The choice that most logically continues the conversation is (B), "Estoy totalmente de acuerdo." Therefore, you should choose answer (B). Now listen to the first conversation.

10. Mark your answer on your answer sheet.
11. Mark your answer on your answer sheet.
12. Mark your answer on your answer sheet.
13. Mark your answer on your answer sheet.
14. Mark your answer on your answer sheet.
15. Mark your answer on your answer sheet.
16. Mark your answer on your answer sheet.
17. Mark your answer on your answer sheet.

GO ON TO THE NEXT PAGE

Part C

Directions: You will now hear a series of selections. For each selection, you will see printed in your test booklet one or more questions with four possible answers. They will not be spoken. Select the best answer to each question from among the four choices printed and fill in the corresponding circle on your answer sheet. You will have twelve seconds to answer each question. There will be no example for this part. Now listen to the first selection.

Selección número 1

18. ¿Qué sugiere hacer el joven para entender mejor la película?

(A) Verla otra vez.
(B) Discutirla con ella.
(C) Ir de compras.
(D) Tomar un helado.

19. ¿Qué deciden hacer con respecto a la película?

(A) Tratar de recordarla.
(B) Entenderla del todo.
(C) No pensar más en ella.
(D) Comprar un video.

Selección número 2

20. ¿Dónde reina la tranquilidad para la narradora?

(A) En la plaza mayor.
(B) En el patio de su casa.
(C) En un parque cercano.
(D) En las calles céntricas.

21. ¿Qué se puede apreciar en este ambiente?

(A) Los coches que van y vienen.
(B) Los pájaros que cantan.
(C) El ruido de los niños.
(D) Las relaciones familiares.

22. ¿De qué hablan los ancianos?

(A) De los árboles del parque.
(B) De las frescas fuentes.
(C) De asuntos del pasado.
(D) Del ambiente sofocante.

Selección número 3

23. ¿Por qué es excepcional este parque zoológico?

(A) Porque tiene animales exóticos.
(B) Porque siempre está abierto.
(C) Porque tiene animales de la región.
(D) Porque tiene todo tipo de peces.

24. ¿Qué se dice en el anuncio de la entrada a este zoológico?

(A) Cuesta cinco dólares.
(B) Cuesta nueve dólares.
(C) Es gratis.
(D) Es libre.

25. ¿Cuándo está abierto el zoológico?

(A) De lunes a domingo.
(B) Todos los días.
(C) De martes a domingo.
(D) Todos los lunes.

GO ON TO THE NEXT PAGE

Selección número 4

26. ¿De qué hablan estas personas?

(A) De una clase.
(B) Del tiempo.
(C) De un horario.
(D) Del día.

27. ¿Qué expresa el joven?

(A) Indiferencia.
(B) Molestia.
(C) Sorpresa.
(D) Alivio.

28. ¿Cómo reacciona Rosaura al final?

(A) Con buen humor.
(B) Con mucha compasión.
(C) Con entusiasmo.
(D) Con admiración.

Selección número 5

29. ¿Qué tiene que hacer Paula?

(A) Llamar a Mariluz.
(B) Salir a la discoteca.
(C) Ayudar a su mamá.
(D) Terminar su tarea.

30. ¿De qué se preocupa la mamá de Paula?

(A) De las vacaciones.
(B) Del trabajo escolar.
(C) De la amiga Mariluz.
(D) De las clases aeróbicas.

END OF SECTION I.
DO NOT GO ON TO SECTION II UNTIL YOU ARE TOLD TO DO SO.

SECTION II

READING

Suggested Time—40 minutes

Questions 31-85

WHEN YOU BEGIN THE READING SECTION, BE SURE THAT YOU MARK YOUR ANSWER TO THE FIRST READING QUESTION BY FILLING IN ONE OF THE CIRCLES NEXT TO NUMBER 31 ON THE ANSWER SHEET.

Part A

Directions: This part consists of a number of incomplete statements, each having four suggested completions. Select the most appropriate completion and fill in the corresponding circle on the answer sheet.

31. Siempre voy al mercado temprano para comprar carne y vegetales -------.

(A) fresco
(B) fresca
(C) frescos
(D) frescas

32. Adopté este sistema de programación porque me pareció ------- al otro.

(A) superior
(B) venturoso
(C) creador
(D) talentoso

33. Si quieres que te ayude, tienes que ------- lo que necesitas.

(A) decirme
(B) escogerme
(C) consultarme
(D) esconderme

34. Como Bárbara no podía ver bien, se ------- al escenario.

(A) amarró
(B) acercó
(C) abrazó
(D) arregló

35. Uno de los ------- más usados en la comida hispanoamericana es el cilantro.

(A) concursos
(B) utensilios
(C) condimentos
(D) colores

36. Francisco me invitó a ver el Ballet Folklórico de Cuba; ¡qué lástima que yo no haya podido ir -------!

(A) consigo
(B) con nosotros
(C) conmigo
(D) con él

37. Hay que ------- los documentos a la embajada hoy o mañana.

(A) lleva
(B) lleve
(C) llevar
(D) llevara

38. Los guerreros españoles fueron ------- valientes como los árabes.

(A) tan
(B) tanto
(C) tantos
(D) todo

GO ON TO THE NEXT PAGE

39. Era invierno y los árboles no tenían -------.

    (A) ramas
    (B) raíces
    (C) grasa
    (D) hojas

40. ¿Has sacado muchas fotos de tu viaje a Guatemala? ¿Cuándo vas a -------?

    (A) enseñárnoslas
    (B) enseñárnoslos
    (C) enseñárnoslo
    (D) enseñárnosla

41. La velocidad de ese corredor es -------.

    (A) indivisible
    (B) asombrosa
    (C) escéptica
    (D) sabrosa

GO ON TO THE NEXT PAGE

Part B

Directions: In each of the following paragraphs, there are numbered blanks indicating that words or phrases have been omitted. For each numbered blank, four completions are provided. First read through the entire paragraph. Then, for each numbered blank, choose the completion that is most appropriate given the context of the entire paragraph and fill in the corresponding circle on the answer sheet.

Aquella ciudad era muy grande. Las casas alineadas __(42)__ la repetición de una sola: ventanas iguales, puertas iguales. Había muchos coches, que no hacían __(43)__ y se alineaban frente a las casas. No existían muchos peatones como Gloria, pero __(44)__ había guardaban el más absoluto silencio. Esta ciudad daba la impresión de __(45)__ sumamente ordenada.

42. (A) parecían
(B) parecer
(C) parecidas
(D) parecieran

43. (A) siesta
(B) soledad
(C) rueda
(D) ruido

44. (A) los que
(B) los cuales
(C) lo que
(D) lo cual

45. (A) mirar
(B) ser
(C) haber
(D) hacer

GO ON TO THE NEXT PAGE

Desde que era muy pequeña a Isabel le __(46)__ las flores y para su octavo cumpleaños pidió un jardín. Su padre decidió que, __(47)__ vivían en un pequeño apartamento en el centro de la Ciudad de México, __(48)__ conseguirle un jardín a su hijita. Él fue en busca de macetas que fueran lo suficientemente grandes para __(49)__ rosas de varios tipos. Al final pudo encontrar una maceta que __(50)__ poner en su pequeño balcón.

46. (A) intentaban
(B) encantaban
(C) ocasionaban
(D) merecían

47. (A) aunque
(B) ni
(C) para que
(D) sin

48. (A) trataría de
(B) trataría con
(C) trataría a
(D) trataría

49. (A) ahorrar
(B) mejorar
(C) esperar
(D) cultivar

50. (A) pudiendo
(B) podido
(C) podría
(D) pueda

GO ON TO THE NEXT PAGE

Hoy en día, nuestro planeta se encuentra __(51)__ un serio dilema. __(52)__, el alarmante crecimiento de la población mundial; por otro lado, la continua destrucción de los recursos naturales y de la herencia natural. A __(53)__ ritmo, nuestro mundo avanza hacia un desastre ecológico. Ésta es la razón por __(54)__ el equilibrio del medio ambiente se ha convertido en una prioridad __(55)__ para la humanidad. Como toda __(56)__ causa, este desafío planetario tiene sus líderes. Presidentes, príncipes y científicos no han dudado en usar su __(57)__, su fama o sus conocimientos, para que nuestro mundo __(58)__ a tomar decisiones urgentes y necesarias.

51. (A) en vez de
    (B) en medio de
    (C) con tal de
    (D) a eso de

52. (A) Por eso
    (B) Por fin
    (C) Por un lado
    (D) Por lo menos

53. (A) este
    (B) el
    (C) cual
    (D) eso

54. (A) la cual
    (B) el cual
    (C) lo cual
    (D) cual

55. (A) residual
    (B) decidida
    (C) esencial
    (D) preliminar

56. (A) bien
    (B) buen
    (C) bueno
    (D) buena

57. (A) poder
    (B) conferencia
    (C) planeta
    (D) retrato

58. (A) empiece
    (B) empezara
    (C) empezará
    (D) empezaría

GO ON TO THE NEXT PAGE

En la oficina nadie hablaba de fútbol. Todo el mundo pasaba su tiempo con la __(59)__ baja atendiendo a su tarea hasta la hora de __(60)__. Por la tarde no se trabajaba, lo cual alegró mucho a Fernando, __(61)__ cada vez más ante la idea de tener tan poco que hacer.

59. (A) calabaza
    (B) pelota
    (C) cabeza
    (D) paleta

60. (A) cierran
    (B) cerrar
    (C) cerrado
    (D) cerrando

61. (A) animándose
    (B) despreciándose
    (C) vistiéndose
    (D) escuchándose

GO ON TO THE NEXT PAGE

Part C

Directions: Read the following texts carefully for comprehension. Each text is followed by a number of questions or incomplete statements. Select the answer or completion that is best according to the text and fill in the corresponding circle on the answer sheet.

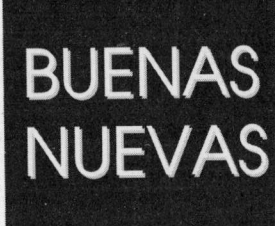

BUENAS NUEVAS

Un nuevo bombero

Ayer, a las cinco de la mañana pasaba una pareja por el cuartel del Cuerpo de Bomberos de Guadalajara rumbo al hospital, y se debieron quedar ahí. Sonia Imelda Santos tuvo a su hijo en el cuartel, con la ayuda de un bombero paramédico. "Hay un nuevo bombero en nuestras filas", dijo el paramédico.

62. El cuartel de bomberos anuncia que hay un nuevo bombero porque

(A) ha asistido en el nacimiento de un niño
(B) la Señora Santos se ha unido al cuartel
(C) se ha incorporado un nuevo miembro
(D) una pareja decidió vivir allí

GO ON TO THE NEXT PAGE

Tres cosas me intrigaban de Pedro Camacho: lo que decía, la austeridad de su vida enteramente consagrada a una obsesión, y su capacidad de trabajo. Esto último, sobre todo. En una biografía sobre Napoleón había leído cómo el emperador seguía dictando mientras sus secretarios se derrumbaban. Yo solía imaginarme al Emperador de los Franceses con la cara nariguda de Camacho y durante algún tiempo lo llamé el Napoleón del Altiplano. Por curiosidad, llegué a establecer su horario de trabajo y, pese a que lo verifiqué muchas veces, siempre me pareció imposible.

Empezó con cuatro radioteatros al día, pero, en vista del éxito, fueron aumentando hasta diez, que se radiaban de lunes a sábado, con una duración de media hora cada capítulo (en realidad, 23 minutos, pues la publicidad acaparaba siete). Como los dirigía e interpretaba todos, debía permanecer en el estudio unas siete horas diarias, calculando que el ensayo y grabación de cada programa durasen cuarenta minutos (entre diez y quince para su arenga y las repeticiones). Escribía los radioteatros a medida que se iban radiando; comprobé que cada capítulo le tomaba apenas el doble de tiempo que su interpretación, una hora. Lo cual significaba, de todos modos, unas diez horas en la máquina de escribir. Esto disminuía algo gracias a los domingos, su día libre, que él, por supuesto, pasaba en su cubículo, adelantando el trabajo de la semana. Su horario era, pues, entre quince y dieciséis horas de lunes a sábado y de ocho a diez los domingos. Todas ellas prácticamente productivas, de rendimiento "artístico" sonante.

Llegaba a Radio Central a las ocho de la mañana y partía cerca de medianoche; sus únicas salidas a la calle las hacía conmigo, al Café Bransa, para tomar las infusiones de té. Almorzaba en su cubículo, un sandwich y un refresco que le iban a comprar. Jamás aceptaba una invitación, jamás le oí decir que había estado en un cine, un teatro, un partido de fútbol o en una fiesta. Jamás lo vi leer un libro, una revista o un periódico, fuera del enorme cuaderno de apuntes y de esos planos que eran sus "instrumentos de trabajo". Aunque miento, un día le descubrí un Boletín de Socios del Club Nacional.

63. El narrador llama a Pedro Camacho el Napoleón del Altiplano por su

(A) dedicación al trabajo
(B) nariz aguileña
(C) vida austera
(D) manera de hablar

64. ¿Cuál es una de las actividades profesionales de Pedro Camacho?

(A) Productor de anuncios comerciales
(B) Escritor de programas de radio
(C) Compositor de canciones populares
(D) Locutor de noticieros regionales

65. ¿Cómo pasaba Pedro los domingos?

(A) Asistiendo a fiestas
(B) Radiando interpretaciones originales
(C) Trabajando en su oficina
(D) Leyendo periódicos

66. ¿Qué usaba a veces Pedro en su trabajo?

(A) Una colección de anotaciones
(B) Artículos periodísticos
(C) Obras de teatro
(D) Biografías

67. ¿Cómo se puede caracterizar la vida de Pedro?

(A) Disciplinada
(B) Divertida
(C) Romántica
(D) Corrupta

68. Se puede concluir que la actitud del narrador hacia Pedro es de

(A) desprecio
(B) indiferencia
(C) envidia
(D) curiosidad

GO ON TO THE NEXT PAGE

OFERTA DE INVIERNO

¡50% MENOS!

Sólo $27^50

una habitación, una noche
una a cuatro personas

A sólo una milla del
parque principal de atracciones

Este cupón ofrece un descuento de 50% sobre la tarifa habitual, desde el 3 de enero hasta el 11 de febrero. Tenemos disponibles 40 habitaciones que dan al jardín. También hay otras tarifas. Limitado a disponibilidad. Válido sólo con reservas hechas por adelantado.

Llame al 1-800-555-0887 en la Florida.

Comfort Inn

MAINGATE
7571 W. Irlo Bronson Memorial Hwy.
(US 192 W)
Kissimmee, FL 34747

69. ¿Cuándo se ofrece este precio especial?
(A) Llegando antes del mediodía
(B) La primera semana de cada mes
(C) Solamente los fines de semana
(D) Durante unas cuantas semanas

70. Para disfrutar de esta oferta hay que
(A) tener cuatro personas en la familia
(B) hacer reservación antes de llegar
(C) pagar en efectivo al llegar
(D) alquilar también un coche

71. Según el anuncio, una gran ventaja de quedarse en este hotel es
(A) que no cobra las llamadas locales
(B) que diariamente ofrece desayuno gratis
(C) su accesibilidad al parque de diversiones
(D) su jardín con juegos para niños

72. ¿A quienes se dirige este anuncio principalmente?
(A) A los vecinos de la zona
(B) A todos los jardineros del parque
(C) A turistas que planean vacaciones
(D) A participantes en convenciones

GO ON TO THE NEXT PAGE

Los mundos de Chile

Puede que haya otros mundos, pero seguro que están en Chile. Y es que, según cuentan sus habitantes, cuando se creó la Tierra, con los restos que sobraron de aquí y de allá, se hizo su país. ¿Dónde si no es posible encontrar semejante contraste de paisajes y gentes? Un desierto como el de Atacama, en el que no cae una gota desde hace medio siglo, pero, también, una de las zonas más lluviosas del planeta, Puerto Montt. Playas paradisíacas a hora y media de cumbres andinas, con nieve perpetua, en las que esquiar todo el año. Enormes y despobladas llanuras verdes en la Patagonia, junto a los impresionantes glaciares de Punta Arenas, en plena Tierra del Fuego, a un paso de la Antártida. Y, por si fuera poco, la Isla de Pascua, perdida en el Pacífico, testigo misterioso del paso de civilizaciones.

73. ¿Cómo se dice que se creó Chile?

(A) Con habitantes de otros mundos
(B) Con partes de varios lugares
(C) Con gentes de la Tierra
(D) Con desiertos inhabitados

74. ¿Qué dice el artículo sobre la zona de Atacama?

(A) Tiene una gran riqueza vegetal.
(B) Ha sido modernizada en las últimas décadas.
(C) Es un lugar lleno de volcanes.
(D) No llueve allí desde hace muchos años.

75. El artículo indica que en los Andes chilenos se puede

(A) disfrutar de la nieve permanentemente
(B) ver un paisaje parecido al de otro planeta
(C) nadar en piscinas termales
(D) conocer civilizaciones misteriosas

76. Según el artículo, ¿cómo es el clima de Chile?

(A) Hace un calor semejante al fuego.
(B) Es principalmente frío y seco.
(C) Exhibe una gran variedad.
(D) Tiene tendencia a la lluvia.

77. Este artículo probablemente proviene de

(A) una novela de aventuras
(B) la introducción de un informe gubernamental
(C) la sección de turismo de un periódico
(D) un anuncio de seguros

GO ON TO THE NEXT PAGE

Reciba Noticias del Mundo de lunes a sábado, en su casa*

Por sólo **25¢ al día**

Póngase al día en lo que sucede en su comunidad, en su país y en el mundo, con **Noticias del Mundo.**

Todos nuestros periodistas son hispanos y saben lo que a usted le interesa.

En **Noticias del Mundo,** usted encontrará: deportes, noticias locales, nacionales e internacionales, entretenimiento, y una extensa sección de clasificados. Además, secciones especiales acerca del mundo de los negocios, la salud, religión y más, mucho más.

PARA SOLICITARLO POR TELÉFONO LLAME GRATIS AL:
1.800.555.6997 EXT. 5

NOTICIAS del MUNDO

***ENTREGA SOLAMENTE DISPONIBLE EN ÁREAS EXCLUSIVAS DE QUEENS.**

78. ¿Cuándo aparece el periódico *Noticias del Mundo* ?

(A) Los siete días de la semana
(B) Sólo los lunes y los sábados
(C) A diario excepto los domingos
(D) Sólo los fines de semana

79. En este anuncio se menciona que una ventaja de recibir *Noticias del Mundo* es que

(A) hay ediciones por la mañana y por la tarde
(B) los periodistas son exclusivamente hispanos
(C) tiene una sección especial sobre viajes
(D) contiene muchos anuncios comerciales

GO ON TO THE NEXT PAGE

Cristóbal Colón partió de España en busca de metales preciosos y especias, sin imaginarse que nunca los encontraría. Lo que sí encontró fue un Nuevo Mundo lleno de frutas y verduras, como el tomate y la papa, que en ese entonces eran exóticas para los europeos.

En sus viajes, Colón equipó sus naves con carne salada, sardinas, anchoas, ajos y cebollas para que sirvieran de alimento a su tripulación. Si hubiera sabido las maravillas culinarias que le esperaban, habría llevado harina, arroz y azúcar, y en vez de marineros recién salidos de las cárceles se habría embarcado con algunos buenos cocineros de la corte real española.

Así, el Nuevo y el Viejo Mundo habrían disfrutado mucho antes platos hoy conocidos por todos nosotros: la carne con papas fritas, las tortas de chocolate, las pastas con salsa de tomate, la pizza. Tal vez Colón en vez de llegar a ser almirante de la mar ahora sería mencionado en los libros de historia como "embajador gastronómico". Y esa misma historia hablaría del humo proveniente no de la pólvora de las armas, sino de los hornos donde se cocinaban tantas delicias.

A la larga, del encuentro de estos dos mundos que no se conocían surgió una fabulosa revolución en el área alimenticia, aunque los chocolates dulces no nos deben permitir olvidar que tantas culturas de las Américas fueron víctimas de amargos sufrimientos.

80. ¿De qué trata este artículo?

(A) De una revolución indígena
(B) Del segundo viaje de Cristóbal Colón
(C) De la grasa en la dieta actual
(D) Del encuentro alimenticio entre dos culturas

81. Según el pasaje, ¿qué encontró Colón en el Nuevo Mundo?

(A) Los condimentos que buscaba
(B) Frutos que no existían en España
(C) Joyas preciosas
(D) Armas para sus marineros

82. Los que acompañaron a Colón eran

(A) navegantes de mala fama
(B) cocineros destacados
(C) embajadores para las Américas
(D) almirantes famosos

83. Un producto que Colón llevó en sus barcos a América era

(A) pescado
(B) oro
(C) hornos
(D) plata

84. Colón no pudo exigir el título de embajador gastronómico porque

(A) a sus marineros sólo les gustaba la comida española
(B) desconocía la comida típica de las Américas
(C) le faltaban expertos en la preparación de la comida
(D) prefería comer pastas con tomates

GO ON TO THE NEXT PAGE

ÉSTA ES SU VIDA

Ya están a la venta
las agendas anuales El País.
Elija el modelo que más se
adapte a sus necesidades:
de Sobremesa, de Bolsillo o Mini.
Rellene hoy mismo este cupón.

Para más información
llamar al teléfono
(91) 555 83 90.

EL PAIS

AGENDA Solicítela enviando este cupón a
DIARIO EL PAÍS, S.A.
APARTADO F.D. 797. 28080 MADRID

Cantidad

- ❒ Agenda de Sobremesa ______
- ❒ Agenda de Bolsillo ______
- ❒ Agenda de Bolsillo Mini ______

FORMAS DE PAGO:

❒ Cheque ❒ Tarjeta de crédito

Nombre y Apellidos ____________________

Dirección ____________________

C.P. ______ Localidad __________ Provincia __________

FIRMA:

85. Para obtener una de estas agendas es necesario

(A) llamar por teléfono
(B) mandar el cupón adjunto
(C) comprar el diario *El País*
(D) ir a la oficina

END OF SECTION II

S T O P

IF YOU FINISH BEFORE TIME IS CALLED, YOU MAY CHECK YOUR WORK ON SECTION II OF THIS TEST.

DO NOT TURN TO ANY OTHER TEST IN THIS BOOK.

NO TEST MATERIAL ON THIS PAGE

How to Score the SAT Subject Test in Spanish with Listening

When you take an actual SAT Subject Test in Spanish with Listening, you receive an overall composite score as well as two subscores: one for the reading section, one for the listening section.

The reading and listening scores are reported on the College Board's 20–80 scale. However the composite score, which is the most significant of the scores reported to the colleges you specify, is in the form of the College Board's 200–800 scale.

Worksheet 1. Finding Your Raw Listening Subscore

STEP 1: Table A on page 1059 lists the correct answers for all the questions on the Subject Test in Spanish with Listening that is reproduced in this book. It also serves as a worksheet for you to calculate your raw Listening subscore.

- Compare your answers with those given in the table.
- Put a check in the column marked "Right" if your answer is correct.
- Put a check in the column marked "Wrong" if your answer is incorrect.
- Leave both columns blank if you omitted the question.

STEP 2: Count the number of right answers for questions 1–30.

Enter the total here: ____________________

STEP 3: Count the number of wrong answers for questions 1–30.

Enter the total here: ____________________

STEP 4: Multiply the number of wrong answers by .333.

Enter the product here: ________________

STEP 5: Subtract the result obtained in Step 4 from the total you obtained in Step 2.

Enter the result here: __________________

STEP 6: Round the number obtained in Step 5 to the nearest whole number.

Enter the result here: __________________

The number you obtained in Step 6 is your raw Listening subscore.

Worksheet 2. Finding Your Raw Reading Subscore

STEP 1: Table A lists the correct answers for all the questions on the Subject Test in Spanish with Listening that is reproduced in this book. It also serves as a worksheet for you to calculate your raw Reading subscore.

STEP 2: Count the number of right answers for questions 31–85.

Enter the total here: ____________________

STEP 3: Count the number of wrong answers for questions 31–85.

Enter the total here: ____________________

STEP 4: Multiply the number of wrong answers by .333.

Enter the product here: ________________

STEP 5: Subtract the result obtained in Step 4 from the total you obtained in Step 2.

Enter the result here: __________________

STEP 6: Round the number obtained in Step 5 to the nearest whole number.

Enter the result here: __________________

The number you obtained in Step 6 is your raw Reading subscore.

Worksheet 3. Finding Your Raw Composite Score

STEP 1: Enter your unrounded raw Reading subscore from Step 5 of Worksheet 2.

Enter the result here: ________________

STEP 2: Enter your unrounded raw Listening subscore from Step 5 of Worksheet 1.

Enter the result here: ________________

STEP 3: Add the result obtained in Step 1 to the result obtained in Step 2.

Enter the result here: ________________

STEP 4: Round the number obtained in Step 3 to the nearest whole number.

Enter the result here: ________________

The number you obtained in Step 4 is your raw composite score.

Table A

Answers to the Subject Test in Spanish with Listening and Percentage of Students Answering Each Question Correctly

Question Number	Correct Answer	Right	Wrong	Percentage of Students Answering the Question Correctly*	Question Number	Correct Answer	Right	Wrong	Percentage of Students Answering the Question Correctly*
1	B			96	33	A			90
2	C			96	34	B			54
3	A			93	35	C			88
4	A			81	36	D			79
5	A			75	37	C			65
6	B			65	38	A			64
7	C			83	39	D			71
8	D			80	40	A			70
9	B			86	41	B			30
10	B			78	42	A			86
11	B			91	43	D			71
12	C			73	44	A			58
13	B			67	45	B			77
14	D			47	46	B			84
15	A			84	47	A			82
16	B			87	48	A			45
17	D			35	49	D			95
18	A			46	50	C			77
19	C			67	51	B			70
20	C			87	52	C			62
21	B			83	53	A			82
22	C			54	54	A			14
23	A			77	55	C			78
24	C			71	56	D			79
25	C			72	57	A			56
26	C			68	58	A			40
27	B			77	59	C			60
28	A			62	60	B			56
29	D			87	61	A			47
30	B			88	62	A			72
31	C			73	63	A			71
32	A			88	64	B			87

Table A continued on next page

Table A continued from previous page

Question Number	Correct Answer	Right	Wrong	Percentage of Students Answering the Question Correctly*	Question Number	Correct Answer	Right	Wrong	Percentage of Students Answering the Question Correctly*
65	C			81	76	C			81
66	A			25	77	C			81
67	A			84	78	C			78
68	D			44	79	B			84
69	D			90	80	D			63
70	B			88	81	B			83
71	C			74	82	A			35
72	C			92	83	A			47
73	B			46	84	C			28
74	D			78	85	B			90
75	A			58					

* These percentages are based on an analysis of the answer sheets of a representative sample of 2,800 students who took the original administration of this test and whose mean composite score was 584. They may be used as an indication of the relative difficulty of a particular question.

Answer explanations for the Subject Test in Spanish with Listening can be found on page 1066.

Finding Your Scaled Score

When you take SAT Subject Tests, the scores sent to the colleges you specify are reported on the College Board scale, which ranges from 200–800. Subscores are reported on a scale which ranges from 20–80. You can convert your practice test scores to scaled scores by using Tables B, C, and D on the following pages. To find your scaled score, locate your raw score in the left-hand column of the table; the corresponding score in the right-hand column is your scaled score. For example, a raw score of 59 on this particular edition of the Subject Test in Spanish with Listening corresponds to a scaled score of 610.

Raw scores are converted to scaled scores to ensure that a score earned on any one edition of a particular Subject Test is comparable to the same scaled score earned on any other edition of the same Subject Test. Because some editions of the tests may be slightly easier or more difficult than others, College Board scaled scores are adjusted so that they indicate the same level of performance regardless of the edition of the test taken and the ability of the group that takes it. Thus, for example, a score of 400 on one edition of a test taken at a particular administration indicates the same level of achievement as a score of 400 on a different edition of the test taken at a different administration.

When you take the SAT Subject Tests during a national administration, your scores are likely to differ somewhat from the scores you obtain on the tests in this book. People perform at different levels at different times for reasons unrelated to the tests themselves. The precision of any test is also limited because it represents only a sample of all the possible questions that could be asked.

Your scaled composite score from Table B is ________________.

Your scaled listening score from Table C is ________________.

Your scaled reading score from Table D is ________________.

Table B

Scaled Score Conversion Table Subject Test in Spanish with Listening Composite Score					
Raw Score	Scaled Score	Raw Score	Scaled Score	Raw Score	Scaled Score
85	800	47	540	9	330
84	800	46	530	8	330
83	800	45	530	7	320
82	800	44	520	6	320
81	790	43	510	5	310
80	780	42	510	4	310
79	780	41	500	3	300
78	770	40	500	2	290
77	760	39	490	1	290
76	750	38	490	0	280
75	740	37	480	-1	280
74	730	36	470	-2	270
73	730	35	470	-3	260
72	720	34	460	-4	250
71	710	33	460	-5	250
70	700	32	450	-6	240
69	690	31	450	-7	240
68	680	30	440	-8	230
67	670	29	430	-9	230
66	660	28	430	-10	220
65	650	27	420	-11	220
64	650	26	420	-12	220
63	640	25	410	-13	210
62	630	24	410	-14	210
61	630	23	400	-15	200
60	620	22	400	-16	200
59	610	21	390	-17	200
58	610	20	390	-18	200
57	600	19	380	-19	200
56	590	18	380	-20	200
55	590	17	370	-21	200
54	580	16	370	-22	200
53	570	15	360	-23	200
52	570	14	360	-24	200
51	560	13	350	-25	200
50	550	12	350	-26	200
49	550	11	340	-27	200
48	540	10	340	-28	200

Table C

Scaled Score Conversion Table
Subject Test in Spanish with Listening
Listening Subscore

Raw Score	Scaled Score	Raw Score	Scaled Score	Raw Score	Scaled Score
30	79	16	50	2	32
29	75	15	49	1	30
28	73	14	48	0	29
27	70	13	46	-1	27
26	67	12	45	-2	25
25	65	11	44	-3	24
24	63	10	42	-4	23
23	61	9	41	-5	22
22	59	8	40	-6	21
21	58	7	39	-7	20
20	56	6	37	-8	20
19	54	5	36	-9	20
18	53	4	35	-10	20
17	52	3	33		

Table D

Scaled Score Conversion Table
Subject Test in Spanish with Listening
Reading Subscore

Raw Score	Scaled Score	Raw Score	Scaled Score	Raw Score	Scaled Score
55	80	30	55	5	35
54	80	29	54	4	34
53	80	28	53	3	33
52	79	27	52	2	32
51	78	26	51	1	31
50	77	25	51	0	30
49	76	24	50	-1	30
48	75	23	49	-2	28
47	74	22	48	-3	27
46	73	21	47	-4	26
45	71	20	46	-5	25
44	70	19	45	-6	24
43	69	18	45	-7	23
42	67	17	44	-8	22
41	66	16	43	-9	21
40	65	15	42	-10	20
39	64	14	41	-11	20
38	63	13	41	-12	20
37	62	12	40	-13	20
36	61	11	39	-14	20
35	60	10	38	-15	20
34	59	9	38	-16	20
33	58	8	37	-17	20
32	57	7	36	-18	20
31	56	6	35		

How Did You Do on the Subject Test in Spanish with Listening?

After you score your test and analyze your performance, think about the following questions:

Did you run out of time before reaching the end of the test?

If so, you may need to pace yourself better. For example, maybe you spent too much time on one or two hard questions. A better approach might be to skip the ones you can't answer right away and try answering all the questions that remain on the test. Then if there's time, go back to the questions you skipped.

Did you take a long time reading the directions?

You will save time when you take the test by learning the directions to the Subject Test in Spanish with Listening ahead of time. Each minute you spend reading directions during the test is a minute that you could use to answer questions.

How did you handle questions you were unsure of?

If you were able to eliminate one or more of the answer choices as wrong and guess from the remaining ones, your approach probably worked to your advantage. On the other hand, making haphazard guesses or omitting questions without trying to eliminate choices could cost you valuable points.

How difficult were the questions for you compared with other students who took the test?

Table A shows you how difficult the multiple-choice questions were for the group of students who took this test during its national administration. The right-hand column gives the percentage of students that answered each question correctly.

A question answered correctly by almost everyone in the group is obviously an easier question. For example, 96 percent of the students answered question 1 correctly. But only 14 percent answered question 54 correctly.

Keep in mind that these percentages are based on just one group of students. They would probably be different with another group of students taking the test.

If you missed several easier questions, go back and try to find out why: Did the questions cover material you haven't yet reviewed? Did you misunderstand the directions?

Answer Explanations for the Spanish with Listening Subject Test

1. Choice (B) is the correct answer. Because there is no food (*comida*) pictured, choice (A) does not make sense. Further, there is no bicycle (*bicicleta*) pictured, so choice (C) is not logical. Choice (D) is incorrect because the picture shows children sitting, and the statement deals with walking (*caminas*).

2. Choice (C) is the correct answer. The picture shows musicians playing instruments on a city street. *Conjunto* means "musical group," *tocar* means "to play an instrument," and *calle* means "street." Choice (A) uses the verb *jugar*, which refers to playing a sport or game rather than an instrument. Choices (B) and (D) are incorrect because they do not refer to what is depicted in the picture. Choice (B) mentions a full auditorium (*auditorio*) and choice (D) states that they have umbrellas because it is raining, but the picture does not show an auditorium, umbrellas, or rain.

3. Choice (A) is the correct answer. The picture shows women and a child speaking with a professional in an office setting. It is possible that the professional is a doctor and that he is writing a prescription (*medicamento*) for the young boy. Choice (B) is incorrect because the picture does not show a classroom setting; it is unlikely that the man is asking that the child bring his homework (*tarea*) to him. Choice (C) is a recommendation to have flan for dessert (*postre*), which does not make sense in this context. Because the people in the picture are already sitting, choice (D), which means "Please be seated," is not a logical choice.

4. Choice (A) is the correct answer. The picture shows a soccer team in front of a stadium full of thousands of fans (*miles de personas*). Choice (B) asks why they are wearing long pants (*pantalones largos*), but the picture does not depict the soccer team wearing long pants. Choice (C) asks why no one has arrived; this question is illogical because it is clear that there are plenty of people there. Choice (D) describes a parade (*desfile*), which is not shown in the picture.

5. Choice (A) is the correct answer. The picture shows an adult male, perhaps the boy's father, relative, or family friend, who appears to be giving the boy advice as they walk along the beach. Choice (A), "Look, son, grades are very important," makes sense in

this context. Choice (B) asks, "When did you say you are retiring?" This question is illogical because it does not make sense that a young boy would be retiring. Neither person in the picture is wearing dark glasses (*anteojos tan oscuros*), so choice (C) does not make sense. Choice (D), "I think we have slept enough, let's get up," does not make sense because both people in the picture are already awake and walking.

6. Choice (B) is the correct answer. The picture shows an elderly man with a thoughtful (*pensativo*) expression sitting on a small, hard chair. The man does not look fearful (*miedo*), as choice (A) suggests. No one is jumping rope (*salta a la cuerda*), so choice (C) does not make sense. Choice (D) refers to a very comfortable chair (*sillón mas cómodo*), which is not an accurate description of the chair in the picture.

7. Choice (C) is the correct answer. The picture shows two very happy girls wearing head coverings and traditional costumes, including interesting ornamentation (*adornos*). Choices (A) and (D) are illogical because they ask "Why didn't they like the joke?" and "Why are they angry?" The girls in the picture are smiling, so there is no reason to suggest that they didn't like the joke or are angry. Choice (B) is incorrect because it states that the girls have beautiful horses (*lindos caballos*) and there are no horses shown in the picture.

8. Choice (D) is the correct answer. The three children on bikes have stopped to pose for a picture (*posar par la foto*). Neither pedestrians (*peatones*), as mentioned in choice (A), nor carts (*carros*), as mentioned in choice (B), are pictured. Choice (C), which refers to a beautiful mural (*lindo mural*) on the wall, is incorrect because there is no mural shown in the picture.

9. Choice (B) is the correct answer. The picture shows many people casually standing or walking around a rustic, old (*muy antiguo*) building. Choice (A) is illogical because the people are not rushing (*apresurado*) and there is no visible damage from an earthquake (*terremoto*). The building does not have arches (*arcos*), as suggested by choice (C). Further, choice (D) describes dances (*bailes*), and no one in the picture is dancing.

10. Choice (B) is the correct answer. The woman in the conversation states that there are only three weeks until summer vacation. The man asks her when she would like to plan something, so it would be logical to respond by saying, "It would be best to decide now." Choice (A) is incorrect because it is irrelevant whether the woman likes the plants (*plantas*). Choice (C) is illogical because there is no connection between passing by a restaurant (*pasamos por el restaurante*) and planning a vacation.

Expressing her desire to iron this afternoon (*planchar esta tarde*), as in choice (D), is also not a logical response.

11. Choice (B) is the correct answer. The man has asked the woman what she wants to buy (*comprar*) at the market (*mercado*). The statement, "I am looking for some tropical fruits," is a logical response. Choice (A) suggests that it is fun to rest in the country, which does not make sense as a response to the man's question. One could certainly buy olives (*aceitunas*) at the market; however, the statement in choice (C), "I am never going to eat olives again," does not answer the man's question. And there is no indication that the woman does not know where Olvera Street market is located, so choice (D) is not the best choice.

12. Choice (C) is the correct answer. The man and woman involved in this conversation are looking for a parking space, and the man asks if there is a place to park nearby. Choice (C) makes sense because the statement indicates that there is space to park in the next block (*en la próxima cuandra*). Choice (A) states, "You cannot cross the street here"; this statement does not provide an answer to the man's question. Choice (B), "The owners live far away," does not make sense in this context. And choice (D) is incorrect because it is illogical to respond by saying that the plaza is full of cars (*llena de autos*).

13. Choice (B) is the correct answer. The first speaker asks if the other person thinks that the Mayan pyramids are very mysterious. The person responds that she has never visited the pyramids. It is logical for the first woman to ask her friend if she would like to go see the pyramids this summer. Choice (A) is incorrect because it does not make sense for the first woman to ask about building other pyramids (*construir otras*). Choice (C), "I feel fine now," is an illogical response in this context. And stating that tourists do not see anything, as in choice (D), does not make sense.

14. Choice (D) is the correct answer. The man, a news reporter, is interviewing a worker about a strike (*huelga*). The reporter asks what the main problem is at the factory (*el mayor problema en la fábrica*). An appropriate response is that their salaries (*sueldos*) have not been raised (*aumentan*). It is unlikely that the owners (*dueños*) do not know each other, as suggested by choice (A); further, the statement in choice (A) would probably not cause a strike. Choices (B) and (C) are not the best choices because both express positive scenarios: workers working well (*trabajadores funcionan bien*) and the union (*el sindicato*) confronting the problem (*se enfrenta con el problema*).

15. Choice (A) is the correct answer. This conversation involves a movie theater employee and a customer. The customer has asked what time the movie starts, and

the employee has told the customer that there are two shows that evening. The most logical response would be, "What time does the first one start?" The other responses are not relevant in this situation. Choice (B) simply asks what the current time is; choice (C) involves traveling, as it is a request for a round-trip ticket (*billete de ida y vuelta*); and choice (D) expresses disappointment because the radio is not working.

16. Choice (B) is the correct answer. In this conversation, the first speaker offers to help the other, who seems to be lost (*perdido*) and asks if there is a bank (*banco*). Choice (B) gives directions: "three blocks from here." Choice (A) says someone "is fine," which does not make sense as a response to a question about a bank. Choice (C) says, "At 2 o'clock sharp," which would be a more logical response if the question were about time. Choice (D), "I don't have change," does not make sense because the person asks about a bank and does not request spare change.

17. Choice (D) is the correct answer. The first speaker tells the second speaker that Maria is on vacation in Venezuela. Choice (D) asks if she is enjoying her trip. Choice (A) is incorrect because it does not make sense to ask, "Did you find her right away?" Choice (B) asks about Maria returning home, and choice (C) asks when Maria is going to leave for Venezuela; choices (B) and (C) do not make sense because it has already been established that Maria is in Venezuela.

18. Choice (A) is the correct answer. Two people are discussing the movie they just saw but did not understand. This question asks what the young man suggests they do to better understand the movie. The young man suggests that they could see it again ("*Quizás viéndola de nuevo. . .*"), as choice (A) describes. Ultimately, the two decide to forget about the movie and go for ice cream (*helado*). Choice (D) refers to having ice cream, but it does not make sense because it does not address the question of understanding the movie better.

19. Choice (C) is the correct answer. After agreeing that they did not understand the movie, they decide to forget about it ("*olvidémonos de ella*") and go for ice cream. In other words, they decide to not think about it any longer, as is stated in choice (C). Choices (A) and (B) suggest continuing their discussion of the movie, and it is clear that the two do not intend to talk about the movie anymore. Choice (D) is incorrect because there is no mention of buying a video in the conversation.

20. Choice (C) is the correct answer. This question asks about where the narrator finds it peaceful. The narrator states that there is nowhere more peaceful than the park near her house, isolated from the suffocating city traffic ("*No hay nada más tranquilo que ir al parquet cerca de mi casa está aislado de todo el tráfico sofocante de la ciudad*").

She reiterates that it would be hard to find as calm an environment as her favorite park anywhere else. Choices (A) and (D) refer to busy places — the main plaza and the central streets — rather than peaceful places.

21. Choice (B) is the correct answer. The narrator mentions the sound of singing birds as part of the calming environment of the park. There is no mention of children or families, as indicated in choices (C) and (D). Choice (A), which refers to the sound of cars, does not make sense; the sound of cars would not be conducive to a peaceful environment, and the narrator mentions that the park is isolated from traffic.

22. Choice (C) is the correct answer. According to the selection, the elderly visitors in the park are chatting about any matter from their past ("*cualquier asunto de su pasado*"). Choices (A), (B), and (D) are incorrect because the selection does not mention the elderly visitors talking about the trees (*árboles*), the fountains (*fuentes*), or the environment (*ambiente*).

23. Choice (A) is the correct answer. The radio announcement suggests that visitors to the zoo can see a rare variety of animals from all over the world. The zoo is not always open, as choice (B) suggests; in fact, the radio announcement specifies the time when the zoo opens and when it closes. Choice (C) is not a logical response because the radio announcement says that visitors can see animals that have never been seen in the region (*jamás vistos en esta region*). There is also no mention of fish (*peces*), as suggested in choice (D).

24. Choice (C) is the correct answer. There is no cost for admission, or entry (*entrada*), into the zoo; it is free (*gratuita* or *gratis*). Choices (A) and (B) are incorrect because they give specific prices. Choice (D) is incorrect; although *libre* means "free," it refers to one's personal freedom rather than something being free with regard to having no monetary cost.

25. Choice (C) is the correct answer. The radio announcement states that the zoo opens at 9 o'clock in the morning and closes at 5 o'clock in the afternoon every day except Monday ("*todos los días excepto el lunes*"). In other words, the zoo is open Tuesday through Sunday. Choices (A), (B), and (D) are incorrect because they all include Monday.

26. Choice (C) is the correct answer. It is the first day of classes, and the two people are discussing the boy's disastrous schedule (*horario*). There is no mention of a specific class, as in choice (A), the weather, as in choice (B), or the day itself, as in choice (D).

27. Choice (B) is the correct answer. The boy considers his schedule a disaster, so it is bothering him; he is complaining about how he will not have time to eat on Monday, Wednesday, and Friday. The boy is certainly not showing indifference, as in choice (A), surprise, as in choice (C), or relief, as in choice (D).

28. Choice (A) is the correct answer. The boy's friend, Rosaura, tells him he should not complain that he does not have time to eat three days a week. She jokes that he can eat for those days during all of his free time on the two days he only has class in the late afternoon ("*Esos días puedes comer por lost otros tres*"). Choice (B) suggests that Rosaura responds with compassion, choice (C) suggests that she responds with enthusiasm, and choice (D) suggests that she responds with admiration; none of these are logical responses, since Rosaura jokes with her friend about his schedule.

29. Choice (D) is the correct answer. Paula is explaining to Mariluz that she cannot go to the dance club (*la discoteca*) because she has homework and her mother will not allow her to go out until she has finished it ("*Tengo que terminar mis deberes. Mi madre no me permite salir hasta que termine. …*"). Choice (A) does not make sense because Paula is leaving a message for Mariluz after calling her. Choice (B) is incorrect because Paula's mother is not letting her go out. And there is no mention of Paula having to help her mother, as suggested by choice (C).

30. Choice (B) is the correct answer. Paula's mother is not allowing Paula to go out until she has finished all of her homework. It makes sense to say that her mother is concerned about Paula's schoolwork. There is no mention of vacation or aerobics classes, as indicated in choices (A) and (D), and there is nothing that indicates that Paula's mother is worried about Mariluz for any reason, as suggested in choice (C).

31. Choice (C) is the correct answer. This sentence involves adjective agreement. The noun *vegetales* is masculine and plural; therefore, a masculine plural adjective is required to agree with the masculine plural noun. *Frescos* is a masculine plural adjective.

32. Choice (A) is the correct answer. This sentence involves a comparative expression. The only adjective that fits the context of the sentence is *superior* because it indicates a comparison. The other choices are logical adjectives to describe the programming system, but they need a modifier such as *más* in order to be followed by *al otro*.

33. Choice (A) is the correct answer. According to the sentence, one must do something in order for the speaker to help him or her. The only verb that fits the context of the

sentence is *decirme*; the speaker can help the other person if he or she tells the speaker what he or she needs. The verbs in the other choices do not specify what is needed in order for the speaker to provide the appropriate help.

34. Choice (B) is the correct answer. According to the sentence, Bárbara cannot see well and needs to do something with respect to the stage (*escenario*). The only verb that fits the context of the sentence is *acercó*, which means "to approach" or "to go closer." Bárbara needs to move closer to the stage in order to see it better. The verbs in the other choices do not make sense in this context.

35. Choice (C) is the correct answer. The only noun that fits the context of the sentence is *condimentos*, or "condiments." The sentence mentions food (*comida*). *Cilantro* is an herb, so it makes sense to describe it as a condiment. The nouns in all of the other choices do not refer to any types of food.

36. Choice (D) is the correct answer. This sentence involves the use of pronouns. According to the first part of the sentence, Francisco invited the speaker to go with him to a ballet. The second part of the sentence says that it was a shame that the speaker was unable to go. Choice (D), *con él*, means "with him" and logically completes the sentence; the phrase refers back to Francisco. Choice (A), *consigo*, is also translated as "with him," but it is only used when it refers back to the subject of the sentence; in this case, the subject of the second part of the sentence is *yo* ("I"). Choices (B) and (C) are incorrect because the phrases *con nosotros* ("with us") and *conmigo* ("with me") do not appropriately refer to Francisco.

37. Choice (C) is the correct answer. This sentence involves sentence structure and use of the expression *hay que*, meaning "to be necessary that." The phrase *hay que* must be followed by a verb in the infinitive. Choice (C), *llevar*, is the only verb that fits the sentence because it is the only choice in the infinitive form.

38. Choice (A) is the correct answer. This sentence involves a comparative expression. According to the sentence, the Spanish warriors were as brave as the Arab warriors. Because *valientes* ("brave") is an adjective, the comparative statement requires the adverbial form *tan* to complete the statement of equality. The other choices would be used for comparisons that used verbs or nouns.

39. Choice (D) is the correct answer. According to the sentence, the trees do not have something in the winter. It is logical to say that the trees do not have leaves (*hojas*) in the winter. Branches (*ramas*) and roots (*raíces*) remain on trees, even in winter, so

choices (A) and (B) are illogical. Choice (C) does not make sense because trees do not have fat (*grasa*) in any season.

40. Choice (A) is the correct answer. These sentences involve sentence structure. The first question asks if the other person has taken many photos of his or her trip to Guatemala; it makes sense that the next question asks when the person will show (*enseñar*) the photos. The word *fotos* is a shortened form of *las fotografías*; therefore, an indirect object with a plural, feminine direct object pronoun is the only correct combination. In choice (A), *enseñárnoslas, las* correctly refers to *las fotografías*.

41. Choice (B) is the correct answer. Choice (B), the adjective *asombrosa* ("amazing"), is the most logical adjective for describing the speed of the runner ("*velocidad de ese corridor*"). Choices (A), (C), and (D) are incorrect because a runner's speed would certainly not be described as indivisible (*indivisible*), skeptical (*escéptica*), or tasty (*sabrosa*).

42. Choice (A) is the correct answer. This sentence involves the use of the appropriate tense based on context clues. The only verb that fits in the context of the sentence is *parecían* ("seemed"). The paragraph describes what the city used to be like; therefore, the verb must be in the third-person plural imperfect tense. Further, all of the other verbs in the paragraph are in the imperfect tense, and choice (A) keeps all the verb tenses consistent.

43. Choice (D) is the correct answer. The only noun that fits the context of the sentence is *ruido* ("noise"). The nouns in the other choices do not make sense with regard to the many cars ("*muchos coches*") that are mentioned in the sentence.

44. Choice (A) is the correct answer. According to the sentence, there were not many pedestrians, but [those that] were there remained absolutely silent. The antecedent, "many pedestrians" ("*muchos peatones*"), requires the plural pronoun *los,* followed by *que,* to comprise the required phrase "those that."

45. Choice (B) is the correct answer. According to the sentence, the city gave the impression of [being] extremely orderly. Although the infinitive verbs in the other choices are appropriate grammatically, they do not fit the context of the sentence.

46. Choice (B) is the correct answer. According to the sentence, Isabel asked for a garden for her eighth birthday. It would make sense, then, to say that Isabel loved flowers

("*le encantaban las flores*") ever since she was a little girl. Choices (A), *intentaban* ("tried"), (C), *ocasionaban* ("caused"), and (D), *merecían* ("deserved"), do not logically complete the sentence.

47. Choice (A) is the correct answer. This sentence involves prepositions. According to the sentence, Isabel's father decided that [even though] they lived in a small apartment . . . he would [try to] get his daughter a garden. The prepositions in the other choices — *ni* ("neither"), *para que* ("in order that"), and *sin* ("without") — do not fit the context of the sentence.

48. Choice (A) is the correct answer. This sentence involves the effect of preposition choice on the meaning of a sentence. According to the sentence, Isabel's father decided that [even though] they lived in a small apartment . . . he would [try to] get his daughter a garden. The missing expression requires *de* before the infinitive *conseguirle* in order for the intended meaning to be correct — "to try to." Choices (B), (C), and (D) do not logically complete the sentence; the meaning of *tratar con* becomes "to deal with," the meaning of *tratar a* becomes "to treat someone," and the verb *tratar* itself means "to treat."

49. Choice (D) is the correct answer. This sentence involves knowledge of vocabulary. According to the sentence, Isabel's father looked for flower pots that were big enough for doing something with a variety of roses. Choice (D), *cultivar* ("to cultivate"), makes sense in this context. Large pots are needed to cultivate a variety of roses. It does not make sense to say that large pots are needed to *save* (A), *improve* (B) or *wait for* (C) a variety of roses.

50. Choice (C) is the correct answer. This sentence involves tense sequence. In this sentence, the relative pronoun *que* connects the preterit form *pudo encontrar* to the next verb form that goes with *poner*. In this case, the future perfect tense is required in order to fit the context of the sentence: Finally, he was able to find a pot that he would be able to (*podría*) put on their small balcony.

51. Choice (B) is the correct answer. This sentence involves prepositional phrases with special meaning. According to the sentence, our planet finds itself [in the middle of] a serious dilemma. The prepositional phrases in the other choices — *en vez de* ("instead of"), *con tal de* ("on the condition of"), and *a eso de* ("approximately") — do not fit the context of the sentence.

52. Choice (C) is the correct answer. This sentence involves the use of vocabulary in context and the use of prepositional phrases with special meaning. The second clause in the sentence begins with the phrase "on the other hand" (*por otro lado*). Therefore, the first clause of the sentence should begin with the phrase "On one hand" (*Por un lado*).

53. Choice (A) is the correct answer. The previous sentence in the passage refers to the destruction of natural resources. This sentence involves the use of a demonstrative pronoun. The demonstrative pronoun "this" (*este*), when used in this sentence, indicates "at this pace," which stresses immediacy. In context, choices (B), *at the pace*, and (C), *at which pace*, do not express the same urgency. Choice (D) is incorrect because the pronoun "that" (*eso*) is not grammatically appropriate in this context.

54. Choice (A) is the correct answer. The antecedent in this sentence is "the reason" (*la razón*). Because this is a feminine noun, the feminine form of the pronoun, *la cual*, is required for correct pronoun–antecedent agreement.

55. Choice (C) is the correct answer. According to the sentence, the balance of the environment has become a priority for humanity. The word that fits the missing blank should describe "priority." The adjective "essential" (*esencial)* is the only logical descriptor to complete the sentence. It does not make sense to describe the priority as *residual* (A), *decided* (B), or *preliminary* (D).

56. Choice (D) is the correct answer. This sentence involves adjective agreement. The word that fits the missing blank modifies the feminine singular noun "cause" (*causa*). Therefore, a feminine singular adjective is required to agree with the noun. *Buena* is the only choice in feminine form.

57. Choice (A) is the correct answer. The word that fits the missing blank should name something used by "presidents, princes and scientists" ("*presidentes, príncipes y científicos*") to protect the environment. The noun "power" (*poder*) best completes the sentence. It does not make sense to say they used their *conference* (B), *planet* (C), or *portrait* (D) to protect the environment.

58. Choice (A) is the correct answer. This sentence involves tense sequence. *Para que* ("in order to") is a conjunction that is always followed by the subjunctive. Because the first clause of the sentence is in the present tense, the present subjunctive (*empiece*) is the only word that correctly completes the sentence.

59. Choice (C) is the correct answer. According to the sentence, while people in the office were attending to their work, they lowered something. The only choice that logically completes the sentence is the noun "head" (*cabeza*); people often lower their heads when they are concentrating on a task. It does not make sense to say that people would lower their *pumpkin* (A), *ball* (B), or *lollipop* (D) while attending to their work.

60. Choice (B) is the correct answer. This sentence involves verb tense. As the object of a preposition, in this case *de*, a verb must be in the infinitive form. *Cerrar* is the only choice that is in the infinitive form.

61. Choice (A) is the correct answer. This sentence involves knowledge of vocabulary. Due to the positive nature communicated through the relative clause "*lo cual alegró mucho a Fernando*," the logical choice is *animándose*, to indicate that he was enlivened about having less and less to do. Choice (B) has a negative connotation, and choices (C) and (D) do not make sense in the context of the sentence.

62. Choice (A) is the correct answer. This question asks why an announcement has been made that there is a new firefighter. The article states that a couple on the way to the hospital only made it as far as the fire station, where a paramedic helped deliver their baby. The article ends with the paramedic referring to the newborn baby as the newest firefighter in their station. Choice (A) is the only response that mentions this scenario. It does not make sense to say that *Mrs. Santos has joined the station* (B), that *a new member has become part of the station* (C) or that *a couple has decided to live there* (D).

63. Choice (A) is the correct answer. This question asks why the narrator has given a coworker a certain nickname ("*el Napoleón del Altiplano*"). In the passage, the narrator states that Pedro Camacho's capacity for work is intriguing. The narrator also mentions that a biography about Napoleon said that the emperor continued to work while his secretaries collapsed. Choice (B) is incorrect; although the narrator mentions Pedro's nose, he was saying that he imagined the emperor with Pedro's nose, not explaining the reasoning behind the nickname. The mention of an *austere life* (C) only refers to Camacho, not to Napoleon. Choice (D) is incorrect because the way Pedro speaks is not mentioned in the text.

64. Choice (B) is the correct answer. This question asks for a description of one of Pedro Camacho's professional activities. The passage states, "*Escribía los radioteatros a medida que se iban radiando . . . Lo cual significaba, de todos modos, unas diez horas en la máquina de escribir.*" In other words, he used to write radio-theater, spending

ten hours at the typewriter daily. This job description does not include *producing commercials* (A), *composing songs* (C) or *reporting regional news* (D).

65. Choice (C) is the correct answer. The passage states, "*. . . los domingos, su día libre, que él, por supuesto, pasaba en su cubículo, adelantando el trabajo de la semana.*" In other words, Pedro spent his Sundays (his day off) in his cubicle, getting a head start on the upcoming week's work. Choice (A) and (D) are incorrect because the passage clearly says, "*jamás le oí decir que había estado en . . . una fiesta. Jamás lo vi leer un libro, una revista o un periódico.*" That is, the narrator never heard Pedro say that he had attended a party and he never saw him read a book, magazine or newspaper.

66. Choice (A) is the correct answer. According to the narrator, "*Jamás lo vi leer un libro, una revista o un periódico, fuera del enorme cuaderno de apuntes y de esos planos que eran sus 'instrumentos de trabajo.'*" The narrator never saw Pedro read a book, magazine or newspaper, except for his enormous notebook with memorandum that was his "work instrument." This statement eliminates all of the other answer choices as logical responses.

67. Choice (A) is the correct answer. Pedro's life can be characterized as *disciplined*. Choices (B), (C), are incorrect because there is nothing *fun* or *romantic* about his life, especially because he has such a grueling work schedule. And there is no indication that his life can be characterized as *corrupt* (D).

68. Choice (D) is the correct answer. This question asks for a description of the narrator's attitude toward Pedro. The narrator begins by saying that he or she is intrigued by, or *curious* about, Pedro Camacho. There is no evidence that the narrator's attitude is one of *disdain* (A), *indifference* (B), or *envy* (C). Their relationship is friendly, established by the fact that they would go together to Café Bransa for tea.

69. Choice (D) is the correct answer. This question asks when the special offer is valid. The advertisement states that the coupon is valid "*desde el 3 de enero hasta el 11 de febrero.*" Early January through mid-February is *a few weeks.*

70. Choice (B) is the correct answer. This question asks what a person must do in order to take advantage of this offer. The advertisement states that the offer is valid only with reservations made in advance ("*con reservas hechas por adelantado*"), so a person must *make a reservation before arriving.*

71. Choice (C) is the correct answer. This question asks for a description of an advantage of staying at this hotel. The advertisement states, *"A solo una milla del parque principal de atracciones."* In other words, the hotel is just a mile from main attractions. Although the advertisement mentions a garden, it does not state that *the garden offers games for children* (D). Additionally, there is no mention of *free local calls* (A) or *free breakfast* (B).

72. Choice (C) is the correct answer. This question asks for a description of the advertisement's target audience. This hotel advertisement is directed to those planning to visit the area attractions for their vacation. There is nothing special mentioned in the advertisement to attract *local people* (A), *gardeners* (B) or *convention attendees* (D).

73. Choice (B) is the correct answer. This question concerns the main idea of the article. According to the inhabitants of Chile, *"cuando se creó la Tierra, con los restos que sobraron de aquí y de allá, se hizo su país."* That is, when the earth was created, the country was made with the leftovers from here and there. The article supports this saying by discussing the varied geographical regions of Chile that can be metaphorically understood, as the saying suggests, to have come from parts of various places. The article only refers to the *varied climate*, not to the people.

74. Choice (D) is the correct answer. This question asks what the article says about the zone of Atacama. The article describes the lack of water in the desert of Atacama, where no rain has fallen for 50 years: *"Un desierto como el de Atacama, en el que no cae una gota desde hace medio siglo. ..."* No other features of the area are mentioned in the article.

75. Choice (A) is the correct answer. This question asks for a description of what people can do in the Andes Mountains. According to the article, the Andean peaks, with continuous snow, allow skiing year-round: *"cumbres andinas, con nieve perpetua, en las que esquiar todo el año."* The activities described in the other answer choices are only applicable to other areas in Chile.

76. Choice (C) is the correct answer. This question asks for a description of the climate in Chile. According to the article, the climate in Chile is *varied*. One type of climate is not dominant.

77. Choice (C) is the correct answer. This question asks where the article probably appears. This article is probably found in the tourism section of a newspaper. It does

not include information that would apply to *an adventure novel* (A), *a government report* (B) or *an advertisement for insurance* (D).

78. Choice (C) is the correct answer. This question asks when you can receive home delivery of *Noticias del Mundo.* According to the advertisement, home delivery takes place "Monday through Saturday" ("*de lunes a sábado*"). Choice (C), *daily except for Sundays,* is another way of saying "Monday through Saturday." Choices (A) and (D) are incorrect because they include Sundays. Choice (B) is incorrect because it indicates Mondays and Saturdays only.

79. Choice (B) is the correct answer. This question asks for a description of an advantage of receiving *Noticias del Mundo.* According to the ad, the newspaper has all Hispanic journalists who know what interests the reader ("*Todos nuestros periodistas son hipanos y saben lo que a usted le interesa*"). There is no mention of *morning and afternoon editions* (A), *a special travel section* (C) or *many business announcements* (D).

80. Choice (D) is the correct answer. This question involves the identification of the main idea of the article. Although there are several references to Christopher Columbus (*Cristóbal Colón*), the article focuses on the many foods that originated in the New World and were combined with foods from Spain, the Old World. As choice (D) states, the article is about *the culinary encounter between two cultures.*

81. Choice (B) is the correct answer. This question asks for a description of what Columbus found in the New World. The article indicates that Columbus found a New World full of fruits and vegetables that were, at that time, exotic for Europeans ("*Lo que sí encontró fue un Nuevo Mundo lleno de frutas y verduras, como el tomate y la papa, que en ese entonces eran exóticas para los europeos*"). Columbus searched for *spices* (A) and *precious metals* (C), but the article states that he never found them. There is no indication that Columbus was looking for *weapons* (D).

82. Choice (A) is the correct answer. This question asks for a description of the people who accompanied Columbus. Although the article mentions that if they had known that they would be finding culinary wonders, they might have traveled with *renowned chefs* (B), the crew actually was made up of newly released prisoners — *disreputable sailors* (A).

83. Choice (A) is the correct answer. This question asks for a description of what Columbus took with him on his voyages to America. According to the article,

Columbus equipped his ships with sardines and anchovies ("*En sus viajes, Colón equipó sus naves con . . . sardinas, anchoas . . .*"). Sardines and anchovies are types of *fish*, not *gold*, *ovens*, or *silver*.

84. Choice (C) is the correct answer. This question asks why Columbus could not demand the title of gastronomic ambassador. The article suggests that perhaps he should be mentioned in history books as such, based on the culinary treasures that he took back to Europe. However, the article implies that Columbus could not historically demand this title because gastronomy was not his interest or his objective for his voyages; he did not bring *experts in the preparation of food*.

85. Choice (B) is the correct answer. This question asks for a description of what a person needs to do in order to obtain one of the planners that is advertised. The advertisement instructs the reader to complete and send the attached coupon ("*Rellene hoy mismo este cupón. ... Solicítela enviando este cupón . . .*").

CollegeBoard

SAT Subject Tests™

COMPLETE MARK ● EXAMPLES OF INCOMPLETE MARKS

You must use a No. 2 pencil and marks must be complete. Do not use a mechanical pencil. It is very important that you fill in the entire circle darkly and completely. If you change your response, erase as completely as possible. Incomplete marks or erasures may affect your score.

1 Your Name: (Print) ______ Last ______ First ______ M.I.

I agree to the conditions on the front and back of the SAT Subject Tests™ book. I also agree with the SAT Test Security and Fairness policies and understand that any violation of these policies will result in score cancellation and may result in reporting of certain violations to law enforcement.

Signature: ______ **Today's Date:** ___/___/___ MM DD YY

Home Address: (Print) ______ Number and Street ______ City ______ State/Country ______ Zip Code

Phone: (   ) ______ **Test Center:** (Print) ______ City ______ State/Country

2 YOUR NAME

Last Name (First 6 Letters) | First Name (First 4 Letters) | Mid. Init.

– ' A B C D E F G H I J K L M N O P Q R S T U V W X Y Z

3 DATE OF BIRTH

MONTH: Jan Feb Mar Apr May Jun Jul Aug Sep Oct Nov Dec

DAY: 0 1 2 3 / 0 1 2 3 4 5 6 7 8 9

YEAR: 0 1 2 3 4 5 6 7 8 9 / 0 1 2 3 4 5 6 7 8 9

4 REGISTRATION NUMBER

(Copy from Admission Ticket.)

0 1 2 3 4 5 6 7 8 9

Important: Fill in items 8 and 9 exactly as shown on the back of test book.

7 TEST BOOK SERIAL NUMBER

(Copy from front of test book.)

0 1 2 3 4 5 6 7 8 9

8 BOOK CODE

(Copy and grid as on back of test book.)

0 1 2 3 4 5 6 7 8 9 / A B C D E F G H I J K L M N O P Q R S T U V W X Y Z / 0 1 2 3 4 5 6 7 8 9

9 BOOK ID

(Copy from back of test book.)

5 ZIP CODE

0 1 2 3 4 5 6 7 8 9

6 TEST CENTER

(Supplied by Test Center Supervisor.)

0 1 2 3 4 5 6 7 8 9

PLEASE MAKE SURE to fill in these fields completely and correctly. If they are not correct, we won't be able to score your test(s)!

FOR OFFICIAL USE ONLY

0 1 2 3 4 5 6

0 1 2 3 4 5 6

0 1 2 3 4 5 6

103648-77191 • NS1114C1085 • Printed in U.S.A.

194415-001 1 2 3 4 5 A B C D E Printed in the USA ISD11312

783175

PLEASE DO NOT WRITE IN THIS AREA

SERIAL #

COMPLETE MARK	EXAMPLES OF INCOMPLETE MARKS

You must use a No. 2 pencil and marks must be complete. Do not use a mechanical pencil. *It is very important that you fill in the entire circle darkly and completely. If you change your response, erase as completely as possible. Incomplete marks or erasures may affect your score.*

○ Literature	○ Mathematics Level 1	○ German	○ Chinese Listening	○ Japanese Listening
○ Biology E	○ Mathematics Level 2	○ Italian	○ French Listening	○ Korean Listening
○ Biology M	○ U.S. History	○ Latin	○ German Listening	○ Spanish Listening
○ Chemistry	○ World History	○ Modern Hebrew		
○ Physics	○ French	○ Spanish		

Background Questions: ① ② ③ ④ ⑤ ⑥ ⑦ ⑧ ⑨

1	Ⓐ Ⓑ Ⓒ Ⓓ Ⓔ	26	Ⓐ Ⓑ Ⓒ Ⓓ Ⓔ	51	Ⓐ Ⓑ Ⓒ Ⓓ Ⓔ	76	Ⓐ Ⓑ Ⓒ Ⓓ Ⓔ
2	Ⓐ Ⓑ Ⓒ Ⓓ Ⓔ	27	Ⓐ Ⓑ Ⓒ Ⓓ Ⓔ	52	Ⓐ Ⓑ Ⓒ Ⓓ Ⓔ	77	Ⓐ Ⓑ Ⓒ Ⓓ Ⓔ
3	Ⓐ Ⓑ Ⓒ Ⓓ Ⓔ	28	Ⓐ Ⓑ Ⓒ Ⓓ Ⓔ	53	Ⓐ Ⓑ Ⓒ Ⓓ Ⓔ	78	Ⓐ Ⓑ Ⓒ Ⓓ Ⓔ
4	Ⓐ Ⓑ Ⓒ Ⓓ Ⓔ	29	Ⓐ Ⓑ Ⓒ Ⓓ Ⓔ	54	Ⓐ Ⓑ Ⓒ Ⓓ Ⓔ	79	Ⓐ Ⓑ Ⓒ Ⓓ Ⓔ
5	Ⓐ Ⓑ Ⓒ Ⓓ Ⓔ	30	Ⓐ Ⓑ Ⓒ Ⓓ Ⓔ	55	Ⓐ Ⓑ Ⓒ Ⓓ Ⓔ	80	Ⓐ Ⓑ Ⓒ Ⓓ Ⓔ
6	Ⓐ Ⓑ Ⓒ Ⓓ Ⓔ	31	Ⓐ Ⓑ Ⓒ Ⓓ Ⓔ	56	Ⓐ Ⓑ Ⓒ Ⓓ Ⓔ	81	Ⓐ Ⓑ Ⓒ Ⓓ Ⓔ
7	Ⓐ Ⓑ Ⓒ Ⓓ Ⓔ	32	Ⓐ Ⓑ Ⓒ Ⓓ Ⓔ	57	Ⓐ Ⓑ Ⓒ Ⓓ Ⓔ	82	Ⓐ Ⓑ Ⓒ Ⓓ Ⓔ
8	Ⓐ Ⓑ Ⓒ Ⓓ Ⓔ	33	Ⓐ Ⓑ Ⓒ Ⓓ Ⓔ	58	Ⓐ Ⓑ Ⓒ Ⓓ Ⓔ	83	Ⓐ Ⓑ Ⓒ Ⓓ Ⓔ
9	Ⓐ Ⓑ Ⓒ Ⓓ Ⓔ	34	Ⓐ Ⓑ Ⓒ Ⓓ Ⓔ	59	Ⓐ Ⓑ Ⓒ Ⓓ Ⓔ	84	Ⓐ Ⓑ Ⓒ Ⓓ Ⓔ
10	Ⓐ Ⓑ Ⓒ Ⓓ Ⓔ	35	Ⓐ Ⓑ Ⓒ Ⓓ Ⓔ	60	Ⓐ Ⓑ Ⓒ Ⓓ Ⓔ	85	Ⓐ Ⓑ Ⓒ Ⓓ Ⓔ
11	Ⓐ Ⓑ Ⓒ Ⓓ Ⓔ	36	Ⓐ Ⓑ Ⓒ Ⓓ Ⓔ	61	Ⓐ Ⓑ Ⓒ Ⓓ Ⓔ	86	Ⓐ Ⓑ Ⓒ Ⓓ Ⓔ
12	Ⓐ Ⓑ Ⓒ Ⓓ Ⓔ	37	Ⓐ Ⓑ Ⓒ Ⓓ Ⓔ	62	Ⓐ Ⓑ Ⓒ Ⓓ Ⓔ	87	Ⓐ Ⓑ Ⓒ Ⓓ Ⓔ
13	Ⓐ Ⓑ Ⓒ Ⓓ Ⓔ	38	Ⓐ Ⓑ Ⓒ Ⓓ Ⓔ	63	Ⓐ Ⓑ Ⓒ Ⓓ Ⓔ	88	Ⓐ Ⓑ Ⓒ Ⓓ Ⓔ
14	Ⓐ Ⓑ Ⓒ Ⓓ Ⓔ	39	Ⓐ Ⓑ Ⓒ Ⓓ Ⓔ	64	Ⓐ Ⓑ Ⓒ Ⓓ Ⓔ	89	Ⓐ Ⓑ Ⓒ Ⓓ Ⓔ
15	Ⓐ Ⓑ Ⓒ Ⓓ Ⓔ	40	Ⓐ Ⓑ Ⓒ Ⓓ Ⓔ	65	Ⓐ Ⓑ Ⓒ Ⓓ Ⓔ	90	Ⓐ Ⓑ Ⓒ Ⓓ Ⓔ
16	Ⓐ Ⓑ Ⓒ Ⓓ Ⓔ	41	Ⓐ Ⓑ Ⓒ Ⓓ Ⓔ	66	Ⓐ Ⓑ Ⓒ Ⓓ Ⓔ	91	Ⓐ Ⓑ Ⓒ Ⓓ Ⓔ
17	Ⓐ Ⓑ Ⓒ Ⓓ Ⓔ	42	Ⓐ Ⓑ Ⓒ Ⓓ Ⓔ	67	Ⓐ Ⓑ Ⓒ Ⓓ Ⓔ	92	Ⓐ Ⓑ Ⓒ Ⓓ Ⓔ
18	Ⓐ Ⓑ Ⓒ Ⓓ Ⓔ	43	Ⓐ Ⓑ Ⓒ Ⓓ Ⓔ	68	Ⓐ Ⓑ Ⓒ Ⓓ Ⓔ	93	Ⓐ Ⓑ Ⓒ Ⓓ Ⓔ
19	Ⓐ Ⓑ Ⓒ Ⓓ Ⓔ	44	Ⓐ Ⓑ Ⓒ Ⓓ Ⓔ	69	Ⓐ Ⓑ Ⓒ Ⓓ Ⓔ	94	Ⓐ Ⓑ Ⓒ Ⓓ Ⓔ
20	Ⓐ Ⓑ Ⓒ Ⓓ Ⓔ	45	Ⓐ Ⓑ Ⓒ Ⓓ Ⓔ	70	Ⓐ Ⓑ Ⓒ Ⓓ Ⓔ	95	Ⓐ Ⓑ Ⓒ Ⓓ Ⓔ
21	Ⓐ Ⓑ Ⓒ Ⓓ Ⓔ	46	Ⓐ Ⓑ Ⓒ Ⓓ Ⓔ	71	Ⓐ Ⓑ Ⓒ Ⓓ Ⓔ	96	Ⓐ Ⓑ Ⓒ Ⓓ Ⓔ
22	Ⓐ Ⓑ Ⓒ Ⓓ Ⓔ	47	Ⓐ Ⓑ Ⓒ Ⓓ Ⓔ	72	Ⓐ Ⓑ Ⓒ Ⓓ Ⓔ	97	Ⓐ Ⓑ Ⓒ Ⓓ Ⓔ
23	Ⓐ Ⓑ Ⓒ Ⓓ Ⓔ	48	Ⓐ Ⓑ Ⓒ Ⓓ Ⓔ	73	Ⓐ Ⓑ Ⓒ Ⓓ Ⓔ	98	Ⓐ Ⓑ Ⓒ Ⓓ Ⓔ
24	Ⓐ Ⓑ Ⓒ Ⓓ Ⓔ	49	Ⓐ Ⓑ Ⓒ Ⓓ Ⓔ	74	Ⓐ Ⓑ Ⓒ Ⓓ Ⓔ	99	Ⓐ Ⓑ Ⓒ Ⓓ Ⓔ
25	Ⓐ Ⓑ Ⓒ Ⓓ Ⓔ	50	Ⓐ Ⓑ Ⓒ Ⓓ Ⓔ	75	Ⓐ Ⓑ Ⓒ Ⓓ Ⓔ	100	Ⓐ Ⓑ Ⓒ Ⓓ Ⓔ

Chemistry *Fill in circle CE only if II is correct explanation of I.

	I	II	CE*		I	II	CE*
101	Ⓣ Ⓕ	Ⓣ Ⓕ	○	109	Ⓣ Ⓕ	Ⓣ Ⓕ	○
102	Ⓣ Ⓕ	Ⓣ Ⓕ	○	110	Ⓣ Ⓕ	Ⓣ Ⓕ	○
103	Ⓣ Ⓕ	Ⓣ Ⓕ	○	111	Ⓣ Ⓕ	Ⓣ Ⓕ	○
104	Ⓣ Ⓕ	Ⓣ Ⓕ	○	112	Ⓣ Ⓕ	Ⓣ Ⓕ	○
105	Ⓣ Ⓕ	Ⓣ Ⓕ	○	113	Ⓣ Ⓕ	Ⓣ Ⓕ	○
106	Ⓣ Ⓕ	Ⓣ Ⓕ	○	114	Ⓣ Ⓕ	Ⓣ Ⓕ	○
107	Ⓣ Ⓕ	Ⓣ Ⓕ	○	115	Ⓣ Ⓕ	Ⓣ Ⓕ	○
108	Ⓣ Ⓕ	Ⓣ Ⓕ	○				

PLEASE MAKE SURE to fill in these fields completely and correctly. If they are not correct, we won't be able to score your test(s)!

7 TEST BOOK SERIAL NUMBER
(Copy from front of test book.)

0	0	0	0	0	0
1	1	1	1	1	1
2	2	2	2	2	2
3	3	3	3	3	3
4	4	4	4	4	4
5	5	5	5	5	5
6	6	6	6	6	6
7	7	7	7	7	7
8	8	8	8	8	8
9	9	9	9	9	9

8 BOOK CODE
(Copy and grid as on back of test book.)

0	A	0
1	B	1
2	C	2
3	D	3
4	E	4
5	F	5
6	G	6
7	H	7
8	I	8
9	J	9
	K	
	L	
	M	
	N	
	O	
	P	
	Q	
	R	
	S	
	T	
	U	
	V	
	W	
	X	
	Y	
	Z	

9 BOOK ID
(Copy from back of test book.)

Quality Assurance Mark

FOR OFFICIAL USE ONLY

R/C	W/S1	FS/S2	CS/S3	WS

CERTIFICATION STATEMENT

Copy the statement below and sign your name as you would an official document.

I hereby agree to the conditions set forth online at sat.collegeboard.org and in any paper registration materials given to me and certify that I am the person whose name, address and signature appear on this answer sheet.

Signature ______________________ Date ______________

COMPLETE MARK ● EXAMPLES OF INCOMPLETE MARKS

You must use a No. 2 pencil and marks must be complete. Do not use a mechanical pencil. It is very important that you fill in the entire circle darkly and completely. If you change your response, erase as completely as possible. Incomplete marks or erasures may affect your score.

○ Literature
○ Biology E
○ Biology M
○ Chemistry
○ Physics
○ Mathematics Level 1
○ Mathematics Level 2
○ U.S. History
○ World History
○ French
○ German
○ Italian
○ Latin
○ Modern Hebrew
○ Spanish
○ Chinese Listening
○ French Listening
○ German Listening
○ Japanese Listening
○ Korean Listening
○ Spanish Listening

Background Questions: ① ② ③ ④ ⑤ ⑥ ⑦ ⑧ ⑨

PLEASE MAKE SURE to fill in these fields completely and correctly. If they are not correct, we won't be able to score your test(s)!

1 Ⓐ Ⓑ Ⓒ Ⓓ Ⓔ	26 Ⓐ Ⓑ Ⓒ Ⓓ Ⓔ	51 Ⓐ Ⓑ Ⓒ Ⓓ Ⓔ	76 Ⓐ Ⓑ Ⓒ Ⓓ Ⓔ
2 Ⓐ Ⓑ Ⓒ Ⓓ Ⓔ	27 Ⓐ Ⓑ Ⓒ Ⓓ Ⓔ	52 Ⓐ Ⓑ Ⓒ Ⓓ Ⓔ	77 Ⓐ Ⓑ Ⓒ Ⓓ Ⓔ
3 Ⓐ Ⓑ Ⓒ Ⓓ Ⓔ	28 Ⓐ Ⓑ Ⓒ Ⓓ Ⓔ	53 Ⓐ Ⓑ Ⓒ Ⓓ Ⓔ	78 Ⓐ Ⓑ Ⓒ Ⓓ Ⓔ
4 Ⓐ Ⓑ Ⓒ Ⓓ Ⓔ	29 Ⓐ Ⓑ Ⓒ Ⓓ Ⓔ	54 Ⓐ Ⓑ Ⓒ Ⓓ Ⓔ	79 Ⓐ Ⓑ Ⓒ Ⓓ Ⓔ
5 Ⓐ Ⓑ Ⓒ Ⓓ Ⓔ	30 Ⓐ Ⓑ Ⓒ Ⓓ Ⓔ	55 Ⓐ Ⓑ Ⓒ Ⓓ Ⓔ	80 Ⓐ Ⓑ Ⓒ Ⓓ Ⓔ
6 Ⓐ Ⓑ Ⓒ Ⓓ Ⓔ	31 Ⓐ Ⓑ Ⓒ Ⓓ Ⓔ	56 Ⓐ Ⓑ Ⓒ Ⓓ Ⓔ	81 Ⓐ Ⓑ Ⓒ Ⓓ Ⓔ
7 Ⓐ Ⓑ Ⓒ Ⓓ Ⓔ	32 Ⓐ Ⓑ Ⓒ Ⓓ Ⓔ	57 Ⓐ Ⓑ Ⓒ Ⓓ Ⓔ	82 Ⓐ Ⓑ Ⓒ Ⓓ Ⓔ
8 Ⓐ Ⓑ Ⓒ Ⓓ Ⓔ	33 Ⓐ Ⓑ Ⓒ Ⓓ Ⓔ	58 Ⓐ Ⓑ Ⓒ Ⓓ Ⓔ	83 Ⓐ Ⓑ Ⓒ Ⓓ Ⓔ
9 Ⓐ Ⓑ Ⓒ Ⓓ Ⓔ	34 Ⓐ Ⓑ Ⓒ Ⓓ Ⓔ	59 Ⓐ Ⓑ Ⓒ Ⓓ Ⓔ	84 Ⓐ Ⓑ Ⓒ Ⓓ Ⓔ
10 Ⓐ Ⓑ Ⓒ Ⓓ Ⓔ	35 Ⓐ Ⓑ Ⓒ Ⓓ Ⓔ	60 Ⓐ Ⓑ Ⓒ Ⓓ Ⓔ	85 Ⓐ Ⓑ Ⓒ Ⓓ Ⓔ
11 Ⓐ Ⓑ Ⓒ Ⓓ Ⓔ	36 Ⓐ Ⓑ Ⓒ Ⓓ Ⓔ	61 Ⓐ Ⓑ Ⓒ Ⓓ Ⓔ	86 Ⓐ Ⓑ Ⓒ Ⓓ Ⓔ
12 Ⓐ Ⓑ Ⓒ Ⓓ Ⓔ	37 Ⓐ Ⓑ Ⓒ Ⓓ Ⓔ	62 Ⓐ Ⓑ Ⓒ Ⓓ Ⓔ	87 Ⓐ Ⓑ Ⓒ Ⓓ Ⓔ
13 Ⓐ Ⓑ Ⓒ Ⓓ Ⓔ	38 Ⓐ Ⓑ Ⓒ Ⓓ Ⓔ	63 Ⓐ Ⓑ Ⓒ Ⓓ Ⓔ	88 Ⓐ Ⓑ Ⓒ Ⓓ Ⓔ
14 Ⓐ Ⓑ Ⓒ Ⓓ Ⓔ	39 Ⓐ Ⓑ Ⓒ Ⓓ Ⓔ	64 Ⓐ Ⓑ Ⓒ Ⓓ Ⓔ	89 Ⓐ Ⓑ Ⓒ Ⓓ Ⓔ
15 Ⓐ Ⓑ Ⓒ Ⓓ Ⓔ	40 Ⓐ Ⓑ Ⓒ Ⓓ Ⓔ	65 Ⓐ Ⓑ Ⓒ Ⓓ Ⓔ	90 Ⓐ Ⓑ Ⓒ Ⓓ Ⓔ
16 Ⓐ Ⓑ Ⓒ Ⓓ Ⓔ	41 Ⓐ Ⓑ Ⓒ Ⓓ Ⓔ	66 Ⓐ Ⓑ Ⓒ Ⓓ Ⓔ	91 Ⓐ Ⓑ Ⓒ Ⓓ Ⓔ
17 Ⓐ Ⓑ Ⓒ Ⓓ Ⓔ	42 Ⓐ Ⓑ Ⓒ Ⓓ Ⓔ	67 Ⓐ Ⓑ Ⓒ Ⓓ Ⓔ	92 Ⓐ Ⓑ Ⓒ Ⓓ Ⓔ
18 Ⓐ Ⓑ Ⓒ Ⓓ Ⓔ	43 Ⓐ Ⓑ Ⓒ Ⓓ Ⓔ	68 Ⓐ Ⓑ Ⓒ Ⓓ Ⓔ	93 Ⓐ Ⓑ Ⓒ Ⓓ Ⓔ
19 Ⓐ Ⓑ Ⓒ Ⓓ Ⓔ	44 Ⓐ Ⓑ Ⓒ Ⓓ Ⓔ	69 Ⓐ Ⓑ Ⓒ Ⓓ Ⓔ	94 Ⓐ Ⓑ Ⓒ Ⓓ Ⓔ
20 Ⓐ Ⓑ Ⓒ Ⓓ Ⓔ	45 Ⓐ Ⓑ Ⓒ Ⓓ Ⓔ	70 Ⓐ Ⓑ Ⓒ Ⓓ Ⓔ	95 Ⓐ Ⓑ Ⓒ Ⓓ Ⓔ
21 Ⓐ Ⓑ Ⓒ Ⓓ Ⓔ	46 Ⓐ Ⓑ Ⓒ Ⓓ Ⓔ	71 Ⓐ Ⓑ Ⓒ Ⓓ Ⓔ	96 Ⓐ Ⓑ Ⓒ Ⓓ Ⓔ
22 Ⓐ Ⓑ Ⓒ Ⓓ Ⓔ	47 Ⓐ Ⓑ Ⓒ Ⓓ Ⓔ	72 Ⓐ Ⓑ Ⓒ Ⓓ Ⓔ	97 Ⓐ Ⓑ Ⓒ Ⓓ Ⓔ
23 Ⓐ Ⓑ Ⓒ Ⓓ Ⓔ	48 Ⓐ Ⓑ Ⓒ Ⓓ Ⓔ	73 Ⓐ Ⓑ Ⓒ Ⓓ Ⓔ	98 Ⓐ Ⓑ Ⓒ Ⓓ Ⓔ
24 Ⓐ Ⓑ Ⓒ Ⓓ Ⓔ	49 Ⓐ Ⓑ Ⓒ Ⓓ Ⓔ	74 Ⓐ Ⓑ Ⓒ Ⓓ Ⓔ	99 Ⓐ Ⓑ Ⓒ Ⓓ Ⓔ
25 Ⓐ Ⓑ Ⓒ Ⓓ Ⓔ	50 Ⓐ Ⓑ Ⓒ Ⓓ Ⓔ	75 Ⓐ Ⓑ Ⓒ Ⓓ Ⓔ	100 Ⓐ Ⓑ Ⓒ Ⓓ Ⓔ

Quality ● Assurance Mark

8 BOOK CODE (Copy and grid as on back of test book.)

⓪	Ⓐ	⓪
①	Ⓑ	①
②	Ⓒ	②
③	Ⓓ	③
④	Ⓔ	④
⑤	Ⓕ	⑤
⑥	Ⓖ	⑥
⑦	Ⓗ	⑦
⑧	Ⓘ	⑧
⑨	Ⓙ	⑨
	Ⓚ	
	Ⓛ	
	Ⓜ	
	Ⓝ	
	Ⓞ	
	Ⓟ	
	Ⓠ	
	Ⓡ	
	Ⓢ	
	Ⓣ	
	Ⓤ	
	Ⓥ	
	Ⓦ	
	Ⓧ	
	Ⓨ	
	Ⓩ	

7 TEST BOOK SERIAL NUMBER (Copy from front of test book.)

⓪	⓪	⓪	⓪	⓪	⓪
①	①	①	①	①	①
②	②	②	②	②	②
③	③	③	③	③	③
④	④	④	④	④	④
⑤	⑤	⑤	⑤	⑤	⑤
⑥	⑥	⑥	⑥	⑥	⑥
⑦	⑦	⑦	⑦	⑦	⑦
⑧	⑧	⑧	⑧	⑧	⑧
⑨	⑨	⑨	⑨	⑨	⑨

9 BOOK ID (Copy from back of test book.)

Chemistry *Fill in circle CE only if II is correct explanation of I.

	I	II	CE*		I	II	CE*
101	Ⓣ Ⓕ	Ⓣ Ⓕ	○	109	Ⓣ Ⓕ	Ⓣ Ⓕ	○
102	Ⓣ Ⓕ	Ⓣ Ⓕ	○	110	Ⓣ Ⓕ	Ⓣ Ⓕ	○
103	Ⓣ Ⓕ	Ⓣ Ⓕ	○	111	Ⓣ Ⓕ	Ⓣ Ⓕ	○
104	Ⓣ Ⓕ	Ⓣ Ⓕ	○	112	Ⓣ Ⓕ	Ⓣ Ⓕ	○
105	Ⓣ Ⓕ	Ⓣ Ⓕ	○	113	Ⓣ Ⓕ	Ⓣ Ⓕ	○
106	Ⓣ Ⓕ	Ⓣ Ⓕ	○	114	Ⓣ Ⓕ	Ⓣ Ⓕ	○
107	Ⓣ Ⓕ	Ⓣ Ⓕ	○	115	Ⓣ Ⓕ	Ⓣ Ⓕ	○
108	Ⓣ Ⓕ	Ⓣ Ⓕ	○				

FOR OFFICIAL USE ONLY

R/C	W/S1	FS/S2	CS/S3	WS

COMPLETE MARK ● EXAMPLES OF INCOMPLETE MARKS

You must use a No. 2 pencil and marks must be complete. Do not use a mechanical pencil. *It is very important that you fill in the entire circle darkly and completely. If you change your response, erase as completely as possible. Incomplete marks or erasures may affect your score.*

- ◯ Literature
- ◯ Biology E
- ◯ Biology M
- ◯ Chemistry
- ◯ Physics
- ◯ Mathematics Level 1
- ◯ Mathematics Level 2
- ◯ U.S. History
- ◯ World History
- ◯ French
- ◯ German
- ◯ Italian
- ◯ Latin
- ◯ Modern Hebrew
- ◯ Spanish
- ◯ Chinese Listening
- ◯ French Listening
- ◯ German Listening
- ◯ Japanese Listening
- ◯ Korean Listening
- ◯ Spanish Listening

Background Questions: ① ② ③ ④ ⑤ ⑥ ⑦ ⑧ ⑨

1	Ⓐ Ⓑ Ⓒ Ⓓ Ⓔ	26	Ⓐ Ⓑ Ⓒ Ⓓ Ⓔ	51	Ⓐ Ⓑ Ⓒ Ⓓ Ⓔ	76	Ⓐ Ⓑ Ⓒ Ⓓ Ⓔ
2	Ⓐ Ⓑ Ⓒ Ⓓ Ⓔ	27	Ⓐ Ⓑ Ⓒ Ⓓ Ⓔ	52	Ⓐ Ⓑ Ⓒ Ⓓ Ⓔ	77	Ⓐ Ⓑ Ⓒ Ⓓ Ⓔ
3	Ⓐ Ⓑ Ⓒ Ⓓ Ⓔ	28	Ⓐ Ⓑ Ⓒ Ⓓ Ⓔ	53	Ⓐ Ⓑ Ⓒ Ⓓ Ⓔ	78	Ⓐ Ⓑ Ⓒ Ⓓ Ⓔ
4	Ⓐ Ⓑ Ⓒ Ⓓ Ⓔ	29	Ⓐ Ⓑ Ⓒ Ⓓ Ⓔ	54	Ⓐ Ⓑ Ⓒ Ⓓ Ⓔ	79	Ⓐ Ⓑ Ⓒ Ⓓ Ⓔ
5	Ⓐ Ⓑ Ⓒ Ⓓ Ⓔ	30	Ⓐ Ⓑ Ⓒ Ⓓ Ⓔ	55	Ⓐ Ⓑ Ⓒ Ⓓ Ⓔ	80	Ⓐ Ⓑ Ⓒ Ⓓ Ⓔ
6	Ⓐ Ⓑ Ⓒ Ⓓ Ⓔ	31	Ⓐ Ⓑ Ⓒ Ⓓ Ⓔ	56	Ⓐ Ⓑ Ⓒ Ⓓ Ⓔ	81	Ⓐ Ⓑ Ⓒ Ⓓ Ⓔ
7	Ⓐ Ⓑ Ⓒ Ⓓ Ⓔ	32	Ⓐ Ⓑ Ⓒ Ⓓ Ⓔ	57	Ⓐ Ⓑ Ⓒ Ⓓ Ⓔ	82	Ⓐ Ⓑ Ⓒ Ⓓ Ⓔ
8	Ⓐ Ⓑ Ⓒ Ⓓ Ⓔ	33	Ⓐ Ⓑ Ⓒ Ⓓ Ⓔ	58	Ⓐ Ⓑ Ⓒ Ⓓ Ⓔ	83	Ⓐ Ⓑ Ⓒ Ⓓ Ⓔ
9	Ⓐ Ⓑ Ⓒ Ⓓ Ⓔ	34	Ⓐ Ⓑ Ⓒ Ⓓ Ⓔ	59	Ⓐ Ⓑ Ⓒ Ⓓ Ⓔ	84	Ⓐ Ⓑ Ⓒ Ⓓ Ⓔ
10	Ⓐ Ⓑ Ⓒ Ⓓ Ⓔ	35	Ⓐ Ⓑ Ⓒ Ⓓ Ⓔ	60	Ⓐ Ⓑ Ⓒ Ⓓ Ⓔ	85	Ⓐ Ⓑ Ⓒ Ⓓ Ⓔ
11	Ⓐ Ⓑ Ⓒ Ⓓ Ⓔ	36	Ⓐ Ⓑ Ⓒ Ⓓ Ⓔ	61	Ⓐ Ⓑ Ⓒ Ⓓ Ⓔ	86	Ⓐ Ⓑ Ⓒ Ⓓ Ⓔ
12	Ⓐ Ⓑ Ⓒ Ⓓ Ⓔ	37	Ⓐ Ⓑ Ⓒ Ⓓ Ⓔ	62	Ⓐ Ⓑ Ⓒ Ⓓ Ⓔ	87	Ⓐ Ⓑ Ⓒ Ⓓ Ⓔ
13	Ⓐ Ⓑ Ⓒ Ⓓ Ⓔ	38	Ⓐ Ⓑ Ⓒ Ⓓ Ⓔ	63	Ⓐ Ⓑ Ⓒ Ⓓ Ⓔ	88	Ⓐ Ⓑ Ⓒ Ⓓ Ⓔ
14	Ⓐ Ⓑ Ⓒ Ⓓ Ⓔ	39	Ⓐ Ⓑ Ⓒ Ⓓ Ⓔ	64	Ⓐ Ⓑ Ⓒ Ⓓ Ⓔ	89	Ⓐ Ⓑ Ⓒ Ⓓ Ⓔ
15	Ⓐ Ⓑ Ⓒ Ⓓ Ⓔ	40	Ⓐ Ⓑ Ⓒ Ⓓ Ⓔ	65	Ⓐ Ⓑ Ⓒ Ⓓ Ⓔ	90	Ⓐ Ⓑ Ⓒ Ⓓ Ⓔ
16	Ⓐ Ⓑ Ⓒ Ⓓ Ⓔ	41	Ⓐ Ⓑ Ⓒ Ⓓ Ⓔ	66	Ⓐ Ⓑ Ⓒ Ⓓ Ⓔ	91	Ⓐ Ⓑ Ⓒ Ⓓ Ⓔ
17	Ⓐ Ⓑ Ⓒ Ⓓ Ⓔ	42	Ⓐ Ⓑ Ⓒ Ⓓ Ⓔ	67	Ⓐ Ⓑ Ⓒ Ⓓ Ⓔ	92	Ⓐ Ⓑ Ⓒ Ⓓ Ⓔ
18	Ⓐ Ⓑ Ⓒ Ⓓ Ⓔ	43	Ⓐ Ⓑ Ⓒ Ⓓ Ⓔ	68	Ⓐ Ⓑ Ⓒ Ⓓ Ⓔ	93	Ⓐ Ⓑ Ⓒ Ⓓ Ⓔ
19	Ⓐ Ⓑ Ⓒ Ⓓ Ⓔ	44	Ⓐ Ⓑ Ⓒ Ⓓ Ⓔ	69	Ⓐ Ⓑ Ⓒ Ⓓ Ⓔ	94	Ⓐ Ⓑ Ⓒ Ⓓ Ⓔ
20	Ⓐ Ⓑ Ⓒ Ⓓ Ⓔ	45	Ⓐ Ⓑ Ⓒ Ⓓ Ⓔ	70	Ⓐ Ⓑ Ⓒ Ⓓ Ⓔ	95	Ⓐ Ⓑ Ⓒ Ⓓ Ⓔ
21	Ⓐ Ⓑ Ⓒ Ⓓ Ⓔ	46	Ⓐ Ⓑ Ⓒ Ⓓ Ⓔ	71	Ⓐ Ⓑ Ⓒ Ⓓ Ⓔ	96	Ⓐ Ⓑ Ⓒ Ⓓ Ⓔ
22	Ⓐ Ⓑ Ⓒ Ⓓ Ⓔ	47	Ⓐ Ⓑ Ⓒ Ⓓ Ⓔ	72	Ⓐ Ⓑ Ⓒ Ⓓ Ⓔ	97	Ⓐ Ⓑ Ⓒ Ⓓ Ⓔ
23	Ⓐ Ⓑ Ⓒ Ⓓ Ⓔ	48	Ⓐ Ⓑ Ⓒ Ⓓ Ⓔ	73	Ⓐ Ⓑ Ⓒ Ⓓ Ⓔ	98	Ⓐ Ⓑ Ⓒ Ⓓ Ⓔ
24	Ⓐ Ⓑ Ⓒ Ⓓ Ⓔ	49	Ⓐ Ⓑ Ⓒ Ⓓ Ⓔ	74	Ⓐ Ⓑ Ⓒ Ⓓ Ⓔ	99	Ⓐ Ⓑ Ⓒ Ⓓ Ⓔ
25	Ⓐ Ⓑ Ⓒ Ⓓ Ⓔ	50	Ⓐ Ⓑ Ⓒ Ⓓ Ⓔ	75	Ⓐ Ⓑ Ⓒ Ⓓ Ⓔ	100	Ⓐ Ⓑ Ⓒ Ⓓ Ⓔ

Chemistry *Fill in circle CE only if II is correct explanation of I.

	I	II	CE*		I	II	CE*
101	Ⓣ Ⓕ	Ⓣ Ⓕ	◯	109	Ⓣ Ⓕ	Ⓣ Ⓕ	◯
102	Ⓣ Ⓕ	Ⓣ Ⓕ	◯	110	Ⓣ Ⓕ	Ⓣ Ⓕ	◯
103	Ⓣ Ⓕ	Ⓣ Ⓕ	◯	111	Ⓣ Ⓕ	Ⓣ Ⓕ	◯
104	Ⓣ Ⓕ	Ⓣ Ⓕ	◯	112	Ⓣ Ⓕ	Ⓣ Ⓕ	◯
105	Ⓣ Ⓕ	Ⓣ Ⓕ	◯	113	Ⓣ Ⓕ	Ⓣ Ⓕ	◯
106	Ⓣ Ⓕ	Ⓣ Ⓕ	◯	114	Ⓣ Ⓕ	Ⓣ Ⓕ	◯
107	Ⓣ Ⓕ	Ⓣ Ⓕ	◯	115	Ⓣ Ⓕ	Ⓣ Ⓕ	◯
108	Ⓣ Ⓕ	Ⓣ Ⓕ	◯				

PLEASE MAKE SURE to fill in these fields completely and correctly. If they are not correct, we won't be able to score your test(s)!

7 TEST BOOK SERIAL NUMBER (Copy from front of test book.)

0	0	0	0	0	0
1	1	1	1	1	1
2	2	2	2	2	2
3	3	3	3	3	3
4	4	4	4	4	4
5	5	5	5	5	5
6	6	6	6	6	6
7	7	7	7	7	7
8	8	8	8	8	8
9	9	9	9	9	9

8 BOOK CODE (Copy and grid as on back of test book.)

0	A	0
1	B	1
2	C	2
3	D	3
4	E	4
5	F	5
6	G	6
7	H	7
8	I	8
9	J	9
	K	
	L	
	M	
	N	
	O	
	P	
	Q	
	R	
	S	
	T	
	U	
	V	
	W	
	X	
	Y	
	Z	

9 BOOK ID (Copy from back of test book.)

Quality Assurance Mark

FOR OFFICIAL USE ONLY				
R/C	W/S1	FS/S2	CS/S3	WS

PLEASE DO NOT WRITE IN THIS AREA

SERIAL #

CollegeBoard

SAT Subject Tests™

COMPLETE MARK ● EXAMPLES OF INCOMPLETE MARKS

You must use a No. 2 pencil and marks must be complete. Do not use a mechanical pencil. It is very important that you fill in the entire circle darkly and completely. If you change your response, erase as completely as possible. Incomplete marks or erasures may affect your score.

1 **Your Name:** (Print)

Last First M.I.

I agree to the conditions on the front and back of the SAT Subject Tests™ book. I also agree with the SAT Test Security and Fairness policies and understand that any violation of these policies will result in score cancellation and may result in reporting of certain violations to law enforcement.

Signature: **Today's Date:** / / (MM DD YY)

Home Address: (Print) Number and Street City State/Country Zip Code

Phone: ( ) **Test Center:** (Print) City State/Country

2 YOUR NAME
Last Name (First 6 Letters) First Name (First 4 Letters) Mid. Init.

3 DATE OF BIRTH
MONTH DAY YEAR
Jan Feb Mar Apr May Jun Jul Aug Sep Oct Nov Dec

4 REGISTRATION NUMBER
(Copy from Admission Ticket.)

Important: Fill in items 8 and 9 exactly as shown on the back of test book.

7 TEST BOOK SERIAL NUMBER
(Copy from front of test book.)

8 BOOK CODE
(Copy and grid as on back of test book.)

9 BOOK ID
(Copy from back of test book.)

5 ZIP CODE

6 TEST CENTER
(Supplied by Test Center Supervisor.)

PLEASE MAKE SURE to fill in these fields completely and correctly. If they are not correct, we won't be able to score your test(s)!

FOR OFFICIAL USE ONLY

103648-77191 • NS1114C1085 • Printed in U.S.A.

194415-001 1 2 3 4 5 A B C D E Printed in the USA ISD11312

783175

PLEASE DO NOT WRITE IN THIS AREA

SERIAL #

OMPLETE MARK ● EXAMPLES OF INCOMPLETE MARKS

You must use a No. 2 pencil and marks must be complete. Do not use a mechanical pencil. *It is very important that you fill in the entire circle darkly and completely. If you change your response, erase as completely as possible. Incomplete marks or erasures may affect your score.*

○ Literature ○ Biology E ○ Biology M ○ Chemistry ○ Physics
○ Mathematics Level 1 ○ Mathematics Level 2 ○ U.S. History ○ World History ○ French
○ German ○ Italian ○ Latin ○ Modern Hebrew ○ Spanish
○ Chinese Listening ○ French Listening ○ German Listening
○ Japanese Listening ○ Korean Listening ○ Spanish Listening

Background Questions: ① ② ③ ④ ⑤ ⑥ ⑦ ⑧ ⑨

1	Ⓐ Ⓑ Ⓒ Ⓓ Ⓔ	26	Ⓐ Ⓑ Ⓒ Ⓓ Ⓔ	51	Ⓐ Ⓑ Ⓒ Ⓓ Ⓔ	76	Ⓐ Ⓑ Ⓒ Ⓓ Ⓔ
2	Ⓐ Ⓑ Ⓒ Ⓓ Ⓔ	27	Ⓐ Ⓑ Ⓒ Ⓓ Ⓔ	52	Ⓐ Ⓑ Ⓒ Ⓓ Ⓔ	77	Ⓐ Ⓑ Ⓒ Ⓓ Ⓔ
3	Ⓐ Ⓑ Ⓒ Ⓓ Ⓔ	28	Ⓐ Ⓑ Ⓒ Ⓓ Ⓔ	53	Ⓐ Ⓑ Ⓒ Ⓓ Ⓔ	78	Ⓐ Ⓑ Ⓒ Ⓓ Ⓔ
4	Ⓐ Ⓑ Ⓒ Ⓓ Ⓔ	29	Ⓐ Ⓑ Ⓒ Ⓓ Ⓔ	54	Ⓐ Ⓑ Ⓒ Ⓓ Ⓔ	79	Ⓐ Ⓑ Ⓒ Ⓓ Ⓔ
5	Ⓐ Ⓑ Ⓒ Ⓓ Ⓔ	30	Ⓐ Ⓑ Ⓒ Ⓓ Ⓔ	55	Ⓐ Ⓑ Ⓒ Ⓓ Ⓔ	80	Ⓐ Ⓑ Ⓒ Ⓓ Ⓔ
6	Ⓐ Ⓑ Ⓒ Ⓓ Ⓔ	31	Ⓐ Ⓑ Ⓒ Ⓓ Ⓔ	56	Ⓐ Ⓑ Ⓒ Ⓓ Ⓔ	81	Ⓐ Ⓑ Ⓒ Ⓓ Ⓔ
7	Ⓐ Ⓑ Ⓒ Ⓓ Ⓔ	32	Ⓐ Ⓑ Ⓒ Ⓓ Ⓔ	57	Ⓐ Ⓑ Ⓒ Ⓓ Ⓔ	82	Ⓐ Ⓑ Ⓒ Ⓓ Ⓔ
8	Ⓐ Ⓑ Ⓒ Ⓓ Ⓔ	33	Ⓐ Ⓑ Ⓒ Ⓓ Ⓔ	58	Ⓐ Ⓑ Ⓒ Ⓓ Ⓔ	83	Ⓐ Ⓑ Ⓒ Ⓓ Ⓔ
9	Ⓐ Ⓑ Ⓒ Ⓓ Ⓔ	34	Ⓐ Ⓑ Ⓒ Ⓓ Ⓔ	59	Ⓐ Ⓑ Ⓒ Ⓓ Ⓔ	84	Ⓐ Ⓑ Ⓒ Ⓓ Ⓔ
10	Ⓐ Ⓑ Ⓒ Ⓓ Ⓔ	35	Ⓐ Ⓑ Ⓒ Ⓓ Ⓔ	60	Ⓐ Ⓑ Ⓒ Ⓓ Ⓔ	85	Ⓐ Ⓑ Ⓒ Ⓓ Ⓔ
11	Ⓐ Ⓑ Ⓒ Ⓓ Ⓔ	36	Ⓐ Ⓑ Ⓒ Ⓓ Ⓔ	61	Ⓐ Ⓑ Ⓒ Ⓓ Ⓔ	86	Ⓐ Ⓑ Ⓒ Ⓓ Ⓔ
12	Ⓐ Ⓑ Ⓒ Ⓓ Ⓔ	37	Ⓐ Ⓑ Ⓒ Ⓓ Ⓔ	62	Ⓐ Ⓑ Ⓒ Ⓓ Ⓔ	87	Ⓐ Ⓑ Ⓒ Ⓓ Ⓔ
13	Ⓐ Ⓑ Ⓒ Ⓓ Ⓔ	38	Ⓐ Ⓑ Ⓒ Ⓓ Ⓔ	63	Ⓐ Ⓑ Ⓒ Ⓓ Ⓔ	88	Ⓐ Ⓑ Ⓒ Ⓓ Ⓔ
14	Ⓐ Ⓑ Ⓒ Ⓓ Ⓔ	39	Ⓐ Ⓑ Ⓒ Ⓓ Ⓔ	64	Ⓐ Ⓑ Ⓒ Ⓓ Ⓔ	89	Ⓐ Ⓑ Ⓒ Ⓓ Ⓔ
15	Ⓐ Ⓑ Ⓒ Ⓓ Ⓔ	40	Ⓐ Ⓑ Ⓒ Ⓓ Ⓔ	65	Ⓐ Ⓑ Ⓒ Ⓓ Ⓔ	90	Ⓐ Ⓑ Ⓒ Ⓓ Ⓔ
16	Ⓐ Ⓑ Ⓒ Ⓓ Ⓔ	41	Ⓐ Ⓑ Ⓒ Ⓓ Ⓔ	66	Ⓐ Ⓑ Ⓒ Ⓓ Ⓔ	91	Ⓐ Ⓑ Ⓒ Ⓓ Ⓔ
17	Ⓐ Ⓑ Ⓒ Ⓓ Ⓔ	42	Ⓐ Ⓑ Ⓒ Ⓓ Ⓔ	67	Ⓐ Ⓑ Ⓒ Ⓓ Ⓔ	92	Ⓐ Ⓑ Ⓒ Ⓓ Ⓔ
18	Ⓐ Ⓑ Ⓒ Ⓓ Ⓔ	43	Ⓐ Ⓑ Ⓒ Ⓓ Ⓔ	68	Ⓐ Ⓑ Ⓒ Ⓓ Ⓔ	93	Ⓐ Ⓑ Ⓒ Ⓓ Ⓔ
19	Ⓐ Ⓑ Ⓒ Ⓓ Ⓔ	44	Ⓐ Ⓑ Ⓒ Ⓓ Ⓔ	69	Ⓐ Ⓑ Ⓒ Ⓓ Ⓔ	94	Ⓐ Ⓑ Ⓒ Ⓓ Ⓔ
20	Ⓐ Ⓑ Ⓒ Ⓓ Ⓔ	45	Ⓐ Ⓑ Ⓒ Ⓓ Ⓔ	70	Ⓐ Ⓑ Ⓒ Ⓓ Ⓔ	95	Ⓐ Ⓑ Ⓒ Ⓓ Ⓔ
21	Ⓐ Ⓑ Ⓒ Ⓓ Ⓔ	46	Ⓐ Ⓑ Ⓒ Ⓓ Ⓔ	71	Ⓐ Ⓑ Ⓒ Ⓓ Ⓔ	96	Ⓐ Ⓑ Ⓒ Ⓓ Ⓔ
22	Ⓐ Ⓑ Ⓒ Ⓓ Ⓔ	47	Ⓐ Ⓑ Ⓒ Ⓓ Ⓔ	72	Ⓐ Ⓑ Ⓒ Ⓓ Ⓔ	97	Ⓐ Ⓑ Ⓒ Ⓓ Ⓔ
23	Ⓐ Ⓑ Ⓒ Ⓓ Ⓔ	48	Ⓐ Ⓑ Ⓒ Ⓓ Ⓔ	73	Ⓐ Ⓑ Ⓒ Ⓓ Ⓔ	98	Ⓐ Ⓑ Ⓒ Ⓓ Ⓔ
24	Ⓐ Ⓑ Ⓒ Ⓓ Ⓔ	49	Ⓐ Ⓑ Ⓒ Ⓓ Ⓔ	74	Ⓐ Ⓑ Ⓒ Ⓓ Ⓔ	99	Ⓐ Ⓑ Ⓒ Ⓓ Ⓔ
25	Ⓐ Ⓑ Ⓒ Ⓓ Ⓔ	50	Ⓐ Ⓑ Ⓒ Ⓓ Ⓔ	75	Ⓐ Ⓑ Ⓒ Ⓓ Ⓔ	100	Ⓐ Ⓑ Ⓒ Ⓓ Ⓔ

Chemistry *Fill in circle CE only if II is correct explanation of I.

	I	II	CE*		I	II	CE*
101	Ⓣ Ⓕ	Ⓣ Ⓕ	○	109	Ⓣ Ⓕ	Ⓣ Ⓕ	○
102	Ⓣ Ⓕ	Ⓣ Ⓕ	○	110	Ⓣ Ⓕ	Ⓣ Ⓕ	○
103	Ⓣ Ⓕ	Ⓣ Ⓕ	○	111	Ⓣ Ⓕ	Ⓣ Ⓕ	○
104	Ⓣ Ⓕ	Ⓣ Ⓕ	○	112	Ⓣ Ⓕ	Ⓣ Ⓕ	○
105	Ⓣ Ⓕ	Ⓣ Ⓕ	○	113	Ⓣ Ⓕ	Ⓣ Ⓕ	○
106	Ⓣ Ⓕ	Ⓣ Ⓕ	○	114	Ⓣ Ⓕ	Ⓣ Ⓕ	○
107	Ⓣ Ⓕ	Ⓣ Ⓕ	○	115	Ⓣ Ⓕ	Ⓣ Ⓕ	○
108	Ⓣ Ⓕ	Ⓣ Ⓕ	○				

PLEASE MAKE SURE to fill in these fields completely and correctly. If they are not correct, we won't be able to score your test(s)!

7 TEST BOOK SERIAL NUMBER
(Copy from front of test book.)

8 BOOK CODE
(Copy and grid as on back of test book.)

9 BOOK ID
(Copy from back of test book.)

Quality Assurance Mark

FOR OFFICIAL USE ONLY

R/C	W/S1	FS/S2	CS/S3	WS

CERTIFICATION STATEMENT

Copy the statement below and sign your name as you would an official document.

I hereby agree to the conditions set forth online at sat.collegeboard.org and in any paper registration materials given to me and certify that I am the person whose name, address and signature appear on this answer sheet.

Signature ______________________ Date ______________

COMPLETE MARK ● EXAMPLES OF INCOMPLETE MARKS

You must use a No. 2 pencil and marks must be complete. Do not use a mechanical pencil. *It is very important that you fill in the entire circle darkly and completely. If you change your response, erase as completely as possible. Incomplete marks or erasures may affect your score.*

◯ Literature	◯ Mathematics Level 1	◯ German	◯ Chinese Listening	◯ Japanese Listening
◯ Biology E	◯ Mathematics Level 2	◯ Italian	◯ French Listening	◯ Korean Listening
◯ Biology M	◯ U.S. History	◯ Latin	◯ German Listening	◯ Spanish Listening
◯ Chemistry	◯ World History	◯ Modern Hebrew		
◯ Physics	◯ French	◯ Spanish		

Background Questions: ① ② ③ ④ ⑤ ⑥ ⑦ ⑧ ⑨

PLEASE MAKE SURE to fill in these fields completely and correctly. If they are not correct, we won't be able to score your test(s)!

1 Ⓐ Ⓑ Ⓒ Ⓓ Ⓔ	26 Ⓐ Ⓑ Ⓒ Ⓓ Ⓔ	51 Ⓐ Ⓑ Ⓒ Ⓓ Ⓔ	76 Ⓐ Ⓑ Ⓒ Ⓓ Ⓔ
2 Ⓐ Ⓑ Ⓒ Ⓓ Ⓔ	27 Ⓐ Ⓑ Ⓒ Ⓓ Ⓔ	52 Ⓐ Ⓑ Ⓒ Ⓓ Ⓔ	77 Ⓐ Ⓑ Ⓒ Ⓓ Ⓔ
3 Ⓐ Ⓑ Ⓒ Ⓓ Ⓔ	28 Ⓐ Ⓑ Ⓒ Ⓓ Ⓔ	53 Ⓐ Ⓑ Ⓒ Ⓓ Ⓔ	78 Ⓐ Ⓑ Ⓒ Ⓓ Ⓔ
4 Ⓐ Ⓑ Ⓒ Ⓓ Ⓔ	29 Ⓐ Ⓑ Ⓒ Ⓓ Ⓔ	54 Ⓐ Ⓑ Ⓒ Ⓓ Ⓔ	79 Ⓐ Ⓑ Ⓒ Ⓓ Ⓔ
5 Ⓐ Ⓑ Ⓒ Ⓓ Ⓔ	30 Ⓐ Ⓑ Ⓒ Ⓓ Ⓔ	55 Ⓐ Ⓑ Ⓒ Ⓓ Ⓔ	80 Ⓐ Ⓑ Ⓒ Ⓓ Ⓔ
6 Ⓐ Ⓑ Ⓒ Ⓓ Ⓔ	31 Ⓐ Ⓑ Ⓒ Ⓓ Ⓔ	56 Ⓐ Ⓑ Ⓒ Ⓓ Ⓔ	81 Ⓐ Ⓑ Ⓒ Ⓓ Ⓔ
7 Ⓐ Ⓑ Ⓒ Ⓓ Ⓔ	32 Ⓐ Ⓑ Ⓒ Ⓓ Ⓔ	57 Ⓐ Ⓑ Ⓒ Ⓓ Ⓔ	82 Ⓐ Ⓑ Ⓒ Ⓓ Ⓔ
8 Ⓐ Ⓑ Ⓒ Ⓓ Ⓔ	33 Ⓐ Ⓑ Ⓒ Ⓓ Ⓔ	58 Ⓐ Ⓑ Ⓒ Ⓓ Ⓔ	83 Ⓐ Ⓑ Ⓒ Ⓓ Ⓔ
9 Ⓐ Ⓑ Ⓒ Ⓓ Ⓔ	34 Ⓐ Ⓑ Ⓒ Ⓓ Ⓔ	59 Ⓐ Ⓑ Ⓒ Ⓓ Ⓔ	84 Ⓐ Ⓑ Ⓒ Ⓓ Ⓔ
10 Ⓐ Ⓑ Ⓒ Ⓓ Ⓔ	35 Ⓐ Ⓑ Ⓒ Ⓓ Ⓔ	60 Ⓐ Ⓑ Ⓒ Ⓓ Ⓔ	85 Ⓐ Ⓑ Ⓒ Ⓓ Ⓔ
11 Ⓐ Ⓑ Ⓒ Ⓓ Ⓔ	36 Ⓐ Ⓑ Ⓒ Ⓓ Ⓔ	61 Ⓐ Ⓑ Ⓒ Ⓓ Ⓔ	86 Ⓐ Ⓑ Ⓒ Ⓓ Ⓔ
12 Ⓐ Ⓑ Ⓒ Ⓓ Ⓔ	37 Ⓐ Ⓑ Ⓒ Ⓓ Ⓔ	62 Ⓐ Ⓑ Ⓒ Ⓓ Ⓔ	87 Ⓐ Ⓑ Ⓒ Ⓓ Ⓔ
13 Ⓐ Ⓑ Ⓒ Ⓓ Ⓔ	38 Ⓐ Ⓑ Ⓒ Ⓓ Ⓔ	63 Ⓐ Ⓑ Ⓒ Ⓓ Ⓔ	88 Ⓐ Ⓑ Ⓒ Ⓓ Ⓔ
14 Ⓐ Ⓑ Ⓒ Ⓓ Ⓔ	39 Ⓐ Ⓑ Ⓒ Ⓓ Ⓔ	64 Ⓐ Ⓑ Ⓒ Ⓓ Ⓔ	89 Ⓐ Ⓑ Ⓒ Ⓓ Ⓔ
15 Ⓐ Ⓑ Ⓒ Ⓓ Ⓔ	40 Ⓐ Ⓑ Ⓒ Ⓓ Ⓔ	65 Ⓐ Ⓑ Ⓒ Ⓓ Ⓔ	90 Ⓐ Ⓑ Ⓒ Ⓓ Ⓔ
16 Ⓐ Ⓑ Ⓒ Ⓓ Ⓔ	41 Ⓐ Ⓑ Ⓒ Ⓓ Ⓔ	66 Ⓐ Ⓑ Ⓒ Ⓓ Ⓔ	91 Ⓐ Ⓑ Ⓒ Ⓓ Ⓔ
17 Ⓐ Ⓑ Ⓒ Ⓓ Ⓔ	42 Ⓐ Ⓑ Ⓒ Ⓓ Ⓔ	67 Ⓐ Ⓑ Ⓒ Ⓓ Ⓔ	92 Ⓐ Ⓑ Ⓒ Ⓓ Ⓔ
18 Ⓐ Ⓑ Ⓒ Ⓓ Ⓔ	43 Ⓐ Ⓑ Ⓒ Ⓓ Ⓔ	68 Ⓐ Ⓑ Ⓒ Ⓓ Ⓔ	93 Ⓐ Ⓑ Ⓒ Ⓓ Ⓔ
19 Ⓐ Ⓑ Ⓒ Ⓓ Ⓔ	44 Ⓐ Ⓑ Ⓒ Ⓓ Ⓔ	69 Ⓐ Ⓑ Ⓒ Ⓓ Ⓔ	94 Ⓐ Ⓑ Ⓒ Ⓓ Ⓔ
20 Ⓐ Ⓑ Ⓒ Ⓓ Ⓔ	45 Ⓐ Ⓑ Ⓒ Ⓓ Ⓔ	70 Ⓐ Ⓑ Ⓒ Ⓓ Ⓔ	95 Ⓐ Ⓑ Ⓒ Ⓓ Ⓔ
21 Ⓐ Ⓑ Ⓒ Ⓓ Ⓔ	46 Ⓐ Ⓑ Ⓒ Ⓓ Ⓔ	71 Ⓐ Ⓑ Ⓒ Ⓓ Ⓔ	96 Ⓐ Ⓑ Ⓒ Ⓓ Ⓔ
22 Ⓐ Ⓑ Ⓒ Ⓓ Ⓔ	47 Ⓐ Ⓑ Ⓒ Ⓓ Ⓔ	72 Ⓐ Ⓑ Ⓒ Ⓓ Ⓔ	97 Ⓐ Ⓑ Ⓒ Ⓓ Ⓔ
23 Ⓐ Ⓑ Ⓒ Ⓓ Ⓔ	48 Ⓐ Ⓑ Ⓒ Ⓓ Ⓔ	73 Ⓐ Ⓑ Ⓒ Ⓓ Ⓔ	98 Ⓐ Ⓑ Ⓒ Ⓓ Ⓔ
24 Ⓐ Ⓑ Ⓒ Ⓓ Ⓔ	49 Ⓐ Ⓑ Ⓒ Ⓓ Ⓔ	74 Ⓐ Ⓑ Ⓒ Ⓓ Ⓔ	99 Ⓐ Ⓑ Ⓒ Ⓓ Ⓔ
25 Ⓐ Ⓑ Ⓒ Ⓓ Ⓔ	50 Ⓐ Ⓑ Ⓒ Ⓓ Ⓔ	75 Ⓐ Ⓑ Ⓒ Ⓓ Ⓔ	100 Ⓐ Ⓑ Ⓒ Ⓓ Ⓔ

Quality Assurance Mark

7 TEST BOOK SERIAL NUMBER
(Copy from front of test book.)

0–9	0–9	0–9	0–9	0–9	0–9

8 BOOK CODE
(Copy and grid as on back of test book.)

0–9	A–Z	0–9

9 BOOK ID
(Copy from back of test book.)

Chemistry *Fill in circle CE only if II is correct explanation of I.

	I	II	CE*		I	II	CE*
101	Ⓣ Ⓕ	Ⓣ Ⓕ	◯	109	Ⓣ Ⓕ	Ⓣ Ⓕ	◯
102	Ⓣ Ⓕ	Ⓣ Ⓕ	◯	110	Ⓣ Ⓕ	Ⓣ Ⓕ	◯
103	Ⓣ Ⓕ	Ⓣ Ⓕ	◯	111	Ⓣ Ⓕ	Ⓣ Ⓕ	◯
104	Ⓣ Ⓕ	Ⓣ Ⓕ	◯	112	Ⓣ Ⓕ	Ⓣ Ⓕ	◯
105	Ⓣ Ⓕ	Ⓣ Ⓕ	◯	113	Ⓣ Ⓕ	Ⓣ Ⓕ	◯
106	Ⓣ Ⓕ	Ⓣ Ⓕ	◯	114	Ⓣ Ⓕ	Ⓣ Ⓕ	◯
107	Ⓣ Ⓕ	Ⓣ Ⓕ	◯	115	Ⓣ Ⓕ	Ⓣ Ⓕ	◯
108	Ⓣ Ⓕ	Ⓣ Ⓕ	◯				

FOR OFFICIAL USE ONLY

R/C	W/S1	FS/S2	CS/S3	WS

COMPLETE MARK ● EXAMPLES OF INCOMPLETE MARKS

You must use a No. 2 pencil and marks must be complete. Do not use a mechanical pencil. It is very important that you fill in the entire circle darkly and completely. If you change your response, erase as completely as possible. Incomplete marks or erasures may affect your score.

- ○ Literature
- ○ Biology E
- ○ Biology M
- ○ Chemistry
- ○ Physics
- ○ Mathematics Level 1
- ○ Mathematics Level 2
- ○ U.S. History
- ○ World History
- ○ French
- ○ German
- ○ Italian
- ○ Latin
- ○ Modern Hebrew
- ○ Spanish
- ○ Chinese Listening
- ○ French Listening
- ○ German Listening
- ○ Japanese Listening
- ○ Korean Listening
- ○ Spanish Listening

Background Questions: ① ② ③ ④ ⑤ ⑥ ⑦ ⑧ ⑨

1 A B C D E	26 A B C D E	51 A B C D E	76 A B C D E
2 A B C D E	27 A B C D E	52 A B C D E	77 A B C D E
3 A B C D E	28 A B C D E	53 A B C D E	78 A B C D E
4 A B C D E	29 A B C D E	54 A B C D E	79 A B C D E
5 A B C D E	30 A B C D E	55 A B C D E	80 A B C D E
6 A B C D E	31 A B C D E	56 A B C D E	81 A B C D E
7 A B C D E	32 A B C D E	57 A B C D E	82 A B C D E
8 A B C D E	33 A B C D E	58 A B C D E	83 A B C D E
9 A B C D E	34 A B C D E	59 A B C D E	84 A B C D E
10 A B C D E	35 A B C D E	60 A B C D E	85 A B C D E
11 A B C D E	36 A B C D E	61 A B C D E	86 A B C D E
12 A B C D E	37 A B C D E	62 A B C D E	87 A B C D E
13 A B C D E	38 A B C D E	63 A B C D E	88 A B C D E
14 A B C D E	39 A B C D E	64 A B C D E	89 A B C D E
15 A B C D E	40 A B C D E	65 A B C D E	90 A B C D E
16 A B C D E	41 A B C D E	66 A B C D E	91 A B C D E
17 A B C D E	42 A B C D E	67 A B C D E	92 A B C D E
18 A B C D E	43 A B C D E	68 A B C D E	93 A B C D E
19 A B C D E	44 A B C D E	69 A B C D E	94 A B C D E
20 A B C D E	45 A B C D E	70 A B C D E	95 A B C D E
21 A B C D E	46 A B C D E	71 A B C D E	96 A B C D E
22 A B C D E	47 A B C D E	72 A B C D E	97 A B C D E
23 A B C D E	48 A B C D E	73 A B C D E	98 A B C D E
24 A B C D E	49 A B C D E	74 A B C D E	99 A B C D E
25 A B C D E	50 A B C D E	75 A B C D E	100 A B C D E

Chemistry *Fill in circle CE only if II is correct explanation of I.

	I	II	CE*		I	II	CE*
101	T F	T F	○	109	T F	T F	○
102	T F	T F	○	110	T F	T F	○
103	T F	T F	○	111	T F	T F	○
104	T F	T F	○	112	T F	T F	○
105	T F	T F	○	113	T F	T F	○
106	T F	T F	○	114	T F	T F	○
107	T F	T F	○	115	T F	T F	○
108	T F	T F	○				

PLEASE MAKE SURE to fill in these fields completely and correctly. If they are not correct, we won't be able to score your test(s)!

7 TEST BOOK SERIAL NUMBER (Copy from front of test book.)

0 1 2 3 4 5 6 7 8 9 (six columns)

8 BOOK CODE (Copy and grid as on back of test book.)

0–9 | A–Z | 0–9

9 BOOK ID (Copy from back of test book.)

Quality Assurance Mark

FOR OFFICIAL USE ONLY

R/C	W/S1	FS/S2	CS/S3	WS

PLEASE DO NOT WRITE IN THIS AREA

SERIAL #

CollegeBoard

SAT Subject Tests™

COMPLETE MARK ● EXAMPLES OF INCOMPLETE MARKS

You must use a No. 2 pencil and marks must be complete. Do not use a mechanical pencil. It is very important that you fill in the entire circle darkly and completely. If you change your response, erase as completely as possible. Incomplete marks or erasures may affect your score.

1 **Your Name:** (Print) ____________________
Last First M.I.

I agree to the conditions on the front and back of the SAT Subject Tests™ book. I also agree with the SAT Test Security and Fairness policies and understand that any violation of these policies will result in score cancellation and may result in reporting of certain violations to law enforcement.

Signature: ____________________ **Today's Date:** ___/___/___
MM DD YY

Home Address: (Print) ____________________
Number and Street City State/Country Zip Code

Phone: ( ) ________ **Test Center:** (Print) ____________________
City State/Country

2 YOUR NAME

Last Name (First 6 Letters) | First Name (First 4 Letters) | Mid. Init.

– ' A B C D E F G H I J K L M N O P Q R S T U V W X Y Z

3 DATE OF BIRTH

MONTH | DAY | YEAR

Jan, Feb, Mar, Apr, May, Jun, Jul, Aug, Sep, Oct, Nov, Dec

0 1 2 3 4 5 6 7 8 9

4 REGISTRATION NUMBER

(Copy from Admission Ticket.)

0 1 2 3 4 5 6 7 8 9

Important: Fill in items 8 and 9 exactly as shown on the back of test book.

7 TEST BOOK SERIAL NUMBER

(Copy from front of test book.)

0 1 2 3 4 5 6 7 8 9

8 BOOK CODE

(Copy and grid as on back of test book.)

0 1 2 3 4 5 6 7 8 9 | A B C D E F G H I J K L M N O P Q R S T U V W X Y Z | 0 1 2 3 4 5 6 7 8 9

9 BOOK ID

(Copy from back of test book.)

5 ZIP CODE

0 1 2 3 4 5 6 7 8 9

6 TEST CENTER

(Supplied by Test Center Supervisor.)

0 1 2 3 4 5 6 7 8 9

PLEASE MAKE SURE to fill in these fields completely and correctly. If they are not correct, we won't be able to score your test(s)!

FOR OFFICIAL USE ONLY

0 1 2 3 4 5 6
0 1 2 3 4 5 6
0 1 2 3 4 5 6

103648-77191 • NS1114C1085 • Printed in U.S.A

194415-001 1 2 3 4 5 A B C D E Printed in the USA ISD11312

783175

PLEASE DO NOT WRITE IN THIS AREA

SERIAL #

COMPLETE MARK ● **EXAMPLES OF INCOMPLETE MARKS**

You must use a No. 2 pencil and marks must be complete. Do not use a mechanical pencil. *It is very important that you fill in the entire circle darkly and completely. If you change your response, erase as completely as possible. Incomplete marks or erasures may affect your score.*

○ Literature	○ Mathematics Level 1	○ German	○ Chinese Listening	○ Japanese Listening
○ Biology E	○ Mathematics Level 2	○ Italian	○ French Listening	○ Korean Listening
○ Biology M	○ U.S. History	○ Latin	○ German Listening	○ Spanish Listening
○ Chemistry	○ World History	○ Modern Hebrew		
○ Physics	○ French	○ Spanish		

Background Questions: (1) (2) (3) (4) (5) (6) (7) (8) (9)

1 Ⓐ Ⓑ Ⓒ Ⓓ Ⓔ	26 Ⓐ Ⓑ Ⓒ Ⓓ Ⓔ	51 Ⓐ Ⓑ Ⓒ Ⓓ Ⓔ	76 Ⓐ Ⓑ Ⓒ Ⓓ Ⓔ
2 Ⓐ Ⓑ Ⓒ Ⓓ Ⓔ	27 Ⓐ Ⓑ Ⓒ Ⓓ Ⓔ	52 Ⓐ Ⓑ Ⓒ Ⓓ Ⓔ	77 Ⓐ Ⓑ Ⓒ Ⓓ Ⓔ
3 Ⓐ Ⓑ Ⓒ Ⓓ Ⓔ	28 Ⓐ Ⓑ Ⓒ Ⓓ Ⓔ	53 Ⓐ Ⓑ Ⓒ Ⓓ Ⓔ	78 Ⓐ Ⓑ Ⓒ Ⓓ Ⓔ
4 Ⓐ Ⓑ Ⓒ Ⓓ Ⓔ	29 Ⓐ Ⓑ Ⓒ Ⓓ Ⓔ	54 Ⓐ Ⓑ Ⓒ Ⓓ Ⓔ	79 Ⓐ Ⓑ Ⓒ Ⓓ Ⓔ
5 Ⓐ Ⓑ Ⓒ Ⓓ Ⓔ	30 Ⓐ Ⓑ Ⓒ Ⓓ Ⓔ	55 Ⓐ Ⓑ Ⓒ Ⓓ Ⓔ	80 Ⓐ Ⓑ Ⓒ Ⓓ Ⓔ
6 Ⓐ Ⓑ Ⓒ Ⓓ Ⓔ	31 Ⓐ Ⓑ Ⓒ Ⓓ Ⓔ	56 Ⓐ Ⓑ Ⓒ Ⓓ Ⓔ	81 Ⓐ Ⓑ Ⓒ Ⓓ Ⓔ
7 Ⓐ Ⓑ Ⓒ Ⓓ Ⓔ	32 Ⓐ Ⓑ Ⓒ Ⓓ Ⓔ	57 Ⓐ Ⓑ Ⓒ Ⓓ Ⓔ	82 Ⓐ Ⓑ Ⓒ Ⓓ Ⓔ
8 Ⓐ Ⓑ Ⓒ Ⓓ Ⓔ	33 Ⓐ Ⓑ Ⓒ Ⓓ Ⓔ	58 Ⓐ Ⓑ Ⓒ Ⓓ Ⓔ	83 Ⓐ Ⓑ Ⓒ Ⓓ Ⓔ
9 Ⓐ Ⓑ Ⓒ Ⓓ Ⓔ	34 Ⓐ Ⓑ Ⓒ Ⓓ Ⓔ	59 Ⓐ Ⓑ Ⓒ Ⓓ Ⓔ	84 Ⓐ Ⓑ Ⓒ Ⓓ Ⓔ
10 Ⓐ Ⓑ Ⓒ Ⓓ Ⓔ	35 Ⓐ Ⓑ Ⓒ Ⓓ Ⓔ	60 Ⓐ Ⓑ Ⓒ Ⓓ Ⓔ	85 Ⓐ Ⓑ Ⓒ Ⓓ Ⓔ
11 Ⓐ Ⓑ Ⓒ Ⓓ Ⓔ	36 Ⓐ Ⓑ Ⓒ Ⓓ Ⓔ	61 Ⓐ Ⓑ Ⓒ Ⓓ Ⓔ	86 Ⓐ Ⓑ Ⓒ Ⓓ Ⓔ
12 Ⓐ Ⓑ Ⓒ Ⓓ Ⓔ	37 Ⓐ Ⓑ Ⓒ Ⓓ Ⓔ	62 Ⓐ Ⓑ Ⓒ Ⓓ Ⓔ	87 Ⓐ Ⓑ Ⓒ Ⓓ Ⓔ
13 Ⓐ Ⓑ Ⓒ Ⓓ Ⓔ	38 Ⓐ Ⓑ Ⓒ Ⓓ Ⓔ	63 Ⓐ Ⓑ Ⓒ Ⓓ Ⓔ	88 Ⓐ Ⓑ Ⓒ Ⓓ Ⓔ
14 Ⓐ Ⓑ Ⓒ Ⓓ Ⓔ	39 Ⓐ Ⓑ Ⓒ Ⓓ Ⓔ	64 Ⓐ Ⓑ Ⓒ Ⓓ Ⓔ	89 Ⓐ Ⓑ Ⓒ Ⓓ Ⓔ
15 Ⓐ Ⓑ Ⓒ Ⓓ Ⓔ	40 Ⓐ Ⓑ Ⓒ Ⓓ Ⓔ	65 Ⓐ Ⓑ Ⓒ Ⓓ Ⓔ	90 Ⓐ Ⓑ Ⓒ Ⓓ Ⓔ
16 Ⓐ Ⓑ Ⓒ Ⓓ Ⓔ	41 Ⓐ Ⓑ Ⓒ Ⓓ Ⓔ	66 Ⓐ Ⓑ Ⓒ Ⓓ Ⓔ	91 Ⓐ Ⓑ Ⓒ Ⓓ Ⓔ
17 Ⓐ Ⓑ Ⓒ Ⓓ Ⓔ	42 Ⓐ Ⓑ Ⓒ Ⓓ Ⓔ	67 Ⓐ Ⓑ Ⓒ Ⓓ Ⓔ	92 Ⓐ Ⓑ Ⓒ Ⓓ Ⓔ
18 Ⓐ Ⓑ Ⓒ Ⓓ Ⓔ	43 Ⓐ Ⓑ Ⓒ Ⓓ Ⓔ	68 Ⓐ Ⓑ Ⓒ Ⓓ Ⓔ	93 Ⓐ Ⓑ Ⓒ Ⓓ Ⓔ
19 Ⓐ Ⓑ Ⓒ Ⓓ Ⓔ	44 Ⓐ Ⓑ Ⓒ Ⓓ Ⓔ	69 Ⓐ Ⓑ Ⓒ Ⓓ Ⓔ	94 Ⓐ Ⓑ Ⓒ Ⓓ Ⓔ
20 Ⓐ Ⓑ Ⓒ Ⓓ Ⓔ	45 Ⓐ Ⓑ Ⓒ Ⓓ Ⓔ	70 Ⓐ Ⓑ Ⓒ Ⓓ Ⓔ	95 Ⓐ Ⓑ Ⓒ Ⓓ Ⓔ
21 Ⓐ Ⓑ Ⓒ Ⓓ Ⓔ	46 Ⓐ Ⓑ Ⓒ Ⓓ Ⓔ	71 Ⓐ Ⓑ Ⓒ Ⓓ Ⓔ	96 Ⓐ Ⓑ Ⓒ Ⓓ Ⓔ
22 Ⓐ Ⓑ Ⓒ Ⓓ Ⓔ	47 Ⓐ Ⓑ Ⓒ Ⓓ Ⓔ	72 Ⓐ Ⓑ Ⓒ Ⓓ Ⓔ	97 Ⓐ Ⓑ Ⓒ Ⓓ Ⓔ
23 Ⓐ Ⓑ Ⓒ Ⓓ Ⓔ	48 Ⓐ Ⓑ Ⓒ Ⓓ Ⓔ	73 Ⓐ Ⓑ Ⓒ Ⓓ Ⓔ	98 Ⓐ Ⓑ Ⓒ Ⓓ Ⓔ
24 Ⓐ Ⓑ Ⓒ Ⓓ Ⓔ	49 Ⓐ Ⓑ Ⓒ Ⓓ Ⓔ	74 Ⓐ Ⓑ Ⓒ Ⓓ Ⓔ	99 Ⓐ Ⓑ Ⓒ Ⓓ Ⓔ
25 Ⓐ Ⓑ Ⓒ Ⓓ Ⓔ	50 Ⓐ Ⓑ Ⓒ Ⓓ Ⓔ	75 Ⓐ Ⓑ Ⓒ Ⓓ Ⓔ	100 Ⓐ Ⓑ Ⓒ Ⓓ Ⓔ

Chemistry *Fill in circle CE only if II is correct explanation of I.

	I	II	CE*		I	II	CE*
101	Ⓣ Ⓕ	Ⓣ Ⓕ	○	109	Ⓣ Ⓕ	Ⓣ Ⓕ	○
102	Ⓣ Ⓕ	Ⓣ Ⓕ	○	110	Ⓣ Ⓕ	Ⓣ Ⓕ	○
103	Ⓣ Ⓕ	Ⓣ Ⓕ	○	111	Ⓣ Ⓕ	Ⓣ Ⓕ	○
104	Ⓣ Ⓕ	Ⓣ Ⓕ	○	112	Ⓣ Ⓕ	Ⓣ Ⓕ	○
105	Ⓣ Ⓕ	Ⓣ Ⓕ	○	113	Ⓣ Ⓕ	Ⓣ Ⓕ	○
106	Ⓣ Ⓕ	Ⓣ Ⓕ	○	114	Ⓣ Ⓕ	Ⓣ Ⓕ	○
107	Ⓣ Ⓕ	Ⓣ Ⓕ	○	115	Ⓣ Ⓕ	Ⓣ Ⓕ	○
108	Ⓣ Ⓕ	Ⓣ Ⓕ	○				

FOR OFFICIAL USE ONLY

R/C	W/S1	FS/S2	CS/S3	WS

PLEASE MAKE SURE to fill in these fields completely and correctly. If they are not correct, we won't be able to score your test(s)!

7 TEST BOOK SERIAL NUMBER
(Copy from front of test book.)

0	0	0	0	0	0
1	1	1	1	1	1
2	2	2	2	2	2
3	3	3	3	3	3
4	4	4	4	4	4
5	5	5	5	5	5
6	6	6	6	6	6
7	7	7	7	7	7
8	8	8	8	8	8
9	9	9	9	9	9

8 BOOK CODE
(Copy and grid as on back of test book.)

0	A	0
1	B	1
2	C	2
3	D	3
4	E	4
5	F	5
6	G	6
7	H	7
8	I	8
9	J	9
	K	
	L	
	M	
	N	
	O	
	P	
	Q	
	R	
	S	
	T	
	U	
	V	
	W	
	X	
	Y	
	Z	

9 BOOK ID
(Copy from back of test book.)

Quality ● Assurance Mark

CERTIFICATION STATEMENT

Copy the statement below and sign your name as you would an official document.

I hereby agree to the conditions set forth online at sat.collegeboard.org and in any paper registration materials given to me and certify that I am the person whose name, address and signature appear on this answer sheet.

____

____

____

____

Signature ____________________ Date ____________________

COMPLETE MARK ● EXAMPLES OF INCOMPLETE MARKS

You must use a No. 2 pencil and marks must be complete. Do not use a mechanical pencil. *It is very important that you fill in the entire circle darkly and completely. If you change your response, erase as completely as possible. Incomplete marks or erasures may affect your score.*

○ Literature	○ Mathematics Level 1	○ German	○ Chinese Listening	○ Japanese Listening
○ Biology E	○ Mathematics Level 2	○ Italian	○ French Listening	○ Korean Listening
○ Biology M	○ U.S. History	○ Latin	○ German Listening	○ Spanish Listening
○ Chemistry	○ World History	○ Modern Hebrew		
○ Physics	○ French	○ Spanish		

Background Questions: ① ② ③ ④ ⑤ ⑥ ⑦ ⑧ ⑨

PLEASE MAKE SURE to fill in these fields completely and correctly. If they are not correct, we won't be able to score your test(s)!

1 Ⓐ Ⓑ Ⓒ Ⓓ Ⓔ	26 Ⓐ Ⓑ Ⓒ Ⓓ Ⓔ	51 Ⓐ Ⓑ Ⓒ Ⓓ Ⓔ	76 Ⓐ Ⓑ Ⓒ Ⓓ Ⓔ
2 Ⓐ Ⓑ Ⓒ Ⓓ Ⓔ	27 Ⓐ Ⓑ Ⓒ Ⓓ Ⓔ	52 Ⓐ Ⓑ Ⓒ Ⓓ Ⓔ	77 Ⓐ Ⓑ Ⓒ Ⓓ Ⓔ
3 Ⓐ Ⓑ Ⓒ Ⓓ Ⓔ	28 Ⓐ Ⓑ Ⓒ Ⓓ Ⓔ	53 Ⓐ Ⓑ Ⓒ Ⓓ Ⓔ	78 Ⓐ Ⓑ Ⓒ Ⓓ Ⓔ
4 Ⓐ Ⓑ Ⓒ Ⓓ Ⓔ	29 Ⓐ Ⓑ Ⓒ Ⓓ Ⓔ	54 Ⓐ Ⓑ Ⓒ Ⓓ Ⓔ	79 Ⓐ Ⓑ Ⓒ Ⓓ Ⓔ
5 Ⓐ Ⓑ Ⓒ Ⓓ Ⓔ	30 Ⓐ Ⓑ Ⓒ Ⓓ Ⓔ	55 Ⓐ Ⓑ Ⓒ Ⓓ Ⓔ	80 Ⓐ Ⓑ Ⓒ Ⓓ Ⓔ
6 Ⓐ Ⓑ Ⓒ Ⓓ Ⓔ	31 Ⓐ Ⓑ Ⓒ Ⓓ Ⓔ	56 Ⓐ Ⓑ Ⓒ Ⓓ Ⓔ	81 Ⓐ Ⓑ Ⓒ Ⓓ Ⓔ
7 Ⓐ Ⓑ Ⓒ Ⓓ Ⓔ	32 Ⓐ Ⓑ Ⓒ Ⓓ Ⓔ	57 Ⓐ Ⓑ Ⓒ Ⓓ Ⓔ	82 Ⓐ Ⓑ Ⓒ Ⓓ Ⓔ
8 Ⓐ Ⓑ Ⓒ Ⓓ Ⓔ	33 Ⓐ Ⓑ Ⓒ Ⓓ Ⓔ	58 Ⓐ Ⓑ Ⓒ Ⓓ Ⓔ	83 Ⓐ Ⓑ Ⓒ Ⓓ Ⓔ
9 Ⓐ Ⓑ Ⓒ Ⓓ Ⓔ	34 Ⓐ Ⓑ Ⓒ Ⓓ Ⓔ	59 Ⓐ Ⓑ Ⓒ Ⓓ Ⓔ	84 Ⓐ Ⓑ Ⓒ Ⓓ Ⓔ
10 Ⓐ Ⓑ Ⓒ Ⓓ Ⓔ	35 Ⓐ Ⓑ Ⓒ Ⓓ Ⓔ	60 Ⓐ Ⓑ Ⓒ Ⓓ Ⓔ	85 Ⓐ Ⓑ Ⓒ Ⓓ Ⓔ
11 Ⓐ Ⓑ Ⓒ Ⓓ Ⓔ	36 Ⓐ Ⓑ Ⓒ Ⓓ Ⓔ	61 Ⓐ Ⓑ Ⓒ Ⓓ Ⓔ	86 Ⓐ Ⓑ Ⓒ Ⓓ Ⓔ
12 Ⓐ Ⓑ Ⓒ Ⓓ Ⓔ	37 Ⓐ Ⓑ Ⓒ Ⓓ Ⓔ	62 Ⓐ Ⓑ Ⓒ Ⓓ Ⓔ	87 Ⓐ Ⓑ Ⓒ Ⓓ Ⓔ
13 Ⓐ Ⓑ Ⓒ Ⓓ Ⓔ	38 Ⓐ Ⓑ Ⓒ Ⓓ Ⓔ	63 Ⓐ Ⓑ Ⓒ Ⓓ Ⓔ	88 Ⓐ Ⓑ Ⓒ Ⓓ Ⓔ
14 Ⓐ Ⓑ Ⓒ Ⓓ Ⓔ	39 Ⓐ Ⓑ Ⓒ Ⓓ Ⓔ	64 Ⓐ Ⓑ Ⓒ Ⓓ Ⓔ	89 Ⓐ Ⓑ Ⓒ Ⓓ Ⓔ
15 Ⓐ Ⓑ Ⓒ Ⓓ Ⓔ	40 Ⓐ Ⓑ Ⓒ Ⓓ Ⓔ	65 Ⓐ Ⓑ Ⓒ Ⓓ Ⓔ	90 Ⓐ Ⓑ Ⓒ Ⓓ Ⓔ
16 Ⓐ Ⓑ Ⓒ Ⓓ Ⓔ	41 Ⓐ Ⓑ Ⓒ Ⓓ Ⓔ	66 Ⓐ Ⓑ Ⓒ Ⓓ Ⓔ	91 Ⓐ Ⓑ Ⓒ Ⓓ Ⓔ
17 Ⓐ Ⓑ Ⓒ Ⓓ Ⓔ	42 Ⓐ Ⓑ Ⓒ Ⓓ Ⓔ	67 Ⓐ Ⓑ Ⓒ Ⓓ Ⓔ	92 Ⓐ Ⓑ Ⓒ Ⓓ Ⓔ
18 Ⓐ Ⓑ Ⓒ Ⓓ Ⓔ	43 Ⓐ Ⓑ Ⓒ Ⓓ Ⓔ	68 Ⓐ Ⓑ Ⓒ Ⓓ Ⓔ	93 Ⓐ Ⓑ Ⓒ Ⓓ Ⓔ
19 Ⓐ Ⓑ Ⓒ Ⓓ Ⓔ	44 Ⓐ Ⓑ Ⓒ Ⓓ Ⓔ	69 Ⓐ Ⓑ Ⓒ Ⓓ Ⓔ	94 Ⓐ Ⓑ Ⓒ Ⓓ Ⓔ
20 Ⓐ Ⓑ Ⓒ Ⓓ Ⓔ	45 Ⓐ Ⓑ Ⓒ Ⓓ Ⓔ	70 Ⓐ Ⓑ Ⓒ Ⓓ Ⓔ	95 Ⓐ Ⓑ Ⓒ Ⓓ Ⓔ
21 Ⓐ Ⓑ Ⓒ Ⓓ Ⓔ	46 Ⓐ Ⓑ Ⓒ Ⓓ Ⓔ	71 Ⓐ Ⓑ Ⓒ Ⓓ Ⓔ	96 Ⓐ Ⓑ Ⓒ Ⓓ Ⓔ
22 Ⓐ Ⓑ Ⓒ Ⓓ Ⓔ	47 Ⓐ Ⓑ Ⓒ Ⓓ Ⓔ	72 Ⓐ Ⓑ Ⓒ Ⓓ Ⓔ	97 Ⓐ Ⓑ Ⓒ Ⓓ Ⓔ
23 Ⓐ Ⓑ Ⓒ Ⓓ Ⓔ	48 Ⓐ Ⓑ Ⓒ Ⓓ Ⓔ	73 Ⓐ Ⓑ Ⓒ Ⓓ Ⓔ	98 Ⓐ Ⓑ Ⓒ Ⓓ Ⓔ
24 Ⓐ Ⓑ Ⓒ Ⓓ Ⓔ	49 Ⓐ Ⓑ Ⓒ Ⓓ Ⓔ	74 Ⓐ Ⓑ Ⓒ Ⓓ Ⓔ	99 Ⓐ Ⓑ Ⓒ Ⓓ Ⓔ
25 Ⓐ Ⓑ Ⓒ Ⓓ Ⓔ	50 Ⓐ Ⓑ Ⓒ Ⓓ Ⓔ	75 Ⓐ Ⓑ Ⓒ Ⓓ Ⓔ	100 Ⓐ Ⓑ Ⓒ Ⓓ Ⓔ

Quality Assurance Mark

7 TEST BOOK SERIAL NUMBER
(Copy from front of test book.)

0	0	0	0	0	0
1	1	1	1	1	1
2	2	2	2	2	2
3	3	3	3	3	3
4	4	4	4	4	4
5	5	5	5	5	5
6	6	6	6	6	6
7	7	7	7	7	7
8	8	8	8	8	8
9	9	9	9	9	9

8 BOOK CODE
(Copy and grid as on back of test book.)

0	A	0
1	B	1
2	C	2
3	D	3
4	E	4
5	F	5
6	G	6
7	H	7
8	I	8
9	J	9
	K	
	L	
	M	
	N	
	O	
	P	
	Q	
	R	
	S	
	T	
	U	
	V	
	W	
	X	
	Y	
	Z	

9 BOOK ID
(Copy from back of test book.)

Chemistry *Fill in circle CE only if II is correct explanation of I.

	I	II	CE*		I	II	CE*
101	Ⓣ Ⓕ	Ⓣ Ⓕ	○	109	Ⓣ Ⓕ	Ⓣ Ⓕ	○
102	Ⓣ Ⓕ	Ⓣ Ⓕ	○	110	Ⓣ Ⓕ	Ⓣ Ⓕ	○
103	Ⓣ Ⓕ	Ⓣ Ⓕ	○	111	Ⓣ Ⓕ	Ⓣ Ⓕ	○
104	Ⓣ Ⓕ	Ⓣ Ⓕ	○	112	Ⓣ Ⓕ	Ⓣ Ⓕ	○
105	Ⓣ Ⓕ	Ⓣ Ⓕ	○	113	Ⓣ Ⓕ	Ⓣ Ⓕ	○
106	Ⓣ Ⓕ	Ⓣ Ⓕ	○	114	Ⓣ Ⓕ	Ⓣ Ⓕ	○
107	Ⓣ Ⓕ	Ⓣ Ⓕ	○	115	Ⓣ Ⓕ	Ⓣ Ⓕ	○
108	Ⓣ Ⓕ	Ⓣ Ⓕ	○				

FOR OFFICIAL USE ONLY

R/C	W/S1	FS/S2	CS/S3	WS

COMPLETE MARK ● EXAMPLES OF INCOMPLETE MARKS

You must use a No. 2 pencil and marks must be complete. Do not use a mechanical pencil. *It is very important that you fill in the entire circle darkly and completely. If you change your response, erase as completely as possible. Incomplete marks or erasures may affect your score.*

○ Literature	○ Mathematics Level 1	○ German	○ Chinese Listening	○ Japanese Listening
○ Biology E	○ Mathematics Level 2	○ Italian	○ French Listening	○ Korean Listening
○ Biology M	○ U.S. History	○ Latin	○ German Listening	○ Spanish Listening
○ Chemistry	○ World History	○ Modern Hebrew		
○ Physics	○ French	○ Spanish		

Background Questions: ① ② ③ ④ ⑤ ⑥ ⑦ ⑧ ⑨

1 A B C D E	26 A B C D E	51 A B C D E	76 A B C D E
2 A B C D E	27 A B C D E	52 A B C D E	77 A B C D E
3 A B C D E	28 A B C D E	53 A B C D E	78 A B C D E
4 A B C D E	29 A B C D E	54 A B C D E	79 A B C D E
5 A B C D E	30 A B C D E	55 A B C D E	80 A B C D E
6 A B C D E	31 A B C D E	56 A B C D E	81 A B C D E
7 A B C D E	32 A B C D E	57 A B C D E	82 A B C D E
8 A B C D E	33 A B C D E	58 A B C D E	83 A B C D E
9 A B C D E	34 A B C D E	59 A B C D E	84 A B C D E
10 A B C D E	35 A B C D E	60 A B C D E	85 A B C D E
11 A B C D E	36 A B C D E	61 A B C D E	86 A B C D E
12 A B C D E	37 A B C D E	62 A B C D E	87 A B C D E
13 A B C D E	38 A B C D E	63 A B C D E	88 A B C D E
14 A B C D E	39 A B C D E	64 A B C D E	89 A B C D E
15 A B C D E	40 A B C D E	65 A B C D E	90 A B C D E
16 A B C D E	41 A B C D E	66 A B C D E	91 A B C D E
17 A B C D E	42 A B C D E	67 A B C D E	92 A B C D E
18 A B C D E	43 A B C D E	68 A B C D E	93 A B C D E
19 A B C D E	44 A B C D E	69 A B C D E	94 A B C D E
20 A B C D E	45 A B C D E	70 A B C D E	95 A B C D E
21 A B C D E	46 A B C D E	71 A B C D E	96 A B C D E
22 A B C D E	47 A B C D E	72 A B C D E	97 A B C D E
23 A B C D E	48 A B C D E	73 A B C D E	98 A B C D E
24 A B C D E	49 A B C D E	74 A B C D E	99 A B C D E
25 A B C D E	50 A B C D E	75 A B C D E	100 A B C D E

Chemistry *Fill in circle CE only if II is correct explanation of I.

	I	II	CE*		I	II	CE*
101	T F	T F	○	109	T F	T F	○
102	T F	T F	○	110	T F	T F	○
103	T F	T F	○	111	T F	T F	○
104	T F	T F	○	112	T F	T F	○
105	T F	T F	○	113	T F	T F	○
106	T F	T F	○	114	T F	T F	○
107	T F	T F	○	115	T F	T F	○
108	T F	T F	○				

PLEASE MAKE SURE to fill in these fields completely and correctly. If they are not correct, we won't be able to score your test(s)!

7 TEST BOOK SERIAL NUMBER
(Copy from front of test book.)

0	0	0	0	0	0
1	1	1	1	1	1
2	2	2	2	2	2
3	3	3	3	3	3
4	4	4	4	4	4
5	5	5	5	5	5
6	6	6	6	6	6
7	7	7	7	7	7
8	8	8	8	8	8
9	9	9	9	9	9

8 BOOK CODE
(Copy and grid as on back of test book.)

0	A	0
1	B	1
2	C	2
3	D	3
4	E	4
5	F	5
6	G	6
7	H	7
8	I	8
9	J	9
	K	
	L	
	M	
	N	
	O	
	P	
	Q	
	R	
	S	
	T	
	U	
	V	
	W	
	X	
	Y	
	Z	

9 BOOK ID
(Copy from back of test book.)

Quality ● Assurance Mark

FOR OFFICIAL USE ONLY

R/C	W/S1	FS/S2	CS/S3	WS

PLEASE DO NOT WRITE IN THIS AREA

SERIAL #

CollegeBoard

SAT Subject Tests™

COMPLETE MARK ● EXAMPLES OF INCOMPLETE MARKS

You must use a No. 2 pencil and marks must be complete. Do not use a mechanical pencil. It is very important that you fill in the entire circle darkly and completely. If you change your response, erase as completely as possible. Incomplete marks or erasures may affect your score.

1 Your Name: (Print) Last First M.I.

I agree to the conditions on the front and back of the SAT Subject Tests™ book. I also agree with the SAT Test Security and Fairness policies and understand that any violation of these policies will result in score cancellation and may result in reporting of certain violations to law enforcement.

Signature: Today's Date: / / MM DD YY

Home Address: (Print) Number and Street City State/Country Zip Code

Phone: ( ) Test Center: (Print) City State/Country

2 YOUR NAME — Last Name (First 6 Letters) | First Name (First 4 Letters) | Mid. Init.

3 DATE OF BIRTH — MONTH | DAY | YEAR — Jan Feb Mar Apr May Jun Jul Aug Sep Oct Nov Dec

4 REGISTRATION NUMBER (Copy from Admission Ticket.)

Important: Fill in items 8 and 9 exactly as shown on the back of test book.

7 TEST BOOK SERIAL NUMBER (Copy from front of test book.)

8 BOOK CODE (Copy and grid as on back of test book.)

9 BOOK ID (Copy from back of test book.)

5 ZIP CODE

6 TEST CENTER (Supplied by Test Center Supervisor.)

PLEASE MAKE SURE to fill in these fields completely and correctly. If they are not correct, we won't be able to score your test(s)!

FOR OFFICIAL USE ONLY

103648-77191 • NS1114C1085 • Printed in U.S.A.

194415-001 1 2 3 4 5 A B C D E Printed in the USA ISD11312

783175

PLEASE DO NOT WRITE IN THIS AREA

SERIAL #

OMPLETE MARK ● EXAMPLES OF INCOMPLETE MARKS

You must use a No. 2 pencil and marks must be complete. Do not use a mechanical pencil. *It is very important that you fill in the entire circle darkly and completely. If you change your response, erase as completely as possible. Incomplete marks or erasures may affect your score.*

◯ Literature	◯ Mathematics Level 1	◯ German	◯ Chinese Listening	◯ Japanese Listening
◯ Biology E	◯ Mathematics Level 2	◯ Italian	◯ French Listening	◯ Korean Listening
◯ Biology M	◯ U.S. History	◯ Latin	◯ German Listening	◯ Spanish Listening
◯ Chemistry	◯ World History	◯ Modern Hebrew		
◯ Physics	◯ French	◯ Spanish		

Background Questions: ① ② ③ ④ ⑤ ⑥ ⑦ ⑧ ⑨

1	A B C D E	26	A B C D E	51	A B C D E	76	A B C D E
2	A B C D E	27	A B C D E	52	A B C D E	77	A B C D E
3	A B C D E	28	A B C D E	53	A B C D E	78	A B C D E
4	A B C D E	29	A B C D E	54	A B C D E	79	A B C D E
5	A B C D E	30	A B C D E	55	A B C D E	80	A B C D E
6	A B C D E	31	A B C D E	56	A B C D E	81	A B C D E
7	A B C D E	32	A B C D E	57	A B C D E	82	A B C D E
8	A B C D E	33	A B C D E	58	A B C D E	83	A B C D E
9	A B C D E	34	A B C D E	59	A B C D E	84	A B C D E
10	A B C D E	35	A B C D E	60	A B C D E	85	A B C D E
11	A B C D E	36	A B C D E	61	A B C D E	86	A B C D E
12	A B C D E	37	A B C D E	62	A B C D E	87	A B C D E
13	A B C D E	38	A B C D E	63	A B C D E	88	A B C D E
14	A B C D E	39	A B C D E	64	A B C D E	89	A B C D E
15	A B C D E	40	A B C D E	65	A B C D E	90	A B C D E
16	A B C D E	41	A B C D E	66	A B C D E	91	A B C D E
17	A B C D E	42	A B C D E	67	A B C D E	92	A B C D E
18	A B C D E	43	A B C D E	68	A B C D E	93	A B C D E
19	A B C D E	44	A B C D E	69	A B C D E	94	A B C D E
20	A B C D E	45	A B C D E	70	A B C D E	95	A B C D E
21	A B C D E	46	A B C D E	71	A B C D E	96	A B C D E
22	A B C D E	47	A B C D E	72	A B C D E	97	A B C D E
23	A B C D E	48	A B C D E	73	A B C D E	98	A B C D E
24	A B C D E	49	A B C D E	74	A B C D E	99	A B C D E
25	A B C D E	50	A B C D E	75	A B C D E	100	A B C D E

PLEASE MAKE SURE to fill in these fields completely and correctly. If they are not correct, we won't be able to score your test(s)!

7 TEST BOOK SERIAL NUMBER
(Copy from front of test book.)

0 1 2 3 4 5 6 7 8 9 (six columns)

8 BOOK CODE
(Copy and grid as on back of test book.)

Column 1: 0 1 2 3 4 5 6 7 8 9
Column 2: A B C D E F G H I J K L M N O P Q R S T U V W X Y Z
Column 3: 0 1 2 3 4 5 6 7 8 9

9 BOOK ID
(Copy from back of test book.)

Quality Assurance Mark

Chemistry *Fill in circle CE only if II is correct explanation of I.

	I	II	CE*		I	II	CE*
101	T F	T F	◯	109	T F	T F	◯
102	T F	T F	◯	110	T F	T F	◯
103	T F	T F	◯	111	T F	T F	◯
104	T F	T F	◯	112	T F	T F	◯
105	T F	T F	◯	113	T F	T F	◯
106	T F	T F	◯	114	T F	T F	◯
107	T F	T F	◯	115	T F	T F	◯
108	T F	T F	◯				

FOR OFFICIAL USE ONLY

R/C	W/S1	FS/S2	CS/S3	WS

CERTIFICATION STATEMENT

Copy the statement below and sign your name as you would an official document.

I hereby agree to the conditions set forth online at sat.collegeboard.org and in any paper registration materials given to me and certify that I am the person whose name, address and signature appear on this answer sheet.

Signature ______________________ Date ______________

COMPLETE MARK ● **EXAMPLES OF INCOMPLETE MARKS**

You must use a No. 2 pencil and marks must be complete. Do not use a mechanical pencil. *It is very important that you fill in the entire circle darkly and completely. If you change your response, erase as completely as possible. Incomplete marks or erasures may affect your score.*

○ Literature	○ Mathematics Level 1	○ German	○ Chinese Listening	○ Japanese Listening
○ Biology E	○ Mathematics Level 2	○ Italian	○ French Listening	○ Korean Listening
○ Biology M	○ U.S. History	○ Latin	○ German Listening	○ Spanish Listening
○ Chemistry	○ World History	○ Modern Hebrew		
○ Physics	○ French	○ Spanish		

Background Questions: ① ② ③ ④ ⑤ ⑥ ⑦ ⑧ ⑨

1 Ⓐ Ⓑ Ⓒ Ⓓ Ⓔ	26 Ⓐ Ⓑ Ⓒ Ⓓ Ⓔ	51 Ⓐ Ⓑ Ⓒ Ⓓ Ⓔ	76 Ⓐ Ⓑ Ⓒ Ⓓ Ⓔ
2 Ⓐ Ⓑ Ⓒ Ⓓ Ⓔ	27 Ⓐ Ⓑ Ⓒ Ⓓ Ⓔ	52 Ⓐ Ⓑ Ⓒ Ⓓ Ⓔ	77 Ⓐ Ⓑ Ⓒ Ⓓ Ⓔ
3 Ⓐ Ⓑ Ⓒ Ⓓ Ⓔ	28 Ⓐ Ⓑ Ⓒ Ⓓ Ⓔ	53 Ⓐ Ⓑ Ⓒ Ⓓ Ⓔ	78 Ⓐ Ⓑ Ⓒ Ⓓ Ⓔ
4 Ⓐ Ⓑ Ⓒ Ⓓ Ⓔ	29 Ⓐ Ⓑ Ⓒ Ⓓ Ⓔ	54 Ⓐ Ⓑ Ⓒ Ⓓ Ⓔ	79 Ⓐ Ⓑ Ⓒ Ⓓ Ⓔ
5 Ⓐ Ⓑ Ⓒ Ⓓ Ⓔ	30 Ⓐ Ⓑ Ⓒ Ⓓ Ⓔ	55 Ⓐ Ⓑ Ⓒ Ⓓ Ⓔ	80 Ⓐ Ⓑ Ⓒ Ⓓ Ⓔ
6 Ⓐ Ⓑ Ⓒ Ⓓ Ⓔ	31 Ⓐ Ⓑ Ⓒ Ⓓ Ⓔ	56 Ⓐ Ⓑ Ⓒ Ⓓ Ⓔ	81 Ⓐ Ⓑ Ⓒ Ⓓ Ⓔ
7 Ⓐ Ⓑ Ⓒ Ⓓ Ⓔ	32 Ⓐ Ⓑ Ⓒ Ⓓ Ⓔ	57 Ⓐ Ⓑ Ⓒ Ⓓ Ⓔ	82 Ⓐ Ⓑ Ⓒ Ⓓ Ⓔ
8 Ⓐ Ⓑ Ⓒ Ⓓ Ⓔ	33 Ⓐ Ⓑ Ⓒ Ⓓ Ⓔ	58 Ⓐ Ⓑ Ⓒ Ⓓ Ⓔ	83 Ⓐ Ⓑ Ⓒ Ⓓ Ⓔ
9 Ⓐ Ⓑ Ⓒ Ⓓ Ⓔ	34 Ⓐ Ⓑ Ⓒ Ⓓ Ⓔ	59 Ⓐ Ⓑ Ⓒ Ⓓ Ⓔ	84 Ⓐ Ⓑ Ⓒ Ⓓ Ⓔ
10 Ⓐ Ⓑ Ⓒ Ⓓ Ⓔ	35 Ⓐ Ⓑ Ⓒ Ⓓ Ⓔ	60 Ⓐ Ⓑ Ⓒ Ⓓ Ⓔ	85 Ⓐ Ⓑ Ⓒ Ⓓ Ⓔ
11 Ⓐ Ⓑ Ⓒ Ⓓ Ⓔ	36 Ⓐ Ⓑ Ⓒ Ⓓ Ⓔ	61 Ⓐ Ⓑ Ⓒ Ⓓ Ⓔ	86 Ⓐ Ⓑ Ⓒ Ⓓ Ⓔ
12 Ⓐ Ⓑ Ⓒ Ⓓ Ⓔ	37 Ⓐ Ⓑ Ⓒ Ⓓ Ⓔ	62 Ⓐ Ⓑ Ⓒ Ⓓ Ⓔ	87 Ⓐ Ⓑ Ⓒ Ⓓ Ⓔ
13 Ⓐ Ⓑ Ⓒ Ⓓ Ⓔ	38 Ⓐ Ⓑ Ⓒ Ⓓ Ⓔ	63 Ⓐ Ⓑ Ⓒ Ⓓ Ⓔ	88 Ⓐ Ⓑ Ⓒ Ⓓ Ⓔ
14 Ⓐ Ⓑ Ⓒ Ⓓ Ⓔ	39 Ⓐ Ⓑ Ⓒ Ⓓ Ⓔ	64 Ⓐ Ⓑ Ⓒ Ⓓ Ⓔ	89 Ⓐ Ⓑ Ⓒ Ⓓ Ⓔ
15 Ⓐ Ⓑ Ⓒ Ⓓ Ⓔ	40 Ⓐ Ⓑ Ⓒ Ⓓ Ⓔ	65 Ⓐ Ⓑ Ⓒ Ⓓ Ⓔ	90 Ⓐ Ⓑ Ⓒ Ⓓ Ⓔ
16 Ⓐ Ⓑ Ⓒ Ⓓ Ⓔ	41 Ⓐ Ⓑ Ⓒ Ⓓ Ⓔ	66 Ⓐ Ⓑ Ⓒ Ⓓ Ⓔ	91 Ⓐ Ⓑ Ⓒ Ⓓ Ⓔ
17 Ⓐ Ⓑ Ⓒ Ⓓ Ⓔ	42 Ⓐ Ⓑ Ⓒ Ⓓ Ⓔ	67 Ⓐ Ⓑ Ⓒ Ⓓ Ⓔ	92 Ⓐ Ⓑ Ⓒ Ⓓ Ⓔ
18 Ⓐ Ⓑ Ⓒ Ⓓ Ⓔ	43 Ⓐ Ⓑ Ⓒ Ⓓ Ⓔ	68 Ⓐ Ⓑ Ⓒ Ⓓ Ⓔ	93 Ⓐ Ⓑ Ⓒ Ⓓ Ⓔ
19 Ⓐ Ⓑ Ⓒ Ⓓ Ⓔ	44 Ⓐ Ⓑ Ⓒ Ⓓ Ⓔ	69 Ⓐ Ⓑ Ⓒ Ⓓ Ⓔ	94 Ⓐ Ⓑ Ⓒ Ⓓ Ⓔ
20 Ⓐ Ⓑ Ⓒ Ⓓ Ⓔ	45 Ⓐ Ⓑ Ⓒ Ⓓ Ⓔ	70 Ⓐ Ⓑ Ⓒ Ⓓ Ⓔ	95 Ⓐ Ⓑ Ⓒ Ⓓ Ⓔ
21 Ⓐ Ⓑ Ⓒ Ⓓ Ⓔ	46 Ⓐ Ⓑ Ⓒ Ⓓ Ⓔ	71 Ⓐ Ⓑ Ⓒ Ⓓ Ⓔ	96 Ⓐ Ⓑ Ⓒ Ⓓ Ⓔ
22 Ⓐ Ⓑ Ⓒ Ⓓ Ⓔ	47 Ⓐ Ⓑ Ⓒ Ⓓ Ⓔ	72 Ⓐ Ⓑ Ⓒ Ⓓ Ⓔ	97 Ⓐ Ⓑ Ⓒ Ⓓ Ⓔ
23 Ⓐ Ⓑ Ⓒ Ⓓ Ⓔ	48 Ⓐ Ⓑ Ⓒ Ⓓ Ⓔ	73 Ⓐ Ⓑ Ⓒ Ⓓ Ⓔ	98 Ⓐ Ⓑ Ⓒ Ⓓ Ⓔ
24 Ⓐ Ⓑ Ⓒ Ⓓ Ⓔ	49 Ⓐ Ⓑ Ⓒ Ⓓ Ⓔ	74 Ⓐ Ⓑ Ⓒ Ⓓ Ⓔ	99 Ⓐ Ⓑ Ⓒ Ⓓ Ⓔ
25 Ⓐ Ⓑ Ⓒ Ⓓ Ⓔ	50 Ⓐ Ⓑ Ⓒ Ⓓ Ⓔ	75 Ⓐ Ⓑ Ⓒ Ⓓ Ⓔ	100 Ⓐ Ⓑ Ⓒ Ⓓ Ⓔ

Quality ● Assurance Mark

PLEASE MAKE SURE to fill in these fields completely and correctly. If they are not correct, we won't be able to score your test(s)!

7 TEST BOOK SERIAL NUMBER (Copy from front of test book.)

0	0	0	0	0	0
1	1	1	1	1	1
2	2	2	2	2	2
3	3	3	3	3	3
4	4	4	4	4	4
5	5	5	5	5	5
6	6	6	6	6	6
7	7	7	7	7	7
8	8	8	8	8	8
9	9	9	9	9	9

8 BOOK CODE (Copy and grid as on back of test book.)

0	A	0
1	B	1
2	C	2
3	D	3
4	E	4
5	F	5
6	G	6
7	H	7
8	I	8
9	J	9
	K	
	L	
	M	
	N	
	O	
	P	
	Q	
	R	
	S	
	T	
	U	
	V	
	W	
	X	
	Y	
	Z	

9 BOOK ID (Copy from back of test book.)

Chemistry *Fill in circle CE only if II is correct explanation of I.

	I	II	CE*		I	II	CE*
101	Ⓣ Ⓕ	Ⓣ Ⓕ	○	109	Ⓣ Ⓕ	Ⓣ Ⓕ	○
102	Ⓣ Ⓕ	Ⓣ Ⓕ	○	110	Ⓣ Ⓕ	Ⓣ Ⓕ	○
103	Ⓣ Ⓕ	Ⓣ Ⓕ	○	111	Ⓣ Ⓕ	Ⓣ Ⓕ	○
104	Ⓣ Ⓕ	Ⓣ Ⓕ	○	112	Ⓣ Ⓕ	Ⓣ Ⓕ	○
105	Ⓣ Ⓕ	Ⓣ Ⓕ	○	113	Ⓣ Ⓕ	Ⓣ Ⓕ	○
106	Ⓣ Ⓕ	Ⓣ Ⓕ	○	114	Ⓣ Ⓕ	Ⓣ Ⓕ	○
107	Ⓣ Ⓕ	Ⓣ Ⓕ	○	115	Ⓣ Ⓕ	Ⓣ Ⓕ	○
108	Ⓣ Ⓕ	Ⓣ Ⓕ	○				

FOR OFFICIAL USE ONLY

R/C	W/S1	FS/S2	CS/S3	WS

OMPLETE MARK ● EXAMPLES OF INCOMPLETE MARKS

You must use a No. 2 pencil and marks must be complete. Do not use a mechanical pencil. It is very important that you fill in the entire circle darkly and completely. If you change your response, erase as completely as possible. Incomplete marks or erasures may affect your score.

○ Literature
○ Biology E
○ Biology M
○ Chemistry
○ Physics
○ Mathematics Level 1
○ Mathematics Level 2
○ U.S. History
○ World History
○ French
○ German
○ Italian
○ Latin
○ Modern Hebrew
○ Spanish
○ Chinese Listening
○ French Listening
○ German Listening
○ Japanese Listening
○ Korean Listening
○ Spanish Listening

Background Questions: ① ② ③ ④ ⑤ ⑥ ⑦ ⑧ ⑨

1 Ⓐ Ⓑ Ⓒ Ⓓ Ⓔ	26 Ⓐ Ⓑ Ⓒ Ⓓ Ⓔ	51 Ⓐ Ⓑ Ⓒ Ⓓ Ⓔ	76 Ⓐ Ⓑ Ⓒ Ⓓ Ⓔ
2 Ⓐ Ⓑ Ⓒ Ⓓ Ⓔ	27 Ⓐ Ⓑ Ⓒ Ⓓ Ⓔ	52 Ⓐ Ⓑ Ⓒ Ⓓ Ⓔ	77 Ⓐ Ⓑ Ⓒ Ⓓ Ⓔ
3 Ⓐ Ⓑ Ⓒ Ⓓ Ⓔ	28 Ⓐ Ⓑ Ⓒ Ⓓ Ⓔ	53 Ⓐ Ⓑ Ⓒ Ⓓ Ⓔ	78 Ⓐ Ⓑ Ⓒ Ⓓ Ⓔ
4 Ⓐ Ⓑ Ⓒ Ⓓ Ⓔ	29 Ⓐ Ⓑ Ⓒ Ⓓ Ⓔ	54 Ⓐ Ⓑ Ⓒ Ⓓ Ⓔ	79 Ⓐ Ⓑ Ⓒ Ⓓ Ⓔ
5 Ⓐ Ⓑ Ⓒ Ⓓ Ⓔ	30 Ⓐ Ⓑ Ⓒ Ⓓ Ⓔ	55 Ⓐ Ⓑ Ⓒ Ⓓ Ⓔ	80 Ⓐ Ⓑ Ⓒ Ⓓ Ⓔ
6 Ⓐ Ⓑ Ⓒ Ⓓ Ⓔ	31 Ⓐ Ⓑ Ⓒ Ⓓ Ⓔ	56 Ⓐ Ⓑ Ⓒ Ⓓ Ⓔ	81 Ⓐ Ⓑ Ⓒ Ⓓ Ⓔ
7 Ⓐ Ⓑ Ⓒ Ⓓ Ⓔ	32 Ⓐ Ⓑ Ⓒ Ⓓ Ⓔ	57 Ⓐ Ⓑ Ⓒ Ⓓ Ⓔ	82 Ⓐ Ⓑ Ⓒ Ⓓ Ⓔ
8 Ⓐ Ⓑ Ⓒ Ⓓ Ⓔ	33 Ⓐ Ⓑ Ⓒ Ⓓ Ⓔ	58 Ⓐ Ⓑ Ⓒ Ⓓ Ⓔ	83 Ⓐ Ⓑ Ⓒ Ⓓ Ⓔ
9 Ⓐ Ⓑ Ⓒ Ⓓ Ⓔ	34 Ⓐ Ⓑ Ⓒ Ⓓ Ⓔ	59 Ⓐ Ⓑ Ⓒ Ⓓ Ⓔ	84 Ⓐ Ⓑ Ⓒ Ⓓ Ⓔ
10 Ⓐ Ⓑ Ⓒ Ⓓ Ⓔ	35 Ⓐ Ⓑ Ⓒ Ⓓ Ⓔ	60 Ⓐ Ⓑ Ⓒ Ⓓ Ⓔ	85 Ⓐ Ⓑ Ⓒ Ⓓ Ⓔ
11 Ⓐ Ⓑ Ⓒ Ⓓ Ⓔ	36 Ⓐ Ⓑ Ⓒ Ⓓ Ⓔ	61 Ⓐ Ⓑ Ⓒ Ⓓ Ⓔ	86 Ⓐ Ⓑ Ⓒ Ⓓ Ⓔ
12 Ⓐ Ⓑ Ⓒ Ⓓ Ⓔ	37 Ⓐ Ⓑ Ⓒ Ⓓ Ⓔ	62 Ⓐ Ⓑ Ⓒ Ⓓ Ⓔ	87 Ⓐ Ⓑ Ⓒ Ⓓ Ⓔ
13 Ⓐ Ⓑ Ⓒ Ⓓ Ⓔ	38 Ⓐ Ⓑ Ⓒ Ⓓ Ⓔ	63 Ⓐ Ⓑ Ⓒ Ⓓ Ⓔ	88 Ⓐ Ⓑ Ⓒ Ⓓ Ⓔ
14 Ⓐ Ⓑ Ⓒ Ⓓ Ⓔ	39 Ⓐ Ⓑ Ⓒ Ⓓ Ⓔ	64 Ⓐ Ⓑ Ⓒ Ⓓ Ⓔ	89 Ⓐ Ⓑ Ⓒ Ⓓ Ⓔ
15 Ⓐ Ⓑ Ⓒ Ⓓ Ⓔ	40 Ⓐ Ⓑ Ⓒ Ⓓ Ⓔ	65 Ⓐ Ⓑ Ⓒ Ⓓ Ⓔ	90 Ⓐ Ⓑ Ⓒ Ⓓ Ⓔ
16 Ⓐ Ⓑ Ⓒ Ⓓ Ⓔ	41 Ⓐ Ⓑ Ⓒ Ⓓ Ⓔ	66 Ⓐ Ⓑ Ⓒ Ⓓ Ⓔ	91 Ⓐ Ⓑ Ⓒ Ⓓ Ⓔ
17 Ⓐ Ⓑ Ⓒ Ⓓ Ⓔ	42 Ⓐ Ⓑ Ⓒ Ⓓ Ⓔ	67 Ⓐ Ⓑ Ⓒ Ⓓ Ⓔ	92 Ⓐ Ⓑ Ⓒ Ⓓ Ⓔ
18 Ⓐ Ⓑ Ⓒ Ⓓ Ⓔ	43 Ⓐ Ⓑ Ⓒ Ⓓ Ⓔ	68 Ⓐ Ⓑ Ⓒ Ⓓ Ⓔ	93 Ⓐ Ⓑ Ⓒ Ⓓ Ⓔ
19 Ⓐ Ⓑ Ⓒ Ⓓ Ⓔ	44 Ⓐ Ⓑ Ⓒ Ⓓ Ⓔ	69 Ⓐ Ⓑ Ⓒ Ⓓ Ⓔ	94 Ⓐ Ⓑ Ⓒ Ⓓ Ⓔ
20 Ⓐ Ⓑ Ⓒ Ⓓ Ⓔ	45 Ⓐ Ⓑ Ⓒ Ⓓ Ⓔ	70 Ⓐ Ⓑ Ⓒ Ⓓ Ⓔ	95 Ⓐ Ⓑ Ⓒ Ⓓ Ⓔ
21 Ⓐ Ⓑ Ⓒ Ⓓ Ⓔ	46 Ⓐ Ⓑ Ⓒ Ⓓ Ⓔ	71 Ⓐ Ⓑ Ⓒ Ⓓ Ⓔ	96 Ⓐ Ⓑ Ⓒ Ⓓ Ⓔ
22 Ⓐ Ⓑ Ⓒ Ⓓ Ⓔ	47 Ⓐ Ⓑ Ⓒ Ⓓ Ⓔ	72 Ⓐ Ⓑ Ⓒ Ⓓ Ⓔ	97 Ⓐ Ⓑ Ⓒ Ⓓ Ⓔ
23 Ⓐ Ⓑ Ⓒ Ⓓ Ⓔ	48 Ⓐ Ⓑ Ⓒ Ⓓ Ⓔ	73 Ⓐ Ⓑ Ⓒ Ⓓ Ⓔ	98 Ⓐ Ⓑ Ⓒ Ⓓ Ⓔ
24 Ⓐ Ⓑ Ⓒ Ⓓ Ⓔ	49 Ⓐ Ⓑ Ⓒ Ⓓ Ⓔ	74 Ⓐ Ⓑ Ⓒ Ⓓ Ⓔ	99 Ⓐ Ⓑ Ⓒ Ⓓ Ⓔ
25 Ⓐ Ⓑ Ⓒ Ⓓ Ⓔ	50 Ⓐ Ⓑ Ⓒ Ⓓ Ⓔ	75 Ⓐ Ⓑ Ⓒ Ⓓ Ⓔ	100 Ⓐ Ⓑ Ⓒ Ⓓ Ⓔ

Chemistry *Fill in circle CE only if II is correct explanation of I.

	I	II	CE*		I	II	CE*
101	Ⓣ Ⓕ	Ⓣ Ⓕ	○	109	Ⓣ Ⓕ	Ⓣ Ⓕ	○
102	Ⓣ Ⓕ	Ⓣ Ⓕ	○	110	Ⓣ Ⓕ	Ⓣ Ⓕ	○
103	Ⓣ Ⓕ	Ⓣ Ⓕ	○	111	Ⓣ Ⓕ	Ⓣ Ⓕ	○
104	Ⓣ Ⓕ	Ⓣ Ⓕ	○	112	Ⓣ Ⓕ	Ⓣ Ⓕ	○
105	Ⓣ Ⓕ	Ⓣ Ⓕ	○	113	Ⓣ Ⓕ	Ⓣ Ⓕ	○
106	Ⓣ Ⓕ	Ⓣ Ⓕ	○	114	Ⓣ Ⓕ	Ⓣ Ⓕ	○
107	Ⓣ Ⓕ	Ⓣ Ⓕ	○	115	Ⓣ Ⓕ	Ⓣ Ⓕ	○
108	Ⓣ Ⓕ	Ⓣ Ⓕ	○				

PLEASE MAKE SURE to fill in these fields completely and correctly. If they are not correct, we won't be able to score your test(s)!

7 TEST BOOK SERIAL NUMBER
(Copy from front of test book.)

0 1 2 3 4 5 6 7 8 9 (six columns)

8 BOOK CODE
(Copy and grid as on back of test book.)

0 1 2 3 4 5 6 7 8 9 | A B C D E F G H I J K L M N O P Q R S T U V W X Y Z | 0 1 2 3 4 5 6 7 8 9

9 BOOK ID
(Copy from back of test book.)

Quality Assurance Mark

FOR OFFICIAL USE ONLY				
R/C	W/S1	FS/S2	CS/S3	WS

PLEASE DO NOT WRITE IN THIS AREA

SERIAL #

CollegeBoard

SAT Subject Tests™

COMPLETE MARK ● EXAMPLES OF INCOMPLETE MARKS

You must use a No. 2 pencil and marks must be complete. Do not use a mechanical pencil. It is very important that you fill in the entire circle darkly and completely. If you change your response, erase as completely as possible. Incomplete marks or erasures may affect your score.

1 **Your Name:** (Print)

Last First M.I.

I agree to the conditions on the front and back of the SAT Subject Tests™ book. I also agree with the SAT Test Security and Fairness policies and understand that any violation of these policies will result in score cancellation and may result in reporting of certain violations to law enforcement.

Signature: **Today's Date:** / / MM DD YY

Home Address: (Print) Number and Street City State/Country Zip Code

Phone: ( ) **Test Center:** (Print) City State/Country

2 YOUR NAME

Last Name (First 6 Letters) | First Name (First 4 Letters) | Mid. Init.

3 DATE OF BIRTH

MONTH | DAY | YEAR

Jan Feb Mar Apr May Jun Jul Aug Sep Oct Nov Dec

4 REGISTRATION NUMBER

(Copy from Admission Ticket.)

Important: Fill in items 8 and 9 exactly as shown on the back of test book.

7 TEST BOOK SERIAL NUMBER

(Copy from front of test book.)

8 BOOK CODE

(Copy and grid as on back of test book.)

9 BOOK ID

(Copy from back of test book.)

5 ZIP CODE

6 TEST CENTER

(Supplied by Test Center Supervisor.)

PLEASE MAKE SURE to fill in these fields completely and correctly. If they are not correct, we won't be able to score your test(s)!

FOR OFFICIAL USE ONLY

103648-77191 • NS1114C1085 • Printed in U.S.A.

194415-001 1 2 3 4 5 A B C D E Printed in the USA ISD11312

783175

PLEASE DO NOT WRITE IN THIS AREA

SERIAL #

COMPLETE MARK ● EXAMPLES OF INCOMPLETE MARKS

You must use a No. 2 pencil and marks must be complete. Do not use a mechanical pencil. *It is very important that you fill in the entire circle darkly and completely. If you change your response, erase as completely as possible. Incomplete marks or erasures may affect your score.*

○ Literature	○ Mathematics Level 1	○ German	○ Chinese Listening	○ Japanese Listening
○ Biology E	○ Mathematics Level 2	○ Italian	○ French Listening	○ Korean Listening
○ Biology M	○ U.S. History	○ Latin	○ German Listening	○ Spanish Listening
○ Chemistry	○ World History	○ Modern Hebrew		
○ Physics	○ French	○ Spanish		

Background Questions: ① ② ③ ④ ⑤ ⑥ ⑦ ⑧ ⑨

Questions 1–100: Ⓐ Ⓑ Ⓒ Ⓓ Ⓔ

PLEASE MAKE SURE to fill in these fields completely and correctly. If they are not correct, we won't be able to score your test(s)!

7 TEST BOOK SERIAL NUMBER (Copy from front of test book.)

8 BOOK CODE (Copy and grid as on back of test book.)

9 BOOK ID (Copy from back of test book.)

Quality Assurance Mark

Chemistry *Fill in circle CE only if II is correct explanation of I.

	I	II	CE*		I	II	CE*
101	Ⓣ Ⓕ	Ⓣ Ⓕ	○	109	Ⓣ Ⓕ	Ⓣ Ⓕ	○
102	Ⓣ Ⓕ	Ⓣ Ⓕ	○	110	Ⓣ Ⓕ	Ⓣ Ⓕ	○
103	Ⓣ Ⓕ	Ⓣ Ⓕ	○	111	Ⓣ Ⓕ	Ⓣ Ⓕ	○
104	Ⓣ Ⓕ	Ⓣ Ⓕ	○	112	Ⓣ Ⓕ	Ⓣ Ⓕ	○
105	Ⓣ Ⓕ	Ⓣ Ⓕ	○	113	Ⓣ Ⓕ	Ⓣ Ⓕ	○
106	Ⓣ Ⓕ	Ⓣ Ⓕ	○	114	Ⓣ Ⓕ	Ⓣ Ⓕ	○
107	Ⓣ Ⓕ	Ⓣ Ⓕ	○	115	Ⓣ Ⓕ	Ⓣ Ⓕ	○
108	Ⓣ Ⓕ	Ⓣ Ⓕ	○				

FOR OFFICIAL USE ONLY

R/C	W/S1	FS/S2	CS/S3	WS

CERTIFICATION STATEMENT

Copy the statement below and sign your name as you would an official document.

I hereby agree to the conditions set forth online at sat.collegeboard.org and in any paper registration materials given to me and certify that I am the person whose name, address and signature appear on this answer sheet.

Signature ______________________ Date ______________

COMPLETE MARK ● EXAMPLES OF INCOMPLETE MARKS

You must use a No. 2 pencil and marks must be complete. Do not use a mechanical pencil. *It is very important that you fill in the entire circle darkly and completely. If you change your response, erase as completely as possible. Incomplete marks or erasures may affect your score.*

○ Literature	○ Mathematics Level 1	○ German	○ Chinese Listening	○ Japanese Listening
○ Biology E	○ Mathematics Level 2	○ Italian	○ French Listening	○ Korean Listening
○ Biology M	○ U.S. History	○ Latin	○ German Listening	○ Spanish Listening
○ Chemistry	○ World History	○ Modern Hebrew		
○ Physics	○ French	○ Spanish		

Background Questions: ① ② ③ ④ ⑤ ⑥ ⑦ ⑧ ⑨

PLEASE MAKE SURE to fill in these fields completely and correctly. If they are not correct, we won't be able to score your test(s)!

1 Ⓐ Ⓑ Ⓒ Ⓓ Ⓔ	26 Ⓐ Ⓑ Ⓒ Ⓓ Ⓔ	51 Ⓐ Ⓑ Ⓒ Ⓓ Ⓔ	76 Ⓐ Ⓑ Ⓒ Ⓓ Ⓔ
2 Ⓐ Ⓑ Ⓒ Ⓓ Ⓔ	27 Ⓐ Ⓑ Ⓒ Ⓓ Ⓔ	52 Ⓐ Ⓑ Ⓒ Ⓓ Ⓔ	77 Ⓐ Ⓑ Ⓒ Ⓓ Ⓔ
3 Ⓐ Ⓑ Ⓒ Ⓓ Ⓔ	28 Ⓐ Ⓑ Ⓒ Ⓓ Ⓔ	53 Ⓐ Ⓑ Ⓒ Ⓓ Ⓔ	78 Ⓐ Ⓑ Ⓒ Ⓓ Ⓔ
4 Ⓐ Ⓑ Ⓒ Ⓓ Ⓔ	29 Ⓐ Ⓑ Ⓒ Ⓓ Ⓔ	54 Ⓐ Ⓑ Ⓒ Ⓓ Ⓔ	79 Ⓐ Ⓑ Ⓒ Ⓓ Ⓔ
5 Ⓐ Ⓑ Ⓒ Ⓓ Ⓔ	30 Ⓐ Ⓑ Ⓒ Ⓓ Ⓔ	55 Ⓐ Ⓑ Ⓒ Ⓓ Ⓔ	80 Ⓐ Ⓑ Ⓒ Ⓓ Ⓔ
6 Ⓐ Ⓑ Ⓒ Ⓓ Ⓔ	31 Ⓐ Ⓑ Ⓒ Ⓓ Ⓔ	56 Ⓐ Ⓑ Ⓒ Ⓓ Ⓔ	81 Ⓐ Ⓑ Ⓒ Ⓓ Ⓔ
7 Ⓐ Ⓑ Ⓒ Ⓓ Ⓔ	32 Ⓐ Ⓑ Ⓒ Ⓓ Ⓔ	57 Ⓐ Ⓑ Ⓒ Ⓓ Ⓔ	82 Ⓐ Ⓑ Ⓒ Ⓓ Ⓔ
8 Ⓐ Ⓑ Ⓒ Ⓓ Ⓔ	33 Ⓐ Ⓑ Ⓒ Ⓓ Ⓔ	58 Ⓐ Ⓑ Ⓒ Ⓓ Ⓔ	83 Ⓐ Ⓑ Ⓒ Ⓓ Ⓔ
9 Ⓐ Ⓑ Ⓒ Ⓓ Ⓔ	34 Ⓐ Ⓑ Ⓒ Ⓓ Ⓔ	59 Ⓐ Ⓑ Ⓒ Ⓓ Ⓔ	84 Ⓐ Ⓑ Ⓒ Ⓓ Ⓔ
10 Ⓐ Ⓑ Ⓒ Ⓓ Ⓔ	35 Ⓐ Ⓑ Ⓒ Ⓓ Ⓔ	60 Ⓐ Ⓑ Ⓒ Ⓓ Ⓔ	85 Ⓐ Ⓑ Ⓒ Ⓓ Ⓔ
11 Ⓐ Ⓑ Ⓒ Ⓓ Ⓔ	36 Ⓐ Ⓑ Ⓒ Ⓓ Ⓔ	61 Ⓐ Ⓑ Ⓒ Ⓓ Ⓔ	86 Ⓐ Ⓑ Ⓒ Ⓓ Ⓔ
12 Ⓐ Ⓑ Ⓒ Ⓓ Ⓔ	37 Ⓐ Ⓑ Ⓒ Ⓓ Ⓔ	62 Ⓐ Ⓑ Ⓒ Ⓓ Ⓔ	87 Ⓐ Ⓑ Ⓒ Ⓓ Ⓔ
13 Ⓐ Ⓑ Ⓒ Ⓓ Ⓔ	38 Ⓐ Ⓑ Ⓒ Ⓓ Ⓔ	63 Ⓐ Ⓑ Ⓒ Ⓓ Ⓔ	88 Ⓐ Ⓑ Ⓒ Ⓓ Ⓔ
14 Ⓐ Ⓑ Ⓒ Ⓓ Ⓔ	39 Ⓐ Ⓑ Ⓒ Ⓓ Ⓔ	64 Ⓐ Ⓑ Ⓒ Ⓓ Ⓔ	89 Ⓐ Ⓑ Ⓒ Ⓓ Ⓔ
15 Ⓐ Ⓑ Ⓒ Ⓓ Ⓔ	40 Ⓐ Ⓑ Ⓒ Ⓓ Ⓔ	65 Ⓐ Ⓑ Ⓒ Ⓓ Ⓔ	90 Ⓐ Ⓑ Ⓒ Ⓓ Ⓔ
16 Ⓐ Ⓑ Ⓒ Ⓓ Ⓔ	41 Ⓐ Ⓑ Ⓒ Ⓓ Ⓔ	66 Ⓐ Ⓑ Ⓒ Ⓓ Ⓔ	91 Ⓐ Ⓑ Ⓒ Ⓓ Ⓔ
17 Ⓐ Ⓑ Ⓒ Ⓓ Ⓔ	42 Ⓐ Ⓑ Ⓒ Ⓓ Ⓔ	67 Ⓐ Ⓑ Ⓒ Ⓓ Ⓔ	92 Ⓐ Ⓑ Ⓒ Ⓓ Ⓔ
18 Ⓐ Ⓑ Ⓒ Ⓓ Ⓔ	43 Ⓐ Ⓑ Ⓒ Ⓓ Ⓔ	68 Ⓐ Ⓑ Ⓒ Ⓓ Ⓔ	93 Ⓐ Ⓑ Ⓒ Ⓓ Ⓔ
19 Ⓐ Ⓑ Ⓒ Ⓓ Ⓔ	44 Ⓐ Ⓑ Ⓒ Ⓓ Ⓔ	69 Ⓐ Ⓑ Ⓒ Ⓓ Ⓔ	94 Ⓐ Ⓑ Ⓒ Ⓓ Ⓔ
20 Ⓐ Ⓑ Ⓒ Ⓓ Ⓔ	45 Ⓐ Ⓑ Ⓒ Ⓓ Ⓔ	70 Ⓐ Ⓑ Ⓒ Ⓓ Ⓔ	95 Ⓐ Ⓑ Ⓒ Ⓓ Ⓔ
21 Ⓐ Ⓑ Ⓒ Ⓓ Ⓔ	46 Ⓐ Ⓑ Ⓒ Ⓓ Ⓔ	71 Ⓐ Ⓑ Ⓒ Ⓓ Ⓔ	96 Ⓐ Ⓑ Ⓒ Ⓓ Ⓔ
22 Ⓐ Ⓑ Ⓒ Ⓓ Ⓔ	47 Ⓐ Ⓑ Ⓒ Ⓓ Ⓔ	72 Ⓐ Ⓑ Ⓒ Ⓓ Ⓔ	97 Ⓐ Ⓑ Ⓒ Ⓓ Ⓔ
23 Ⓐ Ⓑ Ⓒ Ⓓ Ⓔ	48 Ⓐ Ⓑ Ⓒ Ⓓ Ⓔ	73 Ⓐ Ⓑ Ⓒ Ⓓ Ⓔ	98 Ⓐ Ⓑ Ⓒ Ⓓ Ⓔ
24 Ⓐ Ⓑ Ⓒ Ⓓ Ⓔ	49 Ⓐ Ⓑ Ⓒ Ⓓ Ⓔ	74 Ⓐ Ⓑ Ⓒ Ⓓ Ⓔ	99 Ⓐ Ⓑ Ⓒ Ⓓ Ⓔ
25 Ⓐ Ⓑ Ⓒ Ⓓ Ⓔ	50 Ⓐ Ⓑ Ⓒ Ⓓ Ⓔ	75 Ⓐ Ⓑ Ⓒ Ⓓ Ⓔ	100 Ⓐ Ⓑ Ⓒ Ⓓ Ⓔ

Quality ● Assurance Mark

7 TEST BOOK SERIAL NUMBER

(Copy from front of test book.)

0	0	0	0	0	0
1	1	1	1	1	1
2	2	2	2	2	2
3	3	3	3	3	3
4	4	4	4	4	4
5	5	5	5	5	5
6	6	6	6	6	6
7	7	7	7	7	7
8	8	8	8	8	8
9	9	9	9	9	9

8 BOOK CODE

(Copy and grid as on back of test book.)

0	A	0
1	B	1
2	C	2
3	D	3
4	E	4
5	F	5
6	G	6
7	H	7
8	I	8
9	J	9
	K	
	L	
	M	
	N	
	O	
	P	
	Q	
	R	
	S	
	T	
	U	
	V	
	W	
	X	
	Y	
	Z	

9 BOOK ID

(Copy from back of test book.)

Chemistry *Fill in circle CE only if II is correct explanation of I.

	I	II	CE*		I	II	CE*
101	Ⓣ Ⓕ	Ⓣ Ⓕ	○	109	Ⓣ Ⓕ	Ⓣ Ⓕ	○
102	Ⓣ Ⓕ	Ⓣ Ⓕ	○	110	Ⓣ Ⓕ	Ⓣ Ⓕ	○
103	Ⓣ Ⓕ	Ⓣ Ⓕ	○	111	Ⓣ Ⓕ	Ⓣ Ⓕ	○
104	Ⓣ Ⓕ	Ⓣ Ⓕ	○	112	Ⓣ Ⓕ	Ⓣ Ⓕ	○
105	Ⓣ Ⓕ	Ⓣ Ⓕ	○	113	Ⓣ Ⓕ	Ⓣ Ⓕ	○
106	Ⓣ Ⓕ	Ⓣ Ⓕ	○	114	Ⓣ Ⓕ	Ⓣ Ⓕ	○
107	Ⓣ Ⓕ	Ⓣ Ⓕ	○	115	Ⓣ Ⓕ	Ⓣ Ⓕ	○
108	Ⓣ Ⓕ	Ⓣ Ⓕ	○				

FOR OFFICIAL USE ONLY

R/C	W/S1	FS/S2	CS/S3	WS

COMPLETE MARK ● EXAMPLES OF INCOMPLETE MARKS

You must use a No. 2 pencil and marks must be complete. Do not use a mechanical pencil. *It is very important that you fill in the entire circle darkly and completely. If you change your response, erase as completely as possible. Incomplete marks or erasures may affect your score.*

○ Literature	○ Mathematics Level 1	○ German	○ Chinese Listening	○ Japanese Listening
○ Biology E	○ Mathematics Level 2	○ Italian	○ French Listening	○ Korean Listening
○ Biology M	○ U.S. History	○ Latin	○ German Listening	○ Spanish Listening
○ Chemistry	○ World History	○ Modern Hebrew		
○ Physics	○ French	○ Spanish		

Background Questions: ① ② ③ ④ ⑤ ⑥ ⑦ ⑧ ⑨

1 Ⓐ Ⓑ Ⓒ Ⓓ Ⓔ	26 Ⓐ Ⓑ Ⓒ Ⓓ Ⓔ	51 Ⓐ Ⓑ Ⓒ Ⓓ Ⓔ	76 Ⓐ Ⓑ Ⓒ Ⓓ Ⓔ
2 Ⓐ Ⓑ Ⓒ Ⓓ Ⓔ	27 Ⓐ Ⓑ Ⓒ Ⓓ Ⓔ	52 Ⓐ Ⓑ Ⓒ Ⓓ Ⓔ	77 Ⓐ Ⓑ Ⓒ Ⓓ Ⓔ
3 Ⓐ Ⓑ Ⓒ Ⓓ Ⓔ	28 Ⓐ Ⓑ Ⓒ Ⓓ Ⓔ	53 Ⓐ Ⓑ Ⓒ Ⓓ Ⓔ	78 Ⓐ Ⓑ Ⓒ Ⓓ Ⓔ
4 Ⓐ Ⓑ Ⓒ Ⓓ Ⓔ	29 Ⓐ Ⓑ Ⓒ Ⓓ Ⓔ	54 Ⓐ Ⓑ Ⓒ Ⓓ Ⓔ	79 Ⓐ Ⓑ Ⓒ Ⓓ Ⓔ
5 Ⓐ Ⓑ Ⓒ Ⓓ Ⓔ	30 Ⓐ Ⓑ Ⓒ Ⓓ Ⓔ	55 Ⓐ Ⓑ Ⓒ Ⓓ Ⓔ	80 Ⓐ Ⓑ Ⓒ Ⓓ Ⓔ
6 Ⓐ Ⓑ Ⓒ Ⓓ Ⓔ	31 Ⓐ Ⓑ Ⓒ Ⓓ Ⓔ	56 Ⓐ Ⓑ Ⓒ Ⓓ Ⓔ	81 Ⓐ Ⓑ Ⓒ Ⓓ Ⓔ
7 Ⓐ Ⓑ Ⓒ Ⓓ Ⓔ	32 Ⓐ Ⓑ Ⓒ Ⓓ Ⓔ	57 Ⓐ Ⓑ Ⓒ Ⓓ Ⓔ	82 Ⓐ Ⓑ Ⓒ Ⓓ Ⓔ
8 Ⓐ Ⓑ Ⓒ Ⓓ Ⓔ	33 Ⓐ Ⓑ Ⓒ Ⓓ Ⓔ	58 Ⓐ Ⓑ Ⓒ Ⓓ Ⓔ	83 Ⓐ Ⓑ Ⓒ Ⓓ Ⓔ
9 Ⓐ Ⓑ Ⓒ Ⓓ Ⓔ	34 Ⓐ Ⓑ Ⓒ Ⓓ Ⓔ	59 Ⓐ Ⓑ Ⓒ Ⓓ Ⓔ	84 Ⓐ Ⓑ Ⓒ Ⓓ Ⓔ
10 Ⓐ Ⓑ Ⓒ Ⓓ Ⓔ	35 Ⓐ Ⓑ Ⓒ Ⓓ Ⓔ	60 Ⓐ Ⓑ Ⓒ Ⓓ Ⓔ	85 Ⓐ Ⓑ Ⓒ Ⓓ Ⓔ
11 Ⓐ Ⓑ Ⓒ Ⓓ Ⓔ	36 Ⓐ Ⓑ Ⓒ Ⓓ Ⓔ	61 Ⓐ Ⓑ Ⓒ Ⓓ Ⓔ	86 Ⓐ Ⓑ Ⓒ Ⓓ Ⓔ
12 Ⓐ Ⓑ Ⓒ Ⓓ Ⓔ	37 Ⓐ Ⓑ Ⓒ Ⓓ Ⓔ	62 Ⓐ Ⓑ Ⓒ Ⓓ Ⓔ	87 Ⓐ Ⓑ Ⓒ Ⓓ Ⓔ
13 Ⓐ Ⓑ Ⓒ Ⓓ Ⓔ	38 Ⓐ Ⓑ Ⓒ Ⓓ Ⓔ	63 Ⓐ Ⓑ Ⓒ Ⓓ Ⓔ	88 Ⓐ Ⓑ Ⓒ Ⓓ Ⓔ
14 Ⓐ Ⓑ Ⓒ Ⓓ Ⓔ	39 Ⓐ Ⓑ Ⓒ Ⓓ Ⓔ	64 Ⓐ Ⓑ Ⓒ Ⓓ Ⓔ	89 Ⓐ Ⓑ Ⓒ Ⓓ Ⓔ
15 Ⓐ Ⓑ Ⓒ Ⓓ Ⓔ	40 Ⓐ Ⓑ Ⓒ Ⓓ Ⓔ	65 Ⓐ Ⓑ Ⓒ Ⓓ Ⓔ	90 Ⓐ Ⓑ Ⓒ Ⓓ Ⓔ
16 Ⓐ Ⓑ Ⓒ Ⓓ Ⓔ	41 Ⓐ Ⓑ Ⓒ Ⓓ Ⓔ	66 Ⓐ Ⓑ Ⓒ Ⓓ Ⓔ	91 Ⓐ Ⓑ Ⓒ Ⓓ Ⓔ
17 Ⓐ Ⓑ Ⓒ Ⓓ Ⓔ	42 Ⓐ Ⓑ Ⓒ Ⓓ Ⓔ	67 Ⓐ Ⓑ Ⓒ Ⓓ Ⓔ	92 Ⓐ Ⓑ Ⓒ Ⓓ Ⓔ
18 Ⓐ Ⓑ Ⓒ Ⓓ Ⓔ	43 Ⓐ Ⓑ Ⓒ Ⓓ Ⓔ	68 Ⓐ Ⓑ Ⓒ Ⓓ Ⓔ	93 Ⓐ Ⓑ Ⓒ Ⓓ Ⓔ
19 Ⓐ Ⓑ Ⓒ Ⓓ Ⓔ	44 Ⓐ Ⓑ Ⓒ Ⓓ Ⓔ	69 Ⓐ Ⓑ Ⓒ Ⓓ Ⓔ	94 Ⓐ Ⓑ Ⓒ Ⓓ Ⓔ
20 Ⓐ Ⓑ Ⓒ Ⓓ Ⓔ	45 Ⓐ Ⓑ Ⓒ Ⓓ Ⓔ	70 Ⓐ Ⓑ Ⓒ Ⓓ Ⓔ	95 Ⓐ Ⓑ Ⓒ Ⓓ Ⓔ
21 Ⓐ Ⓑ Ⓒ Ⓓ Ⓔ	46 Ⓐ Ⓑ Ⓒ Ⓓ Ⓔ	71 Ⓐ Ⓑ Ⓒ Ⓓ Ⓔ	96 Ⓐ Ⓑ Ⓒ Ⓓ Ⓔ
22 Ⓐ Ⓑ Ⓒ Ⓓ Ⓔ	47 Ⓐ Ⓑ Ⓒ Ⓓ Ⓔ	72 Ⓐ Ⓑ Ⓒ Ⓓ Ⓔ	97 Ⓐ Ⓑ Ⓒ Ⓓ Ⓔ
23 Ⓐ Ⓑ Ⓒ Ⓓ Ⓔ	48 Ⓐ Ⓑ Ⓒ Ⓓ Ⓔ	73 Ⓐ Ⓑ Ⓒ Ⓓ Ⓔ	98 Ⓐ Ⓑ Ⓒ Ⓓ Ⓔ
24 Ⓐ Ⓑ Ⓒ Ⓓ Ⓔ	49 Ⓐ Ⓑ Ⓒ Ⓓ Ⓔ	74 Ⓐ Ⓑ Ⓒ Ⓓ Ⓔ	99 Ⓐ Ⓑ Ⓒ Ⓓ Ⓔ
25 Ⓐ Ⓑ Ⓒ Ⓓ Ⓔ	50 Ⓐ Ⓑ Ⓒ Ⓓ Ⓔ	75 Ⓐ Ⓑ Ⓒ Ⓓ Ⓔ	100 Ⓐ Ⓑ Ⓒ Ⓓ Ⓔ

PLEASE MAKE SURE to fill in these fields completely and correctly. If they are not correct, we won't be able to score your test(s)!

7 TEST BOOK SERIAL NUMBER
(Copy from front of test book.)
0 1 2 3 4 5 6 7 8 9 (six columns)

8 BOOK CODE
(Copy and grid as on back of test book.)
0 1 2 3 4 5 6 7 8 9 | A B C D E F G H I J K L M N O P Q R S T U V W X Y Z | 0 1 2 3 4 5 6 7 8 9

9 BOOK ID
(Copy from back of test book.)

Quality Assurance Mark

Chemistry *Fill in circle CE only if II is correct explanation of I.

	I	II	CE*		I	II	CE*
101	Ⓣ Ⓕ	Ⓣ Ⓕ	○	109	Ⓣ Ⓕ	Ⓣ Ⓕ	○
102	Ⓣ Ⓕ	Ⓣ Ⓕ	○	110	Ⓣ Ⓕ	Ⓣ Ⓕ	○
103	Ⓣ Ⓕ	Ⓣ Ⓕ	○	111	Ⓣ Ⓕ	Ⓣ Ⓕ	○
104	Ⓣ Ⓕ	Ⓣ Ⓕ	○	112	Ⓣ Ⓕ	Ⓣ Ⓕ	○
105	Ⓣ Ⓕ	Ⓣ Ⓕ	○	113	Ⓣ Ⓕ	Ⓣ Ⓕ	○
106	Ⓣ Ⓕ	Ⓣ Ⓕ	○	114	Ⓣ Ⓕ	Ⓣ Ⓕ	○
107	Ⓣ Ⓕ	Ⓣ Ⓕ	○	115	Ⓣ Ⓕ	Ⓣ Ⓕ	○
108	Ⓣ Ⓕ	Ⓣ Ⓕ	○				

FOR OFFICIAL USE ONLY

R/C	W/S1	FS/S2	CS/S3	WS

PLEASE DO NOT WRITE IN THIS AREA

SERIAL #

CollegeBoard

SAT Subject Tests™

COMPLETE MARK | EXAMPLES OF INCOMPLETE MARKS

You must use a No. 2 pencil and marks must be complete. Do not use a mechanical pencil. *It is very important that you fill in the entire circle darkly and completely. If you change your response, erase as completely as possible. Incomplete marks or erasures may affect your score.*

1 Your Name: (Print)

Last First M.I.

I agree to the conditions on the front and back of the SAT Subject Tests™ book. I also agree with the SAT Test Security and Fairness policies and understand that any violation of these policies will result in score cancellation and may result in reporting of certain violations to law enforcement.

Signature: **Today's Date:** / / MM DD YY

Home Address: (Print) Number and Street City State/Country Zip Code

Phone: ( ) **Test Center:** (Print) City State/Country

2 YOUR NAME — Last Name (First 6 Letters) | First Name (First 4 Letters) | Mid. Init.

3 DATE OF BIRTH — MONTH | DAY | YEAR

Jan, Feb, Mar, Apr, May, Jun, Jul, Aug, Sep, Oct, Nov, Dec

4 REGISTRATION NUMBER (Copy from Admission Ticket.)

Important: Fill in items 8 and 9 exactly as shown on the back of test book.

7 TEST BOOK SERIAL NUMBER (Copy from front of test book.)

8 BOOK CODE (Copy and grid as on back of test book.)

5 ZIP CODE

6 TEST CENTER (Supplied by Test Center Supervisor.)

9 BOOK ID (Copy from back of test book.)

PLEASE MAKE SURE to fill in these fields completely and correctly. If they are not correct, we won't be able to score your test(s)!

FOR OFFICIAL USE ONLY

103648-77191 • NS1114C1085 • Printed in U.S.A.

194415-001 1 2 3 4 5 A B C D E Printed in the USA ISD11312

783175

PLEASE DO NOT WRITE IN THIS AREA

SERIAL #

COMPLETE MARK ● EXAMPLES OF INCOMPLETE MARKS

You must use a No. 2 pencil and marks must be complete. Do not use a mechanical pencil. *It is very important that you fill in the entire circle darkly and completely. If you change your response, erase as completely as possible. Incomplete marks or erasures may affect your score.*

○ Literature	○ Mathematics Level 1	○ German	○ Chinese Listening	○ Japanese Listening
○ Biology E	○ Mathematics Level 2	○ Italian	○ French Listening	○ Korean Listening
○ Biology M	○ U.S. History	○ Latin	○ German Listening	○ Spanish Listening
○ Chemistry	○ World History	○ Modern Hebrew		
○ Physics	○ French	○ Spanish		

Background Questions: ① ② ③ ④ ⑤ ⑥ ⑦ ⑧ ⑨

1 Ⓐ Ⓑ Ⓒ Ⓓ Ⓔ	26 Ⓐ Ⓑ Ⓒ Ⓓ Ⓔ	51 Ⓐ Ⓑ Ⓒ Ⓓ Ⓔ	76 Ⓐ Ⓑ Ⓒ Ⓓ Ⓔ
2 Ⓐ Ⓑ Ⓒ Ⓓ Ⓔ	27 Ⓐ Ⓑ Ⓒ Ⓓ Ⓔ	52 Ⓐ Ⓑ Ⓒ Ⓓ Ⓔ	77 Ⓐ Ⓑ Ⓒ Ⓓ Ⓔ
3 Ⓐ Ⓑ Ⓒ Ⓓ Ⓔ	28 Ⓐ Ⓑ Ⓒ Ⓓ Ⓔ	53 Ⓐ Ⓑ Ⓒ Ⓓ Ⓔ	78 Ⓐ Ⓑ Ⓒ Ⓓ Ⓔ
4 Ⓐ Ⓑ Ⓒ Ⓓ Ⓔ	29 Ⓐ Ⓑ Ⓒ Ⓓ Ⓔ	54 Ⓐ Ⓑ Ⓒ Ⓓ Ⓔ	79 Ⓐ Ⓑ Ⓒ Ⓓ Ⓔ
5 Ⓐ Ⓑ Ⓒ Ⓓ Ⓔ	30 Ⓐ Ⓑ Ⓒ Ⓓ Ⓔ	55 Ⓐ Ⓑ Ⓒ Ⓓ Ⓔ	80 Ⓐ Ⓑ Ⓒ Ⓓ Ⓔ
6 Ⓐ Ⓑ Ⓒ Ⓓ Ⓔ	31 Ⓐ Ⓑ Ⓒ Ⓓ Ⓔ	56 Ⓐ Ⓑ Ⓒ Ⓓ Ⓔ	81 Ⓐ Ⓑ Ⓒ Ⓓ Ⓔ
7 Ⓐ Ⓑ Ⓒ Ⓓ Ⓔ	32 Ⓐ Ⓑ Ⓒ Ⓓ Ⓔ	57 Ⓐ Ⓑ Ⓒ Ⓓ Ⓔ	82 Ⓐ Ⓑ Ⓒ Ⓓ Ⓔ
8 Ⓐ Ⓑ Ⓒ Ⓓ Ⓔ	33 Ⓐ Ⓑ Ⓒ Ⓓ Ⓔ	58 Ⓐ Ⓑ Ⓒ Ⓓ Ⓔ	83 Ⓐ Ⓑ Ⓒ Ⓓ Ⓔ
9 Ⓐ Ⓑ Ⓒ Ⓓ Ⓔ	34 Ⓐ Ⓑ Ⓒ Ⓓ Ⓔ	59 Ⓐ Ⓑ Ⓒ Ⓓ Ⓔ	84 Ⓐ Ⓑ Ⓒ Ⓓ Ⓔ
10 Ⓐ Ⓑ Ⓒ Ⓓ Ⓔ	35 Ⓐ Ⓑ Ⓒ Ⓓ Ⓔ	60 Ⓐ Ⓑ Ⓒ Ⓓ Ⓔ	85 Ⓐ Ⓑ Ⓒ Ⓓ Ⓔ
11 Ⓐ Ⓑ Ⓒ Ⓓ Ⓔ	36 Ⓐ Ⓑ Ⓒ Ⓓ Ⓔ	61 Ⓐ Ⓑ Ⓒ Ⓓ Ⓔ	86 Ⓐ Ⓑ Ⓒ Ⓓ Ⓔ
12 Ⓐ Ⓑ Ⓒ Ⓓ Ⓔ	37 Ⓐ Ⓑ Ⓒ Ⓓ Ⓔ	62 Ⓐ Ⓑ Ⓒ Ⓓ Ⓔ	87 Ⓐ Ⓑ Ⓒ Ⓓ Ⓔ
13 Ⓐ Ⓑ Ⓒ Ⓓ Ⓔ	38 Ⓐ Ⓑ Ⓒ Ⓓ Ⓔ	63 Ⓐ Ⓑ Ⓒ Ⓓ Ⓔ	88 Ⓐ Ⓑ Ⓒ Ⓓ Ⓔ
14 Ⓐ Ⓑ Ⓒ Ⓓ Ⓔ	39 Ⓐ Ⓑ Ⓒ Ⓓ Ⓔ	64 Ⓐ Ⓑ Ⓒ Ⓓ Ⓔ	89 Ⓐ Ⓑ Ⓒ Ⓓ Ⓔ
15 Ⓐ Ⓑ Ⓒ Ⓓ Ⓔ	40 Ⓐ Ⓑ Ⓒ Ⓓ Ⓔ	65 Ⓐ Ⓑ Ⓒ Ⓓ Ⓔ	90 Ⓐ Ⓑ Ⓒ Ⓓ Ⓔ
16 Ⓐ Ⓑ Ⓒ Ⓓ Ⓔ	41 Ⓐ Ⓑ Ⓒ Ⓓ Ⓔ	66 Ⓐ Ⓑ Ⓒ Ⓓ Ⓔ	91 Ⓐ Ⓑ Ⓒ Ⓓ Ⓔ
17 Ⓐ Ⓑ Ⓒ Ⓓ Ⓔ	42 Ⓐ Ⓑ Ⓒ Ⓓ Ⓔ	67 Ⓐ Ⓑ Ⓒ Ⓓ Ⓔ	92 Ⓐ Ⓑ Ⓒ Ⓓ Ⓔ
18 Ⓐ Ⓑ Ⓒ Ⓓ Ⓔ	43 Ⓐ Ⓑ Ⓒ Ⓓ Ⓔ	68 Ⓐ Ⓑ Ⓒ Ⓓ Ⓔ	93 Ⓐ Ⓑ Ⓒ Ⓓ Ⓔ
19 Ⓐ Ⓑ Ⓒ Ⓓ Ⓔ	44 Ⓐ Ⓑ Ⓒ Ⓓ Ⓔ	69 Ⓐ Ⓑ Ⓒ Ⓓ Ⓔ	94 Ⓐ Ⓑ Ⓒ Ⓓ Ⓔ
20 Ⓐ Ⓑ Ⓒ Ⓓ Ⓔ	45 Ⓐ Ⓑ Ⓒ Ⓓ Ⓔ	70 Ⓐ Ⓑ Ⓒ Ⓓ Ⓔ	95 Ⓐ Ⓑ Ⓒ Ⓓ Ⓔ
21 Ⓐ Ⓑ Ⓒ Ⓓ Ⓔ	46 Ⓐ Ⓑ Ⓒ Ⓓ Ⓔ	71 Ⓐ Ⓑ Ⓒ Ⓓ Ⓔ	96 Ⓐ Ⓑ Ⓒ Ⓓ Ⓔ
22 Ⓐ Ⓑ Ⓒ Ⓓ Ⓔ	47 Ⓐ Ⓑ Ⓒ Ⓓ Ⓔ	72 Ⓐ Ⓑ Ⓒ Ⓓ Ⓔ	97 Ⓐ Ⓑ Ⓒ Ⓓ Ⓔ
23 Ⓐ Ⓑ Ⓒ Ⓓ Ⓔ	48 Ⓐ Ⓑ Ⓒ Ⓓ Ⓔ	73 Ⓐ Ⓑ Ⓒ Ⓓ Ⓔ	98 Ⓐ Ⓑ Ⓒ Ⓓ Ⓔ
24 Ⓐ Ⓑ Ⓒ Ⓓ Ⓔ	49 Ⓐ Ⓑ Ⓒ Ⓓ Ⓔ	74 Ⓐ Ⓑ Ⓒ Ⓓ Ⓔ	99 Ⓐ Ⓑ Ⓒ Ⓓ Ⓔ
25 Ⓐ Ⓑ Ⓒ Ⓓ Ⓔ	50 Ⓐ Ⓑ Ⓒ Ⓓ Ⓔ	75 Ⓐ Ⓑ Ⓒ Ⓓ Ⓔ	100 Ⓐ Ⓑ Ⓒ Ⓓ Ⓔ

PLEASE MAKE SURE to fill in these fields completely and correctly. If they are not correct, we won't be able to score your test(s)!

7 TEST BOOK SERIAL NUMBER (Copy from front of test book.)

0 1 2 3 4 5 6 7 8 9 (six columns)

8 BOOK CODE (Copy and grid as on back of test book.)

Column 1: 0 1 2 3 4 5 6 7 8 9
Column 2: A B C D E F G H I J K L M N O P Q R S T U V W X Y Z
Column 3: 0 1 2 3 4 5 6 7 8 9

9 BOOK ID (Copy from back of test book.)

Quality Assurance Mark

Chemistry *Fill in circle CE only if II is correct explanation of I.

	I	II	CE*		I	II	CE*
101	Ⓣ Ⓕ	Ⓣ Ⓕ	○	109	Ⓣ Ⓕ	Ⓣ Ⓕ	○
102	Ⓣ Ⓕ	Ⓣ Ⓕ	○	110	Ⓣ Ⓕ	Ⓣ Ⓕ	○
103	Ⓣ Ⓕ	Ⓣ Ⓕ	○	111	Ⓣ Ⓕ	Ⓣ Ⓕ	○
104	Ⓣ Ⓕ	Ⓣ Ⓕ	○	112	Ⓣ Ⓕ	Ⓣ Ⓕ	○
105	Ⓣ Ⓕ	Ⓣ Ⓕ	○	113	Ⓣ Ⓕ	Ⓣ Ⓕ	○
106	Ⓣ Ⓕ	Ⓣ Ⓕ	○	114	Ⓣ Ⓕ	Ⓣ Ⓕ	○
107	Ⓣ Ⓕ	Ⓣ Ⓕ	○	115	Ⓣ Ⓕ	Ⓣ Ⓕ	○
108	Ⓣ Ⓕ	Ⓣ Ⓕ	○				

FOR OFFICIAL USE ONLY

R/C	W/S1	FS/S2	CS/S3	WS

CERTIFICATION STATEMENT

Copy the statement below and sign your name as you would an official document.

I hereby agree to the conditions set forth online at sat.collegeboard.org and in any paper registration materials given to me and certify that I am the person whose name, address and signature appear on this answer sheet.

____

____

____

____

Signature ____________________ Date ______________

COMPLETE MARK ●	EXAMPLES OF INCOMPLETE MARKS

You must use a No. 2 pencil and marks must be complete. Do not use a mechanical pencil. *It is very important that you fill in the entire circle darkly and completely. If you change your response, erase as completely as possible. Incomplete marks or erasures may affect your score.*

○ Literature
○ Biology E
○ Biology M
○ Chemistry
○ Physics
○ Mathematics Level 1
○ Mathematics Level 2
○ U.S. History
○ World History
○ French
○ German
○ Italian
○ Latin
○ Modern Hebrew
○ Spanish
○ Chinese Listening
○ French Listening
○ German Listening
○ Japanese Listening
○ Korean Listening
○ Spanish Listening

Background Questions: ① ② ③ ④ ⑤ ⑥ ⑦ ⑧ ⑨

1 Ⓐ Ⓑ Ⓒ Ⓓ Ⓔ	26 Ⓐ Ⓑ Ⓒ Ⓓ Ⓔ	51 Ⓐ Ⓑ Ⓒ Ⓓ Ⓔ	76 Ⓐ Ⓑ Ⓒ Ⓓ Ⓔ
2 Ⓐ Ⓑ Ⓒ Ⓓ Ⓔ	27 Ⓐ Ⓑ Ⓒ Ⓓ Ⓔ	52 Ⓐ Ⓑ Ⓒ Ⓓ Ⓔ	77 Ⓐ Ⓑ Ⓒ Ⓓ Ⓔ
3 Ⓐ Ⓑ Ⓒ Ⓓ Ⓔ	28 Ⓐ Ⓑ Ⓒ Ⓓ Ⓔ	53 Ⓐ Ⓑ Ⓒ Ⓓ Ⓔ	78 Ⓐ Ⓑ Ⓒ Ⓓ Ⓔ
4 Ⓐ Ⓑ Ⓒ Ⓓ Ⓔ	29 Ⓐ Ⓑ Ⓒ Ⓓ Ⓔ	54 Ⓐ Ⓑ Ⓒ Ⓓ Ⓔ	79 Ⓐ Ⓑ Ⓒ Ⓓ Ⓔ
5 Ⓐ Ⓑ Ⓒ Ⓓ Ⓔ	30 Ⓐ Ⓑ Ⓒ Ⓓ Ⓔ	55 Ⓐ Ⓑ Ⓒ Ⓓ Ⓔ	80 Ⓐ Ⓑ Ⓒ Ⓓ Ⓔ
6 Ⓐ Ⓑ Ⓒ Ⓓ Ⓔ	31 Ⓐ Ⓑ Ⓒ Ⓓ Ⓔ	56 Ⓐ Ⓑ Ⓒ Ⓓ Ⓔ	81 Ⓐ Ⓑ Ⓒ Ⓓ Ⓔ
7 Ⓐ Ⓑ Ⓒ Ⓓ Ⓔ	32 Ⓐ Ⓑ Ⓒ Ⓓ Ⓔ	57 Ⓐ Ⓑ Ⓒ Ⓓ Ⓔ	82 Ⓐ Ⓑ Ⓒ Ⓓ Ⓔ
8 Ⓐ Ⓑ Ⓒ Ⓓ Ⓔ	33 Ⓐ Ⓑ Ⓒ Ⓓ Ⓔ	58 Ⓐ Ⓑ Ⓒ Ⓓ Ⓔ	83 Ⓐ Ⓑ Ⓒ Ⓓ Ⓔ
9 Ⓐ Ⓑ Ⓒ Ⓓ Ⓔ	34 Ⓐ Ⓑ Ⓒ Ⓓ Ⓔ	59 Ⓐ Ⓑ Ⓒ Ⓓ Ⓔ	84 Ⓐ Ⓑ Ⓒ Ⓓ Ⓔ
10 Ⓐ Ⓑ Ⓒ Ⓓ Ⓔ	35 Ⓐ Ⓑ Ⓒ Ⓓ Ⓔ	60 Ⓐ Ⓑ Ⓒ Ⓓ Ⓔ	85 Ⓐ Ⓑ Ⓒ Ⓓ Ⓔ
11 Ⓐ Ⓑ Ⓒ Ⓓ Ⓔ	36 Ⓐ Ⓑ Ⓒ Ⓓ Ⓔ	61 Ⓐ Ⓑ Ⓒ Ⓓ Ⓔ	86 Ⓐ Ⓑ Ⓒ Ⓓ Ⓔ
12 Ⓐ Ⓑ Ⓒ Ⓓ Ⓔ	37 Ⓐ Ⓑ Ⓒ Ⓓ Ⓔ	62 Ⓐ Ⓑ Ⓒ Ⓓ Ⓔ	87 Ⓐ Ⓑ Ⓒ Ⓓ Ⓔ
13 Ⓐ Ⓑ Ⓒ Ⓓ Ⓔ	38 Ⓐ Ⓑ Ⓒ Ⓓ Ⓔ	63 Ⓐ Ⓑ Ⓒ Ⓓ Ⓔ	88 Ⓐ Ⓑ Ⓒ Ⓓ Ⓔ
14 Ⓐ Ⓑ Ⓒ Ⓓ Ⓔ	39 Ⓐ Ⓑ Ⓒ Ⓓ Ⓔ	64 Ⓐ Ⓑ Ⓒ Ⓓ Ⓔ	89 Ⓐ Ⓑ Ⓒ Ⓓ Ⓔ
15 Ⓐ Ⓑ Ⓒ Ⓓ Ⓔ	40 Ⓐ Ⓑ Ⓒ Ⓓ Ⓔ	65 Ⓐ Ⓑ Ⓒ Ⓓ Ⓔ	90 Ⓐ Ⓑ Ⓒ Ⓓ Ⓔ
16 Ⓐ Ⓑ Ⓒ Ⓓ Ⓔ	41 Ⓐ Ⓑ Ⓒ Ⓓ Ⓔ	66 Ⓐ Ⓑ Ⓒ Ⓓ Ⓔ	91 Ⓐ Ⓑ Ⓒ Ⓓ Ⓔ
17 Ⓐ Ⓑ Ⓒ Ⓓ Ⓔ	42 Ⓐ Ⓑ Ⓒ Ⓓ Ⓔ	67 Ⓐ Ⓑ Ⓒ Ⓓ Ⓔ	92 Ⓐ Ⓑ Ⓒ Ⓓ Ⓔ
18 Ⓐ Ⓑ Ⓒ Ⓓ Ⓔ	43 Ⓐ Ⓑ Ⓒ Ⓓ Ⓔ	68 Ⓐ Ⓑ Ⓒ Ⓓ Ⓔ	93 Ⓐ Ⓑ Ⓒ Ⓓ Ⓔ
19 Ⓐ Ⓑ Ⓒ Ⓓ Ⓔ	44 Ⓐ Ⓑ Ⓒ Ⓓ Ⓔ	69 Ⓐ Ⓑ Ⓒ Ⓓ Ⓔ	94 Ⓐ Ⓑ Ⓒ Ⓓ Ⓔ
20 Ⓐ Ⓑ Ⓒ Ⓓ Ⓔ	45 Ⓐ Ⓑ Ⓒ Ⓓ Ⓔ	70 Ⓐ Ⓑ Ⓒ Ⓓ Ⓔ	95 Ⓐ Ⓑ Ⓒ Ⓓ Ⓔ
21 Ⓐ Ⓑ Ⓒ Ⓓ Ⓔ	46 Ⓐ Ⓑ Ⓒ Ⓓ Ⓔ	71 Ⓐ Ⓑ Ⓒ Ⓓ Ⓔ	96 Ⓐ Ⓑ Ⓒ Ⓓ Ⓔ
22 Ⓐ Ⓑ Ⓒ Ⓓ Ⓔ	47 Ⓐ Ⓑ Ⓒ Ⓓ Ⓔ	72 Ⓐ Ⓑ Ⓒ Ⓓ Ⓔ	97 Ⓐ Ⓑ Ⓒ Ⓓ Ⓔ
23 Ⓐ Ⓑ Ⓒ Ⓓ Ⓔ	48 Ⓐ Ⓑ Ⓒ Ⓓ Ⓔ	73 Ⓐ Ⓑ Ⓒ Ⓓ Ⓔ	98 Ⓐ Ⓑ Ⓒ Ⓓ Ⓔ
24 Ⓐ Ⓑ Ⓒ Ⓓ Ⓔ	49 Ⓐ Ⓑ Ⓒ Ⓓ Ⓔ	74 Ⓐ Ⓑ Ⓒ Ⓓ Ⓔ	99 Ⓐ Ⓑ Ⓒ Ⓓ Ⓔ
25 Ⓐ Ⓑ Ⓒ Ⓓ Ⓔ	50 Ⓐ Ⓑ Ⓒ Ⓓ Ⓔ	75 Ⓐ Ⓑ Ⓒ Ⓓ Ⓔ	100 Ⓐ Ⓑ Ⓒ Ⓓ Ⓔ

Quality ● Assurance Mark

Chemistry *Fill in circle CE only if II is correct explanation of I.

	I	II	CE*		I	II	CE*
101	Ⓣ Ⓕ	Ⓣ Ⓕ	○	109	Ⓣ Ⓕ	Ⓣ Ⓕ	○
102	Ⓣ Ⓕ	Ⓣ Ⓕ	○	110	Ⓣ Ⓕ	Ⓣ Ⓕ	○
103	Ⓣ Ⓕ	Ⓣ Ⓕ	○	111	Ⓣ Ⓕ	Ⓣ Ⓕ	○
104	Ⓣ Ⓕ	Ⓣ Ⓕ	○	112	Ⓣ Ⓕ	Ⓣ Ⓕ	○
105	Ⓣ Ⓕ	Ⓣ Ⓕ	○	113	Ⓣ Ⓕ	Ⓣ Ⓕ	○
106	Ⓣ Ⓕ	Ⓣ Ⓕ	○	114	Ⓣ Ⓕ	Ⓣ Ⓕ	○
107	Ⓣ Ⓕ	Ⓣ Ⓕ	○	115	Ⓣ Ⓕ	Ⓣ Ⓕ	○
108	Ⓣ Ⓕ	Ⓣ Ⓕ	○				

FOR OFFICIAL USE ONLY

R/C	W/S1	FS/S2	CS/S3	WS

PLEASE MAKE SURE to fill in these fields completely and correctly. If they are not correct, we won't be able to score your test(s)!

7 TEST BOOK SERIAL NUMBER
(Copy from front of test book.)

0	0	0	0	0	0
1	1	1	1	1	1
2	2	2	2	2	2
3	3	3	3	3	3
4	4	4	4	4	4
5	5	5	5	5	5
6	6	6	6	6	6
7	7	7	7	7	7
8	8	8	8	8	8
9	9	9	9	9	9

8 BOOK CODE
(Copy and grid as on back of test book.)

0	A	0
1	B	1
2	C	2
3	D	3
4	E	4
5	F	5
6	G	6
7	H	7
8	I	8
9	J	9
	K	
	L	
	M	
	N	
	O	
	P	
	Q	
	R	
	S	
	T	
	U	
	V	
	W	
	X	
	Y	
	Z	

9 BOOK ID
(Copy from back of test book.)

COMPLETE MARK ● EXAMPLES OF INCOMPLETE MARKS

You must use a No. 2 pencil and marks must be complete. Do not use a mechanical pencil. *It is very important that you fill in the entire circle darkly and completely. If you change your response, erase as completely as possible. Incomplete marks or erasures may affect your score.*

○ Literature	○ Mathematics Level 1	○ German	○ Chinese Listening	○ Japanese Listening
○ Biology E	○ Mathematics Level 2	○ Italian	○ French Listening	○ Korean Listening
○ Biology M	○ U.S. History	○ Latin	○ German Listening	○ Spanish Listening
○ Chemistry	○ World History	○ Modern Hebrew		
○ Physics	○ French	○ Spanish		

Background Questions: ① ② ③ ④ ⑤ ⑥ ⑦ ⑧ ⑨

PLEASE MAKE SURE to fill in these fields completely and correctly. If they are not correct, we won't be able to score your test(s)!

1 Ⓐ Ⓑ Ⓒ Ⓓ Ⓔ	26 Ⓐ Ⓑ Ⓒ Ⓓ Ⓔ	51 Ⓐ Ⓑ Ⓒ Ⓓ Ⓔ	76 Ⓐ Ⓑ Ⓒ Ⓓ Ⓔ
2 Ⓐ Ⓑ Ⓒ Ⓓ Ⓔ	27 Ⓐ Ⓑ Ⓒ Ⓓ Ⓔ	52 Ⓐ Ⓑ Ⓒ Ⓓ Ⓔ	77 Ⓐ Ⓑ Ⓒ Ⓓ Ⓔ
3 Ⓐ Ⓑ Ⓒ Ⓓ Ⓔ	28 Ⓐ Ⓑ Ⓒ Ⓓ Ⓔ	53 Ⓐ Ⓑ Ⓒ Ⓓ Ⓔ	78 Ⓐ Ⓑ Ⓒ Ⓓ Ⓔ
4 Ⓐ Ⓑ Ⓒ Ⓓ Ⓔ	29 Ⓐ Ⓑ Ⓒ Ⓓ Ⓔ	54 Ⓐ Ⓑ Ⓒ Ⓓ Ⓔ	79 Ⓐ Ⓑ Ⓒ Ⓓ Ⓔ
5 Ⓐ Ⓑ Ⓒ Ⓓ Ⓔ	30 Ⓐ Ⓑ Ⓒ Ⓓ Ⓔ	55 Ⓐ Ⓑ Ⓒ Ⓓ Ⓔ	80 Ⓐ Ⓑ Ⓒ Ⓓ Ⓔ
6 Ⓐ Ⓑ Ⓒ Ⓓ Ⓔ	31 Ⓐ Ⓑ Ⓒ Ⓓ Ⓔ	56 Ⓐ Ⓑ Ⓒ Ⓓ Ⓔ	81 Ⓐ Ⓑ Ⓒ Ⓓ Ⓔ
7 Ⓐ Ⓑ Ⓒ Ⓓ Ⓔ	32 Ⓐ Ⓑ Ⓒ Ⓓ Ⓔ	57 Ⓐ Ⓑ Ⓒ Ⓓ Ⓔ	82 Ⓐ Ⓑ Ⓒ Ⓓ Ⓔ
8 Ⓐ Ⓑ Ⓒ Ⓓ Ⓔ	33 Ⓐ Ⓑ Ⓒ Ⓓ Ⓔ	58 Ⓐ Ⓑ Ⓒ Ⓓ Ⓔ	83 Ⓐ Ⓑ Ⓒ Ⓓ Ⓔ
9 Ⓐ Ⓑ Ⓒ Ⓓ Ⓔ	34 Ⓐ Ⓑ Ⓒ Ⓓ Ⓔ	59 Ⓐ Ⓑ Ⓒ Ⓓ Ⓔ	84 Ⓐ Ⓑ Ⓒ Ⓓ Ⓔ
10 Ⓐ Ⓑ Ⓒ Ⓓ Ⓔ	35 Ⓐ Ⓑ Ⓒ Ⓓ Ⓔ	60 Ⓐ Ⓑ Ⓒ Ⓓ Ⓔ	85 Ⓐ Ⓑ Ⓒ Ⓓ Ⓔ
11 Ⓐ Ⓑ Ⓒ Ⓓ Ⓔ	36 Ⓐ Ⓑ Ⓒ Ⓓ Ⓔ	61 Ⓐ Ⓑ Ⓒ Ⓓ Ⓔ	86 Ⓐ Ⓑ Ⓒ Ⓓ Ⓔ
12 Ⓐ Ⓑ Ⓒ Ⓓ Ⓔ	37 Ⓐ Ⓑ Ⓒ Ⓓ Ⓔ	62 Ⓐ Ⓑ Ⓒ Ⓓ Ⓔ	87 Ⓐ Ⓑ Ⓒ Ⓓ Ⓔ
13 Ⓐ Ⓑ Ⓒ Ⓓ Ⓔ	38 Ⓐ Ⓑ Ⓒ Ⓓ Ⓔ	63 Ⓐ Ⓑ Ⓒ Ⓓ Ⓔ	88 Ⓐ Ⓑ Ⓒ Ⓓ Ⓔ
14 Ⓐ Ⓑ Ⓒ Ⓓ Ⓔ	39 Ⓐ Ⓑ Ⓒ Ⓓ Ⓔ	64 Ⓐ Ⓑ Ⓒ Ⓓ Ⓔ	89 Ⓐ Ⓑ Ⓒ Ⓓ Ⓔ
15 Ⓐ Ⓑ Ⓒ Ⓓ Ⓔ	40 Ⓐ Ⓑ Ⓒ Ⓓ Ⓔ	65 Ⓐ Ⓑ Ⓒ Ⓓ Ⓔ	90 Ⓐ Ⓑ Ⓒ Ⓓ Ⓔ
16 Ⓐ Ⓑ Ⓒ Ⓓ Ⓔ	41 Ⓐ Ⓑ Ⓒ Ⓓ Ⓔ	66 Ⓐ Ⓑ Ⓒ Ⓓ Ⓔ	91 Ⓐ Ⓑ Ⓒ Ⓓ Ⓔ
17 Ⓐ Ⓑ Ⓒ Ⓓ Ⓔ	42 Ⓐ Ⓑ Ⓒ Ⓓ Ⓔ	67 Ⓐ Ⓑ Ⓒ Ⓓ Ⓔ	92 Ⓐ Ⓑ Ⓒ Ⓓ Ⓔ
18 Ⓐ Ⓑ Ⓒ Ⓓ Ⓔ	43 Ⓐ Ⓑ Ⓒ Ⓓ Ⓔ	68 Ⓐ Ⓑ Ⓒ Ⓓ Ⓔ	93 Ⓐ Ⓑ Ⓒ Ⓓ Ⓔ
19 Ⓐ Ⓑ Ⓒ Ⓓ Ⓔ	44 Ⓐ Ⓑ Ⓒ Ⓓ Ⓔ	69 Ⓐ Ⓑ Ⓒ Ⓓ Ⓔ	94 Ⓐ Ⓑ Ⓒ Ⓓ Ⓔ
20 Ⓐ Ⓑ Ⓒ Ⓓ Ⓔ	45 Ⓐ Ⓑ Ⓒ Ⓓ Ⓔ	70 Ⓐ Ⓑ Ⓒ Ⓓ Ⓔ	95 Ⓐ Ⓑ Ⓒ Ⓓ Ⓔ
21 Ⓐ Ⓑ Ⓒ Ⓓ Ⓔ	46 Ⓐ Ⓑ Ⓒ Ⓓ Ⓔ	71 Ⓐ Ⓑ Ⓒ Ⓓ Ⓔ	96 Ⓐ Ⓑ Ⓒ Ⓓ Ⓔ
22 Ⓐ Ⓑ Ⓒ Ⓓ Ⓔ	47 Ⓐ Ⓑ Ⓒ Ⓓ Ⓔ	72 Ⓐ Ⓑ Ⓒ Ⓓ Ⓔ	97 Ⓐ Ⓑ Ⓒ Ⓓ Ⓔ
23 Ⓐ Ⓑ Ⓒ Ⓓ Ⓔ	48 Ⓐ Ⓑ Ⓒ Ⓓ Ⓔ	73 Ⓐ Ⓑ Ⓒ Ⓓ Ⓔ	98 Ⓐ Ⓑ Ⓒ Ⓓ Ⓔ
24 Ⓐ Ⓑ Ⓒ Ⓓ Ⓔ	49 Ⓐ Ⓑ Ⓒ Ⓓ Ⓔ	74 Ⓐ Ⓑ Ⓒ Ⓓ Ⓔ	99 Ⓐ Ⓑ Ⓒ Ⓓ Ⓔ
25 Ⓐ Ⓑ Ⓒ Ⓓ Ⓔ	50 Ⓐ Ⓑ Ⓒ Ⓓ Ⓔ	75 Ⓐ Ⓑ Ⓒ Ⓓ Ⓔ	100 Ⓐ Ⓑ Ⓒ Ⓓ Ⓔ

Chemistry *Fill in circle CE only if II is correct explanation of I.

	I	II	CE*		I	II	CE*
101	Ⓣ Ⓕ	Ⓣ Ⓕ	○	109	Ⓣ Ⓕ	Ⓣ Ⓕ	○
102	Ⓣ Ⓕ	Ⓣ Ⓕ	○	110	Ⓣ Ⓕ	Ⓣ Ⓕ	○
103	Ⓣ Ⓕ	Ⓣ Ⓕ	○	111	Ⓣ Ⓕ	Ⓣ Ⓕ	○
104	Ⓣ Ⓕ	Ⓣ Ⓕ	○	112	Ⓣ Ⓕ	Ⓣ Ⓕ	○
105	Ⓣ Ⓕ	Ⓣ Ⓕ	○	113	Ⓣ Ⓕ	Ⓣ Ⓕ	○
106	Ⓣ Ⓕ	Ⓣ Ⓕ	○	114	Ⓣ Ⓕ	Ⓣ Ⓕ	○
107	Ⓣ Ⓕ	Ⓣ Ⓕ	○	115	Ⓣ Ⓕ	Ⓣ Ⓕ	○
108	Ⓣ Ⓕ	Ⓣ Ⓕ	○				

FOR OFFICIAL USE ONLY

R/C	W/S1	FS/S2	CS/S3	WS

8 BOOK CODE

(Copy and grid as on back of test book.)

⓪	Ⓐ	⓪
①	Ⓑ	①
②	Ⓒ	②
③	Ⓓ	③
④	Ⓔ	④
⑤	Ⓕ	⑤
⑥	Ⓖ	⑥
⑦	Ⓗ	⑦
⑧	Ⓘ	⑧
⑨	Ⓙ	⑨
	Ⓚ	
	Ⓛ	
	Ⓜ	
	Ⓝ	
	Ⓞ	
	Ⓟ	
	Ⓠ	
	Ⓡ	
	Ⓢ	
	Ⓣ	
	Ⓤ	
	Ⓥ	
	Ⓦ	
	Ⓧ	
	Ⓨ	
	Ⓩ	

7 TEST BOOK SERIAL NUMBER

(Copy from front of test book.)

⓪	⓪	⓪	⓪	⓪	⓪
①	①	①	①	①	①
②	②	②	②	②	②
③	③	③	③	③	③
④	④	④	④	④	④
⑤	⑤	⑤	⑤	⑤	⑤
⑥	⑥	⑥	⑥	⑥	⑥
⑦	⑦	⑦	⑦	⑦	⑦
⑧	⑧	⑧	⑧	⑧	⑧
⑨	⑨	⑨	⑨	⑨	⑨

9 BOOK ID

(Copy from back of test book.)

Quality Assurance Mark

PLEASE DO NOT WRITE IN THIS AREA

SERIAL #